KEY TO WORLD MAP PAGES

- Large scale maps (> 1:2 500 000)
- Medium scale maps (1:2 800 000-1:9 000 000)
- Small scale maps (< 1:10 000 000)

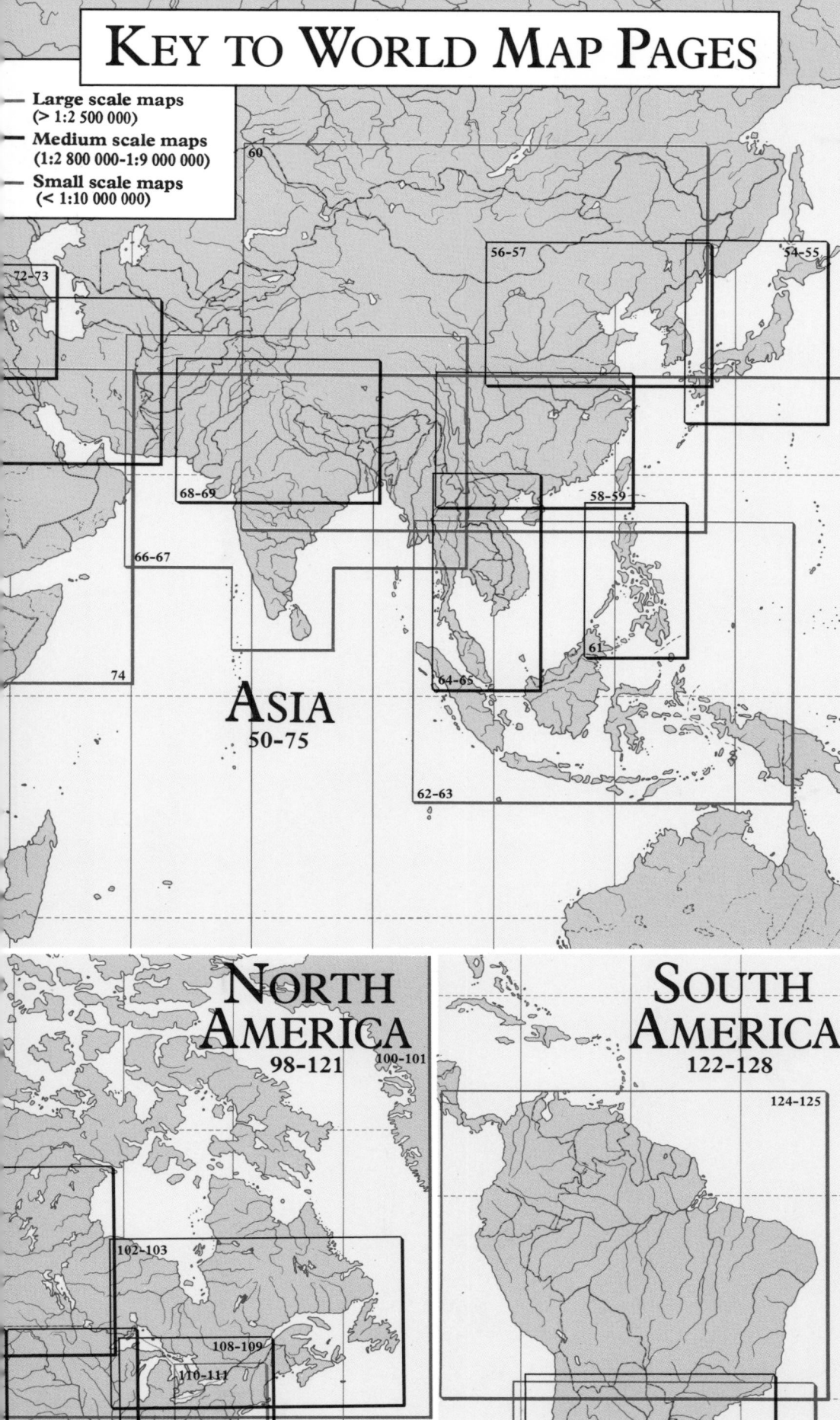

ASIA 50-75

NORTH AMERICA 98-121

SOUTH AMERICA 122-128

COUNTRY INDEX

Afghanistan	66	Kuwait	70–71
Albania	40	Kyrgyzstan	50
Algeria	78		
Angola	84–85	Laos	64
Argentina	126, 128	Latvia	46
Armenia	73	Lebanon	75
Australia	92–95	Lesotho	88–89
Austria	26–27	Liberia	82
Azerbaijan	73	Libya	79
		Lithuania	46
Bahamas	120–121	Luxembourg	17
Bahrain	71		
Bangladesh	67	Macedonia	40
Barbados	121	Madagascar	89
Belarus	46–47	Malawi	87
Belgium	17	Malaysia	62–63
Belize	120	Mali	78, 82–83
Benin	83	Malta	36
Bhutan	67	Mauritania	78, 82
Bolivia	124	Mauritius	77
Bosnia-Herzegovina	29, 40	Mexico	118–119
Botswana	88–89	Moldova	43
Brazil	124–127	Mongolia	60
Brunei	78	Morocco	78
Bulgaria	40–41	Mozambique	85, 87
Burkina Faso	82–83		
Burma	67	Namibia	88
Burundi	86	Nepal	69
		Netherlands	17
Cambodia	64–65	New Zealand	91
Cameroon	84	Nicaragua	120
Canada	100–101	Niger	83
Central African Republic	84	Nigeria	83
Chad	79	Northern Ireland	15
Chile	124, 128	Norway	8–9
China	56–60		
Colombia	124	Oman	74
Congo	84		
Congo, Dem. Rep. of the	84–85	Pakistan	68
Costa Rica	120	Panama	120
Croatia	29, 42	Papua New Guinea	90
Cuba	120–121	Paraguay	126–127
Cyprus	36	Peru	124
Czech Republic	26–27	Philippines	61
		Poland	44–45
Denmark	11	Portugal	34–35
Djibouti	74	Puerto Rico	121
Dominican Republic	121	Qatar	71
Ecuador	124	Romania	42–43
Egypt	80	Russia	50–51
El Salvador	120	Rwanda	86
England	12–13		
Equatorial Guinea	84	Saudi Arabia	74
Eritrea	80–81	Scotland	14
Estonia	46	Senegal	82
Ethiopia	74, 81	Sierra Leone	82
		Singapore	65
Fiji	91	Slovak Republic	27
Finland	8–9	Slovenia	29
France	18–21	Somali Republic	74
French Guiana	125	South Africa	88–89
		Spain	32–35, 37
Gabon	84	Sri Lanka	66
Gambia	82	Sudan	79, 81
Georgia	73	Surinam	124–125
Germany	24–25	Swaziland	89
Ghana	82–83	Sweden	8–9
Greece	38–41	Switzerland	25
Greenland	4	Syria	72–73
Guatemala	120		
Guinea	82	Taiwan	59
Guinea-Bissau	82	Tajikistan	50
Guyana	124	Tanzania	86–87
		Thailand	64–65
Haiti	121	Togo	83
Honduras	120	Trinidad and Tobago	121
Hungary	42	Tunisia	78–79
		Turkey	72–73
Iceland	8	Turkmenistan	50
India	66–69		
Indonesia	62–63	Uganda	86
Iran	70–71	Ukraine	47
Iraq	70–71	United Arab Emirates	71
Irish Republic	15	United Kingdom	12–15
Israel	75	USA	106–117
Italy	28–31	Uruguay	126–127
Ivory Coast	82	Uzbekistan	50
Jamaica	120	Venezuela	124
Japan	54–55	Vietnam	64–65
Jordan	75		
		Wales	12–13
Kazakstan	50		
Kenya	86	Yemen	74
Korea, North	57	Yugoslavia	40, 42
Korea, South	57		
		Zambia	84–85, 87
		Zimbabwe	87

PHILIP'S

CONCISE
WORLD
ATLAS

PHILIP'S

CONCISE WORLD ATLAS

NINTH EDITION

IN ASSOCIATION WITH
THE ROYAL GEOGRAPHICAL SOCIETY
WITH THE INSTITUTE OF BRITISH GEOGRAPHERS

THE EARTH IN SPACE
Cartography by Philip's

Text
Keith Lye

Illustrations
Stefan Chabluk

Star Charts
John Cox
Richard Monkhouse

PICTURE ACKNOWLEDGEMENTS
Robert Harding Picture Library /PHOTRI 13, /Bill Ross 41, /Adam Woolfitt 43
Hutchison Library /Melanie Friend 47, /John Hatt 46
Image Bank /Peter Hendrie 20, /Daniel Hummel 34, /Image Makers 8 top, /Pete Turner 39
Images Colour Library Limited 15
Japan National Tourist Organisation 45
NASA/Galaxy Picture Library 8 bottom left
Panos Pictures /Howard Davies 35
Chris Rayner 19 top
Rex Features /SIPA Press /Scott Andrews 12
Science Photo Library /Martin Bond 14, /CNES, 1992 Distribution Spot Image 27 top, /Luke Dodd 3, 6, /Earth Satellite Corporation 25 bottom, /NASA 9 centre right, 9 top, 22, 23, 24, /David Parker 26, /Peter Ryan 27 below, /Jerry Schad 4, /Space Telescope Science Institute /NASA 9 centre left, 9 bottom right, /US Geological Survey 8 centre right
Space Telescope Science Institute /R. Williams /NASA 2
Starland Picture Library /NASA 8 centre left
Still Pictures /Francois Pierrel 28, /Heine Pedersen 31, 40
Tony Stone Images 33, /Glen Allison 38, /James Balog 16, /John Beatty 21, /Neil Beer 30, /Kristin Finnegan 11, /Jeremy Horner 42, /Gary Norman 36, /Frank Oberle 25 top, /Dennis Oda 17, /Nigel Press 37, /Donovan Reese 18, 19, /Hugh Sitton 32, /Richard Surman 44, /Michael Townsend 29, /World Perspectives 10
Telegraph Colour Library /Space Frontiers 9 bottom left

Published in Great Britain in 1999
by George Philip Limited,
a division of Octopus Publishing Group Limited,
2–4 Heron Quays, London E14 4JP

Cartography by Philip's

ISBN 0–540–07710–0

A CIP catalogue record for this book is available from the British Library.

Printed in China

Details of other Philip's titles and services can be found on our website at:
www.philips-maps.co.uk

Philip's is proud to announce that its World Atlases are now published in association with The Royal Geographical Society (with The Institute of British Geographers).

The Society was founded in 1830 and given a Royal Charter in 1859 for 'the advancement of geographical science'. It holds historical collections of national and international importance, many of which relate to the Society's association with and support for scientific exploration and research from the 19th century onwards. It was pivotal in establishing geography as a teaching and research discipline in British universities close to the turn of the century, and has played a key role in geographical and environmental education ever since.

Today the Society is a leading world centre for geographical learning – supporting education, teaching, research and expeditions, and promoting public understanding of the subject.

The Society welcomes those interested in geography as members. For further information, please visit the website at: www.rgs.org

Philip's World Maps

The reference maps which form the main body of this atlas have been prepared in accordance with the highest standards of international cartography to provide an accurate and detailed representation of the Earth. The scales and projections used have been carefully chosen to give balanced coverage of the world, while emphasizing the most densely populated and economically significant regions. A hallmark of Philip's mapping is the use of hill shading and relief colouring to create a graphic impression of landforms: this makes the maps exceptionally easy to read. However, knowledge of the key features employed in the construction and presentation of the maps will enable the reader to derive the fullest benefit from the atlas.

MAP SEQUENCE

The atlas covers the Earth continent by continent: first Europe; then its land neighbour Asia (mapped north before south, in a clockwise sequence), then Africa, Australia and Oceania, North America and South America. This is the classic arrangement adopted by most cartographers since the 16th century. For each continent, there are maps at a variety of scales. First, physical relief and political maps of the whole continent; then a series of larger-scale maps

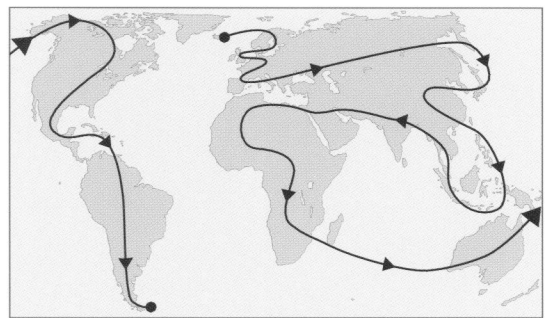

of the regions within the continent, each followed, where required, by still larger-scale maps of the most important or densely populated areas. The governing principle is that by turning the pages of the atlas, the reader moves steadily from north to south through each continent, with each map overlapping its neighbours. A key map showing this sequence, and the area covered by each map, can be found on the endpapers of the atlas.

MAP PRESENTATION

With very few exceptions (e.g. for the Arctic and Antarctic), the maps are drawn with north at the top, regardless of whether they are presented upright or sideways on the page. In the borders will be found the map title; a locator diagram showing the area covered and the page numbers for maps of adjacent areas; the scale; the projection used; the degrees of latitude and longitude; and the letters and figures used in the index for locating place names and geographical features. Physical relief maps also have a height reference panel identifying the colours used for each layer of contouring.

MAP SYMBOLS

Each map contains a vast amount of detail which can only be conveyed clearly and accurately by the use of symbols. Points and circles of varying sizes locate and identify the relative importance of towns and cities; different styles of type are employed for administrative, geographical and regional place names to aid identification. A variety of pictorial symbols denote landscape features such as glaciers, marshes and coral reefs, and man-made structures including roads, railways, airports, canals and dams. International borders are shown by red lines. Where neighbouring countries are in dispute, for example in parts of the Middle East, the maps show the *de facto* boundary between nations, regardless of the legal or historical situation. The symbols are explained on the first page of the World Maps section of the atlas.

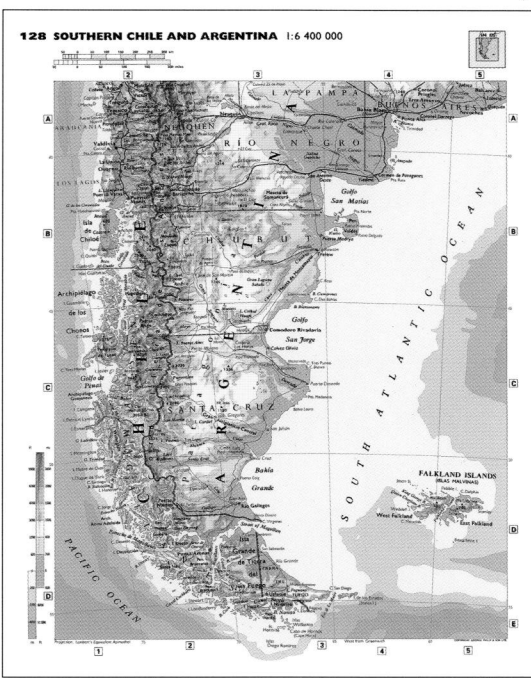

MAP SCALES

1:16 000 000
1 inch = 252 statute miles

The scale of each map is given in the numerical form known as the 'representative fraction'. The first figure is always one, signifying one unit of distance on the map; the second figure, usually in millions, is the number by which the map unit must be multiplied to give the equivalent distance on the Earth's surface. Calculations can easily be made in centimetres and kilometres, by dividing the Earth units figure by 100 000 (i.e. deleting the last five 0s). Thus 1:1 000 000 means 1 cm = 10 km. The calculation for inches and miles is more laborious, but 1 000 000 divided by 63 360 (the number of inches in a mile) shows that 1:1 000 000 means approximately 1 inch = 16 miles. The table below provides distance equivalents for scales down to 1:50 000 000.

LARGE SCALE		
1:1 000 000	1 cm = 10 km	1 inch = 16 miles
1:2 500 000	1 cm = 25 km	1 inch = 39.5 miles
1:5 000 000	1 cm = 50 km	1 inch = 79 miles
1:6 000 000	1 cm = 60 km	1 inch = 95 miles
1:8 000 000	1 cm = 80 km	1 inch = 126 miles
1:10 000 000	1 cm = 100 km	1 inch = 158 miles
1:15 000 000	1 cm = 150 km	1 inch = 237 miles
1:20 000 000	1 cm = 200 km	1 inch = 316 miles
1:50 000 000	1 cm = 500 km	1 inch = 790 miles
SMALL SCALE		

MEASURING DISTANCES

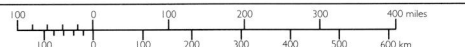

Although each map is accompanied by a scale bar, distances cannot always be measured with confidence because of the distortions involved in portraying the curved surface of the Earth on a flat page. As a general rule, the larger the map scale (i.e. the lower the number of Earth units in the representative fraction), the more accurate and reliable will be the distance measured. On small-scale maps such as those of the world and of entire continents, measurement may only

be accurate along the 'standard parallels', or central axes, and should not be attempted without considering the map projection.

MAP PROJECTIONS

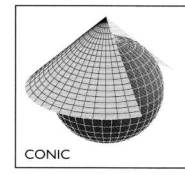

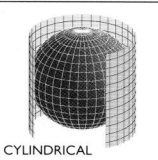

CONIC   AZIMUTHAL   CYLINDRICAL

Unlike a globe, no flat map can give a true scale representation of the world in terms of area, shape and position of every region. Each of the numerous systems that have been devised for projecting the curved surface of the Earth on to a flat page involves the sacrifice of accuracy in one or more of these elements. The variations in shape and position of landmasses such as Alaska, Greenland and Australia, for example, can be quite dramatic when different projections are compared.

For this atlas, the guiding principle has been to select projections that involve the least distortion of size and distance. The projection used for each map is noted in the border. Most fall into one of three categories – conic, cylindrical or azimuthal – whose basic concepts are shown above. Each involves plotting the forms of the Earth's surface on a grid of latitude and longitude lines, which may be shown as parallels, curves or radiating spokes.

LATITUDE AND LONGITUDE

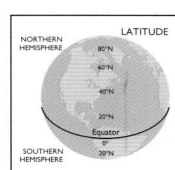
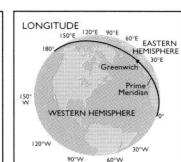
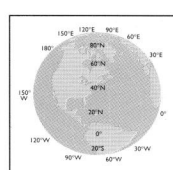

Accurate positioning of individual points on the Earth's surface is made possible by reference to the geometrical system of latitude and longitude. Latitude *parallels* are drawn west–east around the Earth and numbered by degrees north and south of the Equator, which is designated 0° of latitude. Longitude *meridians* are drawn north–south and numbered by degrees east and west of the *prime meridian*, 0° of longitude, which passes through Greenwich in England. By referring to these co-ordinates and their subdivisions of minutes (1/60th of a degree) and seconds (1/60th of a minute), any place on Earth can be located to within a few hundred yards. Latitude and longitude are indicated by blue lines on the maps; they are straight or curved according to the projection employed. Reference to these lines is the easiest way of determining the relative positions of places on different maps, and for plotting compass directions.

NAME FORMS

For ease of reference, both English and local name forms appear in the atlas. Oceans, seas and countries are shown in English throughout the atlas; country names may be abbreviated to their commonly accepted form (e.g. Germany, not The Federal Republic of Germany). Conventional English forms are also used for place names on the smaller-scale maps of the continents. However, local name forms are used on all large-scale and regional maps, with the English form given in brackets only for important cities – the large-scale map of Russia and Central Asia thus shows Moskva (Moscow). For countries which do not use a Roman script, place names have been transcribed according to the systems adopted by the British and US Geographic Names Authorities. For China, the Pin Yin system has been used, with some more widely known forms appearing in brackets, as with Beijing (Peking). Both English and local names appear in the index, the English form being cross-referenced to the local form.

Contents

World Statistics

Countries	x
Cities	xi
Climate	xii
Physical Dimensions	xiv
Regions in the News	xvi

The Earth In Space

The Universe	2–3
Star Charts and Constellations	4–7
The Solar System	8–9
The Earth: Time and Motion	10–11
The Earth From Space	12–13
The Dynamic Earth	14–15
Earthquakes and Volcanoes	16–17
Forces of Nature	18–19
Oceans and Ice	20–21
The Earth's Atmosphere	22–23
Climate and Weather	24–25
Water and Land Use	26–27
The Natural World	28–29
The Human World	30–31
Languages and Religions	32–33
International Organizations	34–35
Agriculture	36–37
Energy and Minerals	38–39
World Economies	40–41
Trade and Commerce	42–43
Travel and Communications	44–45
The World Today	46–47
Glossary of Terms	48

World Maps

Map Symbols	**1**
The World: Political 1:71 100 000	**2–3**
Arctic Ocean 1:31 100 000	**4**
Antarctica 1:31 100 000	**5**

Europe

Europe: Physical
1:17 800 000
6

Europe: Political
1:17 800 000
7

Scandinavia
1:4 400 000

8–9

Denmark and Southern Sweden
1:2 200 000

10–11

England and Wales
1:1 800 000

12–13

Scotland
1:1 800 000

14

Ireland
1:1 800 000

15

British Isles
1:4 400 000

16

Netherlands, Belgium and Luxembourg
1:2 200 000

17

Northern France
1:2 200 000

18–19

Southern France
1:2 200 000

20–21

Middle Europe
1:4 400 000

22–23

Germany and Switzerland
1:2 200 000

24–25

**Austria, Czech Republic
and Slovak Republic**
1:2 200 000

26–27

Northern Italy, Slovenia and Croatia
1:2 200 000

28–29

Southern Italy
1:2 200 000

30–31

Eastern Spain
1:2 200 000

32–33

Western Spain and Portugal
1:2 200 000

34–35

Malta, Crete, Corfu, Rhodes and Cyprus
1:900 000 / 1:1 200 000

36

Balearics, Canaries and Madeira
1:900 000 / 1:1 800 000

37

Southern Greece
1:2 200 000

38–39

Northern Greece, Bulgaria and Albania
1:2 200 000

40–41

Hungary, Romania and the Lower Danube
1:2 200 000

42–43

Poland and the Southern Baltic
1:2 200 000

44–45

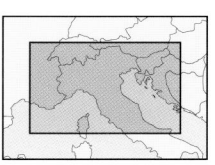
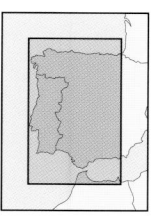
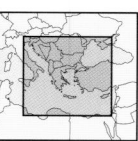
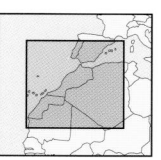
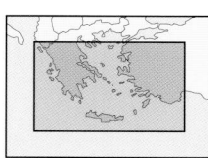
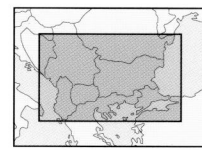
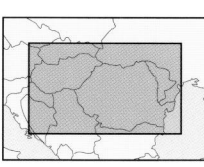
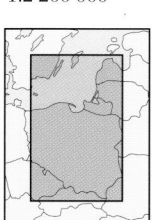

Baltic States, Belarus and Ukraine
1:4 400 000

46–47

Volga Basin and the Caucasus
1:4 400 000

48–49

Asia

Russia and Central Asia
1:17 800 000

50–51

Asia: Physical
1:44 400 000   **52**

Asia: Political
1:44 400 000   **53**

Japan
1:4 400 000

54–55

Northern China and Korea
1:5 300 000

56–57

Southern China
1:5 300 000

58–59

China
1:17 800 000

60

Philippines
1:6 700 000

61

Indonesia and the Philippines
1:11 100 000

62–63

Mainland South-east Asia
1:5 300 000

64–65

South Asia
1:8 900 000

66–67

The Indo-Gangetic Plain
1:5 300 000

68–69

The Middle East
1:6 200 000

70–71

Turkey and Transcaucasia
1:4 400 000

72–73

Arabia and the Horn of Africa
1:13 300 000

74

The Near East
1:2 200 000

75

Africa

Africa: Physical
1:37 300 000   **76**

Africa: Political
1: 37 300 000   **77**

North Africa
1:13 300 000

78–79

The Nile Valley and the Nile Delta
1:7 100 000 / 1:3 600 000

80–81

West Africa
1:7 100 000

82–83

Central and Southern Africa
1:13 300 000

84–85

East Africa
1:7 100 000

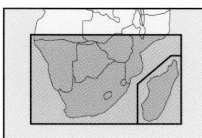

86–87

Southern Africa
1:7 100 000

88–89

Australia and Oceania

**Australia and Oceania:
Physical and Political**
1:44 400 000   90

New Zealand
1:5 300 000

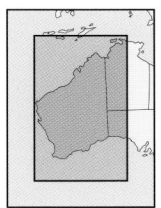

91

Western Australia
1:7 100 000

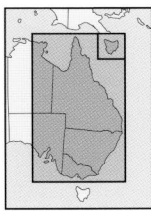

92–93

Eastern Australia
1:7 100 000

94–95

Pacific Ocean
1:48 000 000   96–97

North America

North America: Physical
1:31 100 000   98

North America: Political
1:31 100 000   99

Canada and Alaska
1:13 300 000 / 1:26 700 000

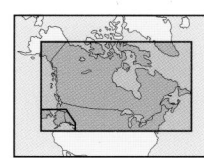

100–101

Eastern Canada
1:6 200 000

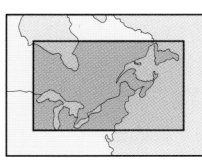

102–103

Western Canada
1:6 200 000

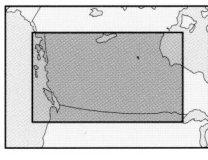

104–105

United States and Hawaii
1:10 700 000 / 1:8 900 000

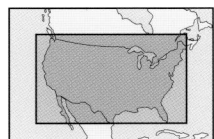

106–107

Eastern United States
1:5 300 000

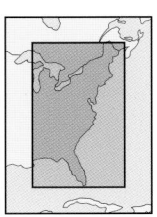

108–109

North-eastern United States
1:2 200 000

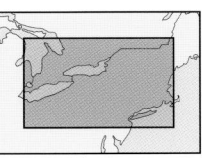

110–111

Middle United States
1:5 300 000

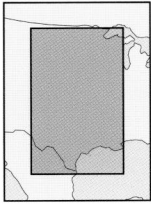

112–113

Western United States
1:5 300 000

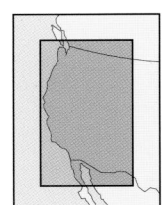

114–115

**Central and Southern California
and Washington**
1:2 200 000

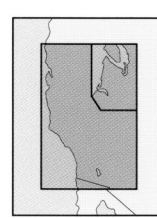

116–117

Mexico
1:7 100 000

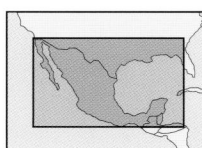

118–119

Central America and the West Indies
1:7 100 000

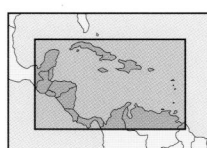

120–121

South America

South America: Physical
1:31 100 000   122

South America: Political
1:31 100 000   123

South America – North
1:14 200 000

124–125

Central South America
1:7 100 000

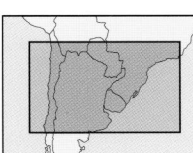

126–127

South America – South
1:14 200 000

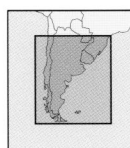

128

Index to World Maps

129–224

World Statistics: Countries

This alphabetical list includes all the countries and territories of the world. If a territory is not completely independent, then the country it is associated with is named. The area figures give the total area of land, inland water and ice.

Units for areas and populations are thousands. The population figures are 1998 estimates. The annual income is the Gross National Product per capita in US dollars. The figures are the latest available, usually 1997.

Country/Territory	Area km² Thousands	Area miles² Thousands	Population Thousands	Capital	Annual Income US $
Afghanistan	652	252	24,792	Kabul	600
Albania	28.8	11.1	3,331	Tirana	750
Algeria	2,382	920	30,481	Algiers	1,490
American Samoa (US)	0.20	0.08	62	Pago Pago	2,600
Andorra	0.45	0.17	75	Andorra La Vella	16,200
Angola	1,247	481	11,200	Luanda	340
Anguilla (UK)	0.1	0.04	11	The Valley	6,800
Antigua & Barbuda	0.44	0.17	64	St John's	7,330
Argentina	2,767	1,068	36,265	Buenos Aires	8,750
Armenia	29.8	11.5	3,422	Yerevan	530
Aruba (Netherlands)	0.19	0.07	69	Oranjestad	15,890
Australia	7,687	2,968	18,613	Canberra	20,540
Austria	83.9	32.4	8,134	Vienna	27,980
Azerbaijan	86.6	33.4	7,856	Baku	510
Azores (Portugal)	2.2	0.87	238	Ponta Delgada	–
Bahamas	13.9	5.4	280	Nassau	11,940
Bahrain	0.68	0.26	616	Manama	7,840
Bangladesh	144	56	125,000	Dhaka	270
Barbados	0.43	0.17	259	Bridgetown	6,560
Belarus	207.6	80.1	10,409	Minsk	2,150
Belgium	30.5	11.8	10,175	Brussels	26,420
Belize	23	8.9	230	Belmopan	2,700
Benin	113	43	6,101	Porto-Novo	380
Bermuda (UK)	0.05	0.02	62	Hamilton	31,870
Bhutan	47	18.1	1,908	Thimphu	390
Bolivia	1,099	424	7,826	La Paz/Sucre	950
Bosnia-Herzegovina	51	20	3,366	Sarajevo	300
Botswana	582	225	1,448	Gaborone	4,381
Brazil	8,512	3,286	170,000	Brasília	4,720
Brunei	5.8	2.2	315	Bandar Seri Begawan	15,800
Bulgaria	111	43	8,240	Sofia	1,140
Burkina Faso	274	106	11,266	Ouagadougou	240
Burma (= Myanmar)	677	261	47,305	Rangoon	1,790
Burundi	27.8	10.7	5,531	Bujumbura	180
Cambodia	181	70	11,340	Phnom Penh	300
Cameroon	475	184	15,029	Yaoundé	650
Canada	9,976	3,852	30,675	Ottawa	19,290
Canary Is. (Spain)	7.3	2.8	1,494	Las Palmas/Santa Cruz	–
Cape Verde Is.	4	1.6	399	Praia	1,010
Cayman Is. (UK)	0.26	0.10	35	George Town	20,000
Central African Republic	623	241	3,376	Bangui	320
Chad	1,284	496	7,360	Ndjaména	240
Chile	757	292	14,788	Santiago	5,020
China	9,597	3,705	1,236,915	Beijing	860
Colombia	1,139	440	38,581	Bogotá	2,280
Comoros	2.2	0.86	545	Moroni	450
Congo	342	132	2,658	Brazzaville	660
Congo (= Zaïre)	2,345	905	49,001	Kinshasa	110
Cook Is. (NZ)	0.24	0.09	20	Avarua	900
Costa Rica	51.1	19.7	3,605	San José	2,640
Croatia	56.5	21.8	4,672	Zagreb	4,610
Cuba	111	43	11,051	Havana	1,300
Cyprus	9.3	3.6	749	Nicosia	13,420
Czech Republic	78.9	30.4	10,286	Prague	5,200
Denmark	43.1	16.6	5,334	Copenhagen	32,500
Djibouti	23.2	9	650	Djibouti	850
Dominica	0.75	0.29	78	Roseau	3,090
Dominican Republic	48.7	18.8	7,999	Santo Domingo	1,670
Ecuador	284	109	12,337	Quito	1,590
Egypt	1,001	387	66,050	Cairo	1,180
El Salvador	21	8.1	5,752	San Salvador	1,810
Equatorial Guinea	28.1	10.8	454	Malabo	530
Eritrea	94	36	3,842	Asmara	570
Estonia	44.7	17.3	1,421	Tallinn	3,330
Ethiopia	1,128	436	58,390	Addis Ababa	110
Faroe Is. (Denmark)	1.4	0.54	41	Tórshavn	23,660
Fiji	18.3	7.1	802	Suva	2,470
Finland	338	131	5,149	Helsinki	24,080
France	552	213	58,805	Paris	26,050
French Guiana (France)	90	34.7	162	Cayenne	10,580
French Polynesia (France)	4	1.5	237	Papeete	7,500
Gabon	268	103	1,208	Libreville	4,230
Gambia, The	11.3	4.4	1,292	Banjul	320
Georgia	69.7	26.9	5,109	Tbilisi	840
Germany	357	138	82,079	Berlin/Bonn	28,260
Ghana	239	92	18,497	Accra	370
Gibraltar (UK)	0.007	0.003	29	Gibraltar Town	5,000
Greece	132	51	10,662	Athens	12,010
Greenland (Denmark)	2,176	840	59	Nuuk (Godthåb)	15,500
Grenada	0.34	0.13	96	St George's	2,880
Guadeloupe (France)	1.7	0.66	416	Basse-Terre	9,200
Guam (US)	0.55	0.21	149	Agana	6,000
Guatemala	109	42	12,008	Guatemala City	1,500
Guinea	246	95	7,477	Conakry	570
Guinea-Bissau	36.1	13.9	1,206	Bissau	240
Guyana	215	83	820	Georgetown	690
Haiti	27.8	10.7	6,781	Port-au-Prince	330
Honduras	112	43	5,862	Tegucigalpa	700
Hong Kong (China)	1.1	0.40	6,707	–	22,990
Hungary	93	35.9	10,208	Budapest	4,430
Iceland	103	40	271	Reykjavik	26,580
India	3,288	1,269	984,000	New Delhi	390
Indonesia	1,905	735	212,942	Jakarta	1,110
Iran	1,648	636	64,411	Tehran	4,700
Iraq	438	169	21,722	Baghdad	2,000
Ireland	70.3	27.1	3,619	Dublin	18,280
Israel	27	10.3	5,644	Jerusalem	15,810
Italy	301	116	56,783	Rome	20,120
Ivory Coast (Côte d'Ivoire)	322	125	15,446	Yamoussoukro	690
Jamaica	11	4.2	2,635	Kingston	1,560
Japan	378	146	125,932	Tokyo	37,850
Jordan	89.2	34.4	4,435	Amman	1,570
Kazakstan	2,717	1,049	16,847	Astana	1,340
Kenya	580	224	28,337	Nairobi	330
Kiribati	0.72	0.28	85	Tarawa	920
Korea, North	121	47	21,234	Pyŏngyang	1,000
Korea, South	99	38.2	46,417	Seoul	10,550
Kuwait	17.8	6.9	1,913	Kuwait City	17,390
Kyrgyzstan	198.5	76.6	4,522	Bishkek	440
Laos	237	91	5,261	Vientiane	400
Latvia	65	25	2,385	Riga	2,430
Lebanon	10.4	4	3,506	Beirut	3,350
Lesotho	30.4	11.7	2,090	Maseru	670
Liberia	111	43	2,772	Monrovia	770
Libya	1,760	679	4,875	Tripoli	6,510
Liechtenstein	0.16	0.06	32	Vaduz	33,000
Lithuania	65.2	25.2	3,600	Vilnius	2,230
Luxembourg	2.6	1	425	Luxembourg	45,360
Macau (China)	0.02	0.006	429	Macau	7,500
Macedonia	25.7	9.9	2,009	Skopje	1,090
Madagascar	587	227	14,463	Antananarivo	250
Madeira (Portugal)	0.81	0.31	253	Funchal	–
Malawi	118	46	9,840	Lilongwe	220
Malaysia	330	127	20,993	Kuala Lumpur	4,680
Maldives	0.30	0.12	290	Malé	1,080
Mali	1,240	479	10,109	Bamako	260
Malta	0.32	0.12	379	Valletta	12,000
Marshall Is.	0.18	0.07	63	Dalap-Uliga-Darrit	1,890
Martinique (France)	1.1	0.42	407	Fort-de-France	10,000
Mauritania	1,030	412	2,511	Nouakchott	450
Mauritius	2.0	0.72	1,168	Port Louis	3,800
Mayotte (France)	0.37	0.14	141	Mamoundzou	1,430
Mexico	1,958	756	98,553	Mexico City	3,680
Micronesia, Fed. States of	0.70	0.27	127	Palikir	2,070
Moldova	33.7	13	4,458	Chişinău	540
Monaco	0.002	0.0001	32	Monaco	25,000
Mongolia	1,567	605	2,579	Ulan Bator	390
Montserrat (UK)	0.10	0.04	12	Plymouth	4,500
Morocco	447	172	29,114	Rabat	1,250
Mozambique	802	309	18,641	Maputo	90
Namibia	825	318	1,622	Windhoek	2,220
Nauru	0.02	0.008	12	Yaren District	10,000
Nepal	141	54	23,698	Katmandu	210
Netherlands	41.5	16	15,731	Amsterdam/The Hague	25,820
Netherlands Antilles (Neths)	0.99	0.38	210	Willemstad	10,400
New Caledonia (France)	18.6	7.2	192	Nouméa	8,000
New Zealand	269	104	3,625	Wellington	16,480
Nicaragua	130	50	4,583	Managua	410
Niger	1,267	489	9,672	Niamey	200
Nigeria	924	357	110,532	Abuja	260
Northern Mariana Is. (US)	0.48	0.18	50	Saipan	11,500
Norway	324	125	4,420	Oslo	36,090
Oman	212	82	2,364	Muscat	4,950
Pakistan	796	307	135,135	Islamabad	490
Palau	0.46	0.18	18	Koror	5,000
Panama	77.1	29.8	2,736	Panama City	3,080
Papua New Guinea	463	179	4,600	Port Moresby	940
Paraguay	407	157	5,291	Asunción	2,010
Peru	1,285	496	26,111	Lima	2,460
Philippines	300	116	77,736	Manila	1,220
Poland	313	121	38,607	Warsaw	3,590
Portugal	92.4	35.7	9,928	Lisbon	10,450
Puerto Rico (US)	9	3.5	3,860	San Juan	7,800
Qatar	11	4.2	697	Doha	11,600
Réunion (France)	2.5	0.97	705	Saint-Denis	4,500
Romania	238	92	22,396	Bucharest	1,420
Russia	17,075	6,592	146,861	Moscow	2,740
Rwanda	26.3	10.2	7,956	Kigali	210
St Kitts & Nevis	0.36	0.14	42	Basseterre	5,870
St Lucia	0.62	0.24	150	Castries	3,500
St Vincent & Grenadines	0.39	0.15	120	Kingstown	2,370
San Marino	0.06	0.02	25	San Marino	20,000
São Tomé & Príncipe	0.96	0.37	150	São Tomé	330
Saudi Arabia	2,150	830	20,786	Riyadh	6,790
Senegal	197	76	9,723	Dakar	550
Seychelles	0.46	0.18	79	Victoria	6,850
Sierra Leone	71.7	27.7	5,080	Freetown	200
Singapore	0.62	0.24	3,490	Singapore	32,940
Slovak Republic	49	18.9	5,393	Bratislava	3,700
Slovenia	20.3	7.8	1,972	Ljubljana	9,680
Solomon Is.	28.9	11.2	441	Honiara	900
Somalia	638	246	6,842	Mogadishu	500
South Africa	1,220	471	42,835	C. Town/Pretoria/Bloem.	3,400
Spain	505	195	39,134	Madrid	14,510
Sri Lanka	65.6	25.3	18,934	Colombo	800
Sudan	2,506	967	33,551	Khartoum	800
Surinam	163	63	427	Paramaribo	1,000
Swaziland	17.4	6.7	966	Mbabane	1,210
Sweden	450	174	8,887	Stockholm	26,220
Switzerland	41.3	15.9	7,260	Bern	44,220
Syria	185	71	16,673	Damascus	1,150
Taiwan	36	13.9	21,908	Taipei	12,400
Tajikistan	143.1	55.2	6,020	Dushanbe	330
Tanzania	945	365	30,609	Dodoma	210
Thailand	513	198	60,037	Bangkok	2,800
Togo	56.8	21.9	4,906	Lomé	330
Tonga	0.75	0.29	107	Nuku'alofa	1,790
Trinidad & Tobago	5.1	2	1,117	Port of Spain	4,230
Tunisia	164	63	9,380	Tunis	2,090
Turkey	779	301	64,568	Ankara	3,130
Turkmenistan	488.1	188.5	4,298	Ashkhabad	630
Turks & Caicos Is. (UK)	0.43	0.17	16	Cockburn Town	5,000
Tuvalu	0.03	0.01	10	Fongafale	600
Uganda	236	91	22,167	Kampala	320
Ukraine	603.7	233.1	50,125	Kiev	1,040
United Arab Emirates	83.6	32.3	2,303	Abu Dhabi	17,360
United Kingdom	243.3	94	58,970	London	20,710
United States of America	9,373	3,619	270,290	Washington, DC	28,740
Uruguay	177	68	3,285	Montevideo	6,020
Uzbekistan	447.4	172.7	23,784	Tashkent	1,010
Vanuatu	12.2	4.7	185	Port-Vila	1,290
Venezuela	912	352	22,803	Caracas	3,450
Vietnam	332	127	76,236	Hanoi	320
Virgin Is. (UK)	0.15	0.06	13	Road Town	–
Virgin Is. (US)	0.34	0.13	118	Charlotte Amalie	12,000
Wallis & Futuna Is. (France)	0.20	0.08	15	Mata-Utu	–
Western Sahara	266	103	280	El Aaiún	300
Western Samoa	2.8	1.1	224	Apia	1,170
Yemen	528	204	16,388	Sana	270
Yugoslavia	102.3	39.5	10,500	Belgrade	2,000
Zambia	753	291	9,461	Lusaka	380
Zimbabwe	391	151	11,044	Harare	750

World Statistics: Cities

This list shows the principal cities with more than 500,000 inhabitants (for Brazil, China and India only cities with more than 1 million inhabitants are included). The figures are taken from the most recent census or population estimate available, and as far as possible are the population of the metropolitan area, e.g. greater New York, Mexico or Paris. All the figures are in thousands. Local name forms have been used for the smaller cities (e.g. Kraków).

AFGHANISTAN
Kabul 1,565
ALGERIA
Algiers 2,168
Oran 916
ANGOLA
Luanda 2,418
ARGENTINA
Buenos Aires 11,256
Córdoba 1,208
Rosario 1,118
Mendoza 773
La Plata 642
San Miguel de Tucumán 622
Mar del Plata 512
ARMENIA
Yerevan 1,248
AUSTRALIA
Sydney 3,770
Melbourne 3,217
Brisbane 1,489
Perth 1,262
Adelaide 1,080
AUSTRIA
Vienna 1,595
AZERBAIJAN
Baku 1,720
BANGLADESH
Dhaka 6,105
Chittagong 2,041
Khulna 877
Rajshahi 517
BELARUS
Minsk 1,700
Homyel 512
BELGIUM
Brussels 948
BENIN
Cotonou 537
BOLIVIA
La Paz 1,126
Santa Cruz 767
BOSNIA-HERZEGOVINA
Sarajevo 526
BRAZIL
São Paulo 16,417
Rio de Janeiro 9,888
Salvador 2,211
Belo Horizonte 2,091
Fortaleza 1,965
Brasília 1,821
Curitiba 1,476
Recife 1,346
Pôrto Alegre 1,288
Manaus 1,157
Belém 1,144
Goiânia 1,004
BULGARIA
Sofia 1,116
BURKINA FASO
Ouagadougou 690
BURMA (MYANMAR)
Rangoon 2,513
Mandalay 533
CAMBODIA
Phnom Penh 920
CAMEROON
Douala 1,200
Yaoundé 800
CANADA
Toronto 4,344
Montréal 3,337
Vancouver 1,831
Ottawa-Hull 1,022
Edmonton 885
Calgary 831
Québec 693
Winnipeg 677
Hamilton 643
CENTRAL AFRICAN REP.
Bangui 553
CHAD
Ndjaména 530
CHILE
Santiago 5,067
CHINA
Shanghai 15,082
Beijing 12,362
Tianjin 10,687
Hong Kong (SAR)* 6,502
Chongqing 3,870
Shenyang 3,860
Wuhan 3,520
Guangzhou 3,114
Harbin 2,505
Nanjing 2,211
Xi'an 2,115
Chengdu 1,933
Dalian 1,855
Changchun 1,810
Jinan 1,660
Taiyuan 1,642
Qingdao 1,584
Fuzhou, Fujian 1,380
Zibo 1,346
Zhengzhou 1,324

Lanzhou 1,296
Anshan 1,252
Fushun 1,246
Kunming 1,242
Changsha 1,198
Hangzhou 1,185
Nanchang 1,169
Shijiazhuang 1,159
Guiyang 1,131
Ürümqi 1,130
Jilin 1,118
Tangshan 1,110
Qiqihar 1,104
Baotou 1,033
Hefei 1,000
COLOMBIA
Bogotá 6,004
Cali 1,985
Medellín 1,970
Barranquilla 1,157
Cartagena 812
CONGO
Brazzaville 937
Pointe-Noire 576
CONGO (ZAÏRE)
Kinshasa 1,655
Lubumbashi 851
Mbuji-Mayi 806
COSTA RICA
San José 1,220
CROATIA
Zagreb 931
CUBA
Havana 2,241
CZECH REPUBLIC
Prague 1,209
DENMARK
Copenhagen 1,362
DOMINICAN REPUBLIC
Santo Domingo 2,135
Santiago 691
ECUADOR
Guayaquil 1,973
Quito 1,487
EGYPT
Cairo 9,900
Alexandria 3,431
El Gîza 2,144
Shubra el Kheima 834
EL SALVADOR
San Salvador 1,522
ETHIOPIA
Addis Ababa 2,112
FINLAND
Helsinki 532
FRANCE
Paris 9,319
Lyon 1,262
Marseille 1,087
Lille 959
Bordeaux 696
Toulouse 650
Nice 516
GEORGIA
Tbilisi 1,300
GERMANY
Berlin 3,470
Hamburg 1,706
Munich 1,240
Cologne 964
Frankfurt 651
Essen 616
Dortmund 600
Stuttgart 587
Düsseldorf 571
Bremen 549
Duisburg 535
Hanover 524
GHANA
Accra 949
GREECE
Athens 3,097
GUATEMALA
Guatemala 1,167
GUINEA
Conakry 1,508
HAITI
Port-au-Prince 1,255
HONDURAS
Tegucigalpa 813
HUNGARY
Budapest 1,885
INDIA
Bombay (Mumbai) 12,572
Calcutta 10,916
Delhi 7,207
Madras (Chennai) 5,361
Hyderabad 4,280
Bangalore 4,087
Ahmadabad 3,298
Pune 2,485
Kanpur 2,111
Nagpur 1,661
Lucknow 1,642
Surat 1,517
Jaipur 1,514

Coimbatore 1,136
Vadodara 1,115
Indore 1,104
Patna 1,099
Madurai 1,094
Bhopal 1,064
Vishakhapatnam 1,052
Varanasi 1,026
Ludhiana 1,012
INDONESIA
Jakarta 11,500
Surabaya 2,701
Bandung 2,368
Medan 1,910
Semarang 1,366
Palembang 1,352
Tangerang 1,198
Ujung Pandang 1,092
Bandar Lampung 832
Malang 763
Padang 721
Pakanbaru 558
Samarinda 536
Banjarmasin 535
Surakarta 516
IRAN
Tehran 6,750
Mashhad 1,964
Esfahan 1,221
Tabriz 1,166
Shiraz 1,043
Ahvaz 828
Qom 780
Bakhtaran 666
Karaj 588
IRAQ
Baghdad 3,841
Diyala 961
As Sulaymaniyah 952
Arbil 770
Al Mawsil 664
Kadhimain 521
IRELAND
Dublin 952
ISRAEL
Tel Aviv-Yafo 1,502
Jerusalem 591
ITALY
Rome 2,775
Milan 1,369
Naples 1,067
Turin 962
Palermo 698
Genoa 678
IVORY COAST
Abidjan 2,500
JAMAICA
Kingston 644
JAPAN
Tokyo-Yokohama 26,836
Osaka 10,601
Nagoya 2,152
Sapporo 1,757
Kyoto 1,464
Kobe 1,424
Fukuoka 1,285
Kawasaki 1,203
Hiroshima 1,109
Kitakyushu 1,020
Sendai 971
Chiba 857
Sakai 803
Kumamoto 650
Okayama 616
Sagamihara 571
Hamamatsu 562
Kagoshima 546
Funabashi 541
Higashiosaka 517
Hachioji 503
JORDAN
Amman 1,300
Az-Zarqā 609
KAZAKSTAN
Almaty 1,150
Qaraghandy 573
KENYA
Nairobi 2,000
Mombasa 600
KOREA, NORTH
Pyŏngyang 2,639
Hamhung 775
Chŏngjin 754
Chinnampo 691
Sinŭiju 500
KOREA, SOUTH
Seoul 11,641
Pusan 3,814
Taegu 2,449
Inchon 2,308
Taejŏn 1,272
Kwangju 1,258
Ulsan 967
Sŏngnam 869
Puch'on 779
Suwŏn 756

Anyang 590
Chŏnju 563
Chŏngju 531
Ansan 510
P'ohang 509
KYRGYZSTAN
Bishkek 584
LATVIA
Riga 846
LEBANON
Beirut 1,900
Tripoli 500
LIBYA
Tripoli 1,083
LITHUANIA
Vilnius 580
MACEDONIA
Skopje 541
MADAGASCAR
Antananarivo 1,053
MALAYSIA
Kuala Lumpur 1,145
MALI
Bamako 800
MAURITANIA
Nouakchott 735
MEXICO
Mexico City 15,048
Guadalajara 2,847
Monterrey 2,522
Puebla 1,055
León 872
Ciudad Juárez 798
Tijuana 743
Culiacán Rosales 602
Mexicali 602
Acapulco de Juárez 592
Mérida 557
Chihuahua 530
San Luis Potosí 526
Aguascalientés 506
MOLDOVA
Chişinău 700
MONGOLIA
Ulan Bator 627
MOROCCO
Casablanca 3,079
Rabat-Salé 1,344
Fès 735
Marrakesh 621
MOZAMBIQUE
Maputo 2,000
NEPAL
Katmandu 535
NETHERLANDS
Amsterdam 1,101
Rotterdam 1,076
The Hague 694
Utrecht 548
NEW ZEALAND
Auckland 997
NICARAGUA
Managua 864
NIGERIA
Lagos 10,287
Ibadan 1,365
Ogbomosho 712
Kano 657
NORWAY
Oslo 714
PAKISTAN
Karachi 9,863
Lahore 5,085
Faisalabad 1,875
Peshawar 1,676
Gujranwala 1,663
Rawalpindi 1,290
Multan 1,257
Hyderabad 1,107
PARAGUAY
Asunción 945
PERU
Lima-Callao 6,601
Callao 638
Arequipa 620
Trujillo 509
PHILIPPINES
Manila 9,280
Quezon City 1,989
Davao 1,191
Caloocan 1,023
Cebu 662
Zamboanga 511
POLAND
Warsaw 1,638
Łódź 825
Kraków 745
Wrocław 642
Poznań 581
PORTUGAL
Lisbon 2,561
Oporto 1,174
ROMANIA
Bucharest 2,060
RUSSIA
Moscow 9,233

Petersburg 4,883
Nizhniy Novgorod 1,425
Novosibirsk 1,400
Yekaterinburg 1,300
Samara 1,200
Omsk 1,200
Chelyabinsk 1,100
Kazan 1,100
Ufa 1,100
Volgograd 1,003
Perm 1,000
Rostov 1,000
Voronezh 908
Saratov 895
Krasnoyarsk 869
Togliatti 689
Simbirsk 678
Izhevsk 654
Krasnodar 645
Vladivostok 632
Yaroslavl 629
Khabarovsk 618
Barnaul 596
Irkutsk 585
Novokuznetsk 572
Ryazan 536
Penza 534
Orenburg 532
Tula 532
Naberezhnyye-Chelny 526
Kemerovo 503
SAUDI ARABIA
Riyadh 1,800
Jedda 1,500
Mecca 630
SENEGAL
Dakar 1,571
SIERRA LEONE
Freetown 505
SINGAPORE
Singapore 3,104
SOMALIA
Mogadishu 1,000
SOUTH AFRICA
Cape Town 2,350
East Rand 1,379
Johannesburg 1,196
Durban 1,137
Pretoria 1,080
West Rand 870
Port Elizabeth 853
Vanderbijlpark-Vereeniging 774
Soweto 597
Sasolburg 540
SPAIN
Madrid 3,029
Barcelona 1,614
Valencia 763
Sevilla 719
Zaragoza 607
Málaga 532
SRI LANKA
Colombo 1,863
SUDAN
Nyala 1,267
Khartoum 925
Sharg el Nil 879
SWEDEN
Stockholm 1,744
Göteburg 775
SWITZERLAND
Zürich 1,175
Bern 942
SYRIA
Aleppo 1,591
Damascus 1,549
Homs 644
TAIWAN
Taipei 2,653
Kaohsiung 1,405
Taichung 817
Tainan 700
Panchiao 544
TAJIKISTAN
Dushanbe 524
TANZANIA
Dar-es-Salaam 1,361
THAILAND
Bangkok 5,572
TOGO
Lomé 590
TUNISIA
Tunis 1,827
TURKEY
Istanbul 7,490
Ankara 3,028
Izmir 2,333
Adana 1,472
Bursa 1,317
Konya 1,040
Gaziantep 930
Icel 908
Antalya 734
Diyarbakir 677
Kocaeli 661
Urfa 649

Kayseri 648
Manisa 641
Hatay 561
Samsun 557
Eskisehir 508
Balikesir 501
TURKMENISTAN
Ashkhabad 536
UGANDA
Kampala 773
UKRAINE
Kiev 2,630
Kharkiv 1,555
Dnipropetrovsk 1,147
Donetsk 1,088
Odesa 1,046
Zaporizhzhya 887
Lviv 802
Kryvyy Rih 720
Mariupol 510
Mykolayiv 508
UNITED KINGDOM
London 8,089
Birmingham 2,373
Manchester 2,353
Liverpool 852
Glasgow 832
Sheffield 661
Nottingham 649
Newcastle 617
Bristol 552
Leeds 529
UNITED STATES
New York 16,329
Los Angeles 12,410
Chicago 7,668
Philadelphia 4,949
Washington, DC 4,466
Detroit 4,307
Houston 3,653
Atlanta 3,331
Boston 3,240
Dallas 2,898
Minneapolis-St Paul 2,688
San Diego 2,632
St Louis 2,536
Phoenix 2,473
Baltimore 2,458
Pittsburgh 2,402
Cleveland 2,222
San Francisco 2,182
Seattle 2,180
Tampa 2,157
Miami 2,025
Newark 1,934
Denver 1,796
Portland (Or.) 1,676
Kansas City (Mo.) 1,647
Cincinnati 1,581
San Jose 1,557
Norfolk 1,529
Indianapolis 1,462
Milwaukee 1,456
Sacramento 1,441
San Antonio 1,437
Columbus (Oh.) 1,423
New Orleans 1,309
Charlotte 1,260
Buffalo 1,189
Salt Lake City 1,178
Hartford 1,151
Oklahoma 1,007
Jacksonville (Fl.) 665
Omaha 663
Memphis 614
El Paso 579
Austin 514
Nashville 505
URUGUAY
Montevideo 1,378
UZBEKISTAN
Tashkent 2,107
VENEZUELA
Caracas 2,784
Maracaibo 1,364
Valencia 1,032
Maracay 800
Barquisimeto 745
Ciudad Guayana 524
VIETNAM
Ho Chi Minh City 4,322
Hanoi 3,056
Haiphong 783
YEMEN
Sana 972
Aden 562
YUGOSLAVIA
Belgrade 1,137
ZAMBIA
Lusaka 982
ZIMBABWE
Harare 1,189
Bulawayo 622

* SAR = Special Administrative Region of China

World Statistics: Climate

Rainfall and temperature figures are provided for more than 70 cities around the world. As climate is affected by altitude, the height of each city is shown in metres beneath its name. For each location, the top row of figures shows the total rainfall or snow in millimetres, and the bottom row the average temperature in degrees Celsius; the average annual temperature and total annual rainfall are at the end of the rows. The map opposite shows the city locations.

CITY	JAN.	FEB.	MAR.	APR.	MAY	JUNE	JULY	AUG.	SEPT.	OCT.	NOV.	DEC.	YEAR
EUROPE													
Athens, Greece	62	37	37	23	23	14	6	7	15	51	56	71	402
107 m	10	10	12	16	20	25	28	28	24	20	15	11	18
Berlin, Germany	46	40	33	42	49	65	73	69	48	49	46	43	603
55 m	-1	0	4	9	14	17	19	18	15	9	5	1	9
Istanbul, Turkey	109	92	72	46	38	34	34	30	58	81	103	119	816
14 m	5	6	7	11	16	20	23	23	20	16	12	8	14
Lisbon, Portugal	111	76	109	54	44	16	3	4	33	62	93	103	708
77 m	11	12	14	16	17	20	22	23	21	18	14	12	17
London, UK	54	40	37	37	46	45	57	59	49	57	64	48	593
5 m	4	5	7	9	12	16	18	17	15	11	8	5	11
Málaga, Spain	61	51	62	46	26	5	1	3	29	64	64	62	474
33 m	12	13	16	17	19	29	25	26	23	20	16	13	18
Moscow, Russia	39	38	36	37	53	58	88	71	58	45	47	54	624
156 m	-13	-10	-4	6	13	16	18	17	12	6	-1	-7	4
Odesa, Ukraine	57	62	30	21	34	34	42	37	37	13	35	71	473
64 m	-3	-1	2	9	15	20	22	22	18	12	9	1	10
Paris, France	56	46	35	42	57	54	59	64	55	50	51	50	619
75 m	3	4	8	11	15	18	20	19	17	12	7	4	12
Rome, Italy	71	62	57	51	46	37	15	21	63	99	129	93	744
17 m	8	9	11	14	18	22	24	25	22	17	13	10	16
Shannon, Ireland	94	67	56	53	61	57	77	79	86	86	96	117	929
2 m	5	5	7	9	12	14	16	16	14	11	8	6	10
Stockholm, Sweden	43	30	25	31	34	45	61	76	60	48	53	48	554
44 m	-3	-3	-1	5	10	15	18	17	12	7	3	0	7
ASIA													
Bahrain	8	18	13	8	<3	0	0	0	0	0	18	18	81
5 m	17	18	21	25	29	32	33	34	31	28	24	19	26
Bangkok, Thailand	8	20	36	58	198	160	160	175	305	206	66	5	1,397
2 m	26	28	29	30	29	29	28	28	28	28	26	25	28
Beirut, Lebanon	191	158	94	53	18	3	<3	<3	5	51	132	185	892
34 m	14	14	16	18	22	24	27	28	26	24	19	16	21
Bombay (Mumbai), India	3	3	3	<3	18	485	617	340	264	64	13	3	1,809
11 m	24	24	26	28	30	29	27	27	27	28	27	26	27
Calcutta, India	10	31	36	43	140	297	325	328	252	114	20	5	1,600
6 m	20	22	27	30	30	30	29	29	29	28	23	19	26
Colombo, Sri Lanka	89	69	147	231	371	224	135	109	160	348	315	147	2,365
7 m	26	26	27	28	28	27	27	27	27	27	26	26	27
Harbin, China	6	5	10	23	43	94	112	104	46	33	8	5	488
160 m	-18	-15	-5	6	13	19	22	21	14	4	-6	-16	3
ASIA (continued)													
Ho Chi Minh, Vietnam	15	3	13	43	221	330	315	269	335	269	114	56	1,984
9 m	26	27	29	30	29	28	28	28	27	27	27	26	28
Hong Kong, China	33	46	74	137	292	394	381	361	257	114	43	31	2,162
33 m	16	15	18	22	26	28	28	28	27	25	21	18	23
Jakarta, Indonesia	300	300	211	147	114	97	64	43	66	112	142	203	1,798
8 m	26	26	27	27	27	27	27	27	27	27	27	26	27
Kabul, Afghanistan	31	36	94	102	20	5	3	3	<3	15	20	10	338
1,815 m	-3	-1	6	13	18	22	25	24	20	14	7	3	12
Karachi, Pakistan	13	10	8	3	3	18	81	41	13	<3	3	5	196
4 m	19	20	24	28	30	31	30	29	28	28	24	20	26
Kazalinsk, Kazakstan	10	10	13	13	15	5	5	8	8	10	13	15	125
63 m	-12	-11	-3	6	18	23	25	23	16	8	-1	-7	7
New Delhi, India	23	18	13	8	13	74	180	172	117	10	3	10	640
218 m	14	17	23	28	33	34	31	30	29	26	20	15	25
Omsk, Russia	15	8	8	13	31	51	51	51	28	25	18	20	318
85 m	-22	-19	-12	-1	10	16	18	16	10	1	-11	-18	-1
Shanghai, China	48	58	84	94	94	180	147	142	130	71	51	36	1,135
7 m	4	5	9	14	20	24	28	28	23	19	12	7	16
Singapore	252	173	193	188	173	173	170	196	178	208	254	257	2,413
10 m	26	27	28	28	28	28	27	27	27	27	27	27	27
Tehran, Iran	46	38	46	36	13	3	3	3	3	8	20	31	246
1,220 m	2	5	9	16	21	26	30	29	25	18	12	6	17
Tokyo, Japan	48	74	107	135	147	165	142	152	234	208	97	56	1,565
6 m	3	4	7	13	17	21	25	26	23	17	11	6	14
Ulan Bator, Mongolia	<3	<3	3	5	10	28	76	51	23	5	5	3	208
1,325 m	-26	-21	-13	-1	6	14	16	14	8	-1	-13	-22	-3
Verkhoyansk, Russia	5	5	3	5	8	23	28	25	13	8	8	5	134
100 m	-50	-45	-32	-15	0	12	14	9	2	-15	-38	-48	-17
AFRICA													
Addis Ababa, Ethiopia	<3	3	25	135	213	201	206	239	102	28	<3	0	1,151
2,450 m	19	20	20	20	19	18	18	19	21	22	21	20	20
Antananarivo, Madag.	300	279	178	53	18	8	8	10	18	61	135	287	1,356
1,372 m	21	21	21	19	18	15	14	15	17	19	21	21	19
Cairo, Egypt	5	5	5	3	3	<3	0	0	<3	<3	3	5	28
116 m	13	15	18	21	25	28	28	28	26	24	20	15	22
Cape Town, S. Africa	15	8	18	48	79	84	89	66	43	31	18	10	508
17 m	21	21	20	17	14	13	12	13	14	16	18	19	17
Jo'burg, S. Africa	114	109	89	38	25	8	8	8	23	56	107	125	709
1,665 m	20	20	18	16	13	10	11	13	16	18	19	20	16

CITY	JAN.	FEB.	MAR.	APR.	MAY	JUNE	JULY	AUG.	SEPT.	OCT.	NOV.	DEC.	YEAR
AFRICA (continued)													
Khartoum, Sudan	<3	<3	<3	<3	3	8	53	71	18	5	<3	0	158
390 m	24	25	28	31	33	34	32	31	32	32	28	25	29
Kinshasa, Congo (Z.)	135	145	196	196	158	8	3	3	31	119	221	142	1,354
325 m	26	26	27	27	26	24	23	24	25	26	26	26	25
Lagos, Nigeria	28	46	102	150	269	460	279	64	140	206	69	25	1,836
3 m	27	28	29	28	28	26	26	25	26	26	28	28	27
Lusaka, Zambia	231	191	142	18	3	<3	<3	0	<3	10	91	150	836
1,277 m	21	22	21	21	19	16	16	18	22	24	23	22	21
Monrovia, Liberia	31	56	97	216	516	973	996	373	744	772	236	130	5,138
23 m	26	26	27	27	26	25	24	25	25	25	26	26	26
Nairobi, Kenya	38	64	125	211	158	46	15	23	31	53	109	86	958
820 m	19	19	19	19	18	16	16	16	18	19	18	18	18
Timbuktu, Mali	<3	<3	3	<3	5	23	79	81	38	3	<3	<3	231
301 m	22	24	28	32	34	35	32	30	32	31	28	23	29
Tunis, Tunisia	64	51	41	36	18	8	3	8	33	51	48	61	419
66 m	10	11	13	16	19	23	26	27	25	20	16	11	18
Walvis Bay, Namibia	<3	5	8	3	3	<3	<3	3	<3	<3	<3	<3	23
7 m	19	19	19	18	17	16	15	14	14	15	17	18	18
AUSTRALIA, NEW ZEALAND AND ANTARCTICA													
Alice Springs, Aust.	43	33	28	10	15	13	8	8	8	18	31	38	252
579 m	29	28	25	20	15	12	12	14	18	23	26	28	21
Christchurch, N.Z.	56	43	48	48	66	66	69	48	46	43	48	56	638
10 m	16	16	14	12	9	6	6	7	9	12	14	16	11
Darwin, Australia	386	312	254	97	15	3	<3	3	13	51	119	239	1,491
30 m	29	29	29	29	28	26	25	26	28	29	30	29	28
Mawson, Antarctica	11	30	20	10	44	180	4	40	3	20	0	0	362
14 m	0	−5	−10	−14	−15	−16	−18	−18	−19	−13	−5	−1	−11
Perth, Australia	8	10	20	43	130	180	170	149	86	56	20	13	881
60 m	23	23	22	19	16	14	13	13	15	16	19	22	18
Sydney, Australia	89	102	127	135	127	117	117	76	73	71	73	73	1,181
42 m	22	22	21	18	15	13	12	13	15	18	19	21	17
NORTH AMERICA													
Anchorage, USA	20	18	15	10	13	18	41	66	66	56	25	23	371
40 m	−11	−8	−5	2	7	12	14	13	9	2	−5	−11	2
Chicago, USA	51	51	66	71	86	89	84	81	79	66	61	51	836
251 m	−4	−3	2	9	14	20	23	22	19	12	5	−1	10
Churchill, Canada	15	13	18	23	32	44	46	58	51	43	39	21	402
13 m	−28	−26	−20	−10	−2	6	12	11	5	−2	−12	−22	−7
Edmonton, Canada	25	19	19	22	43	77	89	78	39	17	16	25	466
676 m	−15	−10	−5	4	11	15	17	16	11	6	−4	−10	3
Honolulu, USA	104	66	79	48	25	18	23	28	36	48	64	104	643
12 m	23	18	19	20	22	24	25	26	26	24	22	19	22
Houston, USA	89	76	84	91	119	117	99	99	104	94	89	109	1,171
12 m	12	13	17	21	24	27	28	29	26	22	16	12	21

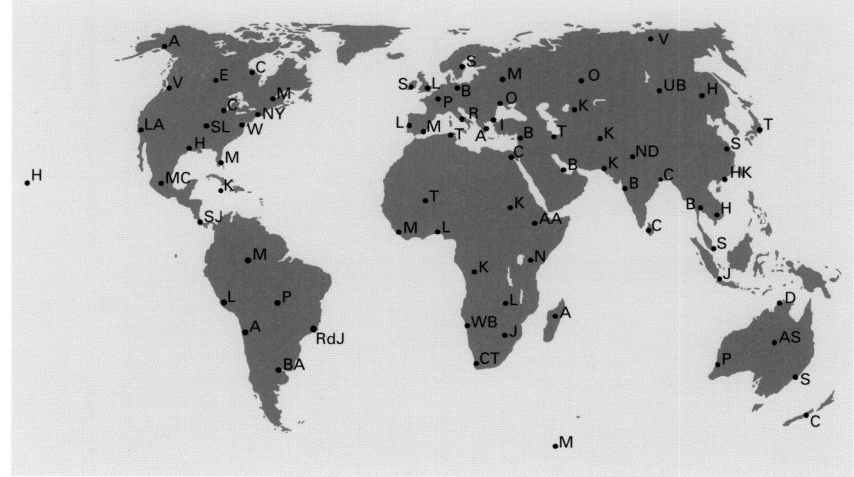

CITY	JAN.	FEB.	MAR.	APR.	MAY	JUNE	JULY	AUG.	SEPT.	OCT.	NOV.	DEC.	YEAR
NORTH AMERICA (continued)													
Kingston, Jamaica	23	15	23	31	102	89	38	91	99	180	74	36	800
34 m	25	25	25	26	26	28	28	28	27	27	26	26	26
Los Angeles, USA	79	76	71	25	10	3	<3	<3	5	15	31	66	381
95 m	13	14	14	16	17	19	21	22	21	18	16	14	17
Mexico City, Mexico	13	5	10	20	53	119	170	152	130	51	18	8	747
2,309 m	12	13	16	18	19	19	17	18	18	16	14	13	16
Miami, USA	71	53	64	81	173	178	155	160	203	234	71	51	1,516
8 m	20	20	22	23	25	27	28	28	27	25	22	21	24
Montréal, Canada	72	65	74	74	66	82	90	92	88	76	81	87	946
57 m	−10	−9	−3	−6	13	18	21	20	15	9	2	−7	6
New York City, USA	94	97	91	81	81	84	107	109	86	89	76	91	1,092
96 m	−1	−1	3	10	16	20	23	23	21	15	7	2	11
St Louis, USA	58	64	89	97	114	114	89	86	81	74	71	64	1,001
173 m	0	1	7	13	19	24	26	26	22	15	8	2	14
San José, Costa Rica	15	5	20	46	229	241	211	241	305	300	145	41	1,798
1,146 m	19	19	21	21	22	21	21	21	21	20	20	19	20
Vancouver, Canada	154	115	101	60	52	45	32	41	67	114	150	182	1,113
14 m	3	5	6	9	12	15	17	17	14	10	6	4	10
Washington, DC, USA	86	76	91	84	94	99	112	109	94	74	66	79	1,064
22 m	1	2	7	12	18	23	25	24	20	14	8	3	13
SOUTH AMERICA													
Antofagasta, Chile	0	0	0	<3	<3	3	5	3	<3	3	<3	0	13
94 m	21	21	20	18	16	15	14	14	15	16	18	19	17
Buenos Aires, Arg.	79	71	109	89	76	61	56	61	79	86	84	99	950
27 m	23	23	21	17	13	9	10	11	13	15	19	22	16
Lima, Peru	3	<3	<3	<3	5	5	8	8	8	3	3	<3	41
120 m	23	24	24	22	19	17	17	16	17	18	19	21	20
Manaus, Brazil	249	231	262	221	170	84	58	38	46	107	142	203	1,811
44 m	28	28	28	27	28	28	28	28	29	29	29	28	28
Paraná, Brazil	287	236	239	102	13	<3	3	5	28	127	231	310	1,582
260 m	23	23	23	23	23	21	21	22	24	24	24	23	23
Rio de Janeiro, Brazil	125	122	130	107	79	53	41	43	66	79	104	137	1,082
61 m	26	26	25	24	22	21	21	21	21	22	23	25	23

World Statistics: Physical Dimensions

Each topic list is divided into continents and within a continent the items are listed in order of size. The order of the continents is as in the atlas, Europe through to South America. The lists down to this mark > are complete; below they are selective. The world top ten are shown in square brackets; in the case of mountains this has not been done because the world top 30 are all in Asia. The figures are rounded as appropriate.

WORLD, CONTINENTS, OCEANS

THE WORLD

	km²	miles²	%
The World	509,450,000	196,672,000	–
Land	149,450,000	57,688,000	29.3
Water	360,000,000	138,984,000	70.7
Asia	44,500,000	17,177,000	29.8
Africa	30,302,000	11,697,000	20.3
North America	24,241,000	9,357,000	16.2
South America	17,793,000	6,868,000	11.9
Antarctica	14,100,000	5,443,000	9.4
Europe	9,957,000	3,843,000	6.7
Australia & Oceania	8,557,000	3,303,000	5.7
Pacific Ocean	179,679,000	69,356,000	49.9
Atlantic Ocean	92,373,000	35,657,000	25.7
Indian Ocean	73,917,000	28,532,000	20.5
Arctic Ocean	14,090,000	5,439,000	3.9

SEAS

South China Sea	2,974,600	1,148,500
Bering Sea	2,268,000	875,000
Sea of Okhotsk	1,528,000	590,000
East China & Yellow	1,249,000	482,000
Sea of Japan	1,008,000	389,000
Gulf of California	162,000	62,500
Bass Strait	75,000	29,000

ATLANTIC	km²	miles²
Caribbean Sea	2,766,000	1,068,000
Mediterranean Sea	2,516,000	971,000
Gulf of Mexico	1,543,000	596,000
Hudson Bay	1,232,000	476,000
North Sea	575,000	223,000
Black Sea	462,000	178,000
Baltic Sea	422,170	163,000
Gulf of St Lawrence	238,000	92,000

INDIAN	km²	miles²
Red Sea	438,000	169,000
The Gulf	239,000	92,000

MOUNTAINS

EUROPE		m	ft
Elbrus	Russia	5,642	18,510
Mont Blanc	France/Italy	4,807	15,771
Monte Rosa	Italy/Switzerland	4,634	15,203
Dom	Switzerland	4,545	14,911
Liskamm	Switzerland	4,527	14,852
Weisshorn	Switzerland	4,505	14,780
Taschorn	Switzerland	4,490	14,730
Matterhorn/Cervino	Italy/Switz.	4,478	14,691
Mont Maudit	France/Italy	4,465	14,649
Dent Blanche	Switzerland	4,356	14,291
Nadelhorn	Switzerland	4,327	14,196
> Grandes Jorasses	France/Italy	4,208	13,806
Jungfrau	Switzerland	4,158	13,642
Barre des Ecrins	France	4,103	13,461
Gran Paradiso	Italy	4,061	13,323
Piz Bernina	Italy/Switzerland	4,049	13,284
Eiger	Switzerland	3,970	13,025
Monte Viso	Italy	3,841	12,602
Grossglockner	Austria	3,797	12,457
Wildspitze	Austria	3,772	12,382
Monte Disgrazia	Italy	3,678	12,066
Mulhacén	Spain	3,478	11,411
Pico de Aneto	Spain	3,404	11,168
Marmolada	Italy	3,342	10,964
Etna	Italy	3,340	10,958
Zugspitze	Germany	2,962	9,718
Musala	Bulgaria	2,925	9,596
Olympus	Greece	2,917	9,570
Triglav	Slovenia	2,863	9,393
Monte Cinto	France (Corsica)	2,710	8,891
Gerlachovka	Slovak Republic	2,655	8,711
Galdhöpiggen	Norway	2,468	8,100
Hvannadalshnúkur	Iceland	2,119	6,952
Ben Nevis	UK	1,343	4,406

ASIA		m	ft
Everest	China/Nepal	8,848	29,029
K2 (Godwin Austen)	China/Kashmir	8,611	28,251
Kanchenjunga	India/Nepal	8,598	28,208
Lhotse	China/Nepal	8,516	27,939
Makalu	China/Nepal	8,481	27,824
Cho Oyu	China/Nepal	8,201	26,906
Dhaulagiri	Nepal	8,172	26,811
Manaslu	Nepal	8,156	26,758
Nanga Parbat	Kashmir	8,126	26,660
Annapurna	Nepal	8,078	26,502
Gasherbrum	China/Kashmir	8,068	26,469
Broad Peak	China/Kashmir	8,051	26,414
Xixabangma	China	8,012	26,286
Kangbachen	India/Nepal	7,902	25,925
Jannu	India/Nepal	7,902	25,925
Gayachung Kang	Nepal	7,897	25,909
Himalchuli	Nepal	7,893	25,896
Disteghil Sar	Kashmir	7,885	25,869
Nuptse	Nepal	7,879	25,849
Khunyang Chhish	Kashmir	7,852	25,761
Masherbrum	Kashmir	7,821	25,659
Nanda Devi	India	7,817	25,646
Rakaposhi	Kashmir	7,788	25,551
Batura	Kashmir	7,785	25,541
Namche Barwa	China	7,756	25,446
Kamet	India	7,756	25,446
Soltoro Kangri	Kashmir	7,742	25,400
Gurla Mandhata	China	7,728	25,354
Trivor	Pakistan	7,720	25,328
> Kongur Shan	China	7,719	25,324
Tirich Mir	Pakistan	7,690	25,229
K'ula Shan	Bhutan/China	7,543	24,747
Pik Kommunizma	Tajikistan	7,495	24,590
Demavend	Iran	5,604	18,386
Ararat	Turkey	5,165	16,945
Gunong Kinabalu	Malaysia (Borneo)	4,101	13,455
Yu Shan	Taiwan	3,997	13,113
Fuji-San	Japan	3,776	12,388

AFRICA		m	ft
Kilimanjaro	Tanzania	5,895	19,340
Mt Kenya	Kenya	5,199	17,057
Ruwenzori (Margherita)	Uganda/Congo (Z.)	5,109	16,762
Ras Dashan	Ethiopia	4,620	15,157
Meru	Tanzania	4,565	14,977
Karisimbi	Rwanda/Congo (Z.)	4,507	14,787
Mt Elgon	Kenya/Uganda	4,321	14,176
Batu	Ethiopia	4,307	14,130
Guna	Ethiopia	4,231	13,882
Toubkal	Morocco	4,165	13,665
Irhil Mgoun	Morocco	4,071	13,356
Mt Cameroon	Cameroon	4,070	13,353
Amba Ferit	Ethiopia	3,875	13,042
Pico del Teide	Spain (Tenerife)	3,718	12,198
Thabana Ntlenyana	Lesotho	3,482	11,424
Emi Koussi	Chad	3,415	11,204
> Mt aux Sources	Lesotho/S. Africa	3,282	10,768
Mt Piton	Réunion	3,069	10,069

OCEANIA		m	ft
Puncak Jaya	Indonesia	5,029	16,499
Puncak Trikora	Indonesia	4,750	15,584
Puncak Mandala	Indonesia	4,702	15,427
Mt Wilhelm	Papua NG	4,508	14,790
> Mauna Kea	USA (Hawaii)	4,205	13,796
Mauna Loa	USA (Hawaii)	4,170	13,681
Mt Cook (Aoraki)	New Zealand	3,753	12,313
Mt Balbi	Solomon Is.	2,439	8,002
Orohena	Tahiti	2,241	7,352
Mt Kosciuszko	Australia	2,237	7,339

NORTH AMERICA		m	ft
Mt McKinley (Denali)	USA (Alaska)	6,194	20,321
Mt Logan	Canada	5,959	19,551
Citlaltepetl	Mexico	5,700	18,701
Mt St Elias	USA/Canada	5,489	18,008
Popocatepetl	Mexico	5,452	17,887

NORTH AMERICA (continued)		m	ft
Mt Foraker	USA (Alaska)	5,304	17,401
Ixtaccihuatl	Mexico	5,286	17,342
Lucania	Canada	5,227	17,149
Mt Steele	Canada	5,073	16,644
Mt Bona	USA (Alaska)	5,005	16,420
Mt Blackburn	USA (Alaska)	4,996	16,391
Mt Sanford	USA (Alaska)	4,940	16,207
Mt Wood	Canada	4,848	15,905
Nevado de Toluca	Mexico	4,670	15,321
Mt Fairweather	USA (Alaska)	4,663	15,298
Mt Hunter	USA (Alaska)	4,442	14,573
Mt Whitney	USA	4,418	14,495
Mt Elbert	USA	4,399	14,432
Mt Harvard	USA	4,395	14,419
Mt Rainier	USA	4,392	14,409
> Blanca Peak	USA	4,372	14,344
Longs Peak	USA	4,345	14,255
Tajumulco	Guatemala	4,220	13,845
Grand Teton	USA	4,197	13,770
Mt Waddington	Canada	3,994	13,104
Mt Robson	Canada	3,954	12,972
Chirripó Grande	Costa Rica	3,837	12,589
Pico Duarte	Dominican Rep.	3,175	10,417

SOUTH AMERICA		m	ft
Aconcagua	Argentina	6,960	22,834
Bonete	Argentina	6,872	22,546
Ojos del Salado	Argentina/Chile	6,863	22,516
Pissis	Argentina	6,779	22,241
Mercedario	Argentina/Chile	6,770	22,211
Huascaran	Peru	6,768	22,204
Llullaillaco	Argentina/Chile	6,723	22,057
Nudo de Cachi	Argentina	6,720	22,047
Yerupaja	Peru	6,632	21,758
N. de Tres Cruces	Argentina/Chile	6,620	21,719
Incahuasi	Argentina/Chile	6,601	21,654
Cerro Galan	Argentina	6,600	21,654
Tupungato	Argentina/Chile	6,570	21,555
> Sajama	Bolivia	6,542	21,463
Illimani	Bolivia	6,485	21,276
Coropuna	Peru	6,425	21,079
Ausangate	Peru	6,384	20,945
Cerro del Toro	Argentina	6,380	20,932
Siula Grande	Peru	6,356	20,853
Chimborazo	Ecuador	6,267	20,561
Alpamayo	Peru	5,947	19,511
Cotapaxi	Ecuador	5,896	19,344
Pico Colon	Colombia	5,800	19,029
Pico Bolivar	Venezuela	5,007	16,427

ANTARCTICA		m	ft
Vinson Massif		4,897	16,066
Mt Kirkpatrick		4,528	14,855
Mt Markham		4,349	14,268

OCEAN DEPTHS

ATLANTIC OCEAN	m	ft	
Puerto Rico (Milwaukee) Deep	9,220	30,249	[7]
Cayman Trench	7,680	25,197	[10]
Gulf of Mexico	5,203	17,070	
Mediterranean Sea	5,121	16,801	
Black Sea	2,211	7,254	
North Sea	660	2,165	
Baltic Sea	463	1,519	
Hudson Bay	258	846	

INDIAN OCEAN	m	ft
Java Trench	7,450	24,442
Red Sea	2,635	8,454
Persian Gulf	73	239

PACIFIC OCEAN	m	ft	
Mariana Trench	11,022	36,161	[1]
Tonga Trench	10,882	35,702	[2]
Japan Trench	10,554	34,626	[3]
Kuril Trench	10,542	34,587	[4]
Mindanao Trench	10,497	34,439	[5]
Kermadec Trench	10,047	32,962	[6]

PACIFIC OCEAN (continued)

		m	ft	
Peru–Chile Trench		8,050	26,410	[8]
Aleutian Trench		7,822	25,662	[9]

ARCTIC OCEAN

	m	ft
Molloy Deep	5,608	18,399

LAND LOWS

		m	ft
Dead Sea	Asia	−403	−1,322
Lake Assal	Africa	−156	−512
Death Valley	N. America	−86	−282
Valdés Peninsula	S. America	−40	−131
Caspian Sea	Europe	−28	−92
Lake Eyre North	Oceania	−16	−52

RIVERS

EUROPE

		km	miles	
Volga	Caspian Sea	3,700	2,300	
Danube	Black Sea	2,850	1,770	
Ural	Caspian Sea	2,535	1,575	
Dnepr (Dnipro)	Black Sea	2,285	1,420	
Kama	Volga	2,030	1,260	
Don	Black Sea	1,990	1,240	
Petchora	Arctic Ocean	1,790	1,110	
Oka	Volga	1,480	920	
Belaya	Kama	1,420	880	
Dnister (Dniester)	Black Sea	1,400	870	
Vyatka	Kama	1,370	850	
Rhine	North Sea	1,320	820	
N. Dvina	Arctic Ocean	1,290	800	
Desna	Dnepr (Dnipro)	1,190	740	
Elbe	North Sea	1,145	710	
> Wisla	Baltic Sea	1,090	675	
Loire	Atlantic Ocean	1,020	635	

ASIA

		km	miles	
Yangtze	Pacific Ocean	6,380	3,960	[3]
Yenisey–Angara	Arctic Ocean	5,550	3,445	[5]
Huang He	Pacific Ocean	5,464	3,395	[6]
Ob–Irtysh	Arctic Ocean	5,410	3,360	[7]
Mekong	Pacific Ocean	4,500	2,795	[9]
Amur	Pacific Ocean	4,400	2,730	[10]
Lena	Arctic Ocean	4,400	2,730	
Irtysh	Ob	4,250	2,640	
Yenisey	Arctic Ocean	4,090	2,540	
Ob	Arctic Ocean	3,680	2,285	
Indus	Indian Ocean	3,100	1,925	
Brahmaputra	Indian Ocean	2,900	1,800	
Syrdarya	Aral Sea	2,860	1,775	
Salween	Indian Ocean	2,800	1,740	
Euphrates	Indian Ocean	2,700	1,675	
Vilyuy	Lena	2,650	1,645	
Kolyma	Arctic Ocean	2,600	1,615	
Amudarya	Aral Sea	2,540	1,575	
Ural	Caspian Sea	2,535	1,575	
Ganges	Indian Ocean	2,510	1,560	
> Si Kiang	Pacific Ocean	2,100	1,305	
Irrawaddy	Indian Ocean	2,010	1,250	
Tarim–Yarkand	Lop Nor	2,000	1,240	
Tigris	Indian Ocean	1,900	1,180	

AFRICA

		km	miles	
Nile	Mediterranean	6,670	4,140	[1]
Congo	Atlantic Ocean	4,670	2,900	[8]
Niger	Atlantic Ocean	4,180	2,595	
Zambezi	Indian Ocean	3,540	2,200	
Oubangi/Uele	Congo (Zaïre)	2,250	1,400	
Kasai	Congo (Zaïre)	1,950	1,210	
Shaballe	Indian Ocean	1,930	1,200	
Orange	Atlantic Ocean	1,860	1,155	
Cubango	Okavango Swamps	1,800	1,120	
> Limpopo	Indian Ocean	1,600	995	
Senegal	Atlantic Ocean	1,600	995	
Volta	Atlantic Ocean	1,500	930	

AUSTRALIA

		km	miles
Murray–Darling	Indian Ocean	3,750	2,330
Darling	Murray	3,070	1,905
Murray	Indian Ocean	2,575	1,600
Murrumbidgee	Murray	1,690	1,050

NORTH AMERICA

		km	miles	
Mississippi–Missouri	Gulf of Mexico	6,020	3,740	[4]
Mackenzie	Arctic Ocean	4,240	2,630	
Mississippi	Gulf of Mexico	3,780	2,350	
Missouri	Mississippi	3,780	2,350	
Yukon	Pacific Ocean	3,185	1,980	
Rio Grande	Gulf of Mexico	3,030	1,880	

NORTH AMERICA (continued)

		km	miles
Arkansas	Mississippi	2,340	1,450
Colorado	Pacific Ocean	2,330	1,445
Red	Mississippi	2,040	1,270
Columbia	Pacific Ocean	1,950	1,210
Saskatchewan	Lake Winnipeg	1,940	1,205
Snake	Columbia	1,670	1,040
Churchill	Hudson Bay	1,600	990
Ohio	Mississippi	1,580	980
Brazos	Gulf of Mexico	1,400	870
> St Lawrence	Atlantic Ocean	1,170	730

SOUTH AMERICA

		km	miles	
Amazon	Atlantic Ocean	6,450	4,010	[2]
Paraná–Plate	Atlantic Ocean	4,500	2,800	
Purus	Amazon	3,350	2,080	
Madeira	Amazon	3,200	1,990	
São Francisco	Atlantic Ocean	2,900	1,800	
Paraná	Plate	2,800	1,740	
Tocantins	Atlantic Ocean	2,750	1,710	
Paraguay	Paraná	2,550	1,580	
Orinoco	Atlantic Ocean	2,500	1,550	
Pilcomayo	Paraná	2,500	1,550	
Araguaia	Tocantins	2,250	1,400	
Juruá	Amazon	2,000	1,240	
Xingu	Amazon	1,980	1,230	
Ucayali	Amazon	1,900	1,180	
> Marañón	Amazon	1,600	990	
Uruguay	Plate	1,600	990	

LAKES

EUROPE

		km²	miles²
Lake Ladoga	Russia	17,700	6,800
Lake Onega	Russia	9,700	3,700
Saimaa system	Finland	8,000	3,100
Vänern	Sweden	5,500	2,100
Rybinskoye Res.	Russia	4,700	1,800

ASIA

		km²	miles²	
Caspian Sea	Asia	371,800	143,550	[1]
Lake Baykal	Russia	30,500	11,780	[8]
Aral Sea	Kazakstan/Uzbekistan	28,687	11,086	[10]
Tonlé Sap	Cambodia	20,000	7,700	
Lake Balqash	Kazakstan	18,500	7,100	
> Lake Dongting	China	12,000	4,600	
Lake Ysyk	Kyrgyzstan	6,200	2,400	
Lake Orumiyeh	Iran	5,900	2,300	
Lake Koko	China	5,700	2,200	
Lake Poyang	China	5,000	1,900	
Lake Khanka	China/Russia	4,400	1,700	
Lake Van	Turkey	3,500	1,400	

AFRICA

		km²	miles²	
Lake Victoria	E. Africa	68,000	26,000	[3]
Lake Tanganyika	C. Africa	33,000	13,000	[6]
Lake Malawi/Nyasa	E. Africa	29,600	11,430	[9]
Lake Chad	C. Africa	25,000	9,700	
Lake Turkana	Ethiopia/Kenya	8,500	3,300	
Lake Volta	Ghana	8,500	3,300	
Lake Bangweulu	Zambia	8,000	3,100	
Lake Rukwa	Tanzania	7,000	2,700	
Lake Mai-Ndombe	Congo (Zaïre)	6,500	2,500	
Lake Kariba	Zambia/Zimbabwe	5,300	2,000	
> Lake Albert	Uganda/Congo (Z.)	5,300	2,000	
Lake Nasser	Egypt/Sudan	5,200	2,000	
Lake Mweru	Zambia/Congo (Z.)	4,900	1,900	
Lake Cabora Bassa	Mozambique	4,500	1,700	
Lake Kyoga	Uganda	4,400	1,700	
Lake Tana	Ethiopia	3,630	1,400	

AUSTRALIA

		km²	miles²
Lake Eyre	Australia	8,900	3,400
Lake Torrens	Australia	5,800	2,200
Lake Gairdner	Australia	4,800	1,900

NORTH AMERICA

		km²	miles²	
Lake Superior	Canada/USA	82,350	31,800	[2]
Lake Huron	Canada/USA	59,600	23,010	[4]
Lake Michigan	USA	58,000	22,400	[5]
Great Bear Lake	Canada	31,800	12,280	[7]
Great Slave Lake	Canada	28,500	11,000	
Lake Erie	Canada/USA	25,700	9,900	
Lake Winnipeg	Canada	24,400	9,400	
Lake Ontario	Canada/USA	19,500	7,500	
Lake Nicaragua	Nicaragua	8,200	3,200	
Lake Athabasca	Canada	8,100	3,100	
> Smallwood Reservoir	Canada	6,530	2,520	
Reindeer Lake	Canada	6,400	2,500	
Nettilling Lake	Canada	5,500	2,100	
Lake Winnipegosis	Canada	5,400	2,100	

SOUTH AMERICA

		km²	miles²
Lake Titicaca	Bolivia/Peru	8,300	3,200
Lake Poopo	Peru	2,800	1,100

ISLANDS

EUROPE

		km²	miles²	
Great Britain	UK	229,880	88,700	[8]
Iceland	Atlantic Ocean	103,000	39,800	
Ireland	Ireland/UK	84,400	32,600	
Novaya Zemlya (N.)	Russia	48,200	18,600	
W. Spitzbergen	Norway	39,000	15,100	
Novaya Zemlya (S.)	Russia	33,200	12,800	
Sicily	Italy	25,500	9,800	
Sardinia	Italy	24,000	9,300	
N.E. Spitzbergen	Norway	15,000	5,600	
Corsica	France	8,700	3,400	
Crete	Greece	8,350	3,200	
Zealand	Denmark	6,850	2,600	

ASIA

		km²	miles²	
Borneo	S. E. Asia	744,360	287,400	[3]
Sumatra	Indonesia	473,600	182,860	[6]
Honshu	Japan	230,500	88,980	[7]
Sulawesi (Celebes)	Indonesia	189,000	73,000	
Java	Indonesia	126,700	48,900	
Luzon	Philippines	104,700	40,400	
Mindanao	Philippines	101,500	39,200	
Hokkaido	Japan	78,400	30,300	
Sakhalin	Russia	74,060	28,600	
Sri Lanka	Indian Ocean	65,600	25,300	
Taiwan	Pacific Ocean	36,000	13,900	
Kyushu	Japan	35,700	13,800	
Hainan	China	34,000	13,100	
Timor	Indonesia	33,600	13,000	
Shikoku	Japan	18,800	7,300	
Halmahera	Indonesia	18,000	6,900	
Ceram	Indonesia	17,150	6,600	
Sumbawa	Indonesia	15,450	6,000	
Flores	Indonesia	15,200	5,900	
Samar	Philippines	13,100	5,100	
> Negros	Philippines	12,700	4,900	
Bangka	Indonesia	12,000	4,600	
Palawan	Philippines	12,000	4,600	
Panay	Philippines	11,500	4,400	
Sumba	Indonesia	11,100	4,300	
Mindoro	Philippines	9,750	3,800	

AFRICA

		km²	miles²	
Madagascar	Indian Ocean	587,040	226,660	[4]
Socotra	Indian Ocean	3,600	1,400	
Réunion	Indian Ocean	2,500	965	
Tenerife	Atlantic Ocean	2,350	900	
Mauritius	Indian Ocean	1,865	720	

OCEANIA

		km²	miles²	
New Guinea	Indon./Papua NG	821,030	317,000	[2]
New Zealand (S.)	Pacific Ocean	150,500	58,100	
New Zealand (N.)	Pacific Ocean	114,700	44,300	
Tasmania	Australia	67,800	26,200	
New Britain	Papua NG	37,800	14,600	
New Caledonia	Pacific Ocean	19,100	7,400	
Viti Levu	Fiji	10,500	4,100	
Hawaii	Pacific Ocean	10,450	4,000	
Bougainville	Papua NG	9,600	3,700	
Guadalcanal	Solomon Is.	6,500	2,500	
> Vanua Levu	Fiji	5,550	2,100	
New Ireland	Papua NG	3,200	1,200	

NORTH AMERICA

		km²	miles²	
Greenland	Atlantic Ocean	2,175,600	839,800	[1]
Baffin Is.	Canada	508,000	196,100	[5]
Victoria Is.	Canada	212,200	81,900	[9]
Ellesmere Is.	Canada	212,000	81,800	[10]
Cuba	Caribbean Sea	110,860	42,800	
Newfoundland	Canada	110,680	42,700	
Hispaniola	Dom. Rep./Haiti	76,200	29,400	
Banks Is.	Canada	67,000	25,900	
Devon Is.	Canada	54,500	21,000	
Melville Is.	Canada	42,400	16,400	
> Vancouver Is.	Canada	32,150	12,400	
Somerset Is.	Canada	24,300	9,400	
Jamaica	Caribbean Sea	11,400	4,400	
Puerto Rico	Atlantic Ocean	8,900	3,400	
Cape Breton Is.	Canada	4,000	1,500	

SOUTH AMERICA

		km²	miles²	
Tierra del Fuego	Argentina/Chile	47,000	18,100	
Falkland Is. (East)	Atlantic Ocean	6,800	2,600	
South Georgia	Atlantic Ocean	4,200	1,600	
Galapagos (Isabela)	Pacific Ocean	2,250	870	

World: Regions in the News

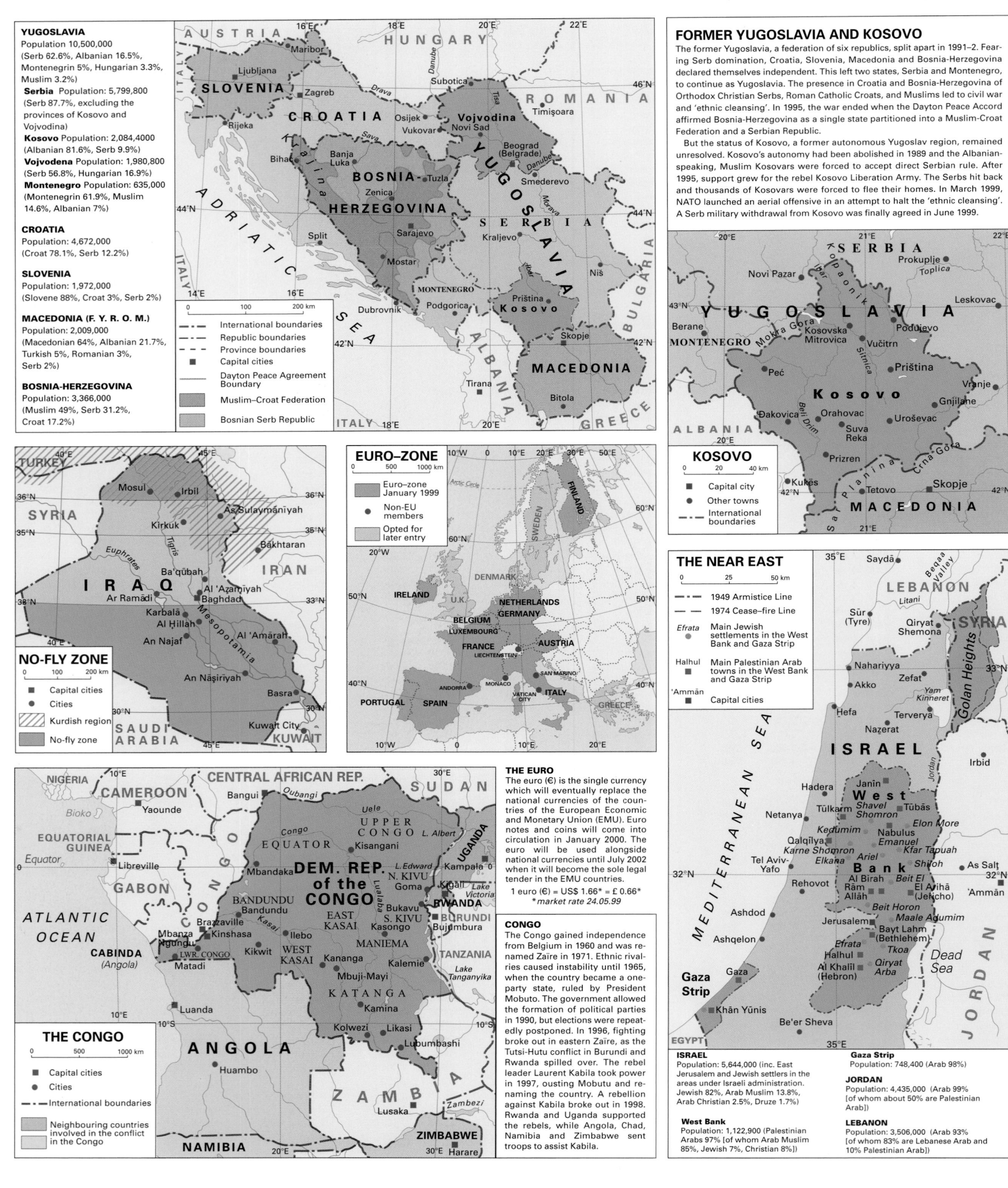

YUGOSLAVIA
Population 10,500,000
(Serb 62.6%, Albanian 16.5%,
Montenegrin 5%, Hungarian 3.3%,
Muslim 3.2%)
Serbia Population: 5,799,800
(Serb 87.7%, excluding the
provinces of Kosovo and
Vojvodina)
Kosovo Population: 2,084,4000
(Albanian 81.6%, Serb 9.9%)
Vojvodena Population: 1,980,800
(Serb 56.8%, Hungarian 16.9%)
Montenegro Population: 635,000
(Montenegrin 61.9%, Muslim
14.6%, Albanian 7%)

CROATIA
Population: 4,672,000
(Croat 78.1%, Serb 12.2%)

SLOVENIA
Population: 1,972,000
(Slovene 88%, Croat 3%, Serb 2%)

MACEDONIA (F. Y. R. O. M.)
Population: 2,009,000
(Macedonian 64%, Albanian 21.7%,
Turkish 5%, Romanian 3%,
Serb 2%)

BOSNIA-HERZEGOVINA
Population: 3,366,000
(Muslim 49%, Serb 31.2%,
Croat 17.2%)

Legend
- ·—·— International boundaries
- -—-— Republic boundaries
- -- -- Province boundaries
- ■ Capital cities
- —— Dayton Peace Agreement Boundary
- Muslim–Croat Federation
- Bosnian Serb Republic

0   100   200 km

FORMER YUGOSLAVIA AND KOSOVO

The former Yugoslavia, a federation of six republics, split apart in 1991–2. Fearing Serb domination, Croatia, Slovenia, Macedonia and Bosnia-Herzegovina declared themselves independent. This left two states, Serbia and Montenegro, to continue as Yugoslavia. The presence in Croatia and Bosnia-Herzegovina of Orthodox Christian Serbs, Roman Catholic Croats, and Muslims led to civil war and 'ethnic cleansing'. In 1995, the war ended when the Dayton Peace Accord affirmed Bosnia-Herzegovina as a single state partitioned into a Muslim-Croat Federation and a Serbian Republic.

But the status of Kosovo, a former autonomous Yugoslav region, remained unresolved. Kosovo's autonomy had been abolished in 1989 and the Albanian-speaking, Muslim Kosovars were forced to accept direct Serbian rule. After 1995, support grew for the rebel Kosovo Liberation Army. The Serbs hit back and thousands of Kosovars were forced to flee their homes. In March 1999, NATO launched an aerial offensive in an attempt to halt the 'ethnic cleansing'. A Serb military withdrawal from Kosovo was finally agreed in June 1999.

KOSOVO
- ■ Capital city
- ● Other towns
- -—-— International boundaries

0   20   40 km

NO-FLY ZONE
- ■ Capital cities
- ● Cities
- ▨ Kurdish region
- No-fly zone

0   100   200 km

EURO–ZONE
- Euro–zone January 1999
- ● Non-EU members
- Opted for later entry

0   500   1000 km

THE EURO

The euro (€) is the single currency which will eventually replace the national currencies of the countries of the European Economic and Monetary Union (EMU). Euro notes and coins will come into circulation in January 2000. The euro will be used alongside national currencies until July 2002 when it will become the sole legal tender in the EMU countries.

1 euro (€) = US$ 1.66* = £ 0.66*
*market rate 24.05.99

THE NEAR EAST

- -—-— 1949 Armistice Line
- -—-— 1974 Cease-fire Line
- *Efrata* ● Main Jewish settlements in the West Bank and Gaza Strip
- *Halhul* ● Main Palestinian Arab towns in the West Bank and Gaza Strip
- *'Ammān* ■ Capital cities

0   25   50 km

THE CONGO
- ■ Capital cities
- ● Cities
- -—-— International boundaries
- Neighbouring countries involved in the conflict in the Congo

0   500   1000 km

CONGO

The Congo gained independence from Belgium in 1960 and was renamed Zaïre in 1971. Ethnic rivalries caused instability until 1965, when the country became a one-party state, ruled by President Mobuto. The government allowed the formation of political parties in 1990, but elections were repeatedly postponed. In 1996, fighting broke out in eastern Zaïre, as the Tutsi-Hutu conflict in Burundi and Rwanda spilled over. The rebel leader Laurent Kabila took power in 1997, ousting Mobutu and renaming the country. A rebellion against Kabila broke out in 1998. Rwanda and Uganda supported the rebels, while Angola, Chad, Namibia and Zimbabwe sent troops to assist Kabila.

ISRAEL
Population: 5,644,000 (inc. East Jerusalem and Jewish settlers in the areas under Israeli administration. Jewish 82%, Arab Muslim 13.8%, Arab Christian 2.5%, Druze 1.7%)

West Bank
Population: 1,122,900 (Palestinian Arabs 97% [of whom Arab Muslim 85%, Jewish 7%, Christian 8%])

Gaza Strip
Population: 748,400 (Arab 98%)

JORDAN
Population: 4,435,000 (Arab 99% [of whom about 50% are Palestinian Arab])

LEBANON
Population: 3,506,000 (Arab 93% [of whom 83% are Lebanese Arab and 10% Palestinian Arab])

The Earth in Space

The Universe 2

Star Charts and Constellations 4

The Solar System 8

The Earth: Time and Motion 10

The Earth from Space 12

The Dynamic Earth 14

Earthquakes and Volcanoes 16

Forces of Nature 18

Oceans and Ice 20

The Earth's Atmosphere 22

Climate and Weather 24

Water and Land Use 26

The Natural World 28

The Human World 30

Languages and Religions 32

International Organizations 34

Agriculture 36

Energy and Minerals 38

World Economies 40

Trade and Commerce 42

Travel and Communications 44

The World Today 46

Glossary of Terms 48

The Universe

The depths of the Universe
This photograph shows some of the 1,500 or more galaxies that were recorded in the montage of photographs taken by the Hubble Space Telescope in 1995.

THE NEAREST STARS

The 20 nearest stars, excluding the Sun, with their distance from the Earth in light-years*.

Star	Distance
Proxima Centauri	4.2
Alpha Centauri A	4.3
Alpha Centauri B	4.3
Barnard's Star	6.0
Wolf 359	7.8
Lalande 21185	8.3
Sirius A	8.7
Sirius B	8.7
UV Ceti A	8.7
UV Ceti B	8.7
Ross 154	9.4
Ross 248	10.3
Epsilon Eridani	10.7
Ross 128	10.9
61 Cygni A	11.1
61 Cygni B	11.1
Epsilon Indi	11.2
Groombridge 34 A	11.2
Groombridge 34 B	11.2
L789-6	11.2

* A light-year equals approximately 9,500 billion km [5,900 billion miles].

Just before Christmas 1995, the Hubble Space Telescope, which is in orbit about 580 km [360 miles] above the Earth, focused on a tiny area in distant space. Over a ten-day period, photographs taken by the telescope revealed unknown galaxies billions of times fainter than the human eye can see.

Because the light from these distant objects has taken so long to reach us, the photographs transmitted from the telescope and released to the media were the deepest look into space that astronomers have ever seen. The features they revealed were in existence when the Universe was less than a billion years old.

The Hubble Space Telescope is operated by the Space Telescope Science Institute in America and was launched in April 1990. The photographs it took of the Hubble Deep Field have been described by NASA as the biggest advance in astronomy since the work of the Italian scientist Galileo in the early 17th century. US scientists have graphically described the astonishing photographs received from the Telescope as 'postcards from the edge of space and time'.

THE BIG BANG

According to the latest theories, the Universe was created, and 'time' began, about 15,000 million (or 15 billion) years ago, though other estimates range from 8 to 24 billion years. Following a colossal explosion, called the 'Big Bang', the Universe expanded in the first millionth of a

The End of the Universe
The diagram shows two theories concerning the fate of the Universe. One theory, top, suggests that the Universe will expand indefinitely, moving into an immense dark graveyard. Another theory, bottom, suggests that the galaxies will fall back until everything is again concentrated in one point in a so-called 'Big Crunch'. This might then be followed by a new 'Big Bang'.

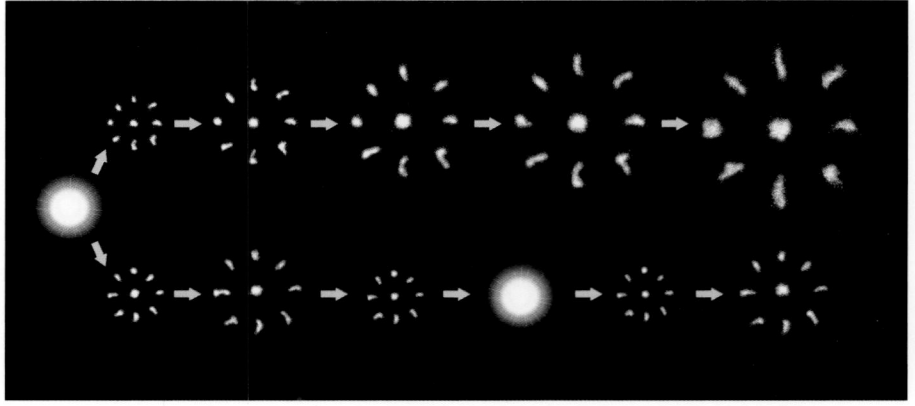

second of its existence from a dimensionless point of infinite mass and density into a fireball, about 30 billion km [19 billion miles] across. The Universe has been expanding ever since, as demonstrated in the 1920s by Edwin Hubble, the American astronomer after whom the Hubble Space Telescope was named.

The temperature at the end of the first second was perhaps 10 billion degrees – far too hot for composite atomic nuclei to exist. As a result, the fireball consisted mainly of radiation mixed with microscopic particles of matter. Almost a million years passed before the Universe was cool enough for atoms to form.

A few billion years later, atoms in regions where matter was relatively dense began, under the influence of gravity, to move together to form proto-galaxies – masses of gas separated by empty space. The proto-galaxies were dark, because the Universe had cooled. But a few billion years later, stars began to form within the proto-galaxies as particles were drawn together. The internal pressure produced as matter condensed created the high temperatures required to cause nuclear fusion. Stars were born and later destroyed. Each generation of stars fed on the debris of extinct ones. Each generation produced larger atoms, increasing the number of different chemical elements.

The Home Galaxy
This schematic plan shows that our Solar System is located in one of the spiral arms of the Milky Way galaxy, a little less than 30,000 light-years from its centre. The centre of the Milky Way galaxy is not visible from Earth. Instead, it is masked by light-absorbing clouds of interstellar dust.

Solar System

THE GALAXIES

At least a billion galaxies are scattered through the Universe, though the discoveries made by the Hubble Space Telescope suggest that there may be far more than once thought, and some estimates are as high as 100 billion. The largest galaxies contain trillions of stars, while small ones contain less than a billion.

Galaxies tend to occur in groups or clusters, while some clusters appear to be grouped in vast superclusters. Our Local Cluster includes the spiral Milky Way galaxy, whose diameter is about 100,000 light-years; one light-year, the distance that light travels in one year, measures about 9,500 billion km [5,900 billion miles]. The Milky Way is a huge galaxy, shaped like a disk with a bulge at the centre. It is larger, brighter and more massive than many other known galaxies. It contains about 100 billion stars which rotate around the centre of the galaxy in the same direction as the Sun does.

One medium-sized star in the Milky Way galaxy is the Sun. After its formation, about 5 billion years ago, there was enough leftover matter around it to create the planets, asteroids,

The Milky Way
This section of the Milky Way is dominated by Sirius, the Dog Star, top centre, in the constellation of Canis Major. Sirius is the brightest star in the sky.

moons and other bodies that together form our Solar System. The Solar System rotates around the centre of the Milky Way galaxy approximately every 225 million years.

Recent discoveries suggest that other stars similar to our Sun have planets orbiting around them, while evidence from the Hubble Space Telescope suggests that the raw materials from which planets are formed is common in dusty disks around many stars. This provokes one of the most intriguing of all the questions that has ever faced humanity. If there are other planets in the Universe, then do living organisms exist elsewhere?

Before the time of Galileo, people thought that the Earth lay at the centre of the Universe. But we now know that our Solar System and even the Milky Way galaxy are tiny specks in the Universe as a whole. Perhaps our planet is also not unique in being the only one to support intelligent life.

Star Charts and Constellations

THE BRIGHTEST STARS

The 15 brightest stars visible from northern Europe. Magnitudes are given to the nearest tenth.

Sirius	−1.5
Arcturus	0.0
Vega	0.0
Capella	0.1
Rigel	0.1
Procyon	0.4
Betelgeuse	0.4
Altair	0.8
Aldebaran	0.8
Antares	1.0
Spica	1.0
Pollux	1.1
Fomalhaut	1.2
Deneb	1.2
Regulus	1.3

The Plough

The Plough, or Big Dipper, above glowing yellow clouds lit by city lights. It is part of a larger group called Ursa Major one of the best-known constellations of the northern hemisphere. The two bright stars to the lower right of the photograph (Merak and Dubhe) are known as the Pointers because they show the way to the Pole Star.

On a clear night, under the best conditions and far away from the glare of city lights, a person in northern Europe can look up and see about 2,500 stars. In a town, however, light pollution can reduce visibility to 200 stars or less. Over the whole celestial sphere it is possible to see about 8,500 stars with the naked eye and it is only when you look through a telescope that you begin to realize that the number of stars is countless.

SMALL AND LARGE STARS

Stars come in several sizes. Some, called neutron stars, are compact, with the same mass as the Sun but with diameters of only about 20 km [12 miles]. Larger than neutron stars are the small white dwarfs. Our Sun is a medium-sized star, but many visible stars in the night sky are giants with diameters between 10 and 100 times that of the Sun, or supergiants with diameters over 100 times that of the Sun.

Two bright stars in the constellation Orion are Betelgeuse (also known as Alpha Orionis) and Rigel (or Beta Orionis). Betelgeuse is an orange-red supergiant, whose diameter is about

400 times that of the Sun. Rigel is also a supergiant. Its diameter is about 50 times that of the Sun, but its luminosity is estimated to be over 100,000 times that of the Sun.

The stars we see in the night sky all belong to our home galaxy, the Milky Way. This name is also used for the faint, silvery band that arches across the sky. This band, a slice through our

THE CONSTELLATIONS

The constellations and their English names. Constellations visible from both hemispheres are listed.

Andromeda	Andromeda	Delphinus	Dolphin	Perseus	Perseus
Antlia	Air Pump	Dorado	Swordfish	Phoenix	Phoenix
Apus	Bird of Paradise	Draco	Dragon	Pictor	Easel
Aquarius	Water Carrier	Equuleus	Little Horse	Pisces	Fishes
Aquila	Eagle	Eridanus	River Eridanus	Piscis Austrinus	Southern Fish
Ara	Altar	Fornax	Furnace	Puppis	Ship's Stern
Aries	Ram	Gemini	Twins	Pyxis	Mariner's Compass
Auriga	Charioteer	Grus	Crane	Reticulum	Net
Boötes	Herdsman	Hercules	Hercules	Sagitta	Arrow
Caelum	Chisel	Horologium	Clock	Sagittarius	Archer
Camelopardalis	Giraffe	Hydra	Water Snake	Scorpius	Scorpion
Cancer	Crab	Hydrus	Sea Serpent	Sculptor	Sculptor
Canes Venatici	Hunting Dogs	Indus	Indian	Scutum	Shield
Canis Major	Great Dog	Lacerta	Lizard	Serpens*	Serpent
Canis Minor	Little Dog	Leo	Lion	Sextans	Sextant
Capricornus	Sea Goat	Leo Minor	Little Lion	Taurus	Bull
Carina	Ship's Keel	Lepus	Hare	Telescopium	Telescope
Cassiopeia	Cassiopeia	Libra	Scales	Triangulum	Triangle
Centaurus	Centaur	Lupus	Wolf	Triangulum Australe	
Cepheus	Cepheus	Lynx	Lynx		Southern Triangle
Cetus	Whale	Lyra	Lyre	Tucana	Toucan
Chamaeleon	Chameleon	Mensa	Table	Ursa Major	Great Bear
Circinus	Compasses	Microscopium	Microscope	Ursa Minor	Little Bear
Columba	Dove	Monoceros	Unicorn	Vela	Ship's Sails
Coma Berenices	Berenice's Hair	Musca	Fly	Virgo	Virgin
Corona Australis	Southern Crown	Norma	Level	Volans	Flying Fish
Corona Borealis	Northern Crown	Octans	Octant	Vulpecula	Fox
Corvus	Crow	Ophiuchus	Serpent Bearer		
Crater	Cup	Orion	Hunter		
Crux	Southern Cross	Pavo	Peacock	** In two halves: Serpens Caput, the*	
Cygnus	Swan	Pegasus	Winged Horse	*head, and Serpens Cauda, the tail.*	

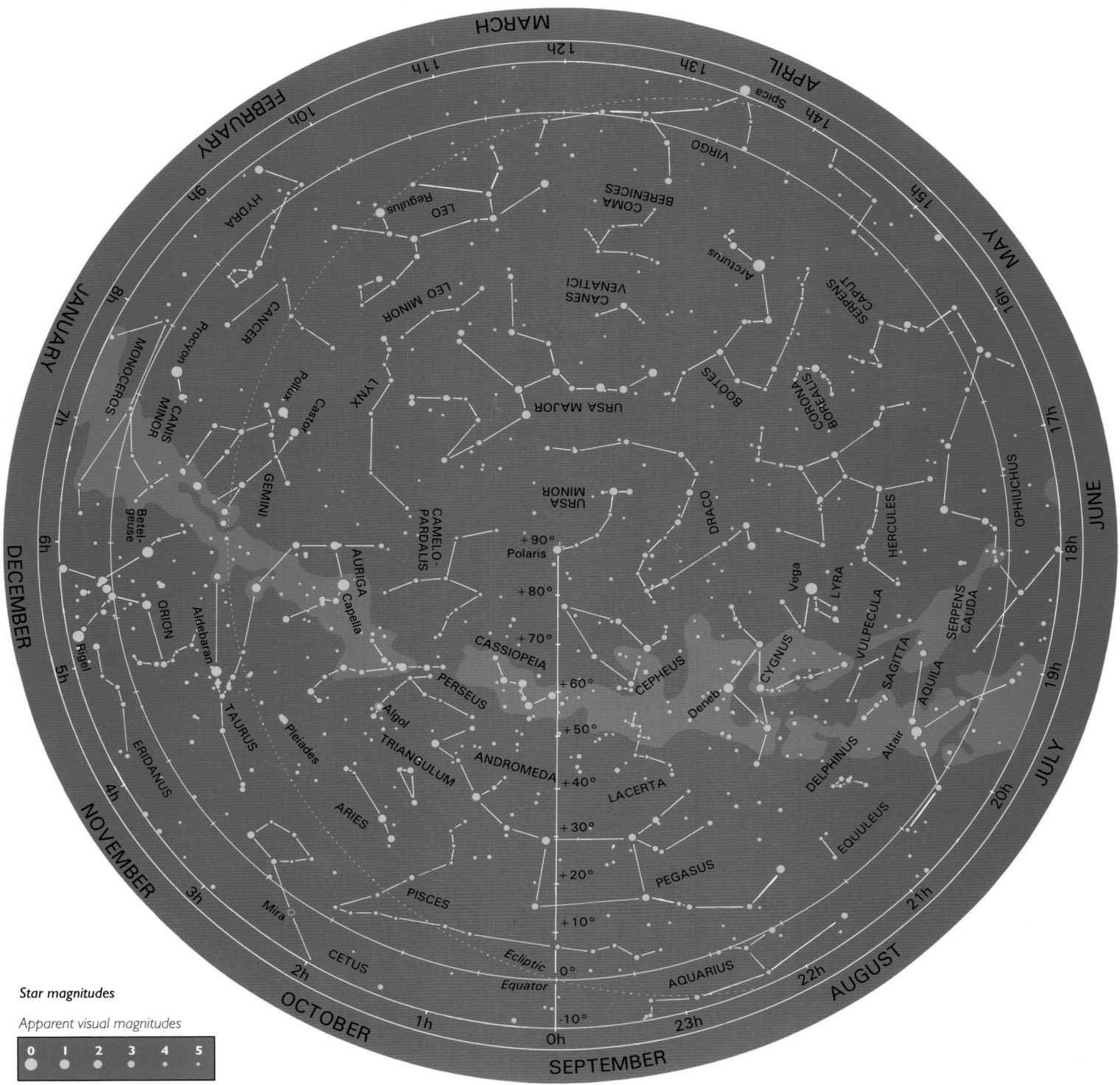

MARCH
FEBRUARY
JANUARY
DECEMBER
NOVEMBER
OCTOBER
SEPTEMBER
AUGUST
JULY
JUNE
MAY
APRIL

12h 11h 13h 10h 14h
9h 15h
8h 16h
7h 17h
6h 18h
5h 19h
4h 20h
3h 21h
2h 22h
1h 23h
0h

HYDRA
Regulus LEO
COMA BERENICES
VIRGO
Spica
CANCER
LEO MINOR
CANES VENATICI
Arcturus
MONOCEROS
Procyon
CANIS MINOR
LYNX
URSA MAJOR
BOÖTES
SERPENS CAPUT
Pollux
Castor GEMINI
CAMELO-PARDALIS
URSA MINOR
DRACO
CORONA BOREALIS
HERCULES
OPHIUCHUS
Betel-geuse
AURIGA
Capella
+90° Polaris
+80°
Vega
LYRA
VULPECULA
SERPENS CAUDA
ORION
Aldebaran
+70°
CASSIOPEIA
CEPHEUS
CYGNUS
SAGITTA
AQUILA
Rigel
+60°
Deneb
Altair
TAURUS
Algol
PERSEUS
+50°
DELPHINUS
EQUULEUS
Pleiades
TRIANGULUM
ANDROMEDA
+40°
LACERTA
ERIDANUS
ARIES
+30°
PEGASUS
+20°
PISCES
+10°
Mira
Ecliptic 0°
Equator
AQUARIUS
CETUS
-10°

Star magnitudes

Apparent visual magnitudes

0	1	2	3	4	5

The Milky Way is shown in light blue on the above chart.

galaxy, contains an enormous number of stars. The nucleus of the Milky Way galaxy cannot be seen from Earth. Lying in the direction of the constellation Sagittarius in the southern hemisphere, it is masked by clouds of dust.

THE BRIGHTNESS OF STARS
Astronomers use a scale of magnitudes to measure the brightness of stars. The brightest visible to the naked eye were originally known as first-magnitude stars, ones not so bright were second-magnitude, down to the faintest visible, which were rated as sixth-magnitude. The brighter the star, the lower the magnitude. With the advent of telescopes and the development of accurate instruments for measuring brightnesses, the magnitude scale has been refined and extended.

Star chart of the northern hemisphere

When you look into the sky, the stars seem to be on the inside of a huge dome. This gives astronomers a way of mapping them. This chart shows the sky as it would appear from the North Pole. To use the star chart above, an observer in the northern hemisphere should face south and turn the chart so that the current month appears at the bottom. The chart will then show the constellations on view at approximately 11pm Greenwich Mean Time. The map should be rotated clockwise 15° for each hour before 11pm and anticlockwise for each hour after 11pm.

Very bright bodies such as Sirius, Venus and the Sun have negative magnitudes. The nearest star is Proxima Centauri, part of a multiple star system, which is 4.2 light-years away. Proxima Centauri is very faint and has a magnitude of 11.3. Alpha Centauri A, one of the two brighter members of the system, is the nearest visible star to Earth. It has a magnitude of 1.7.

These magnitudes are known as apparent magnitudes – measures of the brightnesses of the stars as they appear to us. These are the magnitudes shown on the charts on these pages. But the stars are at very different distances. The star Deneb, in the constellation Cygnus, for example, is over 1,200 light-years away. So astronomers also use absolute magnitudes – measures of how bright the stars really are. A star's absolute magnitude is the apparent magnitude it would have if it could be placed 32.6 light-years away. So Deneb, with an apparent magnitude of 1.2, has an absolute magnitude of −7.2.

The brightest star in the night sky is Sirius, the Dog Star, with a magnitude of −1.5. This medium-sized star is 8.64 light-years distant but it gives out about 20 times as much light as the Sun. After the Sun and the Moon, the brightest objects in the sky are the planets Venus, Mars and Jupiter. For example, Venus has a magnitude of up to −4. The planets have no light of their own however, and shine only because they reflect the Sun's rays. But whilst stars have fixed positions, the planets shift nightly in relation to the constellations, following a path called

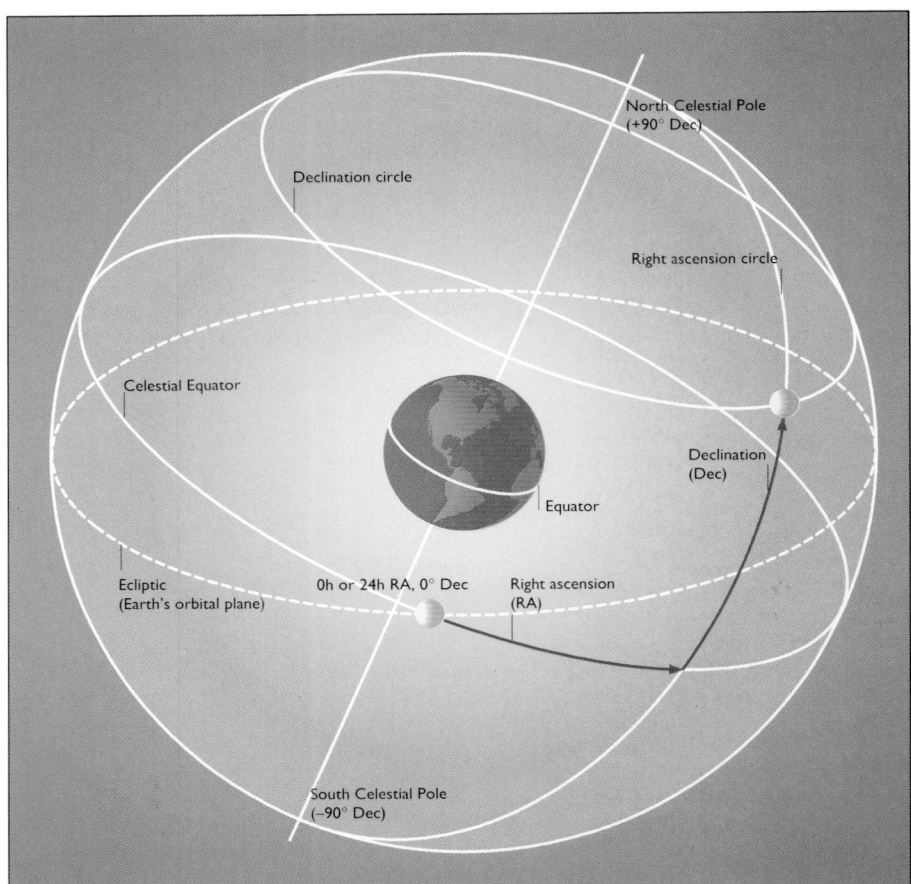

Celestial sphere
The diagram shows the imaginary surface on which astronomical positions are measured. The celestial sphere appears to rotate about the celestial poles, as though an extension of the Earth's own axis. The Earth's axis points towards the celestial poles.

the Ecliptic (shown on the star charts). As they follow their orbits around the Sun, their distances from the Earth vary, and therefore so also do their magnitudes.

While atlas maps record the details of the Earth's surface, star charts are a guide to the heavens. An observer at the Equator can see the entire sky at some time during the year, but an observer at the poles can see only the stars in a single hemisphere. As a result, star charts of both hemispheres are produced. The northern hemisphere chart is centred on the North Celestial Pole, while the southern hemisphere chart is centred on the South Celestial Pole.

In the northern hemisphere, the North Pole is marked by the star Polaris, or North Star. Polaris lies within a degree of the point where an extension of the Earth's axis meets the sky. Polaris appears to be stationary and navigators throughout history have used it as a guide. Unfortunately, the South Pole has no convenient reference point.

Star charts of the two hemispheres are bounded by the Celestial Equator, an imaginary line in the sky directly above the terrestrial Equator. Astronomical co-ordinates, which give the location of stars, are normally stated in terms of right ascension (the equivalent of longitude) and declination (the equivalent of latitude). Because the stars appear to rotate around the Earth every 24 hours, right ascension is measured eastwards in hours and minutes. Declination is measured in degrees north or south of the Celestial Equator.

The Southern Cross
The Southern Cross, or Crux, in the southern hemisphere, was classified as a constellation in the 17th century. It is as familiar to Australians and New Zealanders as the Plough is to people in the northern hemisphere. The vertical axis of the Southern Cross points towards the South Celestial Pole.

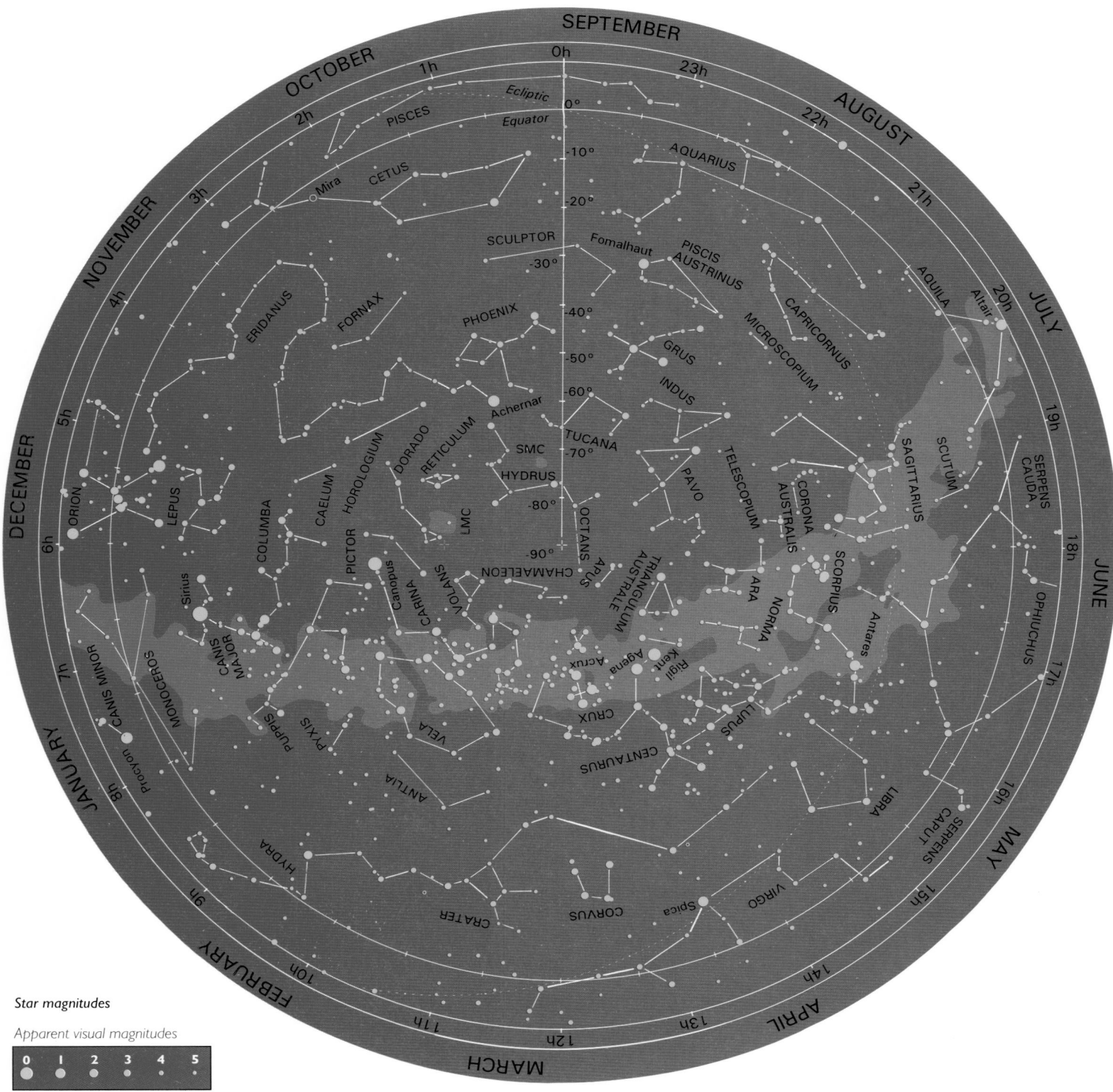

Star magnitudes

Apparent visual magnitudes

0	1	2	3	4	5

The Milky Way is shown in light blue on the above chart.

Star chart of the southern hemisphere

Many constellations in the southern hemisphere were named not by the ancients but by later astronomers. Some, including Antila (Air Pump) and Microscopium (Microscope), have modern names. The Large and Small Magellanic Clouds (LMC, SMC) are small 'satellite' galaxies of the Milky Way. To use the chart, an observer in the southern hemisphere should face north and turn the chart so that the current month appears at the bottom. The map will then show the constellations on view at approximately 11pm Greenwich Mean Time. The chart should be rotated clockwise 15° for each hour before 11pm and anticlockwise for each hour after 11pm.

CONSTELLATIONS

Every star is identifiable as a member of a constellation. The night sky contains 88 constellations, many of which were named by the ancient Greeks, Romans and other early peoples after animals and mythological characters, such as Orion and Perseus. More recently, astronomers invented names for constellations seen in the southern hemisphere, in areas not visible around the Mediterranean Sea.

Some groups of easily recognizable stars form parts of a constellation. For example, seven stars form the shape of the Plough or Big Dipper within the constellation Ursa Major. Such groups are called asterisms.

The stars in constellations lie in the same direction in space, but normally at vastly differ-ent distances. Hence, there is no real connection between them. The positions of stars seem fixed, but in fact the shapes of the constellations are changing slowly over very long periods of time. This is because the stars have their own 'proper motions', which because of the huge distances involved are imperceptible to the naked eye.

The Solar System

Although the origins of the Solar System are still a matter of debate, many scientists believe that it was formed from a cloud of gas and dust, the debris from some long-lost, exploded star. Around 5 billion years ago, material was drawn towards the hub of the rotating disk of gas and dust, where it was compressed to thermonuclear fusion temperatures. A new star, the Sun, was born, containing 99.8% of the mass of the Solar System. The remaining material was later drawn together to form the planets and the other bodies in the Solar System. Spacecraft, manned and unmanned, have greatly increased our knowledge of the Solar System since the start of the Space Age in 1957, when the Soviet Union launched the satellite Sputnik I.

THE PLANETS

Mercury is the closest planet to the Sun and the fastest moving. Space probes have revealed that its surface is covered by craters, and looks much like our Moon. Mercury is a hostile place, with no significant atmosphere and temperatures ranging between 400°C [750°F] by day and −170°C [−275°F] by night. It seems unlikely that anyone will ever want to visit this planet.

Venus is much the same size as Earth, but it is the hottest of the planets, with temperatures reaching 475°C [885°F], even at night. The reason for this scorching heat is the atmosphere, which consists mainly of carbon dioxide, a gas that traps heat thus creating a greenhouse effect. The density of the atmosphere is about 90 times that of Earth and dense clouds permanently mask the surface. Active volcanic regions discharging sulphur dioxide may account for the haze of sulphuric acid droplets in the upper atmosphere.

From planet Earth, Venus is brighter than any other star or planet and is easy to spot. It is often the first object to be seen in the evening sky and the last to be seen in the morning sky. It can even be seen in daylight.

Earth, seen from space, looks blue (because of the oceans which cover more than 70% of the planet) and white (a result of clouds in the atmosphere). The atmosphere and water make Earth the only planet known to support life. The Earth's hard outer layers, including the crust and the top of the mantle, are divided into rigid plates. Forces inside the Earth move the plates, modifying the landscape and causing earthquakes and volcanic activity. Weathering and erosion also change the surface.

Mars has many features in common with Earth, including an atmosphere with clouds and polar caps that partly melt in summer. Scientists once considered that it was the most likely planet on which other life might exist, but the two Viking space probes that went there in the 1970s found only a barren rocky surface with no trace of water. But Mars did have flowing water at one time and there are many dry channels — but these are not the fictitious 'canals'. There are also giant, dormant volcanoes.

PLANETARY DATA

Planet	Mean distance from Sun (million km)	Mass (Earth=1)	Period of orbit (Earth yrs)	Period of rotation (Earth days)	Equatorial diameter (km)	Average density (water=1)	Surface gravity (Earth=1)	Number of known satellites
Sun	–	333,000	–	25.38	1,392,000	1.41	28	–
Mercury	57.9	0.055	0.2406	58.67	4,878	5.43	0.38	0
Venus	108.2	0.815	0.6152	243.0	12,100	5.24	0.90	0
Earth	149.6	1.0	1.00	1.00	12,756	5.52	1.00	1
Mars	227.9	0.107	1.88	1.028	6,794	3.93	0.38	2
Jupiter	778.3	317.8	11.86	0.411	142,800	1.33	2.69	18
Saturn	1,426.8	95.2	29.46	0.427	120,000	0.69	1.19	20
Uranus	2,869.4	14.5	84.01	0.748	52,400	1.25	0.93	15
Neptune	4,496.3	17.1	164.8	0.710	48,400	1.64	0.98	8
Pluto	5,900.1	0.002	2447.7	6.39	2,445	1.40	0.05	1

Asteroids are small, rocky bodies. Most of them orbit the Sun between Mars and Jupiter, but some small ones can approach the Earth. The largest is Ceres, 913 km [567 miles] in diameter. There may be around a million asteroids bigger than 1 km [0.6 miles].

Jupiter, the giant planet, lies beyond Mars and the asteroid belt. Its mass is almost three times as much as all the other planets combined and, because of its size, it shines more brightly than any other planet apart from Venus and, occasionally, Mars. The four largest moons of Jupiter were discovered by Galileo. Jupiter is made up mostly of hydrogen and helium, covered by a layer of clouds. Its Great Red Spot is a high-pressure storm. Jupiter made headline news when it was struck by fragments of Comet Shoemaker–Levy 9 in July 1994. This was the greatest collision ever seen by scientists between a planet and another heavenly body. The fragments of the comet that crashed into Jupiter created huge fireballs that caused scars on the planet that remained visible for months after the event.

Saturn is structurally similar to Jupiter but it is best known for its rings. The rings measure about 270,000 km [170,000 miles] across, yet they are no more than a few hundred metres thick. Seen from Earth, the rings seem divided into three main bands of varying brightness, but photographs sent back by the *Voyager* space probes in 1980 and 1981 showed that they are broken up into thousands of thin ringlets composed of ice particles ranging in size from a snowball to an iceberg. The origin of the rings is still a matter of debate.

Uranus was discovered in 1781 by William Herschel who first thought it was a comet. It is broadly similar to Jupiter and Saturn in composition, though its distance from the Sun makes its surface even colder. Uranus is circled by thin rings which were discovered in 1977. Unlike the rings of Saturn, the rings of Uranus are black, which explains why they cannot be seen from Earth.

Neptune, named after the mythological sea god, was discovered in 1846 as the result of mathematical predictions made by astronomers to explain irregularities in the orbit of Uranus, its near twin. Little was known about this distant body until *Voyager 2* came close to it in 1989. Neptune has thin rings, like those of Uranus. Among its blue-green clouds is a prominent dark spot, which rotates anticlockwise every 18 hours or so.

Pluto is the smallest planet in the Solar System, even smaller than our Moon. The American astronomer Clyde Tombaugh discovered Pluto in 1930. Its orbit is odd and it sometimes comes closer to the Sun than Neptune. The nature of Pluto, a gloomy planet appropriately named after the Greek and Roman god of the underworld, is uncertain. At Pluto's distance and beyond are many small, asteroid-like bodies the first of which was found in 1992.

Comets are small icy bodies that orbit the Sun in highly elliptical orbits. When a comet swings in towards the Sun some of its ice evaporates, and the comet brightens and may become visible from Earth. The best known is Halley's Comet, which takes 76 years to orbit the Sun.

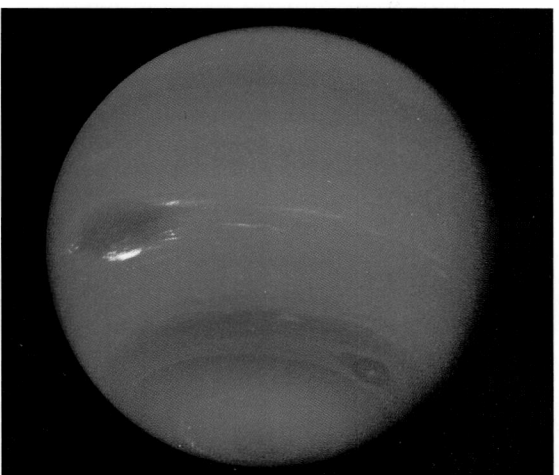

The Earth: Time and Motion

The Earth is constantly moving through space like a huge, self-sufficient spaceship. First, with the rest of the Solar System, it moves around the centre of the Milky Way galaxy. Second, it rotates around the Sun at a speed of more than 100,000 km/h [more than 60,000 mph], covering a distance of nearly 1,000 million km [600 million miles] in a little over 365 days. The Earth also spins on its axis, an imaginary line joining the North and South Poles, via the centre of the Earth, completing one turn in a day. The Earth's movements around the Sun determine our calendar, though accurate observations of

The Earth from the Moon
In 1969, Neil Armstrong and Edwin 'Buzz' Aldrin Junior were the first people to set foot on the Moon. This superb view of the Earth was taken by the crew of Apollo 11.

the stars made by astronomers help to keep our clocks in step with the rotation of the Earth around the Sun.

THE CHANGING YEAR

The Earth takes 365 days, 6 hours, 9 minutes and 9.54 seconds to complete one orbit around the Sun. We have a calendar year of 365 days, so allowance has to be made for the extra time over and above the 365 days. This is allowed for by introducing leap years of 366 days. Leap years are generally those, such as 1992 and 1996, which are divisible by four. Century years, however, are not leap years unless they are divisible by 400. Hence, 1700, 1800 and 1900 were not leap years, but the year 2000 will be one. Leap years help to make the calendar conform with the solar year.

Because the Earth's axis is tilted by 23½°, the middle latitudes enjoy four distinct seasons. On 21 March, the vernal or spring equinox in the northern hemisphere, the Sun is directly overhead at the Equator and everywhere on Earth has about 12 hours of daylight and 12 hours of darkness. But as the Earth continues on its journey around the Sun, the northern hemisphere tilts more and more towards the Sun. Finally, on 21 June, the Sun is overhead at the Tropic of Cancer (latitude 23½° North). This is

The Seasons
The 23½° tilt of the Earth's axis remains constant as the Earth orbits around the Sun. As a result, first the northern and then the southern hemispheres lean towards the Sun. Annual variations in the amount of sunlight received in turn by each hemisphere are responsible for the four seasons experienced in the middle latitudes.

Tides
The daily rises and falls of the ocean's waters are caused by the gravitational pull of the Moon and the Sun. The effect is greatest on the hemisphere facing the Moon, causing a 'tidal bulge'. The diagram below shows that the Sun, Moon and Earth are in line when the spring tides occur. This causes the greatest tidal ranges. On the other hand, the neap tides occur when the pull of the Moon and the Sun are opposed. Neap tides, when tidal ranges are at their lowest, occur near the Moon's first and third quarters.

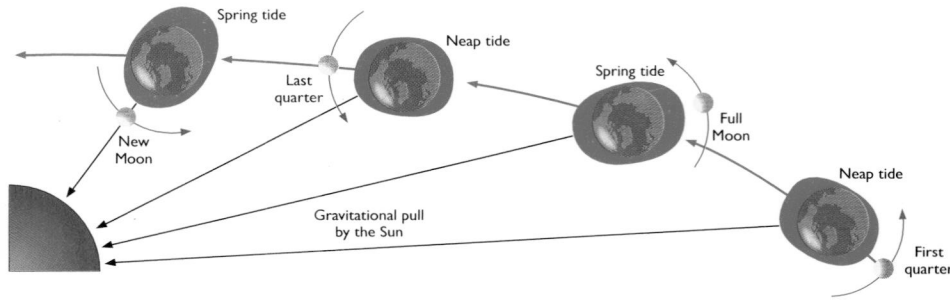

SUN DATA

DIAMETER	1.392×10^6 km
VOLUME	1.412×10^{18} km³
VOLUME (EARTH = 1)	1.303×10^6
MASS	1.989×10^{30} kg
MASS (EARTH = 1)	3.329×10^5
MEAN DENSITY (WATER = 1)	1.409
ROTATION PERIOD	
AT EQUATOR	24.25 days
AT POLES	about 35 days
SURFACE GRAVITY	
(EARTH = 1)	27.9
MAGNITUDE	
APPARENT	−26.9
ABSOLUTE	+4.71
TEMPERATURE	
AT SURFACE	5,400°C [5,700 K]
AT CORE	14×10^{16} K

MOON DATA

DIAMETER	3,476 km
MASS (EARTH = 1)	0.0123
DENSITY (WATER = 1)	3.34
MEAN DISTANCE FROM EARTH	384,402 km
MAXIMUM DISTANCE (APOGEE)	406,740 km
MINIMUM DISTANCE (PERIGEE)	356,410 km
SIDERIAL ROTATION AND REVOLUTION PERIOD	27.322 days
SYNODIC MONTH (NEW MOON TO NEW MOON)	29.531 days
SURFACE GRAVITY (EARTH = 1)	0.165
MAXIMUM SURFACE TEMPERATURE	+130°C [403 K]
MINIMUM SURFACE TEMPERATURE	−158°C [115 K]

Phases of the Moon

The Moon rotates more slowly than the Earth, making one complete turn on its axis in just over 27 days. This corresponds to its period of revolution around the Earth and, hence, the same hemisphere always faces us. The interval between one full Moon and the next (and also between new Moons) is about 29½ days, or one lunar month. The apparent changes in the appearance of the Moon are caused by its changing position in relation to Earth. Like the planets, the Moon produces no light of its own. It shines by reflecting the Sun's rays, varying from a slim crescent to a full circle and back again.

the summer solstice in the northern hemisphere.

The overhead Sun then moves south again until on 23 September, the autumn equinox in the northern hemisphere, the Sun is again overhead at the Equator. The overhead Sun then moves south until, on around 22 December, it is overhead at the Tropic of Capricorn. This is the winter solstice in the northern hemisphere, and the summer solstice in the southern, where the seasons are reversed.

At the poles, there are two seasons. During half of the year, one of the poles leans towards the Sun and has continuous sunlight. For the other six months, the pole leans away from the Sun and is in continuous darkness.

Regions around the Equator do not have marked seasons. Because the Sun is high in the sky throughout the year, it is always hot or warm. When people talk of seasons in the tropics, they are usually referring to other factors, such as rainy and dry periods.

DAY, NIGHT AND TIDES

As the Earth rotates on its axis every 24 hours, first one side of the planet and then the other faces the Sun and enjoys daylight, while the opposite side is in darkness.

The length of daylight varies throughout the year. The longest day in the northern hemisphere falls on the summer solstice, 21 June, while the longest day in the southern hemisphere is on 22 December. At 40° latitude, the length of daylight on the longest day is 14 hours, 30 minutes. At 60° latitude, daylight on that day lasts 18 hours, 30 minutes. On the shortest day, 22 December in the northern hemisphere and 21 June in the southern, daylight hours at 40° latitude total 9 hours and 9 minutes. At latitude 60°, daylight lasts only 5 hours, 30 minutes in the 24-hour period.

Tides are caused by the gravitational pull of the Moon and, to a lesser extent, the Sun on the waters in the world's oceans. Tides occur twice every 24 hours, 50 minutes – one complete orbit

Total eclipse of the Sun
A total eclipse is caused when the Moon passes between the Sun and the Earth. With the Sun's bright disk completely obscured, the Sun's corona, or outer atmosphere, can be viewed.

of the Moon around the Earth.

The highest tides, the spring tides, occur when the Earth, Moon and Sun are in a straight line, so that the gravitational pulls of the Moon and Sun are combined. The lowest, or neap, tides occur when the Moon, Earth and Sun form a right angle. The gravitational pull of the Moon is then opposed by the gravitational pull of the Sun. The greatest tidal ranges occur in the Bay of Fundy in North America. The greatest mean spring range is 14.5 m [47.5 ft].

The speed at which the Earth is spinning on its axis is gradually slowing down, because of the movement of tides. As a result, experts have calculated that, in about 200 million years, the day will be 25 hours long.

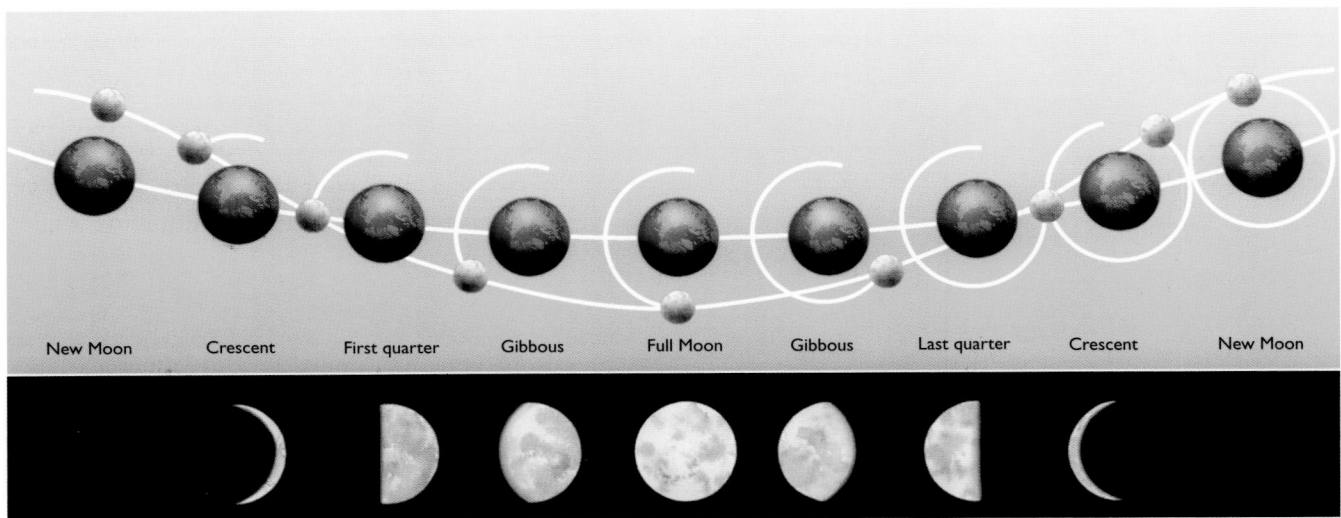

| New Moon | Crescent | First quarter | Gibbous | Full Moon | Gibbous | Last quarter | Crescent | New Moon |

The Earth from Space

Any last doubts about whether the Earth was round or flat were finally resolved by the appearance of the first photographs of our planet taken at the start of the Space Age. Satellite images also confirmed that map- and globe-makers had correctly worked out the shapes of the continents and the oceans.

More importantly, images of our beautiful, blue, white and brown planet from space impressed on many people that the Earth and its resources are finite. They made people realize that if we allow our planet to be damaged by such factors as overpopulation, pollution and irresponsible over-use of resources, then its future and the survival of all the living things upon it may be threatened.

VIEWS FROM ABOVE

The first aerial photographs were taken from balloons in the mid-19th century and their importance in military reconnaissance was recognized as early as the 1860s during the American Civil War.

Launch of the Space Shuttle Atlantis
Space Shuttles transport astronauts and equipment into orbit around the Earth. The American Space Shuttle Atlantis, *shown below, launched the Magellan probe, which undertook a radar mapping programme of the surface of Venus in the early 1990s.*

Since the end of World War II, photographs taken by aircraft have been widely used in map-making. The use of air photographs has greatly speeded up the laborious process of mapping land details and they have enabled cartographers to produce maps of the most remote parts of the world.

Aerial photographs have also proved useful because they reveal features that are not visible at ground level. For example, circles that appear on many air photographs do not correspond to visible features on the ground. Many of these mysterious shapes have turned out to be the sites of ancient settlements previously unknown to archaeologists.

IMAGES FROM SPACE

Space probes equipped with cameras and a variety of remote sensing instruments have sent back images of distant planets and moons. From these images, detailed maps have been produced, rapidly expanding our knowledge of the Solar System.

Photographs from space are also proving invaluable in the study of the Earth. One of the best known uses of space imagery is the study of the atmosphere. Polar-orbiting weather satellites that circle the Earth, together with geostationary satellites, whose motion is synchronized with the Earth's rotation, now regularly transmit images showing the changing patterns of weather systems from above. Forecasters use these images to track the development and the paths taken by hurricanes, enabling them to issue storm warnings to endangered areas, saving lives and reducing damage to property.

Remote sensing devices are now monitoring changes in temperatures over the land and sea, while photographs indicate the melting of ice sheets. Such evidence is vital in the study of global warming. Other devices reveal polluted areas, patterns of vegetation growth, and areas suffering deforestation.

In recent years, remote sensing devices have been used to monitor the damage being done to the ozone layer in the stratosphere, which prevents most of the Sun's harmful ultraviolet radiation from reaching the surface. The discovery of 'ozone holes', where the protective layer of ozone is being thinned by chlorofluorocarbons (CFCs), chemicals used in the manufacture of such things as air conditioners and refrigerators, has enabled governments to take concerted action to save our planet from imminent danger.

EARTH DATA

MAXIMUM DISTANCE FROM SUN
(APHELION)
152,007,016 km

MINIMUM DISTANCE FROM SUN
(PERIHELION)
147,000,830 km

LENGTH OF YEAR – SOLAR
TROPICAL (EQUINOX TO
EQUINOX)
365.24 days

LENGTH OF YEAR – SIDEREAL
(FIXED STAR TO FIXED STAR)
365.26 days

LENGTH OF DAY – MEAN SOLAR
DAY
24 hours, 03 minutes, 56
seconds

LENGTH OF DAY – MEAN SIDEREAL
DAY
23 hours, 56 minutes, 4 seconds

SUPERFICIAL AREA
510,000,000 km²

LAND SURFACE
149,000,000 km² (29.3%)

WATER SURFACE
361,000,000 km² (70.7%)

EQUATORIAL CIRCUMFERENCE
40,077 km

POLAR CIRCUMFERENCE
40,009 km

EQUATORIAL DIAMETER
12,756.8 km

POLAR DIAMETER
12,713.8 km

EQUATORIAL RADIUS
6,378.4 km

POLAR RADIUS
6,356.9 km

VOLUME OF THE EARTH
1,083,230 × 10⁶ km³

MASS OF THE EARTH
5.9 × 10²¹ tonnes

Satellite image of San Francisco Bay

Unmanned scientific satellites called ERTS (Earth Resources Technology Satellites), or Landsats, were designed to collect information about the Earth's resources. The satellites transmitted images of the land using different wavelengths of light in order to identify, in false colours, such subtle features as areas that contain minerals or areas covered with growing crops, that are not identifiable on simple photographs using the visible range of the spectrum. They were also equipped to monitor conditions in the atmosphere and oceans, and also to detect pollution levels. This Landsat image of San Francisco Bay covers an area of great interest to geologists because it lies in an earthquake zone in the path of the San Andreas fault.

The Dynamic Earth

The Earth was formed about 4.6 billion years ago from the ring of gas and dust left over after the formation of the Sun. As the Earth took shape, lighter elements, such as silicon, rose to the surface, while heavy elements, notably iron, sank towards the centre.

Gradually, the outer layers cooled to form a hard crust. The crust enclosed the dense mantle which, in turn, surrounded the even denser liquid outer and solid inner core. Around the Earth was an atmosphere, which contained abundant water

Lulworth Cove, southern England
When undisturbed by earth movements, sedimentary rock strata are generally horizontal. But lateral pressure has squeezed the Jurassic strata at Lulworth Cove into complex folds.

vapour. When the surface cooled, rainwater began to fill hollows, forming the first lakes and seas. Since that time, our planet has been subject to constant change – the result of powerful internal and external forces that still operate today.

THE HISTORY OF THE EARTH

From their study of rocks, geologists have pieced together the history of our planet and the life forms that evolved upon it. They have dated the oldest known crystals, composed of the mineral zircon, at 4.2 billion years. But the oldest rocks are younger, less than 4 billion years old. This is because older rocks have been weathered away by natural processes.

The oldest rocks that contain fossils, which are

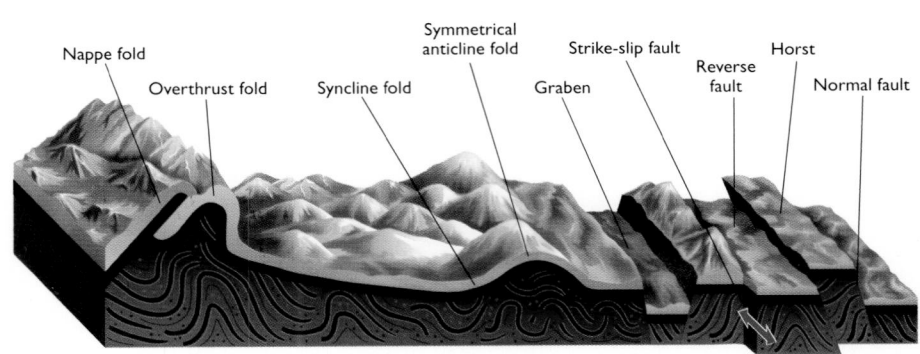

Nappe fold · Overthrust fold · Syncline fold · Symmetrical anticline fold · Graben · Strike-slip fault · Reverse fault · Horst · Normal fault

evidence of once-living organisms, are around 3.5 billion years old. But fossils are rare in rocks formed in the first 4 billion years of Earth history. This vast expanse of time is called the Precambrian. This is because it precedes the Cambrian period, at the start of which, about 590 million years ago, life was abundant in the seas.

The Cambrian is the first period in the Paleozoic (or ancient life) era. The Paleozoic era is followed by the Mesozoic (middle life) era, which witnessed the spectacular rise and fall of the dinosaurs, and the Cenozoic (recent life) era, which was dominated by the evolution of mammals. Each of the eras is divided into periods, and the periods in the Cenozoic era, covering the last 65 million years, are further divided into epochs.

THE EARTH'S CHANGING FACE

While life was gradually evolving, the face of the Earth was constantly changing. By piecing together evidence of rock structures and fossils, geologists have demonstrated that around 250 million years ago, all the world's land areas were grouped together in one huge landmass called Pangaea. Around 180 million years ago, the supercontinent Pangaea, began to break up. New oceans opened up as the continents began to move towards their present positions.

Evidence of how continents drift came from studies of the ocean floor in the 1950s and 1960s. Scientists discovered that the oceans are young features. By contrast with the continents, no part of the ocean floor is more than 200 million years old. The floors of oceans older than 200 million years have completely vanished.

Studies of long undersea ranges, called ocean ridges, revealed that the youngest rocks occur along their centres, which are the edges of huge plates – rigid blocks of the Earth's lithosphere, which is made up of the crust and the solid upper layer of the mantle. The Earth's lithosphere is split into six large and several smaller

Mountain building
Lateral pressure, which occurs when plates collide, squeezes and compresses rocks into folds. Simple symmetrical upfolds are called anticlines, while downfolds are synclines. As the pressure builds up, strata become asymmetrical and they may be tilted over to form recumbent folds. The rocks often crack under the intense pressure and the folds are sheared away and pushed forward over other rocks. These features are called overthrust folds or nappes. Plate movements also create faults along which rocks move upwards, downwards and sideways. The diagram shows a downfaulted graben, or rift valley, and an uplifted horst, or block mountain.

The Himalayas seen from Nepal
The Himalayas are a young fold mountain range formed by a collision between two plates. The earthquakes felt in the region testify that the plate movements are still continuing.

Geological time scale
The geological time scale was first constructed by a study of the stratigraphic, or relative, ages of layers of rock. But the absolute ages of rock strata could not be fixed until the discovery of radioactivity in the early 20th century. Some names of periods, such as Cambrian (Latin for Wales), come from places where the rocks were first studied. Others, such as Carboniferous, refer to the nature of the rocks formed during the period. For example, coal seams (containing carbon) were formed from decayed plant matter during the Carboniferous period.

plates. The ocean ridges are 'constructive' plate margins, because new crustal rock is being formed there from magma that wells up from the mantle as the plates gradually move apart. By contrast, the deep ocean trenches are 'destructive' plate edges. Here, two plates are pushing against each other and one plate is descending beneath the other into the mantle where it is melted and destroyed. Geologists call these areas subduction zones.

A third type of plate edge is called a transform fault. Here two plates are moving alongside each other. The best known of these plate edges is the San Andreas fault in California, which separates the Pacific plate from the North American plate.

Slow-moving currents in the partly molten asthenosphere, which underlies the solid lithosphere, are responsible for moving the plates, a process called plate tectonics.

MOUNTAIN BUILDING

The study of plate tectonics has helped geologists to understand the mechanisms that are responsible for the creation of mountains. Many of the world's greatest ranges were created by the collision of two plates and the bending of the intervening strata into huge loops, or folds. For example, the Himalayas began to rise around 50 million years ago, when a plate supporting India collided with the huge Eurasian plate. Rocks on the floor of the intervening and long-vanished Tethys Sea were squeezed up to form the Himalayan Mountain Range.

Plate movements also create tension that cracks rocks, producing long faults along which rocks move upwards, downwards or sideways. Block mountains are formed when blocks of rock are pushed upwards along faults. Steep-sided rift valleys are formed when blocks of land sink down between faults. For example, the basin and range region of the south-western United States has both block mountains and down-faulted basins, such as Death Valley.

Pre-Cambrian	Lower		Paleozoic (Primary)			Upper		Mesozoic (Secondary)			Cenozoic (Tertiary, Quaternary)		Era
Pre-Cambrian	Cambrian	Ordovician	Silurian	Devonian	Carboniferous	Permian	Triassic	Jurassic	Cretaceous	Paleocene / Eocene / Oligocene / Miocene / Pliocene / Quaternary		System
			CALEDONIAN FOLDING			HERCYNIAN FOLDING				LARAMIDE FOLDING	ALPINE FOLDING	Orogeny
600	550	500	450	400	350	300	250	200	150	100	50	

Millions of years before present

Earthquakes and Volcanoes

On 30 May 1998, an earthquake struck the remote Rostaq region in north-eastern Afghanistan, which was only beginning to recover from a quake on 4 February, when more than 4,200 people died. The death toll in the May earthquake was put at 4,000. Despite a rapid response by aid agencies, many wounded survivors had no food or shelter.

THE RESTLESS EARTH

Earthquakes can occur anywhere, whenever rocks move along faults. But the most severe and most numerous earthquakes occur near the edges of the plates that make up the Earth's lithosphere. Japan, for example, lies in a

San Andreas Fault, United States

Geologists call the San Andreas fault in south-western California a transform, or strike-slip, fault. Sudden movements along it cause earthquakes. In 1906, shifts of about 4.5 metres [15 ft] occurred near San Francisco, causing a massive earthquake.

particularly unstable region above subduction zones, where plates are descending into the Earth's mantle. It lies in a zone encircling the Pacific Ocean, called the 'Pacific ring of fire'.

Plates do not move smoothly. Their edges are jagged and for most of the time they are locked together. However, pressure gradually builds up until the rocks break and the plates lurch forwards, setting off vibrations ranging from tremors that are recorded only by sensitive instruments to terrifying earthquakes. The greater the pressure released, the more destructive the earthquake.

Earthquakes are also common along the ocean trenches where plates are moving apart, but they mostly occur so far from land that they do little damage. Far more destructive are the earthquakes that occur where plates are moving alongside each other. For example, the earthquakes that periodically rock south-western California are caused by movements along the San Andreas Fault.

The spot where an earthquake originates is called the focus, while the point on the Earth's surface directly above the focus is called the epicentre. Two kinds of waves, P-waves or compressional waves and S-waves or shear waves, travel from the focus to the surface where they make the ground shake. P-waves travel faster than S-waves and the time difference between their arrival at recording stations enables scientists to calculate the distance from a station to the epicentre.

Earthquakes are measured on the Richter scale, which indicates the magnitude of the shock. The most destructive earthquakes are shallow-focus, that is, the focus is within 60 km [37 miles] of the surface. A magnitude of 7.0 is a major earthquake, but earthquakes with a somewhat lower magnitude can cause tremendous damage if their epicentres are on or close to densely populated areas.

NOTABLE EARTHQUAKES
(since 1900)

Year	Location	Mag.
1906	San Francisco, USA	8.3
1906	Valparaiso, Chile	8.6
1908	Messina, Italy	7.5
1915	Avezzano, Italy	7.5
1920	Gansu, China	8.6
1923	Yokohama, Japan	8.3
1927	Nan Shan, China	8.3
1932	Gansu, China	7.6
1934	Bihar, India/Nepal	8.4
1935	Quetta, India[†]	7.5
1939	Chillan, Chile	8.3
1939	Erzincan, Turkey	7.9
1964	Anchorage, Alaska	8.4
1968	N. E. Iran	7.4
1970	N. Peru	7.7
1976	Guatemala	7.5
1976	Tangshan, China	8.2
1978	Tabas, Iran	7.7
1980	El Asnam, Algeria	7.3
1980	S. Italy	7.2
1985	Mexico City, Mexico	8.1
1988	N. W. Armenia	6.8
1990	N. Iran	7.7
1993	Maharashtra, India	6.4
1994	Los Angeles, USA	6.6
1995	Kobe, Japan	7.2
1995	Sakhalin Is., Russia	7.5
1996	Yunnan, China	7.0
1997	N. E. Iran	7.1
1998	N. Afghanistan	6.1
1998	N. E. Afghanistan	7.0

[†] *now Pakistan*

Earthquakes in subduction zones

Along subduction zones, one plate is descending beneath another. The plates are locked together until the rocks break and the descending plate lurches forwards. From the point where the plate moves – the origin – seismic waves spread through the lithosphere, making the ground shake. The earthquake in Mexico City in 1985 occurred in this way.

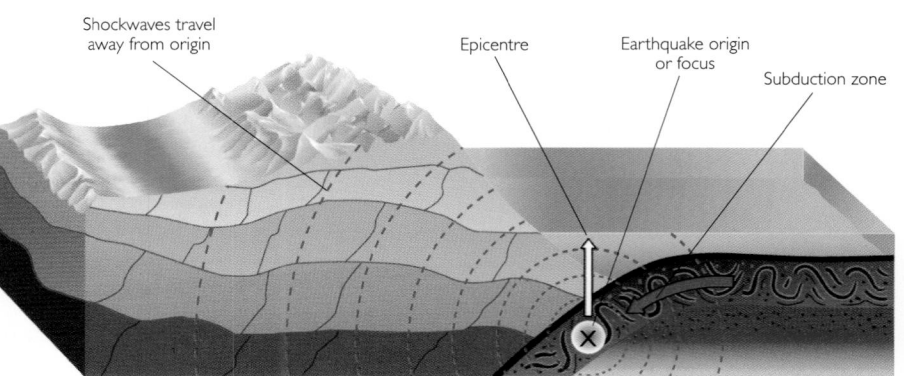

Shockwaves travel away from origin

Epicentre

Earthquake origin or focus

Subduction zone

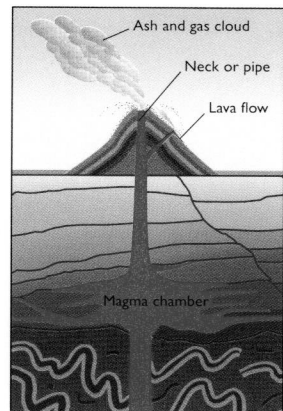

Cross-section of a volcano

Volcanoes are vents in the ground, through which magma reaches the surface. The term volcano is also used for the mountains formed from volcanic rocks. Beneath volcanoes are pockets of magma derived from the semi-molten asthenosphere in the mantle. The magma rises under pressure through the overlying rocks until it reaches the surface. There it emerges through vents as pyroclasts, ranging in size from large lumps of magma, called volcanic bombs, to fine volcanic ash and dust. In quiet eruptions, streams of liquid lava run down the side of the mountain. Side vents sometimes appear on the flanks of existing volcanoes.

Scientists have been working for years to find effective ways of forecasting earthquakes but with very limited success. Following the Kobe earthquake in 1995, many experts argued that they would be better employed developing techniques of reducing the damage caused by earthquakes, rather than pursuing an apparently vain attempt to predict them.

VOLCANIC ERUPTIONS

Most active volcanoes also occur on or near plate edges. Many undersea volcanoes along the ocean ridges are formed from magma that wells up from the asthenosphere to fill the gaps created as the plates, on the opposite sides of the ridges, move apart. Some of these volcanoes reach the surface to form islands. Iceland is a country which straddles the Mid-Atlantic Ocean Ridge. It is gradually becoming wider as magma rises to the surface through faults and vents. Other volcanoes lie alongside subduction zones. The magma that fuels them comes from the melted edges of the descending plates.

A few volcanoes lie far from plate edges. For example, Mauna Loa and Kilauea on Hawaii are situated near the centre of the huge Pacific plate. The molten magma that reaches the surface is created by a source of heat, called a 'hot spot', in the Earth's mantle.

Magma is molten rock at temperatures of about 1,100°C to 1,200°C [2,012°F to 2,192°F]. It contains gases and superheated steam. The chemical composition of magma varies. Viscous magma is rich in silica and superheated steam, while runny magma contains less silica and steam. The chemical composition of the magma affects the nature of volcanic eruptions.

Explosive volcanoes contain thick, viscous magma. When they erupt, they usually hurl clouds of ash (shattered fragments of cooled magma) into the air. By contrast, quiet volcanoes emit long streams of runny magma, or lava. However, many volcanoes are intermediate in type, sometimes erupting explosively and sometimes emitting streams of fluid lava. Explosive and intermediate volcanoes usually have a conical shape, while quiet volcanoes are flattened, resembling upturned saucers. They are often called shield volcanoes.

One dangerous type of eruption is called a *nuée ardente*, or 'glowing cloud'. It occurs when a cloud of intensely hot volcanic gases and dust particles and superheated steam are exploded from a volcano. They move rapidly downhill, burning everything in their path and choking animals and people. The blast that creates the *nuée ardente* may release the pressure inside the volcano, resulting in a tremendous explosion that hurls tall columns of ash into the air.

Kilauea Volcano, Hawaii

The volcanic Hawaiian islands in the North Pacific Ocean were formed as the Pacific plate moved over a 'hot spot' in the Earth's mantle. Kilauea on Hawaii emits blazing streams of liquid lava.

Forces of Nature

When the volcano Mount Pinatubo erupted in the Philippines in 1991, large areas around the mountain were covered by ash. Later, rainwater mixed with the loose ash on sloping land, created lahars, or mudflows, which swept down river valleys burying many areas. Such incidents are not only reminders of the great forces that operate inside our planet but also of those natural forces operating on the surface, which can have dramatic effects on the land.

The chief forces acting on the surface of the Earth are weathering, running water, ice and winds. The forces of erosion seem to act slowly. One estimate suggests that an average of only 3.5 cm [1.4 in] of land is removed by natural processes every 1,000 years. This may not sound much, but over millions of years, it can reduce mountains to almost flat surfaces.

WEATHERING

Weathering occurs in all parts of the world, but the most effective type of weathering in any area depends on the climate and the nature of the rocks. For example, in cold mountain areas,

when water freezes in cracks in rocks, the ice occupies 9% more space than the water. This exerts a force which, when repeated over and over again, can split boulders apart. By contrast, in hot deserts, intense heating by day and cooling by night causes the outer layers of rocks to expand and contract until they break up and peel away like layers of an onion. These are examples of what is called mechanical weathering.

Other kinds of weathering include chemical reactions usually involving water. Rainwater containing carbon dioxide dissolved from the air or the soil is a weak acid which reacts with limestone, wearing out pits, tunnels and networks of caves in layers of limestone rock. Water also combines with some minerals, such as the feldspars in granite, to create kaolin, a white

RATES OF EROSION

	SLOW ◄	WEATHERING RATE ►	FAST
Mineral solubility	low (e.g. quartz)	moderate (e.g. feldspar)	high (e.g. calcite)
Rainfall	low	moderate	heavy
Temperature	cold	temperate	hot
Vegetation	sparse	moderate	lush
Soil cover	bare rock	thin to moderate soil	thick soil

Weathering is the breakdown and decay of rocks in situ. It may be mechanical (physical), chemical or biological.

Rates of erosion
The chart shows that the rates at which weathering takes place depend on the chemistry and hardness of rocks, climatic factors, especially rainfall and temperature, the vegetation and the nature of the soil cover in any area. The effects of weathering are increased by human action, particularly the removal of vegetation and the exposure of soils to the rain and wind.

Grand Canyon, Arizona, at dusk
The Grand Canyon in the United States is one of the world's natural wonders. Eroded by the Colorado River and its tributaries, it is up to 1.6 km [1 mile] deep and 29 km [18 miles] wide.

clay. These are examples of chemical weathering which constantly wears away rock.

RUNNING WATER, ICE AND WIND

In moist regions, rivers are effective in shaping the land. They transport material worn away by weathering and erode the land. They wear out V-shaped valleys in upland regions, while vigorous meanders widen their middle courses. The work of rivers is at its most spectacular when earth movements lift up flat areas and rejuvenate the rivers, giving them a new erosive power capable of wearing out such features as the Grand Canyon. Rivers also have a constructive role. Some of the world's most fertile regions are deltas and flood plains composed of sediments

Glaciers

During Ice Ages, ice spreads over large areas and the effect of glacial erosion on landscapes is enormous. However, during warm periods, the world's ice sheets and glaciers retreat. The chart shows that in recent years, the volumes of many glaciers around the world have been decreasing, possibly as a result of global warming.

ANNUAL FLUCTUATIONS FOR SELECTED GLACIERS

Glacier name and location	Changes in the annual mass balance†		Cumulative total
	1970–1	1990–1	1970–90
Alfotbreen, Norway	+940	+790	+12,110
Wolverine, USA	+770	–410	+2,320
Storglaciaren, Sweden	–190	+170	–120
Djankuat, Russia	–230	–310	–1,890
Grasubreen, Norway	+470	–520	–2,530
Ürümqi, China	+102	–706	–3,828
Golubin, Kyrgyzstan	–90	–722	–7,105
Hintereisferner, Austria	–600	–1,325	–9,081
Gries, Switzerland	–970	–1,480	–10,600
Careser, Italy	–650	–1,730	–11,610
Abramov, Tajikistan	–890	–420	–13,700
Sarennes, France	–1,100	–1,360	–15,020
Place, Canada	–343	–990	–15,175

† *The annual mass balance is defined as the difference between glacier accumulation and ablation (melting) averaged over the whole glacier. Balances are expressed as water equivalent in millimetres. A plus indicates an increase in the depth or length of the glacier; a minus indicates a reduction.*

Juneau Glacier, Alaska

Like huge conveyor belts, glaciers transport weathered debris from mountain regions. Rocks frozen in the ice give the glaciers teeth, enabling them to wear out typical glaciated land features.

periodically dumped there by such rivers as the Ganges, Mississippi and Nile.

Running water in the form of sea waves and currents shapes coastlines, wearing out caves, natural arches, and stacks. The sea also transports and deposits worn material to form such features as spits and bars.

Glaciers in cold mountain regions flow downhill, gradually deepening valleys and shaping dramatic landscapes. They erode steep-sided U-shaped valleys, into which rivers often plunge in large waterfalls. Other features include cirques, armchair-shaped basins bounded by knife-edged ridges called *arêtes*. When several glacial cirques erode to form radial *arêtes*, pyramidal peaks like the Matterhorn are created. Deposits of moraine, rock material dumped by the glacier, are further evidence that ice once covered large areas. The work of glaciers, like other agents of erosion, varies with the climate. In recent years, global warming has been making glaciers retreat in many areas, while several of the ice shelves in Antarctica have been breaking up.

Many land features in deserts were formed by running water at a time when the climate was much rainier than it is today. Water erosion also occurs when flash floods are caused by rare thunderstorms. But the chief agent of erosion in dry areas is wind-blown sand, which can strip the paint from cars, and undercut boulders to create mushroom-shaped rocks.

Oceans and Ice

Since the 1970s, oceanographers have found numerous hot vents on the ocean ridges. Called black smokers, the vents emit dark, mineral-rich water reaching 350°C [662°F]. Around the vents are chimney-like structures formed from minerals deposited from the hot water. The discovery of black smokers did not surprise scientists who already knew that the ridges were plate edges, where new crustal rock was being formed as molten magma welled up to the surface. But what was astonishing was that the hot water contained vast numbers of bacteria, which provided the base of a food chain that included many strange creatures, such as giant worms, eyeless shrimps and white clams. Many species were unknown to science.

Little was known about the dark world beneath the waves until about 50 years ago. But through the use of modern technology such as echo-sounders, magnetometers, research ships equipped with huge drills, submersibles that can carry scientists down to the ocean floor, and satellites, the secrets of the oceans have been gradually revealed.

The study of the ocean floor led to the discovery that the oceans are geologically young features – no more than 200 million years old. It also revealed evidence as to how oceans form and continents drift because of the action of plate tectonics.

THE BLUE PLANET
Water covers almost 71% of the Earth, which makes it look blue when viewed from space. Although the oceans are interconnected, geographers divide them into four main areas: the Pacific, Atlantic, Indian and Arctic oceans. The average depth of the oceans is 3,370 m [12,238 ft], but they are divided into several zones.

Around most continents are gently sloping continental shelves, which are flooded parts of the continents. The shelves end at the continental slope, at a depth of about 200 m [656 ft]. This slope leads steeply down to the abyss. The deepest parts of the oceans are the trenches, which reach a maximum depth of 11,033 m [36,198 ft] in the Mariana Trench in the western Pacific.

Most marine life is found in the top 200 m [656 ft], where there is sufficient sunlight for plants, called phytoplankton, to grow. Below this zone, life becomes more and more scarce, though no part of the ocean, even at the bottom of the deepest trenches, is completely without living things.

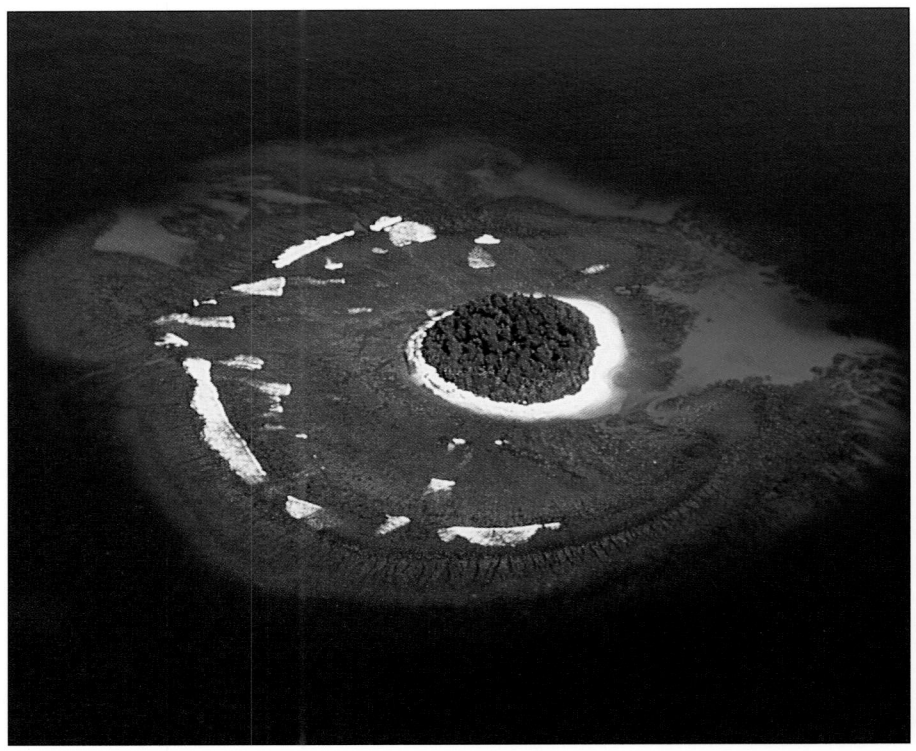

Vava'u Island, Tonga
This small coral atoll in northern Tonga consists of a central island covered by rainforest. Low coral reefs washed by the waves surround a shallow central lagoon.

Continental islands, such as the British Isles, are high parts of the continental shelves. For example, until about 7,500 years ago, when the ice sheets formed during the Ice Ages were melting, raising the sea level and filling the North Sea and the Strait of Dover, Britain was linked to mainland Europe.

By contrast, oceanic islands, such as the Hawaiian chain in the North Pacific Ocean, rise from the ocean floor. All oceanic islands are of volcanic origin, although many of them in warm parts of the oceans have sunk and are capped by layers of coral to form ring- or horseshoe-shaped atolls and coral reefs.

OCEAN WATER
The oceans contain about 97% of the world's water. Seawater contains more than 70 dissolved elements, but chloride and sodium make up 85% of the total. Sodium chloride is common salt and it makes seawater salty. The salinity of the oceans is mostly between 3.3–3.7%. Ocean water fed by icebergs or large rivers is less saline than shallow seas in the tropics, where the evaporation rate is high. Seawater is a source of salt but the water is useless for agriculture or drinking unless it is desalinated. However, land

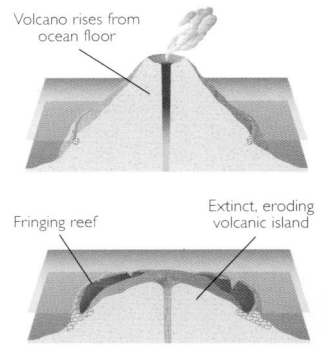

Volcano rises from ocean floor

Fringing reef

Extinct, eroding volcanic island

After subsidence, reef covers buried island

Lagoon

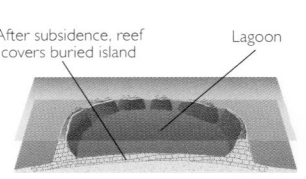

Development of an atoll
Some of the volcanoes that rise from the ocean floor reach the surface to form islands. Some of these islands subside and become submerged. As an island sinks, coral starts to grow around the rim of the volcano, building up layer upon layer of limestone deposits to form fringing reefs. Sometimes coral grows on the tip of a central cone to form an island in the middle of the atoll.

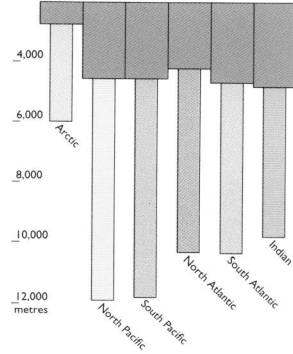

The ocean depths
The diagram shows the average depths (in dark blue) and the greatest depths in the four oceans. The North Pacific Ocean contains the world's deepest trenches, including the Mariana Trench, where the deepest manned descent was made by the bathyscaphe Trieste in 1960. It reached a depth of 10,916 metres [35,813 ft].

Relative sizes of the world's oceans:

PACIFIC   49%   ATLANTIC   26%
INDIAN   21%   ARCTIC   4%

Some geographers distinguish a fifth ocean, the Southern or Antarctic Ocean, but most authorities regard these waters as the southern extension of the Pacific, Atlantic and Indian oceans.

areas get a regular supply of fresh water through the hydrological cycle (see page 26).

The density of seawater depends on its salinity and temperature. Temperatures vary from –2°C [28°F], the freezing point of seawater at the poles, to around 30°C [86°F] in parts of the tropics. Density differences help to maintain the circulation of the world's oceans, especially deep-sea currents. But the main cause of currents within 350 m [1,148 ft] of the surface is the wind. Because of the Earth's rotation, currents are deflected, creating huge circular motions of surface water – clockwise in the northern hemisphere and anticlockwise in the southern hemisphere.

Ocean currents transport heat from the tropics to the polar regions and thus form part of the heat engine that drives the Earth's climates. Ocean currents have an especially marked effect on coastal climates, such as north-western Europe. In the mid-1990s, scientists warned that global warming may be weakening currents, including the warm Gulf Stream which is responsible for the mild winters experienced in north-western Europe.

ICE SHEETS, ICE CAPS AND GLACIERS
Global warming is also a threat to the world's ice sheets, ice caps and glaciers that together account for about 2% of the world's water. There are two ice sheets in the world, the largest covers most of Antarctica. With the ice reaching maximum depths of 4,800 m [15,748 ft], the Antarctic ice sheet contains about 70% of the world's fresh water, with a total volume about nine times greater than the Greenland ice sheet. Smaller bodies of ice include ice caps in northern Canada, Iceland and Scandinavia. Also throughout the world in high ranges are many valley glaciers, which help to shape dramatic mountain scenery.

Only about 11,000 years ago, during the final phase of the Pleistocene Ice Age, ice covered much of the northern hemisphere. The Ice Age, which began about 1.8 million years ago, was not a continuous period of cold. Instead, it consisted of glacial periods when the ice advanced and warmer interglacial periods when temperatures rose and the ice retreated.

Some scientists believe that we are now living in an inter-glacial period, and that glacial conditions will recur in the future. Others fear that global warming, caused mainly by pollution, may melt the world's ice, raising sea levels by up to 55 m [180 ft]. Many fertile and densely populated coastal plains, islands and cities would vanish from the map.

Weddell Sea, Antarctica
Antarctica contains two huge bays, occupied by the Ross and Weddell seas. Ice shelves extend from the ice sheet across parts of these seas. Researchers fear that warmer weather is melting Antarctica's ice sheets at a dangerous rate, after large chunks of the Larsen ice shelf and the Ronne ice shelf broke away in 1997 and 1998, respectively.

The Earth's Atmosphere

Since the discovery in 1985 of a thinning of the ozone layer, creating a so-called 'ozone hole', over Antarctica, many governments have worked to reduce the emissions of ozone-eating substances, notably the chlorofluorocarbons (CFCs) used in aerosols, refrigeration, air conditioning and dry cleaning.

Following forecasts that the ozone layer would rapidly repair itself as a result of controls on these emissions, scientists were surprised in early 1996 when a marked thinning of the ozone layer occurred over the Arctic, northern Europe, Russia and Canada. The damage, which was recorded as far south as southern Britain, was due to pollution combined with intense cold in the stratosphere. It was another sharp reminder of the dangers humanity faces when it interferes with and harms the environment.

The ozone layer in the stratosphere blocks out most of the dangerous ultraviolet B radiation in the Sun's rays. This radiation causes skin cancer and cataracts, as well as harming plants on the land and plankton in the oceans. The ozone layer is only one way in which the atmosphere protects life on Earth. The atmosphere also provides the air we breathe and the carbon dioxide required by plants. It is also a shield against meteors and it acts as a blanket to prevent heat radiated from the Earth escaping into space.

LAYERS OF AIR

The atmosphere is divided into four main layers. The troposphere at the bottom contains about 85% of the atmosphere's total mass, where most weather conditions occur. The troposphere is about 15 km [9 miles] thick over the Equator and 8 km [5 miles] thick at the poles. Temperatures decrease with height by approximately 1°C [2°F] for every 100 m [328 ft]. At the top of the troposphere is a level called the tropopause where temperatures are stable at around −55°C [−67°F]. Above the tropopause is the stratosphere, which contains the ozone layer. Here, at about 50 km [31 miles] above the Earth's surface, temperatures rise to about 0°C [32°F].

The ionosphere extends from the stratopause to about 600 km [373 miles] above the surface. Here temperatures fall up to about 80 km

Moonrise seen from orbit

This photograph taken by an orbiting Shuttle shows the crescent of the Moon. Silhouetted at the horizon is a dense cloud layer. The reddish-brown band is the tropopause, which separates the blue-white stratosphere from the yellow troposphere.

CIRCULATION OF AIR

HIGH PRESSURE
LOW PRESSURE
WARM AIR
COLD AIR
SURFACE WINDS
CLOUDS

The circulation of the atmosphere can be divided into three rotating but interconnected air systems, or cells. The Hadley cell (figure 1 on the above diagram) is in the tropics; the Ferrel cell (2) lies between the subtropics and the mid-latitudes, and the Polar cell (3) is in the high latitudes.

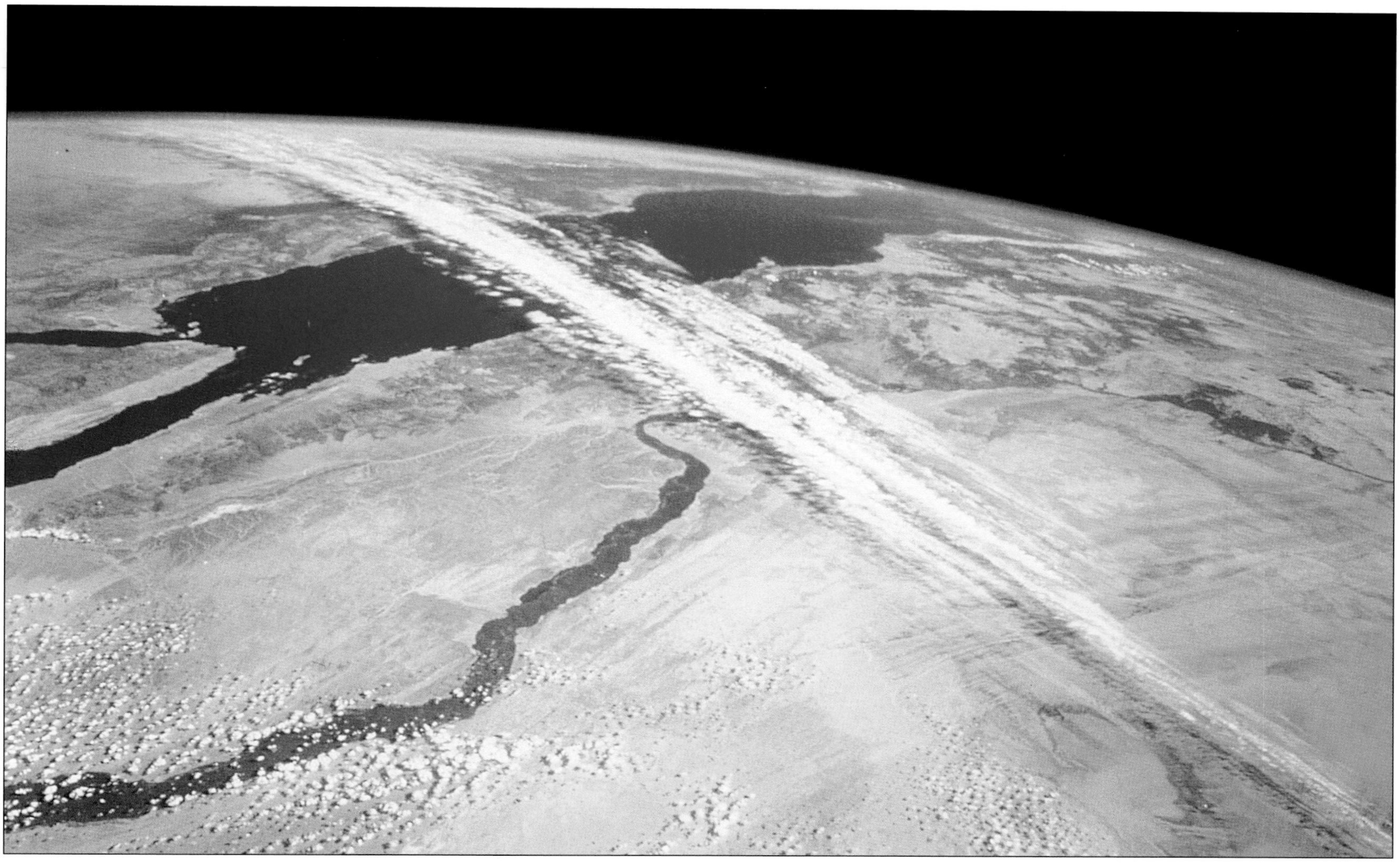

Jetstream from space

Jetstreams are strong winds that normally blow near the tropopause. Cirrus clouds mark the route of the jet stream in this photograph, which shows the Red Sea, North Africa and the Nile valley, which appears as a dark band crossing the desert.

[50 miles], but then rise. The aurorae, which occur in the ionosphere when charged particles from the Sun interact with the Earth's magnetic field, are strongest near the poles. In the exosphere, the outermost layer, the atmosphere merges into space.

CIRCULATION OF THE ATMOSPHERE

The heating of the Earth is most intense around the Equator where the Sun is high in the sky. Here warm, moist air rises in strong currents, creating a zone of low air pressure: the doldrums. The rising air eventually cools and spreads out north and south until it sinks back to the ground around latitudes 30° North and 30° South. This forms two zones of high air pressure called the horse latitudes.

From the horse latitudes, trade winds blow back across the surface towards the Equator, while westerly winds blow towards the poles. The warm westerlies finally meet the polar easterlies (cold dense air flowing from the poles). The line along which the warm and cold air streams meet is called the polar front. Depressions (or cyclones) are low air pressure frontal systems that form along the polar front.

COMPOSITION OF THE ATMOSPHERE

The air in the troposphere is made up mainly of nitrogen (78%) and oxygen (21%). Argon makes up more than 0.9% and there are also minute amounts of carbon dioxide, helium, hydrogen, krypton, methane, ozone and xenon. The atmosphere also contains water vapour, the gaseous form of water, which, when it condenses around minute specks of dust and salt, forms tiny water droplets or ice crystals. Large masses of water droplets or ice crystals form clouds.

Classification of clouds

Clouds are classified broadly into cumuliform, or 'heap' clouds, and stratiform, or 'layer' clouds. Both types occur at all levels. The highest clouds, composed of ice crystals, are cirrus, cirrostratus and cirrocumulus. Medium-height clouds include altostratus, a grey cloud that often indicates the approach of a depression, and altocumulus, a thicker and fluffier version of cirrocumulus. Low clouds include stratus, which forms dull, overcast skies; nimbostratus, a dark grey layer cloud which brings almost continuous rain and snow; cumulus, a brilliant white heap cloud; and stratocumulus, a layer cloud arranged in globular masses or rolls. Cumulonimbus, a cloud associated with thunderstorms, lightning and heavy rain, often extends from low to medium altitudes. It has a flat base, a fluffy outline and often an anvil-shaped top.

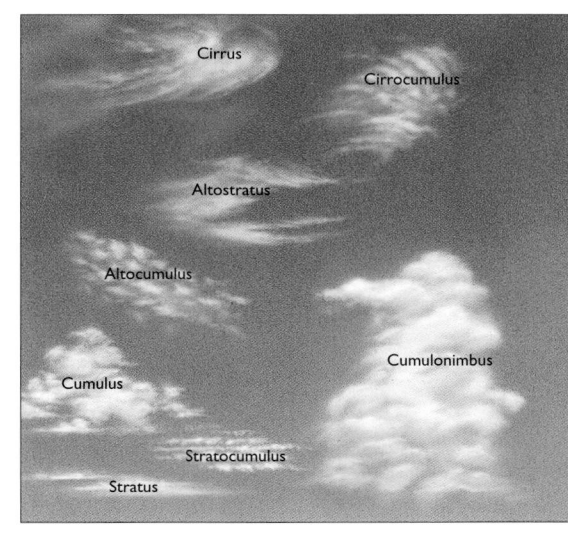

Cirrus

Cirrocumulus

Altostratus

Altocumulus

Cumulonimbus

Cumulus

Stratocumulus

Stratus

Climate and Weather

In April 1989, a tornado destroyed the town of Shaturia in Bangladesh, killing 1,300 people. In 1992, Hurricane Andrew struck the Bahamas, Florida and Louisiana, causing record damage estimated at $30 billion. In September 1998, following heavy monsoon rains, floods submerged about two-thirds of Bangladesh. The same month, in Central America, more than 7,000 people died in floods and mudslides caused by Hurricane Mitch. The economy of Honduras, already crippled by debt, was thought to have been put back by 15 to 20 years.

Every year, exceptional weather conditions cause disasters around the world. Modern forecasting techniques now give people warning of advancing storms, but the toll of human deaths continues as people are powerless in the face of the awesome forces of nature.

Weather is the day-to-day condition of the atmosphere. In some places, the weather is normally stable, but in other areas, especially the middle latitudes, it is highly variable, changing with the passing of a depression. By contrast, climate is the average weather of a place, based on data obtained over a long period.

Hurricane Elena, 1995
Hurricanes form over warm oceans north and south of the Equator. Their movements are tracked by satellites, enabling forecasters to issue storm warnings as they approach land. In North America, forecasters identify them with boys' and girls' names.

CLIMATIC FACTORS

Climate depends basically on the unequal heating of the Sun between the Equator and the poles. But ocean currents and terrain also affect climate. For example, despite their northerly positions, Norway's ports remain ice-free in winter. This is because of the warming effect of the North Atlantic Drift, an extension of the Gulf Stream which flows across the Atlantic Ocean from the Gulf of Mexico.

By contrast, the cold Benguela current which flows up the coast of south-western Africa cools the coast and causes arid conditions. This is because the cold onshore winds are warmed as they pass over the land. The warm air can hold more water vapour than cold air, giving the winds a drying effect.

The terrain affects climate in several ways. Because temperatures fall with altitude, highlands are cooler than lowlands in the same

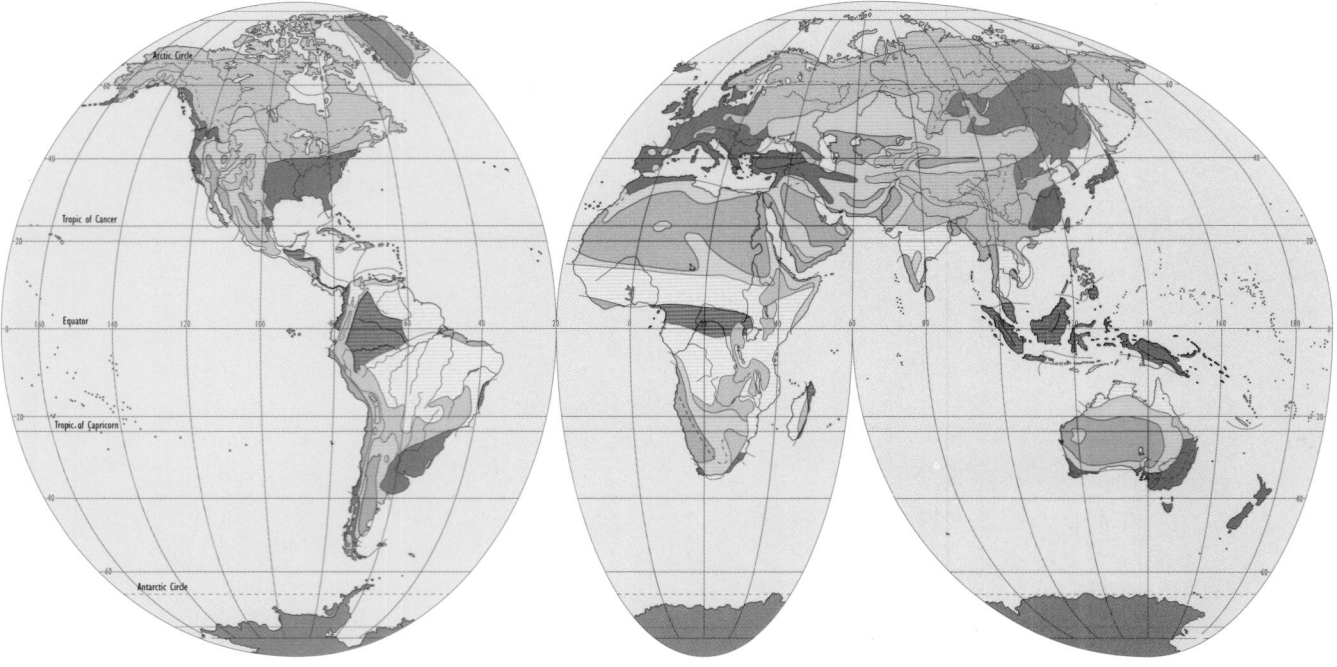

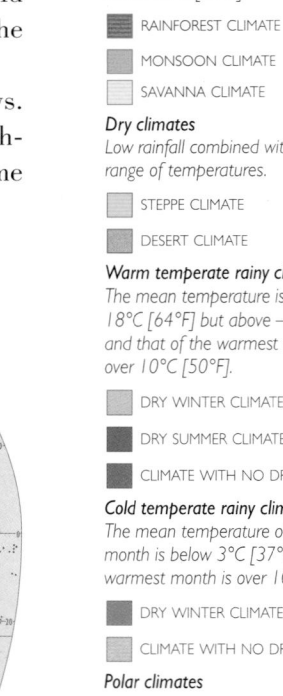

CLIMATIC REGIONS

Tropical rainy climates
All mean monthly temperatures above 18°C [64°F].

■ RAINFOREST CLIMATE
■ MONSOON CLIMATE
□ SAVANNA CLIMATE

Dry climates
Low rainfall combined with a wide range of temperatures.

□ STEPPE CLIMATE
■ DESERT CLIMATE

Warm temperate rainy climates
The mean temperature is below 18°C [64°F] but above −3°C [26°F] and that of the warmest month is over 10°C [50°F].

□ DRY WINTER CLIMATE
■ DRY SUMMER CLIMATE
■ CLIMATE WITH NO DRY SEASON

Cold temperate rainy climates
The mean temperature of the coldest month is below 3°C [37°F] but the warmest month is over 10°C [50°F].

■ DRY WINTER CLIMATE
□ CLIMATE WITH NO DRY SEASON

Polar climates
The temperature of the warmest month is below 10°C [50°F], giving permanently frozen subsoil.

□ TUNDRA CLIMATE
■ POLAR CLIMATE

Floods in St Louis, United States
The satellite image, right, shows the extent of the floods at St Louis at the confluence of the Mississippi and the Missouri rivers in June and July 1993. The floods occurred when very heavy rainfall raised river levels by up to 14 m [46 ft]. The floods reached their greatest extent between Minneapolis in the north and a point approximately 150 km [93 miles] south of St Louis. In places, the width of the Mississippi increased to nearly 11 km [7 miles], while the Missouri reached widths of 32 km [20 miles]. In all, more than 28,000 sq km [10,800 sq miles] were inundated and hundreds of towns and cities were flooded. Damage to crops was estimated at $8 billion. The USA was hit again by flooding in early 1997, when heavy rainfall in North Dakota and Minnesota caused the Red River to flood. The flooding had a catastrophic effect on the city of Grand Forks, which was inundated for months.

Flood damage in the United States
In June and July 1993, the Mississippi River basin suffered record floods. The photograph shows a sunken church in Illinois. The flooding along the Mississippi, Missouri and other rivers caused great damage, amounting to about $12 billion. At least 48 people died in the floods.

CLIMATIC REGIONS

The two major factors that affect climate are temperature and precipitation, including rain and snow. In addition, seasonal variations and other climatic features are also taken into account. Climatic classifications vary because of the weighting given to various features. Yet most classifications are based on five main climatic types: tropical rainy climates; dry climates; warm temperate rainy climates; cold temperate rainy climates; and very cold polar climates. Some classifications also allow for the effect of altitude. The main climatic regions are sub-divided according to seasonal variations and also to the kind of vegetation associated with the climatic conditions. Thus, the rainforest climate, with rain throughout the year, differs from monsoon and savanna climates, which have marked dry seasons. Similarly, parched desert climates differ from steppe climates which have enough moisture for grasses to grow.

latitude. Terrain also affects rainfall. When moist onshore winds pass over mountain ranges, they are chilled as they are forced to rise and the water vapour they contain condenses to form clouds which bring rain and snow. After the winds have crossed the mountains, the air descends and is warmed. These warm, dry winds create rain shadow (arid) regions on the lee side of the mountains.

Water and Land Use

All life on land depends on fresh water. Yet about 80 countries now face acute water shortages. The world demand for fresh water is increasing by about 2.3% a year and this demand will double every 21 years. About a billion people, mainly in developing countries, do not have access to clean drinking water and around 10 million die every year from drinking dirty water. This problem is made worse in many countries by the pollution of rivers and lakes.

In 1995, a World Bank report suggested that wars will be fought over water in the 21st century. Relations between several countries are

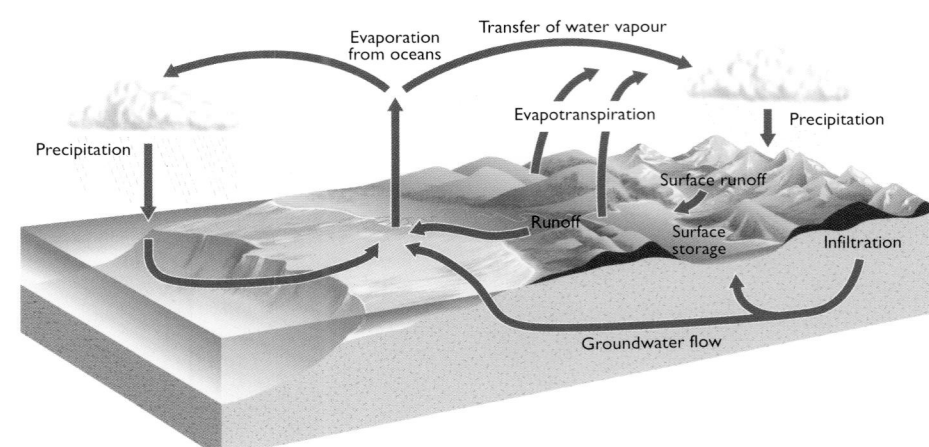

Hoover Dam, United States
The Hoover Dam in Arizona controls the Colorado River's flood waters. Its reservoir supplies domestic and irrigation water to the south-west, while a hydroelectric plant produces electricity.

already soured by disputes over water resources. Egypt fears that Sudan and Ethiopia will appropriate the waters of the Nile, while Syria and Iraq are concerned that Turkish dams will hold back the waters of the Euphrates.

However, experts stress that while individual countries face water crises, there is no global crisis. The chief global problems are the uneven distribution of water and its inefficient and wasteful use.

THE WORLD'S WATER SUPPLY

Of the world's total water supply, 99.4% is in the oceans or frozen in bodies of ice. Most of the rest circulates through the rocks beneath our feet as ground water. Water in rivers and lakes, in the soil and in the atmosphere together make up only 0.013% of the world's water.

The freshwater supply on land is dependent on the hydrological, or water cycle which is driven by the Sun's heat. Water is evaporated from the oceans and carried into the air as invisible water vapour. Although this vapour averages less than 2% of the total mass of the atmosphere, it is the chief component from the standpoint of weather.

When air rises, water vapour condenses into visible water droplets or ice crystals, which eventually fall to earth as rain, snow, sleet, hail or frost. Some of the precipitation that reaches the ground returns directly to the atmosphere through evaporation or transpiration via plants. Much of the rest of the water flows into the rocks to become ground water or across the surface into rivers and, eventually, back to the oceans, so completing the hydrological cycle.

WATER AND AGRICULTURE

Only about a third of the world's land area is used for growing crops, while another third

The hydrological cycle
The hydrological cycle is responsible for the continuous circulation of water around the planet. Water vapour contains and transports latent heat, or latent energy. When the water vapour condenses back into water (and falls as rain, hail or snow), the heat is released. When condensation takes place on cold nights, the cooling effect associated with nightfall is offset by the liberation of latent heat.

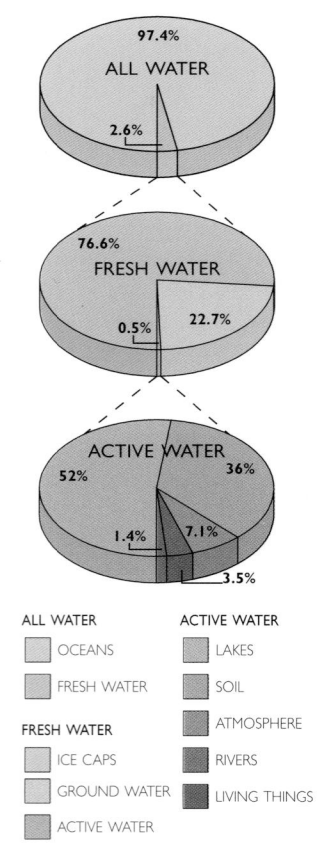

WATER DISTRIBUTION
The distribution of planetary water, by percentage.

ALL WATER	ACTIVE WATER
OCEANS	LAKES
FRESH WATER	SOIL
	ATMOSPHERE
FRESH WATER	RIVERS
ICE CAPS	LIVING THINGS
GROUND WATER	
ACTIVE WATER	

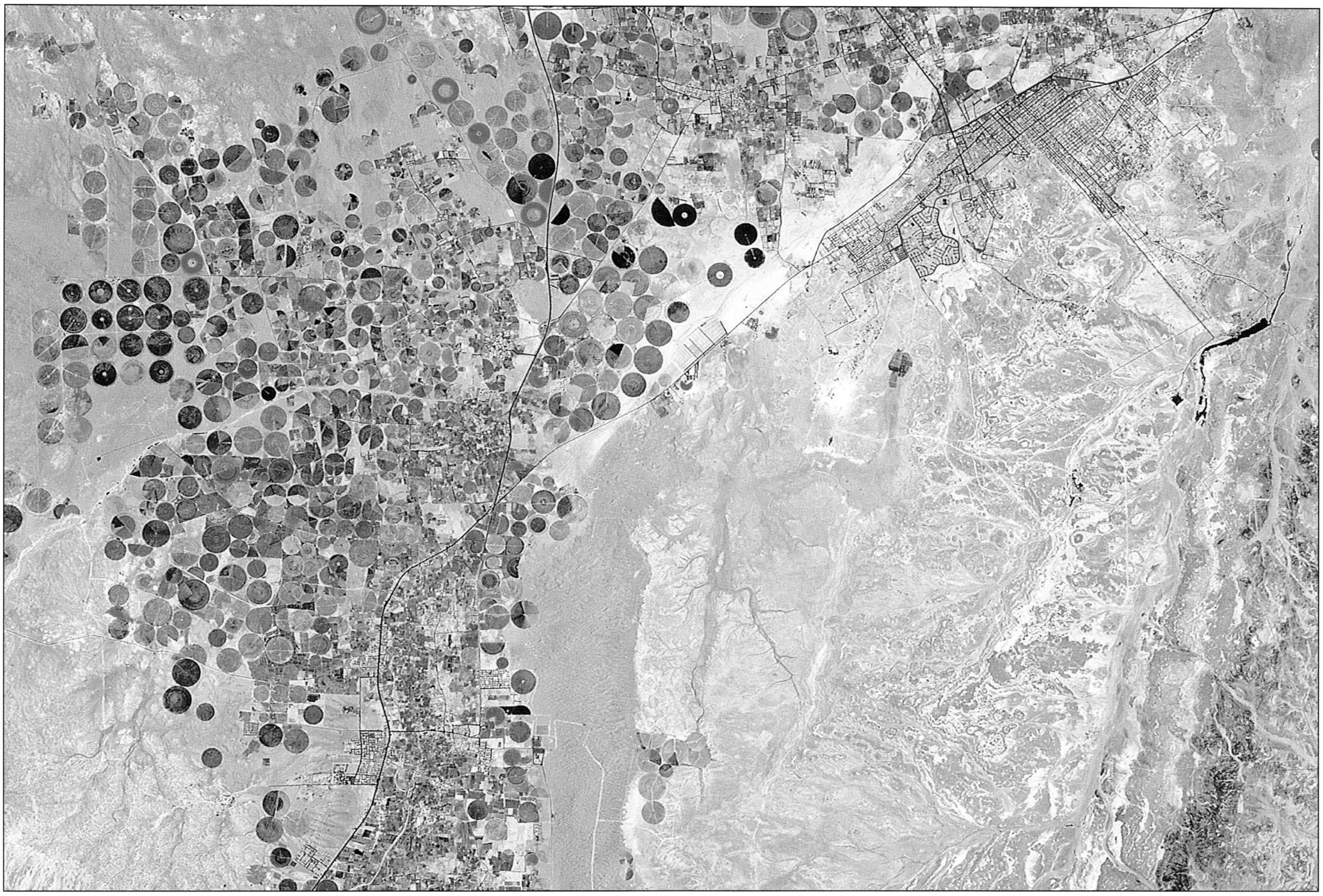

Photographic satellite image of Saudi Arabia irrigation.

Irrigation in Saudi Arabia
Saudi Arabia is a desert country which gets its water from oases, which tap ground water supplies, and desalination plants. The sale of oil has enabled the arid countries of south-western Asia to develop their agriculture. In the above satellite image, vegetation appears brown and red.

Irrigation boom
The photograph shows a pivotal irrigation boom used to sprinkle water over a wheat field in Saudi Arabia. Irrigation in hot countries often takes place at night so that water loss through evaporation is reduced. Irrigation techniques vary from place to place. In monsoon areas with abundant water, the fields are often flooded, or the water is led to the crops along straight furrows. Sprinkler irrigation has become important since the 1940s. In other types of irrigation, the water is led through pipes which are on or under the ground. Underground pipes supply water directly to the plant roots and, as a result, water loss through evaporation is minimized.

consists of meadows and pasture. The rest of the world is unsuitable for farming, being too dry, too cold, too mountainous, or covered by dense forests. Although the demand for food increases every year, problems arise when attempts are made to increase the existing area of farmland. For example, the soils and climates of tropical forest and semi-arid regions of Africa and South America are not ideal for farming. Attempts to work such areas usually end in failure. To increase the world's food supply, scientists now concentrate on making existing farmland more productive rather than farming marginal land.

To grow crops, farmers need fertile, workable land, an equable climate, including a frost-free growing period, and an adequate supply of fresh water. In some areas, the water falls directly as rain. But many other regions depend on irrigation.

Irrigation involves water conservation through the building of dams which hold back storage reservoirs. In some areas, irrigation water comes from underground aquifers, layers of permeable and porous rocks through which ground water percolates. But in many cases, the water in the aquifers has been there for thousands of years, having accumulated at a time when the rainfall

was much greater than it is today. As a result, these aquifers are not being renewed and will, one day, dry up.

Other sources of irrigation water are desalination plants, which remove salt from seawater and pump it to farms. This is a highly expensive process and is employed in areas where water supplies are extremely low, such as the island of Malta, or in the oil-rich desert countries around the Gulf, which can afford to build huge desalination plants.

LAND USE BY CONTINENT

	Forest	Permanent pasture	Permanent crops	Arable	Non-productive
North America	32.2%	17.3%	0.3%	12.6%	37.6%
South America	51.8%	26.7%	1.5%	6.6%	13.4%
Europe	33.4%	17.5%	3.0%	26.8%	19.3%
Africa	23.2%	26.6%	0.6%	5.6%	44.0%
Asia	20.2%	25.0%	1.2%	16.0%	37.8%
Oceania	23.5%	52.2%	0.1%	5.7%	18.5%

The Natural World

In 1995, a United Nations Environment Programme report stated that 11% of all mammal species, 18% of birds and 5% of fish are now threatened with extinction. Furthermore, it predicted that half of all bird and mammal species will become extinct within 300 years, or sooner if current trends continue. This will greatly reduce the biodiversity of our planet, causing the disappearance of unique combinations of genes that could be vital in improving food yields on farms or in the production of drugs to combat diseases.

Extinctions of species have occurred throughout Earth history, but today the extinction rate is estimated to be about 10,000 times the natural average. Some scientists have even compared it with the mass extinction that wiped out the dinosaurs 65 million years ago. However, the main cause of today's high extinction rate is not some natural disaster, such as the impact of an asteroid a few kilometres across, but it is the result of human actions, most notably the destruction of natural habitats for farming and other purposes. In some densely populated areas, such as Western Europe, the natural

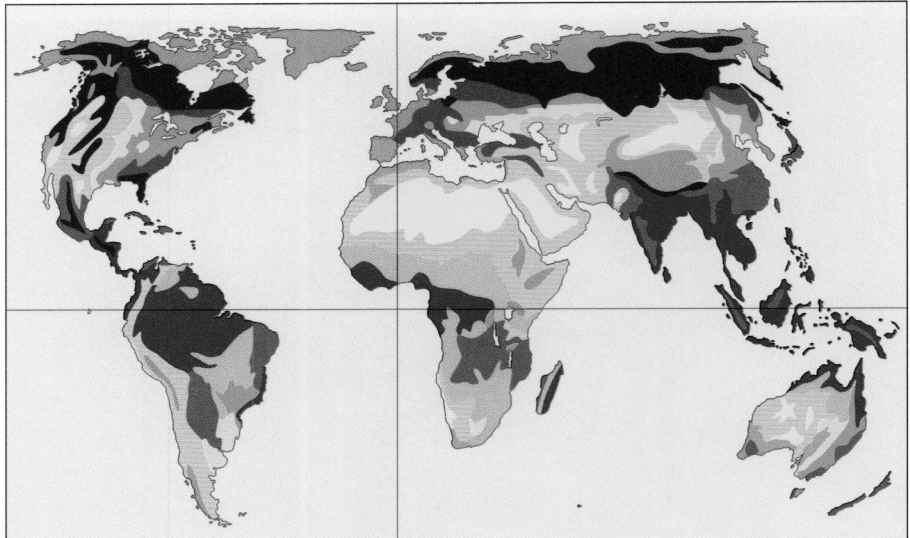

Rainforest in Rwanda
Rainforests are the most threatened of the world's biomes. Effective conservation policies must demonstrate to poor local people that they can benefit from the survival of the forests.

habitats were destroyed long ago. Today, the greatest damage is occurring in tropical rainforests, which contain more than half of the world's known species.

Modern technology has enabled people to live comfortably almost anywhere on Earth. But most plants and many animals are adapted to particular climatic conditions, and they live in association with and dependent on each other. Plant and animal communities that cover large areas are called biomes.

THE WORLD'S BIOMES

The world's biomes are defined mainly by climate and vegetation. They range from the tundra, in polar regions and high mountain regions, to the lush equatorial rainforests.

The Arctic tundra covers large areas in the polar regions of the northern hemisphere. Snow covers the land for more than half of the year and the subsoil, called permafrost, is permanently frozen. Comparatively few species can survive in this harsh, treeless environment. The main plants are hardy mosses, lichens, grasses, sedges and low shrubs. However, in summer, the tundra plays an important part in world animal geography, when its growing plants and swarms of insects provide food for migrating animals and birds that arrive from the south.

The tundra of the northern hemisphere merges in the south into a vast region of needleleaf evergreen forest, called the boreal forest or taiga. Such trees as fir, larch, pine and spruce are adapted to survive the long, bitterly cold winters of this region, but the number of plant and animal species is again small. South of the boreal forests is a zone of mixed needleleaf evergreens and broadleaf deciduous trees, which

NATURAL VEGETATION

- TUNDRA & MOUNTAIN VEGETATION
- NEEDLELEAF EVERGREEN FOREST
- MIXED NEEDLELEAF EVERGREEN & BROADLEAF DECIDUOUS TREES
- BROADLEAF DECIDUOUS WOODLAND
- MID-LATITUDE GRASSLAND
- EVERGREEN BROADLEAF & DECIDUOUS TREES & SHRUBS
- SEMI-DESERT SCRUB
- DESERT
- TROPICAL GRASSLAND (SAVANNA)
- TROPICAL BROADLEAF RAINFOREST & MONSOON FOREST
- SUBTROPICAL BROADLEAF & NEEDLELEAF FOREST

The map shows the world's main biomes. The classification is based on the natural 'climax' vegetation of regions, a result of the climate and the terrain. But human activities have greatly modified this basic division. For example, the original deciduous forests of Western Europe and the eastern United States have largely disappeared. In recent times, human development of some semi-arid areas has turned former dry grasslands into barren desert.

Tundra in subarctic Alaska
The Denali National Park, Alaska, contains magnificent mountain scenery and tundra vegetation which flourishes during the brief summer. The park is open between 1 June and 15 September.

shed their leaves in winter. In warmer areas, this mixed forest merges into broadleaf deciduous forest, where the number and diversity of plant species is much greater.

Deciduous forests are adapted to temperate, humid regions. Evergreen broadleaf and deciduous trees grow in Mediterranean regions, with their hot, dry summers. But much of the original deciduous forest has been cut down and has given way to scrub and heathland. Grasslands occupy large areas in the middle latitudes, where the rainfall is insufficient to support forest

growth. The moister grasslands are often called prairies, while drier areas are called steppe.

The tropics also contain vast dry areas of semi-desert scrub which merges into desert, as well as large areas of savanna, which is grassland with scattered trees. Savanna regions, with their marked dry season, support a wide range of mammals.

Tropical and subtropical regions contain three types of forest biomes. The tropical rainforest, the world's richest biome measured by its plant and animal species, experiences rain and high temperatures throughout the year. Similar forests occur in monsoon regions, which have a season of very heavy rainfall. They, too, are rich in plant species, though less so than the tropical rainforest. A third type of forest is the subtropical broadleaf and needleleaf forest, found in such places as south-eastern China, south-central Africa and eastern Brazil.

NET PRIMARY PRODUCTION OF EIGHT MAJOR BIOMES

- TROPICAL RAINFORESTS
- DECIDUOUS FORESTS
- TROPICAL GRASSLANDS
- CONIFEROUS FORESTS
- MEDITERRANEAN
- TEMPERATE GRASSLANDS
- TUNDRA
- DESERTS

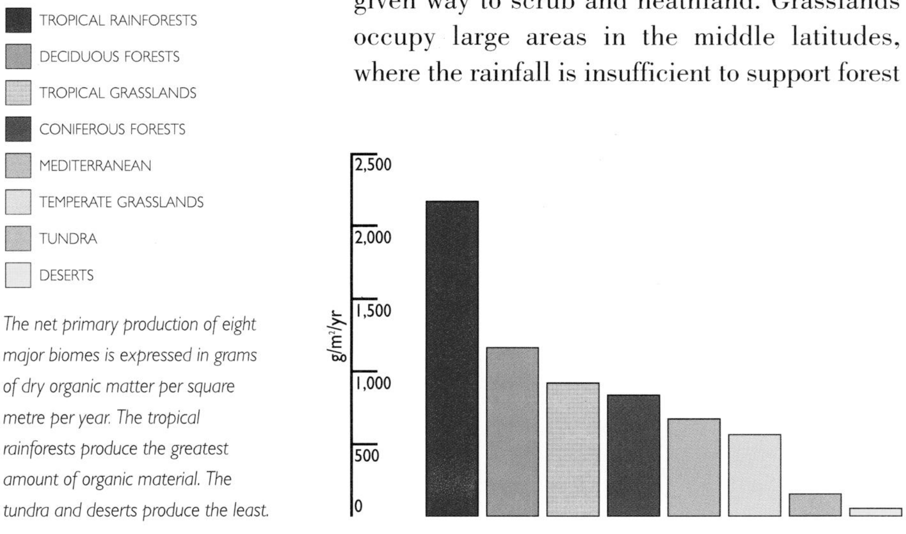

The net primary production of eight major biomes is expressed in grams of dry organic matter per square metre per year. The tropical rainforests produce the greatest amount of organic material. The tundra and deserts produce the least.

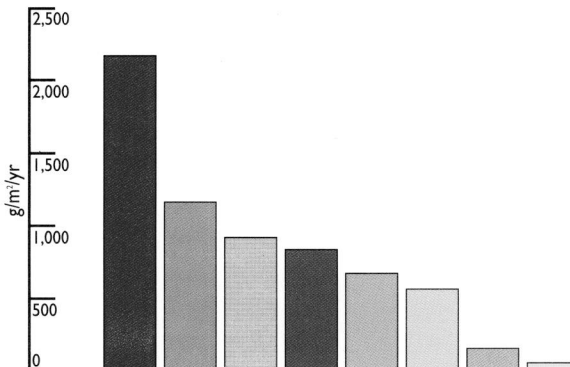

The Human World

Every minute, the world's population increases by between 160 and 170. While forecasts of future growth are difficult to make, most demographers are in agreement that the world's population, which passed the 6 billion mark in October 1999, would reach 8.9 billion by 2050. It was not expected to level out until 2200, when it would peak at around 11 billion. After 2200, it is expected to level out or even decline a little. The fastest rates of increase will take place in the developing countries of Africa, Asia and Latin America – the places least able to afford the enormous costs incurred by such a rapidly expanding population.

Elevated view of Ki Lung Street, Hong Kong
Urban areas of Hong Kong, a Special Administrative Region on the southern coast of China, contain busy streets overlooked by crowded apartments. They reflect the early days of urbanization in China.

Average world population growth rates have declined from about 2% a year in the early 1960s to 1.3% in 1997. This was partly due to a decline in fertility rates – that is, the number of births to the number of women of child-bearing age – especially in developed countries where, as income has risen, the average size of families has fallen.

Declining fertility rates were also evident in many developing countries. Even Africa shows signs of such change, though its population is expected to triple before it begins to fall. Population growth is also dependent on death rates, which are affected by such factors as famine, disease and the quality of medical care.

THE POPULATION EXPLOSION

The world's population has grown steadily throughout most of human history, though certain events triggered periods of population growth. The invention of agriculture around 10,000 years ago, led to great changes in human society. Before then, most people had obtained food by hunting animals and gathering plants. Average life expectancies were probably no more than 20 years and life was hard. However, when farmers began to produce food surpluses, people began to live settled lives. This major milestone in human history led to the development of the first cities and early civilizations.

From an estimated 8 million in 8000 BC, the world population rose to about 300 million by AD 1000. Between 1000 and 1750, the rate of world population increase was around 0.1% per year, but another period of major economic and social change – the Industrial Revolution – began in the late 18th century. The Industrial Revolution led to improvements in farm technology and increases in food production. The world population began to increase quickly as industrialization spread across Europe and into North America. By 1850, it had reached 1.2 billion. The 2 billion mark was passed in the 1920s, and then the population rapidly doubled to 4 billion by the 1970s.

POPULATION FEATURES

Population growth affects the structure of societies. In developing countries with high annual rates of population increase, the large majority of the people are young and soon to become parents themselves. For example, in Kenya, which had until recently an annual rate of population growth of around 4%, just over half

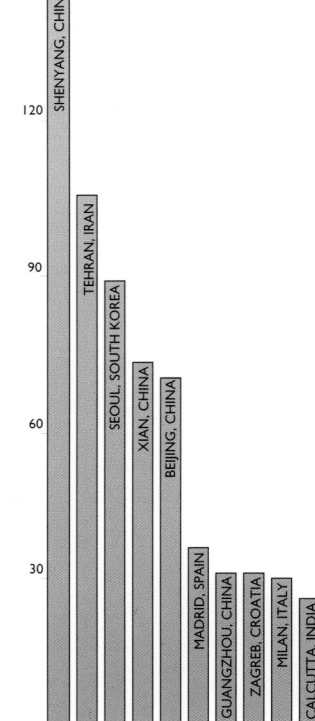

Urban air pollution
This diagram of the world's most polluted cities indicates the number of days per year when sulphur dioxide levels exceed the WHO threshhold of 150 micrograms per cubic metre.

Hong Kong's business district
By contrast with the picturesque old streets of Hong Kong, the business district of Hong Kong City, on the northern shore of Hong Kong Island, is a cluster of modern high-rise buildings. The glittering skyscrapers reflect the success of this tiny region, which has one of the strongest economies in Asia.

of the population is under 15 years of age. On the other hand, the populations of developed countries, with low population growth rates, have a fairly even spread across age groups.

Such differences are reflected in average life expectancies at birth. In rich countries, such as Australia and the United States, the average life expectancy is 77 years (74 years for men and 80 for women; women live longer, on average, than their male counterparts). As a result, an increasing proportion of the people are elderly and retired, contributing little to the economy. The reverse applies in many of the poorer countries, where average life expectancies are below 60 years. In more than a dozen countries in Africa, the average life expectancy is less than 50.

Paralleling the population explosion has been a rapid growth in the number and size of cities and towns, which contained nearly half of the world's people by the 1990s. This proportion is expected to rise to nearly two-thirds by 2025.

Urbanization occurred first in areas undergoing the industrialization of their economies, but today it is also a feature of the developing world. In developing countries, people are leaving impoverished rural areas hoping to gain access to the education, health and other services available in cities. But many cities are unable to provide the housing and other facilities necessitated by rapid population growth. As a result, slums grow up around the cities. Pollution, crime and disease become features of everyday life.

The population explosion poses another probem for the entire world. No one knows how many people the world can support or how consumer demand will damage the fragile environments on our planet. The British economist Thomas Malthus argued in the late 18th century that overpopulation would lead to famine and war. But an increase in farm technology in the 19th and 20th centuries, combined with a green revolution, in which scientists developed high-yield crop varieties, has greatly increased food production since Malthus' time.

However, some modern scientists argue that overpopulation may become a problem in the 21st century. They argue that food shortages leading to disastrous famines will result unless population growth can be halted. Such people argue in favour of birth control programmes. China, the only country with more than a billion people, has introduced a one-child family policy. Their action has slowed the growth of China's huge population, though rising living standards seem to be the most effective brakes on rapid population growth.

POPULATION CHANGE 1990–2000
The predicted population change for the years 1990–2000.

- OVER 40% POPULATION GAIN
- 30–40% POPULATION GAIN
- 20–30% POPULATION GAIN
- 10–20% POPULATION GAIN
- 0–10% POPULATION GAIN
- NO CHANGE OR LOSS

TOP 5 COUNTRIES
Kuwait	+75.0%
Namibia	+62.5%
Afghanistan	+60.1%
Mali	+55.5%
Tanzania	+54.6%

BOTTOM 5 COUNTRIES
Belgium	–0.1%
Hungary	–0.2%
Grenada	–2.4%
Germany	–3.2%
Tonga	–3.2%

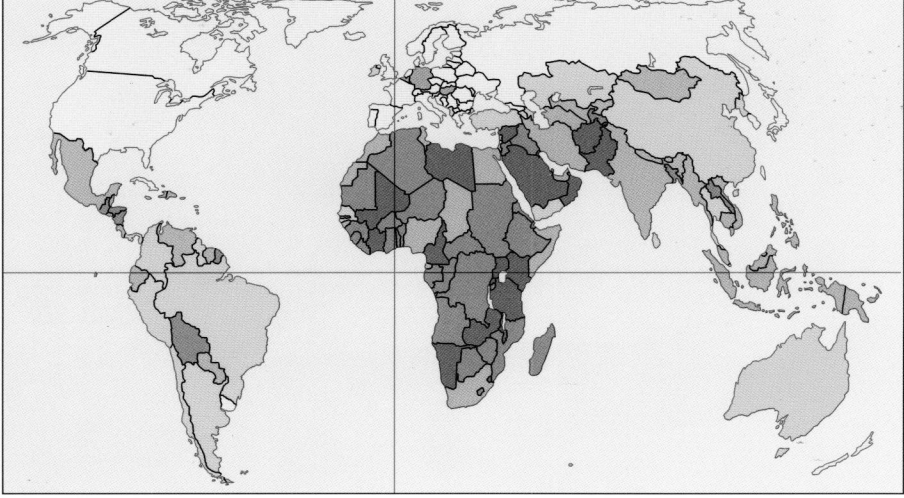

Languages and Religions

In 1995, 90-year-old Edna Guerro died in northern California. She was the last person able to speak Northern Pomo, one of about 50 Native American languages spoken in the state. Her death marked the extinction of one of the world's languages.

This event is not an isolated incident. Language experts regularly report the disappearance of languages and some of them predict that between 20 to 50% of the world's languages will no longer exist by the end of the 21st century. Improved transport and communications are partly to blame, because they bring people from various cultures into closer and closer contact. Many children no longer speak the language of their parents, preferring instead to learn the language used at their schools. The pressures on

children to speak dominant rather than minority languages are often great. In the first part of the 20th century, Native American children were punished if they spoke their native language.

The disappearance of a language represents the extinction of a way of thinking, a unique expression of the experiences and knowledge of a group of people. Language and religion together give people an identity and a sense of belonging. However, there are others who argue that the disappearance of minority languages is a step towards international understanding and economic efficiency.

THE WORLD'S LANGUAGES

Definitions of what is a language or a dialect vary and, hence, estimates of the number of languages spoken around the world range from about 3,000 to 6,000. But whatever the figure, it is clear that the number of languages far exceeds the number of countries.

RELIGIOUS ADHERENTS	
The number of adherents to the world's major religions, in millions.	
Christian	1,667
Roman Catholic	952
Protestant	337
Orthodox	162
Anglican	70
Other Christian	148
Muslim	881
Sunni	841
Shia	40
Hindu	663
Buddhist	312
Chinese Folk	172
Tribal	92
Jewish	18
Sikhs	17

Buddhist monks in Katmandu, Nepal
Hinduism is Nepal's official religion, but the Nepalese observe the festivals of both Hinduism and Buddhism. They also regard Buddhist shrines and Hindu temples as equally sacred.

Countries with only one language tend to be small. For example, in Liechtenstein, everyone speaks German. By contrast, more than 860 languages have been identified in Papua New Guinea, whose population is only about 4.3 million people. Hence, many of its languages are spoken by only small groups of people. In fact, scientists have estimated that about a third of the world's languages are now spoken by less than 1,000 people. By contrast, more than half of the world's population speak just seven languages.

The world's languages are grouped into families. The Indo-European family consists of languages spoken between Europe and the Indian subcontinent. The growth of European empires over the last 300 years led several Indo-European languages, most notably English, French, Portuguese and Spanish, to spread throughout much of North and South America, Africa, Australia and New Zealand.

English has become the official language in many countries which together contain more than a quarter of the world's population. It is now a major international language, surpassing in importance Mandarin Chinese, a member of the Sino-Tibetan family, which is the world's leading first language. Without a knowledge of English, businessmen face many problems when conducting international trade, especially with the United States or other English-speaking countries. But proposals that English, French, Russian or some other language should become a world language seem unlikely to be acceptable to a majority of the world's peoples.

WORLD RELIGIONS

Religion is another fundamental aspect of human culture. It has inspired much of the world's finest architecture, literature, music and painting. It has also helped to shape human cultures since prehistoric times and is responsible for the codes of ethics by which most people live.

The world's major religions were all founded in Asia. Judaism, one of the first faiths to teach that there is only one god, is one of the world's oldest. Founded in south-western Asia, it influenced the more recent Christianity and Islam, two other monotheistic religions which

MOTHER TONGUES
Native speakers of the major languages, in millions (1990).
- MANDARIN CHINESE 834M
- ENGLISH 443M
- HINDI 352M
- SPANISH 341M
- RUSSIAN 293M
- ARABIC 197M
- BENGALI 184M
- PORTUGUESE 173M
- MALAY 142M
- JAPANESE 125M

OFFICIAL LANGUAGES: % OF WORLD POPULATION

English	27.0%
Chinese	19.0%
Hindi	13.5%
Spanish	5.4%
Russian	5.2%
French	4.2%
Arabic	3.3%
Portuguese	3.0%
Malay	3.0%
Bengali	2.9%
Japanese	2.3%

Polyglot nations
The graph, right, shows countries of the world with more than 200 languages. Although it has only about 4.3 million people, Papua New Guinea holds the record for the number of languages spoken.

Brazil (210)
Congo (Z.) (220)
Australia (230)
Mexico (240)
Cameroon (275)
India (410)
Nigeria (470)
Indonesia (701)
Papua New Guinea (862)

The Church of San Giovanni, Dolomites, Italy
Christianity has done much to shape Western civilization. Christian churches were built as places of worship, but many of them are among the finest achievements of world architecture.

now have the greatest number of followers. Hinduism, the third leading faith in terms of the numbers of followers, originated in the Indian subcontinent and most Hindus are now found in India. Another major religion, Buddhism, was founded in the subcontinent partly as a reaction to certain aspects of Hinduism. But unlike Hinduism, it has spread from India throughout much of eastern Asia.

Religion and language are powerful creative forces. They are also essential features of nationalism, which gives people a sense of belonging and pride. But nationalism is often also a cause of rivalry and tension. Cultural differences have led to racial hatred, the persecution of minorities, and to war between national groups.

International Organizations

Twelve days before the surrender of Germany and four months before the final end of World War II, representatives of 50 nations met in San Francisco to create a plan to set up a peace-keeping organization, the United Nations. Since its birth on 24 October 1945, its membership has grown from 51 to 185.

Its first 50 years have been marked by failures as well as successes. While it has helped to prevent some disputes from flaring up into full-scale wars, the Blue Berets, as the UN troops are called, have been forced, because of their policy of neutrality, to stand by when atrocities are committed by rival warring groups.

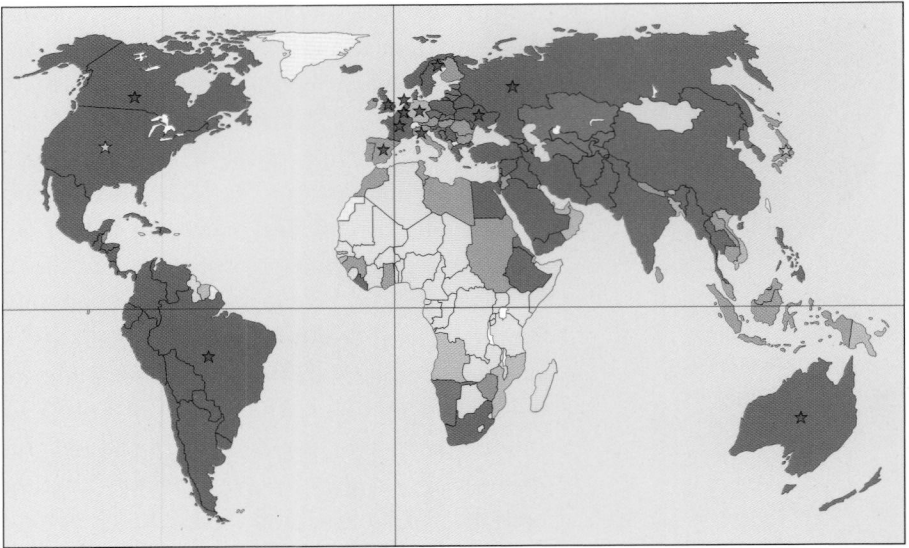

THE WORK OF THE UN

The United Nations has six main organs. They include the General Assembly, where member states meet to discuss issues concerned with peace, security and development. The Security Council, containing 15 members, is concerned with maintaining world peace. The Secretariat, under the Secretary-General, helps the other organs to do their jobs effectively, while the Economic and Social Council works with specialized agencies to implement policies concerned with such matters as development, education and health. The International Court of Justice, or World Court, helps to settle disputes between member nations. The sixth organ of the UN, the Trusteeship Council, was designed to bring 11 UN trust territories to independence. Its task has now been completed.

The specialized agencies do much important work. For example, UNICEF (United Nations International Children's Fund) has provided health care and aid for children in many parts of the world. The ILO (International Labour Organization) has improved working conditions in many areas, while the FAO (Food and Agricultural Organization) has worked to improve the production and distribution of food. Among the other agencies are organizations to help refugees, to further human rights and to control the environment. The latest agency, set up in 1995, is the WTO (World Trade Organization), which took over the work of GATT (General Agreement on Tariffs and Trade).

OTHER ORGANIZATIONS

In a world in which nations have become increasingly interdependent, many other organizations have been set up to deal with a variety of problems. Some, such as NATO (the North Atlantic Treaty Organization), are defence alliances. In the early 1990s, the end of the Cold War suggested that NATO's role might be finished, but the civil war in the former Yugoslavia showed that it still has a role in maintaining peace and security.

Other organizations encourage social and economic co-operation in various regions. Some are NGOs (non-governmental organizations), such as the Red Cross and its Muslim equivalent, the Red Crescent. Other NGOs raise funds to provide aid to countries facing major crises, such as famine.

Some major international organizations aim at economic co-operation and the removal of trade barriers. The best known of these organizations is the European Union, which has 15 members. Its

Food aid

International organizations supply aid to people living in areas suffering from war or famine. In Bosnia-Herzegovina, the UN Protection Force supervised the movements of food aid, as did NATO on the borders of Kosovo a few years later.

MEMBERS OF THE UN
Year of joining.

- 1940s
- 1950s
- 1960s
- 1970s
- 1980s
- 1990s
- NON–MEMBERS
- ★ 1% – 10% CONTRIBUTION TO FUNDING
- ★ OVER 10% CONTRIBUTION TO FUNDING

INTERNATIONAL AID AND GNP
Aid provided as a percentage of GNP, with total aid in brackets (1997).

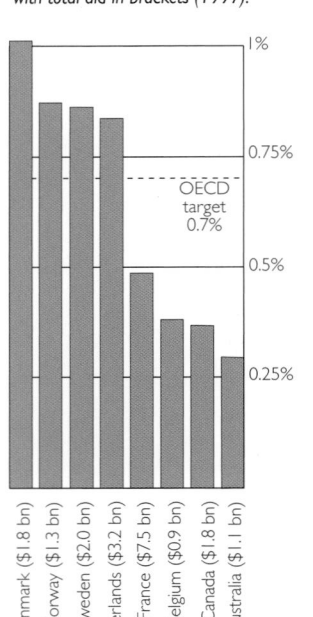

Denmark ($1.8 bn)
Norway ($1.3 bn)
Sweden ($2.0 bn)
Netherlands ($3.2 bn)
France ($7.5 bn)
Belgium ($0.9 bn)
Canada ($1.8 bn)
Australia ($1.1 bn)

OECD target 0.7%

UNHCR-funded jetty, Sri Lanka
In 1994, the UN High Commission for Refugees was responsible for 23 million people. Sometimes, it has to provide transport facilities, such as this jetty, to get aid to the refugees.

economic success has led some people to support the idea of setting up a federal Europe. Others oppose such developments, they fear that a 'United States of Europe' would lead to a loss of national identity among the member states.

Other groupings include ASEAN (the Association of South-east Asian Nations) which aims to reduce trade barriers between its members (Brunei, Burma, Indonesia, Laos, Malaysia, the Philippines, Singapore, Thailand and Vietnam). APEC (the Asia-Pacific Co-operation Group)

was founded in 1989 with the aim of creating a free trade zone between the countries of eastern Asia, North America, Australia and New Zealand by 2020. Meanwhile, Canada, Mexico and the United States have formed NAFTA (the North American Free Trade Agreement), while other economic groupings link most of the countries in Latin America. Another grouping with a more limited but important objective is OPEC (the Organization of Oil-Exporting Countries). OPEC works to unify policies concerning trade in oil on the world markets.

Some organizations exist to discuss matters of common interest between groups of nations. The Commonwealth of Nations, for example, grew out of the links created by the British Empire. In North and South America, the OAS (Organization of American States) aims to increase understanding in the Western hemisphere. The OAU (Organization of African Unity) has a similar role in Africa, while the Arab League represents the Arab nations of North Africa and the Middle East.

COUNTRIES OF THE EUROPEAN UNION

	Total land area (sq km)	Total population (1998)	GNP per capita, US$ (1997)	Unemployment rate, % (1996)	Year of accession to the EU	Seats in EU parliament (1998)
Austria	83,850	8,134,000	27,980	7%	1995	21
Belgium	30,510	10,175,000	26,420	12.7%	1958	25
Denmark	43,070	5,334,000	32,500	8.7%	1973	16
Finland	338,130	5,149,000	24,080	16.3%	1995	16
France	551,500	58,805,000	26,050	12.3%	1958	87
Germany	356,910	82,079,000	28,260	10.4%	1958	99
Greece	131,990	10,662,000	12,010	10.3%	1981	25
Ireland	70,280	3,619,000	18,280	11.9%	1973	15
Italy	301,270	56,783,000	20,120	12.1%	1958	87
Luxembourg	2,590	425,000	45,360	3.3%	1958	6
Netherlands	41,526	15,731,000	25,820	6.6%	1958	31
Portugal	92,390	9,928,000	10,450	7.3%	1986	24
Spain	504,780	39,134,000	14,510	22.2%	1986	64
Sweden	449,960	8,887,000	26,220	8.1%	1995	22
United Kingdom	243,368	58,970,000	20,710	7.6%	1973	87

Agriculture

In 1995, the world production of grains was lower than average – the result mainly of a wet spring in the United States, and bad weather combined with economic turmoil in the former Soviet Union. Downward trends in world food production in the 1990s reopened an old debate – whether food production will be able to keep pace with a rapidly rising world population in the 21st century.

Some experts argue that the lower than expected production figures in the 1990s herald a period of relative scarcity and high prices of food, which will be felt most in the poorer developing countries. Others are more optimistic. They point to the successes of the 'green revolution' which, through the use of new crop varieties produced by scientists, irrigation and the extensive use of fertilizers and pesticides,

Rice harvest, Bali, Indonesia
More than half of the world's people eat rice as their basic food. Rice grows well in tropical and subtropical regions, such as in Indonesia, India and south-eastern China.

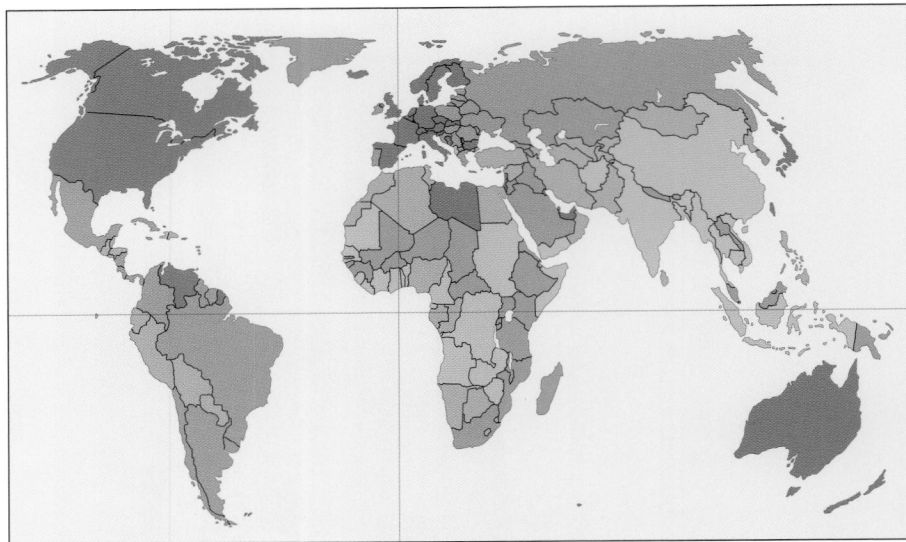

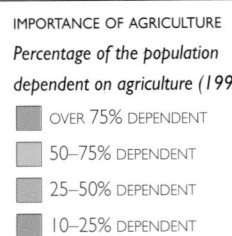

IMPORTANCE OF AGRICULTURE
Percentage of the population dependent on agriculture (1997).
- OVER 75% DEPENDENT
- 50–75% DEPENDENT
- 25–50% DEPENDENT
- 10–25% DEPENDENT
- UNDER 10% DEPENDENT

has revolutionized food production since the 1950s and 1960s.

The green revolution has led to a great expansion in the production of many crops, including such basic foods as rice, maize and wheat. In India, its effects have been spectacular. Between 1955 and 1995, grain production trebled, giving the country sufficient food reserves to prevent famine in years when droughts or floods reduce the harvest. While once India had to import food, it is now self-sufficient.

FOOD PRODUCTION

Agriculture, which supplies most of our food, together with materials to make clothes and other products, is the world's most important economic activity. But its relative importance has declined in comparison with manufacturing and service industries. As a result, the end of the 20th century marked the first time for 10,000 years when the vast majority of the people no longer had to depend for their living on growing crops and herding animals.

However, agriculture remains the dominant economic activity in many developing countries in Africa and Asia. For example, in the late 1990s, 90% or more of the people of Bhutan, Burundi, Nepal and Rwanda depended on farming for their living.

Many people in developing countries eke out the barest of livings by nomadic herding or shifting cultivation, combined with hunting, fishing and gathering plant foods. A large proportion of farmers live at subsistence level, producing little more than they require to provide the basic needs of their families.

The world's largest food producer and exporter is the United States, although agriculture employs

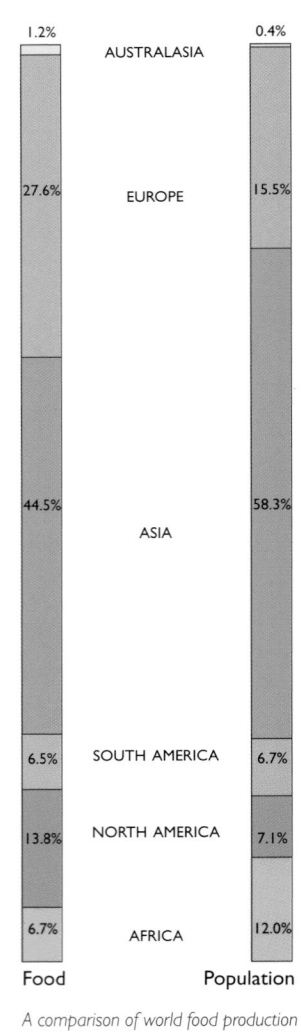

	Food	Population
AUSTRALASIA	1.2%	0.4%
EUROPE	27.6%	15.5%
ASIA	44.5%	58.3%
SOUTH AMERICA	6.5%	6.7%
NORTH AMERICA	13.8%	7.1%
AFRICA	6.7%	12.0%

A comparison of world food production and population by continent.

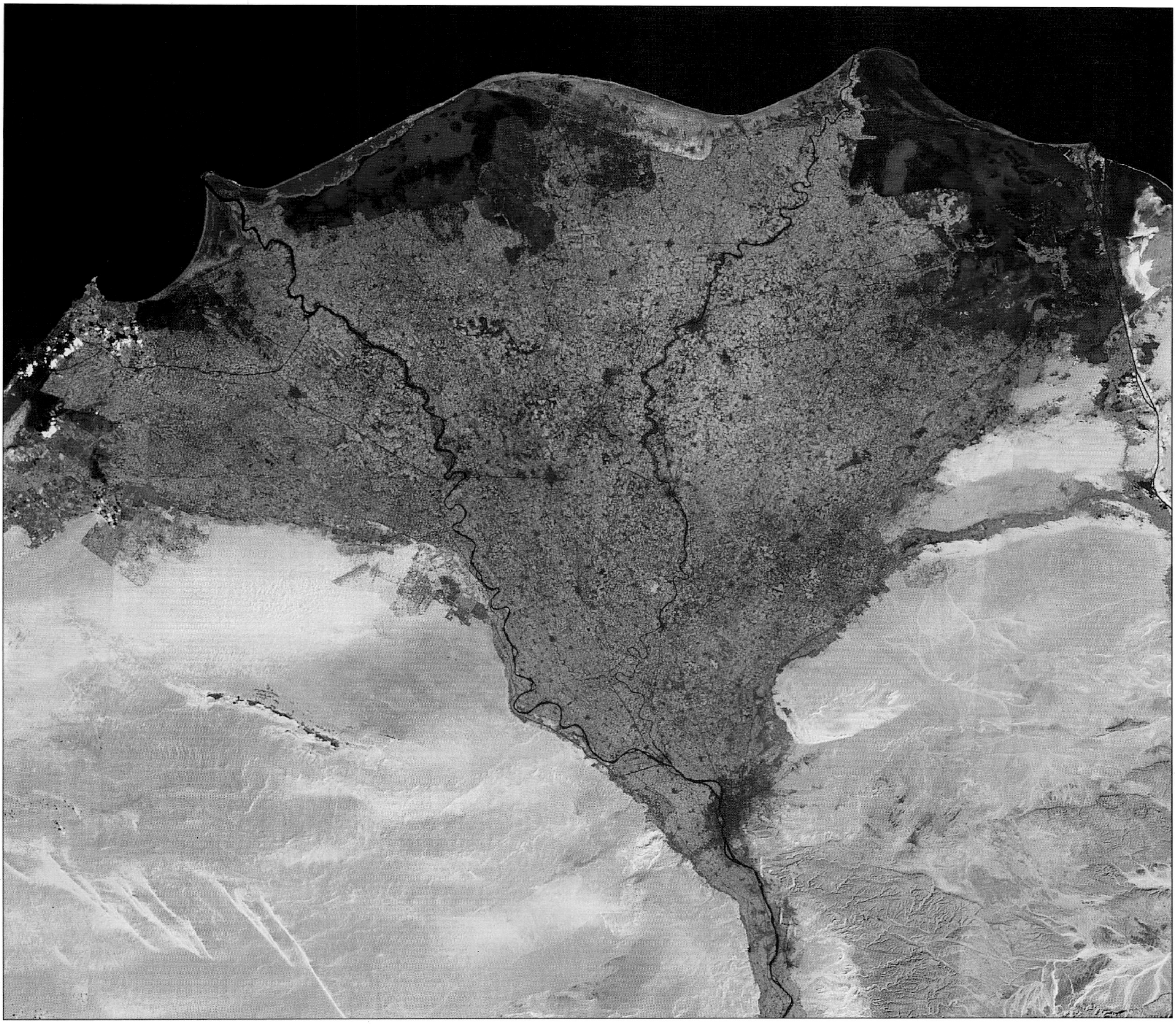

Landsat *image of the Nile delta, Egypt*

Most Egyptians live in the Nile valley and on its delta. Because much of the silt carried by the Nile now ends up on the floor of Lake Nasser, upstream of the Aswan Dam, the delta is now retreating and seawater is seeping inland. This eventuality was not foreseen when the Aswan High Dam was built in the 1960s.

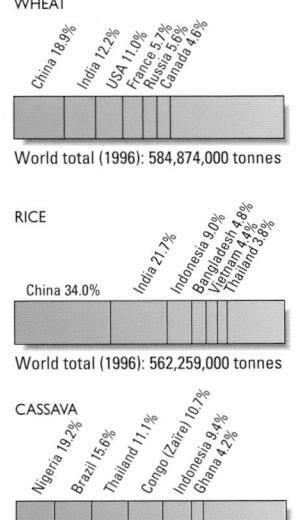

WHEAT

China 18.9% India 12.2% USA 11.0% France 5.7% Russia 5.0% Canada 4.6%

World total (1996): 584,874,000 tonnes

RICE

China 34.0% India 21.7% Indonesia 9.0% Bangladesh 4.8% Vietnam 4.4% Thailand 3.8%

World total (1996): 562,259,000 tonnes

CASSAVA

Nigeria 19.2% Brazil 15.6% Thailand 11.1% Congo (Zaire) 10.7% Indonesia 9.4% Ghana 4.2%

World total (1996): 162,942,000 tonnes

around 3% of its total workforce. The high production of the United States is explained by its use of scientific methods and mechanization, which are features of agriculture throughout the developed world.

INTENSIVE OR ORGANIC FARMING

By the late 20th century, some people were beginning to question the dependence of farmers on chemical fertilizers and pesticides. Many people became concerned that the widespread use of chemicals was seriously polluting and damaging the environment.

Others objected to the intensive farming of animals to raise production and lower prices. For example, the suggestion in Britain in 1996 that BSE, or 'mad cow disease', might be passed

on to people causing CJD (Creuzfeldt-Jakob Disease) caused widespread alarm.

Such problems have led some farmers to return to organic farming, which is based on animal-welfare principles and the banning of chemical fertilizers and pesticides. The costs of organic foods are certainly higher than those produced by intensive farming, but an increasing number of consumers in the Western world are beginning to demand organic products from their retailers.

Energy and Minerals

In March 1996, floods in Ukraine carried radioactive waste dumped near Chernobyl hundreds of kilometres downstream. This was the latest chapter in the disaster caused by the explosion at the Chernobyl nuclear power station in 1986, the worst nuclear accident in history. Nuclear power now provides about 17% of the world's electricity and experts once thought that it would eventually supply much of the world's energy supply. But concern about safety and worries about the high costs involved make this seem unlikely. Several developed countries have already abandoned their nuclear programmes.

FOSSIL FUELS

Huge amounts of energy are needed for heating, generating electricity and for transport. In the early years of the Industrial Revolution, coal

formed from organic matter buried beneath the Earth's surface, was the leading source of energy. It remains important as a raw material in the manufacture of drugs and other products and also as a fuel, despite the fact that burning coal causes air pollution and gives off carbon dioxide, an important greenhouse gas.

However, oil and natural gas, which came into wide use in the 20th century, are cheaper to produce and easier to handle than coal, while, kilogram for kilogram, they give out more heat. Oil is especially important in moving transport, supplying about 97% of the fuel required.

In 1995, proven reserves of oil were sufficient to supply the world, at current rates of production, for 43 years, while supplies of natural gas stood at about 66 years. Coal reserves are more abundant and known reserves would last 200 years at present rates of use. Although these figures must be regarded with caution, because they do not allow for future discoveries, it is clear that fossil fuel reserves will one day run out.

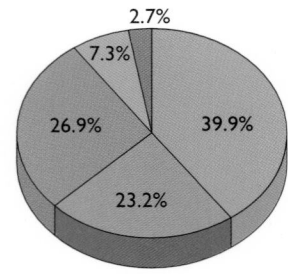

WORLD ENERGY CONSUMPTION

- ☐ OIL
- ☐ GAS
- ☐ COAL
- ☐ NUCLEAR
- ☐ HYDRO

The diagram shows the proportion of world energy consumption in 1997 by form. Total energy consumption was 8,509.2 million tonnes of oil equivalent. Such fuels as wood, peat and animal wastes, together with renewable forms of energy, such as wind and geothermal power, are not included, although they are important in some areas.

Wind farms in California, United States
Wind farms using giant turbines can produce electricity at a lower cost than conventional power stations. But in many areas, winds are too light or too strong for wind farms to be effective.

SELECTED MINERAL PRODUCTION STATISTICS (1995)

Bauxite		Diamonds	
Australia	38%	Australia	38%
Guinea	13%	Congo (Zaïre)	18%
Jamaica	10%	Botswana	16%
Brazil	9%	Russia	12%
China	6%	South Africa	8%

Gold		Iron ore	
South Africa	23%	China	15%
USA	14%	Brazil	12%
Australia	11%	Australia	9%
Canada	7%	Russia	4%
Russia	6%	India	4%

Potash		Zinc	
Canada	37%	China	12%
Germany	13%	Canada	8%
Belarus	11%	Japan	8%
Russia	11%	USA	7%
USA	6%	Germany	5%

MINERAL DISTRIBUTION

Location of the principal mines and deposits.

IRON & FERRO-ALLOYS

 IRON

CHROME

MANGANESE

NICKEL

PRECIOUS METALS

GOLD

SILVER

PRECIOUS STONES

DIAMONDS

LIGHT METALS

BAUXITE

BASE METALS

COPPER

LEAD

MERCURY

TIN

ZINC

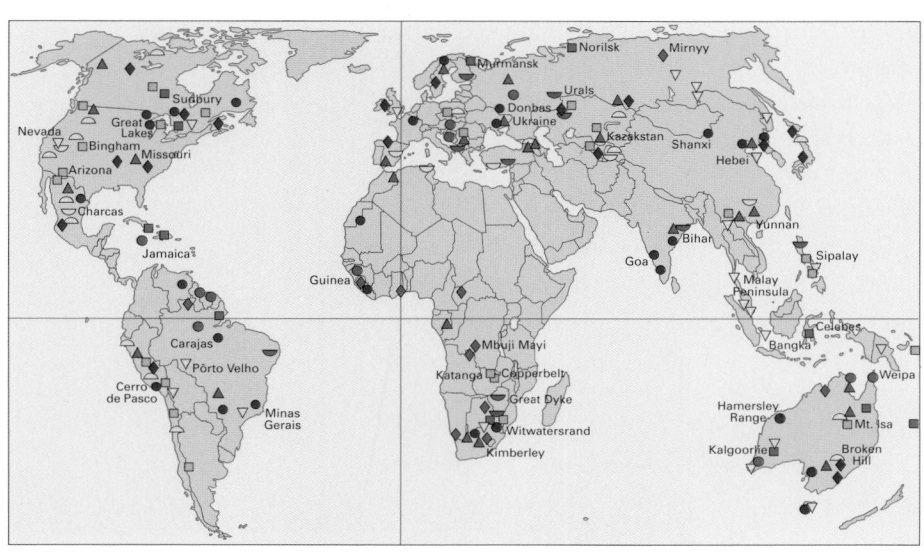

Potash mines in Utah, United States

Potash is a mineral used mainly to make fertilizers. Much of it comes from mines where deposits formed when ancient seas dried up are exploited. Potash is also extracted from salt lakes.

ALTERNATIVE ENERGY

Other sources of energy are therefore required. Besides nuclear energy, the main alternative to fossil fuels is water power. The costs of building dams and hydroelectric power stations is high, though hydroelectric production is comparatively cheap and it does not cause pollution. But the creation of reservoirs uproots people and, in tropical rainforests, it destroys natural habitats. Hydroelectricity is also suitable only in areas with plenty of rivers and steep slopes, such as Norway, while it is unsuitable in flat areas, such as the Netherlands.

In Brazil, alcohol made from sugar has been used to fuel cars. Initially, this government-backed policy met with great success, but it has proved to be extremely expensive. Battery-run, electric cars have also been developed in the United States, but they appear to have limited use, because of the problems involved in regular and time-consuming recharging.

Other forms of energy, which are renewable and cleaner than fossil fuels, are winds, sea waves, the rise and fall of tides, and geothermal power. These forms of energy are already used to some extent. However, their contribution in global terms seems likely to remain small in the immediate future.

MINERALS FOR INDUSTRY

In addition to energy, manufacturing industries need raw materials, including minerals, and these natural resources, like fossil fuels, are being used in such huge quantities that some experts have predicted shortages of some of them before long.

Manufacturers depend on supplies of about 80 minerals. Some, such as bauxite (aluminium ore) and iron, are abundant, but others are scarce or are found only in deposits that are uneconomical to mine. Many experts advocate a policy of recycling scrap metal, including aluminium, chromium, copper, lead, nickel and zinc. This practice would reduce pollution and conserve the energy required for extracting and refining mineral ores.

World Economies

In 1997, Tanzania had a per capita GNP (Gross National Product) of US$210, as compared with Switzerland, whose per capita GNP stood at $44,220. These figures indicate the vast gap between the economies and standards of living of the two countries.

The GNP includes the GDP (Gross Domestic Product), which consists of the total output of goods and services in a country in a given year, plus net exports – that is, the value of goods and services sold abroad less the value of foreign goods and services used in the country in the same year. The GNP divided by the population gives a country's GNP per capita. In low-income developing countries, agriculture makes a high contribution to the GNP. For example, in Tanzania, 56% of the GDP in 1995 came from

Microchip production, Taiwan
Despite its lack of resources, Taiwan is one of eastern Asia's 'tiger' economies. Its high-tech industries have helped it to achieve fast economic growth and to compete on the world market.

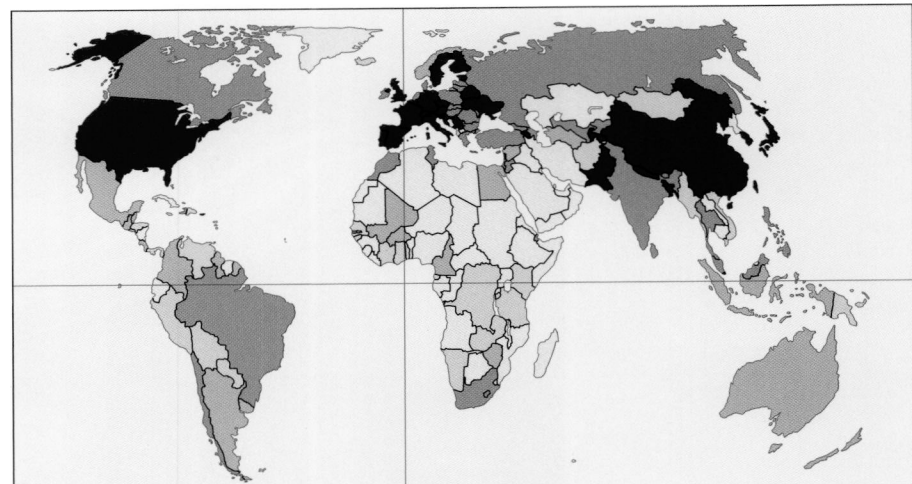

INDUSTRY AND TRADE
Manufactured goods (including machinery and transport) as a percentage of total exports.

■ OVER 75%
■ 50–75%
■ 25–50%
□ 10–25%
□ UNDER 10%

Eastern Asia, including Japan (98.3%), Taiwan (92.7%) and Hong Kong (93.0%), contains countries whose exports are most dominated by manufactures. But some countries in Europe, such as Slovenia (92.5%), are also heavily dependent on manufacturing.

agriculture. On the other hand, manufacturing was small-scale and contributed only 5% of the GDP. By comparison, in high-income economies, the percentage contribution of manufacturing far exceeds that of agriculture.

INDUSTRIALIZATION

The Industrial Revolution began in Britain in the late 18th century. Before that time, most people worked on farms. But with the Industrial Revolution came factories, using machines that could manufacture goods much faster and more cheaply than those made by cottage industries which already existed.

The Industrial Revolution soon spread to several countries in mainland Europe and the United States and, by the late 19th century, it had reached Canada, Japan and Russia. At first, industrial development was based on such areas as coalfields or ironfields. But in the 20th century, the use of oil, which is easy to transport along pipelines, made it possible for industries to be set up anywhere.

Some nations, such as Switzerland, became industrialized even though they lacked natural resources. They depended instead on the specialized skills of their workers. This same pattern applies today. Some countries with rich natural resources, such as Mexico (with a per capita GNP in 1997 of $3,680), lag far behind Japan ($37,850) and Taiwan ($12,400), which lack resources and have to import many of the materials they need for their manufacturing industries.

SERVICE INDUSTRIES

Experts often refer to high-income countries as industrial economies. But manufacturing employs only one in six workers in the United

GROSS NATIONAL PRODUCT PER CAPITA US$ (1997)		
1	Luxembourg	45,360
2	Switzerland	44,220
3	Japan	37,850
4	Norway	36,090
5	Liechtenstein	33,000
6	Singapore	32,940
7	Denmark	32,500
8	Bermuda	31,870
9	USA	28,740
10	Germany	28,260
11	Austria	27,980
12	Iceland	26,580
13	Belgium	26,420
14	Sweden	26,220
15	France	26,050
16	Netherlands	25,820
17	Monaco	25,000
18	Finland	24,080
19	Hong Kong	22,990
20	UK	20,710

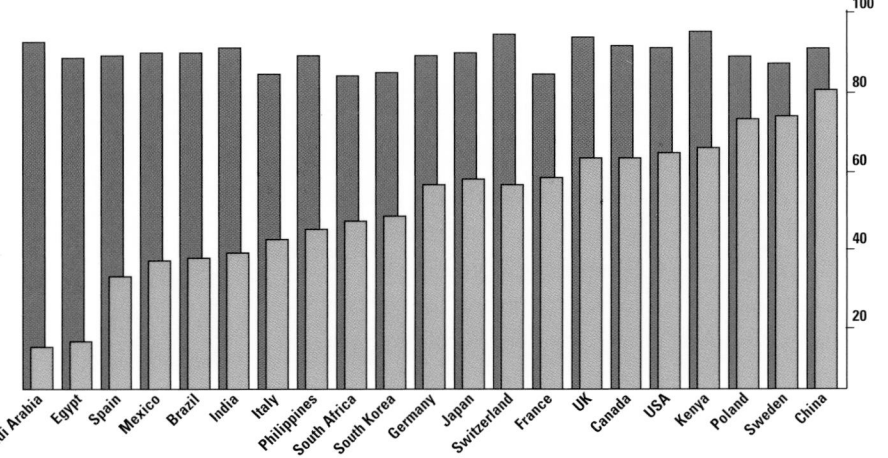

New cars awaiting transportation, Los Angeles, United States
Cars are the most important single manufactured item in world
trade, followed by vehicle parts and engines. The world's leading
car producers are Japan, the United States, Germany and France.

States, one in five in Britain, and one in three in Germany and Japan.

In most developed economies, the percentage of manufacturing jobs has fallen in recent years, while jobs in service industries have risen. For example, in Britain, the proportion of jobs in manufacturing fell from 37% in 1970 to 21% in 1995, while jobs in the service sector rose from just under 50% to 66%. While change in Britain was especially rapid, similar changes were taking place in most industrial economies. By 1995, service industries accounted for well over half the jobs in the generally prosperous countries that made up the OECD (Organization for Economic Co-operation and Development). Instead of being called the 'industrial' economies, these countries might be better named the 'service' economies.

Service industries offer a wide range of jobs and many of them require high educational qualifications. These include finance, insurance and high-tech industries, such as computer programming, entertainment and telecommunications. Service industries also include marketing and advertising, which are essential if the cars and television sets made by manufacturers are to be sold. Another valuable service industry is tourism; in some countries, such as the Gambia, it is the major foreign exchange earner. Trade in services now plays an important part in world economics. The share of services in world trade rose from 17% in 1980 to 22% in 1992.

THE WORKFORCE
Percentage of men and women between 15 and 64 years old in employment, selected countries (latest available year).

MEN
WOMEN

100
80
60
40
20

Saudi Arabia
Egypt
Spain
Mexico
Brazil
India
Italy
Philippines
South Africa
South Korea
Germany
Japan
Switzerland
France
UK
Canada
USA
Kenya
Poland
Sweden
China

Trade and Commerce

The establishment of the WTO (World Trade Organization) on 1 January 1995 was the latest step in the long history of world trade. The WTO was set up by the eighth round of negotiations, popularly called the 'Uruguay round', conducted by the General Agreement on Tariffs and Trade (GATT). This treaty was signed by representatives of 125 governments in April 1994 after many difficulties.

GATT was first established in 1948. Its initial aim was to produce a charter to create a body called the International Trade Organization. This body never came into being. Instead, GATT, acting as an *ad hoc* agency, pioneered a series of agreements aimed at liberalizing world trade by reducing tariffs on imports and other obstacles to free trade.

GATT's objectives were based on the belief

New York City Stock Exchange, United States

Stock exchanges, where stocks and shares are sold and bought, are important in channelling savings and investments to companies and governments. The world's largest stock exchange is in Tokyo, Japan.

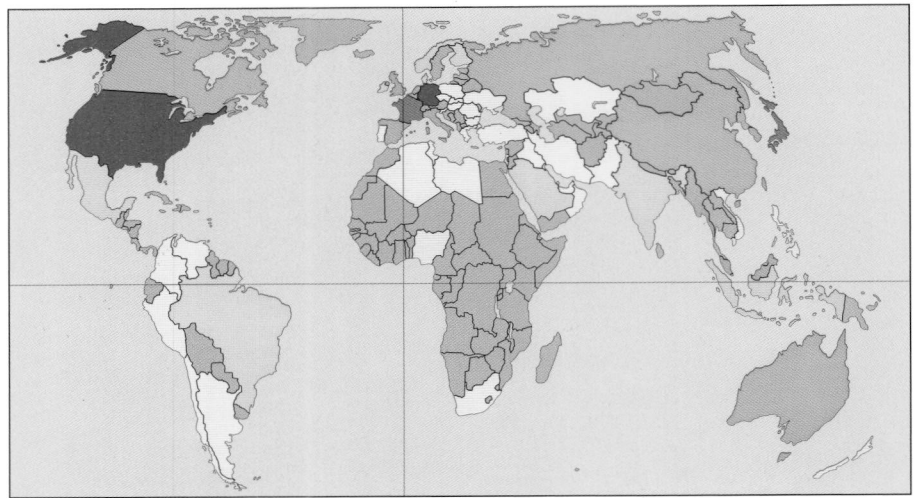

that international trade creates wealth. Trade occurs because the world's resources are not distributed evenly between countries, and, in theory, free trade means that every country should concentrate on what it can do best and purchase from others goods and services that they can supply more cheaply. In practice, however, free trade may cause unemployment when imported goods are cheaper than those produced within the country.

Trade is sometimes an important factor in world politics, especially when trade sanctions are applied against countries whose actions incur the disapproval of the international community. For example, in the 1990s, world-wide trade sanctions were imposed on Serbia because of its involvement in the civil war in Bosnia-Herzegovina.

CHANGING TRADE PATTERNS

The early 16th century, when Europeans began to divide the world into huge empires, opened up a new era in international trade. By the 19th century, the colonial powers, who were among the first industrial powers, promoted trade with their colonies, from which they obtained unprocessed raw materials, such as food, natural fibres, minerals and timber. In return, they shipped clothes, shoes and other cheap items to the colonies.

From the late 19th century until the early 1950s, primary products dominated world trade, with oil becoming the leading item in the later part of this period. Many developing countries still depend heavily on the export of one or two primary products, such as coffee or iron ore, but overall the proportion of primary products in world trade has fallen since the 1950s. Today the most important elements in world trade are

WORLD TRADE

Percentage share of total world exports by value (1996).

- OVER 10% OF WORLD TRADE
- 5–10% OF WORLD TRADE
- 1–5% OF WORLD TRADE
- 0.5–1% OF WORLD TRADE
- 0.1–0.5% OF WORLD TRADE
- UNDER 0.1% OF WORLD TRADE

The world's leading trading nations, according to the combined value of their exports and imports, are the United States, Germany, Japan, France and the United Kingdom.

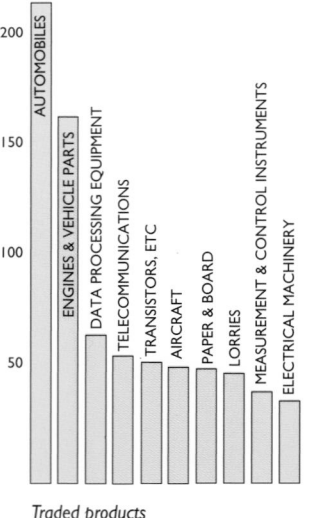

Traded products

Top ten manufactures traded by value in billions of US$ (latest available year).

![Rotterdam harbour scene with ships and barges]

Rotterdam, Netherlands

World trade depends on transport. Rotterdam, the world's largest port, serves not only the Netherlands, but also industrial areas in parts of Germany, France and Switzerland.

DEPENDENCE ON TRADE

Value of exports as a percentage of GDP (Gross Domestic Product) 1997.

- OVER 50% GDP FROM EXPORTS
- 40–50% GDP FROM EXPORTS
- 30–40% GDP FROM EXPORTS
- 20–30% GDP FROM EXPORTS
- 10–20% GDP FROM EXPORTS
- UNDER 10% GDP FROM EXPORTS

- ○ MOST DEPENDENT ON INDUSTRIAL EXPORTS (OVER 75% OF TOTAL)
- ● MOST DEPENDENT ON FUEL EXPORTS (OVER 75% OF TOTAL)
- ● MOST DEPENDENT ON METAL & MINERAL EXPORTS (OVER 75% OF TOTAL)

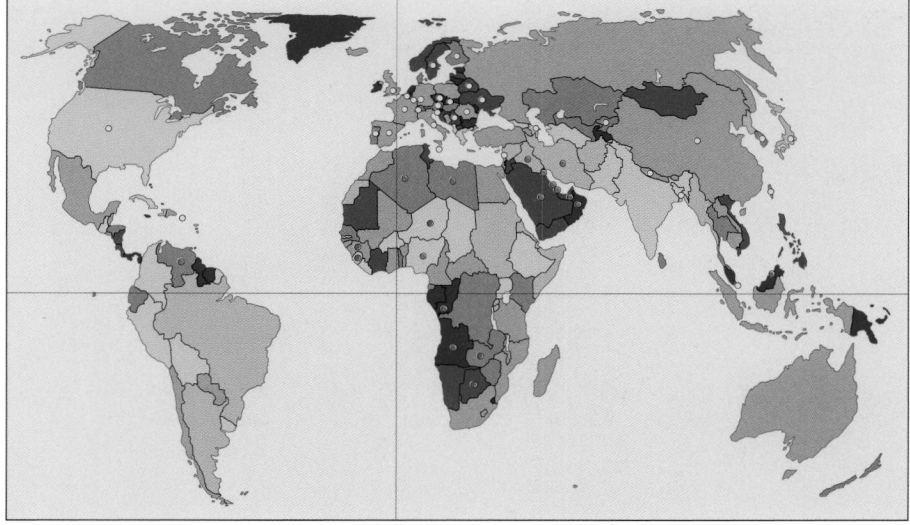

manufactures and semi-manufactures, exchanged mainly between the industrialized nations.

THE WORLD'S MARKETS

Private companies conduct most of world trade, but government policies affect it. Governments which believe that certain industries are strategic, or essential for the country's future, may impose tariffs on imports, or import quotas to limit the volume of imports, if they are thought to be undercutting the domestic industries.

For example, the United States has argued that Japan has greater access to its markets than the United States has to Japan's. This might have led the United States to resort to protectionism, but instead the United States remains committed to free trade.

Other problems in international trade occur when governments give subsidies to its producers, who can then export products at low prices. Another difficulty, called 'dumping', occurs when products are sold at below the market price in order to gain a market share. One of the aims of the newly-created WTO is the phasing out of government subsidies for agricultural products, though the world's poorest countries will be exempt from many of the WTO's most severe regulations.

Governments are also concerned about the volume of imports and exports and most countries keep records of international transactions. When the total value of goods and services imported exceeds the value of goods and services exported, then the country has a deficit in its balance of payments. Large deficits can weaken a country's economy.

Travel and Communications

In the 1990s, millions of people became linked into an 'information superhighway' called the Internet. Equipped with a personal computer, an electricity supply, a telephone and a modem, people are able to communicate with others all over the world. People can now send messages by e-mail (electronic mail), they can engage in electronic discussions, contacting people with similar interests, and engage in 'chat lines', which are the latest equivalent of telephone conferences.

These new developments are likely to affect the working lives of people everywhere, enabling them to work at home whilst having many of the facilities that are available in an office. The Internet is part of an ongoing and astonishingly rapid evolution in the fields of communications and transport.

TRANSPORT

Around 200 years ago, most people never travelled far from their birthplace, but today we are much more mobile. Cars and buses now provide convenient forms of transport for many millions of people, huge ships transport massive cargoes around the world, and jet airliners, some travelling faster than the speed of sound, can transport high-value goods as well as holiday-makers to almost any part of the world.

Land transport of freight has developed greatly

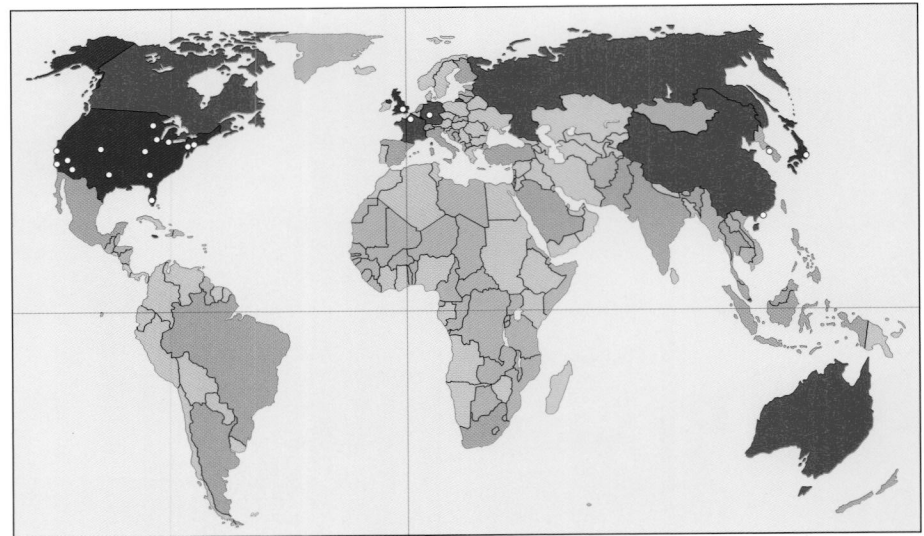

since the start of the Industrial Revolution. Canals, which became important in the 18th century, could not compete with rail transport in the 19th century. Rail transport remains important, but, during the 20th century, it suffered from competition with road transport (especially in the United Kingdom), which is cheaper and has the advantage of carrying materials and goods from door to door.

Road transport causes pollution and the burning of fuels creates greenhouse gases that contribute to global warming. Yet privately owned cars are now the leading form of passenger traffic in developed nations, especially for journeys of less than about 400 km [250 miles]. Car owners do not have to suffer the inconvenience of waiting for public transport, such as buses, though they often have to endure traffic jams at peak travel times.

Ocean passenger traffic is now modest, but ships carry the bulk of international trade. Huge oil tankers and bulk grain carriers now ply the oceans with their cargoes, while container ships

AIR TRAVEL – PASSENGER KILOMETRES* FLOWN (1996).

- ■ OVER 100,000 MILLION
- ■ 50,000–100,000 MILLION
- ▨ 10,000–50,000 MILLION
- ☐ 1,000–10,000 MILLION
- ☐ 500–1,000 MILLION
- ▨ UNDER 500 MILLION
- o MAJOR AIRPORTS (HANDLING OVER 25 MILLION PASSENGERS IN 1996)

* Passenger kilometres are the number of passengers (both international and domestic) multiplied by the distance flown by each passenger from the airport of origin.

Jodrell Bank Observatory, Cheshire, England
The world's first giant radio telescope began operations at Jodrell Bank in 1957. Radio telescopes can explore the Universe as far as 16 billion light-years away.

SELECTED NEWSPAPER CIRCULATION FIGURES (1995)

France			Russia	
Le Monde		357,362	Pravda	1,373,795
Le Figaro		350,000	Ivestia	700,000
Germany			Spain	
Bild		4,500,000	El Pais	407,629
Süddeutsche Zeitung		402,866		
			United Kingdom	
Italy			The Sun	4,061,253
Corriera Della Sella		676,904	Daily Mirror	2,525,000
La Republica		655,321	Daily Express	1,270,642
La Stampa		436,047	The Times	672,802
			The Guardian	402,214
Japan				
Yomiuri Shimbun	(a.m. edition)	9,800,000	United States	
	(p.m. edition)	4,400,000	New York Times	1,724,705
Manichi Shimbun	(a.m. edition)	3,200,000	Chicago Tribune	1,110,552
	(p.m. edition)	1,900,000	Houston Chronicle	605,343

Kansai International Airport, Japan
The new airport, opened in September 1994, is built on an artificial island in Osaka Bay. The island holds the world's biggest airport terminal at nearly 2 km [1.2 miles] long.

carry mixed cargoes. Containers are boxes built to international standards that contain cargo. Containers are easy to handle, and so they reduce shipping costs, speed up deliveries and cut losses caused by breakages. Most large ports now have the facilities to handle containers.

Air transport is suitable for carrying goods that are expensive, light and compact, or perishable. However, because of the high costs of air freight, it is most suitable for carrying passengers along long-distance routes around the world. Through air travel, international tourism, with people sometimes flying considerable distances, has become a major and rapidly expanding industry.

COMMUNICATIONS

After humans first began to communicate by using the spoken word, the next great stage in the development of communications was the invention of writing around 5,500 years ago.

The invention of movable type in the mid 15th century led to the mass production of books and, in the early 17th century, the first newspapers. Newspapers now play an important part in the mass communication of information, although today radio and, even more important, television have led to a decline in the circulation of newspapers in many parts of the world.

The most recent developments have occurred in the field of electronics. Artificial communications satellites now circle the planet, relaying radio, television, telegraph and telephone signals. This enables people to watch events on the

far side of the globe as they are happening. Electronic equipment is also used in many other ways, such as in navigation systems used in air, sea and space, and also in modern weaponry, as shown vividly in the television coverage of the 1991 Gulf War.

THE AGE OF COMPUTERS

One of the most remarkable applications of electronics is in the field of computers. Computers are now making a huge contribution to communications. They are able to process data at incredibly high speeds and can store vast quantities of information. For example, the work of weather forecasters has been greatly improved now that computers can process the enormous amount of data required for a single weather forecast. They also have many other applications in such fields as business, government, science and medicine.

Through the Internet, computers provide a free interchange of news and views around the world. But the dangers of misuse, such as the exchange of pornographic images, have led to calls for censorship. Censorship, however, is a blunt weapon, which can be used by authoritarian governments to suppress the free exchange of information that the new information superhighway makes possible.

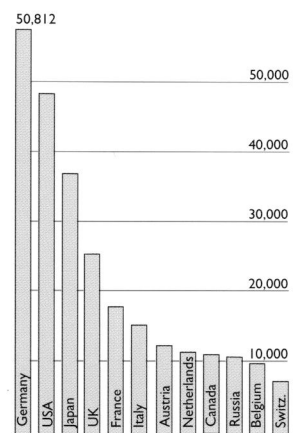

Spending on tourism
Countries spending the most on overseas tourism, US$ million (1996).

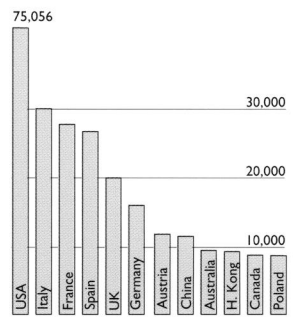

Receipts from tourism
Countries receiving the most from overseas tourism, US$ million (1996).

The World Today

The early years of the 20th century witnessed the exploration of Antarctica, the last uncharted continent. Today, less than 100 years later, tourists are able to take cruises to the icy southern continent, while almost no part of the globe is inaccessible to the determined traveller. Improved transport and images from space have made our world seem smaller.

A DIVIDED WORLD

Between the end of World War II in 1945 and the late 1980s, the world was divided, politically and economically, into three main groups: the developed countries or Western democracies, with their free enterprise or mixed economies; the centrally planned or Communist countries; and the developing countries or Third World.

This division became obsolete when the former Soviet Union and its old European allies, together with the 'special economic zones' in eastern China, began the transition from centrally planned to free enterprise economies. This left the world divided into two broad camps: the prosperous developed countries and the poorer developing countries. The simplest way of distinguishing between the groups is with reference to their per capita Gross National Products (per capita GNPs).

The World Bank divides the developing countries into three main groups. At the bottom are the low-income economies, which include China, India and most of sub-Saharan Africa. This group contains about 56% of the world's population but

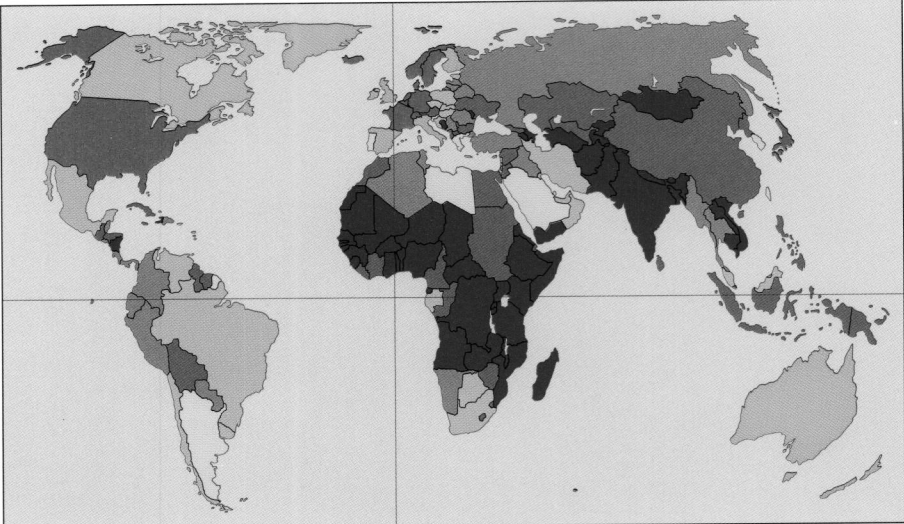

its average per capita GNP in 1994 was only US$390. The other two groups are the lower-middle-income economies with an average GNP per capita of $1,650, and the upper-middle-income economies, with an average GNP per capita of $4,640. By contrast, the high-income economies, also called the developed countries, contain less than 15% of the world's population but have the high (and rising) average GNP per capita of $24,170.

ECONOMIC AND SOCIAL CONTRASTS

Economic differences are coupled with other factors, such as rates of population growth. For example, in 1980–93, the low-income economies had a high rate of population growth of 2% per year, while the populations of the middle-income economies were increasing by 1.7%. By contrast, the populations of countries in the high-income category were increasing by only 0.6%.

Stark contrasts exist worldwide in the quality

GROSS NATIONAL PRODUCT PER CAPITA
The value of total production divided by the population (1997).

- ■ OVER 400% OF WORLD AVERAGE
- ■ 200–400% OF WORLD AVERAGE
- □ 100–200% OF WORLD AVERAGE

[WORLD AVERAGE WEALTH PER PERSON US$6,316]

- ■ 50–100% OF WORLD AVERAGE
- ■ 25–50% OF WORLD AVERAGE
- ■ 10–25% OF WORLD AVERAGE
- ■ UNDER 10% OF WORLD AVERAGE

RICHEST COUNTRIES
Luxembourg	$45,360
Switzerland	$44,220
Japan	$37,850
Norway	$36,090
Liechtenstein	$33,000

POOREST COUNTRIES
Mozambique	$90
Ethiopia	$110
Congo (Dem. Rep.)	$110
Burundi	$180
Sierra Leone	$200

Porters carrying luggage for tourists, Selous Park, Tanzania
Improved and cheaper transport has led to a boom in tourism in many developing countries. Tourism provides jobs and foreign exchange, though it can undermine local cultures.

Birth control poster, China

China is the only country with more than a billion people. Central to its economic development policies is population control. Posters exhort the advantages of one-child families.

of life. Generally, the people in Western Europe and North America are better fed, healthier and have more cars and better homes than the people in low- and middle-income economies.

The average life expectancy at birth in low-income economies in 1993 was 62 years, 15 years less than in the high-income economies. Illiteracy in countries in the low-income category is high, at 42% in 1992, while for women, who get fewer opportunities, the percentage of those who could not read and write stood at 54%. By contrast, illiteracy is relatively rare in the high-income economies.

FUTURE DEVELOPMENT

In the last 50 years, despite all the aid supplied to developing countries, much of the world still suffers from poverty and economic backwardness. Some countries are even poorer now than they were a generation ago while others have become substantially richer.

The most remarkable success has been achieved in eastern Asia. Japan and the 'tiger economies' of Hong Kong, Indonesia, Malaysia, Singapore, South Korea, Thailand and Taiwan had an average annual economic growth rate of 5.5% between 1965 and 1993, while their share in the exports of manufactured goods more than doubled in the same period. In 1997, however,

an Asian market crash temporarily halted this dramatic economic expansion.

Reasons advanced to explain the success of the eastern Asian countries include low wage scales, strong family structures, low state expenditure on welfare and large investment in education for both sexes. Some of the arguments are contradictory. For example, while some argue that the success of Hong Kong is due to free enterprise, the governments of Japan and South Korea have intervened substantially in the development of their economies.

Eastern Asia's economic growth has been exceptional and probably cannot be regarded as a model for the developing world. But several factors suggest that poor countries may find progress easier in the 21st century. For example, technology is now more readily transferable between countries, while improved transport and communications make it easier for countries to take part in the world economy. But industrial development and rising living standards could lead to an increase in global pollution. Hence, any strategy for global economic expansion must also take account of environmental factors.

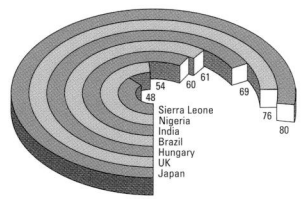

Years of life expectancy at birth, selected countries (1997).

The chart shows the contrasting range of average life expectancies at birth for a range of countries, including both low-income and high-income economies. Generally, improved health services are raising life expectancies. On average, women live longer than men, even in the poorer developing countries.

Glossary

Abyss The lowest part of the oceans, at the foot of the continental slope, which forms the true edge of the continents.

Apparent magnitude The magnitude of a star as seen from Earth; it depends on the absolute magnitude (the apparent magnitude if the star was observed from a standard distance of 32.6 light-years) and the distance of the star from the Earth.

Aquifer A layer of rock which contains water and allows water to percolate through it. It may be porous, as in sandstone, or fissured, as in limestone.

Atmosphere The layer of air which surrounds the Earth, which includes gases, such as nitrogen and oxygen, and water vapour.

Biome A major type of plant and animal community, such as tundra, taiga (boreal forest) or tropical rainforest.

Comet A body in the Solar System consisting of a nucleus and a tail. It is composed of ice particles, gases and dust.

Declination How far north or south a star is above the Celestial Equator, an imaginary line in the sky directly above the Equator. It is measured in degrees.

Delta An area of land at the mouths of some rivers which is made up of sediment deposited there by the river. It gets its name from the triangular Greek letter delta (Δ), though some deltas are not triangular.

Demographers People who study human populations, such as their numbers and distribution.

Developed country A country with a balanced economy, including a major manufacturing sector.

Developing country A poor country in which agriculture (often at subsistence level) is usually the mainstay of the economy.

Element A basic chemical substance which cannot be broken down into other substances by chemical means.

Equinox Two days during the year when the Sun is overhead at the Equator and everywhere on Earth has 12 hours of darkness. The equinoxes occur on or around 21 March and 23 September.

Erosion The processes by which natural forces, including weathering, running water, ice and winds, constantly modify the land.

Fault A crack or fracture in the Earth's crust along which the rocks have moved so that the rocks on either side are displaced.

Fold Bends in rock strata caused by enormous lateral pressure.

Fossil fuel Any non-renewable fuel formed from once-living plant or animal matter, including peat and coal, oil and natural gas.

Glacier A body of ice which flows down a valley. It is composed of compacted snow.

Ice Age A period in history when global temperatures fell and ice covered large areas that are now ice-free.

Ice sheet A huge body of ice covering a large area. The world's two ice sheets cover Antarctica and Greenland. Small ice sheets are called ice caps.

Internet A global network of interconnected computer networks. Until the late 1980s the Internet was used only by governments and universities. By the mid-1990s, millions of home computers were connected.

Lithosphere The hard outer layer of the Earth, consisting of the crust and the hard upper layer of the mantle.

Monsoon A seasonal wind, especially in southern Asia, where the prevailing north-easterly trade winds in winter are replaced in summer by moist south-westerly winds which bring heavy rain.

Moraine Eroded rock ranging from clay to large boulders, that is transported and deposited by glaciers and other bodies of ice.

Neutron star A star made up almost entirely of atomic particles called neutrons.

Nuclear fision The process in stars by which hydrogen nuclei change into helium nuclei, creating energy which escapes in the form of light.

Ozone layer A layer of the gas ozone in the stratosphere that blocks out most of the Sun's harmful ultraviolet radiation.

Population growth A change in human population caused by natural increase (the difference between births and deaths) and migration.

Porous rock A rock, such as sandstone, that contains pores through which water can percolate.

Primary products Raw materials, such as crops, minerals or timber, that have not been processed.

Pyroclasts Fragments of magma thrown out by explosions during volcanic activity.

Right ascension A measure in hours of the position of a star east of the place where the Sun crosses the Celestial Equator on 21 March. One hour represents 15 degrees.

Solstice Two days during the year when the overhead Sun reaches either its northernmost point (the Tropic of Cancer) or its southernmost point (the Tropic of Capricorn).

Special economic zones Areas in eastern China where the government has encouraged foreign investment and where economic growth has been exceptionally rapid.

'Tiger' economies The name given to the developing economies of rapidly industrializing countries of eastern Asia, including Indonesia, Malaysia, South Korea, Singapore, Thailand and Taiwan.

Tornado A small, but violent whirlwind which occurs over land areas.

Trade wind A prevailing wind that blows from the high-pressure horse latitudes towards the low-pressure doldrums around the Equator.

Tropical cyclone A large storm which forms over warm seas north and south of the Equator. It may cause great damage to coastal areas, but it dies out quickly when it reaches land. Other names for this kind of storm are hurricane (in North America), typhoon (in Asia) and willy-willy (in Australia).

WORLD MAPS

SETTLEMENTS

■ PARIS   ■ Berne   ◉ Livorno   ◉ Brugge   ◎ Algeciras   ○ Frejus   ○ Oberammergau   ○ Thira

Settlement symbols and type styles vary according to the scale of each map and indicate the importance
of towns on the map rather than specific population figures

∴ Ruins or Archæological Sites   ˯ Wells in Desert

ADMINISTRATION

──────── International Boundaries

▭ National Parks

Administrative
Area Names

─ ─ ─ ─ International Boundaries
(Undefined or Disputed)

Country Names
NICARAGUA

KENT
CALABRIA

·············· Internal Boundaries

International boundaries show the *de facto* situation where there are rival claims to territory

---

COMMUNICATIONS

──── Principal Roads

⊕ Airfields

──── Other Railways

──── Other Roads

──── Principal Railways

╾┼╌╌┼╼ Railway Tunnels

╾┼╌╌┼╼ Road Tunnels

─ ╌ ─ ╌ Railways
Under Construction

·············· Principal Canals

⋉ Passes

PHYSICAL FEATURES

~~~ Perennial Streams

⬭ Intermittent Lakes

▲ 8848 Elevations in metres

─ ╌ ─ Intermittent Streams

⬭ Swamps and Marshes

▼ 8500 Sea Depths in metres

⬭ Perennial Lakes

▭ Permanent Ice
and Glaciers

1134 Height of Lake Surface
Above Sea Level in metres

ELEVATION AND DEPTH TINTS

Height of Land above Sea Level

Land Below Sea Level

Depth of Sea

| in metres | 6000 | 4000 | 3000 | 2000 | 1500 | 1000 | 400 | 200 | 0 | | | | | | |
| in feet | 18 000 | 12 000 | 9000 | 6000 | 4500 | 3000 | 1200 | 600 | | | | | | | |

| | 6000 | 12 000 | 15 000 | 18 000 | 24 000 | in feet |
| | 0 | 200 | 2000 | 4000 | 5000 | 6000 | 8000 | in metres |

Some of the maps have different contours to highlight and clarify the principal relief features

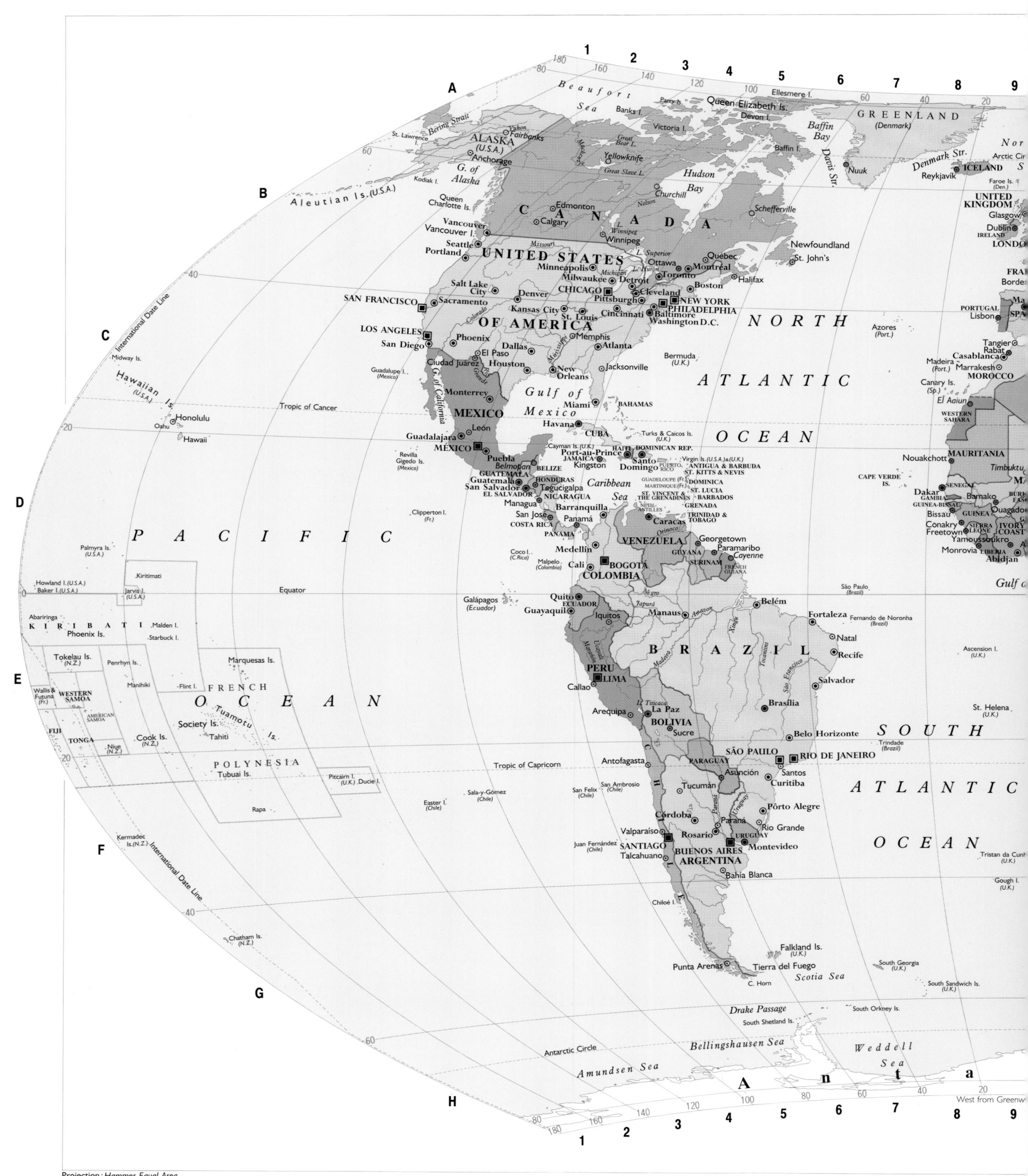

Projection: Hammer Equal Area

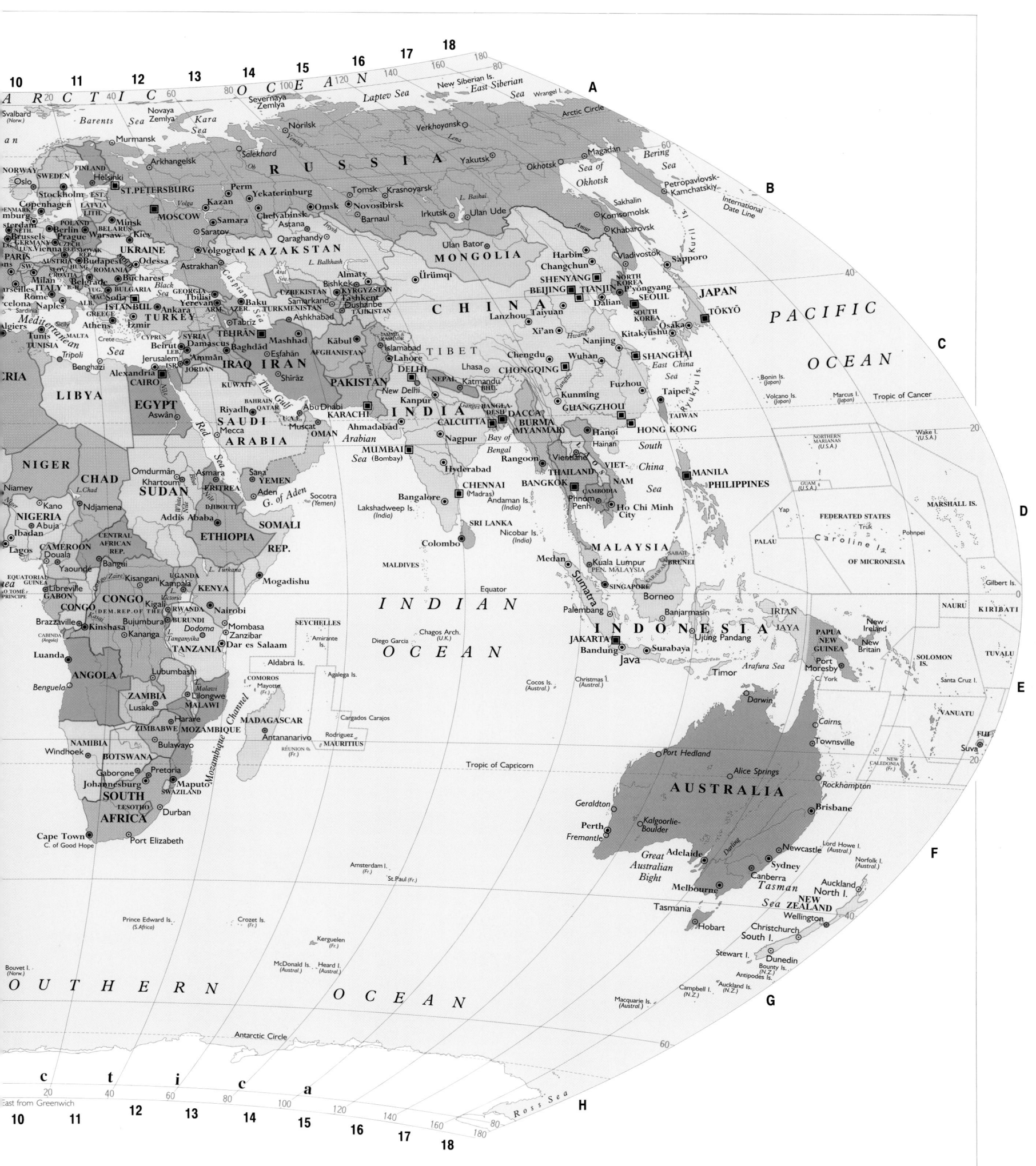

A R C T I C   O C E A N

Svalbard (Norw.)

Barents Novaya *Kara* Severnaya *Laptev Sea* New Siberian Is. East Siberian Wrangel I.
an *Sea* Zemlya *Sea* Zemlya *Sea*
NORWAY SWEDEN FINLAND Murmansk Norilsk Verkhoyansk Arctic Circle
Oslo Helsinki Salekhard Yenisey Lena Yakutsk Magadan Bering
Stockholm EST. ST.PETERSBURG Arkhangelsk Ob Tomsk Krasnoyarsk Okhotsk Sea
DENMARK LATVIA Perm Yekaterinburg L. Baikal Sea of
Copenhagen LITH. MOSCOW Kazan R U S S I A Okhotsk Petropavlovsk-
mburg POLAND BELARUS Samara Omsk Novosibirsk Irkutsk Ulan Ude Sakhalin Kamchatskiy
sterdam Minsk Volga Saratov Astana Barnaul Komsomolsk International
Brussels Berlin Warsaw Kiev Qaraghandy Ulan Bator Amur Khabarovsk Date Line
PARIS GERMANY PRAGUE Volgograd KAZAKSTAN MONGOLIA Harbin Vladivostok Sapporo
AUSTRIA Budapest ROMANIA Astrakhan L. Balkhash Changchun Kuril Is.
Milan CROATIA Belgrade Aral Almaty SHENYANG NORTH JAPAN
Marseilles ITALY YUG. Bucharest Black Sea Bishkek Ürümqi BEIJING TIANJIN KOREA Pyongyang TŌKYŌ
Rome SOFIA BULGARIA GEORGIA UZBEKISTAN KYRGYZSTAN Dalian SEOUL Ōsaka
Barcelona Sardinia ALB. Tbilisi Baku Tashkent Lanzhou Taiyuan SOUTH Kitakyushu PACIFIC
Naples GREECE Yerevan Samarkand C H I N A KOREA
Algiers ISTANBUL ARM. AZER. Dushanbe Xi'an Huang Ho OCEAN
Tunis Athens Izmir TURKEY Ankara TURKMENISTAN TAJIKISTAN Nanjing SHANGHAI Bonin Is.
TUNISIA MALTA Crete CYPRUS SYRIA TEHRAN Ashkhabad TIBET Chengdu Wuhan East China (Japan)
Mediterranean Beirut Damascus Mashhad Kābul Lhasa CHONGQING Sea
Tripoli Sea ISR. Baghdad Esfahan AFGHANISTAN Islamabad Kunming Fuzhou Volcano Is. Marcus I.
Benghazi JORDAN IRAQ IRAN Lahore KASHMIR Guangzhou Taipei (Japan) (Japan) Tropic of Cancer
Alexandria Shiraz PAKISTAN DELHI NEPAL Katmandu GUANGZHOU TAIWAN Wake I.
CAIRO KUWAIT New Delhi BHU. Kanpur BANGLA- HONG KONG NORTHERN (U.S.A.)
LIBYA BAHRAIN The Gulf Abu Dhabi Ganges DESH DACCA MARIANAS
EGYPT QATAR Muscat I N D I A CALCUTTA BURMA Hainan (U.S.A.)
Aswān Riyadh U.A.E. OMAN Nagpur Bay of MYANMAR Hanoi South Marshall Is.
Red Mecca SAUDI Arabian MUMBAI Bengal Rangoon China
NIGER Sea ARABIA Sea (Bombay) Hyderabad THAILAND VIET- Sea MANILA
CHAD Omdurmān Asmara Sana YEMEN Bangalore CHENNAI BANGKOK NAM PHILIPPINES GUAM
Niamey Khartoum ERITREA Aden (Madras) Andaman Is. CAMBODIA (U.S.A.)
NIGERIA SUDAN DJIBOUTI G. of Aden Socotra Lakshadweep Is. (India) Phnom Ho Chi Minh Yap FEDERATED STATES
Kano Ndjamena ADDIS ABABA (Yemen) Penh City Truk Pohnpei
Abuja CENTRAL ETHIOPIA SOMALI SRI LANKA Nicobar Is. MALAYSIA PALAU Caroline Is.
Ibadan AFRICAN REP. MALDIVES Colombo (India) Medan SABAH OF MICRONESIA
Lagos REP. Bangui Kisangani UGANDA KENYA Equator Kuala Lumpur BRUNEI Gilbert Is.
CAMEROON Yaoundé Kampala Mogadishu PEN. MALAYSIA SARAWAK NAURU KIRIBATI
EQUATORIAL Libreville L. Turkana SINGAPORE IRIAN
GUINEA CONGO RWANDA Nairobi Borneo JAYA New
GABON DEM. REP. OF THE Kigali I N D O N E S I A PAPUA Ireland
CONGO Victoria BURUNDI Sumatra Palembang Banjarmasin NEW New
Brazzaville CABINDA Kananga Bujumbura Dodoma SEYCHELLES Ujung Pandang GUINEA Britain
Kinshasa (Angola) Tanganyika TANZANIA JAKARTA Port SOLOMON
Luanda Mombasa Amirante Is. Bandung Moresby IS.
ANGOLA Zanzibar Aldabra Is. Diego Garcia Chagos Arch. Surabaya Timor C. York Santa Cruz I.
Benguela Dar es Salaam (U.K.) Java Arafura Sea
ZAMBIA Malawi COMOROS Mayotte Agalega Is. Cocos Is. Christmas I. VANUATU
Lusaka Lilongwe (Fr.) (Austral.) (Austral.) Darwin
Lubumbashi MALAWI INDIAN Cairns
Harare MADAGASCAR OCEAN Townsville NEW
ZIMBABWE MOZAMBIQUE Cargados Carajos CALEDONIA FIJI
NAMIBIA Bulawayo Antananarivo A U S T R A L I A (Fr.) Suva
Windhoek BOTSWANA Rodriguez Port Hedland Alice Springs Rockhampton
Maputo RÉUNION MAURITIUS Tropic of Capricorn Brisbane
Gaborone Pretoria SWAZILAND (Fr.) Geraldton Lord Howe I.
Johannesburg Mozambique Channel Amsterdam I. Kalgoorlie- Newcastle (Austral.)
SOUTH LESOTHO Durban (Fr.) Perth Boulder Sydney Norfolk I.
AFRICA St.Paul (Fr.) Fremantle Adelaide Canberra (Austral.)
Cape Town Port Elizabeth Great Darling Auckland
C. of Good Hope Prince Edward Is. Crozet Is. Australian Melbourne North I.
(S.Africa) (Fr.) Bight Tasman NEW
Kerguelen Tasmania Sea ZEALAND
(Fr.) Hobart Christchurch Wellington
McDonald Is. Heard I. South I.
(Austral.) (Austral.) Stewart I. Dunedin
Bouvet I. Campbell I. Bounty Is.
(Norw.) (N.Z.) (N.Z.) Antipodes Is.
S O U T H E R N O C E A N Macquarie Is. Auckland Is. (N.Z.)
(Austral.) (N.Z.)
Antarctic Circle
A n t a r c t i c a Ross Sea
East from Greenwich

Hanoi ● Capital Cities

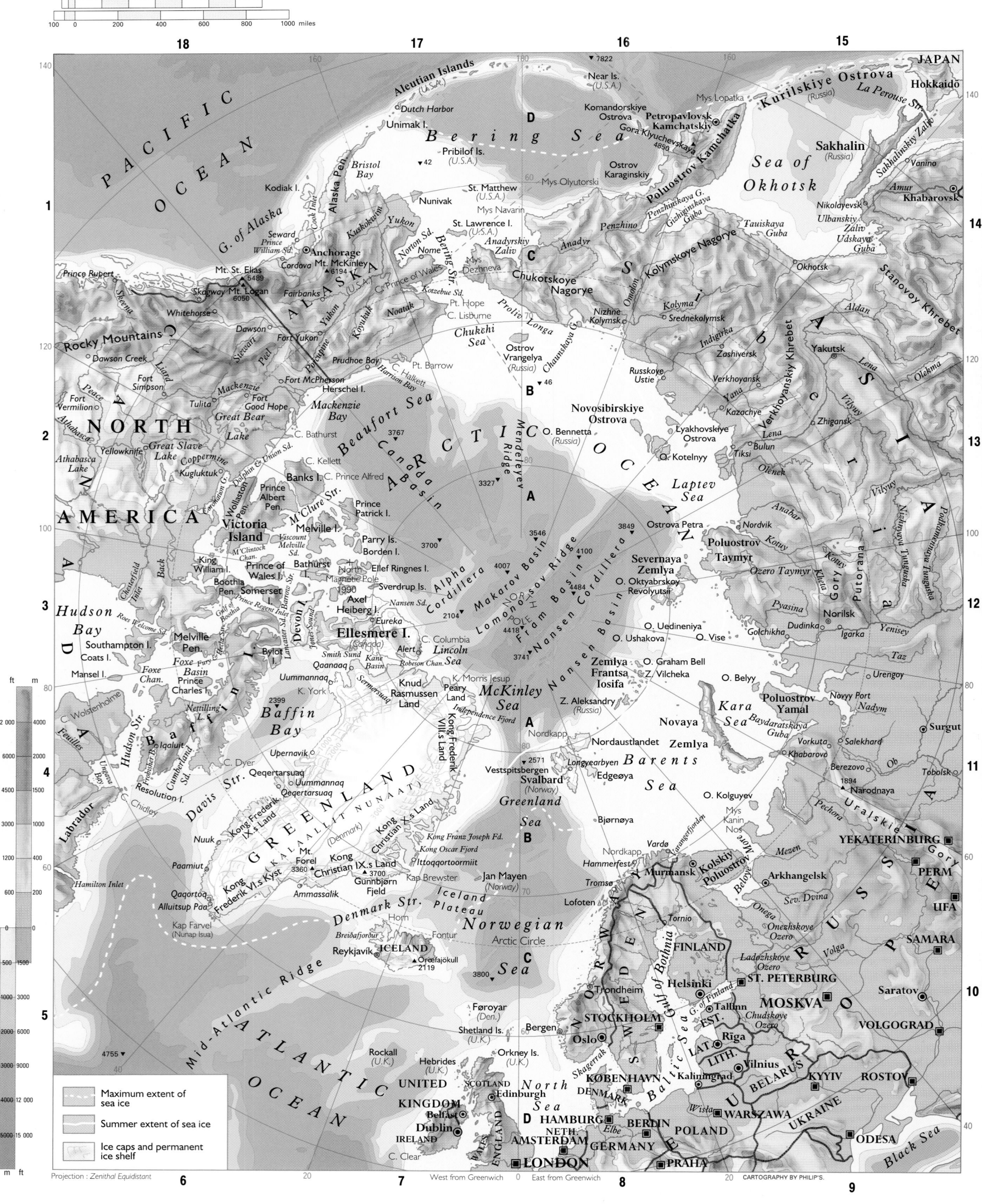

100 0   200   400 600 800 1000 1200 1400 km
100 0   200   400   600   800   1000 miles

18   **17**   **16**   **15**

PACIFIC OCEAN

Aleutian Islands (U.S.A.)
Dutch Harbor
Unimak I.
Bristol Bay
Kodiak I.
G. of Alaska
Seward
Prince William Sd.
Anchorage
Cordova Mt. McKinley 6194
Mt. St. Elias 5489
Skagway Mt. Logan 6050
Fairbanks
Whitehorse
ALASKA (U.S.A.)
Prince Rupert
Rocky Mountains
Dawson
Dawson Creek
Fort Simpson
Fort Vermilion
Peace
Yellowknife Great Slave Lake
Athabasca Lake
Fort Good Hope
Tulita
Great Bear Lake
Coppermine
Kugluktuk

NORTH AMERICA

Victoria Island
Banks I. C. Prince Alfred
Melville I.
Prince Patrick I.
Borden I.
Parry Is.
Ellef Ringnes I.
Axel Heiberg I.
Prince of Wales I.
Bathurst
Somerset
Boothia Pen.
King William I.
Eureka
Ellesmere I. (Canada)
Alert
Devon I.

Hudson Bay
Southampton I.
Coats I.
Mansel I.
Melville Pen.
Foxe Basin
Prince Charles I.
Baffin Island
Iqaluit
Resolution I.
Labrador
Hamilton Inlet

Pribilof Is. (U.S.A.)
St. Matthew
Nunivak
St. Lawrence I. (U.S.A.)
Nome
C. Prince of Wales
Bering Str.
Kotzebue Sd.
Pt. Hope
C. Lisburne
Chukchi Sea
Prudhoe Bay
Pt. Barrow
Herschel I.
Mackenzie Bay
Beaufort Sea
Canada Basin
Alpha Cordillera
NORTH POLE
Lomonosov Ridge
Makarov Basin
Mendeleyev Ridge

Bering Sea
Petropavlovsk Kamchatskiy
Gora Klyuchevskaya 4850
Poluostrov Kamchatka
Anadyr
Anadyrskiy Zaliv
Mys Dezhneva
Chukotskoye Nagorye
Proliv Longa
Ostrov Vrangelya (Russia)

Sea of Okhotsk
Sakhalin (Russia)
Nikolayevsk
Okhotsk

ARCTIC OCEAN

Laptev Sea
Severnaya Zemlya
Novaya Zemlya
Kara Sea
Poluostrov Yamal
Zemlya Frantsa Iosifa (Russia)
Barents Sea
Svalbard (Norway)
Greenland Sea
Norwegian Sea
GREENLAND (KALAALLIT NUNAAT) (Denmark)
Gunnbjørn Fjeld
Ammassalik
Denmark Str.
ICELAND
Mid-Atlantic Ridge
ATLANTIC OCEAN

JAPAN
Hokkaidō
Kurilskiye Ostrova (Russia)
La Perouse Str.

ft m
12 000 4000
6000   2000
4500   1500
3000   1000
1200   400
600   200
0   0
500   1500
1000   3000
2000   6000
3000   9000
4000 12 000
5000 15 000
m ft

Maximum extent of sea ice
Summer extent of sea ice
Ice caps and permanent ice shelf

Projection: Zenithal Equidistant   **6**   **7**   West from Greenwich   0   East from Greenwich   **8**   CARTOGRAPHY BY PHILIP'S.   **9**

FINLAND
Helsinki
SWEDEN
NORWAY
STOCKHOLM
Oslo
København
DENMARK
HAMBURG
BERLIN
GERMANY
AMSTERDAM
NETH.
LONDON
UNITED KINGDOM
IRELAND
Dublin
Edinburgh
SCOTLAND
ENGLAND
WALES
North Sea

ST. PETERBURG
MOSKVA
RUSSIA
YEKATERINBURG
PERM
UFA
SAMARA
SARATOV
VOLGOGRAD
Riga
LAT.
LITH.
Vilnius
BELARUS
KYYIV
UKRAINE
WARSZAWA
POLAND
PRAHA
Kaliningrad
ROSTOV
ODESA
Black Sea

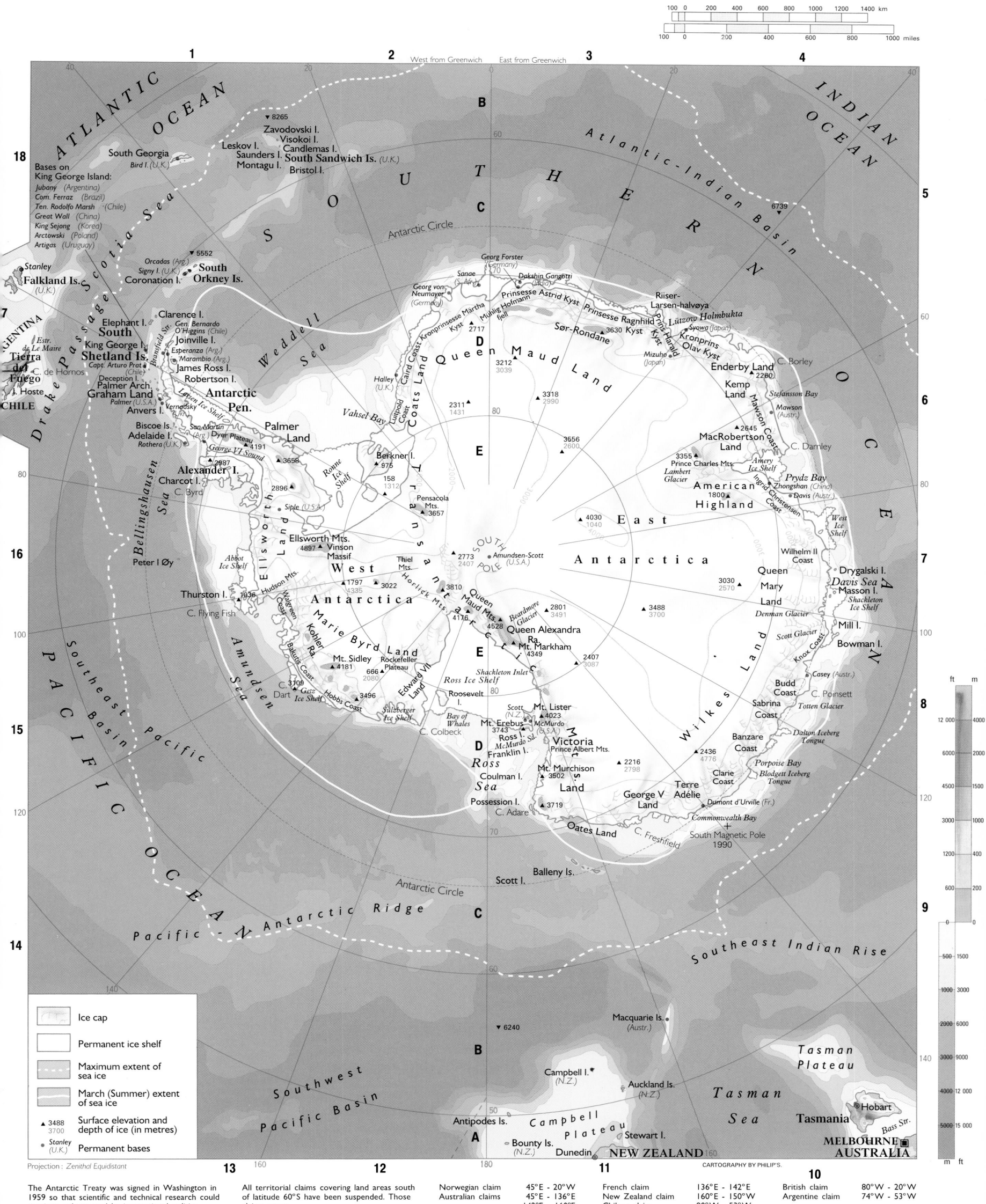

100	0 200 400 600 800 1000 1200	1400 km
100	0 200 400 600	800 1000 miles

Projection : Zenithal Equidistant

CARTOGRAPHY BY PHILIP'S.

Legend:

- Ice cap
- Permanent ice shelf
- Maximum extent of sea ice
- March (Summer) extent of sea ice
- ▲ 3488 / 3700 Surface elevation and depth of ice (in metres)
- ● Stanley (U.K.) Permanent bases

Bases on King George Island:
Jubany (Argentina)
Com. Ferraz (Brazil)
Ten. Rodolfo Marsh (Chile)
Great Wall (China)
King Sejong (Korea)
Arctowski (Poland)
Artigas (Uruguay)

The Antarctic Treaty was signed in Washington in 1959 so that scientific and technical research could continue unhampered by international politics.

All territorial claims covering land areas south of latitude 60°S have been suspended. Those claims were:

Norwegian claim	45°E – 20°W
Australian claims	45°E – 136°E
	142°E – 160°E
French claim	136°E – 142°E
New Zealand claim	160°E – 150°W
Chilean claim	90°W – 53°W
British claim	80°W – 20°W
Argentine claim	74°W – 53°W

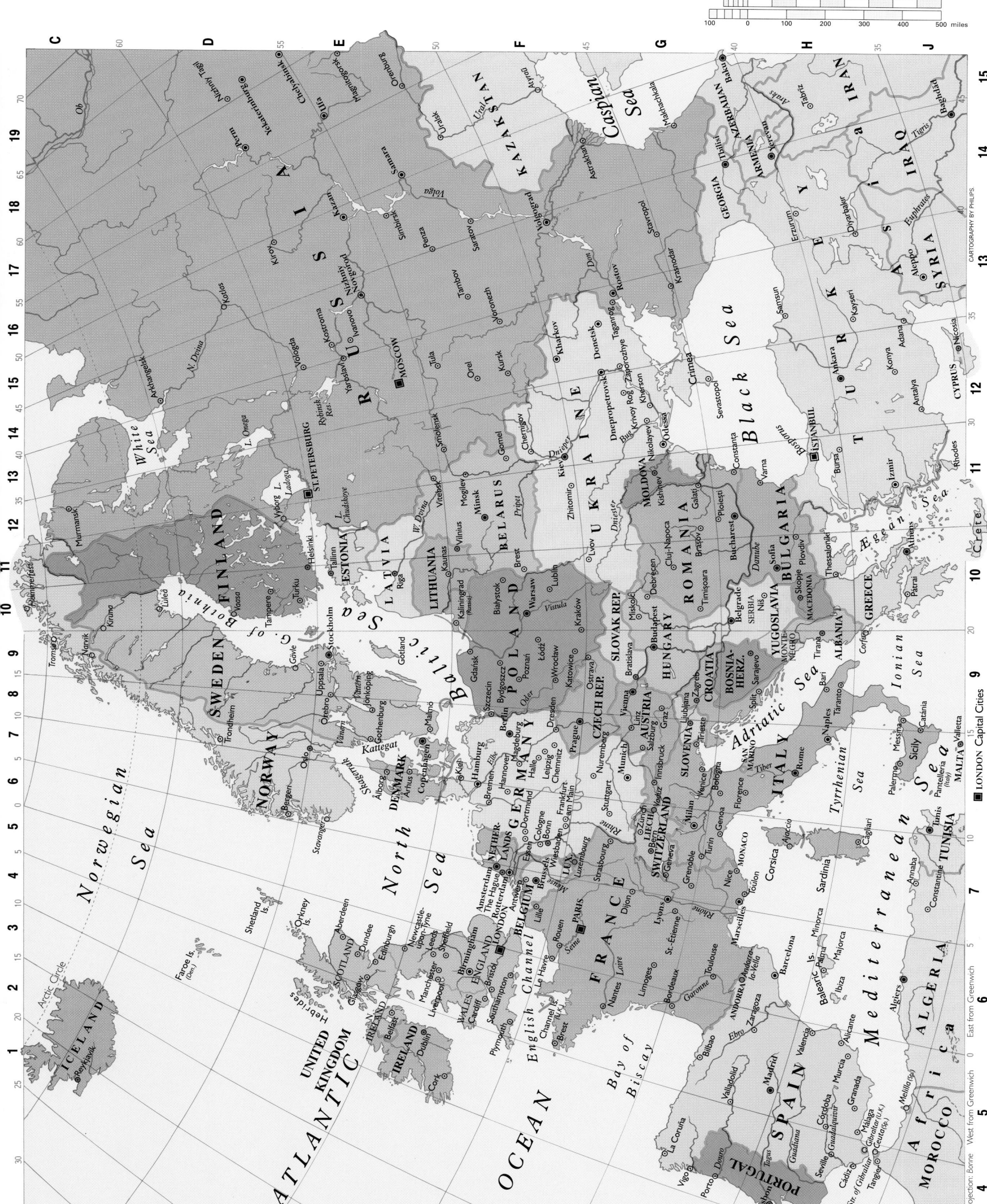

100 0 100 200 300 400 500 600 700 800 km
100 0 100 200 300 400 500 miles

LONDON Capital Cities

Projection: Bonne West from Greenwich 0 East from Greenwich

CARTOGRAPHY BY PHILIPS

SCANDINAVIA 1:4 400 000

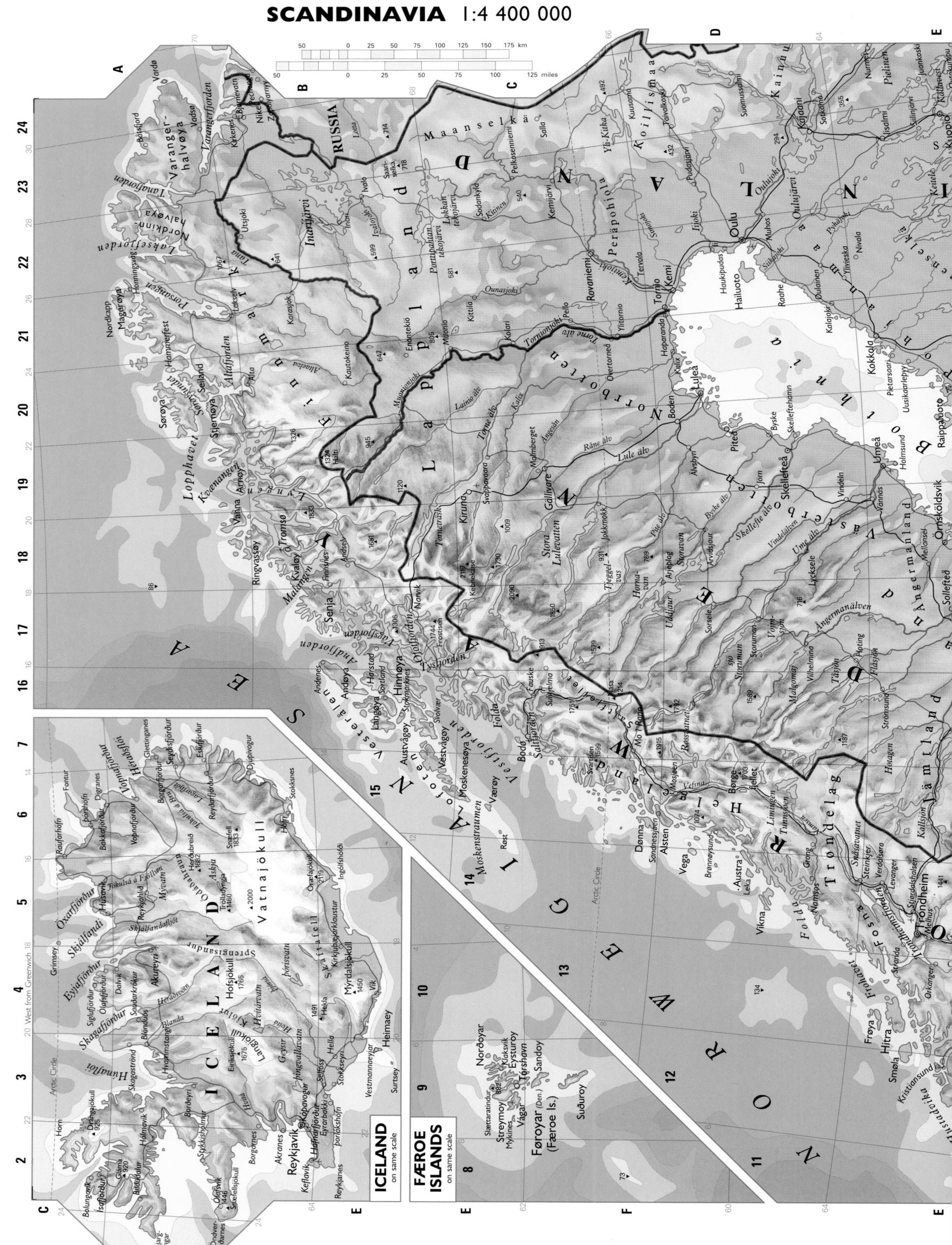

ICELAND
on same scale

FÆROE
ISLANDS
on same scale

ESTONIA
LATVIA
LITHUANIA
FINLAND
SWEDEN
NORWAY
DENMARK
GERMANY
POLAND
RUSSIA
BELARUS

Gulf of Finland
Gulf of Bothnia
Gulf of Riga
BALTIC SEA
Ålands hav
Skagerrak
Kattegat

STOCKHOLM
Helsinki (Helsingfors)
Tallinn
Riga
Vilnius
Kaunas
Oslo
København (Copenhagen)
Göteborg (Gothenburg)

Tampere · Turku (Åbo) · Pori · Rauma · Mikkeli · Jyväskylä · Lappeenranta · Kotka · Kouvola · Espoo · Salo · Lahti
Tartu · Pärnu · Narva
Valmiera · Liepāja · Ventspils · Jelgava · Daugavpils · Šiauliai · Panevėžys · Klaipėda · Kaliningrad (Russia)

Uppsala · Västerås · Eskilstuna · Södertälje · Norrköping · Linköping · Örebro · Karlstad · Gävle · Falun · Mora · Borlänge · Sundsvall · Härnösand · Hudiksvall · Söderhamn · Bollnäs
Jönköping · Växjö · Kalmar · Karlskrona · Kristianstad · Halmstad · Helsingborg · Malmö · Landskrona · Trelleborg · Ystad · Borås · Kristinehamn · Mariestad · Lidköping · Trollhättan · Uddevalla

Ålborg · Århus · Odense · Esbjerg · Randers · Kolding · Horsens · Vejle · Roskilde · Helsingør · Næstved · Slagelse

Gotland · Visby · Öland · Bornholm · Rønne · Rügen · Usedom
Gdańsk · Gdynia · Sopot · Szczecin · Słupsk · Koszalin · Kołobrzeg · Elbląg · Malbork
Rostock · Wismar · Lübeck · Kiel · Flensburg · Neumünster · Cuxhaven

Bergen · Stavanger · Kristiansand · Arendal · Drammen · Tønsberg · Sandefjord · Larvik · Skien · Porsgrunn · Hamar · Lillehammer

Saaremaa (Ösel) · Hiiumaa (Dago) · Åland (Ahvenanmaa) · Fårö · Gotska Sandön · Dalarna · Härjedalen · Jotunheimen · Dovrefjell · Hardangervidda

COPYRIGHT GEORGE PHILIP LTD
Projection: Conical with two standard parallels
East from Greenwich

m / ft elevation scale: 6000 · 4500 · 3000 · 1500 · 600 · 0 — 2000 · 1500 · 1000 · 500 · 200 · 0

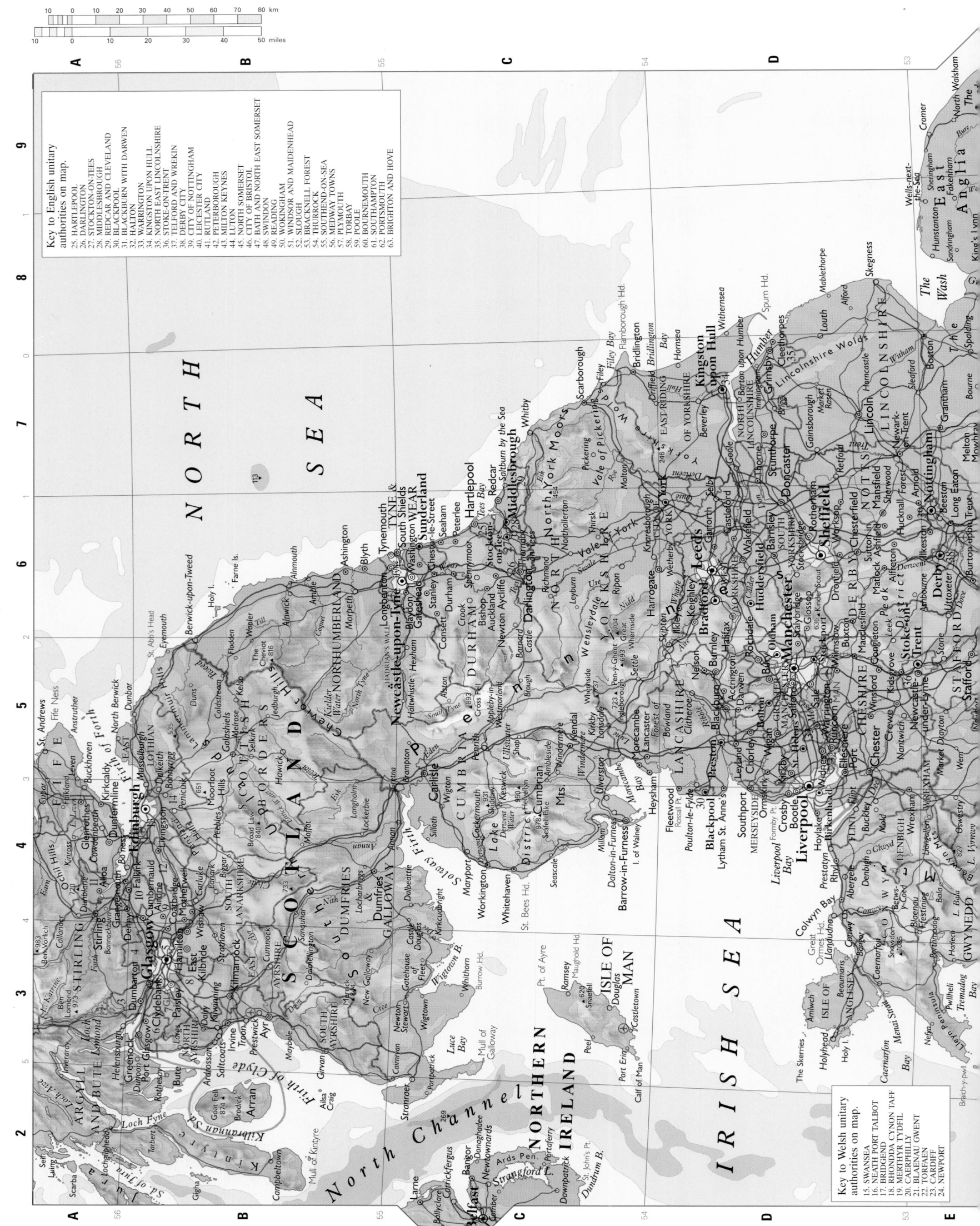

Key to English unitary
authorities on map.

25. HARTLEPOOL
26. DARLINGTON
27. STOCKTON-ON-TEES
28. MIDDLESBROUGH
29. REDCAR AND CLEVELAND
30. BLACKPOOL
31. BLACKBURN WITH DARWEN
32. HALTON
33. WARRINGTON
34. KINGSTON UPON HULL
35. NORTH EAST LINCOLNSHIRE
36. STOKE-ON-TRENT
37. TELFORD AND WREKIN
38. DERBY CITY
39. CITY OF NOTTINGHAM
40. LEICESTER CITY
41. RUTLAND
42. PETERBOROUGH
43. MILTON KEYNES
44. LUTON
45. NORTH SOMERSET
46. CITY OF BRISTOL
47. BATH AND NORTH EAST SOMERSET
48. SWINDON
49. READING
50. WOKINGHAM
51. WINDSOR AND MAIDENHEAD
52. SLOUGH
53. BRACKNELL FOREST
54. THURROCK
55. SOUTHEND-ON-SEA
56. MEDWAY TOWNS
57. TORBAY
58. PLYMOUTH
59. POOLE
60. BOURNEMOUTH
61. SOUTHAMPTON
62. PORTSMOUTH
63. BRIGHTON AND HOVE

Key to Welsh unitary
authorities on map.

15. SWANSEA
16. NEATH PORT TALBOT
17. BRIDGEND
18. RHONDDA CYNON TAFF
19. MERTHYR TYDFIL
20. CAERPHILLY
21. BLAENAU GWENT
22. TORFAEN
23. CARDIFF
24. NEWPORT

ENGLAND

FRANCE

WALES

ENGLISH CHANNEL

Bristol Channel

Cardigan Bay

Baie de la Seine

La Manche

Strait of Dover

Thames Estuary

LONDON

BIRMINGHAM

Bristol

Cardiff

Swansea

Plymouth

Southampton

Portsmouth

Bournemouth

Brighton

Le Havre

Rouen

Caen

Cherbourg

Calais

NORFOLK · SUFFOLK · ESSEX · KENT · EAST SUSSEX · WEST SUSSEX · SURREY · HAMPSHIRE · DORSET · DEVON · CORNWALL · SOMERSET · WILTSHIRE · BERKSHIRE · OXFORDSHIRE · GLOUCESTERSHIRE · HEREFORD · SHROPSHIRE · POWYS · CEREDIGION · PEMBROKESHIRE · CARMARTHENSHIRE · GLAMORGAN · CAMBRIDGE · BUCKS · HERTS · WARWICK · WORCESTER · MONMOUTH

SEINE-MARITIME · EURE · CALVADOS · MANCHE · HAUTE-NORMANDIE · Cotentin

CHANNEL ISLANDS (U.K.) · Jersey · Guernsey · Alderney · Sark · Herm · St. Helier · St. Peter Port

Isles of Scilly — On same scale · St. Mary's · Tresco

Isle of Wight · Newport · Cowes · Ryde · Ventnor

Land's End · Lizard Pt. · St. Ives · Penzance · Newlyn · Truro · Falmouth · Newquay · Redruth · Camborne

Dover · Folkestone · Ramsgate · Margate · Canterbury · Maidstone · Ashford · Hastings · Eastberne · Beachy Head · Deal · Dungeness

Ipswich · Colchester · Chelmsford · Cambridge · Peterborough · Northampton · Oxford · Reading · Gloucester · Cheltenham · Worcester · Hereford · Wolverhampton · Coventry · Leicester

Exeter · Torquay · Barnstaple · Bideford · Bodmin · Launceston

Dieppe · Fécamp · Étretat · Honfleur · Trouville · Deauville · Bayeux · Évreux · Lisieux · St-Lô · Coutances · Granville · Avranches

Projection: Lambert's Conformal Conic

COPYRIGHT GEORGE PHILIP LTD.

East from Greenwich · West from Greenwich

10 0 10 20 30 40 50 60 70 80 km
10 0 10 20 30 40 50 miles

Key to Scottish unitary authorities on map
1. CITY OF ABERDEEN
2. DUNDEE CITY
3. WEST DUNBARTONSHIRE
4. EAST DUNBARTONSHIRE
5. CITY OF GLASGOW
6. INVERCLYDE
7. RENFREWSHIRE
8. EAST RENFREWSHIRE
9. NORTH LANARKSHIRE
10. FALKIRK
11. CLACKMANNANSHIRE
12. WEST LOTHIAN
13. CITY OF EDINBURGH
14. MIDLOTHIAN

ORKNEY IS. On same scale

ORKNEY
North Ronaldsay
Papa Westray
Westray
Sanday
Eday
Rousay
Stronsay
Shapinsay
Stromness
Mainland
Kirkwall
St. Mary's
Burray
Hoy
Scapa Flow
South Ronaldsay
Dunnet Hd.
Stroma
Duncansby Head
John o' Groats
Thurso
Sinclair's Bay
Pentland Firth

Butt of Lewis
Flannan Is.
Gallan Hd.
Stornoway
Broad Bay
Eye Peninsula
LEWIS
WESTERN ISLES
Taransay
Clisham 799
Tarbert
L. Seaforth
Harris
Toe Hd.
Scarp
Pabbay
Berneray
Sound of Harris
North Uist
Lochmaddy
Baleshare
Grimsay
Benbecula
Ardivachar Pt.
Wiay
South Uist
Ben Mhor 620
Lochboisdale
Eriskay
Sound of Barra
Barra
Vatersay
Sandray
Barra Hd. 268

OUTER HEBRIDES
Little Minch
North Minch
Sound of Raasay
C. Wrath
Durness
L. Eriboll
Strathy Pt.
Dounreay
Reay Forest
Ben Hope 927
Tongue
L. Laxford
Eddrachillis B.
Pt. of Stoer
L. Assynt
Ben More Assynt 998
Lochinver
Enard B.
Rubha Coigeach
Ullapool
L. Broom
Gruinard B.
Greenstone Pt.
L. Ewe
L. Maree 1053
L. Fannich
Strathpeffer
Dingwall
Rubha Reidh
Gairloch
Rona
Raasay
Scalpay
Stromeferry
Kyle of Lochalsh
L. Carron
Dornie
Carn Eige 1182
Glen Affric
1068
Cuillin Hills 992
SKYE
Portree
Uig
Rubha Hunish
Inner Sound
Loch Bracadale
Cuillin Sound
Sd. of Sleat
Mallaig
Arisaig
L. Morar
Sound of Mull
Muck
Eigg
Rhum
Canna
Coll
Tiree
Pt. of Ardnamurchan
Tobermory
Ulva
Staffa
Iona
Ben More 966
MULL
Kerrera
Luing
Seil
Scarba
Colonsay
Oronsay
Jura
Islay
Bowmore
Port Ellen
Rhinns Pt.
Ardnave Pt.
Rubh a' Mhail
Gigha
Mull of Oa

Dunnet Hd.
Thurso
Halkirk
Wick
Lybster
Ord of Caithness
Helmsdale
Brora
Golspie
Lairg
L. Shin
Oykel
Bonar Bridge
Dornoch Firth
Dornoch
Tain
Tarbat Ness
Invergordon
Cromarty
Alness
Ben Wyvis 1045
Beauly
Inverness
Nairn
Forres
Elgin
Lossiemouth
Portknockie
Buckie
Cullen
Portsoy
Banff
Macduff
Aberchirder
Turriff
Keith
Rothes
Dufftown
Huntly
Ellon
Oldmeldrum
Inverurie
Alford
Grantown-on-Spey
Tomintoul
Aviemore
Kingussie
Newtonmore
Cairn Gorm 1245
Cairngorm Mts.
Ben Macdhui 1309
Braemar
Ballater
Aboyne
Banchory
Stonehaven
Aberdeen
Girdle Ness
Peterculter
Dyce
Westhill
Peterhead
Buchan Ness
Fraserburgh
Rattray Hd.
Kinnairds Hd.
Buchan
ABERDEENSHIRE
MORAY
Strath Spey
Spey
Findhorn
Deveron
Ythan
Don
Dee
N. Esk
S. Esk
Lochnagar 1154
Forest of Atholl
Blair Atholl
Pitlochry
Kirriemuir
Brechin
Montrose
Forfar
Arbroath
Carnoustie
Monifieth
Dundee
Firth of Tay
Newport
Tayport
St. Andrews
Fife Ness
Cupar
Leven
Anstruther
Buckhaven
Kirkcaldy
FIFE
Glenrothes
Leslie
Falkland
Loch Leven
Kinross
KINROSS
Dunblane
Callander
Crieff
Perth
Scone
Aberfeldy
Dunkeld
Blairgowrie
Alyth
Coupar Angus
L. Tay
Ben Lawers 1214
L. Rannoch
Rannoch Moor
Glen Coe
Ben Nevis 1342
Fort William
Glen Spean
Spean Bridge
L. Lochy
L. Arkaig
L. Eil
L. Shiel
L. Moidart
L. Sunart
Morvern
L. Linnhe
Loch Leven
Ballachulish
Oban
Loch Etive
Ben Cruachan 1126
Loch Awe
ARGYLL AND BUTE
Inveraray
Ben Ime 1011
L. Katrine
Ben More 1174
Ben Vorlich 985
Lochearnhead
Ben Lomond 973
Loch Lomond
Lochgilphead
Tarbert
Kintyre
Sd. of Jura
Loch Fyne
Campbeltown
Mull of Kintyre

SCOTLAND

NORTH SEA

PERTH AND KINROSS
ANGUS
Strathmore
Sidlaw Hills
Ochil Hills
STIRLING
Stirling
Bannockburn
Alloa
Clackmannan
Cowdenbeath
Dunfermline
Firth of Forth
North Berwick
Dunbar
Edinburgh
Musselburgh
Dalkeith
Bonnyrigg
Penicuik
Livingston
Bo'ness
Grangemouth
Denny
Falkirk
Cumbernauld
Airdrie
Coatbridge
Motherwell
Hamilton
Wishaw
Carluke
Lanark
Biggar
Peebles
Moorfoot Hills
Broad Law 840
Galashiels
Melrose
Selkirk
Jedburgh
Hawick
The Cheviot 816
Cheviot Hills
Lammermuir Hills
Duns
Coldstream
Kelso
Berwick-upon-Tweed
Eyemouth
St. Abb's Head
SCOTTISH BORDERS
Tweed
Glasgow
Clydebank
Paisley
Renfrew
Greenock
Port Glasgow
Dumbarton
Helensburgh
Dunoon
Rothesay
Bute
Largs
Ardrossan
Saltcoats
Kilwinning
Irvine
Troon
Prestwick
Ayr
Kilmarnock
Dalry
East Kilbride
Strathaven
NORTH AYRSHIRE
EAST AYRSHIRE
SOUTH AYRSHIRE
SOUTH LANARKSHIRE
Arran
Goat Fell 874
Brodick
Kilbrannan Sd.
Firth of Clyde
Maybole
Girvan
Ailsa Craig
Dalmellington
Cumnock
Sanquhar
Moffat
Dumfries
Lockerbie
Annan
Gretna
Langholm
Merrick 844
New Galloway
Castle Douglas
Dalbeattie
Kirkcudbright
Gatehouse of Fleet
Newton Stewart
Wigtown
Whithorn
Stranraer
Cairnryan
Portpatrick
Luce Bay
Wigtown B.
Burrow Hd.
Mull of Galloway
DUMFRIES & GALLOWAY
Galloway
Solway Firth
Nith
Annan
Esk

ENGLAND
Newcastle-upon-Tyne
Carlisle
Brampton
Haltwhistle
Hexham
Alston
Penrith
Appleby-in-Westmorland
Keswick
Workington
Maryport
Cockermouth
Whitehaven
St. Bees Hd.
Ullswater
Helvellyn 950
Skiddaw 931
Cross Fell 893
CUMBRIA
NORTHUMBERLAND
Kielder Water
Alnwick
Alnmouth
Amble
Morpeth
Wooler
Flodden
Farne Is.
Holy I.
Coquet
North Tyne
South Tyne
Blaydon
Gateshead
Consett
Stanley
Crook
Bishop Auckland
DURHAM
Barnard Castle
Tees

NORTHERN IRELAND
Larne
Carrickfergus
Belfast
Belfast L.
Bangor
Donaghadee
Newtownards
North Channel
Atlantic Ocean

SHETLAND IS. On same scale

SHETLAND
Unst
Haroldswick
Fetlar
Yell
Yell Sound
Ulsta
Whalsay
Mainland
Voe
Esha Ness 453
St. Magnus Bay
Papa Stour
Walls
West Burra
Foula
Scalloway
Lerwick
Bressay
Boddam
Sumburgh Hd.

Projection: Lambert's Conformal Conic
West from Greenwich

ft m
3000 1000
1500 600
900 300
600 200
300 100
0 0
150 50
300 100
600 200
1500 500
3000 1000
m ft

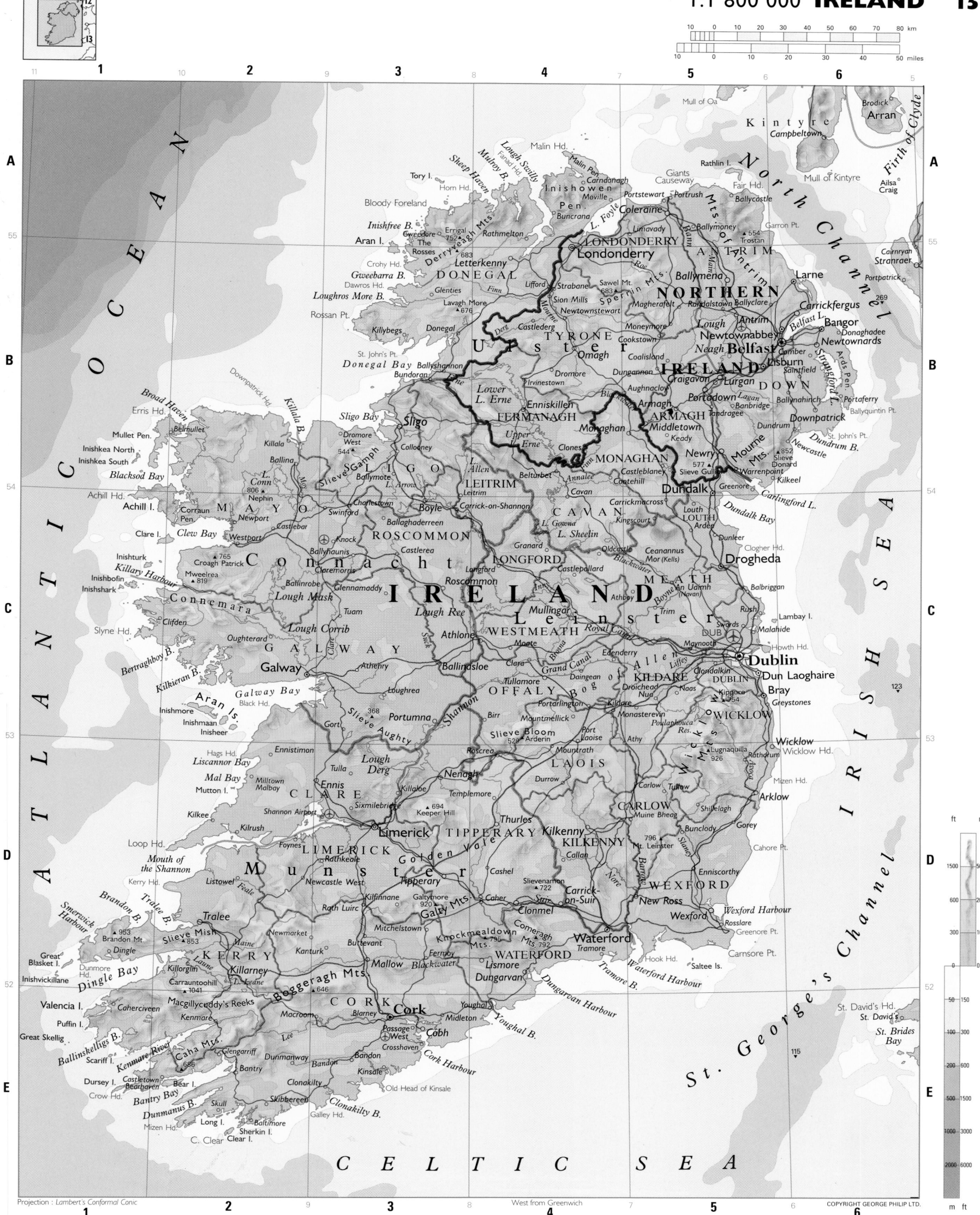

10 0 10 20 30 40 50 60 70 80 km
10 0 10 20 30 40 50 miles

ATLANTIC OCEAN

NORTH CHANNEL

IRISH SEA

St. George's Channel

CELTIC SEA

Mull of Oa
Kintyre
Campbeltown
Brodick
Arran
Firth of Clyde
Ailsa Craig
Cairnryan
Stranraer
Portpatrick

Malin Hd.
Fanad Hd.
Lough Swilly
Malin Pen.
Giants Causeway
Rathlin I.
Mull of Kintyre
Fair Hd.
Ballycastle
Portstewart
Portrush
Coleraine
Limavady
Ballymoney
Garron Pt.
554 Trostan

Tory I.
Horn Hd.
Sheep Haven
Mulroy B.
Carndonagh
Moville
Buncrana
Inishowen Pen.
L. Foyle
Roe
Antrim
Mts. of Antrim
Larne

Bloody Foreland
Inishfree B.
Aran I.
Gweedore
Errigal 752
The Rosses
Crohy Hd.
Gweebarra B.
Dawros Hd.
Rossan Pt.
Killybegs
Derryveagh Mts.
Rathmelton
Letterkenny
DONEGAL
Glenties
Lavagh More 676
Donegal
683
Castlederg
Strabane
Sion Mills
Newtownstewart
Sawel Mt. 683
Spertin Mts.
Magherafelt
Moneymore
Cookstown
Coalisland
Dungannon
TYRONE
Omagh
NORTHERN
Randalstown Ballyclare
Antrim
Ballymena
Lough Neagh
Belfast
Newtownabbey
Craigavon
Lisburn
Comber
Bangor
Donaghadee
Newtownards
Ards Pen.
Carrickfergus
269

St. John's Pt.
Donegal Bay
Ballyshannon
Bundoran
U l s t e r
Erne
Lower L. Erne
Enniskillen
FERMANAGH
Upper L. Erne
IRELAND
Irvinestown
Dromore
Aughnacloy
Armagh
Middletown
Keady
ARMAGH
Portadown
Lurgan
Banbridge
Tandragee
Lagan
DOWN
Downpatrick
Ballynahinch
Dundrum
Saintfield
Ballyquintin Pt.
Portaferry
Strangford L.
Dundrum B.
St. John's Pt.
Newcastle
852 Slieve Donard

Broad Haven
Erris Hd.
Belmullet
Mullet Pen.
Inishkea North
Inishkea South
Blacksod Bay
Killala B.
Downpatrick Hd.
Killala
Ballina
Ballymote
Sligo Bay
Sligo
Dromore West 544
Colloney
SLIGO
L. Arrow
L. Allen
LEITRIM
Leitrim
MONAGHAN
Monaghan
Clones
Belturbet
Annalee
Cootehill
CAVAN
Cavan
Castleblaney
Carrickmacross
Kingscourt
Newry
Slieve Gullion 577
Mourne Mts.
Warrenpoint
Kilkeel
Carlingford L.
Greenore
Dundalk
LOUTH
Ardee
Dunleer
Clogher Hd.
Dundalk Bay

Achill Hd.
Achill I.
Corraun Pen.
Nephin 806
Clare I.
MAYO
Newport
Clew Bay
Westport
Castlebar
Swinford
Charlestown
Ballaghaderreen
Boyle
Carrick-on-Shannon
ROSCOMMON
Castlerea
L. Gowna
Granard
L. Sheelin
Oldcastle
Blackwater
Ceanannus Mor (Kells)
Clogher Hd.
Drogheda
Balbriggan

Inishturk
Inishbofin
Inishshark
Killary Harbour
Croagh Patrick 765
Mweelrea 819
Ballyhaunis
Claremorris
Ballinrobe
Glennamaddy
Castlerea
Roscommon
LONGFORD
Longford
Castlepollard
Lough Ree
MEATH
Trim
Boyne
An Uaimh (Navan)
Athboy
Rush
Lambay I.
C o n n a c h t
Knock
Tuam
Lough Mask
Lough Corrib
Oughterard
IRELAND
Inny
WESTMEATH
Mullingar
Moate
Athlone
L e i n s t e r
Royal Canal
Maynooth
Swords
Malahide
Howth Hd.
DUB
Dublin
Clondalkin
Dun Laoghaire

Clifden
Slyne Hd.
Bertraghboy B.
Kilkieran B.
Connemara
Black Hd.
GALWAY
Galway
Galway Bay
Aran Is.
Inishmore
Inishmaan
Inisheer
Hags Hd.
Liscannor Bay
Mal Bay
Mutton I.
Athenry
Loughrea
Gort
Slieve Aughty 368
Portumna
Shannon
Birr
OFFALY
Tullamore
Clara
Daingean
Portarlington
Bog of Allen
Edenderry
Grand Canal
KILDARE
Droichead Nua
Naas
Kildare
Monasterevin
Port Laoise
Athy
Bog of Allen
Liffey
DUBLIN
Kippure 654
Bray
Greystones
Wicklow Mts.
123

Ennistimon
Tuila
Lough Derg
Roscrea
Nenagh
Templemore
694
Keeper Hill
LAOIS
Mountrath
Arderin 529
Slieve Bloom
Mountmellick
Durrow
Carlow
CARLOW
Tullow
Muine Bheag
Bunclody
Shillelagh
Gorey
WICKLOW
Lugnaquilla 926
Rathdrum
Wicklow
Wicklow Hd.
Arklow
Mizen Hd.

Milltown Malbay
Kilkee
Loop Hd.
Ennis
CLARE
Sixmilebridge
Killaloe
Shannon Airport
Kilrush
Mouth of the Shannon
Foynes
Limerick
Rathkeale
LIMERICK
Newcastle West
Golden Vale
Tipperary
TIPPERARY
Thurles
Kilkenny
KILKENNY
Callan
Mt. Leinster 796
Kilkenny
New Ross
WEXFORD
Enniscorthy
Wexford Harbour
Wexford
Rosslare
Greenore Pt.
Carnsore Pt.
Cahore Pt.

Kerry Hd.
Tralee B.
Smerwick Harbour
Brandon B.
Brandon Mt. 953
953
Slieve Mish 853
Tralee
Dingle
Listowel
Feale
Maine
Newcastle West
Abbeyfeale
Rathluirc
Kilfinnane
Galtymore 920
Galty Mts.
Mitchelstown
Caher
Clonmel
Tipperary
Carrick-on-Suir
Slievenamon 722
Comeragh Mts. 792
Waterford
WATERFORD
Tramore
Waterford Harbour
Hook Hd.
Saltee Is.
Tramore B.
Mt. Leinster

Great Blasket I.
Inishvickillane
Dunmore Hd.
Dingle Bay
KERRY
Killorglin
Killarney
Maine
Laune
Carrauntoohill 1041
Macgillycuddy's Reeks
Kenmare
Newmarket
Kanturk
Buttevant
Mallow
Blackwater
Boggeragh Mts. 646
Fermoy
Knockmealdown Mts. 795
Lismore
Dungarvan
Dungarvan Harbour
115

Valencia I.
Puffin I.
Great Skellig
Caherciveen
Ballinskelligs B.
Scariff I.
Kenmare River
Glengarriff
Caha Mts. 686
Macroom
Lee
CORK
Blarney
Passage West
Cobh
Crosshaven
Cork Harbour
Midleton
Youghal
Youghal B.
Carrickmacross
St. David's Hd.
St. David's
St. Brides Bay

Dursey I.
Crow Hd.
Castletown Bearhaven
Bear I.
Bantry Bay
Dunmanway
Bandon
Bandon
Kinsale
Old Head of Kinsale
Long I.
Skull
Mizen Hd.
Sherkin I.
Baltimore
Clonakilty
Clonakilty B.
Galley Hd.
Skibbereen
Dunmanus B.
C. Clear
Clear I.

West from Greenwich

Projection: *Lambert's Conformal Conic*

COPYRIGHT GEORGE PHILIP LTD.

ft m
1500 500
600 200
300 100
0 0
50 150
100 300
200 600
500 1500
1000 3000
2000 6000
m ft

Projection: Conical with two standard parallels

East from Greenwich
COPYRIGHT GEORGE PHILIP LTD.
West from Greenwich

ATLANTIC OCEAN

NORTH SEA

IRISH SEA

CELTIC SEA

English Channel

St. George's Channel

Bristol Channel

North Channel

Firth of Clyde

Pentland Firth

Moray Firth

UNITED KINGDOM

SCOTLAND

ENGLAND

WALES

IRELAND

NORTHERN IRELAND

Ulster

NORWAY

NETHERLANDS

BELGIUM

FRANCE

Shetland Is.
Yell, Unst, Fetlar, Foula, Mainland, Lerwick, Fair Isle

Orkney Is.
Westray, Sanday, Stronsay, Mainland, Kirkwall, Hoy, South Ronaldsay

Lewis, Stornoway, Harris, St. Kilda, North Uist, Benbecula, South Uist, Barra
Outer Hebrides, Inner Hebrides, North Minch

C. Wrath, Thurso, Wick, Helmsdale, Golspie, Lairg, Ullapool, Tain, Invergordon, Dingwall, Nairn, Inverness, Elgin, Buckie, Banff, Fraserburgh, Peterhead, Huntly, Inverurie, Aberdeen
L. Ness, Aviemore, Grampian Mts., North West Highlands
Skye, Rhum, Eigg, Coll, Maltaig, Fort William, Ben Nevis, Tobermory, Tiree, Mull, Oban, Colonsay, Jura, Islay
Ballater, Stonehaven, Forfar, Arbroath, Montrose, Dundee, St. Andrews, Perth, Glenrothes, Kirkcaldy, Dunfermline, Stirling, L. Lomond, Greenock, Paisley, Glasgow, East Kilbride, Hamilton, Edinburgh, Dunbar, Berwick-upon-Tweed
Campbeltown, Arran, Irvine, Kilmarnock, Ayr, Girvan, Southern Uplands, Galashiels, Jedburgh, Hawick, Cheviot Hills, Alnwick

Malin Hd., Buncrana, Letterkenny, Coleraine, Ballymena, Larne, Antrim, Bangor, Belfast, Lisburn, Lurgan, Portadown, Armagh, Newry, Lough Neagh, Londonderry, Omagh, Enniskillen, Clones, Lower L. Erne, Upper L. Erne
Stranraer, Kirkcudbright, Dumfries, Annan, Carlisle, Workington, Whitehaven, Mull of Galloway
Hexham, Newcastle-upon-Tyne, South Shields, Gateshead, Sunderland, Durham, Hartlepool, Redcar, Darlington, Middlesbrough, Stockton-on-Tees, Cumbrian Mts., Pennines
Barrow-in-Furness, Lancaster, I. of Man, Douglas, Scarborough, Bridlington, Harrogate, York, Beverley, Kingston upon Hull, Scunthorpe, Grimsby, Louth, Boston, Skegness
Blackpool, Preston, Blackburn, Burnley, Keighley, Bradford, Leeds, Halifax, Huddersfield, Barnsley, Doncaster, Rotherham, Sheffield, Lincoln
Bolton, Manchester, Oldham, Liverpool, Warrington, Stockport, Chester, Crewe, Chesterfield, Mansfield, Nottingham, Grantham
Anglesey, Holyhead, Bangor, Colwyn Bay, Wrexham, Stoke-on-Trent, Derby, Stafford, Telford, Leicester, Peterborough, Corby, The Wash, King's Lynn, Norwich, Great Yarmouth, Lowestoft, Cromer
Snowdon, Cambrian Mts., Welshpool, Shrewsbury, Wolverhampton, BIRMINGHAM, Coventry, Nuneaton, Rugby, Northampton, Bedford, Cambridge, Ipswich, Bury St. Edmunds, Thetford, Ely
Pwllheli, Cardigan Bay, Aberystwyth, Redditch, Worcester, Hereford, Royal Leamington Spa, Milton Keynes, Stevenage, Harlow, Colchester, Harwich, Felixstowe
Carmarthen, Merthyr Tydfil, Neath, Brecon, Cheltenham, Gloucester, Oxford, Aylesbury, Hemel Hempstead, Luton, Watford, LONDON, Chelmsford, Southend-on-Sea, Margate
Haverfordwest, Milford Haven, Pembroke, Llanelli, Swansea, Port Talbot, Rhondda, Cwmbran, Newport, Cardiff, Barry, Bristol, Bath, Swindon, Newbury, Reading, Slough, High Wycombe, Basildon, Reigate, Chatham, Canterbury, Dover, Folkestone
Fishguard, Weston-super-Mare, Barnstaple, Exmoor, Taunton, Yeovil, Salisbury, Basingstoke, Guildford, Crawley, Ashford, Maidstone, Hastings, Eastbourne
Bude, Bideford, Exeter, Dartmoor, Torbay, Exmouth, Weymouth, Poole, Bournemouth, Southampton, Winchester, Fareham, Portsmouth, Isle of Wight, Newport, Brighton, Worthing, Havant
Newquay, Truro, St. Austell, Plymouth, Land's End, Penzance, Falmouth, Isles of Scilly

Dublin, Dun Laoghaire, Bray, Drogheda, Dundalk, Castleblaney, Cavan, Ceanannus Mor, Mullingar, Longford, Athlone, Lough Ree, Ballinasloe, Galway, Galway B., Aran Is., Connemara, Lough Corrib, Lough Mask, Westport, Castlebar, Achill, Ballina, L. Conn, Sligo, Bundoran, Donegal, Lifford, Leitrim, Roscommon, Boyne
Ennis, Limerick, Nenagh, Thurles, Tullamore, Port Laoise, Athy, Carlow, Kilkenny, Wexford, Arklow, Rosslare, Wicklow Mts.
Kilrush, Listowel, Tralee, Tipperary, Clonmel, Carrick-on-Suir, Waterford, Dungarvan, Youghal
Dingle, Killarney, Mallow, Blackwater, Cork, Cóbh, Kinsale, Bandon, Bantry, Valencia, Carrauntoohill, Macgillycuddy's Reeks, C. Clear
Shannon, Lee

France / Belgium / Netherlands (south-east):
Bergen, Haugesund, Stord, Bømlo, Kopervik, Åkrahamn, Stavanger, Sandnes, Bryne, Nærbø, Askøy, Osøyro
's-Gravenhage (Den Haag), Rotterdam, Dordrecht, Haarlem, Hoek van Holland, Alkmaar, Den Helder, Vlissingen, Zeebrugge, Oostende, Brugge, Gent, Mechelen, Antwerpen, BRUSSEL (Bruxelles), Tournai, Lille, Roubaix, Tourcoing, Villeneuve-d'Ascq, Lens, Valenciennes, Cambrai, Béthune, Bruay-la-Buissière, Calais, Gris-Nez, Boulogne, St-Omer, Amiens, St-Quentin, Abbeville, Le Tréport, Dieppe, Fécamp, Le Havre, Bolbec, Rouen, Elbeuf, Lisieux, Caen, Bayeux, Valognes, Cherbourg, C. de la Hague, Pte. de Barfleur, Alderney, Guernsey, St. Peter Port, Sark, Jersey, St. Helier, Channel Is. (U.K.), Pays de Caux, Picardie, Seine, Cotentin, Str. of Dover, Le Touquet-Paris-Plage

Str. of Dover

Elevations: 1224, 316, 789, 1182, 1342, 1311, 1214, 973, 840, 816, 893, 978, 635, 238, 16, 36, 33, 1085, 926, 886, 99, 953, 1041, 618

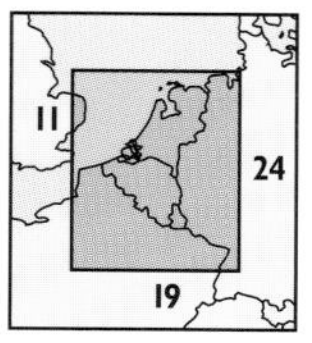

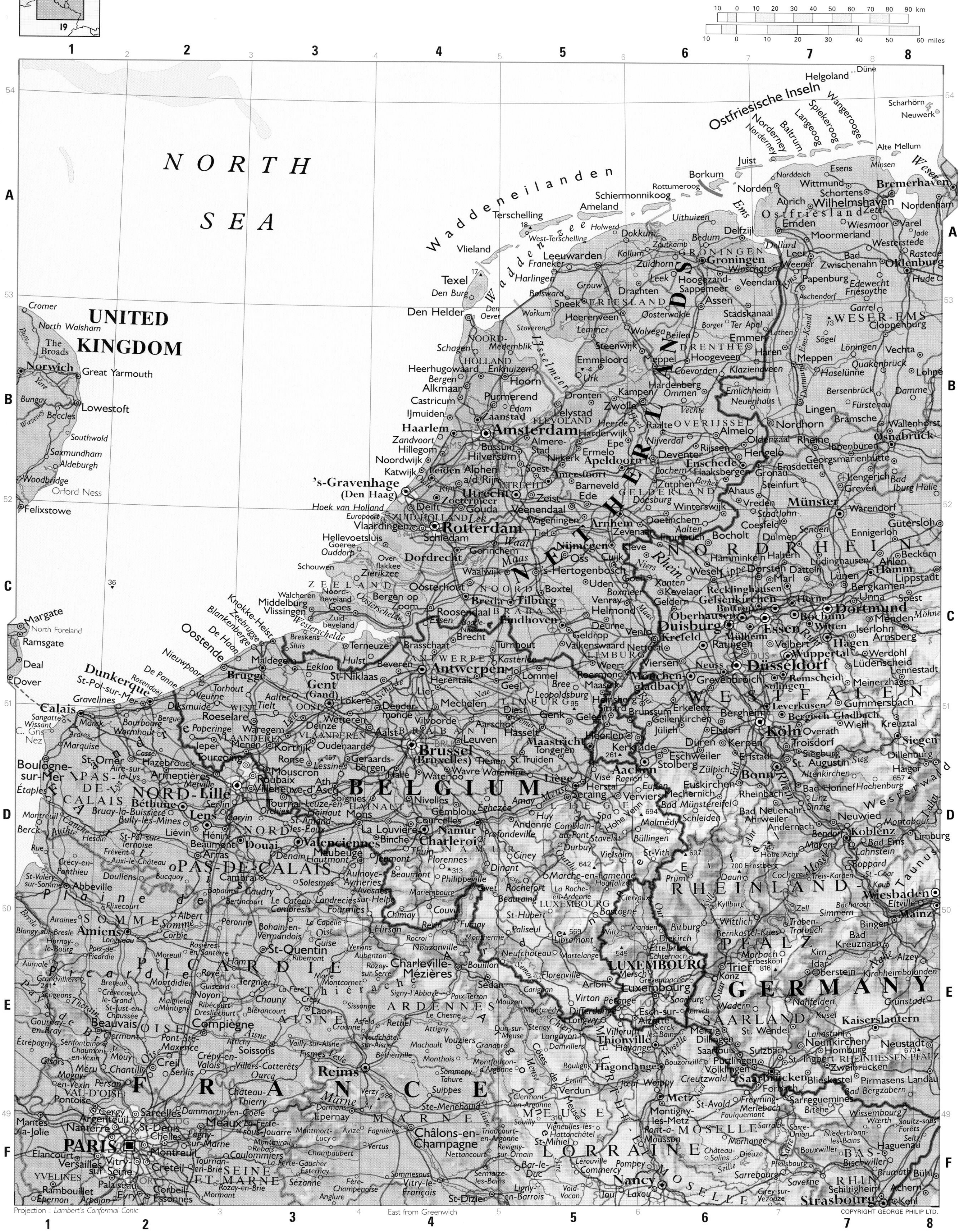

10 0 10 20 30 40 50 60 70 80 90 km
10 0 10 20 30 40 50 60 miles

NORTH SEA

UNITED KINGDOM

NETHERLANDS

BELGIUM

LUXEMBOURG

GERMANY

FRANCE

Projection : Lambert's Conformal Conic

East from Greenwich

COPYRIGHT GEORGE PHILIP LTD.

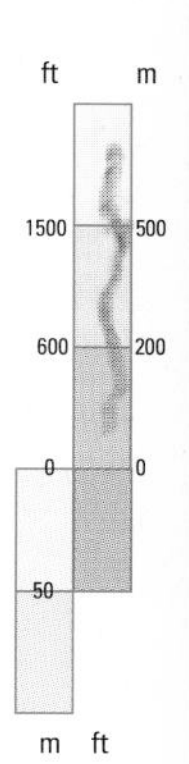

Underlined towns give their name to the administrative area in which they stand.

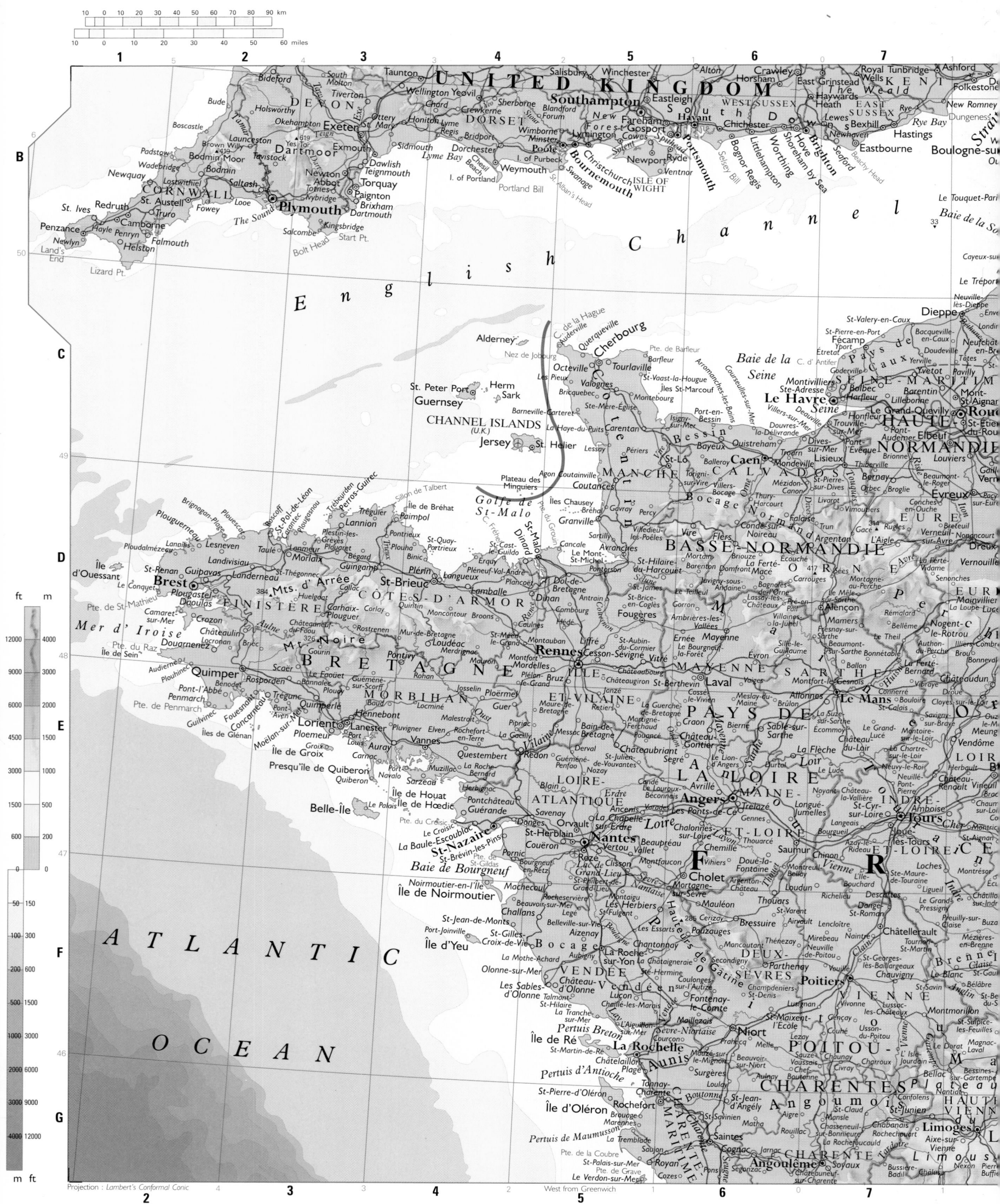

DÉPARTEMENTS IN THE PARIS AREA
1. Ville de Paris   3. Val-de-Marne
2. Seine-St-Denis   4. Hauts-de-Seine

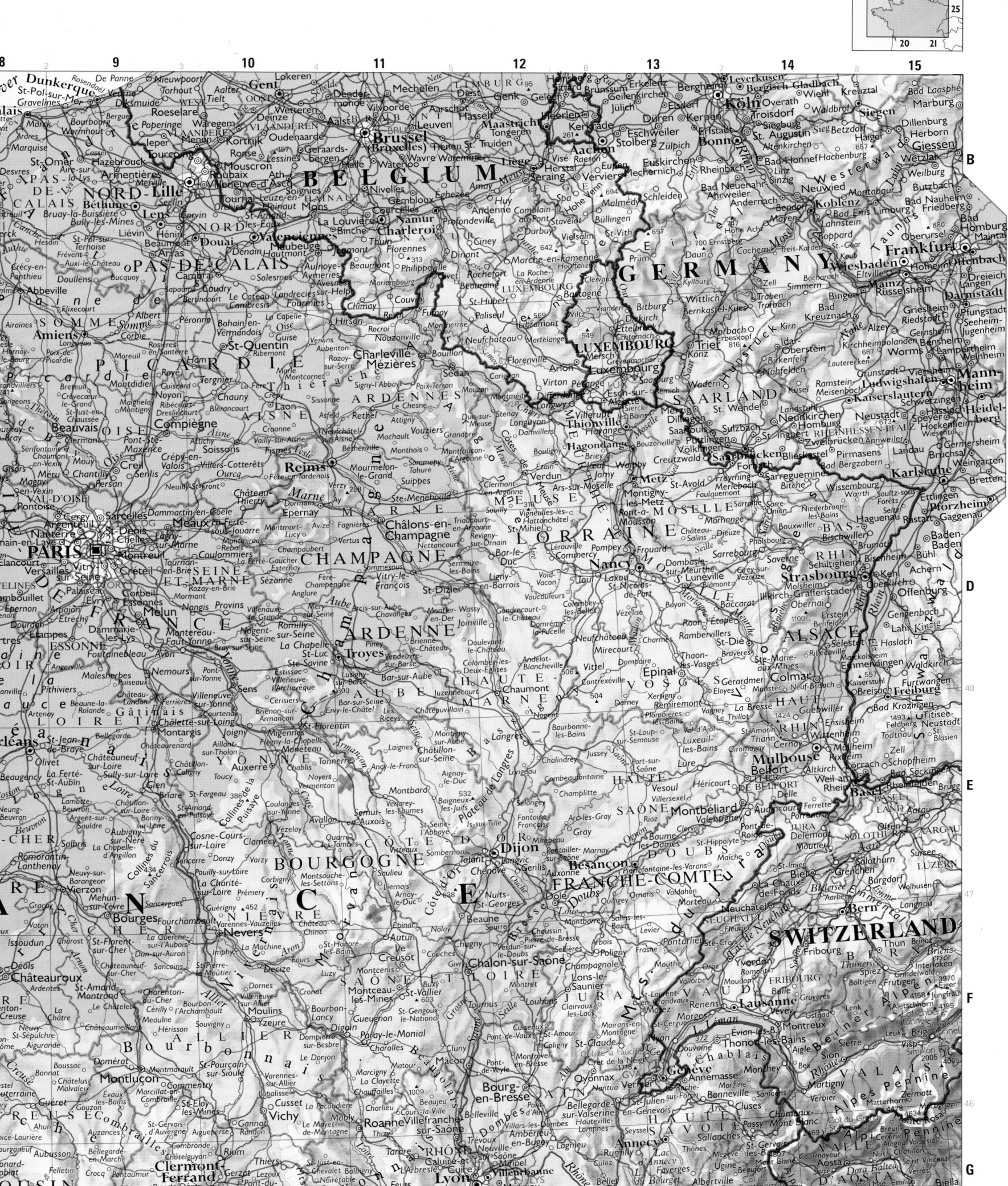

Underlined towns give their name to the
administrative area in which they stand.

East from Greenwich

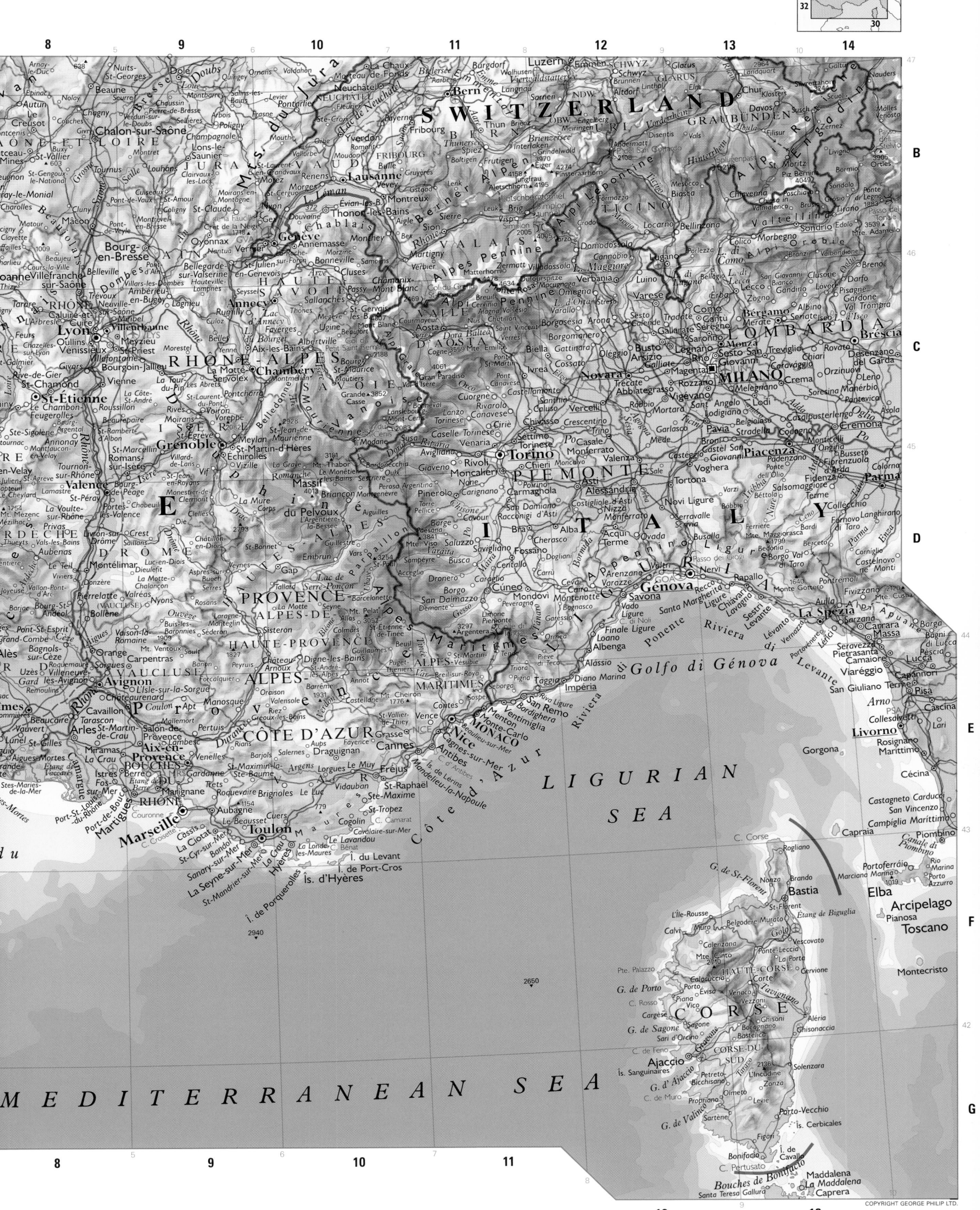

MEDITERRANEAN SEA

LIGURIAN SEA

SWITZERLAND

ITALY

LOMBARDIA

PIEMONTE

LIGURIA

RHÔNE-ALPES

PROVENCE

CÔTE D'AZUR

HAUTE-PROVENCE

ALPES-DE-HAUTE-PROVENCE

CORSE

HAUTE-CORSE

CORSE-DU-SUD

Golfo di Génova

Arcipelago Toscano

COPYRIGHT GEORGE PHILIP LTD.

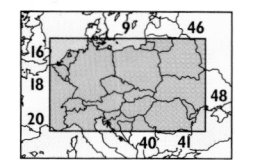

9 18 **10** 20 **11** 22 **12** 24 **13** 26 **14** 28 **15** 30 **16**

54

Zatoka *Baltiysk* Kaliningrad (Russia) *Gusev* Vilnius *Ashmyany* Vileyka *Smarhon* Barysaw *Krupki* Shklow *Mstsislaw* Krychaw 54

Wejherowo Rumia *Gdańska* *Gvardeysk* *Chernyakhovsk* *Marijampolė* 342 Zhodzina LITHUANIA Maladzyechna Smarhon MINSK Cherven Mahilyow Dribin

Lębork *Sopot* Gdynia *Bagrationovsk* *Prienai* 346 Valozhyn Byk haw Slawharad

B

Bytów 329 Gdańsk Tczew Elbląg *Braniewo* Gizycko Suwałki Augustów Druskininkai Lida Navahrudak 323 Nyasvizh Asipovichy Babruysk Rahachow Zhlobin B

morskie Starogard *Gdański* Pojezierze Mazurski Olsztyn Ełk Hrodna Masty Dzyatlava Baranavichy Klyetsk Slutsk Svyetlahorsk Rechytsa

zcinek Chojnice Świecie Grudziądz Brodnica Działdowo Ostrołęka Łomża Białystok Vawkavysk Slonim Salihorsk Glusk Homyel

Bydgoszcz Chełmno Rypin Mława Ciechanów Ostrów Mazowiecka Bielsk Podlaski Hajnówka Pruzhany Bereza Luninyets Pripyats Mazyr Dobrush

znań Toruń Włocławek Płock Pułtusk Narew Sokołów Podlaski Siedlce Biała Podlaska Brest Malaryta Pinsk Dawyd Haradok Stolin Yelsk Loyew

C

Inowrocław Gniezno Września WARSZAWA (Warsaw) Legionowo Mińsk Mazowiecki Międzyrzec Podlaski Łuków Kamin-Kashyrskyy Dubrovytsya Ovruch Chornobyl C

Konin Kutno Łowicz Pruszków Żyrardów Otwock Grójec Włodawa Lyuboml Kovel Olevsk Belokorovichi Korosten Oster

Turek Skierniewice Wieprz Chełm Novovolynsk Rozhyshche Volodymyr- Volynskyy Staryy Chartoryysk Kostopil Novohrad- Volynskyy Malyn Irpin Dymer KYÏV (Kiev)

Kalisz Zduńska Wola ŁÓDŹ Pabianice Tomaszów Mazowiecki Radom Puławy Lublin Świdnik Oleksandriya Kivertsi Sarny Radomyshl Vasylkiv

Ostrów Wielkopolski Sieradz Piotrków Trybunalski Radomsko Kańsk Skarżysko- Kamienna Starachowice Kraśnik Novovolynsk Lutsk Rivne Dubno Zdolbuniv Slavuta Pershotravensk Zhytomyr Korostyshev

Wrocław Oleśnica Kluczbork Częstochowa Kielce 612 Ostrowiec Świętokrzyski Sandomierz Zamość Sokal Horokhiv Ostroh 341 Izyaslav Shepetivka Polonne Berdychiv Bila Tserkva

D

Opole Myszków Zawiercie Jędrzejów Pińczów Tarnobrzeg Stalowa Wola Rava- Ruska Radekhiv Berestechko Kremenets Starokonstyantyniv Khmelnik Kozyatyn Skvyra Tarashcha

Nysa Tarnowskie Góry Bytom Sosnowiec Mielec Nesterov Yavoriv Kamyanka- Buzka Brody Dubno Khmelnytskyy Tetiyiv Zhashkiv

1492 Racibórz Zabrze Gliwice Chorzów Katowice Wisła Tarnów Rzeszów Jarosław Przemyśl Mostyska Lviv (Lvov) Zolochiv Ternopil Zbarazh 384 Vinnytsya Lipovets

Ostrava Opava Tychy Oświęcim Kraków Bochnia Dębica Jasło Krosno Sanok Horodok Sambir Drohobych Berezhany Pidhaytsi Chortkiv Bar Zhmerynka 32 Haysyn

Frýdek- Místek 1324 Havířov Karviná Bielsko-Biała Nowy Sącz 1248 Dukelský Priesmyk 502 Skole Stryy Kalush Rohatyn Terebovlya Kopychyntsi Horodok Skala-Podilska Zalishchyky Mohyliv- Podilskyy 270 Uman

E

Zlín Přerov Žilina Ružomberok 2655 Poprad Prešov Humenné Bolekhiv Ivano-Frankivsk Nadvirna Kolomyya Horodenka Dnister Khotyn Kamyanets- Podilskyy Yampil Bershad Balta

Martin 2043 Nízke Tatry Zvolen 1157 Bardejov Volovets Yaremcha Snyatyn Novoselytsya Lipcani Ocnita Dochia Soroca Kotovsk

768 Trenčín Banská Bystrica 1458 Michalovce Uzhhorod Mukacheve Rakhiv Yasinya Chernivtsi Hlyboka Storozhynets Edinet Fălești Florești Ananyiv

SLOVAK REP. Topoľčany Slovenské Rudohorie Košice Chop Berehove Khust Tyachiv 1881 Rădăuți Dorohoi Bălți Dubăsari Vdkhr. Dubăsari

Nitra Levice Lučenec Ózd Miskolc Sátoraljaújhely Vynohradiv Sighetu Marmatiei Borşa 1565 Suceava Botoşani Fălticeni Cornești Orhei Chişinău Tiraspol

Bratislava Nové Zámky Komárno Salgótarján Eger Nyíregyháza Satu Mare Baia Mare 2303 Pietrosul Vatra-Dornei Piatra Neamţ Roman 418 Ungheni Tighina

F

Győr Tatabánya Vác Gyöngyös Mezőkövesd Hajdúböszörmény Carei 2102 Pietrosul 1864 Bistriţa Iaşi Vaslui Huşi Bârlad Comrat Rozdilna

Mosonmagyaróvár Esztergom Dunakeszi BUDAPEST Jászberény Debrecen Zalău Dej Bistriţa Bacău Tecuci Cahul Bilhorod- Dnistrovskyy Artsyz

Sopron Érd Székesfehérvár Cegléd Karcag Oradea Cluj-Napoca Turda Târgu Mureş 1777 Reghin Odorheiu Secuiesc Miercurea Ciuc Oneşti Bârlad Cădâr-Lunga Izmayil

G

Veszprém Dunaújváros Kecskemét Szolnok Mezőtúr 1836 Munţii Bihor 1848 Abrud Alba-Iulia Sighişoara Mediaş Sfântu Gheorghe 1783 Focşani Vulcanesti Reni Kiliya Ozero Sasyk Vylkove

Nagykanizsa Kaposvár Szekszárd 681 Kiskunfélegyháza Hódmezővásárhely Makó Arad Brad Deva Simeria Hunedoara 1380 Lugoj Sibiu Făgăraş 2543 Braşov Săcele Râmnicu Sărat Galaţi Brăila Tulcea Babadag

Pécs Mohács Baja Szeged Subotica Sânnicolau Mare Timişoara Caransebeş Vf. Peleaga 2509 Petroşani 2507 Vf. Omul Câmpulung Câmpina Buzău Ploieşti Dâmboviţa Brăila Sulina

ATIA 984 Osijek Senta Kikinda Zrenjanin Vršac Reşiţa 1226 Vulcan 2518 Parângul Mare Curtea de Argeş Târgovişte Slobozia Lacul Razelm

Virovitica Vukovar Novi Sad Petrovaradin Bela Crkva Porta Orientalis Porţile de Fier Drobeta- Turnu-Severin Râmnicu Vâlcea Piteşti Ialomiţa Feteşti Năvodari

978 Bosanska Gradiška Sremska Mitrovica Pančevo Smederevo Orşova Drăgăşani Slatina Olteniţa Călăraşi Medgidia Constanţa

Luka Doboj Brčko Bijeljina Zemun BEOGRAD (Belgrade) Požarevac Turnu Severin Craiova Roşiori- de-Vede Vedea Alexandria Giurgiu Silistra Tutrakan Mangalia

G

BOSNIA- YUGOSLAVIA Šabac Valjevo Smederevska Negotin Bor Băileşti Caracal Turnu Măgurele Zimnicea Ruse Razgrad Dobrich Balchik

1943 Zepče Šamac Kragujevac Jagodina Zaječar Vidin Lom Oryakhovo Corabia BUCUREŞTI (Bucharest) BULGARIA Varna Nos Kaliakra

HERZEGOVINA 2006 Cincar 2112 Sarajevo Užice Čačak Kraljevo Kruševac Timok Vidin

9 18 East from Greenwich **10** 20 **11** 22 **12** 24 **13** 26 **14** **15**

COPYRIGHT GEORGE PHILIP LTD.

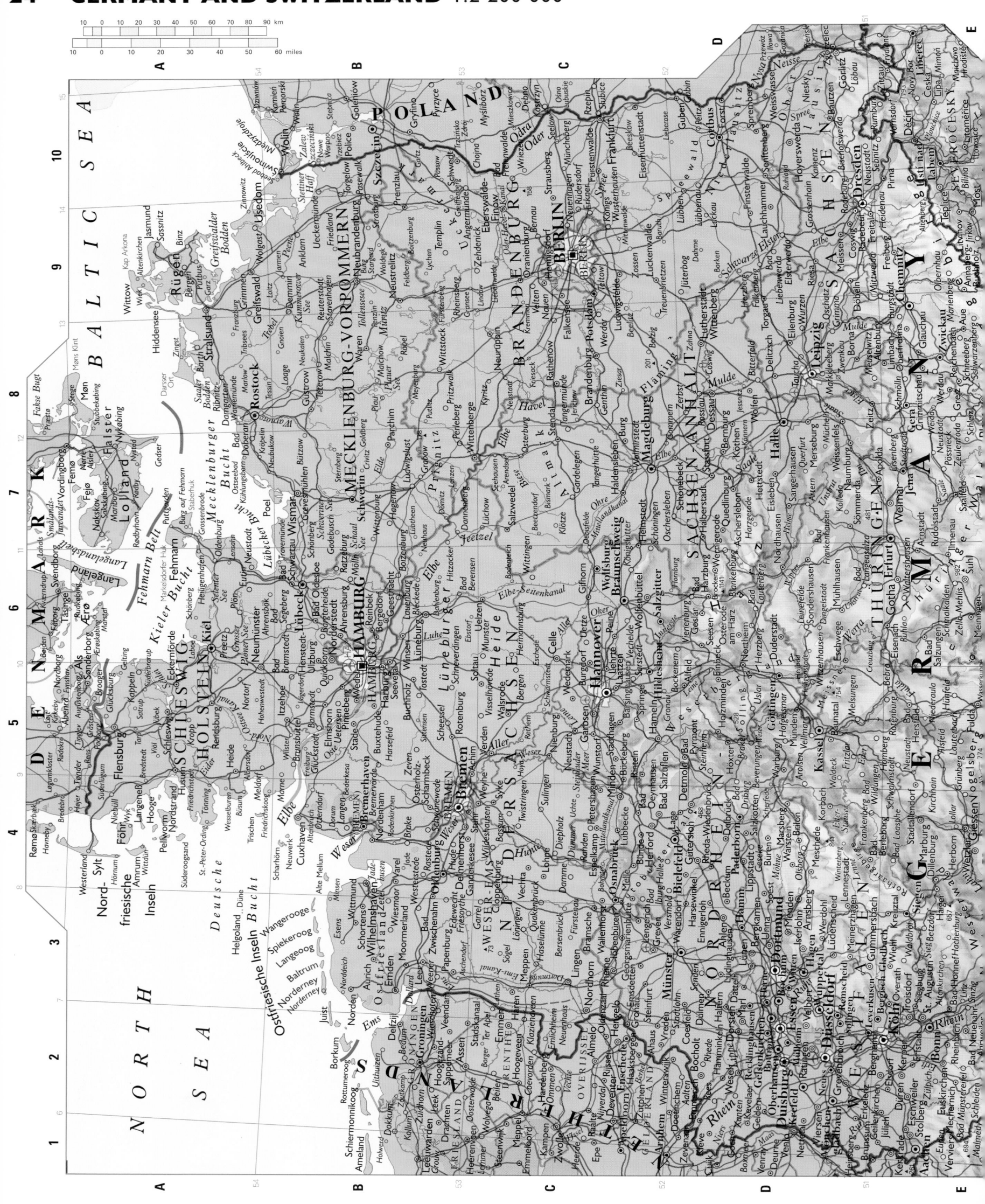

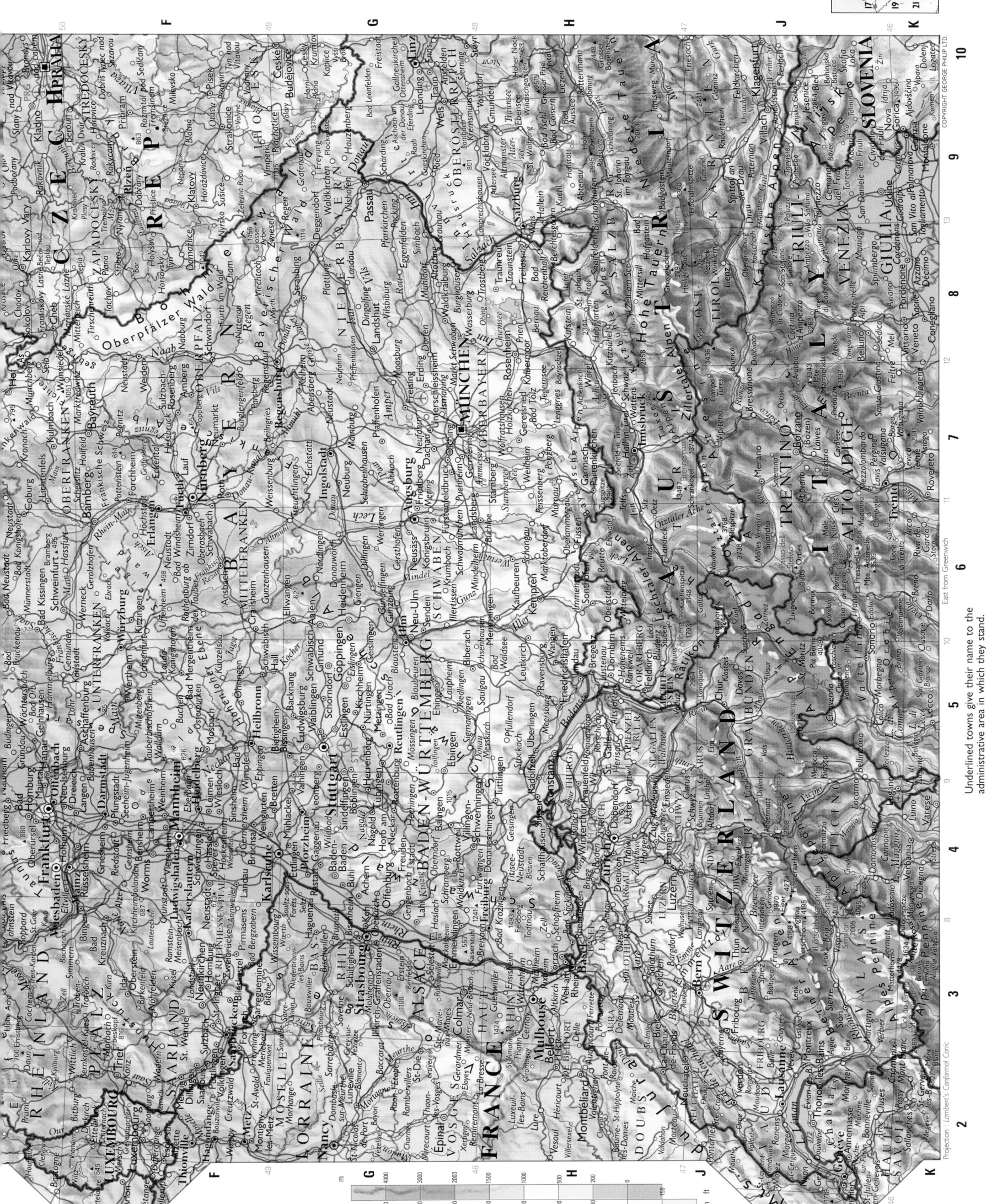

Underlined towns give their name to the
administrative area in which they stand.

East from Greenwich

Projection: Lambert's Conformal Conic

COPYRIGHT GEORGE PHILIP LTD.

Projection: Lambert's Conformal Conic

Underlined towns give their name to the administrative area in which they stand.

East from Greenwich

COPYRIGHT GEORGE PHILIP LTD.

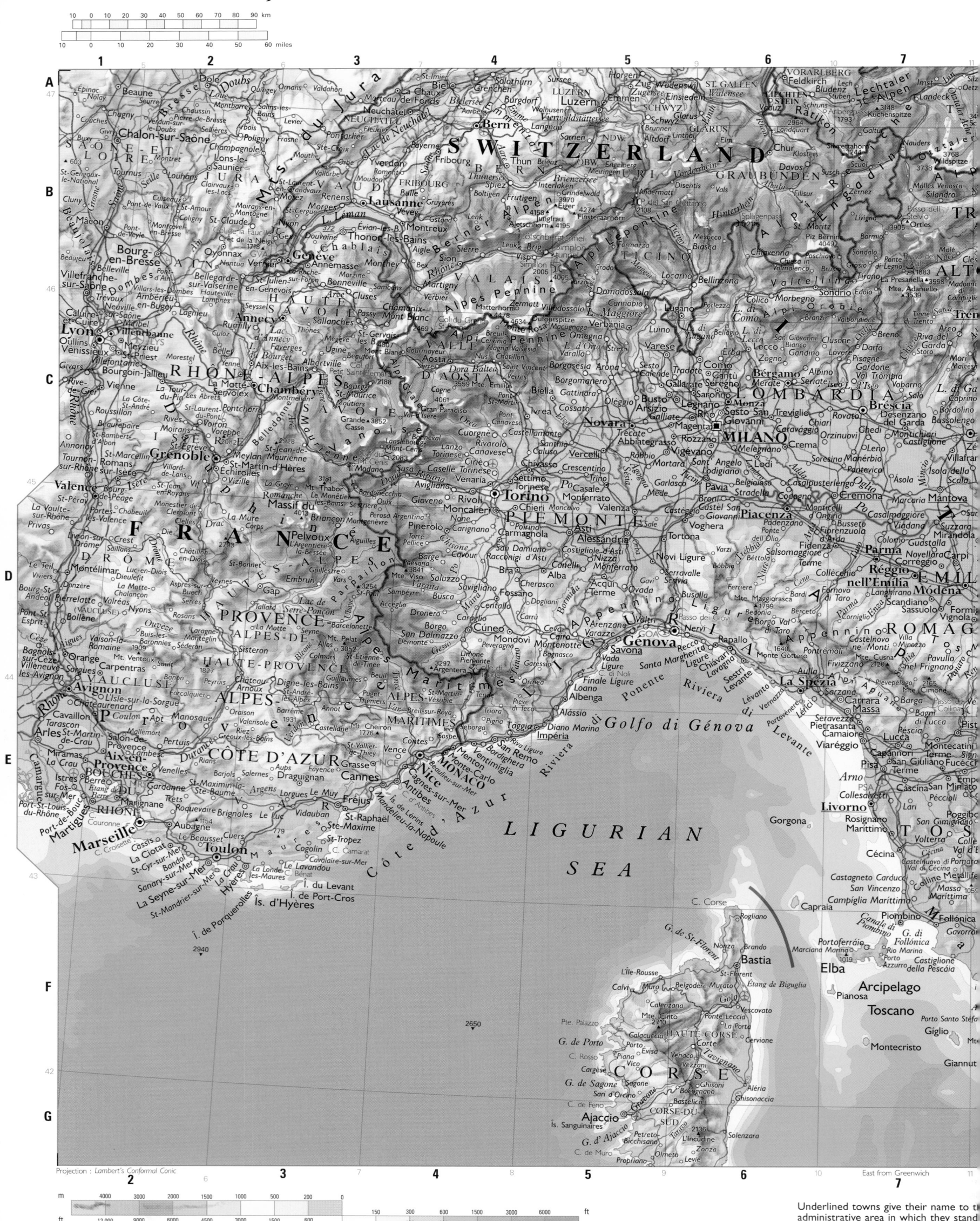

Projection : Lambert's Conformal Conic

Underlined towns give their name to the administrative area in which they stand

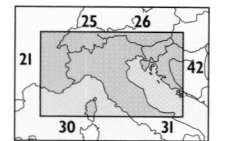

Administrative divisions in Croatia:

1. Brodsko-Posavska
2. Koprivničko-Križevačka
3. Krapinsko-Zagorska
4. Medimurska
6. Požeško-Slavonska
7. Varaždinska
8. Virovitičko-Podravska
10. Zagrebačka

Inter-entity boundaries as agreed
at the 1995 Dayton Peace Agreement.

COPYRIGHT GEORGE PHILIP LTD.

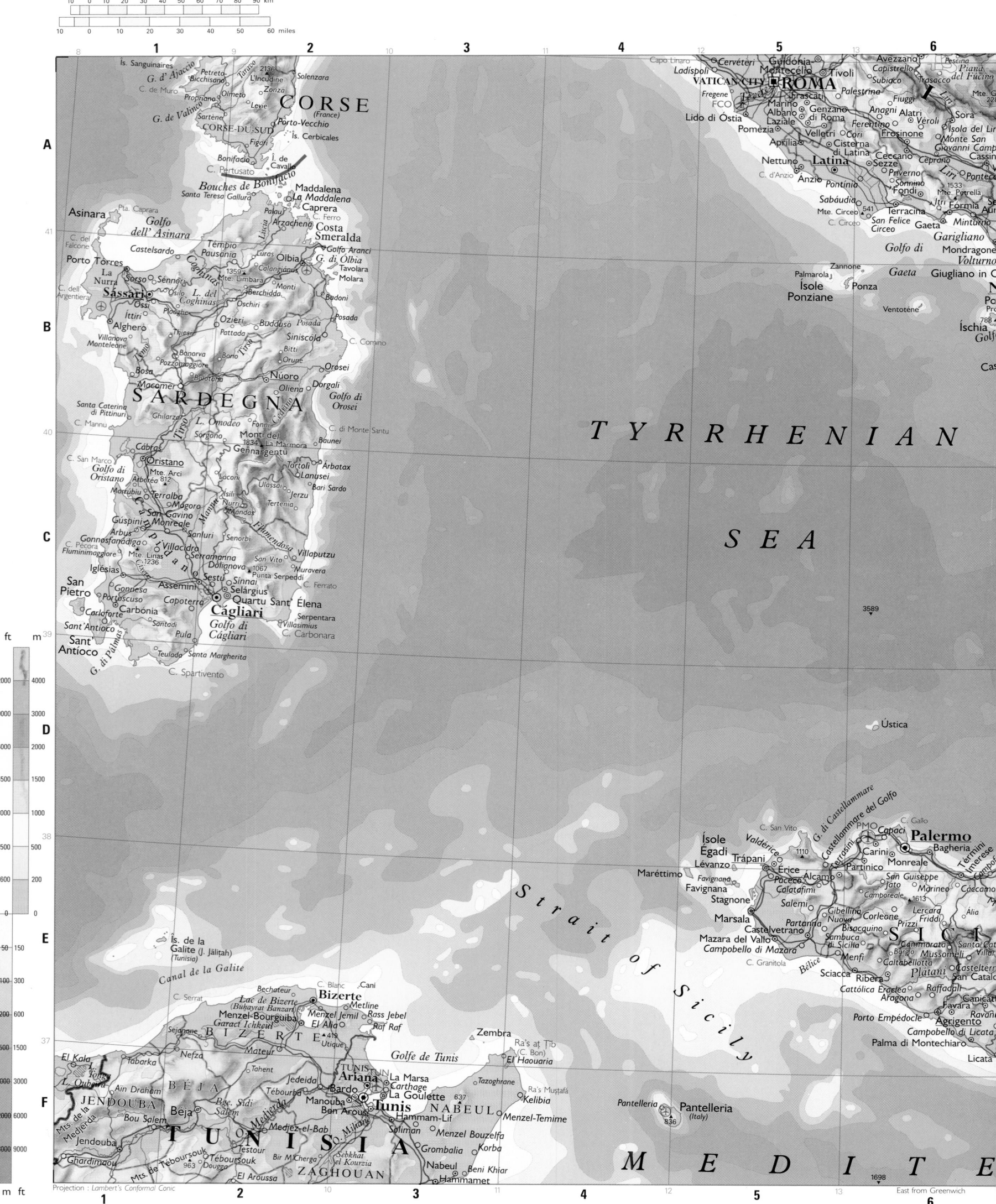

ADRIATIC SEA

Strait of Otranto

ALBANIA

Tiranë
Durrës
Shëngjin
MIRDITE
Rrëshen
Lezhë

Kepi i Rodonit
Bishti i Pallès
Sazani

Vlorë
Fier
Berat
Gjirokaster

GREECE
KÉRKIRA
Kérkira
(Corfu)

IONIAN SEA

ME DI TERRANEAN SEA

MOLISE

Térmoli
Campomarino
L. di Lésina
Vieste
Vico del Gargano

Fóggia
Manfredónia
Golfo di Manfredónia
Monte Sant' Ángelo

Benevento
Barletta
Andria
Bari
Molfetta
Bisceglie

Salerno
Potenza
Matera
Taranto
Brindisi
Lecce
Otranto

BASILICATA

PUGLIA

CALABRIA

Cosenza
Crotone
Catanzaro

Messina
Réggio di Calábria

Ísole Eólie
Strómboli

Etna
Catánia
Siracusa

COPYRIGHT GEORGE PHILIP LTD.

Underlined towns give their name to the
administrative area in which they stand.

MEDITERRANEAN SEA

BALEARIC SEA

Spain region labels: VALENCIA, MURCIA, CASTILLA-LA MANCHA, CIUDAD REAL, ALBACETE, ALICANTE, ALMERÍA, GRANADA

Cities (Spain): Valencia, Torrent, Alicante, Elche, Murcia, Cartagena, Lorca, Almería, Granada, Albacete, Dénia, Benidorm, Gandía, Alcoy, Yecla, Jumilla, Cieza, Hellín, Baza, Guadix, Motril, Adra, Nádor, Melilla

Islands: EIVISSA (IBIZA), FORMENTERA, Cabrera, Alborán (Sp.), Islas Chafarinas

Golfo de Valencia, Costa Blanca, Mar Menor, G. de Mazarrón, G. de Almería, Costa del Sol

Sierra Nevada, Sierra de Segura, Sierra de Cazorla

Algeria: ALGER (Algiers), Blida, Médéa, Mostaganem, Mascara, Oran (Ouahran), Sidi-bel-Abbès, Tiaret, Relizane, Ech Cheliff, Cherchell

Regions (Algeria): MÉDÉA, DJELFA, TIARET, MASCARA, ORAN, RELIZANE, TISSEMSILT, AÏN DEFLA, MOSTAGANEM, ECH CHELIFF, TÉMOUCHENT, AÏN

Golfe d'Arzew, C. Ferrat, C. Ténès

East from Greenwich / West from Greenwich

Projection: Lambert's Conformal Conic

Scale bar: m / ft — 12000 9000 6000 4500 3000 1500 0 ; m 4000 3000 2000 1500 1000 500 200 0 50 150 300 600 1500 3000 6000 9000 ft

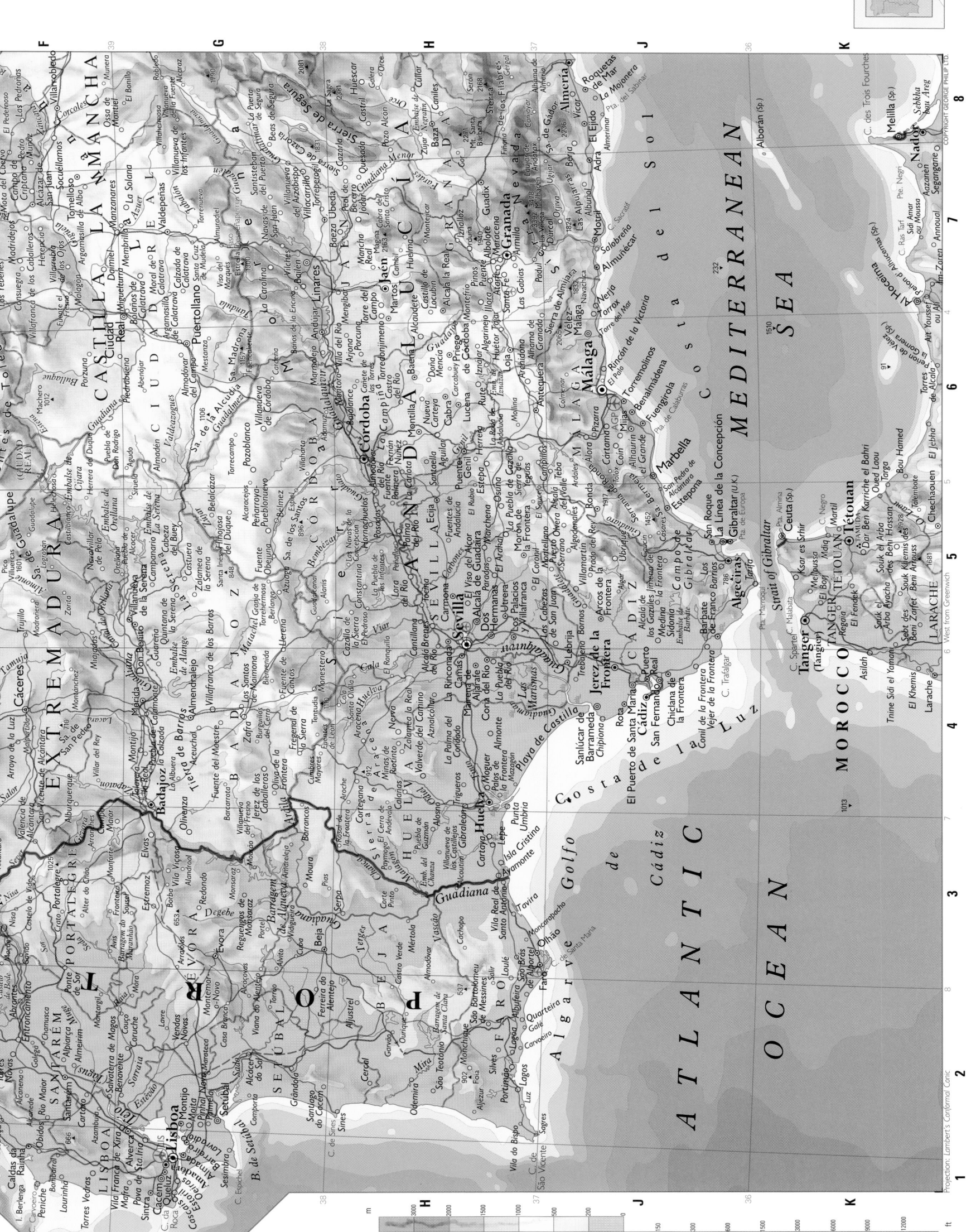

MEDITERRANEAN SEA

ATLANTIC OCEAN

MOROCCO

CRETE
1:1 200 000

MALTA
1:900 000

CORFU
1:900 000

RHODES
1:900 000

CYPRUS
1:1 200 000

CARTOGRAPHY BY PHILIP'S

Projection: Lambert's Conformal Conic

CRETE

SEA OF CRETE

Ákra Sidheros
Vái
Ákra Plaka
Palaiókastron
Zákros
Zíros
Moulianá
Sitía
Skópi
Mókhlos
LASÍTHI
Merabéllou Kólpos
Spinalónga
Psíra
Ayios Nikólaos
Kritsá
Kato Khorió
Ierápetra
Ákra Goúdhoura
Koufonísi
Gaidhouronísi
Yianisádhes
Ákra Ioánnis
Mília
Mílatos
Neápolis
Eloúnda
Dhíkti Óros 2148
Áno Viánnos
Árvi
Mokhós
Tzermiádhes
Lasíthi
Kastéllion
Kato Arkhánai
Knossós
KNOSSOS
Yófiros
Iráklion
IRÁKLION
Dhráni
Káto Khersónisos
Límin Khersonísou
Kólpos Malíon
Mália
Dia
Ákra Stavrós
Óros Ídhi
Anóyia
Tílissos
Rogdhiá
Balí
Ayios Miron
Yioryioúpolis
RÉTHIMNON
Réthimnon
Epískopi
Pánormon
Perama
Lávris
Spíli
Kédhros
Amári
Stavrós 2456
Psiloritis
Tímbakion
PHAISTOS
Vóroi
Mátala
Mélambes
Ayia Gálini
Paximádhia
Ákra Lithinon
Kólpos Mesarás
Moíres
Ayía Varvára
Mirónd
Áno Viánnos
Asteroúsia 1231
GORTIS
Ayioi Dhéka
Ieropetrou
Pómbia
Léndas
Soúda
Khaniá
KHANIÁ
Akrotíri
Khersónisos
Kólpos Khaníon
Stérnes
Kólpos Soúdhas
Mournies
Vámos
Vatólakkos
Lákkoi
Omalós
Le<ka Óros 2453
Askifou
Lívári
Víses
Vryses
Kardános
Rodhopoú
Kandanos
Palaiókhora
Samariá
Khóra Sfakion
Ayia Rouméli
Ákra Spátha
Akra Voúxa
Ákra Kríos
Máleme
Kastélli
Kólpos Kisámou
Stómion
Plátanos
Platániás
Ákra Dhrápanon
Kólpos Almiroú
Almiroú
Sellía
Gávdhos
Gavdhopoúla

MEDITERRANEAN SEA

Kríti

MALTA

Ras San Dimítri 194
Rabat
Nadur
Xlendi
GOZO
Marsalforn
Comino
Marfa Pt.
Mellieħa
Ahrax Pt.
St. Paul's Bay
Bugibba
Mosta
Rabat
Birkirkara
Valletta
Sliema
Paola
Zonqor Pt.
Birżebbuġa
Marsaxlokk
Filfla
MALTA

MEDITERRANEAN SEA

CORFU

ALBANIA
GREECE
Sarándes
(Santi Quaranta)
Ákra Ayía Aikaterini
Ákra Dhráhstis
Sídari
Róda
Magouládhes
Ákra Avlla
Karoúsádhes
Kassiópi
Nissáki
Pandokrátor 906
Ródha
Paleokastrítsa
Erikoúsa
Mathráki
Liapádhes
Érmones
Kérkira
Gouviá
Kondókali
Vidho
Pérama
Andípsis
Gástouri
Benítses
Ákra Lefkímmi
Messonghi
Levkímmi
Kávos
Ákra Asprókavos
Áyios Matthaíos
Sinarádhes
Korakiana
Limni Korissá
Kérkira
Kontoúra
Kérkiras

IONIAN SEA

RHODES

Ákra Koúm-bournoú
Ródhos
Kritiniá
Kaskhinoú
Kremastí
Maritsá
Paradhísi
Triánda
Faliraki
Áfandou
Soroní
Psinthos
Arkhángelos
Kálathos
Putaloudhes
Kámiros
Salakos
Profítis Ilías 798
Ákra Váyia
Embóna
Attáviros 1215
Ayios Isídhoros
Apóllona
Láerma
Ákra Lárdhos
Líndhos
Monólithos
Ormos Lárdhou
Siána
Apolakkiá 563
Mesanagrós
Kattaviá
Ákra Víglas
Ródhos
Alimniá
Khálki
Ormos Apólakkiá
Ákra Prasonísi
Ákra Armenistís

AEGEAN SEA

MEDITERRANEAN SEA

CYPRUS

Klídhes C.
Apóstolos Andréas C.
Rizokárpaso
KARPASÍA
Galinóporni
Komatoú Yialoú
Yialoúsa
Liqadhrísso
Áyios Theódhoros
C. Elea
Trikomo
Ayios Séryios
Kómi Kebir
Famagusta Bay
SALAMIS
Famagusta
Dherínia
Paralímni
Ayía Nápa
C. Gréco
Lápithos
Kyrénia
Akanthou 724
Olymbos 740
Ayios Amvrósios
Lefkóniko
Marathóvouno
MESAORÍA
Vatili
Athná
DHEKELIA SOVEREIGN BASE AREA
Tríkomo
Ayios Sérgios
Xylophágou
C. Pyla
Liopétri
Larnaca
Larnaca Bay
C. Kíti
C. Kórmakiti
Mýrtou
Kazáfani
Livéras
Kythréa
Kýrenia
Lapíthos
Bellapais
NICOSIA
Dhéftera
Palekhóri
Kakopetriá
Kaïmakli
Skilloúra
Kythréa
Pedios
Athalassa
Dháli
Under Turkish Administration
Kórnos
Pyrga
Kóphinou
Léfkara
Péra
Paleometokho
Astromeritis
Morphou Bay
Kato Kopia
Morphou
Karavostasi
Kato Pyrgos
Korovia
Pomos
C. Pomos
C. Kormakíti
Pyrgos
TÍLLIRIA
Pedhoulas
Prodhromos
Troödhos
Mt. Olympus
Chionistra 1951
MARATHÁSA
Kámbos
Kýkko
Panayia
PÍTSILIA 1544
Platanistasa
Pítsyliá
Agros
Ómodhos
Palekhóri
Kyperoúnda
Óra
Asgáta
Zíyi
Límassol
Episkopi
Episkopi Bay
Akrotíri
Akrotíri Bay
AKROTÍRI SOVEREIGN BASE
CURIUM
C. Gáta
C. Kíti
Yeroskípos
Páphos
Timi
Kouklia
Kolossi
Pissoúri
Dhiarizos
Xeropótamos
Choúlou
Pólis
AKÁMAS
Khrysokhoú Bay
C. Arnauti
C. Drépanum
Kathíkas
Peyia
Stroumbi
Kissónerga
Yeróskipos
TRÓODHOS
Aradhíppou
Anglisídhes
Vatyli
Lefkáres
Kalavasós

MEDITERRANEAN SEA

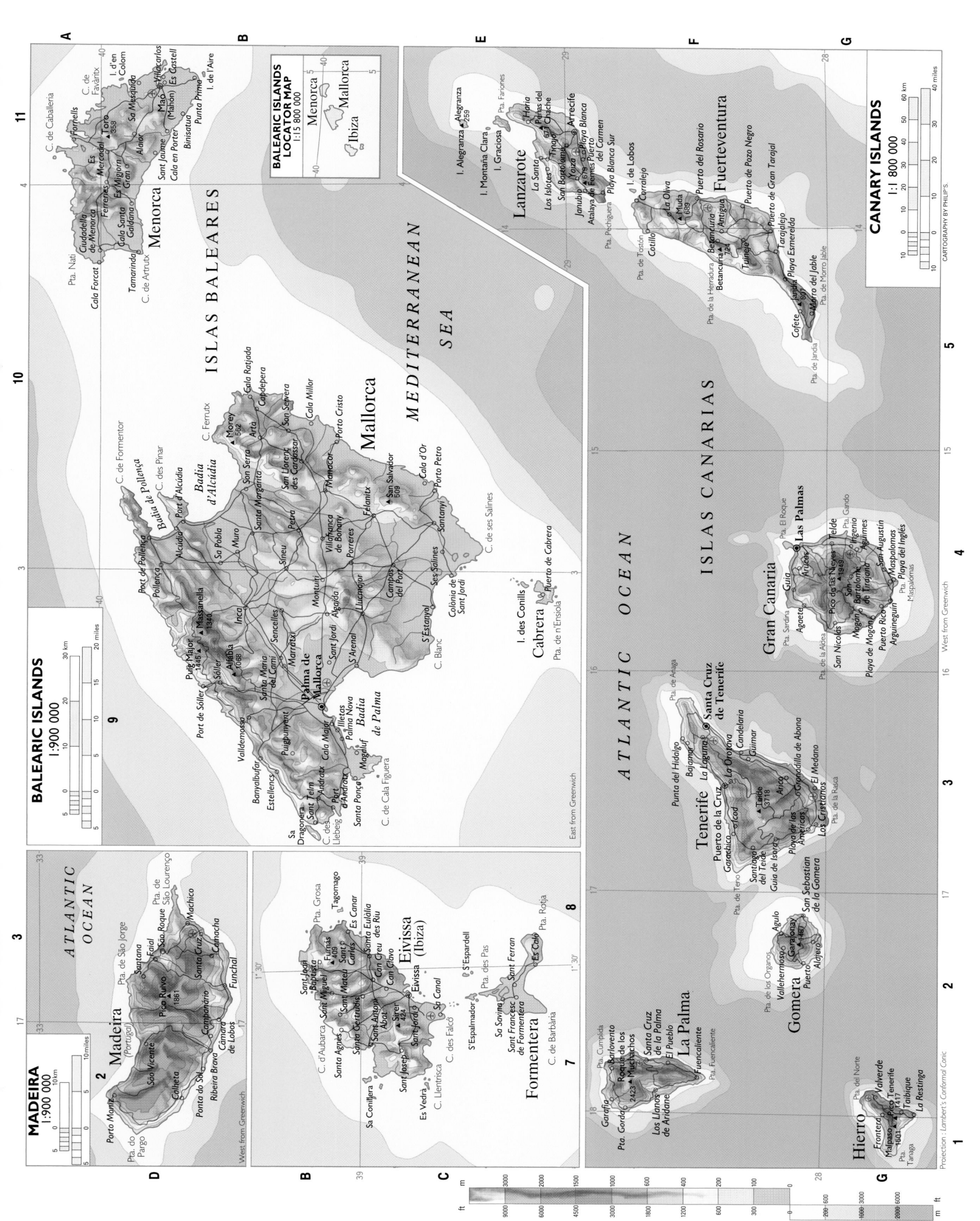

BALEARIC ISLANDS LOCATOR MAP
1:15 800 000

Menorca
Mallorca
Ibiza

MADEIRA
1:900 000

Madeira (Portugal)

ATLANTIC OCEAN

Pta. de São Lourenço
Pta. de São Jorge
Machico
São Roque
Faial
Santana
Pico Ruivo 1861
Santa Cruz
Caniçal
Caniço
Funchal
Câmara de Lobos
Campanário
Ponta do Sol
Ribeira Brava
São Vicente
Calheta
Porto Monte
Pta. do Pargo
Ponta de Lobos

BALEARIC ISLANDS
1:900 000

ISLAS BALEARES

Menorca

C. de Caballeria
Fornells
C. de Favàritx
I. d'en Colom
Ciudadella de Menorca
Es Mercadal
Ferreries
Sa Mesquida
Maó (Mahón)
Toro 358
Alaior
Sant Jaume
Es Castell
Cala en Porter
Binisafua
Punta Prima
I. de l'Aire
Cala Santa Galdana
Es Migjorn Gran
Tamarinda
C. de Arrutx
Pta. Nati
Cala Forcat

Mallorca

Cala Ratjada
Capdepera
Cala Millor
Porto Cristo
C. Ferrutx
Morey 552
Artà
Son Serra
Son Servera
San Llorenç des Cardassar
Manacor
Cala d'Or
Porto Petro
Cala Figuera
San Salvador 509
Felanitx
Santanyí
C. de ses Salines
Petra
Villafranca de Bonany
Porreres
Campos del Port
Ses Salines
Colònia de Sant Jordi
C. des Pinar
Badia d'Alcúdia
Port d'Alcúdia
Alcúdia
C. de Formentor
Port de Pollença
Pollença
Badia de Pollença
Sa Pobla
Muro
Santa Margarita
Sineu
Inca
Sencelles
Santa Maria del Camí
Massanella 1340
Puig Major 1445
Sóller
Alfàbia 1058
Montuiri
Algaida
Llucmajor
Sant Jordi
S'Arenal
Marratxí
Palma de Mallorca
Badia de Palma
Port de Sóller
Valldemossa
Banyalbufar
Estellencs
Puigpunyent
Andratx
Port d'Andratx
Santa Ponça
Magaluf
Palma Nova
Cala Major
Illetas
C. de Cala Figuera
Sant Telm
Sa Dragonera
C. des Llebeig

MEDITERRANEAN SEA

Cabrera
I. des Conills
Puerto de Cabrera
Pta. de n'Ensiola
C. Blanc
S'Estanyol
S'Espalmador

Eivissa (Ibiza)

Pta. Grosa
Tagomago
Pta. de ses Portes
Es Canar
Santa Eulália
Sant Carles
Sant Joan Baptista
Furnes 409
Sant Miquel
Sant Mateu
Con Creu des Riu
Es Canar
Sant Antoni
Santa Agnès
Santa Gertrudis
Sant Josep
Sant Jordi
Eivissa
Siren
Sant Rafel 424
Can Clavo
S'Espardell
S'Espalmador
Sa Conillera
Es Vedrà
Sant Francesc d'Abat
Pta. des Pas
Es Caló
Pta. Rotja

Formentera

Sant Francesc de Formentera
Es Caló
Sa Savina
C. de Barbària

West from Greenwich

ATLANTIC OCEAN

Gomera

Pta. de los Organos
Agulo
Vallehermoso
Hermigua
San Sebastián de la Gomera
Saraguay 1487
Playa de Santiago
Puerto
Aldea
Pta. de la Rasca

La Palma

Pta. Cumplida
Barlovento
Los Muchachos
Roque de los Muchachos 2423
Santa Cruz de la Palma
El Pueblo
Los Llanos de Aridane
El Paso
Fuencaliente
Pta. Gorda
Gardna
Pta. de Fuencaliente

Hierro

Pta. del Norte
Frontera
Valverde
Malpaso 1501
Pico Tenerife 1417
Taibique
La Restinga
Pta. Taraga

Tenerife

Punta del Hidalgo
Pta. de Anaga
Bajamar
La Laguna
Santa Cruz de Tenerife
La Orotava
Candelaria
Puerto de la Cruz
Güímar
Icod
Garachico
Santiago del Teide
Teide 3718
Granadilla de Abona
El Médano
Arico
Los Cristianos
Playa de las Américas
Guía de Isora
Pta. de Teno

ATLANTIC OCEAN

ISLAS CANARIAS

Gran Canaria

Pta. El Roque
Las Palmas
Pta. Sardina
Guía
Agaete
Arucas
Teide
Telde
Pico de las Nieves 1949
Ingenio
San Agustín
Aguimes
San Bartolomé de Tirajana
Maspalomas
Playa del Inglés
Puerto Rico
Playa de Mogán
Mogán
Arguineguín
San Nicolás
La Aldea
Pta. de la Aldea

West from Greenwich

Lanzarote

I. Alegranza
Alegranza 289
I. Montaña Clara
I. Graciosa
La Santa
Los Islotes
Haria
Peñas del Chache 671
Tinajo
Teguise
Arrecife
San Bartolomé
Tahiche
Yaiza
Playa Blanca
Puerto del Carmen
I. de Lobos
Pta. Pechiguera
Playa Blanca Sur
Pta. de Tostón

Fuerteventura

Corralejo
La Oliva
Muda 689
Puerto del Rosario
Betancuria
Antigua 724
Tuineje
Puerto de Pozo Negro
Puerto de Gran Tarajal
Tarajalejo
Jandía Playa Esmeralda
Cofete
Morro del Jable
Pta. de Morro Jable
Pta. de la Herradura
Pta. de Jandía

CANARY ISLANDS
1:1 800 000

Projection: Lambert's Conformal Conic

CARTOGRAPHY BY PHILIP'S

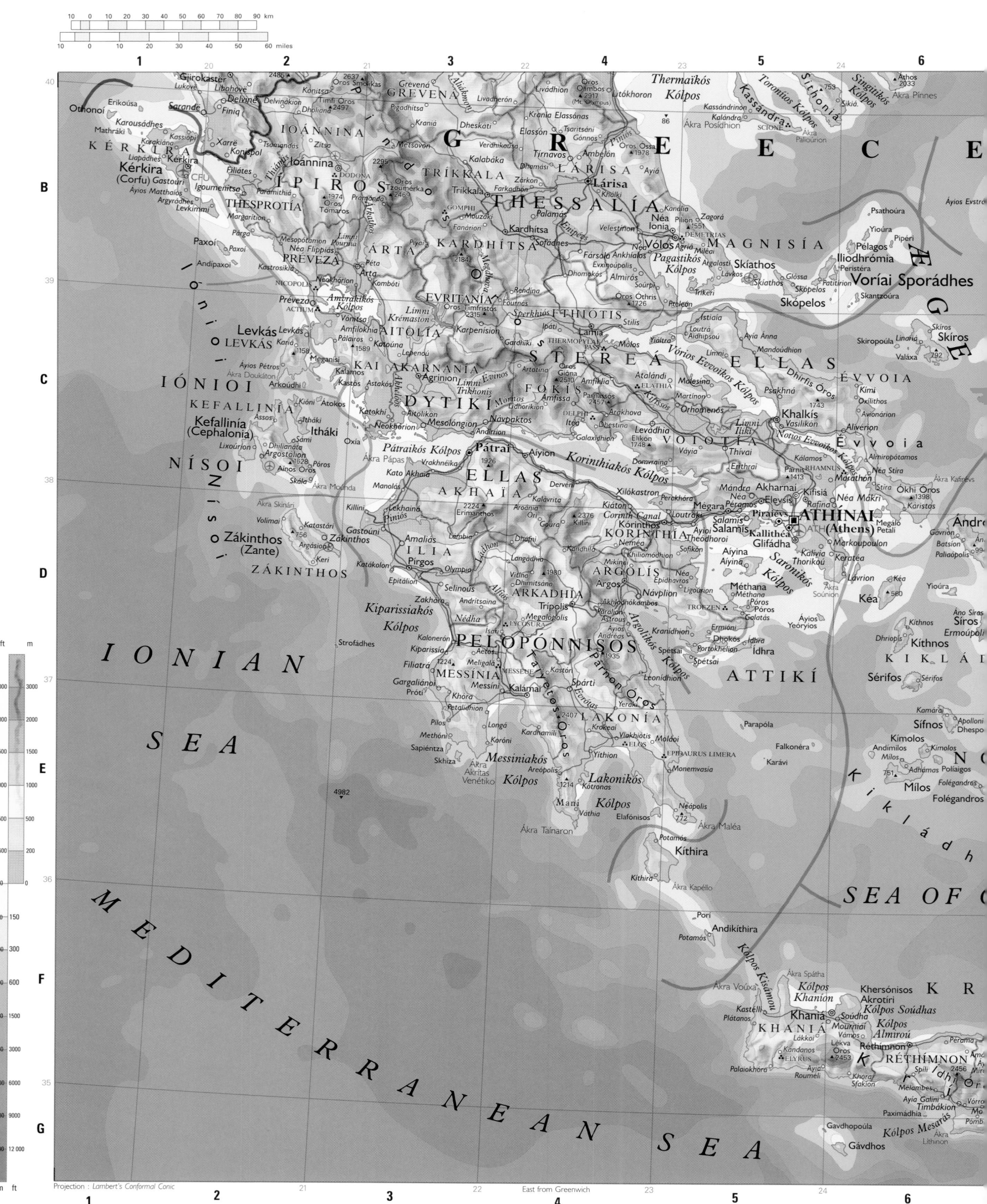

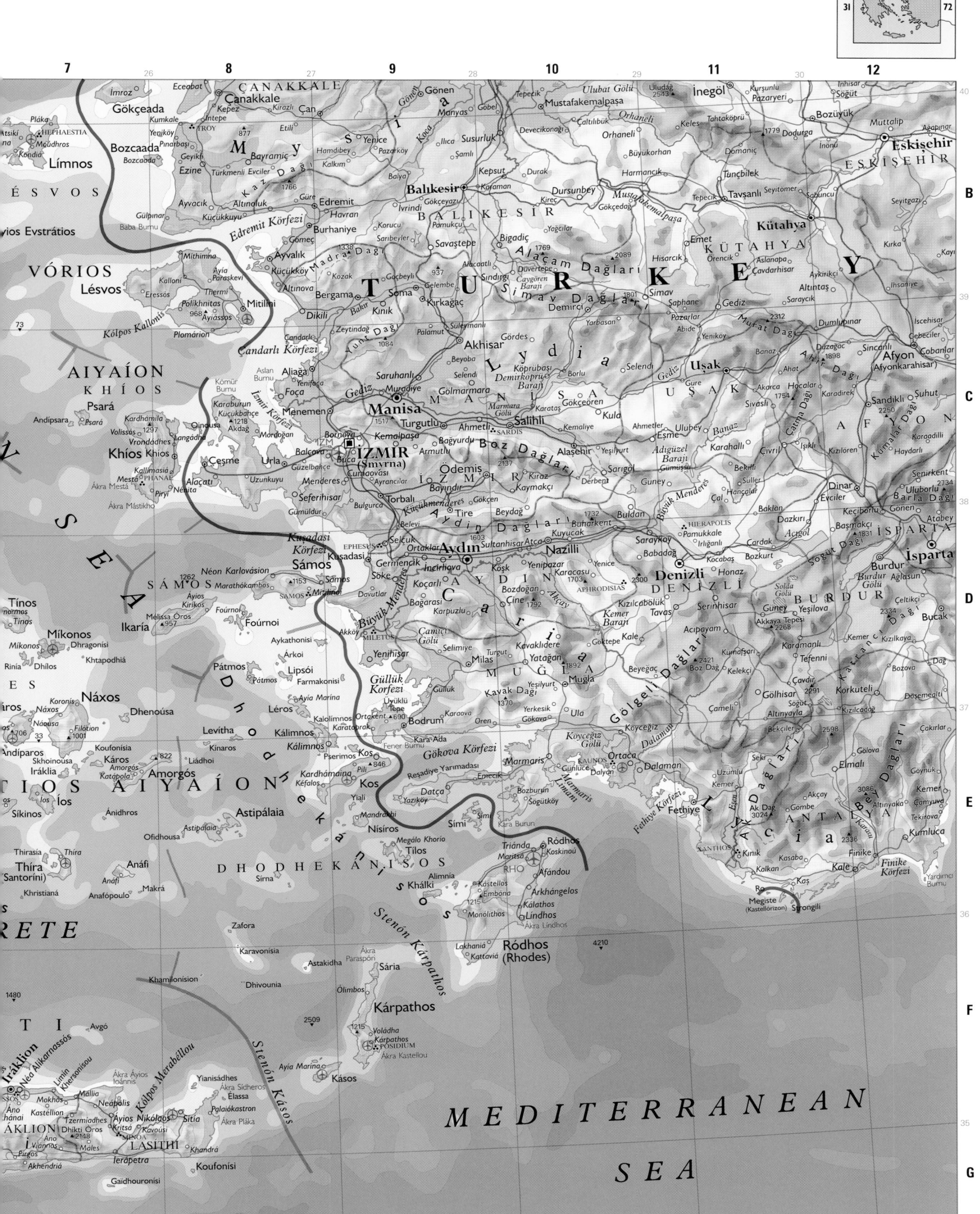

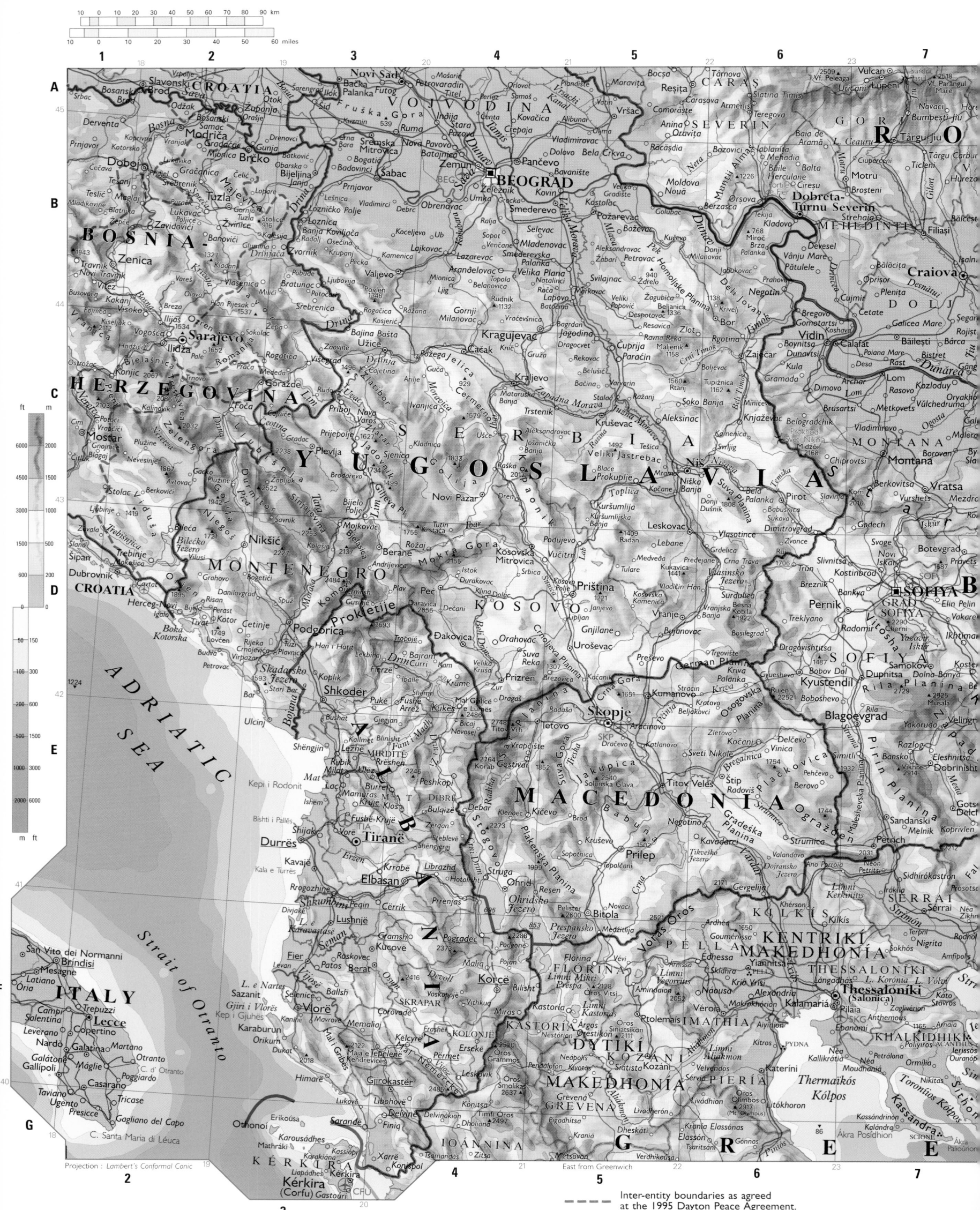

East from Greenwich

Inter-entity boundaries as agreed
at the 1995 Dayton Peace Agreement.

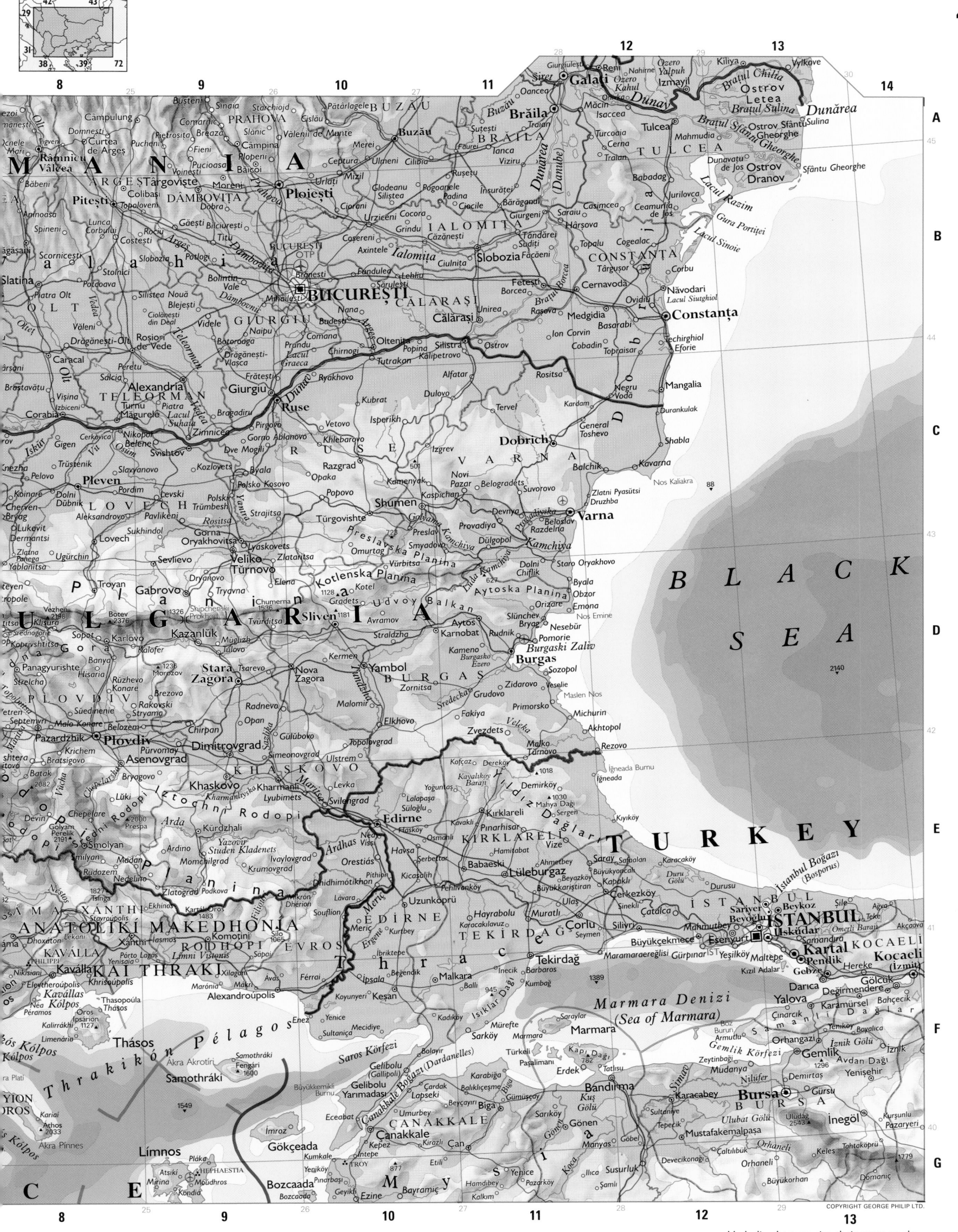

Underlined towns give their name to the
administrative area in which they stand.

COPYRIGHT GEORGE PHILIP LTD.

Administrative divisions in Croatia:
1. Brodsko-Posavska
2. Koprivničko-Križevačka
3. Medimurska
4. Medimurska
5. Osječko-Baranjska
6. Požeško-Slavonska
7. Vukovarsko-Srijemska
8. Virovitičko-Podravska

Inter-entity boundaries as agreed
at the 1995 Dayton Peace Agreement.

Projection: Lambert's Conformal Conic

East from Greenwich

Underlined towns give their name to the
administrative area in which they stand.

45

Underlined towns give their name to the administrative area in which they stand.

COPYRIGHT GEORGE PHILIP LTD.

Projection: Lambert's Conformal Conic

East from Greenwich

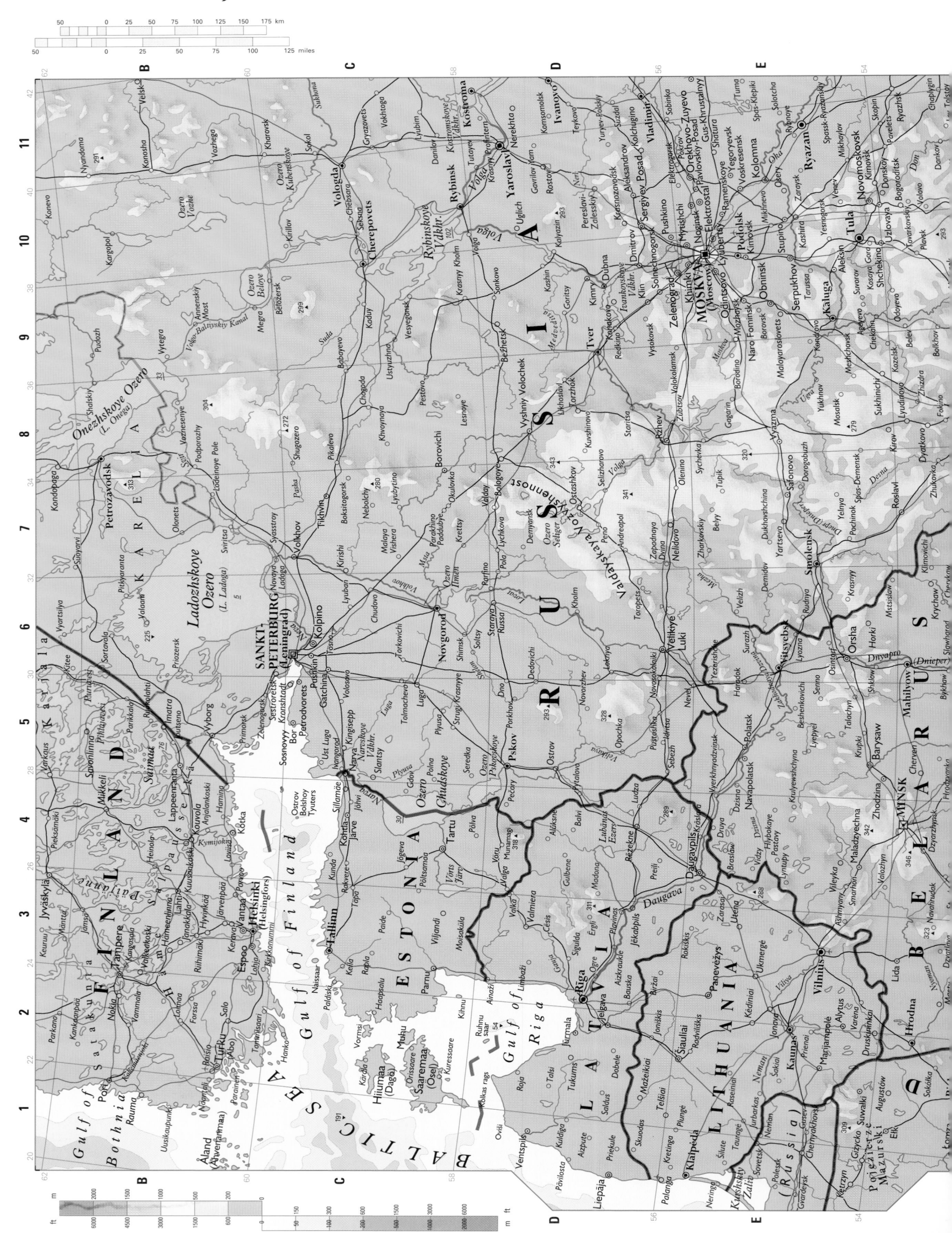

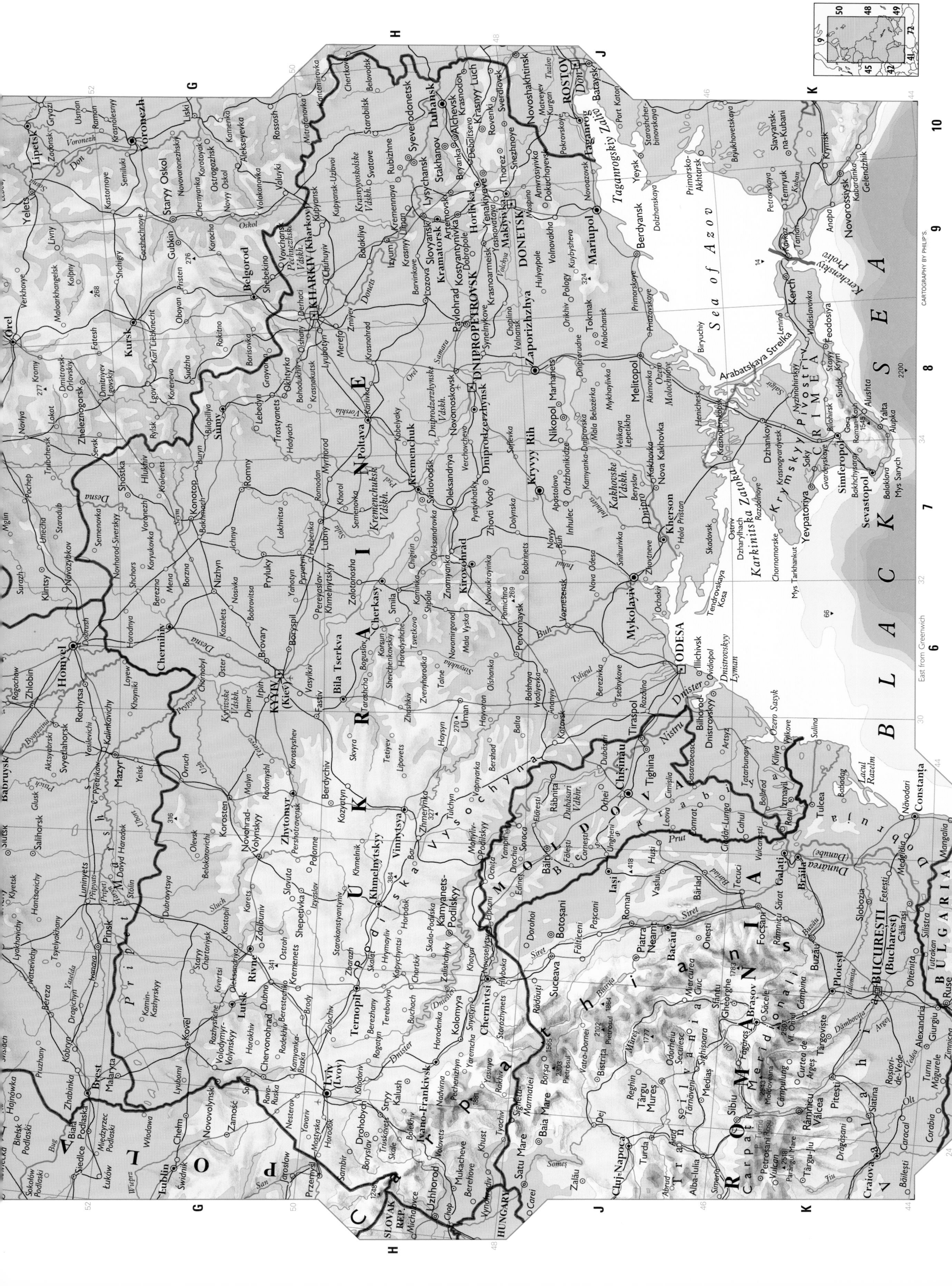

BLACK SEA

Sea of Azov

ROMANIA

MOLDOVA

UKRAINE

BULGARIA

SLOVAK REP.

HUNGARY

CRIMEA

DONETSK

KYIV (Kiev)

KHARKIV (Kharkov)

ODESA

Projection: Conical with two standard parallels

East from Greenwich

CARTOGRAPHY BY PHILIP'S

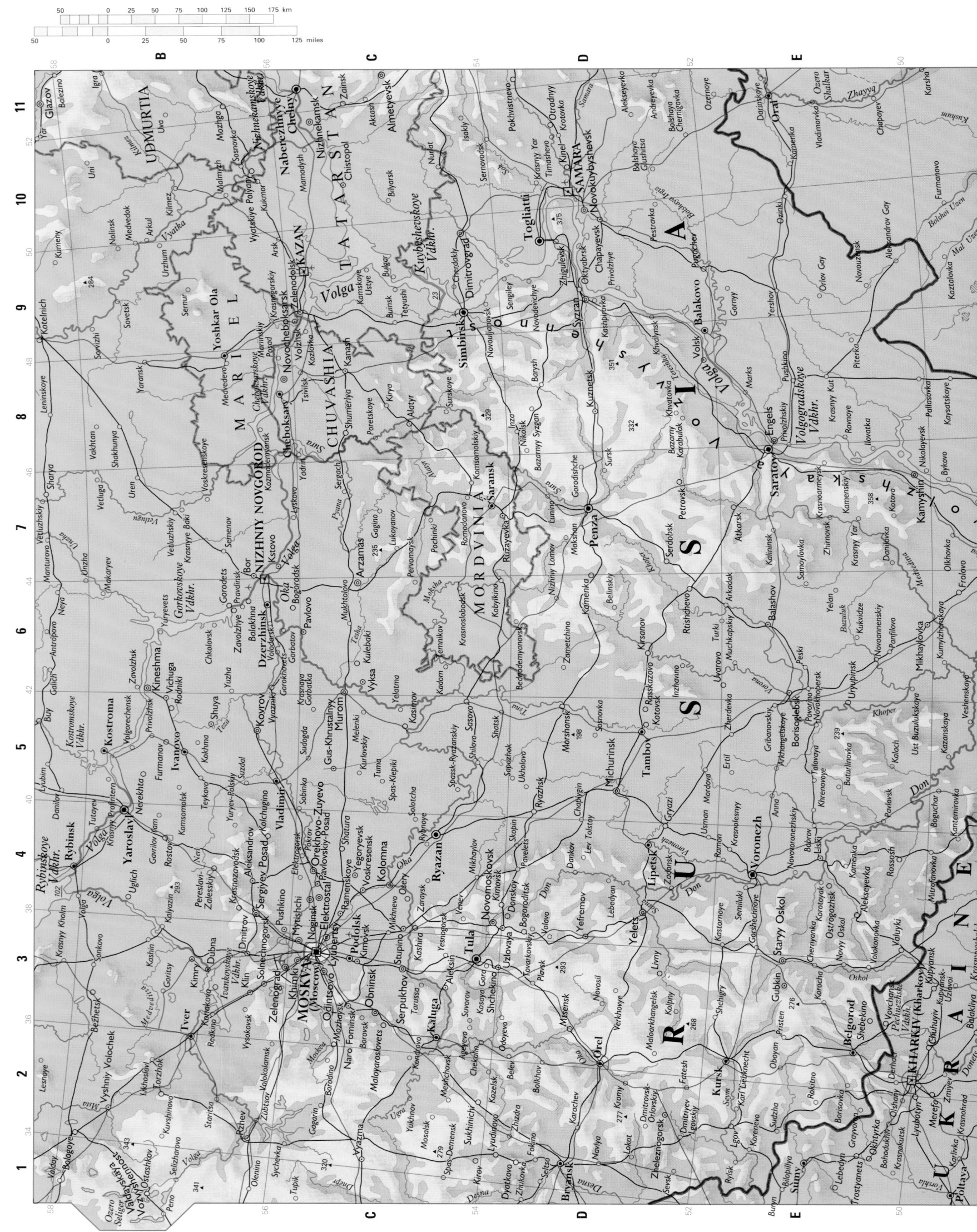

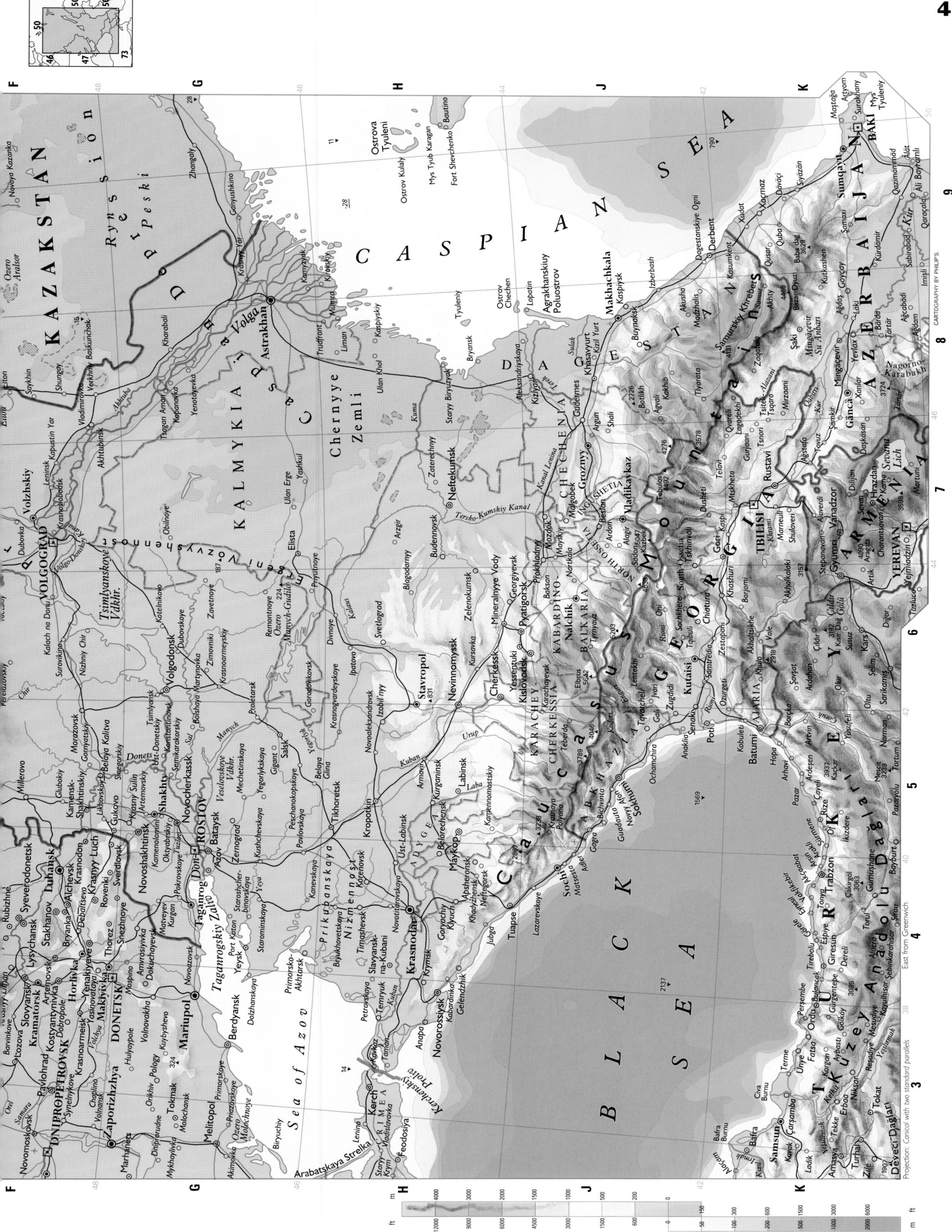

CARTOGRAPHY BY PHILIP'S.

50

F 48 G 46 H 44 J 42 K

KAZAKSTAN

Novaya Kazanka
Ozero Aralsor
Elton
Soykhin
Shungay
Vladimirovka
Akhtubinsk
Verkhniy Baskunchak
Kharabali
Zhanybek
Gonyushkino

Ryn's Peski
De pr es sion

Ostrova Tyuleni

Mys Tyub Karagan
Bautino

Ostrov Kulaly

Mys Shevchenko
Fort Shevchenko

CASPIAN SEA

9

-28

50 50
50
46 47 73

Ozero
Baskunchak
35
Krasnoslobodsk
Leninsk Kapustin Yar

VOLGOGRAD
Dubovka
Volzhskiy

Krasnyy Yar
Astrakhan

Volga

DELTA

Krasnyy Yar
Kamyzyak
Olya

Buzan

Trudfront
Liman
Ulan Khol
Kaspiyskiy

Ostrov
Chechen
Lopatin
Agrakhanskiuy
Poluostrov

8

Kalach na Donu
Voľgo-Donskoy K.
Proletarsky
Tsimlyanskoye Vdkhr.

Chernyye
Zemli

Starry Biryuzyak

Kizlyar
Izberbash

Makhachkala
Kaspiysk

KALMYKIA

Ulan Ege
Yashkul
Kanal Lenina
Kizil Yurt
Khasavyurt
Buynaksk

7

Verkhne-Donskoy

Yenotayevka
Kopanovka

Kuma
Neftekumsk
Tersko-Kumskiy Kanal

Aleksandriyskaya
Sulak
Madzhalis

Akusha

D A G E S T A N
Derbent

Kalach
187 Verkhniy Vozyshenni

Remontnoye
Ozero
Manych-Gudilo

Arzgir
Budennovsk

Terek
Gudermes
Grozny
Argun
Shali

Botlikh
2726
Agvali

6

VOLGODONSK

Elista

Divnoye

Blagodarny
Georgiyevsk

Mozdok
Malgobek
Nazran
Vladikavkaz
4276
Tebulos
4492

Kasumkent
Akhty
4466

Zavetnoye
Zimovniki

Prikumsk

Zelenokumsk
Prokhladny
Nartkala
Beslan

2578

CHECHENIA
INGUSHETIA
NORTH OSSETIA

Akhtyrskaya

Mineralnyye Vody
Pyatigorsk

Nalchik
5203

Kazbek
5047

Mestia

Samuksiy Khrebet
4731

Q u s a r

Baba dag
3629

AZERBAIJAN

Svetlograd

Yessentuki
Kislovodsk

KABARDINO-
BALKARIA

Elbrus
5642

4046

Oni
Ambrolauri

Telavi
Lagodekhi

Qax

Şäki

Qazakh

4

	RUSSIA
1	Adygea
2	Karachey-Cherkessia
3	Kabardino-Balkaria
4	North Ossetia
5	Ingushetia
6	Chechenia
7	Dagestan
8	Mordvinia
9	Chuvashia
10	Mari El
11	Tatarstan
12	Udmurtia
13	Khakassia
	AZERBAIJAN
14	Naxçivan
	GEORGIA UKRAINE
15	Ajaria 17 Crimea
16	Abkhazia

Projection: Conical Orthomorphic with two standard parallels

East from Greenwich

A   B   C

8 9 10 11 12 13 14 15 16 17 18 19

80 90 100 110 120 130 140 150 170

ARCTIC OCEAN

Mys Arkticheskiy

Ostrov Shmidta

Ostrov Komsomolets

Ostrov Pioner

Ostrov Oktyabrskoy Revolyutsii

965▲

Severnaya Zemlya

Ostrov Bolshevik

Proliv Vilkitskogo

Mys Chelyuskin

Laptev Sea

East Siberian Sea

Ostrov Genryetty

Ostrova Zhanetty

Ostrova Delonga

3800▲

Ostrov Bennetta

Ostrova De Long

Ostrov Zhokhova

Ostrov Faddeyevskiy

Ostrov Novaya Sibir

Ostrov Maly Lyakhovskiy

Ostrov Belkovskiy

Ostrov Kotelnyy

Ostrov Stolbovoy

Lyakhovskiye Ostrova

Ostrov Bolshoy Lyakhovskiy

Ostrova Medvezhii

Novosibirskiye Ostrova

374▲

Mys Dezhneva (East C.)

Uelen

Chukchi Sea

19

St. Lawrence I. (U.S.A.)

60

Vankarem

Ostrov Vrangelya

Proliv Dmitriya Lapteva

D

Pevek

Chaun

Ust Chaun

1843▲

Chukotskoye Nagorye

Providenya

Zaliv Lavrentiya

Beringovskiy

Chersky

Bilibino

Ambarchik

Nizhne Kolymsk

Anadyr

Ust Kuyga

Kazachye

Srednekolymsk

Ayan

Omolon

Poren

Bering Sea

Poluostrov Byrranga

Gory

1146▲

Nordvik

Oz. Taymyr

Poluostrov Taymyr

Novorybnoye

Khatanga

Saskylakh

Tit-Ary

Ust Olenek

Tiksi

Bulun

Kyusyur

Zhilinda

Zhigansk

Kystatyam

Sangar

Verkhoyansk

2389▲

Chokurdakh

Deputatskiy

Druzhina

Zyryanka

Khonuu

Pobeda 3147▲

Kolyma

Taskan

Omsukchan

Oratukan

Ust-Nera

2659▲

Oymyakon

Gora Chen 2682▲

Ust-Omchug

Yagodnoye

Susuman

Magadan

Palatka

Kolymskoye Nagorye

Koryakskoye Nagorye

2652▲

Korf

Kamenskoye

Penzhino

Gizhiginskaya Guba

Gizhiga

Ossora

Ostrov Karaginskiy

Sredinnyy Khrebet

Ust-Kamchatsk

Klyuchi

Gora 4750▲ Klyuchevskaya

Poluostrov Kamchatka

Nikolskoye

Komandorskiye Ostrova

Petropavlovsk-Kamchatskiy

3456▲

3621▲

Khrebet Cherskogo

Khatanga

R U S S I A

S A K H A

Norilsk

Gory Putorana

1701▲

Yessey

Volochanka

Kheta

Noginsk

Kotuy

Moyero

Vilyuy

962▲

Arctic Circle

Olenek

Suntar

Nyurba

Vilyuysk

Verkhnevilyuysk

Vilyuy

Namtsy

Sinsk

Pokrovsk

Yakutsk

Mayya

Amga

Ust Mil

Aim

Chagda

Nelkan

Ulya

Maya

Ust Maya

Amga

Aldan

Tommot

2246▲

Neryungri

Nagornyy

2246▲

Ayan

Udya

Chumikan

Tugur

Uda

Sea of Okhotsk

Okhotsk

Ust Khayryuzovo

1780▲

Ust-Bolsheretsk

Kurilskiye Ostrova

Ostrov Paramushir

Ostrov Onekotan

Severo-Kurilsk

50

Yartsevo

Severo-Yeniseyskiy

1104▲

Kuyumba

Mutoray

Vanavara

Yerbogachen

Chernyshevskiy

Mirnyy

Lensk

Olekminsk

Podkamennaya Tunguska

Nizhnyaya Tunguska

Tura

Yukta

Chagda

Ydy Kyuyel

Bodaybo

Yenisey

Yeniseysk

Strelka

Kansk

Boguchany

Ilanskiy

Angara

Chuna

Kondratyevo

Zheleznogorsk-Ilimskiy

Ust-Ilimsk

Makarovo

Ust-Kut

Magistralnyy

Kirensk

Chara 2999▲

Karalon

Ust-Nyukzha

Yenyuka

Tynda

Skovorodino

Zeya

Ushumun

Olekma

Olekma

Dzhalinda

Mogocha

Norsk

Shimanovsk

Zavitinsk

2648▲

Bureya

Selemdzha

Komsomolsk

Amursk

Khrebet Sikhote Alin

Amgu

Terney

Dalnegorsk

Ostrov Iturup

Ostrov Kunashir

Kushiro

Achinsk

Krasnoyarsk

Artemovsk

Vostochnyy Sayan

Chernogorsk

Minusinsk

Abakan

Zapadnyy Sayan

Turan

Chadan

TUVA

Kyzyl

Toora-Khem

Tannu Ola

Samagaltay

Erzin

Uvs Nuur

Hyargas Nuur

Döröö Nuur

362▲

Altay

4266▲

Hami

Gaxun Nur

Yenisey

Kizir

Kansk

2840▲

Nizhneudinsk

Tulun

Zima

Cheremkhovo

Usolye Sibirskoye

Angarsk

1620▲

Irkutsk

Sayan

Slyudyanka

Munku-Sardyk 3491▲

Hövsgöl Nuur

Hatgal

Zakamensk

Darhan

Uliastay

Tsetserleg

M O N G O L I A

Ulaanbaatar

2800▲

Lun

Hentiyn Nuruu

Hangayn Nuruu

Choybalsan

Tamsagbulag

Öndörhaan

1949▲

Linxi

Saynshand

Erenhot

Dalandzadgad

3957▲

G o b i

Xilinhot

Chifeng

Chengde

Baotou

Hohhot

Zhangjiakou

BEIJING

Yingkou

Barguzin

Ulan Ude

Yablonovyy Khrebet

Petrovsk-Zabaykalskiy

Khilok

Bratsk

Tayshet

Bagdarin

Mama

Korshunovo

Vitim

Vitim

456▲

Bukachacha

Chita

Shilka

Sretensk

Nerchinsk

1054▲

Gulian

Da Hinggan Ling

Aginskoye

Oloyannaya

Borzya

Khapcheranga

Zabaykalsk

Hailar

Manzhouli

Hulun Nur

Kyakhta

Gusinoozersk

Orhon

Songhua Jiang

Nenjiang

Nen Jiang

Tao'an

Siping

Tonghua

Nen Jiang

Ang angxi

Hegang

Jiamusi

QIQIHAR

HARBIN

Mudanjiang

JILIN

CHANGCHUN

Songhua Hu

2744▲

Yanji

Tumen

Blagoveshchensk

Svobodnyy

Belogorsk

Chegdomyn

Obluchye

Birobidzhan

Khabarovsk

Smidovich

Bikin

Vyazemskiy

Lesozavodsk

Spassk

Dalniy

Ussuriysk

Artem

Vladivostok

Nakhodka

Kroskino

Chongjin

D o n g b e i

C H I N A

Chengde

Zhangjiakou

FUSHUN

SHENYANG

ANSHAN

Dandong

NORTH KOREA

Wonsan

Kansong

PYONGYANG

Nampo

DALIAN

INCH'ON

SEOUL

Seoul

SOUTH KOREA

TAEJON

TAEGU

PUSAN

Sea of Japan

Hokkaido

SAPPORO

Otaru

Obihiro

3669▲

Wakkanai

2290▲

Abashiri

Hakodate

Aomori

Hachinohe

Akita

Honshu

Niigata

Kanazawa

Fuji-San 3776▲

JAPAN

OSAKA

Yuzhno-Sakhalinsk

Kholmsk

Korsakov

Sakhalin

Aleksandrovsk-Sakhalinskiy

1608▲ Gora Lopatina

Poronaysk

Uglegorsk

Nogliki

Okha

Nikolayevsk-na-Amur

Sakhalinskiy Zaliv

Amur

A   **B**   **C**

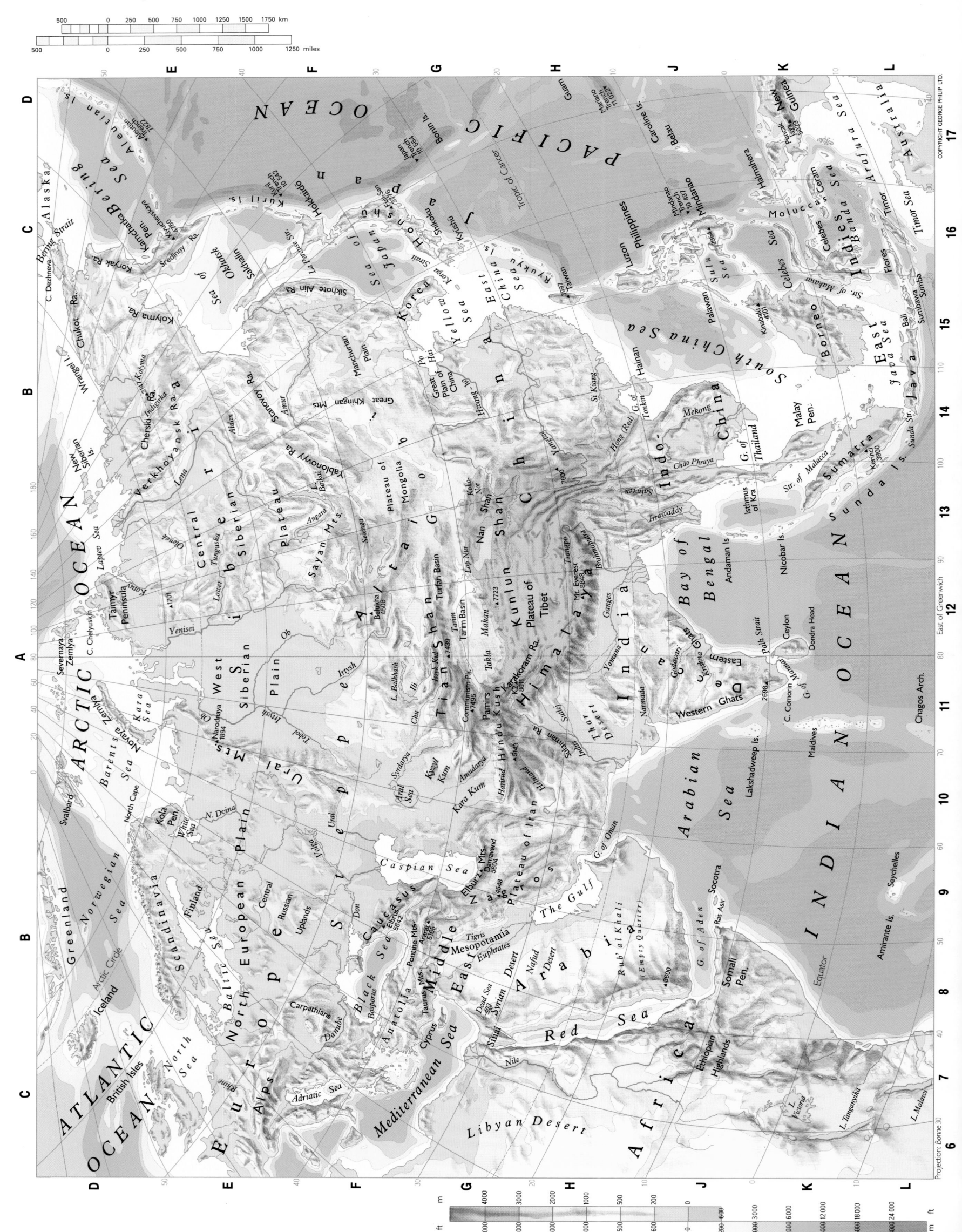

Projection Bonne 30

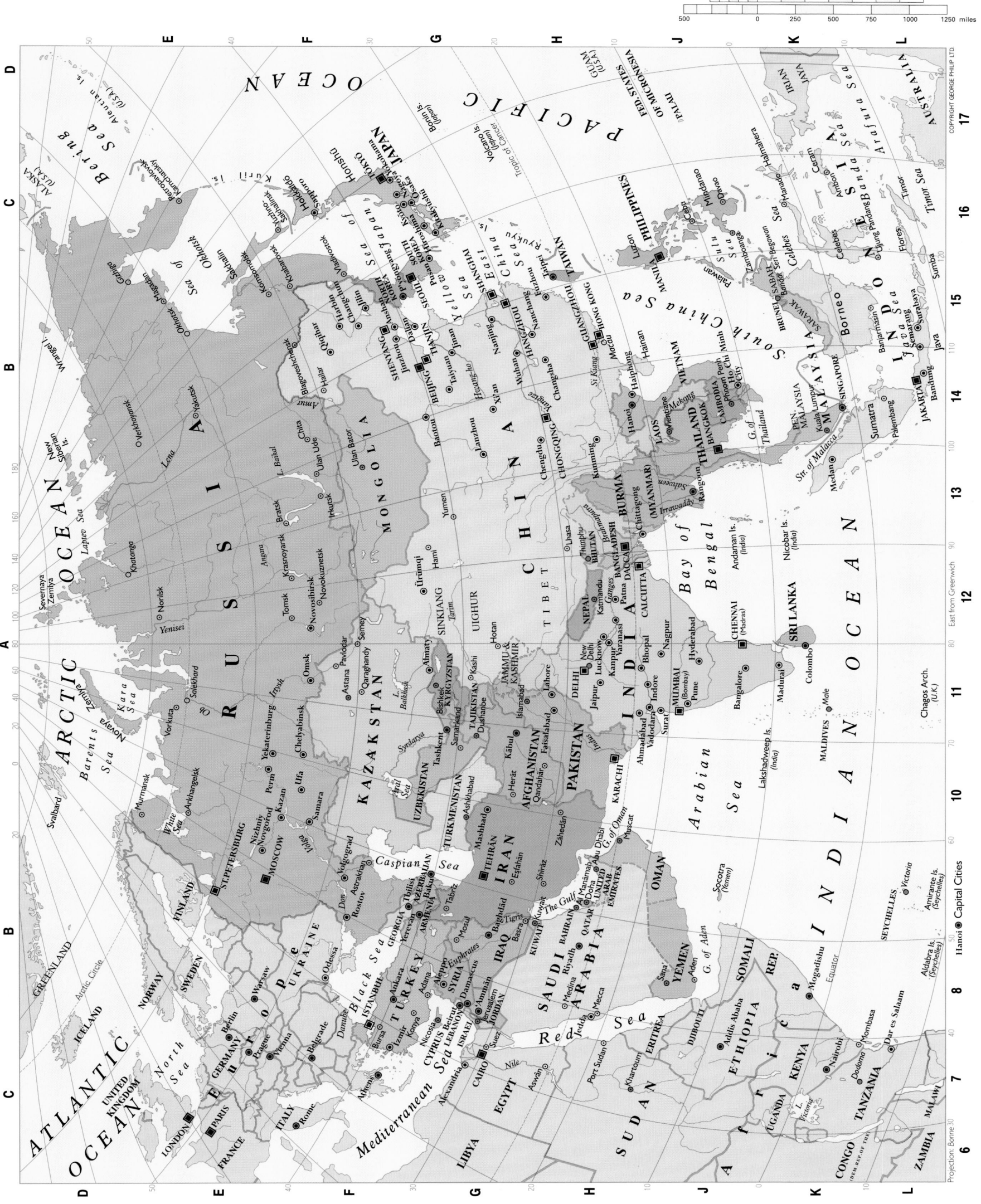

500   0   250   500   750   1000   1250   1500   1750 km

500   0   250   500   750   1000   1250 miles

D

D

O C E A N

Bering
Sea
Aleutian Is.
(USA)

ALASKA
(USA)

C

PACIFIC

JAPAN
TOKYO
Honshu
Hokkaido
Sapporo

C

Wrangel I.
New
Siberian Is.

ARCTIC   OCEAN

Severnaya
Zemlya

Novaya
Zemlya

Svalbard

GREENLAND

B

R U S S I A

Sea of
Okhotsk

Kamchatsky
Petropavlovsk

Magadan
Okhotsk

Yakutsk

Sakhalin
Khabarovsk

Vladivostok

Sea of
Japan

NORTH
KOREA
Nagoya
Kyoto
Osaka

SOUTH
KOREA
SEOUL
Pusan

B

A

ICELAND

ATLANTIC
OCEAN

NORWAY

SWEDEN

FINLAND

Murmansk

White
Sea

Barents
Sea

Kara
Sea

Lena

L. Baikal

Irkutsk

MONGOLIA
Ulan Bator

CHINA

SHENYANG
BEIJING
TANJIN
Dalian

Yellow
Sea

SHANGHAI

East
China
Sea

TAIWAN
Taipei

A

UNITED
KINGDOM

LONDON

FRANCE
PARIS

North
Sea

Berlin
GERMANY
Warsaw

Vienna
Prague

Budapest
Belgrade

Moscow
ST.PETERSBURG

Volga

KAZAKSTAN

Astana

Novosibirsk
Omsk
Tomsk
Krasnoyarsk

Yenisei

Ürümqi

SINKIANG
UIGHUR

Tarim

Hami

Yumen

Lanzhou

Xian

Chengdu

CHONGQING
Kunming

Wuhan

Changsha

Nanchang

Nanjing
HANGZHOU
GUANGZHOU
HONG KONG

Hainan

VIETNAM
Hanoi
Haiphong

LAOS
Vientiane

THAILAND
BANGKOK

BURMA
(MYANMAR)
Rangoon

PHILIPPINES
MANILA
Luzon

Mindanao
Davao

GUAM
(USA)

FED. STATES
OF MICRONESIA

PALAU

INDONESIA

Celebes
Sea

Borneo

SARAWAK
BRUNEI
SABAH

MALAYSIA
Kuala Lumpur
SINGAPORE

Sumatra

JAKARTA
Bandung
Java

Java Sea

Banda Sea

Timor Sea

AUSTRALIA

JAVA

IRAN

Tropic of Cancer

South China Sea

Bay of
Bengal

INDIAN   OCEAN

Arabian
Sea

Hanoi ● Capital Cities

Equator

East from Greenwich

Projection: Bonne

COPYRIGHT GEORGE PHILIP LTD.

JAPAN 1:4 400 000

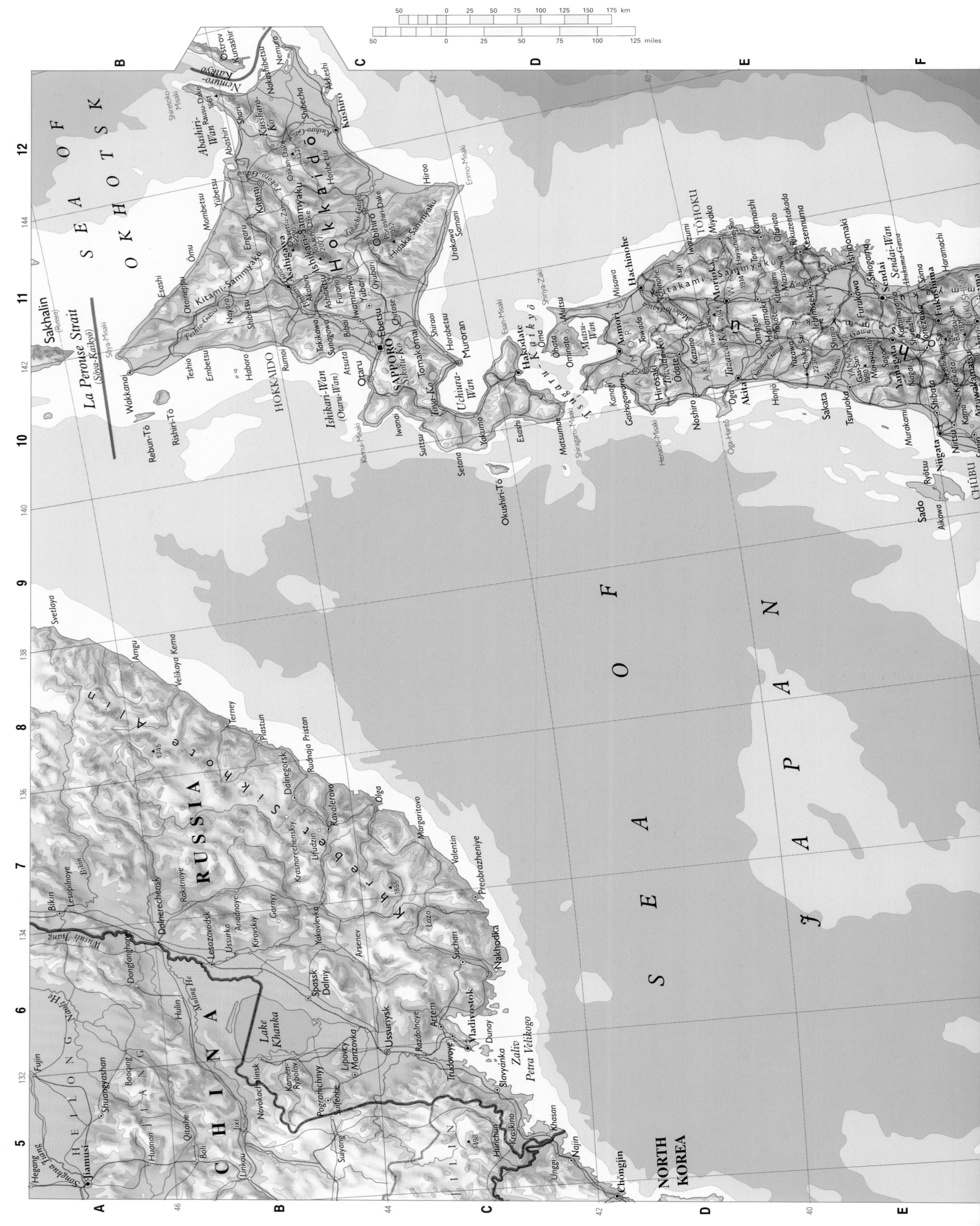

SEA OF OKHOTSK

Ostrov Kunashir

Nemuro-Kaikyō

Sakhalin (Releng)

La Pérouse Strait (Sōya-Kaikyō)

HOKKAIDO

Kitami-Sammyaku

Ishikari-Sammyaku

Hidaka-Sammyaku

SAPPORO

Wakkanai

Rebun-Tō

Rishiri-Tō

Teshio

Embetsu

Haboro

Rumoi

Otaru

Ishikari-Wan
(Otaru-Wan)

Iwanai

Suttsu

Setana

Yokamu

Esashi

Okushiri-Tō

Tsugaru-Kaikyō

Hakodate

Muroran

Uchiura-Wan

Tomakomai

Shiraoi

Horobetsu

TŌHOKU

Hachinohe

Aomori

Hirosaki

Odate

AKITA

Akita

Sakata

Tsuruoka

Niigata

Sado

CHŪBU

Sendai

Sendai-Wan

Fukushima

RUSSIA

Sikhote

Alin

Svetlaya

Terney

Plastun

Dalnegorsk

Olga

Margaritovo

Valentin

Preobrazheniye

Bikin

Dalnerechensk

Spassk Dalniy

Ussuriysk

Vladivostok

Zaliv Petra Velikogo

Nakhodka

Lake Khanka

CHINA

HEILONG JIANG

JILIN

Songhua Jiang

Hegang

Jiamusi

NORTH KOREA

Chŏngjin

S   E   A   O   F   J   A   P   A   N

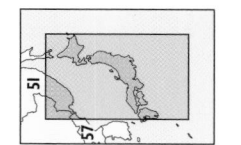

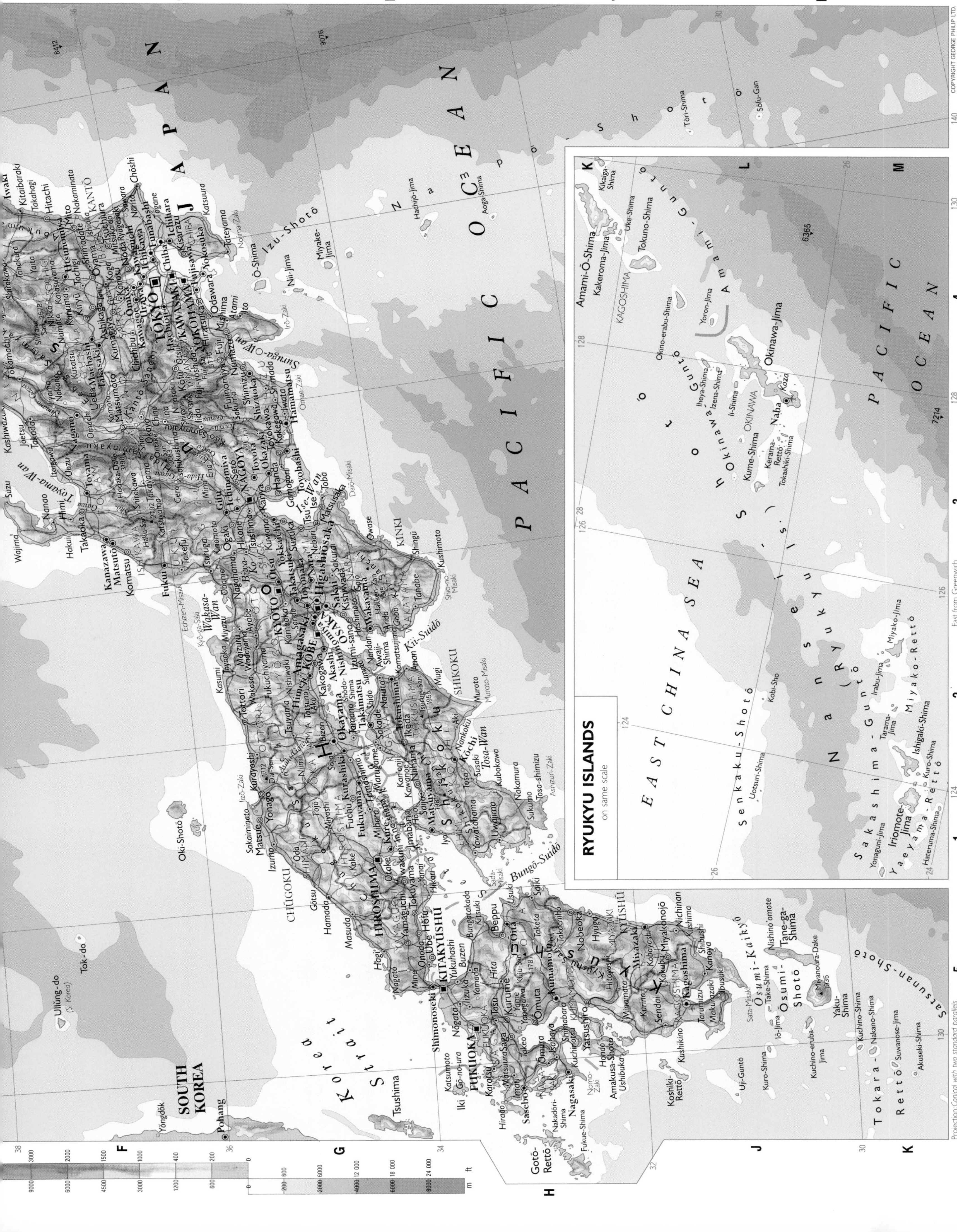

J A P A N

P A C I F I C   O C E A N

TOKYO
KAWASAKI
YOKOHAMA
CHIBA
KANTŌ
Izu-Shotō
Hachijō-Jima
Aoga-Shima

NAGOYA
KYOTO
KOBE
OSAKA
KINKI
Ise-Wan

SHIKOKU
CHŪGOKU
HIROSHIMA
KITAKYŪSHŪ
FUKUOKA
KYŪSHŪ

SOUTH
KOREA

Korea   Strait

Ullung-do
(S. Korea)
Pohang
Tok-do
Tsushima

Bungo-Suidō
Ōsumi-Kaikyō
Yaku-Shima
Tane-ga-Shima
Ōsumi Shotō
Tokara-Rettō
Satsunan-Shotō

RYUKYU ISLANDS
on same scale

E A S T   C H I N A   S E A

P A C I F I C   O C E A N

Amami-Ō-Shima
Kikaiga-Shima
Kakeroma-Shima
Uke-Shima
Tokuno-Shima
KAGOSHIMA
Yoron-Jima
Okino-erabu-Shima
Iheya-Shima
Izena-Shima
Ii-Shima
OKINAWA
Okinawa-Jima
Kume-Shima
Naha
Koza
Kerama-Rettō
Tokashiki-Shima

N a n s e i   (R Y U K Y U)   I s.

Senkaku-Shotō
Uotsuri-Shima
Kobi-Sho
Sakashima-Guntō
Miyako-Rettō
Miyako-Jima
Tarama-Jima
Irabu-Jima
Yaeyama-Rettō
Iriomote-Jima
Ishigaki-Shima
Kuro-Shima
Hateruma-Shima
Yonaguni-Jima

East from Greenwich

Projection: Conical with two standard parallels

ft   m

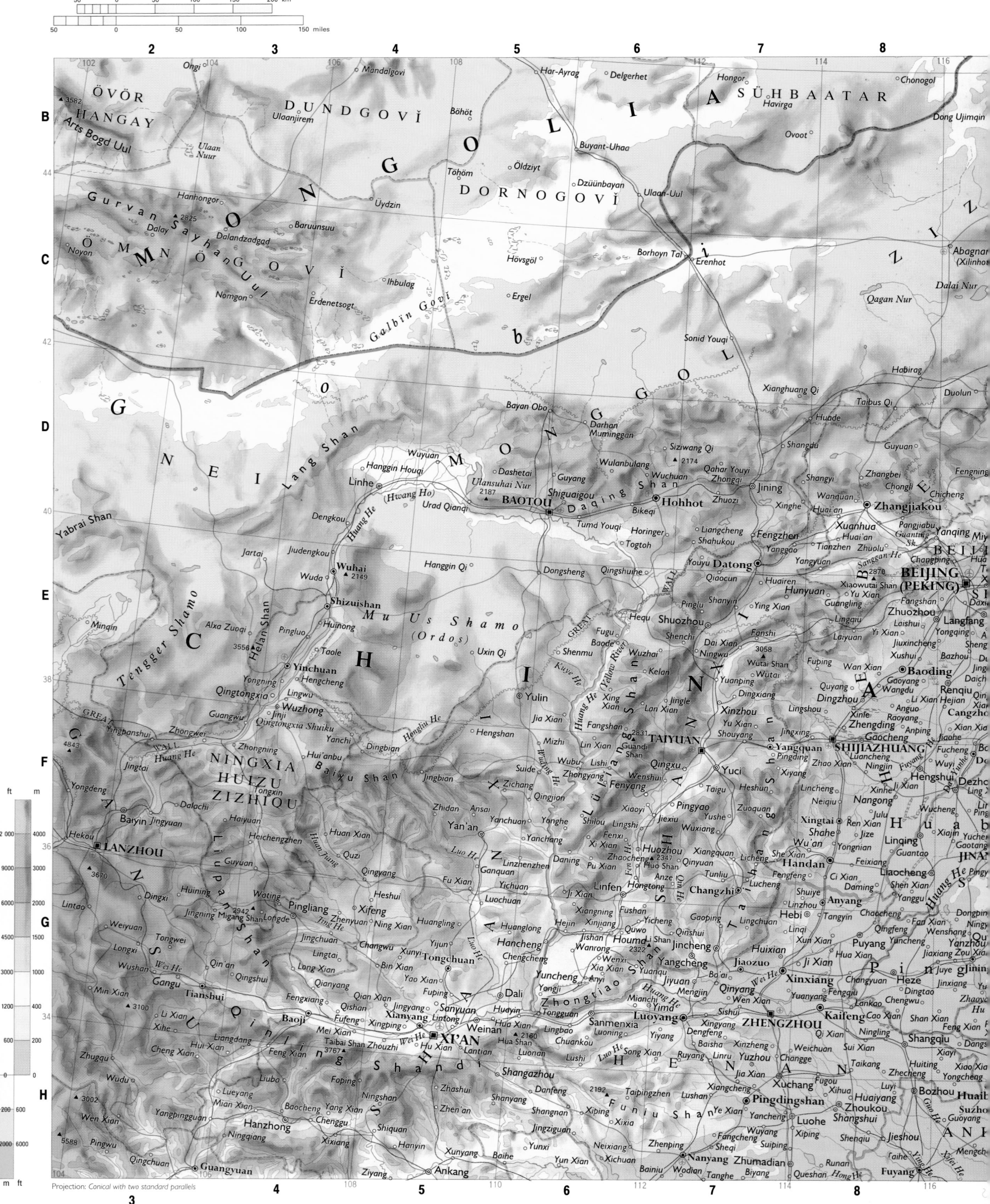

50 0 50 100 150 200 km
50 0 50 100 150 miles

Projection: Conical with two standard parallels

ÖVÖR
HANGAY
Arts Bogd Uul
3582

M
O
N
G

Ongi
Mandalgovi
DUNDGOVI
Har-Ayrag
Delgerhet
Hongor
Chonogol

Böhöt
Havirga
SÜHBAATAR
Ulaanjirem
Buyant-Uhaa
Ovoot
Dong Ujimqin

Hanhongor
Töhöm
Öldziyt
Dzüünbayan
DORNOGOVI
Ulaan-Uul

Ulaan
Nuur
Üydzin
Borhoyn Tal
Erenhot
Abagnar
(Xilinho

Baruunsuu
2825
Dalandzadgad
ZIZ

Ö
Noyon
M
N
Ö
Gurvan Sayhan Uul
Nömgon
Ihbulag
Erdenetsogt
Hövsgöl
Ergel
Qagan Nur
Dalai Nur

G
O
V
I
Galbïn Govi
b
Sonid Youqi
Habirag

Xianghuang Qi
Taibus Qi
Duolun

N
E
I
Bayan Obo
Darhan Muminggan
Huade
Shangdu
Guyuan
Fengning

G
Lang Shan
Wuyuan
Hanggin Houqi
Dashetai
Siziwang Qi
2174
Wulanbulang
Wuchuan
Qahar Youyi Zhongqi
Jining
Shangyi
Zhangbei
Chongli
Chicheng

Linhe
(Hwang Ho)
Ulansuhai Nur
2187
BAOTOU
Guyang
Shiguaigou
Daqing Shan
Hohhot
Bikeqi
Xinghe
Wanquan
Xuanhua
Huai'an
Pangjiabu
Yanqing
BEIJ

Dengkou
Urad Qianqi
Togtoh
Tumd Youqi
Horinger
Shahukou
Yanggao
Tianzhen
Zhuolu
Chaggping
Changping
2870
BEIJING
(PEKING)
SI

Jartai
Jiudengkou
Hanggin Qi
Dongsheng
Qingshuihe
Youyu
Datong
Qiaocun
Huairen
Hunyuan
Guangling
Xiaowutai Shan
Fangshan
Daxi

Wuhai
2149
Wuda
Mu Us Shamo
(Ordos)
Uxin Qi
Hequ
Shuozhou
Pinglu
Shanyin
Ying Xian
Lingqiu
Laishui
Zhuozhou
Langfang

Shizuishan
Alxa Zuoqi
Pingluo
Huinong
Fugu
Guandi
Wuzhai
Shenchi
Kelan
Dai Xian
Ningwu
Fanshi
3058
Wutai
Wutaishan
Fuping
Wan Xian
Laiyuan
Yi Xian
Jiuxincheng
Xushui
Quyang
Baoding

Helan Shan
3556
Taole
Shenmu
Kuye He
(Yellow River)
Yinchuan
Hengcheng
Yulin
Yuanping
Dingxiang
Lingshou
Dingzhou
Gaoyang
Wangdu
Li Xian
Hejian
Renqiu

Yongning
Lingwu
Xing Xian
Lan Xian
Jingle
Xinzhou
Yu Xian
Xinle
Anguo
Raoyang

Qingtongxia
Jia Xian
Mizhi
Lin Xian
Dai Shan
2831
Xinzhou
Yangqu
Xinjixing
Zhengding
SHIJIAZHUANG
Jinxing
Jiahe
Anping

Wuzhong
Hengshan
Suide
Wubu
Lishi
Zhongyang
TAIYUAN
Pingding
Luancheng
Shulu
Ningjin
Shulu

Guangwu
Qingtongxia Shuiku
Yanchi
Dingbian
Zhongwei
Zhongning
Hui'anbu
Jingbian
Zichang
Qingjian
Fenyang
Taigu
Yuci
Zhao Xian
Jize
Fucheng
Wuyi
Hengshui
Dezho

Yingpanshui
4843
Baïxu Shan
Zhidan
Ansai
Yanchuan
Yonghe
Shilou
Lingshi
Jiexiu
Yushe
Zuoquan
Lincheng
Neiqiu
Nangong
Wucheng

Yongdeng
Dalachi
Haiyuan
Huan Xian
Quzi
Yan'an
Yanchang
Fenxi
Huozhou
2347
Zhaocheng
Anze
Tunliu
Lucheng
Xingtai
Ren Xian
Shahe
Jize
Linqing
Guantao

Baiyin
Jingyuan
Heichengzhen
Luo He
Linzhenzhen
Daning
Pu Xian
Qinyuan
Changzhi
Gaoping
Lingchuan
Hebi
Tangyin
Linqi
Fan Xian

Hekou
3670
Dingxi
Weiyuan
Tongwei
Pingliang
Xifeng
Heshui
Qingyang
Yichuan
Ji Xian
Linfen
Hongtong
Fushan
Yicheng
Qinshui
Jincheng
Huixian
Xun Xian
Puyang
Yuncheng
Dongbei

Lintao
Longxi
Jingning
Huangling
Ji Xian
Xiangning
Quwo
Yangcheng
Jiaozuo
Jixian
Changyuan
Yanzhou

Lanzhou
Huining
Migang Shan
Longde
2942
Pingliang
Changwu
Xunyi
Yijun
Luochuan
Huanglong
Hejin
Xinjiang
Wenxi
Houma
2322
Yuanqu
Mianchi
Yima
Xingyang
ZHENGZHOU
Heze
Dingtao
Juye

Wushan
Gangu
Qin'an
Qingshui
Jingchuan
Lingtai
Changwu
Bin Xian
Yao Xian
Tongchuan
Hancheng
Jishan
Wanrong
Xia Shan
Yongji
Sishui
Luoyang
Xinxiang
Kaifeng
Cao Xian
Lankao
Chengwu

Tianshui
3100
Li Xian
Fengxiang
Qishan
Qianyang
Long Xian
Qian Xian
Fuping
Jingyang
Sanyuan
Lintong
Dali
Huayin
Tongguan
Huang He
Mengjin
Qinyang
Yuanyang
Fengqiu
Ningling
Sui Xian
Shan
Feng Xian

Min Xian
Xihe
Hui Xian
Liangdang
Baoji
Mei Xian
Taibai Shan
3767
Zhouzhi
Xianyang
Weinan
Hua Xian
Lingbao
Sanmenxia
Chuankou
Luoning
Yiyang
Dengfeng
Yuzhou
Changge
Weichuan
Huiting
Shangqiu
Dangs

Zhugqu
Wudu
3002
Liuba
Feng Xian
Foping
Zhouzhi
XI'AN
Lantian
2160
Hua Shan
Lushi
Song Xian
Baisha
Linru
Ruyang
Xuchang
Fugou
Luyi
Huaiy
Suzho

Lueyang
Mian Xian
Baocheng
Chenggu
Ningshan
Yang Xian
Shanga
Shangzhou
Danfeng
Shangnan
Xichuan
Neixiang
Zhenping
Sheqi
Suiping
Shenqiu

Hanzhong
5588
Pingwu
Wen Xian
Yangpingguan
Ningqiang
Hanyin
Shiquan
Xixiang
Xunyang
Ankang
Yunxi
Baihe
Yun Xian
Neixiang
Xichuan
Pingdingshan
Ye Xian
Yancheng
Luohe
Wuyang
Fangcheng
Shangshui

Qingchuan
Guangyuan
Ziyang
Ankang
Tanghe
Biyang
Runan
Queshan
Xian Lu
Fuyang

HANGAY | **DUNDGOVI** | **MONGOLIA** | **SÜHBAATAR**

NEI MONGOL

NINGXIA HUIZU ZIZHIQU

GANSU

SHAANXI

SHANXI

HEBEI

SHANDONG

HENAN

ANHUI

ft / m
12 000 / 4000
9000 / 3000
6000 / 2000
4500 / 1500
3000 / 1000
1200 / 400
600 / 200
0 / 0
200 / 600
2000 / 6000
m / ft

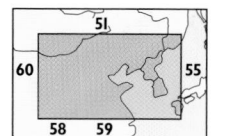

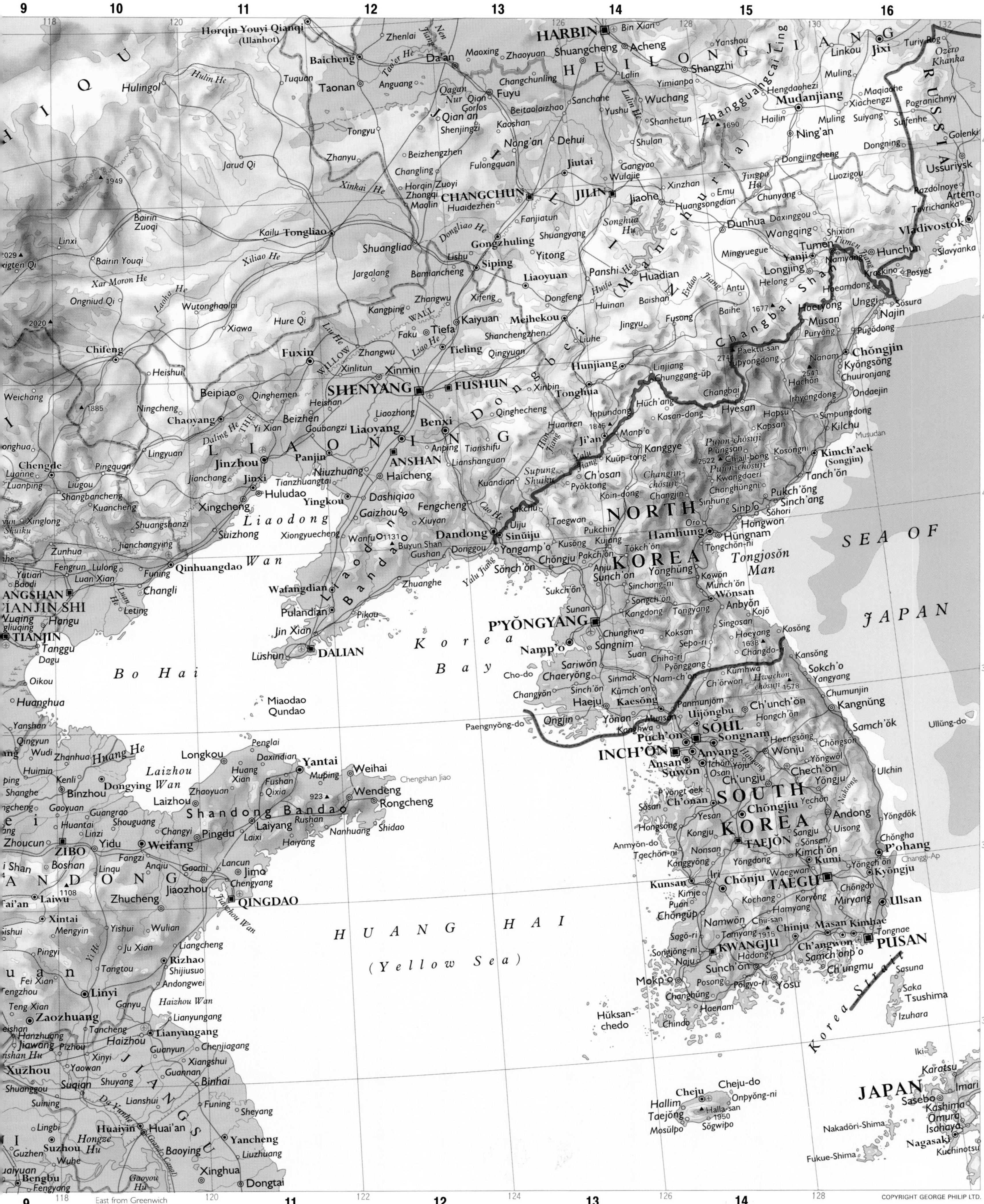

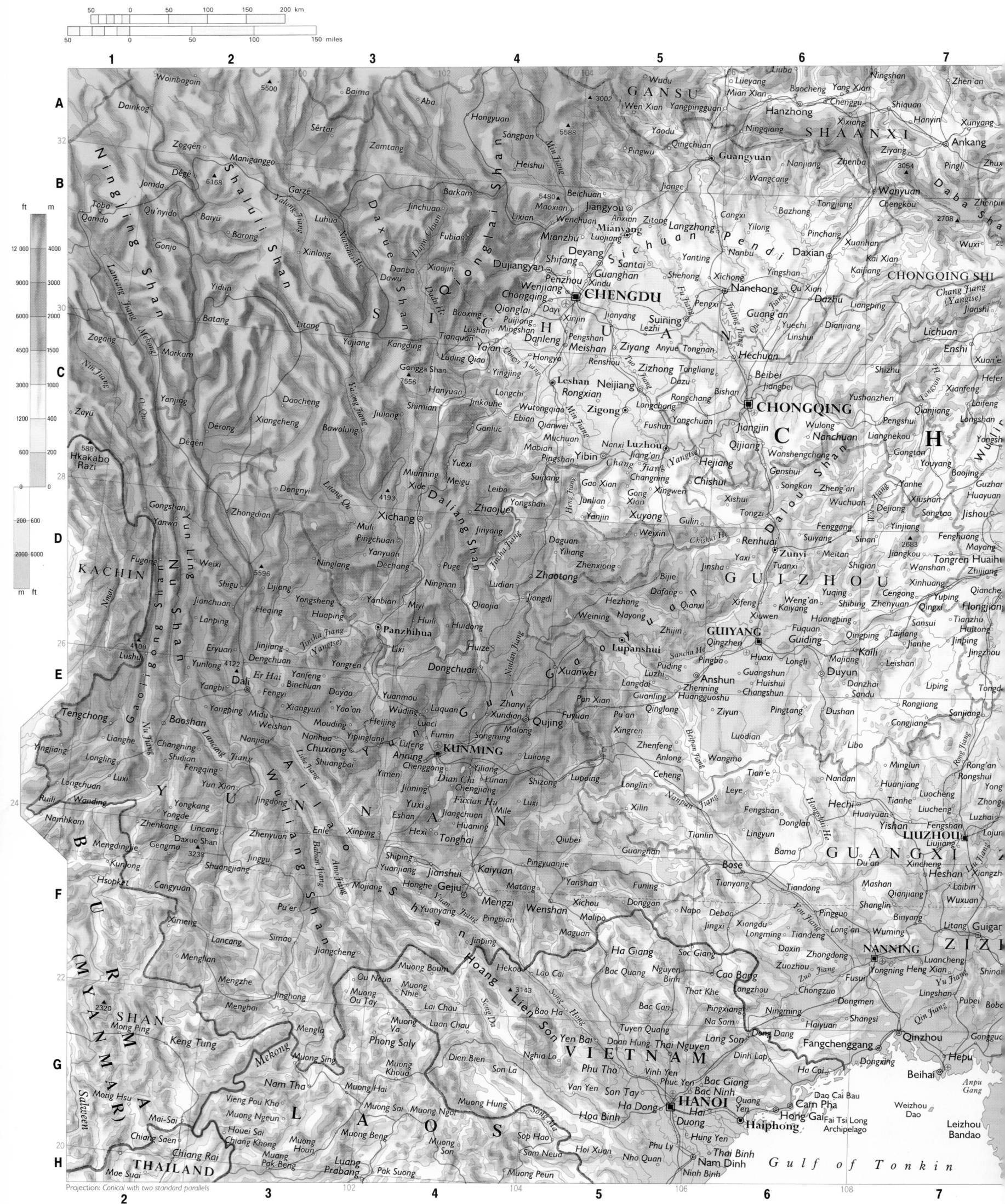

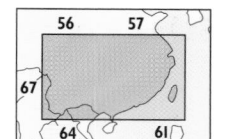

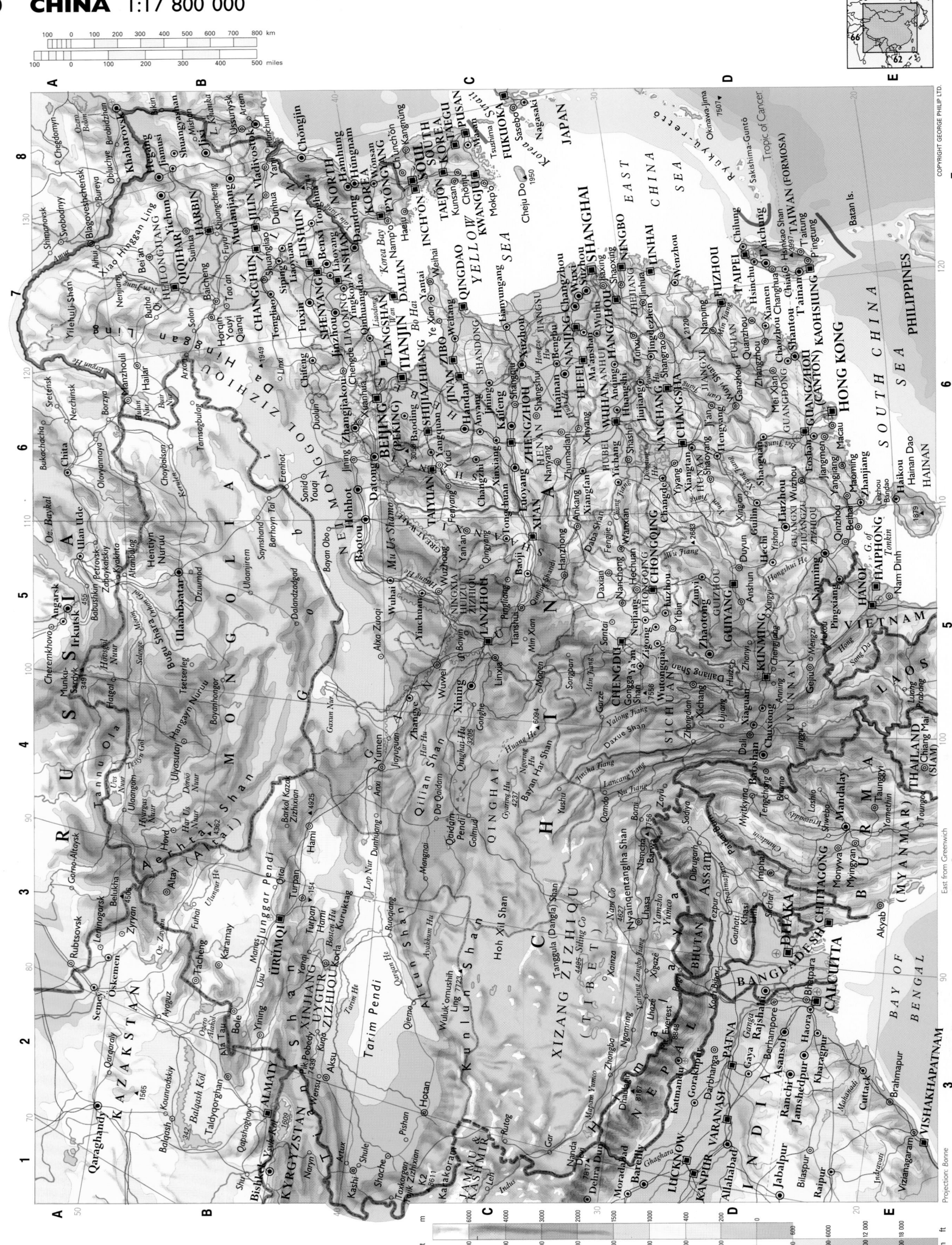

59

62 63

50 0 100 150 200 250 300 km
50 0 50 100 150 200 miles

1 2 3 4 5 6 7 8

116 118 120 122 124 126 128

A Itbayat I.
Batanes Is.
Batan I.

Balintang Channel

B Calayan I. Babuyan I.
Dalupiri I. Babuyan
Islands Camiguin I.
Fuga I.
Mayraira Pt. Babuyan Channel
Claveria
Bacarra Bangui Aparri Santa Ana
San Nicolas Laoag Kabugao Gonzaga
Batac Gattaran

C Vigan Bangued Tuao Tuguegarao
Santa Maria Lubuagan Mt. Cresta
Candon Bontoc Roxas 1685
Tagudin San Mateo Ilagan Palanan Pt.
Balaoan Baguio Santiago Palanan
San Fernando Mt. Pulog Cordon
Bolinao 2928 Solano Cosiguran
Alaminos Rosario Bayombong C. San Ildefonso
Lingayen Dagupan Mt. Anacuao
1852

D Luzon
San Carlos San Manuel Baler Bay
Santa Cruz Bayambang San Jose Baler
Masinloc Camiling Cuyapo
Iba Tarlac Victoria Cabanatuan
Concepcion La Gapan Dingalan
1780 Paz Angeles
Mt. Pinatubo San Fernando
San Antonio Polillo Is.
Olongapo Malabon Patnanongan I.
Bataan Caloocan Jomalig I.
Oroni Quezon City
Manila Bay MANILA
Cavite Pasay Santa Cruz
Dasmariñas Paracale
Nasugbu Tagaytay Lucban Labo
Balayan Lipa San Pablo Atimonan Daet
Lemery Batangas Lucena Calauag Pandan
Lubang Lobo Tayabas Bay Catanauan Viga Catanduanes
Is. Verde I. Pass Boac San Andres Virac
C. Calavite Marin- Naga Lagonoy Gulf
Calapan duque Nabua Iriga Tabaco Rapu Rapu I.
Mamburao Victoria Ligao Mayon Vol.
Mindoro Roxas Pinamalayan Burias I. Legazpi Sorsogon
Mt. Baco Donsol Gubat
Sablayan 2487 Magallanes San Bernardino Str.
Bongabong Tablas Str. Romblon Bulan Irosin Allen
San Jose Roxas Odiongan Ticao I. Laoang
Tablas I. Mondragon Catarman Gamay

E SOUTH
CHINA
SEA
SIBUYAN
SEA

F Busuanga I.
Culion I. Calamian
Linapacan Str. Group
Linapacan I. Pandan Kalibo Roxas Placer Catbalogan Paranas Samar
Cuyo Is. Dao Pilar Bilinan I. Caibiran Santa Rita Borongan
Taytay Cuyo Tibiao 2117 Ajuy Sara VISAYAN Calubian Carigara Basey General MacArthur
Bugasong Passi SEA Palompon Tacloban Guiuan
Panay Cadiz Bogo Ormoc Dulag
San Jose Iloilo Sagay Leyte Abuyog Homonhon I.
Silay Victorias San Carlos Danao Baybay
Palawan Jordan Bacolod Tuburan Camotes Sogod
Guimaras La Carlota 2450 Camotes Bato San Juan Dinagat I.
Hinigaran Binalbagan Mandaue Sea
Himamaylan Cebu Maasin

G Mt. Mantalingajan Kabankalan Carcar Surigao Siargao I. 10 497
2085 Sipalay Argao Bohol I. Panaon I. Placer Bucas Grande I.
Irahuan Honda Bay Bais Negros Siquijor I. Tagbilaran L. Mainit Carrascal
Puerto Princesa Tanjay Oslob BOHOL Cabadbaran 2012 Lanuza
C. Buliluyan Cagayan Is. Dumaguete Camiguin I. Talisayan Butuan Tandag
Bugsuk I. Siaton Zamboanguita SEA Nasipit Bayugan Marihatag
Bayawan Balingasag Esperanza Lianga
Dapitan Talacogan Hinatuan
SULU Dipolog Opo Cagayan de Oro Bislig
SEA Manukan Oroquieta Iligan Bay Iligan 2938 Malaybalay
Balabac I. Sindangan Ozamiz Marawi City Bunawan
Balabac Labason Tubod Cateel
Strait Kabasalan Pagadian Mt. Apo L. Lanao Baganga
Balambangan Siocon Malabang 2815 Panabo Tagum
Bangi Margosatubig Illana Parang Pantukan Manay
Suba Talan Sibuco Bay Cotabato Midsayap Davao
Kudat Jembongan Datu Piang Pikit 2954 Digos San Isidro
Tenghilan Cagayan Sulu I. Moro Gulf Talayan Davao Mati
Langkon Turtle Is. Basilan Kalamansig Lebak Gulf
Kota Belud Pangutaran Group Pilas Isabela Koronadal Malita
G. Kinabalu Pata I. Basilan I. Lamitan Palimbang 2083 General Santos
Kota 4101 Zamboanga Santos C. San Agustin
Kinabalu Jolo Kiamba
Papar Sandakan Parang Jolo Group Samales Group Tinaca Pt.
SABAH Talipao Sarangani Bay
MALAYSIA Siasi Tapul Group
Borneo Teluk Darvel Tapul I. Pata I.
Tawi-tawi Group CELEBES Sarangani Is.
Sibutu Group Sulu Archipelago SEA
Semporna INDONESIA Kep. Talaud

PACIFIC
OCEAN
PHILIPPINES

Mindanao Trench

Mindanao

Projection: Lambert's Conformal Conic
East from Greenwich
COPYRIGHT, GEORGE PHILIP LTD.

ft m
9000 3000
6000 2000
4500 1500
3000 1000
1200 400
600 200
0 0
200 600
4000 12 000
8000 24 000
m ft

100   0   100   200   300   400   500 km
100   0   50   100   150   200   250   300   350 miles

1   **2**   **3**   **4**   **5**

Letpadan
Tharrawaddy
Thoen
BURMA
Insein
Ma-ubin (YANGON) RANGOON
Pyabon
(MYANMAR)
Ye
Uttaradit
Vientiane (Viangchan)
Loei
Nong Khai
Udon Thani
Sakon Nakhon
Nakhon Phanom
Muang Khammouan
Ba Don
Dong Hoi
Quang Tri
Hue
Da Nang
LAOS

A

G. of
Martaban
Moulmein
Kyaikkami
Natkyizin
Tavoy
Maungmagan
Islands
Mali Kyun
Kadan
Kyun
Mergui
Tanintharyi
Letsôk-
aw Kyun
Myeik
Lambi Kyun
Kyunzu Maliwun
Zadetkyi Kyan
Ranong
Ko Phangan
Ko Samui
Phangnga
Nakhon Si Thammarat
Pak Phanang
Phuket
Thung Song
Phatthalung
Trang
Thale Luang
Kantang
Songkhla
Hat Yai
Satun
Yala
Narathiwat
Tumpat
Kota Baharu
Perhentian
Redang

THAILAND
Tak
Mae Sot
Sawankhalok
Phitsanulok
Phong
Phetchabun
Nam Tok
Phra Nakhon
Si Ayutthaya
Kanchanaburi
BANGKOK
Samut
Songkhram
Phet Buri
Hua Hin
Chanthaburi
Prachuap
Khiri Khan
Bang Saphan
Lenya
Chumphon
Kho Khot Kra
Chaiyaphum
Nakhon
Sawan
Saraburi
Nakhon
Ratchasima
Buriram
Khu Khan
Sisaket
Aranyaprathet
Chon Buri
Pattaya
Samut Prakan
Rayong
Trat
Ko Chang
Ko Kut
Khon Kaen
Roi Et
Ubon
Ratchathani
Siemreab
Sisophon
Batdambang
Tonle Sap
Kompong
Thom
Pouthisat
Kompong Chhnang
Kampong Cham
Krong
Koh Kong
Phumi
Sre Ambel
Takeo
Kampot
Chaak Kampong Saom
Kampong Saom
Hon Chong
Dao Phu Quoc
Rach Gia
Sre Ambel

Phnom Dangrek
Kulen
Cheom Ksan
Stoeng Trong
Kracheh
Senmonorom
Da Lat
Buon Me Thuot
Nha Trang
Cam Ranh
Phan Rang
Mui Dinh
Phan Thiet
PHANH BHO HO CHI MINH
My Tho
Sa Dec
Can Tho
Soc Trang
Bac Lieu
Ca Mau
Con Son
Vung Tau
Long
Xuyen
Sway Rieng
Prey Veng
Bien Hoa

CAMBODIA
Phnom Penh
(Phnum Penh)

VIETNAM
Chau O
Quang Ngai
Bong Son
Binh Dinh
Qui Nhon
Song Cau
Kon Tum
Plei Ku
Yun Pa
Muang
Krong
Attapu

Gulf
of
Thailand

B

Mui Ca Mau

Nakhon
Mun
Pakse
2598
2405
1813
2461
3701

1080
2075
1835

Paracel Is.

4424

Nanshan I.

Loaita I.
Itu Aba I.

Sin Cowe I.

Mt. Mantali
C. Buliluyan
Balabac
Kudat
Langkon
Kota Belud
Gunong
Kinabalu
4101

SOUTH   CHINA   SEA

Spratly Is.
Spratly I.
Amboyna Cay

C

ANDAMAN SEA

Strait of Malacca
We
Sabang
Banda Aceh
Meureudu
Bireuen
Sigli
Lhokseumawe
Calang
Idi
Langsa
Peureulak
ACEH
Takengon
Danau Toba
G. Leuser
3381
Meulaboh
Ujung Raja
Tapaktuan
Simeulue
Sinabang
Kepulauan
Banyak
Telukdalem
Gunungsitoli
Nias
Lahewa
Musala
Sibolga
Natal
Tanahmasa
Kepulauan Batu
Tanahbala
Siberut
Sabulubbek
Pulau
Pagai Utara
Kepulauan
Mentawai
Pulau Pagai
Selatan

Langkawi
Alor Setar
Pinang
George Town
Butterworth
Taiping
Ipoh
Teluk
Intan
Kota Kubu
Baharu
Kelang
Port Dickson
KUALA LUMPUR
Seremban
Melaka
Muar
Batu
Pahat
Pasir Mas
Sungai Petani
Kuala Lipis
Kuala Terengganu
Temerloh
Kuantan
Segamat
Keluang
Mersing
Kota Tinggi
Johor Baharu
SINGAPORE
Bintan
Tanjungpinang

PENINSULAR
MALAYSIA
Gunong Tahan
2190
Kampar
Dungun
Kemaman
Tenggol
Pulau
Tioman

Kelang
Kelang

Sungei Petani
Pinang

Perhentian

Kota Baharu

MALAYSIA
Kepulauan
Natuna
Besar
Telukbutun
Natuna
Besar
Matak
Siantan
Midai
Subi
Serasan
Kepulauan
Natuna Selatan
Laut
Binjai
Kepulauan
Anambas

BRUNEI
Kuala Belait
Bandar Seri Begawan
Tutong
Seria
Miri
Niah
Marudi
2938

Pulau
Labuan
Beaufort
Papar
Ranau
SABAH
Melalap
Tenom
Lawas
Limbang
Brassei
Tawa
Banjar

D

Medan
Binjai
Tebingtinggi
Pematangsiantar
Prapat
Tarutung
Rantauprapat
Kabanjahe
Tanjungbalai
Pelabuhan Kelang

S
U
M
A
T
E
R
A
U
T
A
R
A

Port Klang
Bagansiapiapi
Dumai
Bengkalis
Rupat
Pekanbaru
Bangkinang
Siaksriindrapura
Tanjungpinang
Kepulauan
Riau
Bintan
Kepulauan
Badas
Singkawang
Ngabang
Tebakang
Bau
Niut
170
Serian
Bonti
Sanggau
Tayan

SARAWAK
Mukah
Oya
Sibu
Kanowit
Bintulu
Sarikei
Betong
Kapit
Saratok
Kuching
Lundu
Bandar Sri Aman
Tanjung Datu
2240
2988
Gunong Hose
Longnawan
Putussibau
Longiram

KALIMANTAN
Tanjungselor
Tanjung
Sangkulirang
Muarakaman
Tenggarong
Samarinda
Balikpapan

Bornео

B
A
R
A
T

Sekadau
Sintang
Nangapinoh
Semitau
Nangatayap
Ketapang
G. Saran
1758
Pegunungan
Schwaner
2278
Muarajuloi
Purukcahu
Muaratewe
Long Iram

E

0

Kepulauan
Banyak

Lhokkruet

Lubuksikaping
Payakumbuh
Bukittinggi
Padangpanjang
Padang
Solok
Sawahlunto
Muarabungo
Bangko
Sarolangun
Kerinci
3805
Sungaipenuh
Painan
Muaratebo
Muaratembesi
JAMBI
Jambi
Han
Rengat
Tebo
Lingga
Pasirkuning
Lingga
Kepulauan
Lingga
Belinyu
Sungailiat
Pangkalpinang
Bangka
Muntok
Taboali
Manggar
Dendang
Belitung
Tanjungpandan
Selat
Karimata
Nangabulik
Sukamara
Pangkalanbuun
Kumai
Kendawangan
Sampit
Palangkaraya
Buntok
Tanjung
Amuntai
Barabai
Kualakurun
Kualapembuang
Semuda
Kualakapuas
Kangan
1892
Besar

RIAU

BARAT

I
N
D
O
N
E
S
I
A

K
A
M
P
A
R

K

T
E
N
G
A
H

SELATAN
Banjarmasin
Martapura
Pagatan
Pelaihari
Jorong
Satui
Kotabaru
Sebuku
Karamb
Pulau Laut

Amuntai

Tanahgrogot
Tanjung
Balikpapan

Tanjung
Batu

F

INDIAN
OCEAN

Bengkulu
3159
Dempo
Lahat
Muaraenim
Curup
Tebing tinggi
Lubuklinggau
Sekayu
PALEMBANG
Sungaigerong
Perabumulih
Baturaja
Menggala
Manna
Mortabura
Kotabumi
6073
Tanjungkarang
Telukbetung
LAMPUNG
Kotaagung
Kalianda
Merak
Serang
Panaitan
Teluk Pelabuhan
Ratu
JAKARTA
Bogor
Sukabumi
BANDUNG
Tasikmalaya
Cilacap
Garut
Pelabuhanratu
Jatibarang
Purwakarta
Cirebon
Tegal
Pekalongan
Pemalong
Kendal
SEMARANG
Yogyakarta
Magelang
Surakarta
Kebumen
Slamet
3265
Madiun
Kediri
Tulungagung
Blitar
3670
Semeru
Malang
Banyuwangi
Jember
Probolinggo
Pasuruan
SURABAYA
Gresik
Bojonegoro
Bangkalan
Madura
Sampang
Sumenep
Tuban
Java
Trench
6650
2563

B
A
R
A
T

SELATAN

BENGKULU

Java Trench

Greater   Sunda   Islands
JAVA   SEA
Tanjung Puting
Tanjung Sambar
Tg. Selatan
Tg. Lumut
Kepulauan
Karimunjawa
Bawean
Sangkapura
Kepulauan
Kangean
Kepulauan
Masalembo
Kepulauan
Laut Kecil

Kepulauan
Masalembo

TIMUR

BALI
Singaraja
Rinjani
3726
3142
Denpasar
Agung
Proya
Mataram
Lombok
NUSA TENGGARA
BARAT

J   a   v   a
TENGAH
TIMUR

F

Projection: Mercator
1   **2**   **3**   East from Greenwich   **4**   **5**

ft m
12 000 4000
9000 3000
6000 2000
4500 1500
3000 1000
1200 400
600 200
0 0
200 600
2000 6000
4000 12 000
6000 18 000
8000 24 000
m ft

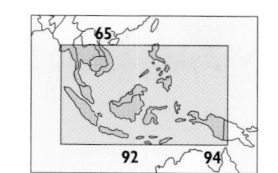

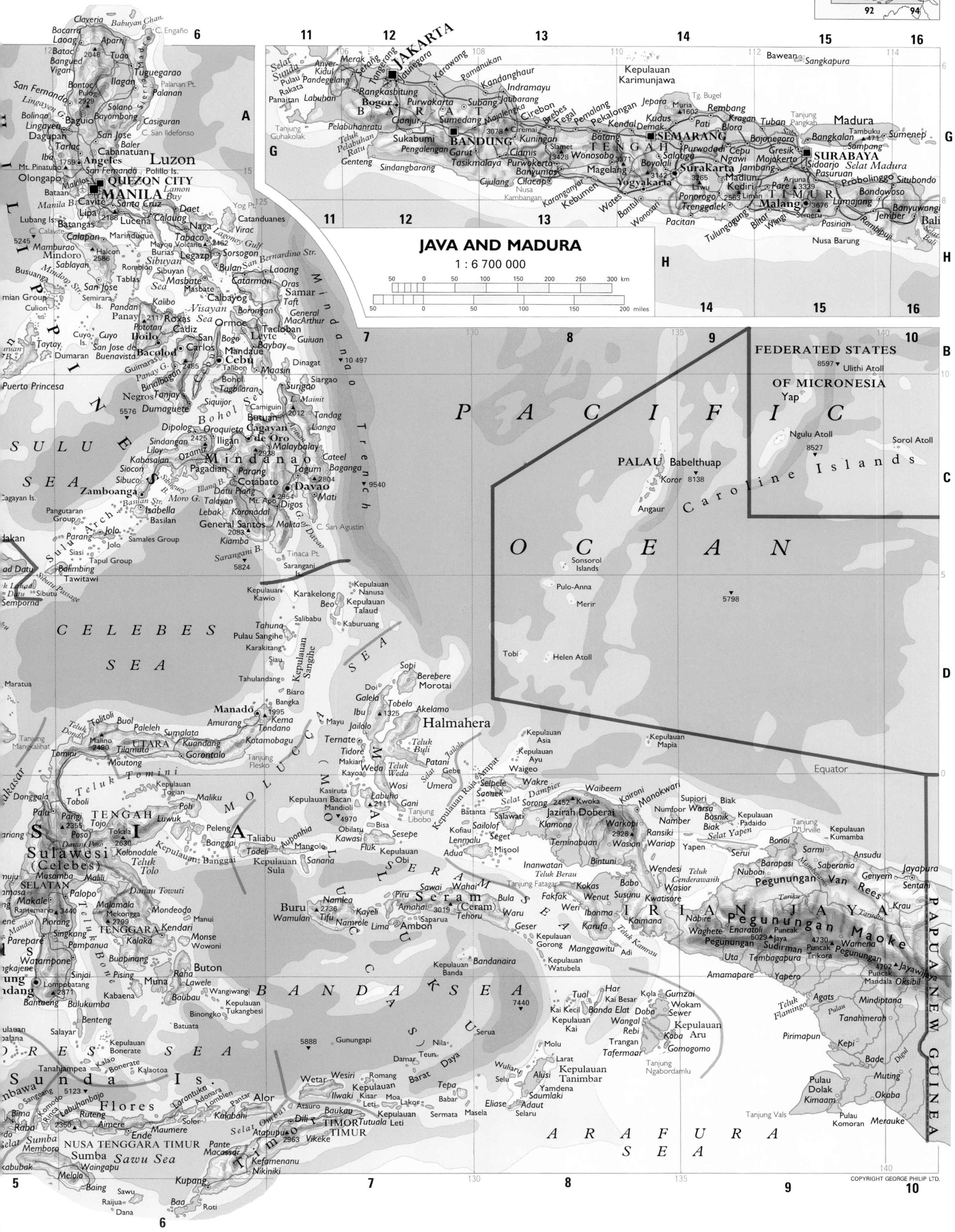

65
92 94

JAVA AND MADURA

1 : 6 700 000

50   0   50   100   150   200   250   300 km
50   0   50   100   150   200 miles

(Inset map – Java and Madura)

JAKARTA · Bogor · Rangkasbitung · Merak · Tangerang · Anyer Kidul · Pulau Rakata · Selat Sunda · Pandeglang · Labuhan · Panaitan · Pelabuhanratu · Teluk Pelabuhan Ratu · Tanjung Guhakolak · Sukabumi · Pengalengan · Genteng · Sindangbarang · BANDUNG · Garut · Tasikmalaya · Cijulang · Cilacap · Banyumas · Purwokerto · Purwakarta · Subang · Karawang · Pamanukan · Kandanghaur · Indramayu · Jatibarang · Majalengka · Sumedang · Cirebon · Kuningan · Ciamis · Ciremai 3078 · Brebes · Tegal · Pemalang · Pekalongan · Slamet 3428 · Wonosobo · Kebumen · Karanganyar · Kambangan · Nusa · Wates · Bantul · BARAT · TENGAH · Kedal · Demak · Kudus · Pati · Muria 1602 · Jepara · Rembang · Blora · Cepu · Ngawi · Purwodadi · Boyolali · Salatiga · SEMARANG · Magelang 3142 · Yogyakarta 3671 · Surakarta · Madiun · Ponorogo · Trenggalek · Pacitan · Tulungagung · Blitar · Kediri · Jambang · Mojokerto · SURABAYA · Gresik · Sidoarjo · Pasuruan · Pare · Arjuna 3339 · Malang 3676 · Semeru · Lumajang · Probolinggo · Bondowoso · Situbondo · Banyuwangi · Jember · Pasirian · TIMUR · Liman 2563 · Lawu 3265 · Bangkalan · Sampang · Tambuku · Sumenep · Madura · Kepulauan Karimunjawa · Bawean · Sangkapura · Tanjung Pangkah · Tuban · Kragan · Bojonegoro · Nusa Barung · Bali · Selat Bali

(Main map)

PHILIPPINE — Luzon · MANILA · QUEZON CITY · Angeles · Cabanatuan · Baguio · Vigan · Laoag · Aparri · Tuguegarao · San Fernando · Dagupan · Olongapo · Batangas · Lipa · Calapan · Mindoro · Naga · Legazpi · Sorsogon · Masbate · Samar · Tacloban · Leyte · Cebu · Bacolod · Iloilo · Panay · Negros · Dumaguete · Cagayan de Oro · Iligan · Mindanao · Cotabato · Davao · General Santos · Zamboanga · Basilan · Jolo · Sulu Arch.

SULU SEA · **CELEBES SEA** · Manado · Gorontalo · Sulawesi (Celebes) · Palu · Kendari · Makasar · Buton · Flores · Sumba · Kupang · TIMUR · TIMUR · Dili · NUSA TENGGARA TIMUR

PACIFIC OCEAN · **FEDERATED STATES OF MICRONESIA** · Yap · PALAU · Babelthuap · Koror · Angaur · Ulithi Atoll · Ngulu Atoll · Sorol Atoll · Caroline Islands · Sonsorol Islands · Pulo-Anna · Merir · Tobi · Helen Atoll · Equator

Halmahera · Ternate · Tidore · MOLUCCA SEA · Morotai · Tobelo · Galela · Buru · Seram (Ceram) · Ambon · SERAM SEA · BANDA SEA · Kepulauan Banda · Kepulauan Kai · Kepulauan Tanimbar · Kepulauan Aru · Dobo

IRIAN JAYA · Jazirah Doberai · Manokwari · Biak · Sorong · Fakfak · Nabire · Teluk Cenderawasih · Jayapura · Sentani · Pegunungan Van Rees · Pegunungan Maoke · Pegunungan Sudirman · Puncak Jaya 5029 · Jayawijaya · Wamena · Merauke · Tanahmerah · Agats · **PAPUA NEW GUINEA**

ARAFURA SEA

COPYRIGHT GEORGE PHILIP LTD.

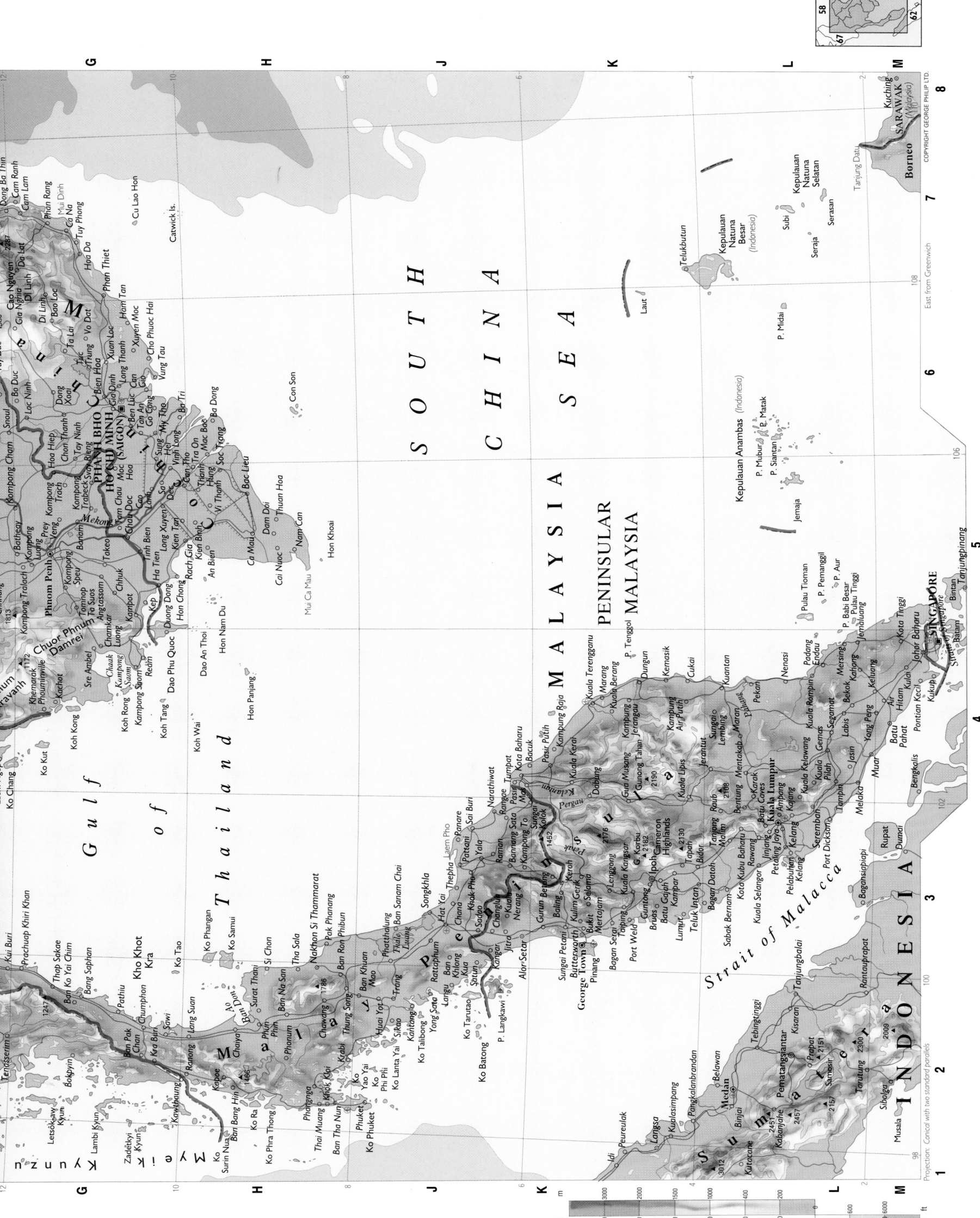

Continuation Southwards
on same scale

Projection: Conical with two standard parallels

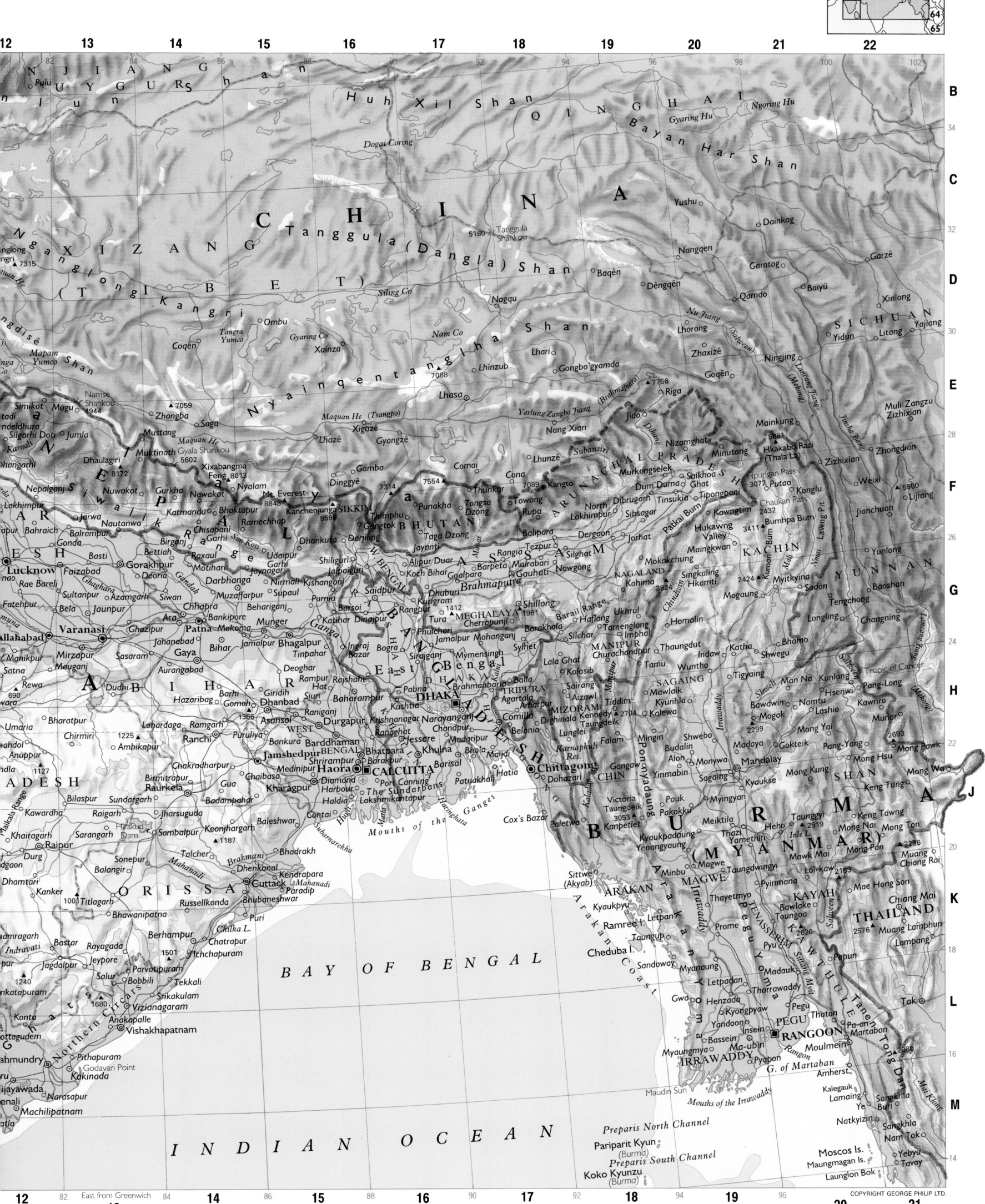

BAY OF BENGAL

INDIAN OCEAN

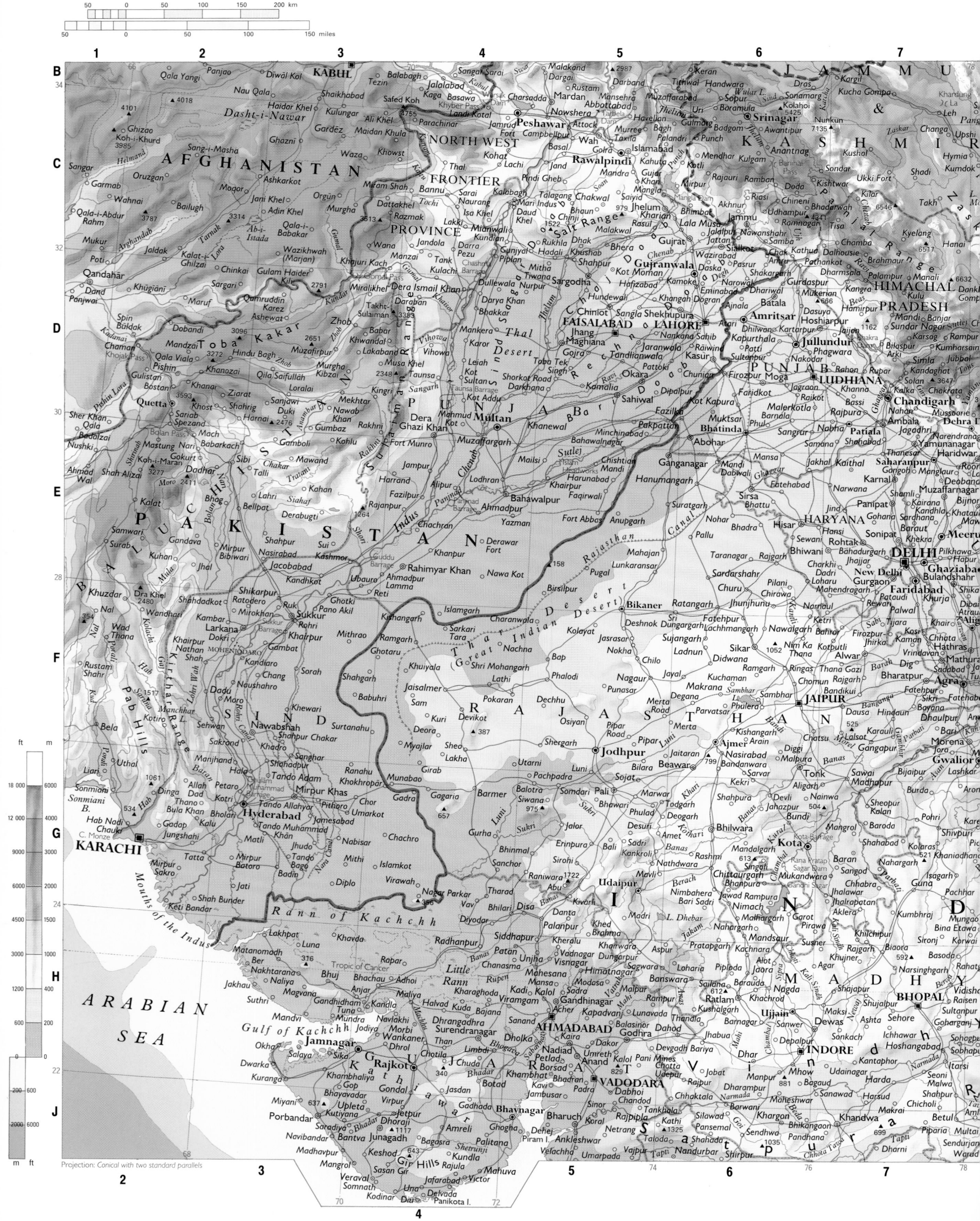

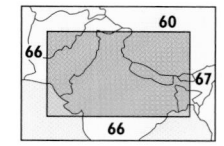

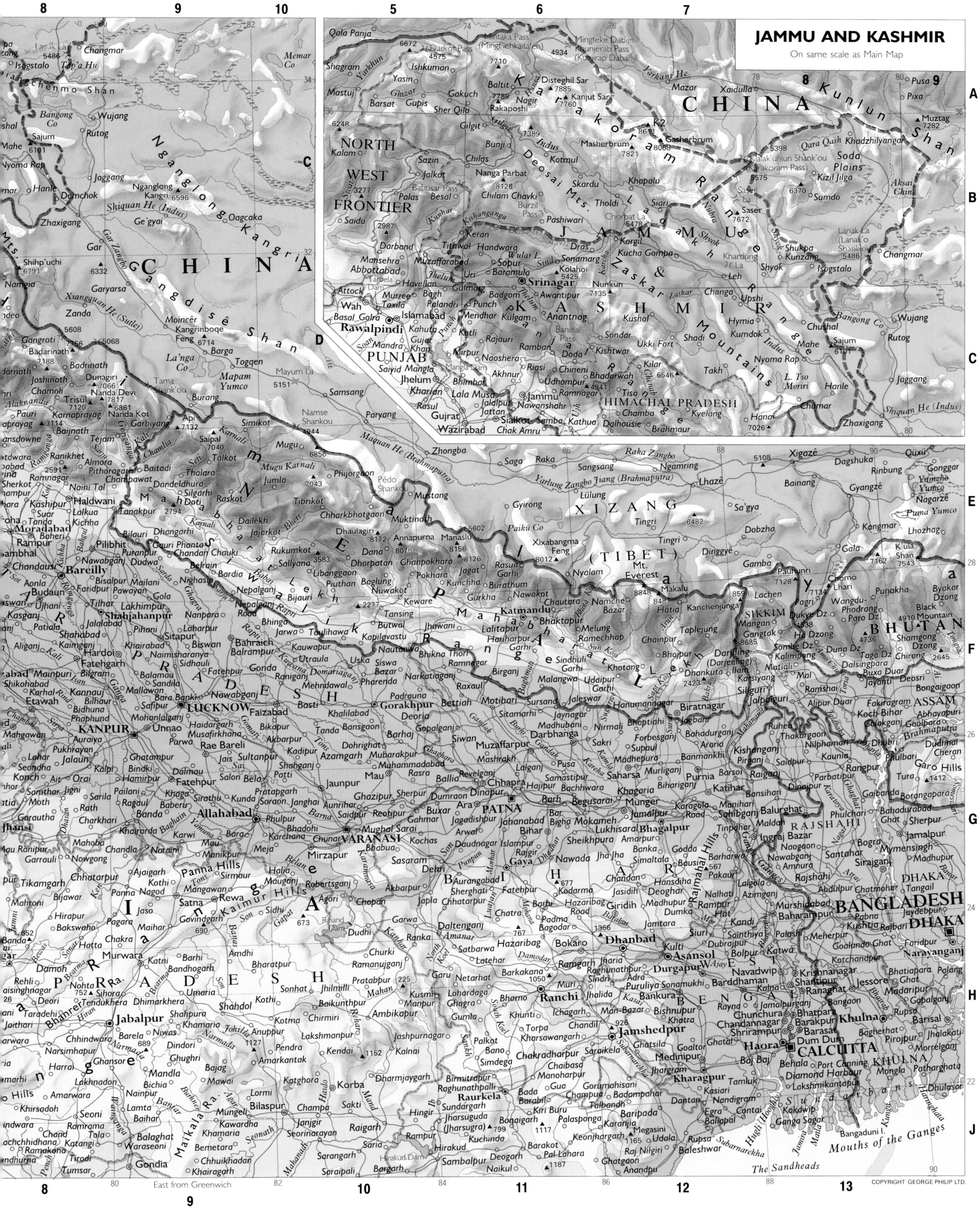

JAMMU AND KASHMIR
On same scale as Main Map

East from Greenwich

COPYRIGHT GEORGE PHILIP LTD.

CHINA

JAMMU & KASHMIR

NORTH WEST FRONTIER

PUNJAB

HIMACHAL PRADESH

XIZANG (TIBET)

NEPAL

UTTAR PRADESH

BIHAR

WEST BENGAL

BANGLADESH

DHAKA

BHUTAN

SIKKIM

ASSAM

RAJSHAHI

KHULNA

INDIA

MADHYA PRADESH

Srinagar
Rawalpindi
Islamabad
Jammu
Sialkot
Lahore

Mt. Everest 8848

K2 8611

Nanga Parbat 8126

Kanchenjunga 8598

Lucknow
Kanpur
Allahabad
Varanasi
Patna
Calcutta
Haora
Jabalpur
Ranchi
Jamshedpur
Dhanbad
Asansol
Durgapur
Khulna
Kharagpur
Raurkela
Bareilly
Moradabad

Mouths of the Ganges

The Sandheads

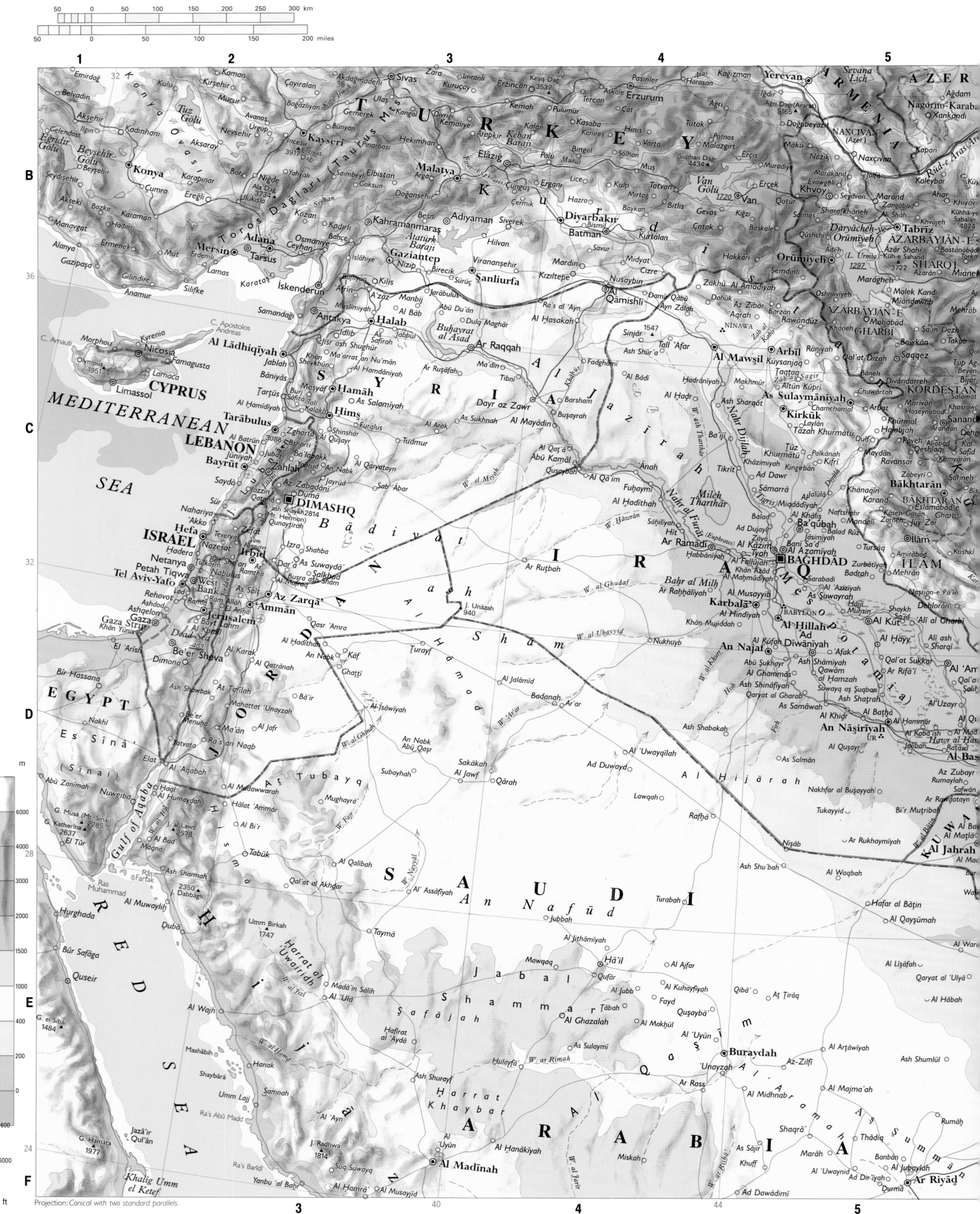

Projection: Conical with two standard parallels

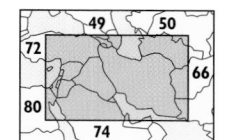

50   0   25   50   75   100 125 150 175 km
50   0   25   50   75   100 125 miles

BULGARIA

B L A C K   S E A

Thrace

Marmara Denizi (Sea of Marmara)

İSTANBUL

İstanbul Boğazı (Bosporus)

Dardanelles

Paphlagonia

Küre Dağları

Bithynia

Köroğlu Dağları

ANKARA

A   n   a   d   o   l   u

Anatolia

Cappadocia

Lydia

Phrygia

Pisidia

Pamphylia

Lycia

Toros Dağları

Cilicia

T   U   R   K

GREECE

Dhodhekánisos

Ródhos (Rhodes)

M E D I T E R R A N E A N
S E A

CYPRUS

Troodos

Olympus

Nicosia

Al Lādhiqīyah (Latakia)

S Y

Ḥamāh

Ḥimṣ (Homs)

Ṭarābulus (Tripoli)

LEBANON

BAYRŪT (Beirut)

DIMASHQ (Damascus)

ISRAEL

Tel Aviv-Yafo

Jerusalem

AMMAN

Az Zarqā

JORDA

Projection: Conical with two standard parallels

Division between Greeks and Turks in Cyprus; Turks to the North.

47 49
41
39 71
80 70
13

CASPIAN SEA

RUSSIA
GEORGIA
Caucasus Mountains
KABARDINO-BALKARIA
NORTH OSSETIA
INGUSHETIA
CHECHENIA
DAGESTAN

ABKHAZIA
ADJARIA
ARMENIA
AZERBAIJAN
NAXCIVAN (Azerbaijan)

TURKEY
IRAN
IRAQ
SYRIA

Sochi
Matsesta
Adler
Gagra
Bichvinta
Guadauta
Novyy Afon
Sokhumi
Ochamchira
Gali
Zugdidi
Anaklia
Senaki
Poti
Kobuleti
Batumi
Hopa
Arhavi
Pazar
Ardeşen
Çayeli
Rize
Of
Trabzon
Tirebolu
Görele
Eynesil
Vakfıkebir
Akçaabat
Sürmene
Araklı
Espiye
Giresun
Dereli
Tonya
İkizdere
Gümüşhane
Anadolu Dağları
Bayburt
Kelkit
Şiran
Refahiye
Erzincan
Kemah
İliç
Kemaliye
Munzur Dağları
Çemişgezek
Keban Barajı
Keban
Pertek
Elâzığ
Maden
Ergani
Çermik
Siverek
Diyarbakır
Bismil
Batman
Kurtalan
Siirt
Kozluk
Silvan
Güneydoğu Toroslar
Hakkâri Dağları
Mardin
Midyat
Cizre
Silopi
Zakhū
Al Qāmishlī
Al Ḥasakah

Teberda
Elbrus 5642
Tyrnyauz
Baksan
Alagir
Ardon
Sadon
Kazbek
Groznyy
Argun
Shali
Khasavyurt
Kizil Yurt
Buynaksk
Makhachkala
Kaspiysk
Izberbash
Derbent

Madikavkaz
South Ossetia
Tskhinvali
Dusheti
Gori
Kaspi
Mtskheta
Telavi
TBILISI
Rustavi
Marneuli
Shulaveri

KUTAISI
Samtredia
Chiatura
Khashuri
Borjomi
Akhaltsikhe
Akhalkalaki
Vale
Khulo
Çıldır
Ardahan
Artvin
Borçka
Şavşat
Ardanuç
Olur
Oltu
Şenkaya
Narman
Kars
Sarıkamış
Selim
Digor
Kağızman
Tuzluca
Iğdır
Ağrı
Eleşkirt
Taşlıçay
Doğubayazıt
Ararat

YEREVAN
Yejmiadzin
Artik
Gyumri
Vanadzor
Dilijan
Sevana Lich
Kamo
Hrazdan
Martuni
Yeghegnadzor
Goris
Kapan
Naxçıvan
Culfa
Ordubad
Jolfa

GÄNCÄ
Mingäçevir
Su Anbarı
Xanlar
Daşkäsän
Bärdä
Tärtär
Nagorno-Karabakh
Xankändi

BAKI
Sumqayıt
Maştağa
Surakhany
Artyom
Qusar
Quba
Däväçi
Siyäzän
Xaçmaz
Xudat
Şäki
Kutkashen
Qäbälä
Göyçay
Şamaxı
Ağsu
Kürdämir
Sabirabad
Äli Bayramlı
Salyan
Neftçala
Bäläsuvar

Van Gölü
Van
Muş
Bitlis
Tatvan
Ahlat
Adilcevaz
Süphan Dağı
Malazgirt
Bulanık
Varto
Hınıs
Ağrı
Muş
Patnos
Erciş
Muradiye
Özalp
Başkale
Hakkâri
Yüksekova
Şemdinli
Çatak
Gürpınar

Khvoy
Marand
Tabriz
Maragheh
Orümiyeh (Urmia)
Daryächeh-ye Orümiyeh (Lake Urmia)
Salmäs
Qotur
Seydvän
Nāzik

Erbil
Al Mawṣil (Mosul)
Tall 'Afar
Sinjar
Al Ḥaḍr
Ash Sharqāt
Makhmūr
Kirkūk
As Sulaymāniyah
Chamchamal
Halabjah
Tāzah Khurmātū
Tūz Khurmātū

Ardabīl
Rasht
Bandar-e Anzalī
Tālesh
Astara
Nīr
Sarāb
Mīāneh
Zanjān
Abhar
Saqqez
Baneh
Sanandaj
Marīvān
Bījār
Bāne
Dīvāndarreh
Qorveh
Bāhar
Hamadān
Bākhtarān
Bīsotūn
Asadābād
Tūysarkān
Malāyer
Nahāvand
Oshtorīnān
Borūjerd
Khorramābād
Īlām
Dezfūl
Andīmeshk
Shūsh

Nahr al Furāt (Euphrates)
Al Jazīrah (Mesopotamia)
Dayr az Zawr
Ar Raqqah
Ma'dīn
Abū Kamāl
Al Qā'im
'Ānah
Hīt
Ramādī
Al Fallūjah
BAGHDĀD
Sāmarrā'
Tikrīt
Bayjī
Ad Dawr
Balad
Ba'qūbah
Karbalā'
An Najaf
Al Ḥillah
Al Kūfah
Ad Dīwānīyah
Al Amārah
Al Kūt
Nahr Dijlah (Tigris)
Mileh Tharthār

Ararat Dağı 5165
Aragats 4090
Kızıl Dağ 3192
Tebulos 4492
Kazbek 5047
Elbrus 5642
4789
4046
5203

East from Greenwich

ft m
9000 3000
6000 2000
4500 1500
3000 1000
1500 500
600 200
200 0
0
50 150
100 300
200 600
500 1500
1000 3000
2000 6000
3000 9000
m ft

8 9 10 11 12 13
A B C D E F G

100 0 100 200 300 400 500 600 km
100 0 100 200 300 400 miles

LEBANON
BAYRŪT
ISRAEL
Tel Aviv-Yafo
Ashdod
Jerusalem
Bûr Sa'îd
Ismâ'iliya
El Suweis
SYRIA
DIMASHQ
Hefa
AMMAN
West Bank
Ma'ān
Al 'Aqabah
Jabal ad Duruz 1801
IRAQ
Ar Rutbah
Karbalā
An Najaf
An Nāşirīyah
BAGHDĀD
Al Amarah
Al Başrah
Ābādān
Khorramshahr
EŞFAHĀN
4548
IRAN
Khvor
Bīrjand
Farāh
AFGHANISTAN
Yazd
Zābol
Daryācheh-ye Seistan

EGYPT
Hurghada
Bûr Safâga
Qena
Quseir
Idfû
Kôm Ombo
Aswân
Sadd el Aali
G. Mûsa 2637
Es Sinâ'
2578
Tabûk
Al Muwaylih
Al Wajh
Ras Bânâs
Bîr Shalatein
Halaib
Ras Hadarba

Al Jawf
Rafhā
Hafar al Bāţin
Hā'il
Buraydah
'Unayzah
An Nafūd
Ḥijāz

SAUDI ARABIA
AR RIYĀḌ
Al Madīnah
Yanbu 'al Bahr
Tropic of Cancer
Makkah
Aţ Ţā'if 2565
Al Līth
Turabah
Muhammad Qol 2259
JIDDAH
As Sulayyil
Laylá
Al 'Ubaylah

KUWAIT
Al Kuwayt
J. Khārk
Būbiyān
Kāzerūn
Būshehr
Deyyer
Jahrom
Shīrāz
Neyrīz
PERSEPOLIS
Bandar 'Abbās
Khamīr
Qeshm
Str. of Hormuz
Ra's Musandam (Oman)
Gābrīk
Bampūr
Kermān
Zāhedān
Bam

Ad Dammām
Al Qaţīf
BAHRAIN
Al Manāmah
QATAR
Al Mubarraz
Al Hufūf
Ad Dawḩah
Harad
Abū Ẓaby
Ra's al-Khaymah
Ash Shāriqah
Dubayy
UNITED ARAB EMIRATES
Gulf of Oman
3019
Nazwá
Maţraḩ
Masqaţ
Şūr
Ras al Hadd
OMAN
Khalūf
Maşīrah
Khalīj Maşīrah

The Gulf

RED SEA

Es Sahrâ en Nûbiy a
Kosha
3rd Cataract
Delgo
Dongola
4th Cataract
Kareima
Ed Debba
Wadi Halfa
Buheirat en Naser
Abu Hamed
Berber
Atbara
5th Cataract
Shendî
6th Cataract
Wad Hamid
Bûr Sûdân
Suakin
Sinkat
Trinkitat
Haiya
Karora 2780
Adarama

SUDAN
Omdurmân
El Khartûm
Kassalâ
Khashm el Girba
Wad Medanî
Gedaref
El Gezira
Ed Dueim
Wad Medanî
Singa
Nil el Azraq
Kôsti
Umm Ruwaba
Ed Damazin
Malakâl
Nekemte
Dembidolo
Metu
Gore
3202
Sûdd
Bahr el Jebel
Pibor Post
Bôr
Tali Post
Juba
Mongalla
Kapoeta
Yei
Kajo Kaji 3187
Torit
UGANDA
Arua
Gulu
Lira
Moroto
Pakwach
Soroti
919
Murchison Falls
L. Albert
L. Kyoga
Masindi
Mbale
Kitale 4321
3206
3084

ERITREA
Akordat
Asmera
Adigrat
Aksum
Adwa
-116
Mekele
Nakfa
Dahlak Kebir
Massawa
Zula
Danakil Desert
Djebel Manar 3550
Aseb

ETHIOPIA
ADDIS ABEBA
Debre Zeyit
Awash
Nazret
3381
Harer
Jijiga
Ras Dashen 4620
Gonder
Lalibela 4190
1830
L. Tana
Debre Tabor
Bahir Dar
Bure
Dese
Debre Markos
Dire Dawa
3686
Jima
Awasa
Yirga Alem
Mt. Batu 4307
Goba
Shashemene
Asela
Ginir
Omo
Dila
Kibre Mengist
Negele
L. Abaya
L. Shamo
Arba Minch
Ziway
Chew Bahir
375
L. Turkana
Mega
Moyale
El Wak
Imi
Kebri Dehar
Scebeli
Ogaden
Ferfer
Dolo
Lugh Ganana
Baidoa
Bur Acaba
Genale
Giuba
Wabi Scebeli

SOMALI REP.
Berbera
Bosaso
Ras Asir
Bereda
Karin
Erigavo
Las Anod
Burao
Hargeisa
Gardo
Bender Beila
El Gal
Dante 2406
Ras Hafun
Garoe
Eil
Galcaio
Sinadogo
Obbia
Belet Uen
El Dere
MUQDISHO
Merca

YEMEN
Sana'
Ta'izz
Al Ḩudaydah
Al Luḩayyah
Kamaran
Hanish
Khamir 2469
Nişāb
Shibām
Ḩadramawt
Sayhūt
Rās Fartak
Al Mukallā
Al Mukhā
Shaqrā
Aḩwar
Bab el Mandeb
Al' Adan
Gulf of Aden
Abd al Kūrī
Hadibu
Socotra (Yemen)

DJIBOUTI
Tadjoura
Djibouti
-155
Dikhil
Zeila
L. Abbé
Tendaho
-116

JORDAN
Badiyat ash Shām
al Mesopotamia
Nahr al Furāt
Nahr Dijlah

Rub' al Khālī (Empty Quarter)
Zufār
Khalīj Masīrah
Ras al Madrakah
J. Khurīyā Murīyā

Abha
Jizān
Farasān

KENYA
Malakâl
Lodwar
Marsabit
Wajir
Dif
South Horn
Bardera
Moyale

Asīr
Hijāz
Dashte Lut

Kûhhā ye Zagros

INDIAN OCEAN

ft m
12 000 4000
9000 3000
6000 2000
4500 1500
3000 1000
1200 400
600 200
0 0
200 600
1000 3000
2000 6000
4000 12 000
m ft

Projection : Sanson-Flamsteed's Sinusoidal

East from Greenwich

COPYRIGHT GEORGE PHILIP LTD.

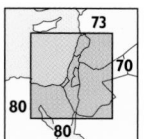

1974 Cease Fire Lines

COPYRIGHT GEORGE PHILIP LTD.

Projection: Polyconic

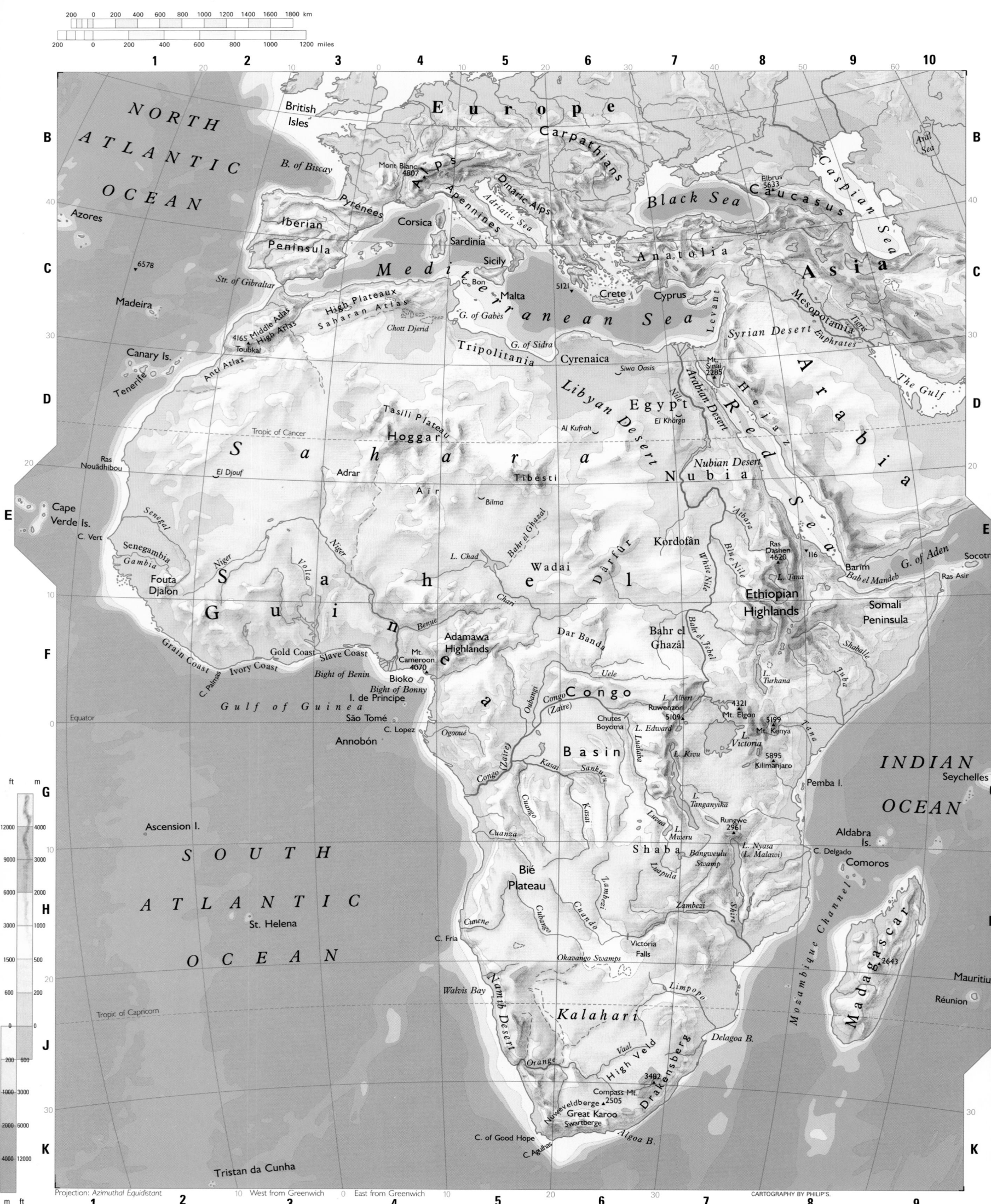

200 0 200 400 600 800 1000 1200 1400 1600 1800 km
200 0 200 400 600 800 1000 1200 miles

NORTH
A T L A N T I C
O C E A N

British
Isles

E u r o p e

Carpathians

B. of Biscay

Mont Blanc
4807

Alps

Dinaric Alps

Adriatic Sea

Apennines

Black Sea

Caucasus

Elbrus
5633

Caspian
Sea

Aral
Sea

Azores

6578

Pyrénées

Iberian
Peninsula

Corsica

Sardinia

Sicily

C. Bon

Anatolia

A s i a

Madeira

Str. of Gibraltar

High Plateaux
Saharan Atlas

Malta

Crete

Cyprus

Levant

Mesopotamia

Tigris

Canary Is.

4165 Middle Atlas
High Atlas
Toubkal

Chott Djerid

G. of Gabès

M e d i t e r r a n e a n   S e a

5121

Euphrates

Tenerife

Ant. Atlas

G. of Sidra

Syrian Desert

A r a b i a

Tripolitania

Cyrenaica

Mt.
Sinai
2285

The Gulf

Ras
Nouâdhibou

Tasili Plateau

Tropic of Cancer

Hoggar

Siwa Oasis

Libyan Desert

Egypt

El Kharga

Nile

Arabian Desert

Hejaz

Red Sea

El Djouf

Adrar

S a h a r a

Air

Bilma

Tibesti

Al Kufrah

Nubian Desert

N u b i a

**Cape
Verde Is.**

C. Vert

Senegal

Senegambia

Gambia

Fouta
Djalon

S
a
G
u
i
n

Niger

Volta

Niger

L. Chad

Bahr el Ghazal

Chari

Wadai

Kordofân

Darfûr

White Nile

Blue Nile

Atbara

Ras
Dashen
4620

116

L. Tana

Barim
Bab el Mandeb

G. of Aden

Socotra

Ras Asir

**Ethiopian
Highlands**

**Somali
Peninsula**

Grain Coast

Gold Coast

Slave Coast

Ivory Coast

C. Palmas

Bight of Benin

Benue

Mt.
Cameroon
4070

Bioko

Adamawa
Highlands

Dar Banda

Uele

Bahr el
Ghazâl

Bahr el Jebel

Shabelle

Jilib

Bight of Bonny

I. de Principe

Oubangui

Congo
(Zaïre)

L. Albert

Ruwenzori
5094

Mt. Elgon

4321

L. Turkana

Gulf   of   Guinea

São Tomé

Equator

C. Lopez

Annobón

Ogooué

Congo

Basin

Congo (Zaïre)

Chutes
Boyoma

Kasai

Sankuru

L. Edward

Lualaba

L. Kivu

L. Victoria

Mt. Kenya
5199

Kilimanjaro
5895

Tana

INDIAN
OCEAN

Seychelles

Ascension I.

Cuango

Kasai

L.
Tanganyika

Pemba I.

Cuanza

Lucua

Rungwe
2961

Aldabra
Is.

S O U T H

A T L A N T I C

St. Helena

Bié
Plateau

Shaba

L. Mweru

Bangweulu
Swamp

L. Nyasa
(L. Malawi)

C. Delgado

Comoros

O C E A N

Cunene

C. Fria

Cubango

Zambezi

Luapula

Zambezi

Shire

Victoria
Falls

Okavango Swamps

Kalahari

Limpopo

Walvis Bay

Namib Desert

Tropic of Capricorn

Cuando

Vaal

High Veld

Drakensberg

Delagoa B.

M a d a g a s c a r

2643

Mauritius

Réunion

Mozambique Channel

Orange

Compass Mt.
3482
2505

Nuweveldberge
Great Karoo
Swartberge

Algoa B.

C. of Good Hope

C. Agulhas

Projection: *Azimuthal Equidistant*

West from Greenwich

East from Greenwich

Tristan da Cunha

CARTOGRAPHY BY PHILIP'S.

ft   m

12000 4000
9000 3000
6000 2000
3000 1000
1500 500
600 200
0 0
200 600
1000 3000
2000 6000
4000 12000

m ft

200 0 200 400 600 800 1000 1200 1400 1600 1800 km
200 0 200 400 600 800 1000 1200 miles

1 2 3 4 5 6 7 8 9 10

NORTH
ATLANTIC
OCEAN

UNITED
KINGDOM
LONDON
NETH.
GERMANY POLAND
Warsaw
BELG.
PARIS
FRANCE
CZECH REP.
Prague
Vienna
SWITZ.
AUSTRIA HUNGARY
SLOVAK REP.
Kiev
UKRAINE
RUSSIA
Volgograd
KAZAKSTAN
Aral Sea

B. of Biscay
CROATIA
BOS.-
HERZ.
ROMANIA
Odessa
GEORGIA
Caspian Sea

Azores
(Port.)
Madrid
PORTUGAL
SPAIN
Lisbon
Corsica
ITALY
Rome
Sardinia
ADRIATIC Sea
ALB.
YUG.
MAC.
BULGARIA
GREECE
Athens
Ankara
TURKEY
ARM.
AZER.
Baku
TURKMEN.
TEHRÃN

Madeira
(Port.)
Rabat
Tetouan
Fès
Casablanca
MOROCCO
Marrakesh
Algiers
Annaba
Constantine
TUNISIA
Tunis
Sfax
MALTA
Crete
CYPRUS
Aleppo
SYRIA
Mosul
Eşfahãn
IRAN

Canary Is.
(Sp.)
Chott Djerid
Tripoli
Misrātah
Benghazi
Alexandria
Port Said
Tel Aviv-Jaffa
LEB.
Damascus
Jerusalem
Baghdãd
IRAQ
Basra

El Aaiún
WESTERN SAHARA
ALGERIA
LIBYA
EGYPT
CAIRO
El Faiyûm
Suez
ISRAEL
JORDAN
Syrian Desert
KUWAIT

Dakhla
Fdérik
In Salah
Marzûq
Al Jawf
Asyût
Aswân
SAUDI
ARABIA
Medina
Riyadh
BAHRAIN
QATAR
The Gulf

Ras Nouâdhibou
Sahara
Wadi Halfa
Port Sudan
Jedda
Mecca

PE VERDE IS.
MAURITANIA
Nouakchott
NIGER
CHAD
Omdurmân
Khartoum
Atbara
'Atbara
Mesewa
ERITREA
Asmera
YEMEN
Socotra
(Yemen)
Ras Asir

St-Louis
C. Vert
Dakar
SENEGAL
GAMBIA
Banjul
GUINEA-BISSAU
Bissau
Senegal
MALI
Tombouctou
Agadès
L. Chad
Abéché
Ndjamena
El Fâsher
SUDAN
El Obeid
Wâd Medani
Blue Nile
White Nile
L. Tana
DJIBOUTI
Djibouti
G. of Aden

Praia
GUINEA
Conakry
Bámako
Niamey
Kano
Maiduguri
Chari
Malakâl
Wau
Addis Ababa
Harer
Berbera

SIERRA LEONE
Freetown
Bobo-Dioulasso
BURKINA FASO
Ouagadougou
BENIN
NIGERIA
Abuja
Bahr el Jebel
ETHIOPIA
L. Turkana
Shabelle
SOMALI REP.

LIBERIA
Monrovia
Yamoussoukro
IVORY COAST
Bouaké
Kumasi
GHANA
TOGO
Lomé
Ibadan
Enugu
Benue
CENTRAL AFRICAN REP.
Bangui
Mogadishu

Abidjan
Sekondi-Takoradi
Accra
Porto Novo
Lagos
BIGHT OF BENIN
Port Harcourt
CAMEROON
Douala
Yaoundé
Congo (Zaïre)
Ubangi
Kisangani
L. Albert
UGANDA
Kampala
KENYA
Kismayu

EQUATORIAL GUINEA
Malabo
Libreville
SÃO TOMÉ & PRÍNCIPE
C. Lopez
GABON
CONGO
CONGO (DEM. REP. OF THE)
Mbandaka
L. Edward
RWANDA
Kigali
L. Kivu
L. Victoria
Kisumu
Nairobi

Gulf of Guinea
Equator
Annobón
Ascension I.
(U.K.)
Brazzaville
Pointe-Noire
CABINDA (Angola)
Kinshasa
Matadi
Kasai
BURUNDI
Bujumbura
L. Tanganyika
TANZANIA
Dodoma
Zanzibar
Mombasa
Dar es Salaam
INDIAN
OCEAN
SEYCHELLES

Luanda
Congo (Zaïre)
Cuango
Karianga
L. Mweru
ANGOLA
Likasi
Lubumbashi
L. Malawi
MALAWI
C. Delgado
Moroni
COMOROS
Antsiranana

SOUTH
ATLANTIC
OCEAN
St. Helena
(U.K.)
Lobito
Huambo
Namibe
Cunene
Cubango
Ndola
ZAMBIA
Lusaka
Lilongwe
Blantyre
Zambezi
MOZAMBIQUE
Moçambique
Mayotte
(Fr.)
Mahajanga
Toamasina

C. Fria
Livingstone
Harare
ZIMBABWE
Bulawayo
Beira
Mozambique Channel
Antananarivo
MADAGASCAR
MAURITIUS
Port Louis

NAMIBIA
Windhoek
BOTSWANA
Limpopo
Fianarantsoa
Réunion
(Fr.)

Tropic of Capricorn
Gaborone
Johannesburg
Pretoria
Vaal
Maputo
SWAZ.
Mbabane
Kimberley
Orange
Maseru
LESOTHO
Durban

SOUTH AFRICA
Cape Town
C. of Good Hope
C. Agulhas
Port Elizabeth
East London

Tristan da Cunha
(U.K.)

Projection: Azimuthal Equidistant
West from Greenwich East from Greenwich
Dakar Capital Cities
COPYRIGHT GEORGE PHILIP LTD.

1 2 3 4 5 6 7 8 9

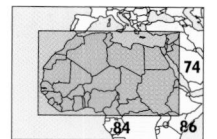

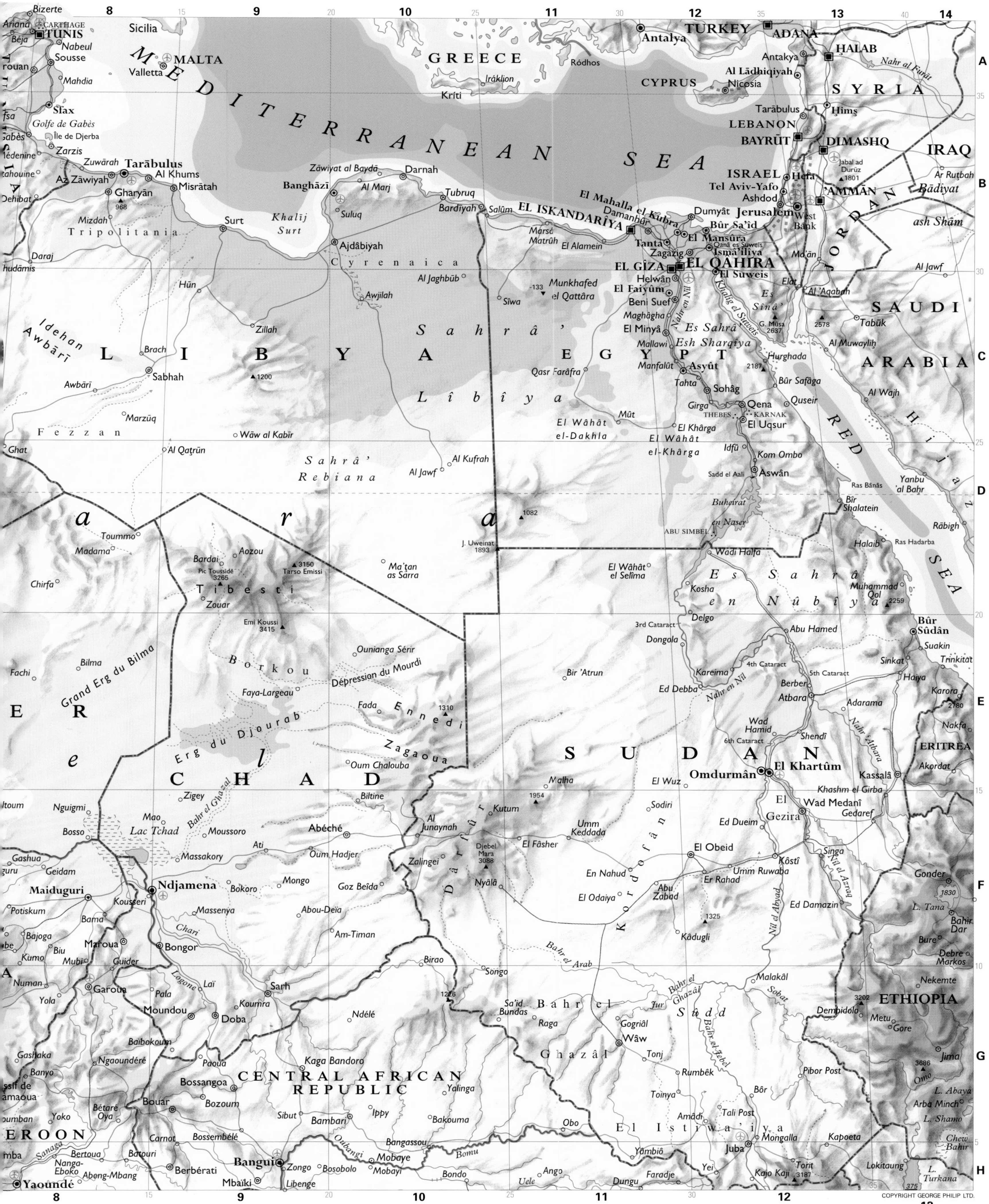

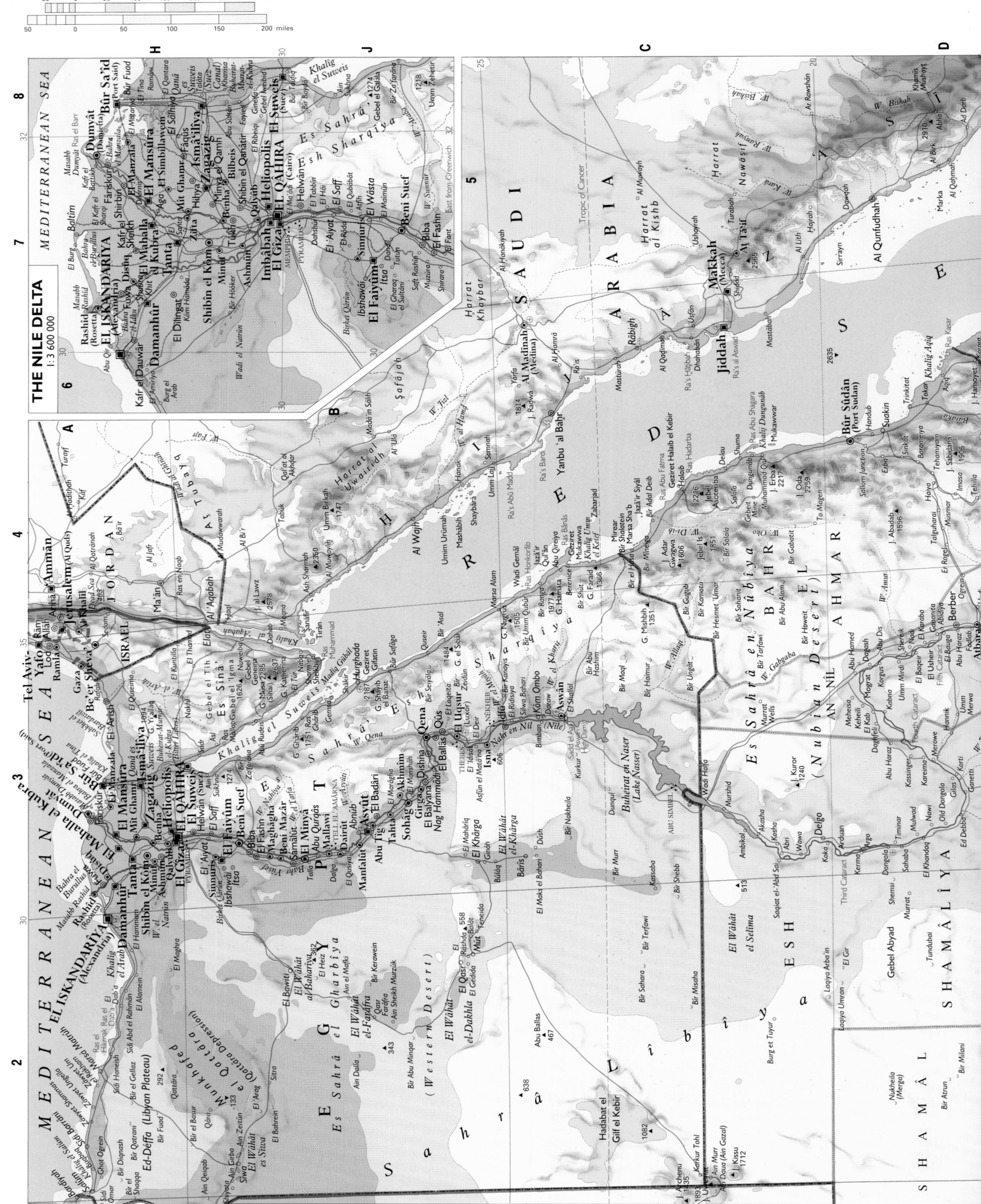

THE NILE DELTA
1:3 600 000

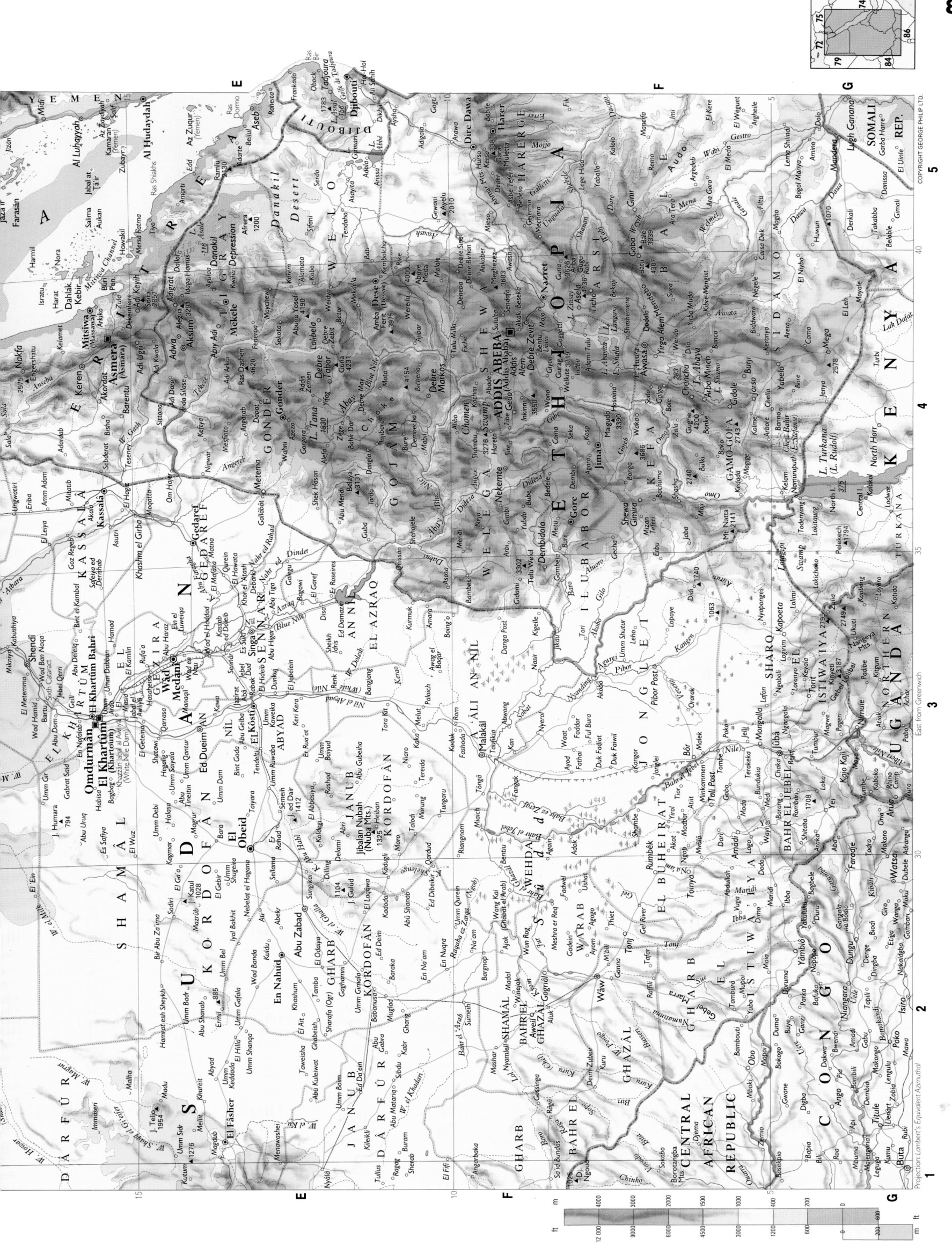

East from Greenwich

Projection: Lambert's Equivalent Azimuthal

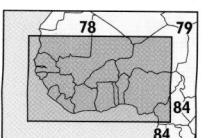

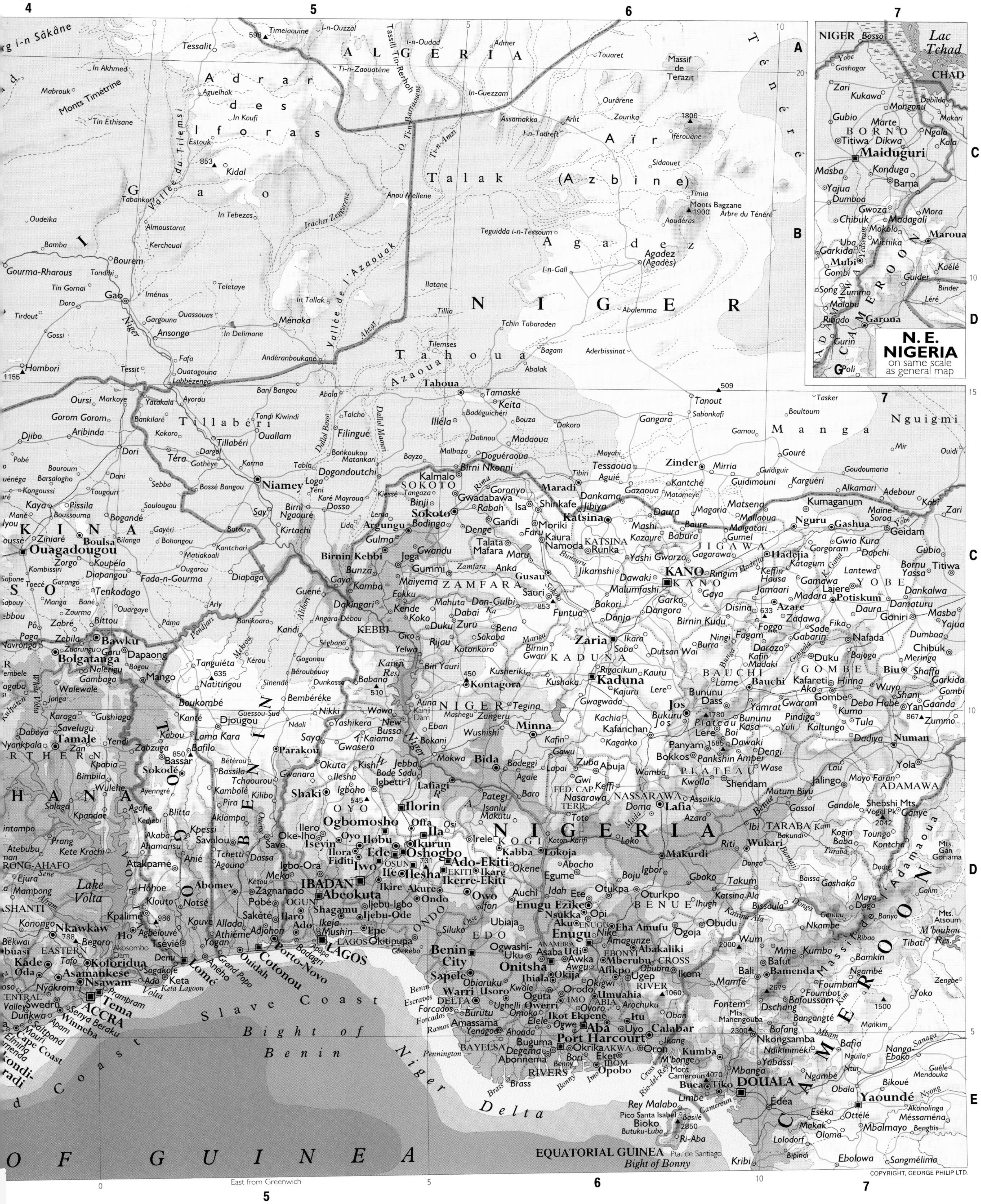

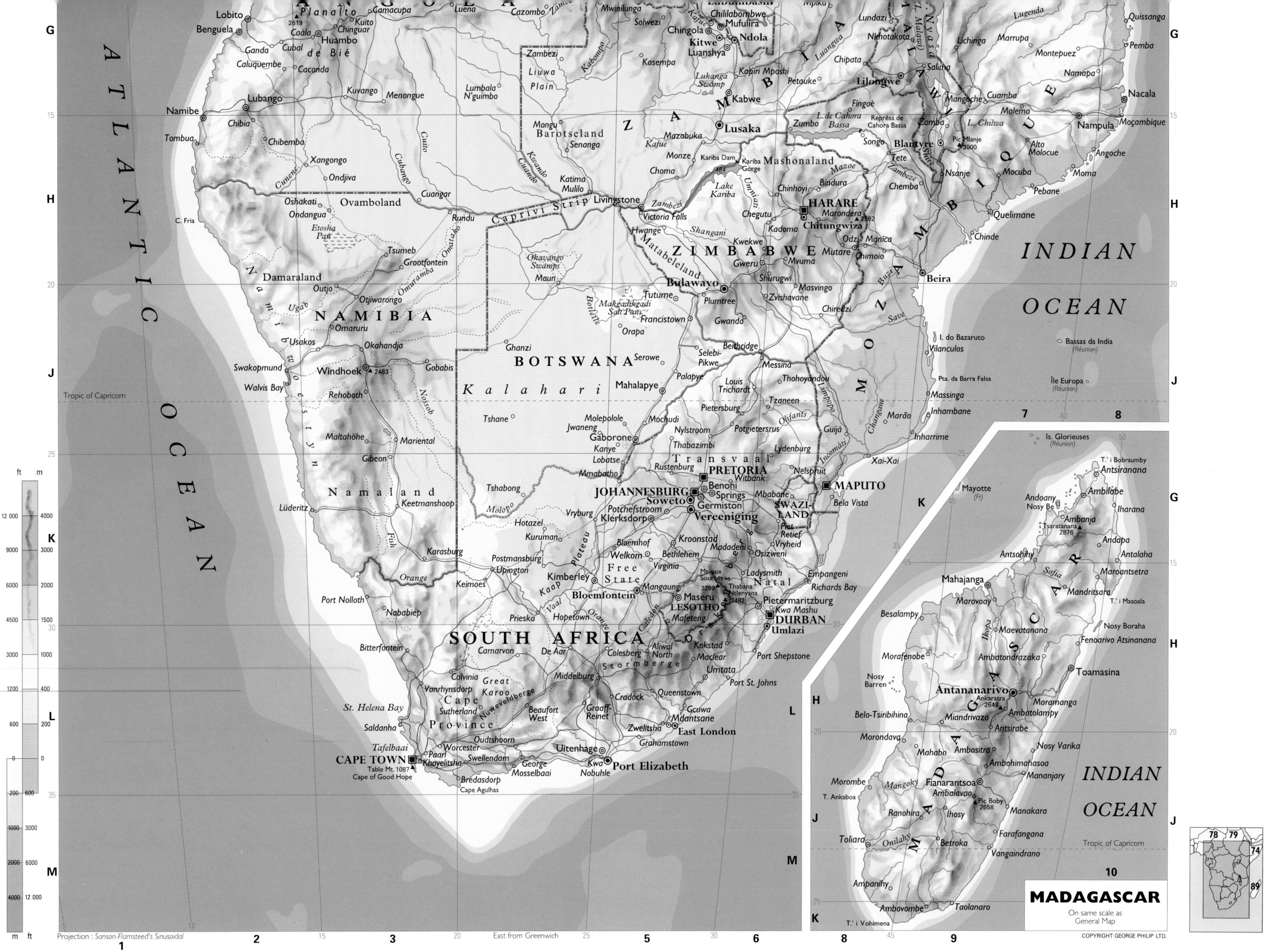

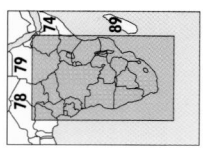

MADAGASCAR
On same scale as
General Map

COPYRIGHT GEORGE PHILIP LTD.

INDIAN OCEAN

ATLANTIC OCEAN

INDIAN OCEAN

ANGOLA

NAMIBIA

BOTSWANA

SOUTH AFRICA

ZIMBABWE

ZAMBIA

MALAWI

MOZAMBIQUE

LESOTHO

SWAZILAND

Transvaal

Natal

Free State

Cape Province

Kalahari

Namaland

Damaraland

Ovamboland

Barotseland

Matabeleland

Mashonaland

Caprivi Strip

Tropic of Capricorn

East from Greenwich

Projection: Sanson Flamsteed's Sinusoidal

CAPE TOWN
Cape of Good Hope
Cape Agulhas
Port Elizabeth
East London
DURBAN
PRETORIA
JOHANNESBURG
Soweto
Vereeniging
MAPUTO
HARARE
Bulawayo
Lusaka
Blantyre
Lilongwe
Beira
Windhoek
Gaborone
Bloemfontein
Kimberley
Maseru
Pietermaritzburg
Victoria Falls
Livingstone
Walvis Bay
Lüderitz
Nacala
Nampula
Quelimane

Antananarivo
Toamasina
Mahajanga
Fianarantsoa
Antsiranana
Toliara
Taolanaro

Tropic of Capricorn

ft m
12 000 4000
9000 3000
6000 2000
4500 1500
3000 1000
1200 400
600 200
0 0
200 - 600
1000 - 3000
2000 - 6000
4000 - 12 000
m ft

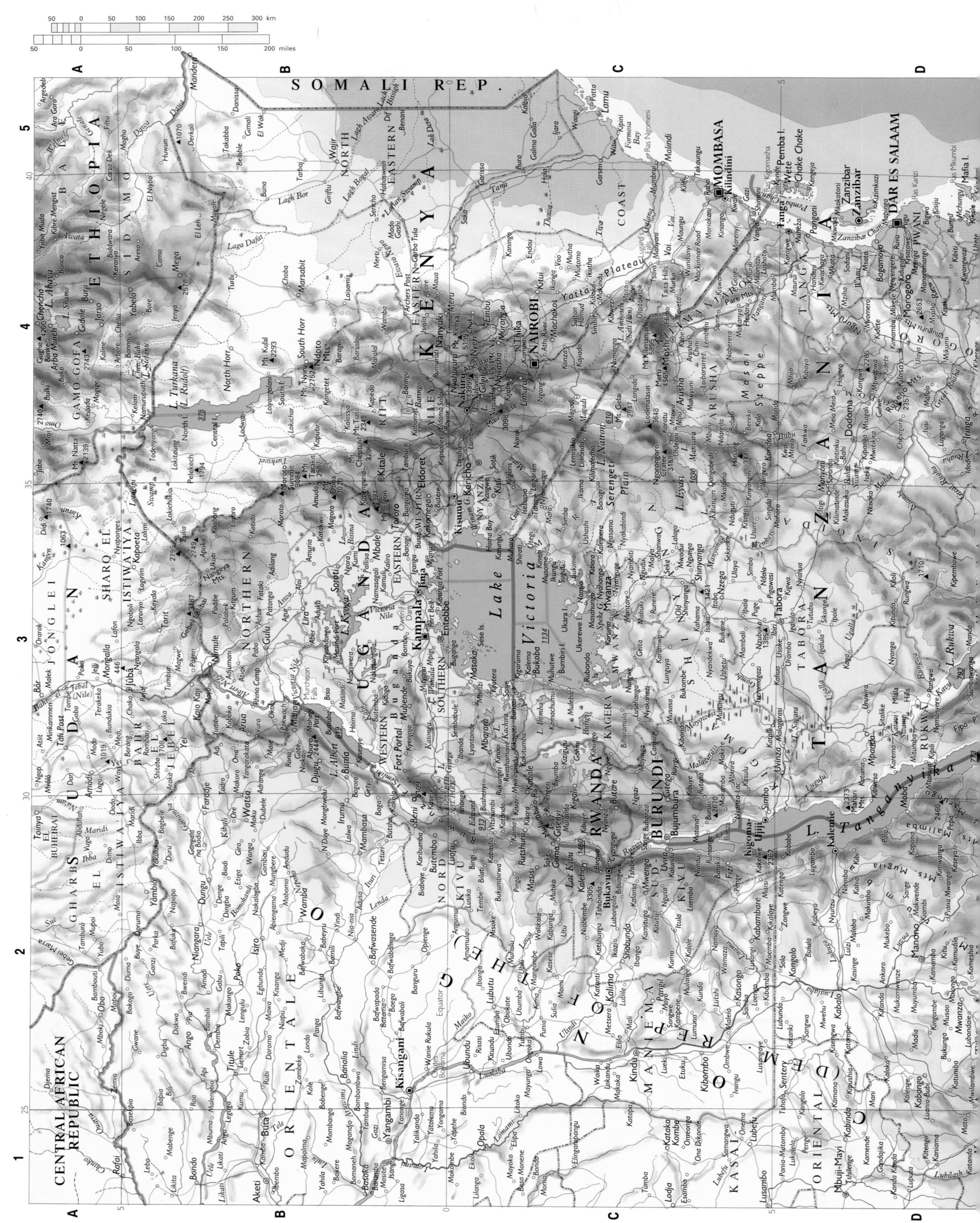

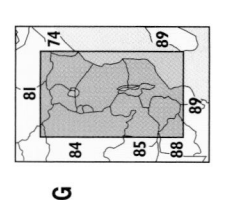

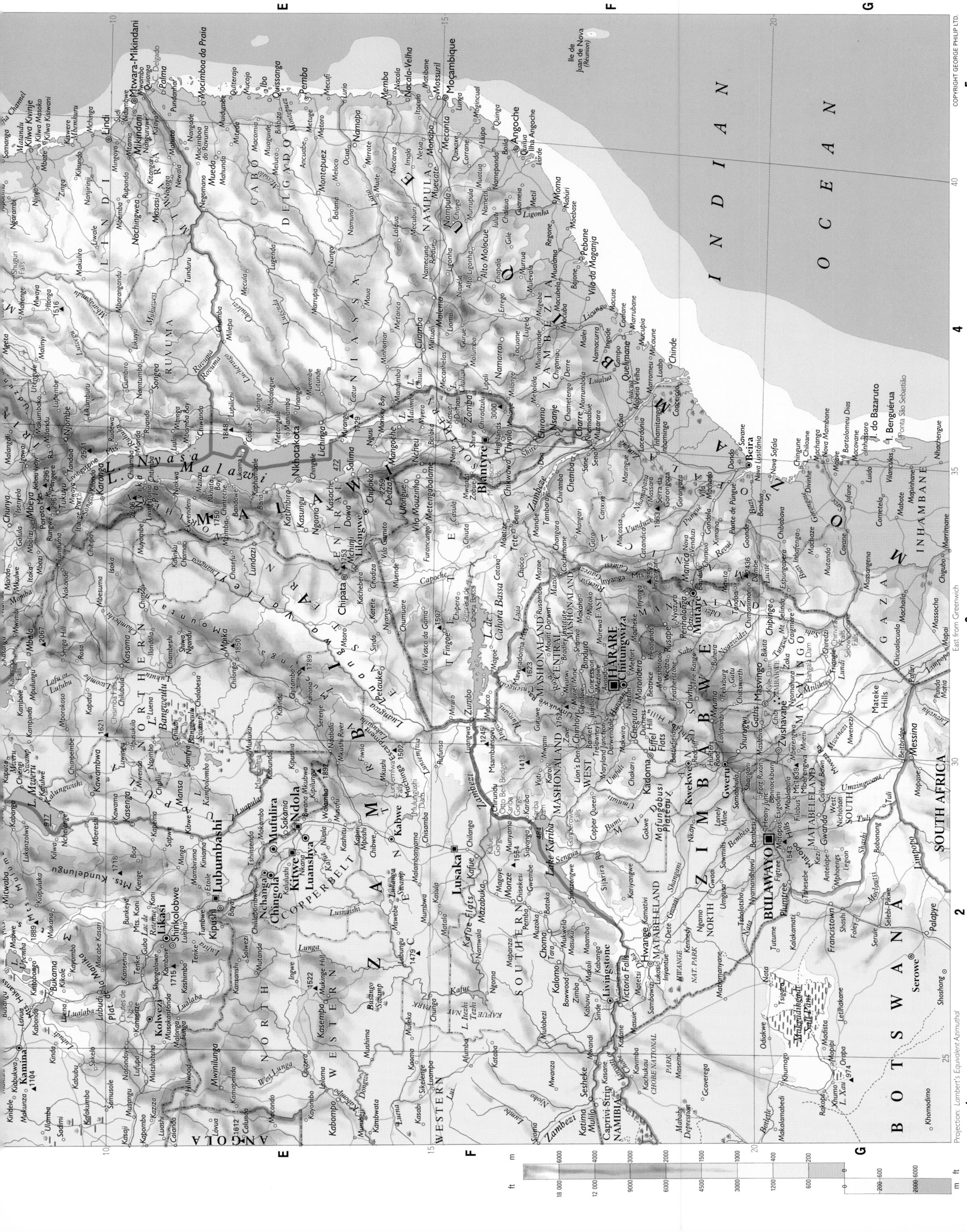

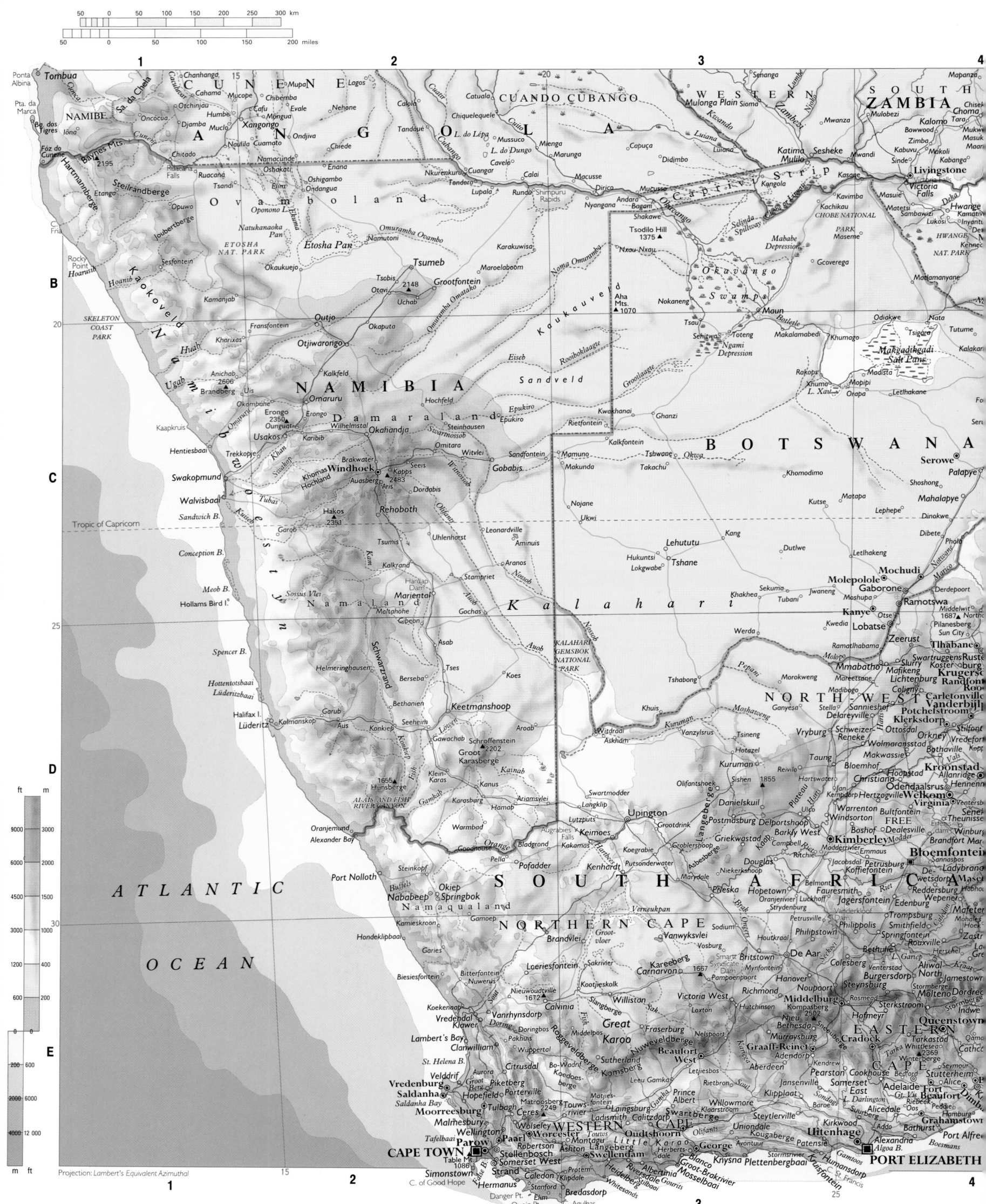

Projection: Lambert's Equivalent Azimuthal

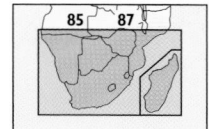

MADAGASCAR

On same scale as General Map

COPYRIGHT GEORGE PHILIP LTD.

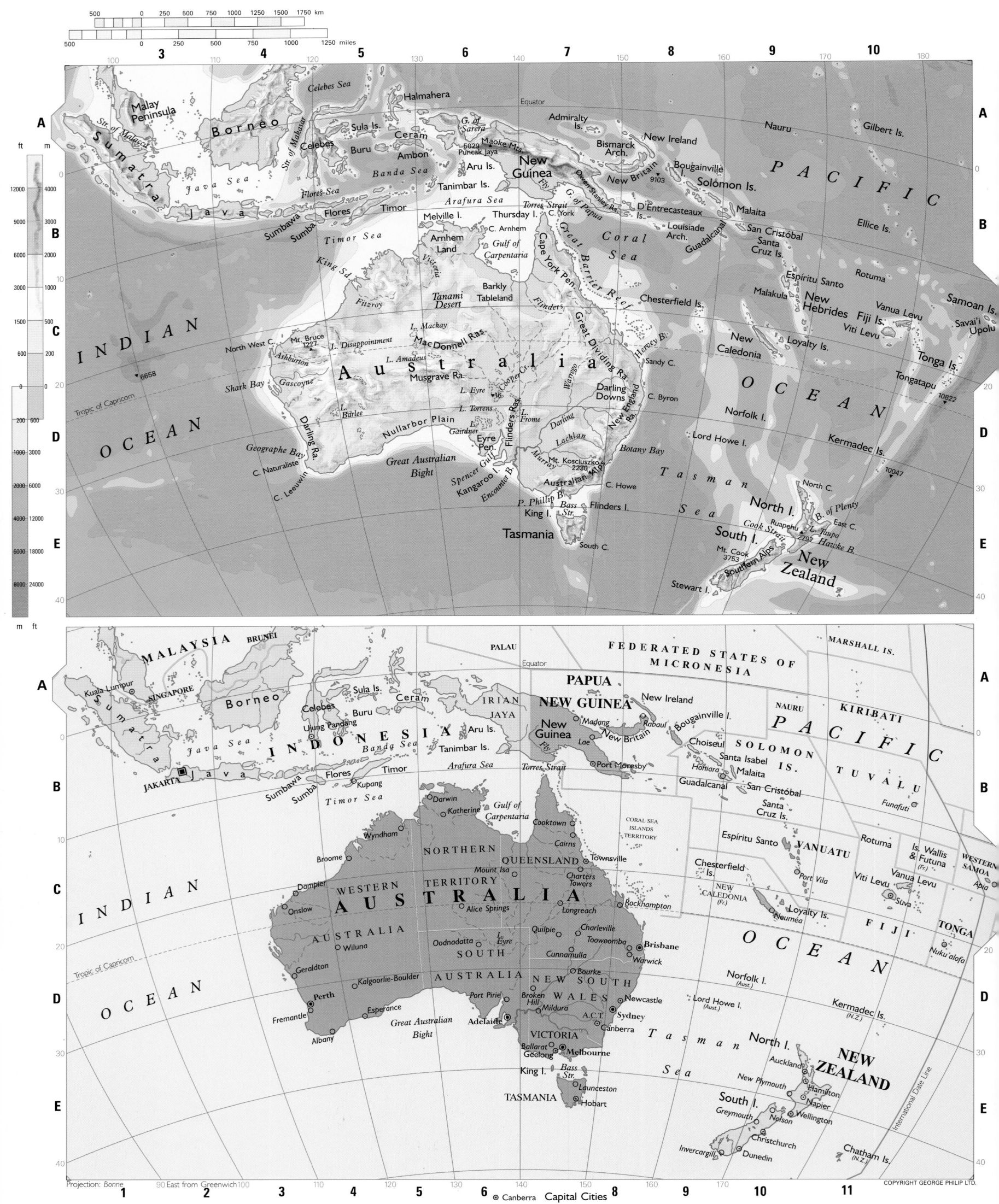

96
96 96 96
96
1

50 0 50 100 150 200 km
50 0 50 100 150 miles

PACIFIC OCEAN

C. Reinga
C. Maria van Diemen
North C.
Rangaunu B.
Houhora Heads
Doubless B.
Mangonui
Whangaroa Harb.
Ahipara B.
Kaitaia
Tauroa Pt.
Okaihau
Opua
C. Brett
Rawene
Kaikohe
Hikurangi
B. of Islands
Hokianga Harbour
Whangarei
Whangarei Harb.
Donnelly's Crossing
Waipu
Bream Hd.
Dargaville
Bream B.
Little Barrier I.
Great Barrier I.
Kaipara Harbour
Warkworth
C. Rodney
C. Colville
Cuvier I.
Helensville
Hauraki Gulf
Coromandel
Takapuna
Devonport
Whitianga
AUCKLAND
Manukau
Papakura
Thames
Mayor I.
Pukekohe
Waihi
Waiuku
Mercer
Paeroa
Tauranga Harb.
Waikato
Huntly
Te Aroha
Mount Maunganui
White I.
C. Runaway
Morrinsville
Tauranga
Bay of Plenty
North Island
Hamilton
Cambridge
Te Puke
Whakatane
East C.
Raglan
Te Awamutu
Opotiki
Raukumara Ra.
Mt Hikurangi 1753
Kawhia Harbour
Putaruru
Kawerau
Taneatua
Otorohanga
Rotorua
Tarawera L.
Murupara
Motu
Waipiro
Mokau
Te Kuiti
Mokau
Kinleith
Kaingaroa Forest
Tolaga Bay
North Taranaki Bight
Wairakei
Mokai
Taupo
Ongarue
Taupo L.
Rangitaiki
Waikaremoana L.
Waitara
Taumarunui
Turangi
Kaimanawa Mts.
Ormond
New Plymouth
Inglewood
Whangamomona
Tarawera
Nuhaka
Gisborne
Mt. Egmont
Stratford
Ruapehu 2797
Poverty Bay
C. Egmont 2518
Opunake
Ohakune
Taihape
Wairoa
Kapuni
Eltham
Raetihi
Waiouru
Waikokopu
Hawera
Waverley
Mahia Pen.
South Taranaki Bight
Mangaweka
Ruahine Ra.
Bay View
Hawke Bay
Patea
Mangaonoho
Wanganui
Marton
Hunterville
Napier
Morton
Feilding
Waipawa
C. Kidnappers
Bulls
Woodville
Hastings
Palmerston North
Dannevirke
Waipukurau
Foxton
Shannon
Pahiatua
C. Turnagain
C. Farewell
Levin
Eketahuna
Collingwood
Golden B.
D'Urville I.
Paraparaumu
Masterton
Takaka
Tasman B.
Otaki
Carterton
Tasman Mts.
Motueka
Pelorus Sd.
Kapiti I.
Greytown
Karamea
Nelson
Upper Hutt
Featherston
Martinborough
Karamea Bight
Richmond
Havelock
Petone
Wairarapa
Seddonville
Tadmor
Wakefield
Picton
Lower Hutt
Granity
Matiri Ra.
Blenheim
WELLINGTON
Lyell
Murchison
Wairau
Seddon
Cook Strait
Westport
Inangahua Junction
Rotoroa L.
Ward
Reefton
Mt Travers 2338
Spenser Mts.
2885 Mt. Tapuaenuku
Blackball
Grey R.
Hanmer Springs
Kaikoura
Runanga
Stillwater
Clarence R.
Greymouth
L. Brunner
Jacksons
Waiau
Kumara
Hokitika
Lewis Pass
Waiau
Hurunui
Ross
Waikari
Culverden
Hanmer R.
Amberley
Waipara
South Island
L. Coleridge
Rangiora
Pegasus Bay
Oxford
Kaiapoi
Springfield
New Brighton
Whitecliffs
Riccarton
Christchurch
Mt Cook 3753
Methven
Lincoln
Lyttelton
Westland Bight
Staveley
Banks Pen.
Southern Alps
Jackson B.
Haast
Rakaia
Akaroa
Little River
Okuru
Tekapo
Ashburton Bight
Rangitata
Fairlie
Ashburton
Mt Aspiring 3027
Pukaki L.
Temuka
St. Andrews
Milford Sd.
Mt. Earnslaw 2818
Wanaka L.
Hawea L.
Ohau L.
Timaru
Bligh Sound
Wanaka
Waimate
George Sound
Arrowtown
Cromwell
Tokarahi
Ngapara
Dunstan Mts.
Oamaru
Secretary I.
Queenstown
Naseby
Kakanui Mts.
Maheno
Doubtful Sd.
Wakatipu L.
Clyde
Alexandra
Hampden
Resolution I.
Kingston
Roxburgh
Palmerston
Dusky Sd.
Te Anau L.
Eyre Mts.
Garvie Mts.
Waikouaiti
Breaksea Sd.
Manapouri L.
Umbrella Mts.
Dunback
Mosgiel
Port Chalmers
Manapouri
Mossburn
Otago
Lawrence
Otago Harbour
Chalky Inlet
Lumsden
Naseby
Kelso
Fairfield
Saunders C.
Preservation Inlet
Clifden
Ohai
Nightcaps
Tapanui
Dunedin
Te Waewae B.
Orepuki
Winton
Clinton
Milton
Riverton
Gore
Balclutha
Invercargill
Hedgehope
Mataura
Kaitangata
Foveaux Str.
Bluff
Wyndham
Owaka
Nugget Pt.
Ruapuke I.
Tahakopa
Halfmoon Bay
Stewart I.
Southwest C.
Port Pegasus

TASMAN SEA

SAMOA ISLANDS
1:10 700 000

WESTERN SAMOA
AMERICAN SAMOA
Savai'i
Apia
Upolu
Pago Pago
Tutuila
West from Greenwich

FIJI AND TONGA ISLANDS
1:10 700 000

Wallis & Futuna (Fr.)
Futuna
Niuafo'ou (Tonga)
Thikombia
Lambasa
Vanua Levu
Yasawa Group
Taveuni
Vanua Mbalavu
Lautoka 1323
Koro
Levuka
FIJI
Nandi
Viti Levu
Ovalau
Lakemba
TONGA (Friendly Is.)
Suva
Gau
Koro Sea
Lau Group
Vava'u
Moala
Kandavu
Moala
Vatoa
Tofua
Tongatapu
Nuku'alofa
East from Greenwich
West from Greenwich

50 0 50 100 150 200 km
50 0 50 100 150 miles

ft m
9000 3000
6000 2000
3000 1000
1200 400
600 200
0 0
200 600
2000 6000
4000 12000
6000 18000
m ft

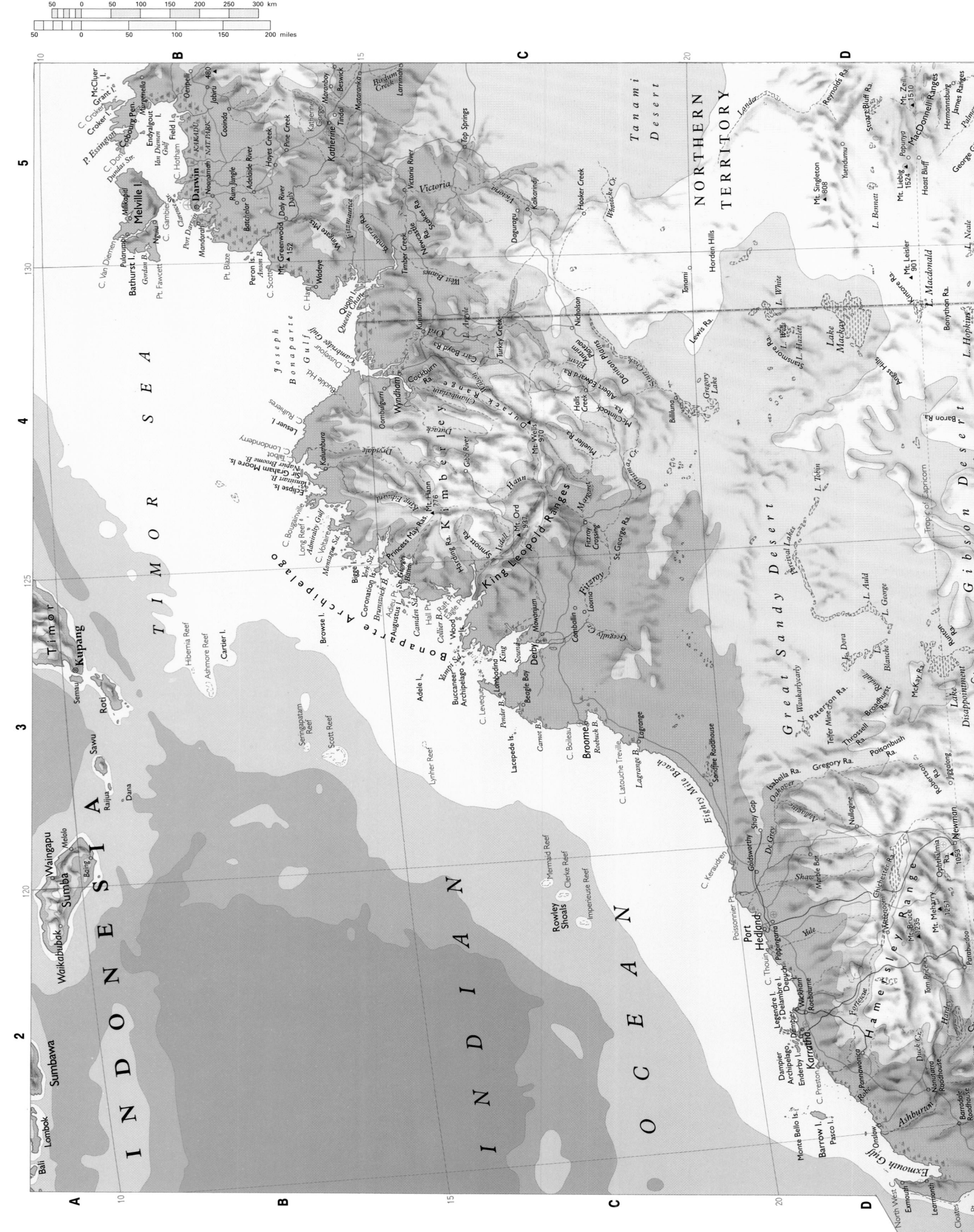

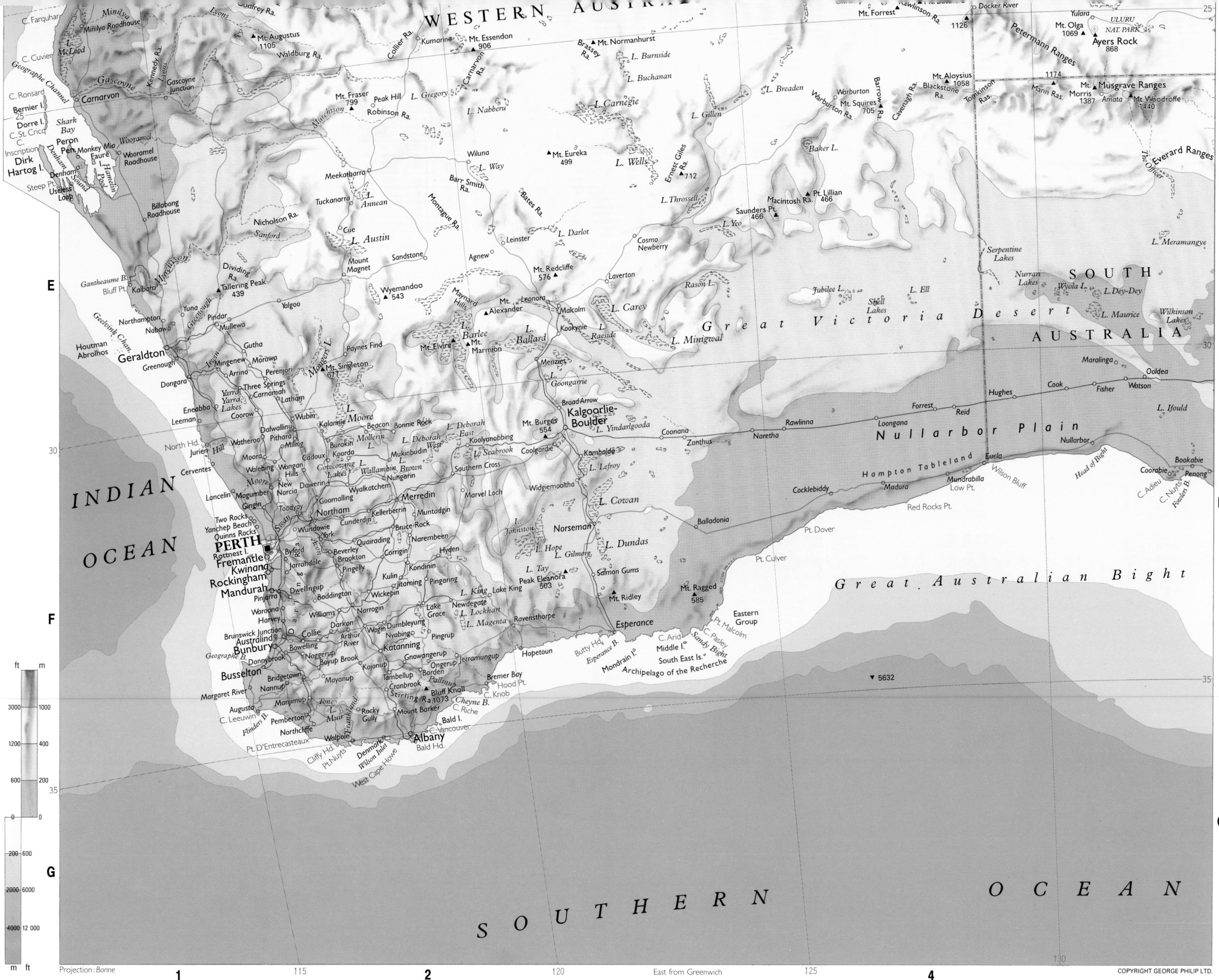

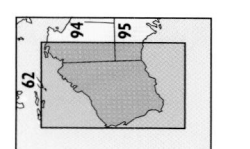

WESTERN AUSTRALIA
SOUTH AUSTRALIA
Great Victoria Desert
Nullarbor Plain
Hampton Tableland
Great Australian Bight
INDIAN OCEAN
SOUTHERN OCEAN
PERTH
Fremantle
Kwinana
Rockingham
Mandurah
Bunbury
Australind
Busselton
Albany
Geraldton
Carnarvon
Kalgoorlie-Boulder
Esperance
Norseman
Coolgardie
Merredin
Northam
Katanning
Collie
Leonora
Laverton
Meekatharra
Wiluna
Cue
Mount Magnet
Southern Cross
Ravensthorpe
Hopetoun
Eucla
Ooldea
Maralinga
Cook
Hughes
Forrest
Rawlinna
Naretha
Zanthus
Coonana
Nullarbor
Madura
Cocklebiddy
Balladonia
Mundrabilla
Ayers Rock 868
Mt. Olga 1069
ULURU NAT. PARK
Yulara
Docker River
Musgrave Ranges
Mt. Woodroffe 1440
Petermann Ranges
Everard Ranges
Mt. Augustus 1105
Mt. Essendon 906
Mt. Fraser 799
Mt. Eureka 499
Mt. Redcliffe 576
Mt. Ragged 585
Bluff Knoll 1073
Stirling Ra.
Dirk Hartog I.
Shark Bay
Houtman Abrolhos
C. Leeuwin
C. Naturaliste
Archipelago of the Recherche
Head of Bight
Red Rocks Pt.
Pt. Dover
Pt. Culver
L. Carnegie
L. Wells
L. Carey
L. Minigwal
L. Barlee
L. Ballard
L. Moore
L. Austin
L. Cowan
L. Dundas
L. Lefroy
L. Yeo
L. Throssell
L. Ifould
▼ 5632
E
F
G
1
2
3
4
5
115
120
125
130
25
30
35
East from Greenwich
Projection: Bonne
COPYRIGHT GEORGE PHILIP LTD.
ft m
3000 1000
1200 400
600 200
0 0
200 600
2000 6000
4000 12 000
m ft

62
94
95

RUSSIA

Yekaterinburg
Tomsk
Novosibirsk
Irkutsk
Chita
Okhotsk
Sea of Okhotsk
Komandorskiye Ostrova *(Russia)*
Ber Se
Near Is. *(U.S.A.)*
Andreane
(U.S.A.)

MOSKVA
Volga
Astana (Aqmola)
Semey
Oz. Baykal
Blagoveshchensk
Sakhalin
Poluostrov Kamchatka
Petropavlovsk-Kamchatskiy
7822
Aleutia

KAZAKSTAN
Aral Sea
Balqash Köl
Ulaanbaatar
Altai
Khabarovsk
Amur
La Perouse Str.
Kuril'skiye Ostrova *(Russia)*
Kuril Trench
Aleutian Trench

Almaty
Toshkent
KYRGYZSTAN
MONGOLIA
Changchun
Harbin
Sapporo
Vladivostok
Hakodate
10,542
Emperor Seamount Chain

TAJIKISTAN
SHENYANG
Sea of Japan
NORTH KOREA
Sendai
Ho

AFGHANISTAN
Kābul
Srinagar
PAKISTAN
Lahore
DELHI
Kanpur
Kunlun Shan
BEIJING
TIANJIN
Taiyuan
Lanzhou
Xi'an
Nanjing
Wuhan
Dalian
SOUTH KOREA
SOUL
Qingdao
Nagoya
Kyoto
Osaka
Kitakyūshū
Shikoku
Kyūshū
Yellow Sea
Fuji-San 3776
TOKYO
Yokohama
JAPAN
10,554
Japan Trench
Midway Is. *(U.S.A.)*

CHINA
Himalaya
Mt Everest
8848
Lhasa
XIZANG
CHONGQING
Changsha
HANGZHOU
SHANGHAI
East China Sea
Ogasawara Gunto *(Japan)*
Minami-Tori-Shima *(Japan)*
Lisianski I. *(U.S.A.)*

Chang J.
Kunming
Fuzhou
Taipei
GUANGZHOU
Ryūkyū-rettō (Japan)
TAIWAN
Kazan-Rettō *(Japan)*
South Honshu Ridge
Marcus
Wake I. *(U.S.A.)*
Necker Rid

BANGLADESH
DHAKA
Mandalay
CALCUTTA
BURMA
LAOS
Hanoi
HONG KONG
Macau
Hainan
C. Engano
Paracel Is.
NORTHERN MARIANAS *(U.S.A.)*
Saipan
MARSHALL IS.
Bikini
International Dateline
P
PA

INDIA
Hyderabad
Bay of Bengal
Rangoon
THAILAND
Irrawaddy
Salween
Mekong
Luzon
MANILA
PHILIPPINES
Samar
Mindoro
GUAM *(U.S.A.)*
11,022
Enewetak Atoll
Mariana Trench

CHENNAI (Madras)
BANGKOK
CAMBODIA
Phnom Penh
G. of Thailand
South China Sea
Palawan
10,497
Yap
Caroline Is.
Truk
Micrones
Mariana Trench
M

SRI LANKA
Nicobar Is. *(India)*
Andaman Is. *(India)*
Phanh Bho Ho Chi Minh
Sulu Sea
Mindanao
Mindanao Trench
Koror
PALAU
FEDERATED STATES OF MICRONESIA
Pohnpei
Palikir
Jaluit I.
Dalap-Uliga-Darrit
Butaritari
O

Colombo
MALAYSIA
Celebes Sea
4101
BRUNEI
SABAH
Mela
nesia
Tarawa
Gilbert Is.
Banaba
Howland I.
Baker I.
KIR

Kuala Lumpur
PEN. MALAYSIA
Borneo
SARAWAK
Halmahera
Sulawesi
Buru
Seram
PAPUA NEW GUINEA
Admiralty Is.
New Ireland
NAURU
Phoenix Is.
Abariring
Enderbu

SINGAPORE
Sumatera
INDONESIA
Ujung Pandang
Puncak Jaya 5029
IRIAN JAYA
New Guinea
Bismarck Arch.
Rabaul
SOLOMON IS.
Fongafale
TUVALU
Is. Wallis & Futuna *(Fr.)*
WESTERN SAMO
Ap

Palembang
Java Sea
JAKARTA
Surabaya
Flores Sea
Banda Sea
7440
New Britain
Bougainville
Lae
Honiara
Guadalcanal
Santa Cruz I. 9165
Rotuma
Espíritu Santo
Vanua Levu
Tokelau *(N.Z)*

Selat Sunda
Jawa
Bali
Sumbawa
Sumba
Flores
Timor
Arafura Sea
Port Moresby
Torres Strait
C. York
VANUATU
Port Vila
Viti Levu
Suva
FIJI
Nuku'alofa
TONG

Java Trench
Christmas Is. *(Austral.)*
C. Arnhem
Darwin
Gulf of Carpentaria
Louisiade Arch.
Is. Chesterfield
Coral Sea
7570
NEW CALEDONIA *(Fr.)*
Is. Loyauté
10,822
Tonga Trench

Cocos Is. *(Austral.)*
North West C.
Broome
Cairns
Townsville
Rockhampton
Nouméa
Lord

INDIAN
Mount Isa
Great Dividing Ra.
Brisbane
Norfolk I. *(Austral.)*
Kermadec Is. *(N.Z.)*

OCEAN
AUSTRALIA
Alice Springs
L. Eyre
Darling
Howe
Lord Howe I. *(Austral.)*
Kermadec Trench 10,047

Geraldton
Perth
Great Australian Bight
Albany
Murray
Adelaide
Sydney
Canberra
Mt. Kosciuszko 2237
Tasman Sea
Auckland
Cook Strait
NEW ZEALAND

Nouvelle Amsterdam *(Fr.)*
I. St. Paul *(Fr.)*
Melbourne
Bass Str.
Tasmania
Hobart
Mt. Cook 3753
Wellington
Christchurch
Chath *(N.Z.)*

Is. Crozet *(Fr.)*
Mid-Indian Ridge
Dunedin
Invercargill
Bounty Is. *(N.Z.)*

Kerguelen *(Fr.)*
Auckland Is. *(N.Z.)*
Antipodes Is. *(N.Z.)*

Heard I. *(Austral.)*
Macquarie I. *(Austral.)*
Campbell I. *(N.Z.)*

Elevation scale (ft / m):
12 000 / 4000
9000 / 3000
6000 / 2000
3000 / 1000
1500 / 500
600 / 200
0 / 0
200 / 600
1000 / 3000
2000 / 6000
4000 / 12000
6000 / 18000
8000 / 24000

11 **12** **13** **14**

160 140

Arctic Circle

15

16 **17** **18** **19** **20**

120 100 80 60 40 20

ALASKA
(U.S.A.)
Anchorage

5959

Bristol Bay

Gulf of Alaska

Juneau

R O C K Y

C A N A D A

Edmonton

L. Winnipeg

Winnipeg

Calgary

Regina

St. Lawrence

Newfoundland

N O R T H

B

Prince of Wales I.
(U.S.A.) Prince Rupert
Queen Charlotte Is.
(Canada)

Vancouver
Vancouver I.
Victoria
Seattle
Portland
Boise

Snake

Minneapolis

Missouri

L. Superior

L. Huron

L. Michigan

Québec
Montréal
Toronto
Ottawa
Detroit
Buffalo
Boston

L. Ontario

L. Erie

St. John's

50

C

C. Mendocino

Sacramento

SAN FRANCISCO

6741

4418

Salt Lake
City

Denver

Colorado

CHICAGO

Kansas City

St. Louis

Cincinnati

Pittsburgh

Appalachian Mts.

NEW YORK CITY
PHILADELPHIA
Baltimore
Washington D.C.

A T L A N T I C

40

D

LOS ANGELES
San Diego

UNITED STATES

Oklahoma City
Phoenix
Dallas
Memphis
Atlanta

C. Hatteras

Guadalupe
(Mex.)

Ciudad
Juárez

Houston
San Antonio

Mississippi

New
Orleans

Jacksonville

Bermuda
(U.K.)

S a r g a s s o   S e a

30

E

Tropic of Cancer

Baja California

Golfo de California

M E X I C O

Monterrey

Gulf of Mexico
Miami

Florida Str.

BAHAMAS

O C E A N

Honolulu
Oahu
4205
HAWAIIAN IS.
(U.S.A.)
Hawaii

C. San Lucas

Guadalajara

MEXICO
5700
Puebla

Mérida

La Habana
CUBA

Canal de Yucatán

West Indies

Johnston I.
(U.S.A.)

I F I C

Is. Revilla Gigedo
(Mex.)

Acapulco

9200
HAITI
JAMAICA
Kingston

DOMINICAN REP.
PUERTO
RICO
(U.S.A.)
Leeward
Is.

20

F

Palmyra Is.
(U.S.A.)

Teraina
Tabuaeran
Kiritimati

I. Clipperton
(Fr.)

GUATEMALA
Guatemala
San Salvador
EL SALVADOR

BELIZE
7680
HONDURAS
NICARAGUA
Managua

Caribbean Sea

BARBADOS
Windward Is.

Barranquilla
Maracaibo
Caracas

C

Jarvis I.
(U.S.A.)

E A N

COSTA
RICA
San José
Colón Panama
PANAMA

Orinoco

VENEZUELA

10

G

B A T I

Malden I.
Starbuck I.

Equator

Galápagos
(Ecuador)

I. del Coco
(Costa Rica)
Medellín
Cali
COLOMBIA

Bogotá

0

Tongareva
Manihiki
Pukapuka

Caroline I.
Vostok I.
Flint I.

I. de Malpelo
(Colombia)

Quito
ECUADOR
Guayaquil

BRAZIL

H

Suwarrow Is.

Is. Marquises

C. Paliñas

Iquitos

Amazonas

10

Is. de la
Société
Papeete Tahiti
Is. Tuamotu

Trujillo

6369
PERU

Cook Is.
(N.Z.)

Rarotonga

FRENCH POLYNESIA

Muru̇roa

Is. Tubuai

LIMA

Cuzco

L. Titicaca

Nevada Ancohuma
6550

J

Arequipa
6866
Peru-
Arica

La Paz
BOLIVIA

20

Tropic of Capricorn

Iquique
Chile

PARAGUAY

Ducie I.

Pitcairn I.
(U.K.)

Sala-y-Gómez
(Chile)

Antofagasta

8050
Trench

San Felix
(Chile)
San Ambrosio
(Chile)

San Miguel
de Tucumán

Asunción

K

Rapa

I. de Pascua
(Chile)

Porto
Alegre

30

Arch. de
Juan Fernández
(Chile)

Córdoba

Aconcagua
6960
Valparaíso
Rosario

SANTIAGO
Concepción

BUENOS
AIRES

URUGUAY
Montevideo

Río de la Plata

L

ARGENTINA

40

S O U T H

M

A T L A N T I C

6212

O C E A N

50

Punta Arenas

Falkland Is.
(U.K.)

South Georgia
(U.K.)

N

Tierra del Fuego

Est. de Magallanes

C. de Hornos

60 West from Greenwich 40

COPYRIGHT GEORGE PHILIP LTD.

11 **12** **13** **14** **15** **16** **17** **18** **19** **20**

160 140 120 100 80

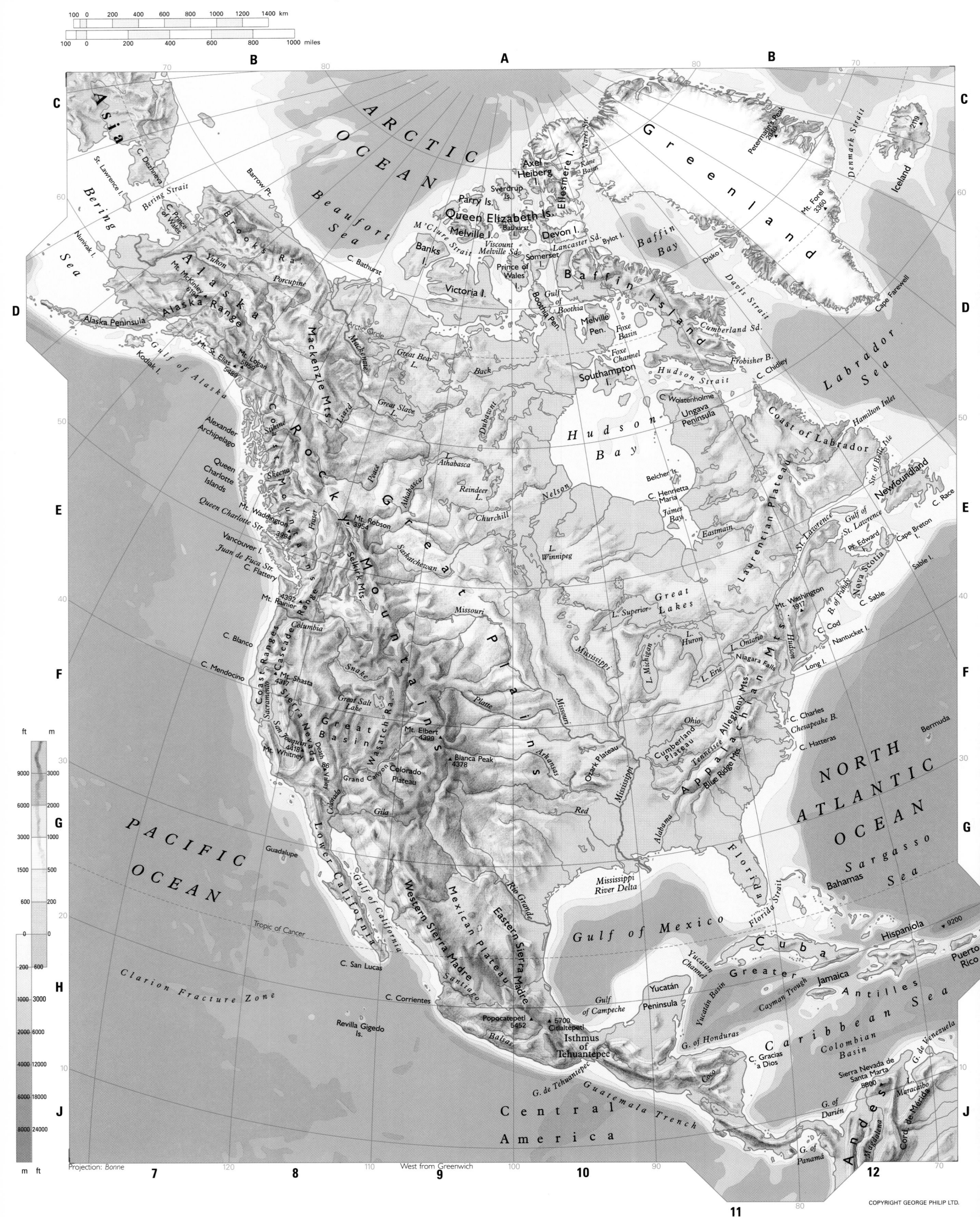

100 0 200 400 600 800 1000 1200 1400 km
100 0 200 400 600 800 1000 miles

ft   m
9000 3000
6000 2000
3000 1000
1500   500
600   200
0   0
200   600
1000 3000
2000 6000
4000 12000
6000 18000
8000 24000
m ft

ASIA

ARCTIC OCEAN

GREENLAND

St. Lawrence I.
C. Dezhneva
Bering Strait
Nunivak I.
C. Prince of Wales
Barrow Pt.
Brooks Ra.
Porcupine
Yukon
Mt. McKinley
6194
Alaska Range
Alaska Peninsula
Kodiak I.
Gulf of Alaska
Mt. S. Elias 5489
Mt. Logan 5959

Beaufort Sea
C. Bathurst
Banks I.
Mackenzie
Mackenzie Mts.
M'Clure Strait
Melville I.
Prince of Wales
Victoria I.
Arctic Circle
Great Bear L.
Back
Great Slave L.

Axel Heiberg I.
Ellesmere I.
Kane Basin
Sverdrup Is.
Parry Is.
Queen Elizabeth Is.
Bathurst
Devon I.
Lancaster Sd.
Viscount Melville Sd.
Somerset
Bylot I.
Disko I.
Baffin Bay
Gulf of Boothia
Boothia Pen.
Melville Pen.
Foxe Basin
Foxe Channel
Baffin Island
Cumberland Sd.
Frobisher B.
C. Chidley

Peterman's Peak
Mt. Forel 3360
Denmark Strait
Iceland
2119

Bering Sea

Alexander Archipelago
Queen Charlotte Islands
Queen Charlotte Str.
Mt. Waddington 3994
Vancouver I.
Juan de Fuca Str.
C. Flattery
Skeena
Stikine
Liard
Peace
Fraser
Rocky Mountains
Selkirk Mts.
Columbia
Mt. Robson 3954
Athabasca
Athabasca
L. Athabasca
Reindeer L.
Saskatchewan
Great Plains
Nelson
Churchill
L. Winnipeg

Dubawnt
Southampton I.
Hudson Bay
Belcher Is.
C. Henrietta Maria
James Bay
Eastmain

C. Wolstenholme
Ungava Peninsula
Hudson Strait
Laurentian Plateau
Coast of Labrador
Labrador Sea
Hamilton Inlet
Cape Farewell

Newfoundland
Str. of Belle Isle
C. Race
Cape Breton I.
Pt. Edward
Gulf of St. Lawrence
St. Lawrence
Nova Scotia
C. Sable
Sable I.
B. of Fundy
Mt. Washington 1917
C. Cod
Nantucket I.

PACIFIC OCEAN

Coast Ranges
Cascade Range
Mt. Rainier 4392
Mt. Shasta 4317
C. Blanco
C. Mendocino
Sacramento
San Joaquin
Sierra Nevada
Mt. Whitney 4418
Death Valley 86
Great Basin
Great Salt Lake
Snake
Wasatch Ra.
Mt. Elbert 4399
Blanca Peak 4378
Colorado Plateau
Grand Canyon
Colorado
Gila

Missouri
Platte
Arkansas
Red
Missouri
Mississippi
Ohio
Alabama

Great Lakes
L. Superior
L. Michigan
L. Huron
L. Erie
L. Ontario
Niagara Falls
Hudson
Long I.

Ozark Plateau
Cumberland Plateau
Tennessee
Allegheny Mts.
Appalachian Mts.
Blue Ridge Mts.
C. Charles
Chesapeake B.
C. Hatteras

NORTH ATLANTIC OCEAN

Bermuda

Guadalupe
Tropic of Cancer
Clarion Fracture Zone
Lower California
Gulf of California
Western Sierra Madre
Mexican Plateau
Eastern Sierra Madre
C. San Lucas
Revilla Gigedo Is.
C. Corrientes
Balsas
Santiago
Popocatepetl 5452
Citlaltepetl 5700
Isthmus of Tehuantepec
G. de Tehuantepec

Rio Grande
Florida
Florida Strait
Mississippi River Delta
Gulf of Mexico
Gulf of Campeche
Yucatán
Yucatán Peninsula
Yucatán Channel
Yucatán Basin
Cuba
Greater Antilles
Cayman Trough
Jamaica
Hispaniola 9200
Puerto Rico
Bahamas
Sargasso Sea
Colombian Basin
Caribbean Sea

Central America
Guatemala Trench
G. of Honduras
C. Gracias a Dios
Coco
G. of Darién
G. of Panamá
Sierra Nevada de Santa Marta
Magdalena
Cord. de Mérida 3800
Andes
G. of Venezuela
L. Maracaibo

West from Greenwich

Projection: Bonne

COPYRIGHT GEORGE PHILIP LTD.

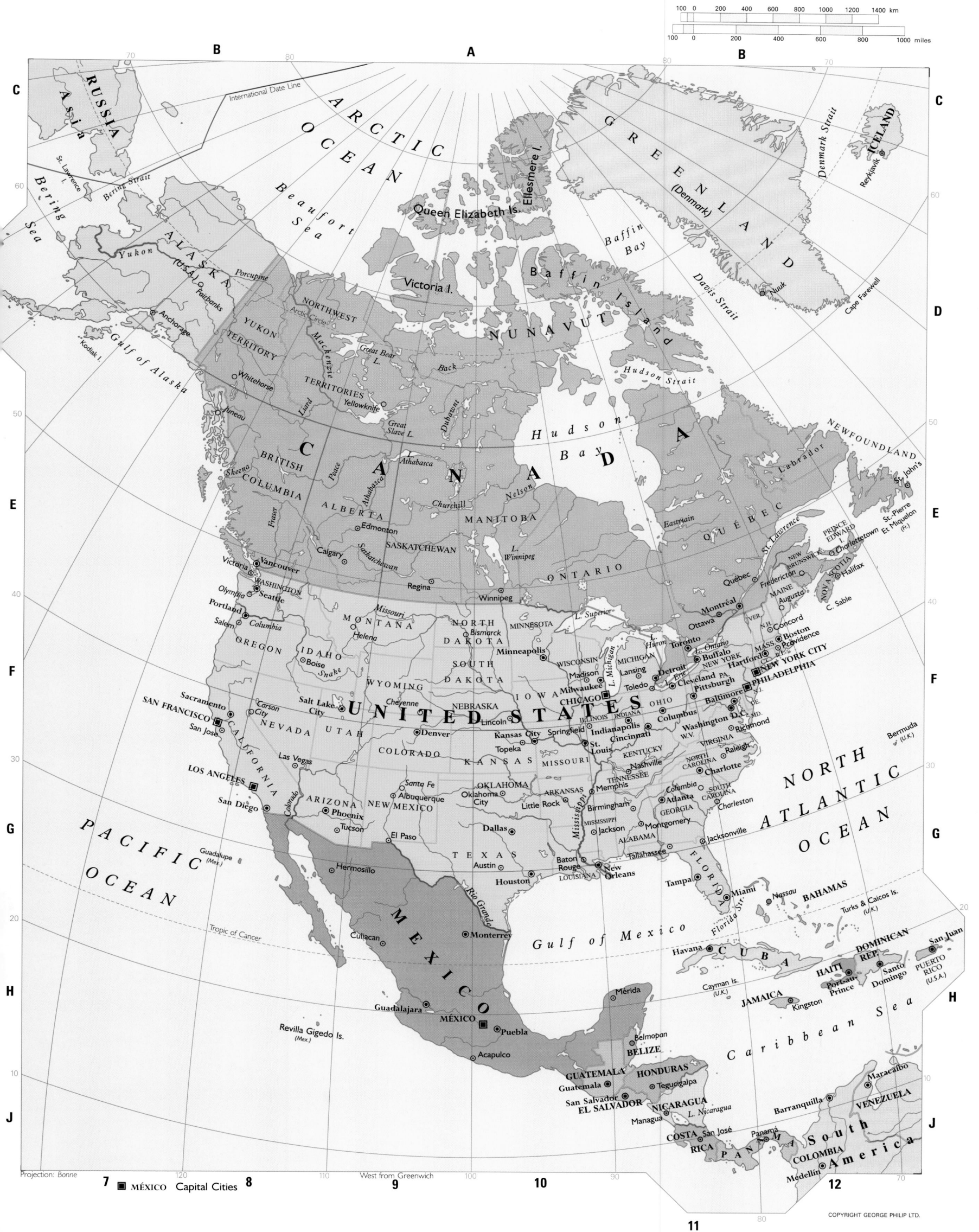

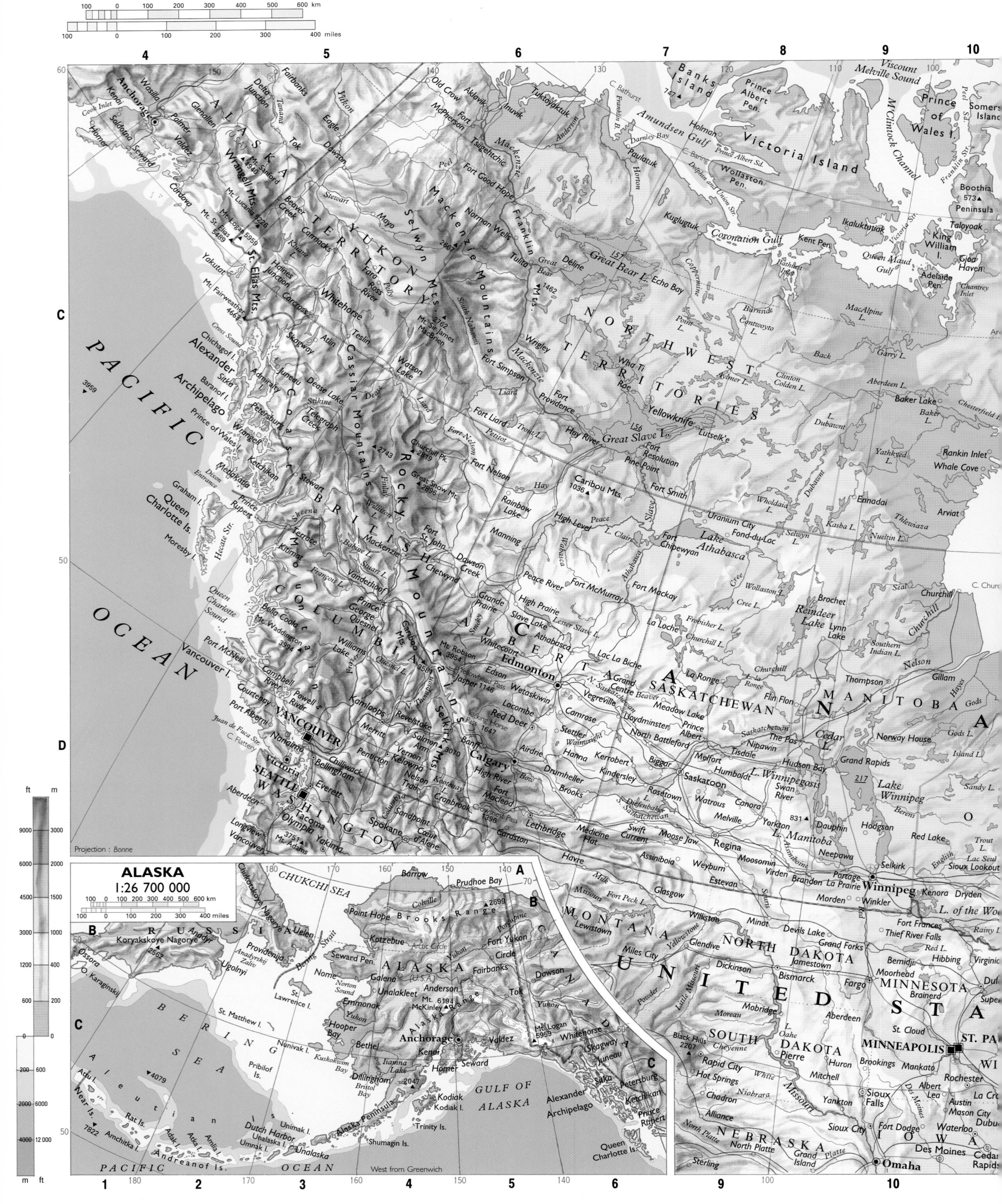

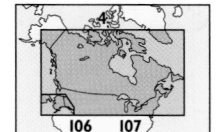

106 107

11 12 13 14 15 16

B

C

D

E

GREENLAND (KALAALLIT NUNAAT) (Denmark)

Baffin Bay

Davis Strait

ATLANTIC OCEAN

Labrador Sea

Devon I.
Lancaster Sound
Arctic Bay
Brodeur Peninsula
Borden Pen.
Bylot I.
Pond Inlet
Clyde River
C. Adair
C. Raper
Home B.
Qeqertarsuaq
Qeqertarsuaq
Nunavik
Uummannaq
Illulissat
Qasigiannguit
Sisimiut
Maniitsoq
Nuuk
Paamiut
Qeqertarsuatsiaat
Nanortalik
Ammassalik

Baffin Island
Fury and Hecla Str.
Igloolik
Simpson Pen.
Pelly Bay
Melville Peninsula
Sanirajak
Prince Charles I.
Air Force I.
Foxe Basin
Nettilling L.
Cumberland Peninsula
Pangnirtung
Hoare B.
Mercy C.
Cumberland Sd.

NUNAVUT
Rae Isthmus
Repulse Bay
C. Dorchester
Foxe Pen.
Amadjuak L.
Cape Dorset
Meta Incognita
Iqaluit
Hall Peninsula
Frobisher Bay
Kimmirut
Resolution I.

Hudson Strait
Southampton I.
Salliq
Bell Pen.
Nottingham I.
Coats I.
Mansel I.
Salisbury I.
Ivujivik
Salluit
Quaqtaq
Akpatok I.
C. Chidley

Hudson Bay
Ottawa Is.
Sleeper Is.
King George Is.
Baker's Dozen Is.
Belcher Is.
Kuujjuarapik
C. Henrietta Maria
Pte. Louis XIV
James Bay
Akimiski I.
Charlton I.

QUÉBEC
Péninsule d'Ungava
Puvirnituq
Inukjuak
Kangiqsujuaq
Kangirsuk
Arnaud
L. Payne
Ungava Bay
Kangiqsualujjuaq
Kuujjuaq
Hebron
Nain
Hopedale
C. Harrison
Rigolet
Cartwright
Port Hope Simpson
Belle Isle
St. Anthony

NEWFOUNDLAND
Smallwood Res.
Schefferville
Esker
Churchill Falls
Churchill
Happy Valley
Goose Bay
Labrador City
Fermont
Wabush
Gagnon
Sept-Îles
St-Augustin
Natashquan
Havre-St-Pierre
Baie Verte
Deer Lake
Grand Falls
Corner Brook
Stephenville
Channel-Port aux Basques
Gander
Bonavista
Carbonear
St. John's
Placentia
C. Race

ONTARIO
Big Trout L.
Winisk
Peawanuck
Attawapiskat
Fort Albany
Moosonee
Nakina
Geraldton
Nipigon
Thunder Bay
Hearst
Kapuskasing
Timmins
Cochrane
Kirkland Lake
Rouyn-Noranda
Val-d'Or
Amos
Chibougamau
Matagami
Chapleau
Wawa
Sault Ste. Marie
Elliot Lake
Sudbury
North Bay
Pembroke
Huntsville
Parry Sound
Lake Superior
Lake Huron
Georgian Bay
Manitoulin
Owen Sound
Barrie
Peterborough
Belleville
Kingston
L. Ontario
Oshawa
TORONTO
Hamilton
Kitchener
London
Sarnia
Windsor
L. Erie

QUÉBEC
La Grande
Chisasibi
Wemindji
Eastmain
Waskaganish
Rupert
Mistassini
Matagami
Lac St-Jean
Roberval
Jonquière
Chicoutimi
La Tuque
Shawinigan
Trois-Rivières
Québec
Lévis
Thetford Mines
MONTRÉAL
Hull
Ottawa
Joliette
St-Hyacinthe
Sherbrooke
Granby
Cornwall

NEW BRUNSWICK
Edmundston
Campbellton
Bathurst
Miramichi
Moncton
Fredericton
Saint John
Woodstock
Grand Falls

NOVA SCOTIA
Amherst
Truro
New Glasgow
Antigonish
Sydney
Glace Bay
Port Hawkesbury
Halifax
Dartmouth
Bridgewater
Liverpool
Yarmouth
Digby
Kentville
Sable I.

PR. EDWARD I.
Summerside
Charlottetown
Cape Breton I.
St-Pierre et Miquelon (Fr)
Gulf of St. Lawrence
Cabot Str.
Î. d'Anticosti
Îs. de la Madeleine

MAINE
Bangor
Augusta
Portland
Lewiston

VERMONT
Montpelier
Burlington
L. Champlain

NEW HAMPSHIRE
Concord
Manchester

MASS.
BOSTON
Springfield
Providence
R.I.

NEW YORK
Albany
Syracuse
Rochester
BUFFALO
Niagara Falls
Binghamton
Elmira
Jamestown
Scranton
HARTFORD
CONN.
New Haven
Bridgeport
NEW YORK
Newark
N.J.
Allentown
Trenton

PENNSYLVANIA
Erie

OHIO
CLEVELAND
Toledo

MICHIGAN
DETROIT
Flint
Saginaw
Lansing
Grand Rapids
Cadillac
Traverse City
Petoskey
Manistique
Escanaba
Menominee
Marquette
Houghton
Ironwood

WISCONSIN
MILWAUKEE
Madison
Racine
Kenosha
Green Bay
Appleton
Sheboygan
Wausau

ILLINOIS
CHICAGO
Rockford

INDIANA
Gary
South Bend

Lake Michigan

West from Greenwich

COPYRIGHT GEORGE PHILIP LTD.

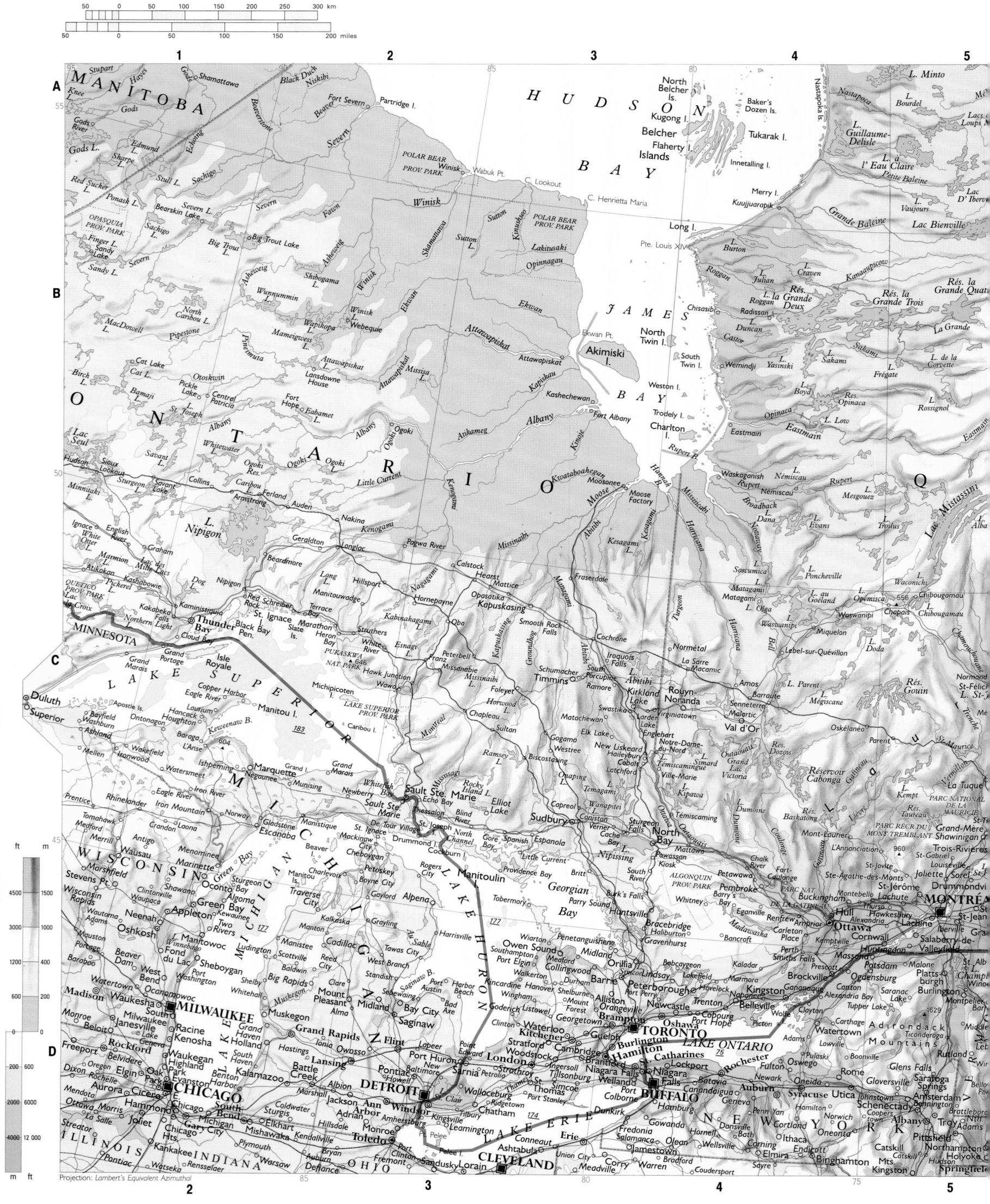

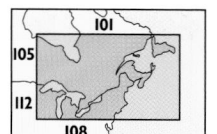

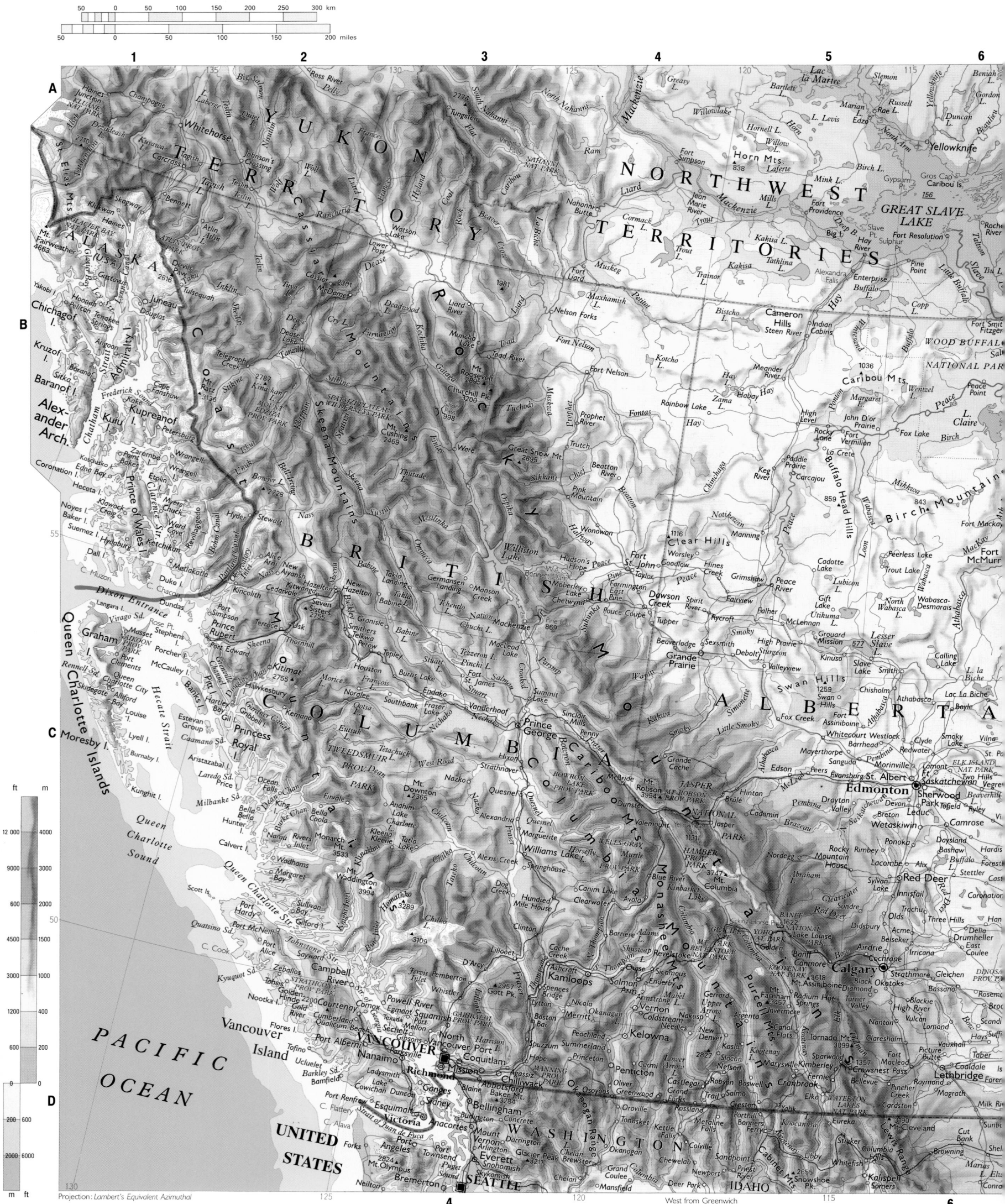

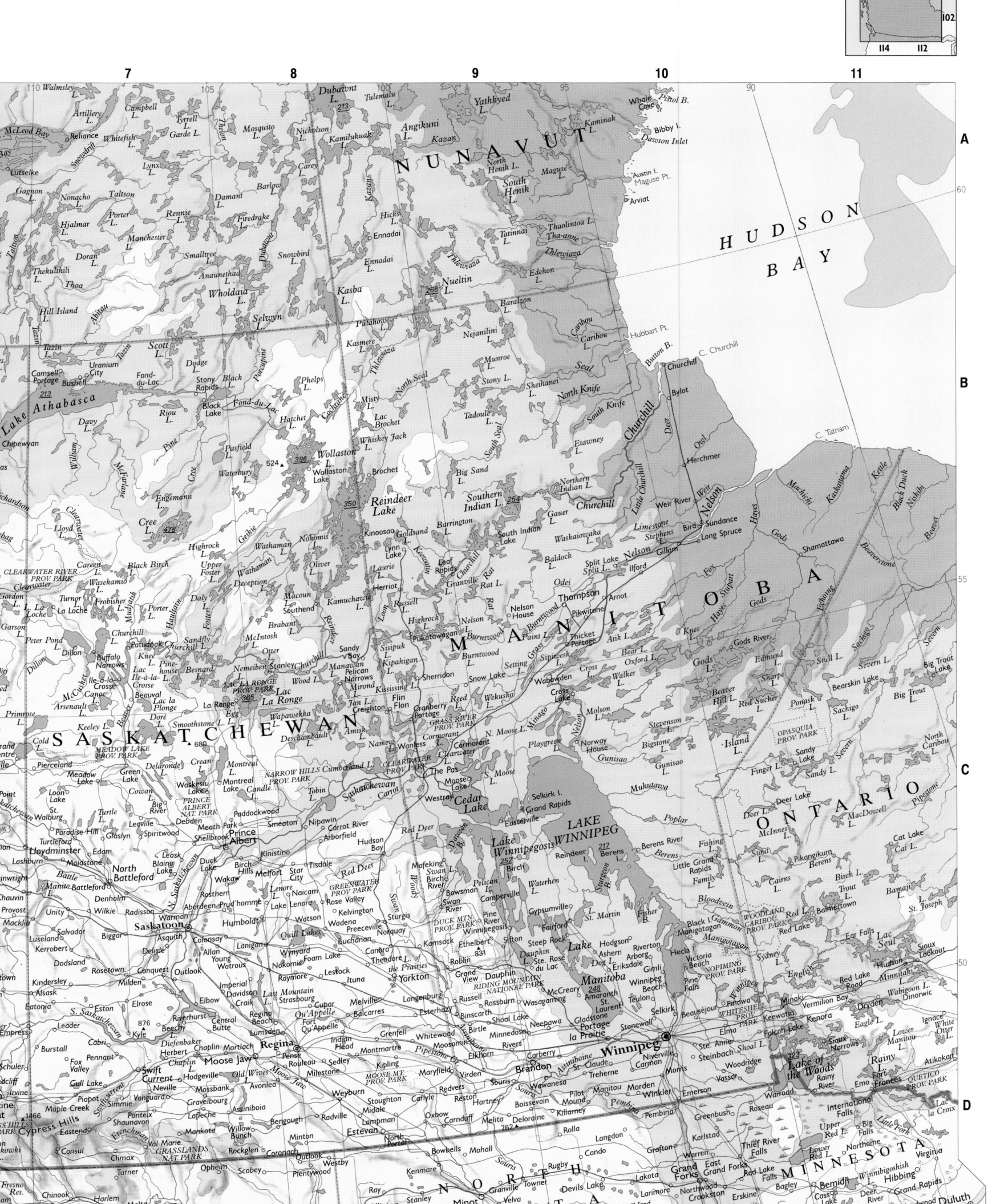

7   8   9   10   11

NUNAVUT

A

HUDSON BAY

60

B

SASKATCHEWAN

MANITOBA

ONTARIO

55

Lake Athabasca

Reindeer Lake

Churchill

Nelson

Gods River

C

LAKE WINNIPEG

Lake Winnipegosis

Cedar Lake

50

Saskatoon

Prince Albert

Regina

Moose Jaw

Winnipeg

Brandon

Lake of the Woods

D

MONTANA   **NORTH DAKOTA**   **MINNESOTA**

110   7   105   8   100   9   95   10

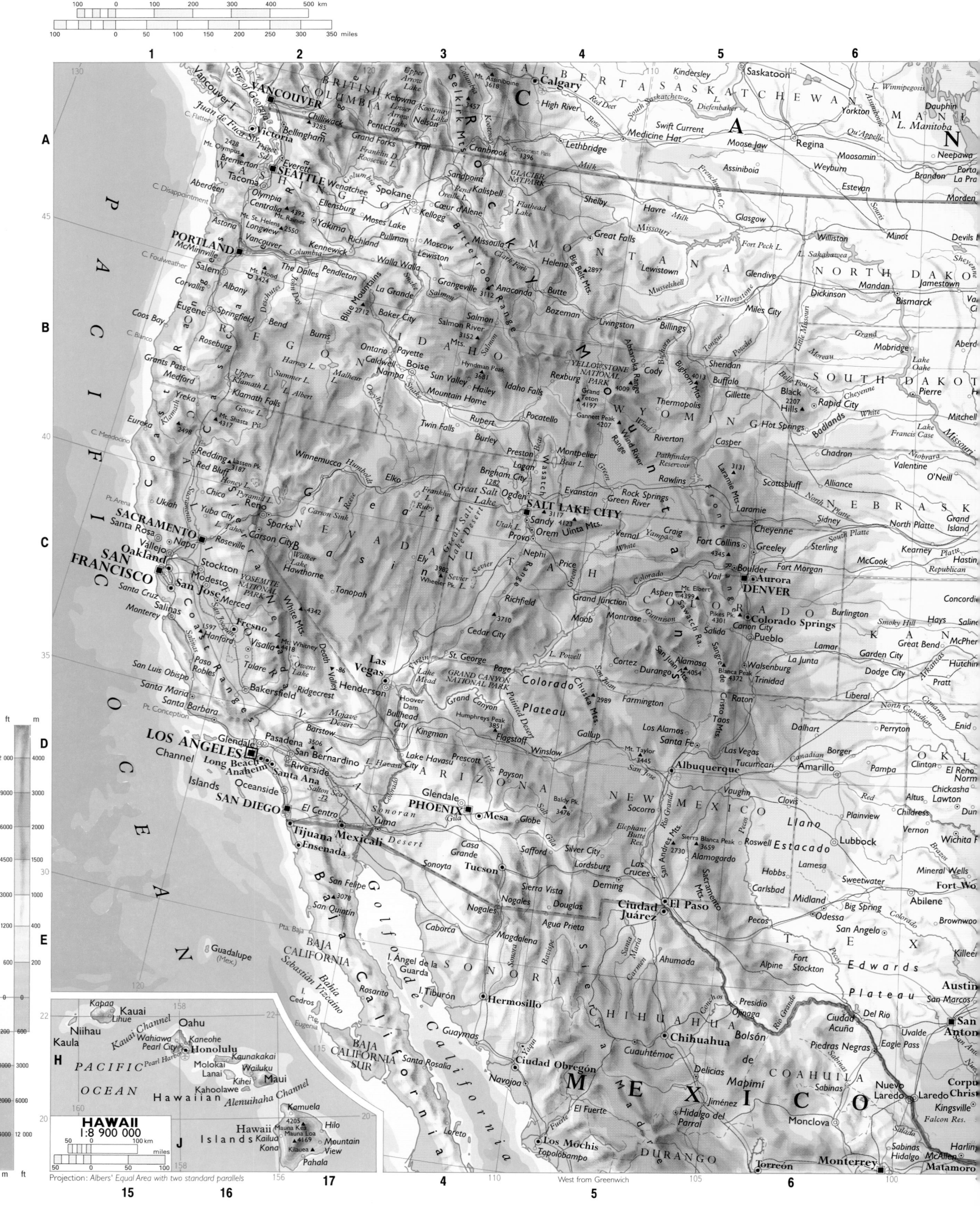

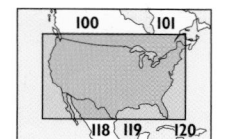

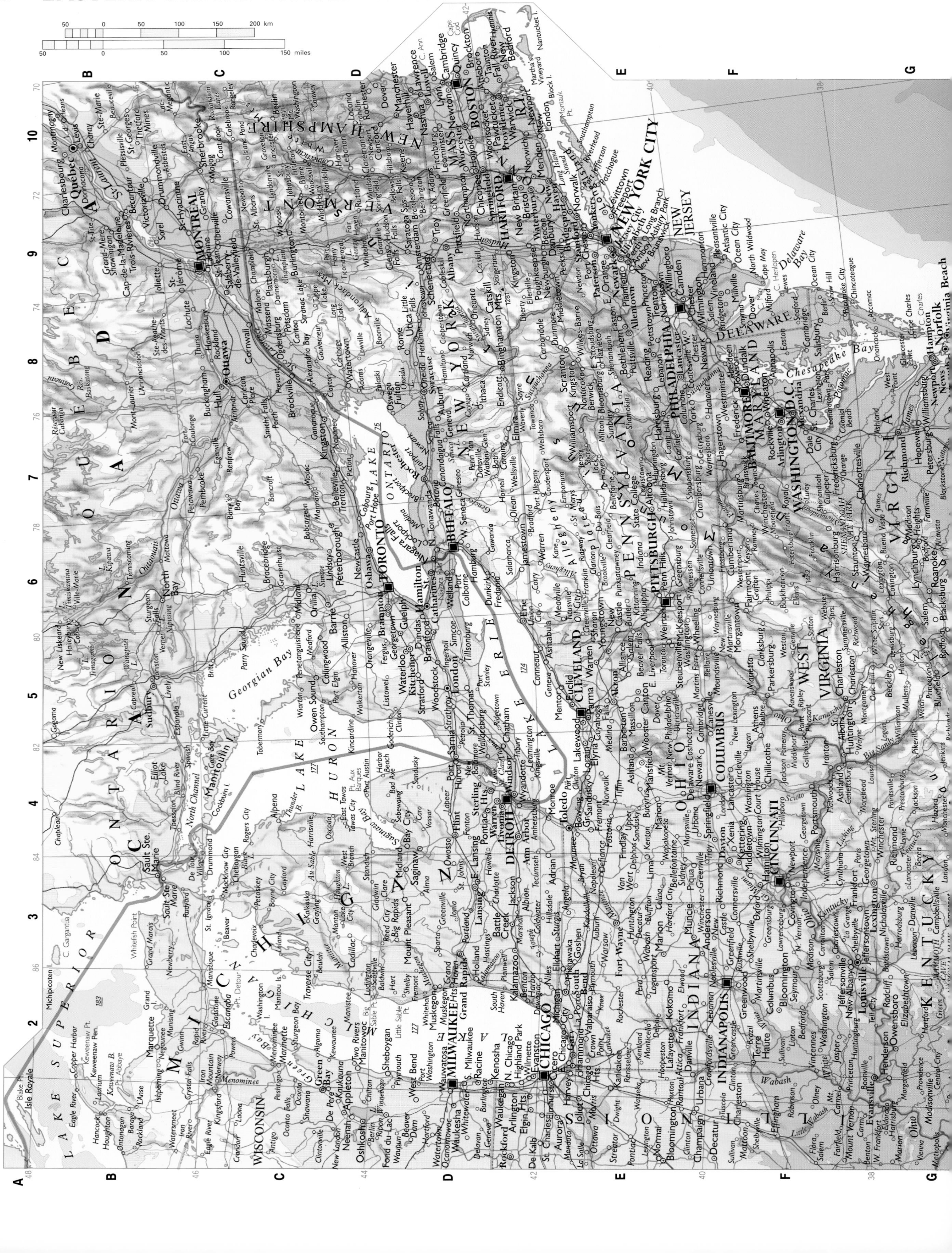

50 0 50 100 150 200 km

50 0 50 100 150 miles

LAKE SUPERIOR

QUÉBEC

ONTARIO

MICHIGAN

WISCONSIN

ILLINOIS

INDIANA

OHIO

KENTUCKY

WEST VIRGINIA

VIRGINIA

PENNSYLVANIA

NEW YORK

VERMONT

NEW HAMPSHIRE

MASS.

R.I.

CONN.

NEW JERSEY

DELAWARE

MARYLAND

MAINE

LAKE MICHIGAN

LAKE HURON

Georgian Bay

LAKE ERIE

LAKE ONTARIO

Chesapeake Bay

MONTREAL

Ottawa

TORONTO

Hamilton

BUFFALO

DETROIT

CHICAGO

MILWAUKEE

INDIANAPOLIS

CINCINNATI

COLUMBUS

CLEVELAND

PITTSBURGH

BOSTON

HARTFORD

NEW YORK CITY

PHILADELPHIA

BALTIMORE

WASHINGTON D.C.

Québec

Continuation Eastwards On same scale.

MAINE

NEW HAMPSHIRE

CANADA

NORTH CAROLINA

SOUTH CAROLINA

TENNESSEE

GEORGIA

ALABAMA

MISSISSIPPI

FLORIDA

BAHAMAS

ATLANTIC OCEAN

GULF OF MEXICO

Nashville
Charlotte
Raleigh
Atlanta
Birmingham
Montgomery
Mobile
Columbia
Charleston
Savannah
Jacksonville
Tampa
Miami
Orlando
Tallahassee
Pensacola
Chattanooga
Knoxville
Asheville
Greenville
Columbus
Macon
Augusta
Wilmington

West from Greenwich

GREAT SMOKY MTS. NAT. PARK
ACADIA NAT. PARK
EVERGLADES NAT. PARK
CYPRESS NAT. PRESERVE

Great Abaco I.
Grand Bahama
Little Abaco I.
Freeport
Hope Town
Southwest Pt.

Florida Keys
Key Largo
Biscayne B.
Coral Gables
Fort Lauderdale
Hollywood
Hialeah
Homestead
Kendall
West Palm Beach
Boca Raton
Delray Beach
Boynton Beach
Pompano Beach
Palm Beach
Lake Worth
Belle Glade
Okeechobee
Lake Okeechobee
Stuart
Fort Pierce
Port St. Lucie
Vero Beach
Melbourne
Titusville
Cocoa
C. Canaveral
Merritt Island
Daytona Beach
New Smyrna Beach
Port Orange
Ormond Beach
St. Augustine
Palm Coast
Gainesville
Ocala
Leesburg
Eustis
Sanford
Winter Park
Orlando
Kissimmee
St. Cloud
Winter Haven
Lakeland
Plant City
Bradenton
Sarasota
Venice
Port Charlotte
Punta Gorda
Cape Coral
Fort Myers
Naples
Marco
Sanibel
St. Petersburg
Clearwater
Largo
Dunedin
Tarpon Springs
New Port Richey
Spring Hill
Brooksville
Inverness
Crystal River

Projection: Albers' Equal Area with two standard parallels

COPYRIGHT GEORGE PHILIP LTD.

m: 2000 1500 1000 400 200 0
ft: 6000 4500 3000 1200 600 0
ft: 12 000 6000 2000 0
m: 4000 2000 600 200

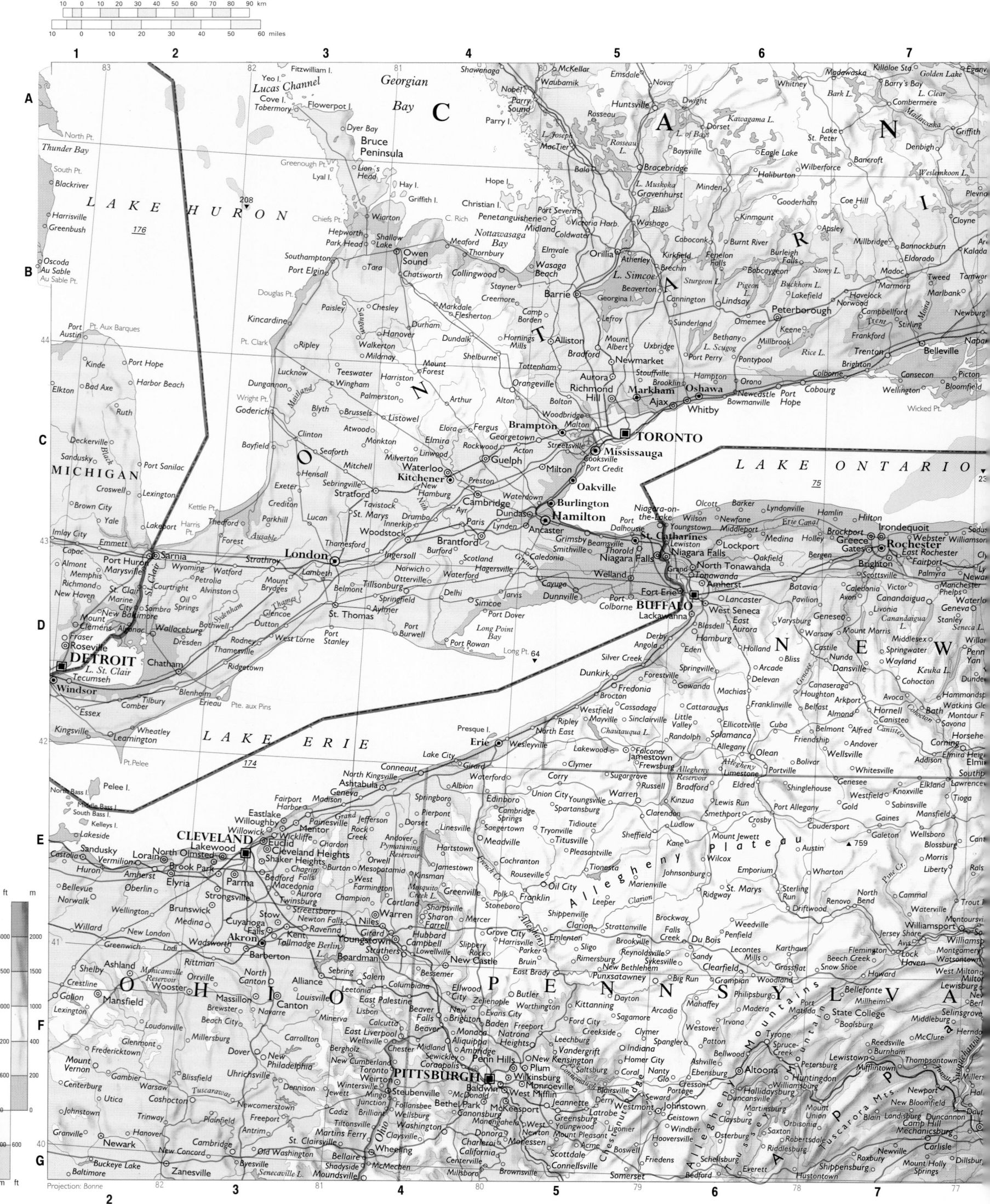

10 0 10 20 30 40 50 60 70 80 90 km
10 0 10 20 30 40 50 60 miles

Projection: Bonne

ft m
6000 2000
4500 1500
3000 1000
1200 400
600 200
0 0
200 600
m ft

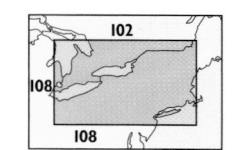

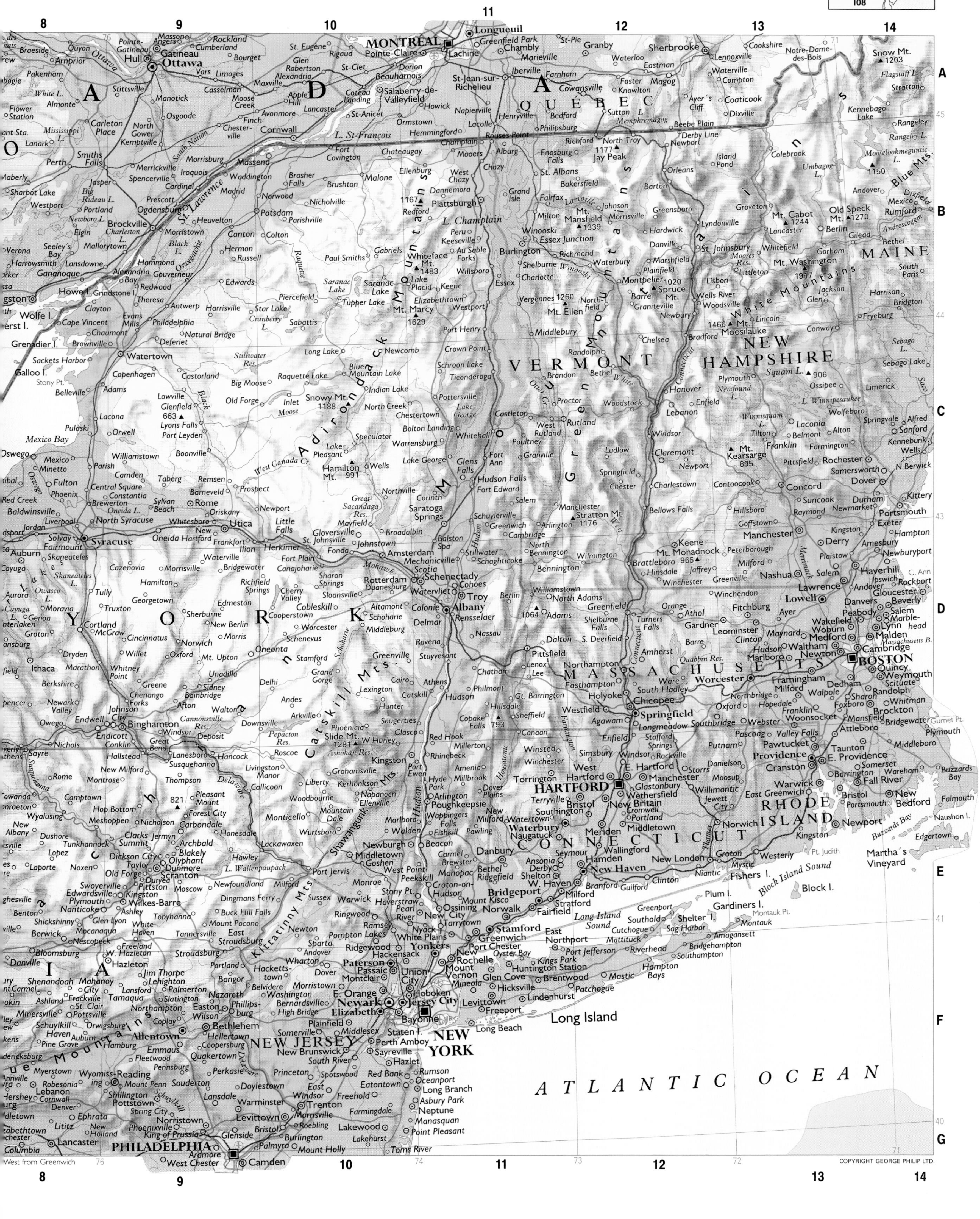

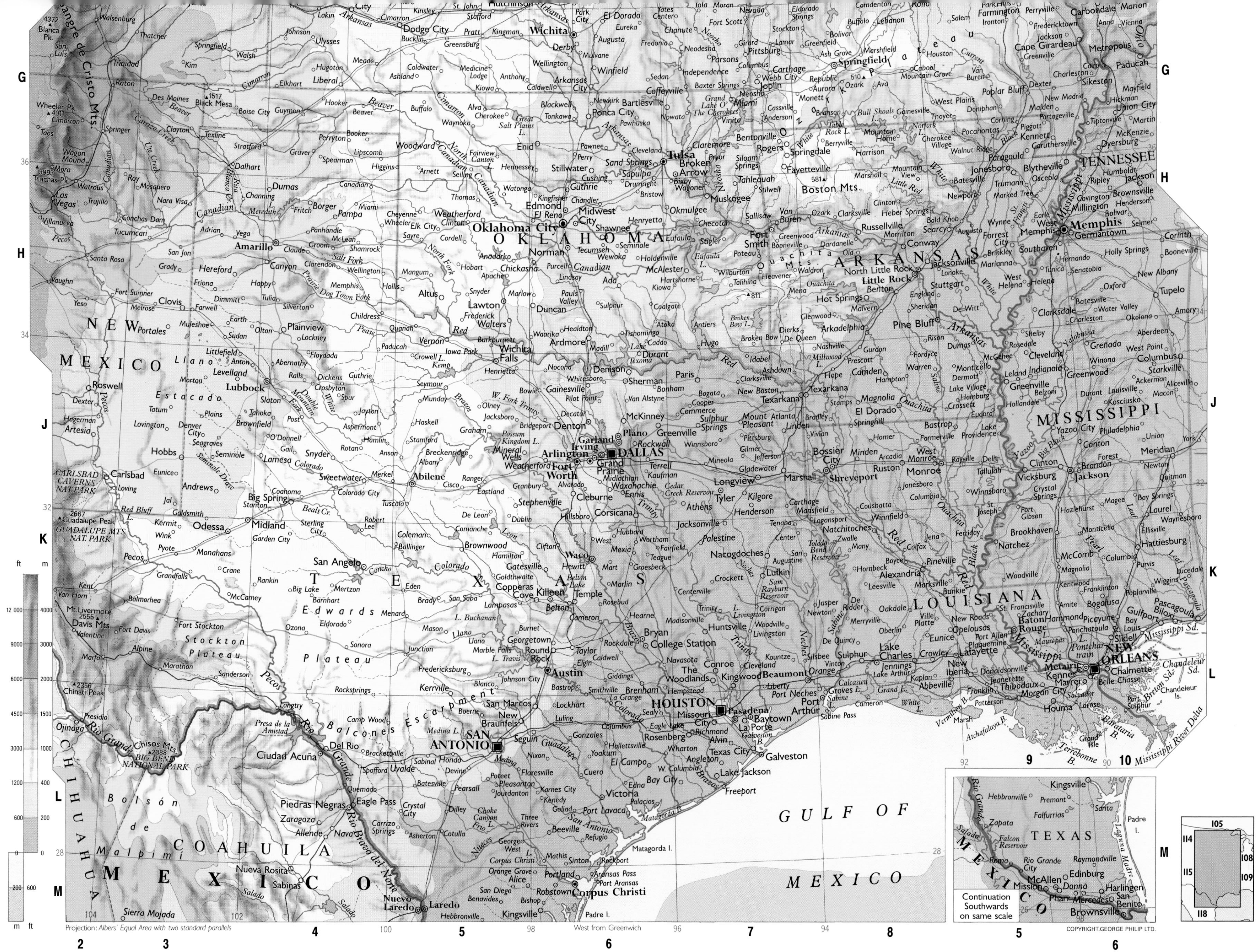

TENNESSEE

MISSISSIPPI

ARKANSAS

LOUISIANA

OKLAHOMA

NEW MEXICO

TEXAS

MEXICO

COAHUILA

CHIHUAHUA

GULF OF MEXICO

Continuation Southwards on same scale

Laguna Madre

Rio Grande

Projection: Albers' Equal Area with two standard parallels

West from Greenwich

COPYRIGHT GEORGE PHILIP LTD.

50   0   50   100   150   200 km
50   0   50   100   150 miles

A   B   C   D   E   F

SASKATCHEWAN

ALBERTA

BRITISH COLUMBIA

MONTANA

WASHINGTON

OREGON

IDAHO

WYOMING

UTAH

NEVADA

R O C K Y   M O U N T A I N S

Bighorn Mountains

Absaroka Range

YELLOWSTONE NATIONAL PARK

GRAND TETON NAT. PARK

Wind River Range

Medicine Bow Mts.

ROCKY MOUNTAIN NAT. PARK

Salmon River Mountains

Sawtooth Range

Lewis Range

Swan Range

Bitterroot Range

Clearwater Mountains

Cabinet Mountains

Blue Mountains

Wallowa Mts.

Harney Basin

Columbia Plateau

Great Salt Lake

Great Salt Lake Desert

Uinta Mountains

Roan Plateau

DINOSAUR NATIONAL MONUMENT

Ruby Mts.

Independence Mts.

Santa Rosa Range

Warner Mts.

Steens Mountain

C A S C A D E   R A N G E

Columbia Basin

OLYMPIC NAT. PARK

Olympic Mts.

NORTH CASCADES NAT. PARK

MOUNT RAINIER NAT. PARK

CRATER LAKE NAT. PARK

LASSEN VOLCANIC NAT. PARK

REDWOOD NAT. PARK

GLACIER NATIONAL PARK

WATERTON LAKES NAT. PARK

C O A S T   R A N G E S

S I E R R A   N E V A D A

VANCOUVER

SEATTLE

PORTLAND

SACRAMENTO

SALT LAKE CITY

Vancouver Island

Strait of Juan de Fuca

Puget Sound

Columbia River

Snake River

Missouri River

Yellowstone River

Green River

Fort Peck Lake

Lake Tahoe

Great Salt Lake

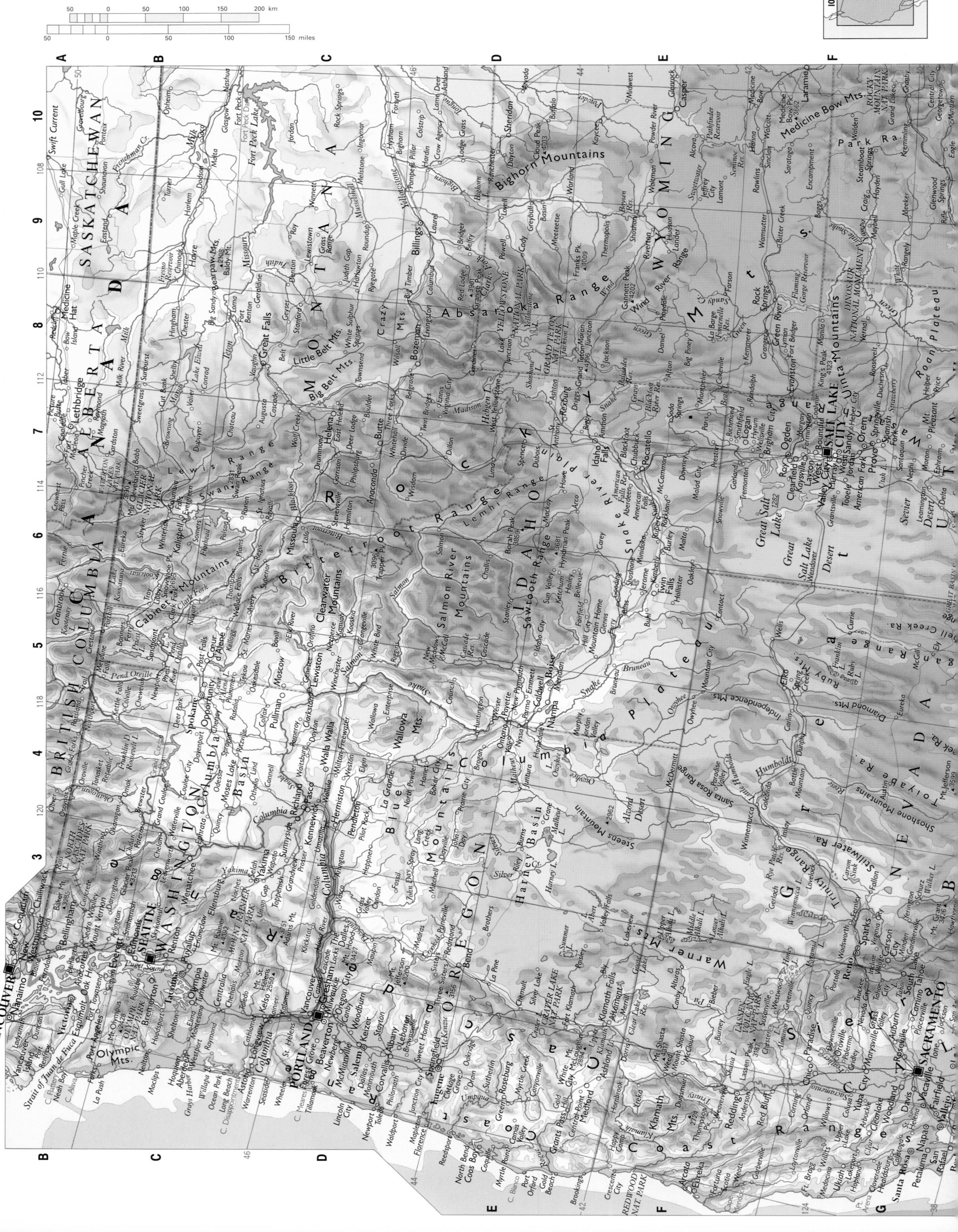

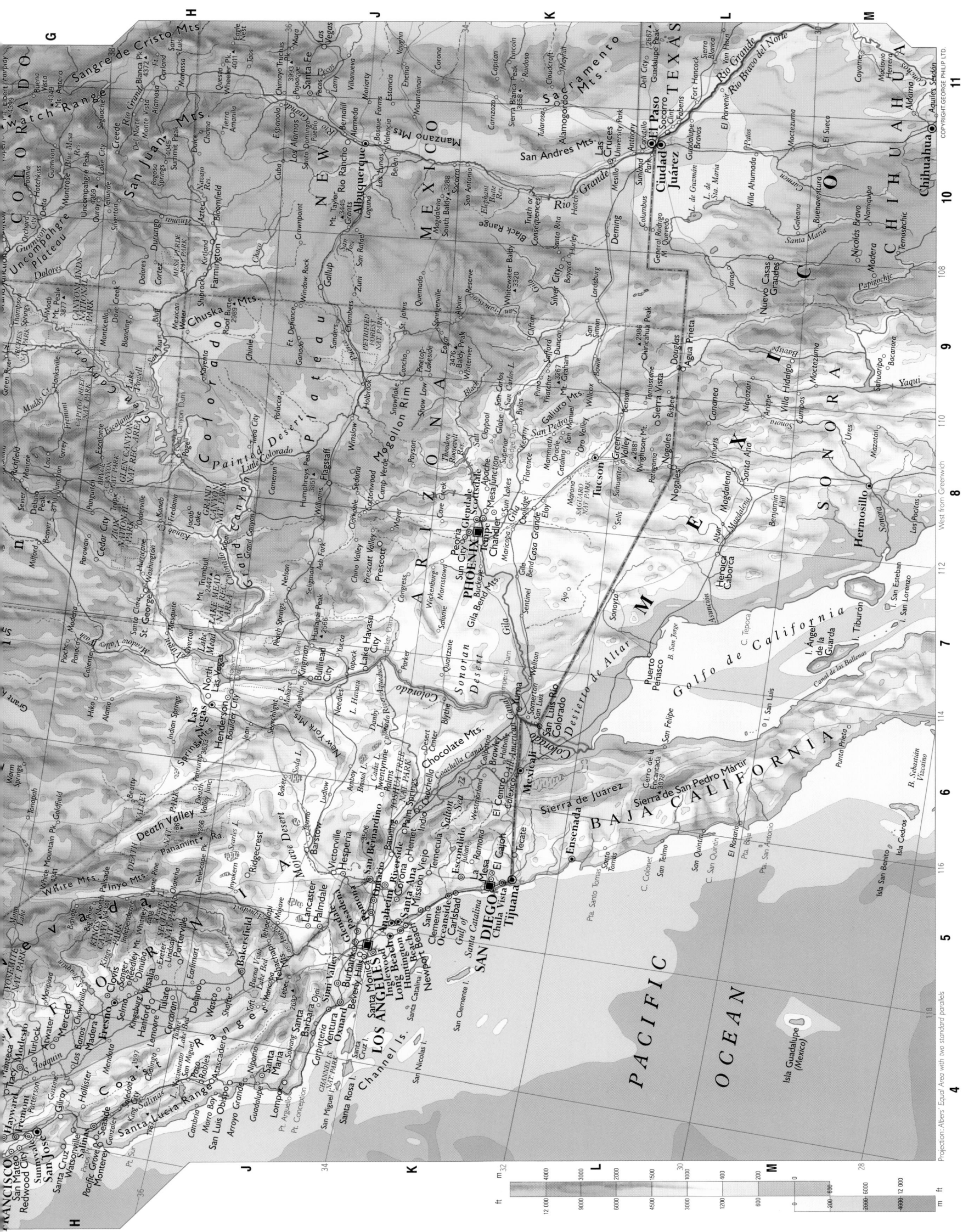

COPYRIGHT GEORGE PHILIP LTD.

Projection: Albers' Equal Area with two standard parallels

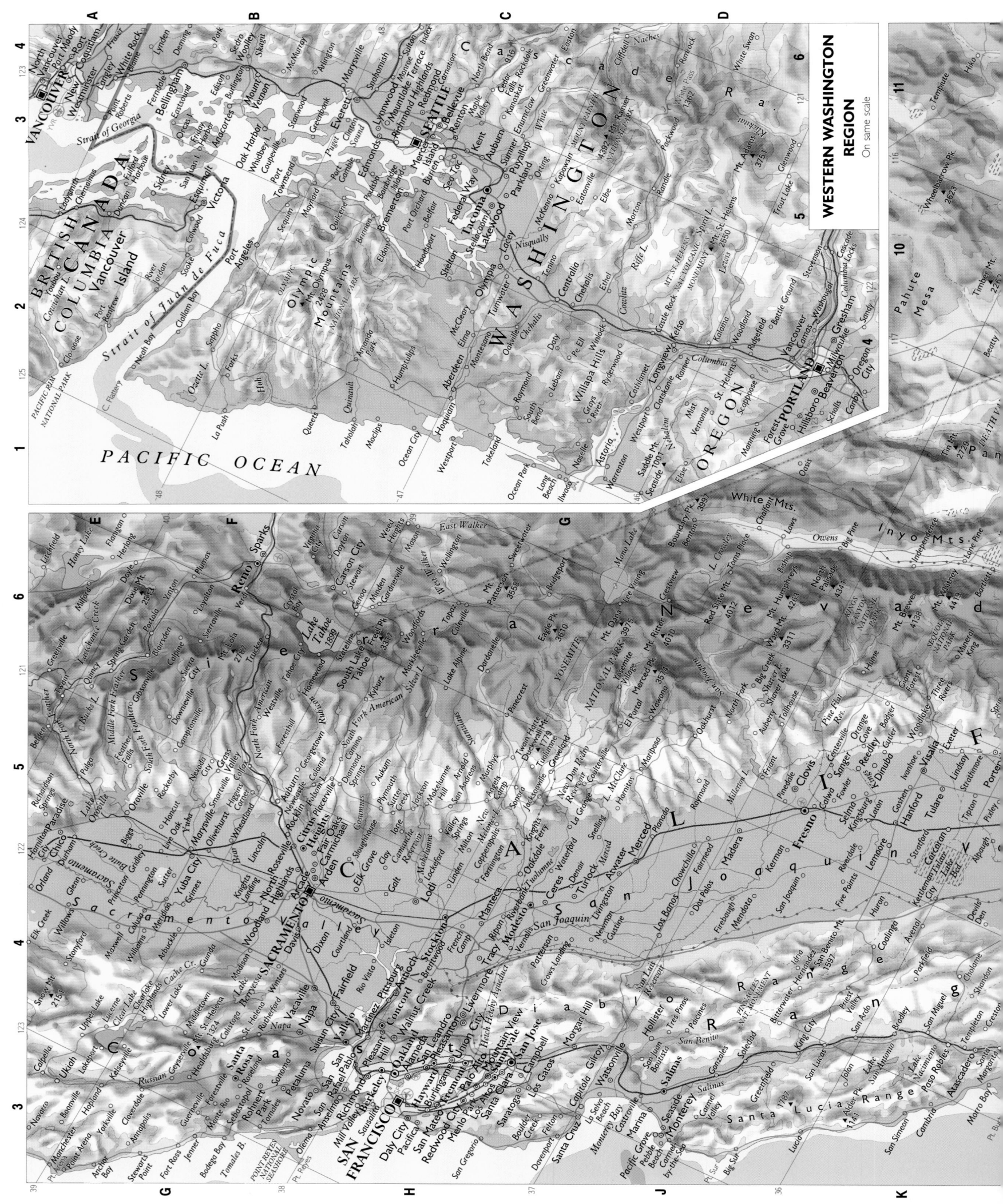

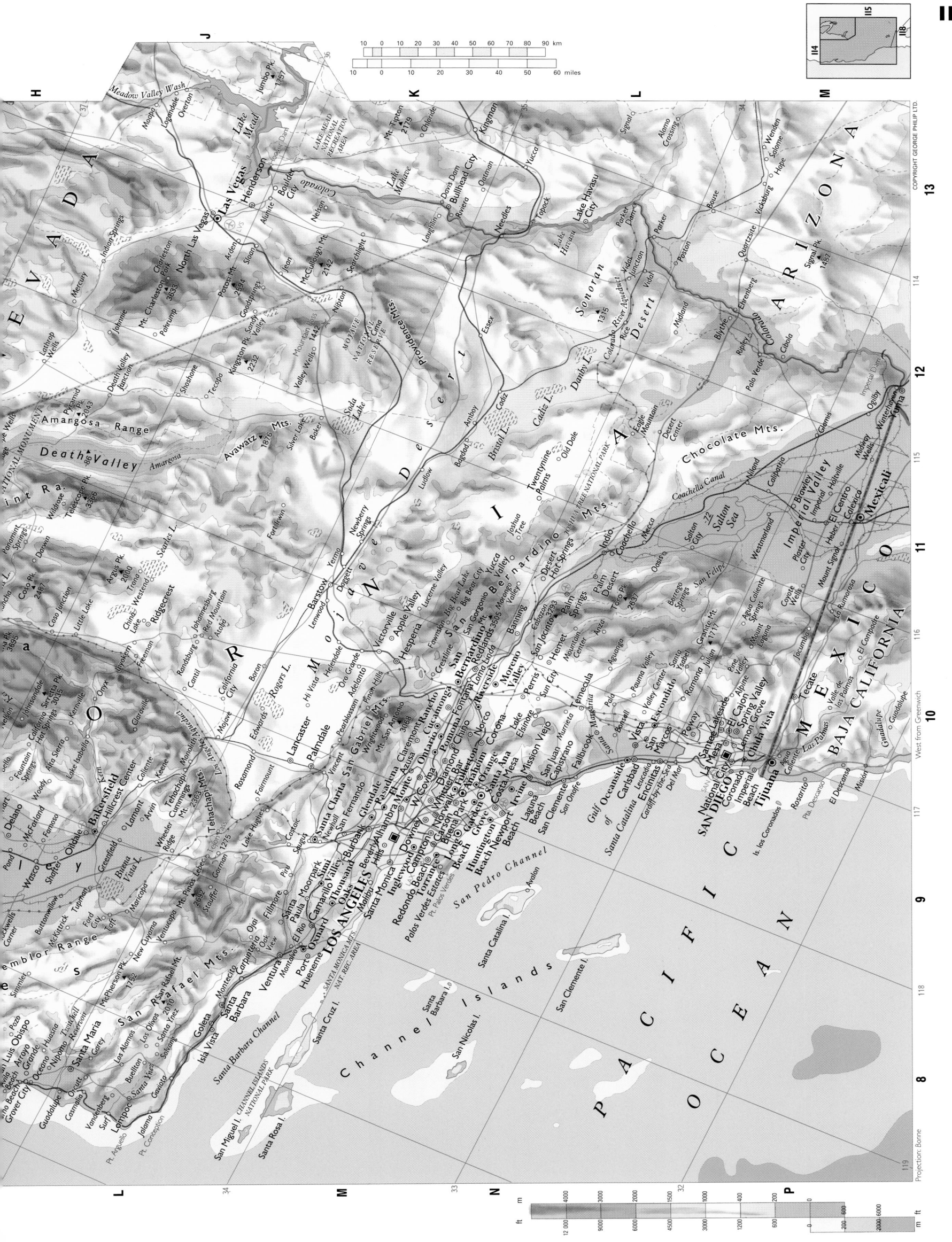

10 0 10 20 30 40 50 60 70 80 90 km
10 0 10 20 30 40 50 60 miles

COPYRIGHT GEORGE PHILIP LTD.

West from Greenwich

Projection: Bonne

NEVADA

ARIZONA

CALIFORNIA

MEXICO

BAJA CALIFORNIA

Meadow Valley Wash
Jumbo Pk. 1457
Overton
Logandale
Moapa
Lake Mead
Hoover Dam
LAKE MEAD NATIONAL RECREATION AREA
Mt. Tipton 2179
Chloride
Signal
Wenden
Hope
Salome
Wendate

Las Vegas
Henderson
Boulder City
Nelson
Davis Dam
Bullhead City
Kingman
Yucca
Alamo Crossing
Signal

North Las Vegas
Arden
Sloan
Jean
McCullough Mt. 2142
Searchlight
Lake Mohave
Riviera
Laughlin
Needles
Topock
Parker Dam
Lake Havasu City
Oatman
Parker
Bouse
Vicksburg

Indian Springs
Charleston Park
Potosi Pk. 2594
Goodsprings
Nipton
Cima
MOJAVE NATIONAL PRESERVE
Essex
Lake Havasu
Vidal
Earp
Poston
Quartzsite
Signal Pk. 1467

Mercury
Mt. Charleston 3633
Pahrump
Sandy Valley
Mountain Pass 1442
PRESERVE
Amboy
Cadiz
Rice
Vidal Junction
Blythe
Ehrenberg
Ripley
Cibola

Johnnie
Kingston Pk. 2232
SONORAN
DESERT
Essex
Danby L.
Cadiz L.
Midland
Palo Verde
Imperial Dam

Death Valley Junction
Shoshone
Tecopa
Valley Wells 1442
Nipton
Ludlow
Bagdad
Bristol L.
Old Dale
Desert Center
Glamis
Ogilby
Yuma
Winterhaven

Amargosa Range
Silver Lake
Baker
Soda Lake
Newberry Springs
Twentynine Palms
JOSHUA TREE NATIONAL PARK
Eagle Mountain
Chocolate Mts.
Midway Wells

Death Valley
Amargosa
Avawatz Mts. 1876
Yermo
Daggett
Barstow
Ludlow
Joshua Tree
Coachella Canal
Niland
Calipatria
Brawley
Calexico
Mexicali

Telescope Pk. 3366
Searles L.
Randsburg
Lenwood
Hinkley
Victorville
Hesperia
San Bernardino Mts.
Desert Hot Springs
Indio
Coachella
Mecca
Salton Sea
Westmorland
Imperial Valley
Imperial
El Centro
Heber
Mexicali

Argus Pk. 2000
Coso Pk. 2481
Trona
China Lake
Ridgecrest
Johannesburg
Red Mountain
Atolia
Boron
California City
Rogers L.
Apple Valley
Lucerne Valley
Big Bear Lake
Yucca Valley
Morongo Valley
San Gorgonio Mt. 3505
Banning
Palm Springs
Desert Center
Borrego Springs
Salton City
Oasis
Coyote Wells
Las Palmas

Kernville
Lake Isabella
Inyokern
Freeman
Mojave
Edwards
Rosamond
Hi Vista
Adelanto
Oro Grande
Helendale
Crestline
Redlands
Loma Linda
Moreno Valley
Perris
Hemet
San Jacinto
Idyllwild
Mountain Center
Anza
Aguanga
Granite Mt. 1711
Pine Valley
Jacumba
Volcano Las Palmas
Mexcate

Bakersfield
Hillcrest Center
Tehachapi
Mojave
Lancaster
Palmdale
Littlerock
Wrightwood
San Gabriel Mts.
Mt. San Antonio 3068
San Bernardino
Riverside
Corona
Lake Elsinore
Sun City
Temecula
Murrieta
Fallbrook
Sunnyside
Pala
Valley Center
Santa Ysabel
Ramona
Julian
Alpine
El Cajon
Spring Valley
Lemon Grove
Guadalupe

Delano
McFarland
Wasco
Shafter
Oildale
Lamont
Arvin
Keene
Tehachapi Mts. 2360
Gorman
Castaic
Saugus
Newhall
Santa Clarita
San Fernando
Glendale
Pasadena
Claremont
Upland
Ontario
Cucamonga
Rancho
Fontana
Pomona
Chino
Norco
Orange
Santa Ana
Mission Viejo
San Juan Capistrano
San Clemente
San Onofre
Oceanside
Carlsbad
Encinitas
Cardiff-by-the-Sea
Del Mar
San Marcos
Escondido
Vista
Poway
Santee
Lakeside
La Mesa
National City
Coronado
Imperial Beach
Chula Vista
Tijuana
Rosarito
Agua Caliente

SAN DIEGO

LOS ANGELES

Santa Monica
Inglewood
Redondo Beach
Torrance
Palos Verdes Estates
Pt. Palos Verdes
San Pedro Channel
Avalon
Santa Catalina I.

Beverly Hills
Burbank
Alhambra
Monterey Park
West Covina
Downey
Compton
Carson
Long Beach
Huntington Beach
Newport Beach
Laguna Beach
Buena Park
Anaheim
Fullerton
Garden Grove
Costa Mesa
Irvine
Gulf of Santa Catalina

Simi Valley
Thousand Oaks
Moorpark
Camarillo
Oxnard
Port Hueneme
Ventura
Fillmore
Santa Paula
Ojai
Oak View
El Rio
Montalvo
Carpinteria
Montecito
Goleta
Santa Barbara
Isla Vista

SANTA MONICA MTS. NAT. REC. AREA
Malibu

Santa Barbara Channel
San Miguel I.
Santa Rosa I.
Santa Cruz I.
Santa Barbara I.
San Nicolas I.
San Clemente I.
CHANNEL ISLANDS NATIONAL PARK

Channel Islands

San Luis Obispo
Pismo Beach
Grover City
Oceano
Guadalupe
Santa Maria
Casmalia
Orcutt
Los Alamos
Buellton
Solvang
Santa Ynez
Lompoc
Surf
Pt. Arguello
Pt. Conception
Gaviota
Nipomo
Arroyo Grande

Temblor Range
San Rafael Mts.
McPherson Pk. 1762
San Emigdio Mts.

PACIFIC OCEAN

Colorado (river)

Valley
Death Valley

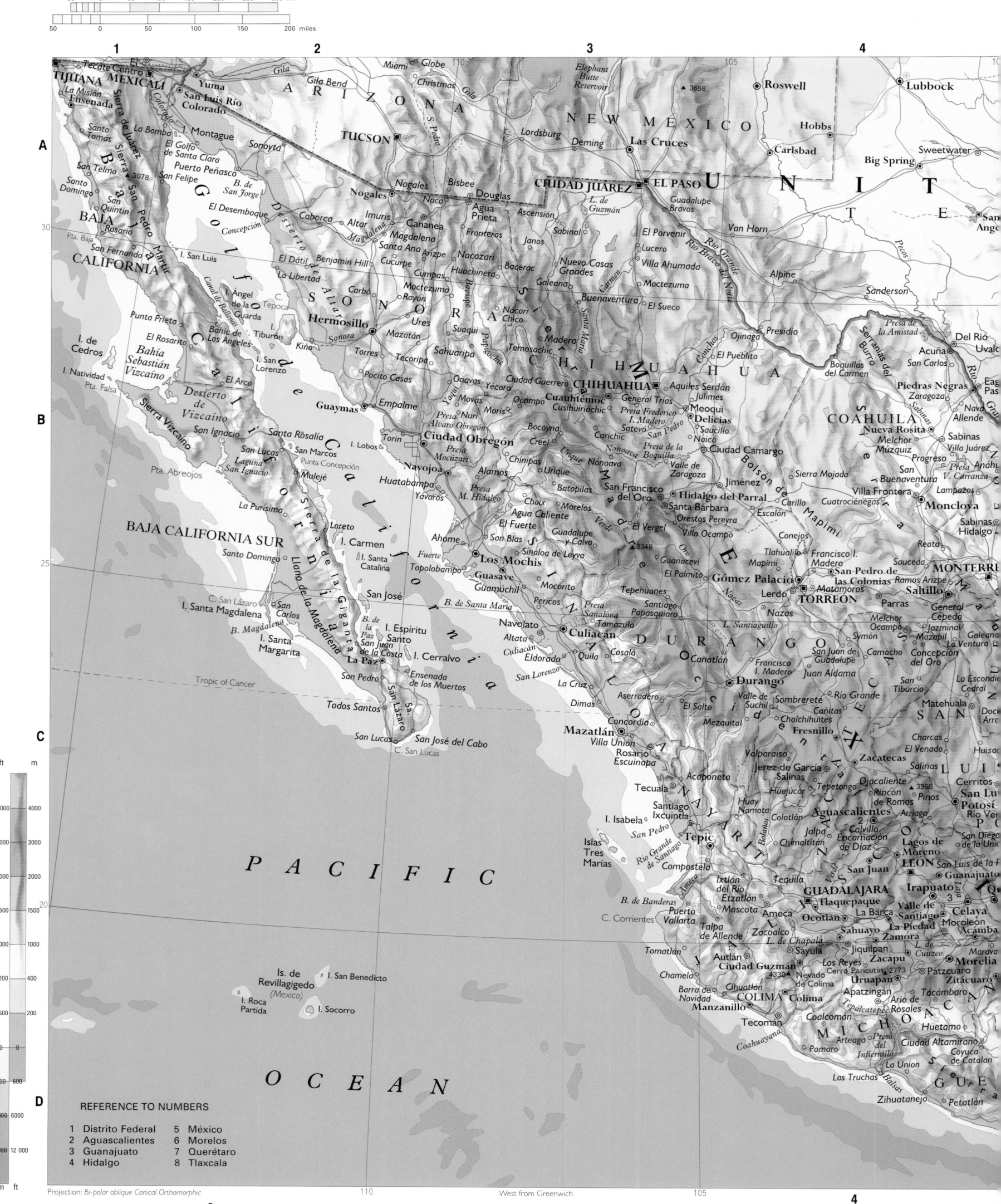

50 0 50 100 150 200 250 300 km
50 0 50 100 150 200 miles

A

B

C

D

Tropic of Cancer

PACIFIC

OCEAN

REFERENCE TO NUMBERS

1 Distrito Federal   5 México
2 Aguascalientes   6 Morelos
3 Guanajuato   7 Querétaro
4 Hidalgo   8 Tlaxcala

Projection: Bi-polar oblique Conical Orthomorphic

West from Greenwich

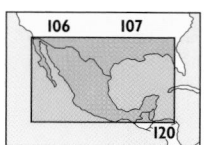

GULF OF MEXICO

PACIFIC OCEAN

CARIBBEAN

U.S.A.
Fort Myers · Naples · West Palm Beach · Fort Lauderdale · Boca Raton · West End · Freeport · Grand Bahama · Hope Town · Little Abaco I. · Great Abaco I.
MIAMI · Hialeah · C. Romano · C. Sable · Everglades
Dry Tortugas (U.S.A.) · Key West · Florida Keys · Straits of Florida
L. Okeechobee
Bimini Is. · Berry Is. · Nicolls Town · Adelaide · New Providence · Nassau · Andros Town · Andros Island · Eleuthera · Dunmore Town · Governor · Great Guana Cay · Great Exuma I. · Exuma Sound · Jumento Cays
Northwest Providence Channel · Northeast Providence Channel · Great Bahama Bank

CUBA
LA HABANA (Havana) · MARIANAO · Guanabacoa · Guanajay · Bahía Honda · La Esperanza · Los Palacios · Pinar del Río · Guane · San Luis · La Fé · Nueva Gerona · I. de la Juventud · Batabanó · San Antonio de los Baños · Güines · Jovellanos · Colón · Jagüey Grande · Matanzas · Cárdenas · Sagua la Grande · Santa Clara · Placetas · Cienfuegos · Trinidad · Sancti Spíritus · Morón · Ciego de Ávila · Júcaro · Tunas de Zaza · Florida · Camagüey · Nuevitas · Santa Cruz del Sur · Victoria de las Tunas · HOLGUÍN · Bayamo · Manzanillo · Golfo de Guacanayabo · Gibara · Puerto Padre · Soria · Sierra Maestra · SANTIAGO DE CUBA · C. Cruz
Santa Cruz del Norte · Canal Nicolás · Canal Viejo de Bahama
Arch. de los Canarreos · Arch. de Jardines de la Reina · Golfo de Ana María

Canal de Yucatán

Cayman Islands (U.K.) · Georgetown · Grand Cayman · Cayman Brac · Little Cayman · 7680

Swan Islands (U.S.A. & Honduras)

JAMAICA
Montego Bay · Lucea · Negril Pt. · South Negril Pt. · Falmouth · St. Ann's Bay · Port Maria · Annotto Bay · Port Antonio · Savanna-la-Mar · Cambridge · Black River · Mandeville · May Pen · Spanish Town · KINGSTON · Port
Pedro Cays (Jamaica)
Bajo Nuevo (Colombia)

MEXICO
I. Desterrada · I. Pérez (Mexico) · Punta Yalkubul · Progreso · Dzilam de Bravo · Dzidzantun · Motul · Temax · Tizimín · El Cuyo · C. Catoche · Río Lagartos · Cancún · Puerto Juárez · Mérida · Izamal · Espita · Valladolid · El Diaz · Maxcanú · Sotuta · Ticul · Peto · Puerto Morelos · Tekax · MAYAPÁN · CHICHEN ITZA · Cozumel · Isla Cozumel · UXMAL · Campeche · Tenabo · Bolonchenticul · Hopelchén · Vigía Chico · B. de la Ascensión · Champotón · San José Carpizo · Felipe Carrillo Puerto · B. del Espíritu Santo · Chenkán · Quintana Roo · Bacalar · Banco Chinchorro · Ciudad del Carmen · I. del Carmen · Campeche · Matamoros · Chetumal · B. de Chetumal · Corozal · Palizada · Balancán · Concepción · Orange Walk · Hondo
YUCATÁN

GUATEMALA
Palenque · Ocosingo · Tenosique · Uaxactún · San Ignacio · TIKAL · L. Petén Itzá · La Libertad · Flores · Benque Viejo · La Independencia · Lacantún · Sebol · Comitán · Sierra de los Cuchumatanes · 3993 · Cuilco · San Marcos · Huehuetenango · Totonicapán · Quezaltenango · Sololá · Cobán · Gualán · Sierra de las Minas · Antigua · GUATEMALA · Jalapa · Chiquimula · Santa Rosa de Copán · Amatitlán · Escuintla · San José · Ayutla · Retalhuleu · Mazatenango · Coatepeque

BELIZE
Ambergris Cay · Belize City · Turneffe Is. · Belmopan · Middlesex · BELIZE · Dangriga · Maya Mts. · Monkey River · San Antonio · Punta Gorda · Livingston · Puerto Barrios · L. de Izabal

HONDURAS
Golfo de Honduras · Is. de la Bahía · Roatán · Puerto Cortés · Tela · La Ceiba · Balfate · Trujillo · Iriona · C. Camarón · Punta Patuca · Brus Laguna · Laguna Caratasca · Mosquitia · C. Falso · C. Gracias a Dios · San Pedro Sula · El Progreso · Santa Bárbara · Yoro · Olanchito · Catacamas · Juticalpa · Comayagua · La Esperanza · La Paz · TEGUCIGALPA · Yuscarán · Danlí · Nacaome · Choluteca

EL SALVADOR
Santa Ana · Ahuachapán · Sonsonate · SAN SALVADOR · Nueva San Salvador · Cojutepeque · Suchitoto · Zacatecoluca · Usulután · San Miguel · La Unión · San José · Acajutla · G. de Fonseca

NICARAGUA
Puerto Cabo Gracias á Dios · Kisalaya · Cayos Miskitos (Nicaragua) · Pta. Gorda · Puerto Cabezas · Bonanza · Siuna · Somoto · Ocotal · Cord. Isabelia · Estelí · Jinotega · Matagalpa · Tuma · Tungla · Prinzapolca · Río Grande · San Pedro del Norte · El Sauce · Muy Muy · Boaco · Santo Domingo · Siquia · Rama · Bluefields · El Bluff · Pta. Mico · Cord. de Yolaina · MANAGUA · Masaya · Juigalpa · León · Chinandega · Corinto · La Paz Centro · L. de Managua · Diriamba · Jinotepe · Granada · Lago de Nicaragua · I. de Ometepe · Rivas · San Carlos · B. de San Juan del Norte · Punta de Perlas · Is. del Maíz (Nicaragua, U.S.A.) · Cayos de Albuquerque (Colombia) · Cayos Roncador (U.S.A. & Colombia) · I. de Providencia (Colombia) · I. de San Andrés (Colombia) · San Juan del Sur · B. de Salinas · C. Santa Elena · G. de Papagayo · C. Velas · San Juan del Norte

COSTA RICA
Liberia · Santa Cruz · Nicoya · Carmona · Pen. de Nicoya · B. Blanco · Puntarenas · Espartza · Alajuela · SAN JOSÉ · Cartago · Guápiles · Siquirres · Limón · Cord. Central · Cord. de Talamanca · 3837 · Chirripó Grande · B. de Coronado · Puerto Quepos · Puerto Cortés · Buenos Aires · San Vito · Golfito · G. Dulce · Puerto Armuelles · Pen. de Osa · Pta. Burica · Bribri · Bocas del Toro · Pandora · Mona

PANAMA
Almirante · Volcán Barú · 3374 · Boquete · David · La Concepción · Remedios · Santiago · Aguadulce · Penonomé · Chitré · Las Tablas · Pocrí · Tonosí · Pta. Mala · Pen. de Azuero · Sona · Río Hato · Arch. de las Perlas · I. del Rey · San Miguel · PANAMÁ · Balboa · L. Gatun · Panama Canal · Colón · Portobelo · Nombre de Dios · Archipiélago de San Blas · Serranía de San Blas · La Chorrera · Chepo · Chimán · Yaviza · El Real · La Palma · Golfo de Panamá · Golfo del Darién · Serranía del Darién · Pta. Manzanillo · I. de Coiba · I. de Cebaco · I. Jicarón · Punta Mariato

CARTAGO · I. de San Bernardo · G. de Morrosquillo

Projection: Conical with two standard parallels

MAS

ATLANTIC

OCEAN

Tropic of Cancer

hur's Town
The Bight
Cat I.
San Salvador I.
Conception I.
Rum Cay
Long I.
Clarence Town
Crooked I. Passage
Samana Cay
Crooked I.
Plana Cays
Albert Town
Snug Corner
Mayaguana I.
Cay Verde
Acklins I.
Mira por vos Cay
Caicos Passage
Turks & Caicos
Caicos Is.
(U.K.)
Hogsty Reef
Little Inagua I.
Turks Island Passage
Turks Is.
Lake Rosa
Great Inagua I.
Matthew Town

MAS

Moa
ayari
Baracoa
Pta. de Maisí
Í. de la Tortue
Monte Cristi
LA ISABELA
Santiago de los Cabelleros
Puerto Rico Trench
uantánamo
Paso de los Vientos
(Windward Passage)
Jean Rabel
Port-de-Paix
Cap-Haïtien
Cap-à-Foux
G. de la Gonâve
Gonaïves
Fort Liberté
Puerto Plata
La Vega
San Francisco de Macorís
Milwaukee Deep 9200
Nagua
Samana
St-Marc
Hinche
Cord. Central
3175
Sánchez
Sabana de la Mar
Bayamón
SAN JUAN
Anegada
Virgin Gorda
Virgin Is.
(U.K.)
Sombrero (U.K.)
HAITI
DOMINICAN
Hato Mayor
Arecibo
Carolina
Tortola
St. Thomas
Road Town
Anguilla (U.K.)
San Juan
REP.
San Pedro de Macorís
Higüey
Aguadilla
1338
Ponce
Fajardo
Carolina
Charlotte-Amalie
Virgin Is.
St. Maarten
St.-Martin (Fr.)
St.-Barthélemy (Fr.)
Jérémie
Í. de la Gonâve
PORT-AU-PRINCE
L. Enriquillo
La Romana
C. Engaño
Caguas
(U.S.A.)
Saba (Neth.)
vassa I.
(U.S.A.)
Marie
Massif de la Hotte
Petit Goâve
2280
Azua de Compostela
B. de Yuma
Guayama
Christiansted
St. Eustatius (Neth.)
Barbuda
Dame
Les Cayes
Aquin
Jacmel
Barahona
Í. Saona
Mayagüez
Frederiksted
St. Croix
Basseterre
ST. KITTS & NEVIS
ANTIGUA & BARBUDA
C. Carcasse
Pointe-à-Gravois
Pedernales
Isla Mona
PUERTO
Nevis
St. John's
Antigua
Hispaniola
Í. Beata
C. Beata
(U.S.A.)
RICO
Redonda
Montserrat
Guadeloupe Passage
H i s p a n i o l a
(U.K.)
Ste.-Rose
Le Moule
La Désirade
A n t i l l e s
Pointe-à-Pitre (Fr.)
GUADELOUPE
(Fr.)
Marie-Galante
Basse-Terre
Grand-Bourg
Í. des Saintes (Fr.)
Dominica Passage
Portsmouth
DOMINICA
Roseau
I. de Aves
(Venezuela)
Martinique Passage
Mt. Pelée
Ste.-Marie
B E A N
S E A
1397
Le François
Fort-de-France
Rivière-Pilote
MARTINIQUE
(Fr.)
St. Lucia Channel
Castries
ST. LUCIA
Soufrière
St. Vincent Passage
La Soufrière 1234
ST. VINCENT
Speightstown
Kingstown
Bridgetown
BARBADOS
Hillsborough
Grenadines
GRENADINES
St. George's
GRENADA

L e s s e r
A n t i l l e s
Aruba (Neth.)
Curaçao
Bonaire
Pta. Gallinas
C. San Román
Willemstad
NETH. ANTILLES
Is. Las Aves
(Ven.)
I. Orchila
(Ven.)
I. Blanquilla (Ven.)
Is. Los Hermanos
(Ven.)
Is. Los Testigos
(Ven.)
Tobago
Scarborough
Pen. de la Guajira
Pta. Espada
Pen. de Paraguaná
Punto Fijo
Punta Cardón
Puerto Cumarebo
Is. Los Roques
(Ven.)
I. de Margarita
La Asunción
NUEVA ESPARTA
Porlamar
I. La Tortuga
(Ven.)
Galera Point
Port of Spain
Trinidad
SANTA MARTA
Ríohacha
Uribia
GUAJIRA
Golfo de Venezuela
Coro
La Vela de Coro
FALCÓN
Tucacas
Maiquetía
La Guaira
CARACAS
DISTRITO FEDERAL
Pen. de Paria
Cumaná
Río Caribe
Güiria
Carúpano
Cariaco
G. de Paria
San Fernando
TRINIDAD & TOBAGO
ARRAN-QUILLA
Barano
Cienaga
San Rafael
Altagracia
Mene de Mauroa
Tocuyo
Puerto Cabello
C. Codera
Guatire
MIRANDA
Los Teques
Río Chico
Puerto La Cruz
Barcelona
Arima
Río Claro
LÁNTICO
Soledad
Sabanalarga
MARACAIBO
Sierra Nevada de Santa Marta
5800
La Concepción
Santa Rita
Baragua
San Felipe
YARACUY
CARABOBO
Valencia
Villa de Cura
Ocumare del Tuy
Caicara
Maturín
Carora
ARAGUA
San Juan de los Morros
SUCRE
Caripito
MONAGAS
Fundación
Valledupar
Agustín Codazzi
Villa del Rosario
Ciudad Ojeda
Machiques
Lago de Maracaibo
Mene Grande
El Tocuyo
Yaritagua de los Morros
San Carlos
Altagracia de Orituco
Aragua de Barcelona
Anaco
Cantaura
DELTA
Tucupita
jona
MAGDALENA
Plato
CÉSAR
Cabimas
LARA
BARQUISIMETO
Acarigua
COJEDES
Calabozo
Valle de la Pascua
El Tigre
AMACURO
Carmen
Zambrano
ZULIA
Trujillo
Betijoque
PORTUGUESA
GUÁRICO
Santa María de Ipire
El Pao
nce
Corozal
Mompós
El Banco
San Carlos del Zulia
Valera
Trujillo
El Baúl
Pariaguán
ANZOÁTEGUI
Ciudad Guayana
Sierra Imataca
San
Sahagún
Magangué
Encontrados
MÉRIDA
Guanare
Portuguesa
Barinas
Soledad
Upata
Planeta
Majagual
NORTE DE OCAÑA
San Carlos
BARINAS
Libertad
Manapire
Orinoco
Ciudad Bolívar
Rica
Codazzi
Mérida
Ciudad Bolivia
Puerto de Nutrias
Mapire
El Callao
BA
BOLÍVAR
Simití
Cord. de Mérida
Santa Bárbara
V E N E Z U E L A
San Fernando de Apure
Caicara
Embalse de Guri
Guasipati
Tumeremo
Caucasia
Cúcuta
TÁCHIRA
Bruzual
Achaguas
Apure

West from Greenwich

COPYRIGHT GEORGE PHILIP LTD

100 0 200 400 600 800 1000 1200 1400 km
100 0 200 400 600 800 1000 miles

Projection: Lambert's Azimuthal Equal Area

30 CARTOGRAPHY BY PHILIP'S. 20

Tropic of Cancer

NORTH ATLANTIC OCEAN

Yucatán Channel
Gulf of Campeche
Yucatán Peninsula
Isthmus of Tehuantepec
Guatemala Trench

Cuba
Greater Antilles
Jamaica
G. de Honduras
C. Gracias a Dios
Coco
L. Nicaragua
Panama Canal
G. of Darién
Gulf of Panamá

Hispaniola
Turks & Caicos Is.
Puerto Rico 9200
Guadeloupe
Dominica
Martinique
St. Lucia
St. Vincent Barbados
Grenada
Tobago
Trinidad
I. Margarita
Lesser Antilles

Caribbean Sea

C. de la Aguja
Sierra Nevada de Santa Marta 5800
L. Maracaibo
Cord. de Mérida

Cordillera Occidental
Cordillera Central
Cordillera Oriental
C. de San Francisco

Llanos
Meta
Orinoco
Guaviare
Guiana Highlands
Mt. Roraima 2810
Sierra Pacaraima
C. Orange

Caquetá
Cotopaxi 5897
Chimborazo 6267
G. of Guayaquil
Pta. Pariñas
Pta. Negra

Napo
Putumayo
Japurá
Negro
Branco
Serra Tumucumaque
Equator
Marajó I.

Marañón
Ucayali
Juruá
Purus
Amazon
Madeira
Iquitos
Tapajós
Xingu
Tocantins
Parnaíba
C. de São Roque

Huascarán 6768
Madre de Dios
Guaporé
Roosevelt
Aripuanã
Araguaia
São Francisco
Plat. of Borborema

Chincha Alta
L. Titicaca
Bolivian Plateau
Nevada Ancohuma 6550
Mamoré
Plateau of Mato Grosso
Brazilian Highlands

PACIFIC OCEAN
Chile Peru Trench

L. de Poopó

Galapagos Is.

Serra da Mantiqueira
Pico da Bandeira 2890
Serra do Mar
Abrolhos Bank
C. Frio

Tropic of Capricorn
San Félix
San Ambrosio

Atacama Desert
8050
Cerro Ojos del Salado 6863
Salinas Grandes
Gran Chaco
Paraguay
Pilcomayo
Paraná
Iguaçu Falls
Uruguay
L. dos Patos

Arch. de Juan Fernández
Mt. Aconcagua 6960
Sierra de Córdoba
L. Mar Chiquita
Saladó
Entre Ríos
Río de la Plata

Andes
Pampas
Colorado
Bahía Blanca
Negro
G. San Matías
Valdés Peninsula 40

SOUTH ATLANTIC OCEAN

Chile Rise
Chiloé I.
Chonos Archipelago
Taitao Peninsula
Gulf of Penas
Mte. San Valentin 4058
Chubut
Patagonia
Gulf of San Jorge
Argentine Basin
6212

Wellington I.
Madre de Dios I.
Magellan's Str.
Santa Inés I.
Canal Cockburn
Canal Beagle
C. Horn
Tierra del Fuego
Staten I.

West Falkland
East Falkland
Falkland Is.
South Georgia

West from Greenwich 50

ft m
12000 4000
9000 3000
6000 2000
3000 1000
1500 500
600 200
0 0
200 600
1000 3000
2000 6000
4000 12000
6000 18000
8000 24000
m ft

Projection: Lambert's Azimuthal Equal Area

■ LIMA Capital Cities

CARTOGRAPHY BY PHILIP'S.

West from Greenwich

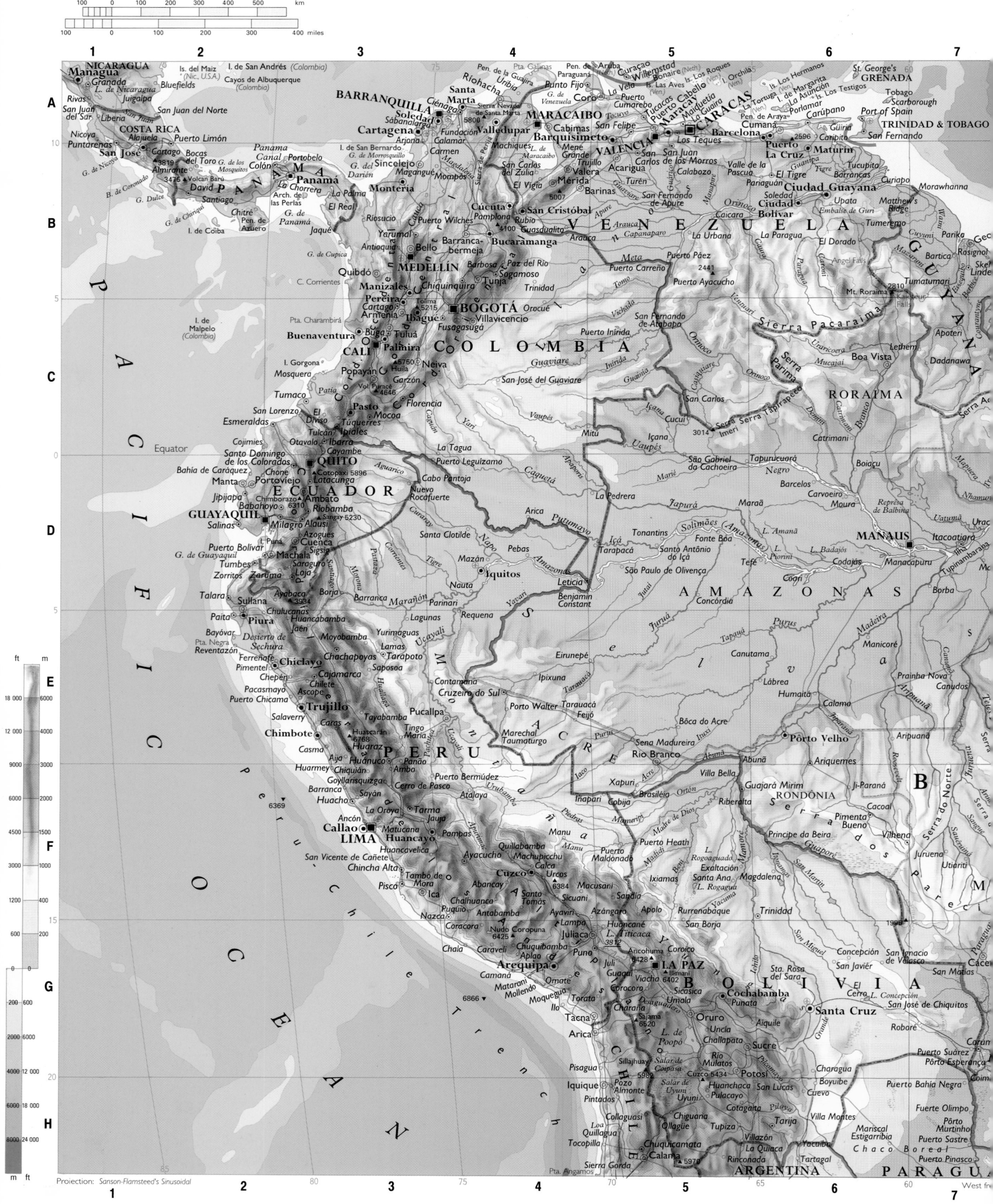

Projection: Sanson-Flamsteed's Sinusoidal

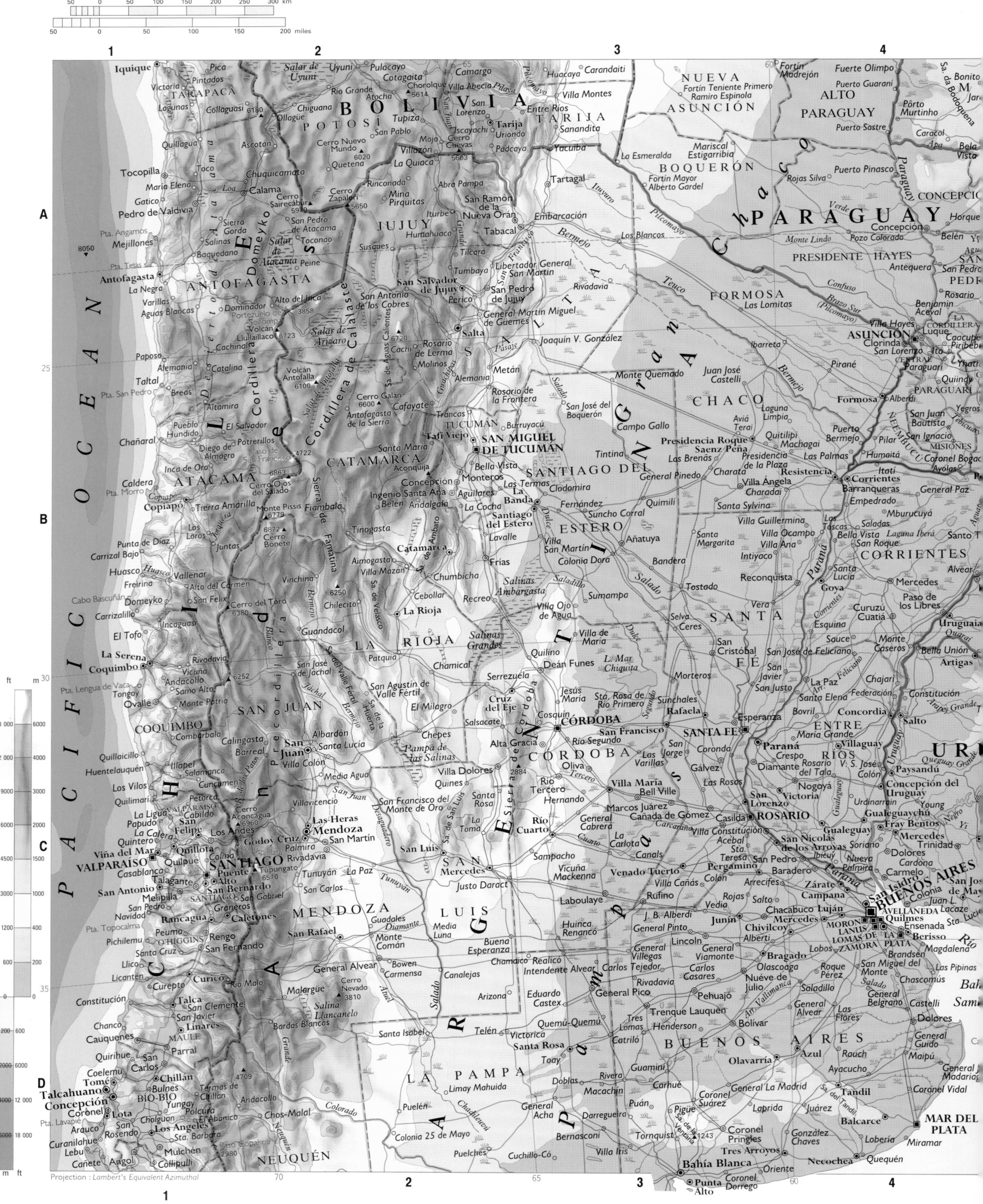

124 125
128

BELO
HORIZONTE
Nova Lima
Itabirito
Congonhas
Conselheiro
Lafaiete
Ouro
Prêto
Ponte Nova
Vitória
Itaquari
Vila
Velha
Guarapari

Passos
Oliveira
Campo Belo
Carangola
Castelo
Cachoeiro
de Itapemirim

Batatais
São Sebastião
do Paraíso
Guaxupé
Alfenas
São João
del Rei
Ubá
Muriaé
Itaperuna
Cambuci
Guarus

MATO GROSSO
DO SUL

Sidrolândia
Nioaque
Três Lagoas
Xavantina
Panorama
Andradina
Mirandópolis
Mirassol
São José
do Rio Prêto
Olímpia
Bebedouro
Ribeirão
Prêto

Três
Pontas
Lavras
Varginha
Poços de
Caldas
Pouso
Alegre
Barbacena
Cataguases
Leopoldina
Paraíba do Sul
CAMPOS

Maracaju
Nova Alvorada
do Sul
Presidente
Epitácio
Adamantina
Santo
Anastácio
São
Araçatuba
Catanduva
Jaboticabal
Mococa
Casa
Branca
Varginha
Três
Corações
Juiz de Fora
RIO DE JANEIRO
Cabo de
São Tomé

Dourados
Rio
Brilhante
Nova
Andradina
Cunha Paulista
Presidente
Prudente
Birigui
Lins
Araraquara
São
Carlos
São João
da Boa Vista
Ouro Fino
Itajubá
Sta Cruz
Volta
Redonda
Barra do Piraí
Nova Friburgo

Ponta Porã
Ivinhema
Rosana
Rancharia
Marília
Garça
Bariri
Rio Claro
Limeira
Mogi-Mirim
Americana
Guaratinguetá
Bragança
Paulista
Barra
Mar
Petrópolis
Macaé

Pedro Juan Caballero
Paranaíba
Assis
Sertanópolis
Cambará
Ourinhos
Botucatu
Tietê
Piracicaba
CAMPINAS
Taubaté
NOVA IGUAÇU
DUQUE DE CAXIAS
SÃO GONÇALO

Amambaí
Navirai
Paranavaí
Nova
Esperança
Londrina
Rolândia
Cornélio
Procópio
Jacarèzinho
Avaré
Tatuí
Itu
Jundiaí
São José dos C.
Angra dos
Reis
Ilha Grande
NITERÓI
RIO DE JANEIRO

CANINDEYU
Curuguaty
Munda Novo
Salto del Guairá
Umuarama
Cianorte
Mandaguari
Apucarana
Joaquim
Távora
Itapetininga
SÃO PAULO
São Bernardo
do Campo
São Vicente
Moji das Cruzes
SANTO ANDRÉ
SANTOS
Guarujá
Ilha de São Sebastião
La de Araruama
Cabo Frio
Tropic of Capricorn

Guaíra
Goio-Erê
PARANÁ
Ibaiti
Itaporanga
Itararé
Itapeva
Paranapiacaba
Itanhaém
Ilha de São Sebastião
Pta. de Boi

Porto Mendes
Ubiratã
Cândido de Abreu
Castro
Apiai
Registro

Toledo
Cascavel
Pitanga
Prudentópolis
Ponta
Grossa
Palmeira
CURITIBA
Juquiá
Iguape
Ilha Comprida

ALTO
Hernandarias
Ciudad
del Este
Irala
Medianeira
Guarapuava
Irati
Antonina
Paranaguá
Matinhos
Ilha do Cardoso

PARANA
Francisco
Beltrão
União da
Vitória
Lapa
Guaratuba

Eldorado
Foz do Iguaçu
Cat. del
Iguaçu
Pato Branco
Clevelândia
Palmas
Porto União
Mafra
Rio Negro
Joinville
São Francisco do Sul

Bernardo
de Irigoyen
Sa. da Fartura
São Mateus
do Sul

MISIONES
San
Pedro
Xanxerê
Caçador
Itajaí

Corpus
Uruguai
Chapecó
São Miguel
do Oeste
1340
Blumenau
Brusque

Encarnación
Obera
Monteagudo
Frederico
Westphalen
Joaçaba
SANTA CATARINA
Santa Cecília
Rio do Sul

Candelaria
Leandro N. Alem
Palmeira
das Missões
Erechim
Campos
Novos
Curitibanos
São
José
Ilha de Santa Catarina
Florianópolis

Apóstoles
San
Javier
Santa Rosa
Carázinho
Passo
Fundo
Lajes
1808

São Luís
Gonzaga
Ijuí
Cruz Alta
Coxilha Grande
São
Joaquim
Vacaria

São Angelo
Santo
Angelo
Guaporé
Laguna

Borja
Sa. do
Espinilho
RIO GRANDE
Bento Gonçalves
Tubarão
Cabo Santa Marta Grande

Santiago
Santa
Maria
Caxias do Sul
Criciúma

Alegrete
Santa Cruz
do Sul
Montenegro
Nôvo Hamburgo
Ararangua
Torres

ário do Sul
Cachoeira do Sul
Taquara

São
Leopoldo
Osorio
Viamão
Canoas
PÔRTO ALEGRE

DO SUL
São
Gabriel
Caçapava
do Sul
Encantadas
Tapes

Santana do
Livramento
Dom Pedrito
Camaquã

Rivera
Santana
Bagé
Sa. do Canguçu
Canguçu
São Lourenço
do Sul
Mostardas

Tacuarembó
Pinheiro
Machado
Pelotas

UAY
Negro
Melo
São José do Norte
Rio Grande

ATLANTIC

Fraile
Muerto
Rio Branco
Jaguarão

San Gregorio
Blanquillo
Cerro
Chato
Vergara
Lagoa Mangueira

Sarandí del Yi
José Batlle
y Ordóñez
Lascano
Treinta y Tres
Santa Vitória do Palmar
Chuy

Aigua
Castillos

elones
Tala
Minas
Rocha

Piedras
San Carlos

ando
Maldonado

MONTEVIDEO

Plata

Antonio

OCEAN

5304

COPYRIGHT GEORGE PHILIP LTD

55   West from Greenwich   50   45   40

A
B
C
D

25
30
35

5   6   7

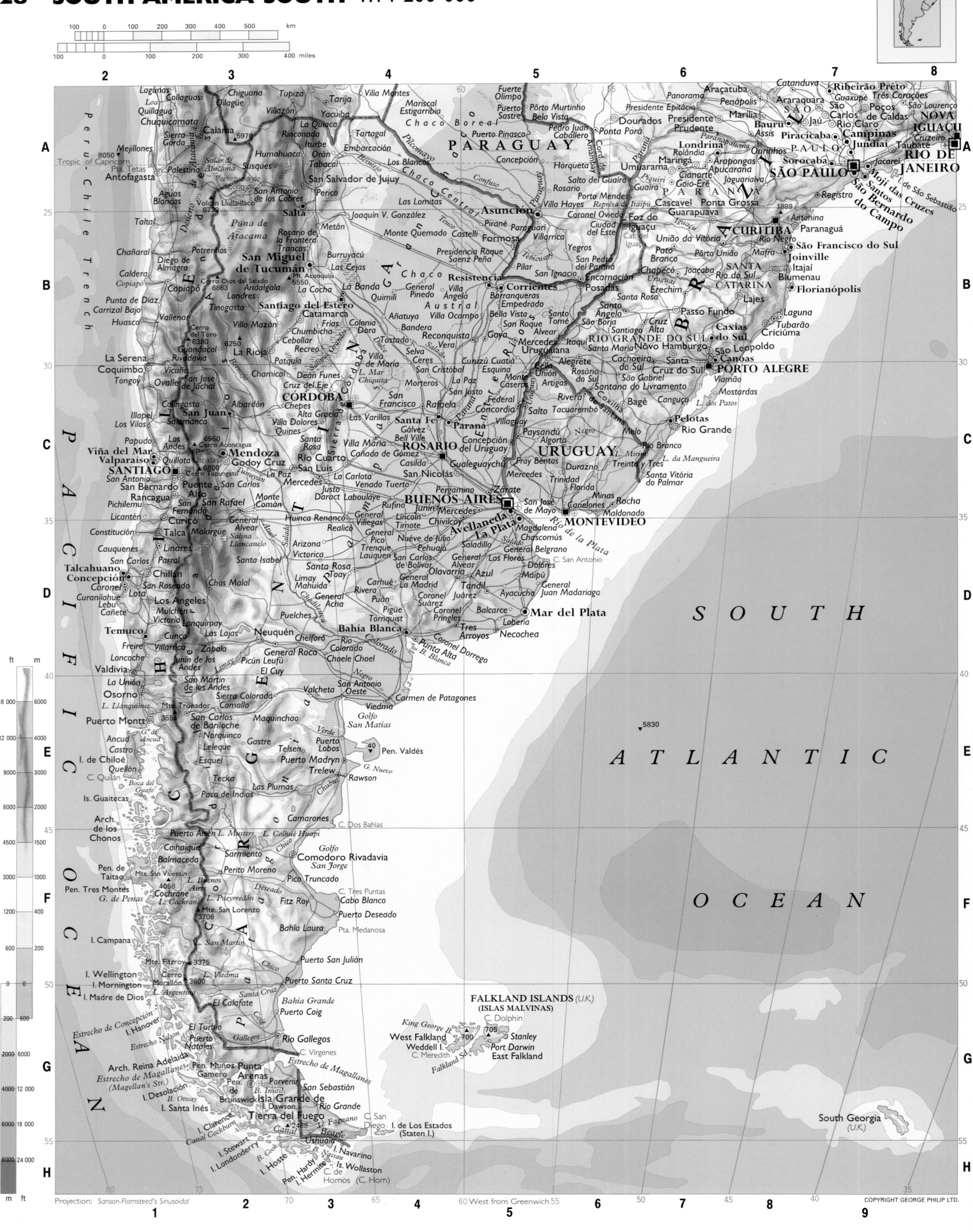

INDEX

The index contains the names of all the principal places and features shown on the World Maps. Each name is followed by an additional entry in italics giving the country or region within which it is located. The alphabetical order of names composed of two or more words is governed primarily by the first word and then by the second. This is an example of the rule:

Mīr Kūh, *Iran* **71** **E8**
Mīr Shahdād, *Iran* **71** **E8**
Mira, *Italy* **29** **C9**
Mira por vos Cay, *Bahamas* . . **121** **B5**
Miraj, *India* **66** **L9**

Physical features composed of a proper name (Erie) and a description (Lake) are positioned alphabetically by the proper name. The description is positioned after the proper name and is usually abbreviated:

Erie, L., *N. Amer.* **110** **D4**

Where a description forms part of a settlement or administrative name however, it is always written in full and put in its true alphabetic position:

Mount Morris, *U.S.A.* **110** **D7**

Names beginning with M' and Mc are indexed as if they were spelled Mac. Names beginning St. are alphabetised under Saint, but Sankt, Sint, Sant', Santa and San are all spelt in full and are alphabetised accordingly. If the same place name occurs two or more times in the index and all are in the same country, each is followed by the name of the administrative subdivision in which it is located. The names are placed in the alphabetical order of the subdivisions. For example:

Jackson, *Ky., U.S.A.* **108** **G4**
Jackson, *Mich., U.S.A.* **108** **D3**
Jackson, *Minn., U.S.A.* **112** **D7**

The number in bold type which follows each name in the index refers to the number of the map page where that feature or place will be found. This is usually the largest scale at which the place or feature appears.

The letter and figure which are in bold type immediately after the page number give the grid square on the map page, within which the feature is situated. The letter represents the latitude and the figure the longitude.

In some cases the feature itself may fall within the specified square, while the name is outside. This is usually the case only with features which are larger than a grid square.

Rivers are indexed to their mouths or confluences, and carry the symbol → after their names. A solid square ■ follows the name of a country, while an open square □ refers to a first order administrative area.

ABBREVIATIONS USED IN THE INDEX

A.C.T. – Australian Capital Territory
Afghan. – Afghanistan
Ala. – Alabama
Alta. – Alberta
Amer. – America(n)
Arch. – Archipelago
Ariz. – Arizona
Ark. – Arkansas
Atl. Oc. – Atlantic Ocean
B. – Baie, Bahía, Bay, Bucht, Bugt
B.C. – British Columbia
Bangla. – Bangladesh
Barr. – Barrage
Bos.-H. – Bosnia-Herzegovina
C. – Cabo, Cap, Cape, Coast
C.A.R. – Central African Republic
C. Prov. – Cape Province
Calif. – California
Cent. – Central
Chan. – Channel
Colo. – Colorado
Conn. – Connecticut
Cord. – Cordillera
Cr. – Creek
Czech. – Czech Republic
D.C. – District of Columbia
Del. – Delaware
Dep. – Dependency
Des. – Desert
Dist. – District
Dj. – Djebel
Domin. – Dominica
Dom. Rep. – Dominican Republic
E. – East

E. Salv. – El Salvador
Eq. Guin. – Equatorial Guinea
Fla. – Florida
Falk. Is. – Falkland Is.
G. – Golfe, Golfo, Gulf, Guba, Gebel
Ga. – Georgia
Gt. – Great, Greater
Guinea-Biss. – Guinea-Bissau
H.K. – Hong Kong
H.P. – Himachal Pradesh
Hants. – Hampshire
Harb. – Harbor, Harbour
Hd. – Head
Hts. – Heights
I.(s). – Île, Ilha, Insel, Isla, Island, Isle
Ill. – Illinois
Ind. – Indiana
Ind. Oc. – Indian Ocean
Ivory C. – Ivory Coast
J. – Jabal, Jebel, Jazira
Junc. – Junction
K. – Kap, Kapp
Kans. – Kansas
Kep. – Kepulauan
Ky. – Kentucky
L. – Lac, Lacul, Lago, Lagoa, Lake, Limni, Loch, Lough
La. – Louisiana
Liech. – Liechtenstein
Lux. – Luxembourg
Mad. P. – Madhya Pradesh
Madag. – Madagascar
Man. – Manitoba
Mass. – Massachusetts

Md. – Maryland
Me. – Maine
Medit. S. – Mediterranean Sea
Mich. – Michigan
Minn. – Minnesota
Miss. – Mississippi
Mo. – Missouri
Mont. – Montana
Mozam. – Mozambique
Mt.(e) – Mont, Monte, Monti, Montaña, Mountain
N. – Nord, Norte, North, Northern, Nouveau
N.B. – New Brunswick
N.C. – North Carolina
N. Cal. – New Caledonia
N. Dak. – North Dakota
N.H. – New Hampshire
N.I. – North Island
N.J. – New Jersey
N. Mex. – New Mexico
N.S. – Nova Scotia
N.S.W. – New South Wales
N.W.T. – North West Territory
N.Y. – New York
N.Z. – New Zealand
Nebr. – Nebraska
Neths. – Netherlands
Nev. – Nevada
Nfld. – Newfoundland
Nic. – Nicaragua
O. – Oued, Ouadi
Occ. – Occidentale
Okla. – Oklahoma
Ont. – Ontario
Or. – Orientale

Oreg. – Oregon
Os. – Ostrov
Oz. – Ozero
P. – Pass, Passo, Pasul, Pulau
P.E.I. – Prince Edward Island
Pa. – Pennsylvania
Pac. Oc. – Pacific Ocean
Papua N.G. – Papua New Guinea
Pass. – Passage
Pen. – Peninsula, Péninsule
Phil. – Philippines
Pk. – Park, Peak
Plat. – Plateau
Prov. – Province, Provincial
Pt. – Point
Pta. – Ponta, Punta
Pte. – Pointe
Qué. – Québec
Queens. – Queensland
R. – Rio, River
R.I. – Rhode Island
Ra.(s). – Range(s)
Raj. – Rajasthan
Reg. – Region
Rep. – Republic
Res. – Reserve, Reservoir
S. – San, South, Sea
Si. Arabia – Saudi Arabia
S.C. – South Carolina
S. Dak. – South Dakota
S.I. – South Island
S. Leone – Sierra Leone
Sa. – Serra, Sierra
Sask. – Saskatchewan
Scot. – Scotland
Sd. – Sound

Sev. – Severnaya
Sib. – Siberia
Sprs. – Springs
St. – Saint
Sta. – Santa, Station
Ste. – Sainte
Sto. – Santo
Str. – Strait, Stretto
Switz. – Switzerland
Tas. – Tasmania
Tenn. – Tennessee
Tex. – Texas
Tg. – Tanjung
Trin. & Tob. – Trinidad & Tobago
U.A.E. – United Arab Emirates
U.K. – United Kingdom
U.S.A. – United States of America
Ut. P. – Uttar Pradesh
Va. – Virginia
Vdkhr. – Vodokhranilishche
Vf. – Virful
Vic. – Victoria
Vol. – Volcano
Vt. – Vermont
W. – Wadi, West
W. Va. – West Virginia
Wash. – Washington
Wis. – Wisconsin
Wlkp. – Wielkopolski
Wyo. – Wyoming
Yorks. – Yorkshire
Yug. – Yugoslavia

A Baña

A

A Baña, *Spain* 34 C2
A Cañiza, *Spain* 34 C2
A Coruña, *Spain* 34 B2
A Estrada, *Spain* 34 C2
A Fonsagrada, *Spain* 34 B3
A Guarda, *Spain* 34 D2
A Gudiña, *Spain* 34 C3
A Rúa, *Spain* 34 C3
Aachen, *Germany* 24 E2
Aalborg = Ålborg, *Denmark* 11 G3
Aalen, *Germany* 25 G6
A'âli an Nîl □, *Sudan* 81 F3
Aalst, *Belgium* 17 D4
Aalten, *Neths.* 17 C6
Aalter, *Belgium* 17 C3
Äänekoski, *Finland* 9 E21
Aarau, *Switz.* 25 H4
Aarberg, *Switz.* 25 H3
Aare →, *Switz.* 25 H4
Aargau □, *Switz.* 25 H4
Aarhus = Århus, *Denmark* 11 H4
Aarschot, *Belgium* 17 D4
Aba, *China* 58 A3
Aba, *Dem. Rep. of the Congo* 86 B3
Aba, *Nigeria* 83 D6
Âbâ, Jazîrat, *Sudan* 81 E3
Abadab, J., *Sudan* 80 D4
Ābādān, *Iran* 71 D6
Abade, *Ethiopia* 81 F4
Ābādeh, *Iran* 71 D7
Abadin, *Spain* 34 B3
Abadla, *Algeria* 78 B5
Abaetetuba, *Brazil* 125 D9
Abagnar Qi, *China* 56 C9
Abai, *Paraguay* 127 B4
Abak, *Nigeria* 83 E6
Abakaliki, *Nigeria* 83 D6
Abakan, *Russia* 51 D10
Abala, *Niger* 83 C5
Abalak, *Niger* 83 B6
Abalemma, *Niger* 83 B6
Abana, *Turkey* 72 B6
Abancay, *Peru* 124 F4
Abano Terme, *Italy* 29 C8
Abarán, *Spain* 33 G3
Abariringa, *Kiribati* 96 H10
Abarqū, *Iran* 71 D7
Abashiri, *Japan* 54 C12
Abashiri-Wan, *Japan* 54 C12
Abaújszántó, *Hungary* 42 B6
Abava →, *Latvia* 44 A8
Ābay = Nîl el Azraq →, *Sudan* 81 D3
Abay, *Kazakstan* 50 E8
Abaya, L., *Ethiopia* 81 F4
Abaza, *Russia* 50 D10
Abbadia San Salvatore, *Italy* 29 F8
'Abbāsābād, *Iran* 71 C8
Abbay = Nîl el Azraq →, *Sudan* 81 D3
Abbaye, Pt., *U.S.A.* 108 B1
Abbé, L., *Ethiopia* 81 E5
Abbeville, *France* 19 B8
Abbeville, *Ala., U.S.A.* 109 K3
Abbeville, *La., U.S.A.* 113 L8
Abbeville, *S.C., U.S.A.* 109 H4
Abbiategrasso, *Italy* 28 C5
Abbot Ice Shelf, *Antarctica* 5 D16
Abbottabad, *Pakistan* 68 B5
Abd al Kūrī, *Ind. Oc.* 74 E5
Ābdar, *Iran* 71 D7
'Abdolābād, *Iran* 71 C8
Abdulpur, *Bangla.* 69 G13
Abéché, *Chad* 79 F10
Abejar, *Spain* 32 D2
Abekr, *Sudan* 81 E2
Abengourou, *Ivory C.* 82 D4
Abenójar, *Spain* 35 G6
Åbenrå, *Denmark* 11 J3
Abensberg, *Germany* 25 G7
Abeokuta, *Nigeria* 83 D5
Aber, *Uganda* 86 B3
Aberaeron, *U.K.* 13 E3
Aberayron = Aberaeron, *U.K.* 13 E3
Aberchirder, *U.K.* 14 D6
Abercorn = Mbala, *Zambia* 87 D3
Abercorn, *Australia* 95 D5
Aberdare, *U.K.* 13 F4
Aberdare Ra., *Kenya* 86 C4
Aberdeen, *Australia* 95 E5
Aberdeen, *Canada* 105 C7
Aberdeen, *S. Africa* 88 E3
Aberdeen, *U.K.* 14 D6
Aberdeen, *Ala., U.S.A.* 109 J1
Aberdeen, *Idaho, U.S.A.* 114 E7
Aberdeen, *Md., U.S.A.* 108 F7
Aberdeen, *S. Dak., U.S.A.* 112 C5
Aberdeen, *Wash., U.S.A.* 116 D3
Aberdeen, City of □, *U.K.* 14 D6
Aberdeenshire □, *U.K.* 14 D6
Aberdovey = Aberdyfi, *U.K.* 13 E3
Aberdyfi, *U.K.* 13 E3
Aberfeldy, *U.K.* 14 E5
Abergavenny, *U.K.* 13 F4
Abergele, *U.K.* 12 D4
Abernathy, *U.S.A.* 113 J4
Abert, L., *U.S.A.* 114 E3
Aberystwyth, *U.K.* 13 E3
Abhā, *Si. Arabia* 74 D3
Abhar, *Iran* 71 B6
Abhayapuri, *India* 69 F14
Abia □, *Nigeria* 83 D6
Abide, *Turkey* 39 C11
Abidiya, *Sudan* 80 D3
Abidjan, *Ivory C.* 82 D4
Abilene, *Kans., U.S.A.* 112 F6
Abilene, *Tex., U.S.A.* 113 J5
Abingdon, *U.K.* 13 F6
Abingdon, *U.S.A.* 109 G5
Abington Reef, *Australia* 94 B4
Abitau →, *Canada* 105 B7
Abitibi →, *Canada* 102 B3
Abitibi, L., *Canada* 102 C4
Abiy Adi, *Ethiopia* 81 E4
Abkhaz Republic = Abkhazia □, *Georgia* 49 J5
Abkhazia □, *Georgia* 49 J5
Abminga, *Australia* 95 D1
Abnûb, *Egypt* 80 B3
Åbo = Turku, *Finland* 9 F20
Abocho, *Nigeria* 83 D6
Abohar, *India* 68 D6
Aboisso, *Ivory C.* 82 D4
Abomey, *Benin* 83 D5
Abong-Mbang, *Cameroon* 84 D2
Abonnema, *Nigeria* 83 E6
Abony, *Hungary* 42 C5
Aboso, *Ghana* 82 D4
Abou-Deïa, *Chad* 79 F9
Aboyne, *U.K.* 14 D6
Abra Pampa, *Argentina* 126 A2
Abraham L., *Canada* 104 C5
Abrantes, *Portugal* 35 F2
Abreojos, Pta., *Mexico* 118 B2
Abri, *Esh Shamâliya, Sudan* 80 C3
Abri, *Janub Kordofân, Sudan* 81 E3
Abrud, *Romania* 42 D8
Abruzzo □, *Italy* 29 F10
Absaroka Range, *U.S.A.* 114 D9
Abtenau, *Austria* 26 D6
Abu, *India* 68 G5
Abū al Abyad, *U.A.E.* 71 E7
Abū al Khaşīb, *Iraq* 71 D6
Abū 'Alī, *Si. Arabia* 71 E6
Abū 'Alī →, *Lebanon* 75 A4
Abu Ballas, *Egypt* 80 C2
Abu Deleiq, *Sudan* 81 D3
Abu Dhabi = Abū Ẓāby, *U.A.E.* 71 E7
Abu Dis, *Sudan* 80 D3
Abu Dom, *Sudan* 81 D3
Abū Du'ān, *Syria* 70 B3
Abu el Gairi, W. →, *Egypt* 75 F2
Abu Fatma, Ras, *Sudan* 80 C4
Abu Gabra, *Sudan* 81 E2
Abu Ga'da, W. →, *Egypt* 75 F1
Abu Gelba, *Sudan* 81 E3
Abu Gubeiha, *Sudan* 81 E3
Abu Habl, Khawr →, *Sudan* 81 E3
Abū Ḩadrīyah, *Si. Arabia* 71 E6
Abu Hamed, *Sudan* 80 D3
Abu Haraz, *An Nîl el Azraq, Sudan* 80 D3
Abu Haraz, *El Gezira, Sudan* 81 E3
Abu Haraz, *Esh Shamâliya, Sudan* 80 D3
Abu Higar, *Sudan* 81 E3
Abū Kamāl, *Syria* 70 C4
Abu Kuleiwat, *Sudan* 81 E2
Abū Madd, Ra's, *Si. Arabia* 70 E3
Abu Matariq, *Sudan* 81 E2
Abu Mendi, *Ethiopia* 81 E4
Abū Mūsā, *U.A.E.* 71 E7
Abu Qir, *Egypt* 80 H7
Abu Qireiya, *Egypt* 80 C4
Abu Qurqâs, *Egypt* 80 B3
Abu Şafāt, W. →, *Jordan* 75 E5
Abu Shagara, Ras, *Sudan* 80 C4
Abu Shanab, *Sudan* 81 E2
Abu Simbel, *Egypt* 80 C3
Abū Şukhayr, *Iraq* 70 D5
Abu Sultân, *Egypt* 80 H8
Abu Tabari, *Sudan* 80 D2
Abu Tig, *Egypt* 80 B3
Abu Tiga, *Sudan* 81 E3
Abu Tineitin, *Sudan* 81 E3
Abu Uruq, *Sudan* 81 D3
Abu Zabad, *Sudan* 81 E2
Abū Ẓāby, *U.A.E.* 71 E7
Abū Zeydābād, *Iran* 71 C6
Abuja, *Nigeria* 83 D6
Abukuma-Gawa →, *Japan* 54 E10
Abukuma-Sammyaku, *Japan* 54 F10
Abunã, *Brazil* 124 E5
Abunã →, *Brazil* 124 E5
Abune Yosef, *Ethiopia* 81 E4
Aburo, *Dem. Rep. of the Congo* 86 B3
Abut Hd., *N.Z.* 91 K3
Abuye Meda, *Ethiopia* 81 E4
Abwong, *Sudan* 81 F3
Åby, *Sweden* 11 F10
Aby, Lagune, *Ivory C.* 82 D4
Abyad, *Sudan* 81 E2
Åbybro, *Denmark* 11 G3
Acadia National Park, *U.S.A.* 109 C11
Açailândia, *Brazil* 125 D9
Acajutla, *El Salv.* 120 D2
Acámbaro, *Mexico* 118 D4
Acanthus, *Greece* 40 F7
Acaponeta, *Mexico* 118 C3
Acapulco, *Mexico* 119 D5
Acarai, Serra, *Brazil* 124 C7
Acarigua, *Venezuela* 124 B5
Acatlán, *Mexico* 119 D5
Acayucan, *Mexico* 119 D6
Accéglio, *Italy* 28 D4
Accomac, *U.S.A.* 108 G8
Accous, *France* 20 E3
Accra, *Ghana* 83 D4
Accrington, *U.K.* 12 D5
Acebal, *Argentina* 126 C3
Aceh □, *Indonesia* 62 D1
Acerra, *Italy* 31 B7
Aceuchal, *Spain* 35 G4
Achalpur, *India* 66 J10
Acheng, *China* 57 B14
Achenkirch, *Austria* 26 D4
Achensee, *Austria* 26 D4
Acher, *India* 68 H5
Achern, *Germany* 25 G4
Achill Hd., *Ireland* 15 C1
Achill I., *Ireland* 15 C1
Achim, *Germany* 24 B5
Achinsk, *Russia* 51 D10
Acıgöl, *Turkey* 39 D11
Acıpayam, *Turkey* 39 D11
Acireale, *Italy* 31 E8
Ackerman, *U.S.A.* 113 J10
Acklins I., *Bahamas* 121 B5
Acme, *Canada* 104 C6
Acme, *U.S.A.* 110 F5
Aconcagua, Cerro, *Argentina* 126 C2
Aconquija, Mt., *Argentina* 126 B2
Açores, Is. dos = Azores, *Atl. Oc.* 78 A1
Acornhoek, *S. Africa* 89 C5
Acquapendente, *Italy* 29 F8
Acquasanta Terme, *Italy* 29 F10
Acquasparta, *Italy* 29 F9
Acquaviva delle Fonti, *Italy* 31 B9
Ácqui Terme, *Italy* 28 D5
Acraman, L., *Australia* 95 E2
Acre = 'Akko, *Israel* 75 C4
Acre □, *Brazil* 124 E4
Acre →, *Brazil* 124 E5
Acri, *Italy* 31 C9
Acs, *Hungary* 42 C3
Actium, *Greece* 38 C2
Acton, *Canada* 110 C4
Acuña, *Mexico* 118 B4
Ad Dammām, *Si. Arabia* 71 E6
Ad Dāmūr, *Lebanon* 75 B4
Ad Dawādimī, *Si. Arabia* 70 E5
Ad Dawḩah, *Qatar* 71 E6
Ad Dawr, *Iraq* 70 C4
Ad Dir'īyah, *Si. Arabia* 70 E5
Ad Dīwānīyah, *Iraq* 70 D5
Ad Dujayl, *Iraq* 70 C5
Ad Duwayd, *Si. Arabia* 70 D4
Ada, *Ghana* 83 D5
Ada, *Serbia, Yug.* 42 E5
Ada, *Minn., U.S.A.* 112 B6
Ada, *Okla., U.S.A.* 113 H6
Adabiya, *Egypt* 75 F1
Adair, C., *Canada* 101 A12
Adaja →, *Spain* 34 D6
Adak I., *U.S.A.* 100 C2
Adamaoua, Massif de l', *Cameroon* 83 D7
Adamawa □, *Nigeria* 83 D7
Adamawa Highlands = Adamaoua, Massif de l', *Cameroon* 83 D7
Adamello, Mte., *Italy* 28 B7
Adami Tulu, *Ethiopia* 81 F4
Adaminaby, *Australia* 95 F4
Adams, *Mass., U.S.A.* 111 D11
Adams, *N.Y., U.S.A.* 111 C8
Adams, *Wis., U.S.A.* 112 D10
Adam's Bridge, *Sri Lanka* 66 Q11
Adams L., *Canada* 104 C5
Adams Mt., *U.S.A.* 116 D5
Adam's Peak, *Sri Lanka* 66 R12
Adamuz, *Spain* 35 G6
Adana, *Turkey* 70 B2
Adanero, *Spain* 34 E6
Adapazarı = Sakarya, *Turkey* 72 B4
Adar Gwagwa, J., *Sudan* 80 C4
Adarama, *Sudan* 81 D3
Adare, C., *Antarctica* 5 D11
Adarte, *Eritrea* 81 E5
Adaut, *Indonesia* 63 F8
Adavale, *Australia* 95 D3
Adda →, *Italy* 28 C6
Addis Ababa = Addis Abeba, *Ethiopia* 81 F4
Addis Abeba, *Ethiopia* 81 F4
Addis Alem, *Ethiopia* 81 F4
Addis Zemen, *Ethiopia* 81 E4
Addison, *U.S.A.* 110 D7
Addo, *S. Africa* 88 E4
Adebour, *Niger* 83 C7
Ādeh, *Iran* 70 B5
Adel, *U.S.A.* 109 K4
Adelaide, *Australia* 95 E2
Adelaide, *Bahamas* 120 A4
Adelaide, *S. Africa* 88 E4
Adelaide I., *Antarctica* 5 C17
Adelaide Pen., *Canada* 100 B10
Adelaide River, *Australia* 92 B5
Adelanto, *U.S.A.* 117 L9
Adele I., *Australia* 92 C3
Adélie, Terre, *Antarctica* 5 C10
Adélie Land = Adélie, Terre, *Antarctica* 5 C10
Ademuz, *Spain* 32 E3
Aden = Al 'Adan, *Yemen* 74 E4
Aden, G. of, *Asia* 74 E4
Adendorp, *S. Africa* 88 E3
Aderbissinat, *Niger* 83 B6
Adh Dhayd, *U.A.E.* 71 E7
Adhoi, *India* 68 H4
Adi, *Indonesia* 63 E8
Adi Arkai, *Ethiopia* 81 E4
Adi Daro, *Ethiopia* 81 E4
Adi Keyih, *Eritrea* 81 E4
Adi Kwala, *Eritrea* 81 E4
Adi Ugri, *Eritrea* 81 E4
Adieu, C., *Australia* 93 F5
Adieu Pt., *Australia* 92 C3
Adigala, *Ethiopia* 81 E5
Adige →, *Italy* 29 C9
Adigrat, *Ethiopia* 81 E4
Adıgüzel Barajı, *Turkey* 39 C11
Adilabad, *India* 66 K11
Adilcevaz, *Turkey* 73 C10
Adin Khel, *Afghan.* 66 C6
Adirondack Mts., *U.S.A.* 111 C10
Adıyaman, *Turkey* 73 D8
Adjohon, *Benin* 83 D5
Adjud, *Romania* 43 D12
Adjumani, *Uganda* 86 B3
Adlavik Is., *Canada* 103 A8
Adler, *Russia* 49 J4
Admer, *Algeria* 83 A6
Admiralty G., *Australia* 92 B4
Admiralty I., *U.S.A.* 104 B2
Admiralty Is., *Papua N. G.* 96 H6
Ado, *Nigeria* 83 D5
Ado-Ekiti, *Nigeria* 83 D6
Adok, *Sudan* 81 F3
Adola, *Ethiopia* 81 E5
Adonara, *Indonesia* 63 F6
Adoni, *India* 66 M10
Adony, *Hungary* 42 C3
Adour →, *France* 20 E2
Adra, *India* 69 H12
Adra, *Spain* 35 J7
Adrano, *Italy* 31 E7
Adrar, *Mauritania* 78 D3
Adrar des Iforas, *Algeria* 76 D4
Ádria, *Italy* 29 C9
Adrian, *Mich., U.S.A.* 108 E3
Adrian, *Tex., U.S.A.* 113 H3
Adriatic Sea, *Medit. S.* 6 G9
Adua, *Indonesia* 63 E7
Adwa, *Ethiopia* 81 E4
Adygea □, *Russia* 49 H5
Adzhar Republic = Ajaria □, *Georgia* 49 K6
Adzopé, *Ivory C.* 82 D4
Ægean Sea, *Medit. S.* 39 C7
Aerhtai Shan, *Mongolia* 60 B4
Ærø, *Denmark* 11 K4
Ærøskøbing, *Denmark* 11 K4
Aëtós, *Greece* 38 D3
'Afak, *Iraq* 70 C5
Afándou, *Greece* 36 C10
Afghanistan ■, *Asia* 66 C4
Afikpo, *Nigeria* 83 D6
Aflou, *Algeria* 78 B6
Afragóla, *Italy* 31 B7
Afram →, *Ghana* 83 D4
Afrera, *Ethiopia* 81 E5
Africa 76 E6
'Afrīn, *Syria* 70 B3
Afşin, *Turkey* 72 C7
Afton, *N.Y., U.S.A.* 111 D9
Afton, *Wyo., U.S.A.* 114 E8
Afuá, *Brazil* 125 D8
'Afula, *Israel* 75 C4
Afyon, *Turkey* 39 C12
Afyon □, *Turkey* 39 C12
Afyonkarahisar = Afyon, *Turkey* 39 C12
Aga, *Egypt* 80 H7
Agadès = Agadez, *Niger* 83 B6
Agadez, *Niger* 83 B6
Agadir, *Morocco* 78 B4
Agaete, *Canary Is.* 37 F4
Agaie, *Nigeria* 83 D6
Again, *Sudan* 81 F2
Ağapınar, *Turkey* 39 B12
Agar, *India* 68 H7
Agaro, *Ethiopia* 81 F4
Agartala, *India* 67 H17
Agăş, *Romania* 43 D11
Agassiz, *Canada* 104 D4
Agats, *Indonesia* 63 F9
Agawam, *U.S.A.* 111 D12
Agbélouvé, *Togo* 83 D5
Agboville, *Ivory C.* 82 D4
Ağcabädi, *Azerbaijan* 49 K8
Ağdam, *Azerbaijan* 49 L8
Ağdaş, *Azerbaijan* 49 K8
Agde, *France* 20 E7
Agde, C. d', *France* 20 E7
Agdzhabedi = Ağcabädi, *Azerbaijan* 49 K8
Agen, *France* 20 D4
Agerbæk, *Denmark* 11 J2
Agersø, *Denmark* 11 J5
Ageyevo, *Russia* 46 E9
Āgh Kand, *Iran* 71 B6
Aghireşu, *Romania* 43 D8
Aginskoye, *Russia* 51 D12
Ağlasun, *Turkey* 39 D12
Agly →, *France* 20 F7
Agnew, *Australia* 93 E3
Agnibilékrou, *Ivory C.* 82 D4
Agnita, *Romania* 43 E9
Agnone, *Italy* 29 G11
Agofie, *Ghana* 83 D5
Agogna →, *Italy* 28 C5
Agogo, *Sudan* 81 F2
Agön, *Sweden* 10 C11
Agon Coutainville, *France* 18 C5
Agordo, *Italy* 29 B9
Agori, *India* 69 G10
Agouna, *Benin* 83 D5
Agout →, *France* 20 E5
Agra, *India* 68 F7
Agrakhanskiy Poluostrov, *Russia* 49 J8
Agramunt, *Spain* 32 D6
Agreda, *Spain* 32 D3
Ağri, *Turkey* 73 C10
Agri →, *Italy* 31 B9
Ağrı Dağı, *Turkey* 70 B5
Agriá, *Greece* 38 B5
Agrigento, *Italy* 30 E6
Agrínion, *Greece* 38 C3
Agrópoli, *Italy* 31 B7
Ağstafa, *Azerbaijan* 49 K7
Agua Caliente, *Baja Calif., Mexico* 117 N10
Agua Caliente, *Sinaloa, Mexico* 118 B3
Agua Caliente Springs, *U.S.A.* 117 N10
Água Clara, *Brazil* 125 H8
Agua Hechicero, *Mexico* 117 N10
Agua Prieta, *Mexico* 118 A3
Aguadilla, *Puerto Rico* 121 C6
Aguadulce, *Panama* 120 E3
Aguanga, *U.S.A.* 117 M10
Aguanish, *Canada* 103 B7
Aguanus →, *Canada* 103 B7
Aguapey →, *Argentina* 126 B4
Aguaray Guazú →, *Paraguay* 126 A4
Aguarico →, *Ecuador* 124 D3
Aguas →, *Spain* 32 D4
Aguas Blancas, *Chile* 126 A2
Aguas Calientes, Sierra de, *Argentina* 126 B2
Aguascalientes, *Mexico* 118 C4
Aguascalientes □, *Mexico* 118 C4
Agudo, *Spain* 35 G6
Águeda, *Portugal* 34 E2
Agueda →, *Spain* 34 D4
Aguelhok, *Mali* 83 B5
Aguié, *Niger* 83 C6
Aguilafuente, *Spain* 34 D6
Aguilar, *Spain* 35 H6
Aguilar de Campóo, *Spain* 34 C6
Aguilares, *Argentina* 126 B2
Aguilas, *Spain* 33 H3
Agüimes, *Canary Is.* 37 G4
Aguja, C. de la, *Colombia* 122 B3
Agulaa, *Ethiopia* 81 E4
Agulhas, C., *S. Africa* 88 E3
Agulo, *Canary Is.* 37 F2
Agung, *Indonesia* 62 F5
Agur, *Uganda* 86 B3
Agusan →, *Phil.* 61 G6
Ağva, *Turkey* 41 E13
Agvali, *Russia* 49 J8
Aha Mts., *Botswana* 88 B3
Ahaggar, *Algeria* 78 D7
Ahamansu, *Ghana* 83 D5
Ahar, *Iran* 70 B5
Ahat, *Turkey* 39 C11
Ahaus, *Germany* 24 C2
Ahipara B., *N.Z.* 91 F4
Ahir Dağı, *Turkey* 39 C12
Ahiri, *India* 66 K12
Ahlat, *Turkey* 73 C10
Ahlen, *Germany* 24 D3
Ahmad Wal, *Pakistan* 68 E1
Ahmadabad, *India* 68 H5
Aḩmadābād, *Khorāsān, Iran* 71 C9
Aḩmadābād, *Khorāsān, Iran* 71 C8
Aḩmadī, *Iran* 71 E8
Ahmadnagar, *India* 66 K9
Ahmadpur, *Pakistan* 68 E4
Ahmadpur Lamma, *Pakistan* 68 E4
Ahmar, *Ethiopia* 81 F5
Ahmedabad = Ahmadabad, *India* 68 H5
Ahmednagar = Ahmadnagar, *India* 66 K9
Ahmetbey, *Turkey* 41 E11
Ahmetler, *Turkey* 39 C11
Ahmetli, *Turkey* 39 C9
Ahoada, *Nigeria* 83 D6
Ahome, *Mexico* 118 B3
Ahoskie, *U.S.A.* 109 G7
Ahr →, *Germany* 24 E3
Ahram, *Iran* 71 D6
Ahrax Pt., *Malta* 36 D1
Ahrensbök, *Germany* 24 A6
Ahrensburg, *Germany* 24 B6
Āhū, *Iran* 71 C6
Ahuachapán, *El Salv.* 120 D2
Ahun, *France* 19 F9
Åhus, *Sweden* 11 J8
Ahvāz, *Iran* 71 D6
Ahvenanmaa = Åland, *Finland* 9 F19
Aḩwar, *Yemen* 74 E4
Ahzar →, *Mali* 83 B5
Ai →, *India* 69 F14
Ai-Ais, *Namibia* 88 D2
Aichach, *Germany* 25 G7
Aichi □, *Japan* 55 G8
Aigle, *Switz.* 25 J2
Aignay-le-Duc, *France* 19 E11
Aigoual, Mt., *France* 20 D7
Aigre, *France* 20 C4
Aigua, *Uruguay* 127 C5
Aigueperse, *France* 19 F10
Aigues →, *France* 21 D8
Aigues-Mortes, *France* 21 E8
Aigues-Mortes, G. d', *France* 21 E8
Aiguilles, *France* 21 D10
Aiguillon, *France* 20 D4
Aigurande, *France* 19 F8
Aihui, *China* 60 A7
Aija, *Peru* 124 E3
Aikawa, *Japan* 54 E9
Aiken, *U.S.A.* 109 J5
Ailao Shan, *China* 58 F3
Aileron, *Australia* 94 C1
Aillant-sur-Tholon, *France* 19 E10
Aillik, *Canada* 103 A8
Ailsa Craig, *U.K.* 14 F3
'Ailūn, *Jordan* 75 C4
Aim, *Russia* 51 D14
Aimere, *Indonesia* 63 F6
Aimogasta, *Argentina* 126 B2
Ain □, *France* 19 F12
Ain →, *France* 21 C9
Aïn Ben Tili, *Mauritania* 78 C4

Aleutian Trench

Ain Dalla, *Egypt* 80 B2
Ain el Mafki, *Egypt* 80 B2
Ain Girba, *Egypt* 80 B2
Ain Murr, *Sudan* 80 C2
Ain Qeiqab, *Egypt* 80 B1
Aïn-Sefra, *Algeria* 78 B5
Ain Sheikh Murzûk, *Egypt* 80 B2
Ain Sudr, *Egypt* 75 F2
Ain Sukhna, *Egypt* 80 J8
Ain Zeitûn, *Egypt* 80 B2
Ainaži, *Latvia* 9 H21
Aínos Óros, *Greece* 38 C2
Ainsworth, *U.S.A.* 112 D5
Aiquile, *Bolivia* 124 G5
Aïr, *Niger* 83 B6
Air Force I., *Canada* 101 B12
Air Hitam, *Malaysia* 65 M4
Airaines, *France* 19 C8
Airdrie, *Canada* 104 C6
Airdrie, *U.K.* 14 F5
Aire →, *France* 19 C11
Aire →, *U.K.* 12 D7
Aire, I. de l', *Spain* 37 B11
Aire-sur-la-Lys, *France* 19 B9
Aire-sur-l'Adour, *France* 20 E3
Airlie Beach, *Australia* 94 C4
Airvault, *France* 18 F6
Aisch →, *Germany* 25 F6
Aisne □, *France* 19 C10
Aisne →, *France* 19 C9
Ait, *India* 69 G8
Aitana, Sierra de, *Spain* 33 G4
Aitkin, *U.S.A.* 112 B8
Aitolía Kai Akarnanía □, *Greece* 38 C3
Aitolikón, *Greece* 38 C3
Aiud, *Romania* 43 D8
Aix-en-Provence, *France* 21 E9
Aix-la-Chapelle = Aachen, *Germany* 24 E2
Aix-les-Bains, *France* 21 C9
Aixe-sur-Vienne, *France* 20 C5
Áíyina, *Greece* 38 D5
Aiyínion, *Greece* 40 F6
Aíyion, *Greece* 38 C4
Aizawl, *India* 67 H18
Aizenay, *France* 18 F5
Aizkraukle, *Latvia* 9 H21
Aizpute, *Latvia* 9 H19
Aizuwakamatsu, *Japan* 54 F9
Ajaccio, *France* 21 G12
Ajaccio, G. d', *France* 21 G12
Ajaigarh, *India* 69 G9
Ajalpan, *Mexico* 119 D5
Ajanta Ra., *India* 66 J9
Ajari Rep. = Ajaria □, *Georgia* 49 K6
Ajaria □, *Georgia* 49 K6
Ajax, *Canada* 110 C5
Ajdâbiyah, *Libya* 79 B10
Ajdovščina, *Slovenia* 29 C10
Ajibar, *Ethiopia* 81 E4
Ajka, *Hungary* 42 C2
'Ajmān, *U.A.E.* 71 E7
Ajmer, *India* 68 F6
Ajnala, *India* 68 D6
Ajo, *U.S.A.* 115 K7
Ajo, C. de, *Spain* 34 B7
Ajok, *Sudan* 81 F2
Ajuy, *Phil.* 61 F5
Ak Dağ, *Turkey* 39 E11
Ak Dağları, *Muğla, Turkey* 39 E11
Ak Dağları, *Sivas, Turkey* 72 C7
Akaba, *Togo* 83 D5
Akabira, *Japan* 54 C11
Akaki Beseka, *Ethiopia* 81 F4
Akala, *Sudan* 81 D4
Akamas □, *Cyprus* 36 D11
Akanthou, *Cyprus* 36 D12
Akarca, *Turkey* 39 C11
Akaroa, *N.Z.* 91 K4
Akasha, *Sudan* 80 C3
Akashi, *Japan* 55 G7
Akbarpur, *Bihar, India* 69 G10
Akbarpur, *Ut. P., India* 69 F10
Akçaabat, *Turkey* 73 B8
Akçadağ, *Turkey* 72 C7
Akçakale, *Turkey* 73 D8
Akçakoca, *Turkey* 72 B4
Akçaova, *Turkey* 41 E13
Akçay, *Turkey* 39 E11
Akçay →, *Turkey* 39 D10
Akdağ, *Turkey* 39 C8
Akdağmadeni, *Turkey* 72 C6
Akelamo, *Indonesia* 63 D7
Åkers styckebruk, *Sweden* 10 E11
Åkersberga, *Sweden* 10 E12
Aketi, *Dem. Rep. of the Congo* 84 D4
Akhaïa □, *Greece* 38 C3
Akhalkalaki, *Georgia* 49 K6
Akhaltsikhe, *Georgia* 49 K6
Akharnaí, *Greece* 38 C5
Akhelóös →, *Greece* 38 C3
Akhendriá, *Greece* 39 G7
Akhisar, *Turkey* 39 C9
Akhladhókambos, *Greece* 38 D4
Akhmîm, *Egypt* 80 B3
Akhnur, *India* 69 C6
Akhtopol, *Bulgaria* 41 D11
Akhtuba →, *Russia* 49 G8
Akhtubinsk, *Russia* 49 F8
Akhty, *Russia* 49 K8
Akhtyrka = Okhtyrka, *Ukraine* 47 G8
Aki, *Japan* 55 H6
Akimiski I., *Canada* 102 B3
Akimovka, *Ukraine* 47 J8
Åkirkeby, *Denmark* 11 J8
Akita, *Japan* 54 E10
Akita □, *Japan* 54 E10
Akjoujt, *Mauritania* 82 B2
Akka, *Mali* 82 B4
Akkaya Tepesi, *Turkey* 39 D11
Akkeshi, *Japan* 54 C12
'Akko, *Israel* 75 C4
Akköy, *Turkey* 39 D9
Aklampa, *Benin* 83 D5
Aklavik, *Canada* 100 B6
Aklera, *India* 68 G7
Akmenė, *Lithuania* 44 B9
Akmenrags, *Latvia* 44 B8
Akmolinsk = Astana, *Kazakstan* 50 D8
Akmonte = Almonte, *Spain* 35 H4
Akō, *Japan* 55 G7
Ako, *Nigeria* 83 C7
Akôbô, *Sudan* 81 F3
Akobo →, *Ethiopia* 81 F3
Akola, *India* 66 J10
Akonolinga, *Cameroon* 83 E7
Akor, *Mali* 82 C3
Akordat, *Eritrea* 81 D4
Akosombo Dam, *Ghana* 83 D5
Akot, *Sudan* 81 F3
Akoupé, *Ivory C.* 82 D4
Akpatok I., *Canada* 101 B13
Åkrahamn, *Norway* 9 G11
Akranes, *Iceland* 8 D2
Akreïjit, *Mauritania* 82 B3
Akrítas Venétiko, Ákra, *Greece* 38 E3
Akron, *Colo., U.S.A.* 112 E3
Akron, *Ohio, U.S.A.* 110 E3
Akrotiri, *Cyprus* 36 E11
Akrotíri, Ákra, *Greece* 41 F9
Akrotiri Bay, *Cyprus* 36 E12
Aksai Chin, *India* 69 B8
Aksaray, *Turkey* 70 B2
Aksay, *Kazakstan* 50 D6
Akşehir, *Turkey* 70 B1
Akşehir Gölü, *Turkey* 72 C4
Akstafa = Ağstafa, *Azerbaijan* 49 K7
Aksu, *China* 60 B3
Aksu →, *Turkey* 72 D4
Aksum, *Ethiopia* 81 E4
Aktash, *Russia* 48 C11
Aktogay, *Kazakstan* 50 E8
Aktsyabrski, *Belarus* 47 F5
Aktyubinsk = Aqtöbe, *Kazakstan* 50 D6
Aku, *Nigeria* 83 D6
Akure, *Nigeria* 83 D6
Akureyri, *Iceland* 8 D4
Akuseki-Shima, *Japan* 55 K4
Akusha, *Russia* 49 J8
Akwa-Ibom □, *Nigeria* 83 E6
Akyab = Sittwe, *Burma* 67 J18
Akyazı, *Turkey* 72 B4
Al 'Adan, *Yemen* 74 E4
Al Aḩsā = Hasa □, *Si. Arabia* 71 E6
Al Ajfar, *Si. Arabia* 70 E4
Al Amādīyah, *Iraq* 70 B4
Al 'Amārah, *Iraq* 70 D5
Al 'Aqabah, *Jordan* 75 F4
Al Arak, *Syria* 70 C3
Al 'Aramah, *Si. Arabia* 70 E5
Al Arṭāwīyah, *Si. Arabia* 70 E5
Al 'Āşimah = 'Ammān □, *Jordan* 75 D5
Al 'Assāfīyah, *Si. Arabia* 70 D3
Al 'Ayn, *Oman* 71 E7
Al 'Ayn, *Si. Arabia* 70 E3
Al 'Azamīyah, *Iraq* 70 C5
Al 'Azīzīyah, *Iraq* 70 C5
Al Bāb, *Syria* 70 B3
Al Bad', *Si. Arabia* 70 D2
Al Bādī, *Iraq* 70 C4
Al Bahrah, *Kuwait* 70 D5
Al Baḩral Mayyit = Dead Sea, *Asia* 75 D4
Al Balqā' □, *Jordan* 75 C4
Al Bārūk, J., *Lebanon* 75 B4
Al Başrah, *Iraq* 70 D5
Al Baţḩā, *Iraq* 70 D5
Al Batrūn, *Lebanon* 75 A4
Al Bayḑā, *Libya* 79 B10
Al Biqā, *Lebanon* 75 A5
Al Bi'r, *Si. Arabia* 70 D3
Al Burayj, *Syria* 75 A5
Al Faḑilī, *Si. Arabia* 71 E6
Al Fallūjah, *Iraq* 70 C4
Al Fāw, *Iraq* 71 D6
Al Fujayrah, *U.A.E.* 71 E8
Al Ghadaf, W. →, *Jordan* 75 D5
Al Ghammās, *Iraq* 70 D5
Al Ghazālah, *Si. Arabia* 70 E4
Al Ḩābah, *Si. Arabia* 70 E5
Al Ḩadīthah, *Iraq* 70 C4
Al Ḩadīthah, *Si. Arabia* 75 D6
Al Ḩaḑr, *Iraq* 70 C4
Al Ḩājānah, *Syria* 75 B5
Al Hajar al Gharbi, *Oman* 71 E8
Al Hāmad, *Si. Arabia* 70 D3
Al Hamdānīyah, *Syria* 70 C3
Al Ḩamīdīyah, *Syria* 75 A4
Al Ḩammār, *Iraq* 70 D5
Al Ḩamrā', *Si. Arabia* 70 E3
Al Ḩanākīyah, *Si. Arabia* 70 E4
Al Harīr, W. →, *Syria* 75 C4
Al Ḩasā, W. →, *Jordan* 75 D4
Al Ḩasakah, *Syria* 70 B4
Al Haydān, W. →, *Jordan* 75 D4
Al Ḩayy, *Iraq* 70 C5
Al Ḩijarah, *Asia* 70 D4
Al Ḩillah, *Iraq* 70 C5
Al Hindīyah, *Iraq* 70 C5
Al Hirmil, *Lebanon* 75 A5
Al Hoceïma, *Morocco* 78 A5
Al Ḩudaydah, *Yemen* 74 E3
Al Hufūf, *Si. Arabia* 71 E6
Al Ḩumayḑah, *Si. Arabia* 70 D2
Al Ḩunayy, *Si. Arabia* 71 E6
Al Īsāwīyah, *Si. Arabia* 70 D3
Al Jafr, *Jordan* 75 E5
Al Jāfūrah, *Si. Arabia* 71 E7
Al Jaghbūb, *Libya* 79 C10
Al Jahrah, *Kuwait* 70 D5
Al Jalāmīd, *Si. Arabia* 70 D3
Al Jamalīyah, *Qatar* 71 E6
Al Janūb □, *Lebanon* 75 B4
Al Jawf, *Libya* 79 D10
Al Jawf, *Si. Arabia* 70 D3
Al Jazirah, *Iraq* 70 C5
Al Jithāmīyah, *Si. Arabia* 70 E4
Al Jubayl, *Si. Arabia* 71 E6
Al Jubaylah, *Si. Arabia* 70 E5
Al Jubb, *Si. Arabia* 70 E4
Al Junaynah, *Sudan* 79 F10
Al Kabā'ish, *Iraq* 70 D5
Al Karak, *Jordan* 75 D4
Al Karak □, *Jordan* 75 E5
Al Kāzim Tyah, *Iraq* 70 C5
Al Khābūra, *Oman* 71 F8
Al Khafji, *Si. Arabia* 71 E6
Al Khalīl, *West Bank* 75 D4
Al Khāliş, *Iraq* 70 C5
Al Kharsānīyah, *Si. Arabia* 71 E6
Al Khaşab, *Oman* 71 E8
Al Khawr, *Qatar* 71 E6
Al Khiḑr, *Iraq* 70 D5
Al Khiyām, *Lebanon* 75 B4
Al Khums, *Libya* 79 B8
Al Kiswah, *Syria* 75 B5
Al Kūfah, *Iraq* 70 C5
Al Kufrah, *Libya* 79 D10
Al Kuhayfīyah, *Si. Arabia* 70 E4
Al Kūt, *Iraq* 70 C5
Al Kuwayt, *Kuwait* 70 D5
Al Labwah, *Lebanon* 75 A5
Al Lādhiqīyah, *Syria* 70 C2
Al Līth, *Si. Arabia* 74 C3
Al Liwā', *Oman* 71 E8
Al Luḩayyah, *Yemen* 74 D3
Al Madīnah, *Iraq* 70 D5
Al Madīnah, *Si. Arabia* 70 E3
Al Mafraq, *Jordan* 75 C5
Al Maḩmūdīyah, *Iraq* 70 C5
Al Majma'ah, *Si. Arabia* 70 E5
Al Makhruq, W. →, *Jordan* 75 D6
Al Makḩūl, *Si. Arabia* 70 E4
Al Manāmah, *Bahrain* 71 E6
Al Maqwa', *Kuwait* 70 D5
Al Marj, *Libya* 79 B10
Al Maţlā, *Kuwait* 70 D5
Al Mawjib, W. →, *Jordan* 75 D4
Al Mawşil, *Iraq* 70 B4
Al Mayādin, *Syria* 70 C4
Al Mazār, *Jordan* 75 D4
Al Midhnab, *Si. Arabia* 70 E5
Al Minā', *Lebanon* 75 A4
Al Miqdādīyah, *Iraq* 70 C5
Al Mubarraz, *Si. Arabia* 71 E6
Al Mudawwarah, *Jordan* 75 F5
Al Mughayrā', *U.A.E.* 71 E7
Al Muḩarraq, *Bahrain* 71 E6
Al Mukallā, *Yemen* 74 E4
Al Mukhā, *Yemen* 74 E3
Al Musayjīd, *Si. Arabia* 70 E3
Al Musayyib, *Iraq* 70 C5
Al Muwayh, *Si. Arabia* 80 C5
Al Muwayliḩ, *Si. Arabia* 70 E2
Al Owuho = Otukpa, *Nigeria* 83 D6
Al Qā'im, *Iraq* 70 C4
Al Qalībah, *Si. Arabia* 70 D3
Al Qāmishlī, *Syria* 70 B4
Al Qaryatayn, *Syria* 75 A6
Al Qaşīm, *Si. Arabia* 70 E4
Al Qaṭ'ā, *Syria* 70 C4
Al Qaţīf, *Si. Arabia* 71 E6
Al Qatrānah, *Jordan* 75 D5
Al Qaţrūn, *Libya* 79 D9
Al Qayşūmah, *Si. Arabia* 70 D5
Al Quds = Jerusalem, *Israel* 75 D4
Al Qunayţirah, *Syria* 75 C4
Al Qunfudhah, *Si. Arabia* 80 D5
Al Qurnah, *Iraq* 70 D5
Al Quşayr, *Iraq* 70 D5
Al Quşayr, *Syria* 75 A5
Al Qutayfah, *Syria* 75 B5
Al 'Ubaylah, *Si. Arabia* 74 C5
Al 'Uḑaylīyah, *Si. Arabia* 71 E6
Al 'Ulā, *Si. Arabia* 70 E3
Al 'Uqayr, *Si. Arabia* 71 E6
Al 'Uthmānīyah, *Si. Arabia* 71 E6
Al 'Uwaynid, *Si. Arabia* 70 E5
Al 'Uwayqīlah, *Si. Arabia* 70 D4
Al 'Uyūn, *Ḩijāz, Si. Arabia* 70 E3
Al 'Uyūn, *Najd, Si. Arabia* 70 E4
Al 'Uzayr, *Iraq* 70 D5
Al Wajh, *Si. Arabia* 70 E3
Al Wakrah, *Qatar* 71 E6
Al Wannān, *Si. Arabia* 71 E6
Al Waqbah, *Si. Arabia* 70 D5
Al Warī'āh, *Si. Arabia* 70 E5
Al Wusayl, *Qatar* 71 E6
Ala, *Italy* 28 C8
Ala Dağ, *Turkey* 70 B2
Ala Dağları, *Turkey* 73 C10
Alabama □, *U.S.A.* 109 J2
Alabama →, *U.S.A.* 109 K2
Alabaster, *U.S.A.* 109 J2
Alaca, *Turkey* 72 B6
Alacaatlı, *Turkey* 39 B10
Alaçam, *Turkey* 72 B6
Alaçam Dağları, *Turkey* 39 B10
Alaçatı, *Turkey* 39 C8
Alachua, *U.S.A.* 109 L4
Alaejos, *Spain* 34 D5
Alaérma, *Greece* 36 C9
Alagir, *Russia* 49 J7
Alagna Valsésia, *Italy* 28 C4
Alagoa Grande, *Brazil* 125 E11
Alagoas □, *Brazil* 125 E11
Alagoinhas, *Brazil* 125 F11
Alagón, *Spain* 32 D3
Alagón →, *Spain* 34 F4
Alaior, *Spain* 37 B11
Alajero, *Canary Is.* 37 F2
Alajuela, *Costa Rica* 120 D3
Alakamisy, *Madag.* 89 C8
Alaknanda →, *India* 69 D8
Alamarvdasht, *Iran* 71 E7
Alamata, *Ethiopia* 81 E4
Alameda, *Calif., U.S.A.* 116 H4
Alameda, *N. Mex., U.S.A.* 115 J10
Alaminos, *Phil.* 61 C3
Alamo, *U.S.A.* 117 J11
Alamo Crossing, *U.S.A.* 117 L13
Alamogordo, *U.S.A.* 115 K11
Alamos, *Mexico* 118 B3
Alamosa, *U.S.A.* 115 H11
Åland, *Finland* 9 F19
Alandroal, *Portugal* 35 G3
Ålands hav, *Sweden* 9 F18
Alandur, *India* 66 N12
Alange, Presa de, *Spain* 35 G4
Alania = North Ossetia □, *Russia* 49 J7
Alanís, *Spain* 35 G5
Alanya, *Turkey* 70 B1
Alaotra, Farihin', *Madag.* 89 B8
Alapayevsk, *Russia* 50 D7
Alar del Rey, *Spain* 34 C6
Alaraz, *Spain* 34 E5
Alarcón, Embalse de, *Spain* 32 F2
Alarobia-Vohiposa, *Madag.* 89 C8
Alaşehir, *Turkey* 39 C10
Alaska □, *U.S.A.* 100 B5
Alaska, G. of, *Pac. Oc.* 100 C5
Alaska Peninsula, *U.S.A.* 100 C4
Alaska Range, *U.S.A.* 100 B4
Alássio, *Italy* 28 E5
Älät, *Azerbaijan* 49 L9
Alatri, *Italy* 29 G10
Alatyr, *Russia* 48 C8
Alatyr →, *Russia* 48 C8
Alausi, *Ecuador* 124 D3
Álava □, *Spain* 32 C2
Alava, C., *U.S.A.* 114 B1
Alaverdi, *Armenia* 49 K7
Alavus, *Finland* 9 E20
Alawoona, *Australia* 95 E3
'Alayh, *Lebanon* 75 B4
Alazani →, *Azerbaijan* 49 K8
Alba, *Italy* 28 D5
Alba □, *Romania* 43 D8
Alba Adriática, *Italy* 29 F10
Alba de Tormes, *Spain* 34 E5
Alba-Iulia, *Romania* 43 D8
Albac, *Romania* 42 D7
Albacete, *Spain* 33 F3
Albacete □, *Spain* 33 G3
Albacutya, L., *Australia* 95 F3
Ålbæk, *Denmark* 11 G4
Ålbæk Bugt, *Denmark* 11 G4
Albaida, *Spain* 33 G4
Albalate de las Nogueras, *Spain* 32 E2
Albalate del Arzobispo, *Spain* 32 D4
Alban, *France* 20 E6
Albanel, L., *Canada* 102 B5
Albania ■, *Europe* 40 E4
Albano Laziale, *Italy* 29 G9
Albany, *Australia* 93 G2
Albany, *Ga., U.S.A.* 109 K3
Albany, *N.Y., U.S.A.* 111 D11
Albany, *Oreg., U.S.A.* 114 D2
Albany, *Tex., U.S.A.* 113 J5
Albany →, *Canada* 102 B3
Albardón, *Argentina* 126 C2
Albarracín, *Spain* 32 E3
Albarracín, Sierra de, *Spain* 32 E3
Albatera, *Spain* 33 G4
Albatross B., *Australia* 94 A3
Albegna →, *Italy* 29 F8
Albemarle, *U.S.A.* 109 H5
Albemarle Sd., *U.S.A.* 109 H7
Albenga, *Italy* 28 D5
Alberche →, *Spain* 34 F6
Alberdi, *Paraguay* 126 B4
Alberes, Mts., *France* 20 F6
Ålberga, *Sweden* 11 F10
Albersdorf, *Germany* 24 A5
Albert, *France* 19 C9
Albert, L., *Australia* 95 F2
Albert Edward Ra., *Australia* 92 C4
Albert L., *Africa* 86 B3
Albert Lea, *U.S.A.* 112 D8
Albert Nile →, *Uganda* 86 B3
Albert Town, *Bahamas* 121 B5
Alberta □, *Canada* 104 C6
Alberti, *Argentina* 126 D3
Albertinia, *S. Africa* 88 E3
Albertirsa, *Hungary* 42 C4
Alberton, *Canada* 103 C7
Albertville = Kalemie, *Dem. Rep. of the Congo* 86 D2
Albertville, *France* 21 C10
Albertville, *U.S.A.* 109 H2
Albi, *France* 20 E6
Albia, *U.S.A.* 112 E8
Albina, *Surinam* 125 B8
Albina, Ponta, *Angola* 88 B1
Albino, *Italy* 28 C6
Albion, *Mich., U.S.A.* 108 D3
Albion, *Nebr., U.S.A.* 112 E6
Albion, *Pa., U.S.A.* 110 E4
Albocácer, *Spain* 32 E5
Albolote, *Spain* 35 H7
Alborán, *Medit. S.* 35 K7
Alborea, *Spain* 33 F3
Ålborg, *Denmark* 11 G3
Ålborg Bugt, *Denmark* 11 H4
Alborz, Reshteh-ye Kūhhā-ye, *Iran* 71 C7
Albox, *Spain* 33 H2
Albufeira, *Portugal* 35 H2
Albula →, *Switz.* 25 J5
Albuñol, *Spain* 35 J7
Albuquerque, *U.S.A.* 115 J10
Albuquerque, Cayos de, *Caribbean* 120 D3
Alburg, *U.S.A.* 111 B11
Alburno, Mte., *Italy* 31 B8
Alburquerque, *Spain* 35 F4
Albury-Wodonga, *Australia* 95 F4
Alcácer do Sal, *Portugal* 35 G2
Alcáçovas, *Portugal* 35 G2
Alcalá de Chivert, *Spain* 32 E5
Alcalá de Guadaira, *Spain* 35 H5
Alcalá de Henares, *Spain* 34 E7
Alcalá de los Gazules, *Spain* 35 J5
Alcalá del Júcar, *Spain* 33 F3
Alcalá del Río, *Spain* 35 H5
Alcalá del Valle, *Spain* 35 J5
Alcalá la Real, *Spain* 35 H7
Álcamo, *Italy* 30 E5
Alcanadre, *Spain* 32 C2
Alcanadre →, *Spain* 32 D4
Alcanar, *Spain* 32 E5
Alcanede, *Portugal* 35 F2
Alcanena, *Portugal* 35 F2
Alcañices, *Spain* 34 D4
Alcañiz, *Spain* 32 D4
Alcântara, *Brazil* 125 D10
Alcántara, *Spain* 34 F4
Alcántara, Embalse de, *Spain* 34 F4
Alcantarilla, *Spain* 33 H3
Alcaracejos, *Spain* 35 G6
Alcaraz, *Spain* 33 G2
Alcaraz, Sierra de, *Spain* 33 G2
Alcaudete, *Spain* 35 H6
Alcázar de San Juan, *Spain* 35 F7
Alchevsk, *Ukraine* 47 H10
Alcira = Alzira, *Spain* 33 F4
Alcobaça, *Portugal* 35 F2
Alcobendas, *Spain* 34 E7
Alcolea del Pinar, *Spain* 32 D2
Alcora, *Spain* 32 E4
Alcorcón, *Spain* 34 E7
Alcoutim, *Portugal* 35 H3
Alcova, *U.S.A.* 114 E10
Alcoy, *Spain* 33 G4
Alcubierre, Sierra de, *Spain* 32 D4
Alcublas, *Spain* 32 F4
Alcúdia, *Spain* 37 B10
Alcúdia, B. d', *Spain* 37 B10
Alcudia, Sierra de la, *Spain* 35 G6
Aldabra Is., *Seychelles* 77 G8
Aldama, *Mexico* 119 C5
Aldan, *Russia* 51 D13
Aldan →, *Russia* 51 C13
Aldea, Pta. de la, *Canary Is.* 37 G4
Aldeburgh, *U.K.* 13 E9
Alder Pk., *U.S.A.* 116 K5
Alderney, *U.K.* 13 H5
Aldershot, *U.K.* 13 F7
Åled, *Sweden* 11 H6
Aledo, *U.S.A.* 112 E9
Alefa, *Ethiopia* 81 E4
Aleg, *Mauritania* 82 B2
Alegranza, *Canary Is.* 37 E6
Alegranza, I., *Canary Is.* 37 E6
Alegre, *Brazil* 127 A7
Alegrete, *Brazil* 127 B4
Aleisk, *Russia* 50 D9
Aleksandriya = Oleksandriya, *Kirovohrad, Ukraine* 47 H7
Aleksandriya = Oleksandriya, *Rivne, Ukraine* 47 G4
Aleksandriyskaya, *Russia* 49 J8
Aleksandrov, *Russia* 46 D10
Aleksandrov Gay, *Russia* 48 E9
Aleksandrovac, *Serbia, Yug.* 40 C5
Aleksandrovac, *Serbia, Yug.* 40 B5
Aleksandrovka = Oleksandrovka, *Ukraine* 47 H7
Aleksandrovo, *Bulgaria* 41 C8
Aleksandrovsk-Sakhalinskiy, *Russia* 51 D15
Aleksandrów Kujawski, *Poland* 45 F5
Aleksandrów Łódzki, *Poland* 45 G6
Alekseyevka, *Samara, Russia* 48 D10
Alekseyevka, *Voronezh, Russia* 47 G10
Aleksin, *Russia* 46 E9
Aleksinac, *Serbia, Yug.* 40 C5
Além Paraíba, *Brazil* 127 A7
Alemania, *Argentina* 126 B2
Alemania, *Chile* 126 B2
Alençon, *France* 18 D7
Alenquer, *Brazil* 125 D8
Alenuihaha Channel, *U.S.A.* 106 H17
Alépé, *Ivory C.* 82 D4
Aleppo = Ḩalab, *Syria* 70 B3
Aléria, *France* 21 F13
Alès, *France* 21 D8
Aleşd, *Romania* 42 C7
Alessándria, *Italy* 28 D5
Ålestrup, *Denmark* 11 H3
Ålesund, *Norway* 9 E12
Alet-les-Bains, *France* 20 F6
Aletschhorn, *Switz.* 25 J4
Aleutian Is., *Pac. Oc.* 100 C2
Aleutian Trench, *Pac. Oc.* 96 C10

Alexander, *U.S.A.* 112 B3
Alexander, Mt., *Australia* .. 93 E3
Alexander Arch., *U.S.A.* ... 100 C6
Alexander Bay, *S. Africa* .. 88 D2
Alexander City, *U.S.A.* 109 J3
Alexander I., *Antarctica* ... 5 C17
Alexandra, *Australia* 95 F4
Alexandra, *N.Z.* 91 L2
Alexandra Falls, *Canada* ... 104 A5
Alexandria = El Iskandarîya,
  Egypt 80 H7
Alexandria, *B.C., Canada* .. 104 C4
Alexandria, *Ont., Canada* .. 102 C5
Alexandria, *Romania* 43 G10
Alexandria, *S. Africa* 88 E4
Alexandria, *U.K.* 14 F4
Alexandria, *La., U.S.A.* 113 K8
Alexandria, *Minn., U.S.A.* . 112 C7
Alexandria, *S. Dak., U.S.A.* 112 D6
Alexandria, *Va., U.S.A.* ... 108 F7
Alexandria Bay, *U.S.A.* 111 B9
Alexandrina, L., *Australia* . 95 F2
Alexandroúpolis, *Greece* ... 41 F9
Alexis →, *Canada* 103 B8
Alexis Creek, *Canada* 104 C4
Alfabia, *Spain* 37 B9
Alfambra, *Spain* 32 E3
Alfândega da Fé, *Portugal* . 34 D4
Alfaro, *Spain* 32 C3
Alfatar, *Bulgaria* 41 C11
Alfaz del Pi, *Spain* 33 G4
Alfeld, *Germany* 24 D5
Alfenas, *Brazil* 127 A6
Alfiós →, *Greece* 38 D3
Alföld, *Hungary* 42 D5
Alfonsine, *Italy* 29 D9
Alford, *Aberds., U.K.* 14 D6
Alford, *Lincs., U.K.* 12 D8
Alfred, *Maine, U.S.A.* 111 C14
Alfred, *N.Y., U.S.A.* 110 D7
Alfreton, *U.K.* 12 D6
Alfta, *Sweden* 10 C10
Alga, *Kazakhstan* 50 E6
Algaida, *Spain* 37 B9
Algar, *Spain* 35 J5
Ålgård, *Norway* 9 G11
Algarinejo, *Spain* 35 H6
Algarve, *Portugal* 35 J2
Algeciras, *Spain* 35 J5
Algemesí, *Spain* 33 F4
Alger, *Algeria* 78 A6
Algeria ■, *Africa* 78 C6
Alghero, *Italy* 30 B1
Älghult, *Sweden* 11 G9
Algiers = Alger, *Algeria* ... 78 A6
Algoa B., *S. Africa* 88 E4
Algodonales, *Spain* 35 J5
Algodor →, *Spain* 34 F7
Algoma, *U.S.A.* 108 C2
Algona, *U.S.A.* 112 D7
Algonac, *U.S.A.* 110 D2
Algonquin Prov. Park,
  Canada 102 C4
Algorta, *Uruguay* 128 C5
Alhama de Almería, *Spain* . 35 J8
Alhama de Aragón, *Spain* . 32 D3
Alhama de Granada, *Spain* . 35 H7
Alhama de Murcia, *Spain* . 33 H3
Alhambra, *U.S.A.* 117 L8
Alhaurín el Grande, *Spain* . 35 J6
Alhucemas = Al Hoceïma,
  Morocco 78 A5
'Alī al Gharbī, *Iraq* 70 C5
'Alī ash Sharqī, *Iraq* 70 C5
Äli Bayramlı, *Azerbaijan* .. 49 L9
'Alī Khēl, *Afghan.* 68 C3
Ali Sahīh, *Djibouti* 81 E5
Alī Shāh, *Iran* 70 B5
Alia, *Italy* 30 E6
'Alīābād, *Khorāsān, Iran* .. 71 C8
'Alīābād, *Kordestān, Iran* . 70 C5
'Alīābād, *Yazd, Iran* 71 D7
Aliaga, *Spain* 32 E4
Aliağa, *Turkey* 39 C8
Aliákmon →, *Greece* 40 F6
Alibo, *Ethiopia* 81 F4
Alibori →, *Benin* 83 C5
Alibunar, *Serbia, Yug.* 42 E5
Alicante, *Spain* 33 G4
Alicante □, *Spain* 33 G4
Alice, *S. Africa* 88 E4
Alice, *U.S.A.* 113 M5
Alice →, *Queens., Australia* 94 C3
Alice →, *Queens., Australia* 94 B3
Alice, Punta, *Italy* 31 C10
Alice Arm, *Canada* 104 B3
Alice Springs, *Australia* ... 94 C1
Alicedale, *S. Africa* 88 E4
Aliceville, *U.S.A.* 109 J1
Alicudi, *Italy* 31 D7
Aliganj, *India* 69 F8
Aligarh, *Raj., India* 68 G7
Aligarh, *Ut. P., India* 68 F8
Alīgūdarz, *Iran* 71 C6
Alijó, *Portugal* 34 D3
Alimnía, *Greece* 36 C9
Alipur, *Pakistan* 68 E4
Alipur Duar, *India* 67 F16
Aliquippa, *U.S.A.* 110 F4
Alishan, *Taiwan* 59 F13
Aliste →, *Spain* 34 D5
Alitus = Alytus, *Lithuania* . 9 J21
Alivérion, *Greece* 38 C6
Aliwal North, *S. Africa* 88 E4
Alix, *Canada* 104 C6
Aljezur, *Portugal* 35 H2
Aljustrel, *Portugal* 35 H2
Alkamari, *Niger* 83 C7
Alkmaar, *Neths.* 17 B4
All American Canal, *U.S.A.* 115 K6

Allada, *Benin* 83 D5
Allagash →, *U.S.A.* 109 B11
Allah Dad, *Pakistan* 68 G2
Allahabad, *India* 69 G9
Allan, *Canada* 105 C7
Allanmyo, *Burma* 67 K19
Allanridge, *S. Africa* 88 D4
Allaqi, Wadi →, *Egypt* ... 80 C3
Allariz, *Spain* 34 C3
Allassac, *France* 20 C5
Ålleberg, *Sweden* 11 F7
Allegany, *U.S.A.* 110 D6
Allegheny →, *U.S.A.* 110 F5
Allegheny Mts., *U.S.A.* ... 108 G6
Allegheny Reservoir, *U.S.A.* 110 E6
Allègre, *France* 20 C7
Allen, Bog of, *Ireland* 15 C5
Allen, L., *Ireland* 15 B3
Allendale, *U.S.A.* 109 J5
Allende, *Mexico* 118 B4
Allentown, *U.S.A.* 111 F9
Allentsteig, *Austria* 26 C8
Alleppey, *India* 66 Q10
Allepuz, *Spain* 32 E4
Aller →, *Germany* 24 C5
Alliance, *Nebr., U.S.A.* ... 112 D3
Alliance, *Ohio, U.S.A.* 110 F3
Allier □, *France* 19 F9
Allier →, *France* 19 F10
Alliford Bay, *Canada* 104 C2
Allinge, *Denmark* 11 J8
Alliston, *Canada* 102 D4
Alloa, *U.K.* 14 E5
Allones, *France* 18 D8
Allora, *Australia* 95 D5
Allos, *France* 21 D10
Alluitsup Paa, *Greenland* .. 4 C5
Alma, *Canada* 103 C5
Alma, *Ga., U.S.A.* 109 K4
Alma, *Kans., U.S.A.* 112 F6
Alma, *Mich., U.S.A.* 108 D3
Alma, *Nebr., U.S.A.* 112 E5
Alma Ata = Almaty,
  Kazakhstan 50 E8
Almacelles, *Spain* 32 D5
Almada, *Portugal* 35 G1
Almaden, *Australia* 94 B3
Almadén, *Spain* 35 G6
Almanor, L., *U.S.A.* 114 F3
Almansa, *Spain* 33 G3
Almanzor, Pico, *Spain* 34 E5
Almanzora →, *Spain* 33 H3
Almaş, Munţii, *Romania* .. 42 F7
Almassora, *Spain* 32 F4
Almaty, *Kazakhstan* 50 E8
Almazán, *Spain* 32 D2
Almeirim, *Brazil* 125 D8
Almeirim, *Portugal* 35 F2
Almelo, *Neths.* 17 B6
Almenar de Soria, *Spain* .. 32 D2
Almenara, *Spain* 32 F4
Almenara, Sierra de la,
  Spain 33 H3
Almendra, Embalse de,
  Spain 34 D4
Almendralejo, *Spain* 35 G4
Almere-Stad, *Neths.* 17 B5
Almería, *Spain* 35 J8
Almería □, *Spain* 33 H2
Almería, G. de, *Spain* 33 J2
Almetyevsk, *Russia* 48 C11
Älmhult, *Sweden* 11 H8
Almirante, *Panama* 120 E3
Almiropótamos, *Greece* ... 38 C6
Almirós, *Greece* 38 B4
Almirou, Kólpos, *Greece* .. 36 D6
Almodôvar, *Portugal* 35 H2
Almodóvar del Campo,
  Spain 35 G6
Almodóvar del Río, *Spain* . 35 H5
Almond, *U.S.A.* 110 D7
Almont, *U.S.A.* 110 D12
Almonte, *Canada* 111 A8
Almonte, *Spain* 35 H4
Almora, *India* 69 E8
Almoradí, *Spain* 33 G4
Almorox, *Spain* 34 E6
Almoustarat, *Mali* 83 B5
Älmsta, *Sweden* 10 E12
Almudévar, *Spain* 32 C4
Almuñécar, *Spain* 35 J7
Almunge, *Sweden* 10 E12
Almuradiel, *Spain* 35 G7
Alness, *U.K.* 14 D4
Alnmouth, *U.K.* 12 B6
Alnwick, *U.K.* 12 B6
Aloi, *Uganda* 86 B3
Alon, *Burma* 67 H19
Alor, *Indonesia* 63 F6
Alor Setar, *Malaysia* 65 J3
Álora, *Spain* 35 J6
Alosno, *Spain* 35 H3
Alot, *India* 68 H6
Aloysius, Mt., *Australia* ... 93 E4
Alpaugh, *U.S.A.* 116 K7
Alpedrinha, *Portugal* 34 E3
Alpena, *U.S.A.* 108 C4
Alpes-de-Haute-Provence □,
  France 21 D10
Alpes-Maritimes □, *France* . 21 E11
Alpha, *Australia* 94 C4
Alphen aan den Rijn, *Neths.* 17 B4
Alpine, *Ariz., U.S.A.* 115 K9
Alpine, *Calif., U.S.A.* 117 N10
Alpine, *Tex., U.S.A.* 113 K3
Alps, *Europe* 6 F7
Alpu, *Turkey* 72 C4

Alqueta, Barragem do,
  Portugal 35 G3
Alrø, *Denmark* 11 J4
Als, *Denmark* 11 K3
Alsace, *France* 19 D14
Alsask, *Canada* 105 C7
Alsasua, *Spain* 32 C2
Alsek →, *U.S.A.* 104 B1
Alsfeld, *Germany* 8 D15
Alsten, *Norway* 8 D15
Alstermo, *Sweden* 11 H9
Alston, *U.K.* 12 C5
Alta, *Norway* 8 B20
Alta, Sierra, *Spain* 32 E3
Alta Gracia, *Argentina* 126 C3
Alta Sierra, *U.S.A.* 117 K8
Altaelva →, *Norway* 8 B20
Altafjorden, *Norway* 8 A20
Altai = Aerhtai Shan,
  Mongolia 60 B4
Altamaha →, *U.S.A.* 109 K5
Altamira, *Brazil* 125 D8
Altamira, *Chile* 126 B2
Altamira, *Mexico* 119 C5
Altamira, Cuevas de, *Spain* 34 B6
Altamont, *U.S.A.* 111 D10
Altamura, *Italy* 31 B9
Altanbulag, *Mongolia* 60 A5
Altar, *Mexico* 118 A2
Altar, Desierto de, *Mexico* . 118 B2
Altata, *Mexico* 118 C3
Altavista, *U.S.A.* 108 G6
Altay, *China* 60 B3
Altdorf, *Switz.* 25 J4
Alte Mellum, *Germany* 24 B4
Altea, *Spain* 33 G4
Altenberg, *Germany* 24 E9
Altenbruch, *Germany* 24 B4
Altenburg, *Germany* 24 E8
Altenkirchen,
  Mecklenburg-Vorpommern,
  Germany 24 A9
Altenkirchen, *Rhld.-Pfz.,*
  Germany 24 E3
Altenmarkt, *Austria* 26 D7
Alter do Chão, *Portugal* ... 35 F3
Altınoluk, *Turkey* 39 B8
Altınova, *Turkey* 39 B8
Altıntaş, *Turkey* 39 B12
Altınyaka, *Turkey* 39 E12
Altınyayla, *Turkey* 39 D11
Altiplano = Bolivian
  Plateau, *S. Amer.* 122 E4
Altkirch, *France* 19 E14
Altmark, *Germany* 24 C7
Altmühl →, *Germany* 25 G7
Altmunster, *Austria* 26 D6
Alto Adige = Trentino-Alto
  Adige □, *Italy* 29 B8
Alto Araguaia, *Brazil* 125 G8
Alto Cuchumatanes =
  Cuchumatanes, Sierra de
  los, *Guatemala* 120 C1
Alto del Carmen, *Chile* 126 B1
Alto del Inca, *Chile* 126 A2
Alto Ligonha, *Mozam.* 87 F4
Alto Molocue, *Mozam.* 87 F4
Alto Paraguai □, *Paraguay* . 126 A4
Alto Paraná □, *Paraguay* .. 127 B5
Alton, *Canada* 110 C4
Alton, *U.K.* 13 F7
Alton, *Ill., U.S.A.* 112 F9
Alton, *N.H., U.S.A.* 111 C13
Altoona, *U.S.A.* 110 F6
Altötting, *Germany* 25 G8
Altstätten, *Switz.* 25 H5
Altun Kūprī, *Iraq* 70 C5
Altun Shan, *China* 60 C3
Alturas, *U.S.A.* 114 F3
Altus, *U.S.A.* 113 H5
Alubijid, *Phil.* 61 G6
Alucra, *Turkey* 73 B8
Aluk, *Sudan* 81 F2
Alunda, *Sweden* 10 D12
Alunite, *U.S.A.* 117 K12
Aluropa →, *Ethiopia* 81 F3
Alupka, *Ukraine* 47 K8
Alushta, *Ukraine* 47 K8
Alusi, *Indonesia* 63 F8
Alustante, *Spain* 32 E3
Alva, *U.S.A.* 113 G5
Alvaiázere, *Portugal* 34 F2
Älvängen, *Sweden* 11 G6
Alvarado, *Mexico* 119 D5
Alvarado, *U.S.A.* 113 J6
Alvaro Obregón, Presa,
  Mexico 118 B3
Älvdalen, *Sweden* 10 C8
Alvear, *Argentina* 126 B4
Alverca, *Portugal* 35 G1
Alvesta, *Sweden* 11 H8
Alvin, *U.S.A.* 113 L7
Alvinston, *Canada* 110 D3
Alvito, *Portugal* 35 G3
Älvkarleby, *Sweden* 10 D11
Alvord Desert, *U.S.A.* 114 E4
Älvros, *Sweden* 10 B8
Älvsborgs län □, *Sweden* .. 11 F6
Älvsbyn, *Sweden* 8 D19
Alwar, *India* 68 F7
Alxa Zuoqi, *China* 56 E3
Alyangula, *Australia* 94 A2
Alyata = Älät, *Azerbaijan* . 49 L9
Alyth, *U.K.* 14 E5
Alytus, *Lithuania* 9 J21
Alzada, *U.S.A.* 112 C2
Alzey, *Germany* 25 F4
Alzira, *Spain* 33 F4
Am-Timan, *Chad* 79 F10
Amadeus, L., *Australia* 93 D5

Amadi,
  Dem. Rep. of the Congo . 86 B2
Amâdi, *Sudan* 81 F3
Amadjuak L., *Canada* 101 B12
Amadora, *Portugal* 35 G1
Amagansett, *U.S.A.* 111 F12
Amagasaki, *Japan* 55 G7
Amager, *Denmark* 11 J6
Amagunze, *Nigeria* 83 D6
Amahai, *Indonesia* 63 E7
Amakusa-Shotō, *Japan* 55 H5
Amål, *Sweden* 11 F6
Amalfi, *Italy* 31 B7
Amaliás, *Greece* 38 D3
Amalner, *India* 66 J9
Amamapare, *Indonesia* 63 E9
Amambaí, *Brazil* 127 A5
Amambaí →, *Brazil* 127 A5
Amambay □, *Paraguay* 127 A4
Amambay, Cordillera de,
  S. Amer. 127 A4
Amami-Guntō, *Japan* 55 L4
Amami-Ō-Shima, *Japan* ... 55 L4
Amaná, L., *Brazil* 124 D6
Amanat →, *India* 69 G11
Amanda Park, *U.S.A.* 116 C3
Amangeldy, *Kazakhstan* ... 50 D7
Amantea, *Italy* 31 C9
Amapá, *Brazil* 125 C8
Amapá □, *Brazil* 125 C8
Amara, *Sudan* 81 E3
Amarante, *Brazil* 125 E10
Amarante, *Portugal* 34 D2
Amaranth, *Canada* 105 C9
Amareleja, *Portugal* 35 G3
Amargosa →, *U.S.A.* 117 J10
Amargosa Range, *U.S.A.* .. 117 J10
Amarillo, *U.S.A.* 113 H4
Amarkantak, *India* 69 H9
Amârna, Tell el', *Sudan* ... 80 B3
Amaro, Mte., *Italy* 29 F11
Amarpur, *India* 69 G12
Amarti, *Eritrea* 81 E5
Amarwara, *India* 69 H8
Amasra, *Turkey* 72 B5
Amassama, *Nigeria* 83 D6
Amasya, *Turkey* 72 B6
Amata, *Australia* 93 E5
Amatikulu, *S. Africa* 89 D5
Amatitlán, *Guatemala* 120 D1
Amatrice, *Italy* 29 F10
Amay, *Belgium* 17 D5
Amazon = Amazonas →,
  S. Amer. 122 D5
Amazonas □, *Brazil* 124 E6
Amazonas →, *S. Amer.* ... 122 D5
Amba Ferit, *Ethiopia* 81 E4
Ambah, *India* 68 F8
Ambahakily, *Madag.* 89 C7
Ambahita, *Madag.* 89 C8
Ambala, *India* 68 D7
Ambalavao, *Madag.* 89 C8
Ambanja, *Madag.* 89 A8
Ambararata, *Madag.* 89 B8
Ambarchik, *Russia* 51 C17
Ambarijeby, *Madag.* 89 A8
Ambaro, Helodranon',
  Madag. 89 A8
Ambato, *Ecuador* 124 D3
Ambato, *Madag.* 89 A8
Ambato, Sierra de,
  Argentina 126 B2
Ambato Boeny, *Madag.* ... 89 B8
Ambatofinandrahana,
  Madag. 89 C8
Ambatolampy, *Madag.* 89 B8
Ambatomainty, *Madag.* ... 89 B8
Ambatomanoina, *Madag.* .. 89 B8
Ambatondrazaka, *Madag.* . 89 B8
Ambatosoratra, *Madag.* ... 89 B8
Ambelón, *Greece* 38 B4
Ambenja, *Madag.* 89 B8
Amberg, *Germany* 25 F7
Ambergris Cay, *Belize* 119 D7
Amberieu-en-Bugey, *France* 21 C9
Amberley, *N.Z.* 91 K4
Ambert, *France* 20 C7
Ambidédi, *Mali* 82 C2
Ambikapur, *India* 69 H10
Ambikol, *Sudan* 80 C3
Ambilobé, *Madag.* 89 A8
Ambinanindrano, *Madag.* . 89 C8
Ambinanitelo, *Madag.* 89 B8
Ambinda, *Madag.* 89 B8
Ambo, *Peru* 124 F3
Amboahangy, *Madag.* 89 C8
Ambodifototra, *Madag.* ... 89 B8
Ambodilazana, *Madag.* ... 89 B8
Ambodiriana, *Madag.* 89 B8
Ambohidratrimo, *Madag.* . 89 B8
Ambohidray, *Madag.* 89 B8
Ambohimahamasina, *Madag.* 89 C8
Ambohimahasoa, *Madag.* . 89 C8
Ambohimanga, *Madag.* ... 89 C8
Ambohimitombo, *Madag.* . 89 C8
Ambohitra, *Madag.* 89 A8
Amboise, *France* 18 E8
Ambon, *Indonesia* 63 E7
Ambondro, *Madag.* 89 D8
Amboseli, L., *Kenya* 86 C4
Ambositra, *Madag.* 89 C8
Ambovombe, *Madag.* 89 D8
Amboy, *U.S.A.* 117 L11
Amboyna Cay, *S. China Sea* 62 C4
Ambridge, *U.S.A.* 110 F4
Ambriz, *Angola* 84 F2
Amchitka I., *U.S.A.* 100 C1

Amdhi, *India* 69 H9
Ameca, *Mexico* 118 C4
Ameca →, *Mexico* 118 C3
Amecameca, *Mexico* 119 D5
Ameland, *Neths.* 17 A5
Amélia, *Italy* 29 F9
Amendolara, *Italy* 31 C9
Amenia, *U.S.A.* 111 E11
American Falls, *U.S.A.* 114 E7
American Falls Reservoir,
  U.S.A. 114 E7
American Fork, *U.S.A.* 114 F8
American Highland,
  Antarctica 5 D6
American Samoa ■,
  Pac. Oc. 91 B13
Americana, *Brazil* 127 A6
Americus, *U.S.A.* 109 K3
Amersfoort, *Neths.* 17 B5
Amersfoort, *S. Africa* 89 D4
Amery Ice Shelf, *Antarctica* 5 C6
Ames, *Spain* 34 C2
Ames, *U.S.A.* 112 E8
Amesbury, *U.S.A.* 111 D14
Amet, *India* 68 G5
Amfíklia, *Greece* 38 C4
Amfilokhía, *Greece* 38 C3
Amfípolis, *Greece* 40 F7
Ámfissa, *Greece* 38 C4
Amga, *Russia* 51 C14
Amga →, *Russia* 51 C14
Amgu, *Russia* 51 E14
Amgun →, *Russia* 51 D14
Amherst, *Burma* 67 L20
Amherst, *Canada* 103 C7
Amherst, *Mass., U.S.A.* ... 111 D12
Amherst, *N.Y., U.S.A.* 110 D6
Amherst, *Ohio, U.S.A.* 110 E2
Amherst I., *Canada* 111 B8
Amherstburg, *Canada* 102 D3
Amiata, Mte., *Italy* 29 F8
Amidon, *U.S.A.* 112 B3
Amiens, *France* 19 C9
Amindaion, *Greece* 40 F5
Åminne, *Sweden* 11 G7
Amino, *Ethiopia* 81 G5
Amīrābād, *Iran* 70 C5
Amirante Is., *Seychelles* ... 52 K9
Amisk L., *Canada* 105 C8
Amistad, Presa de la, *Mexico* 118 B4
Amite, *U.S.A.* 113 K9
Amla, *India* 68 J8
Amlia I., *U.S.A.* 100 C3
Amlwch, *U.K.* 12 D3
Amm Adam, *Sudan* 81 D4
'Ammān, *Jordan* 75 D4
'Ammān □, *Jordan* 75 D5
Ammanford, *U.K.* 13 F4
Ammassalik = Tasiilaq,
  Greenland 4 C6
Ammerån →, *Sweden* 10 A10
Ammersee, *Germany* 25 G7
Ammon, *U.S.A.* 114 E8
Amnat Charoen, *Thailand* . 64 E5
Amo Jiang →, *China* 58 F3
Åmol, *Iran* 71 B7
Amorgós, *Greece* 39 E7
Amory, *U.S.A.* 109 J1
Amos, *Canada* 102 C4
Åmot, *Norway* 9 G13
Åmotfors, *Sweden* 10 E6
Amoy = Xiamen, *China* ... 59 E12
Ampanavoana, *Madag.* 89 B9
Ampang, *Malaysia* 65 L3
Ampangalana,
  Lakandranon', *Madag.* .. 89 C8
Ampanihy, *Madag.* 89 C7
Amparafaravola, *Madag.* .. 89 B8
Ampasinambo, *Madag.* 89 C8
Ampasindava, Helodranon',
  Madag. 89 A8
Ampasindava, Saikanosy,
  Madag. 89 A8
Ampenan, *Indonesia* 62 F5
Amper, *Nigeria* 83 D6
Amper →, *Germany* 25 G7
Ampezzo, *Italy* 29 B9
Ampitsikinana, *Réunion* ... 89 A8
Amposta, *Spain* 32 E5
Ampotaka, *Madag.* 89 D7
Ampoza, *Madag.* 89 C7
Amqui, *Canada* 103 C6
Amravati, *India* 66 J10
Amreli, *India* 68 J4
Amritsar, *India* 68 D6
Amroha, *India* 69 E8
Amrum, *Germany* 24 A4
Amsterdam, *Neths.* 17 B4
Amsterdam, *U.S.A.* 111 D10
Amsterdam, I. = Nouvelle-
  Amsterdam, I., *Ind. Oc.* . 3 F13
Amstetten, *Austria* 26 C7
Amudarya →, *Uzbekistan* . 50 E6
Amundsen Gulf, *Canada* .. 100 A7
Amundsen Sea, *Antarctica* . 5 D15
Amungen, *Sweden* 10 C9
Amuntai, *Indonesia* 62 E5
Amur →, *Russia* 51 D15
Amur, W. →, *Sudan* 80 D3
Amurang, *Indonesia* 63 D6
Amuri Pass, *N.Z.* 91 K4
Amurrio, *Spain* 32 B1
Amursk, *Russia* 51 D14
Amusco, *Spain* 34 C6
Amvrakikós Kólpos, *Greece* 38 C2
Amvrosiyivka, *Ukraine* 47 J10
Amyderya = Amudarya →,
  Uzbekistan 50 E6

An Bien, *Vietnam* 65 H5
An Hoa, *Vietnam* 64 E7
An Nabatīyah at Tahta,
  Lebanon 75 B4
An Nabk, *Si. Arabia* 70 D3
An Nabk, *Syria* 75 A5
An Nabk Abū Qaşr,
  Si. Arabia 70 D3
An Nafūd, *Si. Arabia* 70 D4
An Najaf, *Iraq* 70 C5
An Nāşirīyah, *Iraq* 70 D5
An Nhon, *Vietnam* 64 F7
An Nîl □, *Sudan* 80 D3
An Nîl el Abyad □, *Sudan* . 81 E3
An Nîl el Azraq □, *Sudan* . 81 E3
An Nu'ayrīyah, *Si. Arabia* . 71 E6
An Nu'mānīyah, *Iraq* 73 F11
An Nuwayb'ī, W. →,
  Si. Arabia 75 F3
An Thoi, Dao, *Vietnam* ... 65 H4
An Uaimh, *Ireland* 15 C5
Anabar →, *Russia* 51 B12
'Anabtā, *West Bank* 75 C4
Anaconda, *U.S.A.* 114 C7
Anacortes, *U.S.A.* 116 B4
Anacuao, Mt., *Phil.* 61 C4
Anadarko, *U.S.A.* 113 H5
Anadia, *Portugal* 34 E2
Anadolu, *Turkey* 72 C5
Anadyr, *Russia* 51 C18
Anadyr →, *Russia* 51 C18
Anadyrskiy Zaliv, *Russia* . 51 C19
Anáfi, *Greece* 39 E7
Anafópoulo, *Greece* 39 E7
Anaga, Pta. de, *Canary Is.* 37 F3
Anagni, *Italy* 29 G10
'Ānah, *Iraq* 70 C4
Anaheim, *U.S.A.* 117 M9
Anahim Lake, *Canada* 104 C3
Anáhuac, *Mexico* 118 B4
Anakapalle, *India* 67 L13
Anakie, *Australia* 94 C4
Anaklia, *Georgia* 49 J5
Analalava, *Madag.* 89 A8
Analavoka, *Madag.* 89 C8
Análipsis, *Greece* 36 A3
Anambar →, *Pakistan* 68 D3
Anambas, Kepulauan,
  Indonesia 65 L6
Anambas Is. = Anambas,
  Kepulauan, *Indonesia* .. 65 L6
Anambra □, *Nigeria* 83 D6
Anamosa, *U.S.A.* 112 D9
Anamur, *Turkey* 70 B2
Anamur Burnu, *Turkey* ... 72 D5
Anan, *Japan* 55 H7
Anand, *India* 68 H5
Anánes, *Greece* 38 E6
Anantnag, *India* 69 C6
Ananyiv, *Ukraine* 47 J5
Anapa, *Russia* 47 K9
Anapodháris →, *Greece* .. 36 E7
Anapu →, *Brazil* 125 D8
Anār, *Iran* 71 D7
Anārak, *Iran* 71 C7
Anarisfjällen, *Sweden* ... 10 A7
Anas →, *India* 68 H5
Anatolia = Anadolu, *Turkey* 72 C5
Anatsogno, *Madag.* 89 C7
Añatuya, *Argentina* 126 B3
Anaunethad L., *Canada* ... 105 A8
Anbyŏn, *N. Korea* 57 E14
Ancares, Sierra de, *Spain* . 34 C4
Ancaster, *Canada* 110 C5
Ancenis, *France* 18 E5
Anchor Bay, *U.S.A.* 116 G3
Anchorage, *U.S.A.* 100 B5
Anci, *China* 56 E9
Ancohuma, Nevada, *Bolivia* 122 E4
Ancón, *Peru* 124 F3
Ancona, *Italy* 29 E10
Ancud, *Chile* 128 E2
Ancud, G. de, *Chile* 128 E2
Ancy-le-Franc, *France* ... 19 E11
Andacollo, *Argentina* ... 126 D1
Andacollo, *Chile* 126 C1
Andaingo, *Madag.* 89 B8
Andalgalá, *Argentina* ... 126 B2
Åndalsnes, *Norway* 9 E12
Andalucía □, *Spain* 35 H6
Andalusia = Andalucía □,
  Spain 35 H6
Andalusia, *U.S.A.* 109 K2
Andaman Is., *Ind. Oc.* .. 52 H13
Andaman Sea, *Ind. Oc.* .. 62 B1
Andamooka Opal Fields,
  Australia 95 E2
Andapa, *Madag.* 89 A8
Andara, *Namibia* 88 B3
Andelot-Blancheville, *France* 19 D12
Andenes, *Norway* 8 B17
Andenne, *Belgium* 17 D5
Andéranboukane, *Mali* ... 83 B5
Andermatt, *Switz.* 25 J4
Andernach, *Germany* 24 E3
Andernos-les-Bains, *France* 20 D2
Anderslöv, *Sweden* 11 J7
Anderson, *Alaska, U.S.A.* . 100 B5
Anderson, *Calif., U.S.A.* . 114 F2
Anderson, *Ind., U.S.A.* .. 108 E3
Anderson, *Mo., U.S.A.* ... 113 G7
Anderson, *S.C., U.S.A.* .. 109 H4
Anderson →, *Canada* 100 B7
Anderstorp, *Sweden* 11 G7
Andes, *U.S.A.* 111 D10
Andes, Cord. de los,
  S. Amer. 122 F4
Andfjorden, *Norway* 8 B17
Andhra Pradesh □, *India* . 66 L11
Andijon, *Uzbekistan* 50 E8
Andikíthira, *Greece* 38 F5
Andilamena, *Madag.* 89 B8
Andīmeshk, *Iran* 71 C6
Andímilos, *Greece* 38 E6
Andíparos, *Greece* 39 D7
Andípsara, *Greece* 39 C7
Andírrion, *Greece* 38 C3
Andizhan = Andijon,
  Uzbekistan 50 E8
Andoain, *Spain* 32 B2
Andoany, *Madag.* 89 A8
Andong, *S. Korea* 57 F15
Andongwei, *China* 57 G10
Andoom, *Australia* 94 A3
Andorra ■, *Europe* 20 F5
Andorra La Vella, *Andorra* 20 F5
Andover, *U.K.* 13 F6
Andover, *Maine, U.S.A.* .. 111 B14
Andover, *Mass., U.S.A.* .. 111 D13
Andover, *N.J., U.S.A.* ... 111 F10
Andover, *N.Y., U.S.A.* ... 110 D7
Andover, *Ohio, U.S.A.* ... 110 E4
Andøya, *Norway* 8 B16
Andradina, *Brazil* 125 H8
Andrahary, Mt., *Madag.* .. 89 A8
Andramasina, *Madag.* 89 B8
Andranopasy, *Madag.* 89 C7
Andranovory, *Madag.* 89 C7
Andratx, *Spain* 37 B9
Andreanof Is., *U.S.A.* ... 100 C2
Andreapol, *Russia* 46 D7
Andrews, *S.C., U.S.A.* ... 109 J6
Andrews, *Tex., U.S.A.* ... 113 J3
Andreyevka, *Russia* 48 D10
Ándria, *Italy* 31 A9
Andriamena, *Madag.* 89 B8
Andriandampy, *Madag.* ... 89 C8
Andriba, *Madag.* 89 B8
Andrijevica,
  Montenegro, Yug. 40 D3
Andrítsaina, *Greece* 38 D3
Androka, *Madag.* 89 C7
Andropov = Rybinsk, *Russia* 46 C10
Ándros, *Greece* 38 D6
Andros I., *Bahamas* 120 B4
Andros Town, *Bahamas* .. 120 B4
Androscoggin →, *U.S.A.* . 111 C14
Andrychów, *Poland* 45 J6
Andselv, *Norway* 8 B18
Andújar, *Spain* 35 G6
Andulo, *Angola* 84 G3
Aneby, *Sweden* 11 G8
Anegada I., *Virgin Is.* ... 121 C7
Anegada Passage, *W. Indies* 121 C7
Aného, *Togo* 83 D5
Anenni-Noi, *Moldova* 43 D14
Aneto, Pico de, *Spain* ... 32 C5
Anfu, *China* 59 D10
Ang Thong, *Thailand* 64 E3
Angamos, Punta, *Chile* .. 126 A1
Angara →, *Russia* 51 D10
Angara-Débou, *Benin* 83 C5
Angarab, *Ethiopia* 81 E4
Angarbaka, *Sudan* 81 F1
Angarsk, *Russia* 51 D11
Angas Hills, *Australia* .. 92 D4
Angaston, *Australia* 95 E2
Angaur I., *Pac. Oc.* 63 C8
Ånge, *Sweden* 10 B9
Ángel, Salto = Angel Falls,
  Venezuela 124 B6
Ángel de la Guarda, I.,
  Mexico 118 B2
Angel Falls, *Venezuela* .. 124 B6
Angeles, *Phil.* 61 D4
Ängelholm, *Sweden* 11 H6
Angels Camp, *U.S.A.* 116 G6
Ängelsberg, *Sweden* 10 E10
Anger →, *Ethiopia* 81 F4
Angereb →, *Ethiopia* 81 E4
Ångermanälven →, *Sweden* 10 B11
Ångermanland, *Sweden* ... 8 E18
Angermünde, *Germany* ... 24 B9
Angers, *Canada* 111 A9
Angers, *France* 18 E6
Angerville, *France* 19 D9
Ängesån →, *Sweden* 8 C20
Angikuni L., *Canada* 105 A9
Angkor, *Cambodia* 64 F4
Anglès, *Spain* 32 D7
Anglesey, Isle of □, *U.K.* 12 D3
Anglet, *France* 20 E2
Angleton, *U.S.A.* 113 L7
Anglin →, *France* 20 B4
Anglisidhes, *Cyprus* 36 E12
Anglure, *France* 19 D10
Angmagssalik = Tasiilaq,
  Greenland 4 C6
Ango,
  Dem. Rep. of the Congo . 86 B2
Angoche, *Mozam.* 87 F4
Angoche, I., *Mozam.* 87 F4
Angol, *Chile* 126 D1
Angola, *Ind., U.S.A.* ... 108 E3
Angola, *N.Y., U.S.A.* ... 110 D5
Angola ■, *Africa* 85 G3
Angoulême, *France* 20 C4
Angoumois, *France* 20 C4
Angra dos Reis, *Brazil* .. 127 A7
Angren, *Uzbekistan* 50 E8
Angtassom, *Cambodia* ... 65 G5
Angu,
  Dem. Rep. of the Congo . 86 B1
Anguang, *China* 57 B12
Anguilla ■, *W. Indies* ... 121 C7
Anguo, *China* 56 E8
Angurugu, *Australia* 94 A2
Angus □, *U.K.* 14 E6
Angwa →, *Zimbabwe* 89 B5
Anhanduí →, *Brazil* 127 A5
Anholt, *Denmark* 11 H5
Anhua, *China* 59 C8
Anhui □, *China* 59 B11
Anhwei = Anhui □, *China* . 59 B11
Anichab, *Namibia* 88 C1
Ánidhros, *Greece* 39 E7
Anié, *Togo* 83 D5
Animas →, *U.S.A.* 115 H9
Anina, *Romania* 42 E6
Aninoasa, *Romania* 43 F9
Anivorano, *Madag.* 89 B8
Anjalankoski, *Finland* ... 9 F22
Anjar, *India* 68 H4
Anjidīv I., *India* 66 M9
Anjou, *France* 18 E6
Anjozorobe, *Madag.* 89 B8
Anju, *N. Korea* 57 E13
Anka, *Nigeria* 83 C6
Ankaboa, Tanjona, *Madag.* 89 C7
Ankang, *China* 56 H5
Ankara, *Turkey* 72 C5
Ankaramena, *Madag.* 89 C8
Ankaratra, *Madag.* 89 B8
Ankarsrum, *Sweden* 11 G10
Ankasakasa, *Madag.* 89 B7
Ankavandra, *Madag.* 89 B8
Ankazoabo, *Madag.* 89 C7
Ankazobe, *Madag.* 89 B8
Ankeny, *U.S.A.* 112 E8
Ankilimalinika, *Madag.* .. 89 C7
Ankilizato, *Madag.* 89 C8
Ankisabe, *Madag.* 89 B8
Anklam, *Germany* 24 B9
Ankober, *Ethiopia* 81 F4
Ankoro,
  Dem. Rep. of the Congo . 86 D2
Ankororoka, *Madag.* 89 D8
Anlong, *China* 58 E5
Anlu, *China* 59 B9
Anmyŏn-do, *S. Korea* 57 F14
Ånn, *Sweden* 10 A6
Ann, C., *U.S.A.* 111 D14
Ann Arbor, *U.S.A.* 108 D4
Anna, *Russia* 48 E5
Anna, *U.S.A.* 113 G10
Annaba, *Algeria* 78 A7
Annaberg-Buchholz,
  Germany 24 E9
Annalee →, *Ireland* 15 B4
Annam, *Vietnam* 64 E7
Annamitique, Chaîne, *Asia* 64 D6
Annan, *U.K.* 14 G5
Annan →, *U.K.* 14 G5
Annapolis, *U.S.A.* 108 F7
Annapolis Royal, *Canada* . 103 D6
Annapurna, *Nepal* 69 E10
Annean, L., *Australia* ... 93 E2
Anneberg, *Sweden* 11 G8
Annecy, *France* 21 C10
Annecy, Lac d', *France* .. 21 C10
Annemasse, *France* 19 F13
Annenskiy Most, *Russia* .. 46 B9
Anning, *China* 58 E4
Anniston, *U.S.A.* 109 J3
Annobón, *Atl. Oc.* 77 G4
Annonay, *France* 21 C8
Annot, *France* 21 E10
Annotto Bay, *Jamaica* ... 120 C4
Annville, *U.S.A.* 111 F8
Annweiler, *Germany* 25 F3
Áno Arkhánai, *Greece* ... 39 F7
Áno Porróia, *Greece* 40 E7
Áno Síros, *Greece* 38 D6
Áno Viánnos, *Greece* 36 D7
Anorotsangana, *Madag.* .. 89 A8
Anosibe, *Madag.* 89 B8
Anou Mellene, *Mali* 83 B5
Anoumaba, *Ivory C.* 82 D4
Anóyia, *Greece* 36 D6
Anping, *Hebei, China* ... 56 E8
Anping, *Liaoning, China* . 57 D12
Anpu Gang, *China* 58 G7
Anqing, *China* 59 B11
Anqiu, *China* 57 F10
Anren, *China* 59 D9
Ansager, *Denmark* 11 J2
Ansai, *China* 56 F5
Ansbach, *Germany* 25 F6
Anseba →, *Eritrea* 81 D4
Ansfelden, *Austria* 26 C7
Anshan, *China* 57 D12
Anshun, *China* 58 D5
Ansião, *Portugal* 34 F2
Ansley, *U.S.A.* 112 E5
Ansó, *Spain* 32 C4
Ansoain, *Spain* 32 C3
Anson, *U.S.A.* 113 J5
Anson B., *Australia* 92 B5
Ansongo, *Mali* 83 B5
Ansonia, *U.S.A.* 111 E11
Anstruther, *U.K.* 14 E6
Ansudu, *Indonesia* 63 E9
Antabamba, *Peru* 124 F4
Antakya, *Turkey* 70 B3
Antalaha, *Madag.* 89 A9
Antalya, *Turkey* 72 D4
Antalya □, *Turkey* 39 E12
Antalya Körfezi, *Turkey* . 72 D4
Antambohobe, *Madag.* ... 89 C8
Antanambao-Manampotsy,
  Madag. 89 B8
Antanambe, *Madag.* 89 B8
Antananarivo, *Madag.* ... 89 B8
Antananarivo □, *Madag.* . 89 B8
Antanifotsy, *Madag.* 89 B8
Antanimbaribe, *Madag.* .. 89 C7
Antanimora, *Madag.* 89 C8
Antarctic Pen., *Antarctica* 5 C18
Antarctica 5 E3
Antelope, *Zimbabwe* 87 G2
Antequera, *Paraguay* ... 126 A4
Antequera, *Spain* 35 H6
Antero, Mt., *U.S.A.* 115 G10
Antevamena, *Madag.* 89 C7
Anthemoús, *Greece* 40 F7
Anthony, *Kans., U.S.A.* .. 113 G5
Anthony, *N. Mex., U.S.A.* 115 K10
Anti Atlas, *Morocco* 78 C4
Anti-Lebanon = Ash Sharqi,
  Al Jabal, *Lebanon* 75 B5
Antibes, *France* 21 E11
Antibes, C. d', *France* .. 21 E11
Anticosti, Î. d', *Canada* . 103 C7
Antifer, C. d', *France* .. 18 C7
Antigo, *U.S.A.* 112 C10
Antigonish, *Canada* 103 C7
Antigua, *Canary Is.* 37 F5
Antigua, *W. Indies* 121 C7
Antigua & Barbuda ■,
  W. Indies 121 C7
Antigua Guatemala,
  Guatemala 120 D1
Antilla, *Cuba* 120 B4
Antilles = West Indies,
  Cent. Amer. 121 D7
Antioch, *U.S.A.* 116 G5
Antioche, Pertuis d', *France* 20 B2
Antioquia, *Colombia* 124 B3
Antipodes Is., *Pac. Oc.* . 96 M9
Antlers, *U.S.A.* 113 H7
Antoetra, *Madag.* 89 C8
Antofagasta, *Chile* 126 A1
Antofagasta □, *Chile* ... 126 A2
Antofagasta de la Sierra,
  Argentina 126 B2
Antofalla, *Argentina* ... 126 B2
Antofalla, Salar de,
  Argentina 126 B2
Anton, *U.S.A.* 113 J3
Antongila, Helodrano,
  Madag. 89 B8
Antonibé, *Madag.* 89 B8
Antonibé, Presqu'île d',
  Madag. 89 A8
Antonina, *Brazil* 127 B6
Antrain, *France* 18 D5
Antrim, *U.K.* 15 B5
Antrim, *U.S.A.* 110 F3
Antrim □, *U.K.* 15 B5
Antrim, Mts. of, *U.K.* .. 15 A5
Antrim Plateau, *Australia* 92 C4
Antrodoco, *Italy* 29 F10
Antropovo, *Russia* 48 A6
Antsakabary, *Madag.* 89 B8
Antsalova, *Madag.* 89 B7
Antsenavolo, *Madag.* 89 C8
Antsiafabositra, *Madag.* . 89 B8
Antsirabe, *Antananarivo,
  Madag.* 89 B8
Antsirabe, *Antsiranana,
  Madag.* 89 A8
Antsirabe, *Mahajanga,
  Madag.* 89 B8
Antsiranana, *Madag.* 89 A8
Antsiranana □, *Madag.* .. 89 A8
Antsohihy, *Madag.* 89 A8
Antsohimbondrona
  Seranana, *Madag.* 89 A8
Antu, *China* 57 C15
Antwerp = Antwerpen,
  Belgium 17 C4
Antwerp, *U.S.A.* 111 B9
Antwerpen, *Belgium* 17 C4
Antwerpen □, *Belgium* .. 17 C4
Anupgarh, *India* 68 E5
Anuppur, *India* 69 H9
Anuradhapura, *Sri Lanka* . 66 Q12
Anveh, *Iran* 71 E7
Anvers = Antwerpen,
  Belgium 17 C4
Anvers I., *Antarctica* ... 5 C17
Anwen, *China* 59 C13
Anxi, *Fujian, China* 59 E12
Anxi, *Gansu, China* 60 B4
Anxian, *China* 58 B5
Anxiang, *China* 59 C9
Anxious B., *Australia* ... 95 E1
Anyama, *Ivory C.* 82 D4
Anyang, *China* 56 F8
Anyer-Kidul, *Indonesia* . 63 G11
Anyi, *Jiangxi, China* ... 59 C10
Anyi, *Shanxi, China* 56 G6
Anyuan, *China* 59 E10
Anyue, *China* 58 B5
Anza, *U.S.A.* 117 M10
Anze, *China* 56 F7
Anzhero-Sudzhensk, *Russia* 50 D9
Ánzio, *Italy* 30 A5
Aoga-Shima, *Japan* 55 H9
Aoiz, *Spain* 32 C3
Aomen = Macau, *Asia* ... 59 F9
Aomori, *Japan* 54 D10
Aomori □, *Japan* 54 D10
Aonla, *India* 69 E8
Aosta, *Italy* 28 C4
Aoudéras, *Niger* 83 B6
Aoukâr, *Mauritania* 82 B3
Aozou, *Chad* 79 D9
Apa →, *S. Amer.* 126 A4
Apache, *U.S.A.* 113 H5
Apache Junction, *U.S.A.* . 115 K8
Apalachee B., *U.S.A.* ... 109 L4
Apalachicola, *U.S.A.* ... 109 L3
Apalachicola →, *U.S.A.* . 109 L3
Apam, *Ghana* 83 D4
Apapa, *Nigeria* 83 D5
Apaporis →, *Colombia* ... 124 D5
Aparri, *Phil.* 61 B4
Apateu, *Romania* 42 D6
Apatin, *Serbia, Yug.* ... 42 E4
Apatity, *Russia* 50 C4
Apatzingán, *Mexico* 118 D4
Apeldoorn, *Neths.* 17 B5
Apen, *Germany* 24 B3
Apennines = Appennini,
  Italy 28 E7
Aphrodisias, *Turkey* 39 D10
Apia, *W. Samoa* 91 A13
Apiacás, Serra dos, *Brazil* 124 E7
Apies →, *S. Africa* 89 D4
Apizaco, *Mexico* 119 D5
Aplao, *Peru* 124 G4
Apo, Mt., *Phil.* 63 C7
Apolakkiá, *Greece* 36 C9
Apolakkiá, Ormos, *Greece* 36 C9
Apolda, *Germany* 24 D7
Apollo Bay, *Australia* ... 95 F3
Apollonia, *Greece* 38 E6
Apolo, *Bolivia* 124 F5
Aporé →, *Brazil* 125 G8
Apostle Is., *U.S.A.* 112 B9
Apóstoles, *Argentina* ... 127 B4
Apostolos Andreas, C.,
  Cyprus 36 D13
Apostolovo, *Ukraine* 47 J7
Apoteri, *Guyana* 124 C7
Appalachian Mts., *U.S.A.* 108 G7
Äppelbo, *Sweden* 10 D8
Appennini, *Italy* 28 E7
Appennino Ligure, *Italy* . 28 D6
Appenzell-Ausser
  Rhoden □, *Switz.* 25 H5
Appenzell-Inner Rhoden □,
  Switz. 25 H5
Appiano, *Italy* 29 B8
Apple Hill, *Canada* 111 A10
Apple Valley, *U.S.A.* ... 117 L9
Appleby-in-Westmorland,
  U.K. 12 C5
Appleton, *U.S.A.* 108 C1
Approuague →, *Fr. Guiana* 125 C8
Apricena, *Italy* 29 G12
Aprília, *Italy* 30 A5
Apsheronsk, *Russia* 49 H4
Apsley, *Canada* 110 B6
Apt, *France* 21 E9
Apuane, Alpi, *Italy* 28 D7
Apucarana, *Brazil* 127 A5
Apulia = Púglia □, *Italy* . 31 A9
Apure →, *Venezuela* 124 B5
Apurimac →, *Peru* 124 F4
Apuseni, Munţii, *Romania* 42 D7
Aqā Jarī, *Iran* 71 D6
Aqaba = Al 'Aqabah,
  Jordan 75 F4
Aqaba, G. of, *Red Sea* .. 70 D2
'Aqabah, Khalīj al = Aqaba,
  G. of, *Red Sea* 70 D2
'Aqdā, *Iran* 71 C7
Aqîq, *Sudan* 80 D4
Aqîq, Khalîg, *Sudan* ... 80 D4
Aqmola = Astana,
  Kazakstan 50 D8
Aqrah, *Iraq* 70 B4
Aqtaū, *Kazakstan* 50 E6
Aqtöbe, *Kazakstan* 50 D6
Aquidauana, *Brazil* 125 H7
Aquiles Serdán, *Mexico* . 118 B3
Aquin, *Haiti* 121 C5
Aquitaine □, *France* 20 D3
Ar Rachidiya, *Morocco* .. 78 B5
Ar Rafid, *Syria* 75 C4
Ar Raḥḥālīyah, *Iraq* ... 70 C4
Ar Ramādī, *Iraq* 70 C4
Ar Ramthā, *Jordan* 75 C5
Ar Raqqah, *Syria* 70 C3
Ar Rass, *Si. Arabia* ... 70 E4
Ar Rawshān, *Si. Arabia* . 80 C5
Ar Rifā'ī, *Iraq* 70 D5
Ar Riyāḍ, *Si. Arabia* ... 70 E5
Ar Ru'ays, *Qatar* 71 E6
Ar Rukhaymīyah, *Iraq* .. 70 D5
Ar Ruqayyidah, *Si. Arabia* 71 E6
Ar Ruşāfah, *Syria* 70 C3
Ar Ruţbah, *Iraq* 70 C4
Ara, *India* 69 G11
Ara Goro, *Ethiopia* 81 F5
Ara Tera, *Ethiopia* 81 F5
'Arab, Bahr el →, *Sudan* . 81 F2
Arab, Khalīg el, *Egypt* . 80 A2
'Araba, W. →, *Egypt* ... 80 J8
'Arabābād, *Iran* 71 C8
Araban, *Turkey* 72 D7
Arabatskaya Strelka, *Ukraine* 47 K8
Arabba, *Italy* 29 B8
Arabia, *Asia* 52 G8
Arabian Desert = Es Sahrâ
  Esh Sharqîya, *Egypt* .. 80 B3
Arabian Gulf = Gulf, The,
  Asia 71 E6
Arabian Sea, *Ind. Oc.* .. 52 H10
Araç, *Turkey* 72 B5
Aracaju, *Brazil* 125 F11
Aracati, *Brazil* 125 D11
Araçatuba, *Brazil* 127 A5
Aracena, *Spain* 35 H4
Aracena, Sierra de, *Spain* 35 H4
Aračinovo, *Macedonia* ... 40 D5
Araçuaí, *Brazil* 125 G10
'Arad, *Israel* 75 D4
Arad, *Romania* 42 D6
Arad □, *Romania* 42 D6
Arãdan, *Iran* 71 C7
Aradhippou, *Cyprus* 36 E12
Arafura Sea, *E. Indies* . 52 K17
Aragats, *Armenia* 49 K7
Aragón □, *Spain* 32 D4
Aragón →, *Spain* 32 C3
Aragona, *Italy* 30 E6

Araguacema

Araguacema, *Brazil* 125 E9
Araguaia →, *Brazil* 122 D6
Araguaína, *Brazil* 125 E9
Araguari, *Brazil* 125 G9
Araguari →, *Brazil* 125 C9
Arain, *India* 68 F6
Arak, *Algeria* 78 C6
Arāk, *Iran* 71 C6
Araka, *Sudan* 81 G3
Arakan Coast, *Burma* 67 K19
Arakan Yoma, *Burma* 67 K19
Arákhova, *Greece* 38 C4
Arakli, *Turkey* 73 B8
Araks = Aras, Rūd-e →, *Azerbaijan* 49 K9
Aral, *Kazakstan* 50 E7
Aral Sea, *Asia* 50 E7
Aral Tengizi = Aral Sea, *Asia* 50 E7
Aralsk = Aral, *Kazakstan* 50 E7
Aralskoye More = Aral Sea, *Asia* 50 E7
Aralsor, Ozero, *Kazakstan* 49 F9
Aramac, *Australia* 94 C4
Aran I., *Ireland* 15 A3
Aran Is., *Ireland* 15 C2
Aranda de Duero, *Spain* 34 D7
Arandān, *Iran* 70 C5
Aranđelovac, *Serbia, Yug.* 40 B4
Aranjuez, *Spain* 34 E7
Aranos, *Namibia* 88 C2
Aransas Pass, *U.S.A.* 113 M6
Aranyaprathet, *Thailand* 64 F4
Araouane, *Mali* 82 B4
Arapahoe, *U.S.A.* 112 E5
Arapey Grande →, *Uruguay* 126 C4
Arapgir, *Turkey* 70 B3
Arapiraca, *Brazil* 125 E11
Arapongas, *Brazil* 127 A5
Ar'ar, *Si. Arabia* 70 D4
Araranguá, *Brazil* 127 B6
Araraquara, *Brazil* 125 H9
Ararás, Serra das, *Brazil* 127 B5
Ararat, *Armenia* 73 C11
Ararat, *Australia* 95 F3
Ararat, Mt. = Ağrı Dağı, *Turkey* 70 B5
Araria, *India* 69 F12
Araripe, Chapada do, *Brazil* 125 E11
Araruama, L. de, *Brazil* 127 A7
Aras, Rūd-e →, *Azerbaijan* 49 K9
Aratāne, *Mauritania* 82 B3
Arauca, *Colombia* 124 B4
Arauca →, *Venezuela* 124 B5
Arauco, *Chile* 126 D1
Arawa, *Ethiopia* 81 F5
Araxá, *Brazil* 125 G9
Araya, Pen. de, *Venezuela* 124 A6
Arba Gugu, *Ethiopia* 81 F5
Arba Minch, *Ethiopia* 81 F4
Arbat, *Iraq* 70 C5
Árbatax, *Italy* 30 C2
Arbi, *Ethiopia* 81 F4
Arbīl, *Iraq* 70 B5
Arboga, *Sweden* 10 E9
Arbois, *France* 19 F12
Arbore, *Ethiopia* 81 F4
Arboréa, *Italy* 30 C1
Arborfield, *Canada* 105 C8
Arborg, *Canada* 105 C9
Arbre du Ténéré, *Niger* 83 B7
Arbroath, *U.K.* 14 E6
Arbuckle, *U.S.A.* 116 F4
Arbus, *Italy* 30 C1
Arc →, *France* 21 C10
Arc-lès-Gray, *France* 19 E12
Arcachon, *France* 20 D2
Arcachon, Bassin d', *France* 20 D2
Arcade, *Calif., U.S.A.* 117 L8
Arcade, *N.Y., U.S.A.* 110 D6
Arcadia, *Fla., U.S.A.* 109 M5
Arcadia, *La., U.S.A.* 113 J8
Arcadia, *Pa., U.S.A.* 110 F6
Arcata, *U.S.A.* 114 F1
Arcévia, *Italy* 29 E9
Archangel = Arkhangelsk, *Russia* 50 C5
Archar, *Bulgaria* 40 C6
Archbald, *U.S.A.* 111 E9
Archena, *Spain* 33 G3
Archer →, *Australia* 94 A3
Archer B., *Australia* 94 A3
Archers Post, *Kenya* 86 B4
Arches National Park, *U.S.A.* 115 G9
Archidona, *Spain* 35 H6
Arci, Mte., *Italy* 30 C1
Arcidosso, *Italy* 29 F8
Arcis-sur-Aube, *France* 19 D11
Arckaringa Cr. →, *Australia* 95 D2
Arco, *Italy* 28 C7
Arco, *U.S.A.* 114 E7
Arcos = Arcos de Jalón, *Spain* 32 D2
Arcos de Jalón, *Spain* 32 D2
Arcos de la Frontera, *Spain* 35 J5
Arcos de Valdevez, *Portugal* 34 D2
Arcot, *India* 66 N11
Arcozelo, *Portugal* 34 E3
Arctic Bay, *Canada* 101 A11
Arctic Ocean, *Arctic* 4 B18
Arctic Red River = Tsiigehtchic, *Canada* 100 B6
Arda →, *Bulgaria* 41 E10
Arda →, *Italy* 28 C7
Ardabīl, *Iran* 71 B6
Ardahan, *Turkey* 73 B10
Ardakān = Sepīdān, *Iran* 71 D7
Ardakān, *Iran* 71 C7
Ardala, *Sweden* 11 F7
Ardales, *Spain* 35 J6
Ardèche □, *France* 21 D8
Ardèche →, *France* 21 D8
Ardee, *Ireland* 15 C5
Arden, *Canada* 110 B8
Arden, *Denmark* 11 H3
Arden, *Calif., U.S.A.* 116 G5
Arden, *Nev., U.S.A.* 117 J11
Ardenne, *Belgium* 6 F7
Ardennes = Ardenne, *Belgium* 6 F7
Ardennes □, *France* 19 C11
Ardentes, *France* 19 F8
Arderin, *Ireland* 15 C4
Ardeşen, *Turkey* 73 B9
Ardestān, *Iran* 71 C7
Árdhas →, *Greece* 41 E10
Ardhéa, *Greece* 40 F6
Ardila →, *Portugal* 35 G3
Ardino, *Bulgaria* 41 E9
Ardivachar Pt., *U.K.* 14 D1
Ardlethan, *Australia* 95 E4
Ardmore, *Okla., U.S.A.* 113 H6
Ardmore, *Pa., U.S.A.* 111 G9
Ardnamurchan, Pt. of, *U.K.* 14 E2
Ardnave Pt., *U.K.* 14 F2
Ardon, *Russia* 49 J7
Ardore, *Italy* 31 D9
Ardres, *France* 19 B8
Ardrossan, *Australia* 95 E2
Ardrossan, *U.K.* 14 F4
Ards Pen., *U.K.* 15 B6
Arduan, *Sudan* 80 D3
Ardud, *Romania* 42 C7
Åre, *Sweden* 10 A7
Arecibo, *Puerto Rico* 121 C6
Areia Branca, *Brazil* 125 E11
Arena, Pt., *U.S.A.* 116 G3
Arenal, *Honduras* 120 C2
Arenas = Las Arenas, *Spain* 34 B6
Arenas de San Pedro, *Spain* 34 E5
Arendal, *Norway* 9 G13
Arendsee, *Germany* 24 C7
Arenys de Mar, *Spain* 32 D7
Arenzano, *Italy* 28 D5
Areópolis, *Greece* 38 E4
Arequipa, *Peru* 124 G4
Arero, *Ethiopia* 81 G4
Arès, *France* 20 D2
Arévalo, *Spain* 34 D6
Arezzo, *Italy* 29 E8
Arga, *Turkey* 70 B3
Arga →, *Spain* 32 C3
Argalastí, *Greece* 38 B5
Argamasilla de Alba, *Spain* 35 F7
Argamasilla de Calatrava, *Spain* 35 G6
Arganda, *Spain* 34 E7
Arganil, *Portugal* 34 E2
Argedeb, *Ethiopia* 81 F5
Argelès-Gazost, *France* 20 E3
Argelès-sur-Mer, *France* 20 F7
Argens →, *France* 21 E10
Argent-sur-Sauldre, *France* 19 E9
Argenta, *Canada* 104 C5
Argenta, *Italy* 29 D8
Argentan, *France* 18 D6
Argentário, Mte., *Italy* 29 F8
Argentat, *France* 20 C5
Argentera, *Italy* 28 D4
Argenteuil, *France* 19 D9
Argentia, *Canada* 103 C9
Argentiera, C. dell', *Italy* 30 B1
Argentina ■, *S. Amer.* 128 D3
Argentina Is., *Antarctica* 5 C17
Argentino, L., *Argentina* 128 G2
Argenton-Château, *France* 18 F6
Argenton-sur-Creuse, *France* 19 F8
Argeş □, *Romania* 43 F9
Argeş →, *Romania* 43 F11
Arghandab →, *Afghan.* 68 D1
Argheile, *Ethiopia* 81 F5
Argo, *Sudan* 80 D3
Argolikós Kólpos, *Greece* 38 D4
Argolís □, *Greece* 38 D4
Argonne, *France* 19 C12
Árgos, *Greece* 38 D4
Árgos Orestikón, *Greece* 40 F5
Argostólion, *Greece* 38 C2
Arguedas, *Spain* 32 C3
Arguello, Pt., *U.S.A.* 117 L6
Arguineguín, *Canary Is.* 37 G4
Argun, *Russia* 49 J7
Argun →, *Russia* 51 D13
Argungu, *Nigeria* 83 C5
Argus Pk., *U.S.A.* 117 K9
Argyle, L., *Australia* 92 C4
Argyll & Bute □, *U.K.* 14 E3
Arhavi, *Turkey* 73 B9
Århus, *Denmark* 11 H4
Århus Amtskommune □, *Denmark* 11 H4
Ariadnoye, *Russia* 54 B7
Ariamsvlei, *Namibia* 88 D2
Ariana, *Tunisia* 79 A7
Ariano Irpino, *Italy* 31 A8
Aribinda, *Burkina Faso* 83 C4
Arica, *Chile* 124 G4
Arica, *Colombia* 124 D4
Arico, *Canary Is.* 37 F3
Arid, C., *Australia* 93 F3
Arida, *Japan* 55 G7
Ariège □, *France* 20 F5
Ariège →, *France* 20 E5
Arieş →, *Romania* 43 D8
Arihā, *Israel* 80 A4
Arilje, *Serbia, Yug.* 40 C4
Arílla, Ákra, *Greece* 36 A3
Arima, *Trin. & Tob.* 121 D7
Arinos →, *Brazil* 122 E5
Ario de Rosales, *Mexico* 118 D4
Ariogala, *Lithuania* 44 C10
Aripuanã, *Brazil* 124 E6
Aripuanã →, *Brazil* 122 D4
Ariquemes, *Brazil* 124 E6
Arisaig, *U.K.* 14 E3
Arîsh, W. el →, *Egypt* 80 A3
Arissa, *Ethiopia* 81 E5
Aristazabal I., *Canada* 104 C3
Arivonimamo, *Madag.* 89 B8
Ariza, *Spain* 32 D2
Arizaro, Salar de, *Argentina* 126 A2
Arizona, *Argentina* 126 D2
Arizona □, *U.S.A.* 115 J8
Arizpe, *Mexico* 118 A2
Årjäng, *Sweden* 10 E6
Arjeplog, *Sweden* 8 D18
Arjona, *Colombia* 124 A3
Arjona, *Spain* 35 H6
Arjuna, *Indonesia* 63 G15
Arka, *Russia* 51 C15
Arkadak, *Russia* 48 E6
Arkadelphia, *U.S.A.* 113 H8
Arkadhía □, *Greece* 38 D4
Arkaig, L., *U.K.* 14 E3
Arkalyk = Arqalyk, *Kazakstan* 50 D7
Arkansas □, *U.S.A.* 113 H8
Arkansas →, *U.S.A.* 113 J9
Arkansas City, *U.S.A.* 113 G6
Arkaroola, *Australia* 95 E2
Árkathos →, *Greece* 38 B3
Arkhángelos, *Greece* 36 C10
Arkhangelsk, *Russia* 50 C5
Arkhangelskoye, *Russia* 48 E5
Arki, *India* 68 D7
Arkiko, *Eritrea* 81 D4
Arklow, *Ireland* 15 D5
Árkoi, *Greece* 39 D8
Arkona, Kap, *Germany* 24 A9
Arkösund, *Sweden* 11 F10
Arkoúdhi, *Greece* 38 C2
Arkport, *U.S.A.* 110 D7
Arkticheskiy, Mys, *Russia* 51 A10
Arkul, *Russia* 48 B10
Arkville, *U.S.A.* 111 D10
Årla, *Sweden* 10 E10
Arlanza →, *Spain* 34 C6
Arlanzón →, *Spain* 34 C6
Arlbergpass, *Austria* 26 D3
Arles, *France* 21 E8
Arlington, *S. Africa* 89 D4
Arlington, *N.Y., U.S.A.* 111 E11
Arlington, *Oreg., U.S.A.* 114 D3
Arlington, *S. Dak., U.S.A.* 112 C6
Arlington, *Tex., U.S.A.* 113 J6
Arlington, *Va., U.S.A.* 108 F7
Arlington, *Vt., U.S.A.* 111 C11
Arlington, *Wash., U.S.A.* 116 B4
Arlington Heights, *U.S.A.* 108 D2
Arlit, *Niger* 78 E7
Arlon, *Belgium* 17 E5
Arltunga, *Australia* 94 C1
Arly, *Burkina Faso* 83 C5
Armagh, *U.K.* 15 B5
Armagh □, *U.K.* 15 B5
Armagnac, *France* 20 E4
Armançon →, *France* 19 E10
Armavir, *Russia* 49 H5
Armenia, *Colombia* 124 C3
Armenia ■, *Asia* 49 K7
Armeniş, *Romania* 42 E7
Armenistís, Ákra, *Greece* 36 C9
Armentières, *France* 19 B9
Armidale, *Australia* 95 E5
Armilla, *Spain* 35 H7
Armour, *U.S.A.* 112 D5
Armstrong, *B.C., Canada* 104 C5
Armstrong, *Ont., Canada* 102 B2
Armutlu, *Bursa, Turkey* 41 F12
Armutlu, *İzmir, Turkey* 39 C9
Arnaía, *Greece* 40 F7
Arnarfjörður, *Iceland* 8 D2
Arnaud →, *Canada* 101 B12
Arnauti, C., *Cyprus* 36 D11
Arnay-le-Duc, *France* 19 E11
Arnedillo, *Spain* 32 C2
Arnedo, *Spain* 32 C2
Arnett, *U.S.A.* 113 G5
Arnhem, *Neths.* 17 C5
Arnhem, C., *Australia* 94 A2
Arnhem B., *Australia* 94 A2
Arnhem Land, *Australia* 94 A1
Árnissa, *Greece* 40 F5
Arno →, *Italy* 28 E7
Arno Bay, *Australia* 95 E2
Arnold, *U.K.* 12 D6
Arnold, *U.S.A.* 116 G6
Arnoldstein, *Austria* 26 E6
Arnon →, *France* 19 E9
Arnot, *Canada* 105 B9
Arnøy, *Norway* 8 A19
Arnprior, *Canada* 102 C4
Arnsberg, *Germany* 24 D4
Arnstadt, *Germany* 24 E6
Aroab, *Namibia* 88 D2
Aroánia Óri, *Greece* 38 D4
Aroche, *Spain* 35 H4
Arochuku, *Nigeria* 83 D6
Arolsen, *Germany* 24 D5
Aron, *India* 68 G6
Aron →, *France* 19 F10
Arona, *Italy* 28 C5
Aroroy, *Phil.* 61 E5
Arosa, Ría de, *Spain* 34 C2
Arpajon, *France* 19 D9
Arpajon-sur-Cère, *France* 20 D6
Arpaşu de Jos, *Romania* 43 E9
Arqalyk, *Kazakstan* 50 D7
Arrah = Ara, *India* 69 G11
Arrah, *Ivory C.* 82 D4
Arraiolos, *Portugal* 35 G3
Arran, *U.K.* 14 F3
Arras, *France* 19 B9
Arrasate, *Spain* 32 B2
Arrats →, *France* 20 D4
Arreau, *France* 20 F4
Arrecife, *Canary Is.* 37 F6
Arrecifes, *Argentina* 126 C3
Arrée, Mts. d', *France* 18 D3
Arresø, *Denmark* 11 J6
Arriaga, *Chiapas, Mexico* 119 D6
Arriaga, *San Luis Potosí, Mexico* 118 C4
Arrilalah, *Australia* 94 C3
Arrino, *Australia* 93 E2
Arriondas, *Spain* 34 B5
Arromanches-les-Bains, *France* 18 C6
Arronches, *Portugal* 35 F3
Arros →, *France* 20 E3
Arrow, L., *Ireland* 15 B3
Arrowhead, L., *U.S.A.* 117 L9
Arrowtown, *N.Z.* 91 L2
Arroyo de la Luz, *Spain* 35 F4
Arroyo Grande, *U.S.A.* 117 K6
Års, *Denmark* 11 H3
Ars, *Iran* 70 B5
Ars-sur-Moselle, *France* 19 C13
Arsenault L., *Canada* 105 B7
Arsenev, *Russia* 54 B6
Arsi □, *Ethiopia* 81 F4
Arsiero, *Italy* 29 C8
Arsin, *Turkey* 73 B8
Arsk, *Russia* 48 B9
Årsunda, *Sweden* 10 D10
Árta, *Greece* 38 B3
Artà, *Spain* 37 B10
Árta □, *Greece* 38 B3
Arteaga, *Mexico* 118 D4
Arteche, *Phil.* 61 E6
Arteijo = Arteixo, *Spain* 34 B2
Arteixo, *Spain* 34 B2
Artem = Artyom, *Azerbaijan* 49 K10
Artem, *Russia* 54 C6
Artemovsk, *Russia* 51 D10
Artemovsk, *Ukraine* 47 H9
Artemovskiy, *Russia* 49 G5
Artenay, *France* 19 D8
Artern, *Germany* 24 D7
Artesa de Segre, *Spain* 32 D6
Artesia = Mosomane, *Botswana* 88 C4
Artesia, *U.S.A.* 113 J2
Arthington, *Liberia* 82 D2
Arthur, *Canada* 110 C4
Arthur →, *Australia* 94 G3
Arthur Cr. →, *Australia* 94 C2
Arthur Pt., *Australia* 94 C5
Arthur River, *Australia* 93 F2
Arthur's Pass, *N.Z.* 91 K3
Arthur's Town, *Bahamas* 121 B4
Artigas, *Uruguay* 126 C4
Artik, *Armenia* 49 K6
Artillery L., *Canada* 105 A7
Artois, *France* 19 B9
Artotína, *Greece* 38 C4
Artrutx, C. de, *Spain* 37 B10
Artsyz, *Ukraine* 47 J5
Artvin, *Turkey* 73 B9
Artyom, *Azerbaijan* 49 K10
Aru, Kepulauan, *Indonesia* 63 F8
Aru Is. = Aru, Kepulauan, *Indonesia* 63 F8
Arua, *Uganda* 86 B3
Aruanã, *Brazil* 125 F8
Aruba ■, *W. Indies* 121 D6
Arucas, *Canary Is.* 37 F4
Arudy, *France* 20 E3
Arun →, *Nepal* 69 F12
Arun →, *U.K.* 13 G7
Arunachal Pradesh □, *India* 67 F19
Arusha, *Tanzania* 86 C4
Arusha □, *Tanzania* 86 C4
Arusha Chini, *Tanzania* 86 C4
Aruwimi →, *Dem. Rep. of the Congo* 86 B1
Arvada, *Colo., U.S.A.* 112 F2
Arvada, *Wyo., U.S.A.* 114 D10
Arve →, *France* 19 F13
Árvi, *Greece* 36 E7
Arviat, *Canada* 105 A10
Arvidsjaur, *Sweden* 8 D18
Arvika, *Sweden* 10 E6
Arvin, *U.S.A.* 117 K8
Arwal, *India* 69 G11
Arxan, *China* 60 B6
Åryd, *Sweden* 11 H8
Aryirádhes, *Greece* 36 B3
Aryiroúpolis, *Greece* 36 D6
Arys, *Kazakstan* 50 E7
Arzachena, *Italy* 30 A2
Arzamas, *Russia* 48 C6
Arzgir, *Russia* 49 H7
Arzignano, *Italy* 29 C8
Arzúa, *Spain* 34 C2
Aš, *Czech Rep.* 26 A5
Ås, *Sweden* 10 A8
As Pontes de García Rodríguez, *Spain* 34 B3
Aş Şadr, *U.A.E.* 71 E7
Aş Şafā, *Syria* 75 B6
As Saffānīyah, *Si. Arabia* 71 E6
As Safīrah, *Syria* 70 B3
Aş Şahm, *Oman* 71 E8
As Sājir, *Si. Arabia* 70 E5
As Salamīyah, *Syria* 70 C3
As Salmān, *Iraq* 70 D5
As Salţ, *Jordan* 75 C4
As Sal'w'a, *Qatar* 71 E6
As Samāwah, *Iraq* 70 D5
As Sanamayn, *Syria* 75 B5
As Sohar = Şuḩār, *Oman* 71 E8
As Sukhnah, *Syria* 70 C3
As Sulaymānīyah, *Iraq* 70 C5
As Sulaymī, *Si. Arabia* 70 E4
As Sulayyil, *Si. Arabia* 74 C4
As Summān, *Si. Arabia* 70 E5
As Suwaydā', *Syria* 75 C5
As Suwaydā' □, *Syria* 75 C5
As Suwayq, *Oman* 71 F8
As Şuwayrah, *Iraq* 70 C5
Åsa, *Sweden* 11 G6
Asab, *Namibia* 88 D2
Asaba, *Nigeria* 83 D6
Asad, Buḩayrat al, *Syria* 70 C3
Asadābād, *Iran* 73 E13
Asafo, *Ghana* 82 D4
Asahi-Gawa →, *Japan* 55 G6
Asahigawa, *Japan* 54 C11
Asale, L., *Ethiopia* 81 E5
Asamankese, *Ghana* 83 D4
Asan →, *India* 69 F8
Asansol, *India* 69 H12
Åsarna, *Sweden* 10 B8
Asayita, *Ethiopia* 81 E5
Asbe Teferi, *Ethiopia* 81 F5
Asbesberge, *S. Africa* 88 D3
Asbestos, *Canada* 103 C5
Asbury Park, *U.S.A.* 111 F10
Ascea, *Italy* 31 B8
Ascensión, *Mexico* 118 A3
Ascensión, B. de la, *Mexico* 119 D7
Ascension I., *Atl. Oc.* 77 G2
Aschach an der Donau, *Austria* 26 C7
Aschaffenburg, *Germany* 25 F5
Aschendorf, *Germany* 24 B3
Aschersleben, *Germany* 24 D7
Asciano, *Italy* 29 E8
Áscoli Piceno, *Italy* 29 F10
Áscoli Satriano, *Italy* 31 A8
Ascope, *Peru* 124 E3
Ascotán, *Chile* 126 A2
Aseb, *Eritrea* 81 E5
Åseda, *Sweden* 11 G9
Asela, *Ethiopia* 81 F4
Åsen, *Sweden* 10 C7
Asenovgrad, *Bulgaria* 41 D8
Aserradero, *Mexico* 118 C3
Asfeld, *France* 19 C11
Asfûn el Matâ'na, *Egypt* 80 B3
Asgata, *Cyprus* 36 E12
Ash Fork, *U.S.A.* 115 J7
Ash Grove, *U.S.A.* 113 G8
Ash Shabakah, *Iraq* 70 D4
Ash Shamāl □, *Lebanon* 75 A5
Ash Shāmīyah, *Iraq* 70 D5
Ash Shāriqah, *U.A.E.* 71 E7
Ash Sharmah, *Si. Arabia* 70 D2
Ash Sharqāt, *Iraq* 70 C4
Ash Sharqi, Al Jabal, *Lebanon* 75 B5
Ash Shaţrah, *Iraq* 70 D5
Ash Shawbak, *Jordan* 70 D2
Ash Shawmari, J., *Jordan* 75 E5
Ash Shināfīyah, *Iraq* 70 D5
Ash Shu'bah, *Si. Arabia* 70 D5
Ash Shumlūl, *Si. Arabia* 70 E5
Ash Shūr'a, *Iraq* 70 C4
Ash Shurayf, *Si. Arabia* 70 E3
Ash Shuwayfāt, *Lebanon* 75 B4
Ashanti □, *Ghana* 83 D4
Ashau, *Vietnam* 64 D6
Ashbourne, *U.K.* 12 D6
Ashburn, *U.S.A.* 109 K4
Ashburton, *N.Z.* 91 K3
Ashburton →, *Australia* 92 D1
Ashcroft, *Canada* 104 C4
Ashdod, *Israel* 75 D3
Ashdown, *U.S.A.* 113 J7
Asheboro, *U.S.A.* 109 H6
Ashern, *Canada* 105 C9
Asherton, *U.S.A.* 113 L5
Asheville, *U.S.A.* 109 H4
Ashewat, *Pakistan* 68 D3
Asheweig →, *Canada* 102 B2
Ashford, *Australia* 95 D5
Ashford, *U.K.* 13 F8
Ashgabat, *Turkmenistan* 50 F6
Ashibetsu, *Japan* 54 C11
Ashikaga, *Japan* 55 F9
Ashington, *U.K.* 12 B6
Ashizuri-Zaki, *Japan* 55 H6
Ashkarkot, *Afghan.* 68 C2
Ashkhabad = Ashgabat, *Turkmenistan* 50 F6
Āshkhāneh, *Iran* 71 B8
Ashland, *Kans., U.S.A.* 113 G5
Ashland, *Ky., U.S.A.* 108 F4
Ashland, *Mont., U.S.A.* 114 D10
Ashland, *Ohio, U.S.A.* 110 F2
Ashland, *Oreg., U.S.A.* 114 E2
Ashland, *Pa., U.S.A.* 111 F8
Ashland, *Va., U.S.A.* 108 G7
Ashland, *Wis., U.S.A.* 112 B9
Ashley, *N. Dak., U.S.A.* 112 B5
Ashley, *Pa., U.S.A.* 111 E9
Ashmore Reef, *Australia* 92 B3
Ashmûn, *Egypt* 80 H7
Ashmyany, *Belarus* 9 J21
Ashokan Reservoir, *U.S.A.* 111 E10
Ashqelon, *Israel* 75 D3
Ashta, *India* 68 H7
Ashtabula, *U.S.A.* 110 E4
Ashton, *S. Africa* 88 E3
Ashton, *U.S.A.* 114 D8
Ashuanipi, L., *Canada* 103 B6
Ashville, *U.S.A.* 110 F6
'Āṣī →, *Asia* 72 D6
Asia 52 E11
Asia, Kepulauan, *Indonesia* 63 D8
Āsīā Bak, *Iran* 71 C6
Asiago, *Italy* 29 C8

Asifabad, India 66 K11
Asinara, Italy 30 A1
Asinara, G. dell', Italy ... 30 A1
Asino, Russia 50 D9
Asipovichy, Belarus 46 F5
'Asīr □, Si. Arabia 74 D3
Asir, Ras, Somali Rep. ... 74 E5
Aşkale, Turkey 73 C9
Askersund, Sweden 11 F8
Askham, S. Africa 88 D3
Askim, Norway 9 G14
Askja, Iceland 8 D5
Askøy, Norway 9 F11
Asl, Egypt 80 B3
Aslan Burnu, Turkey 39 C8
Aslanapa, Turkey 39 B11
Asmara = Asmera, Eritrea . 81 D4
Asmera, Eritrea 81 D4
Asnæs, Denmark 11 J4
Åsnen, Sweden 11 H8
Asola, Italy 28 C7
Asosa, Ethiopia 81 E3
Asoteriba, Jebel, Sudan ... 80 C4
Aspe, Spain 33 G4
Aspen, U.S.A. 115 G10
Aspendos, Turkey 72 D4
Aspermont, U.S.A. 113 J4
Aspet, France 20 E4
Aspiring, Mt., N.Z. 91 L2
Aspres-sur-Buëch, France . 21 D9
Asprókavos, Ákra, Greece . 36 B4
Aspromonte, Italy 31 D9
Aspur, India 68 H6
Asquith, Canada 105 C7
Assâba, Massif de l',
  Mauritania 82 B2
Assaikio, Nigeria 83 D6
Assal, L., Djibouti 81 E5
Assam □, India 67 G18
Assamakka, Niger 83 B6
Asse, Belgium 17 D4
Assémini, Italy 30 C1
Assen, Neths. 17 A6
Assens, Denmark 11 J3
Assini, Ivory C. 82 D4
Assiniboia, Canada 105 D7
Assiniboine →, Canada .. 105 D9
Assiniboine, Mt., Canada .. 104 C5
Assis, Brazil 127 A5
Assisi, Italy 29 E9
Ássos, Greece 38 C2
Assynt, L., U.K. 14 C3
Astaffort, France 20 D4
Astakidha, Greece 39 F8
Astakós, Greece 38 C3
Astana, Kazakstan 50 D8
Āstāneh, Iran 71 B6
Astara, Azerbaijan 71 B6
Āstārā, Iran 73 C13
Asterousía, Greece 36 E7
Asti, Italy 28 D5
Astipálaia, Greece 39 E8
Astorga, Spain 34 C4
Astoria, U.S.A. 116 D3
Åstorp, Sweden 11 H6
Astrakhan, Russia 49 G9
Astudillo, Spain 34 C6
Asturias □, Spain 34 B5
Asunción, Paraguay 126 B4
Asunción Nochixtlán, Mexico 119 D5
Åsunden, Sweden 11 F9
Asutri, Sudan 81 D4
Aswa →, Uganda 86 B3
Aswad, Ra's al, Si. Arabia . 80 C4
Aswân, Egypt 80 C3
Aswân High Dam = Sadd el
  Aali, Egypt 80 C3
Asyût, Egypt 80 B3
Asyûti, Wadi →, Egypt .. 80 B3
Aszód, Hungary 42 C4
Aţ Ţafīlah, Jordan 75 E4
Aţ Ţā'if, Si. Arabia 74 C3
Aţ Ţirāq, Si. Arabia ... 70 E5
Aţ Tubayq, Si. Arabia .. 70 D3
Atabey, Turkey 39 D12
Atacama □, Chile 126 B2
Atacama, Desierto de, Chile 126 A2
Atacama, Salar de, Chile .. 126 A2
Atakpamé, Togo 83 D5
Atalándi, Greece 38 C4
Atalaya, Peru 124 F4
Atalaya de Femes,
  Canary Is. 37 F6
Atami, Japan 55 G9
Atapupu, Indonesia 63 F6
Atâr, Mauritania 78 D3
Atarfe, Spain 35 H7
Atari, Pakistan 68 D6
Atascadero, U.S.A. 116 K6
Atasu, Kazakstan 50 E8
Atatürk Baraji, Turkey .. 73 D8
Atauro, Indonesia 63 F7
Atbara, Sudan 80 D3
'Atbara, →, Sudan 80 D3
Atbasar, Kazakstan 50 D7
Atça, Turkey 39 D10
Atchafalaya B., U.S.A. .. 113 L9
Atchison, U.S.A. 112 F7
Atebubu, Ghana 83 D4
Ateca, Spain 32 D3
Aterno →, Italy 29 F10
Åteshān, Iran 71 C7
Atesine, Alpi, Italy 28 B4
Atessa, Italy 29 F11
Atfih, Egypt 80 J7
Ath, Belgium 17 D3
Athabasca, Canada 104 C6
Athabasca →, Canada .. 105 B6
Athabasca, L., Canada .. 105 B7
Athboy, Ireland 15 C5
Athenry, Ireland 15 C3

Athens = Athínai, Greece . 38 D5
Athens, Ala., U.S.A. 109 H2
Athens, Ga., U.S.A. 109 J4
Athens, N.Y., U.S.A. 111 D11
Athens, Ohio, U.S.A. 108 F4
Athens, Pa., U.S.A. 111 E8
Athens, Tenn., U.S.A. ... 109 H3
Athens, Tex., U.S.A. 113 J7
Atherley, Canada 110 B5
Atherton, Australia 94 B4
Athiéme, Benin 83 D5
Athienou, Cyprus 36 D12
Athlone, Ireland 15 C4
Athna, Cyprus 36 D12
Athol, U.S.A. 111 D12
Atholl, Forest of, U.K. .. 14 E5
Atholville, Canada 103 C6
Áthos, Greece 41 F8
Athy, Ireland 15 C5
Ati, Chad 79 F9
Ati, Sudan 81 E2
Atiak, Uganda 86 B3
Atikameg →, Canada ... 102 B3
Atikokan, Canada 102 C1
Atikonak L., Canada ... 103 B7
Atimonan, Phil. 61 E4
Atka, Russia 51 C16
Atka I., U.S.A. 100 C2
Atkarsk, Russia 48 E7
Atkinson, U.S.A. 112 D5
Atlanta, Ga., U.S.A. ... 109 J3
Atlanta, Tex., U.S.A. .. 113 J7
Atlantic, U.S.A. 112 E7
Atlantic City, U.S.A. .. 108 F8
Atlantic Ocean 2 E9
Atlas Mts. = Haut Atlas,
  Morocco 78 B4
Atlin, Canada 104 B2
Atlin, L., Canada 104 B2
Atlin Prov. Park, Canada . 104 B2
Atmore, U.S.A. 109 K2
Atoka, U.S.A. 113 H6
Atokos, Greece 38 C2
Atolia, U.S.A. 117 K9
Atrai →, Bangla. 69 G13
Atrak = Atrek →,
  Turkmenistan 71 B8
Ātran, Sweden 11 G6
Åtran →, Sweden 11 H6
Atrauli, India 68 E8
Atrek →, Turkmenistan ... 71 B8
Atri, Italy 29 F10
Atsiki, Greece 39 B7
Atsoum, Mts., Cameroon . 83 D7
Atsuta, Japan 54 C10
Attalla, U.S.A. 109 H2
Attapu, Laos 64 E6
Attáviros, Greece 36 C9
Attawapiskat, Canada .. 102 B3
Attawapiskat →, Canada . 102 B3
Attawapiskat L., Canada . 102 B2
Attersee, Austria 26 D6
Attica, Ind., U.S.A. ... 108 E2
Attica, Ohio, U.S.A. .. 110 E2
Attichy, France 19 C10
Attigny, France 19 C11
Attikamagen L., Canada . 103 B6
Attikí □, Greece 38 D5
Attleboro, U.S.A. 111 E13
Attock, Pakistan 68 C5
Attopeu = Attapu, Laos . 64 E6
Attu I., U.S.A. 100 C1
Attur, India 66 P11
Atuel →, Argentina ... 126 D2
Atwater, U.S.A. 116 H6
Atwood, Canada 110 C3
Atwood, U.S.A. 112 F4
Atyraū, Kazakstan 50 E6
Au Sable →, U.S.A. ... 110 B1
Au Sable →, U.S.A. ... 108 C4
Au Sable Forks, U.S.A. . 111 B11
Au Sable Pt., U.S.A. .. 110 B1
Aubagne, France 21 E9
Aubarca, C. d', Spain .. 37 B7
Aube □, France 19 D11
Aube →, France 19 D10
Aubenas, France 21 D8
Aubenton, France 19 C11
Auberry, U.S.A. 116 H7
Aubigny-sur-Nère, France 19 E9
Aubin, France 20 D6
Aubrac, Mts. d', France . 20 D7
Auburn, Ala., U.S.A. .. 109 J3
Auburn, Calif., U.S.A. . 116 G5
Auburn, Ind., U.S.A. .. 108 E3
Auburn, Maine, U.S.A. . 109 C10
Auburn, N.Y., U.S.A. .. 111 D8
Auburn, Nebr., U.S.A. . 112 E7
Auburn, Pa., U.S.A. ... 111 F8
Auburn, Wash., U.S.A. . 116 C4
Auburn Ra., Australia . 95 D5
Aubusson, France 20 C6
Auce, Latvia 44 B9
Auch, France 20 E4
Auchi, Nigeria 83 D6
Auckland, N.Z. 91 G5
Auckland Is., Pac. Oc. . 96 N8
Aude □, France 20 E6
Aude →, France 20 E7
Auderville, France ... 18 C5
Audierne, France 18 D2
Audincourt, France .. 19 E13
Audo, Ethiopia 81 F5
Audubon, U.S.A. 112 E7
Aue, Germany 24 E8

Auerbach, Germany 24 E8
Augathella, Australia 95 D4
Aughnacloy, U.K. 15 B5
Augrabies Falls, S. Africa . 88 D3
Augsburg, Germany 25 G6
Augusta, Australia 93 F2
Augusta, Italy 31 E8
Augusta, Ark., U.S.A. .. 113 H9
Augusta, Ga., U.S.A. .. 109 J5
Augusta, Maine, U.S.A. . 101 D13
Augusta, Kans., U.S.A. . 113 G6
Augusta, Mont., U.S.A. . 114 C7
Augustenborg, Denmark . 11 K3
Augustów, Poland 44 E9
Augustus, Mt., Australia . 93 D2
Augustus I., Australia .. 92 C3
Aukan, Eritrea 81 D5
Aukum, U.S.A. 116 G6
Auld, L., Australia 92 D3
Aulla, Italy 28 D6
Aulnay, France 20 B3
Aulne →, France 18 D2
Aulnoye-Aymeries, France 19 B10
Ault, France 18 B8
Ault, U.S.A. 112 E2
Aulus-les-Bains, France . 20 F5
Aumale, France 19 C8
Aumont-Aubrac, France . 20 D7
Auna, Nigeria 83 C5
Auning, Denmark 11 H4
Aunis, France 20 B3
Auponhia, Indonesia .. 63 E7
Aups, France 21 E10
Aur, Pulau, Malaysia .. 65 L5
Auraiya, India 69 F8
Aurangabad, Bihar, India . 69 G11
Aurangabad, Maharashtra,
  India 66 K9
Auray, France 18 E4
Aurich, Germany 24 B3
Auronzo di Cadore, Italy . 29 B9
Aurora, Canada 110 C5
Aurora, S. Africa 88 E2
Aurora, Colo., U.S.A. . 112 F2
Aurora, Ill., U.S.A. ... 108 E1
Aurora, Mo., U.S.A. .. 113 G8
Aurora, N.Y., U.S.A. . 111 D8
Aurora, Nebr., U.S.A. . 112 E6
Aurora, Ohio, U.S.A. . 110 E3
Aurukun, Australia ... 94 A3
Aus, Namibia 88 D2
Ausable →, Canada ... 110 C3
Auschwitz = Oświęcim,
  Poland 45 H6
Austerlitz = Slavkov u Brna,
  Czech Rep. 27 B9
Austin, Minn., U.S.A. . 112 D8
Austin, Nev., U.S.A. .. 114 G5
Austin, Pa., U.S.A. ... 110 E6
Austin, Tex., U.S.A. .. 113 K6
Austin, L., Australia .. 93 E2
Austin I., Canada 105 A10
Austra, Norway 8 D14
Austral Is. = Tubuai Is.,
  Pac. Oc. 97 K13
Austral Seamount Chain,
  Pac. Oc. 97 K13
Australia ■, Oceania .. 96 K5
Australian Capital
  Territory □, Australia . 95 F4
Australind, Australia .. 93 F2
Austria ■, Europe 26 E7
Austvågøy, Norway ... 8 B16
Auterive, France 20 E5
Authie →, France 19 B8
Authon-du-Perche, France . 18 D7
Autlán, Mexico 118 D4
Autun, France 19 F11
Auvergne, France 20 C7
Auvergne, Mts. d', France . 20 C6
Auvézère →, France .. 20 C4
Auxerre, France 19 E10
Auxi-le-Château, France . 19 B9
Auxonne, France 19 E12
Auzances, France 19 F9
Ava, U.S.A. 113 G8
Avallon, France 19 E10
Avalon, U.S.A. 117 M8
Avalon Pen., Canada . 103 C9
Avanos, Turkey 70 B2
Avaré, Brazil 127 A6
Avawatz Mts., U.S.A. . 117 K10
Avdan Dağı, Turkey .. 41 F13
Aveiro, Brazil 125 D7
Aveiro, Portugal 34 E2
Aveiro □, Portugal .. 34 E2
Āvej, Iran 71 C6
Avellaneda, Argentina . 126 C4
Avellino, Italy 31 B7
Avenal, U.S.A. 116 K6
Aversa, Italy 31 B7
Avery, U.S.A. 114 C6
Aves, Is. las, Venezuela . 121 D6
Avesnes-sur-Helpe, France . 19 B10
Avesta, Sweden 10 D10
Aveyron □, France .. 20 D5
Aveyron →, France . 20 D5
Avezzano, Italy 29 F10
Avgó, Greece 39 F7
Aviá Terai, Argentina . 126 B3
Aviano, Italy 29 B9
Aviemore, U.K. 14 D5
Avigliana, Italy 28 C4
Avigliano, Italy 31 B8
Avignon, France ... 21 E8
Ávila, Spain 34 E6
Ávila □, Spain 34 E6
Ávila, Sierra de, Spain . 34 E5
Avila Beach, U.S.A. . 117 K6

Avilés, Spain 34 B5
Avintes, Portugal 34 D2
Avionárion, Greece 38 C6
Avis, Portugal 35 F3
Avis, U.S.A. 110 E7
Avísio →, Italy 28 B8
Aviz = Avis, Portugal ... 35 F3
Avize, France 19 D11
Avlum, Denmark 11 H2
Avoca, Ireland 110 D7
Avoca →, Australia 95 F3
Avoca →, Ireland 15 D5
Avola, Canada 104 C5
Avola, Italy 31 F8
Avon, U.S.A. 110 D7
Avon →, Australia 93 F2
Avon →, Bristol, U.K. .. 13 F5
Avon →, Dorset, U.K. .. 13 G6
Avon →, Warks., U.K. . 13 E6
Avon Park, U.S.A. 109 M5
Avondale, Zimbabwe ... 87 F3
Avonlea, Canada 105 D8
Avonmore, Canada 111 A10
Avramov, Bulgaria 41 D10
Avranches, France 18 D5
Avre →, France 18 D8
Avrig, Romania 43 E9
Avrillé, France 18 E6
Avtovac, Bos.-H. 40 C2
Awag el Baqar, Sudan .. 81 E3
A'waj →, Syria 75 B5
'Awālī, Bahrain 71 E6
Awantipur, India 69 C6
Awasa, Ethiopia 81 F4
Awasa, L., Ethiopia .. 81 F4
Awash, Ethiopia 81 F5
Awash →, Ethiopia .. 81 E5
Awaso, Ghana 82 D4
Awatere →, N.Z. 91 J5
Awbārī, Libya 79 C8
Awe, L., U.K. 14 E3
Aweil, Sudan 81 F2
Awgu, Nigeria 83 D6
Awjilah, Libya 79 C10
Awka, Nigeria 83 D6
Ax-les-Thermes, France . 20 F5
Axat, France 20 F6
Axe →, U.K. 13 F5
Axel Heiberg I., Canada . 4 B3
Axim, Ghana 82 E4
Axintele, Romania .. 43 F11
Axiós →, Greece ... 40 F6
Axminster, U.K. ... 13 G4
Axvall, Sweden 11 F7
Ay, France 19 C11
Ayabaca, Peru 124 D3
Ayabe, Japan 55 G7
Ayacucho, Argentina . 126 D4
Ayacucho, Peru 124 F4
Ayamé, Ivory C. ... 82 D4
Ayamonte, Spain .. 35 H3
Ayan, Russia 51 D14
Ayancık, Turkey ... 72 B6
Ayaviri, Peru 124 F4
Ayas, Turkey 72 B5
Aydın, Turkey 39 D9
Aydın □, Turkey .. 39 D10
Aydın Dağları, Turkey . 39 D10
Ayelu, Ethiopia .. 81 E5
Ayenngré, Togo .. 83 D5
Ayer, U.S.A. 111 D13
Ayerbe, Spain 32 C4
Ayer's Cliff, Canada . 111 A12
Ayers Rock, Australia . 93 E5
Ayía, Greece 38 B4
Ayia Aikateríni, Ákra,
  Greece 36 A3
Ayía Ánna, Greece .. 38 C5
Ayía Dhéka, Greece .. 36 D6
Ayía Gálini, Greece .. 36 D6
Ayía Marína, Kásos, Greece 39 F8
Ayía Marína, Léros, Greece 39 D8
Ayia Napa, Cyprus ... 36 E13
Ayía Paraskeví, Greece . 39 B8
Ayía Phyla, Cyprus .. 36 E12
Ayía Rouméli, Greece . 38 F5
Ayía Varvára, Greece . 36 D7
Ayíássos, Greece 39 B8
Ayíoi Theódhoroi, Greece . 38 D5
Ayíon Óros □, Greece . 41 F8
Áyios Amvrósios, Cyprus . 36 D12
Áyios Andréas, Greece . 38 D4
Áyios Evstrátios, Greece . 38 B6
Áyios Ioánnis, Ákra, Greece 36 D7
Áyios Isídhoros, Greece . 36 C9
Áyios Kiríkos, Greece . 39 D8
Áyios Matthaíos, Greece . 36 B3
Áyios Mírono, Greece . 39 F7
Áyios Nikólaos, Greece . 36 D7
Áyios Pétros, Greece .. 38 C2
Áyios Seryios, Cyprus . 36 D12
Áyios Theodhoros, Cyprus . 36 D13
Áyios Yeóryios, Greece . 38 D5
Aykathonisi, Greece .. 39 D8
Aykirikçi, Turkey 39 B12
Aylesbury, U.K. 13 F7
Aylmer, Canada 110 D4
Aylmer, L., Canada .. 100 B8
'Ayn, Wādī al, Oman . 71 F7
Ayn Dār, Si. Arabia . 71 E7
Ayn Zālah, Iraq 70 B4
Ayna, Spain 33 G2
Ayod, Sudan 81 F3
Ayolas, Paraguay ... 126 B4
Ayom, Sudan 81 F2
Ayon, Ostrov, Russia . 51 C17
Ayora, Spain 33 G3
Ayorou, Niger 83 C5

'Ayoûn el 'Atroûs,
  Mauritania 82 B3
Ayr, Australia 94 B4
Ayr, Canada 110 C4
Ayr, U.K. 14 F4
Ayr →, U.K. 14 F4
Ayrancı, Turkey 72 D5
Ayrancılar, Turkey 39 C9
Ayre, Pt. of, U.K. 12 C3
Aysha, Ethiopia 81 E5
Ayton, Australia 94 B4
Aytos, Bulgaria 41 D11
Aytoska Planina, Bulgaria . 41 D11
Ayu, Kepulauan, Indonesia 63 D8
Ayutla, Guatemala 120 D1
Ayutla, Mexico 119 D5
Ayvacık, Turkey 72 C2
Ayvalık, Turkey 39 B8
Az Zabadānī, Syria .. 75 B5
Az Ẓāhirīyah, West Bank . 75 D3
Az Ẓahrān, Si. Arabia . 71 E6
Az Zarqā, Jordan 75 C5
Az Zarqā', U.A.E. ... 71 E7
Az Zāwiyah, Libya ... 79 B8
Az Zibār, Iraq 70 B5
Az Zilfī, Si. Arabia .. 70 E5
Az Zubayr, Iraq 70 D5
Az Zuqur, Yemen ... 81 E5
Azambuja, Portugal .. 35 F2
Azamgarh, India 69 F10
Azangaro, Peru 124 F4
Azaouad, Mali 82 B4
Azaouak, Vallée de l', Mali 83 B5
Āzar Shahr, Iran 70 B5
Azara, Nigeria 83 D6
Azarān, Iran 70 B5
Azärbayjan = Azerbaijan ■,
  Asia 49 K9
Āzarbāyjān-e Gharbī □, Iran 70 B5
Āzarbāyjān-e Sharqī □, Iran 70 B5
Azare, Nigeria 83 C7
Azay-le-Rideau, France . 18 E7
A'zāz, Syria 70 B3
Azbine = Aïr, Niger .. 83 B6
Azerbaijan ■, Asia ... 49 K9
Azerbaijchan =
  Azerbaijan ■, Asia .. 49 K9
Azezo, Ethiopia 81 E4
Azimganj, India 69 G13
Aznalcóllar, Spain ... 35 H4
Azogues, Ecuador ... 124 D3
Azores, Atl. Oc. 78 A1
Azov, Russia 47 J10
Azov, Sea of, Europe . 47 J9
Azovskoye More = Azov,
  Sea of, Europe 47 J9
Azpeitia, Spain 32 B2
Azraq ash Shīshān, Jordan 75 D5
Aztec, U.S.A. 115 H10
Azúa de Compostela,
  Dom. Rep. 121 C5
Azuaga, Spain 35 G5
Azuara, Spain 32 D4
Azuer →, Spain 35 F7
Azuero, Pen. de, Panama . 120 E3
Azuga, Romania 43 E10
Azul, Argentina 126 D4
Azusa, U.S.A. 117 L9
Azzano Décimo, Italy . 29 C9

B

Ba Don, Vietnam 64 D6
Ba Dong, Vietnam 65 H6
Ba Ngoi = Cam Lam,
  Vietnam 65 G7
Ba Tri, Vietnam 65 G6
Ba Xian = Bazhou, China . 56 E9
Baa, Indonesia 63 F6
Baamonde, Spain 34 B3
Baarle-Nassau, Belgium . 17 C4
Bab el Mandeb, Red Sea . 74 E3
Baba, Bulgaria 40 D7
Baba Burnu, Turkey 39 B8
Baba dag, Azerbaijan ... 49 K9
Bābā Kalū, Iran 71 D6
Babadag, Romania 43 F13
Babadağ, Turkey 39 D10
Babadayhan, Turkmenistan 50 F7
Babaeski, Turkey 41 E11
Babahoyo, Ecuador 124 D3
Babai = Sarju →, India . 69 F9
Babana, Nigeria 83 C5
Babanusa, Sudan 81 E2
Babar, Indonesia 63 F7
Babar, Pakistan 68 D3
Babarkach, Pakistan .. 68 E3
Babayevo, Russia 46 C8
Babb, U.S.A. 114 B7
Babelthuap, Pac. Oc. . 63 C8
Babenhausen, Germany . 25 F4
Bābeni, Romania 43 F9
Baberu, India 69 G9
Babi Besar, Pulau, Malaysia 65 L4
Babia Gora, Europe .. 45 J6
Babian Jiang →, China . 58 F3
Babile, Ethiopia 81 F5
Babimost, Poland ... 45 F2
Babinda, Australia .. 94 B4
Babine, Canada 104 B3
Babine →, Canada .. 104 B3
Babine L., Canada .. 104 C3
Babo, Indonesia ... 63 E8
Babócsa, Hungary .. 42 D2
Bābol, Iran 71 B7
Bābol Sar, Iran 71 B7
Baborów, Poland ... 45 H5

Babruysk, *Belarus* 47 F5
Babuhri, *India* 68 F3
Babuna, *Macedonia* 40 E5
Babura, *Nigeria* 83 C6
Babusar Pass, *Pakistan* ... 69 B5
Babušnica, *Serbia, Yug.* ... 40 C6
Babuyan Chan., *Phil.* 61 B4
Babylon, *Iraq* 70 C5
Bač, *Serbia, Yug.* 42 E4
Bâc →, *Moldova* 43 D14
Bac Can, *Vietnam* 58 F5
Bac Giang, *Vietnam* 58 G6
Bac Lieu, *Vietnam* 65 H5
Bac Ninh, *Vietnam* 58 G6
Bac Phan, *Vietnam* 64 B5
Bac Quang, *Vietnam* 58 F5
Bacabal, *Brazil* 125 D10
Bacalar, *Mexico* 119 D7
Bacan, Kepulauan, *Indonesia* 63 C5
Bacarra, *Phil.* 61 B4
Bacău, *Romania* 43 D11
Bacău □, *Romania* 43 D11
Baccarat, *France* 19 D13
Bacerac, *Mexico* 118 A3
Băcești, *Romania* 43 D12
Bach Long Vi, Dao, *Vietnam* 64 B6
Bacharach, *Germany* 25 E3
Bachelina, *Russia* 50 D7
Bachhwara, *India* 69 G11
Bachuma, *Ethiopia* 81 F4
Bačina, *Serbia, Yug.* 40 C5
Back →, *Canada* 100 B9
Bačka Palanka, *Serbia, Yug.* 42 E4
Bačka Topola, *Serbia, Yug.* 42 E4
Bäckebo, *Sweden* 11 H10
Bäckefors, *Sweden* 11 F6
Bäckhammar, *Sweden* ... 10 E8
Bački Petrovac, *Serbia, Yug.* 42 E4
Backnang, *Germany* 25 G5
Baco, Mt., *Phil.* 61 E4
Bacolod, *Phil.* 61 F5
Bacqueville-en-Caux, *France* 18 C8
Bács-Kiskun □, *Hungary* . 42 D4
Bácsalmás, *Hungary* 42 D4
Bacuag = Placer, *Phil.* ... 61 G6
Bacuk, *Malaysia* 65 J4
Bād, *Iran* 71 C7
Bad →, *U.S.A.* 112 C4
Bad Aussee, *Austria* 26 D6
Bad Axe, *U.S.A.* 110 C2
Bad Bergzabern, *Germany* 25 F3
Bad Berleburg, *Germany* . 24 D4
Bad Bevensen, *Germany* . 24 B6
Bad Bramstedt, *Germany* 24 B5
Bad Brückenau, *Germany* . 25 E5
Bad Doberan, *Germany* ... 24 A7
Bad Driburg, *Germany* ... 24 D5
Bad Ems, *Germany* 25 E3
Bad Frankenhausen,
  Germany 24 D7
Bad Freienwalde, *Germany* 24 C10
Bad Goisern, *Austria* 26 D6
Bad Harzburg, *Germany* .. 24 D6
Bad Hersfeld, *Germany* ... 24 E5
Bad Hofgastein, *Austria* .. 26 D6
Bad Homburg, *Germany* . 25 E4
Bad Honnef, *Germany* ... 24 E3
Bad Iburg, *Germany* 24 C4
Bad Ischl, *Austria* 26 D6
Bad Kissingen, *Germany* . 25 E6
Bad Königshofen, *Germany* 25 E6
Bad Kreuznach, *Germany* . 25 F3
Bad Krozingen, *Germany* . 25 H3
Bad Laasphe, *Germany* ... 24 E4
Bad Lands, *U.S.A.* 112 D3
Bad Langensalza, *Germany* 24 D6
Bad Lauterberg, *Germany* 24 D6
Bad Leonfelden, *Austria* .. 26 C7
Bad Liebenwerda, *Germany* 24 D9
Bad Mergentheim, *Germany* 25 F5
Bad Münstereifel, *Germany* 24 E2
Bad Nauheim, *Germany* .. 25 E4
Bad Neuenahr-Ahrweiler,
  Germany 24 E3
Bad Neustadt, *Germany* .. 25 E6
Bad Oeynhausen, *Germany* 24 C4
Bad Oldesloe, *Germany* .. 24 B6
Bad Orb, *Germany* 25 E5
Bad Pyrmont, *Germany* .. 24 D5
Bad Reichenhall, *Germany* 25 H8
Bad Säckingen, *Germany* . 25 H3
Bad Salzuflen, *Germany* .. 24 C4
Bad Salzungen, *Germany* . 24 E6
Bad Schwartau, *Germany* . 24 B6
Bad Segeberg, *Germany* .. 24 B6
Bad St. Leonhard, *Austria* . 26 E7
Bad Tölz, *Germany* 25 H7
Bad Urach, *Germany* 25 G5
Bad Vöslau, *Austria* 27 D9
Bad Waldsee, *Germany* ... 25 H5
Bad Wildungen, *Germany* . 24 D5
Bad Wimpfen, *Germany* .. 25 F5
Bad Windsheim, *Germany* 25 F6
Bad Zwischenahn, *Germany* 24 B4
Bada Barabil, *India* 69 H11
Badagara, *India* 66 P9
Badagri, *Nigeria* 83 D5
Badajós, L., *Brazil* 124 D6
Badajoz, *Spain* 35 G4
Badajoz □, *Spain* 35 G4
Badalona, *Spain* 32 D7
Badalzai, *Afghan.* 68 E1
Badampahar, *India* 67 H15
Badanah, *Si. Arabia* 70 D4
Badarinath, *India* 69 D8
Badas, Kepulauan, *Indonesia* 62 D3
Baddo →, *Pakistan* 66 F4
Bade, *Indonesia* 63 F9
Badeggi, *Nigeria* 83 D6
Badéguichéri, *Niger* 83 C6
Baden, *Austria* 27 C9

Baden, *Switz.* 25 H4
Baden, *U.S.A.* 110 F4
Baden-Baden, *Germany* .. 25 G4
Baden-Württemberg □,
  Germany 25 G4
Badgastein, *Austria* 26 D6
Badger, *Canada* 103 C8
Badger, *U.S.A.* 116 J7
Bādghīsāt □, *Afghan.* ... 66 B3
Badgom, *India* 69 B6
Badia Polésine, *Italy* 29 C8
Badin, *Pakistan* 68 G3
Badlands National Park,
  U.S.A. 112 D3
Badogo, *Mali* 82 C3
Badoumbé, *Mali* 82 C2
Badrah, *Iraq* 70 C5
Badrinath, *India* 69 D8
Badulla, *Sri Lanka* 66 R12
Baena, *Spain* 35 H6
Baeza, *Spain* 35 H7
Bafang, *Cameroon* 83 D7
Bafatá, *Guinea-Biss.* 82 C2
Baffin B., *Canada* 4 B4
Baffin I., *Canada* 101 B12
Bafia, *Cameroon* 83 E7
Bafilo, *Togo* 83 D5
Bafing →, *Mali* 82 C2
Bafliyūn, *Syria* 70 B3
Bafoulabé, *Mali* 82 C2
Bafoussam, *Cameroon* .. 83 D7
Bāfq, *Iran* 71 D7
Bafra, *Turkey* 72 B6
Bafra Burnu, *Turkey* 72 B7
Bāft, *Iran* 71 D8
Bafut, *Cameroon* 83 D7
Bafwasende,
  Dem. Rep. of the Congo 86 B2
Bagam, *Niger* 83 B6
Bagamoyo, *Tanzania* 86 D4
Bagan Datoh, *Malaysia* .. 65 L3
Bagan Serai, *Malaysia* ... 65 K3
Baganga, *Phil.* 61 H7
Bagani, *Namibia* 88 B3
Bagansiapiapi, *Indonesia* 62 D2
Bagasra, *India* 68 J4
Bagaud, *India* 68 H6
Bagawi, *Sudan* 81 E3
Bagbag, *Sudan* 81 D3
Bagdad, *U.S.A.* 117 L11
Bagdarin, *Russia* 51 D12
Bagé, *Brazil* 127 C5
Bagenalstown = Muine
  Bheag, *Ireland* 15 D5
Baggs, *U.S.A.* 114 F10
Bagh, *Pakistan* 69 C5
Baghain →, *India* 69 G9
Baghdād, *Iraq* 70 C5
Bagheria, *Italy* 30 D6
Baghlān, *Afghan.* 66 A6
Bagley, *U.S.A.* 112 B7
Bagnara Cálabra, *Italy* ... 31 D8
Bagnasco, *Italy* 28 D5
Bagnères-de-Bigorre, *France* 20 E4
Bagnères-de-Luchon, *France* 20 F4
Bagni di Lucca, *Italy* 28 D7
Bagno di Romagna, *Italy* . 29 E8
Bagnols-de-l'Orne, *France* 18 D6
Bagnols-sur-Cèze, *France* . 21 D8
Bagnorégio, *Italy* 29 F9
Bago = Pegu, *Burma* ... 67 L20
Bagodar, *India* 69 G11
Bagrationovsk, *Russia* ... 9 J19
Bagrdan, *Serbia, Yug.* ... 40 B5
Baguio, *Phil.* 61 C4
Bağyurdu, *Turkey* 39 C9
Bagzane, Monts, *Niger* .. 83 B6
Bah, *India* 69 F8
Bahabón de Esgueva, *Spain* 34 D7
Bahadurganj, *India* 69 F12
Bahadurgarh, *India* 68 E7
Bahama, Canal Viejo de,
  W. Indies 120 B4
Bahamas ■, *N. Amer.* ... 121 B5
Bahār, *Iran* 73 E13
Baharampur, *India* 69 G13
Baharîya, El Wâhât al, *Egypt* 80 B2
Bahawalnagar, *Pakistan* . 68 E5
Bahawalpur, *Pakistan* ... 68 E4
Bahçe, *Turkey* 72 D7
Bahçecik, *Turkey* 41 F13
Baheri, *India* 69 E8
Bahgul →, *India* 69 F8
Bahi, *Tanzania* 86 D4
Bahi Swamp, *Tanzania* .. 86 D4
Bahía = Salvador, *Brazil* . 125 F11
Bahía □, *Brazil* 125 F10
Bahía, Is. de la, *Honduras* 120 C2
Bahía Blanca, *Argentina* . 126 D3
Bahía de Caráquez, *Ecuador* 124 D2
Bahía Honda, *Cuba* 120 B3
Bahía Laura, *Argentina* .. 128 F3
Bahía Negra, *Paraguay* .. 124 H7
Bahir Dar, *Ethiopia* 81 E4
Bahmanzād, *Iran* 71 D6
Bahr el Ahmar □, *Sudan* . 80 D4
Bahr el Ghazâl □, *Sudan* . 81 F2
Bahr el Jabal □, *Sudan* .. 81 G3
Bahr Yûsef →, *Egypt* ... 80 B3
Bahraich, *India* 69 F9
Bahrain ■, *Asia* 71 E6
Bahror, *India* 68 F7
Bahū Kalāt, *Iran* 71 E9
Bai, *Mali* 82 C4
Bai Bung, Mui = Ca Mau,
  Mui, *Vietnam* 65 H5
Bai Duc, *Vietnam* 64 C5
Bai Thuong, *Vietnam* ... 64 C5
Baia de Aramă, *Romania* . 42 E7
Baia Mare, *Romania* 43 C8
Baia-Sprie, *Romania* 43 C8

Baião, *Brazil* 125 D9
Baïbokoum, *Chad* 79 G9
Baicheng, *China* 57 B12
Băicoi, *Romania* 43 E10
Baidoa, *Somali Rep.* 74 G3
Baie Comeau, *Canada* .. 103 C6
Baie-St-Paul, *Canada* ... 103 C5
Baie Trinité, *Canada* 103 C6
Baie Verte, *Canada* 103 C8
Baignes-Ste-Radegonde,
  France 20 C3
Baigneux-les-Juifs, *France* . 19 E11
Baihar, *India* 69 H9
Baihe, *China* 56 H6
Ba'ījī, *Iraq* 70 C4
Baijnath, *India* 69 E8
Baikal, L. = Baykal, Oz.,
  Russia 51 D11
Baikunthpur, *India* 69 H10
Baile Atha Cliath = Dublin,
  Ireland 15 C5
Băile Govora, *Romania* .. 43 E9
Băile Herculane, *Romania* 42 F7
Băile Olănești, *Romania* . 43 E9
Băile Tușnad, *Romania* .. 43 D10
Bailén, *Spain* 35 G7
Băilești, *Romania* 43 F8
Baima, *China* 58 A3
Bain-de-Bretagne, *France* . 18 E5
Bainbridge, Ga., *U.S.A.* . 109 K3
Bainbridge, N.Y., *U.S.A.* 111 D9
Baing, *Indonesia* 63 F6
Bainiu, *China* 56 H7
Baiona, *Spain* 34 C2
Ba'ir, *Jordan* 75 E5
Bairin Youqi, *China* 57 C10
Bairin Zuoqi, *China* 57 C10
Bairnsdale, *Australia* ... 95 F4
Bais, *Phil.* 61 G5
Baisha, *China* 56 G7
Baissa, *Nigeria* 83 D7
Baitadi, *Nepal* 69 E9
Baiyin, *China* 56 F3
Baiyu, *China* 58 B2
Baiyu Shan, *China* 56 F4
Baiyuda, *Sudan* 80 D3
Baj Baj, *India* 69 H13
Baja, *Hungary* 42 D3
Baja, Pta., *Mexico* 118 B1
Baja California, *Mexico* . 118 A1
Baja California □, *Mexico* 118 B2
Baja California Sur □,
  Mexico 118 B2
Bajag, *India* 69 H9
Bajamar, *Canary Is.* 37 F3
Bajana, *India* 68 H4
Bājgīrān, *Iran* 71 B8
Bajimba, Mt., *Australia* . 95 D5
Bajina Bašta, *Serbia, Yug.* 40 C3
Bajmok, *Serbia, Yug.* ... 42 E4
Bajo Nuevo, *Caribbean* . 120 C4
Bajoga, *Nigeria* 83 C7
Bajool, *Australia* 94 C5
Bak, *Hungary* 42 D1
Bakar, *Croatia* 29 C11
Bakel, *Senegal* 82 C2
Baker, Calif., *U.S.A.* ... 117 K10
Baker, Mont., *U.S.A.* ... 112 B2
Baker, L., *Canada* 100 B10
Baker City, *U.S.A.* 114 D5
Baker I., *Pac. Oc.* 96 G10
Baker I., *U.S.A.* 104 B2
Baker L., *Australia* 93 E4
Baker Lake, *Canada* 100 B10
Baker Mt., *U.S.A.* 114 B3
Bakers Creek, *Australia* . 94 C4
Baker's Dozen Is., *Canada* 102 A4
Bakersfield, Calif., *U.S.A.* 117 K8
Bakersfield, Vt., *U.S.A.* . 111 B12
Bakhchysaray, *Ukraine* .. 47 K7
Bakhmach, *Ukraine* 47 G7
Bākhtarān, *Iran* 70 C5
Bākhtarān □, *Iran* 70 C5
Bakı, *Azerbaijan* 49 K9
Bakır →, *Turkey* 39 C9
Bakırdaği, *Turkey* 72 C6
Bakkafjörður, *Iceland* ... 8 C6
Bakkan, *Turkey* 39 C11
Bako, *Ethiopia* 81 F4
Bako, *Ivory C.* 82 D3
Bakony, *Hungary* 42 C2
Bakony Forest = Bakony,
  Hungary 42 C2
Bakori, *Nigeria* 83 C6
Bakouma, *C.A.R.* 84 C4
Baksan, *Russia* 49 J6
Bakswaho, *India* 69 G8
Baku = Bakı, *Azerbaijan* 49 K9
Bakundi, *Nigeria* 83 D7
Bakutis Coast, *Antarctica* 5 D15
Baky = Bakı, *Azerbaijan* 49 K9
Bala, *Canada* 110 A5
Bala, *Senegal* 82 C2
Bâla, *Turkey* 72 C5
Bala, *U.K.* 12 E4
Bala, L., *U.K.* 12 E4
Balabac I., *Phil.* 62 C5
Balabac Str., *E. Indies* .. 62 C5
Balabagh, *Afghan.* 68 B4
Bala'lrbak, *Lebanon* 75 B5
Balabalangan, Kepulauan,
  Indonesia 62 E5
Bălăcița, *Romania* 43 F8
Balad, *Iraq* 70 C5
Balad Rūz, *Iraq* 70 C5
Bālādeh, Fārs, *Iran* 71 D6
Bālādeh, Māzandaran, *Iran* 71 B6
Balaghat, *India* 66 J12
Balaghat Ra., *India* 66 K10
Balaguer, *Spain* 32 D5
Balakhna, *Russia* 48 B6

Balaklava, *Ukraine* 47 K7
Balakliya, *Ukraine* 47 H9
Balakovo, *Russia* 48 D8
Bălan, *Romania* 43 D10
Balancán, *Mexico* 119 D6
Balashov, *Russia* 48 E6
Balasinor, *India* 68 H5
Balasore = Baleshwar, *India* 67 J15
Balassagyarmat, *Hungary* 42 B4
Balât, *Egypt* 80 B2
Balaton, *Hungary* 42 D2
Balatonboglár, *Hungary* . 42 D2
Balatonfüred, *Hungary* .. 42 D2
Balatonszentgyörgy, *Hungary* 42 D2
Balayan, *Phil.* 61 E4
Balazote, *Spain* 33 G2
Balbieriškis, *Lithuania* .. 44 D10
Balbigny, *France* 21 C8
Balbina, Reprêsa de, *Brazil* 124 D7
Balboa, *Panama* 120 E4
Balbriggan, *Ireland* 15 C5
Balcarce, *Argentina* 126 D4
Balcarres, *Canada* 105 C8
Bălcești, *Romania* 43 F8
Balchik, *Bulgaria* 41 C12
Balclutha, *N.Z.* 91 M2
Balcones Escarpment,
  U.S.A. 113 L5
Balça, *Turkey* 39 C9
Bald Hd., *Australia* 93 G2
Bald I., *Australia* 93 F2
Bald Knob, *U.S.A.* 113 H9
Baldock L., *Canada* 105 B9
Baldwin, Mich., *U.S.A.* . 108 D3
Baldwin, Pa., *U.S.A.* ... 110 F5
Baldwinsville, *U.S.A.* ... 111 C8
Baldy Mt., *U.S.A.* 114 B9
Baldy Peak, *U.S.A.* 115 K9
Bale, *Croatia* 29 C10
Bale, *Ethiopia* 81 F5
Bale □, *Ethiopia* 81 F5
Baleares, Is., *Spain* 37 B10
Balearic Is. = Baleares, Is.,
  Spain 37 B10
Baleine = Whale →,
  Canada 103 A6
Băleni, *Romania* 43 E12
Baler, *Phil.* 61 D4
Baler Bay, *Phil.* 61 D4
Baleshare, *U.K.* 14 D1
Baleshwar, *India* 67 J15
Balezino, *Russia* 48 B11
Balfate, *Honduras* 120 C2
Balfour, *S. Africa* 89 D4
Balfour, *U.K.* 14 B6
Balharshah, *India* 66 K11
Bali, *Cameroon* 83 D7
Balí, *Greece* 36 D6
Bali, *India* 68 G5
Bali □, *Indonesia* 62 F5
Bali, S. Leone 82 D2
Bali, Selat, *Indonesia* ... 63 H16
Balia, *S. Leone* 82 D2
Baliapal, *India* 69 J12
Baligród, *Poland* 45 J9
Balıkeşir, *Turkey* 39 B9
Balıkeşir □, *Turkey* 39 B9
Balıklıçeşme, *Turkey* 41 F11
Balikpapan, *Indonesia* .. 62 E5
Balimbing, *Phil.* 63 C5
Baling, *Malaysia* 65 K3
Balingen, *Germany* 25 G4
Balingoan, *Phil.* 61 G6
Balinț, *Romania* 42 E6
Balintang Channel, *Phil.* . 61 B4
Balipara, *India* 67 F18
Balkan Mts. = Stara Planina,
  Bulgaria 40 C7
Balkhash = Balqash,
  Kazakstan 50 E8
Balkhash, Ozero = Balqash
  Köl, *Kazakstan* 50 E8
Balla, *Bangla.* 67 G17
Ballachulish, *U.K.* 14 E3
Balladonia, *Australia* ... 93 F3
Ballaghaderreen, *Ireland* . 15 C3
Ballarat, *Australia* 95 F3
Ballard, L., *Australia* 93 E3
Ballater, *U.K.* 14 D5
Ballé, *Mali* 82 B3
Ballenas, Canal de, *Mexico* 118 B2
Balleny Is., *Antarctica* .. 5 C11
Balleroy, *France* 18 C6
Ballerup, *Denmark* 11 J6
Balh, *Turkey* 41 F11
Ballia, *India* 69 G11
Ballina, *Australia* 95 D5
Ballina, *Ireland* 15 B2
Ballinasloe, *Ireland* 15 C3
Ballinger, *U.S.A.* 113 K5
Ballinrobe, *Ireland* 15 C2
Ballinskelligs B., *Ireland* . 15 E1
Ballon, *France* 18 D7
Ballsh, *Albania* 40 F3
Ballston Spa, *U.S.A.* ... 111 D11
Ballycastle, *U.K.* 15 A5
Ballyclare, *U.K.* 15 B5
Ballyhaunis, *Ireland* 15 C3
Ballymena, *U.K.* 15 B5
Ballymoney, *U.K.* 15 A5
Ballymote, *Ireland* 15 B3
Ballynahinch, *U.K.* 15 B6
Ballyquintin Pt., *U.K.* ... 15 B6
Ballyshannon, *Ireland* ... 15 B3
Balmaceda, *Chile* 128 F2
Balmaseda, *Spain* 32 B1
Balmazújváros, *Hungary* . 42 C6
Balmertown, *Canada* ... 105 C10
Balmoral, *Australia* 95 F3
Balmorhea, *U.S.A.* 113 K3
Balonne →, *Australia* ... 95 D4
Balotra, *India* 68 G5
Balqash, *Kazakstan* 50 E8
Balqash Köl, *Kazakstan* . 50 E8
Balrampur, *India* 69 F10

Balranald, *Australia* 95 E3
Balș, *Romania* 43 F9
Balsas, *Mexico* 119 D5
Balsas →, *Brazil* 125 E9
Balsas →, *Mexico* 118 D4
Bålsta, *Sweden* 10 E11
Balston Spa, *U.S.A.* ... 111 D11
Balta, *Romania* 42 F7
Balta, *Ukraine* 47 H5
Baltanás, *Spain* 34 D6
Baltic Sea, *Europe* 9 H18
Baltîm, *Egypt* 80 H7
Baltimore, *Ireland* 15 E2
Baltimore, Md., *U.S.A.* . 108 F7
Baltimore, Ohio, *U.S.A.* 110 G2
Baltit, *Pakistan* 69 A6
Baltiysk, *Russia* 9 J18
Baltrum, *Germany* 24 B3
Baluchistan □, *Pakistan* . 66 C4
Balurghat, *India* 69 G13
Balvi, *Latvia* 9 H22
Balya, *Turkey* 39 B9
Bam, *Iran* 71 D8
Bama, *China* 58 E6
Bama, *Nigeria* 83 C7
Bamaga, *Australia* 94 A3
Bamaji L., *Canada* 102 B1
Bamako, *Mali* 82 C3
Bamba, *Mali* 83 B4
Bambara Maoundé, *Mali* . 82 B4
Bambari, *C.A.R.* 84 C4
Bambaroo, *Australia* 94 B4
Bambaya, *Guinea* 82 D2
Bamberg, *Germany* 25 F6
Bamberg, *U.S.A.* 109 J5
Bambesi, *Ethiopia* 81 F3
Bambey, *Senegal* 82 C1
Bambili,
  Dem. Rep. of the Congo 86 B2
Bamboi, *Ghana* 82 D4
Bamenda, *Cameroon* ... 83 D7
Bamfield, *Canada* 104 D3
Bāmīān □, *Afghan.* 66 B5
Bamiancheng, *China* ... 57 C13
Bamkin, *Cameroon* 83 D7
Bampūr, *Iran* 71 E9
Ban, *Burkina Faso* 82 C4
Ban Ban, *Laos* 64 C4
Ban Bang Hin, *Thailand* . 65 H2
Ban Chiang Klang, *Thailand* 64 C3
Ban Chik, *Laos* 64 D4
Ban Choho, *Thailand* ... 64 E4
Ban Dan Lan Hoi, *Thailand* 64 D2
Ban Don = Surat Thani,
  Thailand 65 H2
Ban Don, *Vietnam* 64 F6
Ban Don, Ao →, *Thailand* 65 H2
Ban Dong, *Thailand* 64 C3
Ban Hong, *Thailand* 64 C2
Ban Kaeng, *Thailand* ... 64 D3
Ban Kantang, *Thailand* .. 65 J2
Ban Keun, *Laos* 64 C4
Ban Khai, *Thailand* 64 F3
Ban Kheun, *Laos* 64 B3
Ban Khlong Kua, *Thailand* 65 J3
Ban Khuan Mao, *Thailand* 65 J2
Ban Ko Yai Chim, *Thailand* 65 G2
Ban Kok, *Thailand* 64 D4
Ban Laem, *Thailand* 64 F2
Ban Lao Ngam, *Laos* ... 64 E6
Ban Le Kathe, *Thailand* . 64 E2
Ban Mae Chedi, *Thailand* 64 C2
Ban Mae Laeng, *Thailand* 64 B2
Ban Mae Sariang, *Thailand* 64 C1
Ban Mê Thuôt = Buon Ma
  Thuot, *Vietnam* 64 F7
Ban Mi, *Thailand* 64 E3
Ban Muong Mo, *Laos* ... 64 C4
Ban Na Mo, *Laos* 64 D5
Ban Na San, *Thailand* ... 65 H2
Ban Na Tong, *Laos* 64 B3
Ban Nam Bac, *Laos* 64 B4
Ban Nam Ma, *Laos* 64 A3
Ban Ngang, *Laos* 64 E6
Ban Nong Bok, *Laos* 64 D5
Ban Nong Boua, *Laos* ... 64 E6
Ban Nong Pling, *Thailand* 64 E3
Ban Pak Chan, *Thailand* . 65 G2
Ban Phai, *Thailand* 64 D4
Ban Pong, *Thailand* 64 F2
Ban Ron Phibun, *Thailand* 65 H2
Ban Sanam Chai, *Thailand* 65 J3
Ban Sangkha, *Thailand* .. 64 E4
Ban Tak, *Thailand* 64 D2
Ban Tako, *Thailand* 64 E4
Ban Tha Dua, *Thailand* .. 64 D2
Ban Tha Li, *Thailand* ... 64 D3
Ban Tha Nun, *Thailand* . 65 H2
Ban Thahine, *Laos* 64 E5
Ban Xien Kok, *Laos* 64 B3
Ban Yen Nhan, *Vietnam* 64 B5
Banaba, *Kiribati* 96 H8
Banalia,
  Dem. Rep. of the Congo 86 B2
Banam, *Cambodia* 65 G5
Banamba, *Mali* 82 C3
Banana Is., *S. Leone* 82 D2
Bananal, I. do, *Brazil* ... 125 F8
Banaras = Varanasi, *India* 69 G10
Banas →, Gujarat, *India* 68 H4
Banas →, Mad. P., *India* 69 G9
Bânâs, Ras, *Egypt* 80 C4
Banaz, *Turkey* 39 C11
Banaz →, *Turkey* 39 C11
Banbân, Si. Arabia 70 E5
Banbridge, *U.K.* 15 B5
Banbury, *U.K.* 13 E6
Banchory, *U.K.* 14 D6
Banco, *Ethiopia* 81 F4

Bancroft, Canada 102 C4
Band, Romania 43 D9
Band Bonī, Iran 71 E8
Band Qīr, Iran 71 D6
Banda, Mad. P., India 69 G8
Banda, Ut. P., India 69 G9
Banda, Kepulauan, Indonesia 63 E7
Banda Aceh, Indonesia 62 C1
Banda Banda, Mt., Australia 95 E5
Banda Elat, Indonesia 63 F8
Banda Is. = Banda, Kepulauan, Indonesia 63 E7
Banda Sea, Indonesia 63 F7
Bandai-San, Japan 54 F10
Bandama →, Ivory C. 82 D3
Bandama Blanc →, Ivory C. 82 D3
Bandama Rouge →, Ivory C. 82 D4
Bandān, Iran 71 D9
Bandanaira, Indonesia 63 E7
Bandanwara, India 68 F6
Bandar = Machilipatnam, India 67 L12
Bandar 'Abbās, Iran 71 E8
Bandar-e Anzalī, Iran 71 B6
Bandar-e Bushehr = Būshehr, Iran 71 D6
Bandar-e Chārak, Iran 71 E7
Bandar-e Deylam, Iran 71 D6
Bandar-e Khomeynī, Iran 71 D6
Bandar-e Lengeh, Iran 71 E7
Bandar-e Maqām, Iran 71 E7
Bandar-e Ma'shur, Iran 71 D6
Bandar-e Nakhīlū, Iran 71 E7
Bandar-e Rīg, Iran 71 D6
Bandar-e Torkeman, Iran 71 B7
Bandar Maharani = Muar, Malaysia 65 L4
Bandar Penggaram = Batu Pahat, Malaysia 65 M4
Bandar Seri Begawan, Brunei 62 C4
Bandar Sri Aman, Malaysia 62 D4
Bandawe, Malawi 87 E3
Bande, Spain 34 C3
Bandeira, Pico da, Brazil 127 A7
Bandera, Argentina 126 B3
Banderas, B. de, Mexico 118 C3
Bandhogarh, India 69 H9
Bandi →, India 68 F6
Bandiagara, Mali 82 C4
Bandikui, India 68 F7
Bandırma, Turkey 41 F11
Bandol, France 21 E9
Bandon, Ireland 15 E3
Bandon →, Ireland 15 E3
Bandula, Mozam. 87 F3
Bandundu, Dem. Rep. of the Congo 84 E3
Bandung, Indonesia 63 G12
Bané, Burkina Faso 83 C4
Băneasa, Romania 43 E12
Bāneh, Iran 70 C5
Bañeres, Spain 33 G4
Banes, Cuba 121 B4
Banff, Canada 104 C5
Banff, U.K. 14 D6
Banff Nat. Park, Canada 104 C5
Banfora, Burkina Faso 82 C4
Bang Fai →, Laos 64 D5
Bang Hieng →, Laos 64 D5
Bang Krathum, Thailand 64 D3
Bang Lamung, Thailand 64 F3
Bang Mun Nak, Thailand 64 D3
Bang Pa In, Thailand 64 E3
Bang Rakam, Thailand 64 D3
Bang Saphan, Thailand 65 G2
Bangaduni I., India 69 J13
Bangala Dam, Zimbabwe 87 G3
Bangalore, India 66 N10
Banganga →, India 68 F6
Bangangté, Cameroon 83 D7
Bangaon, India 69 H13
Bangassou, C.A.R. 84 D4
Banggai, Indonesia 63 E6
Banggai, Kepulauan, Indonesia 63 E6
Banggai Arch. = Banggai, Kepulauan, Indonesia 63 E6
Banggi, Malaysia 62 C5
Banghāzī, Libya 79 B10
Bangjang, Sudan 81 E3
Bangka, Sulawesi, Indonesia 63 D7
Bangka, Sumatera, Indonesia 62 E3
Bangka, Selat, Indonesia 62 E3
Bangkalan, Indonesia 63 G15
Bangkinang, Indonesia 62 D2
Bangko, Indonesia 62 E2
Bangkok, Thailand 64 F3
Bangladesh ■, Asia 67 H17
Bangolo, Ivory C. 82 D3
Bangong Co, India 69 B8
Bangor, Down, U.K. 15 B6
Bangor, Gwynedd, U.K. 12 D3
Bangor, Maine, U.S.A. 101 D13
Bangor, Pa., U.S.A. 111 F9
Bangued, Phil. 61 C4
Bangui, C.A.R. 84 D3
Bangui, Phil. 61 B4
Banguru, Dem. Rep. of the Congo 86 B2
Bangweulu, L., Zambia 87 E3
Bangweulu Swamp, Zambia 87 E3
Bani, Dom. Rep. 121 C5
Bani, Mali 82 C4
Bani Bangou, Niger 83 B5
Banī Sa'd, Iraq 70 C5
Bania, Ivory C. 82 D4
Banihal Pass, India 69 C6
Banikoara, Benin 83 C5
Bāniyās, Syria 70 C3

Banja Luka, Bos.-H. 42 F2
Banjar, India 68 G7
Banjar →, India 69 H9
Banjarmasin, Indonesia 62 E4
Banjul, Gambia 82 C1
Banka, India 69 G12
Bankas, Mali 82 C4
Bankeryd, Sweden 11 G8
Banket, Zimbabwe 87 F3
Bankilaré, Niger 83 C5
Bankipore, India 67 G14
Banks I., B.C., Canada 104 C3
Banks I., N.W.T., Canada 100 A7
Banks Pen., N.Z. 91 K4
Banks Str., Australia 94 G4
Bankura, India 69 H12
Bankya, Bulgaria 40 D7
Banmankhi, India 69 G12
Bann →, Arm., U.K. 15 B5
Bann →, L'derry., U.K. 15 A5
Bannalec, France 18 E3
Bannang Sata, Thailand 65 J3
Banning, U.S.A. 117 M10
Banningville = Bandundu, Dem. Rep. of the Congo 84 E3
Banno, Ethiopia 81 G4
Bannockburn, Canada 110 B7
Bannockburn, U.K. 14 E5
Bannockburn, Zimbabwe 87 G2
Bannu, Pakistan 66 C7
Bano, India 69 H11
Bañolas = Banyoles, Spain 32 C7
Banon, France 21 D9
Baños de la Encina, Spain 35 G4
Baños de Molgas, Spain 34 C3
Bánovce nad Bebravou, Slovak Rep. 27 C11
Banovići, Bos.-H. 42 F3
Bansgaon, India 69 F10
Banská Bystrica, Slovak Rep. 27 C12
Banská Štiavnica, Slovak Rep. 27 C11
Bansko, Bulgaria 40 E7
Banskobystrický □, Slovak Rep. 27 C12
Banswara, India 68 H6
Bantaeng, Indonesia 63 F5
Bantaji, Nigeria 83 D7
Bantayan, Phil. 61 F5
Bantry, Ireland 15 E2
Bantry B., Ireland 15 E2
Bantul, Indonesia 63 G14
Bantva, India 68 J4
Banu, Afghan. 66 B6
Banya, Bulgaria 41 D8
Banyak, Kepulauan, Indonesia 62 D1
Banyalbufar, Spain 37 B9
Banyo, Cameroon 83 D7
Banyoles, Spain 32 C7
Banyuls-sur-Mer, France 20 F7
Banyumas, Indonesia 63 G13
Banyuwangi, Indonesia 63 H16
Banzare Coast, Antarctica 5 C9
Banzyville = Mobayi, Dem. Rep. of the Congo 84 D4
Bao Ha, Vietnam 58 F5
Bao Lac, Vietnam 64 A5
Bao Loc, Vietnam 65 G6
Bao'an = Shenzhen, China 59 F10
Baocheng, China 56 H4
Baode, China 56 E6
Baodi, China 57 E9
Baoding, China 56 E8
Baoji, China 56 G4
Baojing, China 58 C7
Baokang, China 59 B8
Baoshan, Shanghai, China 59 B13
Baoshan, Yunnan, China 58 E2
Baotou, China 56 D6
Baoxing, China 58 B4
Baoying, China 57 H10
Bap, India 68 F5
Bapatla, India 67 M12
Bapaume, France 19 B9
Bāqerābād, Iran 71 C6
Ba'qūbah, Iraq 70 C5
Bar, Montenegro, Yug. 40 D3
Bar, Ukraine 47 H4
Bar Bigha, India 69 G11
Bar Harbor, U.S.A. 109 C11
Bar-le-Duc, France 19 D12
Bar-sur-Aube, France 19 D11
Bar-sur-Seine, France 19 D11
Bara, India 69 G9
Bâra, Romania 43 C12
Bara Banki, India 69 F9
Barabai, Indonesia 62 E5
Baraboo, U.S.A. 112 D10
Baracoa, Cuba 121 B5
Baradā →, Syria 75 B5
Baradero, Argentina 126 C4
Baradine, Australia 95 E4
Baraga, U.S.A. 112 B10
Bărăganul, Romania 43 F12
Barahona, Dom. Rep. 121 C5
Barahona, Spain 32 D2
Barail Range, India 67 G18
Baraka, Sudan 81 E2
Baraka →, Sudan 80 D4
Barakaldo, Spain 32 B2
Barakar →, India 69 G12
Barakhola, India 67 G18
Barakot, India 69 J11
Barakpur, India 69 H13
Baralaba, Australia 94 C4
Baralla, Spain 34 C3
Baralzon L., Canada 105 B9
Barameiya, Sudan 80 D4

Baramula, India 69 B6
Baran, India 68 G7
Baran →, Pakistan 68 G3
Barañain, Spain 32 C3
Baranavichy, Belarus 47 F4
Barani, Burkina Faso 82 C4
Baranof, U.S.A. 104 B2
Baranof I., U.S.A. 100 C6
Baranów Sandomierski, Poland 45 H8
Baranya □, Hungary 42 E3
Baraolt, Romania 43 D10
Barapasi, Indonesia 63 E9
Barasat, India 69 H13
Barat Daya, Kepulauan, Indonesia 63 F7
Barataria B., U.S.A. 113 L10
Barauda, India 68 H6
Baraut, India 68 E7
Barbacena, Brazil 127 A7
Barbados ■, W. Indies 121 D8
Barban, Croatia 29 C11
Barbària, C. de, Spain 37 C7
Barbaros, Turkey 41 F11
Barbastro, Spain 32 C5
Barbate = Barbate de Franco, Spain 35 J5
Barbate de Franco, Spain 35 J5
Barberino di Mugello, Italy 29 E8
Barberton, S. Africa 89 D5
Barberton, U.S.A. 110 E3
Barbezieux-St-Hilaire, France 20 C3
Barbosa, Colombia 124 B4
Barbourville, U.S.A. 109 G4
Barbuda, W. Indies 121 C7
Bârca, Romania 43 G8
Barcaldine, Australia 94 C4
Barcarrota, Spain 35 G4
Barcellona Pozzo di Gotto, Italy 31 D8
Barcelona, Spain 32 D7
Barcelona, Venezuela 124 A6
Barcelona □, Spain 32 D7
Barcelonette, France 21 D10
Barcelos, Brazil 124 D6
Barcin, Poland 45 F4
Barclayville, Liberia 82 E3
Barcoo →, Australia 94 D3
Barcs, Hungary 42 E2
Barczewo, Poland 44 E7
Bärdä, Azerbaijan 49 K8
Bardaï, Chad 79 D9
Bardas Blancas, Argentina 126 D2
Barddhaman, India 69 H12
Bardejov, Slovak Rep. 27 B14
Bardera, Somali Rep. 74 G3
Bardi, Italy 28 D6
Bardīyah, Libya 79 B10
Bardolino, Italy 28 C7
Bardonécchia, Italy 28 C3
Bardsey I., U.K. 12 E3
Bardstown, U.S.A. 108 G3
Bareilly, India 69 E8
Barela, India 69 H9
Barentin, France 18 C7
Barenton, France 18 D6
Barents Sea, Arctic 4 B9
Barentu, Eritrea 81 D4
Barfleur, France 18 C5
Barfleur, Pte. de, France 18 C5
Barga, Italy 28 D7
Bargara, Australia 94 C5
Bargas, Spain 34 F6
Bârgăului Bistrița, Romania 43 C9
Barge, Italy 28 D4
Bargnop, Sudan 81 F2
Bargteheide, Germany 24 B6
Barguzin, Russia 51 D11
Barh, India 69 G11
Barhaj, India 69 F10
Barham, Australia 95 F3
Barharwa, India 69 G12
Barhi, India 69 G11
Bari, India 68 F7
Bari, Italy 31 A9
Bari Doab, Pakistan 68 D5
Bari Sadri, India 68 G6
Bari Sardo, Italy 30 C2
Barīdī, Ra's, Si. Arabia 70 E3
Barīm, Yemen 76 E8
Barinas, Venezuela 124 B4
Baring, C., Canada 100 B8
Baringo, Kenya 86 B4
Baringo, L., Kenya 86 B4
Bârîs, Egypt 80 C3
Barisal, Bangla. 67 H17
Barisan, Bukit, Indonesia 62 E2
Barito →, Indonesia 62 E4
Barjac, France 21 D8
Barjols, France 21 E10
Bark L., Canada 110 A7
Barka = Baraka →, Sudan 80 D4
Barkakana, India 69 H11
Barkam, China 58 B4
Barker, U.S.A. 110 C6
Barkley Sound, Canada 104 D3
Barkly East, S. Africa 88 E4
Barkly Roadhouse, Australia 94 B2
Barkly Tableland, Australia 94 B2
Barkly West, S. Africa 88 D3
Barkol, Wadi →, Sudan 80 D3
Barla Dağı, Turkey 39 C12
Bârlad, Romania 43 D12
Bârlad →, Romania 43 E12
Barlee, L., Australia 93 E2
Barlee, Mt., Australia 93 D4
Barletta, Italy 31 A9
Barlinek, Poland 45 F2
Barlovento, Canary Is. 37 F2
Barlow L., Canada 105 A8

Barmedman, Australia 95 E4
Barmer, India 68 G4
Barmera, Australia 95 E3
Barmouth, U.K. 12 E3
Barmstedt, Germany 24 B5
Barna →, India 69 G10
Barnagar, India 68 H5
Barnala, India 68 D6
Barnard Castle, U.K. 12 C6
Barnaul, Russia 50 D9
Barnesville, U.S.A. 109 J3
Barnet, U.K. 13 F7
Barneveld, Neths. 17 B5
Barneveld, U.S.A. 111 C9
Barneville-Carteret, France 18 C5
Barnhart, U.S.A. 113 K4
Barnsley, U.K. 12 D6
Barnstaple, U.K. 13 F3
Barnstaple Bay = Bideford Bay, U.K. 13 F3
Barnsville, U.S.A. 112 B6
Barnwell, U.S.A. 109 J5
Baro, Nigeria 83 D6
Baro →, Ethiopia 81 F3
Baroda = Vadodara, India 68 H5
Baroda, India 68 G7
Baroe, S. Africa 88 E3
Baron Ra., Australia 92 D4
Barong, China 58 B2
Barotseland, Zambia 85 H4
Barouéli, Mali 82 C3
Barpeta, India 67 F17
Barques, Pt. Aux, U.S.A. 110 B2
Barquísimeto, Venezuela 124 A5
Barr, Ras el, Egypt 80 H7
Barr Smith Range, Australia 93 E3
Barra, Brazil 125 F10
Barra, U.K. 14 E1
Barra, Sd. of, U.K. 14 E1
Barra do Corda, Brazil 125 E9
Barra do Piraí, Brazil 127 A7
Barra Falsa, Pta. da, Mozam. 89 C6
Barra Hd., U.K. 14 E1
Barra Mansa, Brazil 127 A7
Barraba, Australia 95 E5
Barrackpur = Barakpur, India 69 H13
Barradale Roadhouse, Australia 92 D1
Barrafranca, Italy 31 E7
Barraigh = Barra, U.K. 14 E1
Barranca, Lima, Peru 124 F3
Barranca, Loreto, Peru 124 D3
Barrancabermeja, Colombia 124 B4
Barrancas, Venezuela 124 B6
Barrancos, Portugal 35 G4
Barranqueras, Argentina 126 B4
Barranquilla, Colombia 124 A4
Barraute, Canada 102 C4
Barre, Mass., U.S.A. 111 D12
Barre, Vt., U.S.A. 111 B12
Barreal, Argentina 126 C2
Barreiras, Brazil 125 F10
Barreirinhas, Brazil 125 D10
Barreiro, Portugal 35 G1
Barrême, France 21 E10
Barretos, Brazil 125 H9
Barrhead, Canada 104 C6
Barrie, Canada 102 D4
Barrier Ra., Australia 95 E3
Barrière, Canada 104 C4
Barrington, U.S.A. 111 E13
Barrington L., Canada 105 B8
Barrington Tops, Australia 95 E5
Barringun, Australia 95 D4
Barro do Garças, Brazil 125 G8
Barron, U.S.A. 112 C9
Barrow, U.S.A. 100 A4
Barrow →, Ireland 15 D5
Barrow Creek, Australia 94 C1
Barrow I., Australia 92 D2
Barrow-in-Furness, U.K. 12 C4
Barrow Pt., Australia 94 A3
Barrow Pt., U.S.A. 98 B4
Barrow Ra., Australia 93 E4
Barrow Str., Canada 4 B3
Barruecopardo, Spain 34 D4
Barruelo de Santullán, Spain 34 C6
Barry, U.K. 13 F4
Barry's Bay, Canada 102 C4
Barsalogho, Burkina Faso 83 C4
Barsat, Pakistan 69 A5
Barsham, Syria 70 C4
Barsi, India 66 K9
Barsinghausen, Germany 24 C4
Barsoi, India 67 G15
Barstow, U.S.A. 117 L9
Barth, Germany 24 A8
Barthélemy, Col, Vietnam 64 C5
Bartica, Guyana 124 B7
Bartin, Turkey 72 B5
Bartlesville, U.S.A. 113 G7
Bartlett, U.S.A. 116 J8
Bartlett, L., Canada 104 A5
Bartolomeu Dias, Mozam. 89 C6
Barton, Australia 93 F5
Barton upon Humber, U.K. 12 D7
Bartow, U.S.A. 109 M5
Barú, Volcan, Panama 120 E3
Barumba, Dem. Rep. of the Congo 86 B1
Baruth, Germany 24 C9
Baruunsuu, Mongolia 56 C3
Barvinkove, Ukraine 47 H9
Barwani, India 68 H6
Barwice, Poland 44 E3
Barycz →, Poland 45 G3

Barysaw, Belarus 46 E5
Barysh, Russia 48 D8
Barzān, Iraq 70 B5
Bârzava, Romania 42 D6
Bas-Rhin □, France 19 D14
Baša'id, Serbia, Yug. 42 E5
Bāsa'idū, Iran 71 E7
Basal, Pakistan 68 C5
Basankusa, Dem. Rep. of the Congo 84 D3
Basarabeasca, Moldova 43 D13
Basarabi, Romania 43 F13
Basauri, Spain 32 B2
Basawa, Afghan. 68 B4
Bascuñán, C., Chile 126 B1
Basel, Switz. 25 H3
Basel-Landschaft □, Switz. 25 H3
Basento →, Italy 31 B9
Bashākerd, Kūhhā-ye, Iran 71 E8
Bashaw, Canada 104 C6
Bāshī, Iran 71 D6
Bashkir Republic = Bashkortostan □, Russia 50 D6
Bashkortostan □, Russia 50 D6
Basibasy, Madag. 89 C7
Basilan, Phil. 61 H5
Basilan Str., Phil. 61 H5
Basildon, U.K. 13 F8
Basilé, Eq. Guin. 83 E6
Basilicata □, Italy 31 B9
Basim = Washim, India 66 J10
Basin, U.S.A. 114 D9
Basingstoke, U.K. 13 F6
Baška, Croatia 29 D11
Başkale, Turkey 73 C10
Baskatong, Rés., Canada 102 C4
Basle = Basel, Switz. 25 H3
Başmakçı, Turkey 39 D12
Basoda, India 68 H7
Basoka, Dem. Rep. of the Congo 86 B1
Basque, Pays, France 20 E2
Basque Provinces = País Vasco □, Spain 32 C2
Basra = Al Başrah, Iraq 70 D5
Bass Str., Australia 94 F4
Bassano, Canada 104 C6
Bassano del Grappa, Italy 29 C8
Bassar, Togo 83 D5
Bassas da India, Ind. Oc. 85 J7
Basse-Normandie □, France 18 D6
Basse Santa-Su, Gambia 82 C2
Basse-Terre, Guadeloupe 121 C7
Bassein, Burma 67 L19
Basseterre, St. Kitts & Nevis 121 C7
Bassett, U.S.A. 112 D5
Bassi, India 68 G7
Bassigny, France 19 E12
Bassikounou, Mauritania 82 B3
Bassila, Benin 83 D5
Bassum, Germany 24 C4
Båstad, Sweden 11 H6
Bastak, Iran 71 E7
Bastām, Iran 71 B7
Bastar, India 67 K12
Bastelica, France 21 F13
Basti, India 69 F10
Bastia, France 21 F13
Bastogne, Belgium 17 D5
Bastrop, La., U.S.A. 113 J9
Bastrop, Tex., U.S.A. 113 K6
Bat Yam, Israel 75 C3
Bata, Eq. Guin. 84 D1
Bata, Romania 42 D7
Bataan □, Phil. 61 D4
Batabanó, Cuba 120 B3
Batabanó, G. de, Cuba 120 B3
Batac, Phil. 61 B4
Batagai, Russia 51 C14
Batajnica, Serbia, Yug. 40 B4
Batala, India 68 D6
Batalha, Portugal 34 F2
Batama, Dem. Rep. of the Congo 86 B2
Batamay, Russia 51 C13
Batang, China 58 B2
Batang, Indonesia 63 G13
Batangas, Phil. 61 E4
Batanta, Indonesia 63 E8
Batatais, Brazil 127 A6
Batavia, U.S.A. 110 D6
Bataysk, Russia 47 J10
Batchelor, Australia 92 B5
Batdambang, Cambodia 64 F4
Bateman's B., Australia 95 F5
Batemans Bay, Australia 95 F5
Bates Ra., Australia 93 E3
Batesburg, U.S.A. 109 J5
Batesville, Ark., U.S.A. 113 H9
Batesville, Miss., U.S.A. 113 H10
Batesville, Tex., U.S.A. 113 L5
Bath, Canada 111 B8
Bath, U.K. 13 F5
Bath, Maine, U.S.A. 109 D11
Bath, N.Y., U.S.A. 110 D7
Bath & North East Somerset □, U.K. 13 F5
Batheay, Cambodia 65 G5
Bathurst = Banjul, Gambia 82 C1
Bathurst, Australia 95 E4
Bathurst, Canada 103 C6
Bathurst, S. Africa 88 E4
Bathurst, C., Canada 100 A7
Bathurst B., Australia 94 A3
Bathurst Harb., Australia 94 G4
Bathurst I., Australia 92 B5
Bathurst I., Canada 4 B2
Bathurst Inlet, Canada 100 B9
Bati, Ethiopia 81 E5
Batie, Burkina Faso 82 D4

Batlow, *Australia*	95	F4
Batman, *Turkey*	70	B4
Baṭn al Ghūl, *Jordan*	75	F4
Batna, *Algeria*	78	A7
Batobato = San Isidro, *Phil.*	61	H7
Batočina, *Serbia, Yug.*	40	B5
Batoka, *Zambia*	87	F2
Baton Rouge, *U.S.A.*	113	K9
Batong, Ko, *Thailand*	65	J2
Bátonyterenye, *Hungary*	42	C4
Batopilas, *Mexico*	118	B3
Batouri, *Cameroon*	84	D2
Båtsfjord, *Norway*	8	A23
Battambang = Batdambang, *Cambodia*	64	F4
Batticaloa, *Sri Lanka*	66	R12
Battipáglia, *Italy*	31	B7
Battle, *U.K.*	13	G8
Battle →, *Canada*	105	C7
Battle Creek, *U.S.A.*	108	D3
Battle Ground, *U.S.A.*	116	E4
Battle Harbour, *Canada*	103	B8
Battle Lake, *U.S.A.*	112	B7
Battle Mountain, *U.S.A.*	114	F5
Battlefields, *Zimbabwe*	87	F2
Battleford, *Canada*	105	C7
Battonya, *Hungary*	42	D6
Batu, *Ethiopia*	81	F4
Batu, Kepulauan, *Indonesia*	62	E1
Batu Caves, *Malaysia*	65	L3
Batu Gajah, *Malaysia*	65	K3
Batu Is. = Batu, Kepulauan, *Indonesia*	62	E1
Batu Pahat, *Malaysia*	65	M4
Batuata, *Indonesia*	63	F6
Batumi, *Georgia*	49	K5
Baturaja, *Indonesia*	62	E2
Baturité, *Brazil*	125	D11
Bau, *Malaysia*	62	D4
Baubau, *Indonesia*	63	F6
Bauchi, *Nigeria*	83	C6
Bauchi □, *Nigeria*	83	C7
Baud, *France*	18	E3
Baudette, *U.S.A.*	112	A7
Bauer, C., *Australia*	95	E1
Bauhinia, *Australia*	94	C4
Baukau, *Indonesia*	63	F7
Bauld, C., *Canada*	101	C14
Baume-les-Dames, *France*	19	E13
Baunatal, *Germany*	24	D5
Baunei, *Italy*	30	B2
Baure, *Nigeria*	83	C6
Bauru, *Brazil*	127	A6
Bausi, *India*	69	G12
Bauska, *Latvia*	9	H21
Bautino, *Kazakstan*	49	H10
Bautzen, *Germany*	24	D10
Bauya, *S. Leone*	82	D2
Bavānāt, *Iran*	71	D7
Bavanište, *Serbia, Yug.*	42	F5
Bavaria = Bayern □, *Germany*	25	G7
Båven, *Sweden*	10	E10
Bavispe →, *Mexico*	118	B3
Bawdwin, *Burma*	67	H20
Bawean, *Indonesia*	62	F4
Bawku, *Ghana*	83	C4
Bawlake, *Burma*	67	K20
Bawolung, *China*	58	C3
Baxley, *U.S.A.*	109	K4
Baxoi, *China*	58	B1
Baxter, *U.S.A.*	112	B7
Baxter Springs, *U.S.A.*	113	G7
Bay, L. de, *Phil.*	61	D4
Bay City, *Mich., U.S.A.*	108	D4
Bay City, *Tex., U.S.A.*	113	L7
Bay Minette, *U.S.A.*	109	K2
Bay Roberts, *Canada*	103	C9
Bay St. Louis, *U.S.A.*	113	K10
Bay Springs, *U.S.A.*	113	K10
Bay View, *N.Z.*	91	H6
Baya, *Dem. Rep. of the Congo*	87	E2
Bayamo, *Cuba*	120	B4
Bayamón, *Puerto Rico*	121	C6
Bayan Har Shan, *China*	60	C4
Bayan Hot = Alxa Zuoqi, *China*	56	E3
Bayan Obo, *China*	56	D5
Bayan-Ovoo = Erdenetsogt, *Mongolia*	56	C4
Bayana, *India*	68	F7
Bayanaūyl, *Kazakstan*	50	D8
Bayandalay, *Mongolia*	56	C2
Bayanhongor, *Mongolia*	60	B5
Bayard, *N. Mex., U.S.A.*	115	K9
Bayard, *Nebr., U.S.A.*	112	E3
Bayawan, *Phil.*	61	G5
Baybay, *Phil.*	61	F6
Bayburt, *Turkey*	73	B9
Bayelsa □, *Nigeria*	83	E6
Bayerische Alpen, *Germany*	25	H7
Bayerischer Wald, *Germany*	25	G8
Bayern □, *Germany*	25	G7
Bayeux, *France*	18	C6
Bayfield, *Canada*	110	C3
Bayfield, *U.S.A.*	112	B9
Bayındır, *Turkey*	39	C9
Baykal, Oz., *Russia*	51	D11
Baykan, *Turkey*	70	B4
Baykonur = Bayqongyr, *Kazakstan*	50	E7
Baynes Mts., *Namibia*	88	B1
Bayombong, *Phil.*	61	C4
Bayon, *France*	19	D13
Bayona = Baiona, *Spain*	34	C2
Bayonne, *France*	20	E2
Bayonne, *U.S.A.*	111	F10
Bayovar, *Peru*	124	E2
Bayqongyr, *Kazakstan*	50	E7
Bayram-Ali = Bayramaly, *Turkmenistan*	50	F7
Bayramaly, *Turkmenistan*	50	F7
Bayramıç, *Turkey*	39	B8
Bayreuth, *Germany*	25	F7
Bayrischzell, *Germany*	25	H8
Bayrūt, *Lebanon*	75	B4
Bays, L. of, *Canada*	110	A5
Baysville, *Canada*	110	A5
Bayt Lahm, *West Bank*	75	D4
Baytown, *U.S.A.*	113	L7
Bayzo, *Niger*	83	C5
Baza, *Spain*	35	H8
Bazar Dyuzi, *Russia*	49	K8
Bazardüzü = Bazar Dyuzi, *Russia*	49	K8
Bazarny Karabulak, *Russia*	48	D8
Bazarnyy Syzgan, *Russia*	48	D8
Bazaruto, I. do, *Mozam.*	89	C6
Bazas, *France*	20	D3
Bazhong, *China*	58	B6
Bazhou, *China*	56	E9
Bazmān, Kūh-e, *Iran*	71	D9
Beach, *U.S.A.*	112	B3
Beach City, *U.S.A.*	110	F3
Beachport, *Australia*	95	F3
Beachy Hd., *U.K.*	13	G8
Beacon, *Australia*	93	F2
Beacon, *U.S.A.*	111	E11
Beaconsfield, *Australia*	94	G4
Beagle, Canal, *S. Amer.*	122	J4
Beagle Bay, *Australia*	92	C3
Bealanana, *Madag.*	89	A8
Beals Cr. →, *U.S.A.*	113	J4
Beamsville, *Canada*	110	C5
Bear →, *Calif., U.S.A.*	116	G5
Bear →, *Utah, U.S.A.*	106	B4
Béar, C., *France*	20	F7
Bear I., *Ireland*	15	E2
Bear L., *Canada*	105	B9
Bear L., *U.S.A.*	114	F8
Beardmore, *Canada*	102	C2
Beardmore Glacier, *Antarctica*	5	E11
Beardstown, *U.S.A.*	112	F9
Bearma →, *India*	69	G8
Béarn, *France*	20	E3
Bearpaw Mts., *U.S.A.*	114	B9
Bearskin Lake, *Canada*	102	B1
Beas →, *India*	68	D6
Beas de Segura, *Spain*	35	G8
Beasain, *Spain*	32	B2
Beata, C., *Dom. Rep.*	121	C5
Beata, I., *Dom. Rep.*	121	C5
Beatrice, *U.S.A.*	112	E6
Beatrice, *Zimbabwe*	87	F3
Beatrice, C., *Australia*	94	A2
Beatton →, *Canada*	104	B4
Beatton River, *Canada*	104	B4
Beatty, *U.S.A.*	116	J10
Beaucaire, *France*	21	E8
Beauce, Plaine de la, *France*	19	D8
Beauceville, *Canada*	103	C5
Beaudesert, *Australia*	95	D5
Beaufort, *France*	21	C10
Beaufort, *Malaysia*	62	C5
Beaufort, *N.C., U.S.A.*	109	H7
Beaufort, *S.C., U.S.A.*	109	J5
Beaufort Sea, *Arctic*	4	B1
Beaufort West, *S. Africa*	88	E3
Beaugency, *France*	19	E8
Beauharnois, *Canada*	111	A11
Beaujeu, *France*	19	F11
Beaujolais, *France*	19	F11
Beaulieu →, *Canada*	104	A6
Beaulieu-sur-Dordogne, *France*	20	D5
Beaulieu-sur-Mer, *France*	21	E11
Beauly, *U.K.*	14	D4
Beauly →, *U.K.*	14	D4
Beaumaris, *U.K.*	12	D3
Beaumont, *Belgium*	17	D4
Beaumont, *France*	20	D4
Beaumont, *U.S.A.*	113	K7
Beaumont-de-Lomagne, *France*	20	E5
Beaumont-le-Roger, *France*	18	C7
Beaumont-sur-Sarthe, *France*	18	D7
Beaune, *France*	19	E11
Beaune-la-Rolande, *France*	19	D9
Beaupré, *Canada*	103	C5
Beaupréau, *France*	18	E6
Beauraing, *Belgium*	17	D4
Beaurepaire, *France*	21	C9
Beauséjour, *Canada*	105	C9
Beauvais, *France*	19	C9
Beauval, *Canada*	105	B7
Beauvoir-sur-Mer, *France*	18	F4
Beauvoir-sur-Niort, *France*	20	B3
Beaver, *Okla., U.S.A.*	113	G4
Beaver, *Pa., U.S.A.*	110	F4
Beaver, *Utah, U.S.A.*	115	G7
Beaver →, *B.C., Canada*	104	B4
Beaver →, *Ont., Canada*	102	A2
Beaver →, *Sask., Canada*	105	B7
Beaver →, *U.S.A.*	113	G5
Beaver City, *U.S.A.*	112	E5
Beaver Creek, *Canada*	100	B5
Beaver Dam, *U.S.A.*	112	D10
Beaver Falls, *U.S.A.*	110	F4
Beaver Hill L., *Canada*	105	C10
Beaver I., *U.S.A.*	108	C3
Beaverhill L., *Canada*	104	C6
Beaverlodge, *Canada*	104	B5
Beaverstone →, *Canada*	102	B2
Beaverton, *Canada*	110	B5
Beaverton, *U.S.A.*	116	E4
Beawar, *India*	68	F6
Bebedouro, *Brazil*	127	A6
Beboa, *Madag.*	89	B7
Bebra, *Germany*	24	E5
Beccles, *U.K.*	13	E9
Bečej, *Serbia, Yug.*	42	E5
Beceni, *Romania*	43	E11
Becerreá, *Spain*	34	C3
Béchar, *Algeria*	78	B5
Bechyně, *Czech Rep.*	26	B7
Beckley, *U.S.A.*	108	G5
Beckum, *Germany*	24	D4
Beclean, *Romania*	43	C9
Bečov nad Teplou, *Czech Rep.*	26	A5
Bečva →, *Czech Rep.*	27	B10
Bédar, *Spain*	33	H3
Bédarieux, *France*	20	E7
Beddouza, Ras, *Morocco*	78	B4
Bedele, *Ethiopia*	81	F4
Bederkesa, *Germany*	24	B4
Bedeso, *Ethiopia*	81	F5
Bedford, *Brazil*	111	A12
Bedford, *S. Africa*	88	E4
Bedford, *U.K.*	13	E7
Bedford, *Ind., U.S.A.*	108	F2
Bedford, *Iowa, U.S.A.*	112	E7
Bedford, *Ohio, U.S.A.*	110	E3
Bedford, *Pa., U.S.A.*	110	F6
Bedford, *Va., U.S.A.*	108	G6
Bedford, C., *Australia*	94	B4
Bedfordshire □, *U.K.*	13	E7
Będków, *Poland*	45	G6
Bednja →, *Croatia*	29	B13
Bednodemyanovsk, *Russia*	48	D6
Bedónia, *Italy*	28	D6
Bedourie, *Australia*	94	C2
Bedum, *Neths.*	17	A6
Będzin, *Poland*	45	H6
Beebe Plain, *Canada*	111	A12
Beech Creek, *U.S.A.*	110	E7
Beelitz, *Germany*	24	C8
Beenleigh, *Australia*	95	D5
Be'er Menuha, *Israel*	70	D2
Be'er Sheva, *Israel*	75	D3
Beersheba = Be'er Sheva, *Israel*	75	D3
Beeskow, *Germany*	24	C10
Beesteekraal, *S. Africa*	89	D4
Beeston, *U.K.*	12	E6
Beetzendorf, *Germany*	24	C7
Beeville, *U.S.A.*	113	L6
Befale, *Dem. Rep. of the Congo*	84	D4
Befandriana, *Mahajanga, Madag.*	89	B8
Befandriana, *Toliara, Madag.*	89	C7
Befasy, *Madag.*	89	C7
Béfotaka, *Antsiranana, Madag.*	89	A8
Befotaka, *Fianarantsoa, Madag.*	89	C8
Bega, *Australia*	95	F4
Bega, Canalul, *Romania*	42	E5
Bégard, *France*	18	D3
Beğendik, *Turkey*	41	F10
Begoro, *Ghana*	83	D4
Begusarai, *India*	69	G12
Behābād, *Iran*	71	C8
Behala, *India*	69	H13
Behara, *Madag.*	89	C8
Behbehān, *Iran*	71	D6
Behshahr, *Iran*	71	B7
Bei Jiang →, *China*	59	F9
Bei'an, *China*	60	B7
Beibei, *China*	58	C6
Beichuan, *China*	58	B5
Beihai, *China*	58	G7
Beijing, *China*	56	E9
Beijing □, *China*	56	E9
Beilen, *Neths.*	17	B6
Beilngries, *Germany*	25	F7
Beilpajah, *Australia*	95	E3
Beilul, *Eritrea*	81	E5
Beinn na Faoghla = Benbecula, *U.K.*	14	D1
Beipan Jiang →, *China*	58	E5
Beipiao, *China*	57	D11
Beira, *Mozam.*	87	F3
Beirut = Bayrūt, *Lebanon*	75	B4
Beiseker, *Canada*	104	C6
Beitaolaizhao, *China*	57	B13
Beitbridge, *Zimbabwe*	87	G3
Beiuş, *Romania*	42	D7
Beizhen = Binzhou, *China*	57	F10
Beizhen, *China*	57	D11
Beizhengzhen, *China*	57	B12
Beja, *Portugal*	35	G3
Béja, *Tunisia*	79	A7
Beja □, *Portugal*	35	H3
Bejaia, *Algeria*	78	A7
Béjar, *Spain*	34	E5
Bejestān, *Iran*	71	C8
Bekçiler, *Turkey*	39	E11
Békés, *Hungary*	42	D6
Békés □, *Hungary*	42	D6
Békéscsaba, *Hungary*	42	D6
Bekilli, *Turkey*	39	C11
Bekily, *Madag.*	89	C8
Bekisopa, *Madag.*	89	C8
Bekitro, *Madag.*	89	C8
Bekodoka, *Madag.*	89	B8
Bekoji, *Ethiopia*	81	F4
Bekok, *Malaysia*	65	L4
Bekopaka, *Madag.*	89	B7
Bekwai, *Ghana*	83	D4
Bela, *India*	69	G10
Bela, *Pakistan*	68	F2
Bela Crkva, *Serbia, Yug.*	42	F6
Bela Palanka, *Serbia, Yug.*	40	C6
Bela Vista, *Brazil*	126	A4
Bela Vista, *Mozam.*	89	D5
Bélâbre, *France*	20	B5
Belalcázar, *Spain*	35	G5
Belan →, *India*	69	G9
Belanovica, *Serbia, Yug.*	40	B4
Belarus ■, *Europe*	46	F4
Belau = Palau ■, *Pac. Oc.*	52	J17
Belavenona, *Madag.*	89	C8
Belawan, *Indonesia*	62	D1
Belaya, *Ethiopia*	81	E4
Belaya →, *Russia*	50	C6
Belaya Glina, *Russia*	49	G5
Belaya Kalitva, *Russia*	49	F5
Belaya Tserkov = Bila Tserkva, *Ukraine*	47	H6
Belcești, *Romania*	43	C12
Belcher Is., *Canada*	102	A3
Belchite, *Spain*	32	D4
Belden, *U.S.A.*	116	E5
Belém, *Brazil*	125	D9
Belén, *Argentina*	126	B2
Belén, *Paraguay*	126	A4
Belen, *U.S.A.*	115	J10
Belene, *Bulgaria*	41	C9
Beleni, *Turkey*	72	D7
Bélesta, *France*	20	F5
Belet Uen, *Somali Rep.*	74	G4
Belev, *Russia*	46	F9
Belevi, *Turkey*	39	C9
Belfair, *U.S.A.*	116	C4
Belfast, *S. Africa*	89	D5
Belfast, *U.K.*	15	B6
Belfast, *Maine, U.S.A.*	109	C11
Belfast, *N.Y., U.S.A.*	110	D6
Belfast L., *U.K.*	15	B6
Belfield, *U.S.A.*	112	B3
Belfort, *France*	19	E13
Belfort, Territoire de □, *France*	19	E13
Belfry, *U.S.A.*	114	D9
Belgaum, *India*	66	M9
Belgioioso, *Italy*	28	C6
Belgium ■, *Europe*	17	D4
Belgodère, *France*	21	F13
Belgorod, *Russia*	47	G9
Belgorod-Dnestrovskiy = Bilhorod-Dnistrovskyy, *Ukraine*	47	J6
Belgrade = Beograd, *Serbia, Yug.*	40	B4
Belgrade, *U.S.A.*	114	D8
Belhaven, *U.S.A.*	109	H7
Beli Drim →, *Europe*	40	D4
Beli Manastir, *Croatia*	42	E3
Beli Timok →, *Serbia, Yug.*	40	C6
Bélice →, *Italy*	30	E5
Belinskiy, *Russia*	48	D6
Belinyu, *Indonesia*	62	E3
Beliton Is. = Belitung, *Indonesia*	62	E3
Belitung, *Indonesia*	62	E3
Beliu, *Romania*	42	D6
Belize ■, *Cent. Amer.*	119	D7
Belize City, *Belize*	119	D7
Beljakovci, *Macedonia*	40	D5
Beljanica, *Serbia, Yug.*	40	B5
Belkovskiy, Ostrov, *Russia*	51	B14
Bell →, *Canada*	102	C4
Bell I., *Canada*	103	B8
Bell-Irving →, *Canada*	104	B3
Bell Peninsula, *Canada*	101	B11
Bell Ville, *Argentina*	126	C3
Bella, *Italy*	31	B8
Bella Bella, *Canada*	104	C3
Bella Coola, *Canada*	104	C3
Bella Unión, *Uruguay*	126	C4
Bella Vista, *Corrientes, Argentina*	126	B4
Bella Vista, *Tucuman, Argentina*	126	B2
Bellac, *France*	20	B5
Bellágio, *Italy*	28	C6
Bellaire, *U.S.A.*	110	F4
Bellária, *Italy*	29	D9
Bellary, *India*	66	M10
Bellata, *Australia*	95	D4
Belle-Chasse, *U.S.A.*	113	L10
Belle Fourche, *U.S.A.*	112	C3
Belle Fourche →, *U.S.A.*	112	C3
Belle Glade, *U.S.A.*	109	M5
Belle-Île, *France*	18	E3
Belle Isle, *Canada*	103	B8
Belle Isle, Str. of, *Canada*	103	B8
Belle Plaine, *Canada*	112	E8
Belle Yella, *Liberia*	82	D3
Belledonne, *France*	21	C10
Bellefontaine, *U.S.A.*	108	E4
Bellefonte, *U.S.A.*	110	F7
Bellegarde, *France*	19	E9
Bellegarde-en-Marche, *France*	20	C6
Bellegarde-sur-Valserine, *France*	19	F12
Bellême, *France*	18	D7
Belleoram, *Canada*	103	C8
Belleville, *Canada*	102	D4
Belleville, *France*	19	F11
Belleville, *Ill., U.S.A.*	112	F10
Belleville, *Kans., U.S.A.*	112	F6
Belleville, *N.Y., U.S.A.*	111	C8
Belleville-sur-Vie, *France*	18	F5
Bellevue, *Canada*	104	D6
Bellevue, *Idaho, U.S.A.*	114	E6
Bellevue, *Nebr., U.S.A.*	112	E7
Bellevue, *Ohio, U.S.A.*	110	E2
Bellevue, *Wash., U.S.A.*	116	C4
Belley, *France*	19	F12
Bellin = Kangirsuk, *Canada*	101	B13
Bellinge, *Denmark*	11	J4
Bellingen, *Australia*	95	E5
Bellingham, *U.S.A.*	100	D7
Bellingshausen Sea, *Antarctica*	5	C17
Bellinzona, *Switz.*	25	J5
Bello, *Colombia*	124	B3
Bellows Falls, *U.S.A.*	111	C12
Bellpat, *Pakistan*	68	E3
Bellpuig d'Urgell, *Spain*	32	D6
Belluno, *Italy*	29	B9
Bellwood, *U.S.A.*	110	F6
Bélmez, *Spain*	35	G5
Belmont, *Canada*	110	D3
Belmont, *S. Africa*	88	D3
Belmont, *U.S.A.*	110	D6
Belmonte, *Brazil*	125	G11
Belmonte, *Portugal*	34	E3
Belmonte, *Spain*	33	F2
Belmopan, *Belize*	119	D7
Belmullet, *Ireland*	15	B2
Belo Horizonte, *Brazil*	125	G10
Belo-sur-Mer, *Madag.*	89	C7
Belo-Tsiribihina, *Madag.*	89	B7
Belogorsk = Bilohirsk, *Ukraine*	47	K8
Belogorsk, *Russia*	51	D13
Belogradchik, *Bulgaria*	40	C6
Belogradets, *Bulgaria*	41	C11
Beloha, *Madag.*	89	D8
Beloit, *Kans., U.S.A.*	112	F5
Beloit, *Wis., U.S.A.*	112	D10
Belokorovichi, *Ukraine*	47	G5
Belomorsk, *Russia*	50	C4
Belonia, *India*	67	H17
Belopolye = Bilopillya, *Ukraine*	47	G8
Belorechensk, *Russia*	49	H4
Belorussia = Belarus ■, *Europe*	46	F4
Beloslav, *Bulgaria*	41	C11
Belovo, *Bulgaria*	41	D8
Belovo, *Russia*	50	D9
Belovodsk, *Ukraine*	47	H10
Beloye, Ozero, *Russia*	46	B9
Beloye More, *Russia*	50	C4
Belozem, *Bulgaria*	41	D9
Belozersk, *Russia*	46	B9
Belpasso, *Italy*	31	E7
Belpre, *U.S.A.*	108	F4
Belrain, *India*	69	E9
Belt, *U.S.A.*	114	C8
Beltana, *Australia*	95	E2
Belterra, *Brazil*	125	D8
Beltinci, *Slovenia*	29	B13
Belton, *U.S.A.*	113	K6
Belton L., *U.S.A.*	113	K6
Beltsy = Bălţi, *Moldova*	43	C12
Belturbet, *Ireland*	15	B4
Belukha, *Russia*	50	E9
Beluran, *Malaysia*	62	C5
Beluša, *Slovak Rep.*	27	B11
Belušić, *Serbia, Yug.*	40	C5
Belvedere Maríttimo, *Italy*	31	C8
Belvès, *France*	20	D5
Belvidere, *Ill., U.S.A.*	112	D10
Belvidere, *N.J., U.S.A.*	111	F9
Belvis de la Jara, *Spain*	34	F6
Belyando →, *Australia*	94	C4
Belyy, *Russia*	46	E7
Belyy, Ostrov, *Russia*	50	B8
Belyy Yar, *Russia*	50	D9
Bełżec, *Poland*	45	H10
Belzig, *Germany*	24	C8
Belzoni, *U.S.A.*	113	J9
Bełżyce, *Poland*	45	G9
Bemaraha, Lembalemban' i, *Madag.*	89	B7
Bemarivo, *Madag.*	89	C7
Bemarivo →, *Antsiranana, Madag.*	89	A9
Bemarivo →, *Mahajanga, Madag.*	89	C8
Bemavo, *Madag.*	89	C8
Bembéréke, *Benin*	83	C5
Bembesi, *Zimbabwe*	87	F2
Bembesi →, *Zimbabwe*	87	F2
Bembézar →, *Spain*	35	H5
Bembibre, *Spain*	34	C4
Bemetara, *India*	69	J9
Bemidji, *U.S.A.*	112	B7
Bemolanga, *Madag.*	89	B8
Ben, *Iran*	71	C6
Ben Cruachan, *U.K.*	14	E3
Ben Dearg, *U.K.*	14	D4
Ben Hope, *U.K.*	14	C4
Ben Lawers, *U.K.*	14	E4
Ben Lomond, *N.S.W., Australia*	95	E5
Ben Lomond, *Tas., Australia*	94	G4
Ben Lomond, *U.K.*	14	E4
Ben Luc, *Vietnam*	65	G6
Ben Macdhui, *U.K.*	14	D5
Ben Mhor, *U.K.*	14	D1
Ben More, *Arg. & Bute, U.K.*	14	E2
Ben More, *Stirl., U.K.*	14	E4
Ben More Assynt, *U.K.*	14	C4
Ben Nevis, *U.K.*	14	E3
Ben Quang, *Vietnam*	64	D6
Ben Vorlich, *U.K.*	14	E4
Ben Wyvis, *U.K.*	14	D4
Bena, *Nigeria*	83	C6
Benāb, *Iran*	73	D12
Benalla, *Australia*	95	F4
Benalmádena, *Spain*	35	J6
Benares = Varanasi, *India*	69	G10
Bénat, C., *France*	21	E10
Benavente, *Portugal*	35	G2
Benavente, *Spain*	34	C5
Benavides, *U.S.A.*	113	M5
Benavides de Órbigo, *Spain*	34	C5
Benbecula, *U.K.*	14	D1
Benbonyathe, *Australia*	95	E2

Bend, U.S.A. 114 D3
Bendemeer, Australia 95 E5
Bender Beila, Somali Rep. 74 F5
Bendery = Tighina, Moldova 43 D14
Bendigo, Australia 95 F3
Bendorf, Germany 24 E3
Benē Beraq, Israel 75 C3
Bénéna, Mali 82 C4
Benenitra, Madag. 89 C8
Benevento, Italy 31 A7
Benfeld, France 19 D14
Benga, Mozam. 87 F3
Bengal, Bay of, Ind. Oc. 67 M17
Bengbis, Cameroon 83 E7
Bengbu, China 57 H9
Benghazi = Banghāzī, Libya 79 B10
Bengkalis, Indonesia 62 D2
Bengkulu, Indonesia 62 E2
Bengkulu □, Indonesia 62 E2
Bengough, Canada 105 D7
Bengtsfors, Sweden 10 E6
Benguela, Angola 85 G2
Benguérua, I., Mozam. 89 C6
Benha, Egypt 80 H7
Beni,
Dem. Rep. of the Congo 86 B2
Beni →, Bolivia 124 F5
Beni Mazâr, Egypt 80 B3
Beni Mellal, Morocco 78 B4
Beni Suef, Egypt 80 J7
Beniah L., Canada 104 A6
Benicarló, Spain 32 E5
Benicássim, Spain 32 E5
Benicia, U.S.A. 116 G4
Benidorm, Spain 33 G4
Benin ■, Africa 83 D5
Benin →, Nigeria 83 D6
Benin, Bight of, W. Afr. 83 E5
Benin City, Nigeria 83 D6
Benisa, Spain 33 G5
Benitses, Greece 36 A3
Benjamin Aceval, Paraguay 126 A4
Benjamin Constant, Brazil 124 D4
Benjamin Hill, Mexico 118 A2
Benkelman, U.S.A. 112 E4
Benkovac, Croatia 29 D12
Bennett, Canada 104 B2
Bennett, L., Australia 92 D5
Bennetta, Ostrov, Russia 51 B15
Bennettsville, U.S.A. 109 H6
Bennichchāb, Mauritania 82 B1
Bennington, N.H., U.S.A. 111 D11
Bennington, Vt., U.S.A. 111 D11
Bénodet, France 18 E2
Benoni, S. Africa 89 D4
Benque Viejo, Belize 119 D7
Bensheim, Germany 25 F4
Benson, Ariz., U.S.A. 115 L8
Benson, Minn., U.S.A. 112 C7
Bent, Iran 71 E8
Benteng, Indonesia 63 F6
Bentinck I., Australia 94 B2
Bentiu, Sudan 81 F2
Bento Gonçalves, Brazil 127 B5
Benton, Ark., U.S.A. 113 H8
Benton, Calif., U.S.A. 116 H8
Benton, Ill., U.S.A. 112 G10
Benton, Pa., U.S.A. 111 E8
Benton Harbor, U.S.A. 108 D2
Bentonville, U.S.A. 113 G7
Bentu Liben, Ethiopia 81 F4
Bentung, Malaysia 65 L3
Benue □, Nigeria 83 D6
Benue →, Nigeria 83 D6
Benxi, China 57 D12
Beo, Indonesia 63 D7
Beograd, Serbia, Yug. 40 B4
Beoumi, Ivory C. 82 D3
Bepan Jiang →, China 58 E6
Beppu, Japan 55 H5
Beqaa Valley = Al Biqâ,
Lebanon 75 A5
Ber Mota, India 68 H3
Berach →, India 68 G6
Beraketa, Madag. 89 C7
Berane, Montenegro, Yug. 40 D3
Berat, Albania 40 F3
Berau, Teluk, Indonesia 63 E8
Beravina, Madag. 89 B8
Berber, Sudan 80 D3
Berbera, Somali Rep. 74 E4
Berbérati, C.A.R. 84 D3
Berbice →, Guyana 124 B7
Berceto, Italy 28 D6
Berchidda, Italy 30 B2
Berchtesgaden, Germany 25 H8
Berck, France 19 B8
Berdichev = Berdychiv,
Ukraine 47 H5
Berdsk, Russia 50 D9
Berdyansk, Ukraine 47 J9
Berdychiv, Ukraine 47 H5
Berea, U.S.A. 108 G3
Berebere, Indonesia 63 D7
Bereda, Somali Rep. 74 E5
Berehove, Ukraine 47 H2
Berekum, Ghana 82 D4
Berenice, Egypt 80 C4
Berens →, Canada 105 C9
Berens I., Canada 105 C9
Berens River, Canada 105 C9
Beresford, U.S.A. 112 D6
Berestechko, Ukraine 47 G3
Bereşti, Romania 43 D12
Beretău →, Romania 42 C6
Berettyó →, Hungary 42 C6
Berettyóújfalu, Hungary 42 C6
Berevo, Mahajanga, Madag. 89 B7
Berevo, Toliara, Madag. 89 B7
Bereza, Belarus 47 F3

Berezhany, Ukraine 47 H3
Berezina = Byarezina →,
Belarus 47 F6
Berezivka, Ukraine 47 J6
Berezna, Ukraine 47 G6
Berezniki, Russia 50 C5
Berezniki, Russia 50 D6
Berezovo, Russia 50 C7
Berga, Spain 32 C6
Berga, Sweden 11 G10
Bergama, Turkey 39 B9
Bérgamo, Italy 28 C6
Bergara, Spain 32 B2
Bergby, Sweden 10 D11
Bergedorf, Germany 24 B6
Bergeforsen, Sweden 10 B11
Bergen,
Mecklenburg-Vorpommern,
Germany 24 A9
Bergen, Niedersachsen,
Germany 24 C5
Bergen, Neths. 17 B4
Bergen, Norway 9 F11
Bergen op Zoom, Neths. 17 C4
Bergerac, France 20 D4
Bergheim, Germany 24 E2
Bergholz, U.S.A. 110 F4
Bergisch Gladbach, Germany 17 D7
Bergkamen, Germany 24 D3
Bergkvara, Sweden 11 H10
Bergshamra, Sweden 10 E12
Bergsjö, Sweden 10 C11
Bergues, France 19 B9
Bergviken, Sweden 10 C10
Bergville, S. Africa 89 D4
Berhala, Selat, Indonesia 62 E2
Berhampore = Baharampur,
India 69 G13
Berhampur = Brahmapur,
India 67 K14
Berheci →, Romania 43 E12
Bering Sea, Pac. Oc. 100 C1
Bering Strait, Pac. Oc. 100 B3
Beringovskiy, Russia 51 C18
Berisso, Argentina 126 C4
Berja, Spain 35 J8
Berkeley, U.S.A. 116 H4
Berkner I., Antarctica 5 D18
Berkovitsa, Bulgaria 40 C7
Berkshire, U.S.A. 111 D8
Berkshire Downs, U.K. 13 F6
Berlanga, Spain 35 G5
Berlenga, I., Portugal 35 F1
Berlin, Germany 24 C9
Berlin, Md., U.S.A. 108 F8
Berlin, N.H., U.S.A. 111 B13
Berlin, N.Y., U.S.A. 111 D11
Berlin, Wis., U.S.A. 108 D1
Berlin □, Germany 24 C9
Berlin L., U.S.A. 110 E4
Bermeja, Sierra, Spain 35 J5
Bermejo →, Formosa,
Argentina 126 B4
Bermejo →, San Juan,
Argentina 126 C2
Bermen, L., Canada 103 B6
Bermeo, Spain 32 B2
Bermillo de Sayago, Spain 34 D4
Bermuda ■, Atl. Oc. 98 F13
Bern, Switz. 25 J3
Bern □, Switz. 25 J3
Bernalda, Italy 31 B9
Bernalillo, U.S.A. 115 J10
Bernardo de Irigoyen,
Argentina 127 B5
Bernardo O'Higgins □, Chile 126 C1
Bernardsville, U.S.A. 111 F10
Bernasconi, Argentina 126 D3
Bernau, Bayern, Germany 25 H8
Bernau, Brandenburg,
Germany 24 C9
Bernay, France 18 C7
Bernburg, Germany 24 D7
Berndorf, Austria 26 D9
Berne = Bern, Switz. 25 J3
Berne = Bern □, Switz. 25 J3
Berneray, U.K. 14 D1
Bernier I., Australia 93 D1
Bernina, Piz, Switz. 25 J5
Bernkastel-Kues, Germany 25 F3
Beroroha, Madag. 89 C8
Béroubouay, Benin 83 C5
Beroun, Czech Rep. 26 B7
Berounka →, Czech Rep. 26 B7
Berovo, Macedonia 40 E6
Berre, Étang de, France 21 E9
Berre-l'Étang, France 21 E9
Berri, Australia 95 E3
Berriane, Algeria 78 B6
Berrigan, Australia 95 F4
Berry, Australia 95 E5
Berry, France 19 F8
Berry Is., Bahamas 120 A4
Berryessa L., U.S.A. 116 G4
Berryville, U.S.A. 113 G8
Berseba, Namibia 88 D2
Bersenbrück, Germany 24 C3
Bershad, Ukraine 47 H5
Berthold, U.S.A. 112 A4
Berthoud, U.S.A. 112 E2
Bertincourt, France 19 B9
Bertoua, Cameroon 84 D2
Bertraghboy B., Ireland 15 C2
Berwick, U.S.A. 111 E8
Berwick-upon-Tweed, U.K. 12 B6
Berwyn Mts., U.K. 12 E4
Beryslav, Ukraine 47 J7
Berzasca, Romania 42 F6
Berzence, Hungary 42 D2

Besal, Pakistan 69 B5
Besalampy, Madag. 89 B7
Besançon, France 19 E13
Besar, Indonesia 62 E5
Beshenkovichi, Belarus 46 E5
Beška, Serbia, Yug. 42 E5
Beslan, Russia 49 J7
Besna Kobila, Serbia, Yug. 40 D6
Besnard L., Canada 105 B7
Besni, Turkey 70 B3
Besor, N. →, Egypt 75 D3
Bessarabka = Basarabeasca,
Moldova 43 D13
Bessèges, France 21 D8
Bessemer, Ala., U.S.A. 109 J2
Bessemer, Mich., U.S.A. 112 B9
Bessemer, Pa., U.S.A. 110 F4
Bessin, France 18 C6
Bessines-sur-Gartempe,
France 20 B5
Bet She'an, Israel 75 C4
Bet Shemesh, Israel 75 D4
Betafo, Madag. 89 B8
Betancuria, Canary Is. 37 F5
Betanzos, Spain 34 B2
Bétaré Oya, Cameroon 84 C2
Betatao, Madag. 89 B8
Bétera, Spain 33 F4
Bethal, S. Africa 89 D4
Bethanien, Namibia 88 D2
Bethany, Canada 110 B6
Bethany, U.S.A. 112 E7
Bethel, Alaska, U.S.A. 100 B3
Bethel, Conn., U.S.A. 111 E11
Bethel, Maine, U.S.A. 111 B14
Bethel, Vt., U.S.A. 111 C12
Bethel Park, U.S.A. 110 F4
Béthenville, France 19 C11
Bethlehem = Bayt Lahm,
West Bank 75 D4
Bethlehem, S. Africa 89 D4
Bethlehem, U.S.A. 111 F9
Bethulie, S. Africa 88 E4
Béthune, France 19 B9
Béthune →, France 18 C8
Betioky, Madag. 89 C7
Betong, Thailand 65 K3
Betoota, Australia 94 D3
Betor, Ethiopia 81 E4
Betroka, Madag. 89 C8
Betsiamites, Canada 103 C6
Betsiamites →, Canada 103 C6
Betsiboka →, Madag. 89 B8
Bettendorf, U.S.A. 112 E9
Bettiah, India 69 F11
Bettna, Sweden 11 F10
Béttola, Italy 28 D6
Betul, India 66 J10
Betung, Malaysia 62 D4
Betws-y-Coed, U.K. 12 D4
Betxi, Spain 32 F4
Betzdorf, Germany 24 E3
Beulah, Mich., U.S.A. 108 C2
Beulah, N. Dak., U.S.A. 112 B4
Beuvron →, France 18 E8
Beveren, Belgium 17 C4
Beverley, Australia 93 F2
Beverley, U.K. 12 D7
Beverley Hills, U.S.A. 109 L4
Beverly, U.S.A. 111 D14
Beverly Hills, U.S.A. 117 L8
Beverungen, Germany 24 D5
Bevoalavo, Madag. 89 D7
Bewas →, India 69 H8
Bex, Switz. 25 J3
Bexhill, U.K. 13 G8
Bey Dağları, Turkey 39 E12
Beyânlü, Iran 70 C5
Beyazköy, Turkey 41 E11
Beyçayırı, Turkey 41 F10
Beydağ, Turkey 39 C10
Beyeğaç, Turkey 39 D10
Beyin, Ghana 82 D4
Beykoz, Turkey 41 E13
Beyla, Guinea 82 D3
Beynat, France 20 C5
Beyneu, Kazakstan 50 E6
Beyoba, Turkey 39 C9
Beyoğlu, Turkey 41 E12
Beypazarı, Turkey 72 B4
Beyşehir, Turkey 72 D4
Beyşehir Gölü, Turkey 70 B1
Beytüşşebap, Turkey 73 D10
Bezdan, Serbia, Yug. 42 E3
Bezhetsk, Russia 46 D9
Béziers, France 20 E7
Bezwada = Vijayawada,
India 67 L12
Bhabua, India 69 G10
Bhachau, India 66 H7
Bhadar →, Gujarat, India 68 H5
Bhadar →, Gujarat, India 68 J3
Bhadarwah, India 69 C6
Bhadohi, India 69 G10
Bhadra, India 68 E6
Bhadrakh, India 67 J15
Bhadran, India 68 H5
Bhadravati, India 66 N9
Bhag, Pakistan 68 E2
Bhagalpur, India 69 G12
Bhagirathi →, Ut. P., India 69 D8
Bhagirathi →, W. Bengal,
India 69 H13
Bhakkar, Pakistan 68 D4
Bhakra Dam, India 68 D7
Bhamo, Burma 67 G20
Bhandara, India 66 J11

Bhanpura, India 68 G6
Bhanrer Ra., India 69 H8
Bhaptiali, India 69 F12
Bharat = India ■, Asia 66 K11
Bharatpur, Mad. P., India 69 H9
Bharatpur, Raj., India 68 F7
Bharno, India 69 H11
Bhatinda, India 68 D6
Bhatpara, India 69 H13
Bhaun, Pakistan 68 C5
Bhaunagar = Bhavnagar,
India 66 J8
Bhavnagar, India 66 J8
Bhawanipatna, India 67 K12
Bhawari, India 68 G5
Bhayavadar, India 68 J4
Bhera, Pakistan 68 C5
Bhikangaon, India 68 J6
Bhilsa = Vidisha, India 68 H7
Bhilwara, India 68 G6
Bhima →, India 66 L10
Bhimavaram, India 67 L12
Bhimbar, Pakistan 69 C6
Bhind, India 69 F8
Bhinga, India 69 F9
Bhinmal, India 68 G5
Bhiwandi, India 66 K8
Bhiwani, India 68 E7
Bhogava →, India 68 H5
Bhola, Bangla. 67 H17
Bholari, Pakistan 68 G3
Bhopal, India 68 H7
Bhubaneshwar, India 67 J14
Bhuj, India 68 H3
Bhusaval, India 66 J9
Bhutan ■, Asia 67 F17
Biafra, B. of = Bonny, Bight
of, Africa 83 E6
Biak, Indonesia 63 E9
Biała, Poland 45 H4
Biała →, Poland 45 H7
Biała Piska, Poland 44 E9
Biała Podlaska, Poland 45 F10
Biała Rawska, Poland 45 G7
Białobrzegi, Poland 45 G7
Białogard, Poland 44 D2
Białowieża, Poland 45 F10
Biały Bór, Poland 44 E3
Białystok, Poland 45 E10
Biancavilla, Italy 31 E7
Bianco, Italy 31 D9
Biankouma, Ivory C. 82 D3
Biaora, India 68 H7
Biǎrjmand, Iran 71 B7
Biaro, Indonesia 63 D7
Biarritz, France 20 E2
Biasca, Switz. 25 J4
Biba, Egypt 80 J7
Bibai, Japan 54 C10
Bibbiena, Italy 29 E8
Bibby I., Canada 105 A10
Bibel, Spain 34 C3
Biberach, Germany 25 G5
Bibiani, Ghana 82 D4
Bibungwa,
Dem. Rep. of the Congo 86 C2
Bic, Canada 103 C6
Bicaj, Albania 40 E4
Bicaz, Romania 43 D11
Bicazu Ardelean, Romania 43 D10
Bíccari, Italy 31 A8
Bicester, U.K. 13 F6
Bichena, Ethiopia 81 E4
Bicheno, Australia 94 G4
Bichia, India 69 H9
Bichvinta, Georgia 49 J5
Bickerton I., Australia 94 A2
Bicske, Hungary 42 C3
Bida, Nigeria 83 D6
Bidar, India 66 L10
Biddeford, U.S.A. 109 D10
Biddwara, Ethiopia 81 F4
Bideford, U.K. 13 F3
Bideford Bay, U.K. 13 F3
Bidhuna, India 69 F8
Bidor, Malaysia 65 K3
Bie, Sweden 10 E10
Bié, Planalto de, Angola 85 G3
Bieber, U.S.A. 114 F3
Biebrza →, Poland 45 E9
Biecz, Poland 45 J8
Biel, Switz. 25 H3
Bielawa, Poland 45 H3
Bielefeld, Germany 24 C4
Bielersee, Switz. 25 H3
Biella, Italy 28 C5
Bielsk Podlaski, Poland 45 F10
Bielsko-Biała, Poland 45 J6
Bien Hoa, Vietnam 65 G6
Bienne = Biel, Switz. 25 H3
Bienvenida, Spain 35 G4
Bienville, L., Canada 102 A5
Bierné, France 18 E6
Bierun, Poland 45 H6
Bierutów, Poland 45 G4
Biescas, Spain 32 C4
Biese →, Germany 24 C7
Biesiesfontein, S. Africa 88 E2
Bietigheim-Bissingen,
Germany 25 G5
Biezuń, Poland 45 F6
Biferno →, Italy 29 G12
Big →, Canada 103 B8
Big →, U.S.A. 103 A7
Big Bear City, U.S.A. 117 L10
Big Bear Lake, U.S.A. 117 L10
Big Belt Mts., U.S.A. 114 C8
Big Bend, Swaziland 89 D5
Big Bend National Park,
U.S.A. 113 L3

Big Black →, U.S.A. 113 K9
Big Blue →, U.S.A. 112 F6
Big Creek, U.S.A. 116 H7
Big Cypress National
Preserve, U.S.A. 109 M5
Big Cypress Swamp, U.S.A. 109 M5
Big Falls, U.S.A. 112 A8
Big Fork →, U.S.A. 112 A8
Big Horn Mts. = Bighorn
Mts., U.S.A. 114 D10
Big I., Canada 104 A5
Big Lake, U.S.A. 113 K4
Big Moose, U.S.A. 111 C10
Big Muddy Cr. →, U.S.A. 112 A2
Big Pine, U.S.A. 116 H8
Big Piney, U.S.A. 114 E8
Big Rapids, U.S.A. 108 D3
Big Rideau L., Canada 111 B8
Big River, Canada 105 C7
Big Run, U.S.A. 110 F6
Big Sable Pt., U.S.A. 108 C2
Big Salmon →, Canada 104 A2
Big Sand L., Canada 105 B9
Big Sandy, U.S.A. 114 B8
Big Sandy →, U.S.A. 108 F4
Big Sandy Cr. →, U.S.A. 112 F3
Big Sioux →, U.S.A. 112 D6
Big Spring, U.S.A. 113 J4
Big Stone City, U.S.A. 112 C6
Big Stone Gap, U.S.A. 109 G4
Big Stone L., U.S.A. 112 C6
Big Sur, U.S.A. 116 J5
Big Timber, U.S.A. 114 D9
Big Trout L., Canada 102 B2
Big Trout Lake, Canada 102 B2
Biga, Turkey 41 F11
Biga, Turkey 41 F11
Bigadiç, Turkey 39 B10
Biganos, France 20 D3
Biggar, Canada 105 C7
Biggar, U.K. 14 F5
Bigge I., Australia 92 B4
Biggenden, Australia 95 D5
Biggleswade, U.K. 13 E7
Biggs, U.S.A. 116 F5
Bighorn, U.S.A. 114 C10
Bighorn →, U.S.A. 114 C10
Bighorn L., U.S.A. 114 D9
Bighorn Mts., U.S.A. 114 D10
Bignona, Senegal 82 C1
Bigorre, France 20 E4
Bigstone L., Canada 105 C9
Biguglia, Étang de, France 21 F13
Bigwa, Tanzania 86 D4
Bihać, Bos.-H. 29 D12
Bihar, India 69 G11
Bihar □, India 69 G12
Biharamulo, Tanzania 86 C3
Bihariganj, India 69 G12
Biharkeresztes, Hungary 42 C6
Bihor □, Romania 42 D7
Bihor, Munții, Romania 42 D7
Bijagós, Arquipélago dos,
Guinea-Biss. 82 C1
Bijainagar, India 68 G6
Bijapur, Karnataka, India 66 L9
Bijapur, Mad. P., India 67 K12
Bījār, Iran 70 C5
Bijawar, India 69 G8
Bijeljina, Bos.-H. 42 F4
Bijelo Polje,
Montenegro, Yug. 40 C3
Bijie, China 58 D5
Bijnor, India 68 E8
Bikaner, India 68 E5
Bikapur, India 69 F10
Bikeqi, China 56 D6
Bikfayyā, Lebanon 75 B4
Bikin, Russia 51 E14
Bikin →, Russia 54 A7
Bikini Atoll, Marshall Is. 96 F8
Bikita, Zimbabwe 89 C5
Bikoué, Cameroon 83 E7
Bila Tserkva, Ukraine 47 H6
Bilanga, Burkina Faso 83 C4
Bilara, India 68 F5
Bilaspur, Mad. P., India 69 H10
Bilaspur, Punjab, India 68 D7
Biläsuvar, Azerbaijan 73 C13
Bilauk Taungdan, Thailand 64 F2
Bilbao, Spain 32 B2
Bilbeis, Egypt 80 H7
Bilbo = Bilbao, Spain 32 B2
Bilbor, Romania 43 C10
Bilciurești, Romania 43 F10
Bíldudalur, Iceland 8 D2
Bílé Karpaty, Europe 27 B11
Bileća, Bos.-H. 40 D2
Bilecik, Turkey 72 B4
Bilgoraj, Poland 45 H9
Bilgram, India 69 F9
Bilhaur, India 69 F9
Bilhorod-Dnistrovskyy,
Ukraine 47 J6
Bilibino, Russia 51 C17
Biliba, Mozam. 87 E5
Bilishti, Albania 40 F5
Billabalong Roadhouse,
Australia 93 E2
Billdal, Sweden 11 G5
Billiluna, Australia 92 C4
Billings, U.S.A. 114 D9
Billiton Is. = Belitung,
Indonesia 62 E3
Billsta, Sweden 10 A12
Billund, Denmark 11 J3
Bilma, Niger 79 E8
Bilo Gora, Croatia 42 E2
Biloela, Australia 94 C5
Bilohirsk, Ukraine 47 K8
Bilopillya, Ukraine 47 G8

Biloxi, *U.S.A.*	113	K10
Bilpa Morea Claypan, *Australia*	94	D3
Biltine, *Chad*	79	F10
Bilyarsk, *Russia*	48	C10
Bima, *Indonesia*	63	F5
Bimban, *Egypt*	80	C3
Bimbila, *Ghana*	83	D5
Bimini Is., *Bahamas*	120	A4
Bin Xian, *Heilongjiang, China*	57	B14
Bin Xian, *Shaanxi, China*	56	G5
Bin Yauri, *Nigeria*	83	C5
Bina-Etawah, *India*	68	G8
Bināb, *Iran*	71	B6
Binalbagan, *Phil.*	61	F5
Binalong, *Australia*	95	E4
Bīnālūd, Kūh-e, *Iran*	71	B8
Binatang = Bintangor, *Malaysia*	62	D4
Binche, *Belgium*	17	D4
Binchuan, *China*	58	E3
Binder, *Chad*	83	D7
Bindki, *India*	69	F9
Bindslev, *Denmark*	11	G4
Bindura, *Zimbabwe*	87	F3
Binefar, *Spain*	32	D5
Bingara, *Australia*	95	D5
Bingen, *Germany*	25	F3
Bingerville, *Ivory C.*	82	D4
Bingham, *U.S.A.*	109	C11
Binghamton, *U.S.A.*	111	D9
Bingöl, *Turkey*	70	B4
Bingöl Dağları, *Turkey*	73	C9
Bingsjö, *Sweden*	10	C9
Binh Dinh = An Nhon, *Vietnam*	64	F7
Binh Khe, *Vietnam*	64	F7
Binh Son, *Vietnam*	64	E7
Binhai, *China*	57	G10
Binic, *France*	18	D4
Binisatua, *Spain*	37	B11
Binjai, *Indonesia*	62	D3
Binji, *Nigeria*	83	C5
Binnaway, *Australia*	95	E4
Binongko, *Indonesia*	63	F6
Binscarth, *Canada*	105	C8
Bint Goda, *Sudan*	81	E3
Bintan, *Indonesia*	62	D2
Bintangor, *Malaysia*	62	D4
Bintulu, *Malaysia*	62	D4
Bintuni, *Indonesia*	63	E8
Binyang, *China*	58	F7
Binz, *Germany*	24	A9
Binzert = Bizerte, *Tunisia*	79	A7
Binzhou, *China*	57	F10
Bío Bío □, *Chile*	126	D1
Biograd na Moru, *Croatia*	29	E12
Bioko, *Eq. Guin.*	83	E6
Biokovo, *Croatia*	29	E14
Bipindi, *Cameroon*	83	E7
Bir, *India*	66	K9
Bir, Ras, *Djibouti*	81	E5
Bîr Abu Hashim, *Egypt*	80	C3
Bîr Abu Minqar, *Egypt*	80	B2
Bîr Abu Muḥammad, *Egypt*	75	F3
Bi'r ad Dabbāghāt, *Jordan*	75	E4
Bi'r al Butayyihāt, *Jordan*	75	F4
Bi'r al Mārī, *Jordan*	75	E4
Bi'r al Qattār, *Jordan*	75	F4
Bîr 'Asal, *Egypt*	80	B3
Bir Atrun, *Sudan*	80	D2
Bîr Beiḍa, *Egypt*	75	E3
Bîr Diqnash, *Egypt*	80	A2
Bîr el 'Abd, *Egypt*	75	D2
Bîr el Basur, *Egypt*	80	B2
Bîr el Biarât, *Egypt*	75	F3
Bîr el Duweidar, *Egypt*	75	E1
Bîr el Garârât, *Egypt*	75	D2
Bîr el Gellaz, *Egypt*	80	A2
Bîr el Heisi, *Egypt*	75	F3
Bîr el Jafir, *Egypt*	75	E1
Bîr el Mâlḥi, *Egypt*	75	E2
Bîr el Shaqqa, *Egypt*	80	A2
Bîr el Thamâda, *Egypt*	75	E2
Bîr Fuad, *Egypt*	80	A2
Bîr Gebeil Ḥişn, *Egypt*	75	E2
Bi'r Ghadīr, *Syria*	75	A4
Bîr Haimur, *Egypt*	80	C3
Bîr Ḥasana, *Egypt*	75	E2
Bîr Ḥôōker, *Egypt*	80	H7
Bîr Kanayis, *Egypt*	80	C3
Bîr Kaseiba, *Egypt*	75	E2
Bîr Kerawein, *Egypt*	80	B2
Bîr Lahfân, *Egypt*	75	E2
Bîr Madkûr, *Egypt*	75	E1
Bîr Maql, *Egypt*	80	C3
Bîr Mîneiga, *Sudan*	80	C4
Bîr Misaha, *Egypt*	80	C2
Bîr Mogreïn, *Mauritania*	78	C3
Bîr Murr, *Egypt*	80	C3
Bi'r Muṭribah, *Kuwait*	70	D5
Bîr Nakheila, *Egypt*	80	C3
Bîr Qaţia, *Egypt*	75	E1
Bîr Qatrani, *Egypt*	80	A2
Bîr Ranga, *Egypt*	80	C4
Bîr Sahara, *Egypt*	80	C2
Bîr Seiyâla, *Egypt*	80	B3
Bîr Shalatein, *Egypt*	80	C4
Bîr Shebb, *Egypt*	80	C2
Bîr Shût, *Egypt*	80	C2
Bîr Terfawi, *Egypt*	80	C2
Bîr Umm Qubûr, *Egypt*	80	C3
Bîr Ungât, *Egypt*	80	C3
Bîr Za'farâna, *Egypt*	80	J8
Bîr Zeidûn, *Egypt*	80	B3
Biramféro, *Guinea*	82	C3
Biratnagar, *Nepal*	69	F12
Birawa, *Dem. Rep. of the Congo*	86	C2

Birch →, *Canada*	104	B6
Birch Hills, *Canada*	105	C7
Birch I., *Canada*	105	C9
Birch L., *N.W.T., Canada*	104	A5
Birch L., *Ont., Canada*	102	B1
Birch Mts., *Canada*	104	B6
Birch River, *Canada*	105	C8
Birchip, *Australia*	95	F3
Birchiş, *Romania*	42	E7
Bird, *Canada*	105	B10
Bird I. = Las Aves, Is., *W. Indies*	121	C7
Birdsville, *Australia*	94	D2
Birdum Cr., *Australia*	92	C5
Birecik, *Turkey*	70	B3
Birein, *Israel*	75	E3
Bireuen, *Indonesia*	62	C1
Biri →, *Sudan*	81	F2
Birifo, *Gambia*	82	C2
Birigui, *Brazil*	127	A5
Birjand, *Iran*	71	C8
Birkenfeld, *Germany*	25	F3
Birkenhead, *U.K.*	12	D4
Birkerød, *Denmark*	11	J6
Birket Qârûn, *Egypt*	80	J7
Birkfeld, *Austria*	26	D8
Bîrlad = Bârlad, *Romania*	43	D12
Birmingham, *U.K.*	13	E6
Birmingham, *U.S.A.*	109	J2
Birmitrapur, *India*	67	H14
Birni Ngaouré, *Niger*	83	C5
Birni Nkonni, *Niger*	83	C6
Birnin Gwari, *Nigeria*	83	C6
Birnin Kebbi, *Nigeria*	83	C5
Birnin Kudu, *Nigeria*	83	C6
Birobidzhan, *Russia*	51	E14
Birr, *Ireland*	15	C4
Birrie →, *Australia*	95	D4
Birsilpur, *India*	68	E5
Birsk, *Russia*	50	D6
Birštonas, *Lithuania*	44	D11
Birtle, *Canada*	105	C8
Birur, *India*	66	N9
Biryuchiy, *Ukraine*	47	J8
Biržai, *Lithuania*	9	H21
Birzebbugga, *Malta*	36	D2
Bisa, *Indonesia*	63	E7
Bisáccia, *Italy*	31	A8
Bisacquino, *Italy*	30	E6
Bisalpur, *India*	69	E8
Bisbee, *U.S.A.*	115	L9
Biscarrosse, *France*	20	D2
Biscarrosse et de Parentis, Étang de, *France*	20	D2
Biscay, B. of, *Atl. Oc.*	6	F5
Biscayne B., *U.S.A.*	109	N5
Biscéglie, *Italy*	31	A9
Bischheim, *France*	19	D14
Bischofshofen, *Austria*	26	D6
Bischofswerda, *Germany*	24	D10
Bischwiller, *France*	19	D14
Biscoe Bay, *Antarctica*	5	D13
Biscoe Is., *Antarctica*	5	C17
Biscostasing, *Canada*	102	C3
Biševo, *Croatia*	29	F13
Bisha, *Eritrea*	81	D4
Bishah, W. →, *Si. Arabia*	80	C5
Bishan, *China*	58	C6
Bishkek, *Kyrgyzstan*	50	E8
Bishnupur, *India*	69	H12
Bisho, *S. Africa*	89	E4
Bishop, Calif., *U.S.A.*	116	H8
Bishop, Tex., *U.S.A.*	113	M6
Bishop Auckland, *U.K.*	12	C6
Bishop's Falls, *Canada*	103	C8
Bishop's Stortford, *U.K.*	13	F8
Bisignano, *Italy*	31	C9
Bisina, L., *Uganda*	86	B3
Biskra, *Algeria*	78	B7
Biskupiec, *Poland*	44	E7
Bismarck, *U.S.A.*	112	B4
Bismarck Arch., *Papua N. G.*	96	H7
Bismark, *Germany*	24	C7
Bismil, *Turkey*	73	D9
Biso, *Uganda*	86	B3
Bison, *U.S.A.*	112	C3
Bīsotūn, *Iran*	70	C5
Bispgården, *Sweden*	10	A10
Bissagos = Bijagós, Arquipélago dos, Guinea-Biss.	82	C1
Bissau, *Guinea-Biss.*	82	C1
Bissaula, *Nigeria*	83	D7
Bissikrima, *Guinea*	82	C2
Bissorã, *Guinea-Biss.*	82	C1
Bistcho L., *Canada*	104	B5
Bistreţ, *Romania*	43	G8
Bistrica = Ilirska-Bistrica, *Slovenia*	29	C11
Bistriţa, *Romania*	43	C9
Bistriţa →, *Romania*	43	D11
Bistriţa Năsăud □, *Romania*	43	C9
Bistriţei, Munţii, *Romania*	43	C10
Biswan, *India*	69	F9
Bisztynek, *Poland*	44	D7
Bitburg, *Germany*	25	F2
Bitche, *France*	19	C14
Bithynia, *Turkey*	72	B4
Bitlis, *Turkey*	70	B4
Bitola, *Macedonia*	40	E5
Bitolj = Bitola, *Macedonia*	40	E5
Bitonto, *Italy*	31	A9
Bitter Creek, *U.S.A.*	114	F9
Bitter L. = Buheirat-Murrat-el-Kubra, *Egypt*	80	H8
Bitterfeld, *Germany*	24	D8
Bitterfontein, *S. Africa*	88	E2
Bitterroot →, *U.S.A.*	114	C6
Bitterroot Range, *U.S.A.*	114	D6
Bitterwater, *U.S.A.*	116	J6

Bitti, *Italy*	30	B2
Bittou, *Burkina Faso*	83	C4
Biu, *Nigeria*	83	C7
Bivolari, *Romania*	43	C12
Bivolu, Vf., *Romania*	43	C10
Biwa-Ko, *Japan*	55	G8
Biwabik, *U.S.A.*	112	B8
Bixad, *Romania*	43	C8
Bixby, *U.S.A.*	113	H7
Biyang, *China*	56	H7
Biysk, *Russia*	50	D9
Bizana, *S. Africa*	89	E4
Bizen, *Japan*	55	G7
Bizerte, *Tunisia*	79	A7
Bjargtangar, *Iceland*	8	D1
Bjärnum, *Sweden*	11	H7
Bjästa, *Sweden*	10	A12
Bjelasica, *Montenegro, Yug.*	40	D3
Bjelašnica, *Bos.-H.*	42	G3
Bjelovar, *Croatia*	29	C13
Bjerringbro, *Denmark*	11	H3
Björbo, *Sweden*	10	D8
Björneborg, *Sweden*	10	D11
Bjørneborg, *Sweden*	10	E8
Bjørnevatn, *Norway*	8	B23
Bjørnøya, *Arctic*	4	B8
Bjursås, *Sweden*	10	D9
Bjuv, *Sweden*	11	H6
Bla, *Mali*	82	C3
Blace, *Serbia, Yug.*	40	C5
Blachownia, *Poland*	45	H5
Black = Da →, *Vietnam*	58	G5
Black →, *Canada*	110	B5
Black →, *Ariz., U.S.A.*	115	K8
Black →, *Ark., U.S.A.*	113	H9
Black →, *Mich., U.S.A.*	110	D2
Black →, *N.Y., U.S.A.*	111	C8
Black →, *Wis., U.S.A.*	112	D9
Black Bay Pen., *Canada*	102	C2
Black Birch L., *Canada*	105	B7
Black Diamond, *Canada*	104	C6
Black Duck →, *Canada*	102	A2
Black Forest = Schwarzwald, *Germany*	25	G4
Black Forest, *U.S.A.*	112	F2
Black Hd., *Ireland*	15	C2
Black Hills, *U.S.A.*	112	D3
Black I., *Canada*	105	C9
Black L., *Canada*	105	B7
Black L., *Mich., U.S.A.*	108	C3
Black L., *N.Y., U.S.A.*	111	B9
Black Lake, *Canada*	105	B7
Black Mesa, *U.S.A.*	113	G3
Black Mt. = Mynydd Du, *U.K.*	13	F4
Black Mts., *U.K.*	13	F4
Black Range, *U.S.A.*	115	K10
Black River, *Jamaica*	120	C4
Black River Falls, *U.S.A.*	112	C9
Black Sea, *Eurasia*	6	G12
Black Tickle, *Canada*	103	B8
Black Volta →, *Africa*	82	D4
Black Warrior →, *U.S.A.*	109	J2
Blackall, *Australia*	94	C4
Blackball, *N.Z.*	91	K3
Blackbull, *Australia*	94	B3
Blackburn, *U.K.*	12	D5
Blackburn with Darwen □, *U.K.*	12	D5
Blackfoot, *U.S.A.*	114	E7
Blackfoot →, *U.S.A.*	114	C7
Blackfoot River Reservoir, *U.S.A.*	114	E8
Blackie, *Canada*	104	C6
Blackpool, *U.K.*	12	D4
Blackpool □, *U.K.*	12	D4
Blackriver, *U.S.A.*	110	B1
Blacks Harbour, *Canada*	103	C6
Blacksburg, *U.S.A.*	108	G5
Blacksod B., *Ireland*	15	B1
Blackstone, *U.S.A.*	108	G7
Blackstone Ra., *Australia*	93	E4
Blackwater, *Australia*	94	C4
Blackwater →, *Meath, Ireland*	15	C4
Blackwater →, *Waterford, Ireland*	15	D4
Blackwater →, *U.K.*	15	B5
Blackwell, *U.S.A.*	113	G6
Blackwells Corner, *U.S.A.*	117	K7
Blaenau Ffestiniog, *U.K.*	12	E4
Blaenau Gwent □, *U.K.*	13	F4
Blagaj, *Bos.-H.*	40	C1
Blagnac, *France*	20	E5
Blagodarnoye = Blagodarnyy, *Russia*	49	H6
Blagodarnyy, *Russia*	49	H6
Blagoevgrad, *Bulgaria*	40	D7
Blagoveshchensk, *Russia*	51	D13
Blain, *France*	18	E5
Blain, *U.S.A.*	110	F7
Blaine, Minn., *U.S.A.*	112	C8
Blaine, Wash., *U.S.A.*	116	B4
Blaine Lake, *Canada*	105	C7
Blair, *U.S.A.*	112	E6
Blair Athol, *Australia*	94	C4
Blair Atholl, *U.K.*	14	E5
Blairgowrie, *U.K.*	14	E5
Blairsden, *U.S.A.*	116	F6
Blairsville, *U.S.A.*	110	F5
Blaj, *Romania*	43	D8
Blake Pt., *U.S.A.*	112	A3
Blakely, Ga., *U.S.A.*	109	K3
Blakely, Pa., *U.S.A.*	111	E9
Blâmont, *France*	19	D13
Blanc, C., *Spain*	37	B9
Blanc, Mont, *Alps*	21	C10
Blanca, B., *Argentina*	122	D4
Blanca Peak, *U.S.A.*	115	H11
Blanche, C., *Australia*	95	E1

Blanche, L., *S. Austral., Australia*	95	D2
Blanche, L., *W. Austral., Australia*	92	D3
Blanco, *S. Africa*	88	E3
Blanco, *U.S.A.*	113	K5
Blanco →, *Argentina*	126	C2
Blanco, C., *Costa Rica*	120	E2
Blanco, C., *U.S.A.*	114	E1
Blanda →, *Iceland*	8	D3
Blandford Forum, *U.K.*	13	G5
Blanding, *U.S.A.*	115	H9
Blanes, *Spain*	32	D7
Blangy-sur-Bresle, *France*	19	C8
Blanice →, *Czech Rep.*	26	B7
Blankaholm, *Sweden*	11	G10
Blankenberge, *Belgium*	17	C3
Blankenburg, *Germany*	24	D6
Blanquefort, *France*	20	D3
Blanquilla, I., *Venezuela*	121	D7
Blanquillo, *Uruguay*	127	C4
Blansko, *Czech Rep.*	27	B9
Blantyre, *Malawi*	87	F4
Blarney, *Ireland*	15	E3
Blasdell, *U.S.A.*	110	D6
Błaszki, *Poland*	45	G5
Blatná, *Czech Rep.*	26	B6
Blato, *Croatia*	29	F13
Blaubeuren, *Germany*	25	G5
Blaustein, *Germany*	25	G5
Blåvands Huk, *Denmark*	11	J2
Blaydon, *U.K.*	12	C6
Blaye, *France*	20	C3
Blaye-les-Mines, *France*	20	D6
Blayney, *Australia*	95	E4
Blaze, Pt., *Australia*	92	B5
Błażowa, *Poland*	45	J9
Bleckede, *Germany*	24	B6
Bled, *Slovenia*	29	B11
Bleiburg, *Austria*	26	E7
Blejeşti, *Romania*	43	F10
Blekinge, *Sweden*	9	H16
Blekinge län □, *Sweden*	11	H9
Blenheim, *Canada*	110	D3
Blenheim, *N.Z.*	91	J4
Bléone →, *France*	21	D10
Blérancourt, *France*	19	C10
Bletchley, *U.K.*	13	F7
Blida, *Algeria*	78	A6
Blidö, *Sweden*	10	E12
Blidsberg, *Sweden*	11	G7
Bligh Sound, *N.Z.*	91	L1
Blind River, *Canada*	102	C3
Blinisht, *Albania*	40	E3
Bliss, Idaho, *U.S.A.*	114	E6
Bliss, N.Y., *U.S.A.*	110	D6
Blissfield, *U.S.A.*	110	F3
Blitar, *Indonesia*	63	H15
Blitta, *Togo*	83	D5
Block I., *U.S.A.*	111	E13
Block Island Sd., *U.S.A.*	111	E13
Blodgett Iceberg Tongue, *Antarctica*	5	C9
Bloemfontein, *S. Africa*	88	D4
Bloemhof, *S. Africa*	88	D4
Blois, *France*	18	E8
Blomskog, *Sweden*	10	E6
Blomstermåla, *Sweden*	11	H10
Blönduós, *Iceland*	8	D3
Blonie, *Poland*	45	F7
Bloodvein →, *Canada*	105	C9
Bloody Foreland, *Ireland*	15	A3
Bloomer, *U.S.A.*	112	C9
Bloomfield, *Canada*	110	C7
Bloomfield, Iowa, *U.S.A.*	112	E8
Bloomfield, N. Mex., *U.S.A.*	115	H10
Bloomfield, Nebr., *U.S.A.*	112	D6
Bloomington, Ill., *U.S.A.*	112	E10
Bloomington, Ind., *U.S.A.*	108	F2
Bloomington, Minn., *U.S.A.*	112	C8
Bloomsburg, *U.S.A.*	111	F8
Blora, *Indonesia*	63	G14
Blossburg, *U.S.A.*	110	E7
Blouberg, *S. Africa*	89	C4
Blountstown, *U.S.A.*	109	K3
Bludenz, *Austria*	26	D2
Blue Earth, *U.S.A.*	112	D8
Blue Mesa Reservoir, *U.S.A.*	115	G10
Blue Mountain Lake, *U.S.A.*	111	C10
Blue Mts., Maine, *U.S.A.*	111	B14
Blue Mts., Oreg., *U.S.A.*	114	D4
Blue Mts., Pa., *U.S.A.*	111	F8
Blue Mud B., *Australia*	94	A2
Blue Nile = Nîl el Azraq →, *Sudan*	81	D3
Blue Rapids, *U.S.A.*	112	F6
Blue Ridge Mts., *U.S.A.*	109	G5
Blue River, *Canada*	104	C5
Bluefield, *U.S.A.*	108	G5
Bluefields, *Nic.*	120	D3
Bluff, *Australia*	94	C4
Bluff, N.Z.	91	M2
Bluff, *U.S.A.*	115	H9
Bluff Knoll, *Australia*	93	F2
Bluff Pt., *Australia*	93	E1
Bluffton, *U.S.A.*	108	E3
Blumenau, *Brazil*	127	B6
Blunt, *U.S.A.*	112	C5
Bly, *U.S.A.*	114	E3
Blyth, *Canada*	110	C3
Blyth, *U.K.*	12	B6
Blythe, *U.S.A.*	117	M12
Blytheville, *U.S.A.*	113	H10

Bo'ai, *China*	56	G7
Boal, *Spain*	34	B4
Boalsburg, *U.S.A.*	110	F7
Boane, *Mozam.*	89	D5
Boardman, *U.S.A.*	110	E4
Bobadah, *Australia*	95	E4
Bobai, *China*	58	F7
Bobbili, *India*	67	K13
Bóbbio, *Italy*	28	C6
Bobcaygeon, *Canada*	102	D4
Bobo-Dioulasso, *Burkina Faso*	82	C4
Bobolice, *Poland*	44	E3
Boboshevo, *Bulgaria*	40	D7
Bobov Dol, *Bulgaria*	40	D6
Bóbr →, *Poland*	45	F2
Bobraomby, Tanjon' i, *Madag.*	89	A8
Bobrinets, *Ukraine*	47	H7
Bobrov, *Russia*	48	E5
Bobrovitsa, *Ukraine*	47	G6
Bobruysk = Babruysk, *Belarus*	47	F5
Boby, Pic, *Madag.*	85	J9
Bôca do Acre, *Brazil*	124	E5
Boca Raton, *U.S.A.*	109	M5
Bocanda, *Ivory C.*	82	D4
Bocas del Toro, *Panama*	120	E3
Boceguillas, *Spain*	34	D7
Bochnia, *Poland*	45	J7
Bocholt, *Germany*	24	D2
Bochum, *Germany*	24	D3
Bockenem, *Germany*	24	C6
Bočki, *Poland*	45	F10
Bocognano, *France*	21	F13
Bocoyna, *Mexico*	118	B3
Bocşa, *Romania*	42	E6
Böda, Kalmar, *Sweden*	11	G11
Boda, Kopparberg, *Sweden*	10	D6
Boda, Västernorrland, *Sweden*	10	B10
Bodafors, *Sweden*	11	G8
Bodaybo, *Russia*	51	D12
Boddam, *U.K.*	14	B7
Boddington, *Australia*	93	F2
Bode Sadu, *Nigeria*	83	D5
Bodega Bay, *U.S.A.*	116	G3
Boden, *Sweden*	8	D19
Bodensee, *Europe*	25	H5
Bodenteich, *Germany*	24	C6
Bodhan, *India*	66	K10
Bodinga, *Nigeria*	83	C6
Bodmin, *U.K.*	13	G3
Bodmin Moor, *U.K.*	13	G3
Bodø, *Norway*	8	C16
Bodrog →, *Hungary*	42	B6
Bodrum, *Turkey*	39	D9
Bódva →, *Hungary*	42	B5
Boën, *France*	21	C8
Boende, *Dem. Rep. of the Congo*	84	E4
Boerne, *U.S.A.*	113	L5
Boesmans →, *S. Africa*	88	E4
Boffa, *Guinea*	82	C2
Bogalusa, *U.S.A.*	113	K10
Bogan →, *Australia*	95	D4
Bogan Gate, *Australia*	95	E4
Bogandé, *Burkina Faso*	83	C4
Bogantungan, *Australia*	94	C4
Bogata, *U.S.A.*	113	J7
Bogatić, *Serbia, Yug.*	40	B3
Boğazkale, *Turkey*	72	B6
Boğazlıyan, *Turkey*	72	C6
Bogen, *Sweden*	10	D6
Bogense, *Denmark*	11	J4
Bogetići, *Montenegro, Yug.*	40	D2
Boggabilla, *Australia*	95	D5
Boggabri, *Australia*	95	E5
Boggeragh Mts., *Ireland*	15	D3
Boglan = Solhan, *Turkey*	70	B4
Bognor Regis, *U.K.*	13	G7
Bogo, *Phil.*	61	F6
Bogodukhov = Bohodukhiv, *Ukraine*	47	G8
Bogol Manya, *Ethiopia*	81	G5
Bogong, Mt., *Australia*	95	F4
Bogor, *Indonesia*	63	G12
Bogoroditsk, *Russia*	46	F10
Bogorodsk, *Russia*	48	C5
Bogotá, *Colombia*	124	C4
Bogotol, *Russia*	50	D9
Bogou, *Togo*	83	C5
Bogra, *Bangla.*	67	G16
Boguchany, *Russia*	51	D10
Boguchar, *Russia*	48	F5
Bogué, *Mauritania*	82	B2
Boguslav, *Ukraine*	47	H6
Boguszów-Gorce, *Poland*	45	H3
Bohain-en-Vermandois, *France*	19	C10
Bohemian Forest = Böhmerwald, *Germany*	25	F9
Bohinjska Bistrica, *Slovenia*	29	B11
Böhmerwald, *Germany*	25	F9
Bohmte, *Germany*	24	C4
Bohodukhiv, *Ukraine*	47	G8
Bohol □, *Phil.*	61	G6
Bohol Sea, *Phil.*	63	C6
Bohongou, *Burkina Faso*	83	C5
Böhönye, *Hungary*	42	D2
Bohuslän, *Sweden*	11	F5
Boi, *Nigeria*	83	D6
Boi, Pta. de, *Brazil*	127	A6
Boiaçu, *Brazil*	124	D6
Boise, C., *Australia*	92	C3
Boing'o, *Sudan*	81	F3
Boiro, *Spain*	34	C2
Boise, *U.S.A.*	114	E5
Boise City, *U.S.A.*	113	G3

Brakel

Boissevain, Canada 105 D8
Bóite →, Italy 29 B9
Boitzenburg, Germany 24 B9
Boizenburg, Germany 24 B6
Bojador C., W. Sahara 78 C3
Bojana →, Albania 40 E3
Bojano, Italy 31 A7
Bojanowo, Poland 45 G3
Bøjden, Denmark 11 J4
Bojnūrd, Iran 71 B8
Bojonegoro, Indonesia 63 G14
Boju, Nigeria 83 D6
Boka, Serbia, Yug. 42 E5
Boka Kotorska, Montenegro, Yug. 40 D2
Bokala, Ivory C. 82 D4
Bokani, Nigeria 83 D6
Bokaro, India 69 H11
Boké, Guinea 82 C2
Bokhara →, Australia 95 D4
Bokkos, Nigeria 83 D6
Boknafjorden, Norway 9 G11
Bokoro, Chad 79 F9
Bokpyin, Burma 65 G2
Boksitogorsk, Russia 46 C7
Bol, Croatia 29 E13
Bolama, Guinea-Biss. 82 C1
Bolan →, Pakistan 68 E2
Bolan Pass, Pakistan 66 E5
Bolaños →, Mexico 118 C4
Bolaños de Calatrava, Spain 35 G7
Bolayır, Turkey 41 F10
Bolbec, France 18 C7
Boldājī, Iran 71 D6
Boldeşti-Scăeni, Romania 43 E11
Bole, China 60 B3
Bole, Ethiopia 81 F4
Bole, Ghana 82 D4
Bolekhiv, Ukraine 47 H2
Bolesławiec, Poland 45 G2
Bolgatanga, Ghana 83 C4
Bolgrad = Bolhrad, Ukraine 47 K5
Bolhrad, Ukraine 47 K5
Bolinao, Phil. 61 C3
Bolintin-Vale, Romania 43 F10
Bolívar, Argentina 126 D3
Bolivar, Mo., U.S.A. 113 G8
Bolivar, N.Y., U.S.A. 110 D6
Bolivar, Tenn., U.S.A. 113 H10
Bolivia ■, S. Amer. 124 G6
Bolivian Plateau, S. Amer. 122 E4
Boljevac, Serbia, Yug. 40 C5
Bolkhov, Russia 46 F9
Bolków, Poland 45 H3
Bollebygd, Sweden 11 G6
Bollène, France 21 D8
Bollnäs, Sweden 10 C10
Bollon, Australia 95 D4
Bollstabruk, Sweden 10 B11
Bolmen, Sweden 11 H7
Bolobo, Dem. Rep. of the Congo 84 E3
Bologna, Italy 29 D8
Bologoye, Russia 46 D8
Bolonchenticul, Mexico 119 D7
Bolótana, Italy 30 B1
Boloven, Cao Nguyen, Laos 64 E6
Bolpur, India 69 H12
Bolsena, Italy 29 F8
Bolsena, L. di, Italy 29 F8
Bolshaya Chernigovka, Russia 48 D10
Bolshaya Glushitsa, Russia 48 D10
Bolshaya Martynovka, Russia 49 G5
Bolshaya Vradiyevka, Ukraine 47 J6
Bolshevik, Ostrov, Russia 51 B11
Bolshoi Kavkas = Caucasus Mountains, Eurasia 49 J7
Bolshoy Anyuy →, Russia 51 C17
Bolshoy Begichev, Ostrov, Russia 51 B12
Bolshoy Lyakhovskiy, Ostrov, Russia 51 B15
Bolshoy Tokmak = Tokmak, Ukraine 47 J8
Bolshoy Tyuters, Ostrov, Russia 9 G22
Bolsward, Neths. 17 A5
Bolt Head, U.K. 13 G4
Boltaña, Spain 32 C5
Boltigen, Switz. 25 J3
Bolton, Canada 110 C5
Bolton, U.K. 12 D5
Bolton Landing, U.S.A. 111 C11
Bolu, Turkey 72 B4
Bolungavík, Iceland 8 C2
Boluo, China 59 F10
Bolvadin, Turkey 70 B1
Bolzano, Italy 29 B8
Bom Jesus da Lapa, Brazil 125 F10
Boma, Dem. Rep. of the Congo 84 F2
Bombala, Australia 95 F4
Bombarral, Portugal 35 F1
Bombay = Mumbai, India 66 K8
Bomboma, Dem. Rep. of the Congo 84 D3
Bombombwa, Dem. Rep. of the Congo 86 B2
Bomi Hills, Liberia 82 D2
Bomili, Dem. Rep. of the Congo 86 B2
Bømlo, Norway 9 G11
Bomokandi →, Dem. Rep. of the Congo 86 B2
Bomu →, C.A.R. 84 D4
Bon, C., Tunisia 76 C5
Bon Sar Pa, Vietnam 64 F6
Bonaigarh, India 69 J11
Bonaire, Neth. Ant. 121 D6
Bonang, Australia 95 F4
Bonanza, Nic. 120 D3
Bonaparte Arch., Australia 92 B3
Boñar, Spain 34 C5
Bonaventure, Canada 103 C6
Bonavista, Canada 103 C9
Bonavista, C., Canada 103 C9
Bonavista B., Canada 103 C9
Bondeno, Italy 29 D8
Bondo, Dem. Rep. of the Congo 86 B1
Bondoukou, Ivory C. 82 D4
Bondowoso, Indonesia 63 G15
Bone, Teluk, Indonesia 63 E6
Bonerate, Indonesia 63 F6
Bonerate, Kepulauan, Indonesia 63 F6
Bo'ness, U.K. 14 E5
Bonete, Cerro, Argentina 126 B2
Bong Son = Hoai Nhon, Vietnam 64 E7
Bonga, Ethiopia 81 F4
Bongabong, Phil. 61 E4
Bongor, Chad 79 F9
Bongouanou, Ivory C. 82 D4
Bonham, U.S.A. 113 J6
Boni, Mali 82 B4
Bonifacio, France 21 G13
Bonifacio, Bouches de, Medit. S. 30 A2
Bonin Is. = Ogasawara Gunto, Pac. Oc. 52 G18
Bonke, Ethiopia 81 F4
Bonkoukou, Niger 83 C5
Bonn, Germany 24 E3
Bonnat, France 19 F8
Bonne Terre, U.S.A. 113 G9
Bonners Ferry, U.S.A. 114 B5
Bonnétable, France 18 D7
Bonneval, Eure-et-Loir, France 18 D8
Bonneval, Savoie, France 21 C11
Bonneville, France 19 F13
Bonney, L., Australia 95 F3
Bonnie Rock, Australia 93 F2
Bonny, Nigeria 83 E6
Bonny →, Nigeria 83 E6
Bonny, Bight of, Africa 83 E6
Bonny-sur-Loire, France 19 E9
Bonnyrigg, U.K. 14 F5
Bonnyville, Canada 105 C6
Bono, Italy 30 B2
Bonoi, Indonesia 63 E9
Bonorva, Italy 30 B1
Bonsall, U.S.A. 117 M9
Bontang, Indonesia 62 D5
Bonthe, S. Leone 82 D2
Bontoc, Phil. 61 C4
Bonyeri, Ghana 82 D4
Bonyhád, Hungary 42 D3
Bonython Ra., Australia 92 D4
Bookabie, Australia 93 F5
Booker, U.S.A. 113 G4
Boola, Guinea 82 D3
Booligal, Australia 95 E3
Boonah, Australia 95 D5
Boone, Iowa, U.S.A. 112 D8
Boone, N.C., U.S.A. 109 G5
Booneville, Ark., U.S.A. 113 H8
Booneville, Miss., U.S.A. 109 H1
Boonville, Calif., U.S.A. 116 F3
Boonville, Ind., U.S.A. 108 F2
Boonville, Mo., U.S.A. 112 F8
Boonville, N.Y., U.S.A. 111 C9
Boorindal, Australia 95 E4
Boorowa, Australia 95 E4
Boothia, Gulf of, Canada 101 A11
Boothia Pen., Canada 100 A10
Bootle, U.K. 12 D4
Booué, Gabon 84 E2
Boppard, Germany 25 E3
Boquete, Panama 120 E3
Boquilla, Presa de la, Mexico 118 B3
Boquillas del Carmen, Mexico 118 B4
Bor, Czech Rep. 26 B5
Bor, Russia 48 B7
Bor, Serbia, Yug. 40 B6
Bôr, Sudan 81 F3
Bor, Sweden 11 G8
Bor, Turkey 72 D6
Bor Mashash, Israel 75 D3
Borah Peak, U.S.A. 114 D7
Borang, Sudan 81 G3
Borås, Sweden 11 G6
Borāzjān, Iran 71 D6
Borba, Brazil 124 D7
Borba, Portugal 35 G3
Borborema, Planalto da, Brazil 122 D7
Borcea, Romania 43 F12
Borçka, Turkey 73 B9
Bord Khūn-e Now, Iran 71 D6
Borda, C., Australia 95 F2
Bordeaux, France 20 D3
Borden, Australia 93 F2
Borden, Canada 103 C7
Borden I., Canada 4 B2
Borden Pen., Canada 101 A11
Borders = Scottish Borders □, U.K. 14 F6
Bordertown, Australia 95 F3
Borðeyri, Iceland 8 D3
Bordighera, Italy 28 E4
Bordj Fly Ste. Marie, Algeria 78 C5
Bordj-in-Eker, Algeria 78 D7
Bordj Omar Driss, Algeria 78 C7
Bore, Ethiopia 81 G4
Borehamwood, U.K. 13 F7
Borek Wielkopolski, Poland 45 G4
Borensberg, Sweden 11 F9
Borgå = Porvoo, Finland 9 F21
Borgarfjörður, Iceland 8 D7
Borgarnes, Iceland 8 D3
Børgefjellet, Norway 8 D15
Borger, Neths. 17 B6
Borger, U.S.A. 113 H4
Borgholm, Sweden 11 H10
Bórgia, Italy 31 D9
Borgo San Dalmazzo, Italy 28 D4
Borgo San Lorenzo, Italy 29 E8
Borgo Val di Taro, Italy 28 D6
Borgo Valsugana, Italy 29 B8
Borgomanero, Italy 28 C5
Borgorose, Italy 29 F10
Borgosésia, Italy 28 C5
Borhoyn Tal, Mongolia 56 C6
Bori, Nigeria 83 E6
Borikhane, Laos 64 C4
Borisoglebsk, Russia 48 E6
Borisov = Barysaw, Belarus 46 E5
Borisovka, Russia 47 G9
Borja, Peru 124 D3
Borja, Spain 32 D3
Borjas Blancas = Les Borges Blanques, Spain 32 D5
Borjomi, Georgia 49 K6
Borken, Germany 24 D9
Børkop, Denmark 11 J3
Borkou, Chad 79 E9
Borkum, Germany 24 B2
Borlänge, Sweden 10 D9
Borley, C., Antarctica 5 C5
Borlu, Turkey 39 C10
Bormida →, Italy 28 D5
Bórmio, Italy 28 B7
Borna, Germany 24 D8
Borne Sulinowo, Poland 44 E3
Borneo, E. Indies 62 D5
Bornholm, Denmark 11 J8
Bornholms Amtskommune □, Denmark 11 J8
Bornholmsgattet, Europe 11 J8
Borno □, Nigeria 83 C7
Bornos, Spain 35 J5
Bornova, Turkey 39 C9
Bornu Yassa, Nigeria 83 C7
Boro →, Sudan 81 F2
Borodino, Russia 46 E8
Borogontsy, Russia 51 C14
Boromo, Burkina Faso 82 C4
Boron, U.S.A. 117 L9
Borongan, Phil. 61 F6
Borotangba Mts., C.A.R. 81 F2
Borotou, Ivory C. 82 D3
Borovan, Bulgaria 40 C7
Borovichi, Russia 46 C7
Borovsk, Russia 46 E9
Borrby, Sweden 11 J8
Borrego Springs, U.S.A. 117 M10
Borriol, Spain 32 E4
Borroloola, Australia 94 B2
Borşa, Cluj, Romania 43 D8
Borşa, Maramureş, Romania 43 C9
Borsad, India 68 H5
Borsec, Romania 43 D10
Borsod-Abaúj-Zemplén □, Hungary 42 B6
Bort-les-Orgues, France 20 C6
Borth, U.K. 13 E3
Börtnan, Sweden 10 B7
Borūjerd, Iran 71 C6
Boryslav, Ukraine 47 H2
Boryspil, Ukraine 47 G6
Borzhomi = Borjomi, Georgia 49 K6
Borzna, Ukraine 47 G7
Borzya, Russia 51 D12
Bosa, Italy 30 B1
Bosanska Dubica, Bos.-H. 29 C13
Bosanska Gradiška, Bos.-H. 42 E2
Bosanska Kostajnica, Bos.-H. 29 C13
Bosanska Krupa, Bos.-H. 29 D13
Bosanski Brod, Bos.-H. 42 E2
Bosanski Novi, Bos.-H. 29 C13
Bosanski Petrovac, Bos.-H. 29 D13
Bosanski Šamac, Bos.-H. 42 E3
Bosansko Grahovo, Bos.-H. 29 D13
Bosaso, Somali Rep. 74 E4
Boscastle, U.K. 13 G3
Bose, China 58 F6
Boshan, China 57 F9
Boshof, S. Africa 88 D4
Boshrūyeh, Iran 71 C8
Bosilegrad, Serbia, Yug. 40 D6
Boskovice, Czech Rep. 27 B9
Bosna →, Bos.-H. 42 E3
Bosna i Hercegovina = Bosnia-Herzegovina ■, Europe 42 G2
Bosnia-Herzegovina ■, Europe 42 G2
Bosnik, Indonesia 63 E9
Bosobolo, Dem. Rep. of the Congo 84 D3
Bosporus = Istanbul Boğazı, Turkey 41 E13
Bosque Farms, U.S.A. 115 J10
Bossangoa, C.A.R. 84 C3
Bossé Bangou, Niger 83 C5
Bossier City, U.S.A. 113 J8
Bosso, Niger 83 C7
Bosso, Dallol →, Niger 83 C5
Bostan, Pakistan 68 D2
Bostānābād, Iran 70 B5
Bosten Hu, China 60 B3
Boston, U.K. 12 E7
Boston, U.S.A. 111 D13
Boston Bar, Canada 104 D4
Boston Mts., U.S.A. 113 H8
Bosut →, Croatia 42 E3
Boswell, Canada 104 D5
Boswell, U.S.A. 110 F5
Botad, India 68 H4
Botan →, Turkey 73 D10
Botene, Laos 64 D3
Botev, Bulgaria 41 D8
Botevgrad, Bulgaria 40 D7
Bothaville, S. Africa 88 D4
Bothnia, G. of, Europe 8 E19
Bothwell, Australia 94 G4
Bothwell, Canada 110 D3
Boticas, Portugal 34 D3
Botletle →, Botswana 88 C3
Botlikh, Russia 49 J8
Botna →, Moldova 43 D14
Botoroaga, Romania 43 F10
Botoşani, Romania 43 C11
Botoşani □, Romania 43 C11
Botou, Burkina Faso 83 C5
Botricello, Italy 31 D9
Botro, Ivory C. 82 D3
Botswana ■, Africa 88 C3
Bottineau, U.S.A. 112 A4
Bottnaryd, Sweden 11 G7
Bottrop, Germany 17 C6
Botucatu, Brazil 127 A6
Botwood, Canada 103 C8
Bou Djébéha, Mali 82 B4
Bou Rjeïmât, Mauritania 82 B1
Bouaflé, Ivory C. 82 D3
Bouaké, Ivory C. 82 D3
Bouar, C.A.R. 84 C3
Bouârfa, Morocco 78 B5
Boucaut B., Australia 94 A1
Bouches-du-Rhône □, France 21 E9
Bougainville, C., Australia 92 B4
Bougainville I., Papua N. G. 96 H7
Bougainville Reef, Australia 94 B4
Bougie = Bejaia, Algeria 78 A7
Bougouni, Mali 82 C3
Bouillon, Belgium 17 E5
Boukombé, Benin 83 C5
Boulal, Mali 82 B3
Boulazac, France 20 C4
Boulder, Colo., U.S.A. 112 E2
Boulder, Mont., U.S.A. 114 C7
Boulder City, U.S.A. 117 K12
Boulder Creek, U.S.A. 116 H4
Boulder Dam = Hoover Dam, U.S.A. 117 K12
Bouli, Mauritania 82 B2
Boulia, Australia 94 C2
Bouligny, France 19 C12
Boulogne →, France 18 E5
Boulogne-sur-Gesse, France 20 E4
Boulogne-sur-Mer, France 19 B8
Bouloire, France 18 E7
Bouloui, Mali 82 B3
Boulsa, Burkina Faso 83 C4
Boultoum, Niger 83 C7
Boûmdeïd, Mauritania 82 B2
Boun Neua, Laos 64 B3
Boun Tai, Laos 64 B3
Bouna, Ivory C. 82 D4
Boundary Peak, U.S.A. 116 H8
Boundiali, Ivory C. 82 D3
Bountiful, U.S.A. 114 F8
Bounty Is., Pac. Oc. 96 M9
Boura, Mali 82 C4
Bourbon-Lancy, France 19 F10
Bourbon-l'Archambault, France 19 F10
Bourbonnais, France 19 F10
Bourbonne-les-Bains, France 19 E12
Bourbourg, France 19 B9
Bourdel L., Canada 102 A5
Bourem, Mali 83 B4
Bourg, France 20 C3
Bourg-Argental, France 21 C8
Bourg-de-Péage, France 21 C9
Bourg-en-Bresse, France 19 F12
Bourg-Lastic, France 20 C6
Bourg-Madame, France 20 F5
Bourg-St-Andéol, France 21 D8
Bourg-St-Maurice, France 21 C10
Bourganeuf, France 20 C5
Bourges, France 19 E9
Bourget, Canada 111 A9
Bourget, Lac du, France 21 C9
Bourgneuf, B. de, France 18 E4
Bourgneuf-en-Retz, France 18 E5
Bourgogne, France 19 F11
Bourgoin-Jallieu, France 21 C9
Bourgueil, France 18 E7
Bourke, Australia 95 E4
Bourne, U.K. 12 E7
Bournemouth, U.K. 13 G6
Bournemouth □, U.K. 13 G6
Bouroum, Burkina Faso 83 C4
Bouse, U.S.A. 117 M13
Boussac, France 19 F9
Boussé, Burkina Faso 83 C4
Boussouma, Burkina Faso 83 C4
Boutilimit, Mauritania 82 B2
Boutonne →, France 20 C3
Bouvet I. = Bouvetøya, Antarctica 3 G10
Bouvetøya, Antarctica 3 G10
Bouxwiller, France 19 D14
Bouza, Niger 83 C6
Bouzonville, France 19 C13
Bova Marina, Italy 31 E8
Bovalino Marina, Italy 31 D9
Bovec, Slovenia 29 B10
Bovill, U.S.A. 114 C5
Bovino, Italy 31 A8
Bovril, Argentina 126 C4
Bow →, Canada 104 C6
Bow Island, Canada 104 D6
Bowbells, U.S.A. 112 A3
Bowdle, U.S.A. 112 C5
Bowelling, Australia 93 F2
Bowen, Argentina 126 D2
Bowen, Australia 94 C4
Bowen Mts., Australia 95 F4
Bowie, Ariz., U.S.A. 115 K9
Bowie, Tex., U.S.A. 113 J6
Bowkān, Iran 70 B5
Bowland, Forest of, U.K. 12 D5
Bowling Green, Ky., U.S.A. 108 G2
Bowling Green, Ohio, U.S.A. 108 E4
Bowling Green, C., Australia 94 B4
Bowman, U.S.A. 112 B3
Bowman I., Antarctica 5 C8
Bowmanville, Canada 110 C6
Bowmore, U.K. 14 F2
Bowral, Australia 95 E5
Bowraville, Australia 95 E5
Bowron →, Canada 104 C4
Bowron Lake Prov. Park, Canada 104 C4
Bowser L., Canada 104 B3
Bowsman, Canada 105 C8
Bowwood, Zambia 87 F2
Box Cr. →, Australia 95 E3
Boxholm, Sweden 11 F9
Boxmeer, Neths. 17 C5
Boxtel, Neths. 17 C5
Boyabat, Turkey 72 B6
Boyalıca, Turkey 41 F13
Boyang, China 59 C11
Boyce, U.S.A. 113 K8
Boyd L., Canada 102 B4
Boyle, Canada 104 C6
Boyle, Ireland 15 C3
Boyne →, Ireland 15 C5
Boyne City, U.S.A. 108 C3
Boynitsa, Bulgaria 40 C6
Boynton Beach, U.S.A. 109 M5
Boyolali, Indonesia 63 G14
Boyoma, Chutes, Dem. Rep. of the Congo 86 B2
Boysen Reservoir, U.S.A. 114 E9
Boyuibe, Bolivia 124 G6
Boyup Brook, Australia 93 F2
Boz Burun, Turkey 41 F12
Boz Dağ, Turkey 39 D11
Boz Dağları, Turkey 39 C10
Bozburun, Turkey 39 E10
Bozcaada, Turkey 72 C2
Bozdoğan, Turkey 39 D10
Bozeman, U.S.A. 114 D8
Bozen = Bolzano, Italy 29 B8
Boževac, Serbia, Yug. 40 B5
Bozhou, China 56 H8
Bozkır, Turkey 72 D5
Bozkurt, Turkey 39 D11
Bozouls, France 20 D6
Bozoum, C.A.R. 84 C3
Bozova, Antalya, Turkey 39 D12
Bozova, Sanliurfa, Turkey 73 D8
Bozovici, Romania 42 F7
Bozüyük, Turkey 39 B12
Bra, Italy 28 D4
Braås, Sweden 11 G9
Brabant □, Belgium 17 D4
Brabant L., Canada 105 B8
Brabrand, Denmark 11 H4
Brač, Croatia 29 E13
Bracadale, L., U.K. 14 D2
Bracciano, Italy 29 F9
Bracciano, L. di, Italy 29 F9
Bracebridge, Canada 102 C4
Brach, Libya 79 C8
Bracieux, France 18 E8
Bräcke, Sweden 10 B9
Brackettville, U.S.A. 113 L4
Bracki Kanal, Croatia 29 E13
Bracknell, U.K. 13 F7
Bracknell Forest □, U.K. 13 F7
Brad, Romania 42 D7
Brádano →, Italy 31 B9
Bradenton, U.S.A. 109 M4
Bradford, Canada 110 B5
Bradford, U.K. 12 D6
Bradford, Pa., U.S.A. 110 E6
Bradford, Vt., U.S.A. 111 C12
Bradley, Ark., U.S.A. 113 J8
Bradley, Calif., U.S.A. 116 K6
Bradley Institute, Zimbabwe 87 F3
Brady, U.S.A. 113 K5
Brædstrup, Denmark 11 J3
Braemar, U.K. 14 D5
Braeside, Canada 111 A8
Braga, Portugal 34 D2
Braga □, Portugal 34 D2
Bragadiru, Romania 43 G10
Bragado, Argentina 126 D3
Bragança, Brazil 125 D9
Bragança, Portugal 34 D4
Bragança □, Portugal 34 D4
Bragança Paulista, Brazil 127 A6
Brahmanbaria, Bangla. 67 H17
Brahmani →, India 67 J15
Brahmapur, India 67 K14
Brahmaputra →, India 69 H13
Braich-y-pwll, U.K. 12 E3
Braidwood, Australia 95 F4
Brăila, Romania 43 E12
Brăila □, Romania 43 E12
Brainerd, U.S.A. 112 B7
Braintree, U.K. 13 F8
Braintree, U.S.A. 111 D14
Brak →, S. Africa 88 D3
Brake, Germany 24 B4
Brakel, Germany 24 D5

Bräkne-Hoby, *Sweden*	11	H9	
Brakwater, *Namibia*	88	C2	
Brålanda, *Sweden*	11	F6	
Bramberg, *Germany*	25	E6	
Bramdrupdam, *Denmark*	11	J3	
Bramming, *Denmark*	11	J2	
Brämön, *Sweden*	10	B11	
Brampton, *Canada*	102	D4	
Brampton, *U.K.*	12	C5	
Bramsche, *Germany*	24	C3	
Branco →, *Brazil*	122	D4	
Brandberg, *Namibia*	88	B2	
Brande, *Denmark*	11	J3	
Brandenburg =			
Neubrandenburg, *Germany*	24	B9	
Brandenburg, *Germany*	24	C8	
Brandenburg □, *Germany*	24	C9	
Brandfort, *S. Africa*	88	D4	
Brando, *France*	21	F13	
Brandon, *Canada*	105	D9	
Brandon, *U.S.A.*	111	C11	
Brandon B., *Ireland*	15	D1	
Brandon Mt., *Ireland*	15	D1	
Brandsen, *Argentina*	126	D4	
Brandvlei, *S. Africa*	88	E3	
Brandýs nad Labem,			
Czech Rep.	26	A7	
Brăneşti, *Romania*	43	F11	
Branford, *U.S.A.*	111	E12	
Braniewo, *Poland*	44	D6	
Bransfield Str., *Antarctica*	5	C18	
Brańsk, *Poland*	45	F9	
Branson, *U.S.A.*	113	G8	
Brantford, *Canada*	102	D3	
Brantôme, *France*	20	C4	
Branzi, *Italy*	28	B6	
Bras d'Or L., *Canada*	103	C7	
Brasher Falls, *U.S.A.*	111	B10	
Brasil, Planalto, *Brazil*	122	E6	
Brasiléia, *Brazil*	124	F5	
Brasília, *Brazil*	125	G9	
Brasília Legal, *Brazil*	125	D7	
Braslaw, *Belarus*	9	J22	
Braslovče, *Slovenia*	29	B12	
Braşov, *Romania*	43	E10	
Braşov □, *Romania*	43	E10	
Brass, *Nigeria*	83	E6	
Brass →, *Nigeria*	83	E6	
Brassac-les-Mines, *France*	20	C7	
Brasschaat, *Belgium*	17	C4	
Brassey, Banjaran, *Malaysia*	62	D5	
Brassey Ra., *Australia*	93	E3	
Brasstown Bald, *U.S.A.*	109	H4	
Brastad, *Sweden*	11	F5	
Brastavăţu, *Romania*	43	G9	
Bratan = Morozov, *Bulgaria*	41	D9	
Brateş, *Romania*	43	E11	
Bratislava, *Slovak Rep.*	27	C10	
Bratislavský □, *Slovak Rep.*	27	C10	
Bratsigovo, *Bulgaria*	41	D8	
Bratsk, *Russia*	51	D11	
Brattleboro, *U.S.A.*	111	D12	
Bratunac, *Bos.-H.*	42	F4	
Braunau, *Austria*	26	C6	
Braunschweig, *Germany*	24	C6	
Braunton, *U.K.*	13	F3	
Bravicea, *Moldova*	43	C13	
Bråviken, *Sweden*	11	F10	
Bravo del Norte, Rio =			
Grande, Rio →, *U.S.A.*	113	N6	
Brawley, *U.S.A.*	117	N11	
Bray, *Ireland*	15	C5	
Bray, Mt., *Australia*	94	A1	
Bray-sur-Seine, *France*	19	D10	
Brazeau →, *Canada*	104	C5	
Brazil, *U.S.A.*	108	F2	
Brazil ■, *S. Amer.*	125	F9	
Brazilian Highlands = Brasil,			
Planalto, *Brazil*	122	E6	
Brazo Sur →, *S. Amer.*	126	B4	
Brazos →, *U.S.A.*	113	L7	
Brazzaville, *Congo*	84	E3	
Brčko, *Bos.-H.*	42	F3	
Brda →, *Poland*	45	E5	
Brdy, *Czech Rep.*	26	B6	
Breaden, L., *Australia*	93	E4	
Breaksea Sd., *N.Z.*	91	L1	
Bream B., *N.Z.*	91	F5	
Bream Hd., *N.Z.*	91	F5	
Breas, *Chile*	126	B1	
Breaza, *Romania*	43	E10	
Brebes, *Indonesia*	63	G13	
Brechin, *Canada*	110	B5	
Brechin, *U.K.*	14	E6	
Brecht, *Belgium*	17	C4	
Breckenridge, *Colo., U.S.A.*	114	G10	
Breckenridge, *Minn., U.S.A.*	112	B6	
Breckenridge, *Tex., U.S.A.*	113	J5	
Breckland, *U.K.*	13	E8	
Břeclav, *Czech Rep.*	27	C9	
Brecon, *U.K.*	13	F4	
Brecon Beacons, *U.K.*	13	F4	
Breda, *Neths.*	17	C4	
Bredaryd, *Sweden*	11	G7	
Bredasdorp, *S. Africa*	88	E3	
Bredebro, *Denmark*	11	J2	
Bredstedt, *Germany*	24	A4	
Bree, *Belgium*	17	C5	
Bregalnica →, *Macedonia*	40	E5	
Bregenz, *Austria*	26	D2	
Bregovo, *Bulgaria*	40	B6	
Bréhal, *France*	18	D5	
Bréhat, Î. de, *France*	18	D2	
Breiðafjörður, *Iceland*	8	D2	
Breil-sur-Roya, *France*	21	E11	
Breisach, *Germany*	25	G2	
Brejo, *Brazil*	125	D10	
Bremen, *Germany*	24	B4	
Bremen □, *Germany*	24	B4	
Bremer Bay, *Australia*	93	F2	
Bremer I., *Australia*	94	A2	
Bremerhaven, *Germany*	24	B4	
Bremerton, *U.S.A.*	116	C4	
Bremervörde, *Germany*	24	B5	
Brenes, *Spain*	35	H5	
Brenham, *U.S.A.*	113	K6	
Brenne, *France*	20	B5	
Brennerpass, *Austria*	26	D4	
Breno, *Italy*	28	C7	
Brenta →, *Italy*	29	C9	
Brentwood, *U.K.*	13	F8	
Brentwood, *Calif., U.S.A.*	116	H5	
Brentwood, *N.Y., U.S.A.*	111	F11	
Bréscia, *Italy*	28	C7	
Breskens, *Neths.*	17	C3	
Breslau = Wrocław, *Poland*	45	G4	
Bresle →, *France*	18	B8	
Bressanone, *Italy*	29	B8	
Bresse, *France*	19	F12	
Bressuire, *France*	18	F6	
Bressay, *U.K.*	14	A7	
Brest, *Belarus*	47	F2	
Brest, *France*	18	D2	
Brest-Litovsk = Brest,			
Belarus	47	F2	
Bretagne, *France*	18	D3	
Bretçu, *Romania*	43	D11	
Bretenoux, *France*	20	D5	
Breteuil, *Eure, France*	18	D7	
Breteuil, *Oise, France*	19	C9	
Breton, *Canada*	104	C6	
Breton, Pertuis, *France*	20	B2	
Breton Sd., *U.S.A.*	113	L10	
Brett, C., *N.Z.*	91	F5	
Bretten, *Germany*	25	F4	
Breuil-Cervínia, *Italy*	28	C4	
Brevard, *U.S.A.*	109	H4	
Breves, *Brazil*	125	D8	
Brewarrina, *Australia*	95	E4	
Brewer, *U.S.A.*	109	C11	
Brewer, Mt., *U.S.A.*	116	J8	
Brewerville, *Liberia*	82	D2	
Brewster, *N.Y., U.S.A.*	111	E11	
Brewster, *Ohio, U.S.A.*	110	F3	
Brewster, *Wash., U.S.A.*	114	B4	
Brewster, Kap = Kangikajik,			
Greenland	4	B6	
Brewton, *U.S.A.*	109	K2	
Breyten, *S. Africa*	89	D5	
Breza, *Bos.-H.*	42	F3	
Brežice, *Slovenia*	29	C12	
Březnice, *Czech Rep.*	26	B6	
Breznik, *Bulgaria*	40	D6	
Brezno, *Slovak Rep.*	27	C12	
Brezoi, *Romania*	43	E9	
Brezovica, *Kosovo, Yug.*	40	D5	
Brezovo, *Bulgaria*	41	D9	
Briançon, *France*	21	D10	
Briare, *France*	19	E9	
Briático, *Italy*	31	D9	
Bribie I., *Australia*	95	D5	
Bribri, *Costa Rica*	120	E3	
Bricquebec, *France*	18	C5	
Bridgehampton, *U.S.A.*	111	F12	
Bridgend, *U.K.*	13	F4	
Bridgend □, *U.K.*	13	F4	
Bridgeport, *Calif., U.S.A.*	116	G7	
Bridgeport, *Conn., U.S.A.*	111	E11	
Bridgeport, *Nebr., U.S.A.*	112	E3	
Bridgeport, *Tex., U.S.A.*	113	J6	
Bridger, *U.S.A.*	114	D9	
Bridgeton, *U.S.A.*	108	F8	
Bridgetown, *Australia*	93	F2	
Bridgetown, *Barbados*	121	D8	
Bridgetown, *Canada*	103	D6	
Bridgewater, *Canada*	103	D7	
Bridgewater, *Mass., U.S.A.*	111	E14	
Bridgewater, *N.Y., U.S.A.*	111	D9	
Bridgewater, C., *Australia*	95	F3	
Bridgewater-Gagebrook,			
Australia	94	G4	
Bridgnorth, *U.K.*	13	E5	
Bridgton, *U.S.A.*	111	B14	
Bridgwater, *U.K.*	13	F5	
Bridgwater B., *U.K.*	13	F4	
Bridlington, *U.K.*	12	C7	
Bridlington B., *U.K.*	12	C7	
Bridport, *Australia*	94	G4	
Bridport, *U.K.*	13	G5	
Briec, *France*	18	D2	
Brienne-le-Château, *France*	19	D11	
Brienon-sur-Armançon,			
France	19	E10	
Brienz, *Switz.*	25	J4	
Brienzersee, *Switz.*	25	J3	
Brig, *Switz.*	25	J3	
Brigg, *U.K.*	12	D7	
Brigham City, *U.S.A.*	114	F7	
Bright, *Australia*	95	F4	
Brighton, *Australia*	95	F2	
Brighton, *Canada*	110	B7	
Brighton, *U.K.*	13	G7	
Brighton, *Colo., U.S.A.*	112	F2	
Brighton, *N.Y., U.S.A.*	110	C7	
Brignogan-Plage, *France*	18	D2	
Brignoles, *France*	21	E10	
Brihuega, *Spain*	32	E2	
Brikama, *Gambia*	82	C1	
Brilliant, *U.S.A.*	110	F4	
Brilon, *Germany*	24	D4	
Bríndisi, *Italy*	31	B10	
Brinje, *Croatia*	29	D12	
Brinkley, *U.S.A.*	113	H9	
Brinnon, *U.S.A.*	116	C4	
Brion, I., *Canada*	103	C7	
Brionne, *France*	18	C7	
Brionski, *Croatia*	29	D10	
Brioude, *France*	20	C7	
Briouze, *France*	18	D6	
Brisbane, *Australia*	95	D5	
Brisbane →, *Australia*	95	D5	
Brisighella, *Italy*	29	D8	
Bristol, *U.K.*	13	F5	
Bristol, *Conn., U.S.A.*	111	E12	
Bristol, *Pa., U.S.A.*	111	F10	
Bristol, *R.I., U.S.A.*	111	E13	
Bristol, *Tenn., U.S.A.*	109	G4	
Bristol, City of □, *U.K.*	13	F5	
Bristol B., *U.S.A.*	100	C4	
Bristol Channel, *U.K.*	13	F3	
Bristol I., *Antarctica*	5	B1	
Bristol L., *U.S.A.*	115	J5	
Bristow, *U.S.A.*	113	H6	
Britain = Great Britain,			
Europe	6	E5	
British Columbia □, *Canada*	104	C3	
British Indian Ocean Terr. =			
Chagos Arch., *Ind. Oc.*	52	K11	
British Isles, *Europe*	6	E5	
Brits, *S. Africa*	89	D4	
Britstown, *S. Africa*	88	E3	
Britt, *Canada*	102	C3	
Brittany = Bretagne, *France*	18	D3	
Britton, *U.S.A.*	112	C6	
Brive-la-Gaillarde, *France*	20	C5	
Briviesca, *Spain*	34	C7	
Brixen = Bressanone, *Italy*	29	B8	
Brixham, *U.K.*	13	G4	
Brnaze, *Croatia*	29	E13	
Brno, *Czech Rep.*	27	B9	
Broad →, *U.S.A.*	109	J5	
Broad Arrow, *Australia*	93	F3	
Broad B., *U.K.*	14	C2	
Broad Haven, *Ireland*	15	B2	
Broad Law, *U.K.*	14	F5	
Broad Sd., *Australia*	94	C4	
Broadalbin, *U.S.A.*	111	C10	
Broadback →, *Canada*	102	B4	
Broadford, *Australia*	95	F4	
Broadhurst Ra., *Australia*	92	D3	
Broads, The, *U.K.*	12	E9	
Broadus, *U.S.A.*	112	C2	
Broager, *Denmark*	11	K3	
Broby, *Sweden*	11	H8	
Brocēni, *Latvia*	44	B9	
Brochet, *Canada*	105	B8	
Brochet, L., *Canada*	105	B8	
Brocken, *Germany*	24	D6	
Brockport, *U.S.A.*	110	C7	
Brockton, *U.S.A.*	111	D13	
Brockville, *Canada*	102	D4	
Brockway, *Mont., U.S.A.*	112	B2	
Brockway, *Pa., U.S.A.*	110	E6	
Brocton, *U.S.A.*	110	D5	
Brod, *Macedonia*	40	E5	
Brodarevo, *Serbia, Yug.*	40	C3	
Brodeur Pen., *Canada*	101	A11	
Brodhead, Mt., *U.S.A.*	110	E7	
Brodick, *U.K.*	14	F3	
Brodnica, *Poland*	45	E6	
Brody, *Ukraine*	47	G3	
Brogan, *U.S.A.*	114	D5	
Broglie, *France*	18	C7	
Brok, *Poland*	45	F8	
Broken Arrow, *U.S.A.*	113	G7	
Broken Bow, *Nebr., U.S.A.*	112	E5	
Broken Bow, *Okla., U.S.A.*	113	H7	
Broken Bow Lake, *U.S.A.*	113	H7	
Broken Hill = Kabwe,			
Zambia	87	E2	
Broken Hill, *Australia*	95	E3	
Brokind, *Sweden*	11	F9	
Bromley, *U.K.*	13	F8	
Bromölla, *Sweden*	11	H8	
Bromsgrove, *U.K.*	13	E5	
Brønderslev, *Denmark*	11	G3	
Brong-Ahafo □, *Ghana*	82	D4	
Bronkhorstspruit, *S. Africa*	89	D4	
Brønnøysund, *Norway*	8	D15	
Bronte, *Italy*	31	E7	
Brook Park, *U.S.A.*	110	E4	
Brookhaven, *U.S.A.*	113	K9	
Brookings, *Oreg., U.S.A.*	114	E1	
Brookings, *S. Dak., U.S.A.*	112	C6	
Brooklin, *Canada*	110	C6	
Brooklyn Park, *U.S.A.*	112	C8	
Brooks, *Canada*	104	C6	
Brooks Range, *U.S.A.*	100	B5	
Brooksville, *U.S.A.*	109	L4	
Brookton, *Australia*	93	F2	
Brookville, *U.S.A.*	110	E5	
Broom, L., *U.K.*	14	D3	
Broome, *Australia*	92	C3	
Broons, *France*	18	D4	
Brora, *U.K.*	14	C5	
Brora →, *U.K.*	14	C5	
Brørup, *Denmark*	11	J2	
Brösarp, *Sweden*	11	J8	
Brosna →, *Ireland*	15	C4	
Broșteni, *Mehedinţi,*			
Romania	42	F7	
Broșteni, *Suceava, Romania*	43	C10	
Brothers, *U.S.A.*	114	E3	
Brou, *France*	18	D8	
Brouage, *France*	20	C2	
Brough, *U.K.*	12	C5	
Brough Hd., *U.K.*	14	B5	
Broughton Island =			
Qikiqtarjuaq, *Canada*	101	B13	
Broumov, *Czech Rep.*	27	A9	
Brovary, *Ukraine*	47	G6	
Brovst, *Denmark*	11	G3	
Brown, L., *Australia*	93	F2	
Brown, Pt., *Australia*	95	E1	
Brown City, *U.S.A.*	110	C2	
Brown Willy, *U.K.*	13	G3	
Brownfield, *U.S.A.*	113	J3	
Browning, *U.S.A.*	114	B7	
Brownsville, *Oreg., U.S.A.*	114	D2	
Brownsville, *Pa., U.S.A.*	110	F5	
Brownsville, *Tenn., U.S.A.*	113	H10	
Brownsville, *Tex., U.S.A.*	113	N6	
Brownville, *U.S.A.*	111	C9	
Brownwood, *U.S.A.*	113	K5	
Browse I., *Australia*	92	B3	
Bruas, *Malaysia*	65	K3	
Bruay-la-Buissière, *France*	19	B9	
Bruce, Mt., *Australia*	92	D2	
Bruce Pen., *Canada*	110	B3	
Bruce Rock, *Australia*	93	F2	
Bruche →, *France*	19	D14	
Bruchsal, *Germany*	25	F4	
Bruck an der Leitha, *Austria*	27	C9	
Bruck an der Mur, *Austria*	26	D8	
Brue →, *U.K.*	13	F5	
Bruges = Brugge, *Belgium*	17	C3	
Brugg, *Switz.*	25	H4	
Brugge, *Belgium*	17	C3	
Bruin, *U.S.A.*	110	E5	
Brûlé, *Canada*	104	C5	
Brûlon, *France*	18	E6	
Brumado, *Brazil*	125	F10	
Brumath, *France*	19	D14	
Brumunddal, *Norway*	9	F14	
Bruneau, *U.S.A.*	114	E6	
Bruneau →, *U.S.A.*	114	E6	
Bruneck = Brunico, *Italy*	29	B8	
Brunei = Bandar Seri			
Begawan, *Brunei*	62	C4	
Brunei ■, *Asia*	62	D4	
Brunflo, *Sweden*	10	A8	
Brunico, *Italy*	29	B8	
Brunna, *Sweden*	10	E11	
Brunnen, *Switz.*	25	J4	
Brunner, L., *N.Z.*	91	K3	
Brunsbüttel, *Germany*	24	B5	
Brunssum, *Neths.*	17	D5	
Brunswick = Braunschweig,			
Germany	24	C6	
Brunswick, *Ga., U.S.A.*	109	K5	
Brunswick, *Maine, U.S.A.*	109	D11	
Brunswick, *Md., U.S.A.*	108	F7	
Brunswick, *Mo., U.S.A.*	112	F8	
Brunswick, *Ohio, U.S.A.*	110	E3	
Brunswick, Pen. de, *Chile*	128	G2	
Brunswick B., *Australia*	92	C3	
Brunswick Junction,			
Australia	93	F2	
Bruntál, *Czech Rep.*	27	B10	
Bruny I., *Australia*	94	G4	
Brus Laguna, *Honduras*	120	C3	
Brusartsi, *Bulgaria*	40	C7	
Brush, *U.S.A.*	112	E3	
Brushton, *U.S.A.*	111	B10	
Brusio, *Switz.*	25	J6	
Brusque, *Brazil*	127	B6	
Brussel, *Belgium*	17	D4	
Brussels = Brussel, *Belgium*	17	D4	
Brussels, *Canada*	110	C3	
Brusy, *Poland*	44	E4	
Bruthen, *Australia*	95	F4	
Bruxelles = Brussel, *Belgium*	17	D4	
Bruyères, *France*	19	D13	
Bruz, *France*	18	D5	
Brwinów, *Poland*	45	F7	
Bryagovo, *Bulgaria*	41	E9	
Bryan, *Ohio, U.S.A.*	108	E3	
Bryan, *Tex., U.S.A.*	113	K6	
Bryan, Mt., *Australia*	95	E2	
Bryanka, *Ukraine*	47	H10	
Bryansk, *Bryansk, Russia*	47	F8	
Bryansk, *Dagestan, Russia*	49	H8	
Bryanskoye = Bryansk,			
Russia	49	H8	
Bryce Canyon National Park,			
U.S.A.	115	H7	
Bryne, *Norway*	9	G11	
Bryson City, *U.S.A.*	109	H4	
Bryukhovetskaya, *Russia*	47	K10	
Brza Palanka, *Serbia, Yug.*	40	B6	
Brzeg, *Poland*	45	H4	
Brzeg Dolny, *Poland*	45	G3	
Brześć Kujawski, *Poland*	45	F5	
Brzesko, *Poland*	45	J7	
Brzeziny, *Poland*	45	G6	
Brzozów, *Poland*	45	J9	
Bsharri, *Lebanon*	75	A5	
Bū Craa, *W. Sahara*	78	C3	
Bū Ḩasā, *U.A.E.*	71	F7	
Bua, *Sweden*	11	G6	
Bua Yai, *Thailand*	64	E4	
Buapinang, *Indonesia*	63	E6	
Buba, *Guinea-Biss.*	82	C2	
Bubanza, *Burundi*	86	C2	
Bubaque, *Guinea-Biss.*	82	C1	
Bube, *Ethiopia*	81	F4	
Bübiyān, *Kuwait*	71	D6	
Buca, *Turkey*	39	C9	
Bucak, *Turkey*	39	D12	
Bucaramanga, *Colombia*	124	B4	
Bucas Grande I., *Phil.*	61	G6	
Bucasia, *Australia*	94	C4	
Buccaneer Arch., *Australia*	92	C3	
Buccino, *Italy*	31	B8	
Bucecea, *Romania*	43	C11	
Buchach, *Ukraine*	47	H3	
Buchan, *U.K.*	14	D6	
Buchan Ness, *U.K.*	14	D7	
Buchanan, *Canada*	105	C8	
Buchanan, L., *Queens.,*			
Australia	94	C4	
Buchanan, L., *W. Austral.,*			
Australia	93	E3	
Buchanan, L., *U.S.A.*	113	K5	
Buchanan Cr. →, *Australia*	94	B2	
Buchans, *Canada*	103	C8	
Bucharest = Bucureşti,			
Romania	43	F11	
Buchen, *Germany*	25	F5	
Buchholz, *Germany*	24	B5	
Buchloe, *Germany*	25	G6	
Buchon, Pt., *U.S.A.*	116	K5	
Buciumi, *Romania*	42	C8	
Buck Hill Falls, *U.S.A.*	111	E9	
Bückeburg, *Germany*	24	C5	
Buckeye, *U.S.A.*	115	K7	
Buckeye Lake, *U.S.A.*	110	G2	
Buckhannon, *U.S.A.*	108	F5	
Buckhaven, *U.K.*	14	E5	
Buckhorn L., *Canada*	110	B6	
Buckie, *U.K.*	14	D6	
Buckingham, *Canada*	102	C4	
Buckingham, *U.K.*	13	F7	
Buckingham B., *Australia*	94	A2	
Buckinghamshire □, *U.K.*	13	F7	
Buckle Hd., *Australia*	92	B4	
Buckleboo, *Australia*	95	E2	
Buckley, *U.K.*	12	D4	
Buckley →, *Australia*	94	C2	
Bucklin, *U.S.A.*	113	G5	
Bucks L., *U.S.A.*	116	F5	
Bucquoy, *France*	19	B9	
Buctouche, *Canada*	103	C7	
Bucureşti, *Romania*	43	F11	
Bucyrus, *U.S.A.*	108	E4	
Budacu, Vf., *Romania*	43	C10	
Budalin, *Burma*	67	H19	
Budaörs, *Hungary*	42	C3	
Budapest, *Hungary*	42	C4	
Budapest □, *Hungary*	42	C4	
Budaun, *India*	69	E8	
Budd Coast, *Antarctica*	5	C8	
Buddusò, *Italy*	30	B2	
Bude, *U.K.*	13	G3	
Budennovsk, *Russia*	49	H7	
Budeşti, *Romania*	43	F11	
Budge Budge = Baj Baj,			
India	69	H13	
Budgewoi, *Australia*	95	E5	
Budia, *Spain*	32	E2	
Büdingen, *Germany*	25	E5	
Budjala,			
Dem. Rep. of the Congo	84	D3	
Budoni, *Italy*	30	B2	
Búdrio, *Italy*	29	D8	
Budva, *Montenegro, Yug.*	40	D2	
Budzyń, *Poland*	45	F3	
Buea, *Cameroon*	83	E6	
Buellton, *U.S.A.*	117	L6	
Buena Esperanza, *Argentina*	126	C2	
Buena Park, *U.S.A.*	117	M9	
Buena Vista, *Colo., U.S.A.*	115	G10	
Buena Vista, *Va., U.S.A.*	108	G6	
Buena Vista Lake Bed,			
U.S.A.	117	K7	
Buenaventura, *Colombia*	124	C3	
Buenaventura, *Mexico*	118	B3	
Buendía, Embalse de, *Spain*	32	E2	
Buenos Aires, *Argentina*	126	C4	
Buenos Aires, *Costa Rica*	120	E3	
Buenos Aires □, *Argentina*	126	D4	
Buenos Aires, L., *Chile*	128	F2	
Buffalo, *Mo., U.S.A.*	113	G8	
Buffalo, *N.Y., U.S.A.*	110	D6	
Buffalo, *Okla., U.S.A.*	113	G5	
Buffalo, *S. Dak., U.S.A.*	112	C3	
Buffalo, *Wyo., U.S.A.*	114	D10	
Buffalo →, *Canada*	104	A5	
Buffalo →, *S. Africa*	89	D5	
Buffalo Head Hills, *Canada*	104	B5	
Buffalo L., *Alta., Canada*	104	C6	
Buffalo L., *N.W.T., Canada*	104	A5	
Buffalo Narrows, *Canada*	105	B7	
Buffels →, *S. Africa*	88	D2	
Buford, *U.S.A.*	109	H4	
Bug = Buh →, *Ukraine*	47	J6	
Bug →, *Poland*	45	F8	
Buga, *Colombia*	124	C3	
Buganda, *Uganda*	86	C3	
Bugasong, *Phil.*	61	F5	
Bugeat, *France*	20	C5	
Bugel, Tanjung, *Indonesia*	63	G14	
Bugibba, *Malta*	36	D1	
Bugojno, *Bos.-H.*	42	F2	
Bugsuk, *Phil.*	62	C5	
Buguma, *Nigeria*	83	E6	
Bugun Shara, *Mongolia*	60	B5	
Buguruslan, *Russia*	50	D6	
Buh →, *Ukraine*	47	J6	
Buharkent, *Turkey*	39	D10	
Buheirat-Murrat-el-Kubra,			
Egypt	80	H8	
Buhera, *Zimbabwe*	89	B5	
Bühl, *Germany*	25	G4	
Buhl, *U.S.A.*	114	E6	
Buhuşi, *Romania*	43	D11	
Builth Wells, *U.K.*	13	E4	
Buinsk, *Russia*	48	C9	
Buir Nur, *Mongolia*	60	B6	
Buis-les-Baronnies, *France*	21	D9	
Buitrago = Buitrago del			
Lozoya, *Spain*	34	E7	
Buitrago del Lozoya, *Spain*	34	E7	
Bujalance, *Spain*	35	H6	
Bujanovac, *Serbia, Yug.*	40	D5	
Bujaraloz, *Spain*	32	D4	
Buje, *Croatia*	29	C10	
Bujumbura, *Burundi*	86	C2	
Bük, *Hungary*	42	C1	
Buk, *Poland*	45	F3	
Bukachacha, *Russia*	51	D12	
Bukama,			
Dem. Rep. of the Congo	87	D2	

Bukavu,
Dem. Rep. of the Congo . 86 C2
Bukene, Tanzania 86 C3
Bukhara = Bukhoro,
Uzbekistan 50 F7
Bukhoro, Uzbekistan 50 F7
Bukima, Tanzania 86 C3
Bukit Mertajam, Malaysia . 65 K3
Bukittinggi, Indonesia ... 62 E2
Bükk, Hungary 42 B5
Bukoba, Tanzania 86 C3
Bukuru, Nigeria 83 D6
Bukuya, Uganda 86 B3
Būl, Kuh-e, Iran 71 D7
Bula, Guinea-Biss. 82 C1
Bula, Indonesia 63 E8
Būlach, Switz. 25 H4
Bulahdelah, Australia 95 E5
Bulan, Phil. 61 E5
Bulancak, Turkey 73 B8
Bulandshahr, India 68 E7
Bulanık, Turkey 73 C10
Būlāq, Egypt 80 B3
Bulawayo, Zimbabwe 87 G2
Buldan, Turkey 39 C10
Bulgar, Russia 48 C9
Bulgaria ■, Europe 41 D9
Bulgheria, Monte, Italy .. 31 B8
Bulgurca, Turkey 39 C9
Buli, Teluk, Indonesia ... 63 D7
Buliluyan, C., Phil. 61 G2
Bulki, Ethiopia 81 F4
Bulkley →, Canada 104 B3
Bull Shoals L., U.S.A. ... 113 G8
Bullaque →, Spain 35 G6
Bullas, Spain 33 G3
Bulle, Switz. 25 J3
Bullhead City, U.S.A. ... 117 K12
Büllingen, Belgium 17 D6
Bullock Creek, Australia ... 94 B3
Bulloo →, Australia 95 D3
Bulloo L., Australia 95 D3
Bulls, N.Z. 91 J5
Bully-les-Mines, France ... 19 B9
Bulnes, Chile 126 D1
Bulqiza, Albania 40 E4
Bulsar = Valsad, India .. 66 J8
Bultfontein, S. Africa ... 88 D4
Bulukumba, Indonesia ... 63 F6
Bulun, Russia 51 B13
Bumba,
Dem. Rep. of the Congo . 84 D4
Bumbeşti-Jiu, Romania ... 43 E8
Bumbiri I., Tanzania 86 C3
Bumbuna, S. Leone 82 D2
Bumhpa Bum, Burma ... 67 F20
Bumi →, Zimbabwe 87 F2
Buna, Kenya 86 B4
Bunawan, Phil. 61 G6
Bunazi, Tanzania 86 C3
Bunbury, Australia 93 F2
Bunclody, Ireland 15 D5
Buncrana, Ireland 15 A4
Bundaberg, Australia 95 C5
Bünde, Germany 24 C4
Bundey →, Australia ... 94 C2
Bundi, India 68 G6
Bundoran, Ireland 15 B3
Bundukia, Sudan 81 F3
Bung Kan, Thailand 64 C4
Bunga →, Nigeria 83 C6
Bungatakada, Japan 55 H5
Bungay, U.K. 13 E9
Bungil Cr. →, Australia . 95 D4
Bungo-Suidō, Japan 55 H6
Bungoma, Kenya 86 B3
Bungu, Tanzania 86 D4
Bunia,
Dem. Rep. of the Congo . 86 B3
Bunji, Pakistan 69 B6
Bunkie, U.S.A. 113 K8
Buñol, Spain 33 F4
Bunsuru, Nigeria 83 C5
Buntok, Indonesia 62 E4
Bununu Dass, Nigeria ... 83 C6
Bununu Kasa, Nigeria ... 83 D6
Bünyan, Turkey 72 C6
Bunyu, Indonesia 62 D5
Bunza, Nigeria 83 C5
Buol, Indonesia 63 D6
Buon Brieng, Vietnam ... 64 F7
Buon Ma Thuot, Vietnam . 64 F7
Buong Long, Cambodia ... 64 F6
Buorkhaya, Mys, Russia . 51 B14
Buqayq, Si. Arabia 71 E6
Buqbuq, Egypt 80 A2
Bur Acaba, Somali Rep. ... 74 G3
Bûr Fuad, Egypt 80 H8
Bûr Safâga, Egypt 70 E2
Bûr Sa'îd, Egypt 80 H8
Bûr Sûdân, Sudan 80 D4
Bûr Taufiq, Egypt 80 J8
Bura, Kenya 86 C4
Burakin, Australia 93 F2
Buram, Sudan 81 E2
Burao, Somali Rep. 74 F4
Burāq, Syria 75 B5
Buraydah, Si. Arabia ... 70 E5
Burbank, U.S.A. 117 L8
Burda, India 68 G6
Burdekin →, Australia ... 94 B4
Burdur, Turkey 39 D12
Burdur □, Turkey 39 D12
Burdur Gölü, Turkey ... 39 D12
Burdwan = Barddhaman,
India 69 H12
Bure, Gojam, Ethiopia .. 81 E4
Bure, Ilubabor, Ethiopia ... 81 F4
Bure →, U.K. 12 E9
Büren, Germany 24 D4
Bureya →, Russia 51 E13

Burford, Canada 110 C4
Burg, Germany 24 C7
Burg auf Fehmarn, Germany 24 A7
Burg el Arab, Egypt 80 H6
Burg et Tuyur, Sudan ... 80 C2
Burg Stargard, Germany ... 24 B9
Burgas, Bulgaria 41 D11
Burgas □, Bulgaria 41 D10
Burgaski Zaliv, Bulgaria .. 41 D11
Burgdorf, Germany 24 C6
Burgdorf, Switz. 25 H3
Burgenland □, Austria ... 27 D9
Burgeo, Canada 103 C8
Burgersdorp, S. Africa ... 88 E4
Burges, Mt., Australia ... 93 F3
Burghausen, Germany ... 25 G8
Bürgio, Italy 30 E6
Burglengenfeld, Germany ... 25 F8
Burgohondo, Spain 34 E6
Burgos, Spain 34 C7
Burgos □, Spain 34 C7
Burgstädt, Germany 24 E8
Burgsvik, Sweden 11 G12
Burguillos del Cerro, Spain . 35 G4
Burgundy = Bourgogne,
France 19 F11
Burhaniye, Turkey 39 B8
Burhanpur, India 66 J10
Burhi Gandak →, India .. 69 G12
Burhner →, India 69 H9
Buri Pen., Eritrea 81 D4
Burias I., Phil. 61 E5
Burica, Pta., Costa Rica .. 120 E3
Burien, U.S.A. 116 C4
Burigi, L., Tanzania 86 C3
Burin, Canada 103 C8
Buriram, Thailand 64 E4
Burj Şafitā, Syria 70 C3
Burji, Ethiopia 81 F4
Burkburnett, U.S.A. 113 H5
Burke →, Australia 94 C2
Burke Chan., Canada ... 104 C3
Burketown, Australia 94 B2
Burkina Faso ■, Africa .. 82 C4
Burk's Falls, Canada 102 C4
Burlada, Spain 32 C3
Burleigh Falls, Canada ... 110 B6
Burley, U.S.A. 114 E7
Burlingame, U.S.A. 116 H4
Burlington, Canada 102 D4
Burlington, Colo., U.S.A. . 112 F3
Burlington, Iowa, U.S.A. . 112 E9
Burlington, Kans., U.S.A. . 112 F7
Burlington, N.C., U.S.A. .. 109 G6
Burlington, N.J., U.S.A. .. 111 F10
Burlington, Vt., U.S.A. .. 111 B11
Burlington, Wash., U.S.A. . 116 B4
Burlington, Wis., U.S.A. . 108 D1
Burlyu-Tyube, Kazakstan . 50 E8
Burma ■, Asia 67 J20
Burnaby I., Canada 104 C2
Burnet, U.S.A. 113 K5
Burney, U.S.A. 114 F3
Burnham, U.S.A. 110 F7
Burnham-on-Sea, U.K. .. 13 F5
Burnie, Australia 94 G4
Burnley, U.K. 12 D5
Burns, U.S.A. 114 E4
Burns Lake, Canada 104 C3
Burnside →, Canada ... 100 B9
Burnside, L., Australia .. 93 E3
Burnsville, U.S.A. 112 C8
Burnt L., Canada 103 B7
Burnt River, Canada 110 B6
Burntwood →, Canada .. 105 B9
Burntwood L., Canada ... 105 B8
Burqān, Kuwait 70 D5
Burra, Australia 95 E2
Burra, Nigeria 83 C6
Burray, U.K. 14 C6
Burreli, Albania 40 E4
Burren Junction, Australia . 95 E4
Burriana, Spain 32 F4
Burrinjuck Res., Australia . 95 F4
Burro, Serranías del, Mexico 118 B4
Burrow Hd., U.K. 14 G4
Burruyacú, Argentina ... 126 B3
Burry Port, U.K. 13 F3
Bursa, Turkey 41 F13
Burseryd, Sweden 11 G7
Burstall, Canada 105 C7
Burton, Ohio, U.S.A. ... 110 E3
Burton, S.C., U.S.A. 109 J5
Burton, L., Canada 102 B4
Burton upon Trent, U.K. . 12 E6
Buru, Indonesia 63 E7
Burullus, Bahra el, Egypt . 80 H7
Burûn, Râs, Egypt 75 D2
Burundi ■, Africa 86 C3
Bururi, Burundi 86 C2
Burutu, Nigeria 83 D6
Burwell, U.S.A. 112 E5
Burwick, U.K. 14 C5
Bury, U.K. 12 D5
Bury St. Edmunds, U.K. . 13 E8
Buryatia □, Russia 51 D11
Buryn, Ukraine 47 G7
Burzenin, Poland 45 G5
Busalla, Italy 28 D5
Busango Swamp, Zambia . 87 E2
Buşayrah, Syria 70 C4
Busca, Italy 28 D4
Bushati, Albania 40 E3
Büshehr, Iran 71 D6
Büshehr □, Iran 71 D6
Bushell, Canada 105 B7
Bushenyi, Uganda 86 C3
Bushire = Büshehr, Iran . 71 D6
Busie, Ghana 82 C4
Businga,
Dem. Rep. of the Congo . 84 D4

Busko-Zdrój, Poland 45 H7
Busovača, Bos.-H. 42 F7
Buşra ash Shām, Syria ... 75 C5
Busselton, Australia 93 F2
Busseri →, Sudan 81 F2
Busseto, Italy 28 D7
Bussière-Badil, France ... 20 C4
Bussolengo, Italy 28 C7
Bussum, Neths. 17 B5
Buşteni, Romania 43 E10
Busto, C., Spain 34 B4
Busto Arsízio, Italy 28 C5
Busu-Djanoa,
Dem. Rep. of the Congo . 84 D4
Busuanga I., Phil. 61 E3
Büsum, Germany 24 A4
Buta,
Dem. Rep. of the Congo . 86 B1
Butare, Rwanda 86 C2
Butaritari, Kiribati 96 G9
Bute, U.K. 14 F3
Bute Inlet, Canada 104 C4
Butemba, Uganda 86 B3
Butembo,
Dem. Rep. of the Congo . 86 B2
Buteni, Romania 42 D7
Butera, Italy 31 E7
Butha Qi, China 60 B7
Butiaba, Uganda 86 B3
Butler, Mo., U.S.A. 112 F7
Butler, Pa., U.S.A. 110 F5
Buton, Indonesia 63 E6
Butte, Mont., U.S.A. ... 114 C7
Butte, Nebr., U.S.A. 112 D5
Butte Creek →, U.S.A. .. 116 F5
Butterworth = Gcuwa,
S. Africa 89 E4
Butterworth, Malaysia ... 65 K3
Buttevant, Ireland 15 D3
Buttfield, Mt., Australia .. 93 D4
Button B., Canada 105 B10
Buttonwillow, U.S.A. ... 117 K7
Butty Hd., Australia 93 F3
Butuan, Phil. 61 G6
Butuku-Luba, Eq. Guin. .. 83 E6
Butung = Buton, Indonesia 63 E6
Buturlinovka, Russia ... 48 E5
Butzbach, Germany 25 E4
Bützow, Germany 24 B7
Buxa Duar, India 69 F13
Buxar, India 69 G10
Buxtehude, Germany ... 24 B5
Buxton, U.K. 12 D6
Buxy, France 19 F11
Buy, Russia 48 A5
Buynaksk, Russia 49 J8
Buyo, Ivory C. 82 D3
Buyo, L. de, Ivory C. ... 82 D3
Büyük Menderes →, Turkey 39 D9
Büyükçekmece, Turkey .. 41 E12
Büyükkarıştıran, Turkey . 41 E11
Büyükkemikli Burnu, Turkey 41 F10
Büyükorhan, Turkey 39 B10
Büyükyoncalı, Turkey ... 41 E11
Buzançais, France 18 F8
Buzău, Romania 43 E11
Buzău □, Romania 43 E11
Buzău →, Romania 43 E12
Buzău, Pasul, Romania .. 43 E11
Buzen, Japan 55 H5
Buzet, Croatia 29 C10
Buzi →, Mozam. 87 F3
Buziaş, Romania 42 E6
Buzuluk, Russia 50 D6
Buzuluk →, Russia 48 E6
Buzzards B., U.S.A. 111 E14
Buzzards Bay, U.S.A. ... 111 E14
Bwana Mkubwe,
Dem. Rep. of the Congo . 87 E2
Byala, Ruse, Bulgaria ... 41 C9
Byala, Varna, Bulgaria ... 41 D11
Byala Slatina, Bulgaria .. 40 C7
Byarezina →, Belarus ... 47 F6
Bychawa, Poland 45 G9
Byczyna, Poland 45 G5
Bydgoszcz, Poland 45 E5
Byelarus = Belarus ■,
Europe 46 F4
Byelorussia = Belarus ■,
Europe 46 F4
Byers, U.S.A. 112 F2
Byesville, U.S.A. 110 G3
Byford, Australia 93 F2
Bykhaw, Belarus 46 F6
Bykhov = Bykhaw, Belarus 46 F6
Bykovo, Russia 48 E7
Bylas, U.S.A. 115 K8
Bylot, Canada 105 B10
Bylot I., Canada 101 A12
Byrd, C., Antarctica 5 C17
Byrock, Australia 95 E4
Byron Bay, Australia 95 D5
Byrranga, Gory, Russia ... 51 B11
Byrranga Mts. = Byrranga,
Gory, Russia 51 B11
Byrum, Denmark 11 G5
Byske, Sweden 8 D19
Byske älv →, Sweden .. 8 D19
Bystrzyca →, Dolnośląskie,
Poland 45 G3
Bystrzyca →, Lubelskie,
Poland 45 G9
Bystrzyca Kłodzka, Poland . 27 B11
Bytča, Slovak Rep. 27 B11
Bytom, Poland 45 H5
Bytom Odrzański, Poland . 45 G2
Bytów, Poland 44 D3
Byumba, Rwanda 86 C3
Bzenec, Czech Rep. 27 C10
Bzura →, Poland 45 F7

C

Ca →, Vietnam 64 C5
Ca Mau, Vietnam 65 H5
Ca Mau, Mui, Vietnam ... 65 H5
Ca Na, Vietnam 65 G7
Caacupé, Paraguay 126 B4
Caála, Angola 85 G3
Caazapá, Paraguay 126 B4
Caazapá □, Paraguay ... 127 B4
Cabadbaran, Phil. 61 G6
Cabalian = San Juan, Phil. . 61 F6
Cabana, Spain 34 B2
Cabañaquinta, Spain 34 B5
Cabanatuan, Phil. 61 D4
Cabanes, Spain 32 E5
Cabano, Canada 103 C6
Čabar, Croatia 29 C11
Cabazon, U.S.A. 117 M10
Cabedelo, Brazil 125 E12
Cabeza del Buey, Spain .. 35 G5
Cabezón de la Sal, Spain . 34 B6
Cabildo, Chile 126 C1
Cabimas, Venezuela 124 A4
Cabinda, Angola 84 F2
Cabinda □, Angola 84 F2
Cabinet Mts., U.S.A. ... 114 C6
Cabo Blanco, Argentina .. 128 F3
Cabo Frio, Brazil 127 A7
Cabo Pantoja, Peru 124 D3
Cabonga, Réservoir, Canada 102 C4
Cabool, U.S.A. 113 G8
Caboolture, Australia ... 95 D5
Cabora Bassa Dam =
Cahora Bassa, Reprêsa de,
Mozam. 87 F3
Caborca, Mexico 118 A2
Cabot, Mt., U.S.A. 111 B13
Cabot Hd., Canada 110 A3
Cabot Str., Canada 103 C8
Cabra, Spain 35 H6
Cabra del Santo Cristo,
Spain 35 H7
Cábras, Italy 30 C1
Cabrera, Spain 37 B9
Cabrera, Sierra, Spain ... 34 C4
Cabri, Canada 105 C7
Cabriel →, Spain 33 F3
Cabugao, Phil. 61 C4
Cacabelos, Spain 34 C4
Caçador, Brazil 127 B5
Čačak, Serbia, Yug. 40 C4
Caçapava do Sul, Brazil .. 127 C5
Cáccamo, Italy 30 E6
Cacém, Portugal 35 G1
Cáceres, Brazil 124 G7
Cáceres, Spain 35 F4
Cáceres □, Spain 34 F5
Cache Bay, Canada 102 C4
Cache Cr. →, U.S.A. ... 116 G5
Cache Creek, Canada ... 104 C4
Cacheu, Guinea-Biss. ... 82 C1
Cachi, Argentina 126 B2
Cachimbo, Serra do, Brazil 125 E7
Cachinal de la Sierra, Chile 126 A2
Cachoeira, Brazil 125 F11
Cachoeira de Itapemirim,
Brazil 127 A7
Cachoeira do Sul, Brazil .. 127 C5
Cachopo, Portugal 35 H3
Cacine, Guinea-Biss. 82 C1
Cacoal, Brazil 124 F6
Cacólo, Angola 84 G3
Caconda, Angola 85 G3
Caddo, U.S.A. 113 H6
Cader Idris, U.K. 13 E4
Cadereyta, Mexico 118 B5
Cadí, Sierra del, Spain .. 32 C6
Cadibarrawirracanna, L.,
Australia 95 D2
Cadillac, France 20 D3
Cadillac, U.S.A. 108 C3
Cadiz, Phil. 61 F5
Cadiz, Spain 35 J4
Cadiz, Calif., U.S.A. 117 L11
Cadiz, Ohio, U.S.A. 110 F4
Cádiz □, Spain 35 J5
Cádiz, G. de, Spain 35 J3
Cadiz L., U.S.A. 115 J6
Cadney Park, Australia .. 95 D1
Cadomin, Canada 104 C5
Cadotte Lake, Canada ... 104 B5
Cadours, France 20 E5
Cadoux, Australia 93 F2
Caen, France 18 C6
Caernarfon, U.K. 12 D3
Caernarfon B., U.K. 12 D3
Caernarvon = Caernarfon,
U.K. 12 D3
Caerphilly, U.K. 13 F4
Caerphilly □, U.K. 13 F4
Caesarea, Israel 75 C3
Caetité, Brazil 125 F10
Cafayate, Argentina 126 B2
Cafu, Angola 88 B2
Cagayan →, Phil. 61 B4
Cagayan de Oro, Phil. ... 61 G6
Cagayan Is., Phil. 61 G4
Cagayan Sulu I., Phil. ... 61 H3
Cagli, Italy 29 E9
Cágliari, Italy 30 C2
Cágliari, G. di, Italy 30 C2
Cagnano Varano, Italy ... 29 G12
Cagnes-sur-Mer, France .. 21 E11
Caguán →, Colombia ... 124 D4
Caguas, Puerto Rico 121 C6
Caha Mts., Ireland 15 E2
Cahama, Angola 88 B1

Caher, Ireland 15 D4
Caherciveen, Ireland ... 15 E1
Cahora Bassa, Reprêsa de,
Mozam. 87 F3
Cahore Pt., Ireland 15 D5
Cahors, France 20 D5
Cahul, Moldova 43 E13
Caì Bau, Dao, Vietnam .. 58 G6
Cai Nuoc, Vietnam 65 H5
Caia, Mozam. 87 F4
Caianda, Angola 87 E1
Caibarién, Cuba 120 B4
Caibiran, Phil. 61 F6
Caicara, Venezuela 124 B5
Caicó, Brazil 125 E11
Caicos Is., W. Indies ... 121 B5
Caicos Passage, W. Indies . 121 B5
Caidian, China 59 B10
Căinari, Moldova 43 D14
Caird Coast, Antarctica .. 5 D1
Cairn Gorm, U.K. 14 D5
Cairngorm Mts., U.K. ... 14 D5
Cairnryan, U.K. 14 G3
Cairns, Australia 94 B4
Cairns L., Canada 105 C10
Cairo = El Qâhira, Egypt . 80 H7
Cairo, Ga., U.S.A. 109 K3
Cairo, Ill., U.S.A. 113 G10
Cairo, N.Y., U.S.A. 111 D11
Cairo Montenotte, Italy .. 28 D5
Caithness, Ord of, U.K. . 14 C5
Cajamarca, Peru 124 E3
Cajarc, France 20 D5
Cajàzeiras, Brazil 125 E11
Čajetina, Serbia, Yug. .. 40 C3
Çakırgol, Turkey 73 B8
Çakırlar, Turkey 39 E12
Čakovec, Croatia 29 B13
Çal, Turkey 39 C11
Cala, Spain 35 H4
Cala →, Spain 35 H4
Cala Cadolar, Punta de =
Rotja, Pta., Spain 33 G6
Cala d'Or, Spain 37 B10
Cala en Porter, Spain ... 37 B11
Cala Figuera, C. de, Spain . 37 B9
Cala Forcat, Spain 37 B10
Cala Major, Spain 37 B9
Cala Mezquida = Sa
Mesquida, Spain 37 B11
Cala Millor, Spain 37 B10
Cala Ratjada, Spain 37 B10
Cala Santa Galdana, Spain . 37 B10
Calabanga, Phil. 61 E5
Calabar, Nigeria 83 E6
Calabogie, Canada 111 A8
Calabozo, Venezuela 124 B5
Calábria □, Italy 31 C9
Calaburras, Pta. de, Spain . 35 J6
Calaceite, Spain 32 D5
Calacuccia, France 21 F13
Calafat, Romania 42 G7
Calafate, Argentina 128 G2
Calahorra, Spain 32 C3
Calais, France 19 B8
Calais, U.S.A. 109 C12
Calalaste, Cord. de,
Argentina 126 B2
Calama, Brazil 124 E6
Calama, Chile 126 A2
Calamar, Colombia 124 A4
Calamian Group, Phil. ... 61 F3
Calamocha, Spain 32 E3
Calamonte, Spain 35 G4
Calan, Romania 42 E7
Calañas, Spain 35 H4
Calanda, Spain 32 E4
Calang, Indonesia 62 D1
Calangiánus, Italy 30 B2
Calapan, Phil. 61 E4
Călărași, Moldova 43 C13
Călărași, Romania 43 F12
Călărași □, Romania ... 43 F12
Calasparra, Spain 33 G3
Calatafimi, Italy 30 E5
Calatayud, Spain 32 D3
Călățele, Romania 42 D8
Calato = Kálathos, Greece . 39 E10
Calauag, Phil. 61 E5
Calavà, C., Italy 31 D7
Calavite, C., Phil. 61 E4
Calayan, Phil. 61 B4
Calbayog, Phil. 61 E6
Calca, Peru 124 F4
Calcasieu L., U.S.A. 113 L8
Calcutta, India 69 H13
Calcutta, U.S.A. 110 F4
Caldaro, Italy 29 B8
Caldas da Rainha, Portugal 35 F1
Caldas de Reis, Spain ... 34 C2
Calder →, U.K. 12 D6
Caldera, Chile 126 B1
Caldwell, Idaho, U.S.A. . 114 E5
Caldwell, Kans., U.S.A. . 113 G6
Caldwell, Tex., U.S.A. .. 113 K6
Caledon, S. Africa 88 E2
Caledon →, S. Africa .. 88 E4
Caledon B., Australia ... 94 A2
Caledonia, Canada 110 C5
Caledonia, U.S.A. 110 D7
Calella, Spain 32 D7
Calemba, Angola 88 B2
Calen, Australia 94 B4
Calenzana, France 21 F12
Caletones, Chile 126 C1
Calexico, U.S.A. 117 N11
Calf of Man, U.K. 12 C3
Calgary, Canada 104 C6
Calheta, Madeira 37 D2
Calhoun, U.S.A. 109 H3

Cali, Colombia ... 124 C3
Calicut, India ... 66 P9
Caliente, U.S.A. ... 115 H6
California, Mo., U.S.A. ... 112 F8
California, Pa., U.S.A. ... 110 F5
California □, U.S.A. ... 116 H7
California, Baja, Mexico ... 118 A1
California, Baja, T.N. = Baja California □, Mexico ... 118 B2
California, Baja, T.S. = Baja California Sur □, Mexico ... 118 B2
California, G. de, Mexico ... 118 B2
California City, U.S.A. ... 117 K9
California Hot Springs, U.S.A. ... 117 K8
Călimăneşti, Romania ... 43 E9
Călimani, Munţii, Romania ... 43 C10
Calingasta, Argentina ... 126 C2
Calipatria, U.S.A. ... 117 M11
Calistoga, U.S.A. ... 116 G4
Calitri, Italy ... 31 B8
Calitzdorp, S. Africa ... 88 E3
Callabonna, L., Australia ... 95 D3
Callac, France ... 18 D3
Callan, Ireland ... 15 D4
Callander, U.K. ... 14 E4
Callao, Peru ... 124 F3
Calles, Mexico ... 119 C5
Callicoon, U.S.A. ... 111 E9
Calling Lake, Canada ... 104 B6
Calliope, Australia ... 94 C5
Callosa de Ensarriá, Spain ... 33 G4
Callosa de Segura, Spain ... 33 G4
Calne, U.K. ... 13 F6
Calola, Angola ... 88 B2
Calolbon = San Andres, Phil. ... 61 E6
Calonge, Spain ... 32 D8
Caloocan, Phil. ... 61 D4
Calore →, Italy ... 31 A7
Caloundra, Australia ... 95 D5
Calpe, Spain ... 33 G5
Calpella, U.S.A. ... 116 F3
Calpine, U.S.A. ... 116 F6
Calstock, Canada ... 102 C3
Caltabellotta, Italy ... 30 E6
Caltagirone, Italy ... 31 E7
Caltanissetta, Italy ... 31 E7
Çaltılıbük, Turkey ... 41 G12
Caluire-et-Cuire, France ... 19 G11
Calulo, Angola ... 84 G2
Caluso, Italy ... 28 C4
Calvados □, France ... 18 C6
Calvert →, Australia ... 94 B2
Calvert I., Canada ... 104 C3
Calvert Ra., Australia ... 92 D3
Calvi, France ... 21 F12
Calvià, Spain ... 33 F7
Calvillo, Mexico ... 118 C4
Calvinia, S. Africa ... 88 E2
Calvo = Calvo, Mte., Italy ... 29 G12
Calvo, Mte., Italy ... 29 G12
Calwa, U.S.A. ... 116 J7
Calzada Almuradiel = Almuradiel, Spain ... 35 G7
Calzada de Calatrava, Spain ... 35 G7
Cam →, U.K. ... 13 E8
Cam Lam, Vietnam ... 65 G7
Cam Pha, Vietnam ... 58 G6
Cam Ranh, Vietnam ... 65 G7
Cam Xuyen, Vietnam ... 64 C6
Camabatela, Angola ... 84 F3
Camacha, Madeira ... 37 D3
Camacho, Mexico ... 118 C4
Camacupa, Angola ... 85 G3
Camagüey, Cuba ... 120 B4
Camaiore, Italy ... 28 E7
Camaná, Peru ... 124 G4
Camanche Reservoir, U.S.A. ... 116 G6
Camaquã, Brazil ... 127 C5
Camaquã →, Brazil ... 127 C5
Câmara de Lobos, Madeira ... 37 D3
Camarat, C., France ... 21 E10
Camarès, France ... 20 E6
Camaret-sur-Mer, France ... 18 D2
Camargo, Mexico ... 119 B5
Camargue, France ... 21 E8
Camarillo, U.S.A. ... 117 L7
Camariñas, Spain ... 34 B1
Camarón, C., Honduras ... 120 C2
Camarones, Argentina ... 128 E3
Camas, Spain ... 35 H4
Camas, U.S.A. ... 116 E4
Camas Valley, U.S.A. ... 114 E2
Camballin, Australia ... 92 C3
Cambará, Brazil ... 127 A5
Cambay = Khambhat, India ... 68 H5
Cambay, G. of = Khambhat, G. of, India ... 66 J8
Cambil, Spain ... 35 H7
Cambo-les-Bains, France ... 20 E2
Cambodia ■, Asia ... 64 F5
Camborne, U.K. ... 13 G2
Cambrai, France ... 19 B10
Cambre, Spain ... 34 B2
Cambria, U.S.A. ... 116 K5
Cambrian Mts., U.K. ... 13 E4
Cambridge, Canada ... 102 D3
Cambridge, Jamaica ... 120 C4
Cambridge, N.Z. ... 91 G5
Cambridge, U.K. ... 13 E8
Cambridge, Mass., U.S.A. ... 111 D13
Cambridge, Minn., U.S.A. ... 112 C8
Cambridge, N.Y., U.S.A. ... 111 C11
Cambridge, Nebr., U.S.A. ... 112 E4
Cambridge, Ohio, U.S.A. ... 110 F3
Cambridge Bay = Ikaluktutiak, Canada ... 100 B9
Cambridge G., Australia ... 92 B4
Cambridge Springs, U.S.A. ... 110 E4
Cambridgeshire □, U.K. ... 13 E7

Cambrils, Spain ... 32 D6
Cambuci, Brazil ... 127 A7
Cambundi-Catembo, Angola ... 84 G3
Camden, Ala., U.S.A. ... 109 K2
Camden, Ark., U.S.A. ... 113 J8
Camden, Maine, U.S.A. ... 109 C11
Camden, N.J., U.S.A. ... 111 G9
Camden, N.Y., U.S.A. ... 111 C9
Camden, S.C., U.S.A. ... 109 H5
Camden Sd., Australia ... 92 C3
Camdenton, U.S.A. ... 113 F8
Çameli, Turkey ... 39 D11
Camenca, Moldova ... 43 B13
Camerino, Italy ... 29 E10
Cameron, Ariz., U.S.A. ... 115 J8
Cameron, La., U.S.A. ... 113 L8
Cameron, Mo., U.S.A. ... 112 F7
Cameron, Tex., U.S.A. ... 113 K6
Cameron Highlands, Malaysia ... 65 K3
Cameron Hills, Canada ... 104 B5
Camerota, Italy ... 31 B8
Cameroon ■, Africa ... 84 C2
Cameroun →, Cameroon ... 83 E6
Cameroun, Mt., Cameroon ... 83 E6
Cametá, Brazil ... 125 D9
Çamiçi Gölü, Turkey ... 39 D9
Camiguin □, Phil. ... 61 G6
Camiguin I., Phil. ... 61 B4
Camiling, Phil. ... 61 D4
Camilla, U.S.A. ... 109 K3
Caminha, Portugal ... 34 D2
Camino, U.S.A. ... 116 G6
Camira Creek, Australia ... 95 D5
Cammal, U.S.A. ... 110 E7
Cammarata, Italy ... 30 E6
Camocim, Brazil ... 125 D10
Camooweal, Australia ... 94 B2
Camopi, Fr. Guiana ... 125 C8
Camotes Is., Phil. ... 61 F6
Camotes Sea, Phil. ... 61 F6
Camp Borden, Canada ... 110 B5
Camp Hill, U.S.A. ... 110 F8
Camp Nelson, U.S.A. ... 117 J8
Camp Pendleton, U.S.A. ... 117 M9
Camp Verde, U.S.A. ... 115 J8
Camp Wood, U.S.A. ... 113 L5
Campagna, Italy ... 31 B8
Campana, Argentina ... 126 C4
Campana, I., Chile ... 128 F1
Campanário, Madeira ... 37 D2
Campanario, Spain ... 35 G5
Campánia □, Italy ... 31 B7
Campbell, S. Africa ... 88 D3
Campbell, Calif., U.S.A. ... 116 H5
Campbell, Ohio, U.S.A. ... 110 E4
Campbell I., Pac. Oc. ... 96 N8
Campbell L., Canada ... 105 A7
Campbell River, Canada ... 104 C3
Campbell Town, Australia ... 94 G4
Campbellford, Canada ... 110 B7
Campbellpur, Pakistan ... 68 C5
Campbellsville, U.S.A. ... 108 G3
Campbellton, Canada ... 103 C6
Campbelltown, Australia ... 95 E5
Campbeltown, U.K. ... 14 F3
Campeche, Mexico ... 119 D6
Campeche □, Mexico ... 119 D6
Campeche, Golfo de, Mexico ... 119 D6
Campello, Spain ... 33 G4
Câmpeni, Romania ... 42 D8
Camperdown, Australia ... 95 F3
Camperville, Canada ... 105 C8
Campi Salentina, Italy ... 31 B11
Câmpia Turzii, Romania ... 43 D8
Campidano, Italy ... 30 C1
Campíglia Maríttima, Italy ... 28 E7
Campillo de Altobuey, Spain ... 33 F3
Campillos, Spain ... 35 H6
Câmpina, Romania ... 43 E10
Campina Grande, Brazil ... 125 E11
Campinas, Brazil ... 127 A6
Campli, Italy ... 29 F10
Campo, Spain ... 32 C5
Campo de Criptana, Spain ... 35 F7
Campo de Gibraltar, Spain ... 35 J5
Campo Grande, Brazil ... 125 H8
Campo Maior, Brazil ... 125 D10
Campo Maior, Portugal ... 35 F3
Campo Mourão, Brazil ... 127 A5
Campo Túres, Italy ... 29 B8
Campobasso, Italy ... 31 A7
Campobello di Licata, Italy ... 30 E6
Campobello di Mazara, Italy ... 30 E5
Campofelice di Roccella, Italy ... 30 E6
Campomarino, Italy ... 29 G12
Camporeale, Italy ... 30 E6
Camporrobles, Spain ... 32 F3
Campos, Brazil ... 127 A7
Campos Belos, Brazil ... 125 F9
Campos del Puerto, Spain ... 37 B10
Campos Novos, Brazil ... 127 B5
Camprodón, Spain ... 32 C7
Camptonville, U.S.A. ... 116 F5
Camptown, U.S.A. ... 111 E8
Câmpulung, Argeş, Romania ... 43 E10
Câmpulung, Suceava, Romania ... 43 C10
Câmpuri, Romania ... 43 D11
Camrose, Canada ... 104 C6
Camsell Portage, Canada ... 105 B7
Çamyuva, Turkey ... 39 E12
Çan, Turkey ... 41 F11
Can Clavo, Spain ... 37 C7
Can Creu, Spain ... 37 C7
Can Gio, Vietnam ... 65 G6
Can Tho, Vietnam ... 65 G5
Canaan, U.S.A. ... 111 D11
Canada ■, N. Amer. ... 100 C10
Cañada de Gómez, Argentina ... 126 C3

Canadian, U.S.A. ... 113 H4
Canadian →, U.S.A. ... 113 H7
Canajoharie, U.S.A. ... 111 D10
Canal Flats, Canada ... 104 C5
Canalejas, Argentina ... 126 D2
Canals, Argentina ... 126 C3
Canals, Spain ... 33 G4
Canandaigua, U.S.A. ... 110 D7
Canandaigua L., U.S.A. ... 110 D7
Cananea, Mexico ... 118 A2
Canarreos, Arch. de los, Cuba ... 120 B3
Canary Is. = Canarias, Is., Atl. Oc. ... 37 F4
Canaseraga, U.S.A. ... 110 D7
Canatlán, Mexico ... 118 C4
Canaveral, C., U.S.A. ... 109 L5
Cañaverelas, Spain ... 32 E2
Canavieiras, Brazil ... 125 G11
Canberra, Australia ... 95 F4
Canby, Calif., U.S.A. ... 114 F3
Canby, Minn., U.S.A. ... 112 C6
Canby, Oreg., U.S.A. ... 116 E4
Cancale, France ... 18 D5
Cancún, Mexico ... 119 C7
Canche →, France ... 19 B8
Candanchu, Spain ... 32 C4
Çandarlı, Turkey ... 39 C8
Çandarlı Körfezi, Turkey ... 39 C8
Candé, France ... 18 E5
Candela, Italy ... 31 A8
Candelaria, Argentina ... 127 B4
Candelaria, Canary Is. ... 37 F3
Candeleda, Spain ... 34 E5
Candelo, Australia ... 95 F4
Candia = Iráklion, Greece ... 36 D7
Candia, Sea of = Crete, Sea of, Greece ... 39 E7
Candle L., Canada ... 105 C7
Candlemas I., Antarctica ... 5 B1
Cando, U.S.A. ... 112 A5
Candon, Phil. ... 61 C4
Canea = Khaniá, Greece ... 36 D6
Canelli, Italy ... 28 D5
Canelones, Uruguay ... 127 C4
Canet-Plage, France ... 20 F7
Cañete, Chile ... 126 D1
Cañete, Peru ... 124 F3
Cañete, Spain ... 32 E3
Cañete de las Torres, Spain ... 35 H6
Cangas, Spain ... 34 C2
Cangas de Narcea, Spain ... 34 B4
Cangas de Onís, Spain ... 34 B5
Cangnan, China ... 59 D13
Canguaretama, Brazil ... 125 E11
Canguçu, Brazil ... 127 C5
Canguçu, Serra do, Brazil ... 127 C5
Cangwu, China ... 59 F8
Cangxi, China ... 58 B5
Cangyuan, China ... 58 F2
Cangzhou, China ... 56 E9
Caniapiscau →, Canada ... 103 A6
Caniapiscau Rés. de, Canada ... 103 B6
Canicattì, Italy ... 30 E6
Canicattini Bagni, Italy ... 31 E8
Caniles, Spain ... 35 H8
Canim Lake, Canada ... 104 C4
Canindeyu □, Paraguay ... 127 A5
Canino, Italy ... 29 F8
Canistro, U.S.A. ... 110 D7
Canisteo, U.S.A. ... 110 D7
Cañitas, Mexico ... 118 C4
Cañizal, Spain ... 34 D5
Canjáyar, Spain ... 35 H8
Çankırı, Turkey ... 72 B5
Cankuzo, Burundi ... 86 C3
Canmore, Canada ... 104 C5
Cann River, Australia ... 95 F4
Canna, U.K. ... 14 D2
Cannanore, India ... 66 P9
Cannes, France ... 21 E11
Canning Town = Port Canning, India ... 69 H13
Cannington, Canada ... 110 B5
Cannóbio, Italy ... 28 B5
Cannock, U.K. ... 13 E5
Cannon Ball →, U.S.A. ... 112 B4
Cannondale Mt., Australia ... 94 D4
Cannonsville Reservoir, U.S.A. ... 111 D9
Cannonvale, Australia ... 94 C4
Canoas, Brazil ... 127 B5
Canoe L., Canada ... 105 B7
Canon City, U.S.A. ... 112 F2
Canora, Canada ... 105 C8
Canosa di Púglia, Italy ... 31 A9
Canowindra, Australia ... 95 E4
Canso, Canada ... 103 C7
Cantabria □, Spain ... 34 B7
Cantabria, Sierra de, Spain ... 32 C2
Cantabrian Mts. = Cantábrica, Cordillera, Spain ... 34 C5
Cantábrica, Cordillera, Spain ... 34 C5
Cantal □, France ... 20 C6
Cantal, Plomb du, France ... 20 C6
Cantanhede, Portugal ... 34 E2
Cantavieja, Spain ... 32 E4
Čantavir, Serbia, Yug. ... 42 E4
Cantemir, Moldova ... 43 D13
Canterbury, Australia ... 94 D3
Canterbury, U.K. ... 13 F9
Canterbury □, N.Z. ... 91 K3
Canterbury Bight, N.Z. ... 91 L3
Canterbury Plains, N.Z. ... 91 K3
Cantil, U.S.A. ... 117 K9

Cantillana, Spain ... 35 H5
Canton = Guangzhou, China ... 59 F9
Canton, Ga., U.S.A. ... 109 H3
Canton, Ill., U.S.A. ... 112 E9
Canton, Miss., U.S.A. ... 113 J9
Canton, Mo., U.S.A. ... 112 E9
Canton, N.Y., U.S.A. ... 111 B9
Canton, Ohio, U.S.A. ... 110 F3
Canton, S. Dak., U.S.A. ... 112 D6
Canton L., U.S.A. ... 113 G5
Cantù, Italy ... 28 C6
Canudos, Brazil ... 124 E7
Canumã →, Brazil ... 124 D7
Canutama, Brazil ... 124 E6
Canutillo, U.S.A. ... 115 L10
Canvey, U.K. ... 13 F8
Canyon, U.S.A. ... 113 H4
Canyonlands National Park, U.S.A. ... 115 G9
Canyonville, U.S.A. ... 114 E2
Cao Bang, Vietnam ... 58 F6
Cao He →, China ... 57 D13
Cao Lanh, Vietnam ... 65 G5
Cao Xian, China ... 56 G8
Cáorle, Italy ... 29 C9
Cap-aux-Meules, Canada ... 103 C7
Cap-Chat, Canada ... 103 C6
Cap-de-la-Madeleine, Canada ... 102 C5
Cap-Haïtien, Haiti ... 121 C5
Capac, U.S.A. ... 110 C2
Capanaparo →, Venezuela ... 124 B5
Capánnori, Italy ... 28 E7
Capbreton, France ... 20 E2
Capdenac, France ... 20 D6
Capdepera, Spain ... 32 F8
Cape →, Australia ... 94 C4
Cape Barren I., Australia ... 94 G4
Cape Breton Highlands Nat. Park, Canada ... 103 C7
Cape Breton I., Canada ... 103 C7
Cape Charles, U.S.A. ... 108 G8
Cape Coast, Ghana ... 83 D4
Cape Coral, U.S.A. ... 109 M5
Cape Dorset, Canada ... 101 B12
Cape Fear →, U.S.A. ... 109 H6
Cape Girardeau, U.S.A. ... 113 G10
Cape May, U.S.A. ... 108 F8
Cape May Point, U.S.A. ... 108 F8
Cape Province, S. Africa ... 85 L3
Cape Tormentine, Canada ... 103 C7
Cape Town, S. Africa ... 88 E2
Cape Verde Is. ■, Atl. Oc. ... 77 E1
Cape Vincent, U.S.A. ... 111 B8
Cape York Peninsula, Australia ... 94 A3
Capela, Brazil ... 125 F11
Capella, Australia ... 94 C4
Capendu, France ... 20 E7
Capestang, France ... 20 E7
Capim →, Brazil ... 125 D9
Capistrello, Italy ... 29 G10
Capitan, U.S.A. ... 115 K11
Capitol Reef National Park, U.S.A. ... 115 G8
Capitola, U.S.A. ... 116 J5
Capizzi, Italy ... 31 E7
Capoche →, Mozam. ... 87 F3
Capoterra, Italy ... 30 C1
Cappadocia, Turkey ... 72 C6
Capraia, Italy ... 28 E6
Caprara, Pta., Italy ... 30 A1
Caprarola, Italy ... 29 F9
Capreol, Canada ... 102 C3
Caprera, Italy ... 30 A2
Capri, Italy ... 31 B7
Capricorn Group, Australia ... 94 C5
Capricorn Ra., Australia ... 92 D2
Caprino Veronese, Italy ... 28 C7
Caprivi Strip, Namibia ... 88 B3
Captain's Flat, Australia ... 95 F4
Captieux, France ... 20 D3
Caquetá →, Colombia ... 122 D4
Caracal, Romania ... 43 F9
Caracas, Venezuela ... 124 A5
Caracol, Mato Grosso do Sul, Brazil ... 126 A4
Caracol, Piauí, Brazil ... 125 E10
Caráglio, Italy ... 28 D4
Carajas, Brazil ... 125 E8
Carajás, Serra dos, Brazil ... 125 E8
Carangola, Brazil ... 127 A7
Caransebeş, Romania ... 42 E7
Carantec, France ... 18 D3
Caraquet, Canada ... 103 C6
Caras, Peru ... 124 E3
Caraş Severin □, Romania ... 42 E7
Caraşova, Romania ... 42 E6
Caratasca, L., Honduras ... 120 C3
Caratinga, Brazil ... 125 G10
Caraúbas, Brazil ... 125 E11
Caravaca = Caravaca de la Cruz, Spain ... 33 G3
Caravaca de la Cruz, Spain ... 33 G3
Caravággio, Italy ... 28 C6
Caravela, Guinea-Biss. ... 82 C1
Caravelas, Brazil ... 125 G11
Caraveli, Peru ... 124 G4
Caràzinho, Brazil ... 127 B5
Carballino = O Carballiño, Spain ... 34 C2
Carballo, Spain ... 34 B2
Carberry, Canada ... 105 D9
Carbó, Mexico ... 118 B2
Carbon, C., Italy ... 30 C2
Carbonale, Colo., U.S.A. ... 114 G10
Carbondale, Ill., U.S.A. ... 113 G10

Carbondale, Pa., U.S.A. ... 111 E9
Carbonear, Canada ... 103 C9
Carboneras, Spain ... 33 J3
Carboneras de Guadazón, Spain ... 32 F3
Carbónia, Italy ... 30 C1
Carcabuey, Spain ... 35 H6
Carcagente = Carcaixent, Spain ... 33 F4
Carcaixent, Spain ... 33 F4
Carcajou, Canada ... 104 B5
Carcar, Phil. ... 61 F5
Carcarana →, Argentina ... 126 C3
Carcasse, C., Haiti ... 121 C4
Carcross, Canada ... 104 A2
Çardak, Çanakkale, Turkey ... 41 F10
Çardak, Denizli, Turkey ... 39 D11
Cardamon Hills, India ... 66 Q10
Cardeña, Spain ... 35 G6
Cárdenas, Cuba ... 120 B3
Cárdenas, San Luis Potosí, Mexico ... 119 C5
Cárdenas, Tabasco, Mexico ... 119 D6
Cardenete, Spain ... 32 F3
Cardiff, U.K. ... 13 F4
Cardiff □, U.K. ... 13 F4
Cardiff-by-the-Sea, U.S.A. ... 117 M9
Cardigan, U.K. ... 13 E3
Cardigan B., U.K. ... 13 E3
Cardinal, Canada ... 111 B9
Cardona, Spain ... 32 D6
Cardona, Uruguay ... 126 C4
Cardoner →, Spain ... 32 D6
Cardoso, Ilha do, Brazil ... 127 B5
Cardston, Canada ... 104 D6
Cardwell, Australia ... 94 B4
Careen L., Canada ... 105 B7
Carei, Romania ... 42 C7
Careme = Ciremai, Indonesia ... 63 G13
Carentan, France ... 18 C5
Carey, U.S.A. ... 114 E7
Carey, L., Australia ... 93 E3
Carey L., Canada ... 105 A8
Careysburg, Liberia ... 82 D2
Cargèse, France ... 21 F12
Carhaix-Plouguer, France ... 18 D3
Carhué, Argentina ... 126 D3
Caria, Turkey ... 39 D10
Cariacica, Brazil ... 125 H10
Cariati, Italy ... 31 C9
Caribbean Sea, W. Indies ... 121 D5
Cariboo Mts., Canada ... 104 C4
Caribou, U.S.A. ... 109 B12
Caribou →, Man., Canada ... 105 B10
Caribou →, N.W.T., Canada ... 104 A3
Caribou I., Canada ... 102 C2
Caribou Is., Canada ... 104 A6
Caribou L., Man., Canada ... 105 B9
Caribou L., Ont., Canada ... 102 B2
Caribou Mts., Canada ... 104 B5
Carichic, Mexico ... 118 B3
Carigara, Phil. ... 61 F6
Carignan, France ... 19 C12
Carignano, Italy ... 28 D4
Carillo, Mexico ... 118 B4
Carinda, Australia ... 95 E4
Cariñena, Spain ... 32 D3
Carinhanha, Brazil ... 125 F10
Carinhanha →, Brazil ... 125 F10
Carini, Italy ... 30 D6
Cariño, Spain ... 34 B3
Carínola, Italy ... 30 A6
Carinthia = Kärnten □, Austria ... 26 E6
Caripito, Venezuela ... 124 A6
Carlbrod = Dimitrovgrad, Serbia, Yug. ... 40 C7
Carlet, Spain ... 33 F4
Carleton, Mt., Canada ... 103 C6
Carleton Place, Canada ... 102 C4
Carletonville, S. Africa ... 88 D4
Cârlibaba, Romania ... 43 C10
Carlin, U.S.A. ... 114 F5
Carlingford L., U.K. ... 15 B5
Carlinville, U.S.A. ... 112 F10
Carlisle, U.K. ... 12 C5
Carlisle, U.S.A. ... 110 F7
Carlit, Pic, France ... 20 F5
Carloforte, Italy ... 30 C1
Carlos Casares, Argentina ... 126 D3
Carlos Tejedor, Argentina ... 126 D3
Carlow, Ireland ... 15 D5
Carlow □, Ireland ... 15 D5
Carlsbad, Calif., U.S.A. ... 117 M9
Carlsbad, N. Mex., U.S.A. ... 113 J2
Carlsbad Caverns National Park, U.S.A. ... 113 J2
Carluke, U.K. ... 14 F5
Carmacks, Canada ... 100 B6
Carmagnola, Italy ... 28 D4
Carman, Canada ... 105 D9
Carmarthen, U.K. ... 13 F3
Carmarthen B., U.K. ... 13 F3
Carmarthenshire □, U.K. ... 13 F3
Carmaux, France ... 20 D6
Carmel, U.S.A. ... 111 E11
Carmel-by-the-Sea, U.S.A. ... 116 J5
Carmel Valley, U.S.A. ... 116 J5
Carmelo, Uruguay ... 126 C4
Carmen, Colombia ... 124 B3
Carmen, Paraguay ... 127 B4
Carmen →, Mexico ... 118 A3
Carmen, I., Mexico ... 118 B2
Carmen de Patagones, Argentina ... 128 E4
Cármenes, Spain ... 34 C5
Carmensa, Argentina ... 126 D2

Carmi, *Canada* 104 D5
Carmi, *U.S.A.* 108 F1
Carmichael, *U.S.A.* 116 G5
Carmila, *Australia* 94 C4
Carmona, *Costa Rica* 120 E2
Carmona, *Spain* 35 H5
Carn Ban, *U.K.* 14 D4
Carn Eige, *U.K.* 14 D3
Carnamah, *Australia* 93 E2
Carnarvon, *Australia* 93 D1
Carnarvon, *S. Africa* 88 E3
Carnarvon Ra., *Queens.,*
 Australia 94 D4
Carnarvon Ra., *W. Austral.,*
 Australia 93 E3
Carnation, *U.S.A.* 116 C5
Carndonagh, *Ireland* 15 A4
Carnduff, *Canada* 105 D8
Carnegie, *U.S.A.* 110 F4
Carnegie, L., *Australia* ... 93 E3
Carnic Alps = Karnische
 Alpen, *Europe* 26 E6
Carniche Alpi = Karnische
 Alpen, *Europe* 26 E6
Carnot, *C.A.R.* 84 D3
Carnot, C., *Australia* 95 E2
Carnot B., *Australia* 92 C3
Carnoustie, *U.K.* 14 E6
Carnsore Pt., *Ireland* 15 D5
Caro, *U.S.A.* 108 D4
Carol City, *U.S.A.* 109 N5
Carolina, *Brazil* 125 E9
Carolina, *Puerto Rico* 121 C6
Carolina, *S. Africa* 89 D5
Caroline I., *Kiribati* 97 H12
Caroline Is., *Micronesia* ... 52 J17
Caroni →, *Venezuela* 124 B6
Caronie = Nébrodi, Monti,
 Italy 31 E7
Caroona, *Australia* 95 E5
Carpathians, *Europe* 6 F10
Carpații Meridionali,
 Romania 43 E9
Carpentaria, G. of, *Australia* 94 A2
Carpentras, *France* 21 D9
Carpi, *Italy* 28 D7
Cărpineni, *Moldova* 43 D13
Carpinteria, *U.S.A.* 117 L7
Carpio, *Spain* 34 D5
Carr Boyd Ra., *Australia* . 92 C4
Carrabelle, *U.S.A.* 109 L3
Carral, *Spain* 34 B2
Carranza, Presa V., *Mexico* 118 B4
Carrara, *Italy* 28 D7
Carrascal, *Phil.* 61 G6
Carrascosa del Campo, *Spain* 32 E2
Carrauntoohill, *Ireland* ... 15 D2
Carrick-on-Shannon, *Ireland* 15 C3
Carrick-on-Suir, *Ireland* ... 15 D4
Carrickfergus, *U.K.* 15 B6
Carrickmacross, *Ireland* .. 15 C5
Carrieton, *Australia* 95 E2
Carrington, *U.S.A.* 112 B5
Carrión →, *Spain* 34 D6
Carrión de los Condes, *Spain* 34 C6
Carrizal Bajo, *Chile* 126 B1
Carrizalillo, *Chile* 126 B1
Carrizo Cr. →, *U.S.A.* 113 G3
Carrizo Springs, *U.S.A.* ... 113 L5
Carrizozo, *U.S.A.* 115 K11
Carroll, *U.S.A.* 112 D7
Carrollton, *Ga., U.S.A.* ... 109 J3
Carrollton, *Ill., U.S.A.* 112 F9
Carrollton, *Ky., U.S.A.* ... 108 F3
Carrollton, *Mo., U.S.A.* ... 112 F8
Carrollton, *Ohio, U.S.A.* .. 110 F3
Carron →, *U.K.* 14 D4
Carron, L., *U.K.* 14 D3
Carrot →, *Canada* 105 C8
Carrot River, *Canada* 105 C8
Carrouges, *France* 18 D6
Carrù, *Italy* 28 D4
Carruthers, *Canada* 105 C7
Carsa Dek, *Ethiopia* 81 F4
Carşamba, *Turkey* 72 B7
Carsóli, *Italy* 29 F10
Carson, *Calif., U.S.A.* 117 M8
Carson, *N. Dak., U.S.A.* .. 112 B4
Carson →, *U.S.A.* 116 F8
Carson City, *U.S.A.* 116 F7
Carson Sink, *U.S.A.* 114 G4
Cartagena, *Colombia* 124 A3
Cartagena, *Spain* 33 H4
Cartago, *Colombia* 124 C3
Cartago, *Costa Rica* 120 E3
Cártama, *Spain* 35 J6
Cartaxo, *Portugal* 35 F2
Cartaya, *Spain* 35 H3
Cartersville, *U.S.A.* 109 H3
Carterton, *N.Z.* 91 J5
Carthage, *Tunisia* 30 F3
Carthage, *Ill., U.S.A.* 112 E9
Carthage, *Mo., U.S.A.* ... 113 G7
Carthage, *N.Y., U.S.A.* ... 108 D8
Carthage, *Tex., U.S.A.* ... 113 J7
Cartier I., *Australia* 92 B3
Cartwright, *Canada* 103 B8
Caruaru, *Brazil* 125 E11
Carúpano, *Venezuela* 124 A6
Caruthersville, *U.S.A.* 113 G10
Carvin, *France* 19 B9
Carvoeiro, *Brazil* 124 D6
Carvoeiro, C., *Portugal* ... 35 F1
Cary, *U.S.A.* 109 H6
Casa Branca, *Brazil* 35 G2
Casa Grande, *U.S.A.* 115 K8
Casablanca, *Chile* 126 C1
Casablanca, *Morocco* 78 B4
Casacalenda, *Italy* 29 G11
Casalbordino, *Italy* 29 F11
Casale Monferrato, *Italy* ... 28 C5

Casalmaggiore, *Italy* 28 D7
Casalpusterlengo, *Italy* ... 28 C6
Casamance →, *Senegal* ... 82 C1
Casarano, *Italy* 31 B11
Casares, *Spain* 35 J5
Casas Ibáñez, *Spain* 33 F3
Casasimarro, *Spain* 33 F2
Casatejada, *Spain* 34 F5
Casavieja, *Spain* 34 E6
Cascade, *Idaho, U.S.A.* ... 114 D5
Cascade, *Mont., U.S.A.* .. 114 C8
Cascade Locks, *U.S.A.* ... 116 E5
Cascade Ra., *U.S.A.* 116 D5
Cascade Reservoir, *U.S.A.* . 114 D5
Cascais, *Portugal* 35 G1
Cascavel, *Brazil* 127 A5
Cáscina, *Italy* 28 E7
Casco B., *U.S.A.* 109 D10
Caselle Torinese, *Italy* 28 C4
Caserta, *Italy* 31 A7
Cashel, *Ireland* 15 D4
Casiguran, *Phil.* 61 C5
Casilda, *Argentina* 126 C3
Casimcea, *Romania* 43 F13
Casino, *Australia* 95 D5
Casiquiare →, *Venezuela* . 124 C5
Casma, *Peru* 124 E3
Casmalia, *U.S.A.* 117 L6
Cásola Valsénio, *Italy* 29 D8
Cásoli, *Italy* 29 F11
Caspe, *Spain* 32 D4
Casper, *U.S.A.* 114 E10
Caspian Depression, *Eurasia* 49 G9
Caspian Sea, *Eurasia* 50 E6
Cass Lake, *U.S.A.* 112 B7
Cassà de la Selva, *Spain* .. 32 D7
Cassadaga, *U.S.A.* 110 D5
Cassano allo Iónio, *Italy* .. 31 C9
Casse, Grande, *France* ... 21 C10
Cassel, *France* 19 B9
Casselman, *Canada* 111 A9
Casselton, *U.S.A.* 112 B6
Cassiar, *Canada* 104 B3
Cassiar Mts., *Canada* 104 B2
Cassino, *Italy* 30 A6
Cassis, *France* 21 E9
Cassville, *U.S.A.* 113 G8
Castagneto Carducci, *Italy* . 28 E7
Castaic, *U.S.A.* 117 L8
Castalia, *U.S.A.* 110 E2
Castanhal, *Brazil* 125 D9
Castéggio, *Italy* 28 C6
Castejón de Monegros, *Spain* 32 D4
Castèl di Sangro, *Italy* 29 G11
Castèl San Giovanni, *Italy* . 28 C6
Castèl San Pietro Terme,
 Italy 29 D8
Castelbuono, *Italy* 31 E7
Castelfidardo, *Italy* 29 E10
Castelfiorentino, *Italy* 28 E7
Castelfranco Emília, *Italy* .. 28 D8
Castelfranco Véneto, *Italy* . 29 C8
Casteljaloux, *France* 20 D4
Castellabate, *Italy* 31 B7
Castellammare, G. di, *Italy* . 30 D5
Castellammare del Golfo,
 Italy 30 D5
Castellammare di Stábia,
 Italy 31 B7
Castellamonte, *Italy* 28 C4
Castellane, *France* 21 E10
Castellaneta, *Italy* 31 B9
Castelli, *Argentina* 126 D4
Castelló de la Plana, *Spain* . 32 F4
Castellón de la Plana □,
 Spain 32 E4
Castellote, *Spain* 32 E4
Castelmáuro, *Italy* 29 G11
Castelnau-de-Médoc, *France* 20 C3
Castelnau-Magnoac, *France* 20 E4
Castelnaudary, *France* 20 E5
Castelnovo ne' Monti, *Italy* . 28 D7
Castelnuovo di Val di
 Cécina, *Italy* 28 E7
Castelo, *Brazil* 127 A7
Castelo Branco, *Portugal* .. 34 F3
Castelo Branco □, *Portugal* 34 F3
Castelo de Paiva, *Portugal* . 34 D2
Castelo de Vide, *Portugal* .. 35 F3
Castelsardo, *Italy* 30 B1
Castelsarrasin, *France* 20 D5
Casteltérmini, *Italy* 30 E6
Castelvetrano, *Italy* 30 E5
Casterton, *Australia* 95 F3
Castets, *France* 20 E2
Castiglion Fiorentino, *Italy* . 29 E8
Castiglione del Lago, *Italy* . 29 E9
Castiglione della Pescáia,
 Italy 28 F7
Castiglione delle Stiviere,
 Italy 28 C7
Castilblanco, *Spain* 35 F5
Castile, *U.S.A.* 110 D6
Castilla, Playa de, *Spain* .. 35 J4
Castilla-La Mancha □, *Spain* 34 H5
Castilla y León □, *Spain* ... 34 D6
Castillo de Locubín, *Spain* . 35 H7
Castillon-en-Couserans,
 France 20 F5
Castillonès, *France* 20 D4
Castillos, *Uruguay* 127 C5
Castle Dale, *U.S.A.* 114 G8
Castle Douglas, *U.K.* 14 G5
Castle Rock, *Colo., U.S.A.* . 112 F2
Castle Rock, *Wash., U.S.A.* 116 D4
Castlebar, *Ireland* 15 C2
Castleblaney, *Ireland* 15 B5
Castlederg, *U.K.* 15 B4
Castleford, *U.K.* 12 D6
Castlegar, *Canada* 104 D5

Castlemaine, *Australia* 95 F3
Castlepollard, *Ireland* 15 C4
Castlerea, *Ireland* 15 C3
Castlereagh →, *Australia* . 95 E4
Castlereagh B., *Australia* .. 94 A2
Castleton, *U.S.A.* 111 C11
Castletown, *U.K.* 12 C3
Castletown Bearhaven,
 Ireland 15 E2
Castor, *Canada* 104 C6
Castor →, *Canada* 102 B4
Castorland, *U.S.A.* 111 C9
Castres, *France* 20 E6
Castricum, *Neths.* 17 B4
Castries, *St. Lucia* 121 D7
Castril, *Spain* 35 H8
Castro, *Brazil* 127 A6
Castro, *Chile* 128 E2
Castro Alves, *Brazil* 125 F11
Castro del Río, *Spain* 35 H6
Castro-Urdiales, *Spain* 34 B7
Castro Verde, *Portugal* 35 H2
Castrojeriz, *Spain* 34 C6
Castropol, *Spain* 34 B4
Castroreale, *Italy* 31 D8
Castrovíllari, *Italy* 31 C9
Castroville, *U.S.A.* 116 J5
Castuera, *Spain* 35 G5
Çat, *Turkey* 73 C9
Cat Ba, Dao, *Vietnam* 64 B6
Cat I., *Bahamas* 121 B4
Cat L., *Canada* 102 B1
Cat Lake, *Canada* 102 B1
Çata, *Slovak Rep.* 27 D11
Catacamas, *Honduras* 120 D2
Cataguases, *Brazil* 127 A7
Çatak, *Turkey* 73 C10
Catalão, *Brazil* 125 G9
Çatalca, *Turkey* 41 E12
Catalina, *Canada* 103 C9
Catalina, *Chile* 126 B2
Catalina, *U.S.A.* 115 K8
Catalonia = Cataluña □,
 Spain 32 D6
Cataluña □, *Spain* 32 D6
Çatalzeytin, *Turkey* 72 B6
Catamarca, *Argentina* 126 B2
Catamarca □, *Argentina* .. 126 B2
Catanauan, *Phil.* 61 E5
Catanduanes □, *Phil.* 61 E6
Catanduva, *Brazil* 127 A6
Catánia, *Italy* 31 E8
Catánia, G. di, *Italy* 31 E8
Catanzaro, *Italy* 31 D9
Cataram, *Phil.* 61 E6
Catarman, *Phil.* 61 E6
Catbalogan, *Phil.* 61 F6
Cateel, *Phil.* 61 H7
Catembe, *Mozam.* 89 D5
Caterham, *U.K.* 13 F7
Cathcart, *S. Africa* 88 E4
Cathlamet, *U.S.A.* 116 D3
Catio, *Guinea-Biss.* 82 C1
Catlettsburg, *U.S.A.* 108 F4
Çatma Daği, *Turkey* 39 C11
Catoche, C., *Mexico* 119 C7
Cátria, Mte., *Italy* 29 E9
Catrilo, *Argentina* 126 D3
Catrimani, *Brazil* 124 C6
Catrimani →, *Brazil* 124 C6
Catskill, *U.S.A.* 111 D11
Catskill Mts., *U.S.A.* 111 D10
Catt, Mt., *Australia* 94 A1
Cattaraugus, *U.S.A.* 110 D6
Cattólica, *Italy* 29 E9
Cattólica Eraclea, *Italy* 30 E6
Catuala, *Angola* 88 B2
Catuane, *Mozam.* 89 D5
Catur, *Mozam.* 87 E4
Catwick Is., *Vietnam* 65 G7
Cauca →, *Colombia* 124 B4
Caucaia, *Brazil* 125 D11
Caucasus Mountains, *Eurasia* 49 J7
Caudete, *Spain* 33 G3
Caudry, *France* 19 B10
Caulnes, *France* 18 D4
Caulónia, *Italy* 31 D9
Caungula, *Angola* 84 F3
Cauquenes, *Chile* 126 D1
Caura →, *Venezuela* 124 B6
Cauresi →, *Mozam.* 87 F3
Căușani, *Moldova* 43 D14
Causapscal, *Canada* 103 C6
Caussade, *France* 20 D5
Causse-Méjean, *France* ... 20 D7
Cauterets, *France* 20 F3
Caux, Pays de, *France* 18 C7
Cava de' Tirreni, *Italy* 31 B7
Cávado →, *Portugal* 34 D2
Cavaillon, *France* 21 E9
Cavalcante, *Brazil* 125 F9
Cavalese, *Italy* 29 B8
Cavalier, *U.S.A.* 112 A6
Cavalla = Cavally →, *Africa* 82 E3
Cavalleria, C. de, *Spain* ... 37 A11
Cavallo, I. de, *France* 21 G13
Cavally →, *Africa* 82 E3
Cavan, *Ireland* 15 B4
Cavan □, *Ireland* 15 C4
Cavárzere, *Italy* 29 C9
Çavdarhisar, *Turkey* 39 B11
Çavdir, *Turkey* 39 D11
Cave Creek, *U.S.A.* 115 K7
Cavenagh Ra., *Australia* .. 93 E4
Cavendish, *Australia* 95 F3
Caviana, I., *Brazil* 125 C8
Cavite, *Phil.* 61 D4
Cavnic, *Romania* 43 C8
Cavour, *France* 28 D4
Cavtat, *Croatia* 40 D2
Cawndilla L., *Australia* 95 E3

Cawnpore = Kanpur, *India* . 69 F9
Caxias, *Brazil* 125 D10
Caxias do Sul, *Brazil* 127 B5
Çay, *Turkey* 72 C4
Çay Sal Bank, *Bahamas* ... 120 B4
Cayambe, *Ecuador* 124 C3
Çaycuma, *Turkey* 72 B5
Çayeli, *Turkey* 73 B9
Cayenne, *Fr. Guiana* 125 B8
Caygören Barajı, *Turkey* .. 39 B10
Cayıralan, *Turkey* 72 C6
Caylus, *France* 20 D5
Cayman Brac, *Cayman Is.* . 120 C4
Cayman Is. ■, *W. Indies* .. 120 C3
Cayo Romano, *Cuba* 120 B4
Cayres, *France* 20 D7
Cayuga, *Canada* 110 D5
Cayuga, *U.S.A.* 111 D8
Cayuga L., *U.S.A.* 111 D8
Cazalla de la Sierra, *Spain* . 35 H5
Căzănești, *Romania* 43 F12
Cazaubon, *France* 20 E3
Cazaux et de Sanguinet,
 Étang de, *France* 20 D2
Cazenovia, *U.S.A.* 111 D9
Cazères, *France* 20 E5
Cazin, *Bos.-H.* 29 D12
Čazma, *Croatia* 29 C13
Cazombo, *Angola* 85 G4
Cazorla, *Spain* 35 H7
Cazorla, Sierra de, *Spain* .. 35 G8
Cea →, *Spain* 34 C5
Ceamurlia de Jos, *Romania* 43 F13
Ceará = Fortaleza, *Brazil* .. 125 D11
Ceará □, *Brazil* 125 E11
Ceará Mirim, *Brazil* 125 E11
Ceauru, L., *Romania* 43 F8
Cebaco, I. de, *Panama* ... 120 E3
Cebollar, *Argentina* 126 B2
Cebollera, Sierra de, *Spain* . 32 D2
Cebreros, *Spain* 34 E6
Cebu, *Phil.* 61 F5
Čečava, *Bos.-H.* 42 F2
Ceccano, *Italy* 30 A6
Cece, *Hungary* 42 D3
Cechi, *Ivory C.* 82 D4
Cecil Plains, *Australia* 95 D5
Cécina, *Italy* 28 E7
Cécina →, *Italy* 28 E7
Ceclavín, *Spain* 34 F4
Cedar →, *U.S.A.* 112 E9
Cedar City, *U.S.A.* 115 H7
Cedar Creek Reservoir,
 U.S.A. 113 J6
Cedar Falls, *Iowa, U.S.A.* . 112 D8
Cedar Falls, *Wash., U.S.A.* 116 C5
Cedar L., *Canada* 105 C9
Cedar Rapids, *U.S.A.* 112 E9
Cedartown, *U.S.A.* 109 H3
Cedarvale, *Canada* 104 B3
Cedarville, *S. Africa* 89 E4
Cedeira, *Spain* 34 B2
Cedral, *Mexico* 118 C4
Cedrino →, *Italy* 30 B2
Cedro, *Brazil* 125 E11
Cedros, I. de, *Mexico* 118 B1
Ceduna, *Australia* 95 E1
Cedynia, *Poland* 45 F1
Cée, *Spain* 34 C1
Cefalù, *Italy* 31 D7
Cega →, *Spain* 34 D6
Cegléd, *Hungary* 42 C4
Céglie Messápico, *Italy* ... 31 B10
Cehegín, *Spain* 33 G3
Ceheng, *China* 58 E5
Cehu-Silvaniei, *Romania* .. 43 C8
Ceica, *Romania* 42 D7
Ceira →, *Portugal* 34 E2
Čelákovice, *Czech Rep.* ... 26 A7
Celano, *Italy* 29 F10
Celanova, *Spain* 34 C3
Celaya, *Mexico* 118 C4
Celebes Sea, *Indonesia* ... 63 D6
Čelić, *Bos.-H.* 42 F3
Celina, *U.S.A.* 108 E3
Celinac, *Bos.-H.* 42 F2
Celje, *Slovenia* 29 B12
Celldömölk, *Hungary* 42 C2
Celle, *Germany* 24 C6
Celorico da Beira, *Portugal* 34 E3
Çeltikçi, *Turkey* 39 D12
Çemişgezek, *Turkey* 73 C8
Cenderwasih, Teluk,
 Indonesia 63 E9
Cengong, *China* 58 D7
Ceno →, *Italy* 28 D7
Centallo, *Italy* 28 D4
Centelles, *Spain* 32 D7
Center, *N. Dak., U.S.A.* ... 112 B4
Center, *Tex., U.S.A.* 113 K7
Centerburg, *U.S.A.* 110 F2
Centerville, *Calif., U.S.A.* . 116 J7
Centerville, *Iowa, U.S.A.* .. 112 E8
Centerville, *Pa., U.S.A.* ... 110 F5
Centerville, *Tenn., U.S.A.* . 109 H2
Centerville, *Tex., U.S.A.* .. 113 K7
Cento, *Italy* 29 D8
Central □, *Ghana* 83 D4
Central □, *Kenya* 86 C4
Central □, *Malawi* 87 E3
Central □, *Zambia* 87 E2
Central,
 Cordillera, Colombia ... 122 C3
Central, Cordillera,
 Costa Rica 120 D3
Central, Cordillera,
 Dom. Rep. 121 C5
Central, Cordillera, *Phil.* ... 61 C4
Central African Rep. ■,
 Africa 84 C4

Central America, *America* . 98 H11
Central Butte, *Canada* 105 C7
Central City, *Colo., U.S.A.* 114 G11
Central City, *Ky., U.S.A.* .. 108 G2
Central City, *Nebr., U.S.A.* 112 E6
Central I., *Kenya* 86 B4
Central Makran Range,
 Pakistan 66 F4
Central Patricia, *Canada* .. 102 B1
Central Point, *U.S.A.* 114 E2
Central Russian Uplands,
 Europe 6 E13
Central Siberian Plateau,
 Russia 52 C14
Central Square, *U.S.A.* 111 C8
Centralia, *Ill., U.S.A.* 112 F10
Centralia, *Mo., U.S.A.* 112 F8
Centralia, *Wash., U.S.A.* .. 116 D4
Cenxi, *China* 59 F8
Ceotina →, *Bos.-H.* 40 C2
Cephalonia = Kefallinía,
 Greece 38 C2
Čepin, *Croatia* 42 E3
Ceprano, *Italy* 30 A6
Ceptura, *Romania* 43 E11
Cepu, *Indonesia* 63 G14
Ceram = Seram, *Indonesia* 63 E7
Ceram Sea = Seram Sea,
 Indonesia 63 E7
Cerbère, *France* 20 F7
Cerbicales, Is., *France* 21 G13
Cercal, *Portugal* 35 H2
Cerdaña, *Spain* 32 C6
Cère →, *France* 20 D5
Cerea, *Italy* 29 C8
Ceredigion □, *U.K.* 13 E3
Ceres, *Argentina* 126 B3
Ceres, *S. Africa* 88 E2
Ceres, *U.S.A.* 116 H6
Céret, *France* 20 F6
Cergy, *France* 19 C9
Cerignola, *Italy* 31 A8
Cérilly, *France* 19 F9
Cerisiers, *France* 19 D10
Cerizay, *France* 18 F6
Çerkeş, *Turkey* 72 B5
Çerkezköy, *Turkey* 41 E12
Cerknica, *Slovenia* 29 C11
Cermerno, *Serbia, Yug.* ... 40 C4
Çermik, *Turkey* 73 C8
Cerna, *Romania* 43 E13
Cerna →, *Romania* 43 F8
Cernavodă, *Romania* 43 F13
Cernay, *France* 19 E14
Cernik, *Croatia* 42 E2
Cerralvo, I., *Mexico* 118 C3
Cërrik, *Albania* 40 E3
Cerritos, *Mexico* 118 C4
Cerro Chato, *Uruguay* 127 C4
Certaldo, *Italy* 28 E8
Cervaro →, *Italy* 31 A8
Cervati, Monte, *Italy* 31 B8
Cerventes, *Australia* 93 F2
Cervera, *Spain* 32 D6
Cervera de Pisuerga, *Spain* 34 C6
Cervera del Río Alhama,
 Spain 32 C3
Cervéteri, *Italy* 29 F9
Cérvia, *Italy* 29 D9
Cervignano del Friuli, *Italy* 29 C10
Cervinara, *Italy* 31 A7
Cervione, *France* 21 F13
Cervo, *Spain* 34 B3
Cesarò, *Italy* 31 E7
Cesena, *Italy* 29 D9
Cesenático, *Italy* 29 D9
Cēsis, *Latvia* 9 H21
Česká Lípa, *Czech Rep.* ... 26 A7
Česká Třebová, *Czech Rep.* 27 B9
České Budějovice,
 Czech Rep. 26 C7
České Velenice, *Czech Rep.* 26 C7
Českomoravská Vrchovina,
 Czech Rep. 26 B8
Český Brod, *Czech Rep.* ... 26 A7
Český Krumlov, *Czech Rep.* 26 C7
Český Těšín, *Czech Rep.* .. 27 B11
Česma →, *Croatia* 29 C13
Çeşme, *Turkey* 39 C8
Cessnock, *Australia* 95 E5
Cesson-Sévigné, *France* .. 18 D5
Cestas, *France* 20 D3
Cestos →, *Liberia* 82 D3
Cetate, *Romania* 42 F8
Cetin Grad, *Croatia* 29 C12
Cetina →, *Croatia* 29 E13
Cetinje, *Montenegro, Yug.* 40 D2
Cetraro, *Italy* 31 C8
Ceuta, *N. Afr.* 78 A4
Ceva, *Italy* 28 D5
Cévennes, *France* 20 D7
Ceyhan, *Turkey* 70 B2
Ceyhan →, *Turkey* 72 D6
Ceylânpınar, *Turkey* 73 D9
Ceylon = Sri Lanka ■, *Asia* 66 R12
Cèze →, *France* 21 D8
Cha-am, *Thailand* 64 F2
Cha Pa, *Vietnam* 64 A4
Chabanais, *France* 20 C4
Chabeuil, *France* 21 D9
Chablais, *France* 19 F13
Chablis, *France* 19 E10
Chacabuco, *Argentina* 126 C3
Chachapoyas, *Peru* 124 E3
Chachoengsao, *Thailand* .. 64 F3
Chachran, *Pakistan* 66 E7
Chachro, *Pakistan* 68 G4
Chaco □, *Argentina* 126 B3
Chaco □, *Paraguay* 126 B4

Chaco →, U.S.A. 115 H9
Chaco Austral, S. Amer. .. 128 B4
Chaco Boreal, S. Amer. .. 124 H6
Chaco Central, S. Amer. .. 128 A4
Chacon, C., U.S.A. 104 C2
Chad ■, Africa 79 E9
Chad, L. = Tchad, L., Chad 79 F8
Chadan, Russia 51 D10
Chadileuvú →, Argentina .. 126 D2
Chadiza, Zambia 87 E3
Chadron, U.S.A. 112 D3
Chadyr-Lunga = Ciadâr-
  Lunga, Moldova 43 D13
Chae Hom, Thailand 64 C2
Chaem →, Thailand 64 C2
Chaeryŏng, N. Korea 57 E13
Chagai Hills, Afghan. 66 E3
Chagda, Russia 51 D14
Chagny, France 19 F11
Chagoda, Russia 46 C8
Chagos Arch., Ind. Oc. .. 52 K11
Chagrin Falls, U.S.A. 110 E3
Chāh Ākhvor, Iran 71 C8
Chāh Bahār, Iran 71 E9
Chāh-e Kavīr, Iran 71 C8
Chahar Burjak, Afghan. .. 66 D3
Chahar Mahāll va
  Bakhtīarī □, Iran 71 C6
Chaibasa, India 67 H14
Chaillé-les-Marais, France .. 20 B3
Chainat, Thailand 64 E3
Chaiya, Thailand 65 H2
Chaj Doab, Pakistan 68 C5
Chajari, Argentina 126 C4
Chak Amru, Pakistan 68 C6
Chaka, Sudan 81 G3
Chakar →, Pakistan 68 E3
Chakari, Zimbabwe 89 B4
Chake Chake, Tanzania ... 86 D4
Chakhānsūr, Afghan. 66 D3
Chakonipau, L., Canada .. 103 A6
Chakradharpur, India 69 H11
Chakrata, India 68 D7
Chakwal, Pakistan 68 C5
Chala, Peru 124 G4
Chalais, France 20 C4
Chalchihuites, Mexico ... 118 C4
Chalcis = Khalkís, Greece .. 38 C5
Châlette-sur-Loing, France . 19 D9
Chaleur B., Canada 103 C6
Chalfant, U.S.A. 116 H8
Chalhuanca, Peru 124 F4
Chalindrey, France 19 E12
Chaling, China 59 D9
Chalisgaon, India 66 J9
Chalk River, Canada 102 C4
Chalky Inlet, N.Z. 91 M1
Challans, France 18 F5
Challapata, Bolivia 124 G5
Challis, U.S.A. 114 D6
Chalmette, U.S.A. 113 L10
Chalon-sur-Saône, France . 19 F11
Chalonnes-sur-Loire, France 18 E6
Châlons-en-Champagne,
  France 19 D11
Châlus, France 20 C4
Chalyaphum, Thailand ... 64 E4
Cham, Germany 25 F8
Cham, Cu Lao, Vietnam .. 64 E7
Chama, U.S.A. 115 H10
Chamaicó, Argentina 126 D3
Chaman, Pakistan 66 D5
Chamba, India 68 C7
Chamba, Tanzania 87 E4
Chambal →, India 69 F8
Chamberlain, U.S.A. 112 D5
Chamberlain →, Australia . 92 C4
Chamberlain L., U.S.A. .. 109 B11
Chambers, U.S.A. 115 J9
Chambersburg, U.S.A. ... 108 F7
Chambéry, France 21 C9
Chambeshi →, Zambia ... 84 G6
Chambly, Canada 111 A11
Chambord, Canada 103 C5
Chambouliive, France ... 20 C5
Chamchamal, Iraq 70 C5
Chamela, Mexico 118 D3
Chamical, Argentina 126 C2
Chamkar Luong, Cambodia 65 G4
Chamoli, India 69 D8
Chamonix-Mont Blanc,
  France 21 C10
Chamouchouane →, Canada 102 C5
Champa, India 69 H10
Champagne, Canada 104 A1
Champagne, France 19 D11
Champagnole, France ... 19 F12
Champaign, U.S.A. 108 E1
Champassak, Laos 64 E5
Champaubert, France ... 19 D10
Champawat, India 69 E9
Champdeniers-St-Denis,
  France 20 B3
Champdoré, L., Canada .. 103 A6
Champeix, France 20 C7
Champion, U.S.A. 110 B4
Champlain, U.S.A. 111 B11
Champlain, L., U.S.A. ... 111 B11
Champlitte, France 19 E12
Champotón, Mexico 119 D6
Champua, India 69 H11
Chamusca, Portugal 35 F2
Chana, Thailand 65 J3
Chañaral, Chile 126 B1
Chānārān, Iran 71 B8
Chanasma, India 68 H5
Chanco, Chile 126 D1
Chand, India 69 J8
Chandan, India 69 G12
Chandan Chauki, India .. 69 E9
Chandannagar, India 69 H13

Chandausi, India 69 E8
Chandeleur Is., U.S.A. 113 L10
Chandeleur Sd., U.S.A. ... 113 L10
Chandigarh, India 68 D7
Chandil, India 69 H12
Chandler, Australia 95 D1
Chandler, Canada 103 C7
Chandler, Ariz., U.S.A. .. 115 K8
Chandler, Okla., U.S.A. .. 113 H6
Chandod, India 68 J5
Chandpur, Bangla. 67 H17
Chandrapur, India 66 K11
Chānf, Iran 71 E9
Chang, Pakistan 68 F3
Chang, Ko, Thailand 65 F4
Ch'ang Chiang = Chang
  Jiang →, China 59 B13
Chang Jiang →, China ... 59 B13
Changa, India 69 C7
Changanacheri, India 66 Q10
Changane →, Mozam. .. 89 C5
Changbai, China 57 D15
Changbai Shan, China ... 57 C15
Changchiak'ou =
  Zhangjiakou, China ... 56 D8
Ch'angchou = Changzhou,
  China 59 B12
Changchun, China 57 C13
Changchunling, China ... 57 B13
Changde, China 59 C8
Changdo-ri, N. Korea ... 57 E14
Changfeng, China 59 A11
Changhai = Shanghai, China 59 B13
Changhua, China 59 B12
Changhua, Taiwan 59 E13
Changhŭng, S. Korea ... 57 G14
Changhŭngni, N. Korea .. 57 D15
Changjiang, China 64 C7
Changjin, N. Korea 57 D14
Changjin-chŏsuji, N. Korea . 57 D14
Changle, China 59 E12
Changli, China 57 E10
Changling, China 57 B12
Changlun, Malaysia 65 J3
Changning, Hunan, China . 59 D9
Changning, Sichuan, China . 58 C5
Changning, Yunnan, China . 58 E2
Changping, China 56 D9
Changsha, China 59 C9
Changshan, China 59 C12
Changshu, China 59 B13
Changshun, China 58 D6
Changtai, China 59 E11
Changting, China 59 E11
Changwu, China 56 G4
Changxing, China 59 B12
Changyang, China 59 B8
Changyi, China 57 F10
Changyŏn, N. Korea ... 57 E13
Changyuan, China 56 G8
Changzhi, China 56 F7
Changzhou, China 59 B12
Chanhanga, Angola 88 B1
Chanlar = Xanlar,
  Azerbaijan 49 K8
Channapatna, India 66 N10
Channel Is., U.K. 13 H5
Channel Is., U.S.A. 117 M7
Channel Islands National
  Park, U.S.A. 117 M8
Channel-Port aux Basques,
  Canada 103 C8
Channel Tunnel, Europe .. 13 F9
Channing, U.S.A. 113 H3
Chantada, Spain 34 C3
Chanthaburi, Thailand ... 64 F4
Chantilly, France 19 C9
Chantonnay, France 18 F5
Chantrey Inlet, Canada .. 100 B10
Chanute, U.S.A. 113 G7
Chanza →, Spain 35 H3
Chao Hu, China 59 B11
Chao Phraya →, Thailand . 64 F3
Chao Phraya Lowlands,
  Thailand 64 E3
Chaocheng, China 56 F8
Chaohu, China 59 B11
Chaoyang, Guangdong,
  China 59 F11
Chaoyang, Liaoning, China . 57 D11
Chaozhou, China 59 F11
Chapais, Canada 102 C5
Chapala, Mozam. 87 F4
Chapala, L. de, Mexico .. 118 C4
Chapayev, Kazakstan ... 48 E10
Chapayevsk, Russia 48 D9
Chapecó, Brazil 127 B5
Chapel Hill, U.S.A. 109 H6
Chapleau, Canada 102 C3
Chaplin, Canada 105 C7
Chaplin L., Canada 105 C7
Chaplino, Ukraine 47 H9
Chaplygin, Russia 46 F11
Chappell, U.S.A. 112 E3
Chapra = Chhapra, India . 69 G11
Chara, Russia 51 D12
Charadai, Argentina 126 B4
Charagua, Bolivia 124 G6
Charambirá, Punta,
  Colombia 124 C3
Charaña, Bolivia 124 G5
Charantsavan, Armenia .. 49 K7
Charanwala, India 68 F5
Charata, Argentina 126 B3
Charcas, Mexico 118 C4
Chard, U.K. 13 G5
Chardon, U.S.A. 110 E3
Chardzhou = Chärjew,
  Turkmenistan 50 F7
Charente □, France 20 C4
Charente →, France ... 20 C2

Charente-Maritime □,
  France 20 C3
Charenton-du-Cher, France 19 F9
Chari →, Chad 79 F8
Chārīkār, Afghan. 66 B6
Chariton →, U.S.A. 112 F8
Chärjew, Turkmenistan ... 50 F7
Charkhari, India 69 G8
Charkhi Dadri, India 68 E7
Charleroi, Belgium 17 D4
Charleroi, U.S.A. 110 F5
Charles, C., U.S.A. 108 G8
Charles City, U.S.A. 112 D8
Charles L., Canada 105 B6
Charles Town, U.S.A. ... 108 F7
Charleston, Ill., U.S.A. .. 108 F1
Charleston, Miss., U.S.A. . 113 H9
Charleston, Mo., U.S.A. .. 113 G10
Charleston, S.C., U.S.A. . 109 J6
Charleston, W. Va., U.S.A. 108 F5
Charleston L., Canada ... 111 B9
Charleston Peak, U.S.A. .. 117 J11
Charlestown, Ireland 15 C3
Charlestown, S. Africa ... 89 D4
Charlestown, Ind., U.S.A. . 108 F3
Charlestown, N.H., U.S.A. . 111 C12
Charleville = Rath Luirc,
  Ireland 15 D3
Charleville, Australia ... 95 D4
Charleville-Mézières, France 19 C11
Charlevoix, U.S.A. 108 C3
Charlieu, France 19 F11
Charlotte, Mich., U.S.A. .. 108 D3
Charlotte, N.C., U.S.A. .. 109 H5
Charlotte, Vt., U.S.A. ... 111 B11
Charlotte Amalie, Virgin Is. 121 C7
Charlotte Harbor, U.S.A. . 109 M4
Charlotte L., Canada ... 104 C3
Charlottenberg, Sweden .. 10 E6
Charlottesville, U.S.A. ... 108 F6
Charlottetown, Nfld.,
  Canada 103 B8
Charlottetown, P.E.I.,
  Canada 103 C7
Charlton, Australia 95 F3
Charlton, U.S.A. 112 E8
Charlton I., Canada 102 B4
Charmes, France 19 D13
Charny, Canada 103 C5
Charolles, France 19 F11
Chârost, France 19 F9
Charouine, Algeria 78 C5
Charre, Mozam. 87 F4
Charroux, France 20 B4
Charsadda, Pakistan ... 68 B4
Charters Towers, Australia 94 C4
Chartres, France 18 D8
Chascomús, Argentina ... 126 D4
Chasefu, Zambia 87 E3
Chashma Barrage, Pakistan 68 C4
Chasseneuil-sur-Bonnieure,
  France 20 C4
Chāt, Iran 71 B7
Chatal Balkan = Udvoy
  Balkan, Bulgaria 41 D10
Château-Arnoux, France .. 21 D10
Château-Chinon, France .. 19 E10
Château-d'Olonne, France . 20 B2
Château-du-Loir, France .. 18 E7
Château-Gontier, France . 18 E6
Château-la-Vallière, France 18 E7
Château-Landon, France . 19 D9
Château-Renault, France . 18 E7
Château-Salins, France .. 19 D13
Château-Thierry, France . 19 C10
Châteaubourg, France ... 18 D5
Châteaubriant, France ... 18 E5
Châteaudun, France 18 D8
Chateaugay, U.S.A. 111 B10
Châteaugiron, France ... 18 D5
Châteauguay, L., Canada . 103 A5
Châteaulin, France 18 D2
Châteaumeillant, France . 19 F9
Châteauneuf-du-Faou,
  France 18 D3
Châteauneuf-sur-Charente,
  France 20 C3
Châteauneuf-sur-Cher,
  France 19 F9
Châteauneuf-sur-Loire,
  France 19 E9
Châteaurenard,
  Bouches-du-Rhône, France 21 E8
Châteaurenard, Loiret,
  France 19 E9
Châteauroux, France ... 19 F8
Châteauvillain, France ... 19 D11
Châtelaillon-Plage, France . 20 B2
Châtelguyon, France ... 20 C7
Châtellerault, France ... 18 F7
Châtelus-Malvaleix, France . 19 F9
Chatham = Miramichi,
  Canada 103 C6
Chatham, Canada 102 D3
Chatham, U.K. 13 F8
Chatham, U.S.A. 111 D11
Chatham Is., Pac. Oc. ... 96 M10
Châtillon, Italy 28 C4
Châtillon-Coligny, France . 19 E9
Châtillon-en-Diois, France . 21 D9
Châtillon-sur-Indre, France . 18 F8
Châtillon-sur-Loire, France . 19 E9
Châtillon-sur-Seine, France . 19 E11
Chatmohar, Bangla. 69 G13
Chatra, India 69 G11
Chatrapur, India 67 K14
Chats, L. des, Canada ... 111 A8
Chatsu, India 68 F6
Chatsworth, Canada 110 B4
Chatsworth, Zimbabwe .. 87 F3
Chattahoochee, U.S.A. .. 109 K3
Chattahoochee →, U.S.A. . 109 K3

Chattanooga, U.S.A. 109 H3
Chatteris, U.K. 13 E8
Chaturat, Thailand 64 E3
Chau Doc, Vietnam 65 G5
Chaudes-Aigues, France .. 20 D7
Chauffailles, France 19 F11
Chauk, Burma 67 J19
Chaukan La, Burma 67 F20
Chaumont, France 19 D12
Chaumont, U.S.A. 111 B8
Chaumont-en-Vexin, France 19 C8
Chaumont-sur-Loire, France 18 E8
Chaunay, France 20 B4
Chauny, France 19 C10
Chausey, Îs., France ... 18 D5
Chaussin, France 19 F12
Chautauqua L., U.S.A. .. 110 D5
Chauvigny, France 18 F7
Chauvin, Canada 105 C6
Chavanges, France 19 D11
Chaves, Brazil 125 D9
Chaves, Portugal 34 D3
Chawang, Thailand 65 H2
Chazelles-sur-Lyon, France 21 C8
Chazy, U.S.A. 111 B11
Cheb, Czech Rep. 26 A5
Cheboksarskoye Vdkhr.,
  Russia 48 B8
Cheboksary, Russia 48 B8
Cheboygan, U.S.A. 108 C3
Chebsara, Russia 46 C10
Chech, Erg, Africa 78 D5
Chechen, Ostrov, Russia . 49 H8
Chechenia □, Russia ... 49 J7
Checheno-Ingush Republic =
  Chechenia □, Russia .. 49 J7
Chechnya = Chechenia □,
  Russia 49 J7
Chech'ŏn, S. Korea 57 F15
Chęciny, Poland 45 H7
Checotah, U.S.A. 113 H7
Chedabucto B., Canada .. 103 C7
Cheduba I., Burma 67 K18
Cheepie, Australia 95 D4
Chef-Boutonne, France .. 20 B3
Chegdomyn, Russia 51 D14
Chegga, Mauritania 78 C4
Chegutu, Zimbabwe ... 87 F3
Chehalis, U.S.A. 116 D4
Chehalis →, U.S.A. ... 116 D3
Cheiron, Mt., France ... 21 E10
Cheju do, S. Korea 57 H14
Chekalin, Russia 46 E9
Chekiang = Zhejiang □,
  China 59 C13
Chel = Kuru, Bahr el →,
  Sudan 81 F2
Chela, Sa. da, Angola ... 88 B1
Chelan, U.S.A. 114 C4
Chelan, L., U.S.A. 114 B3
Cheleken, Turkmenistan ... 50 F6
Cheleken Yarymadasy,
  Turkmenistan 71 B7
Chelforó, Argentina 128 D3
Chelkar = Shalqar,
  Kazakstan 50 E6
Chelkar Tengiz, Solonchak,
  Kazakstan 50 E7
Chella, Ethiopia 81 F4
Chelles, France 19 D9
Chełm, Poland 45 G10
Chełmno, Poland 45 E5
Chelmsford, U.K. 13 F8
Chełmza, Poland 45 E5
Chelsea, U.S.A. 111 C12
Cheltenham, U.K. 13 F5
Chelva, Spain 32 F4
Chelyabinsk, Russia ... 50 D7
Chelyuskin, C., Russia .. 52 B14
Chemainus, Canada ... 116 B3
Chemba, Mozam. 85 H6
Chembar = Belinskiy, Russia 48 D6
Chemillé, France 18 E6
Chemnitz, Germany ... 24 E8
Chemult, U.S.A. 114 E3
Chen, Gora, Russia ... 51 C15
Chenab →, Pakistan ... 68 D4
Chenango Forks, U.S.A. . 111 D9
Chencha, Ethiopia 81 F4
Chenchiang = Zhenjiang,
  China 59 A12
Cheney, U.S.A. 114 C5
Cheng Xian, China 56 H3
Chengbu, China 59 D8
Chengcheng, China 56 G5
Chengchou = Zhengzhou,
  China 56 G7
Chengde, China 57 D9
Chengdong Hu, China .. 59 A11
Chengdu, China 58 B5
Chenggong, China 58 E4
Chenggu, China 56 H4
Chenghai, China 59 F11
Chengjiang, China 58 E4
Chengkou, China 58 B7
Ch'engtu = Chengdu, China 58 B5
Chengwu, China 56 G8
Chengxi Hu, China 59 A11
Chengyang, China 57 F11
Chenjiagang, China ... 57 G10
Chenkán, Mexico 119 D6
Chenôve, France 19 E12
Chenxi, China 59 C8
Chenzhou, China 59 E9
Cheo Reo, Vietnam ... 62 B3
Cheom Ksan, Cambodia . 64 E5
Chepelare, Bulgaria ... 41 E8
Chepén, Peru 124 E3
Chepes, Argentina 126 C2

Chepo, Panama 120 E4
Chepstow, U.K. 13 F5
Cheptulil, Mt., Kenya ... 86 B4
Chequamegon B., U.S.A. . 112 B9
Cher □, France 19 E9
Cher →, France 18 E7
Chéradi, Italy 31 B10
Cherasco, Italy 28 D4
Cheraw, U.S.A. 109 H6
Cherbourg, France 18 C5
Cherdakly, Russia 48 C9
Cherdyn, Russia 50 C6
Cheremkhovo, Russia .. 51 D11
Cherepanovo, Russia .. 50 D9
Cherepovets, Russia .. 46 C9
Chergui, Chott ech, Algeria 78 B6
Cherikov = Cherykaw,
  Belarus 46 F6
Cherkasy, Ukraine 47 H7
Cherkessk, Russia 49 H6
Cherlak, Russia 50 D8
Chernaya, Russia 51 B9
Cherni, Bulgaria 40 D7
Chernigov = Chernihiv,
  Ukraine 47 G6
Chernihiv, Ukraine 47 G6
Chernivtsi, Ukraine ... 47 H3
Chernobyl = Chornobyl,
  Ukraine 47 G6
Chernogorsk, Russia .. 51 D10
Chernomorskoye =
  Chornomorske, Ukraine . 47 K7
Chernovtsy = Chernivtsi,
  Ukraine 47 H3
Chernyakhovsk, Russia .. 9 J19
Chernyanka, Russia ... 47 G9
Chernyshevskiy, Russia . 51 C12
Chernyye Zemli, Russia .. 49 H8
Cherokee, Iowa, U.S.A. .. 112 D7
Cherokee, Okla., U.S.A. .. 113 G5
Cherokee Village, U.S.A. . 113 G9
Cherokees, Grand Lake O'
  The, U.S.A. 113 G7
Cherrapunji, India 67 G17
Cherry Valley, Calif., U.S.A. 117 M10
Cherry Valley, N.Y., U.S.A. 111 D10
Cherskiy, Russia 51 C17
Cherskogo Khrebet, Russia . 51 C15
Chertkovo, Russia 47 H11
Cherven, Belarus 46 F5
Cherven-Bryag, Bulgaria . 41 C8
Chervonohrad, Ukraine .. 47 G3
Cherwell →, U.K. ... 13 F6
Cherykaw, Belarus 46 F6
Chesapeake, U.S.A. ... 108 G7
Chesapeake B., U.S.A. .. 108 G7
Cheshire □, U.K. 12 D5
Cheshskaya Guba, Russia . 50 C5
Cheshunt, U.K. 13 F7
Chesil Beach, U.K. 13 G5
Chesley, Canada 110 B3
Cheste, Spain 33 F4
Chester, U.K. 12 D5
Chester, Calif., U.S.A. .. 114 F3
Chester, Ill., U.S.A. ... 113 G10
Chester, Mont., U.S.A. .. 114 B8
Chester, Pa., U.S.A. ... 108 F8
Chester, S.C., U.S.A. ... 109 H5
Chester, Vt., U.S.A. ... 111 C12
Chester, W. Va., U.S.A. .. 110 F4
Chester-le-Street, U.K. .. 12 C6
Chesterfield, U.K. 12 D6
Chesterfield, Is., N. Cal. .. 96 J7
Chesterfield Inlet, Canada . 100 B10
Chesterton Ra., Australia . 95 D4
Chestertown, U.S.A. ... 111 C11
Chesterville, Canada ... 111 A9
Chestnut Ridge, U.S.A. .. 110 F5
Chesuncook L., U.S.A. .. 109 C11
Chéticamp, Canada 103 C7
Chetrosu, Moldova ... 43 B12
Chetumal, Mexico 119 D7
Chetumal, B. de, Mexico . 119 D7
Chetwynd, Canada 104 B4
Chevanceaux, France .. 20 C3
Cheviot, The, U.K. 12 B5
Cheviot Hills, U.K. 12 B5
Cheviot Ra., Australia .. 94 D3
Chew Bahir, Ethiopia .. 81 G4
Chewelah, U.S.A. 114 B5
Cheyenne, Okla., U.S.A. . 113 H5
Cheyenne, Wyo., U.S.A. . 112 E2
Cheyenne →, U.S.A. ... 112 C4
Cheyenne Wells, U.S.A. . 112 F3
Cheyne B., Australia ... 93 F2
Chhabra, India 68 G7
Chhaktala, India 68 H6
Chhapra, India 69 G11
Chhata, India 68 F7
Chhatarpur, Bihar, India . 69 G11
Chhatarpur, Mad. P., India 69 G8
Chhep, Cambodia 64 F5
Chhindwara, Mad. P., India 69 H8
Chhindwara, Mad. P., India 69 H8
Chhlong, Cambodia ... 65 F5
Chhota Tawa →, India .. 68 H7
Chhoti Kali Sindh →, India 68 G6
Chhuikhadan, India ... 69 J9
Chhuk, Cambodia 65 G5
Chi →, Thailand 64 E5
Chiai, Taiwan 59 F13
Chiali, Taiwan 59 F13
Chiamboni, Somali Rep. .. 84 C4
Chiamussu = Jiamusi, China 60 B8
Chianciano Terme, Italy .. 29 E8
Chiang Dao, Thailand ... 64 C2
Chiang Kham, Thailand .. 64 C3
Chiang Khan, Thailand .. 64 D3
Chiang Khong, Thailand . 58 G3
Chiang Mai, Thailand ... 64 C2
Chiang Rai, Thailand ... 58 H2

Chiang Saen, Thailand	58	G3
Chiapa →, Mexico	119	D6
Chiapa de Corzo, Mexico	119	D6
Chiapas □, Mexico	119	D6
Chiaramonte Gulfi, Italy	31	E7
Chiaravalle, Italy	29	E10
Chiaravalle Centrale, Italy	31	D9
Chiari, Italy	28	C6
Chiatura, Georgia	49	J6
Chiautla, Mexico	119	D5
Chiávari, Italy	28	D6
Chiavenna, Italy	28	B6
Chiba, Japan	55	G10
Chiba □, Japan	55	G10
Chibabava, Mozam.	89	C5
Chibemba, Cunene, Angola	85	H2
Chibemba, Huila, Angola	88	B2
Chibi, Zimbabwe	89	C5
Chibia, Angola	85	H2
Chibougamau, Canada	102	C5
Chibougamau, L., Canada	102	C5
Chibuk, Nigeria	83	C7
Chibuto, Mozam.	89	C5
Chic-Chocs, Mts., Canada	103	C6
Chicacole = Srikakulam, India	67	K13
Chicago, U.S.A.	108	E2
Chicago Heights, U.S.A.	108	E2
Chichagof I., U.S.A.	100	C6
Chichén-Itzá, Mexico	119	C7
Chicheng, China	56	D8
Chichester, U.K.	13	G7
Chichester Ra., Australia	92	D2
Chichibu, Japan	55	F9
Ch'ich'ihaerh = Qiqihar, China	51	E13
Chicholi, India	68	H8
Chickasha, U.S.A.	113	H6
Chiclana de la Frontera, Spain	35	J4
Chiclayo, Peru	124	E3
Chico, U.S.A.	116	F5
Chico →, Chubut, Argentina	128	E3
Chico →, Santa Cruz, Argentina	128	G3
Chicomo, Mozam.	89	C5
Chicontepec, Mexico	119	C5
Chicopee, U.S.A.	111	D12
Chicoutimi, Canada	103	C5
Chicualacuala, Mozam.	89	C5
Chidambaram, India	66	P11
Chidenguele, Mozam.	89	C5
Chidley, C., Canada	101	B13
Chiducuane, Mozam.	89	C5
Chiede, Angola	88	B2
Chiefs Pt., Canada	110	B3
Chiem Hoa, Vietnam	64	A5
Chiemsee, Germany	25	H8
Chiengi, Zambia	87	D2
Chiengmai = Chiang Mai, Thailand	64	C2
Chienti →, Italy	29	E10
Chieri, Italy	28	C4
Chiers →, France	19	C11
Chiesa in Valmalenco, Italy	28	B6
Chiese →, Italy	28	C7
Chieti, Italy	29	F11
Chifeng, China	57	C10
Chigirin, Ukraine	47	H7
Chignecto B., Canada	103	C7
Chiguana, Bolivia	126	A2
Chigwell, U.K.	13	F8
Chiha-ri, N. Korea	57	E14
Chihli, G. of = Bo Hai, China	57	E10
Chihuahua, Mexico	118	B3
Chihuahua □, Mexico	118	B3
Chiili, Kazakstan	50	E7
Chik Bollapur, India	66	N10
Chikmagalur, India	66	N9
Chikwawa, Malawi	87	F3
Chilac, Mexico	119	D5
Chilam Chavki, Pakistan	69	B6
Chilanga, Zambia	87	F2
Chilapa, Mexico	119	D5
Chilas, Pakistan	69	B6
Chilaw, Sri Lanka	66	R11
Chilcotin →, Canada	104	C4
Childers, Australia	95	D5
Childress, U.S.A.	113	H4
Chile ■, S. Amer.	128	D2
Chile Rise, Pac. Oc.	97	L18
Chilecito, Argentina	126	B2
Chilete, Peru	124	E3
Chilia, Brațul →, Romania	43	E14
Chililabombwe, Zambia	87	E2
Chilin = Jilin, China	57	C14
Chilka L., India	67	K14
Chilko →, Canada	104	C4
Chilko L., Canada	104	C4
Chillagoe, Australia	94	B3
Chillán, Chile	126	D1
Chillicothe, Ill., U.S.A.	112	E10
Chillicothe, Mo., U.S.A.	112	F8
Chillicothe, Ohio, U.S.A.	108	F4
Chilliwack, Canada	104	D4
Chilo, India	68	F5
Chiloane, I., Mozam.	89	C5
Chiloé, I. de, Chile	122	H3
Chilpancingo, Mexico	119	D5
Chiltern Hills, U.K.	13	F7
Chilton, U.S.A.	108	C1
Chilubi, Zambia	87	E2
Chilubula, Zambia	87	E2
Chilumba, Malawi	87	E3
Chilung, Taiwan	59	E13
Chilwa, L., Malawi	87	F4
Chimaltitán, Mexico	118	C4
Chimán, Panama	120	E4
Chimanimani, Zimbabwe	89	B5
Chimay, Belgium	17	D4
Chimayo, U.S.A.	115	H11
Chimbay, Uzbekistan	50	E6
Chimborazo, Ecuador	122	D3
Chimbote, Peru	124	E3
Chimkent = Shymkent, Kazakstan	50	E7
Chimoio, Mozam.	87	F3
Chimpembe, Zambia	87	D2
Chin □, Burma	67	J18
Chin Ling Shan = Qinling Shandi, China	56	H5
China, Mexico	119	B5
China ■, Asia	60	D6
China Lake, U.S.A.	117	K9
Chinan = Jinan, China	56	F9
Chinandega, Nic.	120	D2
Chinati Peak, U.S.A.	113	L2
Chincha Alta, Peru	122	E3
Chinchaga →, Canada	104	B5
Chinchilla, Australia	95	D5
Chinchilla de Monte Aragón, Spain	33	G3
Chinchorro, Banco, Mexico	119	D7
Chinchou = Jinzhou, China	57	D11
Chincoteague, U.S.A.	108	G8
Chinde, Mozam.	87	F4
Chindo, S. Korea	57	G14
Chindwin →, Burma	67	J19
Chineni, India	69	C6
Chinga, Mozam.	87	F4
Chingola, Zambia	87	E2
Chingole, Malawi	87	E3
Ch'ingtao = Qingdao, China	57	F11
Chinguetti, Mauritania	78	D3
Chingune, Mozam.	89	C5
Chinhae, S. Korea	57	G15
Chinhanguanine, Mozam.	89	D5
Chinhoyi, Zimbabwe	87	F3
Chini, India	68	D8
Chiniot, Pakistan	68	D5
Chinju, S. Korea	57	G15
Chinle, U.S.A.	115	H9
Chinmen, Taiwan	59	E13
Chinmen Tao, Taiwan	59	E13
Chinnampo = Namp'o, N. Korea	57	E13
Chino, Japan	55	G9
Chino, U.S.A.	117	L9
Chino Valley, U.S.A.	115	J7
Chinon, France	18	E7
Chinook, U.S.A.	114	B9
Chinsali, Zambia	87	E3
Chióggia, Italy	29	C9
Chíos = Khíos, Greece	39	C8
Chipata, Zambia	87	E3
Chiperceni, Moldova	43	C13
Chipinge, Zimbabwe	87	G3
Chipiona, Spain	35	J4
Chipley, U.S.A.	109	K3
Chipman, Canada	103	C6
Chipoka, Malawi	87	E3
Chippenham, U.K.	13	F5
Chippewa →, U.S.A.	112	C8
Chippewa Falls, U.S.A.	112	C9
Chipping Norton, U.K.	13	F6
Chiprovtsi, Bulgaria	40	C6
Chiputneticook Lakes, U.S.A.	109	C11
Chiquián, Peru	124	F3
Chiquimula, Guatemala	120	D2
Chiquinquira, Colombia	124	B4
Chir →, Russia	49	F6
Chirala, India	66	M12
Chiramba, Mozam.	87	F3
Chirawa, India	68	E6
Chirchiq, Uzbekistan	50	E7
Chiredzi, Zimbabwe	89	C5
Chirfa, Niger	79	D8
Chiricahua Peak, U.S.A.	115	L9
Chiriquí, G. de, Panama	120	E3
Chiriquí, L. de, Panama	120	E3
Chirivira Falls, Zimbabwe	87	G3
Chirmiri, India	67	H13
Chirnogi, Romania	43	F11
Chirpan, Bulgaria	41	D9
Chirripó Grande, Cerro, Costa Rica	120	E3
Chirundu, Zimbabwe	89	B4
Chisamba, Zambia	87	E2
Chisapani Garhi, Nepal	67	F14
Chisasibi, Canada	102	B4
Ch'ishan, Taiwan	59	F13
Chisholm, Canada	104	C6
Chisholm, U.S.A.	112	B8
Chishtian Mandi, Pakistan	68	E5
Chishui, China	58	C5
Chishui He →, China	58	C5
Chisimaio, Somali Rep.	77	G8
Chisimba Falls, Zambia	87	E3
Chişinău, Moldova	43	C13
Chişineu Criş, Romania	42	D6
Chisone →, Italy	28	D4
Chisos Mts., U.S.A.	113	L3
Chistopol, Russia	48	C10
Chita, Russia	51	D12
Chitipa, Malawi	87	D3
Chitose, Japan	54	C10
Chitral, Pakistan	66	B7
Chitré, Panama	120	E3
Chittagong, Bangla.	67	H17
Chittagong □, Bangla.	67	G17
Chittaurgarh, India	68	G6
Chittoor, India	66	N11
Chitungwiza, Zimbabwe	87	F3
Chiusi, Italy	29	E8
Chiva, Spain	33	F4
Chivasso, Italy	28	C4
Chivhu, Zimbabwe	87	F3
Chivilcoy, Argentina	126	C4
Chiwanda, Tanzania	87	E3
Chixi, China	59	G9
Chizera, Zambia	87	E2
Chkalov = Orenburg, Russia	50	D6
Chkolovsk, Russia	48	B6
Chloride, U.S.A.	117	K12
Chlumec nad Cidlinou, Czech Rep.	26	A8
Chmielnik, Poland	45	H7
Cho Bo, Vietnam	58	G5
Cho-do, N. Korea	57	E13
Cho Phuoc Hai, Vietnam	65	G6
Choba, Kenya	86	B4
Chobe National Park, Botswana	88	B4
Choch'iwŏn, S. Korea	57	F14
Chocianów, Poland	45	G2
Chociwel, Poland	44	E2
Chocolate Mts., U.S.A.	117	M11
Choctawatchee →, U.S.A.	109	K3
Chodecz, Poland	45	F6
Chodov, Czech Rep.	26	A5
Chodziez, Poland	45	F3
Choele Choel, Argentina	128	D3
Choix, Mexico	118	B3
Chojna, Poland	45	F1
Chojnice, Poland	44	E4
Chojnów, Poland	45	G2
Chōkai-San, Japan	54	E10
Choke, Ethiopia	81	E4
Choke Canyon L., U.S.A.	113	L5
Chokurdakh, Russia	51	B15
Cholame, U.S.A.	116	K6
Cholet, France	18	E6
Cholguan, Chile	126	D1
Choluteca, Honduras	120	D2
Choluteca →, Honduras	120	D2
Chom Bung, Thailand	64	F2
Chom Thong, Thailand	64	C2
Choma, Zambia	87	F2
Chomen Swamp, Ethiopia	81	F4
Chomun, India	68	F6
Chomutov, Czech Rep.	26	A6
Chon Buri, Thailand	64	F3
Chon Thanh, Vietnam	65	G6
Ch'onan, S. Korea	57	F14
Chone, Ecuador	124	D3
Chong Kai, Cambodia	64	F4
Chong Mek, Thailand	64	E5
Chongde, China	59	B13
Chŏngdo, S. Korea	57	G15
Chŏngha, S. Korea	57	F15
Chŏngjin, N. Korea	57	D15
Chŏngju, S. Korea	57	F14
Chŏngju, N. Korea	57	E13
Chongli, China	56	D8
Chongming, China	59	B13
Chongming Dao, China	59	B13
Chongqing, Chongqing, China	58	C6
Chongqing, Sichuan, China	58	B4
Chongqing □, China	60	C5
Chongqing Shi □, China	58	C6
Chongren, China	59	D11
Chonguene, Mozam.	89	C5
Chŏngup, S. Korea	57	G14
Chongyi, China	59	E10
Chongzuo, China	58	F6
Chŏnju, S. Korea	57	G14
Chonos, Arch. de los, Chile	122	H3
Chop, Ukraine	47	H2
Chopim →, Brazil	127	B5
Chor, Pakistan	68	G3
Chorbat La, India	69	B7
Chorley, U.K.	12	D5
Chornobyl, Ukraine	47	G10
Chornomorske, Ukraine	47	K7
Chorolque, Cerro, Bolivia	126	A2
Choroszcz, Poland	45	E9
Chorregon, Australia	94	C3
Chortkiv, Ukraine	47	H3
Ch'orwon, S. Korea	57	E14
Chorzele, Poland	45	E7
Chorzów, Poland	45	H5
Chos-Malal, Argentina	126	D1
Chosan, N. Korea	57	D13
Choszczno, Poland	45	E2
Choteau, U.S.A.	114	C7
Chotila, India	68	H4
Chotta Udepur, India	68	H6
Chowchilla, U.S.A.	116	H6
Choybalsan, Mongolia	60	B6
Christchurch, N.Z.	91	K4
Christchurch, U.K.	13	G6
Christian I., Canada	110	B4
Christiana, S. Africa	88	D4
Christiansfeld, Denmark	11	J3
Christiansted, Virgin Is.	121	C7
Christie B., Canada	105	A6
Christina →, Canada	105	B6
Christmas Cr. →, Australia	92	C4
Christmas I. = Kiritimati, Kiribati	97	G12
Christmas I., Ind. Oc.	96	J2
Christopher L., Australia	93	D4
Chrudim, Czech Rep.	26	B8
Chrzanów, Poland	45	H6
Chtimba, Malawi	87	E3
Chu = Shu, Kazakstan	50	E8
Chu →, Shu →, Kazakstan	50	E10
Chu →, Vietnam	64	C5
Chu Lai, Vietnam	64	E7
Ch'uanchou = Quanzhou, China	59	E12
Chuankou, China	56	G6
Chubbuck, U.S.A.	114	E7
Chūbu □, Japan	55	F8
Chubut →, Argentina	122	H4
Chuchi L., Canada	104	B4
Chuda, India	68	H4
Chudovo, Russia	46	C6
Chudskoye, Ozero, Russia	9	G22
Chūgoku □, Japan	55	G6
Chūgoku-Sanchi, Japan	55	G6
Chuguyev = Chuhuyiv, Ukraine	47	H9
Chugwater, U.S.A.	112	E2
Chuhuyiv, Ukraine	47	H9
Chukchi Sea, Russia	51	C19
Chukotskoye Nagorye, Russia	51	C18
Chula Vista, U.S.A.	117	N9
Chulman, Russia	51	D13
Chulucanas, Peru	124	E2
Chulym →, Russia	50	D9
Chum Phae, Thailand	64	D4
Chum Saeng, Thailand	64	E3
Chumar, India	69	C8
Chumbicha, Argentina	126	B2
Chumerna, Bulgaria	41	D9
Chumikan, Russia	51	D14
Chumphon, Thailand	65	G2
Chumuare, Mozam.	87	E3
Chumunjin, S. Korea	57	F15
Chuna →, Russia	51	D10
Chun'an, China	59	C12
Ch'unch'ŏn, S. Korea	57	F14
Chunchura, India	69	H13
Chunga, Zambia	87	F2
Chunggang-ŭp, N. Korea	57	D14
Chunghwa, N. Korea	57	E13
Ch'ungju, S. Korea	57	F14
Chungking = Chongqing, China	58	C6
Chungli, Taiwan	59	E13
Ch'ungmu, S. Korea	57	G15
Chungt'iaoshan = Zhongtiao Shan, China	56	G6
Chungyang Shanmo, Taiwan	59	F13
Chunian, Pakistan	68	D6
Chunya, Tanzania	87	D3
Chunyang, China	57	C15
Chuquibamba, Peru	124	G4
Chuquicamata, Chile	126	A2
Chur, Switz.	25	J5
Churachandpur, India	67	G18
Churchill, Canada	105	B10
Churchill →, Man., Canada	105	B10
Churchill →, Nfld., Canada	103	B7
Churchill, C., Canada	105	B10
Churchill Falls, Canada	103	B7
Churchill L., Canada	105	B7
Churchill Pk., Canada	104	B3
Churki, India	69	H10
Churu, India	68	E6
Churún Merú = Angel Falls, Venezuela	124	B6
Chushal, India	69	C8
Chuska Mts., U.S.A.	115	H9
Chusovoy, Russia	50	D6
Chute-aux-Outardes, Canada	103	C6
Chuuronjang, N. Korea	57	D15
Chuvash Republic = Chuvashia □, Russia	48	C8
Chuvashia □, Russia	48	C8
Chuwārtah, Iraq	70	C5
Chuxiong, China	58	E3
Chuy, Uruguay	127	C5
Chuzhou, China	59	A12
Ci Xian, China	56	F8
Ciacova, Romania	42	E6
Ciadâr-Lunga, Moldova	43	D13
Ciamis, Indonesia	63	G13
Cianjur, Indonesia	63	G12
Cianorte, Brazil	127	A5
Cibola, U.S.A.	117	M12
Cicero, U.S.A.	108	E2
Cidacos →, Spain	32	C3
Cide, Turkey	72	B5
Ciechanów, Poland	45	F7
Ciechanowiec, Poland	45	F9
Ciechocinek, Poland	45	F5
Ciego de Avila, Cuba	120	B4
Ciénaga, Colombia	124	A4
Cienfuegos, Cuba	120	B3
Cierp, France	20	F4
Cíes, Is., Spain	34	C2
Cieszanów, Poland	45	H10
Cieszyn, Poland	45	J5
Cieza, Spain	33	G3
Cifuentes, Spain	32	E2
Cihanbeyli, Turkey	72	C5
Cihuatlán, Mexico	118	D4
Cijara, Embalse de, Spain	35	F6
Cijulang, Indonesia	63	G13
Cilacap, Indonesia	63	G13
Çıldır, Turkey	73	B10
Çıldır Gölü, Turkey	73	B10
Cili, China	59	C8
Cilibia, Romania	43	E12
Cilicia, Turkey	72	D5
Cill Chainnigh = Kilkenny, Ireland	15	D4
Cilo Dağı, Turkey	73	D10
Cima, U.S.A.	117	K11
Cimarron, Kans., U.S.A.	113	G4
Cimarron, N. Mex., U.S.A.	113	G2
Cimarron →, U.S.A.	113	G6
Cimişlia, Moldova	43	D13
Cimone, Mte., Italy	28	D7
Çinar, Turkey	73	D9
Çinarcık, Turkey	41	F13
Cinca →, Spain	32	D5
Cincar, Bos.-H.	42	G2
Cincinnati, U.S.A.	108	F3
Cincinnatus, U.S.A.	111	D9
Çine, Turkey	39	D10
Ciney, Belgium	17	D5
Cíngoli, Italy	29	E10
Cinigiano, Italy	29	F8
Cinto, Mte., France	21	F12
Cintruénigo, Spain	32	C3
Ciocile, Romania	43	F12
Ciolănești din Deal, Romania	43	F10
Ciorani, Romania	43	F11
Ciovo, Croatia	29	E13
Circeo, Mte., Italy	30	A6
Çirçir, Turkey	72	C7
Circle, Alaska, U.S.A.	100	B5
Circle, Mont., U.S.A.	112	B2
Circleville, U.S.A.	108	F4
Cirebon, Indonesia	63	G13
Ciremai, Indonesia	63	G13
Cirencester, U.K.	13	F6
Cireșu, Romania	42	F7
Cirey-sur-Vezouze, France	19	D13
Ciriè, Italy	28	C4
Cirium, Cyprus	36	E11
Cirò, Italy	31	C10
Cirò Marina, Italy	31	C10
Ciron →, France	20	D3
Cisco, U.S.A.	113	J5
Cislău, Romania	43	E11
Cisna, Poland	45	J9
Cisnădie, Romania	43	E9
Cisterna di Latina, Italy	30	A5
Cisternino, Italy	31	B10
Cistierna, Spain	34	C5
Citeli-Ckaro = Tsiteli-Tsqaro, Georgia	49	K8
Citlaltépetl, Mexico	119	D5
Citrus Heights, U.S.A.	116	G5
Citrusdal, S. Africa	88	E2
Città della Pieve, Italy	29	F9
Città di Castello, Italy	29	E9
Città Sant' Angelo, Italy	29	F11
Cittadella, Italy	29	C8
Cittaducale, Italy	29	F9
Cittanova, Italy	31	D9
Ciuc, Munții, Romania	43	D11
Ciucaș, Vf., Romania	43	E10
Ciucea, Romania	42	D7
Ciuciulea, Moldova	43	C12
Ciuciuleni, Moldova	43	C13
Ciudad Altamirano, Mexico	118	D4
Ciudad Bolívar, Venezuela	124	B6
Ciudad Camargo, Mexico	118	B3
Ciudad de Valles, Mexico	119	C5
Ciudad del Carmen, Mexico	119	D6
Ciudad del Este, Paraguay	127	B5
Ciudad Delicias = Delicias, Mexico	118	B3
Ciudad Guayana, Venezuela	124	B6
Ciudad Guerrero, Mexico	118	B3
Ciudad Guzmán, Mexico	118	D4
Ciudad Juárez, Mexico	118	A3
Ciudad Madero, Mexico	119	C5
Ciudad Mante, Mexico	119	C5
Ciudad Obregón, Mexico	118	B3
Ciudad Real, Spain	35	G7
Ciudad Real □, Spain	35	G7
Ciudad Rodrigo, Spain	34	E4
Ciudad Trujillo = Santo Domingo, Dom. Rep.	121	C6
Ciudad Victoria, Mexico	119	C5
Ciudadela, Spain	37	B10
Ciulnița, Romania	43	F12
Ciumeghiu, Romania	42	D6
Ciuperceni, Romania	42	F8
Civa Burnu, Turkey	72	B7
Cividale del Friuli, Italy	29	B10
Cívita Castellana, Italy	29	F9
Civitanova Marche, Italy	29	E10
Civitavécchia, Italy	29	F8
Civray, France	20	B4
Çivril, Turkey	39	C11
Cixerri →, Italy	30	C1
Cixi, China	59	B13
Cizre, Turkey	70	B4
Cizur Mayor, Spain	32	C3
Clackmannanshire □, U.K.	14	E5
Clacton-on-Sea, U.K.	13	F9
Clain →, France	18	F7
Claire, L., Canada	104	B6
Clairton, U.S.A.	110	F5
Clairvaux-les-Lacs, France	19	F12
Claise →, France	18	F7
Clallam Bay, U.S.A.	116	B2
Clamecy, France	19	E10
Clanton, U.S.A.	109	J2
Clanwilliam, S. Africa	88	E2
Clara, Ireland	15	C4
Claraville, U.S.A.	117	K8
Clare, Australia	95	E2
Clare, U.S.A.	108	D3
Clare □, Ireland	15	D3
Clare →, Ireland	15	C2
Clare I., Ireland	15	C1
Claremont, Calif., U.S.A.	117	L9
Claremont, N.H., U.S.A.	111	C12
Claremont Pt., Australia	94	A3
Claremore, U.S.A.	113	G7
Claremorris, Ireland	15	C3
Clarence →, Australia	95	D5
Clarence →, N.Z.	91	K4
Clarence, I., Chile	128	G2
Clarence Str., Australia	92	B5
Clarence Town, Bahamas	121	B5
Clarendon, Pa., U.S.A.	110	E5
Clarendon, Tex., U.S.A.	113	H4
Clarenville, Canada	103	C9
Claresholm, Canada	104	D6
Clarie Coast, Antarctica	5	C9
Clarinda, U.S.A.	112	E7
Clarion, Iowa, U.S.A.	112	D8
Clarion, Pa., U.S.A.	110	E5
Clarion →, U.S.A.	110	E5
Clark, U.S.A.	112	C6
Clark, Pt., Canada	110	B3
Clark Fork, U.S.A.	114	B5
Clark Fork →, U.S.A.	114	B5

Clark Hill L., *U.S.A.* 109 J4
Clarkdale, *U.S.A.* 115 J7
Clarke City, *Canada* 103 B6
Clarke I., *Australia* 94 G4
Clarke Ra., *Australia* 94 C4
Clark's Fork →, *U.S.A.* 114 D9
Clark's Harbour, *Canada* 103 D6
Clarks Summit, *U.S.A.* 111 E9
Clarksburg, *U.S.A.* 108 F5
Clarksdale, *U.S.A.* 113 H9
Clarksville, *Ark., U.S.A.* 113 H8
Clarksville, *Tenn., U.S.A.* 109 G2
Clarksville, *Tex., U.S.A.* 113 J7
Clatskanie, *U.S.A.* 116 D3
Claude, *U.S.A.* 113 H4
Claveria, *Phil.* 61 B4
Clay, *U.S.A.* 116 G5
Clay Center, *U.S.A.* 112 F6
Claypool, *U.S.A.* 115 K8
Claysburg, *U.S.A.* 110 F6
Claysville, *U.S.A.* 110 F4
Clayton, *N. Mex., U.S.A.* 113 G3
Clayton, *N.Y., U.S.A.* 111 B8
Clear, C., *Ireland* 15 E2
Clear, L., *Canada* 110 A7
Clear Hills, *Canada* 104 B5
Clear I., *Ireland* 15 E2
Clear L., *U.S.A.* 116 F4
Clear Lake, *Iowa, U.S.A.* 112 D8
Clear Lake, *S. Dak., U.S.A.* 112 C6
Clear Lake Reservoir, *U.S.A.* 114 F3
Clearfield, *Pa., U.S.A.* 110 E6
Clearfield, *Utah, U.S.A.* 114 F8
Clearlake, *U.S.A.* 114 G2
Clearlake Highlands, *U.S.A.* 116 G4
Clearwater, *Canada* 104 C4
Clearwater, *U.S.A.* 109 M4
Clearwater →, *Alta., Canada* 104 C6
Clearwater →, *Alta., Canada* 105 B6
Clearwater L., *Canada* 105 C9
Clearwater Mts., *U.S.A.* 114 C6
Clearwater Prov. Park, *Canada* 105 C8
Clearwater River Prov. Park, *Canada* 105 B7
Cleburne, *U.S.A.* 113 J6
Clee Hills, *U.K.* 13 E5
Cleethorpes, *U.K.* 12 D7
Cleeve Cloud, *U.K.* 13 F6
Clelles, *France* 21 D9
Clemson, *U.S.A.* 109 H4
Clerke Reef, *Australia* 92 C2
Clermont, *Australia* 94 C4
Clermont, *France* 19 C9
Clermont, *U.S.A.* 109 L5
Clermont-en-Argonne, *France* 19 C12
Clermont-Ferrand, *France* 20 C7
Clermont-l'Hérault, *France* 20 E7
Clerval, *France* 19 E13
Clervaux, *Lux.* 17 D6
Cles, *Italy* 28 B8
Cleve, *Australia* 95 E2
Clevedon, *U.K.* 13 F5
Cleveland, *Miss., U.S.A.* 113 J9
Cleveland, *Ohio, U.S.A.* 110 E3
Cleveland, *Okla., U.S.A.* 113 G6
Cleveland, *Tenn., U.S.A.* 109 H3
Cleveland, *Tex., U.S.A.* 113 K7
Cleveland, C., *Australia* 94 B4
Cleveland, Mt., *U.S.A.* 114 B7
Cleveland Heights, *U.S.A.* 110 E3
Clevelândia, *Brazil* 127 B5
Clew B., *Ireland* 15 C2
Clewiston, *U.S.A.* 109 M5
Clifden, *Ireland* 15 C1
Clifden, *N.Z.* 91 M1
Cliffdell, *U.S.A.* 116 D5
Cliffy Hd., *Australia* 93 G2
Clifton, *Australia* 95 D5
Clifton, *Ariz., U.S.A.* 115 K9
Clifton, *Colo., U.S.A.* 115 G9
Clifton, *Tex., U.S.A.* 113 K6
Clifton Beach, *Australia* 94 B4
Climax, *Canada* 105 D7
Clinch →, *U.S.A.* 109 H3
Clingmans Dome, *U.S.A.* 109 H4
Clint, *U.S.A.* 115 L10
Clinton, *B.C., Canada* 104 C4
Clinton, *Ont., Canada* 102 D3
Clinton, *N.Z.* 91 M2
Clinton, *Ark., U.S.A.* 113 H8
Clinton, *Conn., U.S.A.* 111 E12
Clinton, *Ill., U.S.A.* 112 E10
Clinton, *Ind., U.S.A.* 108 F2
Clinton, *Iowa, U.S.A.* 112 E9
Clinton, *Mass., U.S.A.* 111 D13
Clinton, *Miss., U.S.A.* 113 J9
Clinton, *Mo., U.S.A.* 112 F8
Clinton, *N.C., U.S.A.* 109 H6
Clinton, *Okla., U.S.A.* 113 H5
Clinton, *S.C., U.S.A.* 109 H5
Clinton, *Tenn., U.S.A.* 109 G3
Clinton, *Wash., U.S.A.* 116 C4
Clinton C., *Australia* 94 C5
Clinton Colden L., *Canada* 100 B9
Clintonville, *U.S.A.* 112 C10
Clipperton, I., *Pac. Oc.* 97 F17
Clisham, *U.K.* 14 D2
Clisson, *France* 18 E5
Clitheroe, *U.K.* 12 D5
Clo-oose, *Australia* 116 B2
Cloates, Pt., *Australia* 92 D1
Clocolan, *S. Africa* 89 D4
Clodomira, *Argentina* 126 B3
Clogher Hd., *Ireland* 15 C5
Clonakilty, *Ireland* 15 E3
Clonakilty B., *Ireland* 15 E3

Cloncurry, *Australia* 94 C3
Cloncurry →, *Australia* 94 B3
Clondalkin, *Ireland* 15 C5
Clones, *Ireland* 15 B4
Clonmel, *Ireland* 15 D4
Cloppenburg, *Germany* 24 C4
Cloquet, *U.S.A.* 112 B8
Clorinda, *Argentina* 126 B4
Cloud Bay, *Canada* 102 C2
Cloud Peak, *U.S.A.* 114 D10
Cloudcroft, *U.S.A.* 115 K11
Cloverdale, *U.S.A.* 116 G4
Clovis, *Calif., U.S.A.* 116 J7
Clovis, *N. Mex., U.S.A.* 113 H3
Cloyes-sur-le-Loir, *France* 18 E8
Cloyne, *Canada* 110 B7
Cluj □, *Romania* 43 D8
Cluj-Napoca, *Romania* 43 D8
Clunes, *Australia* 95 F3
Cluny, *France* 19 F11
Cluses, *France* 19 F13
Clusone, *Italy* 28 C6
Clutha →, *N.Z.* 91 M2
Clwyd →, *U.K.* 12 D4
Clyde, *Canada* 104 C6
Clyde, *N.Z.* 91 L2
Clyde, *U.S.A.* 110 C8
Clyde →, *U.K.* 14 F4
Clyde, Firth of, *U.K.* 14 F3
Clyde River, *Canada* 101 A13
Clydebank, *U.K.* 14 F4
Clymer, *N.Y., U.S.A.* 110 D5
Clymer, *Pa., U.S.A.* 110 D5
Ćmielów, *Poland* 45 H8
Côa →, *Portugal* 34 D3
Coachella, *U.S.A.* 117 M10
Coachella Canal, *U.S.A.* 117 N12
Coahoma, *U.S.A.* 113 J4
Coahuayana →, *Mexico* 118 D4
Coahuila □, *Mexico* 118 B4
Coal →, *Canada* 104 B3
Coalane, *Mozam.* 87 F4
Coalcomán, *Mexico* 118 D4
Coaldale, *Canada* 104 D6
Coalgate, *U.S.A.* 113 H6
Coalinga, *U.S.A.* 116 J6
Coalisland, *U.K.* 15 B5
Coalville, *U.K.* 12 E6
Coalville, *U.S.A.* 114 F8
Coari, *Brazil* 124 D6
Coast □, *Kenya* 86 C4
Coast Mts., *Canada* 104 C3
Coast Ranges, *U.S.A.* 116 G4
Coatbridge, *U.K.* 14 F4
Coatepec, *Mexico* 119 D5
Coatepeque, *Guatemala* 120 D1
Coatesville, *U.S.A.* 108 F8
Coaticook, *Canada* 103 C5
Coats I., *Canada* 101 B11
Coats Land, *Antarctica* 5 D1
Coatzacoalcos, *Mexico* 119 D6
Cobadin, *Romania* 43 F13
Cobalt, *Canada* 102 C4
Cobán, *Guatemala* 120 C1
Çobanlar, *Turkey* 39 C12
Cobar, *Australia* 95 E4
Cobargo, *Australia* 95 F4
Cóbh, *Ireland* 15 E3
Cobija, *Bolivia* 124 F5
Cobleskill, *U.S.A.* 111 D10
Coboconk, *Canada* 110 B6
Cobourg, *Canada* 102 D4
Cobourg Pen., *Australia* 92 B5
Cobram, *Australia* 95 F4
Cóbué, *Mozam.* 87 E3
Coburg, *Germany* 25 E6
Coca, *Spain* 34 D6
Cocanada = Kakinada, *India* 67 L13
Cocentaina, *Spain* 33 G4
Cochabamba, *Bolivia* 124 G5
Cochem, *Germany* 25 E3
Cochemane, *Mozam.* 87 F3
Cochin, *India* 66 Q10
Cochin China, *Vietnam* 65 G6
Cochran, *U.S.A.* 109 J4
Cochrane, *Alta., Canada* 104 C6
Cochrane, *Ont., Canada* 102 C3
Cochrane, *Chile* 128 F2
Cochrane →, *Canada* 105 B8
Cochrane, L., *Chile* 128 F2
Cochranton, *U.S.A.* 110 E4
Cockburn, *Australia* 95 E3
Cockburn, Canal, *Chile* 122 J3
Cockburn I., *Canada* 102 C3
Cockburn Ra., *Australia* 92 C4
Cockermouth, *U.K.* 12 C4
Cocklebiddy, *Australia* 93 F4
Coco →, *Cent. Amer.* 120 D3
Coco, I. del, *Pac. Oc.* 97 G19
Cocoa, *U.S.A.* 109 L5
Cocobeach, *Gabon* 84 D1
Cocora, *Romania* 43 F12
Cocos Is., *Ind. Oc.* 96 J1
Cod, C., *U.S.A.* 108 D10
Codajás, *Brazil* 124 D6
Codigoro, *Italy* 29 D9
Codlea, *Romania* 43 E10
Codó, *Brazil* 125 D10
Codogno, *Italy* 28 C6
Codróipo, *Italy* 29 C10
Codru, Munții, *Romania* 42 D7
Cody, *U.S.A.* 114 D9
Coe Hill, *Canada* 110 B7
Coelemu, *Chile* 126 D1
Coen, *Australia* 94 A3
Coesfeld, *Germany* 24 D3
Cœur d'Alene, *U.S.A.* 114 C5
Cœur d'Alene L., *U.S.A.* 114 C5
Coevorden, *Neths.* 17 B6
Cofete, *Canary Is.* 37 F5
Coffeyville, *U.S.A.* 113 G7

Coffin B., *Australia* 95 E2
Coffin Bay, *Australia* 95 E2
Coffin Bay Peninsula, *Australia* 95 E2
Coffs Harbour, *Australia* 95 E5
Cofrentes, *Spain* 33 F3
Cogealac, *Romania* 43 F13
Coghinas →, *Italy* 30 B1
Coghinas, L. del, *Italy* 30 B2
Cognac, *France* 20 C3
Cogne, *Italy* 28 C4
Cogolin, *France* 21 E10
Cogolludo, *Spain* 32 E1
Cohocton, *U.S.A.* 110 D7
Cohocton →, *U.S.A.* 110 D7
Cohoctan →, *U.S.A.* 111 D11
Cohuna, *Australia* 95 F3
Coig →, *Argentina* 128 G3
Coigeach, Rubha, *U.K.* 14 C3
Coihaique, *Chile* 128 F2
Coimbatore, *India* 66 P10
Coimbra, *Brazil* 124 G7
Coimbra, *Portugal* 34 E2
Coimbra □, *Portugal* 34 E2
Coín, *Spain* 35 J6
Coipasa, Salar de, *Bolivia* 124 G5
Cojimíes, *Ecuador* 124 C3
Cojocna, *Romania* 43 D8
Cojutepequé, *El Salv.* 120 D2
Čoka, *Serbia, Yug.* 42 E5
Cokeville, *U.S.A.* 114 E8
Colac, *Australia* 95 F3
Colatina, *Brazil* 125 G10
Colbeck, C., *Antarctica* 5 D13
Colborne, *Canada* 110 C7
Colby, *U.S.A.* 112 F4
Colchester, *U.K.* 13 F8
Cold L., *Canada* 105 C7
Coldstream, *Canada* 104 C5
Coldstream, *U.K.* 14 F6
Coldwater, *Canada* 110 B5
Coldwater, *Kans., U.S.A.* 113 G5
Coldwater, *Mich., U.S.A.* 108 E3
Coleambally, *Australia* 95 E4
Colebrook, *U.S.A.* 111 B13
Coleman, *U.S.A.* 113 K5
Coleman →, *Australia* 94 B3
Colenso, *S. Africa* 89 D4
Coleraine, *Australia* 95 F3
Coleraine, *U.K.* 15 A5
Coleridge, L., *N.Z.* 91 K3
Colesberg, *S. Africa* 88 E4
Coleville, *U.S.A.* 116 G7
Colfax, *Calif., U.S.A.* 116 F6
Colfax, *La., U.S.A.* 113 K8
Colfax, *Wash., U.S.A.* 114 C5
Colhué Huapi, L., *Argentina* 128 F3
Colibași, *Moldova* 43 E13
Colibași, *Romania* 43 F9
Cólico, *Italy* 28 B6
Coligny, *France* 19 F12
Coligny, *S. Africa* 89 D4
Colima, *Mexico* 118 D4
Colima □, *Mexico* 118 D4
Colima, Nevado de, *Mexico* 118 D4
Colina, *Chile* 126 C1
Colina do Norte, *Guinea-Biss.* 82 C2
Colinas, *Brazil* 125 E10
Colindres, *Spain* 34 B7
Coll, *U.K.* 14 E2
Collaguasi, *Chile* 126 A2
Collarada, Peña, *Spain* 32 C4
Collarenebri, *Australia* 95 D4
Colle di Val d'Elsa, *Italy* 28 E8
Collécchio, *Italy* 28 D7
Colleen Bawn, *Zimbabwe* 87 G2
College Park, *U.S.A.* 109 J3
College Station, *U.S.A.* 113 K6
Collesalvetti, *Italy* 28 E7
Collie, *Australia* 93 F2
Collier B., *Australia* 92 C3
Collier Ra., *Australia* 93 D2
Collina, Passo di, *Italy* 28 D7
Collingwood, *Canada* 102 D3
Collingwood, *N.Z.* 91 J4
Collins, *Canada* 102 B2
Collinsville, *Australia* 94 C4
Collipulli, *Chile* 126 D1
Collooney, *Ireland* 15 B3
Colmar, *France* 19 D14
Colmars, *France* 21 D10
Colmenar, *Spain* 35 J6
Colmenar de Oreja, *Spain* 34 E7
Colmenar Viejo, *Spain* 34 E7
Colo →, *Australia* 95 E5
Cologne = Köln, *Germany* 24 E2
Colom, I. d'en, *Spain* 37 B11
Coloma, *U.S.A.* 116 G6
Colomb-Béchar = Béchar, *Algeria* 78 B5
Colombey-les-Belles, *France* 19 D12
Colombey-les-Deux-Églises, *France* 19 D11
Colombia ■, *S. Amer.* 124 C4
Colombian Basin, *S. Amer.* 98 H12
Colombo, *Sri Lanka* 66 R11
Colón, *Buenos Aires, Argentina* 126 C3
Colón, *Entre Ríos, Argentina* 126 C4
Colón, *Cuba* 120 B3
Colón, *Panama* 120 E4
Colonia de Sant Jordi, *Spain* 37 B9
Colonia del Sacramento, *Uruguay* 126 C4
Colonia Dora, *Argentina* 126 B3
Colonial Beach, *U.S.A.* 108 F7
Colonie, *U.S.A.* 111 D11

Colonna, C., *Italy* 31 C10
Colonsay, *Canada* 105 C7
Colonsay, *U.K.* 14 E2
Colorado □, *U.S.A.* 115 G10
Colorado →, *Argentina* 128 D4
Colorado →, *N. Amer.* 115 L6
Colorado →, *U.S.A.* 113 L7
Colorado City, *U.S.A.* 113 J4
Colorado Plateau, *U.S.A.* 115 H8
Colorado River Aqueduct, *U.S.A.* 117 L12
Colorado Springs, *U.S.A.* 112 F2
Colorno, *Italy* 28 D7
Colotlán, *Mexico* 118 C4
Colstrip, *U.S.A.* 114 D10
Colton, *U.S.A.* 111 B10
Columbia, *Ky., U.S.A.* 108 G3
Columbia, *La., U.S.A.* 113 J8
Columbia, *Miss., U.S.A.* 113 K10
Columbia, *Mo., U.S.A.* 112 F8
Columbia, *Pa., U.S.A.* 111 F8
Columbia, *S.C., U.S.A.* 109 J5
Columbia, *Tenn., U.S.A.* 109 H2
Columbia →, *N. Amer.* 116 D2
Columbia, C., *Canada* 4 A4
Columbia, District of □, *U.S.A.* 108 F7
Columbia, Mt., *Canada* 104 C5
Columbia Basin, *U.S.A.* 114 C4
Columbia Falls, *U.S.A.* 114 B6
Columbia Mts., *Canada* 104 C5
Columbia Plateau, *U.S.A.* 114 D5
Columbiana, *U.S.A.* 110 F4
Columbretes, Is., *Spain* 32 F5
Columbus, *Ga., U.S.A.* 109 J3
Columbus, *Ind., U.S.A.* 108 F3
Columbus, *Kans., U.S.A.* 113 G7
Columbus, *Miss., U.S.A.* 109 J1
Columbus, *Mont., U.S.A.* 114 D9
Columbus, *N. Mex., U.S.A.* 115 L10
Columbus, *Nebr., U.S.A.* 112 E6
Columbus, *Ohio, U.S.A.* 108 F4
Columbus, *Tex., U.S.A.* 113 L6
Colunga, *Spain* 34 B5
Colusa, *U.S.A.* 116 F4
Colville, *U.S.A.* 114 B5
Colville →, *U.S.A.* 100 A4
Colville, C., *N.Z.* 91 G5
Colwood, *Canada* 116 B3
Colwyn Bay, *U.K.* 12 D4
Coma, *Ethiopia* 81 F4
Comácchio, *Italy* 29 D9
Comalcalco, *Mexico* 119 D6
Comallo, *Argentina* 128 E2
Comana, *Romania* 43 F11
Comanche, *U.S.A.* 113 K5
Comănești, *Romania* 43 D11
Comarnic, *Romania* 43 E10
Comayagua, *Honduras* 120 D2
Combahee →, *U.S.A.* 109 J5
Combarbalá, *Chile* 126 C1
Combeaufontaine, *France* 19 E12
Comber, *Canada* 110 D2
Comber, *U.K.* 15 B6
Combermere, *Canada* 110 A7
Comblain-au-Pont, *Belgium* 17 D5
Combourg, *France* 18 D5
Combrailles, *France* 19 F9
Combronde, *France* 20 C7
Comeragh Mts., *Ireland* 15 D4
Comet, *Australia* 94 C4
Comilla, *Bangla.* 67 H17
Comino, *Malta* 36 C1
Comino, C., *Italy* 30 B2
Cómiso, *Italy* 31 F7
Comitán, *Mexico* 119 D6
Commentry, *France* 19 F9
Commerce, *Ga., U.S.A.* 109 H4
Commerce, *Tex., U.S.A.* 113 J7
Commercy, *France* 19 D12
Committee B., *Canada* 101 B11
Commonwealth B., *Antarctica* 5 C10
Commoron Cr. →, *Australia* 95 D5
Communism Pk. = Kommunizma, Pik, *Tajikistan* 50 F8
Como, *Italy* 28 C6
Como, Lago di, *Italy* 28 B6
Comodoro Rivadavia, *Argentina* 128 F3
Comorâște, *Romania* 42 E6
Comorin, C., *India* 66 Q10
Comoro Is. = Comoros ■, *Ind. Oc.* 77 H8
Comoros ■, *Ind. Oc.* 77 H8
Comox, *Canada* 104 D4
Compiègne, *France* 19 C9
Comporta, *Portugal* 35 G2
Compostela, *Mexico* 118 C4
Comprida, I., *Brazil* 127 A6
Compton, *Canada* 111 A13
Compton, *U.S.A.* 117 M8
Comrat, *Moldova* 43 D13
Con Cuong, *Vietnam* 64 C5
Con Son, *Vietnam* 65 H6
Conakry, *Guinea* 82 D2
Conara, *Australia* 94 G4
Concarneau, *France* 18 E3
Conceição, *Mozam.* 87 F4
Conceição da Barra, *Brazil* 125 G11
Conceição do Araguaia, *Brazil* 125 E9

Concepción, L., *Bolivia* 124 G6
Concepción, Punta, *Mexico* 118 B2
Concepción del Oro, *Mexico* 118 C4
Concepción del Uruguay, *Argentina* 126 C4
Conception, Pt., *U.S.A.* 117 L6
Conception B., *Canada* 103 C9
Conception B., *Namibia* 88 C1
Conception I., *Bahamas* 121 B4
Concession, *Zimbabwe* 87 F3
Conchas Dam, *U.S.A.* 113 H2
Conches-en-Ouche, *France* 18 D7
Concho, *U.S.A.* 115 J9
Concho →, *U.S.A.* 113 K5
Conchos →, *Chihuahua, Mexico* 118 B4
Conchos →, *Tamaulipas, Mexico* 119 B5
Concord, *Calif., U.S.A.* 116 H4
Concord, *N.C., U.S.A.* 109 H5
Concord, *N.H., U.S.A.* 111 C13
Concordia, *Argentina* 126 C4
Concórdia, *Brazil* 124 D5
Concordia, *Mexico* 118 C3
Concordia, *U.S.A.* 112 F6
Concrete, *U.S.A.* 114 B3
Condamine, *Australia* 95 D5
Condat, *France* 20 C6
Conde, *U.S.A.* 112 C5
Condé-sur-Noireau, *France* 18 D6
Condeúba, *Brazil* 125 F10
Condobolin, *Australia* 95 E4
Condom, *France* 20 E4
Condon, *U.S.A.* 114 D3
Conegliano, *Italy* 29 C9
Conejera, I. = Conills, I. des, *Spain* 37 B9
Conejos, *Mexico* 118 B4
Confolens, *France* 20 B4
Confuso →, *Paraguay* 126 B4
Congaz, *Moldova* 43 D13
Conghua, *China* 59 F9
Congjiang, *China* 58 E7
Congleton, *U.K.* 12 D5
Congo (Kinshasa) = Congo, Dem. Rep. of the ■, *Africa* 84 E4
Congo ■, *Africa* 84 E3
Congo →, *Africa* 84 F2
Congo, Dem. Rep. of the ■, *Africa* 84 E4
Congo Basin, *Africa* 84 E4
Congonhas, *Brazil* 127 A7
Congress, *U.S.A.* 115 J7
Conil = Conil de la Frontera, *Spain* 35 J4
Conil de la Frontera, *Spain* 35 J4
Conills, I. des, *Spain* 37 B9
Coniston, *Canada* 102 C3
Conjeeveram = Kanchipuram, *India* 66 N11
Conklin, *Canada* 105 B6
Conklin, *U.S.A.* 111 D9
Conn, L., *Ireland* 15 B2
Connacht □, *Ireland* 15 C2
Conneaut, *U.S.A.* 110 E4
Connecticut □, *U.S.A.* 111 E12
Connecticut →, *U.S.A.* 111 E12
Connell, *U.S.A.* 114 C4
Connellsville, *U.S.A.* 110 F5
Connemara, *Ireland* 15 C2
Connemaugh →, *U.S.A.* 110 F5
Connersville, *U.S.A.* 108 F3
Connors Ra., *Australia* 94 C4
Conques, *France* 20 D6
Conquest, *Canada* 105 C7
Conrad, *U.S.A.* 114 B8
Conran, C., *Australia* 95 F4
Conroe, *U.S.A.* 113 K7
Consecon, *Canada* 110 C7
Conselheiro Lafaiete, *Brazil* 127 A7
Conselve, *Italy* 29 C8
Consett, *U.K.* 12 C6
Consort, *Canada* 105 C6
Constance = Konstanz, *Germany* 25 H5
Constance, L. = Bodensee, *Europe* 25 H5
Constanța, *Romania* 43 F13
Constanța □, *Romania* 43 F13
Constantia, *U.S.A.* 111 C8
Constantina, *Spain* 35 H5
Constantine, *Algeria* 78 A7
Constitución, *Chile* 126 D1
Constitución, *Uruguay* 126 C4
Consuegra, *Spain* 35 F7
Consul, *Canada* 105 D7
Contact, *U.S.A.* 114 F6
Contai, *India* 69 J12
Contamana, *Peru* 124 E4
Contarina, *Italy* 29 C9
Contas →, *Brazil* 125 F11
Contes, *France* 21 E11
Contoocook, *U.S.A.* 111 C13
Contra Costa, *Mozam.* 89 D5
Contres, *France* 18 E8
Contrexéville, *France* 19 D12
Contwoyto L., *Canada* 100 B8
Conversano, *Italy* 31 B10
Conway = Conwy, *U.K.* 12 D4
Conway = Conwy →, *U.K.* 12 D4
Conway, *Ark., U.S.A.* 113 H8
Conway, *N.H., U.S.A.* 111 C13
Conway, *S.C., U.S.A.* 109 J6
Conway, L., *Australia* 95 D2
Conwy, *U.K.* 12 D4
Conwy □, *U.K.* 12 D4
Conwy →, *U.K.* 12 D4
Coober Pedy, *Australia* 95 D1

Cuillin Sd.

Cooch Behar = Koch Bihar, *India* 67 F16
Cooinda, *Australia* 92 B5
Cook, *Australia* 93 F5
Cook, *U.S.A.* 112 B8
Cook, B., *Chile* 128 H3
Cook, C., *Canada* 104 C3
Cook, Mt., *N.Z.* 91 K3
Cook Inlet, *U.S.A.* 100 C4
Cook Is., *Pac. Oc.* 97 J12
Cook Strait, *N.Z.* 91 J5
Cookeville, *U.S.A.* 109 G3
Cookhouse, *S. Africa* 88 E4
Cookshire, *Canada* 111 A13
Cookstown, *U.K.* 15 B5
Cooksville, *Canada* 110 C5
Cooktown, *Australia* 94 B4
Coolabah, *Australia* 95 E4
Cooladdi, *Australia* 95 D4
Coolah, *Australia* 95 E4
Coolamon, *Australia* 95 E4
Coolgardie, *Australia* 93 F3
Coolidge, *U.S.A.* 115 K8
Coolidge Dam, *U.S.A.* 115 K8
Cooma, *Australia* 95 F4
Coon Rapids, *U.S.A.* 112 C8
Coonabarabran, *Australia* 95 E4
Coonalpyn, *Australia* 95 F2
Coonamble, *Australia* 95 E4
Coonana, *Australia* 93 F3
Coondapoor, *India* 66 N9
Cooninie, L., *Australia* 95 D2
Cooper, *U.S.A.* 113 J7
Cooper Cr. →, *Australia* 95 D2
Cooperstown, *N. Dak., U.S.A.* 112 B5
Cooperstown, *N.Y., U.S.A.* 111 D10
Coorabie, *Australia* 93 F5
Coorow, *Australia* 93 E2
Cooroy, *Australia* 95 D5
Coos Bay, *U.S.A.* 114 E1
Coosa →, *U.S.A.* 109 J2
Cootamundra, *Australia* 95 E4
Cootehill, *Ireland* 15 B4
Copahue Paso, *Argentina* 126 D1
Copainalá, *Mexico* 119 D6
Copake Falls, *U.S.A.* 111 D11
Copalnic Mănăştur, *Romania* 43 C8
Copán, *Honduras* 120 D2
Cope, *U.S.A.* 112 F3
Cope, C., *Spain* 33 H3
Copenhagen = København, *Denmark* 11 J6
Copenhagen, *U.S.A.* 111 C9
Copertino, *Italy* 31 B11
Copiapó, *Chile* 126 B1
Copiapó →, *Chile* 126 B1
Coplay, *U.S.A.* 111 F9
Copp L., *Canada* 104 A6
Copparo, *Italy* 29 D8
Coppename →, *Surinam* 125 B7
Copper Harbor, *U.S.A.* 108 B2
Copper Queen, *Zimbabwe* 87 F2
Copperas Cove, *U.S.A.* 113 K6
Copperbelt □, *Zambia* 87 E2
Coppermine = Kugluktuk, *Canada* 100 B8
Coppermine →, *Canada* 100 B8
Copperopolis, *U.S.A.* 116 H6
Copşa Mică, *Romania* 43 D9
Coquet →, *U.K.* 12 B6
Coquilhatville = Mbandaka, *Dem. Rep. of the Congo* 84 D3
Coquille, *U.S.A.* 114 E1
Coquimbo, *Chile* 126 C1
Coquimbo □, *Chile* 126 C1
Corabia, *Romania* 43 G9
Coracora, *Peru* 124 G4
Coraki, *Australia* 95 D5
Coral, *U.S.A.* 110 F5
Coral Gables, *U.S.A.* 109 N5
Coral Harbour = Salliq, *Canada* 101 B11
Coral Sea, *Pac. Oc.* 96 J7
Coral Springs, *U.S.A.* 109 M5
Coraopolis, *U.S.A.* 110 F4
Corato, *Italy* 31 A9
Corbeil-Essonnes, *France* 19 D9
Corbie, *France* 19 C9
Corbières, *France* 20 F6
Corbigny, *France* 19 E10
Corbin, *U.S.A.* 108 G3
Corbones →, *Spain* 35 H5
Corbu, *Romania* 43 F13
Corby, *U.K.* 13 E7
Corcaigh = Cork, *Ireland* 15 E3
Corcoran, *U.S.A.* 116 J7
Cordele, *U.S.A.* 109 K4
Cordell, *U.S.A.* 113 H5
Cordenòns, *Italy* 29 C9
Cordes, *France* 20 D5
Córdoba, *Argentina* 126 C3
Córdoba, *Mexico* 119 D5
Córdoba, *Spain* 35 H6
Córdoba □, *Argentina* 126 C3
Córdoba □, *Spain* 35 G6
Córdoba, Sierra de, *Argentina* 126 C3
Cordon, *Phil.* 61 C4
Cordova, *U.S.A.* 100 B5
Corella, *Spain* 32 C3
Corella →, *Australia* 94 B3
Corfield, *Australia* 94 C3
Corfu = Kérkira, *Greece* 36 A3
Corfu, Str. of, *Greece* 36 A4
Corgo = O Corgo, *Spain* 34 C3
Cori, *Italy* 30 A5
Coria, *Spain* 34 F4
Coria del Río, *Spain* 35 H4
Corigliano Cálabro, *Italy* 31 C9
Coringa Is., *Australia* 94 B4
Corinth = Kórinthos, *Greece* 38 D4
Corinth, *Miss., U.S.A.* 109 H1
Corinth, *N.Y., U.S.A.* 111 C11
Corinth, *N.Y., U.S.A.* 111 C11
Corinth, G. of = Korinthiakós Kólpos, *Greece* 38 C4
Corinth Canal, *Greece* 38 D4
Corinto, *Brazil* 125 G10
Corinto, *Nic.* 120 D2
Cork, *Ireland* 15 E3
Cork □, *Ireland* 15 E3
Cork Harbour, *Ireland* 15 E3
Corlay, *France* 18 D3
Corleone, *Italy* 30 E6
Corleto Perticara, *Italy* 31 B9
Çorlu, *Turkey* 41 E11
Cormack L., *Canada* 104 A4
Cormòns, *Italy* 29 C10
Cormorant, *Canada* 105 C8
Cormorant L., *Canada* 105 C8
Corn Is. = Maiz, Is. del, *Nic.* 120 D3
Cornélio Procópio, *Brazil* 127 A5
Corner Brook, *Canada* 103 C8
Corneşti, *Moldova* 43 C13
Corníglio, *Italy* 28 D7
Corning, *Ark., U.S.A.* 113 G9
Corning, *Calif., U.S.A.* 114 G2
Corning, *Iowa, U.S.A.* 112 E7
Corning, *N.Y., U.S.A.* 110 D7
Corno Grande, *Italy* 29 F10
Cornwall, *Canada* 102 C5
Cornwall, *U.S.A.* 111 F8
Cornwall □, *U.K.* 13 G3
Corny Pt., *Australia* 95 E2
Coro, *Venezuela* 124 A5
Coroatá, *Brazil* 125 D10
Corocoro, *Bolivia* 124 G5
Coroico, *Bolivia* 124 G5
Coromandel, *N.Z.* 91 G5
Coromandel Coast, *India* 66 N12
Corona, *Calif., U.S.A.* 117 M9
Corona, *N. Mex., U.S.A.* 115 J11
Coronach, *Canada* 105 D7
Coronado, *U.S.A.* 117 N9
Coronado, B. de, *Costa Rica* 120 E3
Coronados, Is. los, *U.S.A.* 117 N9
Coronation, *Canada* 104 C6
Coronation Gulf, *Canada* 100 B8
Coronation I., *Antarctica* 5 C18
Coronation Is., *Australia* 92 B3
Coronda, *Argentina* 126 C3
Coronel, *Chile* 126 D1
Coronel Bogado, *Paraguay* 126 B4
Coronel Dorrego, *Argentina* 126 D3
Coronel Oviedo, *Paraguay* 126 B4
Coronel Pringles, *Argentina* 126 D3
Coronel Suárez, *Argentina* 126 D3
Coronel Vidal, *Argentina* 126 D4
Coropuna, Nevado, *Peru* 124 G4
Çorovoda, *Albania* 40 F4
Corowa, *Australia* 95 F4
Corozal, *Belize* 119 D7
Corps, *France* 21 D9
Corpus, *Argentina* 127 B4
Corpus Christi, *U.S.A.* 113 M6
Corpus Christi, L., *U.S.A.* 113 L6
Corral de Almaguer, *Spain* 34 F7
Corralejo, *Canary Is.* 37 F6
Corraun Pen., *Ireland* 15 C2
Corréggio, *Italy* 28 D7
Correntes, C. das, *Mozam.* 89 C6
Corrèze □, *France* 20 C5
Corrèze →, *France* 20 C5
Corrib, L., *Ireland* 15 C2
Corridónia, *Italy* 29 E10
Corrientes, *Argentina* 126 B4
Corrientes □, *Argentina* 126 B4
Corrientes →, *Argentina* 126 C4
Corrientes →, *Peru* 124 D4
Corrientes, C., *Colombia* 124 B3
Corrientes, C., *Cuba* 120 B3
Corrientes, C., *Mexico* 118 C3
Corrigan, *U.S.A.* 113 K7
Corrigin, *Australia* 93 F2
Corry, *U.S.A.* 110 E5
Corryong, *Australia* 95 F4
Corse, *France* 21 G13
Corse, C., *France* 21 E13
Corse-du-Sud □, *France* 21 G13
Corsica = Corse, *France* 21 G13
Corsicana, *U.S.A.* 113 J6
Corte, *France* 21 F13
Corte Pinto, *Portugal* 35 H3
Cortegana, *Spain* 35 H4
Cortez, *U.S.A.* 115 H9
Cortina d'Ampezzo, *Italy* 29 B9
Cortland, *N.Y., U.S.A.* 111 D8
Cortland, *Ohio, U.S.A.* 110 E4
Cortona, *Italy* 29 E8
Corubal →, *Guinea-Biss.* 82 C2
Coruche, *Portugal* 35 G2
Çoruh →, *Turkey* 49 K5
Çorum, *Turkey* 72 B6
Corumbá, *Brazil* 124 G7
Corund, *Romania* 43 D10
Corunna = A Coruña, *Spain* 34 B2
Corvallis, *U.S.A.* 114 D2
Corvette, L. de la, *Canada* 102 B5
Corydon, *U.S.A.* 112 E8
Cosalá, *Mexico* 118 C3
Cosamaloapan, *Mexico* 119 D5
Cosenza, *Italy* 31 C9
Coşereni, *Romania* 43 F11
Coshocton, *U.S.A.* 110 F3
Cosmo Newberry, *Australia* 93 E3
Cosne-Cours-sur-Loire, *France* 19 E9
Coso Junction, *U.S.A.* 117 J9
Coso Pk., *U.S.A.* 117 J9
Cospeito, *Spain* 34 B3
Cosquín, *Argentina* 126 C3
Cossato, *Italy* 28 C5
Cossé-le-Vivien, *France* 18 E6
Cosson →, *France* 18 E8
Costa Blanca, *Spain* 33 G4
Costa Brava, *Spain* 32 D8
Costa del Sol, *Spain* 35 J6
Costa Dorada, *Spain* 32 D6
Costa Mesa, *U.S.A.* 117 M9
Costa Rica ■, *Cent. Amer.* 120 E3
Costa Smeralda, *Italy* 30 A2
Costeşti, *Romania* 43 F9
Costigliole d'Asti, *Italy* 28 D5
Cosumnes →, *U.S.A.* 116 G5
Coswig, *Sachsen, Germany* 24 D9
Coswig, *Sachsen-Anhalt, Germany* 24 D8
Cotabato, *Phil.* 61 H6
Cotagaita, *Bolivia* 126 A2
Côte d'Azur, *France* 21 E11
Côte-d'Ivoire = Ivory Coast ■, *Africa* 82 D4
Côte d'Or, *France* 19 E11
Côte-d'Or □, *France* 19 E11
Coteau des Prairies, *U.S.A.* 112 C6
Coteau du Missouri, *U.S.A.* 112 B4
Coteau Landing, *Canada* 111 A10
Cotentin, *France* 18 C5
Côtes-d'Armor □, *France* 18 D4
Côtes de Meuse, *France* 19 C12
Côtes-du-Nord = Côtes-d'Armor □, *France* 18 D4
Cotiella, *Spain* 32 C5
Cotillo, *Canary Is.* 37 F5
Cotiujeni, *Moldova* 43 C13
Cotonou, *Benin* 83 D5
Cotopaxi, *Ecuador* 122 D3
Cotronei, *Italy* 31 C9
Cotswold Hills, *U.K.* 13 F5
Cottage Grove, *U.S.A.* 114 E2
Cottbus, *Germany* 24 D10
Cottonwood, *U.S.A.* 115 J7
Cotulla, *U.S.A.* 113 L5
Coubre, Pte. de la, *France* 20 C2
Couches, *France* 19 F11
Couço, *Portugal* 35 G2
Coudersport, *U.S.A.* 110 E6
Couedic, C. du, *Australia* 95 F2
Couëron, *France* 18 E5
Couesnon →, *France* 18 D5
Couhé, *France* 20 B4
Coulanges-sur-Yonne, *France* 19 E10
Coulee City, *U.S.A.* 114 C4
Coulman I., *Antarctica* 5 D11
Coulommiers, *France* 19 D10
Coulon →, *France* 21 E9
Coulonge →, *Canada* 102 C4
Coulonges-sur-l'Autize, *France* 20 B3
Coulounieix-Chamiers, *France* 20 C4
Coulterville, *U.S.A.* 116 H6
Council, *U.S.A.* 114 D5
Council Bluffs, *U.S.A.* 112 E7
Council Grove, *U.S.A.* 112 F6
Coupeville, *U.S.A.* 116 B4
Courantyne →, *S. Amer.* 122 C5
Courcelles, *Belgium* 17 D4
Courçon, *France* 20 B3
Courmayeur, *Italy* 28 C3
Couronne, C., *France* 21 E9
Cours-la-Ville, *France* 19 F11
Coursan, *France* 20 E7
Courseulles-sur-Mer, *France* 18 C6
Courtenay, *Canada* 104 D4
Courtenay, *France* 19 D10
Courtland, *U.S.A.* 116 G5
Courtrai = Kortrijk, *Belgium* 17 D3
Courtright, *Canada* 110 D2
Coushatta, *U.S.A.* 113 J8
Coutances, *France* 18 C5
Coutras, *France* 20 C3
Coutts Crossing, *Australia* 95 D5
Couvin, *Belgium* 17 D4
Covarrubias, *Spain* 34 C7
Covasna, *Romania* 43 E11
Covasna □, *Romania* 43 E10
Cove I., *Canada* 110 A3
Coventry, *U.K.* 13 E6
Covilhã, *Portugal* 34 E3
Covington, *Ga., U.S.A.* 109 J4
Covington, *Ky., U.S.A.* 108 F3
Covington, *Okla., U.S.A.* 113 G6
Covington, *Tenn., U.S.A.* 113 H10
Covington, *Va., U.S.A.* 108 G5
Cowal, L., *Australia* 95 E4
Cowan, L., *Australia* 93 F3
Cowan L., *Canada* 105 C7
Cowangie, *Australia* 95 F3
Cowansville, *Canada* 102 C5
Coward Springs, *Australia* 95 D2
Cowcowing Lakes, *Australia* 93 F2
Cowdenbeath, *U.K.* 14 E5
Cowell, *Australia* 95 E2
Cowes, *U.K.* 13 G6
Cowichan L., *Canada* 116 B2
Cowlitz →, *U.S.A.* 116 D4
Cowra, *Australia* 95 E4
Cox, *Spain* 33 G4
Coxilha Grande, *Brazil* 127 B5
Coxim, *Brazil* 125 G8
Cox's Bazar, *Bangla.* 67 J17
Coyote Wells, *U.S.A.* 117 N11
Coyuca de Benítez, *Mexico* 119 D4
Coyuca de Catalan, *Mexico* 118 D4
Cozad, *U.S.A.* 112 E5
Cozes, *France* 20 C3
Cozumel, *Mexico* 119 C7
Cozumel, Isla, *Mexico* 119 C7
Cracow = Kraków, *Poland* 45 H6
Cracow, *Australia* 95 D5
Cradock, *Australia* 95 E2
Cradock, *S. Africa* 88 E4
Craig, *U.S.A.* 114 F10
Craigavon, *U.K.* 15 B5
Craigmore, *Zimbabwe* 87 G3
Craik, *Canada* 105 C7
Crailsheim, *Germany* 25 F6
Craiova, *Romania* 43 F8
Cramsie, *Australia* 94 C3
Cranberry L., *U.S.A.* 111 B10
Cranberry Portage, *Canada* 105 C8
Cranbrook, *Australia* 93 F2
Cranbrook, *Canada* 104 D5
Crandon, *U.S.A.* 112 C10
Crane, *Oreg., U.S.A.* 114 E4
Crane, *Tex., U.S.A.* 113 K3
Cranston, *U.S.A.* 111 E13
Craon, *France* 18 E6
Craonne, *France* 19 C10
Craponne-sur-Arzon, *France* 20 C7
Crasna, *Romania* 43 D12
Crasna →, *Romania* 42 C7
Crasnei, Munţii, *Romania* 43 C8
Crater L., *U.S.A.* 114 E2
Crater Lake National Park, *U.S.A.* 114 E2
Crateús, *Brazil* 125 E10
Crati →, *Italy* 31 C9
Crato, *Brazil* 125 E11
Crato, *Portugal* 35 F3
Craven, L., *Canada* 102 B4
Crawford, *U.S.A.* 112 D3
Crawfordsville, *U.S.A.* 108 E2
Crawley, *U.K.* 13 F7
Crazy Mts., *U.S.A.* 114 C8
Crean L., *Canada* 105 C7
Crécy-en-Ponthieu, *France* 19 B8
Crediton, *Canada* 110 C3
Cree →, *Canada* 105 B7
Cree →, *U.K.* 14 G4
Cree L., *Canada* 105 B7
Creede, *U.S.A.* 115 H10
Creekside, *U.S.A.* 110 F5
Creel, *Mexico* 118 B3
Creemore, *Canada* 110 B4
Creighton, *Canada* 105 C8
Creighton, *U.S.A.* 112 D6
Creil, *France* 19 C9
Crema, *Italy* 28 C6
Cremona, *Italy* 28 C7
Crepaja, *Serbia, Yug.* 42 E5
Crépy, *France* 19 C10
Crépy-en-Valois, *France* 19 C9
Cres, *Croatia* 29 D11
Crescent City, *U.S.A.* 114 F1
Crescentino, *Italy* 28 C5
Crespo, *Argentina* 126 C3
Cresson, *U.S.A.* 110 F6
Crest, *France* 21 D9
Cresta, Mt., *Phil.* 61 C5
Crestline, *Calif., U.S.A.* 117 L9
Crestline, *Ohio, U.S.A.* 110 F2
Creston, *Canada* 104 D5
Creston, *Calif., U.S.A.* 116 K6
Creston, *Iowa, U.S.A.* 112 E7
Crestview, *Calif., U.S.A.* 116 H8
Crestview, *Fla., U.S.A.* 109 K2
Crêt de la Neige, *France* 19 F12
Crete = Kríti, *Greece* 36 D7
Crete, *U.S.A.* 112 E6
Crete, Sea of, *Greece* 39 E7
Créteil, *France* 19 D9
Creus, C. de, *Spain* 32 C8
Creuse □, *France* 19 F9
Creuse →, *France* 20 B4
Creutzwald, *France* 19 C13
Creuzburg, *Germany* 24 D6
Crèvecœur-le-Grand, *France* 19 C9
Crevillente, *Spain* 33 G4
Crewe, *U.K.* 12 D5
Crewkerne, *U.K.* 13 G5
Criciúma, *Brazil* 127 B6
Cricova, *Moldova* 43 C13
Crieff, *U.K.* 14 E5
Crikvenica, *Croatia* 29 C11
Crimea □, *Ukraine* 47 K8
Crimean Pen. = Krymskyy Pivostriv, *Ukraine* 47 K8
Crimmitschau, *Germany* 24 E8
Cristuru Secuiesc, *Romania* 43 D10
Crişul Alb →, *Romania* 42 D6
Crişul Negru →, *Romania* 42 D6
Crişul Repede →, *Romania* 42 D5
Criuleni, *Moldova* 43 C14
Crivitz, *Germany* 24 B7
Crna →, *Macedonia* 40 E5
Crna Gora = Montenegro □, *Yugoslavia* 40 D3
Crna Gora, *Macedonia* 40 D5
Crna Reka = Crna →, *Macedonia* 40 E5
Crna Trava, *Serbia, Yug.* 40 D6
Crni Drim →, *Macedonia* 40 E4
Crni Timok →, *Serbia, Yug.* 40 C6
Crnoljeva Planina, *Kosovo, Yug.* 40 D5
Črnomelj, *Slovenia* 29 C12
Croagh Patrick, *Ireland* 15 C2
Croatia ■, *Europe* 29 C13
Crocker, Banjaran, *Malaysia* 62 C5
Crockett, *U.S.A.* 113 K7
Crocodile = Krokodil →, *Mozam.* 89 D5
Crocodile Is., *Australia* 94 A1
Crocq, *France* 20 C6
Crodo, *Italy* 28 B5
Crohy Hd., *Ireland* 15 B3
Croisette, C., *France* 21 E9
Croisic, Pte. du, *France* 18 E4
Croix, L. La, *Canada* 102 C1
Croker, C., *Australia* 92 B5
Croker, C., *Canada* 110 B4
Croker I., *Australia* 92 B5
Cromarty, *U.K.* 14 D4
Cromer, *U.K.* 12 E9
Cromwell, *N.Z.* 91 L2
Cromwell, *U.S.A.* 111 E12
Cronat, *France* 19 F10
Crook, *U.K.* 12 C6
Crooked →, *Canada* 104 C4
Crooked →, *U.S.A.* 114 D3
Crooked I., *Bahamas* 121 B5
Crooked Island Passage, *Bahamas* 121 B5
Crookston, *Minn., U.S.A.* 112 B6
Crookston, *Nebr., U.S.A.* 112 D4
Crookwell, *Australia* 95 E4
Crosby, *U.K.* 12 D4
Crosby, *N. Dak., U.S.A.* 112 A3
Crosby, *Pa., U.S.A.* 110 E6
Crosbyton, *U.S.A.* 113 J4
Crosía, *Italy* 31 C9
Cross →, *Nigeria* 83 E6
Cross City, *U.S.A.* 109 L4
Cross Fell, *U.K.* 12 C5
Cross L., *Canada* 105 C9
Cross Lake, *Canada* 105 C9
Cross River □, *Nigeria* 83 D6
Cross Sound, *U.S.A.* 100 C6
Crossett, *U.S.A.* 113 J9
Crosshaven, *Ireland* 15 E3
Crossville, *U.S.A.* 109 G3
Croswell, *U.S.A.* 110 C2
Croton-on-Hudson, *U.S.A.* 111 E11
Crotone, *Italy* 31 C10
Crow →, *Canada* 104 B4
Crow Agency, *U.S.A.* 114 D10
Crow Hd., *Ireland* 15 E1
Crowell, *U.S.A.* 113 J5
Crowley, *U.S.A.* 113 K8
Crowley, L., *U.S.A.* 116 H8
Crown Point, *Ind., U.S.A.* 108 E2
Crown Point, *N.Y., U.S.A.* 111 C11
Crownpoint, *U.S.A.* 115 J9
Crows Landing, *U.S.A.* 116 H5
Crows Nest, *Australia* 95 D5
Crowsnest Pass, *Canada* 104 D6
Croydon, *Australia* 94 B3
Croydon, *U.K.* 13 F7
Crozet, Is., *Ind. Oc.* 3 G12
Crozon, *France* 18 D2
Cruz, C., *Cuba* 120 C4
Cruz Alta, *Brazil* 127 B5
Cruz de Incio, *Spain* 34 C3
Cruz del Eje, *Argentina* 126 C3
Cruzeiro, *Brazil* 127 A7
Cruzeiro do Oeste, *Brazil* 127 A5
Cruzeiro do Sul, *Brazil* 124 E4
Cry L., *Canada* 104 B3
Crystal Bay, *U.S.A.* 116 F7
Crystal Brook, *Australia* 95 E2
Crystal City, *U.S.A.* 113 L5
Crystal Falls, *U.S.A.* 108 B1
Crystal River, *U.S.A.* 109 L4
Crystal Springs, *U.S.A.* 113 K9
Csenger, *Hungary* 42 C7
Csongrád, *Hungary* 42 D5
Csongrád □, *Hungary* 42 D5
Csorna, *Hungary* 42 C2
Csurgo, *Hungary* 42 D2
Cu Lao Hon, *Vietnam* 65 G7
Cua Rao, *Vietnam* 64 C5
Cuácua →, *Mozam.* 87 F4
Cuamato, *Angola* 88 B2
Cuamba, *Mozam.* 87 E4
Cuando →, *Angola* 85 H4
Cuando Cubango □, *Angola* 88 B3
Cuangar, *Angola* 88 B2
Cuanza →, *Angola* 76 G5
Cuarto →, *Argentina* 126 C3
Cuatrociénegas, *Mexico* 118 B4
Cuauhtémoc, *Mexico* 118 B3
Cuba, *Portugal* 35 G3
Cuba, *N. Mex., U.S.A.* 115 J10
Cuba, *N.Y., U.S.A.* 110 D6
Cuba ■, *W. Indies* 120 B4
Cubango →, *Africa* 88 B3
Çubuk, *Turkey* 72 B5
Cuchumatanes, Sierra de los, *Guatemala* 120 C1
Cuckfield, *U.K.* 13 F7
Cucuí, *Brazil* 124 C5
Cucurpe, *Mexico* 118 A2
Cúcuta, *Colombia* 124 B4
Cudalbi, *Romania* 43 E12
Cuddalore, *India* 66 P11
Cuddapah, *India* 66 M11
Cuddapan, L., *Australia* 94 D3
Cudillero, *Spain* 34 B4
Cue, *Australia* 93 E2
Cuéllar, *Spain* 34 D6
Cuenca, *Ecuador* 124 D3
Cuenca, *Spain* 32 E2
Cuenca □, *Spain* 32 F3
Cuenca, Serranía de, *Spain* 32 F3
Cuerdo del Pozo, Embalse de la, *Spain* 32 D2
Cuernavaca, *Mexico* 119 D5
Cuero, *U.S.A.* 113 L6
Cuers, *France* 21 E10
Cuevas del Almanzora, *Spain* 33 H3
Cuevo, *Bolivia* 124 H6
Cugir, *Romania* 43 E8
Cugnaux, *France* 20 E5
Cuhai-Bakony →, *Hungary* 42 C2
Cuiabá, *Brazil* 125 G7
Cuiabá →, *Brazil* 125 G7
Cuijk, *Neths.* 17 C5
Cuilco, *Guatemala* 120 C1
Cuillin Hills, *U.K.* 14 D2
Cuillin Sd., *U.K.* 14 D2

Cuiseaux

Cuiseaux, *France* 19 F12
Cuito →, *Angola* 88 B3
Cuitzeo, L. de, *Mexico* 118 D4
Cujmir, *Romania* 42 F7
Cukai, *Malaysia* 65 K4
Culbertson, *U.S.A.* 112 A2
Culcairn, *Australia* 95 F4
Culebra, Sierra de la, *Spain* 34 D4
Culfa, *Azerbaijan* 73 C11
Culgoa →, *Australia* 95 D4
Culiacán, *Mexico* 118 C3
Culiacán →, *Mexico* 118 C3
Culion, *Phil.* 61 F4
Cúllar, *Spain* 35 H8
Cullarin Ra., *Australia* 95 E4
Cullen, *U.K.* 14 D6
Cullen Pt., *Australia* 94 A3
Cullera, *Spain* 33 F4
Cullman, *U.S.A.* 109 H2
Culoz, *France* 21 C9
Culpeper, *U.S.A.* 108 F7
Culuene →, *Brazil* 125 F8
Culver, Pt., *Australia* 93 F3
Culverden, *N.Z.* 91 K4
Cumaná, *Venezuela* 124 A6
Cumaovası, *Turkey* 39 C9
Cumberland, *B.C., Canada* 104 D4
Cumberland, *Ont., Canada* 111 A9
Cumberland, *U.S.A.* 108 F6
Cumberland →, *U.S.A.* 109 G2
Cumberland, L., *U.S.A.* 109 G3
Cumberland I., *U.S.A.* 109 K5
Cumberland Is., *Australia* 94 C4
Cumberland L., *Canada* 105 C8
Cumberland Pen., *Canada* 101 B13
Cumberland Plateau, *U.S.A.* 109 H3
Cumberland Sd., *Canada* 101 B13
Cumbernauld, *U.K.* 14 F5
Cumborah, *Australia* 95 D4
Cumbres Mayores, *Spain* 35 G4
Cumbria □, *U.K.* 12 C5
Cumbrian Mts., *U.K.* 12 C5
Cumbum, *India* 66 M11
Cuminá →, *Brazil* 125 D7
Cummings Mt., *U.S.A.* 117 K8
Cummins, *Australia* 95 E2
Cumnock, *Australia* 95 E4
Cumnock, *U.K.* 14 F4
Cumpas, *Mexico* 118 B3
Cumplida, Pta., *Canary Is.* 37 F2
Çumra, *Turkey* 72 D5
Cunco, *Chile* 128 D2
Cuncumén, *Chile* 126 C1
Cunderdin, *Australia* 93 F2
Cunene →, *Angola* 88 B1
Cúneo, *Italy* 28 D4
Çüngüş, *Turkey* 70 B3
Cunillera, I. = Sa Conillera, *Spain* 37 C7
Cunlhat, *France* 20 C7
Cunnamulla, *Australia* 95 D4
Cuorgnè, *Italy* 28 C4
Cupar, *Canada* 105 C8
Cupar, *U.K.* 14 E5
Cupcini, *Moldova* 43 B12
Cupica, G. de, *Colombia* 124 B3
Ćuprija, *Serbia, Yug.* 40 C5
Curaçao, *Neth. Ant.* 121 D6
Curanilahue, *Chile* 126 D1
Curaray →, *Peru* 124 D4
Cure →, *France* 19 E10
Curepto, *Chile* 126 D1
Curiapo, *Venezuela* 124 B6
Curicó, *Chile* 126 C1
Curinga, *Italy* 31 D9
Curitiba, *Brazil* 127 B6
Curitibanos, *Brazil* 127 B5
Currabubula, *Australia* 95 E5
Currais Novos, *Brazil* 125 E11
Curralinho, *Brazil* 125 D9
Currant, *U.S.A.* 114 G6
Current →, *U.S.A.* 113 G9
Currie, *Australia* 94 F3
Currie, *U.S.A.* 114 F6
Curtea de Argeş, *Romania* 43 E9
Curtici, *Romania* 42 D6
Curtis, *U.S.A.* 112 E4
Curtis Group, *Australia* 94 F4
Curtis I., *Australia* 94 C5
Curuápanema →, *Brazil* 125 D7
Curuçá, *Brazil* 125 D9
Curuguaty, *Paraguay* 127 A4
Curup, *Indonesia* 62 E2
Cururupu, *Brazil* 125 D10
Curuzú Cuatiá, *Argentina* 126 B4
Curvelo, *Brazil* 125 G10
Cushing, *U.S.A.* 113 H6
Cushing, Mt., *Canada* 104 B3
Cusihuiriáchic, *Mexico* 118 B3
Cusna, Mte., *Italy* 28 D7
Cusset, *France* 19 F10
Custer, *U.S.A.* 112 D3
Cut Bank, *U.S.A.* 114 B7
Cutchogue, *U.S.A.* 111 E12
Cuthbert, *U.S.A.* 109 K3
Cutler, *U.S.A.* 116 J7
Cutro, *Italy* 31 C9
Cuttaburra →, *Australia* 95 D3
Cuttack, *India* 67 J14
Cuvier, C., *Australia* 93 D1
Cuvier I., *N.Z.* 91 G5
Cuxhaven, *Germany* 24 B4
Cuyahoga Falls, *U.S.A.* 110 E3
Cuyapo, *Phil.* 61 D4
Cuyo, *Phil.* 61 F4
Cuyo East Pass, *Phil.* 61 F4
Cuyo West Pass, *Phil.* 61 F4
Cuyuni →, *Guyana* 124 B7
Cuzco, *Bolivia* 124 H5
Cuzco, *Peru* 124 F4
Čvrsnica, *Bos.-H.* 42 G2
Cwmbran, *U.K.* 13 F4
Cyangugu, *Rwanda* 86 C2
Cybinka, *Poland* 45 F1
Cyclades = Kikládhes, *Greece* 38 E6
Cygnet, *Australia* 94 G4
Cynthiana, *U.S.A.* 108 F3
Cypress Hills, *Canada* 105 D7
Cypress Hills Prov. Park, *Canada* 105 D7
Cyprus ■, *Asia* 36 E12
Cyrenaica, *Libya* 79 C10
Czaplinek, *Poland* 44 E3
Czar, *Canada* 105 C6
Czarna →, *Łódzkie, Poland* 45 G6
Czarna →, *Świętokrzyskie, Poland* 45 H8
Czarna Białostocka, *Poland* 45 E10
Czarna Woda, *Poland* 44 E5
Czarne, *Poland* 44 E3
Czarnków, *Poland* 45 F3
Czech Rep. ■, *Europe* 26 B8
Czechowice-Dziedzice, *Poland* 45 J5
Czempiń, *Poland* 45 F3
Czeremcha, *Poland* 45 F10
Czerniejewo, *Poland* 45 F4
Czersk, *Poland* 44 E4
Czerwieńsk, *Poland* 45 F2
Czerwionka-Leszczyny, *Poland* 45 H5
Częstochowa, *Poland* 45 H6
Człopa, *Poland* 45 E3
Człuchów, *Poland* 44 E4
Czyżew-Osada, *Poland* 45 F9

D

Da →, *Vietnam* 58 G5
Da Hinggan Ling, *China* 60 B7
Da Lat, *Vietnam* 65 G7
Da Nang, *Vietnam* 64 D7
Da Qaidam, *China* 60 C4
Da Yunhe →, *China* 57 G11
Da'an, *China* 57 B13
Dab'a, Ras el, *Egypt* 80 H6
Daba Shan, *China* 58 B7
Dabai, *Nigeria* 83 C6
Dabakala, *Ivory C.* 82 D4
Dabas, *Hungary* 42 C4
Dabat, *Ethiopia* 81 E4
Dabbagh, Jabal, *Si. Arabia* 70 E2
Dabhoi, *India* 68 H5
Dąbie, *Poland* 45 F5
Dabie Shan, *China* 59 B10
Dabilda, *Cameroon* 83 C7
Dabnou, *Niger* 83 C6
Dabo = Pasirkuning, *Indonesia* 62 E2
Dabola, *Guinea* 82 C2
Dabou, *Ivory C.* 82 D4
Daboya, *Ghana* 83 D4
Dąbrowa Białostocka, *Poland* 44 E10
Dąbrowa Górnicza, *Poland* 45 H6
Dąbrowa Tarnowska, *Poland* 45 H7
Dabu, *China* 59 E11
Dabung, *Malaysia* 65 K4
Dabus →, *Ethiopia* 81 E4
Dacato →, *Ethiopia* 81 F5
Dacca = Dhaka, *Bangla.* 69 H14
Dacca = Dhaka □, *Bangla.* 69 G14
Dachau, *Germany* 25 G7
Dachstein, Hoher, *Austria* 26 D6
Dačice, *Czech Rep.* 26 B8
Dadanawa, *Guyana* 124 C7
Daday, *Turkey* 72 B5
Dade City, *U.S.A.* 109 L4
Dadhar, *Pakistan* 68 E2
Dadiya, *Nigeria* 83 D7
Dadra & Nagar Haveli □, *India* 66 J8
Dadri = Charkhi Dadri, *India* 68 E7
Dadu, *Pakistan* 68 F2
Dadu He →, *China* 58 C4
Daet, *Phil.* 61 D5
Dafang, *China* 58 D5
Dağ, *Turkey* 39 D12
Dagana, *Senegal* 82 B1
Dagash, *Sudan* 80 D3
Dagestan □, *Russia* 49 J8
Dagestanskiye Ogni, *Russia* 49 J9
Daggett, *U.S.A.* 117 L10
Daghestan Republic = Dagestan □, *Russia* 49 J8
Daghfeli, *Sudan* 80 D3
Dağlıq Qarabağ = Nagorno-Karabakh, *Azerbaijan* 70 B5
Dagö = Hiiumaa, *Estonia* 9 G20
Dagu, *China* 57 E9
Daguan, *China* 58 D4
Dagupan, *Phil.* 61 C4
Daguragu, *Australia* 92 C5
Dahab, *Egypt* 80 B3
Dahlak Kebir, *Eritrea* 81 D5
Dahlenburg, *Germany* 24 B6
Dahlonega, *U.S.A.* 109 H4
Dahme, *Germany* 24 D9
Dahod, *India* 68 H6
Dahomey = Benin ■, *Africa* 83 D5
Dahong Shan, *China* 59 B9
Dahra, *Senegal* 82 B1
Dahshûr, *Egypt* 80 J7
Dahūk, *Iraq* 70 B3
Dai Hao, *Vietnam* 64 C6
Dai-Sen, *Japan* 55 G6
Dai Shan, *China* 59 B14
Dai Xian, *China* 56 E7
Daicheng, *China* 56 E9
Daimiel, *Spain* 35 F7
Daingean, *Ireland* 15 C4
Dainkog, *China* 58 A1
Daintree, *Australia* 94 B4
Daiō-Misaki, *Japan* 55 G8
Dair, J. ed, *Sudan* 81 E3
Dairût, *Egypt* 80 B3
Daisetsu-Zan, *Japan* 54 C11
Dajarra, *Australia* 94 C2
Dajin Chuan →, *China* 58 B3
Dak Dam, *Cambodia* 64 F6
Dak Nhe, *Vietnam* 64 E6
Dak Pek, *Vietnam* 64 E6
Dak Song, *Vietnam* 65 F6
Dak Sui, *Vietnam* 64 E6
Dakar, *Senegal* 82 C1
Dakhla, *W. Sahara* 78 D2
Dakhla, El Wâhât el-, *Egypt* 80 B2
Dakingari, *Nigeria* 83 C5
Dakor, *India* 68 H5
Dakoro, *Niger* 83 C6
Dakota City, *U.S.A.* 112 D6
Đakovica, *Kosovo, Yug.* 40 D4
Đakovo, *Croatia* 42 E3
Dalaba, *Guinea* 82 C2
Dalachi, *China* 56 F3
Dalai Nur, *China* 56 C9
Dālakī, *Iran* 71 D6
Dalälven, *Sweden* 10 D10
Dalaman, *Turkey* 39 E10
Dalaman →, *Turkey* 39 E10
Dalandzadgad, *Mongolia* 56 C3
Dalap-Uliga-Darrit, *Marshall Is.* 96 G9
Dalarna, *Sweden* 10 D8
Dālbandīn, *Pakistan* 66 E4
Dalbeattie, *U.K.* 14 G5
Dalbeg, *Australia* 94 C4
Dalbosjön, *Sweden* 11 F6
Dalby, *Australia* 95 D5
Dalby, *Sweden* 11 J7
Dale City, *U.S.A.* 108 F7
Dale Hollow L., *U.S.A.* 109 G3
Dalga, *Egypt* 80 B3
Dalgān, *Iran* 71 E8
Dalhart, *U.S.A.* 113 G3
Dalhousie, *Canada* 103 C6
Dalhousie, *India* 68 C6
Dali, *Shaanxi, China* 56 G5
Dali, *Yunnan, China* 58 E3
Dalian, *China* 57 E11
Daliang Shan, *China* 58 D4
Daling He →, *China* 57 D11
Dāliyat el Karmel, *Israel* 75 C4
Dalj, *Croatia* 42 E3
Dalkeith, *U.K.* 14 F5
Dallas, *Oreg., U.S.A.* 114 D2
Dallas, *Tex., U.S.A.* 113 J6
Dallol, *Ethiopia* 81 E5
Dalmā, *U.A.E.* 71 E7
Dalmacija, *Croatia* 29 E13
Dalmas, L., *Canada* 103 B5
Dalmatia = Dalmacija, *Croatia* 29 E13
Dalmau, *India* 69 F9
Dalmellington, *U.K.* 14 F4
Dalnegorsk, *Russia* 51 E14
Dalnerechensk, *Russia* 51 E14
Daloa, *Ivory C.* 82 D3
Dalou Shan, *China* 58 C6
Dalry, *U.K.* 14 F4
Dalrymple, L., *Australia* 94 C4
Dals Långed, *Sweden* 11 F6
Dalsjöfors, *Sweden* 11 G7
Dalsland, *Sweden* 11 F6
Daltenganj, *India* 69 H11
Dalton, *Ga., U.S.A.* 109 H3
Dalton, *Mass., U.S.A.* 111 D11
Dalton, *Nebr., U.S.A.* 112 E3
Dalton Iceberg Tongue, *Antarctica* 5 C9
Dalton-in-Furness, *U.K.* 12 C4
Dalupiri I., *Phil.* 61 B4
Dalvík, *Iceland* 8 D4
Dalwallinu, *Australia* 93 F2
Daly →, *Australia* 92 B5
Daly City, *U.S.A.* 116 H4
Daly L., *Canada* 105 B7
Daly River, *Australia* 92 B5
Daly Waters, *Australia* 94 B1
Dalyan, *Turkey* 39 E10
Dam Doi, *Vietnam* 65 H5
Dam Ha, *Vietnam* 64 B6
Daman, *India* 66 J8
Dāmaneh, *Iran* 71 C6
Damanhûr, *Egypt* 80 H7
Damant L., *Canada* 105 A7
Damanzhuang, *China* 56 E9
Damar, *Indonesia* 63 F7
Damaraland, *Namibia* 88 C2
Damascus = Dimashq, *Syria* 75 B5
Damaturu, *Nigeria* 83 C7
Damāvand, *Iran* 71 C7
Damāvand, Qolleh-ye, *Iran* 71 C7
Damba, *Angola* 84 F3
Dâmboviţa □, *Romania* 43 F10
Dâmboviţa →, *Romania* 43 F11
Dâmbovnic →, *Romania* 43 F10
Dame Marie, *Haiti* 121 C5
Dāmghān, *Iran* 71 B7
Dămienesti, *Romania* 43 D11
Damietta = Dumyât, *Egypt* 80 H7
Daming, *China* 56 F8
Damīr Qābū, *Syria* 70 B4
Dammam = Ad Dammām, *Si. Arabia* 71 E6
Dammarie-les-Lys, *France* 19 D9
Dammartin-en-Goële, *France* 19 C9
Damme, *Germany* 24 C4
Damodar →, *India* 69 H12
Damoh, *India* 69 H8
Dampier, *Australia* 92 D2
Dampier, Selat, *Indonesia* 63 E8
Dampier Arch., *Australia* 92 D2
Damrei, Chuor Phnum, *Cambodia* 65 G4
Damvillers, *France* 19 C12
Dan-Gulbi, *Nigeria* 83 C6
Dan Xian, *China* 64 C7
Dana, *Indonesia* 63 F6
Dana, L., *Canada* 102 B4
Dana, Mt., *U.S.A.* 116 H7
Danakil Depression, *Ethiopia* 81 E5
Danakil Desert, *Ethiopia* 81 E5
Danané, *Ivory C.* 82 D3
Danao, *Phil.* 61 F6
Danau Poso, *Indonesia* 63 E6
Danba, *China* 58 B3
Danbury, *U.S.A.* 111 E11
Danby L., *U.S.A.* 115 J6
Dand, *Afghan.* 68 D1
Dandeldhura, *Nepal* 69 E9
Dandeli, *India* 66 M9
Dandenong, *Australia* 95 F4
Dandīl, *Egypt* 80 J7
Dandong, *China* 57 D13
Danfeng, *China* 56 H6
Dangan Liedao, *China* 59 F10
Dangé-St-Roman, *France* 20 B4
Dângeni, *Romania* 43 C11
Danger Is. = Pukapuka, *Cook Is.* 97 J11
Danger Pt., *S. Africa* 88 E2
Dangla, *Ethiopia* 81 E4
Dangla Shan = Tanggula Shan, *China* 60 C4
Dangora, *Nigeria* 83 C6
Dangouadougou, *Burkina Faso* 82 D4
Dangrek, Phnom, *Thailand* 64 E5
Dangriga, *Belize* 119 D7
Dangshan, *China* 56 G9
Dangtu, *China* 59 B12
Dangyang, *China* 59 B8
Dani, *Burkina Faso* 83 C4
Daniel, *U.S.A.* 114 E8
Daniel's Harbour, *Canada* 103 B8
Danielskuil, *S. Africa* 88 D3
Danielson, *U.S.A.* 111 E13
Danilov, *Russia* 46 C11
Danilovgrad, *Montenegro, Yug.* 40 D3
Danilovka, *Russia* 48 E7
Daning, *China* 56 F6
Danissa, *Kenya* 86 B5
Danja, *Nigeria* 83 C6
Danjiangkou, *China* 59 A8
Danjiangkou Shuiku, *China* 59 A8
Ḑank, *Oman* 71 F8
Dankalwa, *Nigeria* 83 C7
Dankama, *Nigeria* 83 C6
Dankhar Gompa, *India* 66 C11
Dankov, *Russia* 46 F10
Danleng, *China* 58 B4
Danlí, *Honduras* 120 D2
Dannemora, *U.S.A.* 111 B11
Dannenberg, *Germany* 24 B7
Dannevirke, *N.Z.* 91 J6
Dannhauser, *S. Africa* 89 D5
Dansville, *U.S.A.* 110 D7
Danta, *India* 68 G5
Dantan, *India* 69 J12
Dante, *Somali Rep.* 74 E5
Danube = Dunărea →, *Europe* 43 E14
Danvers, *U.S.A.* 111 D14
Danville, *Ill., U.S.A.* 108 E2
Danville, *Ky., U.S.A.* 108 G3
Danville, *Pa., U.S.A.* 111 F8
Danville, *Va., U.S.A.* 109 G6
Danville, *Vt., U.S.A.* 111 B12
Danyang, *China* 59 B12
Danzhai, *China* 58 D6
Danzig = Gdańsk, *Poland* 44 D5
Dão →, *Portugal* 34 E2
Dao Xian, *China* 59 E8
Daocheng, *China* 58 C3
Daoukro, *Ivory C.* 82 D4
Dapaong, *Togo* 83 C5
Dapchi, *Nigeria* 83 C7
Dapitan, *Phil.* 61 G5
Daqing Shan, *China* 56 D6
Daqu Shan, *China* 59 B14
Dar Banda, *Africa* 76 F6
Dar el Beida = Casablanca, *Morocco* 78 B4
Dar es Salaam, *Tanzania* 86 D4
Dar Mazār, *Iran* 71 D8
Dar'ā, *Syria* 75 C5
Dar'ā □, *Syria* 75 C5
Dārāb, *Iran* 71 D7
Daraban, *Pakistan* 68 D4
Darabani, *Romania* 43 B11
Daraina, *Madag.* 89 A8
Daraj, *Libya* 79 B8
Dārān, *Iran* 71 C6
Daravica, *Kosovo, Yug.* 40 D4
Daraw, *Egypt* 80 C3
Dārayyā, *Syria* 75 B5
Darazo, *Nigeria* 83 C7
Darband, *Pakistan* 68 B5
Darband, Kūh-e, *Iran* 71 D8
Darbhanga, *India* 69 F11
D'Arcy, *Canada* 104 C4
Darda, *Croatia* 42 E3
Dardanelle, *Ark., U.S.A.* 113 H8
Dardanelle, *Calif., U.S.A.* 116 G7
Dardanelles = Çanakkale Boğazı, *Turkey* 41 F10
Dare →, *Ethiopia* 81 F5
Darende, *Turkey* 72 C7
Dārestān, *Iran* 71 D8
Darfo, *Italy* 28 C7
Dârfûr, *Sudan* 79 F10
Dargai, *Pakistan* 68 B4
Dargan Ata, *Uzbekistan* 50 E7
Dargaville, *N.Z.* 91 F4
Dargol, *Niger* 83 C5
Darhan Muminggan Lianheqi, *China* 56 D6
Dari, *Sudan* 81 F3
Darıca, *Turkey* 72 B3
Darién, G. del, *Colombia* 122 C3
Dariganga = Ovoot, *Mongolia* 56 B7
Darinskoye, *Kazakstan* 48 E10
Darjeeling = Darjiling, *India* 69 F13
Darjiling, *India* 69 F13
Darkan, *Australia* 93 F2
Darkhana, *Pakistan* 68 D5
Darkhazīneh, *Iran* 71 D6
Darkot Pass, *Pakistan* 69 A5
Darling →, *Australia* 95 E3
Darling Downs, *Australia* 95 D5
Darling Ra., *Australia* 93 F2
Darlington, *U.K.* 12 C6
Darlington, *U.S.A.* 109 H6
Darlington □, *U.K.* 12 C6
Darlington, L., *S. Africa* 88 E4
Darlington Point, *Australia* 95 E4
Darlot, L., *Australia* 93 E3
Darłowo, *Poland* 44 D3
Dărmăneşti, *Bacău, Romania* 43 D11
Dărmăneşti, *Suceava, Romania* 43 C11
Darmstadt, *Germany* 25 F4
Darnah, *Libya* 79 B10
Darnall, *S. Africa* 89 D5
Darney, *France* 19 D13
Darnley, C., *Antarctica* 5 C6
Darnley B., *Canada* 100 B7
Daroca, *Spain* 32 D3
Darou-Mousti, *Senegal* 82 B1
Darr →, *Australia* 94 C3
Darra Pezu, *Pakistan* 68 C4
Darrequeira, *Argentina* 126 D3
Darrington, *U.S.A.* 114 B3
Darsser Ort, *Germany* 24 A8
Dart →, *U.K.* 13 G4
Dart, C., *Antarctica* 5 D14
Dartford, *U.K.* 13 F8
Dartmoor, *U.K.* 13 G4
Dartmouth, *Canada* 103 D7
Dartmouth, *U.K.* 13 G4
Dartmouth, L., *Australia* 95 D4
Dartuch, C. = Artrutx, C. de, *Spain* 37 B10
Daruvar, *Croatia* 42 E2
Darvaza, *Turkmenistan* 50 E6
Darvel, Teluk = Lahad Datu, Teluk, *Malaysia* 63 D5
Darwen, *U.K.* 12 D5
Darwendale, *Zimbabwe* 89 B5
Darwha, *India* 66 J10
Darwin, *Australia* 92 B5
Darwin, *U.S.A.* 117 J9
Darya Khan, *Pakistan* 68 D4
Daryoi Amu = Amudarya →, *Uzbekistan* 50 E6
Dās, *U.A.E.* 71 E7
Dashen, Ras, *Ethiopia* 81 E4
Dashetai, *China* 56 D5
Dashhowuz, *Turkmenistan* 50 E6
Dashkesan = Daşkäsän, *Azerbaijan* 49 K7
Dashköpri, *Turkmenistan* 71 B9
Dasht, *Iran* 71 B8
Dasht →, *Pakistan* 66 G2
Daska, *Pakistan* 68 C6
Daşkäsän, *Azerbaijan* 49 K7
Dassa, *Benin* 83 D5
Dasuya, *India* 68 D6
Datça, *Turkey* 39 E9
Datia, *India* 69 G8
Datian, *China* 59 E11
Datong, *Anhui, China* 59 B11
Datong, *Shanxi, China* 56 D7
Dattakhel, *Pakistan* 68 C3
Datteln, *Germany* 24 D3
Datu, Tanjung, *Indonesia* 62 D3
Datu Piang, *Phil.* 61 H6
Daud Khel, *Pakistan* 68 C4
Daudnagar, *India* 69 G11
Daugava →, *Latvia* 9 H21
Daugavpils, *Latvia* 9 J22
Daulpur, *India* 68 F7
Daun, *Germany* 25 E2
Dauphin, *Canada* 105 C8
Dauphin, *U.S.A.* 110 F8
Dauphin L., *Canada* 105 C9
Dauphiné, *France* 21 C9
Daura, *Borno, Nigeria* 83 C7
Daura, *Katsina, Nigeria* 83 C6
Dausa, *India* 68 F7
Däväçi, *Azerbaijan* 49 K9
Davangere, *India* 66 M9
Davao, *Phil.* 61 H6
Davao G., *Phil.* 61 H6
Dāvar Panāh, *Iran* 71 E9
Davenport, *Calif., U.S.A.* 116 H4
Davenport, *Iowa, U.S.A.* 112 E9
Davenport, *Wash., U.S.A.* 114 C4
Davenport Ra., *Australia* 94 C1
Daventry, *U.K.* 13 E6
David, *Panama* 120 E3
David City, *U.S.A.* 112 E6
David Gorodok = Davyd Haradok, *Belarus* 47 F4
Davidson, *Canada* 105 C7
Davis, *U.S.A.* 116 G5
Davis Dam, *U.S.A.* 117 K12

Davis Inlet, Canada 103 A7
Davis Mts., U.S.A. 113 K2
Davis Sea, Antarctica 5 C7
Davis Str., N. Amer. 101 B14
Davo →, Ivory C. 82 D3
Davos, Switz. 25 J5
Davutlar, Turkey 39 D9
Davy L., Canada 105 B7
Davyd Haradok, Belarus ... 47 F4
Dawa →, Ethiopia 81 G5
Dawaki, Bauchi, Nigeria ... 83 D6
Dawaki, Kano, Nigeria 83 C6
Dawei, Burma 64 E2
Dawes Ra., Australia 94 C5
Dawlish, U.K. 13 G4
Dawros Hd., Ireland 15 B3
Dawson, Canada 100 B6
Dawson, U.S.A. 109 K3
Dawson, I., Chile 128 G2
Dawson B., Canada 105 C8
Dawson Creek, Canada 104 B4
Dawson Inlet, Canada 105 A10
Dawson Ra., Australia 94 C4
Dawu, Hubei, China 59 B9
Dawu, Sichuan, China 58 B3
Dax, France 20 E2
Daxian, China 58 B6
Daxin, China 58 F6
Daxindian, China 57 F11
Daxinggou, China 57 C15
Daxue Shan, Sichuan, China 58 B3
Daxue Shan, Yunnan, China 58 F2
Dayao, China 58 E3
Daye, China 59 B10
Dayet en Naharat, Mali ... 82 B4
Dayi, China 58 B4
Daylesford, Australia 95 F3
Dayong, China 59 C8
Dayr az Zawr, Syria 70 C4
Daysland, Canada 104 C6
Dayton, Nev., U.S.A. 116 F7
Dayton, Ohio, U.S.A. 108 F3
Dayton, Pa., U.S.A. 110 F5
Dayton, Tenn., U.S.A. 109 H3
Dayton, Wash., U.S.A. 114 C4
Dayton, Wyo., U.S.A. 114 D10
Daytona Beach, U.S.A. 109 L5
Dayu, China 59 E10
Dayville, U.S.A. 114 D4
Dazhu, China 58 B6
Dazkırı, Turkey 39 D11
Dazu, China 58 C5
De Aar, S. Africa 88 E3
De Funiak Springs, U.S.A. . 109 K2
De Grey →, Australia 92 D2
De Haan, Belgium 17 C3
De Kalb, U.S.A. 112 E10
De Land, U.S.A. 109 L5
De Leon, U.S.A. 113 J5
De Panne, Belgium 17 C2
De Pere, U.S.A. 108 C1
De Queen, U.S.A. 113 H7
De Quincy, U.S.A. 113 K8
De Ridder, U.S.A. 113 K8
De Smet, U.S.A. 112 C6
De Soto, U.S.A. 112 F9
De Tour Village, U.S.A. ... 108 C4
De Witt, U.S.A. 113 H9
Dead Sea, Asia 75 D4
Deadwood, U.S.A. 112 C3
Deadwood L., Canada 104 B3
Deal, U.K. 13 F9
Deal I., Australia 94 F4
Dealesville, S. Africa 88 D4
De'an, China 59 C10
Dean →, Canada 104 C3
Dean, Forest of, U.K. 13 F5
Dean Chan., Canada 104 C3
Deán Funes, Argentina ... 126 C3
Dease →, Canada 104 B3
Dease L., Canada 104 B2
Dease Lake, Canada 104 B2
Death Valley, U.S.A. 117 J10
Death Valley Junction,
  U.S.A. 117 J10
Death Valley National Park,
  U.S.A. 117 J10
Deauville, France 18 C7
Deba, Spain 32 B2
Deba Habe, Nigeria 83 C7
Debao, China 58 F6
Debar, Macedonia 40 E4
Debden, Canada 105 C7
Dębica, Poland 45 H8
Dęblin, Poland 45 G8
Dębno, Poland 45 F1
Débo, L., Mali 82 B4
Debolt, Canada 104 B5
Deborah East, L., Australia 93 F2
Deborah West, L., Australia 93 F2
Debrc, Serbia, Yug. 40 B3
Debre Birhan, Ethiopia ... 81 F4
Debre Markos, Ethiopia ... 81 E4
Debre May, Ethiopia 81 E4
Debre Sina, Ethiopia 81 E4
Debre Tabor, Ethiopia 81 E4
Debre Zevit, Ethiopia 81 E4
Debre Zeyit, Ethiopia 81 F4
Debrecen, Hungary 42 C6
Debrzno, Poland 44 E4
Dečani, Kosovo, Yug. 40 D4
Decatur, Ala., U.S.A. 109 H2
Decatur, Ga., U.S.A. 109 J3
Decatur, Ill., U.S.A. 112 F10
Decatur, Ind., U.S.A. 108 E3
Decatur, Tex., U.S.A. 113 J6
Decazeville, France 20 D6
Deccan, India 66 L11
Deception Bay, Australia .. 95 D5
Deception L., Canada 105 B8

Dechang, China 58 D4
Dechhu, India 68 F5
Děčín, Czech Rep. 26 A7
Decize, France 19 F10
Deckerville, U.S.A. 110 C2
Decollatura, Italy 31 C9
Decorah, U.S.A. 112 D9
Deda, Romania 43 D9
Dedéagach =
  Alexandroúpolis, Greece 41 F9
Deder, Ethiopia 81 F5
Dedham, U.S.A. 111 D13
Dédougou, Burkina Faso .. 82 C4
Dedovichi, Russia 46 D5
Dedza, Malawi 87 E3
Dee →, Aberds., U.K. 14 D6
Dee →, Dumf. & Gall.,
  U.K. 14 G4
Dee →, Wales, U.K. 12 D4
Deep B., Canada 104 A5
Deepwater, Australia 95 D5
Deer →, Canada 105 B10
Deer L., Canada 105 C10
Deer Lake, Nfld., Canada . 103 C8
Deer Lake, Ont., Canada .. 105 C10
Deer Lodge, U.S.A. 114 C7
Deer Park, U.S.A. 114 C5
Deer River, U.S.A. 112 B8
Deeragun, Australia 94 B4
Deerdepoort, S. Africa ... 88 C4
Deferiet, U.S.A. 111 B9
Defiance, U.S.A. 108 E3
Degana, India 68 F6
Dêgê, China 58 B2
Degebe →, Portugal 35 G3
Degeberga, Sweden 11 J8
Dégelis, Canada 103 C6
Degema, Nigeria 83 E6
Degerfors, Sweden 10 E8
Degerhamn, Sweden 11 H10
Deggendorf, Germany 25 G8
Degh →, Pakistan 68 D5
Değirmendere, Turkey ... 41 F13
Deh Bīd, Iran 71 D7
Deh-e Shīr, Iran 71 D7
Dehaj, Iran 71 D7
Dehak, Iran 71 E9
Dehdez, Iran 71 D6
Dehej, India 68 J5
Dehestān, Iran 71 D7
Dehgolān, Iran 70 C5
Dehi Titan, Afghan. 66 C3
Dehibat, Tunisia 79 B8
Dehlorān, Iran 70 C5
Dehnow-e Kühestān, Iran .. 71 E8
Dehra Dun, India 68 D8
Dehri, India 69 G11
Dehua, China 59 E12
Dehui, China 57 B13
Deim Zubeir, Sudan 81 F2
Deinze, Belgium 17 D3
Dej, Romania 43 C8
Deje, Sweden 10 E7
Dejiang, China 58 C7
Deka →, S. Africa 88 B4
Dekemhare, Eritrea 81 D4
Dekese,
  Dem. Rep. of the Congo . 84 E4
Del Mar, U.S.A. 117 N9
Del Norte, U.S.A. 115 H10
Del Rio, U.S.A. 113 L4
Delai, Sudan 80 D4
Delambre I., Australia ... 92 D2
Delami, Sudan 81 E3
Delano, U.S.A. 117 K7
Delano Peak, U.S.A. 115 G7
Delareyville, S. Africa ... 88 D4
Delaronde L., Canada 105 C7
Delavan, U.S.A. 112 D10
Delaware, U.S.A. 108 E4
Delaware □, U.S.A. 108 F8
Delaware →, U.S.A. 111 G9
Delaware B., U.S.A. 108 F8
Delay →, Canada 103 A5
Delbrück, Germany 24 D4
Delčevo, Macedonia 40 E6
Delegate, Australia 95 F4
Delémont, Switz. 25 H3
Delevan, U.S.A. 110 D6
Delft, Neths. 17 B4
Delfzijl, Neths. 17 A6
Delgado, C., Mozam. 87 E5
Delgerhet, Mongolia 56 B6
Delgo, Sudan 80 C3
Delhi, Canada 110 D4
Delhi, India 68 E7
Delhi, La., U.S.A. 113 J9
Delhi, N.Y., U.S.A. 111 D10
Deli Jovan, Serbia, Yug. .. 40 B6
Delia, Canada 104 C6
Delice, Turkey 72 C6
Delicias, Mexico 118 B3
Delījān, Iran 71 C6
Deline, Canada 100 B7
Delisle, Canada 105 C7
Delitzsch, Germany 24 D8
Dell City, U.S.A. 115 L11
Dell Rapids, U.S.A. 112 D6
Delle, France 19 E14
Delmar, U.S.A. 111 D11
Delmenhorst, Germany ... 24 B4
Delnice, Croatia 29 C11
Delong, Ostrova, Russia .. 51 B15
Deloraine, Australia 94 G4
Deloraine, Canada 105 D8
Delphi, Greece 38 C4
Delphi, U.S.A. 108 E2
Delphos, U.S.A. 108 E3
Delportshoop, S. Africa ... 88 D3
Delray Beach, U.S.A. 109 M5
Delsbo, Sweden 10 C10

Delta, Colo., U.S.A. 115 G9
Delta, Utah, U.S.A. 114 G7
Delta □, Nigeria 83 D6
Delta Junction, U.S.A. ... 100 B5
Deltona, U.S.A. 109 L5
Delungra, Australia 95 D5
Delvada, India 68 J4
Delvinákion, Greece 38 B2
Delvinë, Albania 40 G4
Demanda, Sierra de la, Spain 32 C2
Demavand = Damāvand,
  Iran 71 C7
Dembecha, Ethiopia 81 E4
Dembi, Ethiopia 81 F4
Dembia,
  Dem. Rep. of the Congo . 86 B2
Dembidolo, Ethiopia 81 F3
Demchok, India 69 C8
Demer →, Belgium 17 D4
Demetrias, Greece 38 B5
Demidov, Russia 46 E6
Deming, N. Mex., U.S.A. . 115 K10
Deming, Wash., U.S.A. ... 116 B4
Demini →, Brazil 124 D6
Demirci, Turkey 39 B10
Demirköprü Baraji, Turkey 39 C10
Demirköy, Turkey 41 E11
Demmin, Germany 24 B9
Demonte, Italy 28 D4
Demopolis, U.S.A. 109 J2
Dempo, Indonesia 62 E2
Demyansk, Russia 46 D7
Den Burg, Neths. 17 A4
Den Chai, Thailand 64 D3
Den Haag = 's-Gravenhage,
  Neths. 17 B4
Den Helder, Neths. 17 B4
Den Oever, Neths. 17 B5
Denain, France 19 B10
Denair, U.S.A. 116 H6
Denau, Uzbekistan 50 F7
Denbigh, Canada 110 A7
Denbigh, U.K. 12 D4
Denbighshire □, U.K. 12 D4
Dendang, Indonesia 62 E3
Dendermonde, Belgium .. 17 C4
Deneba, Ethiopia 81 F4
Dengchuan, China 58 E3
Denge, Nigeria 83 C6
Dengfeng, China 56 G7
Dengi, Nigeria 83 D6
Dengkou, China 56 D4
Dengzhou, China 59 A9
Denham, Australia 93 E1
Denham Ra., Australia ... 94 C4
Denham Sd., Australia ... 93 E1
Denholm, Canada 105 C7
Denia, Spain 33 G5
Denial B., Australia 95 E1
Deniliquin, Australia 95 F3
Denison, Iowa, U.S.A. ... 112 E7
Denison, Tex., U.S.A. ... 113 J6
Denison Plains, Australia . 92 C4
Denizli, Turkey 39 D11
Denizli □, Turkey 39 D11
Denman Glacier, Antarctica 5 C7
Denmark, Australia 93 F2
Denmark ■, Europe 11 J3
Denmark Str., Atl. Oc. ... 4 C6
Dennison, U.S.A. 110 F3
Denny, U.K. 14 E5
Denpasar, Indonesia 62 F5
Denton, Mont., U.S.A. ... 114 C9
Denton, Tex., U.S.A. 113 J6
D'Entrecasteaux, Pt.,
  Australia 93 F2
Denu, Ghana 83 D5
Denver, Colo., U.S.A. 112 F2
Denver, Pa., U.S.A. 111 F8
Denver City, U.S.A. 113 J3
Deoband, India 68 E7
Deogarh, India 68 G5
Deoghar, India 69 G12
Deolali, India 66 K8
Deoli = Devli, India 68 G6
Déols, France 19 F8
Deora, India 68 F4
Deori, India 69 H8
Deoria, India 69 F10
Deosai Mts., Pakistan 69 B6
Deosri, India 69 F14
Depalpur, India 68 H6
Deping, China 57 F9
Deposit, U.S.A. 111 D9
Depuch I., Australia 92 D2
Deputatskiy, Russia 51 C14
Dêqên, China 58 C2
Deqing, China 59 F8
Dera Ghazi Khan, Pakistan 68 D4
Dera Ismail Khan, Pakistan 68 D4
Derabugti, Pakistan 68 E3
Derawar Fort, Pakistan ... 68 E4
Derbent, Russia 49 J9
Derbent, Turkey 39 C10
Derby, Australia 92 C3
Derby, U.K. 12 E6
Derby, Conn., U.S.A. 111 E11
Derby, Kans., U.S.A. 113 G6
Derby, N.Y., U.S.A. 110 D6
Derby City □, U.K. 12 E6
Derby Line, U.S.A. 111 B12
Derbyshire □, U.K. 12 D6
Derecske, Hungary 42 C6
Dereköy, Turkey 41 E11
Dereli, Turkey 73 B8
Derg →, Ireland 15 B4
Derg, L., Ireland 15 D3
Dergachi = Derhaci,
  Ukraine 47 G9
Dergaon, India 67 F19
Derhaci, Ukraine 47 G9

Derik, Turkey 73 D9
Derinkuyu, Turkey 72 C6
Dermantsi, Bulgaria 41 C8
Dermott, U.S.A. 113 J9
Dêrong, China 58 C2
Derry = Londonderry, U.K. 15 B4
Derry = Londonderry □,
  U.K. 15 B4
Derry, N.H., U.S.A. 111 D13
Derry, Pa., U.S.A. 110 F5
Derryveagh Mts., Ireland . 15 B3
Derudub, Sudan 80 D4
Derval, France 18 E5
Dervéni, Greece 38 C4
Derventa, Bos.-H. 42 F2
Derwent →, Cumb., U.K. . 12 C4
Derwent →, Derby, U.K. . 12 E6
Derwent →, N. Yorks.,
  U.K. 12 D7
Derwent Water, U.K. 12 C4
Des Moines, Iowa, U.S.A. . 112 E8
Des Moines, N. Mex.,
  U.S.A. 113 G3
Des Moines →, U.S.A. ... 112 E9
Desa, Romania 42 G8
Desaguadero →, Argentina 126 C2
Desaguadero →, Bolivia .. 124 G5
Descanso, Pta., Mexico ... 117 N9
Descartes, France 20 B4
Deschaillons, Canada 103 C5
Deschambault L., Canada . 105 C8
Deschutes →, U.S.A. 114 D3
Dese, Ethiopia 81 E4
Deseado →, Argentina ... 128 F3
Desenzano del Garda, Italy 28 C7
Desert Center, U.S.A. 117 M11
Desert Hot Springs, U.S.A. 117 M10
Deshnok, India 68 F5
Desna →, Ukraine 47 G6
Desnăţui →, Romania ... 43 G8
Desolación, I., Chile 128 G2
Despeñaperros, Paso, Spain 35 G7
Despotovac, Serbia, Yug. . 40 B5
Dessau, Germany 24 D8
Dessye = Dese, Ethiopia .. 81 E4
D'Estrees B., Australia ... 95 F2
Desuri, India 68 G5
Desvres, France 19 B8
Det Udom, Thailand 64 E5
Deta, Romania 42 E6
Dete, Zimbabwe 87 F2
Đetinja →, Serbia, Yug. .. 40 C4
Detmold, Germany 24 D4
Detour, Pt., U.S.A. 108 C2
Detroit, U.S.A. 110 D1
Detroit Lakes, U.S.A. 112 B7
Detva, Slovak Rep. 27 C12
Deurne, Neths. 17 C5
Deutsche Bucht, Germany . 24 A4
Deutschlandsberg, Austria . 26 E8
Deux-Sèvres □, France ... 18 F6
Deva, Romania 42 E7
Devakottai, India 66 Q11
Devaprayag, India 69 D8
Dévaványa, Hungary 42 C5
Deveci Dağları, Turkey ... 72 B7
Devecser, Hungary 42 C2
Develi, Turkey 72 C6
Deventer, Neths. 17 B6
Deveron →, U.K. 14 D6
Devesel, Romania 42 F7
Devgadh Bariya, India ... 68 H5
Devikot, India 68 F4
Devils Den, U.S.A. 116 K7
Devils Lake, U.S.A. 112 A5
Devils Paw, Canada 104 B2
Devils Tower Junction,
  U.S.A. 112 C2
Devin, Bulgaria 41 E8
Devine, U.S.A. 113 L5
Devizes, U.K. 13 F6
Devli, India 68 G6
Devnya, Bulgaria 41 C11
Devoll →, Albania 40 F4
Devon, Canada 104 C6
Devon □, U.K. 13 G4
Devon I., Canada 4 B3
Devonport, Australia 94 G4
Devonport, N.Z. 91 G5
Devrek, Turkey 72 B4
Devrekâni, Turkey 72 B5
Devrez →, Turkey 72 B6
Dewas, India 68 H7
Dewetsdorp, S. Africa 88 D4
Dexing, China 59 C11
Dexter, Maine, U.S.A. ... 109 C11
Dexter, Mo., U.S.A. 113 G10
Dexter, N. Mex., U.S.A. .. 113 J2
Dey-Dey, L., Australia ... 93 E5
Deyang, China 58 B5
Deyhūk, Iran 71 C8
Deyyer, Iran 71 E6
Dezadeash L., Canada ... 104 A1
Dezfūl, Iran 71 C6
Dezhneva, Mys, Russia ... 51 C19
Dezhou, China 56 F9
Dhadhar →, India 69 G11
Dhafni, Kríti, Greece 38 D7
Dháfni, Pelópónnisos, Greece 38 D4
Dhahaban, Si. Arabia 80 C4
Dhahiriya = Aẓ Ẓāhirīyah,
  West Bank 75 D3
Dhahran = Aẓ Ẓahrān,
  Si. Arabia 71 E6
Dhak, Pakistan 68 C5
Dhaka, Bangla. 69 H14
Dhaka □, Bangla. 69 G14
Dhali, Cyprus 36 D12
Dhamási, Greece 38 B4

Dhampur, India 69 E8
Dhamtari, India 67 J12
Dhanbad, India 69 H12
Dhangarhi, Nepal 67 E12
Dhankuta, Nepal 69 F12
Dhar, India 68 H6
Dharampur, India 68 H6
Dharamsala = Dharmsala,
  India 68 C7
Dhariwal, India 68 D6
Dharla →, Bangla. 69 G13
Dharmapuri, India 66 N11
Dharmavaram, India 66 M10
Dharmjaygarh, India 69 H10
Dharmsala, India 68 C7
Dharni, India 68 J7
Dhasan →, India 69 G8
Dhaulagiri, Nepal 69 E10
Dhebar, L., India 68 G6
Dheftera, Cyprus 36 D12
Dhenkanal, India 67 J14
Dhenoúsa, Greece 39 D7
Dherinia, Cyprus 36 D12
Dheskáti, Greece 40 G5
Dhespotikó, Greece 38 E6
Dhestina, Greece 38 C4
Dhiarrizos →, Cyprus ... 36 E11
Dhíbān, Jordan 75 D4
Dhidhimótikhon, Greece .. 41 E10
Dhíkti Óros, Greece 36 D7
Dhilianáta, Greece 38 C2
Dhílos, Greece 39 D7
Dhilwan, India 68 D6
Dhimarkhera, India 69 H9
Dhimitsána, Greece 38 D4
Dhírfis = Dhírfis Óros,
  Greece 38 C5
Dhírfis Óros, Greece 38 C5
Dhodhekánisos, Greece .. 39 E8
Dhodhekánisos □, Greece .. 39 E8
Dhokós, Greece 38 D5
Dholiana, Greece 38 B2
Dholka, India 68 H5
Dhomokós, Greece 38 B4
Dhoraji, India 68 J4
Dhoxáton, Greece 41 E8
Dhragonísi, Greece 39 D7
DhrÁhstis, Ákra, Greece .. 36 A3
Dhrápanon, Ákra, Greece . 36 D6
Dhripís, Greece 38 D6
Dhrol, India 68 H4
Dhuburi, India 67 F16
Dhule, India 66 J9
Di-ib, W. →, Sudan 80 C4
Di Linh, Vietnam 65 G7
Di Linh, Cao Nguyen,
  Vietnam 65 G7
Día, Greece 36 D7
Diabakania, Guinea 82 C2
Diablo, Mt., U.S.A. 116 H5
Diablo Range, U.S.A. 116 J5
Diafarabé, Mali 82 C4
Diala, Mali 82 C3
Dialakoro, Mali 82 C3
Dialakoto, Senegal 82 C2
Diallassagou, Mali 82 C4
Diamante, Argentina 126 C3
Diamante, Italy 31 C8
Diamante →, Argentina .. 126 C2
Diamantina, Brazil 125 G10
Diamantina →, Australia . 95 D2
Diamantino, Brazil 125 F7
Diamond Bar, U.S.A. 117 L9
Diamond Harbour, India . 69 H13
Diamond Is., Australia ... 94 B5
Diamond Mts., U.S.A. ... 114 G6
Diamond Springs, U.S.A. . 116 G6
Dian Chi, China 58 E4
Dianalund, Denmark 11 J5
Dianbai, China 59 G8
Diancheng, China 59 G8
Dianjiang, China 58 B6
Diano Marina, Italy 28 E5
Dianra, Ivory C. 82 D3
Diapaga, Burkina Faso ... 83 C5
Diapangou, Burkina Faso . 83 C5
Diariguila, Guinea 82 C2
Dibâ, Oman 71 E8
Dibai, India 68 E8
Dibaya-Lubue,
  Dem. Rep. of the Congo . 84 E3
Dibete, Botswana 88 C4
Dibrugarh, India 67 F19
Dickens, U.S.A. 113 J4
Dickinson, U.S.A. 112 B3
Dickson = Dikson, Russia . 50 B9
Dickson, U.S.A. 109 G2
Dickson City, U.S.A. 111 E9
Dicle Nehri →, Turkey ... 73 D9
Dicomano, Italy 29 E8
Didesa, W. →, Ethiopia .. 81 E4
Didi, Sudan 81 F3
Didiéni, Mali 82 C3
Didsbury, Canada 104 C6
Didwana, India 68 F6
Die, France 21 D9
Diébougou, Burkina Faso . 82 C4
Diecke, Guinea 82 D3
Diefenbaker, L., Canada .. 105 C7
Diego de Almagro, Chile . 126 B1
Diego Garcia, Ind. Oc. ... 3 E13
Diekirch, Lux. 17 E6
Diéma, Mali 82 C3
Diembéring, Senegal 82 C1
Dien Ban, Vietnam 64 E7
Dien Bien, Vietnam 58 G4
Dien Khanh, Vietnam 65 F7
Diepholz, Germany 24 C4
Dieppe, France 18 C8
Dierks, U.S.A. 113 H8
Diest, Belgium 17 D5

Dietikon

Dietikon, Switz. 25 H4
Dieulefit, France 21 D9
Dieuze, France 19 D13
Dif, Somali Rep. 74 G3
Differdange, Lux. 17 E5
Dig, India 68 F7
Digba,
  Dem. Rep. of the Congo . 86 B2
Digby, Canada 103 D6
Diggi, India 68 F6
Dighinala, Bangla. 67 H18
Dighton, U.S.A. 112 F4
Digna, Mali 82 C3
Digne-les-Bains, France ... 21 D10
Digoin, France 19 F11
Digor, Turkey 73 B10
Digos, Phil. 61 H6
Digranes, Iceland 8 C6
Digul →, Indonesia 63 F9
Dihang →, India 67 F19
Dijlah, Nahr →, Asia 70 D5
Dijon, France 19 E12
Dikhil, Djibouti 81 E5
Dikili, Turkey 39 B8
Dikirnis, Egypt 80 H7
Dikkil = Dikhil, Djibouti 81 E5
Diksmuide, Belgium 17 C2
Dikson, Russia 50 B9
Dikwa, Nigeria 83 C7
Dila, Ethiopia 81 F4
Dili, Indonesia 63 F7
Dilijan, Armenia 49 K7
Dilizhan = Dilijan, Armenia ... 49 K7
Dilj, Croatia 42 E3
Dillenburg, Germany 24 E4
Dilley, U.S.A. 113 L5
Dilling, Sudan 81 E2
Dillingen, Bayern, Germany ... 25 G6
Dillingen, Saarland,
  Germany 25 F2
Dillingham, U.S.A. 100 C4
Dillon, Canada 105 B7
Dillon, Mont., U.S.A. 114 D7
Dillon, S.C., U.S.A. 109 H6
Dillon →, Canada 105 B7
Dillsburg, U.S.A. 110 F7
Dilly, Mali 82 C3
Dilolo,
  Dem. Rep. of the Congo . 84 G4
Dimas, Mexico 118 C3
Dimashq, Syria 75 B5
Dimashq □, Syria 75 B5
Dimbaza, S. Africa 89 E4
Dimbokro, Ivory C. 82 D4
Dimboola, Australia 95 F3
Dîmbovița = Dâmbovița →,
  Romania 43 F11
Dimbulah, Australia 94 B4
Dimitrovgrad, Bulgaria 41 D9
Dimitrovgrad, Russia 48 C9
Dimitrovgrad, Serbia, Yug. ... 40 C6
Dimitrovo = Pernik,
  Bulgaria 40 D7
Dimmitt, U.S.A. 113 H3
Dimo, Sudan 81 F2
Dimona, Israel 75 D4
Dimovo, Bulgaria 40 C6
Dinagat, Phil. 61 F6
Dinajpur, Bangla. 67 G16
Dinan, France 18 D4
Dīnān Āb, Iran 71 C8
Dinant, Belgium 17 D4
Dinapur, India 69 G11
Dinar, Turkey 39 C12
Dīnār, Kūh-e, Iran 71 D6
Dinara Planina, Croatia 29 D13
Dinard, France 18 D4
Dinaric Alps = Dinara
  Planina, Croatia 29 D13
Dindanko, Mali 82 C3
Dinder, Nahr ed →, Sudan ... 81 E3
Dindigul, India 66 P11
Dindori, India 69 H9
Ding Xian = Dingzhou,
  China 56 E8
Dinga, Pakistan 68 G2
Dingalan, Phil. 61 D4
Dingbian, China 56 F4
Dingelstädt, Germany 24 D6
Dingle, Ireland 15 D1
Dingle, Sweden 11 F5
Dingle B., Ireland 15 D1
Dingmans Ferry, U.S.A. ... 111 E10
Dingnan, China 59 E10
Dingo, Australia 94 C4
Dingolfing, Germany 25 G8
Dingtao, China 56 G8
Dinguira, Mali 82 C2
Dinguiraye, Guinea 82 C2
Dingwall, U.K. 14 D4
Dingxi, China 56 G3
Dingxiang, China 56 E7
Dingyuan, China 59 A11
Dingzhou, China 56 E8
Dinh, Mui, Vietnam 65 G7
Dinh Lap, Vietnam 58 G6
Dinokwe, Botswana 88 C4
Dinorwic, Canada 105 D10
Dinosaur National
  Monument, U.S.A. 114 F9
Dinosaur Prov. Park, Canada 104 C6
Dinuba, U.S.A. 116 J7
Diö, Sweden 11 H8
Dioïla, Mali 82 C3
Dioka, Mali 82 C2
Diongoï, Mali 82 C2
Diósgyör, Hungary 42 B5
Diosig, Romania 42 C7
Diougani, Mali 82 C4
Diouloulou, Senegal 82 C1

Dioura, Mali 82 C3
Diourbel, Senegal 82 C1
Dipalpur, Pakistan 68 D5
Diplo, Pakistan 68 G3
Dipolog, Phil. 61 G5
Dir, Pakistan 66 B7
Diré, Mali 82 B4
Dire Dawa, Ethiopia 81 F5
Diriamba, Nic. 120 D2
Dirk Hartog I., Australia ... 93 E1
Dirranbandi, Australia 95 D4
Disa, India 68 G5
Disa, Sudan 81 E3
Disappointment, C., U.S.A. ... 114 C2
Disappointment, L.,
  Australia 92 D3
Disaster B., Australia 95 F4
Discovery B., Australia 95 F3
Disentis Muster, Switz. 25 J4
Dishna, Egypt 80 B3
Disina, Nigeria 83 C6
Disko = Qeqertarsuaq,
  Greenland 4 C5
Disko Bugt, Greenland 4 C5
Disna = Dzisna →, Belarus ... 46 E5
Diss, U.K. 13 E9
Disteghil Sar, Pakistan 69 A6
Distrito Federal □, Brazil ... 125 G9
Distrito Federal □, Mexico ... 119 D5
Disûq, Egypt 80 H7
Diu, India 68 J4
Dīvāndarreh, Iran 70 C5
Dives →, France 18 C6
Dives-sur-Mer, France 18 C6
Divichi = Däväçi, Azerbaijan 49 K9
Divide, U.S.A. 114 D7
Dividing Ra., Australia 93 E2
Divinópolis, Brazil 125 H10
Divjake, Albania 40 F3
Divnoye, Russia 49 H6
Divo, Ivory C. 82 D3
Divriği, Turkey 73 C8
Dīwāl Kol, Afghan. 68 B2
Dixie Mt., U.S.A. 116 F6
Dixon, Calif., U.S.A. 116 G5
Dixon, Ill., U.S.A. 112 E10
Dixon Entrance, U.S.A. 100 C6
Dixville, Canada 111 A13
Diyadin, Turkey 73 C10
Diyālā →, Iraq 70 C5
Diyarbakır, Turkey 70 B4
Diyodar, India 68 G4
Djakarta = Jakarta,
  Indonesia 63 G12
Djamba, Angola 88 B1
Djambala, Congo 84 E2
Djanet, Algeria 78 D7
Djawa = Jawa, Indonesia ... 63 G14
Djelfa, Algeria 78 B6
Djema, C.A.R. 86 A2
Djenné, Mali 82 C4
Djerba, I. de, Tunisia 79 B8
Djerid, Chott, Tunisia 78 B7
Djibo, Burkina Faso 83 C4
Djibouti, Djibouti 81 E5
Djibouti ■, Africa 81 E5
Djolu,
  Dem. Rep. of the Congo . 84 D4
Djougou, Benin 83 D5
Djoum, Cameroon 84 D2
Djourab, Erg du, Chad 79 E9
Djugu,
  Dem. Rep. of the Congo . 86 B3
Djúpivogur, Iceland 8 D6
Djurås, Sweden 10 D9
Djursland, Denmark 11 H4
Dmitriya Lapteva, Proliv,
  Russia 51 B15
Dmitriyev Lgovskiy, Russia ... 47 F8
Dmitrov, Russia 46 D9
Dmitrovsk-Orlovskiy, Russia 47 F8
Dnepr →= Dnipro →,
  Ukraine 47 J7
Dneprodzerzhinsk =
  Dniprodzerzhynsk,
  Ukraine 47 H8
Dneprodzerzhinskoye
  Vdkhr. =
  Dniprodzerzhynske
  Vdskh., Ukraine 47 H8
Dnepropetrovsk =
  Dnipropetrovsk, Ukraine ... 47 H8
Dneprorudnoye =
  Dniprorudne, Ukraine 47 J8
Dnestr →= Dnister →,
  Europe 47 J6
Dnestrovski = Belgorod,
  Russia 47 G9
Dnieper = Dnipro →,
  Ukraine 47 J7
Dniester = Dnister →,
  Europe 47 J6
Dnipro →, Ukraine 47 J7
Dniprodzerzhynsk, Ukraine ... 47 H8
Dniprodzerzhynske Vdskh.,
  Ukraine 47 H8
Dnipropetrovsk, Ukraine ... 47 H8
Dniprorudne, Ukraine 47 J8
Dnister →, Europe 47 J6
Dnistrovskyy Lyman,
  Ukraine 47 J6
Dno, Russia 46 D5
Dnyapro = Dnipro →,
  Ukraine 47 J7
Doaktown, Canada 103 C6
Doan Hung, Vietnam 58 G5
Doany, Madag. 89 A8
Doba, Chad 79 G9
Dobandi, Pakistan 68 D2
Dobbiaco, Italy 29 B9
Dobbyn, Australia 94 B3

Dobczyce, Poland 45 J7
Dobele, Latvia 9 H20
Dobele □, Latvia 44 B10
Döbeln, Germany 24 D9
Doberai, Jazirah, Indonesia ... 63 E8
Dobiegniew, Poland 45 F2
Doblas, Argentina 126 D3
Dobo, Indonesia 63 F8
Doboj, Bos.-H. 42 F3
Dobra, Wielkopolskie,
  Poland 45 G5
Dobra,
  Zachodnio-Pomorskie,
  Poland 44 E2
Dobra, Dîmbovita, Romania ... 43 F10
Dobra, Hunedoara, Romania ... 42 E7
Dobre Miasto, Poland 44 E7
Dobrești, Romania 42 D7
Dobrich, Bulgaria 41 C11
Dobrinishta, Bulgaria 40 E7
Dobříš, Czech Rep. 26 B7
Dobrodzień, Poland 45 H5
Dobropole, Ukraine 47 H9
Dobrush, Belarus 47 F6
Dobrzany, Poland 44 E2
Dobrzyń nad Wisłą, Poland ... 45 F6
Doc, Mui, Vietnam 64 D6
Docker River, Australia 93 D4
Docksta, Sweden 10 A12
Doctor Arroyo, Mexico ... 118 C4
Doda, India 69 C6
Doda, L., Canada 102 C4
Dodecanese =
  Dhodhekánisos, Greece .. 39 E8
Dodge City, U.S.A. 113 G5
Dodge L., Canada 105 B7
Dodgeville, U.S.A. 112 D9
Dodo, Cameroon 83 D7
Dodo, Sudan 81 F2
Dodola, Ethiopia 81 F4
Dodoma, Tanzania 86 D4
Dodoma □, Tanzania 86 D4
Dodona, Greece 38 B2
Dodsland, Canada 105 C7
Dodson, U.S.A. 114 B9
Doduarga, Latvia 39 H11
Doesburg, Neths. 17 B6
Doetinchem, Neths. 17 C6
Dog Creek, Canada 104 C4
Dog L., Man., Canada 105 C9
Dog L., Ont., Canada 102 C2
Doğanşehir, Turkey 72 C7
Dogi, Afghan. 66 C3
Dogliani, Italy 28 D4
Dogondoutchi, Niger 83 C5
Dogran, Pakistan 68 D5
Doğubayazıt, Turkey 70 B5
Doguéraoua, Niger 83 C6
Doha = Ad Dawḥah, Qatar ... 71 E6
Dohazari, Bangla. 67 H18
Dohrighat, India 69 F10
Doi, Indonesia 63 D7
Doi Luang, Thailand 64 C3
Doi Saket, Thailand 64 C2
Dois Irmãos, Sa., Brazil ... 125 E10
Dojransko Jezero,
  Macedonia 40 E6
Dokkum, Neths. 17 A5
Dokri, Pakistan 68 F3
Dokuchayevsk, Ukraine 47 J9
Dol-de-Bretagne, France ... 18 D5
Dolac, Kosovo, Yug. 40 D4
Dolak, Pulau, Indonesia 63 F9
Dolbeau, Canada 103 C5
Dole, France 19 E12
Doleib, Wadi →, Sudan 81 E3
Dolenji Logatec, Slovenia ... 29 C11
Dolgellau, U.K. 12 E4
Dolgelley = Dolgellau, U.K. ... 12 E4
Dolhasca, Romania 43 C10
Dolianova, Italy 30 C2
Dolina = Dolyna, Ukraine ... 47 H7
Dolinskaya = Dolynska,
  Ukraine 47 H7
Dolj □, Romania 43 F8
Dollard, Neths. 17 A7
Dolna Banya, Bulgaria 40 D7
Dolni Chiflik, Bulgaria 41 D11
Dolni Dŭbnik, Bulgaria 41 C8
Dolnośląskie □, Poland 45 G3
Dolný Kubín, Slovak Rep. ... 27 B12
Dolo, Ethiopia 81 G5
Dolo, Italy 29 C9
Dolomites = Dolomiti, Italy ... 29 B8
Dolomiti, Italy 29 B8
Dolores, Argentina 126 D4
Dolores, Uruguay 126 C4
Dolores, U.S.A. 115 G9
Dolores →, U.S.A. 115 G9
Dolovo, Serbia, Yug. 42 F5
Dolphin, C., Falk. Is. 128 G5
Dolphin and Union Str.,
  Canada 100 B8
Dolsk, Poland 45 G4
Dolynska, Ukraine 47 H7
Dolzhanskaya, Russia 47 J9
Dom Pedrito, Brazil 127 C5
Domaila, Nigeria 83 D6
Domaniç, Turkey 39 B11
Domariaganj →, India 69 F10
Domasi, Malawi 87 F4
Domažlice, Czech Rep. 26 B5
Dombarovskiy, Russia 50 D6
Dombås, Norway 9 E13
Dombasle-sur-Meurthe,
  France 19 D13
Dombes, France 21 C9
Dombóvár, Hungary 42 D3
Dombrád, Hungary 42 B6

Domel I. = Letsôk-aw Kyun,
  Burma 65 G2
Domérat, France 19 F9
Domeyko, Chile 126 B1
Domeyko, Cordillera, Chile 126 A2
Domfront, France 18 D6
Dominador, Chile 126 A2
Dominica ■, W. Indies 121 C7
Dominica Passage, W. Indies 121 C7
Dominican Rep. ■,
  W. Indies 121 C5
Dömitz, Germany 24 B7
Domme, France 20 D5
Domnești, Romania 43 E9
Domodóssola, Italy 28 B5
Dompaire, France 19 D13
Dompierre-sur-Besbre,
  France 19 F10
Dompim, Ghana 82 D4
Domrémy-la-Pucelle, France ... 19 D12
Domville, Mt., Australia 95 D5
Domvraína, Greece 38 C4
Domžale, Slovenia 29 B11
Don →, Russia 47 J10
Don →, Aberds., U.K. 14 D6
Don →, S. Yorks., U.K. 12 D7
Don, C., Australia 92 B5
Don Benito, Spain 35 G5
Dona Ana = Nhamaabué,
  Mozam. 87 F4
Doña Mencía, Spain 35 H6
Donaghadee, U.K. 15 B6
Donald, Australia 95 F3
Donaldsonville, U.S.A. 113 K9
Donalsonville, U.S.A. 109 K3
Donau = Dunărea →,
  Europe 43 E14
Donau →, Austria 17 D3
Donaueschingen, Germany ... 25 H4
Donauwörth, Germany 25 G6
Doncaster, U.K. 12 D6
Dondo, Mozam. 87 F3
Dondo, Teluk, Indonesia 63 D6
Dondra Head, Sri Lanka 66 S12
Dondușeni, Moldova 43 B12
Donegal, Ireland 15 B3
Donegal □, Ireland 15 B4
Donegal B., Ireland 15 B3
Donets →, Russia 49 G5
Donetsk, Ukraine 47 J9
Dong Ba Thin, Vietnam 65 F7
Dong Dang, Vietnam 58 G6
Dong Giam, Vietnam 64 C5
Dong Ha, Vietnam 64 D6
Dong Hene, Laos 64 D5
Dong Hoi, Vietnam 64 D6
Dong Jiang →, China 59 F10
Dong Khe, Vietnam 64 A6
Dong Ujimqin Qi, China 56 B9
Dong Van, Vietnam 64 A5
Dong Xoai, Vietnam 65 G6
Donga, Nigeria 83 D7
Donga →, Nigeria 83 D7
Dong'an, China 59 D8
Dongara, Australia 93 E1
Dongbei, China 57 D13
Dongchuan, China 58 D4
Donges, France 18 E4
Dongfang, China 64 C7
Dongfeng, China 57 C13
Donggala, Indonesia 63 E5
Donggan, China 58 F5
Donggou, China 57 E13
Dongguan, China 59 F9
Dongguang, China 56 F9
Donghai Dao, China 59 G8
Dongjingcheng, China 57 B15
Dongkou, China 59 D8
Donglan, China 58 E6
Dongliu, China 59 B11
Dongmen, China 58 F6
Dongning, China 57 B16
Dongnyi, China 58 C3
Dongola, Sudan 80 D3
Dongping, China 56 G9
Dongshan, China 59 F11
Dongsheng, China 56 E6
Dongtai, China 57 H11
Dongting Hu, China 59 C9
Dongtou, China 59 D13
Dongxiang, China 59 C11
Dongxing, China 58 G7
Dongyang, China 59 C13
Dongzhi, China 59 B11
Donington, C., Australia 95 E2
Doniphan, U.S.A. 113 G9
Donja Stubica, Croatia 29 C12
Donji Dušnik, Serbia, Yug. ... 40 C6
Donji Miholjac, Croatia 42 E3
Donji Milanovac,
  Serbia, Yug. 40 B6
Donji Vakuf, Bos.-H. 42 F2
Dønna, Norway 8 C15
Donna, U.S.A. 113 M5
Donnaconna, Canada 103 C5
Donnelly's Crossing, N.Z. ... 91 F4
Donnybrook, Australia 93 F2
Donnybrook, S. Africa 89 D4
Donora, U.S.A. 110 F5
Donostia = Donostia-San
  Sebastián, Spain 32 B3
Donostia-San Sebastián,
  Spain 32 B3
Donskoy, Russia 46 F10
Donsol, Phil. 61 E5
Donzère, France 21 D8
Donzy, France 19 E10
Doon →, U.K. 14 F4

Doran L., Canada 105 A7
Dorchester, U.K. 13 G5
Dorchester, C., Canada ... 101 B12
Dordabis, Namibia 88 C2
Dordogne □, France 20 C4
Dordogne →, France 20 C3
Dordrecht, Neths. 17 C4
Dordrecht, S. Africa 88 E4
Dore →, France 20 C7
Doré L., Canada 105 C7
Doré Lake, Canada 105 C7
Dorfen, Germany 25 G8
Dorgali, Italy 30 B2
Dori, Burkina Faso 83 C4
Doring →, S. Africa 88 E2
Doringbos, S. Africa 88 E2
Dorion, Canada 111 A10
Dormaa-Ahenkro, Ghana 82 D4
Dormans, France 19 C10
Dormo, Ras, Eritrea 81 E5
Dornbirn, Austria 26 D2
Dornești, Romania 43 C11
Dornie, U.K. 14 D3
Dornoch, U.K. 14 D4
Dornoch Firth, U.K. 14 D4
Dornogovĭ □, Mongolia 56 C6
Doro, Mali 83 B4
Dorog, Hungary 42 C3
Dorogobuzh, Russia 46 E7
Dorohoi, Romania 43 C11
Döröö Nuur, Mongolia 60 B4
Dorr, Iran 71 C6
Dorre I., Australia 93 E1
Dorrigo, Australia 95 E5
Dorris, U.S.A. 114 F3
Dorset, Canada 110 A6
Dorset, U.K. 110 E4
Dorset □, U.K. 13 G5
Dorsten, Germany 24 D2
Dortmund, Germany 24 D3
Dortmund-Ems-Kanal →,
  Germany 24 D3
Dörtyol, Turkey 72 D7
Dorum, Germany 24 B4
Doruma,
  Dem. Rep. of the Congo . 86 B2
Dorūneh, Iran 71 C8
Dos Bahías, C., Argentina ... 128 E3
Dos Hermanas, Spain 35 H5
Dos Palos, U.S.A. 116 J6
Döşemealtı, Turkey 39 D12
Dosso, Niger 83 C5
Dothan, U.S.A. 109 K3
Doty, U.S.A. 116 D3
Douai, France 19 B10
Douako, Guinea 82 D2
Douala, Cameroon 83 E6
Douarnenez, France 18 D2
Doubabougou, Mali 82 C3
Double Island Pt., Australia ... 95 D5
Double Mountain Fork →,
  U.S.A. 113 J4
Doubrava →, Czech Rep. 26 A8
Doubs □, France 19 E13
Doubs →, France 19 F12
Doubtful Sd., N.Z. 91 L1
Doubtless B., N.Z. 91 F4
Doudeville, France 18 C7
Doué-la-Fontaine, France .. 18 E6
Douentza, Mali 82 C4
Douglas, S. Africa 88 D3
Douglas, U.K. 12 C3
Douglas, Ariz., U.S.A. 115 L9
Douglas, Ga., U.S.A. 109 K4
Douglas, Wyo., U.S.A. 112 D2
Douglas Chan., Canada 104 C3
Douglas Pt., Canada 110 B3
Douglastown, Canada 103 C7
Douglasville, U.S.A. 109 J3
Doukáton, Ákra, Greece 38 C2
Doulevant-le-Château,
  France 19 D11
Doullens, France 19 B9
Doumen, China 59 F9
Douna, Mali 82 C3
Douna, Mali 83 C4
Dounreay, U.K. 14 C5
Dourada, Serra, Brazil 125 F9
Dourados, Brazil 127 A5
Dourados →, Brazil 127 A5
Dourados, Serra dos, Brazil 127 A5
Dourdan, France 19 D9
Douro →, Europe 34 D2
Douvaine, France 19 F13
Douvres-la-Délivrande,
  France 18 C6
Douze →, France 20 E3
Dove →, U.K. 12 E6
Dove Creek, U.S.A. 115 H9
Dover, Australia 94 G4
Dover, U.K. 13 F9
Dover, Del., U.S.A. 108 F8
Dover, N.H., U.S.A. 111 C14
Dover, N.J., U.S.A. 111 F10
Dover, Ohio, U.S.A. 110 F3
Dover, Pt., Australia 93 F4
Dover, Str. of, Europe 13 G9
Dover-Foxcroft, U.S.A. 109 C11
Dover Plains, U.S.A. 111 E11
Dovey = Dyfi →, U.K. 13 E3
Dovrefjell, Norway 9 E13
Dow Rūd, Iran 71 C6
Dowa, Malawi 87 E3
Dowagiac, U.S.A. 108 E2
Dowerin, Australia 93 F2
Dowgha'i, Iran 71 B8
Dowlatābād, Iran 71 D8
Down □, U.K. 15 B5
Downey, Calif., U.S.A. 117 M8
Downey, Idaho, U.S.A. 114 E7

Downham Market, *U.K.* ... 13 E8
Downieville, *U.S.A.* 116 F6
Downpatrick, *U.K.* 15 B6
Downpatrick Hd., *Ireland* .. 15 B2
Downsville, *U.S.A.* 111 D10
Downton, Mt., *Canada* ... 104 C4
Dowsārī, *Iran* 71 D8
Doyle, *U.S.A.* 116 E6
Doylestown, *U.S.A.* 111 F9
Dozois, Rés., *Canada* 102 C4
Dra Khel, *Pakistan* 68 F2
Drac →, *France* 21 C9
Dračevo, *Macedonia* 40 E5
Drachten, *Neths.* 17 A6
Drăgănești, *Moldova* 43 C13
Drăgănești-Olt, *Romania* .. 43 F9
Drăgănești-Vlașca, *Romania* 43 F10
Dragaš, *Kosovo, Yug.* 40 D4
Drăgășani, *Romania* 43 F9
Dragichyn, *Belarus* 47 F3
Dragocvet, *Serbia, Yug.* .. 40 C5
Dragovishtitsa, *Bulgaria* .. 40 D6
Draguignan, *France* 21 E10
Drain, *U.S.A.* 114 E2
Drake, *U.S.A.* 112 B4
Drake Passage, *S. Ocean* .. 5 B17
Drakensberg, *S. Africa* ... 89 D4
Dráma, *Greece* 41 E8
Dráma □, *Greece* 41 E8
Drammen, *Norway* 9 G14
Drangajökull, *Iceland* 8 C2
Dranov, Ostrov, *Romania* .. 43 F14
Dras, *India* 69 B6
Drau = Drava →, *Croatia* . 42 E3
Drava →, *Croatia* 42 E3
Dravograd, *Slovenia* 29 B12
Drawa →, *Poland* 45 F2
Drawno, *Poland* 45 E2
Drawsko Pomorskie, *Poland* 44 E2
Drayton Valley, *Canada* ... 104 C6
Dreieich, *Germany* 25 E4
Dren, *Kosovo, Yug.* 40 C4
Drenthe □, *Neths.* 17 B6
Drepanum, C., *Cyprus* 36 E11
Dresden, *Canada* 110 D2
Dresden, *Germany* 24 D9
Dreux, *France* 18 D8
Drezdenko, *Poland* 45 F2
Driffield, *U.K.* 12 C7
Driftwood, *U.S.A.* 110 E6
Driggs, *U.S.A.* 114 E8
Drin i Zi →, *Albania* 40 E4
Drina →, *Bos.-H.* 40 B3
Drincea →, *Romania* 42 F7
Drini →, *Albania* 40 D3
Drinjača →, *Bos.-H.* 42 F4
Drissa = Vyerkhnyadzvinsk,
    Belarus 46 E4
Drniš, *Croatia* 29 E13
Drøbak, *Norway* 9 G14
Drobin, *Poland* 45 F6
Drochia, *Moldova* 43 B12
Drogheda, *Ireland* 15 C5
Drogichin = Dragichyn,
    Belarus 47 F3
Drogobych = Drohobych,
    Ukraine 47 H2
Drohiczyn, *Poland* 45 F9
Drohobych, *Ukraine* 47 H2
Droichead Atha =
    Drogheda, *Ireland* 15 C5
Droichead Nua, *Ireland* ... 15 C5
Droitwich, *U.K.* 13 E5
Drôme □, *France* 21 D9
Drôme →, *France* 21 D8
Dromedary, C., *Australia* . 95 F5
Dromore, *U.K.* 15 B4
Dromore West, *Ireland* ... 15 B3
Dronero, *Italy* 28 D4
Dronfield, *U.K.* 12 D6
Dronne →, *France* 20 C3
Dronninglund, *Denmark* .. 11 G4
Dronten, *Neths.* 17 B5
Dropt →, *France* 20 D3
Drosendorf, *Austria* 26 C8
Droué, *France* 18 D8
Drumbo, *Canada* 110 C4
Drumheller, *Canada* 104 C6
Drummond, *U.S.A.* 114 C7
Drummond I., *U.S.A.* 108 C4
Drummond Pt., *Australia* . 95 E2
Drummond Ra., *Australia* . 94 C4
Drummondville, *Canada* .. 102 C5
Drumright, *U.S.A.* 113 H6
Druskininkai, *Lithuania* ... 9 J20
Drut →, *Belarus* 47 F6
Druya, *Belarus* 46 E4
Druzhba, *Bulgaria* 41 C12
Druzhina, *Russia* 51 C15
Drvar, *Bos.-H.* 29 D13
Drvenik, *Croatia* 29 E13
Drwęca →, *Poland* 45 E5
Dry Tortugas, *U.S.A.* 120 B3
Dryanovo, *Bulgaria* 41 D9
Dryden, *Canada* 105 D10
Dryden, *U.S.A.* 111 D8
Drygalski I., *Antarctica* ... 5 C7
Drysdale →, *Australia* 92 B4
Drysdale I., *Australia* 94 A2
Drzewica, *Poland* 45 G7
Drzewiczka →, *Poland* 45 G7
Dschang, *Cameroon* 83 D7
Du Bois, *U.S.A.* 110 E6
Du Gué →, *Canada* 102 A5
Du He, *China* 59 A8
Du Quoin, *U.S.A.* 112 G10
Du'an, *China* 58 F7
Duanesburg, *U.S.A.* 111 D10
Duaringa, *Australia* 94 C4
Dubā, *Si. Arabia* 70 E2
Dubai = Dubayy, *U.A.E.* .. 71 E7

Dubăsari, *Moldova* 43 C14
Dubăsari Vdkhr., *Moldova* . 43 C13
Dubawnt →, *Canada* 105 A8
Dubawnt, L., *Canada* 105 A8
Dubayy, *U.A.E.* 71 E7
Dubbo, *Australia* 95 E4
Dubele,
    Dem. Rep. of the Congo . 86 B2
Dübendorf, *Switz.* 25 H4
Dubica, *Croatia* 29 C13
Dublin, *Ireland* 15 C5
Dublin, *Ga., U.S.A.* 109 J4
Dublin, *Tex., U.S.A.* 113 J5
Dublin □, *Ireland* 15 C5
Dubna, *Russia* 46 D9
Dubnica nad Váhom,
    Slovak Rep. 27 C11
Dubno, *Ukraine* 47 G3
Dubois, *U.S.A.* 114 D7
Dubossary = Dubăsari,
    Moldova 43 C14
Dubossary Vdkhr. =
    Dubăsari Vdkhr., *Moldova* 43 C13
Dubovka, *Russia* 49 F7
Dubovskoye, *Russia* 49 G6
Dubrajpur, *India* 69 H12
Dubréka, *Guinea* 82 D2
Dubrovitsa = Dubrovytsya,
    Ukraine 47 G4
Dubrovnik, *Croatia* 40 D2
Dubrovytsya, *Ukraine* 47 G4
Dubuque, *U.S.A.* 112 D9
Dubysa →, *Lithuania* 44 C10
Duchang, *China* 59 C11
Duchesne, *U.S.A.* 114 F8
Duchess, *Australia* 94 C2
Ducie I., *Pac. Oc.* 97 K15
Duck →, *U.S.A.* 109 G2
Duck Cr. →, *Australia* 92 D2
Duck Lake, *Canada* 105 C7
Duck Mountain Prov. Park,
    Canada 105 C8
Duckwall, Mt., *U.S.A.* 116 H6
Duderstadt, *Germany* 24 D6
Dudhi, *India* 67 G13
Dudinka, *Russia* 51 C9
Dudley, *U.K.* 13 E5
Dudwa, *India* 69 E9
Duékoué, *Ivory C.* 82 D3
Dueñas, *Spain* 34 D6
Duero = Douro →, *Europe* 34 D2
Dufftown, *U.K.* 14 D5
Dufourspitz, *Switz.* 25 K3
Dugi Otok, *Croatia* 29 D11
Dugo Selo, *Croatia* 29 C13
Duifken Pt., *Australia* 94 A3
Duisburg, *Germany* 24 D2
Duiwelskloof, *S. Africa* 89 C5
Dujiangyan, *China* 58 B4
Duk Fadiat, *Sudan* 81 F3
Duk Faiwil, *Sudan* 81 F3
Dukati, *Albania* 40 F3
Dükdamīn, *Iran* 71 C8
Dukelský Průsmyk,
    Slovak Rep. 27 B14
Dukhān, *Qatar* 71 E6
Dukhovshchina, *Russia* ... 46 E7
Duki, *Pakistan* 66 D6
Dukla, *Poland* 45 J8
Duku, *Bauchi, Nigeria* 83 C7
Duku, *Sokoto, Nigeria* 83 C5
Dulag, *Phil.* 61 F6
Dulce, *U.S.A.* 115 H10
Dulce →, *Argentina* 126 C3
Dulce, G., *Costa Rica* 120 E3
Dulf, *Iraq* 70 C5
Dŭlgopol, *Bulgaria* 41 C11
Dulit, Banjaran, *Malaysia* . 62 D4
Duliu, *China* 56 E9
Dullewala, *Pakistan* 68 D4
Dullstroom, *S. Africa* 89 D5
Dülmen, *Germany* 24 D3
Dulovo, *Bulgaria* 41 C11
Dulq Maghār, *Syria* 70 B3
Duluth, *U.S.A.* 112 B8
Dum Dum, *India* 69 H13
Dum Duma, *India* 67 F19
Dūmā, *Syria* 75 B5
Dumaguete, *Phil.* 61 G5
Dumai, *Indonesia* 62 D2
Dumaran, *Phil.* 61 F3
Dumas, *Ark., U.S.A.* 113 J9
Dumas, *Tex., U.S.A.* 113 H4
Dumayr, *Syria* 75 B5
Dumbarton, *U.K.* 14 F4
Dumbier, *Slovak Rep.* 27 C12
Dumbleyung, *Australia* 93 F2
Dumboa, *Nigeria* 83 C7
Dumbrăveni, *Romania* 43 D9
Dumfries, *U.K.* 14 F5
Dumfries & Galloway □,
    U.K. 14 F5
Dumitrești, *Romania* 43 E11
Dumka, *India* 69 G12
Dumlupınar, *Turkey* 39 C12
Dümmer, *Germany* 24 C4
Dumoine →, *Canada* 102 C4
Dumoine, L., *Canada* 102 C4
Dumraon, *India* 69 G11
Dumyât, *Egypt* 80 H7
Dumyât, Masabb, *Egypt* .. 80 H7
Dún Dealgan = Dundalk,
    Ireland 15 B5
Dun Laoghaire, *Ireland* ... 15 C5
Dun-le-Palestel, *France* ... 19 F8
Dun-sur-Auron, *France* ... 19 F9
Dun-sur-Meuse, *France* ... 19 C12
Duna = Dunărea →,
    Europe 43 E14
Duna →, *Hungary* 42 E3
Duna-völgyi-főcsatorna,
    Hungary 42 D4

Dunaföldvár, *Hungary* 42 D3
Dunagiri, *India* 69 D8
Dunaj = Dunărea →,
    Europe 43 E14
Dunaj →, *Slovak Rep.* 27 D11
Dunajec →, *Poland* 45 H7
Dunajská Streda,
    Slovak Rep. 27 C10
Dunakeszi, *Hungary* 42 C4
Dunapataj, *Hungary* 42 D4
Dunărea →, *Europe* 43 E14
Dunaszekcső, *Hungary* 42 D3
Dunaújváros, *Hungary* 42 D3
Dunav = Dunărea →,
    Europe 43 E14
Dunavațu de Jos, *Romania* . 43 F14
Dunavtsi, *Bulgaria* 40 C6
Dunay, *Russia* 54 C6
Dunback, *N.Z.* 91 L3
Dunbar, *U.K.* 14 E6
Dunblane, *U.K.* 14 E5
Duncan, *Canada* 104 D4
Duncan, *Ariz., U.S.A.* 115 K9
Duncan, *Okla., U.S.A.* 113 H6
Duncan, L., *Canada* 102 B4
Duncan L., *Canada* 104 A6
Duncan Town, *Bahamas* .. 120 B4
Duncannon, *U.S.A.* 110 F7
Duncansby Head, *U.K.* 14 C5
Duncansville, *U.S.A.* 110 F6
Dundaga, *Latvia* 44 A9
Dundalk, *Canada* 110 B4
Dundalk, *Ireland* 15 B5
Dundalk, *U.S.A.* 108 F7
Dundalk Bay, *Ireland* 15 C5
Dundas, *Canada* 110 C5
Dundas, L., *Australia* 93 F3
Dundas I., *Canada* 104 C2
Dundas Str., *Australia* 92 B5
Dundee, *S. Africa* 89 D5
Dundee, *U.K.* 14 E6
Dundee, *U.S.A.* 110 D8
Dundee City □, *U.K.* 14 E6
Dundgovĭ □, *Mongolia* ... 56 B4
Dundrum, *U.K.* 15 B6
Dundrum B., *U.K.* 15 B6
Dunedin, *N.Z.* 91 L3
Dunedin, *U.S.A.* 109 L4
Dunedoo, *Australia* 95 E4
Dunfermline, *U.K.* 14 E5
Dungannon, *Canada* 110 C3
Dungannon, *U.K.* 15 B5
Dungarpur, *India* 68 H5
Dungarvan, *Ireland* 15 D4
Dungarvan Harbour, *Ireland* 15 D4
Dungeness, *U.K.* 13 G8
Dungo, L. do, *Angola* 88 B2
Dungog, *Australia* 95 E5
Dungu,
    Dem. Rep. of the Congo . 86 B2
Dungun, *Malaysia* 65 K4
Dungunâb, *Sudan* 80 C4
Dungunâb, Khalij, *Sudan* . 80 C4
Dunhua, *China* 57 C15
Dunhuang, *China* 60 B4
Dunk I., *Australia* 94 B4
Dunkassa, *Benin* 83 C5
Dunkeld, *Australia* 95 E4
Dunkeld, *U.K.* 14 E5
Dunkerque, *France* 19 A9
Dunkery Beacon, *U.K.* ... 13 F4
Dunkirk = Dunkerque,
    France 19 A9
Dunkirk, *U.S.A.* 110 D5
Dunkuj, *Sudan* 81 E3
Dunkwa, *Central, Ghana* . 82 D4
Dunkwa, *Central, Ghana* . 83 D4
Dúnleary = Dun Laoghaire,
    Ireland 15 C5
Dunleer, *Ireland* 15 C5
Dunmanus B., *Ireland* 15 E2
Dunmanway, *Ireland* 15 E2
Dunmara, *Australia* 94 B1
Dunmore, *U.S.A.* 111 E9
Dunmore Town, *Bahamas* . 120 A4
Dunn, *U.S.A.* 109 H6
Dunnet Hd., *U.K.* 14 C5
Dunning, *U.S.A.* 112 E4
Dunnville, *Canada* 110 D5
Dunolly, *Australia* 95 F3
Dunoon, *U.K.* 14 F4
Dunphy, *U.S.A.* 114 F5
Dunqul, *Egypt* 80 C3
Duns, *U.K.* 14 F6
Dunseith, *U.S.A.* 112 A4
Dunsmuir, *U.S.A.* 114 F2
Dunstable, *U.K.* 13 F7
Dunstan Mts., *N.Z.* 91 L2
Dunster, *Canada* 104 C5
Dunvegan L., *Canada* 105 A7
Duolun, *China* 56 C9
Duong Dong, *Vietnam* 65 G4
Dupree, *U.S.A.* 112 C4
Dupuyer, *U.S.A.* 114 B7
Duque de Caxias, *Brazil* .. 127 A7
Durack →, *Australia* 92 C4
Durack Ra., *Australia* 92 C4
Durağan, *Turkey* 72 B6
Durak, *Turkey* 39 B10
Đurakovac, *Kosovo, Yug.* . 40 D4
Durance →, *France* 21 E8
Durand, *U.S.A.* 112 C9
Durango, *Mexico* 118 C4
Durango □, *Mexico* 118 C4
Durankulak, *Bulgaria* 41 C12
Durant, *Miss., U.S.A.* 113 J10
Durant, *Okla., U.S.A.* 113 J6
Duratón →, *Spain* 34 D6
Durazno, *Uruguay* 126 C4

Durazzo = Durrësi, *Albania* 40 E3
Durban, *France* 20 F6
Durban, *S. Africa* 89 D5
Durbuy, *Belgium* 17 D5
Dúrcal, *Spain* 35 J7
Đurđevac, *Croatia* 42 D2
Düren, *Germany* 24 E2
Durg, *India* 67 J12
Durgapur, *India* 69 H12
Durham, *Canada* 102 D3
Durham, *U.K.* 12 C6
Durham, *N.C., U.S.A.* 109 H6
Durham, *N.H., U.S.A.* 111 C14
Durham □, *U.K.* 12 C6
Durlești, *Moldova* 43 C13
Durmā, *Si. Arabia* 70 E5
Durmitor, *Montenegro, Yug.* 40 C2
Durness, *U.K.* 14 C4
Durrësi, *Albania* 40 E3
Durrow, *Ireland* 15 D4
Dursey I., *Ireland* 15 E1
Dursunbey, *Turkey* 39 B10
Durtal, *France* 18 E6
Duru,
    Dem. Rep. of the Congo . 86 B2
Duru Gölü, *Turkey* 41 E12
Durusu, *Turkey* 41 E12
Durūz, Jabal ad, *Jordan* ... 75 C5
D'Urville, Tanjung,
    Indonesia 63 E9
D'Urville I., *N.Z.* 91 J4
Duryea, *U.S.A.* 111 E9
Dûsh, *Egypt* 80 C3
Dushak, *Turkmenistan* 50 F7
Dushan, *China* 58 E6
Dushanbe, *Tajikistan* 50 F7
Dusheti, *Georgia* 49 J7
Dushore, *U.S.A.* 111 E8
Dusky Sd., *N.Z.* 91 L1
Dussejour, C., *Australia* .. 92 B4
Düsseldorf, *Germany* 24 D2
Duszniki-Zdrój, *Poland* ... 45 H3
Dutch Harbor, *U.S.A.* 100 C3
Dutlwe, *Botswana* 88 C3
Dutsan Wai, *Nigeria* 83 C6
Dutton, *Canada* 110 D3
Dutton →, *Australia* 94 C3
Duved, *Sweden* 10 A6
Düvertepe, *Turkey* 39 B10
Duwayhin, Khawr, *U.A.E.* . 71 E6
Duyun, *China* 58 D6
Düzağac, *Turkey* 39 C12
Düzce, *Turkey* 72 B4
Duzdab = Zāhedān, *Iran* .. 71 D9
Dve Mogili, *Bulgaria* 41 C9
Dvina, Severnaya →, *Russia* 50 C5
Dvinsk = Daugavpils, *Latvia* 9 J22
Dvor, *Croatia* 29 C13
Dvůr Králové nad Labem,
    Czech Rep. 26 A8
Dwarka, *India* 68 H3
Dwellingup, *Australia* 93 F2
Dwight, *Canada* 110 A5
Dwight, *U.S.A.* 108 E1
Dyatkovo, *Russia* 46 F8
Dyatlovo = Dzyatlava,
    Belarus 46 F3
Dyce, *U.K.* 14 D6
Dyer, C., *Canada* 101 B13
Dyer Bay, *Canada* 110 A3
Dyer Plateau, *Antarctica* .. 5 D17
Dyersburg, *U.S.A.* 113 G10
Dyfi →, *U.K.* 13 E3
Dyje →, *Czech Rep.* 27 C9
Dymer, *Ukraine* 47 G6
Dynów, *Poland* 45 J9
Dysart, *Australia* 94 C4
Dzamin Üüd = Borhoyn Tal,
    Mongolia 56 C6
Dzerzhinsk, *Russia* 48 B6
Dzhalinda, *Russia* 51 D13
Dzhambul = Zhambyl,
    Kazakstan 50 E8
Dzhankoy, *Ukraine* 47 K8
Dzhanybek, *Kazakstan* 48 F8
Dzharylhach, Ostriv, *Ukraine* 47 J7
Dzhezkazgan =
    Zhezqazghan, *Kazakstan* . 50 E7
Dzhizak = Jizzakh,
    Uzbekistan 50 E7
Dzhugdzur, Khrebet, *Russia* 51 D14
Dzhvari = Jvari, *Georgia* .. 49 J6
Działdowo, *Poland* 45 E7
Działoszyce, *Poland* 45 H7
Działoszyn, *Poland* 45 G5
Dzibilchaltun, *Mexico* 119 C7
Dzierzgoń, *Poland* 44 E6
Dzierżoniów, *Poland* 45 H3
Dzilam de Bravo, *Mexico* . 119 C7
Dzisna, *Belarus* 46 E5
Dzisna →, *Belarus* 46 E5
Dziwnów, *Poland* 44 D1
Dzungaria = Junggar Pendi,
    China 60 B3
Dzuumod, *Mongolia* 60 B5
Dzyarzhynsk, *Belarus* 46 F4
Dzyatlava, *Belarus* 46 F3

E

Eabamet L., *Canada* 102 B2
Eads, *U.S.A.* 112 F3
Eagar, *U.S.A.* 115 J9
Eagle, *Alaska, U.S.A.* 100 B5
Eagle, *Colo., U.S.A.* 114 G10
Eagle →, *Canada* 103 B8
Eagle Butte, *U.S.A.* 112 C4

Eagle Grove, *U.S.A.* 112 D8
Eagle L., *Canada* 105 D10
Eagle L., *Calif., U.S.A.* ... 114 F3
Eagle L., *Maine, U.S.A.* .. 109 B11
Eagle Lake, *Canada* 110 A6
Eagle Lake, *Maine, U.S.A.* . 109 B11
Eagle Lake, *Tex., U.S.A.* .. 113 L6
Eagle Mountain, *U.S.A.* .. 117 M11
Eagle Nest, *U.S.A.* 115 H11
Eagle Pass, *U.S.A.* 113 L4
Eagle Pk., *U.S.A.* 116 G7
Eagle Pt., *Australia* 92 C3
Eagle River, *Mich., U.S.A.* 108 B1
Eagle River, *Wis., U.S.A.* . 112 C10
Eaglehawk, *Australia* 95 F3
Eagles Mere, *U.S.A.* 111 E8
Ealing □, *U.K.* 13 F7
Ear Falls, *Canada* 105 C10
Earle, *U.S.A.* 113 H9
Earlimart, *U.S.A.* 117 K7
Earn →, *U.K.* 14 E5
Earn, L., *U.K.* 14 E4
Earnslaw, Mt., *N.Z.* 91 L2
Earth, *U.S.A.* 113 H3
Easley, *U.S.A.* 109 H4
East Angus, *Canada* 103 C5
East Anglia, *U.K.* 12 E9
East Aurora, *U.S.A.* 110 D6
East Ayrshire □, *U.K.* 14 F4
East Bengal, *Bangla.* 67 H17
East Beskids = Východné
    Beskydy, *Europe* 27 B15
East Brady, *U.S.A.* 110 F5
East C., *N.Z.* 91 G7
East Chicago, *U.S.A.* 108 E2
East China Sea, *Asia* 60 C7
East Coulee, *Canada* 104 C6
East Dereham, *U.K.* 13 E8
East Dunbartonshire □,
    U.K. 14 F4
East Falkland, *Falk. Is.* ... 122 J5
East Grand Forks, *U.S.A.* . 112 B6
East Greenwich, *U.S.A.* .. 111 E13
East Grinstead, *U.K.* 13 F8
East Hartford, *U.S.A.* 111 E12
East Helena, *U.S.A.* 114 C8
East Indies, *Asia* 52 K15
East Kilbride, *U.K.* 14 F4
East Lansing, *U.S.A.* 108 D3
East Liverpool, *U.S.A.* ... 110 F4
East London, *S. Africa* ... 89 E4
East Lothian □, *U.K.* 14 F6
East Main = Eastmain,
    Canada 102 B4
East Northport, *U.S.A.* ... 111 F11
East Orange, *U.S.A.* 111 F10
East Pacific Ridge, *Pac. Oc.* 97 J17
East Palestine, *U.S.A.* 110 F4
East Pine, *Canada* 104 B4
East Point, *U.S.A.* 109 J3
East Providence, *U.S.A.* .. 111 E13
East Pt., *Canada* 103 C7
East Renfrewshire □, *U.K.* 14 F4
East Retford = Retford,
    U.K. 12 D7
East Riding of Yorkshire □,
    U.K. 12 D7
East Rochester, *U.S.A.* ... 110 C7
East St. Louis, *U.S.A.* 112 F9
East Schelde =
    Oosterschelde →, *Neths.* 17 C4
East Siberian Sea, *Russia* . 51 B17
East Stroudsburg, *U.S.A.* . 111 E9
East Sussex □, *U.K.* 13 G8
East Tawas, *U.S.A.* 108 C4
East Timor = Timor
    Timur □, *Indonesia* 63 F7
East Toorale, *Australia* ... 95 E4
East Walker →, *U.S.A.* ... 116 G7
East Windsor, *U.S.A.* 111 F10
Eastbourne, *N.Z.* 91 J5
Eastbourne, *U.K.* 13 G8
Eastend, *Canada* 105 D7
Easter I. = Pascua, I. de,
    Pac. Oc. 97 K17
Eastern →, *Ghana* 83 D4
Eastern →, *Kenya* 86 C4
Eastern →, *Uganda* 86 B3
Eastern Cape □, *S. Africa* . 88 E4
Eastern Cr. →, *Australia* .. 94 C3
Eastern Ghats, *India* 66 N11
Eastern Group = Lau
    Group, *Fiji* 91 C9
Eastern Group, *Australia* . 93 F3
Eastern Province □,
    S. Leone 82 D2
Eastern Transvaal =
    Mpumalanga □, *S. Africa* 89 B5
Easterville, *Canada* 105 C9
Easthampton, *U.S.A.* 111 D12
Eastlake, *U.S.A.* 110 E3
Eastland, *U.S.A.* 113 J5
Eastleigh, *U.K.* 13 G6
Eastmain, *Canada* 102 B4
Eastmain →, *Canada* 102 B4
Eastman, *Canada* 111 A12
Eastman, *U.S.A.* 109 J4
Easton, *Md., U.S.A.* 108 F7
Easton, *Pa., U.S.A.* 111 F9
Easton, *Wash., U.S.A.* ... 116 C5
Eastpointe, *U.S.A.* 110 D2
Eastport, *U.S.A.* 109 C12
Eastsound, *U.S.A.* 116 B4
Eaton, *U.S.A.* 112 E2
Eatonia, *Canada* 105 C7
Eatonton, *U.S.A.* 109 J4
Eatontown, *U.S.A.* 111 F10
Eatonville, *U.S.A.* 116 D4
Eau Claire, *U.S.A.* 112 C9
Eau Claire, L. à l', *Canada* 102 A5
Eauze, *France* 20 E4

Eban, *Nigeria* 83 D5
Ebbw Vale, *U.K.* 13 F4
Ebeltoft, *Denmark* 11 H4
Ebeltoft Vig, *Denmark* 11 H4
Ebensburg, *U.S.A.* 110 F6
Ebensee, *Austria* 26 D6
Eber Gölü, *Turkey* 72 C4
Eberbach, *Germany* 25 F4
Eberswalde-Finow, *Germany* .. 24 C9
Ebetsu, *Japan* 54 C10
Ebian, *China* 58 C4
Ebingen, *Germany* 25 G5
Éboli, *Italy* 31 B8
Ebolowa, *Cameroon* 83 E7
Ebonyi □, *Nigeria* 83 D6
Ebrach, *Germany* 25 F6
Ébrié, Lagune, *Ivory C.* .. 82 D4
Ebro →, *Spain* 32 E5
Ebro, Embalse del, *Spain* .. 34 C7
Ebstorf, *Germany* 24 B6
Eceabat, *Turkey* 41 F10
Ech Cheliff, *Algeria* ... 78 A6
Echigo-Sammyaku, *Japan* .. 55 F9
Échirolles, *France* 21 C9
Echizen-Misaki, *Japan* 55 G7
Echmiadzin = Yejmiadzin,
  Armenia 49 K7
Echo Bay, *N.W.T., Canada* .. 100 B8
Echo Bay, *Ont., Canada* .. 102 C3
Echoing →, *Canada* 102 B10
Echternach, *Lux.* 17 E6
Echuca, *Australia* 95 F3
Ecija, *Spain* 35 H5
Eckental, *Germany* 25 F7
Eckernförde, *Germany* ... 24 A5
Eclipse Is., *Australia* ... 92 B4
Eclipse Sd., *Canada* 101 A11
Écommoy, *France* 18 E7
Écouché, *France* 18 D6
Ecuador ■, *S. Amer.* 124 D3
Écueillé, *France* 18 E8
Ed, *Sweden* 11 F5
Ed Dabbura, *Sudan* 80 D3
Ed Da'ein, *Sudan* 81 E2
Ed Damazin, *Sudan* 79 F12
Ed Dâmer, *Sudan* 80 D3
Ed Debba, *Sudan* 80 D3
Ed-Déffa, *Egypt* 80 A2
Ed Deim, *Sudan* 81 E2
Ed Dueim, *Sudan* 81 E3
Edam, *Canada* 105 C7
Edam, *Neths.* 17 B5
Edane, *Sweden* 10 E6
Eday, *U.K.* 14 B6
Edd, *Eritrea* 81 E5
Eddrachillis B., *U.K.* ... 14 C3
Eddystone Pt., *Australia* .. 94 G4
Ede, *Neths.* 17 B5
Ede, *Nigeria* 83 D5
Edéa, *Cameroon* 83 E7
Edebäck, *Sweden* 10 D7
Edehon L., *Canada* 105 A9
Edelény, *Hungary* 42 B5
Eden, *Australia* 95 F4
Eden, *N.C., U.S.A.* 109 G6
Eden, *N.Y., U.S.A.* 110 D6
Eden, *Tex., U.S.A.* 113 K5
Eden →, *U.K.* 12 C4
Edenburg, *S. Africa* 88 D4
Edendale, *S. Africa* 89 D5
Edenderry, *Ireland* 15 C4
Edenhope, *Australia* 95 F3
Edenton, *U.S.A.* 109 G7
Edenville, *S. Africa* 89 D4
Eder →, *Germany* 24 D5
Eder-Stausee, *Germany* .. 24 D4
Edewecht, *Germany* 24 B3
Edgar, *U.S.A.* 112 E6
Edgartown, *U.S.A.* 111 E14
Edge Hill, *U.K.* 13 E6
Edgefield, *U.S.A.* 109 J5
Edgeley, *U.S.A.* 112 B5
Edgemont, *U.S.A.* 112 D3
Edgeøya, *Svalbard* 4 B9
Édhessa, *Greece* 40 F6
Ediévale, *N.Z.* 91 L2
Edina, *Liberia* 82 D2
Edina, *U.S.A.* 112 E8
Edinboro, *U.S.A.* 110 E4
Edinburg, *U.S.A.* 113 M5
Edinburgh, *U.K.* 14 F5
Edinburgh, City of □, *U.K.* .. 14 F5
Edineţ, *Moldova* 43 B12
Edirne, *Turkey* 41 E10
Edirne □, *Turkey* 41 E10
Edison, *U.S.A.* 116 B4
Edithburgh, *Australia* ... 95 F2
Edmeston, *U.S.A.* 111 D9
Edmond, *U.S.A.* 113 H6
Edmonds, *U.S.A.* 116 C4
Edmonton, *Australia* 94 B4
Edmonton, *Canada* 104 C6
Edmund L., *Canada* 102 B1
Edmundston, *Canada* 103 C6
Edna, *U.S.A.* 113 L6
Edo □, *Nigeria* 83 D6
Edolo, *Italy* 28 B7
Edremit, *Turkey* 39 B9
Edremit Körfezi, *Turkey* .. 39 B8
Edsbro, *Sweden* 10 E12
Edsbyn, *Sweden* 10 C9
Edson, *Canada* 104 C5
Eduardo Castex, *Argentina* .. 126 D3
Edward →, *Australia* 95 F3
Edward →, *Africa* 86 C2
Edward River, *Australia* .. 94 A3
Edward VII Land, *Antarctica* .. 5 E13
Edwards, *Calif., U.S.A.* .. 117 L9
Edwards, *N.Y., U.S.A.* .. 111 B9
Edwards Air Force Base,
  U.S.A. 117 L9

Edwards Plateau, *U.S.A.* .. 113 K4
Edwardsville, *U.S.A.* ... 111 E9
Edzo, *Canada* 104 A5
Eeklo, *Belgium* 17 C3
Eferding, *Austria* 26 C7
Effingham, *U.S.A.* 108 F1
Eforie, *Romania* 43 F13
Ega →, *Spain* 32 C3
Égadi, Ísole, *Italy* 30 E5
Egan Range, *U.S.A.* 114 G6
Eganville, *Canada* 102 C4
Eger = Cheb, *Czech Rep.* .. 26 A5
Eger, *Hungary* 42 C5
Eger →, *Hungary* 42 C5
Egersund, *Norway* 9 G12
Egg L., *Canada* 105 B7
Eggenburg, *Austria* 26 C8
Eggenfelden, *Germany* ... 25 G8
Éghezée, *Belgium* 17 D4
Égletons, *France* 20 C6
Egmont, *Canada* 104 D4
Egmont, C., *N.Z.* 91 H4
Egmont, Mt., *N.Z.* 91 H5
Egra, *India* 69 J12
Eğridir, *Turkey* 72 D4
Eğridir Gölü, *Turkey* ... 70 B1
Egtved, *Denmark* 11 J3
Egume, *Nigeria* 83 D6
Éguzon-Chantôme, *France* .. 19 F8
Egvekinot, *Russia* 51 C19
Egyek, *Hungary* 42 C5
Egypt ■, *Africa* 80 B3
Eha Amufu, *Nigeria* 83 D6
Ehime □, *Japan* 55 H6
Ehingen, *Germany* 25 G5
Ehrenberg, *U.S.A.* 117 M12
Ehrwald, *Austria* 26 D3
Eibar, *Spain* 32 B2
Eichstätt, *Germany* 25 G7
Eickhelberg, *Germany* ... 24 A4
Eider →, *Germany* 24 A4
Eidsvold, *Australia* 95 D5
Eidsvoll, *Norway* 9 F14
Eifel, *Germany* 25 E2
Eiffel Flats, *Zimbabwe* .. 87 F3
Eiger, *Switz.* 28 B5
Eigg, *U.K.* 14 E2
Eighty Mile Beach, *Australia* .. 92 C3
Eil, *Somali Rep.* 74 F4
Eil, L., *U.K.* 14 E3
Eildon, *Australia* 95 F4
Eildon, L., *Australia* ... 95 F4
Eilenburg, *Germany* 24 D8
Ein el Luweiqa, *Sudan* .. 81 E3
Einasleigh, *Australia* ... 94 B3
Einasleigh →, *Australia* .. 94 B3
Einbeck, *Germany* 24 D5
Eindhoven, *Neths.* 17 C5
Einsiedeln, *Switz.* 25 H4
Eire = Ireland ■, *Europe* .. 15 C4
Eiríksjökull, *Iceland* ... 8 D3
Eirunepé, *Brazil* 124 E5
Eiseb →, *Namibia* 88 C2
Eisenach, *Germany* 24 E6
Eisenberg, *Germany* 24 E7
Eisenerz, *Austria* 26 D7
Eisenhüttenstadt, *Germany* .. 24 C10
Eisenkappel, *Austria* ... 26 E7
Eisenstadt, *Austria* 27 D9
Eisfeld, *Germany* 25 E6
Eisleben, *Germany* 24 D7
Eislingen, *Germany* 25 G5
Eivissa, *Spain* 37 C7
Eixe, Serra do, *Spain* ... 34 C4
Ejea de los Caballeros, *Spain* .. 32 C3
Ejeda, *Madag.* 89 C7
Ejura, *Ghana* 83 D4
Ejutla, *Mexico* 119 D5
Ekalaka, *U.S.A.* 112 C2
Ekenässjön, *Sweden* 11 G9
Ekerö, *Sweden* 10 E11
Eket, *Nigeria* 83 E6
Eketahuna, *N.Z.* 91 J5
Ekhínos, *Greece* 41 E9
Ekibastuz, *Kazakstan* ... 50 D8
Ekoli,
  Dem. Rep. of the Congo .. 86 C1
Ekoln, *Sweden* 10 E11
Ekshärad, *Sweden* 10 D7
Eksjö, *Sweden* 11 G8
Ekuma →, *Namibia* 88 B2
Ekwan →, *Canada* 102 B3
Ekwan Pt., *Canada* 102 B3
El Aaiún, *W. Sahara* 78 C3
El Abanico, *Chile* 126 D1
El Abbasiya, *Sudan* 81 E3
El 'Agrûd, *Egypt* 75 E3
El Ait, *Sudan* 81 E2
El 'Aiyat, *Egypt* 80 J7
El Alamein, *Egypt* 80 A2
El 'Aqaba, W. →, *Egypt* .. 75 E2
El 'Arag, *Egypt* 80 B2
El Arahal, *Spain* 35 H5
El 'Arîḥâ, *West Bank* ... 75 D4
El 'Arîsh, *Egypt* 75 D2
El 'Arîsh, W. →, *Egypt* .. 75 D2
El Asnam = Ech Cheliff,
  Algeria 78 A6
El Astillero, *Spain* 34 B7
El Badâri, *Egypt* 80 B3
El Bahrein, *Egypt* 80 B2
El Ballâs, *Egypt* 80 B3
El Balyana, *Egypt* 80 B3
El Baqeir, *Sudan* 80 D3
El Barco de Ávila, *Spain* .. 34 E5
El Barco de Valdeorras = O
  Barco, *Spain* 34 C4
El Bauga, *Sudan* 80 D3
El Bawiti, *Egypt* 80 B2
El Bayadh, *Algeria* 78 B6
El Bierzo, *Spain* 34 C4

El Bluff, *Nic.* 120 D3
El Bonillo, *Spain* 33 G2
El Brûk, W. →, *Egypt* .. 75 E2
El Buheirat □, *Sudan* ... 81 F3
El Burgo de Osma, *Spain* .. 32 D1
El Cajon, *U.S.A.* 117 N10
El Campo, *U.S.A.* 113 L6
El Centro, *U.S.A.* 117 N11
El Cerro, *Bolivia* 124 G6
El Cerro de Andévalo, *Spain* .. 35 H4
El Compadre, *Mexico* ... 117 N10
El Coronil, *Spain* 35 H5
El Cuy, *Argentina* 128 D3
El Cuyo, *Mexico* 119 C7
El Dab'a, *Egypt* 80 H6
El Daheir, *Egypt* 75 D3
El Dátil, *Mexico* 118 B2
El Deir, *Egypt* 80 B3
El Dere, *Somali Rep.* ... 74 G4
El Descanso, *Mexico* 117 N10
El Desemboque, *Mexico* .. 118 A2
El Dilingat, *Egypt* 80 H7
El Diviso, *Colombia* 124 C3
El Djouf, *Mauritania* ... 78 D4
El Dorado, *Ark., U.S.A.* .. 113 J8
El Dorado, *Kans., U.S.A.* .. 113 G6
El Dorado, *Venezuela* ... 124 B6
El 'Ein, *Sudan* 81 D2
El Ejido, *Spain* 35 J8
El Escorial, *Spain* 34 E6
El Espinar, *Spain* 34 E6
El Faiyûm, *Egypt* 80 J7
El Fâsher, *Sudan* 81 E2
El Fashn, *Egypt* 80 J7
El Ferrol = Ferrol, *Spain* .. 34 B2
El Fifi, *Sudan* 81 E2
El Fuerte, *Mexico* 118 B3
El Ga'a, *Sudan* 81 D2
El Gal, *Somali Rep.* 74 E5
El Garef, *Sudan* 81 E3
El Gebir, *Sudan* 81 E2
El Gedida, *Egypt* 80 B2
El Geneina = Al Junaynah,
  Sudan 79 F10
El Geteina, *Sudan* 81 E3
El Gezira □, *Sudan* 81 E3
El Gir, *Sudan* 80 D2
El Gîza, *Egypt* 80 J7
El Goléa, *Algeria* 78 B6
El Grau, *Spain* 33 G4
El Hagiz, *Sudan* 81 D4
El Hâi, *Egypt* 80 J7
El Hammam, *Egypt* 80 A2
El Hawata, *Sudan* 81 E3
El Heiz, *Egypt* 80 B2
El Hideib, *Sudan* 81 E3
El Hilla, *Sudan* 81 E2
El 'Idisât, *Egypt* 80 B3
El Iskandarîya, *Egypt* .. 80 H7
El Istiwa'iya, *Sudan* ... 81 F2
El Jadida, *Morocco* 78 B4
El Jardal, *Honduras* 120 D2
El Jebelein, *Sudan* 81 E3
El Kab, *Sudan* 80 D3
El Kabrît, G., *Egypt* ... 75 F2
El Kafr el Sharqi, *Egypt* .. 80 H7
El Kamlin, *Sudan* 81 D3
El Karaba, *Sudan* 80 D3
El Kere, *Ethiopia* 81 F5
El Khandaq, *Sudan* 80 D3
El Khârga, *Egypt* 80 B3
El Khartûm, *Sudan* 81 D3
El Khartûm □, *Sudan* ... 81 D3
El Khartûm Bahrî, *Sudan* .. 81 D3
El Kuntilla, *Egypt* 75 F3
El Laqâwa, *Sudan* 81 E2
El Laqeita, *Egypt* 80 B3
El Leh, *Ethiopia* 81 G4
El Leiya, *Sudan* 81 D4
El Maestrazgo, *Spain* ... 32 E4
El Mafâza, *Sudan* 81 E3
El Maghra, *Egypt* 80 A2
El Mahalla el Kubra, *Egypt* .. 80 H7
El Mahârîq, *Egypt* 80 B3
El Maîmûn, *Egypt* 80 J7
El Maks el Bahari, *Egypt* .. 80 C3
El Manshâh, *Egypt* 80 B3
El Mansûra, *Egypt* 80 H7
El Manzala, *Egypt* 80 H7
El Marâgha, *Egypt* 80 B3
El Masid, *Sudan* 81 D3
El Masnou, *Spain* 32 D7
El Matariya, *Egypt* 80 H8
El Meda, *Ethiopia* 81 F5
El Medano, *Canary Is.* .. 37 F3
El Metemma, *Sudan* 81 D3
El Milagro, *Argentina* .. 126 C2
El Minyâ, *Egypt* 80 B3
El Monte, *U.S.A.* 117 L8
El Montseny, *Spain* 32 D7
El Mreyye, *Mauritania* .. 82 B3
El Niybo, *Ethiopia* 81 G4
El Obeid, *Sudan* 81 E3
El Odaiya, *Sudan* 81 E2
El Oro, *Mexico* 119 D4
El Oued, *Algeria* 78 B7
El Palmito, Presa, *Mexico* .. 118 B3
El Paso, *U.S.A.* 115 L10
El Paso Robles, *U.S.A.* .. 116 K6
El Pedernoso, *Spain* 33 F2
El Pedroso, *Spain* 35 H5
El Pobo de Dueñas, *Spain* .. 32 E3
El Portal, *U.S.A.* 116 H7
El Porvenir, *Mexico* 118 A3
El Prat de Llobregat, *Spain* .. 32 D7
El Progreso, *Honduras* .. 120 C2
El Pueblito, *Mexico* 118 B3
El Pueblo, *Canary Is.* .. 37 F2
El Puente del Arzobispo,
  Spain 34 F5

El Puerto de Santa María,
  Spain 35 J4
El Qâhira, *Egypt* 80 H7
El Qantara, *Egypt* 75 E1
El Qasr, *Egypt* 80 B2
El Qubâbât, *Egypt* 80 J7
El Quseima, *Egypt* 75 E3
El Qusîya, *Egypt* 80 B3
El Râshda, *Egypt* 80 B2
El Real, *Panama* 124 B3
El Reno, *U.S.A.* 113 H6
El Rîdisiya, *Egypt* 80 C3
El Rio, *U.S.A.* 117 L7
El Ronquillo, *Spain* 35 H4
El Roque, Pta., *Canary Is.* .. 37 F4
El Rosarito, *Mexico* 118 B2
El Rubio, *Spain* 35 H5
El Saff, *Egypt* 80 J7
El Saheira, W. →, *Egypt* .. 75 E2
El Salto, *Mexico* 118 C3
El Salvador ■, *Cent. Amer.* .. 120 D2
El Sauce, *Nic.* 120 D2
El Saucejo, *Spain* 35 H5
El Shallal, *Egypt* 80 C3
El Simbillawein, *Egypt* .. 80 H7
El Sueco, *Mexico* 118 B3
El Suweis, *Egypt* 80 J8
El Tamarâni, W. →, *Egypt* .. 75 E3
El Thamad, *Egypt* 75 F3
El Tigre, *Venezuela* 124 B6
El Tîh, Gebal, *Egypt* ... 75 F2
El Tîna, *Egypt* 80 H8
El Tîna, Khalîg, *Egypt* .. 75 D1
El Tofo, *Chile* 126 B1
El Tránsito, *Chile* 126 B1
El Tûr, *Egypt* 70 D2
El Turbio, *Argentina* ... 128 G2
El Uqsur, *Egypt* 80 B3
El Venado, *Mexico* 118 C4
El Vendrell, *Spain* 32 D6
El Vergel, *Mexico* 118 B3
El Vigía, *Venezuela* 124 B4
El Viso del Alcor, *Spain* .. 35 H5
El Wabeira, *Egypt* 75 F2
El Wak, *Kenya* 86 B5
El Waqf, *Egypt* 80 B3
El Weguet, *Ethiopia* 81 F5
El Wuz, *Sudan* 81 D3
Elafónisos, *Greece* 38 E4
Élancourt, *France* 19 D8
Élassa, *Greece* 39 F8
Elassón, *Greece* 38 B4
Elat, *Israel* 75 F3
Eláthia, *Greece* 38 C4
Elâzığ, *Turkey* 70 B3
Elba, *Italy* 28 F7
Elba, *U.S.A.* 109 K2
Elbasani, *Albania* 40 E4
Elbe, *U.S.A.* 116 D4
Elbe →, *Europe* 24 B5
Elbe-Seitenkanal, *Germany* .. 24 C6
Elbert, Mt., *U.S.A.* 115 G10
Elberton, *U.S.A.* 109 H4
Elbeuf, *France* 18 C8
Elbidtan, *Turkey* 70 B3
Elbing = Elbląg, *Poland* .. 44 D6
Elbistan, *Turkey* 72 C7
Elbląg, *Poland* 44 D6
Elbow, *Canada* 105 C7
Elbrus, *Asia* 49 J6
Elburz Mts. = Alborz,
  Reshteh-ye Kūhhā-ye, *Iran* .. 71 C7
Elche, *Spain* 33 G4
Elche de la Sierra, *Spain* .. 33 G2
Elcho I., *Australia* 94 A2
Elda, *Spain* 33 G4
Elde →, *Germany* 24 B7
Eldon, *Mo., U.S.A.* 112 F8
Eldon, *Wash., U.S.A.* ... 116 C3
Eldora, *U.S.A.* 112 D8
Eldorado, *Argentina* 127 B5
Eldorado, *Canada* 110 B7
Eldorado, *Mexico* 118 C3
Eldorado, *Ill., U.S.A.* .. 108 G1
Eldorado, *Tex., U.S.A.* .. 113 K4
Eldorado Springs, *U.S.A.* .. 113 G8
Eldoret, *Kenya* 86 B4
Eldred, *U.S.A.* 110 E6
Elea, C., *Cyprus* 36 D13
Eleanora, Pk., *Australia* .. 93 F3
Elefantes →, *Mozam.* ... 89 C5
Elektrogorsk, *Russia* ... 46 E10
Elektrostal, *Russia* 46 E10
Elele, *Nigeria* 83 D6
Elena, *Bulgaria* 41 D9
Elephant Butte Reservoir,
  U.S.A. 115 K10
Elephant I., *Antarctica* .. 5 C18
Eleshnitsa, *Bulgaria* ... 40 E7
Eleşkirt, *Turkey* 73 C10
Eleuthera, *Bahamas* 120 B4
Elevsís, *Greece* 38 C5
Elevtheroúpolis, *Greece* .. 41 F8
Elgin, *Canada* 111 B8
Elgin, *U.K.* 14 D5
Elgin, *Ill., U.S.A.* 108 D1
Elgin, *N. Dak., U.S.A.* .. 112 B4
Elgin, *Oreg., U.S.A.* ... 114 D5
Elgin, *Tex., U.S.A.* 113 K6
Elgoibar, *Spain* 32 B2
Elgon, Mt., *Africa* 86 B3
Eliase, *Indonesia* 63 F8
Elikón, *Greece* 38 C4
Elim, *Namibia* 88 B2
Elim, *S. Africa* 88 E2
Elin Pelin, *Bulgaria* ... 40 D7
Elisabethville =
  Lubumbashi,
  Dem. Rep. of the Congo .. 87 E2
Elista, *Russia* 49 G7

Elizabeth, *Australia* ... 95 E2
Elizabeth, *N.J., U.S.A.* .. 111 F10
Elizabeth, *N.J., U.S.A.* .. 111 F10
Elizabeth City, *U.S.A.* .. 109 G7
Elizabethton, *U.S.A.* ... 109 G4
Elizabethtown, *Ky., U.S.A.* .. 108 G3
Elizabethtown, *N.Y., U.S.A.* .. 111 B11
Elizabethtown, *Pa., U.S.A.* .. 111 F8
Elizondo, *Spain* 32 B3
Elk, *Poland* 44 E9
Elk →, *Canada* 104 C5
Elk →, *Poland* 44 E9
Elk →, *U.S.A.* 109 H2
Elk City, *U.S.A.* 113 H5
Elk Creek, *U.S.A.* 116 F4
Elk Grove, *U.S.A.* 116 G5
Elk Island Nat. Park,
  Canada 104 C6
Elk Lake, *Canada* 102 C3
Elk Point, *Canada* 105 C6
Elk River, *Idaho, U.S.A.* .. 114 C5
Elk River, *Minn., U.S.A.* .. 112 C8
Elkedra →, *Australia* ... 94 C2
Elkhart, *Ind., U.S.A.* .. 108 E3
Elkhart, *Kans., U.S.A.* .. 113 G4
Elkhorn, *Canada* 105 D8
Elkhorn →, *U.S.A.* 112 E6
Elkhovo, *Bulgaria* 41 D10
Elkin, *U.S.A.* 109 G5
Elkins, *U.S.A.* 108 F6
Elkland, *U.S.A.* 110 E7
Elko, *Canada* 104 D5
Elko, *U.S.A.* 114 F6
Elkton, *U.S.A.* 110 C1
Ell, L., *Australia* 93 E4
Ellef Ringnes I., *Canada* .. 4 B2
Ellen, Mt., *U.S.A.* 111 B12
Ellenburg, *U.S.A.* 111 B11
Ellendale, *U.S.A.* 112 B5
Ellensburg, *U.S.A.* 114 C3
Ellenville, *U.S.A.* 111 E10
Ellery, Mt., *Australia* .. 95 F4
Ellesmere, L., *N.Z.* 91 M4
Ellesmere I., *Canada* ... 4 B4
Ellesmere Port, *U.K.* ... 12 D5
Ellice Is. = Tuvalu ■,
  Pac. Oc. 96 H9
Ellicottville, *U.S.A.* ... 110 D6
Elliot, *Australia* 94 B1
Elliot, *S. Africa* 89 E4
Elliot Lake, *Canada* 102 C3
Elliotdale = Xhora, *S. Africa* .. 89 E4
Ellis, *U.S.A.* 112 F5
Elliston, *Australia* 95 E1
Ellisville, *U.S.A.* 113 K10
Ellon, *U.K.* 14 D6
Ellore = Eluru, *India* .. 67 L12
Ellsworth, *Kans., U.S.A.* .. 112 F5
Ellsworth, *Maine, U.S.A.* .. 109 C11
Ellsworth Land, *Antarctica* .. 5 D16
Ellsworth Mts., *Antarctica* .. 5 D16
Ellwangen, *Germany* 25 G6
Ellwood City, *U.S.A.* ... 110 F4
Elm, *Switz.* 25 J5
Elma, *Canada* 105 D9
Elma, *U.S.A.* 116 D3
Elmadağ, *Turkey* 72 C5
Elmalı, *Turkey* 39 E11
Elmhurst, *U.S.A.* 108 E2
Elmina, *Ghana* 83 D4
Elmira, *Canada* 110 C4
Elmira, *U.S.A.* 110 D8
Elmira Heights, *U.S.A.* .. 110 D8
Elmore, *Australia* 95 F3
Elmore, *U.S.A.* 117 M11
Elmshorn, *Germany* 24 B5
Elmvale, *Canada* 110 B5
Elne, *France* 20 F6
Elora, *Canada* 110 C4
Elos, *Greece* 38 E4
Eloúnda, *Greece* 36 D7
Eloy, *U.S.A.* 115 K8
Éloyes, *France* 19 D13
Elrose, *Canada* 105 C7
Elsdorf, *Germany* 24 E2
Elsie, *U.S.A.* 110 D3
Elsinore = Helsingør,
  Denmark 11 H6
Elster →, *Germany* 24 D7
Elsterwerda, *Germany* ... 24 D9
Eltham, *N.Z.* 91 H5
Elton, *Russia* 49 F8
Elton, Ozero, *Russia* ... 49 F8
Eltville, *Germany* 25 E4
Eluru, *India* 67 L12
Elvas, *Portugal* 35 G3
Elven, *France* 18 E4
Elverum, *Norway* 9 F14
Elvire →, *Australia* 92 C4
Elvire, Mt., *Australia* .. 93 E2
Elvo →, *Italy* 28 C5
Elwell, L., *U.S.A.* 114 B8
Elwood, *Ind., U.S.A.* ... 108 E3
Elwood, *Nebr., U.S.A.* .. 112 E5
Elx = Elche, *Spain* 33 G4
Ely, *U.K.* 13 E8
Ely, *Minn., U.S.A.* 112 B9
Ely, *Nev., U.S.A.* 114 G6
Elyria, *U.S.A.* 110 E2
Elyrus, *Greece* 38 F5
Elz →, *Germany* 25 G3
Emådalen, *Sweden* 10 C8
Emāmrūd, *Iran* 71 B7
Emån →, *Sweden* 11 G10
Emba, *Kazakstan* 50 E6
Emba →, *Kazakstan* 50 E6
Embarcación, *Argentina* .. 126 A3
Embarras Portage, *Canada* .. 105 B6
Embetsu, *Japan* 54 B10
Embi = Emba, *Kazakstan* .. 50 E6

Embi = Emba →, Kazakstan ... 50 E6
Embóna, Greece ... 36 C9
Embrun, France ... 21 D10
Embu, Kenya ... 86 C4
Emden, Germany ... 24 B3
Emecik, Turkey ... 39 E9
Emerald, Australia ... 94 C4
Emerson, Canada ... 105 D9
Emet, Turkey ... 39 B11
Emi Koussi, Chad ... 79 E9
Emília-Romagna □, Italy ... 28 D8
Emilius, Mte., Italy ... 28 C4
Eminabad, Pakistan ... 68 C6
Emine, Nos, Bulgaria ... 41 D11
Emirdağ, Turkey ... 72 C4
Emlenton, U.S.A. ... 110 E5
Emlichheim, Germany ... 24 C2
Emmaboda, Sweden ... 11 H9
Emmaus, S. Africa ... 88 D4
Emmaus, U.S.A. ... 111 F9
Emme →, Switz. ... 25 H3
Emmeloord, Neths. ... 17 B5
Emmen, Neths. ... 17 B6
Emmen, Switz. ... 25 H4
Emmendingen, Germany ... 25 G3
Emmental, Switz. ... 25 J3
Emmerich, Germany ... 24 D2
Emmet, Australia ... 94 C3
Emmetsburg, U.S.A. ... 112 D7
Emmett, Idaho, U.S.A. ... 114 E5
Emmett, Mich., U.S.A. ... 110 D2
Emmonak, U.S.A. ... 100 B3
Emo, Canada ... 105 D10
Emőd, Hungary ... 42 C5
Emona, Bulgaria ... 41 D11
Empalme, Mexico ... 118 B2
Empangeni, S. Africa ... 89 D5
Empedrado, Argentina ... 126 B4
Emperor Seamount Chain, Pac. Oc. ... 96 D9
Empoli, Italy ... 28 E7
Emporia, Kans., U.S.A. ... 112 F6
Emporia, Va., U.S.A. ... 109 G7
Emporium, U.S.A. ... 110 E6
Empress, Canada ... 105 C7
Empty Quarter = Rub' al Khālī, Si. Arabia ... 74 D4
Ems →, Germany ... 24 B3
Emsdale, Canada ... 110 A5
Emsdetten, Germany ... 24 C3
Emu, China ... 57 C15
Emu Park, Australia ... 94 C5
'En 'Avrona, Israel ... 75 F4
En Nahud, Sudan ... 81 E2
En Nofalab, Sudan ... 81 D3
Ena, Japan ... 55 G8
Enana, Namibia ... 88 B2
Enånger, Sweden ... 10 C11
Enaratoli, Indonesia ... 63 E9
Enard B., U.K. ... 14 C3
Enare = Inarijärvi, Finland ... 8 B22
Encampment, U.S.A. ... 114 F10
Encantadas, Serra, Brazil ... 127 C5
Encarnación, Paraguay ... 127 B4
Encarnación de Diaz, Mexico ... 118 C4
Enchi, Ghana ... 82 D4
Encinitas, U.S.A. ... 117 M9
Encino, U.S.A. ... 115 J11
Encounter B., Australia ... 95 F2
Encs, Hungary ... 42 B6
Endako, Canada ... 104 C3
Ende, Indonesia ... 63 F6
Endeavour Str., Australia ... 94 A3
Endelave, Denmark ... 11 J4
Enderbury I., Kiribati ... 96 H10
Enderby, Canada ... 104 C5
Enderby I., Australia ... 92 D2
Enderby Land, Antarctica ... 5 C5
Enderlin, U.S.A. ... 112 B6
Endicott, U.S.A. ... 111 D8
Endwell, U.S.A. ... 111 D8
Endyalgout I., Australia ... 92 B5
Eneabba, Australia ... 93 E2
Enewetak Atoll, Marshall Is. ... 96 F8
Enez, Turkey ... 41 F10
Enfield, Canada ... 103 D7
Enfield, Conn., U.S.A. ... 111 E12
Enfield, N.H., U.S.A. ... 111 C12
Engadin, Switz. ... 25 J6
Engaño, C., Dom. Rep. ... 121 C6
Engaño, C., Phil. ... 63 A6
Engaru, Japan ... 54 B11
Engcobo, S. Africa ... 89 E4
Engelberg, Switz. ... 25 J4
Engels, Russia ... 48 E8
Engemann L., Canada ... 105 B7
Engershatu, Eritrea ... 81 D4
Enggano, Indonesia ... 62 F2
England, U.S.A. ... 113 H9
England □, U.K. ... 13 D7
Englee, Canada ... 103 B8
Englehart, Canada ... 102 C4
Englewood, U.S.A. ... 112 F2
English →, Canada ... 105 C10
English Bazar = Ingraj Bazar, India ... 69 G13
English Channel, Europe ... 13 G6
English River, Canada ... 102 C1
Engures ezers, Latvia ... 44 A10
Enguri →, Georgia ... 49 J5
Enid, U.S.A. ... 113 G6
Enipévs →, Greece ... 38 B4
Enkhuizen, Neths. ... 17 B5
Enle, China ... 58 F3
Enna, Italy ... 31 E7
Ennadai, Canada ... 105 A8
Ennadai L., Canada ... 105 A8
Ennedi, Chad ... 79 E10
Enngonia, Australia ... 95 D4

Ennigerloh, Germany ... 24 D4
Ennis, Ireland ... 15 D3
Ennis, Mont., U.S.A. ... 114 D8
Ennis, Tex., U.S.A. ... 113 J6
Enniscorthy, Ireland ... 15 D5
Enniskillen, U.K. ... 15 B4
Ennistimon, Ireland ... 15 D2
Enns, Austria ... 26 C7
Enns →, Austria ... 26 C7
Enontekiö, Finland ... 8 B20
Enosburg Falls, U.S.A. ... 111 B12
Enping, China ... 59 F9
Enriquillo, L., Dom. Rep. ... 121 C5
Enschede, Neths. ... 17 B6
Ensenada, Argentina ... 126 C4
Ensenada, Mexico ... 118 A1
Ensenada de los Muertos, Mexico ... 118 C2
Enshi, China ... 58 B7
Ensiola, Pta. de n', Spain ... 37 B9
Ensisheim, France ... 19 E14
Entebbe, Uganda ... 86 B3
Enterprise, Canada ... 104 A5
Enterprise, Ala., U.S.A. ... 109 K3
Enterprise, Oreg., U.S.A. ... 114 D5
Entraygues-sur-Truyère, France ... 20 D6
Entre Ríos, Bolivia ... 126 A3
Entre Ríos □, Argentina ... 126 C4
Entrepeñas, Embalse de, Spain ... 32 E2
Entroncamento, Portugal ... 35 F2
Enugu, Nigeria ... 83 D6
Enugu □, Nigeria ... 83 D6
Enugu Ezike, Nigeria ... 83 D6
Enumclaw, U.S.A. ... 116 C5
Envermeu, France ... 18 C8
Enviken, Sweden ... 10 D9
Enying, Hungary ... 42 D3
Enza →, Italy ... 28 D7
Eólie, Ís., Italy ... 31 D7
Epanomí, Greece ... 40 F6
Epe, Neths. ... 17 B5
Epe, Nigeria ... 83 D5
Épernay, France ... 19 C10
Épernon, France ... 19 D8
Ephesus, Turkey ... 39 D9
Ephraim, U.S.A. ... 114 G8
Ephrata, Pa., U.S.A. ... 111 F8
Ephrata, Wash., U.S.A. ... 114 C4
Epidaurus Limera, Greece ... 38 E5
Épila, Spain ... 32 D3
Épinac, France ... 19 F11
Épinal, France ... 19 D13
Episkopi, Cyprus ... 36 E11
Episkopí, Greece ... 36 D6
Episkopi Bay, Cyprus ... 36 E11
Epitálion, Greece ... 38 D3
Eppan = Appiano, Italy ... 29 B8
Eppingen, Germany ... 25 F4
Epsom, U.K. ... 13 F7
Epukiro, Namibia ... 88 C2
Equatorial Guinea ■, Africa ... 84 D1
Er Hai, China ... 58 E3
Er Rahad, Sudan ... 81 E3
Er Rif, Morocco ... 78 A5
Er Rogel, Sudan ... 80 D4
Er Roseires, Sudan ... 81 E3
Er Rua'at, Sudan ... 81 E3
Eraclea, Italy ... 29 C9
Erāwadī Myit = Irrawaddy →, Burma ... 67 M19
Erba, Italy ... 28 C6
Erba, Sudan ... 80 D4
Erba, J., Sudan ... 80 C4
Erbaa, Turkey ... 72 B7
Erbeskopf, Germany ... 25 F3
Erbil = Arbīl, Iraq ... 70 B5
Erbu, Ethiopia ... 81 E3
Erçek, Turkey ... 70 B4
Erçiş, Turkey ... 73 C10
Erçiyaş Dağı, Turkey ... 70 B2
Érd, Hungary ... 42 C3
Erdao Jiang →, China ... 57 C14
Erdek, Turkey ... 41 F11
Erdemli, Turkey ... 72 D6
Erdene = Ulaan-Uul, Mongolia ... 56 B6
Erdenetsogt, Mongolia ... 56 C4
Erding, Germany ... 25 G7
Erdre →, France ... 18 E5
Erebus, Mt., Antarctica ... 5 D11
Erechim, Brazil ... 127 B5
Ereğli, Konya, Turkey ... 70 D6
Ereğli, Zonguldak, Turkey ... 72 B4
Erei, Monti, Italy ... 31 E7
Erenhot, China ... 56 C7
Eresma →, Spain ... 34 D6
Eressós, Greece ... 39 B7
Erewadi Myitwanya, Burma ... 67 M19
Erfenisdam, S. Africa ... 88 D4
Erfstadt, Germany ... 24 E2
Erft →, Germany ... 24 D2
Erfurt, Germany ... 24 E7
Erg Iguidi, Africa ... 78 C4
Ergani, Turkey ... 70 B3
Ergel, Mongolia ... 56 C5
Ergene →, Turkey ... 41 E10
Ergeni Vozvyshennost, Russia ... 49 G7
Ērgli, Latvia ... 9 H21
Erhlin, Taiwan ... 59 F13
Eria →, Spain ... 34 C5
Eriba, Sudan ... 81 D4
Eriboll, L., U.K. ... 14 C4
Érice, Italy ... 30 D5
Erie, U.S.A. ... 110 D4
Erie, L., N. Amer. ... 110 D4
Erie Canal, U.S.A. ... 110 C7
Erieau, Canada ... 110 D3
Erigavo, Somali Rep. ... 74 E4

Erikoúsa, Greece ... 36 A3
Eriksdale, Canada ... 105 C9
Erímanthos, Greece ... 38 D3
Erimo-misaki, Japan ... 54 D11
Erinpura, India ... 68 G5
Erithraí, Greece ... 38 C5
Eritrea ■, Africa ... 81 E4
Erjas →, Portugal ... 34 F3
Erkelenz, Germany ... 24 D2
Erkner, Germany ... 24 C9
Erlangen, Germany ... 25 F6
Erldunda, Australia ... 94 D1
Ermelo, Neths. ... 17 B5
Ermelo, S. Africa ... 89 D4
Ermenek, Turkey ... 70 D5
Ermil, Sudan ... 81 E2
Ermióni, Greece ... 38 D5
Ermones, Greece ... 36 A3
Ermoúpolis = Síros, Greece ... 38 D6
Ernakulam = Cochin, India ... 66 Q10
Erne →, Ireland ... 15 B3
Erne, Lower L., U.K. ... 15 B4
Erne, Upper L., U.K. ... 15 B4
Ernée, France ... 18 D6
Ernest Giles Ra., Australia ... 93 E3
Ernstberg, Germany ... 25 E2
Erode, India ... 66 P10
Eromanga, Australia ... 95 D3
Erongo, Namibia ... 88 C2
Erquy, France ... 18 D4
Erramala Hills, India ... 66 M11
Errer →, Ethiopia ... 81 F5
Errigal, Ireland ... 15 A3
Erris Hd., Ireland ... 15 B1
Erseka, Albania ... 40 F4
Erskine, U.S.A. ... 112 B7
Erstein, France ... 19 D14
Ertholmene, Denmark ... 11 J9
Ertil, Russia ... 48 E5
Ertis = Irtysh →, Russia ... 50 C7
Eruh, Turkey ... 73 D10
Eruwa, Nigeria ... 83 D5
Ervy-le-Châtel, France ... 19 D10
Erwin, U.S.A. ... 109 G4
Eryuan, China ... 58 D2
Erzgebirge, Germany ... 24 E8
Erzin, Russia ... 51 D10
Erzincan, Turkey ... 70 B3
Erzurum, Turkey ... 70 B4
Es Caló, Spain ... 37 C7
Es Canar, Spain ... 37 B8
Es Mercadal, Spain ... 37 B11
Es Migjorn Gran, Spain ... 37 B11
Es Safiya, Sudan ... 81 D3
Es Sahrâ' Esh Sharqîya, Egypt ... 80 B3
Es Sînâ', Egypt ... 75 F3
Es Sûkî, Sudan ... 81 E3
Es Vedrà, Spain ... 37 C7
Esambo, Dem. Rep. of the Congo ... 86 C1
Esan-Misaki, Japan ... 54 D10
Esashi, Hokkaidō, Japan ... 54 B11
Esashi, Hokkaidō, Japan ... 54 D10
Esbjerg, Denmark ... 11 J2
Escalante, U.S.A. ... 115 H8
Escalante →, U.S.A. ... 115 H8
Escalón, Mexico ... 118 B4
Escambia →, U.S.A. ... 109 K2
Escanaba, U.S.A. ... 108 C2
Esch-sur-Alzette, Lux. ... 17 E6
Eschede, Germany ... 24 C6
Eschwege, Germany ... 24 D6
Eschweiler, Germany ... 24 E2
Escondido, U.S.A. ... 117 M9
Escravos →, Nigeria ... 83 D6
Escuinapa, Mexico ... 118 C3
Escuintla, Guatemala ... 120 D1
Eséka, Cameroon ... 83 E7
Eşen →, Turkey ... 39 E11
Esenguly, Turkmenistan ... 50 F6
Esens, Germany ... 24 B3
Esenyurt, Turkey ... 41 E12
Esera →, Spain ... 32 C5
Eşfahān, Iran ... 71 C6
Eşfahān □, Iran ... 71 C6
Esfarāyen, Iran ... 71 B8
Esfideh, Iran ... 71 C8
Esguevas →, Spain ... 34 D6
Esh Sham = Dimashq, Syria ... 75 B5
Esh Shamâlîya □, Sudan ... 80 D2
Esha Ness, U.K. ... 14 A7
Eshan, China ... 58 E4
Esher, U.K. ... 13 F7
Eshowe, S. Africa ... 89 D5
Esiama, Ghana ... 82 E4
Esigodini, Zimbabwe ... 89 C4
Esil = Ishim →, Russia ... 50 D8
Esino →, Italy ... 29 E10
Esira, Madag. ... 89 C8
Esk →, Cumb., U.K. ... 14 G5
Esk →, N. Yorks., U.K. ... 12 C7
Eskān, Iran ... 71 D9
Esker, Canada ... 103 B6
Eskifjörður, Iceland ... 8 D7
Eskilsäter, Sweden ... 11 F7
Eskilstuna, Sweden ... 10 E10
Eskimalatya, Turkey ... 73 C8
Eskimo Pt., Canada ... 100 B10
Eskişehir, Turkey ... 39 B12
Eskişehir □, Turkey ... 39 B12
Esla →, Spain ... 34 D4
Eslāmābād-e Gharb, Iran ... 70 C5
Eslāmshahr, Iran ... 71 C6
Eslöv, Sweden ... 11 J7
Eşme, Turkey ... 39 C10
Esmeraldas, Ecuador ... 124 C3
Esnagi L., Canada ... 102 C3
Espalion, France ... 20 D6

Espanola, Canada ... 102 C3
Espanola, U.S.A. ... 115 H10
Esparreguera, Spain ... 32 D6
Esparta, Costa Rica ... 120 E3
Espelkamp, Germany ... 24 C4
Esperance, Australia ... 93 F3
Esperance B., Australia ... 93 F3
Esperanza, Argentina ... 126 C3
Esperanza, Phil. ... 61 G6
Espéraza, France ... 20 F6
Espichel, C., Portugal ... 35 G1
Espiel, Spain ... 35 G5
Espigão, Serra do, Brazil ... 127 B5
Espinaço, Serra do = Espinhaço, Serra do, Brazil ... 125 G10
Espinazo, Sierra del = Espinhaço, Serra do, Brazil ... 125 G10
Espinho, Portugal ... 34 D2
Espinilho, Serra do, Brazil ... 127 B5
Espinosa de los Monteros, Spain ... 34 B7
Espírito Santo □, Brazil ... 125 H10
Espiritu Santo, Vanuatu ... 96 J8
Espíritu Santo, B. del, Mexico ... 119 D7
Espíritu Santo, I., Mexico ... 118 C2
Espita, Mexico ... 119 C7
Espiye, Turkey ... 73 B8
Espluga de Francolí, Spain ... 32 D6
Espoo, Finland ... 9 F21
Espuña, Sierra de, Spain ... 33 H3
Espungabera, Mozam. ... 89 C5
Esquel, Argentina ... 128 E2
Esquimalt, Canada ... 104 D4
Esquina, Argentina ... 126 C4
Essaouira, Morocco ... 78 B4
Essebie, Dem. Rep. of the Congo ... 86 B3
Essen, Belgium ... 17 C4
Essen, Germany ... 24 D3
Essendon, Mt., Australia ... 93 E3
Essequibo →, Guyana ... 122 C5
Essex, Canada ... 110 D2
Essex, Calif., U.S.A. ... 117 L11
Essex, N.Y., U.S.A. ... 111 B11
Essex □, U.K. ... 13 F8
Essex Junction, U.S.A. ... 111 B11
Esslingen, Germany ... 25 G5
Essonne □, France ... 19 D9
Estaca de Bares, C. de, Spain ... 34 B3
Estadilla, Spain ... 32 C5
Estados, I. de Los, Argentina ... 122 J4
Estagel, France ... 20 F6
Eşţahbānāt, Iran ... 71 D7
Estância, Brazil ... 125 F11
Estancia, U.S.A. ... 115 J10
Estārm, Iran ... 71 D8
Estarreja, Portugal ... 34 E2
Estcourt, S. Africa ... 89 D4
Este, Italy ... 29 C8
Estelí, Nic. ... 120 D2
Estella, Spain ... 32 C2
Estellencs, Spain ... 37 B9
Estena →, Spain ... 35 F6
Estepa, Spain ... 35 H6
Estepona, Spain ... 35 J5
Esterhazy, Canada ... 105 C8
Esternay, France ... 19 D10
Esterri d'Aneu, Spain ... 32 C6
Estevan, Canada ... 105 D8
Estevan Group, Canada ... 104 C3
Estherville, U.S.A. ... 112 D7
Estissac, France ... 19 D10
Eston, Canada ... 105 C7
Estonia ■, Europe ... 9 G21
Estoril, Portugal ... 35 G1
Estouk, Mali ... 83 B5
Estreito, Brazil ... 125 E9
Estrela, Serra da, Portugal ... 34 E3
Estrella, Spain ... 35 G7
Estremoz, Portugal ... 35 G3
Estrondo, Serra do, Brazil ... 125 E9
Esztergom, Hungary ... 42 C3
Et Tîdra, Mauritania ... 82 B1
Etah, India ... 69 F8
Étain, France ... 19 C12
Étampes, France ... 19 D9
Etanga, Namibia ... 88 B1
Étaples, France ... 19 B8
Etawah, India ... 69 F8
Etawney L., Canada ... 105 B9
Ete, Nigeria ... 83 D6
Ethel, U.S.A. ... 116 D4
Ethelbert, Canada ... 105 C8
Ethiopia ■, Africa ... 74 F3
Ethiopian Highlands, Ethiopia ... 52 J7
Etili, Turkey ... 41 G10
Etive, L., U.K. ... 14 E3
Etna, Italy ... 31 E7
Etoile, Dem. Rep. of the Congo ... 87 E2
Etosha Nat. Park, Namibia ... 88 B2
Etosha Pan, Namibia ... 88 B2
Etowah, U.S.A. ... 109 H3
Etuku, Dem. Rep. of the Congo ... 86 C2
Etulia, Moldova ... 43 E13
Etzatlán, Mexico ... 118 C4
Etzná, Mexico ... 119 D6
Eu, France ... 18 B8

Euboea = Évvoia, Greece ... 38 C6
Eucla, Australia ... 93 F4
Euclid, U.S.A. ... 110 E3
Eucumbene, L., Australia ... 95 F4
Eudora, U.S.A. ... 113 J9
Eufaula, Ala., U.S.A. ... 109 K3
Eufaula, Okla., U.S.A. ... 113 H7
Eufaula L., U.S.A. ... 113 H7
Eugene, U.S.A. ... 114 E2
Eugowra, Australia ... 95 E4
Eulo, Australia ... 95 D4
Eunice, La., U.S.A. ... 113 K8
Eunice, N. Mex., U.S.A. ... 113 J3
Eupen, Belgium ... 17 D6
Euphrates = Furāt, Nahr al →, Asia ... 70 D5
Eure □, France ... 18 C8
Eure →, France ... 18 C8
Eure-et-Loir □, France ... 18 D8
Eureka, Canada ... 4 B3
Eureka, Calif., U.S.A. ... 114 F1
Eureka, Kans., U.S.A. ... 113 G6
Eureka, Mont., U.S.A. ... 114 B6
Eureka, Nev., U.S.A. ... 114 G5
Eureka, S. Dak., U.S.A. ... 112 C5
Eureka, Mt., Australia ... 93 E3
Euroa, Australia ... 95 F4
Europa, Île, Ind. Oc. ... 85 J8
Europa, Picos de, Spain ... 34 B6
Europa, Pta. de, Gib. ... 35 J5
Europe ... 6 E10
Europoort, Neths. ... 17 C4
Euskirchen, Germany ... 24 E2
Eustis, U.S.A. ... 109 L5
Euston, Australia ... 95 E3
Eutin, Germany ... 24 A6
Eutsuk L., Canada ... 104 C3
Evale, Angola ... 88 B2
Evans, U.S.A. ... 112 E2
Evans, L., Canada ... 102 B4
Evans City, U.S.A. ... 110 F4
Evans Head, Australia ... 95 D5
Evans Mills, U.S.A. ... 111 B9
Evansburg, Canada ... 104 C5
Evanston, Ill., U.S.A. ... 108 E2
Evanston, Wyo., U.S.A. ... 114 F8
Evansville, U.S.A. ... 108 G2
Évaux-les-Bains, France ... 19 F9
Evaz, Iran ... 71 E7
Evciler, Afyon, Turkey ... 39 C11
Evciler, Çanakkale, Turkey ... 39 B8
Eveleth, U.S.A. ... 112 B8
Evensk, Russia ... 51 C16
Everard, L., Australia ... 95 E2
Everard Ranges, Australia ... 93 E5
Everest, Mt., Nepal ... 69 E12
Everett, Pa., U.S.A. ... 110 F6
Everett, Wash., U.S.A. ... 116 C4
Everglades, The, U.S.A. ... 109 N5
Everglades National Park, U.S.A. ... 109 N5
Evergreen, Ala., U.S.A. ... 109 K2
Evergreen, Mont., U.S.A. ... 114 B6
Everöd, Sweden ... 11 J8
Evertsberg, Sweden ... 10 C7
Evesham, U.K. ... 13 E6
Évian-les-Bains, France ... 19 F13
Évinos →, Greece ... 38 C3
Évisa, France ... 21 F12
Evje, Norway ... 9 G12
Évora, Portugal ... 35 G3
Évora □, Portugal ... 35 G3
Evowghlī, Iran ... 70 B5
Évreux, France ... 18 C8
Evritanía □, Greece ... 38 B3
Évron, France ... 18 D6
Évros □, Greece ... 41 E10
Évros →, Bulgaria ... 72 B2
Evrótas →, Greece ... 38 E4
Évry, France ... 19 D9
Évvoia, Greece ... 38 C6
Évvoia □, Greece ... 38 C6
Evxinoúpolis, Greece ... 38 B4
Ewe, L., U.K. ... 14 D3
Ewing, U.S.A. ... 112 D5
Ewo, Congo ... 84 E2
Exaltación, Bolivia ... 124 F5
Excelsior Springs, U.S.A. ... 112 F7
Excideuil, France ... 20 C5
Exe →, U.K. ... 13 G4
Exeter, Canada ... 110 C3
Exeter, U.K. ... 13 G4
Exeter, Calif., U.S.A. ... 116 J7
Exeter, N.H., U.S.A. ... 111 D14
Exmoor, U.K. ... 13 F4
Exmouth, Australia ... 92 D1
Exmouth, U.K. ... 13 G4
Exmouth G., Australia ... 92 D1
Expedition Ra., Australia ... 94 C4
Extremadura □, Spain ... 35 F4
Exuma Sound, Bahamas ... 120 B4
Eyasi, L., Tanzania ... 86 C4
Eye, Cambs., U.K. ... 13 E7
Eye, Pen., U.K. ... 14 C2
Eyemouth, U.K. ... 14 F6
Eygurande, France ... 19 C9
Eyjafjörður, Iceland ... 8 C4
Eymet, France ... 20 D4
Eymoutiers, France ... 20 C5
Eynesil, Turkey ... 73 B8
Eyre (North), L., Australia ... 95 D2
Eyre (South), L., Australia ... 95 D2
Eyre Mts., N.Z. ... 91 L2
Eyre Pen., Australia ... 95 E2
Eysturoy, Færoe Is. ... 8 E9
Eyvānkī, Iran ... 71 C6
Ez Zeidab, Sudan ... 80 D3
Ezcaray, Spain ... 32 C1
Ežerėlis, Lithuania ... 44 D10
Ezhou, China ... 59 B10
Ezine, Turkey ... 39 B8
Ezouza →, Cyprus ... 36 E11

F

F.Y.R.O.M. =
  Macedonia ■, Europe ... 40 E5
Fabala, Guinea 82 D3
Fabens, U.S.A. 115 L10
Fabero, Spain 34 C4
Fåborg, Denmark 11 J4
Fabriano, Italy 29 E9
Făcăeni, Romania 43 F12
Fachi, Niger 79 E8
Fada, Chad 79 E10
Fada-n-Gourma,
  Burkina Faso 83 C5
Fadd, Hungary 42 D3
Faddeyevskiy, Ostrov, Russia 51 B15
Faddor, Sudan 81 F3
Fadghāmī, Syria 70 C4
Fadlab, Sudan 80 D3
Faenza, Italy 29 D8
Færoe Is. = Føroyar,
  Atl. Oc. 8 F9
Fafa, Mali 83 B5
Fafe, Portugal 34 D2
Fagam, Nigeria 83 C7
Făgăras, Romania 43 E9
Făgăras, Munţii, Romania 43 E9
Fågelmara, Sweden 11 H9
Fagerhult, Sweden 11 G9
Fagersta, Sweden 10 D9
Făget, Romania 42 E7
Făget, Munţii, Romania .. 43 C8
Fagnano, L., Argentina .. 128 G3
Fagnières, France 19 D11
Faguibine, L., Mali 82 B4
Fahlīān, Iran 71 D6
Fahraj, Kermān, Iran ... 71 D8
Fahraj, Yazd, Iran 71 D7
Fai Tsi Long Archipelago,
  Vietnam 58 G6
Faial, Madeira 37 D3
Fair Haven, U.S.A. 108 D9
Fair Hd., U.K. 15 A5
Fair Oaks, U.S.A. 116 G5
Fairbanks, U.S.A. 100 B5
Fairbury, U.S.A. 112 E6
Fairfax, U.S.A. 111 B11
Fairfield, Ala., U.S.A. . 109 J2
Fairfield, Calif., U.S.A. 116 G4
Fairfield, Conn., U.S.A. 111 E11
Fairfield, Idaho, U.S.A. 114 E6
Fairfield, Ill., U.S.A. . 108 F1
Fairfield, Iowa, U.S.A. . 112 E9
Fairfield, Tex., U.S.A. . 113 K7
Fairford, Canada 105 C9
Fairhope, U.S.A. 109 K2
Fairlie, N.Z. 91 L3
Fairmead, U.S.A. 116 H6
Fairmont, Minn., U.S.A. 112 D7
Fairmont, W. Va., U.S.A. 108 F5
Fairmount, Calif., U.S.A. 117 L8
Fairmount, N.Y., U.S.A. 111 C8
Fairplay, U.S.A. 115 G11
Fairport, U.S.A. 110 C7
Fairport Harbor, U.S.A. 110 E3
Fairview, Canada 104 B5
Fairview, Mont., U.S.A. 112 B2
Fairview, Okla., U.S.A. 113 G5
Fairweather, Mt., U.S.A. 104 B1
Faisalabad, Pakistan ... 68 D5
Faith, U.S.A. 112 C3
Faizabad, India 69 F10
Fajardo, Puerto Rico ... 121 C6
Fajr, W. →, Si. Arabia . 70 D3
Fakenham, U.K. 12 E8
Fåker, Sweden 10 A8
Fakfak, Indonesia 63 E8
Fakiya, Bulgaria 41 D11
Fakobli, Ivory C. 82 D3
Fakse, Denmark 11 J6
Fakse Bugt, Denmark 11 J6
Fakse Ladeplads, Denmark 11 J6
Faku, China 57 C12
Falaba, S. Leone 82 D2
Falaise, France 18 D6
Falaise, Mui, Vietnam .. 64 C5
Falakrón Óros, Greece .. 40 E7
Falam, Burma 67 H18
Falces, Spain 32 C3
Fălciu, Romania 43 D13
Falcó, C. des, Spain ... 37 C7
Falcón, Presa, Mexico .. 119 B5
Falcon Lake, Canada 105 D9
Falcon Reservoir, U.S.A. 113 M5
Falconara Maríttima, Italy 29 E10
Falcone, C. del, Italy .. 30 B1
Falconer, U.S.A. 110 D5
Faléa, Mali 82 C2
Falémé →, Senegal 82 C2
Falerum, Sweden 11 F10
Faleshty = Fălesti, Moldova 43 C12
Fălesti, Moldova 43 C12
Falfurrias, U.S.A. 113 M5
Falher, Canada 104 B5
Falirakí, Greece 36 C10
Falkenberg, Germany 24 D9
Falkenberg, Sweden 11 H6
Falkensee, Germany 24 C9
Falkirk, U.K. 14 F5
Falkirk □, U.K. 14 F5
Falkland, U.K. 14 E5
Falkland Is. □, Atl. Oc. 128 G5
Falkland Sd., Falk. Is. . 128 G5
Falkonéra, Greece 38 E5
Falköping, Sweden 11 F7
Fall River, U.S.A. 111 E13
Fallbrook, U.S.A. 117 M9
Fallon, U.S.A. 114 G4
Falls City, U.S.A. 112 E7
Falls Creek, U.S.A. 110 E6

Falmouth, Jamaica 120 C4
Falmouth, U.K. 13 G2
Falmouth, U.S.A. 111 E14
Falsa, Pta., Mexico 118 B1
False B., S. Africa 88 E2
Falso, C., Honduras 120 C3
Falster, Denmark 11 K5
Falsterbo, Sweden 9 J15
Fălticeni, Romania 43 C11
Falun, Sweden 10 D9
Famagusta, Cyprus 36 D12
Famagusta Bay, Cyprus .. 36 D13
Famalé, Niger 78 F6
Famatina, Sierra de,
  Argentina 126 B2
Family L., Canada 105 C9
Famoso, U.S.A. 117 K7
Fan Xian, China 56 G8
Fana, Mali 82 C3
Fanad Hd., Ireland 15 A4
Fanárion, Greece 38 B3
Fandriana, Madag. 89 C8
Fang, Thailand 58 H2
Fang Xian, China 59 A8
Fangaga, Sudan 80 D4
Fangak, Sudan 81 F3
Fangchang, China 59 B12
Fangcheng, China 56 H7
Fangchenggang, China ... 58 G7
Fangliao, Taiwan 59 F13
Fangshan, China 56 E6
Fangzi, China 57 F10
Fani i Madh →, Albania 40 E4
Fanjakana, Madag. 89 C8
Fanjiatun, China 57 C13
Fannich, L., U.K. 14 D4
Fannūj, Iran 71 E8
Fanø, Denmark 11 J2
Fano, Italy 29 E10
Fanshi, China 56 E7
Fao = Al Fāw, Iraq 71 D6
Faqirwali, Pakistan ... 68 E5
Fâqûs, Egypt 80 H7
Fara in Sabina, Italy .. 29 F9
Faradje,
  Dem. Rep. of the Congo 86 B2
Farafangana, Madag. 89 C8
Farâfra, El Wâhât el-, Egypt 80 B2
Farāh, Afghan. 66 C3
Farāh □, Afghan. 66 C3
Farahalana, Madag. 89 A9
Faraid, Gebel, Egypt .. 80 C4
Farako, Ivory C. 82 D4
Faramana, Burkina Faso . 82 C4
Faranah, Guinea 82 C2
Farasān, Jazā'ir, Si. Arabia 74 D3
Farasan Is. = Farasān,
  Jazā'ir, Si. Arabia .. 74 D3
Faratsiho, Madag. 89 B8
Fardes →, Spain 35 H7
Fareham, U.K. 13 G6
Farewell, C., N.Z. 91 J4
Farewell C. = Nunap Isua,
  Greenland 4 D5
Färgelanda, Sweden 11 F5
Farghona, Uzbekistan ... 50 E8
Fargo, U.S.A. 112 B6
Fär'iah, W. al →,
  West Bank 75 C4
Faribault, U.S.A. 112 C8
Faridabad, India 68 E6
Faridkot, India 68 D6
Faridpur, Bangla. 69 H13
Faridpur, India 69 E8
Färila, Sweden 10 C9
Farim, Guinea-Biss. 82 C1
Farīmān, Iran 71 C8
Farina, Australia 95 E2
Fariones, Pta., Canary Is. 37 E6
Fâriskûr, Egypt 80 H7
Färjestaden, Sweden 11 H10
Farkadhón, Greece 38 B4
Farmakonisi, Greece 39 D9
Farmerville, U.S.A. 113 J8
Farmingdale, U.S.A. 111 F10
Farmington, Canada 104 B4
Farmington, Calif., U.S.A. 116 H6
Farmington, Maine, U.S.A. 109 C10
Farmington, Mo., U.S.A. 113 G9
Farmington, N.H., U.S.A. 111 C13
Farmington, N. Mex.,
  U.S.A. 115 H9
Farmington, Utah, U.S.A. 114 F8
Farmington →, U.S.A. .. 111 E12
Farmville, U.S.A. 108 G6
Färnäs, Sweden 10 D8
Farne Is., U.K. 12 B6
Farnham, Canada 111 A12
Farnham, Mt., Canada ... 104 C5
Faro, Brazil 125 D7
Faro, Canada 100 B6
Faro, Portugal 35 H3
Fårö, Sweden 9 H18
Faro □, Portugal 35 H2
Fårösund, Sweden 11 G13
Farquhar, C., Australia 93 D1
Farrars Cr. →, Australia 94 D3
Farrāshband, Iran 71 D7
Farrell, U.S.A. 110 E4
Farrokhī, Iran 71 C8
Farruch, C. = Ferrutx, C.,
  Spain 37 B10
Farrukhabad-cum-Fatehgarh,
  India 66 F11
Fārs □, Iran 71 D7
Fársala, Greece 38 B4
Farsø, Denmark 11 H3
Farson, U.S.A. 114 E9
Farsund, Norway 9 G12
Fartak, Râs, Si. Arabia 70 D2
Fartak, Ra's, Yemen ... 74 D5

Fârţăneşti, Romania 43 E12
Fartura, Serra da, Brazil 127 B5
Faru, Nigeria 83 C6
Fārūj, Iran 71 B8
Fårup, Denmark 11 H3
Farvel, Kap = Nunap Isua,
  Greenland 4 D5
Farwell, U.S.A. 113 H3
Fasā, Iran 71 D7
Fasano, Italy 31 B10
Fashoda, Sudan 81 F3
Fassa, Mali 82 C3
Fastiv, Ukraine 47 G5
Fastov = Fastiv, Ukraine 47 G5
Fatagar, Tanjung, Indonesia 63 E8
Fatehabad, Haryana, India 68 E6
Fatehabad, Ut. P., India 68 F8
Fatehgarh, India 69 F8
Fatehpur, Bihar, India . 69 G11
Fatehpur, Raj., India .. 68 F6
Fatehpur, Ut. P., India 69 G9
Fatehpur, Ut. P., India 69 F9
Fatehpur Sikri, India .. 68 F6
Fatesh, Russia 47 F8
Fathai, Sudan 81 F3
Fatick, Senegal 82 C1
Fatima, Canada 103 C7
Fátima, Portugal 35 F2
Fatoya, Guinea 82 C3
Fatsa, Turkey 72 B7
Faucille, Col de la, France 19 F13
Faulkton, U.S.A. 112 C5
Faulquemont, France ... 19 C13
Faure I., Australia 93 E1
Fauresmith, S. Africa .. 88 D4
Fauske, Norway 8 C16
Favara, Italy 30 E6
Favárito, C. de, Spain . 37 B11
Faverges, France 21 C10
Favignana, Italy 30 E5
Favignana, I., Italy ... 30 E5
Fawcett, Pt., Australia 92 B5
Fawn →, Canada 102 A2
Fawnskin, U.S.A. 117 L10
Faxaflói, Iceland 8 D2
Faxälven →, Sweden ... 10 A10
Faya-Largeau, Chad 79 E9
Fayd, Si. Arabia 70 E4
Fayence, France 21 E10
Fayette, Ala., U.S.A. .. 109 J2
Fayette, Mo., U.S.A. .. 112 F8
Fayetteville, Ark., U.S.A. 113 G7
Fayetteville, N.C., U.S.A. 109 H6
Fayetteville, Tenn., U.S.A. 109 H2
Fayied, Egypt 80 H8
Fayón, Spain 32 D5
Fazilka, India 68 D6
Fazilpur, Pakistan 68 E4
Fdérik, Mauritania 78 D3
Feale →, Ireland 15 D2
Fear, C., U.S.A. 109 J7
Feather →, U.S.A. 114 G3
Feather Falls, U.S.A. .. 116 F5
Featherston, N.Z. 91 J5
Featherstone, Zimbabwe 87 F3
Fécamp, France 18 C7
Fedala = Mohammedia,
  Morocco 78 B4
Federación, Argentina .. 126 C4
Féderal, Argentina 128 C5
Federal Capital Terr. □,
  Nigeria 83 D6
Federal Way, U.S.A. ... 116 C4
Fedeshkūh, Iran 71 D7
Fehérgyarmat, Hungary .. 42 C7
Fehmarn, Germany 24 A7
Fehmarn Bælt, Europe .. 11 K5
Fehmarn Belt = Fehmarn
  Bælt, Europe 11 K5
Fei Xian, China 57 G9
Feijó, Brazil 124 E4
Feilding, N.Z. 91 J5
Feira de Santana, Brazil 125 F11
Feixi, China 59 B11
Feixiang, China 56 F8
Fejér □, Hungary 42 C3
Fejø, Denmark 11 K5
Feke, Turkey 72 D6
Fekete →, Hungary 42 E3
Felanitx, Spain 37 B10
Feldbach, Austria 26 E8
Feldberg, Baden-W.,
  Germany 25 H3
Feldberg,
  Mecklenburg-Vorpommern,
  Germany 24 B9
Feldkirch, Austria 26 D2
Feldkirchen, Austria .. 26 E7
Felipe Carrillo Puerto,
  Mexico 119 D7
Felixburg, Zimbabwe ... 89 B5
Felixstowe, U.K. 13 F9
Felletin, France 20 C6
Fellingsbro, Sweden ... 10 E9
Felton, U.S.A. 116 H4
Feltre, Italy 29 B8
Femer Bælt = Fehmarn
  Bælt, Europe 11 K5
Femø, Denmark 11 K5
Femunden, Norway 9 E14
Fen He →, China 56 G6
Fene, Spain 34 B2
Fenelon Falls, Canada .. 110 B6
Fener Burnu, Turkey ... 39 E9
Feneroa, Ethiopia 81 E4
Feng Xian, Jiangsu, China 56 G9
Feng Xian, Shaanxi, China 56 H4
Fengári, Greece 41 F9
Fengcheng, Jiangxi, China 59 C10
Fengcheng, Liaoning, China 57 D13

Fengfeng, China 56 F8
Fenggang, China 58 D6
Fenghua, China 59 C13
Fenghuang, China 58 D7
Fengkai, China 59 F8
Fengkang, Taiwan 59 F13
Fengle, China 59 B9
Fenglin, Taiwan 59 F13
Fengning, China 56 D9
Fengqing, China 58 E2
Fengqiu, China 56 G8
Fengrun, China 57 E10
Fengshan,
  Guangxi Zhuangzu, China 58 E7
Fengshan,
  Guangxi Zhuangzu, China 58 E6
Fengshan, Taiwan 59 F13
Fengshun, China 59 F11
Fengtai, Anhui, China . 59 A11
Fengtai, Beijing, China 56 E9
Fengxian, China 59 B13
Fengxiang, China 56 G4
Fengxin, China 59 C10
Fengyang, China 57 H9
Fengyi, China 58 E3
Fengyüan, Taiwan 59 E13
Fengzhen, China 56 D7
Feno, C. de, France ... 21 G12
Fenoarivo, Fianarantsoa,
  Madag. 89 C8
Fenoarivo, Fianarantsoa,
  Madag. 89 C8
Fenoarivo Afovoany, Madag. 89 B8
Fenoarivo Atsinanana,
  Madag. 89 B8
Fens, The, U.K. 12 E7
Fensmark, Denmark 11 J5
Fenton, U.S.A. 108 D4
Fenxi, China 56 F6
Fenyang, China 56 F6
Fenyi, China 59 D10
Feodosiya, Ukraine 47 K8
Ferdows, Iran 71 C8
Fère-Champenoise, France 19 D10
Fère-en-Tardenois, France 19 C10
Ferentino, Italy 29 G10
Ferfer, Somali Rep. ... 74 F4
Fergana = Farghona,
  Uzbekistan 50 E8
Fergus, Canada 110 C4
Fergus Falls, U.S.A. .. 112 B6
Feričanci, Croatia 42 E2
Ferkéssédougou, Ivory C. 82 D3
Ferlach, Austria 26 E7
Ferland, Canada 102 B2
Ferlo, Vallée du, Senegal 82 B2
Fermanagh □, U.K. 15 B4
Ferment, Canada 103 B6
Fermo, Italy 29 E10
Fermont, Canada 103 B6
Fermoselle, Spain 34 D4
Fermoy, Ireland 15 D3
Fernán Núñez, Spain ... 35 H6
Fernández, Argentina .. 126 B3
Fernandina Beach, U.S.A. 109 K5
Fernando de Noronha, Brazil 125 D12
Fernando Póo = Bioko,
  Eq. Guin. 83 E6
Ferndale, U.S.A. 116 B4
Fernie, Canada 104 D5
Fernlees, Australia ... 94 C4
Fernley, U.S.A. 114 G4
Ferozepore = Firozpur,
  India 68 D6
Férrai, Greece 41 F10
Ferrandina, Italy 31 B9
Ferrara, Italy 29 D8
Ferrato, C., Italy 30 C2
Ferreira do Alentejo,
  Portugal 35 G2
Ferreñafe, Peru 124 E3
Ferrerías, Spain 37 B11
Ferret, C., France 20 D2
Ferrette, France 19 E14
Ferriday, U.S.A. 113 K9
Ferriere, Italy 28 D6
Ferrières, France 19 D9
Ferro, Capo, Italy 30 A2
Ferrol, Spain 34 B2
Ferron, U.S.A. 115 G8
Ferrutx, C., Spain 37 B10
Ferryland, Canada 103 C9
Fertile, U.S.A. 112 B6
Fertőszentmiklós, Hungary 42 C1
Fès, Morocco 78 B5
Fessenden, U.S.A. 112 B5
Festus, U.S.A. 112 F9
Feté Bowé, Senegal 82 C2
Fetesti, Romania 43 F12
Fethiye, Turkey 39 E11
Fethiye Körfezi, Turkey 39 E10
Fetlar, U.K. 14 A8
Feuilles →, Canada ... 101 C12
Feurs, France 21 C8
Fez = Fès, Morocco 78 B5
Fezzan, Libya 79 C8
Fiambalá, Argentina ... 126 B2
Fianarantsoa, Madag. .. 89 C8
Fianarantsoa □, Madag. 89 B8
Fiche, Ethiopia 81 F4
Fichtelgebirge, Germany 25 E7
Ficksburg, S. Africa .. 89 D4
Fidenza, Italy 28 D7
Fiditi, Nigeria 83 D5
Field, Canada 102 C3
Field I., Australia ... 92 B5
Fier, Romania 43 E10
Fier, Albania 40 F3
Fierzë, Albania 40 D4
Fife □, U.K. 14 E5
Fife Ness, U.K. 14 E6
Fifth Cataract, Sudan . 80 D3

Figari, France 21 G13
Figeac, France 20 D6
Figeholm, Sweden 11 G10
Figline Valdarno, Italy 29 E8
Figtree, Zimbabwe 87 G2
Figueira Castelo Rodrigo,
  Portugal 34 E4
Figueira da Foz, Portugal 34 E2
Figueiró dos Vinhos,
  Portugal 34 F2
Figueres, Spain 32 C7
Figuig, Morocco 78 B5
Fihaonana, Madag. 89 B8
Fiherenana, Madag. 89 C8
Fiherenana →, Madag. . 89 C7
Fiji ■, Pac. Oc. 91 C8
Fik, Ethiopia 81 F5
Fika, Nigeria 83 C7
Filabres, Sierra de los, Spain 35 H8
Filabusi, Zimbabwe 89 C4
Filadélfia, Italy 31 D9
Fil'akovo, Slovak Rep. . 27 C12
Filey, U.K. 12 C7
Filey B., U.K. 12 C7
Filfla, Malta 36 D1
Filiaşi, Romania 43 F8
Filiátes, Greece 38 B2
Filiatrá, Greece 38 D3
Filicudi, Italy 31 D7
Filingué, Niger 83 C5
Filiouri →, Greece ... 41 E9
Filipstad, Sweden 10 E8
Filisur, Switz. 25 J5
Fillmore, Calif., U.S.A. 117 L8
Fillmore, Utah, U.S.A. 115 G7
Filótion, Greece 39 D7
Filottrano, Italy 29 E10
Filtu, Ethiopia 81 F5
Finale Emília, Italy .. 29 D8
Finale Lígure, Italy .. 28 D5
Fiñana, Spain 35 H8
Finch, Canada 111 A9
Findhorn →, U.K. 14 D5
Findlay, U.S.A. 108 E4
Finger L., Canada 102 B1
Finger Lakes, U.S.A. .. 111 D8
Fíngoè, Mozam. 87 E3
Finike, Turkey 39 E12
Finike Körfezi, Turkey 39 E12
Finiq, Albania 40 G4
Finistère □, France .. 18 D3
Finisterre, C. = Fisterra, C.,
  Spain 34 C1
Finke, Australia 94 D1
Finland ■, Europe 8 E22
Finland, G. of, Europe 9 G21
Finlay →, Canada 104 B3
Finley, Australia 95 F4
Finley, U.S.A. 112 B6
Finn →, Ireland 15 B4
Finnerödja, Sweden 11 F8
Finnigan, Mt., Australia 94 B4
Finniss, C., Australia 95 E1
Finnmark, Norway 8 B20
Finnsnes, Norway 8 B18
Finspång, Sweden 11 F9
Finsteraarhorn, Switz. 25 J4
Finsterwalde, Germany . 24 D9
Fiora →, Italy 29 F8
Fiorenzuola d'Arda, Italy 28 D6
Fīq, Syria 75 C4
Firat = Furāt, Nahr al →,
  Asia 70 D5
Firebag →, Canada 105 B6
Firebaugh, U.S.A. 116 J6
Firedrake L., Canada .. 105 A8
Firenze, Italy 29 E8
Firenzuola, Italy 29 D8
Firk →, Iraq 70 D5
Firmi, France 20 D6
Firminy, France 21 C8
Firozabad, India 69 F8
Firozpur, India 68 D6
Firozpur-Jhirka, India 68 F7
Fīrūzābād, Iran 71 D7
Fīrūzkūh, Iran 71 C7
Firvale, Canada 104 C3
Fish →, Namibia 88 D2
Fish →, S. Africa 88 E3
Fish River Canyon, Namibia 88 D2
Fisher, Australia 93 F5
Fisher, Canada 105 C9
Fishers I., U.S.A. 111 E13
Fishguard, U.K. 13 E3
Fishing L., Canada 105 C9
Fishkill, U.S.A. 111 E11
Fismes, France 19 C10
Fisterra, Spain 34 C1
Fisterra, C., Spain ... 34 C1
Fitchburg, U.S.A. 111 D13
Fitz Roy, Argentina ... 128 F3
Fitzgerald, Canada 104 B6
Fitzgerald, U.S.A. 109 K4
Fitzmaurice →, Australia 92 B5
Fitzroy →, Queens.,
  Australia 94 C5
Fitzroy →, W. Austral.,
  Australia 92 C3
Fitzroy, Mte., Argentina 128 F2
Fitzroy Crossing, Australia 92 C4
Fitzwilliam I., Canada 110 A3
Fiuggi, Italy 29 G10
Fiume = Rijeka, Croatia 29 C11
Five Points, U.S.A. ... 116 J6
Fivizzano, Italy 28 D7
Fizi, Dem. Rep. of the Congo 86 C2
Fjällbacka, Sweden 11 F5
Fjærland, Norway 10 E10
Fjellerup, Denmark 11 H4
Fjerritslev, Denmark .. 11 G3

Fritch

Fjugesta, *Sweden* 10 E8
Flagstaff, *U.S.A.* 115 J8
Flagstaff L., *U.S.A.* 109 C10
Flaherty I., *Canada* 102 A4
Flåm, *Norway* 9 F12
Flambeau →, *U.S.A.* 112 C9
Flamborough Hd., *U.K.* 12 C7
Fläming, *Germany* 24 C8
Flaming Gorge Reservoir, *U.S.A.* 114 F9
Flamingo, Teluk, *Indonesia* 63 F9
Flanders = Flandre, *Europe* 19 B9
Flandre, *Europe* 19 B9
Flandre Occidentale = West-Vlaanderen □, *Belgium* 17 D2
Flandre Orientale = Oost-Vlaanderen □, *Belgium* 17 C3
Flandreau, *U.S.A.* 112 C6
Flanigan, *U.S.A.* 116 E7
Flannan Is., *U.K.* 14 C1
Flåsjön, *Sweden* 8 D16
Flat →, *Canada* 104 A3
Flathead L., *U.S.A.* 114 C7
Flattery, C., *Australia* 94 A4
Flattery, C., *U.S.A.* 116 B2
Flatwoods, *U.S.A.* 108 F4
Fleetwood, *U.K.* 12 D4
Fleetwood, *U.S.A.* 111 F9
Flekkefjord, *Norway* 9 G12
Flemington, *U.S.A.* 110 E7
Flen, *Sweden* 10 E10
Flensburg, *Germany* 24 A5
Flers, *France* 18 D6
Flesherton, *Canada* 110 B4
Flesko, Tanjung, *Indonesia* 63 D6
Fleurance, *France* 20 E4
Fleurier, *Switz.* 25 J2
Fleurieu Pen., *Australia* 95 F2
Flevoland □, *Neths.* 17 B5
Flin Flon, *Canada* 105 C8
Flinders →, *Australia* 94 B3
Flinders B., *Australia* 93 F2
Flinders Group, *Australia* 94 A3
Flinders I., *S. Austral., Australia* 95 E1
Flinders I., *Tas., Australia* 94 G4
Flinders Ranges, *Australia* 95 E2
Flinders Reefs, *Australia* 94 B4
Flint, *U.K.* 12 D4
Flint, *U.S.A.* 108 D4
Flint →, *U.S.A.* 109 K3
Flint I., *Kiribati* 97 J12
Flintshire □, *U.K.* 12 D4
Fliseryd, *Sweden* 11 G10
Flix, *Spain* 32 D5
Flixecourt, *France* 19 B9
Floby, *Sweden* 11 F7
Floda, *Sweden* 11 G6
Flodden, *U.K.* 12 B5
Flogny-la-Chapelle, *France* 19 E10
Floodwood, *U.S.A.* 112 B8
Flora, *U.S.A.* 108 F1
Florac, *France* 20 D7
Florala, *U.S.A.* 109 K2
Florence = Firenze, *Italy* 29 E8
Florence, *Ala., U.S.A.* 109 H2
Florence, *Ariz., U.S.A.* 115 K8
Florence, *Colo., U.S.A.* 112 F2
Florence, *Oreg., U.S.A.* 114 E1
Florence, *S.C., U.S.A.* 109 H6
Florence, L., *Australia* 95 D2
Florencia, *Colombia* 124
Florennes, *Belgium* 17 D4
Florensac, *France* 20 E7
Florenville, *Belgium* 17 E5
Flores, *Guatemala* 120 C2
Flores, *Indonesia* 63 F6
Flores I., *Canada* 104 D3
Flores Sea, *Indonesia* 63 F6
Florești, *Moldova* 43 C13
Floresville, *U.S.A.* 113 L5
Floriano, *Brazil* 125 E10
Florianópolis, *Brazil* 127 B6
Florida, *Cuba* 120 B4
Florida, *Uruguay* 127 C4
Florida □, *U.S.A.* 109 L5
Florida, Straits of, *U.S.A.* 120 B4
Florida B., *U.S.A.* 120 B3
Florida Keys, *U.S.A.* 109 N5
Florídia, *Italy* 31 E8
Flórina, *Greece* 40 F5
Flórina □, *Greece* 40 F5
Florø, *Norway* 9 F11
Flower Station, *Canada* 111 A8
Flowerpot I., *Canada* 110 A3
Floydada, *U.S.A.* 113 J4
Fluk, *Indonesia* 63 E7
Flúmen →, *Spain* 32 D4
Flumendosa →, *Italy* 30 C2
Fluminimaggiore, *Italy* 30 C1
Flushing = Vlissingen, *Neths.* 17 C3
Fluviá →, *Spain* 32 C8
Flying Fish, C., *Antarctica* 5 D15
Foam Lake, *Canada* 105 C8
Foča, *Bos.-H.* 40 C2
Foça, *Turkey* 39 C8
Focșani, *Romania* 43 E12
Fodécontéa, *Guinea* 82 C2
Fogang, *China* 59 F9
Fóggia, *Italy* 31 A8
Foggo, *Nigeria* 83 C6
Foglia →, *Italy* 29 E9
Fogo, *Canada* 103 C9
Fogo I., *Canada* 103 C9
Fohnsdorf, *Austria* 26 D7
Föhr, *Germany* 24 A4
Foia, *Portugal* 35 H2
Foix, *France* 20 E5
Fojnica, *Bos.-H.* 42 G2
Fokino, *Russia* 46 F8
Fokís □, *Greece* 38 C4
Fokku, *Nigeria* 83 C5
Folda, *Nord-Trøndelag, Norway* 8 D14
Folda, *Nordland, Norway* 8 C16
Főldeák, *Hungary* 42 D5
Folégandros, *Greece* 38 E6
Foley, *Botswana* 88 C4
Foley, *U.S.A.* 109 K2
Foleyet, *Canada* 102 C3
Folgefonni, *Norway* 9 F12
Foligno, *Italy* 29 F9
Folkestone, *U.K.* 13 F9
Folkston, *U.S.A.* 109 K5
Follansbee, *U.S.A.* 110 F4
Follónica, *Italy* 28 F7
Follónica, G. di, *Italy* 28 F7
Folsom L., *U.S.A.* 116 G5
Foltești, *Romania* 43 E13
Fond-du-Lac, *Canada* 105 B7
Fond du Lac, *U.S.A.* 112 D10
Fond-du-Lac →, *Canada* 105 B7
Fonda, *U.S.A.* 111 D10
Fondi, *Italy* 30 A6
Fonfría, *Spain* 34 D4
Fongafale, *Tuvalu* 96 H9
Fonni, *Italy* 30 B2
Fonsagrada = A Fonsagrada, *Spain* 34 B3
Fonseca, G. de, *Cent. Amer.* 120 D2
Font-Romeu, *France* 20 F5
Fontaine-Française, *France* 19 E12
Fontainebleau, *France* 19 D9
Fontana, *U.S.A.* 117 L9
Fontas →, *Canada* 104 B4
Fonte Boa, *Brazil* 124 D5
Fontem, *Cameroon* 83 D6
Fontenay-le-Comte, *France* 20 B3
Fontenelle Reservoir, *U.S.A.* 114 E8
Fontur, *Iceland* 8 C6
Fonyód, *Hungary* 42 D2
Foochow = Fuzhou, *China* 59 D12
Foping, *China* 56 H5
Forbach, *France* 19 C13
Forbes, *Australia* 95 E4
Forbesganj, *India* 69 F12
Forcados, *Nigeria* 83 D6
Forcados →, *Nigeria* 83 D6
Forcalquier, *France* 21 E9
Forchheim, *Germany* 25 F7
Ford City, *Calif., U.S.A.* 117 K7
Ford City, *Pa., U.S.A.* 110 F5
Førde, *Norway* 9 F11
Ford's Bridge, *Australia* 95 D4
Fordyce, *U.S.A.* 113 J8
Forécariah, *Guinea* 82 D2
Forel, Mt., *Greenland* 4 C6
Foremost, *Canada* 104 D6
Forest, *Canada* 110 C3
Forest, *U.S.A.* 113 J10
Forest City, *Iowa, U.S.A.* 112 D8
Forest City, *N.C., U.S.A.* 109 H5
Forest City, *Pa., U.S.A.* 111 E9
Forest Grove, *U.S.A.* 116 E3
Forestburg, *Canada* 104 C6
Foresthill, *U.S.A.* 116 F6
Forestier Pen., *Australia* 94 G4
Forestville, *Canada* 103 C6
Forestville, *Calif., U.S.A.* 116 G4
Forestville, *N.Y., U.S.A.* 110 D5
Forez, Mts. du, *France* 20 C7
Forfar, *U.K.* 14 E6
Forks, *U.S.A.* 116 C2
Forksville, *U.S.A.* 111 E8
Forlì, *Italy* 29 D9
Forman, *U.S.A.* 112 B6
Formazza, *Italy* 28 B5
Formby Pt., *U.K.* 12 D4
Formentera, *Spain* 37 C7
Formentor, C. de, *Spain* 37 B10
Former Yugoslav Republic of Macedonia = Macedonia ■, *Europe* 40 E5
Fórmia, *Italy* 30 A6
Formígine, *Italy* 28 D7
Formosa = Taiwan ■, *Asia* 59 F13
Formosa, *Argentina* 126 B4
Formosa, *Brazil* 125 G9
Formosa □, *Argentina* 126 B4
Formosa, Serra, *Brazil* 125 F8
Formosa Bay, *Kenya* 86 C5
Formosa Strait = Taiwan Strait, *Asia* 59 E12
Fornells, *Spain* 37 A11
Fornos de Algodres, *Portugal* 34 E3
Fornovo di Taro, *Italy* 28 D7
Føroyar, *Atl. Oc.* 8 F9
Forres, *U.K.* 14 D5
Forrest, *Australia* 93 F4
Forrest, Mt., *Australia* 93 D4
Forrest City, *U.S.A.* 113 H9
Fors, *Sweden* 10 D10
Forsayth, *Australia* 94 B3
Forshaga, *Sweden* 10 E7
Förslöv, *Sweden* 11 H6
Forsmo, *Sweden* 10 A11
Forssa, *Finland* 9 F20
Forst, *Germany* 24 D10
Forsvik, *Sweden* 11 F8
Forsyth, *U.S.A.* 114 C10
Fort Abbas, *Pakistan* 68 E5
Fort Albany, *Canada* 102 B3
Fort Ann, *U.S.A.* 111 C11
Fort Assiniboine, *Canada* 104 C6
Fort Augustus, *U.K.* 14 D4
Fort Beaufort, *S. Africa* 88 E4
Fort Benton, *U.S.A.* 114 C8
Fort Bragg, *U.S.A.* 114 G2
Fort Bridger, *U.S.A.* 114 F8
Fort Chipewyan, *Canada* 105 B6
Fort Collins, *U.S.A.* 112 E2
Fort-Coulonge, *Canada* 102 C4
Fort Covington, *U.S.A.* 111 B10
Fort Davis, *U.S.A.* 113 K3
Fort-de-France, *Martinique* 121 D7
Fort Defiance, *U.S.A.* 115 J9
Fort Dodge, *U.S.A.* 112 D7
Fort Edward, *U.S.A.* 111 C11
Fort Erie, *Canada* 110 D6
Fort Fairfield, *U.S.A.* 109 B12
Fort Frances, *Canada* 105 D10
Fort Garland, *U.S.A.* 115 H11
Fort George = Chisasibi, *Canada* 102 B4
Fort Good-Hope, *Canada* 100 B7
Fort Hancock, *U.S.A.* 115 L11
Fort Hertz = Putao, *Burma* 67 F20
Fort Hope, *Canada* 102 B2
Fort Irwin, *U.S.A.* 117 K10
Fort Jameson = Chipata, *Zambia* 87 E3
Fort Kent, *U.S.A.* 109 B11
Fort Klamath, *U.S.A.* 114 E3
Fort-Lamy = Ndjamena, *Chad* 79 F8
Fort Laramie, *U.S.A.* 112 D2
Fort Lauderdale, *U.S.A.* 109 M5
Fort Liard, *Canada* 104 A4
Fort Liberté, *Haiti* 121 C5
Fort Lupton, *U.S.A.* 112 E2
Fort Mackay, *Canada* 104 B6
Fort Macleod, *Canada* 104 D6
Fort McMurray, *Canada* 104 B6
Fort McPherson, *Canada* 100 B6
Fort Madison, *U.S.A.* 112 E9
Fort Meade, *U.S.A.* 109 M5
Fort Morgan, *U.S.A.* 112 E3
Fort Munro, *Pakistan* 68 E3
Fort Myers, *U.S.A.* 109 M5
Fort Nelson, *Canada* 104 B4
Fort Nelson →, *Canada* 104 B4
Fort Norman = Tulita, *Canada* 100 B7
Fort Payne, *U.S.A.* 109 H3
Fort Peck, *U.S.A.* 114 B10
Fort Peck Dam, *U.S.A.* 114 C10
Fort Peck L., *U.S.A.* 114 C10
Fort Pierce, *U.S.A.* 109 M5
Fort Pierre, *U.S.A.* 112 C4
Fort Plain, *U.S.A.* 111 D10
Fort Portal, *Uganda* 86 B3
Fort Providence, *Canada* 104 A5
Fort Qu'Appelle, *Canada* 105 C8
Fort Resolution, *Canada* 104 A6
Fort Rixon, *Zimbabwe* 87 G2
Fort Rosebery = Mansa, *Zambia* 87 E2
Fort Ross, *U.S.A.* 116 G3
Fort Rupert = Waskaganish, *Canada* 102 B4
Fort St. James, *Canada* 104 C4
Fort St. John, *Canada* 104 B4
Fort Sandeman = Zhob, *Pakistan* 68 D3
Fort Saskatchewan, *Canada* 104 C6
Fort Scott, *U.S.A.* 113 G7
Fort Severn, *Canada* 102 A2
Fort Shevchenko, *Kazakstan* 49 H10
Fort Simpson, *Canada* 104 A4
Fort Smith, *Canada* 104 B6
Fort Smith, *U.S.A.* 113 H7
Fort Stockton, *U.S.A.* 113 K3
Fort Sumner, *U.S.A.* 113 H2
Fort Thompson, *U.S.A.* 112 C5
Fort Trinquet = Bir Mogreïn, *Mauritania* 78 C3
Fort Valley, *U.S.A.* 109 J4
Fort Vermilion, *Canada* 104 B5
Fort Walton Beach, *U.S.A.* 109 K2
Fort Wayne, *U.S.A.* 108 E3
Fort William, *U.K.* 14 E3
Fort Worth, *U.S.A.* 113 J6
Fort Yates, *U.S.A.* 112 B4
Fort Yukon, *U.S.A.* 100 B5
Fortaleza, *Brazil* 125 D11
Forteau, *Canada* 103 B8
Fortescue →, *Australia* 92 D2
Forth →, *U.K.* 14 E5
Forth, Firth of, *U.K.* 14 E6
Fortore →, *Italy* 29 G12
Fortrose, *U.K.* 14 D4
Fortuna, *Spain* 33 G3
Fortuna, *Calif., U.S.A.* 114 F1
Fortuna, *N. Dak., U.S.A.* 112 A3
Fortune, *Canada* 103 C8
Fortune B., *Canada* 103 C8
Forūr, *Iran* 71 E7
Fos-sur-Mer, *France* 21 E8
Foshan, *China* 59 F9
Fosna, *Norway* 8 E14
Fosnavåg, *Norway* 9 E11
Foso, *Ghana* 83 D4
Fossano, *Italy* 28 D4
Fossil, *U.S.A.* 114 D3
Fossombrone, *Italy* 29 E9
Foster, *Australia* 95 F4
Foster, *Canada* 111 A12
Foster →, *Canada* 105 B7
Fosters Ra., *Australia* 94 C1
Fostoria, *U.S.A.* 108 E4
Fotadrevo, *Madag.* 89 C8
Fouesnant, *France* 18 E2
Fougères, *France* 18 D5
Foul Pt., *Sri Lanka* 66 Q12
Foula, *U.K.* 14 A6
Foulalaba, *Mali* 82 C3
Foulness I., *U.K.* 13 F8
Foulpointe, *Madag.* 89 B8
Foulweather, C., *U.S.A.* 106 B2
Foumban, *Cameroon* 83 D7
Foumbot, *Cameroon* 83 D7
Foundiougne, *Senegal* 82 C1
Fountain, *U.S.A.* 112 F2
Fountain Springs, *U.S.A.* 117 K8
Fourchambault, *France* 19 E10
Fouriesburg, *S. Africa* 88 D4
Fourmies, *France* 19 B11
Fournás, *Greece* 38 B3
Foúrnoi, *Greece* 39 D8
Fours, *France* 19 F10
Fourth Cataract, *Sudan* 80 D3
Fouta Djalon, *Guinea* 82 C2
Foux, Cap-à-, *Haiti* 121 C5
Foveaux Str., *N.Z.* 91 M2
Fowey, *U.K.* 13 G3
Fowler, *Calif., U.S.A.* 116 J7
Fowler, *Colo., U.S.A.* 112 F3
Fowlers B., *Australia* 93 F5
Fowman, *Iran* 71 B6
Fox →, *Canada* 105 B10
Fox Creek, *Canada* 104 C5
Fox Lake, *Canada* 104 B6
Fox Valley, *Canada* 105 C7
Foxboro, *U.S.A.* 111 D13
Foxe Basin, *Canada* 101 B12
Foxe Chan., *Canada* 101 B11
Foxe Pen., *Canada* 101 B12
Foxen, *Sweden* 10 E5
Foxton, *N.Z.* 91 J5
Foyle, Lough, *U.K.* 15 A4
Foynes, *Ireland* 15 D2
Foz, *Spain* 34 B3
Fóz do Cunene, *Angola* 88 B1
Foz do Iguaçu, *Brazil* 127 B5
Frackville, *U.S.A.* 111 F8
Fraga, *Spain* 32 D5
Fraile Muerto, *Uruguay* 127 C5
Framingham, *U.S.A.* 111 D13
Frampol, *Poland* 45 H9
Franca, *Brazil* 125 H9
Francavilla al Mare, *Italy* 29 F11
Francavilla Fontana, *Italy* 31 B10
France ■, *Europe* 7 F6
Frances, *Australia* 95 F3
Frances →, *Canada* 104 A3
Frances L., *Canada* 104 A3
Franceville, *Gabon* 84 E2
Franche-Comté, *France* 19 F12
Francis Case, L., *U.S.A.* 112 D5
Francisco Beltrão, *Brazil* 127 B5
Francisco I. Madero, *Coahuila, Mexico* 118 B4
Francisco I. Madero, *Durango, Mexico* 118 C4
Francistown, *Botswana* 89 C4
Francofonte, *Italy* 31 E7
François, *Canada* 103 C8
François L., *Canada* 104 C3
Franeker, *Neths.* 17 A5
Frankado, *Djibouti* 81 E5
Frankenberg, *Germany* 24 D4
Frankenwald, *Germany* 25 E7
Frankford, *Canada* 110 B7
Frankfort, *S. Africa* 89 D4
Frankfort, *Ind., U.S.A.* 108 E2
Frankfort, *Kans., U.S.A.* 112 F6
Frankfort, *Ky., U.S.A.* 108 F3
Frankfort, *N.Y., U.S.A.* 111 C9
Frankfurt, *Brandenburg, Germany* 24 C10
Frankfurt, *Hessen, Germany* 25 E4
Fränkische Alb, *Germany* 25 F7
Fränkische Rezat →, *Germany* 25 F7
Fränkische Saale →, *Germany* 25 E5
Fränkische Schweiz, *Germany* 25 F7
Frankland →, *Australia* 93 G2
Franklin, *Ky., U.S.A.* 109 G2
Franklin, *La., U.S.A.* 113 L9
Franklin, *Mass., U.S.A.* 111 D13
Franklin, *N.H., U.S.A.* 111 C13
Franklin, *Nebr., U.S.A.* 112 E5
Franklin, *Pa., U.S.A.* 110 E5
Franklin, *Va., U.S.A.* 109 G7
Franklin, *W. Va., U.S.A.* 108 F6
Franklin B., *Canada* 100 B7
Franklin D. Roosevelt L., *U.S.A.* 114 B4
Franklin I., *Antarctica* 5 D11
Franklin L., *U.S.A.* 114 F6
Franklin Mts., *Canada* 100 B7
Franklin Str., *Canada* 100 A10
Franklinton, *U.S.A.* 113 K9
Franklinville, *U.S.A.* 110 D6
Franks Pk., *U.S.A.* 114 E9
Frankston, *Australia* 95 F4
Frånö, *Sweden* 10 B11
Fransfontein, *Namibia* 88 C2
Fränsta, *Sweden* 10 B10
Frantsa Iosifa, Zemlya, *Russia* 50 A6
Franz, *Canada* 102 C3
Franz Josef Land = Frantsa Iosifa, Zemlya, *Russia* 50 A6
Franzburg, *Germany* 24 A8
Frascati, *Italy* 29 G9
Fraser, *U.S.A.* 110 D2
Fraser →, *B.C., Canada* 104 D4
Fraser →, *Nfld., Canada* 103 A7
Fraser, Mt., *Australia* 93 E2
Fraser I., *Australia* 95 D5
Fraser Lake, *Canada* 104 C4
Fraserburg, *S. Africa* 88 E3
Fraserburgh, *U.K.* 14 D6
Fraserdale, *Canada* 102 C3
Frashëri, *Albania* 40 F4
Frasne, *France* 19 F13
Frătești, *Romania* 43 G10
Frauenfeld, *Switz.* 25 H4
Fray Bentos, *Uruguay* 126 C4
Frechilla, *Spain* 34 C6
Fredericia, *Denmark* 11 J3
Frederick, *Md., U.S.A.* 108 F7
Frederick, *Okla., U.S.A.* 113 H5
Frederick, *S. Dak., U.S.A.* 112 C5
Fredericksburg, *Pa., U.S.A.* 111 F8
Fredericksburg, *Tex., U.S.A.* 113 K5
Fredericksburg, *Va., U.S.A.* 108 F7
Fredericktown, *Mo., U.S.A.* 113 G9
Fredericktown, *Ohio, U.S.A.* 110 F2
Frederico I. Madero, Presa, *Mexico* 118 B3
Frederico Westphalen, *Brazil* 127 B5
Fredericton, *Canada* 103 C6
Fredericton Junction, *Canada* 103 C6
Frederiksborg Amtskommune □, *Denmark* 11 J6
Frederikshåb = Paamiut, *Greenland* 4 C5
Frederikshavn, *Denmark* 11 G4
Frederikssund, *Denmark* 11 J6
Frederiksted, *Virgin Is.* 121 C7
Frederiksværk, *Denmark* 11 J6
Fredonia, *Ariz., U.S.A.* 115 H7
Fredonia, *Kans., U.S.A.* 113 G7
Fredonia, *N.Y., U.S.A.* 110 D5
Fredriksberg, *Sweden* 10 D8
Fredrikstad, *Norway* 9 G14
Free State □, *S. Africa* 88 D4
Freehold, *U.S.A.* 111 F10
Freel Peak, *U.S.A.* 116 G7
Freeland, *U.S.A.* 111 E9
Freels, C., *Canada* 103 C9
Freeman, *Calif., U.S.A.* 117 K9
Freeman, *S. Dak., U.S.A.* 112 D6
Freeport, *Bahamas* 120 A4
Freeport, *Ill., U.S.A.* 112 D10
Freeport, *N.Y., U.S.A.* 111 F11
Freeport, *Ohio, U.S.A.* 110 F3
Freeport, *Pa., U.S.A.* 110 F5
Freeport, *Tex., U.S.A.* 113 L7
Freetown, *S. Leone* 82 D2
Frégate, L., *Canada* 102 B5
Fregenal de la Sierra, *Spain* 35 G4
Fregene, *Italy* 29 G9
Fréhel, C., *France* 18 D4
Freiberg, *Germany* 24 E9
Freibourg = Fribourg, *Switz.* 25 J3
Freiburg, *Baden-W., Germany* 25 H3
Freiburg, *Niedersachsen, Germany* 24 B5
Freilassing, *Germany* 25 H8
Freire, *Chile* 128 D2
Freirina, *Chile* 126 B1
Freising, *Germany* 25 G7
Freistadt, *Austria* 26 C7
Freital, *Germany* 24 D9
Fréjus, *France* 21 E10
Fremantle, *Australia* 93 F2
Fremont, *Calif., U.S.A.* 116 H4
Fremont, *Mich., U.S.A.* 108 D3
Fremont, *Nebr., U.S.A.* 112 E6
Fremont, *Ohio, U.S.A.* 108 E4
Fremont →, *U.S.A.* 115 G8
French Camp, *U.S.A.* 116 H5
French Creek →, *U.S.A.* 110 E5
French Guiana ■, *S. Amer.* 125 C8
French Pass, *N.Z.* 91 J4
French Polynesia ■, *Pac. Oc.* 97 K13
Frenchman Cr. →, *N. Amer.* 114 B10
Frenchman Cr. →, *U.S.A.* 112 E4
Frenštát pod Radhoštěm, *Czech Rep.* 27 B11
Fresco, *Ivory C.* 82 D3
Fresco →, *Brazil* 125 E8
Freshfield, C., *Antarctica* 5 C10
Fresnay-sur-Sarthe, *France* 18 D7
Fresnillo, *Mexico* 118 C4
Fresno, *U.S.A.* 116 J7
Fresno Alhandiga, *Spain* 34 E5
Fresno Reservoir, *U.S.A.* 114 B9
Freudenstadt, *Germany* 25 G4
Frévent, *France* 19 B9
Frew →, *Australia* 94 C2
Frewsburg, *U.S.A.* 110 D5
Freycinet Pen., *Australia* 94 G4
Freyming-Merlebach, *France* 19 C13
Freyung, *Germany* 25 G9
Fria, *Guinea* 82 C2
Fria, C., *Namibia* 88 B1
Friant, *U.S.A.* 116 J7
Frías, *Argentina* 126 B2
Fribourg, *Switz.* 25 J3
Fribourg □, *Switz.* 25 J3
Fridafors, *Sweden* 11 H8
Friday Harbor, *U.S.A.* 116 B3
Friedberg, *Bayern, Germany* 25 G6
Friedberg, *Hessen, Germany* 25 E4
Friedens, *U.S.A.* 110 F6
Friedland, *Germany* 24 B9
Friedrichshafen, *Germany* 25 H5
Friedrichskoog, *Germany* 24 A4
Friedrichstadt, *Germany* 24 A5
Friendly Is. = Tonga ■, *Pac. Oc.* 91 D11
Friendship, *U.S.A.* 110 D6
Friesach, *Austria* 26 E7
Friesack, *Germany* 24 C8
Friesland □, *Neths.* 17 A5
Friesoythe, *Germany* 24 B3
Friggesund, *Sweden* 10 C10
Frillesås, *Sweden* 11 G6
Frinnaryd, *Sweden* 11 G8
Frio →, *U.S.A.* 113 L5
Frio, C., *Brazil* 122 F6
Friol, *Spain* 34 B3
Friona, *U.S.A.* 113 H3
Fristad, *Sweden* 11 G6
Fritch, *U.S.A.* 113 H4

Fritsla, *Sweden* 11 G6
Fritzlar, *Germany* 24 D5
Friuli-Venézia Giulia □, *Italy* 29 B9
Frobisher B., *Canada* 101 B13
Frobisher Bay = Iqaluit,
  Canada 101 B13
Frobisher L., *Canada* 105 B7
Frohavet, *Norway* 8 E13
Frohnleiten, *Austria* 26 D8
Frolovo, *Russia* 48 F6
Frombork, *Poland* 44 D6
Frome, *U.K.* 13 F5
Frome →, *U.K.* 13 G5
Frome, L., *Australia* 95 E2
Frómista, *Spain* 34 C6
Front Range, *U.S.A.* 106 C5
Front Royal, *U.S.A.* 108 F6
Fronteira, *Portugal* 35 F3
Frontera, *Canary Is.* 37 G2
Frontera, *Mexico* 119 D6
Fronteras, *Mexico* 118 A3
Frontignan, *France* 20 E7
Frosinone, *Italy* 30 A6
Frostburg, *U.S.A.* 108 F6
Frostisen, *Norway* 8 B17
Frouard, *France* 19 D13
Frövi, *Sweden* 10 E9
Frøya, *Norway* 8 E13
Frumoasa, *Romania* 43 D10
Frunze = Bishkek,
  Kyrgyzstan 50 E8
Fruška Gora, *Serbia, Yug.* 42 E4
Frutal, *Brazil* 125 H9
Frutigen, *Switz.* 25 J3
Frýdek-Místek, *Czech Rep.* 27 B11
Frýdlant, *Czech Rep.* 26 A8
Fryeburg, *U.S.A.* 111 B14
Fryvaldov = Jeseník,
  Czech Rep. 27 A10
Fthiótis □, *Greece* 38 C4
Fu Jiang →, *China* 58 C6
Fu Xian = Wafangdian,
  China 57 E11
Fu Xian, *China* 56 G5
Fu'an, *China* 59 D12
Fubian, *China* 58 B4
Fucécchio, *Italy* 28 E7
Fucheng, *China* 56 F9
Fuchou = Fuzhou, *China* 59 D12
Fuchū, *Japan* 55 G6
Fuchuan, *China* 59 E8
Fuchun Jiang →, *China* 59 B13
Fúcino, Piana del, *Italy* 29 F10
Fuding, *China* 59 D13
Fuencaliente, *Canary Is.* 37 F2
Fuengirola, *Spain* 35 J7
Fuenlabrada, *Spain* 34 E7
Fuensalida, *Spain* 34 E6
Fuente-Álamo, *Spain* 33 G3
Fuente-Álamo de Murcia,
  Spain 33 H3
Fuente de Cantos, *Spain* 35 G4
Fuente del Maestre, *Spain* 35 G4
Fuente el Fresno, *Spain* 35 F7
Fuente Obejuna, *Spain* 35 G5
Fuente Palmera, *Spain* 35 H5
Fuentes de Andalucía, *Spain* 35 H5
Fuentes de Ebro, *Spain* 32 D4
Fuentes de León, *Spain* 35 G4
Fuentes de Oñoro, *Spain* 34 E4
Fuentesaúco, *Spain* 34 D5
Fuerte →, *Mexico* 118 B3
Fuerte Olimpo, *Paraguay* 126 A4
Fuerteventura, *Canary Is.* 37 F6
Fufeng, *China* 56 G5
Fuga I., *Phil.* 61 B4
Fugong, *China* 58 D2
Fugou, *China* 56 G8
Fugu, *China* 56 E6
Fuhai, *China* 60 B3
Fuḥaymī, *Iraq* 70 C4
Fuji, *Japan* 55 G9
Fuji-San, *Japan* 55 G9
Fuji-yoshida, *Japan* 55 G9
Fujian □, *China* 59 E12
Fujinomiya, *Japan* 55 G9
Fujisawa, *Japan* 55 G9
Fujiyama, Mt. = Fuji-San,
  Japan 55 G9
Fukien = Fujian □, *China* 59 E12
Fukuchiyama, *Japan* 55 G7
Fukue-Shima, *Japan* 55 H4
Fukui, *Japan* 55 F8
Fukui □, *Japan* 55 G8
Fukuoka, *Japan* 55 H5
Fukuoka □, *Japan* 55 H5
Fukushima, *Japan* 54 F10
Fukushima □, *Japan* 54 F10
Fukuyama, *Japan* 55 G6
Fulacunda, *Guinea-Biss.* 82 C1
Fulda, *Germany* 24 E5
Fulda →, *Germany* 24 D5
Fulford Harbour, *Canada* 116 B3
Fuliang, *China* 59 C11
Fullerton, *Calif., U.S.A.* 117 M9
Fullerton, *Nebr., U.S.A.* 112 E6
Fulongquan, *China* 57 B13
Fülöpszállás, *Hungary* 42 D4
Fulton, *Mo., U.S.A.* 112 F9
Fulton, *N.Y., U.S.A.* 111 C8
Fuluálven →, *Sweden* 10 C7
Fulufjället, *Sweden* 10 C6
Fumay, *France* 19 C11
Fumel, *France* 20 D4
Fumin, *China* 58 E4
Funabashi, *Japan* 55 G10
Funäsdalen, *Sweden* 10 B6
Funchal, *Madeira* 37 D3

Fundación, *Colombia* 124 A4
Fundão, *Portugal* 34 E3
Fundu Moldovei, *Romania* 43 C10
Fundulea, *Romania* 43 F11
Fundy, B. of, *Canada* 103 D6
Funhalouro, *Mozam.* 89 C5
Funing, *Hebei, China* 57 E10
Funing, *Jiangsu, China* 57 H10
Funing, *Yunnan, China* 58 F5
Funiu Shan, *China* 56 H7
Funsi, *Ghana* 82 C4
Funtua, *Nigeria* 83 C6
Fuping, *Hebei, China* 56 E8
Fuping, *Shaanxi, China* 56 G5
Fuqing, *China* 59 E12
Fuquan, *China* 58 D6
Furano, *Japan* 54 C11
Furāt, Nahr al →, *Asia* 70 D5
Fûrg, *Iran* 71 D7
Furmanov, *Russia* 48 B5
Furmanovo, *Kazakstan* ... 48 F9
Furnás, *Spain* 37 B8
Furnas, Reprêsa de, *Brazil* 127 A6
Furneaux Group, *Australia* 94 G4
Furqlus, *Syria* 75 A6
Fürstenau, *Germany* 24 C3
Fürstenberg, *Germany* 24 B9
Fürstenfeld, *Austria* 26 D9
Fürstenfeldbruck, *Germany* 25 G7
Fürstenwalde, *Germany* 24 C10
Fürth, *Germany* 25 F6
Furth im Wald, *Germany* 25 F8
Furtwangen, *Germany* 25 G4
Furudal, *Sweden* 10 C9
Furukawa, *Japan* 54 E10
Furulund, *Sweden* 11 J7
Fury and Hecla Str., *Canada* 101 B11
Fusagasuga, *Colombia* 124 C4
Fuscaldo, *Italy* 31 C9
Fushan, *Shandong, China* 57 F11
Fushan, *Shanxi, China* 56 G6
Fushë Arrëzi, *Albania* 40 D4
Fushë-Krujë, *Albania* 40 E3
Fushun, *Liaoning, China* 57 D12
Fushun, *Sichuan, China* 58 C5
Fusong, *China* 57 C14
Füssen, *Germany* 25 H6
Fusui, *China* 58 F6
Futog, *Yugoslavia* 42 E4
Fuxian Hu, *China* 58 E4
Fuxin, *China* 57 C11
Fuyang, *Anhui, China* 56 H8
Fuyang, *Zhejiang, China* 59 B12
Fuyang He →, *China* 56 E9
Fuying Dao, *China* 59 D13
Fuyu, *China* 57 B13
Fuyuan, *China* 58 E5
Füzesgyarmat, *Hungary* 42 C6
Fuzhou, *China* 59 D12
Fylde, *U.K.* 12 D5
Fyn, *Denmark* 11 J4
Fyne, L., *U.K.* 14 F3
Fyns Amtskommune □,
  Denmark 11 J4
Fynshav, *Denmark* 11 K3

G

Ga, *Ghana* 82 D4
Gaanda, *Nigeria* 83 C7
Gabarin, *Nigeria* 83 C7
Gabas →, *France* 20 E3
Gabela, *Angola* 84 G2
Gabès, *Tunisia* 79 B8
Gabès, G. de, *Tunisia* 79 B8
Gabgaba, W. →, *Egypt* 80 C3
Gąbin, *Poland* 45 F6
Gabon ■, *Africa* 84 E2
Gaborone, *Botswana* 88 C4
Gabriels, *U.S.A.* 111 B10
Gábrík, *Iran* 71 E8
Gabrovo, *Bulgaria* 41 D9
Gacé, *France* 18 D7
Gäch Sär, *Iran* 71 B6
Gachsärän, *Iran* 71 D6
Gacko, *Bos.-H.* 40 C2
Gadag, *India* 66 M9
Gadamai, *Sudan* 81 D4
Gadap, *Pakistan* 68 G2
Gadarwara, *India* 69 H8
Gadein, *Sudan* 81 F2
Gadhada, *India* 68 J4
Gádor, Sierra de, *Spain* 35 J8
Gadra, *Pakistan* 68 G4
Gadsden, *U.S.A.* 109 H3
Gadwal, *India* 66 L10
Gadyach = Hadyach,
  Ukraine 47 G8
Găeşti, *Romania* 43 F10
Gaeta, *Italy* 30 A6
Gaeta, G. di, *Italy* 30 A6
Gaffney, *U.S.A.* 109 H5
Gafsa, *Tunisia* 78 B7
Gagarawa, *Nigeria* 83 C6
Gagaria, *India* 68 G4
Gagarin, *Russia* 46 E8
Gaggenau, *Germany* 25 G4
Gaghamni, *Sudan* 81 E2
Gagino, *Russia* 48 C7
Gagliano del Capo, *Italy* 31 C11
Gagnef, *Sweden* 10 D9
Gagnoa, *Ivory C.* 82 D3
Gagnon, *Canada* 103 B6
Gagnon, L., *Canada* 105 A6
Gagra, *Georgia* 49 J5

Gahini, *Rwanda* 86 C3
Gahmar, *India* 69 G10
Gai Xian = Gaizhou, *China* 57 D12
Gaïdhouronísi, *Greece* 36 E7
Gail, *U.S.A.* 113 J4
Gail →, *Austria* 26 E6
Gaillac, *France* 20 E5
Gaillimh = Galway, *Ireland* 15 C2
Gaillon, *France* 18 C8
Gaines, *U.S.A.* 110 E7
Gainesville, *Fla., U.S.A.* 109 L4
Gainesville, *Ga., U.S.A.* 109 H4
Gainesville, *Mo., U.S.A.* 113 G8
Gainesville, *Tex., U.S.A.* 113 J6
Gainsborough, *U.K.* 12 D7
Gairdner, L., *Australia* ... 95 E2
Gairloch, L., *U.K.* 14 D3
Gaizhou, *China* 57 D12
Gaj, *Croatia* 42 E2
Gaj →, *Pakistan* 68 F2
Gakuch, *Pakistan* 69 A5
Galala, Gebel el, *Egypt* 80 J8
Galán, Cerro, *Argentina* 126 B2
Galana →, *Kenya* 86 C5
Galanta, *Slovak Rep.* 27 C10
Galápagar, *Spain* 34 E7
Galápagos, *Pac. Oc.* 122 D1
Galashiels, *U.K.* 14 F6
Galatás, *Greece* 38 D5
Galaţi, *Romania* 43 E13
Galaţi □, *Romania* 43 E12
Galatia, *Turkey* 72 C5
Galatina, *Italy* 31 B11
Galátone, *Italy* 31 B11
Galax, *U.S.A.* 109 G5
Galaxídhion, *Greece* 38 C4
Galcaio, *Somali Rep.* 74 F4
Galdhøpiggen, *Norway* 9 F12
Galeana, *Chihuahua, Mexico* 118 A3
Galeana, *Nuevo León,
  Mexico* 118 A3
Galegu, *Sudan* 81 E4
Galela, *Indonesia* 63 D7
Galena, *U.S.A.* 100 B4
Galera, *Spain* 33 H2
Galera Point, *Trin. & Tob.* 121 D7
Galesburg, *U.S.A.* 112 E9
Galeton, *U.S.A.* 110 E7
Galga →, *Ethiopia* 81 F4
Gali, *Georgia* 49 J5
Galicea Mare, *Romania* 43 F8
Galich, *Russia* 48 A6
Galiche, *Bulgaria* 40 C7
Galicia □, *Spain* 34 C3
Galilee = Hagalil, *Israel* 75 C4
Galilee, L., *Australia* 94 C4
Galilee, Sea of = Yam
  Kinneret, *Israel* 75 C4
Galim, *Cameroon* 83 D7
Galinoporni, *Cyprus* 36 D13
Galion, *U.S.A.* 110 F2
Galiuro Mts., *U.S.A.* 115 K8
Galiwinku, *Australia* 94 A2
Gallabat, *Sudan* 81 E4
Gallan Hd., *U.K.* 14 C1
Gallarate, *Italy* 28 C5
Gallatin, *U.S.A.* 109 G2
Galle, *Sri Lanka* 66 R12
Gállego →, *Spain* 32 D4
Gallegos →, *Argentina* 128 G3
Galletti →, *Ethiopia* 81 F5
Galley Hd., *Ireland* 15 E3
Galliate, *Italy* 28 C5
Gallinas, Pta., *Colombia* 124 A4
Gallípoli = Gelibolu, *Turkey* 41 F10
Gallípoli, *Italy* 31 B10
Gallipolis, *U.S.A.* 108 F4
Gällivare, *Sweden* 8 C19
Gallneukirchen, *Austria* 26 C7
Gällö, *Sweden* 10 B9
Gallo →, *Spain* 32 D3
Gallóo I., *U.S.A.* 111 C8
Galloway, *U.K.* 14 F4
Galloway, Mull of, *U.K.* 14 G4
Gallup, *U.S.A.* 115 J9
Gallur, *Spain* 32 D3
Galoya, *Sri Lanka* 66 Q12
Galt, *U.S.A.* 116 G5
Galten, *Denmark* 11 H3
Galtür, *Austria* 26 E3
Galty Mts., *Ireland* 15 D3
Galtymore, *Ireland* 15 D3
Galva, *U.S.A.* 112 E9
Galve de Sorbe, *Spain* 32 D1
Galveston, *U.S.A.* 113 L7
Galveston B., *U.S.A.* 113 L7
Gálvez, *Argentina* 126 C3
Galway, *Ireland* 15 C2
Galway □, *Ireland* 15 C2
Galway B., *Ireland* 15 C2
Gam →, *Vietnam* 64 B5
Gamagori, *Japan* 55 G8
Gamari, L., *Ethiopia* 81 E5
Gamawa, *Nigeria* 83 C7
Gamay, *Phil.* 61 E6
Gambaga, *Ghana* 83 C4
Gambat, *Pakistan* 68 F3
Gambhir →, *India* 68 F6
Gambia ■, *W. Afr.* 82 C1
Gambia →, *W. Afr.* 82 C1
Gambier, *U.S.A.* 110 F2
Gambier, C., *Australia* 92 B5
Gambier Is., *Australia* 95 F2
Gambo, *Canada* 103 C9
Gamboli, *Pakistan* 68 E3
Gamboma, *Congo* 84 E3
Gamka →, *S. Africa* 88 E3
Gamkab →, *Namibia* 88 D2
Gamla Uppsala, *Sweden* 10 E11

Gamlakarleby = Kokkola,
  Finland 8 E20
Gamleby, *Sweden* 11 G10
Gammon →, *Canada* 105 C9
Gamo-Gofa □, *Ethiopia* 81 F4
Gamou, *Niger* 83 C6
Gamtoos →, *S. Africa* 88 E4
Gan, *France* 20 E3
Gan Goriama, Mts.,
  Cameroon 83 D7
Gan Jiang →, *China* 59 C11
Ganado, *U.S.A.* 115 J9
Gananita, *Sudan* 80 D3
Gananoque, *Canada* 102 D4
Ganāveh, *Iran* 71 D6
Gäncä, *Azerbaijan* 49 K8
Gancheng, *China* 64 C7
Gand = Gent, *Belgium* 17 C3
Ganda, *Angola* 85 G2
Gandajika,
  Dem. Rep. of the Congo 84 F4
Gandak →, *India* 69 G11
Gandava, *Pakistan* 68 E2
Gander, *Canada* 103 C9
Gander L., *Canada* 103 C9
Ganderkesee, *Germany* 24 B4
Ganderowe Falls, *Zimbabwe* 87 F2
Gandesa, *Spain* 32 D5
Gandhi Sagar, *India* 68 G6
Gandhinagar, *India* 68 H5
Gandi, *Nigeria* 83 C6
Gandía, *Spain* 33 G4
Gandino, *Italy* 28 C6
Gando, Pta., *Canary Is.* 37 G4
Gandole, *Nigeria* 83 D7
Gâneb, *Mauritania* 82 B2
Ganedidalem = Gani,
  Indonesia 63 E7
Ganetti, *Sudan* 80 D3
Ganga →, *India* 69 H14
Ganga Sagar, *India* 69 J13
Gangafani, *Mali* 82 C4
Gangan →, *India* 69 E8
Ganganagar, *India* 68 E5
Gangapur, *India* 68 F7
Gangara, *Niger* 83 C6
Gangaw, *Burma* 67 H19
Gangdisê Shan, *China* 67 D12
Ganges = Ganga →, *India* 69 H14
Ganges, *Canada* 104 D4
Ganges, *France* 20 E7
Ganges, Mouths of the, *India* 69 J14
Gånghester, *Sweden* 11 G7
Gangi, *Italy* 31 E7
Gângiova, *Romania* 43 G8
Gangoh, *India* 68 E7
Gangroti, *India* 69 D8
Gangtok, *India* 67 F16
Gangu, *China* 56 G3
Gangyao, *China* 57 B14
Gani, *Indonesia* 63 E7
Ganj, *India* 69 F8
Ganluc, *China* 58 C4
Gannat, *France* 19 F10
Gannett Peak, *U.S.A.* 114 E9
Ganquan, *China* 56 F5
Gänserdorf, *Austria* 27 C9
Ganshui, *China* 58 C6
Gansu □, *China* 56 G3
Ganta, *Liberia* 82 D3
Gantheaume, C., *Australia* 95 F2
Gantheaume B., *Australia* 93 E1
Gantsevichi = Hantsavichy,
  Belarus 47 F4
Ganye, *Nigeria* 83 D7
Ganyem = Genyem,
  Indonesia 63 E10
Ganyu, *China* 57 G10
Ganyushkino, *Kazakstan* 49 G9
Ganzhou, *China* 59 E10
Gao, *Mali* 83 B4
Gao, *Mali* 83 B5
Gao Xian, *China* 58 C5
Gao'an, *China* 59 C10
Gaochun, *China* 59 B12
Gaohe, *China* 59 F9
Gaohebu, *China* 59 B11
Gaokeng, *China* 59 D9
Gaolan Dao, *China* 59 G9
Gaoligong Shan, *China* 58 E2
Gaomi, *China* 57 F10
Gaoming, *China* 59 F9
Gaotang, *China* 56 F9
Gaoua, *Burkina Faso* 82 C4
Gaoual, *Guinea* 82 C2
Gaoxiong = Kaohsiung,
  Taiwan 59 F13
Gaoyang, *China* 56 E8
Gaoyao, *China* 59 F9
Gaoyou, *China* 59 A12
Gaoyou Hu, *China* 57 H10
Gaoyuan, *China* 57 F9
Gaozhou, *China* 59 G8
Gap, *France* 21 D10
Gapan, *Phil.* 61 D4
Gapat →, *India* 69 G10
Gapuwiyak, *Australia* 94 A2
Gar, *China* 60 C2
Garabogazköl Aylagy,
  Turkmenistan 50 E6
Garachico, *Canary Is.* 37 F3
Garachiné, *Panama* 120 E4
Garafia, *Canary Is.* 37 F2
Garah, *Australia* 95 D4
Garajonay, *Canary Is.* 37 F2
Garango, *Burkina Faso* 83 C4
Garanhuns, *Brazil* 125 E11
Garautha, *India* 69 G8
Garawe, *Liberia* 82 E3
Garba Tula, *Kenya* 86 B4

Garberville, *U.S.A.* 114 F2
Garbiyang, *India* 69 D9
Garbsen, *Germany* 24 C5
Gard □, *France* 21 D8
Gard →, *France* 21 E8
Garda, L. di, *Italy* 28 C7
Gardanne, *France* 21 E9
Gårdby, *Sweden* 11 H10
Garde L., *Canada* 105 A7
Gardelegen, *Germany* 24 C7
Garden City, *Ga., U.S.A.* 109 J5
Garden City, *Kans., U.S.A.* 113 G4
Garden City, *Tex., U.S.A.* 113 K4
Garden Grove, *U.S.A.* 117 M9
Gardēz, *Afghan.* 68 C3
Gardhíki, *Greece* 38 C3
Gardiner, *Maine, U.S.A.* 109 C11
Gardiner, *Mont., U.S.A.* 114 D8
Gardiners I., *U.S.A.* 111 E12
Gardner, *U.S.A.* 111 D13
Gardner Canal, *Canada* 104 C3
Gardnerville, *U.S.A.* 116 G7
Gardno, Jezioro, *Poland* 44 D4
Gardo, *Somali Rep.* 74 F4
Gardone Val Trómpia, *Italy* 28 C7
Gárdony, *Hungary* 42 C3
Garešnica, *Croatia* 29 C13
Garéssio, *Italy* 28 D5
Garey, *U.S.A.* 117 L6
Garfield, *U.S.A.* 114 C5
Garforth, *U.K.* 12 D6
Gargaliánoi, *Greece* 38 D3
Gargan, Mt., *France* 20 C5
Gargouna, *Mali* 83 B5
Gargždai, *Lithuania* 44 C8
Garibaldi Prov. Park,
  Canada 104 D4
Gariep, L., *S. Africa* 88 E4
Garies, *S. Africa* 88 E2
Garigliano →, *Italy* 30 A6
Garissa, *Kenya* 86 C4
Garkida, *Nigeria* 83 C7
Garko, *Nigeria* 83 C6
Garland, *Tex., U.S.A.* 113 J6
Garland, *Utah, U.S.A.* 114 F7
Garlasco, *Italy* 28 C5
Garliava, *Lithuania* 44 D10
Garlin, *France* 20 E3
Garm, *Tajikistan* 50 F8
Garmāb, *Iran* 71 C8
Garmisch-Partenkirchen,
  Germany 25 H7
Garmsār, *Iran* 71 C7
Garner, *U.S.A.* 112 D8
Garnett, *U.S.A.* 112 F7
Garo Hills, *India* 69 G14
Garoe, *Somali Rep.* 74 F4
Garonne →, *France* 20 C3
Garonne, Canal Latéral à la,
  France 20 D4
Garot, *India* 68 G6
Garoua, *Cameroon* 83 D7
Garpenberg, *Sweden* 10 D10
Garphyttan, *Sweden* 10 E8
Garrauli, *India* 69 G8
Garrel, *Germany* 24 C4
Garrigue = Garrigues,
  France 20 E7
Garrigues, *France* 20 E7
Garrison, *Mont., U.S.A.* 114 C7
Garrison, *N. Dak., U.S.A.* 112 B4
Garrison Res. = Sakakawea,
  L., *U.S.A.* 112 B4
Garron Pt., *U.K.* 15 A6
Garrovillas, *Spain* 35 F4
Garrucha, *Spain* 33 H3
Garry →, *U.K.* 14 E5
Garry, L., *Canada* 100 B9
Garsen, *Kenya* 86 C5
Gärsnäs, *Sweden* 11 J8
Garson L., *Canada* 105 B6
Gartempe →, *France* 20 B4
Gartz, *Germany* 24 B10
Garu, *Ghana* 83 C5
Garut, *India* 69 H11
Garub, *Namibia* 88 D2
Garut, *Indonesia* 63 G12
Garvão, *Portugal* 35 H2
Garvie Mts., *N.Z.* 91 L2
Garwa = Garoua, *Cameroon* 83 D7
Garwa, *India* 69 G10
Garwolin, *Poland* 45 G8
Gary, *U.S.A.* 108 E2
Garz, *Germany* 24 A9
Garze, *China* 58 B3
Garzón, *Colombia* 124 C3
Gas-San, *Japan* 54 E10
Gasan Kuli = Esenguly,
  Turkmenistan 50 F6
Gascogne, *France* 20 E4
Gascogne, G. de, *Europe* 20 E2
Gascony = Gascogne, *France* 20 E4
Gascoyne →, *Australia* 93 D1
Gascoyne Junction, *Australia* 93 E2
Gascueña, *Spain* 32 E2
Gash, Wadi →, *Ethiopia* 81 D4
Gashagar, *Nigeria* 83 C7
Gashaka, *Nigeria* 83 D7
Gasherbrum, *Pakistan* 69 B7
Gashua, *Nigeria* 83 C7
Gaspé, *Canada* 103 C7
Gaspé, C. de, *Canada* 103 C7
Gaspé, Pén. de, *Canada* 103 C6
Gaspésie, Parc de
  Conservation de la,
  Canada 103 C6
Gassan, *Burkina Faso* 82 C4
Gassol, *Nigeria* 83 D7
Gasteiz = Vitoria-Gasteiz,
  Spain 32 C2
Gastonia, *U.S.A.* 109 H5

Gastoúni, *Greece* 38 D3
Gastoúri, *Greece* 38 B1
Gastre, *Argentina* 128 E3
Gästrikland, *Sweden* 10 D10
Gata, C., *Cyprus* 36 E12
Gata, C. de, *Spain* 33 J2
Gata, Sierra de, *Spain* 34 E4
Gataga →, *Canada* 104 B3
Gătaia, *Romania* 42 E6
Gatchina, *Russia* 46 C6
Gatehouse of Fleet, *U.K.* . 14 G4
Gates, *U.S.A.* 110 C7
Gateshead, *U.K.* 12 C6
Gatesville, *U.S.A.* 113 K6
Gaths, *Zimbabwe* 87 G3
Gatico, *Chile* 126 A1
Gâtinais, *France* 19 D9
Gâtine, Hauteurs de, *France* 18 B3
Gatineau, *Canada* 111 A9
Gatineau →, *Canada* 102 C4
Gatineau, Parc Nat. de la,
    Canada 102 C4
Gattaran, *Phil.* 61 B4
Gattinara, *Italy* 28 C5
Gatton, *Australia* 95 D5
Gatun, L., *Panama* 120 E4
Gatyana, *S. Africa* 89 E4
Gau, *Fiji* 91 D8
Gaucín, *Spain* 35 J5
Gauer L., *Canada* 105 B9
Gauhati, *India* 67 F17
Gauja →, *Latvia* 9 H21
Gaula →, *Norway* 8 E14
Gauri Phanta, *India* 69 E9
Gausta, *Norway* 9 G13
Gauteng □, *S. Africa* 89 D4
Gāv Koshī, *Iran* 71 D8
Gāvakān, *Iran* 71 D7
Gavarnie, *France* 20 F3
Gavāter, *Iran* 71 E9
Gāvbandī, *Iran* 71 E7
Gavdhopoúla, *Greece* 36 E6
Gávdhos, *Greece* 36 E6
Gavi, *Italy* 28 D5
Gavião, *Portugal* 35 F3
Gaviota, *U.S.A.* 117 L6
Gāvkhūnī, Bāṭlāq-e, *Iran* . 71 C7
Gävle, *Sweden* 10 D11
Gävleborgs län □, *Sweden* . 10 C10
Gävlebukten, *Sweden* 10 D11
Gavorrano, *Italy* 28 F7
Gavray, *France* 18 D5
Gavrilov Yam, *Russia* 46 D10
Gávrion, *Greece* 38 D6
Gawachab, *Namibia* 88 D2
Gawilgarh Hills, *India* 66 J10
Gawler, *Australia* 95 E2
Gawu, *Nigeria* 83 D6
Gaxun Nur, *China* 60 B5
Gaya, *India* 69 G11
Gaya, *Niger* 83 C5
Gaya, *Nigeria* 83 C6
Gaylord, *U.S.A.* 108 C3
Gayndah, *Australia* 95 D5
Gaysin = Haysyn, *Ukraine* . 47 H5
Gayvoron = Hayvoron,
    Ukraine 47 H5
Gaza, *Gaza Strip* 75 D3
Gaza □, *Mozam.* 89 C5
Gaza Strip □, *Asia* 75 D3
Gazanjyk, *Turkmenistan* ... 71 B7
Gazaoua, *Niger* 83 C6
Gāzbor, *Iran* 71 D8
Gazi,
    Dem. Rep. of the Congo . 86 B1
Gaziantep, *Turkey* 70 B3
Gazipaşa, *Turkey* 72 D5
Gbarnga, *Liberia* 82 D3
Gbekebo, *Nigeria* 83 D5
Gboko, *Nigeria* 83 D6
Gbongan, *Nigeria* 83 D5
Gcoverega, *Botswana* 88 B3
Gcuwa, *S. Africa* 89 E4
Gdańsk, *Poland* 44 D5
Gdańska, Zatoka, *Poland* .. 44 D6
Gdov, *Russia* 9 G22
Gdynia, *Poland* 44 D5
Geba →, *Guinea-Biss.* 82 C1
Gebe, *Indonesia* 63 D7
Gebeciler, *Turkey* 39 C12
Gebeit Mine, *Sudan* 80 C4
Gebel Abyad, *Sudan* 80 D2
Gebel Iweibid, *Egypt* 80 H8
Gebze, *Turkey* 41 F13
Gecha, *Ethiopia* 81 F4
Gedaref, *Sudan* 81 E4
Gedaref □, *Sudan* 81 E4
Gediz, *Turkey* 39 B11
Gediz →, *Turkey* 39 C8
Gedo, *Ethiopia* 81 F4
Gèdre, *France* 20 F4
Gedser, *Denmark* 11 K5
Geegully Cr. →, *Australia* . 92 C3
Geel, *Belgium* 17 C4
Geelong, *Australia* 95 F3
Geelvink B. = Cenderwasih,
    Teluk, *Indonesia* 63 E9
Geelvink Chan., *Australia* . 93 E1
Geesthacht, *Germany* 24 B6
Geidam, *Nigeria* 83 C7
Geikie →, *Canada* 105 B8
Geilenkirchen, *Germany* ... 24 E2
Geili, *Sudan* 81 D3
Geisingen, *Germany* 25 H4
Geislingen, *Germany* 25 G5
Geistown, *U.S.A.* 110 F6
Geita, *Tanzania* 86 C3
Gejiu, *China* 58 F4
Gel →, *Sudan* 81 F2
Gel, Meydān-e, *Iran* 71 D7

Gel River, *Sudan* 81 F2
Gela, *Italy* 31 E7
Gela, G. di, *Italy* 31 F7
Gelahun, *Liberia* 82 D2
Gelderland □, *Neths.* 17 B6
Geldern, *Germany* 24 D2
Geldrop, *Neths.* 17 C5
Geleen, *Neths.* 17 D5
Gelehun, *S. Leone* 82 D2
Gelembe, *Turkey* 39 B9
Gelemso, *Ethiopia* 81 F5
Gelendost, *Turkey* 72 C4
Gelendzhik, *Russia* 47 K10
Gelibolu, *Turkey* 41 F10
Gelibolu Yarımadası, *Turkey* 41 F10
Gelidonya Burnu, *Turkey* .. 72 D4
Gelnhausen, *Germany* 25 E5
Gelnica, *Slovak Rep.* 27 C13
Gelsenkirchen, *Germany* ... 24 D3
Gelting, *Germany* 24 A5
Gemas, *Malaysia* 65 L4
Gembloux, *Belgium* 17 D4
Gembu, *Nigeria* 83 D7
Gemena,
    Dem. Rep. of the Congo . 84 D3
Gemerek, *Turkey* 70 B3
Gemla, *Sweden* 11 H8
Gemlik, *Turkey* 41 F13
Gemlik Körfezi, *Turkey* 41 F12
Gemona del Friuli, *Italy* .. 29 B10
Gemsa, *Egypt* 80 B3
Gemünden, *Germany* 25 E5
Genç, *Turkey* 73 C9
Gençay, *France* 20 B4
Geneina, Gebel, *Egypt* 80 B3
General Acha, *Argentina* .. 126 D3
General Alvear,
    Buenos Aires, Argentina . 126 D4
General Alvear, *Mendoza,
    Argentina* 126 D2
General Artigas, *Paraguay* . 126 B4
General Belgrano, *Argentina* 126 D4
General Cabrera, *Argentina* 126 C3
General Cepeda, *Mexico* ... 118 B4
General Guido, *Argentina* . 126 D4
General Juan Madariaga,
    Argentina 126 D4
General La Madrid,
    Argentina 126 D3
General MacArthur, *Phil.* .. 61 F6
General Martín Miguel de
    Güemes, *Argentina* 126 A3
General Paz, *Argentina* 126 B4
General Pico, *Argentina* ... 126 D3
General Pinedo, *Argentina* . 126 B3
General Pinto, *Argentina* .. 126 C3
General Roca, *Argentina* ... 128 D3
General Santos, *Phil.* 61 H6
General Toshevo, *Bulgaria* . 41 C12
General Trevino, *Mexico* ... 119 B5
General Trías, *Mexico* 118 B3
General Viamonte, *Argentina* 126 D3
General Villegas, *Argentina* 126 D3
Genesee, *Idaho, U.S.A.* 114 C5
Genesee, *Pa., U.S.A.* 110 E7
Genesee →, *U.S.A.* 110 C7
Geneseo, *Ill., U.S.A.* 112 E9
Geneseo, *N.Y., U.S.A.* 110 D7
Geneva = Genève, *Switz.* .. 25 J2
Geneva, *Ala., U.S.A.* 109 K3
Geneva, *N.Y., U.S.A.* 110 D8
Geneva, *Nebr., U.S.A.* 112 E6
Geneva, *Ohio, U.S.A.* 110 E4
Geneva, L. = Léman, L.,
    Europe 19 F13
Geneva, L., *U.S.A.* 108 D1
Genève, *Switz.* 25 J2
Gengenbach, *Germany* 25 G4
Gengma, *China* 58 F2
Genichesk = Henichesk,
    Ukraine 47 J8
Genil →, *Spain* 35 H5
Genk, *Belgium* 17 D5
Genlis, *France* 19 E12
Gennargentu, Mti. del, *Italy* 30 B2
Gennes, *France* 18 E6
Genoa = Génova, *Italy* 28 D5
Genoa, *Australia* 95 F4
Genoa, *N.Y., U.S.A.* 111 D8
Genoa, *Nebr., U.S.A.* 112 E6
Genoa, *Nev., U.S.A.* 116 F7
Génova, *Italy* 28 D5
Génova, G. di, *Italy* 28 E6
Genriyetty, Ostrov, *Russia* . 51 B16
Gent, *Belgium* 17 C3
Genteng, *Indonesia* 63 G12
Genthin, *Germany* 24 C8
Genyem, *Indonesia* 63 E10
Genzano di Lucánia, *Italy* . 31 B9
Genzano di Roma, *Italy* ... 29 G9
Geoagiu, *Romania* 43 E8
Geographe B., *Australia* ... 93 F2
Geographe Chan., *Australia* 93 D1
Geokchay =Göyçay,
    Azerbaijan 49 K8
Georga, Zemlya, *Russia* ... 50 A5
George, *S. Africa* 88 E3
George →, *Canada* 103 A6
George, L., *N.S.W.,
    Australia* 95 F4
George, L., *S. Austral.,
    Australia* 95 F3
George, L., *W. Austral.,
    Australia* 92 D3
George, L., *Uganda* 86 B3
George, L., *Fla., U.S.A.* ... 109 L5
George, L., *N.Y., U.S.A.* ... 111 C11
George Gill Ra., *Australia* . 92 D5
Kangiqsualujjuaq, *Canada* 101 C13

George Sound, *N.Z.* 91 L1
George Town, *Australia* ... 94 G4
George Town, *Bahamas* ... 120 B4
George Town, *Malaysia* ... 65 K3
George V Land, *Antarctica* . 5 C10
George VI Sound, *Antarctica* 5 D17
George West, *U.S.A.* 113 L5
Georgetown, *Australia* 94 B3
Georgetown, *Ont., Canada* . 102 D4
Georgetown, *P.E.I., Canada* 103 C7
Georgetown, *Cayman Is.* .. 120 C3
Georgetown, *Gambia* 82 C2
Georgetown, *Guyana* 124 B7
Georgetown, *Calif., U.S.A.* 116 G6
Georgetown, *Colo., U.S.A.* 114 G11
Georgetown, *Ky., U.S.A.* .. 108 F3
Georgetown, *N.Y., U.S.A.* . 111 D9
Georgetown, *Ohio, U.S.A.* . 108 F4
Georgetown, *S.C., U.S.A.* . 109 J6
Georgetown, *Tex., U.S.A.* . 113 K6
Georgia □, *U.S.A.* 109 K5
Georgia ■, *Asia* 49 J6
Georgia, Str. of, *Canada* .. 104 D4
Georgian B., *Canada* 102 C3
Georgina →, *Australia* 94 C2
Georgina I., *Canada* 110 B5
Georgiu-Dezh = Liski,
    Russia 47 G10
Georgiyevsk, *Russia* 49 H6
Georgsmarienhütte,
    Germany 24 C4
Gera, *Germany* 24 E8
Geraardsbergen, *Belgium* .. 17 D3
Geral, Serra, *Brazil* 127 B6
Geral de Goiás, Serra, *Brazil* 125 F9
Geraldine, *U.S.A.* 114 C8
Geraldton, *Australia* 93 E1
Geraldton, *Canada* 102 C2
Gérardmer, *France* 19 D13
Gercüş, *Turkey* 73 D9
Gerede, *Turkey* 72 B5
Gerês, Sierra do, *Portugal* . 34 D3
Gereshk, *Afghan.* 66 D4
Geretsried, *Germany* 25 H7
Gérgal, *Spain* 33 H2
Gerik, *Malaysia* 65 K3
Gering, *U.S.A.* 112 E3
Gerlach, *U.S.A.* 114 F4
Gerlachovský štít,
    Slovak Rep. 27 B13
German Planina, *Macedonia* 40 D6
Germansen Landing, *Canada* 104 B4
Germantown, *U.S.A.* 113 M10
Germany ■, *Europe* 24 E6
Germencik, *Turkey* 39 D9
Germering, *Germany* 25 G7
Germersheim, *Germany* ... 25 F4
Germī, *Iran* 71 B6
Germiston, *S. Africa* 89 D4
Gernika-Lumo, *Spain* 32 B2
Gernsheim, *Germany* 25 F4
Gero, *Japan* 55 G8
Gerolzhofen, *Germany* 25 F6
Gerona = Girona, *Spain* ... 32 D7
Gerrard, *Canada* 104 C5
Gers □, *France* 20 E4
Gers →, *France* 20 D4
Gersfeld, *Germany* 24 E5
Gersthofen, *Germany* 25 G6
Gerzat, *France* 20 C7
Gerze, *Turkey* 72 B6
Geseke, *Germany* 24 D4
Geser, *Indonesia* 63 E8
Gesso →, *Italy* 28 D4
Gestro, Wabi →, *Ethiopia* . 81 G5
Getafe, *Spain* 34 E7
Getinge, *Sweden* 11 H6
Gettysburg, *Pa., U.S.A.* ... 108 F7
Gettysburg, *S. Dak., U.S.A.* 112 C5
Getxo, *Spain* 32 B2
Getz Ice Shelf, *Antarctica* . 5 D14
Gevaş, *Turkey* 73 C10
Gévaudan, *France* 20 D7
Gevgelija, *Macedonia* 40 E6
Gévora →, *Spain* 35 G4
Gewani, *Ethiopia* 81 E5
Gex, *France* 19 F13
Geyikli, *Turkey* 39 B8
Geyser, *U.S.A.* 114 C8
Geyserville, *U.S.A.* 116 G4
Geyve, *Turkey* 72 B4
Ghâbat el Arab = Wang
    Kai, *Sudan* 81 F2
Ghabeish, *Sudan* 81 E2
Ghaggar →, *India* 68 E6
Ghaghara →, *India* 69 G11
Ghaghat →, *Bangla.* 69 G13
Ghagra, *India* 69 H11
Ghagra →, *India* 69 F9
Ghalla, Wadi el →, *Sudan* . 81 E2
Ghana ■, *W. Afr.* 83 D4
Ghansor, *India* 69 H9
Ghanzi, *Botswana* 88 C3
Gharb el Istiwa'iya □, *Sudan* 81 F2
Gharb Kordofân □, *Sudan* . 81 E2
Gharbîya, Es Sahrâ el, *Egypt* 80 B2
Ghardaïa, *Algeria* 78 B6
Ghârib, G., *Egypt* 80 B3
Ghat, *Libya* 79 D8
Ghatal, *India* 69 H12
Ghatampur, *India* 69 F9
Ghatsila, *India* 69 H12
Ghaṭṭī, *Si. Arabia* 70 D3
Ghawdex = Gozo, *Malta* .. 36 C1
Ghazal, Bahr el →, *Chad* .. 79 F9
Ghazâl, Bahr el →, *Sudan* . 81 F3
Ghaziabad, *India* 68 E7
Ghazipur, *India* 69 G10
Ghaznī, *Afghan.* 68 C3

Ghaznī □, *Afghan.* 66 C6
Ghedi, *Italy* 28 C7
Ghelari, *Romania* 42 E7
Ghent = Gent, *Belgium* ... 17 C3
Gheorghe Gheorghiu-Dej =
    Oneşti, *Romania* 43 D11
Gheorgheni, *Romania* 43 D10
Gherla, *Romania* 43 C8
Ghidigeni, *Romania* 43 D12
Ghilarza, *Italy* 30 B1
Ghimeş-Făget, *Romania* ... 43 D11
Ghīnah, Wādī al →,
    Si. Arabia 70 D3
Ghīnah, Wādī al →,
    Si. Arabia 80 B4
Ghisonaccia, *France* 21 F13
Ghisoni, *France* 21 F13
Ghizao, *Afghan.* 68 C1
Ghizar →, *Pakistan* 69 A5
Ghot Ogrein, *Egypt* 80 A2
Ghotaru, *India* 68 F4
Ghotki, *Pakistan* 68 E3
Ghowr □, *Afghan.* 66 C4
Ghudaf, W. al →, *Iraq* 70 C4
Ghughri, *India* 69 H9
Ghugus, *India* 66 K11
Ghulam Mohammad
    Barrage, *Pakistan* 68 G3
Ghūrīān, *Afghan.* 66 B2
Gia Dinh, *Vietnam* 65 G6
Gia Lai = Plei Ku, *Vietnam* 64 F7
Gia Nghia, *Vietnam* 65 G6
Gia Ngoc, *Vietnam* 64 E7
Gia Vuc, *Vietnam* 64 E7
Giannutri, *Italy* 28 F8
Giant Forest, *U.S.A.* 116 J8
Giant Mts. = Krkonoše,
    Czech Rep. 26 A8
Giants Causeway, *U.K.* 15 A5
Giarabub = Al Jaghbūb,
    Libya 79 C10
Giarre, *Italy* 31 E8
Giaveno, *Italy* 28 C4
Gibara, *Cuba* 120 B4
Gibb River, *Australia* 92 C4
Gibbon, *U.S.A.* 112 E5
Gibe →, *Ethiopia* 81 F4
Gibellina Nuova, *Italy* 30 E5
Gibeon, *Namibia* 88 D2
Gibraléon, *Spain* 35 H4
Gibraltar ■, *Europe* 35 J5
Gibraltar, Str. of, *Medit. S.* 35 K5
Gibson Desert, *Australia* .. 92 D4
Gibsons, *Canada* 104 D4
Gibsonville, *U.S.A.* 116 F6
Giddings, *U.S.A.* 113 K6
Gidole, *Ethiopia* 81 F4
Gien, *France* 19 E9
Giengen, *Germany* 25 G6
Giessen, *Germany* 24 E4
Gīfān, *Iran* 71 B8
Gifatin, Geziret, *Egypt* 80 B3
Gifhorn, *Germany* 24 C6
Gift Lake, *Canada* 104 B5
Gifu, *Japan* 55 G8
Gifu □, *Japan* 55 G8
Gigant, *Russia* 49 G5
Giganta, Sa. de la, *Mexico* . 118 B2
Gigen, *Bulgaria* 41 C8
Gigha, *U.K.* 14 F3
Gíglio, *Italy* 28 F7
Gignac, *France* 20 E7
Gigüela →, *Spain* 35 F7
Gijón, *Spain* 34 B5
Gil I., *Canada* 104 C3
Gila →, *U.S.A.* 115 K6
Gila Bend, *U.S.A.* 115 K7
Gila Bend Mts., *U.S.A.* ... 115 K7
Gīlān □, *Iran* 71 B6
Gilău, *Romania* 43 D8
Gilbert →, *Australia* 94 B3
Gilbert Is., *Kiribati* 96 G9
Gilbert River, *Australia* ... 94 B3
Gilead, *U.S.A.* 111 B14
Gilf el Kebîr, Hadabat el,
    Egypt 80 C2
Gilford I., *Canada* 104 C3
Gilgandra, *Australia* 95 E4
Gilgil, *Kenya* 86 C4
Gilgit, *India* 69 B6
Gilgit →, *Pakistan* 69 B6
Gilgunnia, *Australia* 95 E4
Giljeva Planina, *Serbia, Yug.* 40 C3
Gillam, *Canada* 105 B10
Gilleleje, *Denmark* 11 H6
Gillen, L., *Australia* 93 E3
Gilles, L., *Australia* 95 E2
Gillette, *U.S.A.* 112 C2
Gilliat, *Australia* 94 C3
Gillingham, *U.K.* 13 F8
Gilmer, *U.S.A.* 113 J7
Gilmore, L., *Australia* 93 F3
Gilo →, *Ethiopia* 81 F3
Gilort →, *Romania* 43 F8
Gilroy, *U.S.A.* 116 H5
Gimbi, *Ethiopia* 81 F4
Gimli, *Canada* 105 C9
Gimo, *Sweden* 10 D12
Gimone →, *France* 20 E5
Gimont, *France* 20 E4
Gin Gin, *Australia* 95 D5
Ginâh, *Egypt* 80 B3
Gineifa, *Egypt* 80 H8
Gingin, *Australia* 93 F2
Gingindlovu, *S. Africa* 89 D5
Ginir, *Ethiopia* 81 F5
Ginosa, *Italy* 31 B9
Ginzo de Limia = Xinzo de
    Limia, *Spain* 34 C3
Gióia, G. di, *Italy* 31 D8

Gióia del Colle, *Italy* 31 B9
Gióia Táuro, *Italy* 31 D8
Gioiosa Iónica, *Italy* 31 D9
Gioiosa Marea, *Italy* 31 D7
Gióna, Óros, *Greece* 38 C4
Giovinazzo, *Italy* 31 A9
Gippsland, *Australia* 95 F4
Gir Hills, *India* 68 J4
Girab, *India* 68 F4
Girâfi, W. →, *Egypt* 75 F3
Giraltovce, *Slovak Rep.* ... 27 B14
Girard, *Kans., U.S.A.* 113 G7
Girard, *Ohio, U.S.A.* 110 E4
Girard, *Pa., U.S.A.* 110 D4
Girardot, *Colombia* 124 C4
Girdle Ness, *U.K.* 14 D6
Giresun, *Turkey* 73 B8
Girga, *Egypt* 80 B3
Giri →, *India* 68 D7
Giridih, *India* 69 G12
Girifalco, *Italy* 31 D9
Girne = Kyrenia, *Cyprus* .. 36 D12
Giro, *Nigeria* 83 C5
Giromagny, *France* 19 E13
Girona, *Spain* 32 D7
Girona □, *Spain* 32 C7
Gironde □, *France* 20 D3
Gironde →, *France* 20 C2
Gironella, *Spain* 32 C6
Giru, *Australia* 94 B4
Girvan, *U.K.* 14 F4
Gisborne, *N.Z.* 91 H7
Gisenyi, *Rwanda* 86 C2
Gislaved, *Sweden* 11 G7
Gisors, *France* 19 C8
Gitega, *Burundi* 86 C2
Giuba →, *Somali Rep.* 74 G3
Giugliano in Campania, *Italy* 31 B7
Giulianova, *Italy* 29 F10
Giurgeni, *Romania* 43 F12
Giurgiu, *Romania* 43 G10
Giurgiu □, *Romania* 43 F10
Giurgiuleşti, *Moldova* 43 E13
Give, *Denmark* 11 J3
Givet, *France* 19 B11
Givors, *France* 21 C8
Givry, *France* 19 F11
Giyon, *Ethiopia* 81 F4
Giza = El Gîza, *Egypt* 80 J7
Gizhiga, *Russia* 51 C17
Gizhiginskaya Guba, *Russia* 51 C16
Giżycko, *Poland* 44 D8
Gizzeria, *Italy* 31 D9
Gjalicës e Lumës, Mal,
    Albania 40 D4
Gjegjani, *Albania* 40 E4
Gjirokastra, *Albania* 40 F4
Gjoa Haven, *Canada* 100 B10
Gjøvik, *Norway* 9 F14
Gjuhës, Kep i, *Albania* 40 F3
Glace Bay, *Canada* 103 C8
Glacier Bay National Park
    and Preserve, *U.S.A.* .. 104 B1
Glacier National Park,
    Canada 104 C5
Glacier National Park,
    U.S.A. 114 B7
Glacier Peak, *U.S.A.* 114 B3
Gladewater, *U.S.A.* 113 J7
Gladstone, *Queens.,
    Australia* 94 C5
Gladstone, *S. Austral.,
    Australia* 95 E2
Gladstone, *Canada* 105 C9
Gladstone, *U.S.A.* 108 C2
Gladwin, *U.S.A.* 108 D3
Glafsfjorden, *Sweden* 10 E6
Głogów Małopolski, *Poland* 45 H8
Glâma = Glomma →,
    Norway 9 G14
Gláma, *Iceland* 8 D2
Glamis, *U.S.A.* 117 N11
Glamoč, *Bos.-H.* 29 D13
Glamsbjerg, *Denmark* 11 J4
Glarus, *Switz.* 25 H5
Glarus □, *Switz.* 25 J5
Glasco, *Kans., U.S.A.* 112 F6
Glasco, *N.Y., U.S.A.* 111 D11
Glasgow, *U.K.* 14 F4
Glasgow, *Ky., U.S.A.* 108 G3
Glasgow, *Mont., U.S.A.* ... 114 B10
Glasgow, City of □, *U.K.* .. 14 F4
Glaslyn, *Canada* 105 C7
Glastonbury, *U.K.* 13 F5
Glastonbury, *U.S.A.* 111 E12
Glauchau, *Germany* 24 E8
Glava, *Sweden* 10 E6
Glavice, *Croatia* 29 E13
Glazov, *Russia* 48 A11
Gleichen, *Canada* 104 C6
Gleisdorf, *Austria* 26 D8
Gleiwitz = Gliwice, *Poland* 45 H5
Glen, *U.S.A.* 111 B13
Glen Affric, *U.K.* 14 D3
Glen Canyon, *U.S.A.* 115 H8
Glen Canyon Dam, *U.S.A.* 115 H8
Glen Canyon National
    Recreation Area, *U.S.A.* 115 H8
Glen Coe, *U.K.* 14 E3
Glen Cove, *U.S.A.* 111 F11
Glen Garry, *U.K.* 14 D3
Glen Innes, *Australia* 95 D5
Glen Lyon, *U.S.A.* 111 E8
Glen Mor, *U.K.* 14 D4
Glen Moriston, *U.K.* 14 D4
Glen Robertson, *Canada* .. 111 A10
Glen Spean, *U.K.* 14 E4
Glen Ullin, *U.S.A.* 112 B4
Glénan, Îs. de, *France* 18 E3

Glencoe, Canada 110 D3
Glencoe, S. Africa 89 D5
Glencoe, U.S.A. 112 C7
Glendale, Ariz., U.S.A. .. 115 K7
Glendale, Calif., U.S.A. .. 117 L8
Glendale, Zimbabwe 87 F3
Glendive, U.S.A. 112 B2
Glendo, U.S.A. 112 D2
Glenelg →, Australia 95 F3
Glenfield, U.S.A. 111 C9
Glengarriff, Ireland 15 E2
Glenmont, U.S.A. 110 F2
Glenmorgan, Australia 95 D4
Glenn, U.S.A. 116 F4
Glennallen, U.S.A. 100 B5
Glennamaddy, Ireland 15 C3
Glenns Ferry, U.S.A. 114 E6
Glenore, Australia 94 B3
Glenreagh, Australia 95 E5
Glenrock, U.S.A. 114 E11
Glenrothes, U.K. 14 E5
Glens Falls, U.S.A. 111 C11
Glenside, U.S.A. 111 F9
Glenties, Ireland 15 B3
Glenville, U.S.A. 108 F5
Glenwood, Canada 103 C9
Glenwood, Ark., U.S.A. . 113 H8
Glenwood, Hawaii, U.S.A. 106 J17
Glenwood, Iowa, U.S.A. . 112 E7
Glenwood, Minn., U.S.A. 112 C7
Glenwood, Wash., U.S.A. 116 D5
Glenwood Springs, U.S.A. 114 G10
Glettinganes, Iceland 8 D7
Glifádha, Greece 38 D5
Glimåkra, Sweden 11 H8
Glina, Croatia 29 C13
Glinojeck, Poland 45 F7
Gliwice, Poland 45 H5
Globe, U.S.A. 115 K8
Glodeanu Siliştea, Romania 43 F11
Glodeni, Moldova 43 C12
Glödnitz, Austria 26 E7
Głogów, Poland 45 G3
Głogówek, Poland 45 H4
Glomma →, Norway 9 G14
Glorieuses, Is., Ind. Oc. . 89 A8
Glóssa, Greece 38 B5
Glossop, U.K. 12 D6
Gloucester, Australia 95 E5
Gloucester, U.K. 13 F5
Gloucester, U.S.A. 111 D14
Gloucester I., Australia ... 94 C4
Gloucester Point, U.S.A. . 108 G7
Gloucestershire □, U.K. .. 13 F5
Gloversville, U.S.A. 111 C10
Glovertown, Canada 103 C9
Głowno, Poland 45 G6
Głubczyce, Poland 45 H4
Glubokiy, Russia 49 F5
Glubokoye = Hlybokaye,
  Belarus 46 E4
Głuchołazy, Poland 45 H4
Glücksburg, Germany 24 A5
Glückstadt, Germany 24 B5
Glukhov = Hlukhiv, Ukraine 47 G7
Glusk, Belarus 47 F5
Głuszyca, Poland 45 H3
Glyngøre, Denmark 11 H2
Gmünd, Kärnten, Austria . 26 E6
Gmünd, Niederösterreich,
  Austria 26 C8
Gmunden, Austria 26 D6
Gnarp, Sweden 10 B11
Gnesta, Sweden 10 E11
Gniew, Poland 44 E5
Gniewkowo, Poland 45 F5
Gniezno, Poland 45 F4
Gnjilane, Kosovo, Yug. ... 40 D5
Gnoien, Germany 24 B8
Gnosjö, Sweden 11 G7
Gnowangerup, Australia ... 93 F2
Go Cong, Vietnam 65 G6
Gō-no-ura, Japan 55 H4
Goa, India 66 M8
Goa □, India 66 M8
Goalen Hd., Australia 95 F5
Goalpara, India 67 F17
Goaltor, India 69 H12
Goalundo Ghat, Bangla. .. 69 H13
Goaso, Ghana 82 D4
Goat Fell, U.K. 14 F3
Goba, Ethiopia 81 F4
Goba, Mozam. 89 D5
Gobabis, Namibia 88 C2
Göbel, Turkey 41 F12
Gobi, Asia 56 C6
Gobō, Japan 55 H7
Gobo, Sudan 81 F3
Göçbeyli, Turkey 39 B9
Goch, Germany 24 D2
Gochas, Namibia 88 C2
Godavari →, India 67 L13
Godavari Pt., India 67 L13
Godbout, Canada 103 C6
Godda, India 69 G12
Godech, Bulgaria 40 C7
Goderich, Canada 102 D3
Goderville, France 18 C4
Godfrey Ra., Australia ... 93 D2
Godhavn = Qeqertarsuaq,
  Greenland 4 C5
Godhra, India 68 H5
Gödöllő, Hungary 42 C4
Godoy Cruz, Argentina ... 126 C2
Gods →, Canada 102 A1
Gods L., Canada 102 B1
Gods River, Canada 105 C10
Godthåb = Nuuk, Greenland 101 B14
Godwin Austen = K2,
  Pakistan 69 B7

Goeie Hoop, Kaap die =
Good Hope, C. of,
  S. Africa 88 E2
Goéland, L. au, Canada .. 102 C4
Goeree, Neths. 17 C3
Goes, Neths. 17 C3
Goffstown, U.S.A. 111 C13
Gogama, Canada 102 C3
Gogebic, L., U.S.A. 112 B10
Goggetti, Ethiopia 81 F4
Gogolin, Poland 45 H5
Gogonou, Benin 83 C5
Gogra = Ghaghara →,
  India 69 G11
Gogriâl, Sudan 81 F2
Gogti, Ethiopia 81 E5
Gohana, India 68 E7
Goharganj, India 68 H7
Goi →, India 68 H6
Goiânia, Brazil 125 G9
Goiás, Brazil 125 G8
Goiás □, Brazil 125 F9
Goio-Ere, Brazil 127 A5
Góis, Portugal 34 E2
Gojam □, Ethiopia 81 E4
Gojeb, Wabi →, Ethiopia 81 F4
Gojō, Japan 55 G7
Gojra, Pakistan 68 D5
Gökçeada, Turkey 41 F9
Gökçedağ, Turkey 39 B10
Gökçen, Turkey 39 C9
Gökçeören, Turkey 39 C10
Gökçeyazı, Turkey 39 B9
Gökırmak →, Turkey 72 B6
Gökova, Turkey 39 D10
Gökova Körfezi, Turkey .. 39 E9
Göksu →, Turkey 72 D6
Göksun, Turkey 72 C7
Gökteik, Burma 67 H20
Göktepe, Turkey 39 D10
Gokurt, Pakistan 68 E2
Gokwe, Zimbabwe 89 B4
Gol Gol, Australia 95 E3
Gola, India 69 E9
Golakganj, India 69 F13
Golan Heights = Hagolan,
  Syria 75 C4
Gołańcz, Poland 45 F4
Golāshkerd, Iran 71 E8
Golaya Pristen = Hola
  Pristan, Ukraine 47 J7
Gölbaşı, Adıyaman, Turkey 72 D7
Gölbaşı, Ankara, Turkey .. 72 C5
Golchikha, Russia 4 B12
Golconda, U.S.A. 114 F5
Gölcük, Kocaeli, Turkey . 41 F13
Gölcük, Niğde, Turkey .. 72 C6
Gold, U.S.A. 110 E7
Gold Beach, U.S.A. 114 E1
Gold Coast, W. Afr. 83 E4
Gold Hill, U.S.A. 114 E2
Gold River, Canada 104 D3
Gołdap, Poland 44 D9
Goldberg, Germany 24 B8
Golden, Canada 104 C5
Golden B., N.Z. 91 J4
Golden Gate, U.S.A. 114 H2
Golden Hinde, Canada ... 104 D3
Golden Lake, Canada 110 A7
Golden Vale, Ireland 15 D3
Goldendale, U.S.A. 114 D3
Goldfield, U.S.A. 115 H5
Goldsand L., Canada 105 B8
Goldsboro, U.S.A. 109 H7
Goldsmith, U.S.A. 113 K3
Goldsworthy, Australia ... 92 D2
Goldthwaite, U.S.A. 113 K5
Golegã, Portugal 35 F2
Goleniów, Poland 44 E1
Golestānak, Iran 71 D7
Goleta, U.S.A. 117 L7
Golfito, Costa Rica 120 E3
Golfo Aranci, Italy 30 B2
Goliad, U.S.A. 113 L6
Golija, Montenegro, Yug. . 40 C2
Golija, Serbia, Yug. 40 C4
Golina, Poland 45 F5
Gölköy, Turkey 72 B7
Göllersdorf, Austria 26 C9
Gölmarmara, Turkey 39 C9
Golo →, France 21 F13
Gölova, Turkey 39 E12
Golpāyegān, Iran 71 C6
Gölpazarı, Turkey 72 B4
Golra, Pakistan 68 C5
Golspie, U.K. 14 D5
Golub-Dobrzyń, Poland .. 45 E6
Golubac, Serbia, Yug. ... 40 B5
Golyam Perelik, Bulgaria . 41 E8
Golyama Kamchiya →,
  Bulgaria 41 C11
Goma,
  Dem. Rep. of the Congo 86 C2
Gomal Pass, Pakistan 68 D3
Gomati →, India 69 G10
Gombari,
  Dem. Rep. of the Congo 86 B2
Gombe, Nigeria 83 C7
Gömbe, Turkey 39 E11
Gombe □, Nigeria 83 C7
Gombe →, Tanzania 86 C3
Gombi, Nigeria 83 C7
Gomel = Homyel, Belarus 47 F6
Gomera, Canary Is. 37 F2
Gómez Palacio, Mexico .. 118 B4
Gomīshān, Iran 71 B7
Gommern, Germany 24 C7
Gomogomo, Indonesia ... 63 F8
Gomoh, India 67 H15

Gomotartsi, Bulgaria 40 B6
Gompa = Ganta, Liberia . 82 D3
Gomphi, Greece 38 B3
Gonābād, Iran 71 C8
Gonaïves, Haiti 121 C5
Gonâve, G. de la, Haiti .. 121 C5
Gonâve, I. de la, Haiti ... 121 C5
Gonbad-e Kāvūs, Iran ... 71 B7
Gönc, Hungary 42 B6
Gonda, India 69 F9
Gondal, India 68 J4
Gonder, Ethiopia 81 E4
Gonder □, Ethiopia 81 E4
Gondia, India 66 J12
Gondola, Mozam. 87 F3
Gondomar, Portugal 34 D2
Gondrecourt-le-Château,
  France 19 D12
Gönen, Balıkesir, Turkey . 41 F11
Gönen, Isparta, Turkey .. 39 D12
Gönen →, Turkey 41 F11
Gong Xian, China 58 C5
Gong'an, China 59 B9
Gongcheng, China 59 E8
Gongga Shan, China 58 C3
Gongguan, China 58 G7
Gonghe, China 60 C5
Gongola →, Nigeria 83 D7
Gongolgon, Australia 95 E4
Gongshan, China 58 D2
Gongtan, China 58 C7
Gongzhuling, China 57 C13
Goniri, Nigeria 83 C7
Gonjo, China 58 B2
Gonnesa, Italy 30 C1
Gónnos, Greece 38 B4
Gonnosfanádiga, Italy 30 C1
Gonzaga, Phil. 61 B5
Gonzales, Calif., U.S.A. . 116 J5
Gonzales, Tex., U.S.A. .. 113 L6
González Chaves, Argentina 126 D3
Good Hope, C. of, S. Africa 88 E2
Gooderham, Canada 110 B6
Goodhouse, S. Africa 88 D2
Gooding, U.S.A. 114 E6
Goodland, U.S.A. 112 F4
Goodlow, Canada 104 B4
Goodooga, Australia 95 D4
Goodsprings, U.S.A. 117 K11
Goole, U.K. 12 D7
Goolgowi, Australia 95 E4
Goolwa, Australia 95 F2
Goomalling, Australia 93 F2
Goomeri, Australia 95 D5
Goonda, Mozam. 87 F3
Goondiwindi, Australia ... 95 D5
Goongarrie, L., Australia . 93 F3
Goonyella, Australia 94 C4
Goose →, Canada 103 B7
Goose Creek, U.S.A. 109 J5
Goose L., U.S.A. 114 F3
Gop, India 66 H6
Gopalganj, India 69 F11
Göppingen, Germany 25 G5
Gor, Spain 35 H8
Góra, Dolnośląskie, Poland 45 G3
Góra, Mazowieckie, Poland 45 F7
Góra Kalwaria, Poland ... 45 G8
Gorakhpur, India 69 F10
Goražde, Bos.-H. 42 G3
Gorbatov, Russia 48 B6
Gorbea, Peña, Spain 32 B2
Gorda, U.S.A. 116 K5
Gorda, Pta., Canary Is. .. 37 F2
Gorda, Pta., Nic. 120 D3
Gordan B., Australia 92 B5
Gördes, Turkey 39 C10
Gordon, U.S.A. 112 D3
Gordon →, Australia 94 G4
Gordon L., Alta., Canada 105 B6
Gordon L., N.W.T., Canada 104 A6
Gordonvale, Australia ... 94 B4
Gore, Ethiopia 81 F4
Gore, N.Z. 91 M2
Gore Bay, Canada 102 C3
Görele, Turkey 73 B8
Goreme, Turkey 72 C6
Gorey, Ireland 15 D5
Gorg, Iran 71 D8
Gorgān, Iran 71 B7
Gorgona, Italy 28 E6
Gorgona, I., Colombia ... 124 C3
Gorgora, Ethiopia 81 E4
Gorgoram, Nigeria 83 C7
Gorham, U.S.A. 111 B13
Gori, Georgia 49 J7
Goriganga →, India 69 E9
Gorinchem, Neths. 17 C4
Goris, Armenia 73 C12
Goritsy, Russia 46 D9
Gorízia, Italy 29 C10
Gorj □, Romania 43 E8
Gorki = Horki, Belarus .. 46 E6
Gorki = Nizhniy Novgorod,
  Russia 48 B7
Gorkiy = Nizhniy Novgorod,
  Russia 48 B7
Gorkovskoye Vdkhr., Russia 48 B6
Gorlice, Poland 45 J8
Görlitz, Germany 24 D10
Gorlovka = Horlivka,
  Ukraine 47 H10
Gorman, U.S.A. 117 L8
Gorna Dzhumaya =
Blagoevgrad, Bulgaria .. 40 D7
Gorna Oryakhovitsa,
  Bulgaria 41 C9
Gornja Radgona, Slovenia 29 B13
Gornja Tuzla, Bos.-H. ... 42 F3
Gornji Grad, Slovenia ... 29 B11

Gornji Milanovac,
  Serbia, Yug. 40 B4
Gornji Vakuf, Bos.-H. ... 42 G2
Gorno Ablanovo, Bulgaria 41 C9
Gorno-Altay □, Russia .. 50 D9
Gorno-Altaysk, Russia ... 50 D9
Gornyatskiy, Russia 49 F5
Gornyy, Saratov, Russia . 48 E9
Gornyy, Sib., Russia 54 B6
Gorodenka = Horodenka,
  Ukraine 47 H3
Gorodets, Russia 48 B6
Gorodishche =
Horodyshche, Ukraine . 47 H6
Gorodishche, Russia 48 D7
Gorodnya = Horodnya,
  Ukraine 47 G6
Gorodok = Haradok,
  Belarus 46 E6
Gorodok = Horodok,
  Ukraine 47 H2
Gorodovikovsk, Russia ... 49 G5
Gorokhov = Horokhiv,
  Ukraine 47 G3
Gorokhovets, Russia 48 B6
Gorom Gorom,
  Burkina Faso 83 C4
Goromonzi, Zimbabwe ... 87 F3
Gorong, Kepulauan,
  Indonesia 63 E8
Gorongose →, Mozam. .. 89 C5
Gorongoza, Mozam. 87 F3
Gorongoza, Sa. da, Mozam. 87 F3
Gorontalo, Indonesia 63 D6
Goronyo, Nigeria 83 C6
Górowo Iławeckie, Poland 44 D7
Gorron, France 18 D6
Gorshechnoye, Russia ... 47 G10
Gort, Ireland 15 C3
Gortis, Greece 36 D6
Góry Bystrzyckie, Poland 45 H3
Goryachiy Klyuch, Russia 49 H4
Gorzkowice, Poland 45 G6
Górzno, Poland 45 E6
Gorzów Śląski, Poland ... 45 G5
Gorzów Wielkopolski,
  Poland 45 F2
Gosford, Australia 95 E5
Goshen, Calif., U.S.A. .. 116 J7
Goshen, Ind., U.S.A. ... 108 E3
Goshen, N.Y., U.S.A. .. 111 E10
Goshogawara, Japan 54 D10
Goslar, Germany 24 D6
Gospič, Croatia 29 D12
Gosport, U.K. 13 G6
Gossas, Senegal 82 C1
Gosse →, Australia 94 B1
Gossi, Mali 83 B4
Gossinga, Sudan 81 F2
Gostivar, Macedonia 40 E4
Gostyń, Poland 45 G4
Gostynin, Poland 45 F6
Göta älv →, Sweden 11 G5
Göta kanal, Sweden 11 F9
Götaland, Sweden 11 G8
Göteborg, Sweden 11 G5
Göteborgs och Bohus län □,
  Sweden 11 F5
Götene, Sweden 11 F7
Goteşti, Moldova 43 D13
Gotha, Germany 24 E6
Gothenburg = Göteborg,
  Sweden 11 G5
Gothenburg, U.S.A. 112 E4
Gothèye, Niger 83 C5
Gotland, Sweden 11 G12
Gotlands län □, Sweden . 11 G12
Gotō-Rettō, Japan 55 H4
Gotse Delchev, Bulgaria . 40 E7
Gotska Sandön, Sweden . 9 G18
Götsu, Japan 55 G6
Gott Pk., Canada 104 C4
Götteborg, Monte, Italy .. 28 D6
Göttingen, Germany 24 D5
Gottwald = Zmiyev, Ukraine 47 H9
Gottwaldov = Zlín,
  Czech Rep. 27 B10
Goubangzi, China 57 D11
Gouda, Neths. 17 B4
Goúdhoura, Ákra, Greece 36 E8
Goudiry, Senegal 82 C2
Goudoumaria, Niger 83 C7
Gouéké, Guinea 82 D3
Gough I., Atl. Oc. 2 G9
Gouin, Rés., Canada 102 C5
Goulburn, Australia 95 E4
Goulburn Is., Australia .. 94 A1
Goulia, Ivory C. 82 C3
Goulimine, Morocco 78 C3
Goumbou, Mali 82 B3
Gouménissa, Greece 40 F6
Goundam, Mali 82 B4
Goúra, Greece 38 D4
Gourbassi, Mali 82 C2
Gourdon, France 20 D5
Gouré, Niger 83 C7
Gourin, France 18 D3
Gourits →, S. Africa ... 88 E3
Gourma-Rharous, Mali .. 83 B4
Goúrnais, Greece 36 D7
Gournay-en-Bray, France 19 C8
Goursi, Burkina Faso ... 82 C4
Gouverneur, U.S.A. 111 B9
Gouviá, Greece 36 A3
Gouzon, France 19 F9
Governador Valadares,
  Brazil 125 G10
Governor's Harbour,
  Bahamas 120 A4
Govindgarh, India 69 G9

Gowan Ra., Australia 94 D4
Gowanda, U.S.A. 110 D6
Gowd-e Zirreh, Afghan. . 66 E3
Gower, U.K. 13 F3
Gowna, L., Ireland 15 C4
Goya, Argentina 126 B4
Göyçay, Azerbaijan 49 K8
Goyder Lagoon, Australia . 95 D2
Goyllarisquisga, Peru ... 124 F3
Göynük, Antalya, Turkey . 39 E12
Göynük, Bolu, Turkey ... 72 B4
Goz Beîda, Chad 79 F10
Goz Regeb, Sudan 81 D4
Gozdnica, Poland 45 G2
Gozo, Malta 36 C1
Graaff-Reinet, S. Africa .. 88 E3
Grabo, Ivory C. 82 D3
Grabow, Germany 24 B7
Grabów nad Prosną, Poland 45 G5
Gračac, Croatia 29 D12
Gračanica, Bos.-H. 42 F3
Graçay, France 19 E8
Gracias a Dios, C.,
  Honduras 120 D3
Graciosa, I., Canary Is. .. 37 E6
Grad Sofiya □, Bulgaria . 40 D7
Gradac, Montenegro, Yug. 40 C3
Gradačac, Bos.-H. 42 F3
Gradeška Planina,
  Macedonia 40 E6
Gradets, Bulgaria 41 D10
Gradišče, Slovenia 29 B12
Grădiştea de Munte,
  Romania 43 E8
Grado, Italy 29 C10
Grado, Spain 34 B4
Grady, U.S.A. 113 H3
Graeca, Lacul, Romania . 43 F11
Grafenau, Germany 25 G9
Gräfenberg, Germany ... 25 F7
Grafham Water, U.K. ... 13 E7
Grafton, Australia 95 D5
Grafton, N. Dak., U.S.A. 112 A6
Grafton, W. Va., U.S.A. . 108 F5
Graham, Canada 102 C1
Graham, U.S.A. 113 J5
Graham, Mt., U.S.A. ... 115 K9
Graham Bell, Ostrov =
Greem-Bell, Ostrov,
  Russia 50 A7
Graham I., B.C., Canada . 104 C2
Graham I., N.W.T., Canada 100 C6
Graham Land, Antarctica . 5 C17
Grahamstown, S. Africa . 88 E4
Grahamsville, U.S.A. ... 111 E10
Grahovo, Montenegro, Yug. 40 D2
Graie, Alpi, Europe 21 C11
Grain Coast, W. Afr. ... 82 E3
Grajaú, Brazil 125 E9
Grajaú →, Brazil 125 D10
Grajewo, Poland 44 E9
Gramada, Bulgaria 40 C6
Gramat, France 20 D5
Grammichele, Italy 31 E7
Grámmos, Óros, Greece . 40 F4
Grampian, U.S.A. 110 F6
Grampian Highlands =
Grampian Mts., U.K. .. 14 E5
Grampian Mts., U.K. ... 14 E5
Grampians, The, Australia 95 F3
Gramsh, Albania 40 F4
Gran Canaria, Canary Is. 37 G4
Gran Chaco, S. Amer. .. 126 B3
Gran Paradiso, Italy 28 C4
Gran Sasso d'Itália, Italy . 29 F10
Granada, Nic. 120 D2
Granada, Spain 35 H7
Granada, U.S.A. 113 F3
Granada □, Spain 35 H7
Granadilla de Abona,
  Canary Is. 37 F3
Granard, Ireland 15 C4
Granbury, U.S.A. 113 J6
Granby, Canada 102 C5
Granby, U.S.A. 114 F11
Grand →, Canada 110 D5
Grand →, Mo., U.S.A. . 112 F8
Grand →, S. Dak., U.S.A. 112 C4
Grand Bahama, Bahamas 120 A4
Grand Bank, Canada 103 C8
Grand Bassam, Ivory C. . 82 D4
Grand Béréby, Ivory C. . 82 E3
Grand-Bourg, Guadeloupe 121 C7
Grand Canal = Yun Ho →,
  China 57 E9
Grand Canyon, U.S.A. .. 115 H7
Grand Canyon National
  Park, U.S.A. 115 H7
Grand Cayman, Cayman Is. 120 C3
Grand Centre, Canada ... 105 C6
Grand Cess, Liberia 82 E3
Grand Coulee, U.S.A. .. 114 C4
Grand Coulee Dam, U.S.A. 114 C4
Grand Erg du Bilma, Niger 79 E8
Grand Erg Occidental,
  Algeria 78 B6
Grand Erg Oriental, Algeria 78 B7
Grand Falls, Canada 103 C6
Grand Falls-Windsor,
  Canada 103 C8
Grand Forks, Canada ... 104 D5
Grand Forks, U.S.A. ... 112 B6
Grand Gorge, U.S.A. .. 111 D10
Grand Haven, U.S.A. ... 108 D2
Grand I., Mich., U.S.A. . 108 B2
Grand I., N.Y., U.S.A. . 110 D6
Grand Island, U.S.A. ... 112 E5
Grand Isle, La., U.S.A. . 113 L9
Grand Isle, Vt., U.S.A. . 111 B11
Grand Junction, U.S.A. . 115 G9
Grand L., N.B., Canada . 103 C6

Grand L., *Nfld., Canada* ... 103 C8
Grand L., *Nfld., Canada* ... 103 B7
Grand L., *U.S.A.* 113 L8
Grand Lahou, *Ivory C.* 82 D3
Grand Lake, *Canada* 114 F11
Grand-Lieu, L. de, *France* .. 18 E5
Grand Manan I., *Canada* ... 103 D6
Grand Marais, *Canada* 112 B9
Grand Marais, *U.S.A.* 108 B3
Grand-Mère, *Canada* 102 C5
Grand Popo, *Benin* 83 D5
Grand Portage, *U.S.A.* 112 B10
Grand Prairie, *U.S.A.* 113 J6
Grand Rapids, *Canada* 105 C9
Grand Rapids, *Mich., U.S.A.* ... 108 D2
Grand Rapids, *Minn., U.S.A.* ... 112 B8
Grand St-Bernard, Col du, *Europe* 25 K3
Grand Teton, *U.S.A.* 114 E8
Grand Teton National Park, *U.S.A.* 114 D8
Grand Union Canal, *U.K.* .. 13 E7
Grand View, *Canada* 105 C8
Grandas de Salime, *Spain* .. 34 B4
Grande →, *Jujuy, Argentina* 126 A2
Grande →, *Mendoza, Argentina* 126 D2
Grande →, *Bolivia* 124 G6
Grande →, *Bahia, Brazil* .. 125 F10
Grande →, *Minas Gerais, Brazil* 125 H8
Grande, B., *Argentina* 128 G3
Grande, Rio →, *U.S.A.* ... 113 N6
Grande Baleine, R. de la →, *Canada* 102 A4
Grande Cache, *Canada* 104 C5
Grande-Entrée, *Canada* ... 103 C7
Grande Prairie, *Canada* ... 104 B5
Grande-Rivière, *Canada* ... 103 C7
Grande-Vallée, *Canada* ... 103 C6
Grandfalls, *U.S.A.* 113 K3
Grândola, *Portugal* 35 G2
Grandpré, *France* 19 C11
Grandview, *U.S.A.* 114 C4
Grandvilliers, *France* 19 C8
Graneros, *Chile* 126 C1
Grangemouth, *U.K.* 14 E5
Granger, *U.S.A.* 114 F9
Grängesberg, *Sweden* 10 D9
Grangeville, *U.S.A.* 114 D5
Granisle, *Canada* 104 C3
Granite City, *U.S.A.* 112 F9
Granite Falls, *U.S.A.* 112 C7
Granite L., *Canada* 103 C8
Granite Mt., *U.S.A.* 117 M10
Granite Pk., *U.S.A.* 114 D9
Graniteville, *U.S.A.* 111 B12
Granity, *N.Z.* 91 J3
Granja, *Brazil* 125 D10
Granja de Moreruela, *Spain* 34 D5
Granja de Torrehermosa, *Spain* 35 G5
Gränna, *Sweden* 11 F8
Granollers, *Spain* 32 D7
Gransee, *Germany* 24 B9
Grant, *U.S.A.* 112 E4
Grant, Mt., *U.S.A.* 114 G4
Grant City, *U.S.A.* 112 E7
Grant I., *Australia* 92 B5
Grant Range, *U.S.A.* 115 G6
Grantham, *U.K.* 12 E7
Grantown-on-Spey, *U.K.* .. 14 D5
Grants, *U.S.A.* 115 J10
Grants Pass, *U.S.A.* 114 E2
Grantsville, *U.S.A.* 114 F7
Granville, *France* 18 D5
Granville, *N. Dak., U.S.A.* 112 A4
Granville, *N.Y., U.S.A.* ... 111 C11
Granville, *Ohio, U.S.A.* ... 110 F2
Granville L., *Canada* 105 B8
Graskop, *S. Africa* 89 C5
Gräsö, *Sweden* 10 D12
Grass →, *Canada* 105 B9
Grass Range, *U.S.A.* 114 C9
Grass River Prov. Park, *Canada* 105 C8
Grass Valley, *Calif., U.S.A.* 116 F6
Grass Valley, *Oreg., U.S.A.* 114 D3
Grassano, *Italy* 31 B9
Grasse, *France* 21 E10
Grassflat, *U.S.A.* 110 F6
Grasslands Nat. Park, *Canada* 105 D7
Grassy, *Australia* 94 G3
Gråsten, *Denmark* 11 K3
Grästorp, *Sweden* 11 F6
Gratkorn, *Austria* 26 D8
Graubünden □, *Switz.* ... 25 J5
Graulhet, *France* 20 E5
Graus, *Spain* 32 C5
Grave, Pte. de, *France* ... 20 C2
Gravelbourg, *Canada* 105 D7
Gravelines, *France* 19 A9
's-Gravenhage, *Neths.* 17 B4
Gravenhurst, *Canada* 102 B4
Gravesend, *Australia* 95 D5
Gravesend, *U.K.* 13 F8
Gravina in Púglia, *Italy* ... 31 B9
Gravois, Pointe-à-, *Haiti* .. 121 C5
Gravone →, *France* 21 G12
Gray, *France* 19 E12
Grayling, *U.S.A.* 108 C3
Grays Harbor, *U.S.A.* 114 C1
Grays L., *U.S.A.* 114 E8
Grays River, *U.S.A.* 116 D3
Grayvoron, *Russia* 47 G8
Graz, *Austria* 26 D8
Grdelica, *Serbia, Yug.* 40 D6

Greasy L., *Canada* 104 A4
Great Abaco I., *Bahamas* .. 120 A4
Great Artesian Basin, *Australia* 94 C3
Great Australian Bight, *Australia* 93 F5
Great Bahama Bank, *Bahamas* 120 B4
Great Barrier I., *N.Z.* 91 G5
Great Barrier Reef, *Australia* 94 B4
Great Barrington, *U.S.A.* .. 111 D11
Great Basin, *U.S.A.* 114 G5
Great Basin Nat. Park, *U.S.A.* 114 G6
Great Bear →, *Canada* ... 100 B7
Great Bear L., *Canada* ... 100 B7
Great Belt = Store Bælt, *Denmark* 11 J4
Great Bend, *Kans., U.S.A.* 112 F5
Great Bend, *Pa., U.S.A.* .. 111 E9
Great Blasket I., *Ireland* .. 15 D1
Great Britain, *Europe* 6 E5
Great Codroy, *Canada* ... 103 C8
Great Dividing Ra., *Australia* 94 C4
Great Driffield = Driffield, *U.K.* 12 C7
Great Exuma I., *Bahamas* . 120 B4
Great Falls, *U.S.A.* 114 C8
Great Fish = Groot Vis →, *S. Africa* 88 E4
Great Guana Cay, *Bahamas* 120 B4
Great Inagua I., *Bahamas* . 121 B5
Great Indian Desert = Thar Desert, *India* 68 F5
Great Karoo, *S. Africa* ... 88 E3
Great Lake, *Australia* 94 G4
Great Lakes, *N. Amer.* ... 98 E11
Great Malvern, *U.K.* 13 E5
Great Miami →, *U.S.A.* .. 108 F3
Great Ormes Head, *U.K.* .. 12 D4
Great Ouse →, *U.K.* 12 E8
Great Palm I., *Australia* .. 94 B4
Great Plains, *N. Amer.* ... 106 A6
Great Ruaha →, *Tanzania* . 86 D4
Great Sacandaga Res. . 111 C10
Great Saint Bernard Pass = Grand St-Bernard, Col du, *Europe* 25 K3
Great Salt L., *U.S.A.* 114 F7
Great Salt Lake Desert, *U.S.A.* 114 F7
Great Salt Plains L., *U.S.A.* 113 G5
Great Sandy Desert, *Australia* 92 D3
Great Sangi = Sangihe, Pulau, *Indonesia* 63 D7
Great Scarcies →, *S. Leone* 82 D2
Great Skellig, *Ireland* 15 E1
Great Slave L., *Canada* ... 104 A5
Great Smoky Mts. Nat. Park, *U.S.A.* 109 H4
Great Snow Mt., *Canada* .. 104 B4
Great Stour = Stour →, *U.K.* 13 F9
Great Victoria Desert, *Australia* 93 E4
Great Wall, *China* 56 E5
Great Whernside, *U.K.* ... 12 C6
Great Yarmouth, *U.K.* ... 13 E9
Greater Antilles, *W. Indies* 121 C5
Greater London □, *U.K.* .. 13 F7
Greater Manchester □, *U.K.* 12 D5
Greater Sunda Is., *Indonesia* 62 F4
Grebbestad, *Sweden* 11 F5
Grebenka = Hrebenka, *Ukraine* 47 G7
Greco, C., *Cyprus* 36 E13
Greco, Mte., *Italy* 29 G10
Gredos, Sierra de, *Spain* .. 34 E6
Greece, *U.S.A.* 110 C7
Greece ■, *Europe* 38 B3
Greeley, *Colo., U.S.A.* ... 112 E2
Greeley, *Nebr., U.S.A.* ... 112 E5
Greem-Bell, Ostrov, *Russia* 50 A7
Green, *U.S.A.* 114 E2
Green →, *Ky., U.S.A.* ... 108 G2
Green →, *Utah, U.S.A.* .. 115 G9
Green B., *U.S.A.* 108 C2
Green Bay, *U.S.A.* 108 C2
Green C., *Australia* 95 F5
Green Cove Springs, *U.S.A.* 109 L5
Green Lake, *Canada* 105 C7
Green Mts., *U.S.A.* 111 C12
Green River, *Utah, U.S.A.* 115 G8
Green River, *Wyo., U.S.A.* 114 F9
Green Valley, *U.S.A.* 115 L8
Greenbank, *U.S.A.* 116 B4
Greenbush, *Mich., U.S.A.* . 110 B1
Greenbush, *Minn., U.S.A.* . 112 A6
Greencastle, *U.S.A.* 108 F2
Greene, *U.S.A.* 111 D9
Greenfield, *Calif., U.S.A.* . 116 J5
Greenfield, *Calif., U.S.A.* . 117 K8
Greenfield, *Ind., U.S.A.* .. 108 F3
Greenfield, *Iowa, U.S.A.* .. 112 E7
Greenfield, *Mass., U.S.A.* . 111 D12
Greenfield, *Mo., U.S.A.* .. 113 G8
Greenfield Park, *Canada* .. 111 A11
Greenland ■, *N. Amer.* ... 4 C5
Greenland Sea, *Arctic* 4 B7
Greenock, *U.K.* 14 F4
Greenore, *Ireland* 15 B5
Greenore Pt., *Ireland* 15 D5
Greenough, *Australia* 93 E1
Greenough →, *Australia* .. 93 E1
Greenough Pt., *Canada* ... 110 B3
Greenport, *U.S.A.* 111 E12
Greensboro, *N.C., U.S.A.* . 109 J4
Greensboro, *N.C., U.S.A.* . 109 G6

Greensboro, *Vt., U.S.A.* .. 111 B12
Greensburg, *Ind., U.S.A.* . 108 F3
Greensburg, *Kans., U.S.A.* 113 G5
Greensburg, *Pa., U.S.A.* .. 110 F5
Greenstone Pt., *U.K.* 14 D3
Greenvale, *Australia* 94 B4
Greenville, *Liberia* 82 D3
Greenville, *Ala., U.S.A.* .. 109 K2
Greenville, *Calif., U.S.A.* . 116 E6
Greenville, *Maine, U.S.A.* . 109 C11
Greenville, *Mich., U.S.A.* . 108 D3
Greenville, *Miss., U.S.A.* . 113 J9
Greenville, *Mo., U.S.A.* .. 113 G9
Greenville, *N.C., U.S.A.* .. 109 H7
Greenville, *N.H., U.S.A.* .. 111 D13
Greenville, *N.Y., U.S.A.* .. 111 D10
Greenville, *Ohio, U.S.A.* .. 108 E3
Greenville, *Pa., U.S.A.* ... 110 E4
Greenville, *S.C., U.S.A.* .. 109 H4
Greenville, *Tenn., U.S.A.* . 109 G4
Greenville, *Tex., U.S.A.* .. 113 J6
Greenwater Lake Prov. Park, *Canada* 105 C8
Greenwich, *U.K.* 13 F8
Greenwich, *Conn., U.S.A.* 111 E11
Greenwich, *N.Y., U.S.A.* . 111 C11
Greenwich, *Ohio, U.S.A.* . 110 E2
Greenwood, *Canada* 104 D5
Greenwood, *Ark., U.S.A.* . 113 H7
Greenwood, *Ind., U.S.A.* . 108 F2
Greenwood, *Miss., U.S.A.* 113 J9
Greenwood, *S.C., U.S.A.* . 109 H4
Greenwood, Mt., *Australia* 92 B5
Gregbe, *Ivory C.* 82 D3
Gregory, *U.S.A.* 112 D5
Gregory →, *Australia* 94 B2
Gregory, L., *S. Austral., Australia* 95 D2
Gregory, L., *W. Austral., Australia* 93 E2
Gregory Downs, *Australia* . 94 B2
Gregory L., *Australia* 92 D4
Gregory Ra., *Queens., Australia* 94 B3
Gregory Ra., *W. Austral., Australia* 92 D3
Greiffenberg, *Germany* ... 24 B9
Greifswald, *Germany* 24 A9
Greifswalder Bodden, *Germany* 24 A9
Grein, *Austria* 26 C7
Greiz, *Germany* 24 E8
Gremikha, *Russia* 50 C6
Grená, *Denmark* 11 H4
Grenada, *U.S.A.* 113 J10
Grenada ■, *W. Indies* ... 121 D7
Grenade, *France* 20 E5
Grenadier I., *U.S.A.* 111 B8
Grenadines, *W. Indies* ... 121 D7
Grenchen, *Switz.* 25 H3
Grenen, *Denmark* 11 G4
Grenfell, *Australia* 95 E4
Grenfell, *Canada* 105 C8
Grenoble, *France* 21 C9
Grenora, *U.S.A.* 112 A2
Grenville, C., *Australia* ... 94 A3
Grenville Chan., *Canada* .. 104 C3
Gréoux-les-Bains, *France* . 21 E9
Gresham, *U.S.A.* 116 E4
Gresik, *Indonesia* 63 G15
Gretna, *U.K.* 14 F5
Greven, *Germany* 24 C3
Grevená, *Greece* 40 F5
Grevená □, *Greece* 40 F5
Grevenbroich, *Germany* .. 24 D2
Grevenmacher, *Lux.* 17 E6
Grevesmühlen, *Germany* .. 24 B7
Grevestrand, *Denmark* ... 11 J6
Grey →, *Canada* 103 C8
Grey →, *N.Z.* 91 K3
Grey, C., *Australia* 94 A2
Grey Ra., *Australia* 95 D3
Greybull, *U.S.A.* 114 D9
Greymouth, *N.Z.* 91 K3
Greystones, *Ireland* 15 C5
Greytown, *N.Z.* 91 J5
Greytown, *S. Africa* 89 D5
Gribanovskiy, *Russia* 48 E5
Gribbell I., *Canada* 104 C3
Gribës, Mal i, *Albania* ... 40 F3
Gridley, *U.S.A.* 116 F5
Griekwastad, *S. Africa* ... 88 D3
Griesheim, *Germany* 25 F4
Grieskirchen, *Austria* 26 C6
Griffin, *U.S.A.* 109 J3
Griffith, *Australia* 95 E4
Griffith, *Canada* 110 A7
Griffith I., *Canada* 110 B4
Grignols, *France* 20 D3
Grigoriopol, *Moldova* ... 43 C14
Grimaylov = Hrymayliv, *Ukraine* 47 H4
Grimes, *U.S.A.* 116 F5
Grimma, *Germany* 24 D8
Grimmen, *Germany* 24 A9
Grimsay, *U.K.* 14 D1
Grimsby, *Canada* 110 C5
Grimsby, *U.K.* 12 D7
Grímsey, *Iceland* 8 C5
Grimshaw, *Canada* 104 B5
Grimslöv, *Sweden* 11 H8
Grimstad, *Norway* 9 G13
Grindelwald, *Switz.* 25 J4
Grindsted, *Denmark* 11 J2
Grindstone I., *Canada* ... 111 B8
Grindu, *Romania* 43 F11
Grinnell, *U.S.A.* 112 E8
Grintavec, *Slovenia* 29 B11
Gris-Nez, C., *France* 19 B8
Grisolles, *France* 20 E5
Grisons = Graubünden □, *Switz.* 25 J5

Grisslehamn, *Sweden* 10 D12
Grmeč Planina, *Bos.-H.* .. 29 D13
Groais I., *Canada* 103 B8
Grobiņa, *Latvia* 44 B8
Groblersdal, *S. Africa* ... 89 D4
Groblershoop, *S. Africa* .. 88 D3
Grocka, *Serbia, Yug.* 40 B4
Gródek, *Poland* 45 E10
Grodków, *Poland* 45 H4
Grodno = Hrodna, *Belarus* 46 F2
Grodzisk Mazowiecki, *Poland* 45 F7
Grodzisk Wielkopolski, *Poland* 45 F3
Grodzyanka = Hrodzyanka, *Belarus* 46 F5
Groesbeck, *U.S.A.* 113 K6
Groix, *France* 18 E3
Groix, Î. de, *France* 18 E3
Grójec, *Poland* 45 G7
Gronau, *Niedersachsen, Germany* 24 C5
Gronau, *Nordrhein-Westfalen, Germany* 24 C3
Grong, *Norway* 8 D15
Grönhögen, *Sweden* 11 H10
Groningen, *Neths.* 17 A6
Groningen □, *Neths.* 17 A6
Groom, *U.S.A.* 113 H4
Groot →, *S. Africa* 88 E3
Groot Berg →, *S. Africa* . 88 E2
Groot-Brakrivier, *S. Africa* 88 E3
Groot Karasberge, *Namibia* 88 D2
Groot-Kei →, *S. Africa* .. 89 E4
Groot Vis →, *S. Africa* .. 88 E4
Grootdrink, *S. Africa* 88 D3
Groote Eylandt, *Australia* . 94 A2
Grootfontein, *Namibia* ... 88 B2
Grootlaagte →, *Africa* ... 88 C3
Grootvloer →, *S. Africa* .. 88 E3
Gros C., *Canada* 104 A6
Gros Morne Nat. Park, *Canada* 103 C8
Grósio, *Italy* 28 B7
Grosne →, *France* 19 F11
Grossa, Pta., *Spain* 37 B8
Grossenbrode, *Germany* .. 24 A7
Grossenhain, *Germany* ... 24 D9
Grosser Arber, *Germany* . 25 F9
Grosser Plöner See, *Germany* 24 A6
Grosseto, *Italy* 29 F8
Grossgerungs, *Austria* ... 26 C7
Grossglockner, *Austria* ... 26 D5
Groswater B., *Canada* 103 B8
Groton, *Conn., U.S.A.* ... 111 E12
Groton, *N.Y., U.S.A.* 111 D8
Groton, *S. Dak., U.S.A.* .. 112 C5
Grottáglie, *Italy* 31 B10
Grottaminarda, *Italy* 31 A8
Grottammare, *Italy* 29 F11
Grouard Mission, *Canada* . 104 B5
Grouin, Pte. du, *France* .. 18 D5
Groundhog →, *Canada* .. 102 C3
Grouw, *Neths.* 17 A5
Grove City, *U.S.A.* 110 E4
Grove Hill, *U.S.A.* 109 K2
Groveland, *U.S.A.* 116 H6
Grover City, *U.S.A.* 117 K6
Groves, *U.S.A.* 113 L8
Groveton, *U.S.A.* 111 B13
Groznjan, *Croatia* 29 C10
Groznyy, *Russia* 49 J7
Grubišno Polje, *Croatia* .. 42 C2
Grudovo, *Bulgaria* 41 D11
Grudusk, *Poland* 45 E7
Grudziądz, *Poland* 44 E5
Gruinard B., *U.K.* 14 D3
Gruissan, *France* 20 E7
Grumo Áppula, *Italy* 31 A9
Grums, *Sweden* 10 E7
Grünberg, *Germany* 24 E4
Gründau, *Germany* 25 E5
Grundy Center, *U.S.A.* .. 112 D8
Grünstadt, *Germany* 25 F4
Grünwerget, *Sweden* 10 C10
Gruver, *U.S.A.* 113 G4
Gruyères, *Switz.* 25 J3
Gruža, *Serbia, Yug.* 40 C4
Gryazi, *Russia* 47 F10
Gryazovets, *Russia* 46 C11
Grybów, *Poland* 45 J7
Grycksbo, *Sweden* 10 D9
Gryfice, *Poland* 44 E2
Gryfino, *Poland* 44 E1
Gryfów Śląski, *Poland* ... 45 G2
Grythyttan, *Sweden* 10 E8

Guadalupe, *U.S.A.* 117 L6
Guadalupe →, *Mexico* ... 117 N10
Guadalupe →, *U.S.A.* ... 113 L6
Guadalupe, Sierra de, *Spain* 35 F5
Guadalupe Bravos, *Mexico* 118 A3
Guadalupe I., *Pac. Oc.* ... 98 G8
Guadalupe Mts. Nat. Park, *U.S.A.* 113 K2
Guadalupe Peak, *U.S.A.* .. 113 K2
Guadalupe y Calvo, *Mexico* 118 B3
Guadarrama, Sierra de, *Spain* 34 E7
Guadaloupe ■, *W. Indies* . 121 C7
Guadeloupe Passage, *W. Indies* 121 C7
Guadiamar →, *Spain* 35 J4
Guadiana →, *Portugal* ... 35 H3
Guadiana Menor →, *Spain* 35 H5
Guadiaro →, *Spain* 35 J5
Guadiato →, *Spain* 35 H5
Guadiela →, *Spain* 32 E2
Guadix, *Spain* 35 H7
Guafo, Boca del, *Chile* ... 128 E2
Guainía →, *Colombia* 124 C5
Guaíra, *Brazil* 127 A5
Guaitecas, Is., *Chile* 128 E2
Guajará-Mirim, *Brazil* ... 124 F5
Guajira, Pen. de la, *Colombia* 124 A4
Gualán, *Guatemala* 120 C2
Gualdo Tadino, *Italy* 29 E9
Gualeguay, *Argentina* ... 126 C4
Gualeguaychú, *Argentina* . 126 C4
Gualequay →, *Argentina* . 126 C4
Guam ■, *Pac. Oc.* 96 F6
Guaminí, *Argentina* 126 D3
Guamúchil, *Mexico* 118 B3
Guanabacoa, *Cuba* 120 B3
Guanacaste, Cordillera del, *Costa Rica* 120 D2
Guanaceví, *Mexico* 118 B3
Guanahani = San Salvador I., *Bahamas* 121 B5
Guanajay, *Cuba* 120 B3
Guanajuato, *Mexico* 118 C4
Guanajuato □, *Mexico* ... 118 C4
Guandacol, *Argentina* ... 126 B2
Guane, *Cuba* 120 B3
Guang'an, *China* 58 B6
Guangchang, *China* 59 D11
Guangde, *China* 59 B12
Guangdong □, *China* 59 F9
Guangfeng, *China* 59 C12
Guanghan, *China* 58 B5
Guanghua, *China* 58 E5
Guangling, *China* 56 E8
Guangnan, *China* 58 E5
Guangning, *China* 59 F9
Guangrao, *China* 57 F10
Guangshui, *China* 59 B9
Guangshun, *China* 58 D6
Guangwu, *China* 56 F3
Guangxi Zhuangzu Zizhiqu □, *China* 58 F7
Guangyuan, *China* 58 A5
Guangze, *China* 59 D11
Guangzhou, *China* 59 F9
Guanipa →, *Venezuela* .. 124 B6
Guanling, *China* 58 E5
Guanta, *Venezuela* 124 A5
Guantánamo, *Cuba* 121 B4
Guantao, *China* 56 F8
Guanyang, *China* 59 E8
Guanyun, *China* 57 G10
Guápiles, *Costa Rica* 120 D3
Guaporé, *Brazil* 127 B5
Guaporé →, *Brazil* 122 E4
Guaqui, *Bolivia* 124 G5
Guara, Sierra de, *Spain* .. 32 C4
Guarapari, *Brazil* 127 A7
Guarapuava, *Brazil* 127 B5
Guaratinguetá, *Brazil* ... 127 A6
Guaratuba, *Brazil* 127 B6
Guarda, *Portugal* 34 E3
Guarda □, *Portugal* 34 E3
Guardafui, C. = Asir, Ras, *Somali Rep.* 74 E5
Guardamar del Segura, *Spain* 33 G4
Guardavalle, *Italy* 31 D9
Guárdia Sanframondi, *Italy* 31 A7
Guardiagrele, *Italy* 29 F11
Guardo, *Spain* 34 C6
Guareña, *Spain* 35 G4
Guareña →, *Spain* 34 D5
Guárico □, *Venezuela* ... 124 B5
Guarujá, *Brazil* 127 A6
Guarus, *Brazil* 127 A7
Guasave, *Mexico* 118 B3
Guasdualito, *Venezuela* .. 124 B4
Guastalla, *Italy* 28 D7
Guatemala, *Guatemala* ... 120 D1
Guatemala ■, *Cent. Amer.* 120 C1
Guatire, *Venezuela* 124 A5
Guaviare →, *Colombia* .. 124 C5
Guaxupé, *Brazil* 127 A6
Guayama, *Puerto Rico* ... 121 C6
Guayaquil, *Ecuador* 124 D3
Guayaquil, G. de, *Ecuador* 124 D2
Guaymas, *Mexico* 118 B2
Guazhou, *China* 59 A12
Guba, *Dem. Rep. of the Congo* 87 E2
Guba, *Ethiopia* 81 E4
Gúbakha, *Russia* 50 D6
Gûbâl, Madîq, *Egypt* 80 B3
Gubat, *Phil.* 61 E6
Gúbbio, *Italy* 29 E9
Guben, *Germany* 24 D10
Gubin, *Poland* 45 G1
Gubio, *Nigeria* 83 C7
Gubkin, *Russia* 47 G9
Guča, *Serbia, Yug.* 40 C4

Gucheng, *China* 59 A8
Gudata = Guadauta,
  Georgia 49 J5
Gudbrandsdalen, *Norway* .. 9 F14
Guddu Barrage, *Pakistan* .. 66 E6
Gudenå →, *Denmark* 11 H4
Gudermes, *Russia* 49 J8
Gudhjem, *Denmark* 11 J8
Gudivada, *India* 67 L12
Gudur, *India* 66 M11
Guebwiller, *France* 19 E14
Guecho = Getxo, *Spain* ... 32 B2
Guékédou, *Guinea* 82 D2
Guéle Mendouka, *Cameroon* 83 E7
Guelph, *Canada* 102 D3
Guéméné-Penfao, *France* .. 18 E5
Guéméné-sur-Scorff, *France* 18 D3
Guéné, *Benin* 83 C5
Guer, *France* 18 E4
Guérande, *France* 18 E4
Guéret, *France* 19 F8
Guérigny, *France* 19 E10
Guerneville, *U.S.A.* 116 G4
Guernica = Gernika-Lumo,
  Spain 32 B2
Guernsey, *U.K.* 13 H5
Guernsey, *U.S.A.* 112 D2
Guerrero □, *Mexico* 119 D5
Guessou-Sud, *Benin* 83 C5
Gueugnon, *France* 19 F11
Guéyo, *Ivory C.* 82 D3
Gughe, *Ethiopia* 81 F4
Gügher, *Iran* 71 D8
Guglionesi, *Italy* 29 G11
Guhakolak, Tanjung,
  Indonesia 63 G11
Gui Jiang →, *China* 59 F8
Guia, *Canary Is.* 37 F4
Guia de Isora, *Canary Is.* . 37 F3
Guia Lopes da Laguna,
  Brazil 127 A4
Guiana, *S. Amer.* 122 C4
Guibéroua, *Ivory C.* 82 D3
Guichi, *China* 59 B11
Guider, *Cameroon* 83 D7
Guidiguir, *Niger* 83 C6
Guidimouni, *Niger* 83 C6
Guiding, *China* 58 D6
Guidong, *China* 59 D9
Guidónia-Montecélio, *Italy* 29 F9
Guiers, L. de, *Senegal* 82 B1
Guigang, *China* 58 F7
Guiglo, *Ivory C.* 82 D3
Guihulñgan, *Phil.* 61 F6
Guijá, *Mozam.* 89 C5
Guijuelo, *Spain* 34 E5
Guildford, *U.K.* 13 F7
Guilford, *U.S.A.* 111 E12
Guilin, *China* 59 E8
Guillaume-Delisle L.,
  Canada 102 A4
Guillaumes, *France* 21 D10
Guillestre, *France* 21 D10
Guilvinec, *France* 18 E2
Güimar, *Canary Is.* 37 F3
Guimarães, *Portugal* 34 D2
Guimaras □, *Phil.* 61 F5
Guinda, *U.S.A.* 116 G4
Guinea, *Africa* 76 F4
Guinea ■, *W. Afr.* 82 C2
Guinea, Gulf of, *Atl. Oc.* . 83 E5
Guinea-Bissau ■, *Africa* .. 82 C2
Güines, *Cuba* 120 B3
Guingamp, *France* 18 D3
Guinguinéo, *Senegal* 82 C1
Guipavas, *France* 18 D2
Guiping, *China* 59 F8
Guipúzcoa □, *Spain* 32 B2
Guir, *Mali* 82 B4
Guirel, *Mauritania* 82 B3
Güiria, *Venezuela* 124 A6
Guiscard, *France* 19 C10
Guise, *France* 19 C10
Guitiriz, *Spain* 34 B3
Guitri, *Ivory C.* 82 D3
Guiuan, *Phil.* 61 F6
Guixi, *China* 59 C11
Guiyang, *Guizhou, China* . 58 D6
Guiyang, *Hunan, China* ... 59 E9
Guizhou □, *China* 58 D6
Gujan-Mestras, *France* ... 20 D2
Gujar Khan, *Pakistan* 68 C5
Gujarat □, *India* 68 H4
Gujiang, *China* 59 D10
Gujranwala, *Pakistan* 68 C6
Gujrat, *Pakistan* 68 C6
Gukovo, *Russia* 49 F5
Gulargambone, *Australia* . 95 E4
Gulbarga, *India* 66 L10
Gulbene, *Latvia* 9 H22
Gulf, The, *Asia* 71 E6
Gulfport, *U.S.A.* 113 K10
Gulgong, *Australia* 95 E4
Gulin, *China* 58 C5
Gulistan, *Pakistan* 68 D2
Gull Lake, *Canada* 105 C7
Gullbrandstorp, *Sweden* .. 11 H6
Gullspång, *Sweden* 11 F8
Güllük, *Turkey* 39 D9
Güllük Korfezi, *Turkey* ... 39 D9
Gulma, *Nigeria* 83 C5
Gulmarg, *India* 69 B6
Gülnar, *Turkey* 72 D5
Gülpınar, *Turkey* 39 B8
Gülşehir, *Turkey* 72 C6
Gulshad, *Kazakhstan* 50 E8
Gulu, *Uganda* 86 B3
Gŭlŭbovo, *Bulgaria* 41 D9
Gulud, J., *Sudan* 81 E2
Gulwe, *Tanzania* 86 D4

Gulyaypole = Hulyaypole,
  Ukraine 47 J9
Gumal →, *Pakistan* 68 D3
Gumbaz, *Pakistan* 68 D3
Gumel, *Nigeria* 83 C6
Gumiel de Hizán, *Spain* .. 34 D7
Gumla, *India* 69 H11
Gumlu, *Australia* 94 B4
Gumma □, *Japan* 55 F9
Gummersbach, *Germany* .. 24 D3
Gummi, *Nigeria* 83 C6
Gümüldür, *Turkey* 39 C9
Gümüşçay, *Turkey* 41 F11
Gümüşhacıköy, *Turkey* ... 72 B6
Gümüşhane, *Turkey* 73 B8
Gümüşsu, *Turkey* 39 C11
Gumzai, *Indonesia* 63 F8
Guna, *Ethiopia* 81 F4
Guna, *India* 68 G7
Gundelfingen, *Germany* .. 25 G6
Güney, *Burdur, Turkey* ... 39 D11
Güney, *Denizli, Turkey* ... 39 C11
Güneydoğu Toroslar, *Turkey* 73 C9
Gunisao →, *Canada* 105 C9
Gunisao L., *Canada* 105 C9
Gunjyal, *Pakistan* 68 C4
Günlüce, *Turkey* 39 E10
Gunnarskog, *Sweden* 10 E6
Gunnbjørn Fjeld, *Greenland* 4 C6
Gunnebo, *Sweden* 11 G10
Gunnedah, *Australia* 95 E5
Gunnewin, *Australia* 95 D4
Gunningbar Cr. →,
  Australia 95 E4
Gunnison, *Colo., U.S.A.* .. 115 G10
Gunnison, *Utah, U.S.A.* ... 114 G8
Gunnison →, *U.S.A.* 115 G9
Gunpowder, *Australia* 94 B2
Guntakal, *India* 66 M10
Guntersville, *U.S.A.* 109 H2
Guntong, *Malaysia* 65 K3
Guntur, *India* 67 L12
Gunungapi, *Indonesia* 63 F7
Gunungsitoli, *Indonesia* .. 62 D1
Günz →, *Germany* 25 G6
Gunza, *Angola* 84 G2
Günzburg, *Germany* 25 G6
Gunzenhausen, *Germany* .. 25 F6
Guo He →, *China* 57 H9
Guoyang, *China* 56 H9
Gupis, *Pakistan* 69 A5
Gura Humorului, *Romania* 43 C10
Gura-Teghii, *Romania* 43 E11
Gurag, *Ethiopia* 81 F4
Gurahonţ, *Romania* 42 D7
Gurdaspur, *India* 68 C6
Gurdon, *U.S.A.* 113 J8
Güre, *Balıkesir, Turkey* ... 39 B8
Güre, *Uşak, Turkey* 39 C11
Gurgaon, *India* 68 E7
Gürgentepe, *Turkey* 72 B7
Gurghiu, Munţii, *Romania* 43 D10
Gurgueia →, *Brazil* 125 E10
Gurha, *India* 68 G4
Guri, Embalse de, *Venezuela* 124 B6
Gurin, *Nigeria* 83 D7
Gurjaani, *Georgia* 49 K7
Gurk →, *Austria* 26 E7
Gurkha, *Nepal* 69 E11
Gurley, *Australia* 95 D4
Gurnet Point, *U.S.A.* 111 D14
Gürpınar, *İst., Turkey* 41 F12
Gürpınar, *Van, Turkey* ... 73 C10
Gürsu, *Turkey* 41 F13
Gurué, *Mozam.* 87 F4
Gurun, *Malaysia* 65 K3
Gürün, *Turkey* 72 C7
Gurupá, *Brazil* 125 D8
Gurupá, I. Grande de, *Brazil* 125 D8
Gurupi, *Brazil* 125 F9
Gurupi →, *Brazil* 125 D9
Guruwe, *Zimbabwe* 89 B5
Guryev = Atyraū, *Kazakstan* 50 E6
Gus-Khrustalnyy, *Russia* .. 48 C5
Gusau, *Nigeria* 83 C6
Gusev, *Russia* 9 J20
Gushan, *China* 57 E12
Gushgy, *Turkmenistan* 50 F7
Gushi, *China* 59 A10
Gushiago, *Ghana* 83 D4
Gusinje, *Montenegro, Yug.* 40 D3
Gusinoozersk, *Russia* 51 D11
Gúspini, *Italy* 30 C1
Güssing, *Austria* 27 D9
Gustavsberg, *Sweden* 10 E12
Gustavus, *U.S.A.* 104 B1
Gustine, *U.S.A.* 116 H6
Güstrow, *Germany* 24 B8
Gusum, *Sweden* 11 F10
Guta = Kolárovo,
  Slovak Rep. 27 D10
Gütersloh, *Germany* 24 D4
Gutha, *Australia* 93 E2
Guthalungra, *Australia* ... 94 B4
Guthrie, *Okla., U.S.A.* ... 113 H6
Guthrie, *Tex., U.S.A.* 113 J4
Gutian, *China* 59 D12
Guttenberg, *U.S.A.* 112 D9
Gutu, *Zimbabwe* 89 B5
Guyana ■, *S. Amer.* 124 C7
Guyane française = French
  Guiana ■, *S. Amer.* 125 C8
Guyang, *China* 56 D6
Guyenne, *France* 20 D4
Guymon, *U.S.A.* 113 G4
Guyra, *Australia* 95 E5
Guyuan, *Hebei, China* 56 D8
Guyuan, *Ningxia Huizu,
  China* 56 G4
Güzelbahçe, *Turkey* 39 C8
Guzhang, *China* 58 C7

Guzhen, *China* 57 H9
Guzmán, L. de, *Mexico* ... 118 A3
Gvardeysk, *Russia* 9 J19
Gvardeyskoye, *Ukraine* ... 47 K8
Gwa, *Burma* 67 L19
Gwaai, *Zimbabwe* 87 F2
Gwabegar, *Australia* 95 E4
Gwadabawa, *Nigeria* 83 C6
Gwādar, *Pakistan* 66 G3
Gwagwada, *Nigeria* 83 C6
Gwalior, *India* 68 F8
Gwanara, *Nigeria* 83 D5
Gwanda, *Zimbabwe* 87 G2
Gwandu, *Nigeria* 83 C5
Gwane,
  Dem. Rep. of the Congo 86 B2
Gwaram, *Nigeria* 83 C7
Gwarzo, *Nigeria* 83 C6
Gwasero, *Nigeria* 83 D5
Gwda →, *Poland* 45 E3
Gweebarra B., *Ireland* 15 B3
Gweedore, *Ireland* 15 A3
Gweru, *Zimbabwe* 87 F2
Gwi, *Nigeria* 83 D6
Gwinn, *U.S.A.* 108 B2
Gwio Kura, *Nigeria* 83 C7
Gwoza, *Nigeria* 83 C7
Gwydir →, *Australia* 95 D4
Gwynedd □, *U.K.* 12 E3
Gyandzha = Gäncä,
  Azerbaijan 49 K8
Gyaring Hu, *China* 60 C4
Gydanskiy Poluostrov,
  Russia 50 C8
Gympie, *Australia* 95 D5
Gyomaendrőd, *Hungary* .. 42 D5
Gyöngyös, *Hungary* 42 C4
Győr, *Hungary* 42 C2
Győr-Moson-Sopron □,
  Hungary 42 C2
Gypsum Pt., *Canada* 104 A6
Gypsumville, *Canada* 105 C9
Gyueshevo, *Bulgaria* 40 D6
Gyula, *Hungary* 42 D6
Gyumri, *Armenia* 49 K6
Gyzylarbat, *Turkmenistan* . 50 F6
Gyzyletrek, *Turkmenistan* . 71 B7
Gzhatsk = Gagarin, *Russia* . 46 E8

H

Ha 'Arava →, *Israel* 75 E4
Ha Coi, *Vietnam* 58 G6
Ha Dong, *Vietnam* 58 G5
Ha Giang, *Vietnam* 58 F5
Ha Tien, *Vietnam* 65 G5
Ha Tinh, *Vietnam* 64 C5
Ha Trung, *Vietnam* 64 C5
Haaksbergen, *Neths.* 17 B6
Haapsalu, *Estonia* 9 G20
Haarlem, *Neths.* 17 B4
Haast →, *N.Z.* 91 K2
Haast Bluff, *Australia* 92 D5
Hab →, *Pakistan* 68 G3
Hab Nadi Chauki, *Pakistan* 68 G2
Habaswein, *Kenya* 86 B4
Habay, *Canada* 104 B5
Ḥabbānīyah, *Iraq* 70 C4
Ḥabbānīyah, Hawr al, *Iraq* . 73 F10
Habo, *Sweden* 11 G8
Haboro, *Japan* 54 B10
Ḥabshān, *U.A.E.* 71 F7
Hachenburg, *Germany* 24 E3
Hachijō-Jima, *Japan* 55 H9
Hachinohe, *Japan* 54 D10
Hachiōji, *Japan* 55 G9
Hachŏn, *N. Korea* 57 D15
Hacıbektaş, *Turkey* 72 C6
Hacılar, *Turkey* 72 C6
Hackås, *Sweden* 10 B8
Hackensack, *U.S.A.* 111 F10
Hackettstown, *U.S.A.* 111 F10
Hadali, *Pakistan* 68 C5
Hadarba, Ras, *Sudan* 80 C4
Hadarom □, *Israel* 75 E4
Hadd, Ra's al, *Oman* 74 C6
Hadejia, *Nigeria* 83 C7
Hadejia →, *Nigeria* 83 C7
Hadera, *Israel* 75 C3
Hadera, N. →, *Israel* 75 C3
Haderslev, *Denmark* 11 J3
Hadhramaut = Ḥaḍramawt,
  Yemen 74 D4
Hadibu, *Yemen* 74 E5
Hadım, *Turkey* 72 D5
Hadong, S. *Korea* 57 G14
Ḥaḍramawt, *Yemen* 74 D4
Ḥadrāniyah, *Iraq* 70 C4
Hadrian's Wall, *U.K.* 12 B5
Hadsten, *Denmark* 11 H4
Hadsund, *Denmark* 11 H4
Hadyach, *Ukraine* 47 G8
Haeju, N. *Korea* 57 E13
Haenam, S. *Korea* 57 G14
Haenertsburg, S. *Africa* ... 89 C4
Haerhpin = Harbin, *China* . 57 B14
Hafar al Bāṭin, *Si. Arabia* .. 70 D5
Hafirat al 'Aydā, *Si. Arabia* . 70 E3
Hafit, *Oman* 71 F7
Ḥafit, Jabal, *Oman* 71 E7
Hafizabad, *Pakistan* 68 C5
Haflong, *India* 67 G18
Hafnarfjörður, *Iceland* 8 D3
Haft Gel, *Iran* 71 D6
Hafun, Ras, *Somali Rep.* .. 74 E5
Hagalil, *Israel* 75 C4
Hagby, *Sweden* 11 H10

Hagen, *Germany* 24 D3
Hagenow, *Germany* 24 B7
Hagerman, *U.S.A.* 113 J2
Hagerstown, *U.S.A.* 108 F7
Hagersville, *Canada* 110 D4
Hagetmau, *France* 20 E3
Hagfors, *Sweden* 10 D7
Hagi, *Japan* 55 G5
Hagolan, *Syria* 75 C4
Hagondange, *France* 19 C13
Hags Hd., *Ireland* 15 D2
Hague, C. de la, *France* ... 18 C5
Hague, The = 's-
  Gravenhage, *Neths.* 17 B4
Haguenau, *France* 19 D14
Hai Duong, *Vietnam* 58 G6
Hai'an, *Guangdong, China* . 59 G8
Hai'an, *Jiangsu, China* 59 A13
Haicheng, *Fujian, China* ... 59 E11
Haicheng, *Liaoning, China* . 57 D12
Haidar Khel, *Afghan.* 68 C3
Haidargarh, *India* 69 F9
Haifa = Hefa, *Israel* 75 C4
Haifeng, *China* 59 F10
Haiger, *Germany* 24 E4
Haikou, *China* 60 D6
Ḥā'il, *Si. Arabia* 70 E4
Ḥā'il □, *Si. Arabia* 70 E4
Hailar, *China* 60 B6
Hailey, *U.S.A.* 114 E6
Haileybury, *Canada* 102 C4
Hailin, *China* 57 B15
Hailing Dao, *China* 59 G8
Hailong, *China* 57 C13
Hailuoto, *Finland* 8 D21
Haimen, *Guangdong, China* 59 F11
Haimen, *Jiangsu, China* ... 59 B13
Hainan □, *China* 60 E5
Hainaut □, *Belgium* 17 D4
Hainburg, *Austria* 27 C9
Haines, *Alaska, U.S.A.* 104 B1
Haines, *Oreg., U.S.A.* 114 D5
Haines City, *U.S.A.* 109 L5
Haines Junction, *Canada* .. 104 A1
Hainfeld, *Austria* 26 C8
Haining, *China* 59 B13
Haiphong, *Vietnam* 58 G6
Haitan Dao, *China* 59 E12
Haiti ■, *W. Indies* 121 C5
Haiya, *Sudan* 80 D4
Haiyan, *China* 59 B13
Haiyang, *China* 57 F11
Haiyuan,
  Guangxi Zhuangzu, China 58 F6
Haiyuan, *Ningxia Huizu,
  China* 56 F3
Haizhou, *China* 57 G10
Haizhou Wan, *China* 57 G10
Hajdú-Bihar □, *Hungary* .. 42 C6
Hajdúböszörmény, *Hungary* 42 C6
Hajdúdurog, *Hungary* 42 C6
Hajdúhadház, *Hungary* ... 42 C6
Hajdúnánás, *Hungary* 42 C6
Hajdúsámson, *Hungary* ... 42 C6
Hajdúszoboszló, *Hungary* . 42 C6
Hajipur, *India* 69 G11
Hājjī Muḥsin, *Iraq* 70 C5
Ḥājjīābād, *Iran* 71 D7
Ḥājjīābād-e Zarrīn, *Iran* .. 71 C7
Hajnówka, *Poland* 45 F10
Hakansson, Mts.,
  Dem. Rep. of the Congo 87 D2
Hakkâri, *Turkey* 70 B4
Hakkâri Dağları, *Turkey* .. 73 C10
Hakken-Zan, *Japan* 55 G7
Hakodate, *Japan* 54 D10
Hakos, *Namibia* 88 C2
Håksberg, *Sweden* 10 D9
Haku-San, *Japan* 55 F8
Hakui, *Japan* 55 F8
Hala, *Pakistan* 68 G3
Halab, *Syria* 70 B3
Halabjah, *Iraq* 70 C5
Halaib, *Sudan* 80 C4
Halasa, *Sudan* 81 E3
Ḥalāt 'Ammār, *Si. Arabia* . 70 D3
Halba, *Lebanon* 75 A5
Halberstadt, *Germany* 24 D7
Halcombe, *N.Z.* 91 J5
Halcon, *Phil.* 63 B6
Halden, *Norway* 9 G14
Haldensleben, *Germany* ... 24 C7
Haldia, *India* 67 H16
Haldwani, *India* 69 E8
Hale →, *Australia* 94 C2
Haleakala Crater, *U.S.A.* .. 106 H16
Halesowen, *U.K.* 13 E5
Haleyville, *U.S.A.* 109 H2
Half Assini, *Ghana* 82 D4
Halfway →, *Canada* 104 B4
Halia, *India* 69 G10
Haliburton, *Canada* 102 C4
Halifax, *Australia* 94 B4
Halifax, *Canada* 103 D7
Halifax, *U.K.* 12 D6
Halifax, *U.S.A.* 110 F8
Halifax B., *Australia* 94 B4
Halifax I., *Namibia* 88 D2
Ḥalīl →, *Iran* 71 E8
Halkirk, *U.K.* 14 C5
Hall Beach = Sanirajak,
  Canada 101 B11
Hall in Tirol, *Austria* 26 D4
Hall Pen., *Canada* 101 B13
Hall Pt., *Australia* 92 C3
Hallabro, *Sweden* 11 H9
Halland, *Sweden* 9 H15
Hallands län □, *Sweden* ... 11 H6
Hallands Väderö, *Sweden* . 11 H6
Hallandsås, *Sweden* 11 H7
Hällbybrunn, *Sweden* 10 E10
Halle, *Belgium* 17 D4

Halle, *Nordrhein-Westfalen,
  Germany* 24 C4
Halle, *Sachsen-Anhalt,
  Germany* 24 D7
Hällefors, *Sweden* 10 E8
Hälleforsnäs, *Sweden* 10 E10
Hallein, *Austria* 26 D6
Hällekis, *Sweden* 11 F7
Hallen, *Sweden* 10 A8
Hallett, *Australia* 95 E2
Hallettsville, *U.S.A.* 113 L6
Hallim, S. *Korea* 57 H14
Hallingdalselvi →, *Norway* 9 F13
Hallock, *U.S.A.* 112 A6
Halls Creek, *Australia* 92 C4
Hallsberg, *Sweden* 10 E9
Hallstahammar, *Sweden* .. 10 E10
Hallstatt, *Austria* 26 D6
Hallstavik, *Sweden* 10 D12
Hallstead, *U.S.A.* 111 E9
Halmahera, *Indonesia* 63 D7
Halmeu, *Romania* 42 C8
Halmstad, *Sweden* 11 H6
Hals, *Denmark* 11 H4
Hälsingborg = Helsingborg,
  Sweden 11 H6
Hälsingland, *Sweden* 10 C10
Halstead, *U.K.* 13 F8
Haltern, *Germany* 24 D3
Halti, *Finland* 8 B19
Halton □, *U.K.* 12 D5
Haltwhistle, *U.K.* 12 C5
Halul, *Qatar* 71 E7
Halvad, *India* 68 H4
Halvān, *Iran* 71 C8
Ham, *France* 19 C10
Ham Tan, *Vietnam* 65 G6
Ham Yen, *Vietnam* 64 A5
Hamab, *Namibia* 88 D2
Hamad, *Sudan* 81 D3
Hamada, *Japan* 55 G6
Hamadān, *Iran* 71 C6
Hamadān □, *Iran* 70 C5
Hamāh, *Syria* 70 C3
Hamamatsu, *Japan* 55 G8
Hamar, *Norway* 9 F14
Hamâta, Gebel, *Egypt* 70 C3
Hambantota, *Sri Lanka* ... 66 R12
Hamber Prov. Park, *Canada* 104 C5
Hamburg, *Germany* 24 B5
Hamburg, *Ark., U.S.A.* ... 113 J9
Hamburg, *N.Y., U.S.A.* ... 110 D6
Hamburg, *Pa., U.S.A.* 111 F9
Hamburg □, *Germany* 24 B5
Ḥamḍ, W. al →, *Si. Arabia* 70 E3
Hamden, *U.S.A.* 111 E12
Hamdibey, *Turkey* 39 B9
Häme, *Finland* 9 F20
Hämeenlinna, *Finland* 9 F21
Hamélé, *Ghana* 82 C4
Hamelin Pool, *Australia* .. 93 E1
Hameln, *Germany* 24 C5
Hamerkaz □, *Israel* 75 C3
Hamersley Ra., *Australia* .. 92 D2
Hamhung, *N. Korea* 57 E14
Hami, *China* 60 B4
Hamilton, *Australia* 95 F3
Hamilton, *Canada* 102 D4
Hamilton, *N.Z.* 91 G5
Hamilton, *U.K.* 14 F4
Hamilton, *Ala., U.S.A.* ... 109 H1
Hamilton, *Mont., U.S.A.* . 114 C6
Hamilton, *N.Y., U.S.A.* ... 111 D9
Hamilton, *Ohio, U.S.A.* .. 108 F3
Hamilton, *Tex., U.S.A.* ... 113 K5
Hamilton →, *Australia* ... 94 C2
Hamilton City, *U.S.A.* 116 F4
Hamilton Inlet, *Canada* ... 103 B8
Hamilton Mt., *U.S.A.* 111 C10
Hamina, *Finland* 9 F22
Hamirpur, *H.P., India* 68 D7
Hamirpur, *Ut. P., India* ... 69 G9
Hamitabat, *Turkey* 41 E11
Hamlet, *U.S.A.* 109 H6
Hamley Bridge, *Australia* . 95 E2
Hamlin = Hameln, *Germany* 24 C5
Hamlin, *N.Y., U.S.A.* 110 C7
Hamlin, *Tex., U.S.A.* 113 J4
Hamm, *Germany* 24 D3
Ḥammār, Hawr al, *Iraq* ... 70 D5
Hammarstrand, *Sweden* ... 10 A10
Hammelburg, *Germany* ... 25 E5
Hammeren, *Denmark* 11 J8
Hammerfest, *Norway* 8 A20
Hammerum, *Denmark* 11 H3
Hamminkeln, *Germany* ... 24 D2
Hammond, *Ind., U.S.A.* .. 108 E2
Hammond, *La., U.S.A.* ... 113 K9
Hammond, *N.Y., U.S.A.* .. 111 B9
Hammondsport, *U.S.A.* ... 110 D7
Hammonton, *U.S.A.* 108 F8
Hamneda, *Sweden* 11 H7
Hamoyet, Jebel, *Sudan* ... 80 D4
Hampden, *N.Z.* 91 L3
Hampshire □, *U.K.* 13 F6
Hampshire Downs, *U.K.* .. 13 F6
Hampton, *N.B., Canada* .. 103 C6
Hampton, *Ont., Canada* .. 110 C6
Hampton, *Ark., U.S.A.* ... 113 J8
Hampton, *Iowa, U.S.A.* .. 112 D8
Hampton, *N.H., U.S.A.* .. 111 D14
Hampton, *S.C., U.S.A.* ... 109 J5
Hampton, *Va., U.S.A.* 108 G7
Hampton Bays, *U.S.A.* ... 111 F12
Hampton Tableland,
  Australia 93 F4
Hamra, *Sweden* 10 C8
Hamrat esh Sheykh, *Sudan* 81 E2
Hamur, *Turkey* 73 C10
Hamyang, S. *Korea* 57 G14
Han Jiang →, *China* 59 F11

Hérault

Han Shui, China 58 A7
Han Shui →, China 59 B10
Hana, U.S.A. 106 H17
Hanak, Si. Arabia 70 E3
Hanamaki, Japan 54 E10
Hanang, Tanzania 86 C4
Hanau, Germany 25 E4
Hanbogd = Ihbulag, Mongolia 56 C4
Hançalar, Turkey 39 C11
Hânceşti, Moldova 43 D13
Hancheng, China 56 G6
Hanchuan, China 59 B9
Hancock, Mich., U.S.A. 112 B10
Hancock, N.Y., U.S.A. 111 E9
Handa, Japan 55 G8
Handan, China 56 F8
Handeni, Tanzania 86 D4
Handlová, Slovak Rep. 27 C11
Handub, Sudan 80 D4
Handwara, India 69 B6
Hanegev, Israel 75 E4
Hanford, U.S.A. 116 J7
Hang Chat, Thailand 64 C2
Hang Dong, Thailand 64 C2
Hangang →, S. Korea 57 F14
Hangayn Nuruu, Mongolia 60 B4
Hangchou = Hangzhou, China 59 B13
Hanggin Houqi, China 56 D4
Hanggin Qi, China 56 E5
Hangu, China 57 E9
Hangzhou, China 59 B13
Hangzhou Wan, China 59 B13
Hanhongor, Mongolia 56 C3
Ḩanīdh, Si. Arabia 71 E6
Ḩanīsh, Yemen 74 E3
Haniska, Slovak Rep. 27 C14
Hanjiang, China 59 E12
Hankinson, U.S.A. 112 B6
Hanko, Finland 9 G20
Hankou, China 59 B10
Hanksville, U.S.A. 115 G8
Hanle, India 69 C8
Hanmer Springs, N.Z. 91 K4
Hann →, Australia 92 C4
Hann, Mt., Australia 92 C4
Hanna, Canada 104 C6
Hanna, U.S.A. 114 F10
Hannah B., Canada 102 B4
Hannibal, Mo., U.S.A. 112 F9
Hannibal, N.Y., U.S.A. 111 C8
Hannik, Sudan 80 D3
Hannover, Germany 24 C5
Hanö, Sweden 11 H8
Hanöbukten, Sweden 11 J8
Hanoi, Vietnam 58 G5
Hanover = Hannover, Germany 24 C5
Hanover, Canada 102 D3
Hanover, S. Africa 88 E3
Hanover, N.H., U.S.A. 111 C12
Hanover, Ohio, U.S.A. 110 F2
Hanover, Pa., U.S.A. 108 F7
Hanover, I., Chile 128 G2
Hansdiha, India 69 G12
Hanshou, China 59 C8
Hansi, India 68 E6
Hanson, L., Australia 95 E2
Hanstholm, Denmark 11 G2
Hantsavichy, Belarus 47 F4
Hanumangarh, India 68 E6
Hanyin, China 58 A7
Hanyuan, China 58 C4
Hanzhong, China 56 H4
Hanzhuang, China 57 G9
Haora, India 69 H13
Haoxue, China 59 B9
Haparanda, Sweden 8 D21
Happy, U.S.A. 113 H4
Happy Camp, U.S.A. 114 F2
Happy Valley-Goose Bay, Canada 103 B7
Hapsu, N. Korea 57 D15
Hapur, India 68 E7
Ḩaql, Si. Arabia 75 F3
Har, Indonesia 63 F8
Har-Ayrag, Mongolia 56 B5
Har Hu, China 60 C4
Har Us Nuur, Mongolia 60 B4
Har Yehuda, Israel 75 D3
Ḩaraḑ, Si. Arabia 74 C4
Haradok, Belarus 46 E6
Häradsbäck, Sweden 11 H8
Haranomachi, Japan 54 F10
Harare, Zimbabwe 87 F3
Harat, Eritrea 81 D4
Harbin, China 57 B14
Harbiye, Turkey 72 D7
Harbo, Sweden 10 D11
Harboør, Denmark 11 H2
Harbor Beach, U.S.A. 110 C2
Harbour Breton, Canada 103 C8
Harbour Deep, Canada 103 B8
Harburg, Germany 24 B5
Hårby, Denmark 11 J4
Harda, India 68 H7
Hardangerfjorden, Norway 9 F12
Hardangervidda, Norway 9 F12
Hardap Dam, Namibia 88 C2
Hardenberg, Neths. 17 B6
Harderwijk, Neths. 17 B5
Hardey →, Australia 92 D2
Hardin, U.S.A. 114 D10
Harding, S. Africa 89 E4
Harding Ra., Australia 92 C3
Hardisty, Canada 104 C6
Hardoi, India 69 F9
Hardwar = Haridwar, India 68 E8
Hardwick, U.S.A. 111 B12
Hardy, Pen., Chile 128 H3
Hare B., Canada 103 B8
Hareid, Norway 9 E12
Haren, Germany 24 C3
Harer, Ethiopia 81 F5
Harerge □, Ethiopia 81 F5
Hareto, Ethiopia 81 F4
Harfleur, France 18 C7
Hargeisa, Somali Rep. 74 F3
Harghita □, Romania 43 D10
Harghita, Munţii, Romania 43 D10
Hargshamn, Sweden 10 D12
Hari →, Indonesia 62 E2
Haria, Canary Is. 37 E6
Haridwar, India 68 E8
Harim, Jabal al, Oman 71 E8
Haringhata →, Bangla. 67 J16
Harīrūd →, Asia 66 A2
Härjedalen, Sweden 10 B7
Harlan, Iowa, U.S.A. 112 E7
Harlan, Ky., U.S.A. 109 G4
Hârlău, Romania 43 C11
Harlech, U.K. 12 E3
Harlem, U.S.A. 114 B9
Hårlev, Denmark 11 J6
Harlingen, Neths. 17 A5
Harlingen, U.S.A. 113 M6
Harlow, U.K. 13 F8
Harlowton, U.S.A. 114 C9
Harmancık, Turkey 39 B11
Harmånger, Sweden 10 C11
Harmil, Eritrea 81 D5
Harnai, Pakistan 68 D2
Harney Basin, U.S.A. 114 E4
Harney L., U.S.A. 114 E4
Harney Peak, U.S.A. 112 D3
Härnön, Sweden 10 B12
Härnösand, Sweden 10 B11
Haro, Spain 32 C2
Haroldswick, U.K. 14 A8
Harp L., Canada 103 A7
Harper, Liberia 82 E3
Harplinge, Sweden 11 H6
Harr, Mauritania 82 B2
Harrai, India 69 H8
Harrand, Pakistan 68 E4
Ḩarrat Khaybar, Si. Arabia 80 B5
Ḩarrat Nawāşīf, Si. Arabia 80 C5
Harricana →, Canada 102 B4
Harriman, U.S.A. 109 H3
Harrington Harbour, Canada 103 B8
Harris, U.K. 14 D2
Harris, Sd. of, U.K. 14 D1
Harris L., Australia 95 E2
Harris Pt., Canada 110 C2
Harrisburg, Ill., U.S.A. 113 G10
Harrisburg, Nebr., U.S.A. 112 E3
Harrisburg, Pa., U.S.A. 110 F8
Harrismith, S. Africa 89 D4
Harrison, Ark., U.S.A. 113 G8
Harrison, Maine, U.S.A. 111 B14
Harrison, Nebr., U.S.A. 112 D3
Harrison, C., Canada 103 B8
Harrison L., Canada 104 D4
Harrisonburg, U.S.A. 108 F6
Harrisonville, U.S.A. 112 F7
Harriston, Canada 110 C4
Harrisville, Mich., U.S.A. 110 B1
Harrisville, N.Y., U.S.A. 111 B9
Harrisville, Pa., U.S.A. 110 E5
Harrodsburg, U.S.A. 108 G3
Harrogate, U.K. 12 C6
Harrow, U.K. 13 F7
Harrowsmith, Canada 111 B8
Harry S. Truman Reservoir, U.S.A. 112 F7
Harsefeld, Germany 24 B5
Harsewinkel, Germany 24 D4
Harsīn, Iran 70 C5
Hârşova, Romania 43 F12
Harstad, Norway 8 B17
Harsud, India 68 H7
Hart, U.S.A. 108 D2
Hart, L., Australia 95 E2
Hartbees →, S. Africa 88 D3
Hartberg, Austria 26 D8
Hartford, Conn., U.S.A. 111 E12
Hartford, Ky., U.S.A. 108 G2
Hartford, S. Dak., U.S.A. 112 D6
Hartford, Wis., U.S.A. 112 D10
Hartford City, U.S.A. 108 E3
Hartland, Canada 103 C6
Hartland Pt., U.K. 13 F3
Hartlepool, U.K. 12 C6
Hartlepool □, U.K. 12 C6
Hartley Bay, Canada 104 C3
Hartmannberge, Namibia 88 B1
Hartney, Canada 105 D8
Hârtop, Moldova 43 D13
Harts →, S. Africa 88 D3
Hartselle, U.S.A. 109 H2
Hartshorne, U.S.A. 113 H7
Hartstown, U.S.A. 110 E4
Hartsville, U.S.A. 109 H5
Hartswater, S. Africa 88 D3
Hartwell, U.S.A. 109 H4
Harunabad, Pakistan 68 E5
Harvand, Iran 71 D7
Harvey, Australia 93 F2
Harvey, Ill., U.S.A. 108 E2
Harvey, N. Dak., U.S.A. 112 B5
Harwich, U.K. 13 F9
Haryana □, India 68 E7
Haryn →, Belarus 47 F4
Harz, Germany 24 D6
Harzgerode, Germany 24 D7
Hasa □, Si. Arabia 71 E6
Hasaheisa, Sudan 81 E3
Ḩasanābād, Iran 71 C7
Hasdo →, India 69 J10
Haselünne, Germany 24 C3
Hashimoto, Japan 55 G7
Hashtjerd, Iran 71 C6
Haskell, U.S.A. 113 J5
Hasköy, Turkey 41 E10
Haslach, Germany 25 G4
Hasle, Denmark 11 J8
Haslemere, U.K. 13 F7
Haslev, Denmark 11 J5
Hasparren, France 20 E2
Hassa, Turkey 72 D7
Hassela, Sweden 10 B10
Hasselt, Belgium 17 D5
Hassfurt, Germany 25 E6
Hassi Messaoud, Algeria 78 B7
Hässleholm, Sweden 11 H7
Hassloch, Germany 25 F4
Hästholmen, Sweden 11 F8
Hastings, N.Z. 91 H6
Hastings, U.K. 13 G8
Hastings, Mich., U.S.A. 108 D3
Hastings, Minn., U.S.A. 112 C8
Hastings, Nebr., U.S.A. 112 E5
Hastings Ra., Australia 95 E5
Hästveda, Sweden 11 H7
Hat Yai, Thailand 65 J3
Hatanbulag = Ergel, Mongolia 56 C5
Hatay = Antalya, Turkey 72 D4
Hatch, U.S.A. 115 K10
Hatchet L., Canada 105 B8
Haţeg, Romania 42 E7
Hateruma-Shima, Japan 55 M1
Hatfield P.O., Australia 95 E3
Hatgal, Mongolia 60 A5
Hathras, India 68 F8
Hatia, Bangla. 67 H17
Ḩāţibah, Ra's, Si. Arabia 80 C4
Hato Mayor, Dom. Rep. 121 C6
Hatta, India 69 G8
Hattah, Australia 95 E3
Hatteras, C., U.S.A. 109 H8
Hattiesburg, U.S.A. 113 K10
Hatvan, Hungary 42 C4
Hau Bon = Cheo Reo, Vietnam 62 B3
Hau Duc, Vietnam 64 E7
Haugesund, Norway 9 G11
Haukipudas, Finland 8 D21
Haultain →, Canada 105 B7
Hauraki G., N.Z. 91 G5
Hausruck, Austria 26 C6
Haut Atlas, Morocco 78 B4
Haut-Rhin □, France 19 E14
Haut-Zaïre = Orientale □, Dem. Rep. of the Congo 86 B2
Haute-Corse □, France 21 F13
Haute-Garonne □, France 20 E5
Haute-Loire □, France 20 C7
Haute-Marne □, France 19 D12
Haute-Normandie □, France 18 C7
Haute-Saône □, France 19 E13
Haute-Savoie □, France 21 C10
Haute-Vienne □, France 20 C5
Hautes-Alpes □, France 21 D10
Hautes Fagnes = Hohe Venn, Belgium 17 D6
Hautes-Pyrénées □, France 20 F4
Hauteville-Lompnès, France 21 C9
Hautmont, France 19 B10
Hauts-de-Seine □, France 19 D9
Hauts Plateaux, Algeria 76 C4
Hauzenberg, Germany 25 G9
Havana = La Habana, Cuba 120 B3
Havana, U.S.A. 112 E9
Havant, U.K. 13 G7
Havârna, Romania 43 B11
Havasu, L., U.S.A. 117 L12
Havdhem, Sweden 11 G12
Havel →, Germany 24 C8
Havelian, Pakistan 68 B5
Havelock, Canada 102 D4
Havelock, N.Z. 91 J4
Havelock, U.S.A. 109 H7
Haverfordwest, U.K. 13 F3
Haverhill, U.S.A. 111 D13
Haverstraw, U.S.A. 111 E11
Håverud, Sweden 11 F6
Havirga, Mongolia 56 B7
Havířov, Czech. 27 B11
Havlíčkův Brod, Czech Rep. 26 B8
Havneby, Denmark 11 J2
Havran, Turkey 39 B9
Havre, U.S.A. 114 B9
Havre-Aubert, Canada 103 C7
Havre-St.-Pierre, Canada 103 B7
Havsa, Turkey 41 E10
Havza, Turkey 72 B6
Haw →, U.S.A. 109 H6
Hawaii □, U.S.A. 106 H16
Hawaii I., Pac. Oc. 106 J17
Hawaiian Is., Pac. Oc. 106 H17
Hawaiian Ridge, Pac. Oc. 97 E11
Hawarden, U.S.A. 112 D6
Hawea, L., N.Z. 91 L2
Hawera, N.Z. 91 H5
Hawick, U.K. 14 F6
Hawk Junction, Canada 102 C3
Hawke B., N.Z. 91 H6
Hawker, Australia 95 E2
Hawkesbury, Canada 102 C5
Hawkesbury I., Canada 104 C3
Hawkesbury Pt., Australia 94 A1
Hawkinsville, U.S.A. 109 J4
Hawley, Minn., U.S.A. 112 B6
Hawley, Pa., U.S.A. 111 E9
Ḩawrān, W. →, Iraq 70 C4
Ḩawsh Mūssá, Lebanon 75 B4
Hawthorne, U.S.A. 114 G4
Hay, Australia 95 E3
Hay →, Australia 94 C2
Hay →, Canada 104 A5
Hay, C., Australia 92 B4
Hay I., Canada 110 B4
Hay L., Canada 104 B5
Hay-on-Wye, U.K. 13 E4
Hay River, Canada 104 A5
Hay Springs, U.S.A. 112 D3
Haya = Tehoru, Indonesia 63 E7
Hayachine-San, Japan 54 E10
Hayange, France 19 C13
Haydarlı, Turkey 39 C12
Hayden, U.S.A. 114 F10
Haydon, Australia 94 B3
Hayes, U.S.A. 112 C4
Hayes →, Canada 102 A1
Hayes Creek, Australia 92 B5
Hayle, U.K. 13 G2
Hayling I., U.K. 13 G7
Haymana, Turkey 72 C5
Hayrabolu, Turkey 41 E11
Hays, Canada 104 C6
Hays, U.S.A. 112 F5
Haysyn, Ukraine 47 H5
Hayvoron, Ukraine 47 H5
Hayward, Calif., U.S.A. 116 H4
Hayward, Wis., U.S.A. 112 B9
Haywards Heath, U.K. 13 G7
Haẕafon □, Israel 75 C4
Hazārān, Kūh-e, Iran 71 D8
Hazard, U.S.A. 108 G4
Hazaribag, India 69 H11
Hazaribag Road, India 69 G11
Hazebrouck, France 19 B9
Hazelton, Canada 104 B3
Hazelton, U.S.A. 112 B4
Hazen, U.S.A. 112 B4
Hazlehurst, Ga., U.S.A. 109 K4
Hazlehurst, Miss., U.S.A. 113 K9
Hazlet, U.S.A. 111 F10
Hazleton, U.S.A. 111 F9
Hazlett, L., Australia 92 D4
Hazro, Turkey 70 B4
He Xian, Anhui, China 59 B12
He Xian, Guangxi Zhuangzu, China 59 E8
Head of Bight, Australia 93 F5
Headlands, Zimbabwe 87 F3
Healdsburg, U.S.A. 116 G4
Healdton, U.S.A. 113 H6
Healesville, Australia 95 F4
Heany Junction, Zimbabwe 89 C4
Heard I., Ind. Oc. 3 G13
Hearne, U.S.A. 113 K6
Hearst, Canada 102 C3
Heart →, U.S.A. 112 B4
Heart's Content, Canada 103 C9
Heath Pt., Canada 103 C7
Heavener, U.S.A. 113 H7
Hebbronville, U.S.A. 113 M5
Hebei □, China 56 E9
Hebel, Australia 95 D4
Heber, U.S.A. 117 N11
Heber City, U.S.A. 114 F8
Heber Springs, U.S.A. 113 H9
Hebert, Canada 105 C7
Hebgen L., U.S.A. 114 D8
Hebi, China 56 G8
Hebrides, U.K. 6 D4
Hebron = Al Khalīl, West Bank 75 D4
Hebron, Canada 101 C13
Hebron, N. Dak., U.S.A. 112 B3
Hebron, Nebr., U.S.A. 112 E6
Heby, Sweden 10 E10
Hecate Str., Canada 104 C2
Heceta I., U.S.A. 104 B2
Hechi, China 58 E7
Hechingen, Germany 25 G4
Hechuan, China 58 B6
Hecla, U.S.A. 112 C5
Hecla I., Canada 105 C9
Hédé, France 18 D5
Hede, Sweden 10 B7
Hedemora, Sweden 10 D9
Hedensted, Denmark 11 J3
Hedesunda, Sweden 10 D10
Heerde, Neths. 17 B6
Heerenveen, Neths. 17 B5
Heerhugowaard, Neths. 17 B4
Heerlen, Neths. 17 D5
Ḩefa, Israel 75 C4
Ḩefa □, Israel 75 C4
Hefei, China 59 B11
Hefeng, China 59 C8
Hegalig, Sudan 81 E3
Hegang, China 60 B8
Heiban, Sudan 81 E3
Heichengzhen, China 56 F4
Heide, Germany 24 A5
Heidelberg, Germany 25 F4
Heidelberg, S. Africa 88 E3
Heidenau, Germany 24 E9
Heidenheim, Germany 25 G6
Heijing, China 58 E3
Heilbad Heiligenstadt, Germany 24 D6
Heilbron, S. Africa 89 D4
Heilbronn, Germany 25 F5
Heiligenblut, Austria 26 D5
Heiligenhafen, Germany 24 A6
Heilongjiang □, China 60 B7
Heilunkiang = Heilongjiang □, China 60 B7
Heimaey, Iceland 8 E3
Heinola, Finland 9 F22
Heinsberg, Germany 24 D2
Heinze Is., Burma 67 M20
Heishan, China 57 D12
Heishui, Liaoning, China 57 C10
Heishui, Sichuan, China 58 A4
Hejaz = Ḩijāz □, Si. Arabia 70 E3
Hejian, China 56 E9
Hejiang, China 58 C5
Hejin, China 56 G6
Hekımhan, Turkey 70 B3
Hekla, Iceland 8 E4
Hekou, Guangdong, China 59 F9
Hekou, Yunnan, China 58 F4
Hel, Poland 44 D5
Helagsfjället, Sweden 10 B6
Helan Shan, China 56 E3
Helechosa, Spain 35 F6
Helen Atoll, Pac. Oc. 63 D8
Helena, Ark., U.S.A. 113 H9
Helena, Mont., U.S.A. 114 C7
Helendale, U.S.A. 117 L9
Helensburgh, U.K. 14 E4
Helensville, N.Z. 91 G5
Helenvale, Australia 94 B4
Helgasjön, Sweden 11 H8
Helgeland, Norway 8 C15
Helgoland, Germany 24 A3
Heligoland = Helgoland, Germany 24 A3
Heligoland B. = Deutsche Bucht, Germany 24 A4
Heliopolis, Egypt 80 H7
Hella, Iceland 8 E3
Hellertown, U.S.A. 111 F9
Hellespont = Çanakkale Boğazı, Turkey 41 F10
Hellevoetsluis, Neths. 17 C4
Hellín, Spain 33 G3
Helmand □, Afghan. 66 D4
Helmand →, Afghan. 66 D2
Helme →, Germany 24 D7
Helmeringhausen, Namibia 88 D2
Helmond, Neths. 17 C5
Helmsdale, U.K. 14 C5
Helmsdale →, U.K. 14 C5
Helmstedt, Germany 24 C7
Helong, China 57 C15
Helper, U.S.A. 114 G8
Helsingborg, Sweden 11 H6
Helsinge, Denmark 11 H6
Helsingfors = Helsinki, Finland 9 F21
Helsingør, Denmark 11 H6
Helsinki, Finland 9 F21
Helska, Mierzeja, Poland 44 D5
Helston, U.K. 13 G2
Helvellyn, U.K. 12 C4
Helwân, Egypt 80 J7
Hemel Hempstead, U.K. 13 F7
Hemet, U.S.A. 117 M10
Hemingford, U.S.A. 112 D3
Hemmingford, Canada 111 A11
Hempstead, U.S.A. 113 K6
Hemse, Sweden 11 G12
Hemsön, Sweden 10 B12
Henån, Sweden 11 F5
Henan □, China 56 H8
Henares →, Spain 34 E7
Henashi-Misaki, Japan 54 D9
Hendaye, France 20 E2
Hendek, Turkey 72 B4
Henderson, Argentina 126 D3
Henderson, Ky., U.S.A. 108 G2
Henderson, N.C., U.S.A. 109 G6
Henderson, Nev., U.S.A. 117 J12
Henderson, Tenn., U.S.A. 109 H1
Henderson, Tex., U.S.A. 113 J7
Hendersonville, N.C., U.S.A. 109 H4
Hendersonville, Tenn., U.S.A. 109 G2
Hendījān, Iran 71 D6
Hendorābī, Iran 71 E7
Heng Jiang, China 58 C5
Heng Xian, China 58 F7
Hengcheng, China 56 E4
Hengchun, Taiwan 59 F13
Hengdaohezi, China 57 B15
Hengelo, Neths. 17 B6
Hengfeng, China 59 C10
Hengshan, Hunan, China 59 D9
Hengshan, Shaanxi, China 56 F5
Hengshui, China 56 F8
Hengyang, Hunan, China 59 D9
Hengyang, Hunan, China 59 D9
Henichesk, Ukraine 47 J8
Hénin-Beaumont, France 19 B9
Henlopen, C., U.S.A. 108 F8
Hennan, Sweden 10 B9
Hennebont, France 18 E3
Hennenman, S. Africa 88 D4
Hennessey, U.S.A. 113 G6
Hennigsdorf, Germany 24 C9
Henrietta, U.S.A. 113 J5
Henrietta, Ostrov = Genriyetty, Ostrov, Russia 51 B16
Henrietta Maria, C., Canada 102 A3
Henry, U.S.A. 112 E10
Henryetta, U.S.A. 113 H7
Henryville, Canada 111 A11
Hensall, Canada 110 C3
Henstedt-Ulzburg, Germany 24 B6
Hentiesbaai, Namibia 88 C1
Hentiyn Nuruu, Mongolia 60 B5
Henty, Australia 95 F4
Henzada, Burma 67 L19
Hephaestia, Greece 39 B7
Heping, China 59 E10
Heppner, U.S.A. 114 D4
Hepu, China 58 G7
Hepworth, Canada 110 B3
Heqing, China 58 D3
Hequ, China 56 E6
Héraðsflói, Iceland 8 D6
Héraðsvötn →, Iceland 8 D4
Herald Cays, Australia 94 B4
Herāt, Afghan. 66 B3
Herāt □, Afghan. 66 B3
Hérault □, France 20 E7

Hérault →, France	20	E7
Herbault, France	18	E8
Herbert →, Australia	94	B4
Herberton, Australia	94	B4
Herbertsdale, S. Africa	88	E3
Herbignac, France	18	E4
Herborn, Germany	24	E4
Herby, Poland	45	H5
Herceg-Novi, Montenegro, Yug.	40	D2
Herchmer, Canada	105	B10
Herðubreið, Iceland	8	D5
Hereford, U.K.	13	E5
Hereford, U.S.A.	113	H3
Herefordshire □, U.K.	13	E5
Hereke, Turkey	41	F13
Herencia, Spain	35	F7
Herentals, Belgium	17	C4
Herford, Germany	24	C4
Héricourt, France	19	E13
Herington, U.S.A.	112	F6
Herisau, Switz.	25	H5
Hérisson, France	19	F9
Herkimer, U.S.A.	111	D10
Herlong, U.S.A.	116	E6
Herm, U.K.	13	H5
Hermann, U.S.A.	112	F9
Hermannsburg, Australia	92	D5
Hermannsburg, Germany	24	C6
Hermanus, S. Africa	88	E2
Herment, France	20	C6
Hermidale, Australia	95	E4
Hermiston, U.S.A.	114	D4
Hermitage, N.Z.	91	K3
Hermite, I., Chile	128	H3
Hermon, U.S.A.	111	B9
Hermon, Mt. = Shaykh, J. ash, Lebanon	75	B4
Hermosillo, Mexico	118	B2
Hernád →, Hungary	42	C6
Hernandarias, Paraguay	127	B5
Hernandez, U.S.A.	116	J6
Hernando, Argentina	126	C3
Hernando, U.S.A.	113	H10
Hernani, Spain	32	B3
Herndon, U.S.A.	110	F8
Herne, Germany	24	C3
Herne Bay, U.K.	13	F9
Herning, Denmark	11	H2
Heroica = Caborca, Mexico	118	A2
Heroica Nogales = Nogales, Mexico	118	A2
Heron Bay, Canada	102	C2
Herradura, Pta. de la, Canary Is.	37	F5
Herreid, U.S.A.	112	C4
Herrenberg, Germany	25	G4
Herrera, Spain	35	H6
Herrera de Alcántara, Spain	35	F3
Herrera de Pisuerga, Spain	34	C6
Herrera del Duque, Spain	35	F5
Herrestad, Sweden	11	F5
Herrin, U.S.A.	113	G10
Herriot, Canada	105	B8
Herrljunga, Sweden	11	F7
Hersbruck, Germany	25	F7
Hershey, U.S.A.	111	F8
Hersonissos, Greece	36	D7
Herstal, Belgium	17	D5
Hertford, U.K.	13	F7
Hertfordshire □, U.K.	13	F7
's-Hertogenbosch, Neths.	17	C5
Hertzogville, S. Africa	88	D4
Hervás, Spain	34	E5
Hervey B., Australia	94	C5
Herzberg, Brandenburg, Germany	24	D9
Herzberg, Niedersachsen, Germany	24	D6
Herzliyya, Israel	75	C3
Herzogenaurach, Austria	26	C8
Heşār, Fārs, Iran	71	D6
Heşār, Markazī, Iran	71	C6
Hesdin, France	19	B9
Heshan, China	58	F7
Heshui, China	56	G5
Heshun, China	56	F7
Hesperia, U.S.A.	117	L9
Hesse = Hessen □, Germany	24	E4
Hessen □, Germany	24	E4
Hestra, Sweden	11	G7
Hetch Hetchy Aqueduct, U.S.A.	116	H5
Hettinger, U.S.A.	112	C3
Hettstedt, Germany	24	D7
Heuvelton, U.S.A.	111	B9
Heves, Hungary	42	C5
Heves □, Hungary	42	C5
Hewitt, U.S.A.	113	K6
Hexham, U.K.	12	C5
Hexi, Yunnan, China	58	E4
Hexi, Zhejiang, China	59	D12
Hexigten Qi, China	57	C9
Ḥeydarābād, Iran	71	D7
Heysham, U.K.	12	C5
Heyuan, China	59	F10
Heywood, Australia	95	F3
Heze, China	56	G8
Hezhang, China	58	D5
Hi Vista, U.S.A.	117	L9
Hialeah, U.S.A.	109	N5
Hiawatha, U.S.A.	112	F7
Hibbing, U.S.A.	112	B8
Hibbs B., Australia	94	G4
Hibernia Reef, Australia	92	B3
Hickman, U.S.A.	113	G10
Hickory, U.S.A.	109	H5
Hicks, Pt., Australia	95	F4
Hicks L., Canada	105	A9
Hicksville, U.S.A.	111	F11
Hida, Romania	43	C8

Hida-Gawa →, Japan	55	G8
Hida-Sammyaku, Japan	55	F8
Hidaka-Sammyaku, Japan	54	C11
Hidalgo, Mexico	119	C5
Hidalgo □, Mexico	119	C5
Hidalgo, Presa M., Mexico	118	B3
Hidalgo, Pta. del, Canary Is.	37	F3
Hidalgo del Parral, Mexico	118	B3
Hiddensee, Germany	24	A9
Hieflau, Austria	26	D7
Hiendelaencina, Spain	32	D2
Hierro, Canary Is.	37	G1
Higashijima-San, Japan	54	F10
Higashiōsaka, Japan	55	G7
Higgins, U.S.A.	113	G4
Higgins Corner, U.S.A.	116	F5
High Atlas = Haut Atlas, Morocco	78	B4
High Bridge, U.S.A.	111	F10
High Level, Canada	104	B5
High Point, U.S.A.	109	H6
High Prairie, Canada	104	B5
High River, Canada	104	C6
High Tatra = Tatry, Slovak Rep.	27	B13
High Veld, Africa	76	J6
High Wycombe, U.K.	13	F7
Highland □, U.K.	14	D4
Highland Park, U.S.A.	108	D2
Highmore, U.S.A.	112	C5
Highrock L., Man., Canada	105	B8
Highrock L., Sask., Canada	105	B7
Higüey, Dom. Rep.	121	C6
Hihya, Egypt	80	H7
Hiiumaa, Estonia	9	G20
Híjar, Spain	32	D4
Ḥijāz □, Si. Arabia	70	E3
Hijo = Tagum, Phil.	61	H6
Hikari, Japan	55	H5
Hikmak, Ras el, Egypt	80	A2
Hiko, U.S.A.	116	H11
Hikone, Japan	55	G8
Hikurangi, N.Z.	91	F5
Hikurangi, Mt., N.Z.	91	H6
Hildburghausen, Germany	24	E6
Hildesheim, Germany	24	C5
Hill →, Australia	93	F2
Hill City, Idaho, U.S.A.	114	E6
Hill City, Kans., U.S.A.	112	F5
Hill City, S. Dak., U.S.A.	112	D3
Hill Island L., Canada	105	A7
Hillared, Sweden	11	G7
Hillcrest Center, U.S.A.	117	K8
Hillegom, Neths.	17	B4
Hillerød, Denmark	11	J6
Hillerstorp, Sweden	11	G7
Hillsboro, Kans., U.S.A.	112	F6
Hillsboro, N. Dak., U.S.A.	112	B6
Hillsboro, N.H., U.S.A.	111	C13
Hillsboro, Ohio, U.S.A.	108	F4
Hillsboro, Oreg., U.S.A.	116	E4
Hillsboro, Tex., U.S.A.	113	J6
Hillsborough, Grenada	121	D7
Hillsdale, Mich., U.S.A.	108	E3
Hillsdale, N.Y., U.S.A.	111	D11
Hillsport, Canada	102	C2
Hillston, Australia	95	E4
Hilo, U.S.A.	106	J17
Hilton, U.S.A.	110	C7
Hilton Head Island, U.S.A.	109	J5
Hilvan, Turkey	73	D8
Hilversum, Neths.	17	B5
Himachal Pradesh □, India	68	D7
Himalaya, Asia	69	E11
Himamaylan, Phil.	61	F5
Himara, Albania	40	F3
Himatnagar, India	66	H8
Himeji, Japan	55	G7
Himi, Japan	55	F8
Himmerland, Denmark	11	H3
Ḥimş, Syria	75	A5
Ḥimş □, Syria	75	A6
Hinche, Haiti	121	C5
Hinchinbrook I., Australia	94	B4
Hinckley, U.K.	13	E6
Hinckley, U.S.A.	112	B8
Hindaun, India	68	F7
Hindmarsh, L., Australia	95	F3
Hindsholm, Denmark	11	J4
Hindu Bagh, Pakistan	68	D2
Hindu Kush, Asia	66	B7
Hindubagh, Pakistan	66	D5
Hindupur, India	66	N10
Hines Creek, Canada	104	B5
Hinesville, U.S.A.	109	K5
Hinganghat, India	66	J11
Hingham, U.S.A.	114	B8
Hingir, India	69	J10
Hingoli, India	66	K10
Hinigaran, Phil.	61	F5
Hinis, Turkey	73	C9
Hinna = Imi, Ethiopia	81	F5
Hinna, Nigeria	83	C7
Hinnerup, Denmark	11	H4
Hinnøya, Norway	8	B16
Hinojosa del Duque, Spain	35	G5
Hinsdale, U.S.A.	111	D12
Hinterrhein →, Switz.	25	J5
Hinton, Canada	104	C5
Hinton, U.S.A.	108	G5
Hınzır Burnu, Turkey	72	D6
Hirado, Japan	55	H4
Hirakud Dam, India	67	J13
Hiran →, India	69	H8
Hirapur, India	69	G8
Hiratsuka, Japan	55	G9
Hirfanlı Baraji, Turkey	72	C5
Hiroo, Japan	54	C11
Hirosaki, Japan	54	D10
Hiroshima, Japan	55	G6
Hiroshima □, Japan	55	G6

Hirson, France	19	C11
Hirtshals, Denmark	11	G3
Hisar, India	68	E6
Hisarcık, Turkey	39	B11
Hisaria, Bulgaria	41	D8
Hisb →, Iraq	70	D5
Ḥismá, Si. Arabia	70	D3
Hispaniola, W. Indies	121	C5
Ḥīt, Iraq	70	C4
Hita, Japan	55	H5
Hitachi, Japan	55	F10
Hitchin, U.K.	13	F7
Hitoyoshi, Japan	55	H5
Hitra, Norway	8	E13
Hitzacker, Germany	24	B7
Hixon, Canada	104	C4
Hiyyon, N. →, Israel	75	E4
Hjalmar L., Canada	105	A7
Hjälmaren, Sweden	10	E9
Hjältevad, Sweden	11	G9
Hjo, Sweden	11	F8
Hjørring, Denmark	11	G3
Hjortkvarn, Sweden	11	F9
Hlinsko, Czech Rep.	26	B8
Hlobane, S. Africa	89	D5
Hlohovec, Slovak Rep.	27	C10
Hlučín, Czech Rep.	27	B11
Hluhluwe, S. Africa	89	D5
Hlukhiv, Ukraine	47	G7
Hlyboka, Ukraine	47	H3
Hlybokaye, Belarus	46	E4
Hnúšťa, Slovak Rep.	27	C12
Ho, Ghana	83	D5
Ho Chi Minh City = Phanh Bho Ho Chi Minh, Vietnam	65	G6
Ho Thuong, Vietnam	64	C5
Hoa Binh, Vietnam	58	G5
Hoa Da, Vietnam	65	G7
Hoa Hiep, Vietnam	65	G5
Hoai Nhon, Vietnam	64	E7
Hoang Lien Son, Vietnam	58	F4
Hoanib →, Namibia	88	B2
Hoare B., Canada	101	B13
Hoarusib →, Namibia	88	B2
Hobart, Australia	94	G4
Hobart, U.S.A.	113	H5
Hobbs, U.S.A.	113	J3
Hobbs Coast, Antarctica	5	D14
Hobe Sound, U.S.A.	109	M5
Hoboken, U.S.A.	111	F10
Hobro, Denmark	11	H3
Hoburgen, Sweden	11	H12
Hocalar, Turkey	39	C11
Hochfeld, Namibia	88	C2
Hochschwab, Austria	26	D8
Höchstadt, Germany	25	F6
Hockenheim, Germany	25	F4
Hodaka-Dake, Japan	55	F8
Hodgeville, Canada	105	C7
Hodgson, Canada	105	C9
Hódmezővásárhely, Hungary	42	D5
Hodna, Chott el, Algeria	78	A6
Hodonín, Czech Rep.	27	C10
Hoeamdong, N. Korea	57	C16
Hœdic, Î. de, France	18	E4
Hoek van Holland, Neths.	17	C4
Hoengsŏng, S. Korea	57	F14
Hoeryong, N. Korea	57	C15
Hoeyang, N. Korea	57	E14
Hof, Germany	25	E7
Hofgeismar, Germany	24	D5
Hofheim, Germany	25	E4
Hofmeyr, S. Africa	88	E4
Höfn, Iceland	8	D6
Hofors, Sweden	10	D10
Hofsjökull, Iceland	8	D4
Hōfu, Japan	55	G5
Hogan Group, Australia	95	F4
Höganäs, Sweden	11	H6
Hogarth, Mt., Australia	94	C2
Hoggar = Ahaggar, Algeria	78	D7
Högsäter, Sweden	11	F6
Högsby, Sweden	11	G10
Högsjö, Sweden	10	E9
Hogsty Reef, Bahamas	121	B5
Hoh →, U.S.A.	116	C2
Hohe Acht, Germany	25	E3
Hohe Tauern, Austria	26	D5
Hohe Venn, Belgium	17	D6
Hohenau, Austria	27	C9
Hohenems, Austria	26	D2
Hohenloher Ebene, Germany	25	F5
Hohenwald, U.S.A.	109	H2
Hohenwestedt, Germany	24	A5
Hoher Rhön = Rhön, Germany	24	E5
Hohhot, China	56	D6
Hóhlakas, Greece	36	D9
Hohoe, Ghana	83	D5
Hoi An, Vietnam	64	E7
Hoi Xuan, Vietnam	58	G5
Hoisington, U.S.A.	112	F5
Højer, Denmark	11	K2
Hōjō, Japan	55	H6
Hok, Sweden	11	G8
Hökensås, Sweden	11	G8
Hökerum, Sweden	11	G7
Hokianga Harbour, N.Z.	91	F4
Hokitika, N.Z.	91	K3
Hokkaidō □, Japan	54	C11
Hol-Hol, Djibouti	81	E5
Hola Pristan, Ukraine	47	J7
Holbæk, Denmark	11	J5
Holbrook, Australia	95	F4
Holbrook, U.S.A.	115	J8
Holden, U.S.A.	114	G7
Holdenville, U.S.A.	113	H6
Holdrege, U.S.A.	112	E5
Holešov, Czech Rep.	27	B10
Holguín, Cuba	120	B4

Holíč, Slovak Rep.	27	C10
Holice, Czech Rep.	26	A8
Höljes, Sweden	10	D6
Hollabrunn, Austria	26	C9
Hollams Bird I., Namibia	88	C1
Holland, Mich., U.S.A.	108	D2
Holland, N.Y., U.S.A.	110	D6
Hollandale, U.S.A.	113	J9
Hollandia = Jayapura, Indonesia	63	E10
Holley, U.S.A.	110	C6
Hollfeld, Germany	25	F7
Hollidaysburg, U.S.A.	110	F6
Hollis, U.S.A.	113	H5
Hollister, Calif., U.S.A.	116	J5
Hollister, Idaho, U.S.A.	114	E6
Höllviken, Sweden	11	J6
Holly Hill, U.S.A.	109	L5
Holly Springs, U.S.A.	113	H10
Hollywood, Calif., U.S.A.	106	D3
Hollywood, Fla., U.S.A.	109	N5
Holman, Canada	100	A8
Hólmavík, Iceland	8	D3
Holmen, U.S.A.	112	D9
Holmes Reefs, Australia	94	B4
Holmsjö, Sweden	11	H9
Holmsjön, Västernorrland, Sweden	10	B10
Holmsjön, Västernorrland, Sweden	10	B9
Holmsland Klit, Denmark	11	J2
Holmsund, Sweden	8	E19
Holod, Romania	42	D7
Holon, Israel	75	C3
Holroyd →, Australia	94	A3
Holstebro, Denmark	11	H2
Holsworthy, U.K.	13	G3
Holton, Canada	103	B8
Holton, U.S.A.	112	F7
Holtville, U.S.A.	117	N11
Holwerd, Neths.	17	A5
Holy I., Angl., U.K.	12	D3
Holy I., Northumb., U.K.	12	B6
Holyhead, U.K.	12	D3
Holyoke, Colo., U.S.A.	112	E3
Holyoke, Mass., U.S.A.	111	D12
Holyrood, Canada	103	C9
Holzkirchen, Germany	25	H7
Holzminden, Germany	24	D5
Homa Bay, Kenya	86	C3
Homalin, Burma	67	G19
Homand, Iran	71	C8
Homathko →, Canada	104	C4
Hombori, Mali	83	B4
Homburg, Germany	25	F3
Home B., Canada	101	B13
Home Hill, Australia	94	B4
Homedale, U.S.A.	114	E5
Homer, Alaska, U.S.A.	100	C4
Homer, La., U.S.A.	113	J8
Homer City, U.S.A.	110	F5
Homestead, Australia	94	C4
Homestead, U.S.A.	109	N5
Homewood, U.S.A.	116	F6
Homoine, Mozam.	89	C6
Homoljske Planina, Serbia, Yug.	40	B5
Homorod, Romania	43	D10
Homs = Ḥimş, Syria	75	A5
Homyel, Belarus	47	F6
Hon Chong, Vietnam	65	G5
Hon Me, Vietnam	64	C5
Honan = Henan □, China	56	H8
Honaz, Turkey	39	D11
Honbetsu, Japan	54	C11
Honcut, U.S.A.	116	F5
Honda Bay, Phil.	61	G3
Hondarribia, Spain	32	B3
Hondeklipbaai, S. Africa	88	E2
Hondo, Japan	55	H5
Hondo, U.S.A.	113	L5
Hondo →, Belize	119	D7
Honduras ■, Cent. Amer.	120	D2
Honduras, G. de, Caribbean	120	C2
Hønefoss, Norway	9	F14
Honesdale, U.S.A.	111	E9
Honey L., U.S.A.	116	E6
Honfleur, France	18	C7
Høng, Denmark	11	J5
Hong →, Vietnam	58	F5
Hong Gai, Vietnam	58	G6
Hong He →, China	56	H8
Hong Hu, China	59	C9
Hong Kong □, China	59	F10
Hong'an, China	59	B10
Hongch'ŏn, S. Korea	57	F14
Honghai Wan, China	59	F10
Honghe, China	58	F4
Honghu, China	59	C9
Hongjiang, China	58	D7
Hongliu He →, China	56	F5
Hongor, Mongolia	56	B7
Hongsa, Laos	64	C3
Hongshui He →, China	58	F7
Hongtong, China	56	F6
Honguedo, Détroit d', Canada	103	C7
Hongwon, N. Korea	57	E14
Hongya, China	58	C4
Hongze Hu, China	57	H10
Honiara, Solomon Is.	96	H7
Honiton, U.K.	13	G4
Honjō, Japan	54	E10
Honkorâb, Ras, Egypt	80	C4
Honningsvåg, Norway	8	A21
Honō, Sweden	11	G5
Honolulu, U.S.A.	106	H16
Honshū, Japan	55	G9
Hontoria del Pinar, Spain	32	D1

Hood, Mt., U.S.A.	114	D3
Hood, Pt., Australia	93	F2
Hood River, U.S.A.	114	D3
Hoodsport, U.S.A.	116	C3
Hooge, Germany	24	A4
Hoogeveen, Neths.	17	B6
Hoogezand-Sappemeer, Neths.	17	A6
Hooghly = Hugli →, India	69	J13
Hooghly-Chinsura = Chunchura, India	69	H13
Hook Hd., Ireland	15	D5
Hook I., Australia	94	C4
Hook of Holland = Hoek van Holland, Neths.	17	C4
Hooker, U.S.A.	113	G4
Hooker Creek, Australia	92	C5
Hoonah, U.S.A.	104	B1
Hooper Bay, U.S.A.	100	B3
Hoopeston, U.S.A.	108	E2
Hoopstad, S. Africa	88	D4
Höör, Sweden	11	J7
Hoorn, Neths.	17	B5
Hoover, U.S.A.	109	J2
Hoover Dam, U.S.A.	117	K12
Hooversville, U.S.A.	110	F6
Hop Bottom, U.S.A.	111	E9
Hopa, Turkey	73	B9
Hope, Canada	104	D4
Hope, Ariz., U.S.A.	117	M13
Hope, Ark., U.S.A.	113	J8
Hope, L., S. Austral., Australia	95	D2
Hope, L., W. Austral., Australia	93	F3
Hope I., Canada	110	B4
Hope Town, Bahamas	120	A4
Hopedale, Canada	103	A7
Hopedale, U.S.A.	111	D13
Hopefield, S. Africa	88	E2
Hopei = Hebei □, China	56	E9
Hopelchén, Mexico	119	D7
Hopetoun, Vic., Australia	95	F3
Hopetoun, W. Austral., Australia	93	F3
Hopetown, S. Africa	88	D3
Hopevale, Australia	94	B4
Hopewell, U.S.A.	108	G7
Hopfgarten, Austria	26	D5
Hopkins, L., Australia	92	D4
Hopkinsville, U.S.A.	109	G2
Hopland, U.S.A.	116	G3
Horasan, Turkey	73	B10
Horaždovice, Czech Rep.	26	B6
Horb, Germany	25	G4
Hörby, Sweden	11	J7
Horcajo de Santiago, Spain	32	F1
Horden Hills, Australia	92	D5
Horezu, Romania	43	E8
Horgen, Switz.	25	H4
Horgoš, Serbia, Yug.	42	D4
Hořice, Czech Rep.	26	A8
Horinger, China	56	D6
Horki, Belarus	46	E6
Horlick Mts., Antarctica	5	E15
Horlivka, Ukraine	47	H10
Hormak, Iran	71	D9
Hormoz, Iran	71	E7
Hormoz, Jaz.-ye, Iran	71	E8
Hormozgān □, Iran	71	E8
Hormuz, Kūh-e, Iran	71	E7
Hormuz, Str. of, The Gulf	71	E8
Horn, Austria	26	C8
Horn, Iceland	8	C2
Horn, Sweden	11	G9
Horn →, Canada	104	A5
Horn, Cape = Hornos, C. de, Chile	122	J4
Horn Head, Ireland	15	A3
Horn I., Australia	94	A3
Horn Mts., Canada	104	A5
Hornachuelos, Spain	35	H5
Hornavan, Sweden	8	C17
Hornbeck, U.S.A.	113	K8
Hornbrook, U.S.A.	114	F2
Hornburg, Germany	24	C6
Horncastle, U.K.	12	D7
Horndal, Sweden	10	D10
Hornell, U.S.A.	110	D7
Hornell L., Canada	104	A5
Hornepayne, Canada	102	C3
Horní Planá, Czech Rep.	26	C7
Hornings Mills, Canada	110	B4
Hornitos, U.S.A.	116	H6
Hornos, C. de, Chile	122	J4
Hornoy-le-Bourg, France	19	C8
Hornsea, U.K.	12	D7
Hornslandet, Sweden	10	C11
Hörnum, Germany	24	A4
Horobetsu, Japan	54	C10
Horodenka, Ukraine	47	H3
Horodnya, Ukraine	47	G6
Horodok, Khmelnytskyy, Ukraine	47	H4
Horodok, Lviv, Ukraine	47	H2
Horodyshche, Ukraine	47	H6
Horokhiv, Ukraine	47	G3
Horovice, Czech Rep.	26	B6
Horqin Youyi Qianqi, China	57	A12
Horqueta, Paraguay	126	A4
Horred, Sweden	11	G6
Horse Creek, U.S.A.	112	E3
Horse Is., Canada	103	B8
Horsefly L., Canada	104	C4
Horseheads, U.S.A.	110	D8
Horsens, Denmark	11	J3
Horsham, Australia	95	F3
Horsham, U.K.	13	F7
Horšovský Týn, Czech Rep.	26	B5
Horten, Norway	9	G14

Hortobágy →, Hungary ... 42 C6
Horton, U.S.A. 112 F7
Horton →, Canada 100 B7
Horwood L., Canada 102 C3
Hosaina, Ethiopia 81 F4
Hose, Gunung-Gunung,
  Malaysia 62 D4
Ḩoseynābād, Khuzestān, Iran 71 C6
Ḩoseynābād, Kordestān, Iran 70 C5
Hoshangabad, India 68 H7
Hoshiarpur, India 68 D6
Hospet, India 66 M10
Hoste, I., Chile 128 H3
Hostens, France 20 D3
Hot, Thailand 64 C2
Hot Creek Range, U.S.A. .. 114 G6
Hot Springs, Ark., U.S.A. . 113 H8
Hot Springs, S. Dak., U.S.A. 112 D3
Hotagen, Sweden 8 E16
Hotan, China 60 C2
Hotazel, S. Africa 88 D3
Hotchkiss, U.S.A. 115 G10
Hotham, C., Australia 92 B5
Hoting, Sweden 8 D17
Hotolishti, Albania 40 E4
Hotte, Massif de la, Haiti . 121 C5
Hottentotsbaai, Namibia .. 88 D1
Houat, Î. de, France 18 E4
Houdan, France 19 D8
Houei Sai, Laos 58 G3
Houeillès, France 20 D4
Houffalize, Belgium 17 D5
Houghton, Mich., U.S.A. . 112 B10
Houghton, N.Y., U.S.A. .. 110 D6
Houghton L., U.S.A. 108 C3
Houhora Heads, N.Z. 91 F4
Houlton, U.S.A. 109 B12
Houma, U.S.A. 113 L9
Houndé, Burkina Faso 82 C4
Hourtin, France 20 C2
Hourtin-Carcans, Étang d',
  France 20 C2
Housatonic →, U.S.A. ... 111 E11
Houston, Canada 104 C3
Houston, Mo., U.S.A. 113 G9
Houston, Tex., U.S.A. ... 113 L7
Hout →, S. Africa 89 C4
Houtkraal, S. Africa 88 E3
Houtman Abrolhos,
  Australia 93 E1
Hovd, Mongolia 60 B4
Hove, U.K. 13 G7
Hoveyzeh, Iran 71 D6
Hovmantorp, Sweden 11 H9
Hövsgöl, Mongolia 56 C5
Hövsgöl Nuur, Mongolia .. 60 A5
Hovsta, Sweden 10 E9
Howakil, Eritrea 81 D5
Howar, Wadi →, Sudan .. 81 D2
Howard, Australia 95 D5
Howard, Pa., U.S.A. 110 F7
Howard, S. Dak., U.S.A. . 112 C6
Howe, U.S.A. 114 E7
Howe, C., Australia 95 F5
Howe I., Canada 111 B8
Howell, U.S.A. 108 D4
Howick, Canada 111 A11
Howick, S. Africa 89 D5
Howick Group, Australia . 94 A4
Howitt, L., Australia 95 D2
Howland I., Pac. Oc. 96 G10
Howrah = Haora, India ... 69 H13
Howth Hd., Ireland 15 C5
Höxter, Germany 24 D5
Hoy, U.K. 14 C5
Hoya, Germany 24 C5
Høyanger, Norway 9 F12
Hoyerswerda, Germany ... 24 D10
Hoylake, U.K. 12 D4
Hoyos, Spain 34 E4
Hpa-an = Pa-an, Burma .. 67 L20
Hpungan Pass, Burma 67 F20
Hradec Králové, Czech Rep. 26 A8
Hrádek, Czech Rep. 27 C9
Hranice, Czech Rep. 27 B10
Hrazdan, Armenia 49 K7
Hrebenka, Ukraine 47 G7
Hrodna, Belarus 46 F2
Hrodzyanka, Belarus 46 F5
Hron →, Slovak Rep. 27 D11
Hrubieszów, Poland 45 H10
Hrubý Jeseník, Czech Rep. 27 A10
Hrvatska = Croatia ■,
  Europe 29 C13
Hrymayliv, Ukraine 47 H4
Hsenwi, Burma 67 H20
Hsiamen = Xiamen, China . 59 E12
Hsian = Xi'an, China 56 G5
Hsinchu, Taiwan 59 E13
Hsinhailien = Lianyungang,
  China 57 G10
Hsinying, Taiwan 59 F13
Hsopket, Burma 58 F2
Hsüchou = Xuzhou, China 57 G9
Hu Xian, China 56 G5
Hua Hin, Thailand 64 F2
Hua Xian, Henan, China .. 56 G8
Hua Xian, Shaanxi, China . 56 G5
Hua'an, China 59 E11
Huab →, Namibia 88 B2
Huacheng, China 59 E10
Huachinera, Mexico 118 A3
Huacho, Peru 124 F3
Huade, China 56 D7
Huadian, China 57 C14
Huadu, China 59 F9
Huai He →, China 59 A12
Huai Yot, Thailand 65 J2
Huai'an, Hebei, China 56 D8
Huai'an, Jiangsu, China ... 57 H10
Huaibei, China 56 G9

Huaibin, China 59 A10
Huaide = Gongzhuling,
  China 57 C13
Huaidezhen, China 57 C13
Huaihua, China 58 D7
Huaiji, China 59 F9
Huainan, China 59 A11
Huaining, China 59 B11
Huairen, China 56 E7
Huairou, China 56 D9
Huaiyang, China 56 H8
Huaiyin, China 57 H10
Huaiyuan, Anhui, China .. 57 H9
Huaiyuan,
  Guangxi Zhuangzu, China 58 E7
Huajianzi, China 57 D13
Huajuapan de Leon, Mexico 119 D5
Hualapai Peak, U.S.A. ... 115 J7
Hualien, Taiwan 59 E13
Huallaga →, Peru 124 E3
Huambo, Angola 85 G3
Huan Jiang →, China 56 G5
Huan Xian, China 56 F4
Huancabamba, Peru 124 E3
Huancane, Peru 124 G5
Huancavelica, Peru 124 F3
Huancayo, Peru 124 F3
Huanchaca, Bolivia 124 H5
Huang Hai = Yellow Sea,
  China 57 G12
Huang He →, China 57 F10
Huang Xian, China 57 F11
Huangchuan, China 59 A10
Huanggang, China 59 B10
Huangguoshu, China 58 E5
Huangling, China 56 G5
Huanglong, China 56 G5
Huanglongtan, China 59 A8
Huangmei, China 59 B10
Huangpi, China 59 B10
Huangping, China 58 D6
Huangshan, China 59 C12
Huangshi, China 59 B10
Huangsongdian, China ... 57 C14
Huangyan, China 59 C13
Huangyangsi, China 59 D8
Huaning, China 58 E4
Huanjiang, China 58 E7
Huantai, China 57 F9
Huánuco, Peru 124 E3
Huaping, China 58 D3
Huaraz, Peru 124 E3
Huarmey, Peru 124 F3
Huarong, China 59 C9
Huascarán, Peru 122 D3
Huasco, Chile 126 B1
Huasco →, Chile 126 B1
Huasna, U.S.A. 117 K6
Huatabampo, Mexico 118 B3
Huauchinango, Mexico ... 119 C5
Huautla de Jiménez, Mexico 119 D5
Huaxi, China 58 D6
Huay Namota, Mexico ... 118 C4
Huayin, China 56 G6
Huayuan, China 58 C7
Huayun, China 58 B6
Huazhou, China 59 G8
Hubbard, Ohio, U.S.A. ... 110 E4
Hubbard, Tex., U.S.A. ... 113 K6
Hubbart Pt., Canada 105 B10
Hubei □, China 59 B9
Hubli, India 66 M9
Huch'ang, N. Korea 57 D14
Hucknall, U.K. 12 D6
Huddersfield, U.K. 12 D6
Hude, Germany 24 B4
Hudi, Sudan 80 D3
Hudiksvall, Sweden 10 C11
Hudson, Canada 102 B1
Hudson, Mass., U.S.A. ... 111 D13
Hudson, N.Y., U.S.A. ... 111 D11
Hudson, Wis., U.S.A. ... 112 C8
Hudson, Wyo., U.S.A. ... 114 E9
Hudson →, U.S.A. 111 F10
Hudson Bay, N.W.T.,
  Canada 101 C11
Hudson Bay, Sask., Canada 105 C8
Hudson Falls, U.S.A. 111 C11
Hudson Mts., Antarctica . 5 D16
Hudson Str., Canada 101 B13
Hudson's Hope, Canada .. 104 B4
Hue, Vietnam 64 D6
Huebra →, Spain 34 D4
Huedin, Romania 42 D8
Huehuetenango, Guatemala 120 C1
Huejúcar, Mexico 118 C4
Huélamo, Spain 32 E3
Huelgoat, France 18 D3
Huelma, Spain 35 H7
Huelva, Spain 35 H4
Huelva □, Spain 35 H4
Huelva →, Spain 35 H5
Huentelauquén, Chile ... 126 C1
Huércal-Overa, Spain ... 33 H3
Huerta, Sa. de la, Argentina 126 C2
Huertas, C. de las, Spain . 33 G4
Huerva →, Spain 32 D4
Huesca, Spain 32 C5
Huesca □, Spain 32 C5
Huéscar, Spain 33 H2
Huetamo, Mexico 118 D4
Huete, Spain 32 E2
Hugh →, Australia 94 D1
Hughenden, Australia ... 94 C3
Hughes, Australia 93 F4
Hughesville, U.S.A. 111 E8
Hugli →, India 69 J13
Hugo, Colo., U.S.A. 112 F3
Hugo, Okla., U.S.A. 113 H7
Hugoton, U.S.A. 113 G4
Hui Xian = Huixian, China 56 G7

Hui Xian, China 56 H4
Hui'an, China 59 E12
Hui'anbu, China 56 F4
Huichang, China 59 E10
Huichapán, Mexico 119 C5
Huidong, Guangdong, China 59 F10
Huidong, Sichuan, China . 58 D4
Huifa He →, China 57 C14
Huila, Nevado del, Colombia 124 C3
Huilai, China 59 F11
Huili, China 58 D4
Huimin, China 57 F9
Huinan, China 57 C14
Huinca Renancó, Argentina 126 C3
Huining, China 56 G3
Huisache, Mexico 118 C4
Huishui, China 58 D6
Huisne →, France 18 E7
Huiting, China 56 G9
Huitong, China 58 D7
Huixian, China 56 G7
Huixtla, Mexico 119 D6
Huize, China 58 D4
Huizhou, China 59 F10
Hukawng Valley, Burma . 67 F20
Hukou, China 59 C11
Hukuntsi, Botswana 88 C3
Hulayfā', Si. Arabia 70 E4
Huld = Ulaanjirem,
  Mongolia 56 B3
Hulin He →, China 57 B12
Hull = Kingston upon Hull,
  U.K. 12 D7
Hull, Canada 102 C4
Hull →, U.K. 12 D7
Hulst, Neths. 17 C4
Hultsfred, Sweden 11 G9
Hulun Nur, China 60 B6
Hulyaypole, Ukraine 47 J9
Humahuaca, Argentina .. 126 A2
Humaitá, Brazil 124 E6
Humaitá, Paraguay 126 B4
Humansdorp, S. Africa .. 88 E3
Humbe, Angola 88 B1
Humber →, U.K. 12 D7
Humboldt, Canada 105 C2
Humboldt, Iowa, U.S.A. . 112 D7
Humboldt, Tenn., U.S.A. 113 H10
Humboldt →, U.S.A. ... 114 F4
Humboldt Gletscher,
  Greenland 4 B4
Hume, U.S.A. 116 J8
Hume, L., Australia 95 F4
Humenné, Slovak Rep. .. 27 C14
Hummelsta, Sweden 10 E10
Humphreys, Mt., U.S.A. . 116 H8
Humphreys Peak, U.S.A. . 115 J8
Humpolec, Czech Rep. ... 26 B8
Humptulips, U.S.A. 116 C3
Hūn, Libya 79 C9
Hun Jiang →, China 57 D13
Hunan □, China 59 D9
Hunchun, China 57 C16
Hundested, Denmark ... 11 J4
Hundewali, Pakistan 68 D5
Hundred Mile House,
  Canada 104 C4
Hunedoara, Romania ... 42 F7
Hunedoara □, Romania . 42 E7
Hünfeld, Germany 24 E5
Hung Yen, Vietnam 58 G6
Hungary ■, Europe 27 D12
Hungary, Plain of, Europe 6 F10
Hungerford, Australia ... 95 D3
Hŭngnam, N. Korea 57 E14
Hungt'ou Hsü, Taiwan .. 59 F13
Huni Valley, Ghana 82 D4
Hunneberg, Sweden 11 F6
Hunnebostrand, Sweden . 11 F5
Hunsberge, Namibia 88 D2
Hunsrück, Germany 25 F3
Hunstanton, U.K. 12 E8
Hunte →, Germany 24 B4
Hunter →, Australia 95 E5
Hunter I., Australia 94 G3
Hunter I., Canada 104 C3
Hunter Ra., Australia ... 95 E5
Hunters Road, Zimbabwe . 87 F2
Hunterville, N.Z. 91 H5
Huntingburg, U.S.A. 108 F2
Huntingdon, Canada 102 C5
Huntingdon, U.K. 13 E7
Huntington, Ind., U.S.A. 108 E3
Huntington, Oreg., U.S.A. 114 D5
Huntington, Utah, U.S.A. 114 G8
Huntington, W. Va., U.S.A. 108 F4
Huntington Beach, U.S.A. 117 M9
Huntington Station, U.S.A. 111 F11
Huntly, N.Z. 91 G5
Huntly, U.K. 14 D6
Huntsville, Canada 102 C4
Huntsville, Ala., U.S.A. . 109 H2
Huntsville, Tex., U.S.A. . 113 K7
Hunyani →, Zimbabwe . 87 F3
Hunyuan, China 56 E7
Hunza →, India 69 B6
Huo Xian = Huozhou,
  China 56 F6
Huo Hoa, Vietnam 64 D6
Huong Khe, Vietnam ... 64 C5
Huonville, Australia 94 G4
Huoqiu, China 59 A11
Huoshan, Anhui, China . 59 A12
Huoshan, Anhui, China . 59 B11
Huoshao Dao = Lü-Tao,
  Taiwan 59 F13
Huozhou, China 56 F6

Hupeh = Hubei □, China . 59 B9
Ḩūr, Iran 71 D9
Hurbanovo, Slovak Rep. . 27 D11
Hurd, C., Canada 110 A3
Hure Qi, China 57 C11
Hurezani, Romania 43 F8
Hurghada, Egypt 80 B3
Hurley, N. Mex., U.S.A. . 115 K9
Hurley, Wis., U.S.A. 112 B9
Huron, Calif., U.S.A. ... 116 J6
Huron, Ohio, U.S.A. 110 E2
Huron, S. Dak., U.S.A. . 112 C5
Huron, L., U.S.A. 110 B2
Hurricane, U.S.A. 115 H7
Hurso, Ethiopia 81 F5
Hurunui →, N.Z. 91 K4
Hurup, Denmark 11 H2
Húsavík, Iceland 8 C5
Huşi, Romania 43 D13
Huskvarna, Sweden 11 G8
Hustadvika, Norway 8 E12
Hustontown, U.S.A. 110 F6
Hustopeče, Czech Rep. .. 27 C9
Husum, Germany 24 A5
Husum, Sweden 10 A13
Hutchinson, Kans., U.S.A. 113 F6
Hutchinson, Minn., U.S.A. 112 C7
Hutte Sauvage, L. de la,
  Canada 103 A7
Hüttenberg, Austria 26 E7
Hutton, Mt., Australia .. 95 D4
Huwun, Ethiopia 81 G5
Huy, Belgium 17 D5
Huzhou, China 59 B13
Hvalpsund, Denmark ... 11 H3
Hvammstangi, Iceland .. 8 D3
Hvar, Croatia 29 E13
Hvarski Kanal, Croatia . 29 E13
Hvítá →, Iceland 8 D3
Hwachŏn-chŏsuji, S. Korea 57 E14
Hwang Ho = Huang He →,
  China 57 F10
Hwange, Zimbabwe 87 F2
Hwange Nat. Park,
  Zimbabwe 88 B4
Hyannis, Mass., U.S.A. . 108 E14
Hyannis, Nebr., U.S.A. . 112 E4
Hyargas Nuur, Mongolia . 60 B4
Hybo, Sweden 10 C10
Hydaburg, U.S.A. 104 B2
Hyde Park, U.S.A. 111 E11
Hyden, Australia 93 F2
Hyder, U.S.A. 104 B2
Hyderabad, India 66 L11
Hyderabad, Pakistan ... 68 G3
Hyères, France 21 E10
Hyères, Îs. d', France ... 21 F10
Hyesan, N. Korea 57 D15
Hyland →, Canada 104 B3
Hyltebruk, Sweden 11 H7
Hymia, India 69 C8
Hyndman Peak, U.S.A. . 114 E6
Hyōgo □, Japan 55 G7
Hyrum, U.S.A. 114 F8
Hysham, U.S.A. 114 C10
Hythe, U.K. 13 F9
Hyūga, Japan 55 H5
Hyvinge = Hyvinkää,
  Finland 9 F21
Hyvinkää, Finland 9 F21

I

I-n-Gall, Niger 83 B6
I-n-Oudad, Algeria 83 A5
I-n-Ouzzal, Algeria 83 A5
I-n-Tadreft, Niger 83 B6
Iablaniţa, Romania 42 F7
Iaco →, Brazil 124 E5
Iacobeni, Romania 43 C10
Iakora, Madag. 89 C8
Ialomiţa □, Romania ... 43 F12
Ialomiţa →, Romania .. 43 F12
Ialoveni, Moldova 43 D13
Ialpug →, Moldova ... 43 E13
Ianca, Romania 43 E12
Iara, Romania 43 D8
Iarda, Ethiopia 81 E4
Iargara, Moldova 43 D13
Iaşi, Romania 43 C12
Iaşi □, Romania 43 C12
Íasmos, Greece 41 E9
Ib →, India 69 J10
Iba, Phil. 61 D3
Ibadan, Nigeria 83 D5
Ibagué, Colombia 124 C3
Iballja, Albania 40 D4
Ibănești, Botoșani, Romania 43 B11
Ibănești, Mureș, Romania 43 D9
Ibar →, Serbia, Yug. .. 40 C4
Ibaraki □, Japan 55 F10
Ibarra, Ecuador 124 C3
Ibba, Sudan 81 G2
Ibba, Bahr el →, Sudan 81 F2
Ibbenbüren, Germany .. 24 C3
Ibembo,
  Dem. Rep. of the Congo 86 B1
Ibera, L., Argentina ... 126 B4
Iberian Peninsula, Europe 6 H5
Iberville, Canada 102 C5
Iberville, Lac d', Canada 102 A5
Ibi, Nigeria 83 D6
Ibi, Spain 33 G4
Ibiá, Brazil 125 G9
Ibicaraí, Brazil 127 B4
Ibicuy, Argentina 126 C4
Ibioapaba, Sa. da, Brazil 125 D10
Ibiza = Eivissa, Spain . 37 C7

Íblei, Monti, Italy 31 E7
Ibo, Mozam. 87 E5
Ibonma, Indonesia 63 E8
Ibotirama, Brazil 125 F10
Ibrāhīm →, Lebanon .. 75 A4
'Ibrī, Oman 71 F8
Ibriktepe, Turkey 41 E10
Ibshawâi, Egypt 80 J7
Ibu, Indonesia 63 D7
Ibusuki, Japan 55 J5
Ica, Peru 124 F3
Içá →, Brazil 124 D5
Içana, Brazil 124 C5
Içana →, Brazil 124 C5
İçel = Mersin, Turkey .. 70 B2
Iceland ■, Europe 8 D4
Ich'ang = Yichang, China 59 B8
Ichchapuram, India 67 K14
Ichhawar, India 68 H7
Ichihara, Japan 55 G10
Ichikawa, Japan 55 G9
Ichilo →, Bolivia 124 G6
Ichinohe, Japan 54 D10
Ichinomiya, Japan 55 G8
Ichinoseki, Japan 54 E10
Ichnya, Ukraine 47 G7
Ichŏn, S. Korea 57 F14
Icod, Canary Is. 37 F3
Ida Grove, U.S.A. 112 D7
Idabel, U.S.A. 113 J7
Idaga Hamus, Ethiopia . 81 E4
Idah, Nigeria 83 D6
Idaho □, U.S.A. 114 D7
Idaho City, U.S.A. 114 E6
Idaho Falls, U.S.A. 114 E7
Idanha-a-Nova, Portugal 34 F3
Idar-Oberstein, Germany 25 F3
Idfû, Egypt 80 C3
Ídhi Óros, Greece 36 D6
Ídhra, Greece 38 D5
Idi, Indonesia 62 C1
Idiofa,
  Dem. Rep. of the Congo 84 E3
Idkerberget, Sweden ... 10 D9
Idlib, Syria 70 C3
Idre, Sweden 10 C6
Idria, U.S.A. 116 J6
Idrija, Slovenia 29 C11
Idritsa, Russia 46 D5
Idutywa, S. Africa 89 E4
Ieper, Belgium 17 D2
Ierápetra, Greece 36 E7
Ierissós, Greece 40 F7
Ierissoú Kólpos, Greece 40 F7
Iernut, Romania 43 D9
Iesi, Italy 29 E10
Iésolo, Italy 29 C9
Ifach, Peñón de, Spain . 33 G5
Ifakara, Tanzania 84 F7
'Ifāl, W. al →, Si. Arabia 70 D2
Ifanadiana, Madag. ... 89 C8
Ife, Nigeria 83 D5
Iférouâne, Niger 83 B6
Iffley, Australia 94 B3
Ifni, Morocco 78 C3
Ifon, Nigeria 83 D6
Iforas, Adrar des, Mali . 83 B5
Ifould, L., Australia ... 93 F5
Iganga, Uganda 86 B3
Igarapava, Brazil 125 H9
Igarka, Russia 50 C9
Igatimi, Paraguay 127 A4
Igbetti, Nigeria 83 D5
Igbo-Ora, Nigeria 83 D5
Igboho, Nigeria 83 D5
Igbor, Nigeria 83 D6
Iğdır, Turkey 73 C11
Igelfors, Sweden 11 F9
Iggesund, Sweden 10 C11
Iglésias, Italy 30 C1
Igloolik, Canada 101 B11
Igluligaarjuk, Canada .. 101 B10
'Igma, Gebel el, Egypt . 80 B3
Ignace, Canada 102 C1
Iğneada, Turkey 41 E11
Iğneada Burnu, Turkey . 41 E12
Igoumenítsa, Greece ... 38 C2
Igra, Russia 48 B11
Iguaçu →, Brazil 127 B5
Iguaçu, Cat. del, Brazil . 127 B5
Iguaçu Falls = Iguaçu, Cat.
  del, Brazil 127 B5
Iguala, Mexico 119 D5
Igualada, Spain 32 D6
Iguassu = Iguaçu →, Brazil 127 B5
Iguatu, Brazil 125 E11
Iharana, Madag. 89 A9
Ihbulag, Mongolia 56 C4
Iheya-Shima, Japan ... 55 L3
Ihiala, Nigeria 83 D6
Ihosy, Madag. 89 C8
Ihotry, Farihy, Madag. . 89 C7
Ihugh, Nigeria 83 D6
Ii, Finland 8 D21
Ii-Shima, Japan 55 L3
Iida, Japan 55 G8
Iijoki →, Finland 8 D21
Iisalmi, Finland 8 E22
Iiyama, Japan 55 F9
Iizuka, Japan 55 H5
Ijebu-Igbo, Nigeria ... 83 D5
Ijebu-Ode, Nigeria 83 D5
IJmuiden, Neths. 17 B4
IJssel →, Neths. 17 B5
IJsselmeer, Neths. 17 B5
Ijuí, Brazil 127 B5
Ijuí →, Brazil 127 B4
Ikalamavony, Madag. .. 89 C8
Ikale, Nigeria 83 D6
Ikaluktutiak, Canada .. 100 B9

165

Ikang, Nigeria ... 83 E6
Ikara, Nigeria ... 83 C6
Ikare, Nigeria ... 83 D6
Ikaría, Greece ... 39 D8
Ikast, Denmark ... 11 H3
Ikeda, Japan ... 55 G6
Ikeja, Nigeria ... 83 D5
Ikela,
  Dem. Rep. of the Congo . 84 E4
Ikerre-Ekiti, Nigeria ... 83 D6
Ikhtiman, Bulgaria ... 40 D7
Iki, Japan ... 55 H4
Ikimba L., Tanzania ... 86 C3
Ikire, Nigeria ... 83 D5
Ikizdere, Turkey ... 73 B9
Ikom, Nigeria ... 83 D6
Ikongo, Madag. ... 89 C8
Ikopa →, Madag. ... 89 B8
Ikot Ekpene, Nigeria ... 83 D6
Ikungu, Tanzania ... 86 C3
Ikurun, Nigeria ... 83 D5
Ila, Nigeria ... 83 D5
Ilagan, Phil. ... 61 C4
Ilaka, Madag. ... 89 B8
Ilâm, Iran ... 70 C5
Ilam, Nepal ... 69 F12
Ilam □, Iran ... 70 C5
Ilan, Taiwan ... 59 E13
Ilanskiy, Russia ... 51 D10
Ilaro, Nigeria ... 83 D5
Ilatane, Niger ... 83 B5
Iława, Poland ... 44 E6
Ile-à-la-Crosse, Canada ... 105 B7
Ile-à-la-Crosse, Lac, Canada 105 B7
Île-de-France □, France ... 19 D9
Ileanda, Romania ... 43 C8
Ilebo,
  Dem. Rep. of the Congo . 84 E4
Ilek, Russia ... 50 D6
Ilero, Nigeria ... 83 D5
Ilesha, Kwara, Nigeria ... 83 D5
Ilesha, Oyo, Nigeria ... 83 D5
Ilford, Canada ... 105 B9
Ilfracombe, Australia ... 94 C3
Ilfracombe, U.K. ... 13 F3
Ilgaz, Turkey ... 72 B5
Ilgaz Dağları, Turkey ... 72 B5
Ilgın, Turkey ... 72 C4
Ílhavo, Portugal ... 34 E2
Ilhéus, Brazil ... 125 F11
Ili →, Kazakstan ... 50 E8
Ilia, Romania ... 42 E7
Ilía □, Greece ... 38 D3
Iliamna L., U.S.A. ... 100 C4
Iliç, Turkey ... 73 C8
Ilıca, Turkey ... 39 B9
Ilichevsk, Azerbaijan ... 73 C11
Iligan, Phil. ... 61 G6
Iligan Bay, Phil. ... 61 G6
Ilíki, L., Greece ... 38 C5
Ilin I., Phil. ... 61 E4
Iliodhrómia, Greece ... 38 B5
Ilion, U.S.A. ... 111 D9
Ilirska-Bistrica, Slovenia ... 29 C11
Ilkeston, U.K. ... 12 E6
Ilkley, U.K. ... 12 D6
Illampu = Ancohuma,
  Nevada, Bolivia ... 122 E4
Illana B., Phil. ... 61 H5
Illapel, Chile ... 126 C1
Ille-et-Vilaine □, France ... 18 D5
Ille-sur-Têt, France ... 20 F6
Illéla, Niger ... 83 C6
Iller →, Germany ... 25 G5
Illertissen, Germany ... 25 G6
Illescas, Spain ... 34 E7
Illetas, Spain ... 37 B9
Illichivsk, Ukraine ... 47 J6
Illiers-Combray, France ... 18 D8
Illimani, Nevado, Bolivia ... 124 G5
Illinois □, U.S.A. ... 112 E10
Illinois →, U.S.A. ... 107 C8
Illium = Troy, Turkey ... 39 B8
Illizi, Algeria ... 78 C7
Illkirch-Graffenstaden,
  France ... 19 D14
Illoqqortoormiit, Greenland . 4 B6
Íllora, Spain ... 35 H7
Ilm →, Germany ... 24 D7
Ilmajoki, Finland ... 9 E20
Ilmen, Ozero, Russia ... 46 C6
Ilmenau, Germany ... 24 E6
Ilo, Peru ... 124 G4
Ilobu, Nigeria ... 83 D5
Iloilo, Phil. ... 61 F5
Ilora, Nigeria ... 83 D5
Ilorin, Nigeria ... 83 D5
Ilovatka, Russia ... 48 E7
Ilovlya, Russia ... 49 F7
Ilovlya →, Russia ... 49 F7
Iłowa, Poland ... 45 G2
Ilubabor □, Ethiopia ... 81 F4
Ilva Mică, Romania ... 43 C9
Ilwaco, U.S.A. ... 116 D2
Ilwaki, Indonesia ... 63 F7
Ilyichevsk = Illichivsk,
  Ukraine ... 47 J6
Iłża, Poland ... 45 G8
Izanka →, Poland ... 45 G8
Imabari, Japan ... 55 G6
Imaloto →, Madag. ... 89 C8
Imamoğlu, Turkey ... 72 D6
Imandra, Ozero, Russia ... 50 C4
Imanombo, Madag. ... 89 C8
Imari, Japan ... 55 H4
Imasa, Sudan ... 80 D4
Imathía □, Greece ... 40 F6
Imatra, Finland ... 46 B5
Imbil, Australia ... 95 D5
Iménas, Mali ... 83 B5

imeni 26 Bakinskikh
  Komissarov = Neftçala,
  Azerbaijan ... 71 B6
imeni 26 Bakinskikh
  Komissarov, Turkmenistan 71 B7
Imeri, Serra, Brazil ... 124 C5
Imerimandroso, Madag. ... 89 B8
Imi, Ethiopia ... 81 F5
Imishly = Imişli, Azerbaijan 49 L9
Imişli, Azerbaijan ... 49 L9
Imlay, U.S.A. ... 114 F4
Imlay City, U.S.A. ... 110 D1
Immaseri, Sudan ... 81 D2
Immenstadt, Germany ... 25 H6
Immingham, U.K. ... 12 D7
Immokalee, U.S.A. ... 109 M5
Imo □, Nigeria ... 83 D6
Imo →, Nigeria ... 83 D6
Imola, Italy ... 29 D8
Imotski, Croatia ... 29 E14
Imperatriz, Brazil ... 125 E9
Impéria, Italy ... 28 E5
Imperial, Canada ... 105 C7
Imperial, Calif., U.S.A. ... 117 N11
Imperial, Nebr., U.S.A. ... 112 E4
Imperial Beach, U.S.A. ... 117 N9
Imperial Dam, U.S.A. ... 117 N12
Imperial Reservoir, U.S.A. 117 N12
Imperial Valley, U.S.A. ... 117 N11
Imperieuse Reef, Australia . 92 C2
Impfondo, Congo ... 84 D3
Imphal, India ... 67 G18
Imphy, France ... 19 F10
Imranlı, Turkey ... 73 C8
Imroz = Gökçeada, Turkey 41 F9
Imroz, Turkey ... 41 F9
Imst, Austria ... 26 D3
Imuris, Mexico ... 118 A2
Imuruan B., Phil. ... 63 B5
In Akhmed, Mali ... 83 B4
In-Aleï, Mali ... 82 B4
In Delimane, Mali ... 83 B5
In-Guezzam, Niger ... 83 B6
In Koufi, Mali ... 83 B5
In Salah, Algeria ... 78 C6
In Tallak, Mali ... 83 B5
In Tebezas, Mali ... 83 B5
Ina, Japan ... 55 G8
Inangahua Junction, N.Z. ... 91 J3
Inanwatan, Indonesia ... 63 E8
Iñapari, Peru ... 124 F5
Inari, Finland ... 8 B22
Inarijärvi, Finland ... 8 B22
Inawashiro-Ko, Japan ... 54 F10
Inca, Spain ... 37 B9
Inca de Oro, Chile ... 126 B2
Incaguasi, Chile ... 126 B1
Ince Burun, Turkey ... 72 A6
Incekum Burnu, Turkey ... 72 D5
Incesu, Turkey ... 70 B2
Inch'ŏn, S. Korea ... 57 F14
Incio = Cruz de Incio, Spain 34 C3
Incirliova, Turkey ... 39 D9
Incline Village, U.S.A. ... 114 G4
Incomáti →, Mozam. ... 89 D5
Inda Silase, Ethiopia ... 81 E4
Indal, Sweden ... 10 B11
Indalsälven →, Sweden ... 10 B11
Indaw, Burma ... 67 G20
Indbir, Ethiopia ... 81 F4
Independence, Calif., U.S.A. 116 J8
Independence, Iowa, U.S.A. 112 D9
Independence, Kans., U.S.A. 113 G7
Independence, Ky., U.S.A. 108 F3
Independence, Mo., U.S.A. 112 F7
Independence Fjord,
  Greenland ... 4 A6
Independence Mts., U.S.A. 114 F5
Independența, Romania ... 43 E12
Index, U.S.A. ... 116 C5
India ■, Asia ... 66 K11
Indian →, U.S.A. ... 109 M5
Indian Cabins, Canada ... 104 B5
Indian Harbour, Canada ... 103 B8
Indian Head, Canada ... 105 C8
Indian Lake, U.S.A. ... 111 C10
Indian Ocean ... 52 K11
Indian Springs, U.S.A. ... 117 J11
Indiana, U.S.A. ... 110 F5
Indiana □, U.S.A. ... 108 F3
Indianapolis, U.S.A. ... 108 F2
Indianola, Iowa, U.S.A. ... 112 E8
Indianola, Miss., U.S.A. ... 113 J9
Indigirka →, Russia ... 51 B15
Indija, Serbia, Yug. ... 42 E5
Indio, U.S.A. ... 117 M10
Indo-China, Asia ... 52 H14
Indonesia ■, Asia ... 62 F5
Indore, India ... 68 H6
Indramayu, Indonesia ... 63 G13
Indravati →, India ... 67 K12
Indre □, France ... 19 F8
Indre →, France ... 18 E7
Indre-et-Loire □, France ... 18 E7
Indulkana, Australia ... 95 D1
Indus →, Pakistan ... 68 G2
Indus, Mouth of the,
  Pakistan ... 68 H3
İnebolu, Turkey ... 72 B5
İnecik, Turkey ... 41 F11
İnegöl, Turkey ... 41 F13
Ineu, Romania ... 42 D6
Infantes = Villanueva de los
  Infantes, Spain ... 35 G7
Infiernillo, Presa del, Mexico 118 D4
Infiesto, Spain ... 34 B5
Ingelstad, Sweden ... 11 H8
Ingenio, Canary Is. ... 37 G4
Ingenio Santa Ana,
  Argentina ... 126 B2
Ingersoll, Canada ... 102 D3

Ingham, Australia ... 94 B4
Ingleborough, U.K. ... 12 C5
Inglewood, Queens.,
  Australia ... 95 D5
Inglewood, Vic., Australia .. 95 F3
Inglewood, N.Z. ... 91 H5
Inglewood, U.S.A. ... 117 M8
Ingólfshöfði, Iceland ... 8 E5
Ingolstadt, Germany ... 25 G7
Ingomar, U.S.A. ... 114 C10
Ingonish, Canada ... 103 C7
Ingore, Guinea-Biss. ... 82 C1
Ingraj Bazar, India ... 69 G13
Ingrid Christensen Coast,
  Antarctica ... 5 C6
Ingul = Inhul →,
  Ukraine ... 47 J7
Ingulec = Inhulec →, Ukraine 47 J7
Ingulets = Inhulets →,
  Ukraine ... 47 J7
Inguri = Enguri →,
  Georgia ... 49 J5
Ingushetia □, Russia ... 49 J7
Ingwavuma, S. Africa ... 89 D5
Inhaca, Mozam. ... 89 D5
Inhafenga, Mozam. ... 89 C5
Inhambane, Mozam. ... 89 C6
Inhambane □, Mozam. ... 89 C5
Inhaminga, Mozam. ... 87 F4
Inharrime, Mozam. ... 89 C6
Inharrime →, Mozam. ... 89 C6
Inhisar, Turkey ... 39 A12
Inhul →, Ukraine ... 47 J7
Inhulec →, Ukraine ... 47 J7
Inhulets →, Ukraine ... 47 J7
Iniesta, Spain ... 33 F3
Inishbofin, Ireland ... 15 C1
Inisheer, Ireland ... 15 C2
Inishfree B., Ireland ... 15 A3
Inishkea North, Ireland ... 15 B1
Inishkea South, Ireland ... 15 B1
Inishmaan, Ireland ... 15 C2
Inishmore, Ireland ... 15 C2
Inishowen Pen., Ireland ... 15 A4
Inishshark, Ireland ... 15 C1
Inishturk, Ireland ... 15 C1
Inishvickillane, Ireland ... 15 D1
Injibara, Ethiopia ... 81 E4
Injune, Australia ... 95 D4
Inklin →, Canada ... 104 B2
Inle L., Burma ... 67 J20
Inlet, U.S.A. ... 111 C10
Inn →, Austria ... 26 C6
Innamincka, Australia ... 95 D3
Inner Hebrides, U.K. ... 14 E2
Inner Mongolia = Nei
  Mongol Zizhiqu □, China 56 D7
Inner Sound, U.K. ... 14 D3
Innerkip, Canada ... 110 C4
Innetalling I., Canada ... 102 A4
Innisfail, Australia ... 94 B4
Innisfail, Canada ... 104 C6
In'no-shima, Japan ... 55 G6
Innsbruck, Austria ... 26 D4
Inny →, Ireland ... 15 C4
Inongo,
  Dem. Rep. of the Congo . 84 E3
İnönü, Turkey ... 39 B12
Inoucdjouac = Inukjuak,
  Canada ... 101 C12
Inowrocław, Poland ... 45 F5
Inpundong, N. Korea ... 57 D14
Inscription, C., Australia ... 93 E1
Insein, Burma ... 67 L20
Insjön, Sweden ... 10 D9
İnşko, Poland ... 44 E2
Însurăței, Romania ... 43 F12
Inta, Russia ... 50 C6
Intendente Alvear, Argentina 126 D3
Intepe, Turkey ... 39 A8
Interlaken, Switz. ... 25 J3
Interlaken, U.S.A. ... 111 D8
International Falls, U.S.A. . 112 A8
Intiyaco, Argentina ... 126 B3
Întorsura Buzăului, Romania 43 E11
Inukjuak, Canada ... 101 C12
Inútil, B., Chile ... 128 G2
Inuvik, Canada ... 100 B6
Inveraray, U.K. ... 14 E3
Inverbervie, U.K. ... 14 E6
Invercargill, N.Z. ... 91 M2
Inverclyde □, U.K. ... 14 F4
Inverell, Australia ... 95 D5
Invergordon, U.K. ... 14 D4
Inverloch, Australia ... 95 F4
Invermere, Canada ... 104 C5
Inverness, Canada ... 103 C7
Inverness, U.K. ... 14 D4
Inverness, U.S.A. ... 109 L4
Inverurie, U.K. ... 14 D6
Investigator Group, Australia 95 E1
Investigator Str., Australia . 95 F2
Inya, Russia ... 50 D9
Inyanga, Zimbabwe ... 87 F3
Inyangani, Zimbabwe ... 87 F3
Inyantue, Zimbabwe ... 88 B4
Inyo Mts., U.S.A. ... 116 J9
Inyokern, U.S.A. ... 117 K9
Inza, Russia ... 48 D8
Inzhavino, Russia ... 48 D6
Iō-Jima, Japan ... 55 J5
Ioánnina, Greece ... 38 B2
Ioánnina □, Greece ... 38 B2
Ion Corvin, Romania ... 43 F12
Iona, U.K. ... 14 E2
Ione, U.S.A. ... 116 G6
Ionia, U.S.A. ... 108 D3

Ionian Is. = Iónioi Nísoi,
  Greece ... 38 C2
Ionian Sea, Medit. S. ... 6 H9
Iónioi Nísoi, Greece ... 38 C2
Iónioi Nísoi □, Greece ... 38 C2
Íos, Greece ... 39 D7
Iowa □, U.S.A. ... 112 E9
Iowa →, U.S.A. ... 112 E9
Iowa City, U.S.A. ... 112 E9
Iowa Falls, U.S.A. ... 112 D8
Iowa Park, U.S.A. ... 113 J5
Ipala, Tanzania ... 86 C3
Ipameri, Brazil ... 125 G9
Ipáti, Greece ... 38 C4
Ipatinga, Brazil ... 125 G10
Ipatovo, Russia ... 49 H6
Ipel' →, Europe ... 27 D11
Ipiales, Colombia ... 124 C3
Ipin = Yibin, China ... 58 C5
Ipixuna, Brazil ... 124 E4
Ipoh, Malaysia ... 65 K3
Ippy, C.A.R. ... 84 C4
Ipsala, Turkey ... 41 F10
Ipsárion, Óros, Greece ... 41 F8
Ipswich, Australia ... 95 D5
Ipswich, U.K. ... 13 E9
Ipswich, Mass., U.S.A. ... 111 D14
Ipswich, S. Dak., U.S.A. .. 112 C5
Ipu, Brazil ... 125 D10
Iqaluit, Canada ... 101 B13
Iquique, Chile ... 124 H4
Iquitos, Peru ... 124 D4
Irabu-Jima, Japan ... 55 M2
Iracoubo, Fr. Guiana ... 125 B8
Irafshān, Iran ... 71 E9
Irahuan, Phil. ... 61 G3
Iráklia, Kikládhes, Greece . 39 E7
Iráklia, Sérrai, Greece ... 40 E7
Iráklion, Greece ... 36 D7
Iráklion □, Greece ... 36 D7
Irala, Paraguay ... 127 B5
Iran ■, Asia ... 71 C7
Iran, Gunung-Gunung,
  Malaysia ... 62 D4
Iran, Plateau of, Asia ... 52 F9
Iran Ra. = Iran, Gunung-
  Gunung, Malaysia ... 62 D4
Īrānshahr, Iran ... 71 E9
Irapuato, Mexico ... 118 C4
Iraq ■, Asia ... 70 C5
Irati, Brazil ... 127 B5
Irbes saurums, Latvia ... 44 A9
Irbid, Jordan ... 75 C4
Irbid □, Jordan ... 75 C5
Irebu,
  Dem. Rep. of the Congo . 84 E3
Irele, Nigeria ... 83 D6
Irgiz, Bolshaya →, Russia . 48 D9
Irhyangdong, N. Korea ... 57 D15
Iri, S. Korea ... 57 G14
Irian Jaya □, Indonesia ... 63 E9
Irié, Guinea ... 82 D3
Iriga, Phil. ... 61 E5
Iringa, Tanzania ... 86 D4
Iringa □, Tanzania ... 86 D4
Iriomote-Jima, Japan ... 55 M1
Iriona, Honduras ... 120 C2
Iriri →, Brazil ... 125 D8
Irish Republic ■, Europe .. 15 C3
Irish Sea, U.K. ... 12 D3
Irkutsk, Russia ... 51 D11
Irlığanlı, Turkey ... 39 D11
Irma, Canada ... 105 C6
Irō-Zaki, Japan ... 55 G9
Iroise, Mer d', France ... 18 D2
Iron Baron, Australia ... 95 E2
Iron Gate = Portile de Fier,
  Europe ... 42 F7
Iron Knob, Australia ... 95 E2
Iron Mountain, U.S.A. ... 108 C1
Iron River, U.S.A. ... 112 B10
Irondequoit, U.S.A. ... 110 C7
Ironton, Mo., U.S.A. ... 113 G9
Ironton, Ohio, U.S.A. ... 108 F4
Ironwood, U.S.A. ... 112 B9
Iroquois, Canada ... 111 B9
Iroquois Falls, Canada ... 102 C3
Irosin, Phil. ... 61 E6
Irpin, Ukraine ... 47 G6
Irrara Cr. →, Australia ... 95 D4
Irrawaddy □, Burma ... 67 L19
Irrawaddy →, Burma ... 67 M19
Irricana, Canada ... 104 C6
Irsina, Italy ... 31 B9
Irtysh →, Russia ... 50 C7
Irumu,
  Dem. Rep. of the Congo . 86 B2
Irún, Spain ... 32 B3
Irunea = Pamplona, Spain . 32 C3
Irurzun, Spain ... 32 C3
Irvine, Canada ... 105 D6
Irvine, U.K. ... 14 F4
Irvine, Calif., U.S.A. ... 117 M9
Irvine, Ky., U.S.A. ... 108 G4
Irvinestown, U.K. ... 15 B4
Irvona, U.S.A. ... 110 F6
Irymple, Australia ... 95 E3
Is, Jebel, Sudan ... 80 C4
Is-sur-Tille, France ... 19 E12
Isa, Nigeria ... 83 C6
Isa Khel, Pakistan ... 68 C4
Isaac →, Australia ... 94 C4
Isaac, U.S.A. ... 112 C4
Isabel, I., Mexico ... 118 C3
Isabela, Phil. ... 61 H5
Isabela, I., Mexico ... 118 C3
Isabelia, Cord., Nic. ... 120 D2
Isabella Ra., Australia ... 92 D3

Isaccea, Romania ... 43 E13
Ísafjarðardjúp, Iceland ... 8 C2
Ísafjörður, Iceland ... 8 C2
Isagarh, India ... 68 G7
Isahaya, Japan ... 55 H5
Isaka, Tanzania ... 86 C3
Isakly, Russia ... 48 C10
Isalnița, Romania ... 43 F8
Isan →, India ... 69 F9
Isana = Içana →, Brazil . 124 C5
Isanlu Makutu, Nigeria ... 83 D6
Isar →, Germany ... 25 G8
Ísarco →, Italy ... 29 B8
Isari, Greece ... 38 D3
Íscar, Spain ... 34 D6
Iscehisar, Turkey ... 39 C12
Íschia, Italy ... 30 B6
Isdell →, Australia ... 92 C3
Ise, Japan ... 55 G8
Ise-Wan, Japan ... 55 G8
Isefjord, Denmark ... 11 J5
Isel →, Austria ... 26 E5
Iseo, Italy ... 28 C7
Iseo, L. d', Italy ... 28 C7
Iseramagazi, Tanzania ... 86 C3
Isère □, France ... 21 C9
Isère →, France ... 21 D8
Iserlohn, Germany ... 24 D3
Isérnia, Italy ... 31 A7
Iseyin, Nigeria ... 83 D5
Isfahan = Eşfahān, Iran ... 71 C6
Ishigaki-Shima, Japan ... 55 M2
Ishikari-Gawa →, Japan .. 54 C10
Ishikari-Sammyaku, Japan . 54 C11
Ishikari-Wan, Japan ... 54 C10
Ishikawa □, Japan ... 55 F8
Ishim, Russia ... 50 D7
Ishim →, Russia ... 50 D8
Ishinomaki, Japan ... 54 E10
Ishioka, Japan ... 55 F10
Ishkuman, Pakistan ... 69 A5
Ishmi, Albania ... 40 E3
Ishpeming, U.S.A. ... 108 B2
Isigny-sur-Mer, France ... 18 C5
Isıklar Dağı, Turkey ... 41 F11
Işıklı, Turkey ... 39 C11
Isil Kul, Russia ... 50 D8
Isili, Italy ... 30 C2
Isiolo, Kenya ... 86 B4
Isiro,
  Dem. Rep. of the Congo . 86 B2
Isisford, Australia ... 94 C3
Iskenderun, Turkey ... 70 B3
Iskenderun Körfezi, Turkey 72 D6
Iskilip, Turkey ... 72 B6
İskür →, Bulgaria ... 41 C8
İskür, Yazovir, Bulgaria ... 40 D7
Iskut →, Canada ... 104 B2
Isla →, U.K. ... 14 E5
Isla Cristina, Spain ... 35 H3
Isla Vista, U.S.A. ... 117 L7
Islāhiye, Turkey ... 72 D7
Islam Headworks, Pakistan . 68 E5
Islamabad, Pakistan ... 68 C5
Islamgarh, Pakistan ... 68 F4
Islamkot, Pakistan ... 68 G4
Islampur, India ... 69 G11
Island L., Canada ... 105 C10
Island Lagoon, Australia ... 95 E2
Island Pond, U.S.A. ... 111 B13
Islands, B. of, Canada ... 103 C8
Islay, U.K. ... 14 F2
Isle →, France ... 20 D3
Isle aux Morts, Canada ... 103 C8
Isle of Wight □, U.K. ... 13 G6
Isle Royale, U.S.A. ... 112 B10
Isle Royale National Park,
  U.S.A. ... 112 B10
Isleton, U.S.A. ... 116 G5
Ismail = Izmayil, Ukraine . 47 K5
Ismâ'ilîya, Egypt ... 80 H8
Ismaning, Germany ... 25 G7
Isna, Egypt ... 80 B3
Isoanala, Madag. ... 89 C8
Isogstadu, India ... 69 B8
Ísola del Liri, Italy ... 29 G10
Ísola della Scala, Italy ... 28 C7
Ísola di Capo Rizzuto, Italy 31 D10
Isparta, Turkey ... 39 D12
İsperikh, Bulgaria ... 41 C10
Íspica, Italy ... 31 F7
Israel ■, Asia ... 75 D3
Isratu, Eritrea ... 81 D4
Issia, Ivory C. ... 82 D3
Issoire, France ... 20 C7
Issoudun, France ... 19 F8
Issyk-Kul, Ozero = Ysyk-
  Köl, Ozero, Kyrgyzstan . 50 E8
Ist, Croatia ... 29 D11
Istállós-kő, Hungary ... 42 B5
İstanbul, Turkey ... 41 E12
İstanbul □, Turkey ... 41 E12
İstanbul Boğazı, Turkey ... 41 E13
Istiaía, Greece ... 38 C5
Istok, Kosovo, Yug. ... 40 D4
Istokpoga, L., U.S.A. ... 109 M5
Istra, Croatia ... 29 C10
Istra, Russia ... 46 E9
Istres, France ... 21 E8
Istria = Istra, Croatia ... 29 C10
Itá, Paraguay ... 126 B4
Itaberaba, Brazil ... 125 F10
Itabira, Brazil ... 125 G10
Itabirito, Brazil ... 127 A7
Itabuna, Brazil ... 125 F11
Itacaunas →, Brazil ... 125 E9
Itacoatiara, Brazil ... 125 D7
Itaipú, Reprêsa de, Brazil . 127 B5
Itaituba, Brazil ... 125 D7
Itajaí, Brazil ... 127 B6
Itajubá, Brazil ... 127 A6

Itaka, *Tanzania* 87 D3
Italy ■, *Europe* 7 G8
Itamaraju, *Brazil* 125 G11
Itampolo, *Madag.* 89 C7
Itandrano, *Madag.* 89 C8
Itapecuru-Mirim, *Brazil* ... 125 D10
Itaperuna, *Brazil* 127 A7
Itapetininga, *Brazil* 127 A6
Itapeva, *Brazil* 127 A6
Itapicuru →, *Bahia, Brazil* 125 F11
Itapicuru →, *Maranhão,*
  Brazil 125 D10
Itapipoca, *Brazil* 125 D11
Itapuá □, *Paraguay* 127 B4
Itaquari, *Brazil* 127 A7
Itaquí, *Brazil* 126 B4
Itararé, *Brazil* 127 A6
Itarsi, *India* 68 H7
Itatí, *Argentina* 126 B4
Itbayat, *Phil.* 61 A4
Itchen →, *U.K.* 13 G6
Itéa, *Greece* 38 C4
Itezhi Tezhi, L., *Zambia* .. 87 F2
Ithaca = Itháki, *Greece* ... 38 C2
Ithaca, *U.S.A.* 111 D8
Itháki, *Greece* 38 C2
Itiquira →, *Brazil* 125 G7
Ito, *Japan* 55 G9
Ito Aba I., *S. China Sea* .. 62 B4
Itoigawa, *Japan* 55 F8
Iton →, *France* 18 C8
Itonamas →, *Bolivia* 124 F6
Itri, *Italy* 30 A6
Itsa, *Egypt* 80 J7
Ittiri, *Italy* 30 B1
Itu, *Brazil* 127 A6
Itu, *Nigeria* 83 D6
Ituiutaba, *Brazil* 125 G9
Itumbiara, *Brazil* 125 G9
Ituna, *Canada* 105 C8
Itunge Port, *Tanzania* 87 D3
Iturbe, *Argentina* 126 A2
Ituri →,
  Dem. Rep. of the Congo . 86 B2
Iturup, Ostrov, *Russia* ... 51 E15
Ituxi →, *Brazil* 124 E6
Ituyuro →, *Argentina* 126 A3
Itzehoe, *Germany* 24 B5
Ivahona, *Madag.* 89 C8
Ivaí →, *Brazil* 127 A5
Ivalo, *Finland* 8 B22
Ivalojoki →, *Finland* 8 B22
Ivanava, *Belarus* 47 F3
Ivančice, *Czech Rep.* 27 B9
Ivănești, *Romania* 43 D12
Ivangorod, *Russia* 46 C5
Ivanhoe, *Australia* 95 E3
Ivanhoe, *Calif., U.S.A.* ... 116 J7
Ivanhoe, *Minn., U.S.A.* ... 112 C6
Ivanić Grad, *Croatia* 29 C13
Ivanjica, *Serbia, Yug.* 40 C4
Ivanjska, *Bos.-H.* 42 F2
Ivankoyskoye Vdkhr., *Russia* 46 D9
Ivano-Frankivsk, *Ukraine* .. 47 H3
Ivano-Frankovsk = Ivano-
  Frankivsk, *Ukraine* 47 H3
Ivanovo, *Russia* 46 D11
Ivanščica, *Croatia* 29 B13
Ivato, *Madag.* 89 C8
Ivatsevichy, *Belarus* 47 F3
Ivaylovgrad, *Bulgaria* 41 E10
Ivinheima, *Brazil* 127 A5
Ivínhema, *Brazil* 127 A5
Ivohibe, *Madag.* 89 C8
Ivory Coast, *W. Afr.* 82 E4
Ivory Coast ■, *Africa* 82 D4
Ivösjön, *Sweden* 11 H8
Ivrea, *Italy* 28 C4
Ivrindi, *Turkey* 39 B9
Ivujivik, *Canada* 101 B12
Ivybridge, *U.K.* 13 G4
Iwaizumi, *Japan* 54 E10
Iwaki, *Japan* 55 F10
Iwakuni, *Japan* 55 G6
Iwamizawa, *Japan* 54 C10
Iwanai, *Japan* 54 C10
Iwata, *Japan* 55 G8
Iwate □, *Japan* 54 E10
Iwate-San, *Japan* 54 E10
Iwo, *Nigeria* 83 D5
Iwonicz-Zdrój, *Poland* 45 J8
Ixiamas, *Bolivia* 124 F5
Ixopo, *S. Africa* 89 E5
Ixtepec, *Mexico* 119 D5
Ixtlán del Río, *Mexico* 118 C4
Iyal Bakhit, *Sudan* 81 E2
Iyo, *Japan* 55 H6
Izabal, L. de, *Guatemala* . 120 C2
Izamal, *Mexico* 119 C7
Izberbash, *Russia* 49 J8
Izbica, *Poland* 45 H10
Izbica Kujawska, *Poland* .. 45 F5
Izberceni, *Romania* 43 G9
Izena-Shima, *Japan* 55 L3
Izgrev, *Bulgaria* 41 C10
Izhevsk, *Russia* 50 D6
Izmayil, *Ukraine* 47 K5
İzmir, *Turkey* 39 C9
İzmir □, *Turkey* 39 C9
İzmit = Kocaeli, *Turkey* .. 41 F13
Iznájar, *Spain* 35 H6
Iznalloz, *Spain* 35 H7
İznik, *Turkey* 72 B3
İznik Gölü, *Turkey* 41 F13
Izola, *Slovenia* 29 C10
Izra, *Syria* 75 C5
Iztochni Rodopi, *Bulgaria* . 41 E9

Izu-Shotō, *Japan* 55 G10
Izúcar de Matamoros,
  Mexico 119 D5
Izumi-sano, *Japan* 55 G7
Izumo, *Japan* 55 G6
Izyaslav, *Ukraine* 47 G4
Izyum, *Ukraine* 47 H9

J

Jaba, *Ethiopia* 81 F4
Jabal al Awliyā, *Sudan* ... 81 D3
Jabal at Ta'ir, *Eritrea* 81 D5
Jabalón →, *Spain* 35 G6
Jabalpur, *India* 69 H8
Jabbūl, *Syria* 70 B3
Jabiru, *Australia* 92 B5
Jablah, *Syria* 70 C3
Jablanac, *Croatia* 29 D11
Jablanica, *Bos.-H.* 42 G2
Jablonec nad Nisou,
  Czech Rep. 26 A8
Jablonica, *Slovak Rep.* ... 27 C10
Jabłonowo Pomorskie,
  Poland 44 E6
Jablunkov, *Czech Rep.* 27 B11
Jaboatão, *Brazil* 125 E11
Jaboticabal, *Brazil* 127 A6
Jabukovac, *Serbia, Yug.* .. 40 B6
Jaca, *Spain* 32 C4
Jacareí, *Brazil* 127 A6
Jacarèzinho, *Brazil* 127 A6
Jackman, *U.S.A.* 109 C10
Jacksboro, *U.S.A.* 113 J5
Jackson, *Ala., U.S.A.* 109 K2
Jackson, *Calif., U.S.A.* ... 116 G6
Jackson, *Ky., U.S.A.* 108 G4
Jackson, *Mich., U.S.A.* ... 108 D3
Jackson, *Minn., U.S.A.* ... 112 D7
Jackson, *Miss., U.S.A.* ... 113 J9
Jackson, *Mo., U.S.A.* 113 G10
Jackson, *N.H., U.S.A.* 111 B13
Jackson, *Ohio, U.S.A.* 108 F4
Jackson, *Tenn., U.S.A.* ... 109 H1
Jackson, *Wyo., U.S.A.* ... 114 E8
Jackson B., *N.Z.* 91 K2
Jackson L., *U.S.A.* 114 E8
Jacksons, *N.Z.* 91 K3
Jackson's Arm, *Canada* ... 103 C8
Jacksonville, *Ala., U.S.A.* . 109 J3
Jacksonville, *Ark., U.S.A.* . 113 H8
Jacksonville, *Calif., U.S.A.* 116 H6
Jacksonville, *Fla., U.S.A.* . 109 K5
Jacksonville, *Ill., U.S.A.* .. 112 F9
Jacksonville, *N.C., U.S.A.* 109 H7
Jacksonville, *Tex., U.S.A.* 113 K7
Jacksonville Beach, *U.S.A.* 109 K5
Jacmel, *Haiti* 121 C5
Jacob Lake, *U.S.A.* 115 H7
Jacobabad, *Pakistan* 68 E3
Jacobina, *Brazil* 125 F10
Jacques Cartier, Dét. de,
  Canada 103 C7
Jacques-Cartier, Mt., *Canada* 103 C6
Jacques Cartier, Parc Prov.,
  Canada 103 C5
Jacqueville, *Ivory C.* 82 D4
Jacuí →, *Brazil* 127 C5
Jacumba, *U.S.A.* 117 N10
Jacundá →, *Brazil* 125 D8
Jade, *Germany* 24 B4
Jadebusen, *Germany* 24 B4
Jadotville = Likasi,
  Dem. Rep. of the Congo . 87 E2
Jadovnik, *Serbia, Yug.* ... 40 C3
Jadraque, *Spain* 32 E2
Jaén, *Peru* 124 E3
Jaén, *Spain* 35 H7
Jaén □, *Spain* 35 H7
Jafarabad, *India* 68 J4
Jaffa = Tel Aviv-Yafo, *Israel* 75 C3
Jaffa, C., *Australia* 95 F2
Jaffna, *Sri Lanka* 66 Q12
Jaffrey, *U.S.A.* 111 D12
Jagadhri, *India* 68 D7
Jagadishpur, *India* 69 G11
Jagdalpur, *India* 67 K13
Jagersfontein, *S. Africa* .. 88 D4
Jaghīn →, *Iran* 71 E8
Jagodina, *Serbia, Yug.* ... 40 B5
Jagraon, *India* 66 D9
Jagst →, *Germany* 25 F5
Jagtial, *India* 66 K11
Jaguariaíva, *Brazil* 127 A6
Jaguaribe, *Brazil* 125 D11
Jagüey Grande, *Cuba* 120 B3
Jahanabad, *India* 69 G11
Jahazpur, *India* 68 G6
Jahrom, *Iran* 71 D7
Jaijon, *India* 68 D7
Jailolo, *Indonesia* 63 D7
Jailolo, Selat, *Indonesia* .. 63 D7
Jaipur, *India* 68 F6
Jais, *India* 69 F9
Jaisalmer, *India* 68 F4
Jaisinghnagar, *India* 69 H8
Jaitaran, *India* 68 F5
Jaithari, *India* 69 H8
Jājarm, *Iran* 71 B8
Jajce, *Bos.-H.* 42 F2
Jakam →, *India* 68 H6
Jakarta, *Indonesia* 63 G12
Jakhal, *India* 68 E6
Jakhau, *India* 68 H3
Jakobstad = Pietarsaari,
  Finland 8 E20
Jakupica, *Macedonia* 40 E5
Jal, *U.S.A.* 113 J3

Jalalabad, *Afghan.* 68 B4
Jalalabad, *India* 69 F8
Jalalpur Jattan, *Pakistan* . 68 C6
Jalama, *U.S.A.* 117 L6
Jalapa, *Guatemala* 120 D2
Jalapa Enríquez, *Mexico* .. 119 D5
Jalasjärvi, *Finland* 9 E20
Jalaun, *India* 69 F8
Jaldhaka →, *Bangla.* 69 F13
Jalesar, *India* 68 F8
Jaleswar, *Nepal* 69 F11
Jalgaon, *Maharashtra, India* 66 J10
Jalgaon, *Maharashtra, India* 66 J9
Jalībah, *Iraq* 70 D5
Jalingo, *Nigeria* 83 D7
Jalisco □, *Mexico* 118 D4
Jalkot, *Pakistan* 69 B5
Jallas →, *Spain* 34 C1
Jalna, *India* 66 K9
Jalón →, *Spain* 32 D3
Jalor, *India* 68 G5
Jalpa, *Mexico* 118 C4
Jalpaiguri, *India* 67 F16
Jalūlā, *Iraq* 70 C5
Jamaari, *Nigeria* 83 C6
Jamaica ■, *W. Indies* 120 C4
Jamalpur, *Bangla.* 67 G16
Jamalpur, *India* 69 G12
Jamalpurganj, *India* 69 H13
Jamanxim →, *Brazil* 125 D7
Jambi, *Indonesia* 62 E2
Jambi □, *Indonesia* 62 E2
Jambusar, *India* 68 H5
James →, *S. Dak., U.S.A.* 112 D6
James →, *Va., U.S.A.* 108 G7
James B., *Canada* 102 B3
James Ranges, *Australia* .. 92 D5
James Ross I., *Antarctica* . 5 C18
Jamesabad, *Pakistan* 68 G3
Jamestown, *Australia* 95 E2
Jamestown, *S. Africa* 88 E4
Jamestown, *N. Dak., U.S.A.* 112 B5
Jamestown, *N.Y., U.S.A.* . 110 D5
Jamestown, *Pa., U.S.A.* .. 110 E4
Jamīlābād, *Iran* 71 C6
Jamiltepec, *Mexico* 119 D5
Jamira →, *India* 69 J13
Jämjö, *Sweden* 11 H9
Jamkhandi, *India* 66 L9
Jammerbugt, *Denmark* 11 G3
Jammu, *India* 68 C6
Jammu & Kashmir □, *India* 69 B7
Jamnagar, *India* 68 H4
Jamni →, *India* 69 G8
Jampur, *Pakistan* 68 E4
Jamrud, *Pakistan* 68 C4
Jämsä, *Finland* 9 F21
Jamshedpur, *India* 69 H12
Jamtara, *India* 69 H12
Jämtland, *Sweden* 8 E15
Jämtlands län □, *Sweden* . 10 B7
Jan L., *Canada* 105 C8
Jan Mayen, *Arctic* 4 B7
Janakkala, *Finland* 9 F21
Janaúba, *Brazil* 125 G10
Jand, *Pakistan* 68 C5
Jandaq, *Iran* 71 C7
Jandia, *Canary Is.* 37 F5
Jandia, Pta. de, *Canary Is.* 37 F5
Jandola, *Pakistan* 68 C4
Jandowae, *Australia* 95 D5
Jándula →, *Spain* 35 G6
Janesville, *U.S.A.* 112 D10
Janga, *Ghana* 83 C4
Jangamo, *Mozam.* 89 C6
Janghai, *India* 69 G10
Janīn, *West Bank* 75 C4
Janja, *Bos.-H.* 42 F4
Janjgir, *India* 69 J10
Janjina, *Croatia* 29 F14
Janjina, *Madag.* 89 C8
Janos, *Mexico* 118 A3
Jánoshalma, *Hungary* 42 D4
Jánosháza, *Hungary* 42 C2
Jánossomorja, *Hungary* .. 42 C2
Janów, *Poland* 45 H6
Janów Lubelski, *Poland* .. 45 H9
Janów Podlaski, *Poland* .. 45 F10
Janowiec Wielkopolski,
  Poland 45 F4
Januária, *Brazil* 125 G10
Janub Dârfûr □, *Sudan* .. 81 E2
Janub Kordofân □, *Sudan* 81 E3
Janubio, *Canary Is.* 37 F6
Janville, *France* 19 D8
Janzé, *France* 18 E5
Jaora, *India* 68 H6
Japan ■, *Asia* 55 G8
Japan, Sea of, *Asia* 54 E7
Japan Trench, *Pac. Oc.* .. 52 F18
Japen = Yapen, *Indonesia* 63 E9
Japla, *India* 69 G11
Japurá →, *Brazil* 122 D4
Jaquarão, *Brazil* 127 C5
Jaqué, *Panama* 120 E4
Jarābulus, *Syria* 70 B3
Jaraicejo, *Spain* 35 F5
Jaraíz de la Vera, *Spain* .. 34 E5
Jarama →, *Spain* 34 E7
Jaramānah, *Syria* 75 B5
Jarandilla, *Spain* 34 E5
Jaranwala, *Pakistan* 68 D5
Jarash, *Jordan* 75 C4
Järbo, *Sweden* 10 D10
Jardim, *Brazil* 126 A4
Jardín →, *Spain* 33 G2

Jardines de la Reina, Arch.
  de los, *Cuba* 120 B4
Jargalang, *China* 57 C12
Jargalant = Hovd, *Mongolia* 60 B4
Jari →, *Brazil* 125 D8
Jarīr, W. al →, *Si. Arabia* . 70 E4
Järlåsa, *Sweden* 10 E11
Jarmen, *Germany* 24 B9
Järna, *Kopparberg, Sweden* 10 D8
Järna, *Stockholm, Sweden* . 10 E11
Jarnac, *France* 20 C3
Jarny, *France* 19 C12
Jarocin, *Poland* 45 G4
Jaroměř, *Czech Rep.* 26 A8
Jarosław, *Poland* 45 H9
Jarrahdale, *Australia* 93 F2
Jarrahi →, *Iran* 71 D6
Jarso, *Ethiopia* 81 F4
Jartai, *China* 56 E3
Jarud Qi, *China* 57 B11
Jarvis, *Canada* 110 D4
Jarvis I., *Pac. Oc.* 97 H12
Jarvornik, *Czech Rep.* 27 A10
Järvsö, *Sweden* 10 C10
Jarwa, *India* 69 F10
Jaša Tomić, *Serbia, Yug.* . 42 E5
Jasdan, *India* 68 H4
Jashpurnagar, *India* 69 H11
Jasidih, *India* 69 G12
Jasień, *Poland* 45 G2
Jāsimīyah, *Iraq* 70 C5
Jasin, *Malaysia* 65 L4
Jāsk, *Iran* 71 E8
Jasło, *Poland* 45 J8
Jasmund, *Germany* 24 A9
Jaso, *India* 69 G9
Jasper, *Alta., Canada* 104 C5
Jasper, *Ont., Canada* 111 B9
Jasper, *Ala., U.S.A.* 109 J2
Jasper, *Fla., U.S.A.* 109 K4
Jasper, *Ind., U.S.A.* 108 F2
Jasper, *Tex., U.S.A.* 113 K8
Jasper Nat. Park, *Canada* . 104 C5
Jasrasar, *India* 68 F5
Jastarnia, *Poland* 44 D5
Jastrebarsko, *Croatia* 29 C12
Jastrowie, *Poland* 44 E3
Jastrzębie Zdrój, *Poland* .. 45 J5
Jász-Nagykun-Szolnok □,
  Hungary 42 C5
Jászapáti, *Hungary* 42 C5
Jászárokszállás, *Hungary* . 42 C4
Jászberény, *Hungary* 42 C4
Jászkisér, *Hungary* 42 C5
Jászladány, *Hungary* 42 C5
Jataí, *Brazil* 125 G8
Jatibarang, *Indonesia* 63 G13
Jatinegara, *Indonesia* 63 G12
Játiva = Xátiva, *Spain* ... 33 G4
Jättendal, *Sweden* 10 C11
Jaú, *Brazil* 127 A6
Jauja, *Peru* 124 F3
Jaunpur, *India* 69 G10
Java = Jawa, *Indonesia* .. 63 G14
Java Barat □, *Indonesia* .. 63 G12
Java Sea, *Indonesia* 62 E3
Java Tengah □, *Indonesia* 63 G14
Java Timur □, *Indonesia* . 63 G15
Java Trench, *Ind. Oc.* 62 F3
Javalambre, Sa. de, *Spain* . 32 E4
Jávea, *Spain* 33 G5
Javhlant = Uliastay,
  Mongolia 60 B4
Jawa, *Indonesia* 63 G14
Jawad, *India* 68 G6
Jawor, *Poland* 45 G3
Jaworzno, *Poland* 45 H6
Jaworzyna Śląska, *Poland* . 45 H3
Jay Peak, *U.S.A.* 111 B12
Jaya, Puncak, *Indonesia* .. 63 E9
Jayanti, *India* 67 F16
Jayapura, *Indonesia* 63 E10
Jayawijaya, Pegunungan,
  Indonesia 63 E9
Jaynagar, *India* 67 F15
Jayrūd, *Syria* 70 C3
Jayton, *U.S.A.* 113 J4
Jāz Mūrīān, Hāmūn-e, *Iran* 71 E8
Jazīreh-ye Shīf, *Iran* 71 D6
Jazminal, *Mexico* 118 C4
Jazzīn, *Lebanon* 75 B4
Jean, *U.S.A.* 117 K11
Jean Marie River, *Canada* . 104 A4
Jean Rabel, *Haiti* 121 C5
Jeanerette, *U.S.A.* 113 L9
Jeanette, Ostrov =
  Zhannetty, Ostrov, *Russia* 51 B16
Jeannette, *U.S.A.* 110 F5
Jebäl Bärez, Kūh-e, *Iran* .. 71 D8
Jebba, *Nigeria* 83 D5
Jebel, Bahr el →, *Sudan* .. 81 F3
Jebel Dud, *Sudan* 81 E3
Jebel Qerri, *Sudan* 81 D3
Jedburgh, *U.K.* 14 F6
Jedda = Jiddah, *Si. Arabia* 74 C2
Jeddore L., *Canada* 103 C8
Jedlicze, *Poland* 45 J8
Jędrzejów, *Poland* 45 H7
Jedwabne, *Poland* 45 E9
Jeetzel →, *Germany* 24 B7
Jefferson, *Iowa, U.S.A.* .. 112 D7
Jefferson, *Ohio, U.S.A.* .. 110 E4
Jefferson, *Tex., U.S.A.* ... 113 J7
Jefferson, Mt., *Nev., U.S.A.* 114 G5
Jefferson, Mt., *Oreg.,*
  U.S.A. 114 D3

Jefferson City, *Mo., U.S.A.* 112 F8
Jefferson City, *Tenn., U.S.A.* 109 G4
Jeffersontown, *U.S.A.* 108 F3
Jeffersonville, *U.S.A.* 108 F3
Jeffrey City, *U.S.A.* 114 E10
Jega, *Nigeria* 83 C5
Jēkabpils, *Latvia* 9 H21
Jekyll I., *U.S.A.* 109 K5
Jelcz-Laskowice, *Poland* .. 45 G4
Jelenia Góra, *Poland* 45 H2
Jelgava, *Latvia* 9 H20
Jelica, *Serbia, Yug.* 40 C4
Jelli, *Sudan* 81 F3
Jelšava, *Slovak Rep.* 27 C13
Jemaja, *Indonesia* 65 L5
Jemaluang, *Malaysia* 65 L4
Jember, *Indonesia* 63 H15
Jembongan, *Malaysia* 62 C5
Jena, *Germany* 24 E7
Jena, *U.S.A.* 113 K8
Jenbach, *Austria* 26 D4
Jenkins, *U.S.A.* 108 G4
Jenner, *U.S.A.* 116 G3
Jennings, *U.S.A.* 113 K8
Jepara, *Indonesia* 63 G14
Jeparit, *Australia* 95 F3
Jequié, *Brazil* 125 F10
Jequitinhonha, *Brazil* 125 G10
Jequitinhonha →, *Brazil* . 125 G11
Jerantut, *Malaysia* 65 L4
Jérémie, *Haiti* 121 C5
Jerez, Punta, *Mexico* 119 C5
Jerez de García Salinas,
  Mexico 118 C4
Jerez de la Frontera, *Spain* . 35 J4
Jerez de los Caballeros,
  Spain 35 G4
Jericho = El Arīḥā,
  West Bank 75 D4
Jericho, *Australia* 94 C4
Jerichow, *Germany* 24 C8
Jerilderie, *Australia* 95 F4
Jermyn, *U.S.A.* 111 E9
Jerome, *U.S.A.* 114 E6
Jerramungup, *Australia* .. 93 F2
Jersey, *U.K.* 13 H5
Jersey City, *U.S.A.* 111 F10
Jersey Shore, *U.S.A.* 110 E7
Jerseyville, *U.S.A.* 112 F9
Jerusalem, *Israel* 75 D4
Jervis B., *Australia* 95 F5
Jervis Inlet, *Canada* 104 C4
Jerzu, *Italy* 30 C2
Jesenice, *Slovenia* 29 B11
Jeseník, *Czech Rep.* 27 A10
Jesenké, *Slovak Rep.* 27 C13
Jesselton = Kota Kinabalu,
  Malaysia 62 C5
Jessnitz, *Germany* 24 D8
Jessore, *Bangla.* 67 H16
Jesup, *U.S.A.* 109 K5
Jesús Carranza, *Mexico* .. 119 D5
Jesús María, *Argentina* ... 126 C3
Jetmore, *U.S.A.* 113 F5
Jetpur, *India* 68 J4
Jeumont, *France* 19 B11
Jevnaker, *Norway* 9 F14
Jewett, *U.S.A.* 113 K7
Jewett City, *U.S.A.* 111 E13
Jeyḥūnābād, *Iran* 71 C6
Jeypore, *India* 67 K13
Jeziorak, Jezioro, *Poland* . 44 E6
Jeziorany, *Poland* 44 E7
Jeziorka →, *Poland* 45 F8
Jha Jha, *India* 69 G12
Jhabua, *India* 68 H6
Jhajjar, *India* 68 E7
Jhal, *Pakistan* 68 E2
Jhal Jhao, *Pakistan* 66 F4
Jhalawar, *India* 68 G7
Jhalida, *India* 69 H11
Jhalrapatan, *India* 68 G7
Jhang Maghiana, *Pakistan* 68 D5
Jhansi, *India* 69 G8
Jhargram, *India* 69 H12
Jharia, *India* 69 H12
Jharsuguda, *India* 67 J14
Jhelum, *Pakistan* 68 C5
Jhelum →, *Pakistan* 68 D5
Jhilmilli, *India* 69 H10
Jhudo, *Pakistan* 68 G3
Jhunjhunu, *India* 68 E6
Ji-Paraná, *Brazil* 124 F6
Ji Xian, *Hebei, China* 56 F8
Ji Xian, *Henan, China* 56 G8
Ji Xian, *Shanxi, China* ... 56 F6
Jia Xian, *Henan, China* ... 56 H7
Jia Xian, *Shaanxi, China* . 56 E6
Jiading, *China* 59 B13
Jiahe, *China* 59 E9
Jialing Jiang →, *China* ... 58 C6
Jiamusi, *China* 60 B8
Ji'an, *Jiangxi, China* 59 D10
Ji'an, *Jilin, China* 57 D14
Jianchang, *China* 57 D11
Jianchangying, *China* 57 D10
Jiande, *China* 59 C12
Jiang'an, *China* 58 C5
Jiangbei, *China* 58 C6
Jiangcheng, *China* 58 F3
Jiangdi, *China* 58 D4
Jiangdu, *China* 59 A12
Jiange, *China* 58 A5
Jianghua, *China* 59 E8
Jiangjin, *China* 58 C6
Jiangkou, *China* 58 D7
Jiangle, *China* 59 D11
Jiangling, *China* 59 B9

Jiangmen

Jiangmen, *China* 59 F9
Jiangning, *China* 59 B12
Jiangshan, *China* 59 C12
Jiangsu □, *China* 57 H11
Jiangxi □, *China* 59 D11
Jiangyan, *China* 59 A13
Jiangyin, *China* 59 B13
Jiangyong, *China* 59 E8
Jiangyou, *China* 58 B5
Jianhe, *China* 58 D7
Jianli, *China* 59 C9
Jianning, *China* 59 D11
Jian'ou, *China* 59 D12
Jianshi, *China* 58 B7
Jianshui, *China* 58 F4
Jianyang, *Fujian, China* 59 D12
Jianyang, *Sichuan, China* 58 B5
Jiao Xian = Jiaozhou, *China* 57 F11
Jiaohe, *Hebei, China* 56 E9
Jiaohe, *Jilin, China* 57 C14
Jiaojiang, *China* 59 C13
Jiaoling, *China* 59 E11
Jiaozhou, *China* 57 F11
Jiaozhou Wan, *China* 57 F11
Jiaozuo, *China* 56 G7
Jiashan, *China* 59 B13
Jiawang, *China* 57 G9
Jiaxiang, *China* 56 G9
Jiaxing, *China* 59 B13
Jiayi = Chiai, *Taiwan* 59 F13
Jiayu, *China* 59 C9
Jibiya, *Nigeria* 83 C6
Jibou, *Romania* 43 C8
Jibuti = Djibouti ■, *Africa* 81 E5
Jicarón, I., *Panama* 120 E3
Jičín, *Czech Rep.* 26 A8
Jiddah, *Si. Arabia* 74 C2
Jido, *India* 67 E19
Jieshou, *China* 56 H8
Jiexiu, *China* 56 F6
Jieyang, *China* 59 F11
Jigawa □, *Nigeria* 83 C6
Jiggalong, *Australia* 92 D3
Jigni, *India* 69 G8
Jihlava, *Czech Rep.* 26 B8
Jihlava →, *Czech Rep.* 27 C9
Jihočeský □, *Czech Rep.* 26 B7
Jihomoravský □, *Czech Rep.* 27 B9
Jijiga, *Ethiopia* 74 F3
Jikamshi, *Nigeria* 83 C6
Jikau, *Sudan* 81 F3
Jilin, *China* 57 C14
Jilin □, *China* 57 C14
Jiloca →, *Spain* 32 D3
Jilong = Chilung, *Taiwan* 59 E13
Jim Thorpe, *U.S.A.* 111 F9
Jima, *Ethiopia* 81 F4
Jimbolia, *Romania* 42 E5
Jimena de la Frontera, *Spain* 35 J5
Jiménez, *Mexico* 118 B4
Jimo, *China* 57 F11
Jin Jiang →, *China* 59 C10
Jin Xian = Jinzhou, *China* 56 E8
Jin Xian, *China* 57 E11
Jinan, *China* 56 F9
Jincheng, *China* 56 G7
Jinchuan, *China* 58 B4
Jind, *India* 68 E7
Jindabyne, *Australia* 95 F4
Jindřichův Hradec, *Czech Rep.* 26 B8
Jing He →, *China* 56 G5
Jing Shan, *China* 59 B8
Jing Xian, *China* 59 B12
Jing'an, *China* 59 C10
Jingbian, *China* 56 F5
Jingchuan, *China* 56 G4
Jingde, *China* 59 B12
Jingdezhen, *China* 59 C11
Jingdong, *China* 58 E3
Jinggangshan, *China* 59 D10
Jinggu, *China* 58 F3
Jinghai, *China* 56 E9
Jinghong, *China* 58 G3
Jingjiang, *China* 59 A13
Jingle, *China* 56 E6
Jingmen, *China* 59 B9
Jingning, *China* 56 G3
Jingpo Hu, *China* 57 C15
Jingshan, *China* 59 B9
Jingtai, *China* 56 F3
Jingxi, *China* 58 F6
Jingxing, *China* 56 E8
Jingyang, *China* 56 G5
Jingyu, *China* 57 C14
Jingyuan, *China* 56 F3
Jingzhou, *China* 58 D7
Jingziguan, *China* 56 H6
Jinhua, *China* 59 C12
Jining, *Nei Mongol Zizhiqu, China* 56 D7
Jining, *Shandong, China* 56 G9
Jinja, *Uganda* 86 B3
Jinjang, *Malaysia* 65 L3
Jinji, *China* 56 F4
Jinjiang, *Fujian, China* 59 E12
Jinjiang, *Yunnan, China* 58 D3
Jinjie, *China* 58 F6
Jinjini, *Ghana* 82 D4
Jinkou, *China* 59 B10
Jinkouhe, *China* 58 C4
Jinmen Dao, *China* 59 E12
Jinnah Barrage, *Pakistan* 66 C7
Jinning, *China* 58 E4
Jinotega, *Nic.* 120 D2
Jinotepe, *Nic.* 120 D2
Jinping, *Guizhou, China* 58 D7
Jinping, *Yunnan, China* 58 F4
Jinsha, *China* 58 D6
Jinsha Jiang →, *China* 58 C5
Jinshan, *China* 59 B13
Jinshi, *China* 59 C8
Jintan, *China* 59 B12
Jinxi, *Jiangxi, China* 59 D11
Jinxi, *Liaoning, China* 57 D11
Jinxian, *China* 59 C11
Jinxiang, *China* 56 G9
Jinyang, *China* 58 D4
Jinyun, *China* 59 C13
Jinzhai, *China* 59 B10
Jinzhou, *Hebei, China* 56 E8
Jinzhou, *Liaoning, China* 57 D11
Jiparaná →, *Brazil* 124 E6
Jipijapa, *Ecuador* 124 D2
Jiquilpan, *Mexico* 118 D4
Jishan, *China* 56 G6
Jishou, *China* 58 C7
Jishui, *China* 59 D10
Jisr ash Shughūr, *Syria* 70 C3
Jitarning, *Australia* 93 F2
Jitra, *Malaysia* 65 J3
Jiu →, *Romania* 43 G8
Jiudengkou, *China* 56 E4
Jiujiang, *Guangdong, China* 59 F9
Jiujiang, *Jiangxi, China* 59 C10
Jiuling Shan, *China* 59 C10
Jiulong, *China* 58 C3
Jiutai, *China* 57 B13
Jiuxiangcheng, *China* 56 H8
Jiuxincheng, *China* 56 E8
Jiuyuhang, *China* 59 B12
Jixi, *Anhui, China* 59 B12
Jixi, *Heilongjiang, China* 57 B16
Jiyang, *China* 57 F9
Jiyuan, *China* 56 G7
Jīzān, *Si. Arabia* 74 D3
Jize, *China* 56 F8
Jizera →, *Czech Rep.* 26 A7
Jizl, W. →, *Si. Arabia* 80 B4
Jizl, Wādī al, *Si. Arabia* 70 E3
Jizō-Zaki, *Japan* 55 G6
Jizzakh, *Uzbekistan* 50 E7
Joaçaba, *Brazil* 127 B5
Joal Fadiout, *Senegal* 82 C1
João Pessoa, *Brazil* 125 E12
Joaquín V. González, *Argentina* 126 B3
Jobat, *India* 68 H6
Jobourg, Nez de, *France* 18 C5
Jódar, *Spain* 35 H7
Jodhpur, *India* 68 F5
Jodiya, *India* 68 H4
Jōetsu, *Japan* 55 F9
Jœuf, *France* 19 C12
Jofane, *Mozam.* 89 C5
Jogbani, *India* 69 F12
Jõgeva, *Estonia* 9 G22
Jogjakarta = Yogyakarta, *Indonesia* 63 G14
Johannesburg, *S. Africa* 89 D4
Johannesburg, *U.S.A.* 117 K9
Johansfors, *Sweden* 11 H9
Johilla →, *India* 69 H9
John Day, *U.S.A.* 114 D4
John Day →, *U.S.A.* 114 D3
John D'Or Prairie, *Canada* 104 B5
John H. Kerr Reservoir, *U.S.A.* 109 G6
John o' Groats, *U.K.* 14 C5
Johnnie, *U.S.A.* 117 J10
John's Ra., *Australia* 94 C1
Johnson, *Kans., U.S.A.* 113 G4
Johnson, *Vt., U.S.A.* 111 B12
Johnson City, *N.Y., U.S.A.* 111 D9
Johnson City, *Tenn., U.S.A.* 109 G4
Johnson City, *Tex., U.S.A.* 113 K5
Johnsonburg, *U.S.A.* 110 E6
Johnsondale, *U.S.A.* 117 K8
Johnson's Crossing, *Canada* 104 A2
Johnston, L., *Australia* 93 F3
Johnston Falls = Mambilima Falls, *Zambia* 87 E2
Johnston I., *Pac. Oc.* 97 F11
Johnstone Str., *Canada* 104 C3
Johnstown, *N.Y., U.S.A.* 111 C10
Johnstown, *Ohio, U.S.A.* 110 F2
Johnstown, *Pa., U.S.A.* 110 F6
Johor Baharu, *Malaysia* 65 M4
Jõhvi, *Estonia* 9 G22
Joigny, *France* 19 E10
Joinville, *Brazil* 127 B6
Joinville, *France* 19 D12
Joinville I., *Antarctica* 5 C18
Jojutla, *Mexico* 119 D5
Jokkmokk, *Sweden* 8 C18
Jökulsá á Bru →, *Iceland* 8 D6
Jökulsá á Fjöllum →, *Iceland* 8 C5
Jolfā, *Āzarbājān-e Sharqī, Iran* 70 B5
Jolfā, *Eşfahan, Iran* 71 C6
Joliet, *U.S.A.* 108 E1
Joliette, *Canada* 102 C5
Jolo, *Phil.* 61 J4
Jolon, *U.S.A.* 116 K5
Jomalig I., *Phil.* 61 D5
Jombang, *Indonesia* 63 G15
Jomda, *China* 58 B2
Jonava, *Lithuania* 9 J21
Jones Sound, *Canada* 4 B3
Jonesboro, *Ark., U.S.A.* 113 H9
Jonesboro, *La., U.S.A.* 113 J8
Jong →, *S. Leone* 82 D2
Jonglei, *Sudan* 81 F3
Jonglei □, *Sudan* 81 F3
Joniškis, *Lithuania* 9 H20
Jönköping, *Sweden* 11 G8
Jönköpings län □, *Sweden* 11 G8
Jonquière, *Canada* 103 C5
Jonsered, *Sweden* 11 G6
Jonzac, *France* 20 C3
Joplin, *U.S.A.* 113 G7
Jora, *India* 68 F6
Jordan, *Mont., U.S.A.* 114 C10
Jordan, *N.Y., U.S.A.* 111 C8
Jordan ■, *Asia* 75 E5
Jordan →, *Asia* 75 D4
Jordan Valley, *U.S.A.* 114 E5
Jordanów, *Poland* 45 J6
Jorhat, *India* 67 F19
Jörn, *Sweden* 8 D19
Jorong, *Indonesia* 62 E4
Jørpeland, *Norway* 9 G11
Jorquera →, *Chile* 126 B2
Jos, *Nigeria* 83 D6
Jos Plateau, *Nigeria* 83 D6
Jošanička Banja, *Serbia, Yug.* 40 C4
José Batlle y Ordóñez, *Uruguay* 127 C4
Joseni, *Romania* 43 D10
Joseph, L., *Nfld., Canada* 103 B6
Joseph, L., *Ont., Canada* 110 A5
Joseph Bonaparte G., *Australia* 92 B4
Joshinath, *India* 69 D8
Joshua Tree, *U.S.A.* 117 L10
Joshua Tree National Park, *U.S.A.* 117 M10
Josselin, *France* 18 E4
Jostedalsbreen, *Norway* 9 F12
Jotunheimen, *Norway* 9 F13
Joubertberge, *Namibia* 88 B1
Joué-lès-Tours, *France* 18 E7
Jourdanton, *U.S.A.* 113 L5
Joutseno, *Finland* 46 B5
Jovellanos, *Cuba* 120 B3
Joyeuse, *France* 21 D8
Józefów, *Lubelskie, Poland* 45 H10
Józefów, *Mazowieckie, Poland* 45 F8
Ju Xian, *China* 57 F10
Juan Aldama, *Mexico* 118 C4
Juan Bautista Alberdi, *Argentina* 126 C3
Juan de Fuca Str., *Canada* 116 B3
Juan de Nova, *Ind. Oc.* 89 B7
Juan Fernández, Arch. de, *Pac. Oc.* 122 G2
Juan José Castelli, *Argentina* 126 B3
Juan L. Lacaze, *Uruguay* 126 C4
Juankoski, *Finland* 8 E23
Juárez, *Argentina* 126 D4
Juárez, *Mexico* 117 N11
Juárez, Sierra de, *Mexico* 118 A1
Juàzeiro, *Brazil* 125 E10
Juàzeiro do Norte, *Brazil* 125 E11
Juba, *Sudan* 81 G3
Jubayl, *Lebanon* 75 A4
Jubbah, *Si. Arabia* 70 D4
Jubbal, *India* 68 D7
Jubbulpore = Jabalpur, *India* 69 H8
Jübek, *Germany* 24 A5
Jubga, *Russia* 49 H4
Jubilee L., *Australia* 93 E4
Juby, C., *Morocco* 78 C3
Júcar = Xúquer →, *Spain* 33 F4
Júcaro, *Cuba* 120 B4
Juchitán, *Mexico* 119 D5
Judaea = Har Yehuda, *Israel* 75 D3
Judenburg, *Austria* 26 D7
Judith →, *U.S.A.* 114 C9
Judith, Pt., *U.S.A.* 111 E13
Judith Gap, *U.S.A.* 114 C9
Juelsminde, *Denmark* 11 J4
Jugoslavia = Yugoslavia ■, *Europe* 40 C4
Juigalpa, *Nic.* 120 D2
Juillac, *France* 20 C5
Juist, *Germany* 24 B2
Juiz de Fora, *Brazil* 127 A7
Jujuy □, *Argentina* 126 A2
Julesburg, *U.S.A.* 112 E3
Juli, *Peru* 124 G5
Julia Cr. →, *Australia* 94 C3
Julia Creek, *Australia* 94 C3
Juliaca, *Peru* 124 G4
Julian, *U.S.A.* 117 M10
Julian Alps = Julijske Alpe, *Slovenia* 29 B11
Julian L., *Canada* 102 B4
Julianatop, *Surinam* 125 C7
Julianehåb = Qaqortoq, *Greenland* 4 C5
Jülich, *Germany* 24 E2
Julijske Alpe, *Slovenia* 29 B11
Julimes, *Mexico* 118 B3
Jullundur, *India* 68 D6
Julu, *China* 56 F8
Jumbo, *Zimbabwe* 87 F3
Jumbo Pk., *U.S.A.* 117 J12
Jumentos Cays, *Bahamas* 120 B4
Jumilla, *Spain* 33 G3
Jumla, *Nepal* 69 E10
Jumna = Yamuna →, *India* 69 G9
Junagadh, *India* 68 J4
Junction, *Tex., U.S.A.* 113 K5
Junction, *Utah, U.S.A.* 115 G7
Junction B., *Australia* 94 A1
Junction City, *Kans., U.S.A.* 112 F6
Junction City, *Oreg., U.S.A.* 114 D2
Junction Pt., *Australia* 94 A1
Jundah, *Australia* 94 C3
Jundiaí, *Brazil* 127 A6
Juneau, *U.S.A.* 104 B2
Junee, *Australia* 95 E4
Jungfrau, *Switz.* 25 J3
Junggar Pendi, *China* 60 B3
Jungshahi, *Pakistan* 68 G2
Juniata →, *U.S.A.* 110 F7
Junín, *Argentina* 126 C3
Junín de los Andes, *Argentina* 128 D2
Jūniyah, *Lebanon* 75 B4
Junlian, *China* 58 C5
Juntas, *Chile* 126 B2
Juntura, *U.S.A.* 114 E4
Jur, Nahr el →, *Sudan* 81 F2
Jura = Jura, Mts. du, *Europe* 19 F13
Jura = Schwäbische Alb, *Germany* 25 G5
Jura, *U.K.* 14 F3
Jura □, *France* 19 F12
Jura □, *Switz.* 25 H3
Jūra →, *Lithuania* 44 C9
Jura, Mts. du, *Europe* 19 F13
Jura, Sd. of, *U.K.* 14 F3
Jurbarkas, *Lithuania* 9 J20
Jurien, *Australia* 93 F2
Jurilovca, *Romania* 43 F13
Jūrmala, *Latvia* 9 H20
Jurong, *China* 59 B12
Juruá →, *Brazil* 122 D4
Juruena, *Brazil* 124 F7
Juruena →, *Brazil* 124 E7
Juruti, *Brazil* 125 D7
Jussey, *France* 19 E12
Justo Daract, *Argentina* 126 C2
Jutaí →, *Brazil* 124 D5
Jüterbog, *Germany* 24 D9
Juticalpa, *Honduras* 120 D2
Jutland = Jylland, *Denmark* 11 H3
Juventud, I. de la, *Cuba* 120 B3
Juvigny-sous-Andaine, *France* 18 D6
Juwain, *Afghan.* 66 D2
Jūy Zar, *Iran* 70 C5
Juye, *China* 56 G9
Juzennecourt, *France* 19 D11
Jvari, *Georgia* 49 J6
Jwaneng, *Botswana* 85 J4
Jyderup, *Denmark* 11 J5
Jylland, *Denmark* 11 H3
Jyväskylä, *Finland* 9 E21

K

K2, *Pakistan* 69 B7
Ka →, *Nigeria* 83 C5
Kaap Plateau, *S. Africa* 88 D3
Kaapkruis, *Namibia* 88 C1
Kaapstad = Cape Town, *S. Africa* 88 E2
Kaba, *Guinea* 82 C2
Kabaena, *Indonesia* 63 F6
Kabala, *S. Leone* 82 D2
Kabale, *Uganda* 86 C3
Kabalo, *Dem. Rep. of the Congo* 86 D2
Kabambare, *Dem. Rep. of the Congo* 86 C2
Kabango, *Dem. Rep. of the Congo* 87 D2
Kabanjahe, *Indonesia* 62 D1
Kabankalan, *Phil.* 61 G5
Kabara, *Mali* 82 B4
Kabardinka, *Russia* 47 K10
Kabardino-Balkar Republic = Kabardino-Balkaria □, *Russia* 49 J6
Kabardino-Balkaria □, *Russia* 49 J6
Kabarega Falls = Murchison Falls, *Uganda* 86 B3
Kabasalan, *Phil.* 61 H5
Kabba, *Nigeria* 83 D6
Kabetogama, *U.S.A.* 112 A8
Kabi, *Niger* 83 C7
Kabin Buri, *Thailand* 64 F3
Kabinakagami L., *Canada* 102 C3
Kabinda, *Dem. Rep. of the Congo* 84 F4
Kabna, *Sudan* 80 D3
Kabompo, *Zambia* 87 E1
Kabompo →, *Zambia* 85 G4
Kabondo, *Dem. Rep. of the Congo* 87 D2
Kabongo, *Dem. Rep. of the Congo* 86 D2
Kabot, *Guinea* 82 C2
Kabou, *Togo* 83 D5
Kabr, *Sudan* 81 E2
Kabūd Gonbad, *Iran* 71 B8
Kabugao, *Phil.* 61 B4
Kābul, *Afghan.* 68 B3
Kābul □, *Afghan.* 66 B6
Kabul →, *Pakistan* 68 C5
Kabunga, *Dem. Rep. of the Congo* 86 C2
Kaburuang, *Indonesia* 63 D7
Kabushiya, *Sudan* 81 D3
Kabwe, *Zambia* 87 E2
Kačanik, *Kosovo, Yug.* 40 D5
Kačerginė, *Lithuania* 44 D10
Kachchh, Gulf of, *India* 68 H3
Kachchh, Rann of, *India* 68 H4
Kachchhidhana, *India* 69 J8
Kachebera, *Zambia* 87 E3
Kachia, *Nigeria* 83 D6
Kachikau, *Botswana* 88 B3
Kachin □, *Burma* 58 D1
Kachira, L., *Uganda* 86 C3
Kachiry, *Kazakstan* 50 D8
Kachisi, *Ethiopia* 81 F4
Kachnara, *India* 68 H6
Kachot, *Cambodia* 65 G4
Kaçkar, *Turkey* 73 B9
Kadan, *Czech Rep.* 26 A6
Kadan Kyun, *Burma* 64 F2
Kadanai →, *Afghan.* 68 D1
Kadarkút, *Hungary* 42 D2
Kade, *Ghana* 83 D4
Kadi, *India* 68 H5
Kadina, *Australia* 95 E2
Kadınhanı, *Turkey* 72 C5
Kadiolo, *Mali* 82 C3
Kadipur, *India* 69 F10
Kadirli, *Turkey* 70 B3
Kadiyevka = Stakhanov, *Ukraine* 47 H10
Kadodo, *Sudan* 81 E2
Kadoka, *U.S.A.* 112 D4
Kadom, *Russia* 48 C6
Kadoma, *Zimbabwe* 87 F2
Kâdugli, *Sudan* 81 E2
Kaduna, *Nigeria* 83 C6
Kaduna □, *Nigeria* 83 C6
Kaduy, *Russia* 46 C9
Kaédi, *Mauritania* 82 B2
Kaélé, *Cameroon* 83 C7
Kaeng Khoï, *Thailand* 64 E3
Kaesŏng, *N. Korea* 57 F14
Kāf, *Si. Arabia* 70 D3
Kafan = Kapan, *Armenia* 70 B5
Kafanchan, *Nigeria* 83 D6
Kafareti, *Nigeria* 83 C7
Kaffrine, *Senegal* 82 C1
Kafin, *Nigeria* 83 D6
Kafin Madaki, *Nigeria* 83 C6
Kafinda, *Zambia* 87 E3
Kafirévs, Ákra, *Greece* 38 C6
Kafr el Battikh, *Egypt* 80 H7
Kafr el Dauwâr, *Egypt* 80 H7
Kafr el Sheikh, *Egypt* 80 H7
Kafue, *Zambia* 87 F2
Kafue →, *Zambia* 85 H5
Kafue Flats, *Zambia* 87 F2
Kafue Nat. Park, *Zambia* 87 F2
Kafulwe, *Zambia* 87 D2
Kaga, *Afghan.* 68 B4
Kaga Bandoro, *C.A.R.* 84 C3
Kagan, *Uzbekistan* 50 F7
Kagarko, *Nigeria* 83 D6
Kagawa □, *Japan* 55 G7
Kagera □, *Tanzania* 86 C3
Kagera →, *Uganda* 86 C3
Kağızman, *Turkey* 70 B4
Kagmar, *Sudan* 81 E3
Kagoshima, *Japan* 55 J5
Kagoshima □, *Japan* 55 J5
Kagul = Cahul, *Moldova* 43 E13
Kahak, *Iran* 71 B6
Kahama, *Tanzania* 86 C3
Kahan, *Pakistan* 68 E3
Kahang, *Malaysia* 65 L4
Kahayan →, *Indonesia* 62 E4
Kahe, *Tanzania* 86 C4
Kahnūj, *Iran* 71 E8
Kahoka, *U.S.A.* 112 E9
Kahoolawe, *U.S.A.* 106 H16
Kahramanmaraş, *Turkey* 70 B3
Kâhta, *Turkey* 73 D8
Kahuta, *Pakistan* 68 C5
Kai, Kepulauan, *Indonesia* 63 F8
Kai Besar, *Indonesia* 63 F8
Kai Is. = Kai, Kepulauan, *Indonesia* 63 F8
Kai Kecil, *Indonesia* 63 F8
Kai Xian, *China* 58 B7
Kaiama, *Nigeria* 83 D5
Kaiapoi, *N.Z.* 91 K4
Kaieteur Falls, *Guyana* 124 B7
Kaifeng, *China* 56 G8
Kaihua, *China* 59 C12
Kaijiang, *China* 58 B6
Kaikohe, *N.Z.* 91 F4
Kaikoura, *N.Z.* 91 K4
Kaikoura Ra., *N.Z.* 91 J4
Kailahun, *S. Leone* 82 D2
Kaili, *China* 58 D6
Kailu, *China* 57 C11
Kailua Kona, *U.S.A.* 106 J17
Kaimana, *Indonesia* 63 E8
Kaimanawa Mts., *N.Z.* 91 H5
Kaimganj, *India* 69 F8
Kaimur Hills, *India* 69 G10
Kainab →, *Namibia* 88 D2
Kaingaroa Forest, *N.Z.* 91 H6
Kainji Dam, *Nigeria* 83 D5
Kainji Res., *Nigeria* 83 C5
Kainuu, *Finland* 8 D23
Kaipara Harbour, *N.Z.* 91 G5
Kaiping, *China* 59 F9
Kaipokok B., *Canada* 103 B8
Kaira, *India* 68 H5
Kairana, *India* 68 E7
Kaironi, *Indonesia* 63 E8
Kairouan, *Tunisia* 79 A8
Kaiserslautern, *Germany* 25 F3
Kaiserstuhl, *Germany* 25 G3
Kaitaia, *N.Z.* 91 F4
Kaitangata, *N.Z.* 91 M2
Kaithal, *India* 68 E7
Kaitu →, *Pakistan* 68 C4
Kaiwi Channel, *U.S.A.* 106 H16
Kaiyang, *China* 58 D6
Kaiyuan, *Liaoning, China* 57 C13
Kaiyuan, *Yunnan, China* 58 F4
Kajaani, *Finland* 8 D22
Kajabbi, *Australia* 94 C3
Kajana = Kajaani, *Finland* 8 D22
Kajang, *Malaysia* 65 L3
Kajaran, *Armenia* 73 C12
Kajiado, *Kenya* 86 C4
Kajo Kaji, *Sudan* 81 G3
Kajuru, *Nigeria* 83 C6
Kaka, *Sudan* 81 E3
Kakabeka Falls, *Canada* 102 C2
Kakadu Nat. Park, *Australia* 92 B5
Kakamas, *S. Africa* 88 D3
Kakamega, *Kenya* 86 B3

Kakanj, Bos.-H. 42 F3
Kakanui Mts., N.Z. 91 L3
Kakata, Liberia 82 D2
Kakdwip, India 69 J13
Kake, Japan 55 G6
Kake, U.S.A. 104 B2
Kakegawa, Japan 55 G9
Kakeroma-Jima, Japan 55 K4
Kakhib, Russia 49 J8
Kakhovka, Ukraine 47 J7
Kakhovske Vdskh., Ukraine 47 J7
Kakinada, India 67 L13
Kakisa →, Canada . 104 A5
Kakisa L., Canada 104 A5
Kakogawa, Japan 55 G7
Kakwa →, Canada 104 C5
Kāl Gūsheh, Iran 71 D8
Kal Safīd, Iran 70 C5
Kala, Nigeria 83 C7
Kalaallit Nunaat =
  Greenland ■, N. Amer. . 4 C5
Kalabagh, Pakistan 68 C4
Kalabahi, Indonesia 63 F6
Kalabáka, Greece 38 B3
Kalabana, Mali 82 C3
Kalach, Russia 48 E5
Kalach na Donu, Russia ... 49 F6
Kaladan →, Burma 67 J18
Kaladar, Canada 102 D4
Kalahari, Africa 88 C3
Kalahari Gemsbok Nat.
  Park, S. Africa 88 D3
Kalajoki, Finland 8 D20
Kālak, Iran 71 E8
Kalakamati, Botswana 89 C4
Kalakan, Russia 51 D12
K'alak'unlun Shank'ou =
  Karakoram Pass, Pakistan 69 B7
Kalam, Pakistan 69 B5
Kalama,
  Dem. Rep. of the Congo . 86 C2
Kalama, U.S.A. 116 E4
Kalámai, Greece 38 D4
Kalamariá, Greece 40 F6
Kalamata = Kalámai, Greece 38 D4
Kalamazoo, U.S.A. 108 D3
Kalamazoo →, U.S.A. 108 D2
Kalambo Falls, Tanzania .. 87 D3
Kálamos, Attikí, Greece ... 38 C5
Kálamos, Íonioi Nísoi,
  Greece 38 C2
Kalan, Turkey 70 B3
Kalankalan, Guinea 82 C3
Kalannie, Australia 93 F2
Kalántarī, Iran 71 C7
Kalao, Indonesia 63 F6
Kalaotoa, Indonesia 63 F6
Kälarne, Sweden 10 B10
Kalasin, Thailand 64 D4
Kalat, Pakistan 66 E5
Kalāteh, Iran 71 B7
Kalāteh-ye Ganj, Iran ... 71 E8
Kálathos, Greece 39 E10
Kalaus →, Russia 49 H7
Kalávrita, Greece 38 C4
Kalbarri, Australia 93 E1
Kale, Antalya, Turkey 39 E12
Kale, Denizli, Turkey 39 D10
Kalecik, Turkey 72 B5
Kalegauk Kyun, Burma ... 67 M20
Kalehe,
  Dem. Rep. of the Congo . 86 C2
Kalema, Tanzania 86 C3
Kalemie,
  Dem. Rep. of the Congo . 86 D2
Kalety, Poland 45 H5
Kalewa, Burma 67 H19
Kaleybar, Iran 70 B5
Kalgan = Zhangjiakou,
  China 56 D8
Kalgoorlie-Boulder, Australia 93 F3
Kali →, India 69 F8
Kali Sindh →, India 68 G6
Kaliakra, Nos, Bulgaria 41 C12
Kalianda, Indonesia 62 F3
Kalibo, Phil. 61 F5
Kalima,
  Dem. Rep. of the Congo . 86 C2
Kalimantan □, Indonesia ... 62 E4
Kalimantan Barat □,
  Indonesia 62 E4
Kalimantan Selatan □,
  Indonesia 62 E5
Kalimantan Tengah □,
  Indonesia 62 E4
Kalimantan Timur □,
  Indonesia 62 D5
Kálimnos, Greece 39 D8
Kalimpong, India 69 F13
Kalinin = Tver, Russia 46 D8
Kaliningrad, Russia 9 J19
Kalininsk, Russia 48 E7
Kalinkavichy, Belarus 47 F5
Kalinkovichi = Kalinkavichy,
  Belarus 47 F5
Kalinovik, Bos.-H. 40 C2
Kalipetrovo, Bulgaria 41 B11
Kaliro, Uganda 86 B3
Kalirrákhi, Greece 41 F8
Kalispell, U.S.A. 114 B6
Kalisz, Poland 45 G5
Kalisz Pomorski, Poland .. 45 E2
Kaliua, Tanzania 86 D3
Kalívia Thorikoú, Greece .. 38 D5
Kalix, Sweden 8 D20
Kalix →, Sweden 8 D20
Kalka, India 68 D7
Kalkan, Turkey 39 E11
Kalkarindji, Australia 92 C5
Kalkaska, U.S.A. 108 C3
Kalkfeld, Namibia 88 C2

Kalkfontein, Botswana 88 C3
Kalkım, Turkey 39 B9
Kalkrand, Namibia 88 C2
Kållandsö, Sweden 11 F7
Kallavesi, Finland 8 E22
Källby, Sweden 11 F7
Kållered, Sweden 11 G6
Kallimasiá, Greece 39 C8
Kallinge, Sweden 11 H9
Kallithéa, Greece 38 D5
Kallmeti, Albania 40 E3
Kalloní, Greece 39 B8
Kallonís, Kólpos, Greece .. 39 B8
Kallsjön, Sweden 8 E15
Kalmalo, Nigeria 83 C6
Kalmar, Sweden 11 H10
Kalmar län □, Sweden 11 G10
Kalmar sund, Sweden 11 H10
Kalmyk Republic =
  Kalmykia □, Russia 49 G8
Kalmykia □, Russia 49 G8
Kalmykovo, Kazakstan 50 E6
Kalna, India 69 H13
Kalnai, India 69 H10
Kalocsa, Hungary 42 D4
Kalofer, Bulgaria 41 D8
Kalokhorio, Cyprus 36 E12
Kaloko,
  Dem. Rep. of the Congo . 86 D2
Kalol, Gujarat, India 68 H5
Kalol, Gujarat, India 68 H5
Kalolímnos, Greece 39 D9
Kalomo, Zambia 87 F2
Kalonerón, Greece 38 D3
Kalpi, India 69 F8
Kaltern = Caldaro, Italy ... 29 B8
Kaltungo, Nigeria 83 D7
Kalu, Pakistan 68 G2
Kaluga, Russia 46 E9
Kalulushi, Zambia 87 E2
Kalundborg, Denmark 11 J5
Kalush, Ukraine 47 H3
Kałuszyn, Poland 45 F8
Kalutara, Sri Lanka 66 R12
Kalvarija, Lithuania 44 D10
Kalyazin, Russia 46 D9
Kam →, Nigeria 83 D7
Kama,
  Dem. Rep. of the Congo . 86 C2
Kama →, Russia 6 D16
Kamachumu, Tanzania ... 86 C3
Kamaishi, Japan 54 E10
Kamalia, Pakistan 68 D5
Kaman, India 68 F6
Kaman, Turkey 72 C5
Kamanjab, Namibia 88 B2
Kamapanda, Zambia 87 E1
Kamaran, Yemen 74 D3
Kamativi, Zimbabwe 88 B4
Kamba, Nigeria 83 C5
Kambalda, Australia 93 F3
Kambar, Pakistan 68 F3
Kambia, S. Leone 82 D2
Kambolé, Togo 83 D5
Kambolé, Zambia 87 D3
Kambos, Cyprus 36 D11
Kambove,
  Dem. Rep. of the Congo . 87 E2
Kamchatka, Poluostrov,
  Russia 51 D16
Kamchatka Pen. =
  Kamchatka, Poluostrov,
  Russia 51 D16
Kamchiya →, Bulgaria ... 41 C11
Kamen, Russia 50 D9
Kamen-Rybolov, Russia ... 54 B6
Kamenica, Serbia, Yug. .. 40 C6
Kamenica, Serbia, Yug. .. 40 B3
Kamenice nad Lipou,
  Czech Rep. 26 B8
Kamenjak, Rt., Croatia ... 29 D10
Kamenka = Kaminka,
  Ukraine 47 H7
Kamenka, Kazakstan 48 E10
Kamenka, Penza, Russia .. 48 D6
Kamenka, Voronezh, Russia 47 G10
Kamenka Bugskaya =
  Kamyanka-Buzka, Ukraine 47 G3
Kamenka Dneprovskaya =
  Kamyanka-Dniprovska,
  Ukraine 47 J8
Kamennomostskiy, Russia .. 49 H5
Kameno, Bulgaria 41 D11
Kamenolomni, Russia 49 G5
Kamensk-Shakhtinskiy,
  Russia 49 F5
Kamensk Uralskiy, Russia .. 50 D7
Kamenskiy, Russia 48 E7
Kamenskoye, Russia 51 C17
Kamenyak, Bulgaria 41 C10
Kamenz, Germany 24 D10
Kameoka, Japan 55 G7
Kami, Albania 40 D4
Kamiah, U.S.A. 114 C5
Kamień Krajeński, Poland .. 44 E4
Kamień Pomorski, Poland . 44 E1
Kamienna →, Poland 45 G8
Kamienna Góra, Poland ... 45 H3
Kamieńsk, Poland 45 G6
Kamieskroon, S. Africa ... 88 E2
Kamilukuak, L., Canada .. 105 A8
Kamin-Kashyrskyy, Ukraine 47 G3
Kamina,
  Dem. Rep. of the Congo . 87 D2
Kaminak L., Canada 105 A10
Kaministiquia, Canada ... 102 C1
Kaminka, Ukraine 47 H7
Kaminoyama, Japan 54 E10
Kamiros, Greece 36 C9
Kamituga,
  Dem. Rep. of the Congo . 86 C2

Kamla →, India 69 G12
Kamloops, Canada 104 C4
Kamnik, Slovenia 29 B11
Kamo, Armenia 49 K7
Kamo, Japan 54 F9
Kamoke, Pakistan 68 C6
Kamp →, Austria 26 C8
Kampala, Uganda 86 B3
Kampang Chhnang,
  Cambodia 65 F5
Kampar, Malaysia 65 K3
Kampar →, Indonesia 62 D2
Kampen, Neths. 17 B5
Kampene,
  Dem. Rep. of the Congo . 84 E5
Kamphaeng Phet, Thailand . 64 D2
Kampolombo, L., Zambia . 87 E2
Kampong Saom, Cambodia 65 G4
Kampong Saom, Chaak,
  Cambodia 65 G4
Kampong To, Thailand 65 J3
Kampot, Cambodia 65 G5
Kampti, Burkina Faso 82 C4
Kampuchea = Cambodia ■,
  Asia 64 F5
Kampung Air Putih,
  Malaysia 65 K4
Kampung Jerangau, Malaysia 65 K4
Kampung Raja, Malaysia .. 65 K4
Kampungbaru = Tolitoli,
  Indonesia 63 D6
Kamrau, Teluk, Indonesia . 63 E8
Kamsack, Canada 105 C8
Kamsai, Guinea 82 C2
Kamskoye Ustye, Russia .. 48 C9
Kamuchawie L., Canada .. 105 B8
Kamuela, U.S.A. 106 H17
Kamui-Misaki, Japan 54 C10
Kamyanets-Podilskyy,
  Ukraine 47 H4
Kamyanka-Buzka, Ukraine 47 G3
Kamyanka-Dniprovska,
  Ukraine 47 J8
Kāmyārān, Iran 70 C5
Kamyshin, Russia 48 E7
Kamyzyak, Russia 49 G9
Kan, Sudan 81 F3
Kanaaupscow, Canada 102 B4
Kanaaupscow →, Canada . 101 C12
Kanab, U.S.A. 115 H7
Kanab →, U.S.A. 115 H7
Kanagi, Japan 54 D10
Kanairiktok →, Canada ... 103 A7
Kanália, Greece 38 B4
Kananga,
  Dem. Rep. of the Congo . 84 F4
Kanash, Russia 48 C8
Kanaskat, U.S.A. 116 C5
Kanastraíon, Ákra =
  Palioúrion, Ákra, Greece . 40 G7
Kanawha →, U.S.A. 108 F4
Kanazawa, Japan 55 F8
Kanchanaburi, Thailand .. 64 E2
Kanchenjunga, Nepal 69 F13
Kanchipuram, India 66 N11
Kańczuga, Poland 45 J9
Kandaghat, India 68 D7
Kandahar = Qandahār,
  Afghan. 66 D4
Kandalaksha, Russia 50 C4
Kandalu, Afghan. 66 E3
Kandangan, Indonesia 62 E5
Kandanghaur, Indonesia .. 63 G13
Kandanos, Greece 36 D5
Kandava, Latvia 44 A9
Kandhíla, Greece 38 D4
Kandhkot, Pakistan 68 E3
Kandhla, India 68 E7
Kandi, Benin 83 C5
Kandi, India 69 H13
Kandiaro, Pakistan 68 F3
Kandra, Turkey 72 B4
Kandla, India 68 H4
Kandos, Australia 95 E4
Kandreho, Madag. 89 B8
Kandy, Sri Lanka 66 R12
Kane, U.S.A. 110 E6
Kane Basin, Greenland ... 4 B4
Kanel, Senegal 82 B2
Kaneohe, U.S.A. 106 H16
Kanevskaya, Russia 49 G4
Kanfanar, Croatia 29 C10
Kang, Botswana 88 C3
Kangaba, Mali 82 C3
Kangal, Turkey 72 C7
Kangān, Fārs, Iran 71 E7
Kangān, Hormozgān, Iran . 71 E8
Kangar, Malaysia 65 J3
Kangaré, Mali 82 C3
Kangaroo I., Australia 95 F2
Kangaroo Mts., Australia .. 94 C3
Kangasala, Finland 9 F21
Kangāvar, Iran 71 C6
Kangding, China 58 B3
Kangdong, N. Korea 57 E14
Kangean, Kepulauan,
  Indonesia 62 F5
Kangean Is. = Kangean,
  Kepulauan, Indonesia ... 62 F5
Kangen →, Sudan 81 F3
Kanggye, N. Korea 57 D14
Kanggyŏng, S. Korea 57 F14
Kanghwa, S. Korea 57 F14
Kangikajik, Greenland ... 4 B6
Kangiqsualujjuaq, Canada . 101 C13
Kangiqsujuaq, Canada 101 B12
Kangirsuk, Canada 101 B13
Kangnŭng, S. Korea 57 F15
Kangping, China 57 C12
Kangra, India 68 C7
Kangto, India 67 F18

Kanhar →, India 69 G10
Kani, Ivory C. 82 D3
Kaniama,
  Dem. Rep. of the Congo . 86 D1
Kaniapiskau =
  Caniapiscau →, Canada . 103 A6
Kaniapiskau, Res. =
  Caniapiscau Rés. de,
  Canada 103 B6
Kanin, Poluostrov, Russia . 50 C5
Kanin Nos, Mys, Russia .. 50 C5
Kanin Pen. = Kanin,
  Poluostrov, Russia 50 C5
Kanina, Albania 40 F3
Kaniva, Australia 95 F3
Kanjiža, Serbia, Yug. 42 D5
Kanjut Sar, Pakistan 69 A6
Kankaanpää, Finland 9 F20
Kankakee, U.S.A. 108 E2
Kankakee →, U.S.A. 108 E1
Kankan, Guinea 82 C3
Kankendy = Xankändi,
  Azerbaijan 70 B5
Kanker, India 67 J12
Kankossa, Mauritania 82 B2
Kankroli, India 68 G5
Kannapolis, U.S.A. 109 H5
Kannauj, India 69 F8
Kannod, India 66 H10
Kano, Nigeria 83 C6
Kano □, Nigeria 83 C6
Kan'onji, Japan 55 G6
Kanoroba, Ivory C. 82 D3
Kanowit, Malaysia 62 D4
Kanoya, Japan 55 J5
Kanpetlet, Burma 67 J18
Kanpur, India 69 F9
Kansas □, U.S.A. 112 F6
Kansas →, U.S.A. 112 F7
Kansas City, Kans., U.S.A. . 112 F7
Kansas City, Mo., U.S.A. . 112 F7
Kansenia,
  Dem. Rep. of the Congo . 87 E2
Kansk, Russia 51 D10
Kansŏng, S. Korea 57 E15
Kansu = Gansu □, China . 56 G3
Kantaphor, India 68 H7
Kantchari, Burkina Faso .. 83 C5
Kantché, Niger 83 C6
Kanté, Togo 83 D5
Kantemirovka, Russia 47 H10
Kantharalak, Thailand 64 E5
Kantli →, India 68 E6
Kantō □, Japan 55 F9
Kantō-Sanchi, Japan 55 G9
Kanturk, Ireland 15 D3
Kanuma, Japan 55 F9
Kanus, Namibia 88 D2
Kanye, Botswana 88 C4
Kanzenze,
  Dem. Rep. of the Congo . 87 E2
Kanzi, Ras, Tanzania 86 D4
Kaohsiung, Taiwan 59 F13
Kaokoveld, Namibia 88 B1
Kaolack, Senegal 82 C1
Kaoshan, China 57 B13
Kapaa, U.S.A. 106 G15
Kapadvanj, India 68 H5
Kapan, Armenia 70 B5
Kapanga,
  Dem. Rep. of the Congo . 84 F4
Kapchagai = Qapshaghay,
  Kazakstan 50 E8
Kapela = Velika Kapela,
  Croatia 29 C12
Kapéllo, Ákra, Greece 38 E5
Kapema,
  Dem. Rep. of the Congo . 87 E2
Kapfenberg, Austria 26 D8
Kapı Dağı, Turkey 41 F11
Kapiri Mposhi, Zambia ... 87 E2
Kapiskau →, Canada 102 B3
Kapit, Malaysia 62 D4
Kapiti I., N.Z. 91 J5
Kaplan, U.S.A. 113 K8
Kaplice, Czech Rep. 26 C7
Kapoe, Thailand 65 H2
Kapoeta, Sudan 81 G3
Kápolnásnyék, Hungary ... 42 C3
Kapos →, Hungary 42 D3
Kaposvár, Hungary 42 D2
Kapowsin, U.S.A. 116 D4
Kappeln, Germany 24 A5
Kappelshamn, Sweden 11 G12
Kapps, Namibia 88 C2
Kaprije, Croatia 29 E12
Kapsan, N. Korea 57 D15
Kapsukas = Marijampolé,
  Lithuania 9 J20
Kapuas →, Indonesia 62 E3
Kapuas Hulu, Pegunungan,
  Malaysia 62 D4
Kapuas Hulu Ra. = Kapuas
  Hulu, Pegunungan,
  Malaysia 62 D4
Kapulo,
  Dem. Rep. of the Congo . 87 D2
Kapunda, Australia 95 E2
Kapuni, N.Z. 91 H5
Kapurthala, India 68 D6
Kapuskasing, Canada 102 C3
Kapuskasing →, Canada .. 102 C3
Kapustin Yar, Russia 49 F7
Kaputar, Australia 95 E5
Kaputir, Kenya 86 B4
Kapuvár, Hungary 42 C2
Kara, Russia 50 C7
Karā, W. →, Si. Arabia .. 80 C5
Kara Ada, Turkey 39 E9

Kara Bogaz Gol, Zaliv =
  Garabogazköl Aylagy,
  Turkmenistan 50 E6
Kara Burun, Turkey 39 E9
Kara Kum, Turkmenistan .. 50 F6
Kara Kalpak Republic =
  Karakalpakstan □,
  Uzbekistan 50 E6
Kara Sea, Russia 50 B7
Karaadilli, Turkey 39 C12
Karabiğa, Turkey 41 F11
Karabük, Turkey 72 B5
Karaburun, Turkey 39 C8
Karaburuni, Albania 40 F3
Karabutak = Qarabutaq,
  Kazakstan 50 E7
Karacabey, Turkey 41 F12
Karacakılavuz, Turkey 41 E11
Karacaköy, Turkey 41 E12
Karachala = Qaraçala,
  Azerbaijan 49 L9
Karachayevsk, Russia 49 J5
Karachev, Russia 47 F8
Karachey-Cherkessia □,
  Russia 49 J5
Karachi, Pakistan 68 G2
Karad, India 66 L9
Karadirek, Turkey 39 C12
Karaga, Ghana 83 D4
Karaganda = Qaraghandy,
  Kazakstan 50 E8
Karagayly, Kazakstan 50 E8
Karaginskiy, Ostrov, Russia 51 D17
Karagola Road, India 69 G12
Karagüney Dağları, Turkey 72 B6
Karahallı, Turkey 39 C11
Karaikal, India 66 P11
Karaikkudi, India 66 P11
Karaisalı, Turkey 72 D6
Karaj, Iran 71 C6
Karak, Malaysia 65 L4
Karakalpakstan □,
  Uzbekistan 50 E6
Karakelong, Indonesia 63 D7
Karakitang, Indonesia 63 D7
Karaklis = Vanadzor,
  Armenia 49 K7
Karakoçan, Turkey 73 C9
Karakoram Pass, Pakistan 69 B7
Karakoram Ra., Pakistan . 69 B7
Karakurt, Turkey 73 B10
Karakuwisa, Namibia 88 B2
Karalon, Russia 51 D12
Karama, Jordan 75 D4
Karaman, Balıkesir, Turkey 39 B9
Karaman, Konya, Turkey . 70 B2
Karamanlı, Turkey 39 D11
Karamay, China 60 B3
Karambu, Indonesia 62 E5
Karamea Bight, N.Z. 91 J3
Karamnasa →, India 69 G10
Karamürsel, Turkey 41 F13
Karand, Iran 70 C5
Karanganyar, Indonesia .. 63 G13
Karanjia, India 69 J11
Karankasso, Burkina Faso . 82 C4
Karaova, Turkey 39 D9
Karapınar, Turkey 72 D5
Karasburg, Namibia 88 D2
Karasino, Russia 50 C9
Karasjok, Norway 8 B21
Karasu, Turkey 72 B4
Karasu →, Turkey 39 E12
Karasuk, Russia 50 D8
Karasuyama, Japan 55 F10
Karataş, Adana, Turkey .. 72 D6
Karataş, Manisa, Turkey . 39 C10
Karataş Burnu, Turkey 72 D6
Karatau = Qarataū,
  Kazakstan 50 E8
Karatau, Khrebet, Kazakstan 50 E7
Karatoprak, Turkey 39 D9
Karatsu, Japan 55 H5
Karaul, Russia 50 B9
Karauli, India 68 F7
Karavastasë, L. e, Albania . 40 F3
Kárávi, Greece 38 E5
Karavostasi, Cyprus 36 D11
Karawang, Indonesia 63 G12
Karawanken, Europe 26 E7
Karayazı, Turkey 73 C10
Karazhal, Kazakstan 50 E8
Karbalā', Iraq 70 C5
Kårböle, Sweden 10 C9
Karcag, Hungary 42 C5
Karcha →, Pakistan 69 B7
Karchana, India 69 G9
Karczew, Poland 45 F8
Kardam, Bulgaria 41 C12
Kardeljevo = Ploče, Croatia 29 E14
Kardhámila, Greece 39 C8
Kardhámli, Greece 38 E4
Kardhítsa, Greece 38 B3
Kardhítsa □, Greece 38 B3
Kärdla, Estonia 9 G20
Kareeberge, S. Africa 88 E3
Kareha →, India 69 G12
Kareima, Sudan 80 D3
Karelia □, Russia 50 C4
Karelian Republic =
  Karelia □, Russia 50 C4
Karera, India 68 G8
Kārevāndar, Iran 71 E9
Kargasok, Russia 50 D9
Kargat, Russia 50 D9
Kargı, Turkey 72 B6
Kargil, India 69 B7
Kargopol, Russia 46 B10
Kargowa, Poland 45 F2

Karguéri, Niger ... 83 C7
Karhal, India ... 69 F8
Kariá, Greece ... 38 C2
Kariaí, Greece ... 41 F8
Karīān, Iran ... 71 E8
Karianga, Madag. ... 89 C8
Kariba, Zimbabwe ... 87 F2
Kariba, L., Zimbabwe ... 87 F2
Kariba Dam, Zimbabwe ... 87 F2
Kariba Gorge, Zambia ... 87 F2
Karibib, Namibia ... 88 C2
Karimata, Kepulauan, Indonesia ... 62 E3
Karimata, Selat, Indonesia ... 62 E3
Karimata Is. = Karimata, Kepulauan, Indonesia ... 62 E3
Karimnagar, India ... 66 K11
Karimunjawa, Kepulauan, Indonesia ... 62 F4
Karin, Somali Rep. ... 74 E4
Káristos, Greece ... 38 C6
Karīt, Iran ... 71 C8
Kariya, Japan ... 55 G8
Kariyangwe, Zimbabwe ... 89 B4
Karjala, Finland ... 46 A5
Karkaralinsk = Qarqaraly, Kazakhstan ... 50 E8
Karkheh →, Iran ... 70 D5
Karkinitska Zatoka, Ukraine ... 47 K7
Karkinitskiy Zaliv = Karkinitska Zatoka, Ukraine ... 47 K7
Karkur Tohl, Egypt ... 80 C2
Karl Liebknecht, Russia ... 47 G8
Karl-Marx-Stadt = Chemnitz, Germany ... 24 E8
Karlholmsbruk, Sweden ... 10 D11
Karlino, Poland ... 44 D2
Karlivka, Ukraine ... 47 H8
Karlobag, Croatia ... 29 D12
Karlovac, Croatia ... 29 C12
Karlovka = Karlivka, Ukraine ... 47 H8
Karlovo, Bulgaria ... 41 D8
Karlovy Vary, Czech Rep. ... 26 A5
Karlsbad = Karlovy Vary, Czech Rep. ... 26 A5
Karlsborg, Sweden ... 11 F8
Karlshamn, Sweden ... 11 H8
Karlskoga, Sweden ... 10 E8
Karlskrona, Sweden ... 11 H9
Karlsruhe, Germany ... 25 F4
Karlstad, Sweden ... 10 E8
Karlstad, U.S.A. ... 112 A6
Karlstadt, Germany ... 25 F5
Karma, Niger ... 83 C5
Karmélava, Lithuania ... 44 D11
Karmi'el, Israel ... 75 C4
Karnak, Egypt ... 79 C12
Karnal, India ... 68 E7
Karnali →, Nepal ... 69 E9
Karnaphuli Res., Bangla. ... 67 H18
Karnaprayag, India ... 69 D8
Karnataka □, India ... 66 N10
Karnes City, U.S.A. ... 113 L6
Karnische Alpen, Europe ... 26 E6
Karnobat, Bulgaria ... 41 D10
Kärnten □, Austria ... 26 E6
Karo, Mali ... 82 C4
Karoi, Zimbabwe ... 87 F2
Karonga, Malawi ... 87 D3
Karoonda, Australia ... 95 F2
Karor, Pakistan ... 68 D4
Karora, Sudan ... 80 D4
Káros, Greece ... 39 E7
Karousádhes, Greece ... 38 B1
Karpacz, Poland ... 45 H2
Karpasia □, Cyprus ... 36 D13
Kárpathos, Greece ... 39 F9
Kárpathos, Stenón, Greece ... 39 F9
Karpenísion, Greece ... 38 C3
Karpuz Burnu = Apostolos Andreas, C., Cyprus ... 36 D13
Karpuzlu, Turkey ... 39 D9
Karratha, Australia ... 92 D2
Kars, Turkey ... 73 B10
Karsakpay, Kazakhstan ... 50 E7
Karsha, Kazakhstan ... 48 F10
Karshi = Qarshi, Uzbekistan ... 50 F7
Karsiyang, India ... 69 F13
Karsog, India ... 68 D7
Karst = Kras, Croatia ... 29 C10
Kartal, Turkey ... 41 F13
Kartál Óros, Greece ... 41 E9
Kartaly, Russia ... 50 D7
Kartapur, India ... 68 D6
Karthaus, U.S.A. ... 110 E6
Kartuzy, Poland ... 44 D5
Karufa, Indonesia ... 63 E8
Karumba, Australia ... 94 B3
Karumo, Tanzania ... 86 C3
Karumwa, Tanzania ... 86 C3
Karūn →, Iran ... 71 D6
Karungu, Kenya ... 86 C3
Karup, Denmark ... 11 H3
Karviná, Czech Rep. ... 27 B11
Karwan →, India ... 68 F8
Karwar, India ... 66 M9
Karwi, India ... 69 G9
Kaş, Turkey ... 39 E11
Kasaba, Turkey ... 39 E11
Kasache, Malawi ... 87 E3
Kasai →, Dem. Rep. of the Congo ... 84 E3
Kasaï-Oriental □, Dem. Rep. of the Congo ... 86 D1
Kasaji, Dem. Rep. of the Congo ... 87 E1
Kasama, Zambia ... 87 E3
Kasan-dong, N. Korea ... 57 D14

Kasane, Namibia ... 88 B3
Kasanga, Tanzania ... 87 D3
Kasar, Ras, Sudan ... 80 D4
Kasaragod, India ... 66 N9
Kasba L., Canada ... 105 A8
Kāseh Garān, Iran ... 70 C5
Kasempa, Zambia ... 87 E2
Kasenga, Dem. Rep. of the Congo ... 87 E2
Kasese, Uganda ... 86 B3
Kasewa, Zambia ... 87 E2
Kasganj, India ... 69 F8
Kashabowie, Canada ... 102 C1
Kashaf, Iran ... 71 C9
Kāshān, Iran ... 71 C6
Kashechewan, Canada ... 102 B3
Kashi, China ... 60 C2
Kashimbo, Dem. Rep. of the Congo ... 87 E2
Kashin, Russia ... 46 D9
Kashipur, India ... 69 E8
Kashira, Russia ... 46 E10
Kashiwazaki, Japan ... 55 F9
Kashk-e Kohneh, Afghan. ... 66 B3
Kashkū'īyeh, Iran ... 71 D7
Kāshmar, Iran ... 71 C8
Kashmir, Asia ... 69 C7
Kashmor, Pakistan ... 68 E3
Kashpirovka, Russia ... 48 D9
Kashun Noerh = Gaxun Nur, China ... 60 B5
Kasiari, India ... 69 H12
Kasimov, Russia ... 48 C5
Kasinge, Dem. Rep. of the Congo ... 86 D2
Kasiruta, Indonesia ... 63 E7
Kaskaskia →, U.S.A. ... 112 G10
Kaskattama →, Canada ... 105 B10
Kaskinen, Finland ... 9 E19
Kaslo, Canada ... 104 D5
Kasmere L., Canada ... 105 B8
Kasongo, Dem. Rep. of the Congo ... 86 C2
Kasongo Lunda, Dem. Rep. of the Congo ... 84 F3
Kásos, Greece ... 39 F8
Kásos, Stenón, Greece ... 39 F8
Kaspi, Georgia ... 49 K7
Kaspichan, Bulgaria ... 41 C11
Kaspiysk, Russia ... 49 J8
Kaspiyskiy, Russia ... 49 H8
Kassab ed Doleib, Sudan ... 81 E3
Kassaba, Egypt ... 80 C2
Kassalâ, Sudan ... 81 D4
Kassalâ □, Sudan ... 81 D4
Kassándra, Greece ... 40 F7
Kassándrinon, Greece ... 40 F7
Kassel, Germany ... 24 D5
Kassinger, Sudan ... 80 D3
Kassiópi, Greece ... 36 A3
Kasson, U.S.A. ... 112 C8
Kastamonu, Turkey ... 72 B5
Kastav, Croatia ... 29 C11
Kastélli, Greece ... 36 D5
Kastéllion, Greece ... 36 D7
Kastellórizon = Megiste, Greece ... 39 E11
Kástellos, Greece ... 39 E9
Kastellou, Ákra, Greece ... 39 F9
Kasterlee, Belgium ... 17 C4
Kastlösa, Sweden ... 11 H10
Kastóri, Greece ... 38 D4
Kastoría, Greece ... 40 F5
Kastoría □, Greece ... 40 F5
Kastorías, Límni, Greece ... 40 F5
Kastornoye, Russia ... 47 G10
Kastós, Greece ... 38 C2
Kastrosikiá, Greece ... 38 B2
Kastsyukovichy, Belarus ... 46 F7
Kasulu, Tanzania ... 86 C3
Kasumi, Japan ... 55 G7
Kasumkent, Russia ... 49 K9
Kasungu, Malawi ... 87 E3
Kasur, Pakistan ... 68 D6
Kataba, Zambia ... 87 F2
Katagum, Nigeria ... 83 C7
Katahdin, Mt., U.S.A. ... 109 C11
Katako Kombe, Dem. Rep. of the Congo ... 86 C1
Katákolon, Greece ... 38 D3
Katale, Tanzania ... 86 C3
Katanda, Katanga, Dem. Rep. of the Congo ... 86 D1
Katanda, Nord-Kivu, Dem. Rep. of the Congo ... 86 C2
Katanga □, Dem. Rep. of the Congo ... 86 D2
Katangi, India ... 66 J11
Katanning, Australia ... 93 F2
Katastári, Greece ... 38 D2
Katavi Swamp, Tanzania ... 86 D3
Kateríni, Greece ... 40 F6
Katghora, India ... 69 H10
Katha, Burma ... 67 G20
Katherîna, Gebel, Egypt ... 70 D2
Katherine, Australia ... 92 B5
Katherine Gorge, Australia ... 92 B5
Kathi, India ... 68 J6
Kathiawar, India ... 68 H4
Kathikas, Cyprus ... 36 E11
Kathua, India ... 68 C6
Kati, Mali ... 82 C3
Katihar, India ... 69 G12
Katima Mulilo, Zambia ... 88 B3
Katimbira, Malawi ... 87 E3
Katingan = Mendawai →, Indonesia ... 62 E4
Katiola, Ivory C. ... 82 D3
Katlanovo, Macedonia ... 40 E5
Katmandu, Nepal ... 69 F11
Katni, India ... 69 H9

Kato Akhaïa, Greece ... 38 C3
Káto Arkhánai, Greece ... 36 D7
Káto Khorió, Greece ... 36 D7
Kato Pyrgos, Cyprus ... 36 D11
Káto Stavros, Greece ... 40 F7
Katokhí, Greece ... 38 C3
Katompe, Dem. Rep. of the Congo ... 86 D2
Katonga →, Uganda ... 86 B3
Katoomba, Australia ... 95 E5
Katoúna, Greece ... 38 C3
Katowice, Poland ... 45 H6
Katrancı Dağı, Turkey ... 39 D12
Katrine, L., U.K. ... 14 E4
Katrineholm, Sweden ... 11 E10
Katsepe, Madag. ... 89 B8
Katsina, Nigeria ... 83 C6
Katsina □, Nigeria ... 83 C6
Katsina Ala, Nigeria ... 83 D6
Katsina Ala →, Nigeria ... 83 D6
Katsumoto, Japan ... 55 H4
Katsuura, Japan ... 55 G10
Katsuyama, Japan ... 55 F8
Kattaviá, Greece ... 36 D9
Kattegat, Denmark ... 11 H5
Katthammarsvik, Sweden ... 11 G12
Katul, J., Sudan ... 81 E2
Katumba, Dem. Rep. of the Congo ... 86 D2
Katungu, Kenya ... 86 C5
Katwa, India ... 69 H13
Katwijk, Neths. ... 17 B4
Kauai, U.S.A. ... 106 H15
Kauai Channel, U.S.A. ... 106 H15
Kaub, Germany ... 25 E3
Kaufbeuren, Germany ... 25 H6
Kaufman, U.S.A. ... 113 J6
Kauhajoki, Finland ... 9 E20
Kaukauna, U.S.A. ... 108 C1
Kaukauveld, Namibia ... 88 C3
Kaunakakai, U.S.A. ... 106 H16
Kaunas, Lithuania ... 9 J20
Kaunia, Bangla. ... 69 G13
Kaunos, Turkey ... 39 E10
Kaura Namoda, Nigeria ... 83 C6
Kauru, Nigeria ... 83 C6
Kautokeino, Norway ... 8 B20
Kauwapur, India ... 69 F10
Kavacha, Russia ... 51 C17
Kavadarci, Macedonia ... 40 E6
Kavaja, Albania ... 40 E3
Kavak, Turkey ... 72 B7
Kavak Dağı, Turkey ... 39 D10
Kavaklı, Turkey ... 41 E11
Kavaklıdere, Turkey ... 39 D10
Kavalerovo, Russia ... 54 B7
Kavali, India ... 66 M12
Kavála, Greece ... 41 F8
Kavála □, Greece ... 41 E8
Kavála Kólpos, Greece ... 41 F8
Kavār, Iran ... 71 D7
Kavarna, Bulgaria ... 41 C12
Kavi, India ... 68 H5
Kavimba, Botswana ... 88 B3
Kavīr, Dasht-e, Iran ... 71 C7
Kavkaz, Russia ... 47 K9
Kavos, Greece ... 36 B4
Kavoúsi, Greece ... 36 D7
Kaw, Fr. Guiana ... 125 C8
Kawa, Sudan ... 81 E3
Kawagama L., Canada ... 110 A6
Kawagoe, Japan ... 55 G9
Kawaguchi, Japan ... 55 G9
Kawaihae, U.S.A. ... 106 H17
Kawambwa, Zambia ... 87 D2
Kawanoe, Japan ... 55 G6
Kawardha, India ... 69 J9
Kawasaki, Japan ... 55 G9
Kawasi, Indonesia ... 63 E7
Kawerau, N.Z. ... 91 H6
Kawhia Harbour, N.Z. ... 91 H5
Kawio, Kepulauan, Indonesia ... 63 D7
Kawnro, Burma ... 67 H21
Kawthaung, Burma ... 65 H2
Kawthoolei = Kawthule □, Burma ... 67 L20
Kawthule □, Burma ... 67 L20
Kaxholmen, Sweden ... 11 G8
Kaya, Burkina Faso ... 83 C4
Kayah □, Burma ... 67 K20
Kayalıköy Baraji, Turkey ... 41 E11
Kayan →, Indonesia ... 62 D5
Kaycee, U.S.A. ... 114 E10
Kayeli, Indonesia ... 63 E7
Kayenta, U.S.A. ... 115 H8
Kayes, Mali ... 82 C2
Kayı, Turkey ... 39 B12
Kayima, S. Leone ... 82 D2
Kayin = Kawthule □, Burma ... 67 L20
Kayımakçı, Turkey ... 39 C10
Kayoa, Indonesia ... 63 D7
Kayomba, Zambia ... 87 E1
Kaysatskoye, Russia ... 48 F8
Kayseri, Turkey ... 70 B2
Kaysville, U.S.A. ... 114 F8
Kaz Dağı, Turkey ... 39 B8
Kazachye, Russia ... 51 B14
Kazakhstan ■, Asia ... 50 E7
Kazan, Russia ... 48 C9
Kazan →, Canada ... 105 A9
Kazan-Rettō, Pac. Oc. ... 96 E6
Kazanskaya, Russia ... 48 F5
Kazatin = Kozyatyn, Ukraine ... 47 H5
Kazaure, Nigeria ... 83 C6
Kazbek, Russia ... 49 J7
Kāzerūn, Iran ... 71 D6

Kazi Magomed = Qazimämmäd, Azerbaijan ... 49 K9
Kazimierz Dolny, Poland ... 45 G8
Kazimierza Wielka, Poland ... 45 H7
Kazincbarcika, Hungary ... 42 B5
Kazlų Rūda, Lithuania ... 44 D10
Kaztalovka, Kazakhstan ... 48 F9
Kazuno, Japan ... 54 D10
Kazym →, Russia ... 50 C7
Kcynia, Poland ... 45 F4
Keady, U.K. ... 15 B5
Kearney, U.S.A. ... 112 E5
Kearny, U.S.A. ... 115 K8
Kearsarge, Mt., U.S.A. ... 111 C13
Keban, Turkey ... 73 C8
Keban Baraji, Turkey ... 70 B3
Kebbi □, Nigeria ... 83 C5
Kébi, Ivory C. ... 82 D3
Kebnekaise, Sweden ... 8 C18
Kebri Dehar, Ethiopia ... 74 F3
Kebumen, Indonesia ... 63 G13
Kecel, Hungary ... 42 D4
Kechika →, Canada ... 104 B3
Kecskemét, Hungary ... 42 D4
Kedada, Ethiopia ... 81 F4
Kėdainiai, Lithuania ... 9 J21
Kedarnath, India ... 69 D8
Kedgwick, Canada ... 103 C6
Kédhros Óros, Greece ... 36 D6
Kediri, Indonesia ... 63 G15
Kedjebi, Ghana ... 83 D5
Kédougou, Senegal ... 82 C2
Kędzierzyn-Koźle, Poland ... 45 H5
Keeler, U.S.A. ... 116 J9
Keeley L., Canada ... 105 C7
Keeling Is. = Cocos Is., Ind. Oc. ... 96 J1
Keelung = Chilung, Taiwan ... 59 E13
Keene, Canada ... 110 B6
Keene, Calif., U.S.A. ... 117 K8
Keene, N.H., U.S.A. ... 111 D12
Keene, N.Y., U.S.A. ... 111 B11
Keeper Hill, Ireland ... 15 D3
Keer-Weer, C., Australia ... 94 A3
Keeseville, U.S.A. ... 111 B11
Keetmanshoop, Namibia ... 88 D2
Keewatin, Canada ... 105 D10
Keewatin →, Canada ... 105 B8
Kefa □, Ethiopia ... 81 F4
Kefallinía, Greece ... 38 C2
Kefallinía □, Greece ... 38 C2
Kéfalos, Greece ... 39 E8
Kefamenanu, Indonesia ... 63 F6
Kefar Sava, Israel ... 75 C3
Keffi, Nigeria ... 83 D6
Keffin Hausa, Nigeria ... 83 C6
Keflavík, Iceland ... 8 D2
Keftya, Ethiopia ... 81 E4
Keg River, Canada ... 104 B5
Kegaska, Canada ... 103 B7
Keheili, Sudan ... 80 D3
Kehl, Germany ... 25 G3
Keighley, U.K. ... 12 D6
Keila, Estonia ... 9 G21
Keimoes, S. Africa ... 88 D3
Keita, Niger ... 83 C6
Keitele, Finland ... 8 E22
Keith, Australia ... 95 F3
Keith, U.K. ... 14 D6
Keizer, U.S.A. ... 114 D2
Kejimkujik Nat. Park, Canada ... 103 D6
Kejser Franz Joseph Fd., Greenland ... 4 B6
Kekri, India ... 68 G6
Kelam, Ethiopia ... 81 G4
Kelamet, Eritrea ... 81 D4
Kelan, China ... 56 E6
Kelang, Malaysia ... 65 L3
Kelantan □, Malaysia ... 65 J4
Kelantan →, Malaysia ... 65 J4
Kělcyra, Albania ... 40 F4
Kelekçi, Turkey ... 39 D11
Keles, Turkey ... 41 G13
Keleti-főcsatorna, Hungary ... 42 C6
Kelheim, Germany ... 25 G7
Kelkit, Turkey ... 73 B8
Kelkit →, Turkey ... 72 B7
Kellerberrin, Australia ... 93 F2
Kellett, C., Canada ... 4 B1
Kelleys I., U.S.A. ... 110 E2
Kellogg, U.S.A. ... 114 C5
Kells = Ceannanus Mor, Ireland ... 15 C5
Kelmė, Lithuania ... 44 C9
Kelokedhara, Cyprus ... 36 E11
Kelowna, Canada ... 104 D5
Kelseyville, U.S.A. ... 116 G4
Kelso, N.Z. ... 91 L2
Kelso, U.K. ... 14 F6
Kelso, U.S.A. ... 116 D4
Keluang, Malaysia ... 65 L4
Kelvington, Canada ... 105 C8
Kem, Russia ... 50 C4
Kema, Indonesia ... 63 D7
Kemah, Turkey ... 73 C8
Kemaliye, Erzincan, Turkey ... 73 C8
Kemaliye, Manisa, Turkey ... 39 C10
Kemalpaşa, Turkey ... 39 C9
Kemaman, Malaysia ... 62 D2
Kemano, Canada ... 104 C3
Kemasik, Malaysia ... 65 K4
Kembolcha, Ethiopia ... 81 E4
Kemer, Antalya, Turkey ... 39 E12
Kemer, Burdur, Turkey ... 39 D11
Kemer, Muğla, Turkey ... 39 E11
Kemer Baraji, Turkey ... 39 D10
Kemerovo, Russia ... 50 D9
Kemi, Finland ... 8 D21

Kemi älv = Kemijoki →, Finland ... 8 D21
Kemijärvi, Finland ... 8 C22
Kemijoki →, Finland ... 8 D21
Kemmerer, U.S.A. ... 114 F8
Kemmuna = Comino, Malta ... 36 C1
Kemp, L., U.S.A. ... 113 J5
Kemp Land, Antarctica ... 5 C5
Kempsey, Australia ... 95 E5
Kempt, L., Canada ... 102 C5
Kempten, Germany ... 25 H6
Kempton, Australia ... 94 G4
Kemptville, Canada ... 102 D4
Ken →, India ... 69 G9
Kenai, U.S.A. ... 100 B4
Kendal, Indonesia ... 63 G14
Kendal, U.K. ... 12 C5
Kendall, Australia ... 95 E5
Kendall, U.S.A. ... 109 N5
Kendall →, Australia ... 94 A3
Kendallville, U.S.A. ... 108 E3
Kendari, Indonesia ... 63 E6
Kendawangan, Indonesia ... 62 E4
Kende, Nigeria ... 83 C5
Kendrapara, India ... 67 J15
Këndrevicës, Maja e, Albania ... 40 F3
Kendrew, S. Africa ... 88 E3
Kene Thao, Laos ... 64 D3
Kenedy, U.S.A. ... 113 L6
Kenema, S. Leone ... 82 D2
Keng Kok, Laos ... 64 D5
Keng Tawng, Burma ... 67 J21
Keng Tung, Burma ... 58 G2
Kengeja, Tanzania ... 86 D4
Kenhardt, S. Africa ... 88 D3
Kéniéba, Mali ... 82 C2
Kenitra, Morocco ... 78 B4
Kenli, China ... 57 F10
Kenmare, Ireland ... 15 E2
Kenmare, U.S.A. ... 112 A3
Kenmare River, Ireland ... 15 E2
Kennebago Lake, U.S.A. ... 111 A14
Kennebec, U.S.A. ... 112 D5
Kennebec →, U.S.A. ... 109 D11
Kennebunk, U.S.A. ... 111 C14
Kennedy, Zimbabwe ... 88 B4
Kennedy Ra., Australia ... 93 D2
Kennedy Taungdeik, Burma ... 67 H18
Kenner, U.S.A. ... 113 L9
Kennet →, U.K. ... 13 F7
Kenneth Ra., Australia ... 93 D2
Kennett, U.S.A. ... 113 G9
Kennewick, U.S.A. ... 114 C4
Kenogami →, Canada ... 102 B3
Kenora, Canada ... 105 D10
Kenosha, U.S.A. ... 108 D2
Kensington, Canada ... 103 C7
Kent, Ohio, U.S.A. ... 110 E3
Kent, Tex., U.S.A. ... 113 K2
Kent, Wash., U.S.A. ... 116 C4
Kent □, U.K. ... 13 F8
Kent Group, Australia ... 94 F4
Kent Pen., Canada ... 100 B9
Kentau, Kazakhstan ... 50 E7
Kentland, U.S.A. ... 108 E2
Kenton, U.S.A. ... 108 E4
Kentucky □, U.S.A. ... 108 G3
Kentucky →, U.S.A. ... 108 F3
Kentucky L., U.S.A. ... 109 G2
Kentville, Canada ... 103 C7
Kentwood, U.S.A. ... 113 K9
Kenya ■, Africa ... 86 C4
Kenya, Mt., Kenya ... 86 C4
Keo Neua, Deo, Vietnam ... 64 C5
Keokuk, U.S.A. ... 112 E9
Keonjhargarh, India ... 69 J11
Kep, Cambodia ... 65 G5
Kep, Vietnam ... 64 B6
Kepez, Turkey ... 41 F10
Kepi, Indonesia ... 63 F9
Kepice, Poland ... 44 D3
Kępno, Poland ... 45 G4
Kepsut, Turkey ... 39 B10
Kerala □, India ... 66 P10
Kerama-Rettō, Japan ... 55 L3
Keran, Pakistan ... 69 B5
Kerang, Australia ... 95 F3
Keranyo, Ethiopia ... 81 F4
Kerao →, Sudan ... 81 E3
Keratéa, Greece ... 38 D5
Keraudren, C., Australia ... 92 C2
Kerava, Finland ... 9 F21
Kerch, Ukraine ... 47 K9
Kerchenskiy Proliv, Black Sea ... 47 K9
Kerchoual, Mali ... 83 B5
Kerempe Burnu, Turkey ... 72 A5
Keren, Eritrea ... 81 D4
Kerewan, Gambia ... 82 C1
Kerguelen, Ind. Oc. ... 3 G13
Keri, Greece ... 38 D2
Keri Kera, Sudan ... 81 E3
Kerki, Turkmenistan ... 50 F7
Kerkínitis, Límni, Greece ... 40 E7
Kérkira, Greece ... 36 A3
Kérkira □, Greece ... 38 B1
Kerkrade, Neths. ... 17 D6
Kerma, Sudan ... 80 D3
Kermadec Is., Pac. Oc. ... 96 L10
Kermadec Trench, Pac. Oc. ... 96 L10
Kermān, Iran ... 71 D8
Kermān, U.S.A. ... 116 J6
Kermān □, Iran ... 71 D8
Kermān, Bīābān-e, Iran ... 71 D8
Kermānshāh = Bākhtarān, Iran ... 70 C5
Kermen, Bulgaria ... 41 D10

Kermit, *U.S.A.* ... 113 K3
Kern →, *U.S.A.* ... 117 K7
Kernhof, *Austria* ... 26 D8
Kernville, *U.S.A.* ... 117 K8
Keroh, *Malaysia* ... 65 K3
Kérou, *Benin* ... 83 C5
Kérouane, *Guinea* ... 82 D3
Kerpen, *Germany* ... 24 E2
Kerrera, *U.K.* ... 14 E3
Kerrobert, *Canada* ... 105 C7
Kerrville, *U.S.A.* ... 113 K5
Kerry □, *Ireland* ... 15 D2
Kerry Hd., *Ireland* ... 15 D2
Kersa, *Ethiopia* ... 81 F5
Kerzaz, *Algeria* ... 78 C5
Kesagami →, *Canada* ... 102 B4
Kesagami L., *Canada* ... 102 B3
Keşan, *Turkey* ... 41 F10
Kesennuma, *Japan* ... 54 E10
Keshit, *Iran* ... 71 D8
Keşiş Dağ, *Turkey* ... 73 C8
Keskin, *Turkey* ... 72 C5
Kestell, *S. Africa* ... 89 D4
Kestenga, *Russia* ... 50 C4
Keswick, *U.K.* ... 12 C4
Keszthely, *Hungary* ... 42 D2
Ket →, *Russia* ... 50 D9
Keta, *Ghana* ... 83 D5
Keta Lagoon, *Ghana* ... 83 D5
Ketapang, *Indonesia* ... 62 E4
Ketchikan, *U.S.A.* ... 104 B2
Ketchum, *U.S.A.* ... 114 E6
Kete Krachi, *Ghana* ... 83 D4
Ketef, Khalig Umm el, *Egypt* ... 70 F2
Keti Bandar, *Pakistan* ... 68 G2
Kétou, *Benin* ... 83 D5
Ketri, *India* ... 68 E6
Kętrzyn, *Poland* ... 44 D8
Kettering, *U.K.* ... 13 E7
Kettering, *U.S.A.* ... 108 F3
Kettle →, *Canada* ... 105 B11
Kettle Falls, *U.S.A.* ... 114 B4
Kettle Pt., *Canada* ... 110 C2
Kettleman City, *U.S.A.* ... 116 J7
Kęty, *Poland* ... 45 J6
Keuka L., *U.S.A.* ... 110 D7
Keuruu, *Finland* ... 9 E21
Kevelaer, *Germany* ... 24 D2
Kewanee, *U.S.A.* ... 112 E10
Kewaunee, *U.S.A.* ... 108 C2
Keweenaw B., *U.S.A.* ... 108 B1
Keweenaw Pen., *U.S.A.* ... 108 B2
Keweenaw Pt., *U.S.A.* ... 108 B2
Key L., *U.S.A.* ... 109 N5
Key West, *U.S.A.* ... 107 F10
Keyala, *Sudan* ... 81 G3
Keynsham, *U.K.* ... 13 F5
Keyser, *U.S.A.* ... 108 F6
Kezhma, *Russia* ... 51 D11
Kezi, *Zimbabwe* ... 89 C4
Kežmarok, *Slovak Rep.* ... 27 B13
Khabarovsk, *Russia* ... 51 E14
Khabr, *Iran* ... 71 D8
Khābūr →, *Syria* ... 70 C4
Khachmas = Xaçmaz, *Azerbaijan* ... 49 K9
Khachrod, *India* ... 68 H6
Khadari, W. el →, *Sudan* ... 81 E2
Khadro, *Pakistan* ... 68 F3
Khadyzhensk, *Russia* ... 49 H4
Khadzhilyangar, *India* ... 69 B8
Khaga, *India* ... 69 G9
Khagaria, *India* ... 69 G12
Khaipur, *Pakistan* ... 68 E5
Khair, *India* ... 68 F7
Khairabad, *India* ... 69 F9
Khairagarh, *India* ... 69 J9
Khairpur, *Pakistan* ... 68 F3
Khairpur Nathan Shah, *Pakistan* ... 68 F2
Khairwara, *India* ... 68 H5
Khaisor →, *Pakistan* ... 68 D3
Khajuri Kach, *Pakistan* ... 68 C3
Khakassia □, *Russia* ... 50 D9
Khakhea, *Botswana* ... 88 C3
Khalafābād, *Iran* ... 71 D6
Khalilabad, *India* ... 69 F10
Khalīlī, *Iran* ... 71 E7
Khalkhāl, *Iran* ... 71 B6
Khálki, *Dhodhekánisos, Greece* ... 39 E9
Khálki, *Thessalía, Greece* ... 38 B4
Khalkidhikí □, *Greece* ... 40 F7
Khalkís, *Greece* ... 38 C5
Khalmer-Sede = Tazovskiy, *Russia* ... 50 C8
Khalmer Yu, *Russia* ... 50 C7
Khalūf, *Oman* ... 74 C6
Kham Keut, *Laos* ... 64 C5
Khamaria, *India* ... 69 H9
Khambhaliya, *India* ... 68 H3
Khambhat, *India* ... 68 H5
Khambhat, G. of, *India* ... 66 J8
Khamilonísion, *Greece* ... 39 F8
Khamir, *Iran* ... 71 E7
Khamir, *Yemen* ... 74 D3
Khamsa, *Egypt* ... 75 E1
Khan →, *Namibia* ... 88 C2
Khān Abū Shāmat, *Syria* ... 75 B5
Khān Azād, *Iraq* ... 70 C5
Khan Mujiddah, *Iraq* ... 70 C4
Khān Shaykhūn, *Syria* ... 70 C3
Khān Yūnis, *Gaza Strip* ... 75 D3
Khanai, *Pakistan* ... 68 D2
Khānaqīn, *Iraq* ... 70 C5
Khānbāghī, *Iran* ... 71 B7
Khandra, *Greece* ... 39 F8
Khandwa, *India* ... 66 J10
Khandyga, *Russia* ... 51 C14
Khāneh, *Iran* ... 70 B5

Khanewal, *Pakistan* ... 68 D4
Khangah Dogran, *Pakistan* ... 68 D5
Khanh Duong, *Vietnam* ... 64 F7
Khaniá, *Greece* ... 36 D6
Khaniá □, *Greece* ... 36 D6
Khaníon, Kólpos, *Greece* ... 36 D5
Khanka, L., *Asia* ... 51 E14
Khankendy = Xankändi, *Azerbaijan* ... 70 B5
Khanna, *India* ... 68 D7
Khanozai, *Pakistan* ... 68 D2
Khanpur, *Pakistan* ... 68 E4
Khanty-Mansiysk, *Russia* ... 50 C7
Khapalu, *Pakistan* ... 69 B7
Khapcheranga, *Russia* ... 51 E12
Kharaghoda, *India* ... 68 H4
Kharagpur, *India* ... 69 H12
Khárakas, *Greece* ... 36 D7
Kharan Kalat, *Pakistan* ... 66 E4
Kharānaq, *Iran* ... 71 C7
Kharda, *India* ... 66 K9
Khardung La, *India* ... 69 B7
Khârga, El Wâhât-el, *Egypt* ... 80 B3
Khargon, *India* ... 66 J9
Khari →, *India* ... 68 G6
Kharian, *Pakistan* ... 68 C5
Kharit, Wadi el →, *Egypt* ... 80 C3
Khārk, Jazīreh-ye, *Iran* ... 71 D6
Kharkiv, *Ukraine* ... 47 H9
Kharkov = Kharkiv, *Ukraine* ... 47 H9
Kharmanli, *Bulgaria* ... 41 E9
Kharovsk, *Russia* ... 46 C11
Kharsawangarh, *India* ... 69 H11
Kharta, *Turkey* ... 72 B3
Khartoum = El Khartûm, *Sudan* ... 81 D3
Khasan, *Russia* ... 54 C5
Khasavyurt, *Russia* ... 49 J8
Khāsh, *Iran* ... 66 E2
Khashm el Girba, *Sudan* ... 81 E4
Khashum, *Sudan* ... 81 E2
Khashuri, *Georgia* ... 49 J6
Khaskovo, *Bulgaria* ... 41 E9
Khaskovo □, *Bulgaria* ... 41 E9
Khatanga, *Russia* ... 51 B11
Khatanga →, *Russia* ... 51 B11
Khatauli, *India* ... 68 E7
Khatra, *India* ... 69 H12
Khātūnābād, *Iran* ... 71 D7
Khatyrka, *Russia* ... 51 C18
Khavda, *India* ... 68 H3
Khaybar, Harrat, *Si. Arabia* ... 70 E4
Khayelitsha, *S. Africa* ... 85 L3
Khāzimiyah, *Iraq* ... 70 C4
Khazzân Jabal al Awliyâ, *Sudan* ... 81 D3
Khe Bo, *Vietnam* ... 64 C5
Khe Long, *Vietnam* ... 64 B5
Khed Brahma, *India* ... 66 G8
Khekra, *India* ... 68 E7
Khemarak Phouminville, *Cambodia* ... 65 G4
Khemisset, *Morocco* ... 78 B4
Khemmarat, *Thailand* ... 64 D5
Khenāmān, *Iran* ... 71 D8
Khenchela, *Algeria* ... 78 A7
Kherson →, *Iran* ... 71 D6
Khérson, *Greece* ... 40 E6
Kherson, *Ukraine* ... 47 J7
Khersónisos Akrotíri, *Greece* ... 36 D6
Kheta →, *Russia* ... 51 B11
Khewari, *Pakistan* ... 68 F3
Khilchipur, *India* ... 68 G7
Khiliomódhion, *Greece* ... 38 D4
Khilok, *Russia* ... 51 D12
Khimki, *Russia* ... 46 E9
Khíos, *Greece* ... 39 C8
Khíos □, *Greece* ... 39 C8
Khirsadoh, *India* ... 69 H8
Khiuma = Hiiumaa, *Estonia* ... 9 G20
Khiva, *Uzbekistan* ... 50 E7
Khīyāv, *Iran* ... 70 B5
Khlebarovo, *Bulgaria* ... 41 C10
Khlong Khlung, *Thailand* ... 64 D2
Khmelnik, *Ukraine* ... 47 H4
Khmelnitskiy = Khmelnytskyy, *Ukraine* ... 47 H4
Khmelnytskyy, *Ukraine* ... 47 H4
Khmer Rep. = Cambodia ■, *Asia* ... 64 F5
Khoai, Hon, *Vietnam* ... 65 H5
Khodoriv, *Ukraine* ... 47 H3
Khodzent = Khudzhand, *Tajikistan* ... 50 E7
Khojak Pass, *Afghan.* ... 68 D2
Khok Kloi, *Thailand* ... 65 H2
Khok Pho, *Thailand* ... 65 J3
Kholm, *Russia* ... 46 D6
Kholmsk, *Russia* ... 51 E15
Khomas Hochland, *Namibia* ... 88 C2
Khombole, *Senegal* ... 82 C1
Khomeyn, *Iran* ... 71 C6
Khomeynī Shahr, *Iran* ... 71 C6
Khomodino, *Botswana* ... 88 C3
Khon Kaen, *Thailand* ... 64 D4
Khong →, *Cambodia* ... 64 F5
Khong Sedone, *Laos* ... 64 E5
Khonuu, *Russia* ... 51 C15
Khoper →, *Russia* ... 48 F6
Khor el 'Atash, *Sudan* ... 81 E3
Khóra, *Greece* ... 38 D3
Khóra Sfakíon, *Greece* ... 36 D6
Khorāsān □, *Iran* ... 71 C8
Khorat = Nakhon Ratchasima, *Thailand* ... 64 E4
Khorat, Cao Nguyen, *Thailand* ... 64 E4
Khorixas, *Namibia* ... 88 C1
Khorol, *Ukraine* ... 47 H7

Khorramābād, *Khorāsān, Iran* ... 71 C8
Khorramābād, *Lorestān, Iran* ... 71 C6
Khorrāmshahr, *Iran* ... 71 D6
Khorugh, *Tajikistan* ... 50 F8
Khosravī, *Iran* ... 71 D6
Khosrowābād, *Khuzestān, Iran* ... 71 D6
Khosrowābād, *Kordestān, Iran* ... 70 C5
Khost, *Pakistan* ... 68 D2
Khosūyeh, *Iran* ... 71 D7
Khotyn, *Ukraine* ... 47 H4
Khouribga, *Morocco* ... 78 B4
Khowai, *Bangla.* ... 67 G17
Khowst, *Afghan.* ... 68 C3
Khoyniki, *Belarus* ... 47 G5
Khrami →, *Georgia* ... 49 K7
Khrenovoye, *Russia* ... 48 E5
Khrisoúpolis, *Greece* ... 41 F8
Khristianá, *Greece* ... 39 E7
Khrysokhou B., *Cyprus* ... 36 D11
Khtapodhiá, *Greece* ... 39 D7
Khu Khan, *Thailand* ... 64 E5
Khudzhand, *Tajikistan* ... 50 E7
Khuff, *Si. Arabia* ... 70 E5
Khūgīānī, *Afghan.* ... 68 D1
Khuis, *Botswana* ... 88 D3
Khuiyala, *India* ... 68 F4
Khujner, *India* ... 68 H7
Khulna, *Bangla.* ... 67 H16
Khulna □, *Bangla.* ... 67 H16
Khulo, *Georgia* ... 49 K6
Khumago, *Botswana* ... 88 C3
Khūnsorkh, *Iran* ... 71 E8
Khunti, *India* ... 69 H11
Khūr, *Iran* ... 71 C8
Khurai, *India* ... 68 G8
Khurays, *Si. Arabia* ... 71 E6
Khureit, *Sudan* ... 81 E2
Khurīyā Murīyā, Jazā 'ir, *Oman* ... 74 D6
Khurja, *India* ... 68 E7
Khūrmāl, *Iraq* ... 70 C5
Khurr, Wādī al, *Iraq* ... 70 C4
Khūsf, *Iran* ... 71 C8
Khush, *Afghan.* ... 66 C3
Khushab, *Pakistan* ... 68 C5
Khust, *Ukraine* ... 47 H2
Khuzdar, *Pakistan* ... 68 F2
Khūzestān □, *Iran* ... 71 D6
Khvāf, *Iran* ... 71 C9
Khvājeh, *Iran* ... 70 B5
Khvalynsk, *Russia* ... 48 D9
Khvānsār, *Iran* ... 71 D7
Khvatovka, *Russia* ... 48 D8
Khvor, *Iran* ... 71 C7
Khvorgū, *Iran* ... 71 E8
Khvormūj, *Iran* ... 71 D6
Khvoy, *Iran* ... 70 B5
Khvoynaya, *Russia* ... 46 C8
Khyber Pass, *Afghan.* ... 68 B4
Kiabukwa, *Dem. Rep. of the Congo* ... 87 D1
Kiama, *Australia* ... 95 E5
Kiamba, *Phil.* ... 61 H6
Kiambi, *Dem. Rep. of the Congo* ... 86 D2
Kiambu, *Kenya* ... 86 C4
Kiangara, *Madag.* ... 89 B8
Kiangsi = Jiangxi □, *China* ... 59 D11
Kiangsu = Jiangsu □, *China* ... 57 H11
Kiáton, *Greece* ... 38 C4
Kibæk, *Denmark* ... 11 H2
Kibanga Port, *Uganda* ... 86 B3
Kibara, *Tanzania* ... 86 C3
Kibare, Mts., *Dem. Rep. of the Congo* ... 86 D2
Kibombo, *Dem. Rep. of the Congo* ... 86 C2
Kibondo, *Tanzania* ... 86 C3
Kibre Mengist, *Ethiopia* ... 81 F4
Kibumbu, *Burundi* ... 86 C2
Kibungo, *Rwanda* ... 86 C3
Kibuye, *Burundi* ... 86 C2
Kibuye, *Rwanda* ... 86 C2
Kibwesa, *Tanzania* ... 86 D2
Kibwezi, *Kenya* ... 86 C4
Kicasalih, *Turkey* ... 41 E10
Kičevo, *Macedonia* ... 40 E4
Kichha, *India* ... 69 E8
Kichha →, *India* ... 69 E8
Kicking Horse Pass, *Canada* ... 104 C5
Kidal, *Mali* ... 83 B5
Kidderminster, *U.K.* ... 13 E5
Kidete, *Tanzania* ... 86 D4
Kidira, *Senegal* ... 82 C2
Kidnappers, C., *N.Z.* ... 91 H6
Kidsgrove, *U.K.* ... 12 D5
Kidston, *Australia* ... 94 B3
Kidugallo, *Tanzania* ... 86 D4
Kiel, *Germany* ... 24 A6
Kiel Canal = Nord-Ostsee-Kanal, *Germany* ... 24 A5
Kielce, *Poland* ... 45 H7
Kielder Water, *U.K.* ... 12 B5
Kieler Bucht, *Germany* ... 24 A6
Kiembara, *Burkina Faso* ... 82 C4
Kien Binh, *Vietnam* ... 65 H5
Kien Tan, *Vietnam* ... 65 G5
Kienge, *Dem. Rep. of the Congo* ... 87 E2
Kiessé, *Niger* ... 83 C5
Kiev = Kyyiv, *Ukraine* ... 47 G6
Kifaya, *Guinea* ... 82 C2
Kiffa, *Mauritania* ... 82 B2
Kifisiá, *Greece* ... 38 C5
Kifissós →, *Greece* ... 38 C5
Kifrī, *Iraq* ... 70 C5
Kigali, *Rwanda* ... 86 C3
Kigarama, *Tanzania* ... 86 C3

Kigelle, *Sudan* ... 81 F3
Kigoma □, *Tanzania* ... 86 D3
Kigoma-Ujiji, *Tanzania* ... 86 C2
Kigomasha, Ras, *Tanzania* ... 86 C4
Kığzı, *Turkey* ... 70 B4
Kihei, *U.S.A.* ... 106 H16
Kihnu, *Estonia* ... 9 G21
Kii-Sanchi, *Japan* ... 55 G8
Kii-Suidō, *Japan* ... 55 H7
Kikaiga-Shima, *Japan* ... 55 K4
Kikinda, *Serbia, Yug.* ... 42 E5
Kikládhes, *Greece* ... 38 E6
Kikládhes □, *Greece* ... 38 D6
Kikwit, *Dem. Rep. of the Congo* ... 84 E3
Kil, *Sweden* ... 10 E7
Kilafors, *Sweden* ... 10 C10
Kilar, *India* ... 68 C7
Kilauea, *U.S.A.* ... 106 J14
Kilauea Crater, *U.S.A.* ... 106 J17
Kilbrannan Sd., *U.K.* ... 14 F3
Kilchu, *N. Korea* ... 57 D15
Kilcoy, *Australia* ... 95 D5
Kildare, *Ireland* ... 15 C5
Kildare □, *Ireland* ... 15 C5
Kileikli, *Sudan* ... 81 E2
Kilfinnane, *Ireland* ... 15 D3
Kilgore, *U.S.A.* ... 113 J7
Kilibo, *Benin* ... 83 D5
Kilifi, *Kenya* ... 86 C4
Kilimanjaro, *Tanzania* ... 86 C4
Kilimanjaro □, *Tanzania* ... 86 C4
Kilimli, *Turkey* ... 72 B4
Kilindini, *Kenya* ... 86 C4
Kilis, *Turkey* ... 70 B3
Kiliya, *Ukraine* ... 47 K5
Kilkee, *Ireland* ... 15 D2
Kilkeel, *U.K.* ... 15 B5
Kilkenny, *Ireland* ... 15 D4
Kilkenny □, *Ireland* ... 15 D4
Kilkieran B., *Ireland* ... 15 C2
Kilkís, *Greece* ... 40 F6
Kilkís □, *Greece* ... 40 E6
Killala, *Ireland* ... 15 B2
Killala B., *Ireland* ... 15 B2
Killaloe, *Ireland* ... 15 D3
Killaloe Sta., *Canada* ... 110 A7
Killarney, *Australia* ... 95 D5
Killarney, *Canada* ... 105 D9
Killarney, *Ireland* ... 15 D2
Killary Harbour, *Ireland* ... 15 C2
Killdeer, *Canada* ... 112 B3
Killeberg, *Sweden* ... 11 H8
Killeen, *U.S.A.* ... 113 K6
Killin, *U.K.* ... 14 E4
Killíni, *Ilía, Greece* ... 38 D3
Killíni, *Korinthía, Greece* ... 38 D4
Killorglin, *Ireland* ... 15 D2
Killybegs, *Ireland* ... 15 B3
Kilmarnock, *U.K.* ... 14 F4
Kilmez, *Russia* ... 48 B10
Kilmez →, *Russia* ... 48 B10
Kilmore, *Australia* ... 95 F3
Kilondo, *Tanzania* ... 87 D3
Kilosa, *Tanzania* ... 86 D4
Kilrush, *Ireland* ... 15 D2
Kilwa Kisiwani, *Tanzania* ... 87 D4
Kilwa Kivinje, *Tanzania* ... 87 D4
Kilwa Masoko, *Tanzania* ... 87 D4
Kilwinning, *U.K.* ... 14 F4
Kim, *U.S.A.* ... 113 G3
Kim →, *Cameroon* ... 83 D7
Kimaam, *Indonesia* ... 63 F9
Kimamba, *Tanzania* ... 86 D4
Kimba, *Australia* ... 95 E2
Kimball, *Nebr., U.S.A.* ... 112 E3
Kimball, *S. Dak., U.S.A.* ... 112 D5
Kimberley, *Australia* ... 92 C4
Kimberley, *Canada* ... 104 D5
Kimberley, *S. Africa* ... 88 D3
Kimberly, *U.S.A.* ... 114 E6
Kimch'aek, *N. Korea* ... 57 D15
Kimch'ŏn, *S. Korea* ... 57 F15
Kími, *Greece* ... 38 C6
Kimje, *S. Korea* ... 57 G14
Kimmirut, *Canada* ... 101 B13
Kímolos, *Greece* ... 38 E6
Kimovsk, *Moskva, Russia* ... 46 E9
Kimovsk, *Tula, Russia* ... 46 E10
Kimparana, *Mali* ... 82 C4
Kimpese, *Dem. Rep. of the Congo* ... 84 F2
Kimry, *Russia* ... 46 D9
Kimstad, *Sweden* ... 11 F9
Kinabalu, Gunong, *Malaysia* ... 62 C5
Kinaskan L., *Canada* ... 104 B2
Kinbasket L., *Canada* ... 104 C5
Kincardine, *Canada* ... 102 D3
Kincolith, *Canada* ... 104 B3
Kinda, *Dem. Rep. of the Congo* ... 87 D2
Kindberg, *Austria* ... 26 D8
Kinde, *U.S.A.* ... 110 C2
Kinder Scout, *U.K.* ... 12 D6
Kindersley, *Canada* ... 105 C7
Kindia, *Guinea* ... 82 D2
Kindu, *Dem. Rep. of the Congo* ... 86 C2
Kinel, *Russia* ... 48 D10
Kineshma, *Russia* ... 48 B6
Kinesi, *Tanzania* ... 86 C3
King, L., *Australia* ... 93 F2
King, Mt., *Australia* ... 94 D4
King City, *U.S.A.* ... 116 J5
King Cr. →, *Australia* ... 94 C2
King Edward →, *Australia* ... 92 B4
King Frederick VI Land = Kong Frederik VI Kyst, *Greenland* ... 4 C5
King George B., *Falk. Is.* ... 128 G4

King George I., *Antarctica* ... 5 C18
King George Is., *Canada* ... 101 C11
King I. = Kadan Kyun, *Burma* ... 64 F2
King I., *Australia* ... 94 F3
King I., *Canada* ... 104 C3
King Leopold Ranges, *Australia* ... 92 C4
King of Prussia, *U.S.A.* ... 111 F9
King Sd., *U.S.A.* ... 92 C3
King William I., *Canada* ... 100 B10
King William's Town, *S. Africa* ... 88 E4
Kingaroy, *Australia* ... 95 D5
Kingfisher, *U.S.A.* ... 113 H6
Kingirbān, *Iraq* ... 70 C5
Kingisepp = Kuressaare, *Estonia* ... 9 G20
Kingisepp, *Russia* ... 46 C5
Kingman, *Ariz., U.S.A.* ... 117 K12
Kingman, *Kans., U.S.A.* ... 113 G5
Kingoonya, *Australia* ... 95 E2
Kingri, *Pakistan* ... 68 D3
Kings →, *U.S.A.* ... 116 J7
Kings Canyon National Park, *U.S.A.* ... 116 J8
King's Lynn, *U.K.* ... 12 E8
Kings Mountain, *U.S.A.* ... 109 H5
Kings Park, *U.S.A.* ... 111 F11
King's Peak, *U.S.A.* ... 114 F8
Kingsbridge, *U.K.* ... 13 G4
Kingsburg, *U.S.A.* ... 116 J7
Kingscote, *Australia* ... 95 F2
Kingscourt, *Ireland* ... 15 C5
Kingsford, *U.S.A.* ... 108 C1
Kingsland, *U.S.A.* ... 109 K5
Kingsley, *U.S.A.* ... 112 D7
Kingsport, *U.S.A.* ... 109 G4
Kingston, *Canada* ... 102 D4
Kingston, *Jamaica* ... 120 C4
Kingston, *N.Z.* ... 91 L2
Kingston, *N.H., U.S.A.* ... 111 D13
Kingston, *N.Y., U.S.A.* ... 111 E11
Kingston, *Pa., U.S.A.* ... 111 E9
Kingston, *R.I., U.S.A.* ... 111 E13
Kingston Pk., *U.S.A.* ... 117 K11
Kingston South East, *Australia* ... 95 F2
Kingston upon Hull, *U.K.* ... 12 D7
Kingston upon Hull □, *U.K.* ... 12 D7
Kingston-upon-Thames, *U.K.* ... 13 F7
Kingstree, *U.S.A.* ... 109 J6
Kingsville, *Canada* ... 102 D3
Kingsville, *U.S.A.* ... 113 M6
Kingussie, *U.K.* ... 14 D4
Kingwood, *U.S.A.* ... 113 K7
Kınık, *Antalya, Turkey* ... 39 E11
Kınık, *İzmir, Turkey* ... 39 B9
Kinistino, *Canada* ... 105 C7
Kinkala, *Congo* ... 84 E2
Kinki □, *Japan* ... 55 H8
Kinleith, *N.Z.* ... 91 H5
Kinmount, *Canada* ... 110 B6
Kinna, *Sweden* ... 11 G6
Kinnairds Hd., *U.K.* ... 14 D6
Kinnared, *Sweden* ... 11 G7
Kinnarodden, *Norway* ... 6 A11
Kinnarp, *Sweden* ... 11 F7
Kinneviken, *Sweden* ... 11 F7
Kino, *Mexico* ... 118 B2
Kinoje →, *Canada* ... 102 B3
Kinomoto, *Japan* ... 55 G8
Kinoni, *Uganda* ... 86 C3
Kinoosao, *Canada* ... 105 B8
Kinross, *U.K.* ... 14 E5
Kinsale, *Ireland* ... 15 E3
Kinsale, Old Hd. of, *Ireland* ... 15 E3
Kinsha = Chang Jiang →, *China* ... 59 B13
Kinshasa, *Dem. Rep. of the Congo* ... 84 E3
Kinsley, *U.S.A.* ... 113 G5
Kinsman, *U.S.A.* ... 110 E4
Kinston, *U.S.A.* ... 109 H7
Kintampo, *Ghana* ... 83 D4
Kintore Ra., *Australia* ... 92 D4
Kintyre, *Australia* ... 14 F3
Kintyre, Mull of, *U.K.* ... 14 F3
Kinushseo →, *Canada* ... 102 A3
Kinuso, *Canada* ... 104 B5
Kinyangiri, *Tanzania* ... 86 C3
Kinyeti, *Sudan* ... 81 G3
Kinzig →, *Germany* ... 25 G3
Kinzua, *U.S.A.* ... 110 E6
Kinzua Dam, *U.S.A.* ... 110 E6
Kióni, *Greece* ... 38 C2
Kiosk, *Canada* ... 102 C4
Kiowa, *Kans., U.S.A.* ... 113 G5
Kiowa, *Okla., U.S.A.* ... 113 H7
Kipahigan L., *Canada* ... 105 B8
Kipanga, *Tanzania* ... 86 D4
Kiparissía, *Greece* ... 38 D3
Kiparissiakós Kólpos, *Greece* ... 38 D3
Kipawa, L., *Canada* ... 102 C4
Kipembawe, *Tanzania* ... 86 D3
Kipengere Ra., *Tanzania* ... 87 D3
Kipili, *Tanzania* ... 86 D3
Kipini, *Kenya* ... 86 C5
Kipling, *Canada* ... 105 C8
Kippure, *Ireland* ... 15 C5
Kipushi, *Dem. Rep. of the Congo* ... 87 E2
Kirane, *Mali* ... 82 B2
Kiranomena, *Madag.* ... 89 B8
Kiraz, *Turkey* ... 39 C10
Kirazlı, *Turkey* ... 41 F10
Kirchhain, *Germany* ... 24 E4
Kirchheim, *Germany* ... 25 G5
Kirchheimbolanden, *Germany* ... 25 F3

Kirchschlag, Austria 27 D9
Kireç, Turkey 39 B10
Kirensk, Russia 51 D11
Kirghizia = Kyrgyzstan ■, Asia 50 E8
Kirghizstan = Kyrgyzstan ■, Asia 50 E8
Kiribati ■, Pac. Oc. 96 H10
Kırıkhan, Turkey 72 D7
Kırıkkale, Turkey 72 C5
Kirillov, Russia 46 C10
Kirin = Jilin, China 57 C14
Kirishi, Russia 46 C7
Kiritimati, Kiribati 97 G12
Kırka, Turkey 39 B12
Kirkağaç, Turkey 39 B9
Kirkby, U.K. 12 D5
Kirkby Lonsdale, U.K. 12 C5
Kirkcaldy, U.K. 14 E5
Kirkcudbright, U.K. 14 G4
Kirkee, India 66 K8
Kirkenes, Norway 8 B23
Kirkfield, Canada 110 B6
Kirkjubæjarklaustur, Iceland 8 E4
Kirkkonummi, Finland 9 F21
Kirkland, Canada 102 C3
Kirkland Lake, Canada 102 C3
Kırklareli, Turkey 41 E11
Kırklareli □, Turkey 41 E11
Kirksville, U.S.A. 112 E8
Kirkük, Iraq 70 C5
Kirkwall, U.K. 14 C6
Kirkwood, S. Africa 88 E4
Kirn, Germany 25 F3
Kirov, Kaluga, Russia 46 E8
Kirov, Kirov, Russia 50 D5
Kirovabad = Gäncä, Azerbaijan 49 K8
Kirovakan = Vanadzor, Armenia 49 K7
Kirovograd = Kirovohrad, Ukraine 47 H7
Kirovohrad, Ukraine 47 H7
Kirovsk = Babadayhan, Turkmenistan 50 F7
Kirovskiy, Astrakhan, Russia 49 H9
Kirovskiy, Kamchatka, Russia 51 D16
Kirovskiy, Primorsk, Russia 54 B6
Kirriemuir, U.K. 14 E5
Kirsanov, Russia 48 D6
Kırşehir, Turkey 70 B2
Kirtachi, Niger 83 C5
Kirthar Range, Pakistan 68 F2
Kirtland, U.S.A. 115 H9
Kiruna, Sweden 8 C19
Kirundu, Dem. Rep. of the Congo 86 C2
Kirya, Russia 48 C8
Kiryū, Japan 55 F9
Kisa, Sweden 11 G9
Kisaga, Tanzania 86 C3
Kisalaya, Nic. 120 D3
Kisalföld, Hungary 42 C2
Kisámou, Kólpos, Greece 36 D5
Kisanga, Dem. Rep. of the Congo 86 B2
Kisangani, Dem. Rep. of the Congo 86 B2
Kisar, Indonesia 63 F7
Kisarawe, Tanzania 86 D4
Kisarazu, Japan 55 G9
Kisbér, Hungary 42 C3
Kishanganga →, Pakistan 69 B5
Kishanganj, India 69 F13
Kishangarh, Raj., India 68 F6
Kishangarh, Raj., India 68 F4
Kishi, Nigeria 83 D5
Kishinev = Chişinău, Moldova 43 C13
Kishiwada, Japan 55 G7
Kishtwar, India 69 C6
Kisielice, Poland 44 E6
Kisii, Kenya 86 C3
Kisiju, Tanzania 86 D4
Kisir, Turkey 73 B10
Kisizi, Uganda 86 C2
Kiskomárom = Zalakomár, Hungary 42 C2
Kiskörei-víztároló, Hungary 42 C5
Kiskőrös, Hungary 42 D4
Kiskundorozsma, Hungary 42 D5
Kiskunfélegyháza, Hungary 42 D4
Kiskunhalas, Hungary 42 D4
Kiskunmajsa, Hungary 42 D4
Kislovodsk, Russia 49 J6
Kismayu = Chisimaio, Somali Rep. 77 G8
Kiso-Gawa →, Japan 55 G8
Kiso-Sammyaku, Japan 55 G8
Kisofukushima, Japan 55 G8
Kisoro, Uganda 86 C2
Kissidougou, Guinea 82 D2
Kissimmee, U.S.A. 109 L5
Kissimmee →, U.S.A. 109 M5
Kississing L., Canada 105 B8
Kissónerga, Cyprus 36 E11
Kissu, J., Sudan 80 C2
Kistanje, Croatia 29 E12
Kisújszállás, Hungary 42 C5
Kisumu, Kenya 86 C3
Kisvárda, Hungary 42 B7
Kiswani, Tanzania 86 C4
Kiswere, Tanzania 87 D4
Kit Carson, U.S.A. 112 F3
Kita, Mali 82 C3
Kitaibaraki, Japan 55 F10
Kitakami, Japan 54 E10
Kitakami-Gawa →, Japan 54 E10
Kitakami-Sammyaku, Japan 54 E10
Kitakata, Japan 54 F9
Kitakyūshū, Japan 55 H5

Kitale, Kenya 86 B4
Kitami, Japan 54 C11
Kitami-Sammyaku, Japan 54 B11
Kitangiri, L., Tanzania 86 C3
Kitaya, Tanzania 87 E5
Kitchener, Canada 102 D3
Kitee, Finland 46 A6
Kitega = Gitega, Burundi 86 C2
Kitengo, Dem. Rep. of the Congo 86 D1
Kitgum, Uganda 86 B3
Kíthira, Greece 38 E5
Kíthnos, Greece 38 D6
Kiti, Cyprus 36 E12
Kiti, C., Cyprus 36 E12
Kitimat, Canada 104 C3
Kitinen →, Finland 8 C22
Kitiyab, Sudan 81 D3
Kítros, Greece 40 F6
Kitsuki, Japan 55 H5
Kittakittaooloo, L., Australia 95 D2
Kittanning, U.S.A. 110 F5
Kittatinny Mts., U.S.A. 111 F10
Kittery, U.S.A. 109 D10
Kittilä, Finland 8 C21
Kitui, Kenya 86 C4
Kitwanga, Canada 104 B3
Kitwe, Zambia 87 E2
Kitzbühel, Austria 26 D5
Kitzbüheler Alpen, Austria 26 D5
Kitzingen, Germany 25 F6
Kivarli, India 68 G5
Kivertsi, Ukraine 47 G3
Kividhes, Cyprus 36 E11
Kivik, Sweden 11 J8
Kivotós, Greece 40 F5
Kivu, L., Dem. Rep. of the Congo 86 C2
Kiyev = Kyyiv, Ukraine 47 G6
Kiyevskoye = Kyyivske Vdskh., Ukraine 47 G6
Kıyıköy, Turkey 41 E12
Kizil Adalar, Turkey 41 F13
Kizil Irmak →, Turkey 72 B6
Kizil Jilga, India 69 B8
Kizil Yurt, Russia 49 J8
Kızılcabölük, Turkey 39 D11
Kızılcadağ, Turkey 39 D11
Kızılcahamam, Turkey 72 B5
Kızılhisar, Turkey 72 D3
Kızılırmak, Turkey 72 B5
Kızılkaya, Turkey 39 D12
Kızılören, Turkey 39 C12
Kızıltepe, Turkey 70 B4
Kizimkazi, Tanzania 86 D4
Kizlyar, Russia 49 J8
Kizyl-Arvat = Gyzylarbat, Turkmenistan 50 F6
Kjellerup, Denmark 11 H3
Kjölur, Iceland 8 D4
Kladanj, Bos.-H. 42 F3
Kladnica, Serbia, Yug. 40 C4
Kladno, Czech Rep. 26 A7
Kladovo, Serbia, Yug. 40 B6
Klaeng, Thailand 64 F3
Klagenfurt, Austria 26 E7
Klaipėda, Lithuania 9 J19
Klaipėda □, Lithuania 44 C8
Klaksvík, Faroe Is. 8 E9
Klamath →, U.S.A. 114 F1
Klamath Falls, U.S.A. 114 E3
Klamath Mts., U.S.A. 114 F2
Klamono, Indonesia 63 E8
Klanjec, Croatia 29 B12
Klappan →, Canada 104 B3
Klarälven →, Sweden 10 E7
Klässbol, Sweden 10 E6
Klatovy, Czech Rep. 26 B6
Klawer, S. Africa 88 E2
Klazienaveen, Neths. 17 B6
Klé, Mali 82 C3
Klecko, Poland 45 F4
Kleczew, Poland 45 F5
Kleena Kleene, Canada 104 C4
Klein-Karas, Namibia 88 D2
Klekovača, Bos.-H. 29 D13
Klenoec, Macedonia 40 E4
Klenovec, Slovak Rep. 27 C12
Klerksdorp, S. Africa 88 D4
Kleszczele, Poland 45 F10
Kletnya, Russia 46 F7
Kletsk = Klyetsk, Belarus 47 F4
Kletskiy, Russia 49 F6
Kleve, Germany 24 D2
Klickitat, U.S.A. 114 D3
Klickitat →, U.S.A. 116 E5
Klidhes, Cyprus 36 D13
Klimovichi, Belarus 46 F6
Klin, Russia 46 D9
Klina, Kosovo, Yug. 40 D4
Klinaklini →, Canada 104 C3
Klintehamn, Sweden 11 G12
Klintsy, Russia 47 F7
Klip →, S. Africa 89 D4
Klipdale, S. Africa 88 E2
Klipplaat, S. Africa 88 E4
Klisura, Bulgaria 41 D8
Kljajićevo, Serbia, Yug. 42 E4
Ključ, Bos.-H. 29 D13
Kłobuck, Poland 45 H5
Klockestrand, Sweden 10 B11
Kłodawa, Poland 45 F5
Kłodzko, Poland 45 H3
Klosi, Albania 40 E4
Klosterneuburg, Austria 27 C9
Klosters, Switz. 25 J5
Klötze, Germany 24 C7
Klouto, Togo 83 D5
Kluane L., Canada 100 E6

Kluane Nat. Park, Canada 104 A1
Kluczbork, Poland 45 H5
Klukwan, U.S.A. 104 B1
Klyetsk, Belarus 47 F4
Klyuchevskaya, Gora, Russia 51 D17
Knäred, Sweden 11 H7
Knaresborough, U.K. 12 C6
Knee L., Man., Canada 102 A1
Knee L., Sask., Canada 105 B7
Knezha, Bulgaria 41 C8
Knić, Serbia, Yug. 40 C4
Knight Inlet, Canada 104 C3
Knighton, U.K. 13 E4
Knights Ferry, U.S.A. 116 H6
Knights Landing, U.S.A. 116 G5
Knin, Croatia 29 D13
Knislinge, Sweden 11 H8
Knittelfeld, Austria 26 D7
Knivsta, Sweden 10 E11
Knjaževac, Serbia, Yug. 40 C6
Knob, C., Australia 93 F2
Knock, Ireland 15 C3
Knockmealdown Mts., Ireland 15 D4
Knokke-Heist, Belgium 17 C3
Knossós, Greece 36 D7
Knowlton, Canada 111 A12
Knox, U.S.A. 108 E2
Knox Coast, Antarctica 5 C8
Knoxville, Iowa, U.S.A. 112 E8
Knoxville, Tenn., U.S.A. 109 H4
Knysna, S. Africa 88 E3
Knyszyn, Poland 44 E9
Ko Ka, Thailand 64 C2
Koartac = Quaqtaq, Canada 101 B13
Koba, Indonesia 63 F8
Kobarid, Slovenia 29 B10
Kobayashi, Japan 55 J5
Kobdo = Hovd, Mongolia 60 B4
Kōbe, Japan 55 G7
Kobelyaky, Ukraine 47 H8
København, Denmark 11 J6
København Amtskommune □, Denmark 11 J6
Kobenni, Mauritania 82 B3
Kōbi-Sho, Japan 55 M1
Koblenz, Germany 25 E3
Kobo, Ethiopia 81 E4
Kobryn, Belarus 47 F3
Kobuleti, Georgia 49 K5
Kobylin, Poland 45 G4
Kobyłka, Poland 45 F8
Kobylkino, Russia 48 C6
Kocabaş, Turkey 39 D11
Kocaeli, Turkey 41 F13
Kocaeli □, Turkey 41 F13
Kočane, Serbia, Yug. 40 C5
Kočani, Macedonia 40 E6
Koçarlı, Turkey 39 D9
Koceljevo, Serbia, Yug. 40 B3
Kočevje, Slovenia 29 C11
Koch Bihar, India 67 F16
Kochang, S. Korea 57 G14
Kochas, India 69 G10
Kocher →, Germany 25 F5
Kōchi, Japan 55 H6
Kōchi □, Japan 55 H6
Kochiu = Gejiu, China 58 F4
Kock, Poland 45 G9
Kodarma, India 69 G11
Kode, Sweden 11 G5
Kodiak, U.S.A. 100 C4
Kodiak I., U.S.A. 100 C4
Kodinar, India 68 J4
Kodok, Sudan 81 F3
Kodori →, Georgia 49 J5
Koedoesberge, S. Africa 88 E3
Koes, Namibia 88 D2
Kofçaz, Turkey 41 E11
Koffiefontein, S. Africa 88 D4
Kofiau, Indonesia 63 E7
Köflach, Austria 26 D8
Koforidua, Ghana 83 D4
Kōfu, Japan 55 G9
Koga, Japan 55 F9
Kogaluk →, Canada 103 A7
Køge, Denmark 11 J6
Køge Bugt, Denmark 11 J6
Kogi □, Nigeria 83 D6
Kogin Baba, Nigeria 83 D7
Koh-i-Bābā, Afghan. 66 B5
Koh-i-Khurd, Afghan. 66 C1
Koh-i-Maran, Pakistan 68 E2
Kohat, Pakistan 68 C4
Kohima, India 67 G19
Kohkīlūyeh va Būyer Aḥmadi □, Iran 71 D6
Kohler Ra., Antarctica 5 D15
Kohlu, Pakistan 68 E3
Kohtla-Järve, Estonia 9 G22
Koillismaa, Finland 8 D23
Koin-dong, N. Korea 57 D14
Koinare, Bulgaria 41 C8
Koindu, S. Leone 82 D2
Kojetín, Czech Rep. 27 B10
Kojŏ, N. Korea 57 E14
Kojonup, Australia 93 F2
Kojūr, Iran 71 B6
Koka, Sudan 80 C3
Kokand = Qŭqon, Uzbekistan 50 E8
Kokas, Indonesia 63 E8
Kokava, Slovak Rep. 27 C12
Kokchetav = Kökshetaū, Kazakstan 50 D7
Kokemäenjoki →, Finland 9 F19
Kokhma, Russia 48 B5
Koki, Senegal 82 B1

Kokkola, Finland 8 E20
Koko, Nigeria 83 C5
Koko Kyunzu, Burma 67 M18
Kokolopozo, Ivory C. 82 D3
Kokomo, U.S.A. 108 E2
Kokoro, Niger 83 C5
Koksan, N. Korea 57 E14
Kökshetaū, Kazakstan 50 D7
Koksoak →, Canada 101 C13
Kokstad, S. Africa 89 E4
Kokubu, Japan 55 J5
Kola, Indonesia 63 F8
Kola, Russia 50 C4
Kola Pen. = Kolskiy Poluostrov →, Russia 50 C4
Kolachi →, Pakistan 68 F2
Kolahoi, India 69 B6
Kolahun, Liberia 82 D2
Kolaka, Indonesia 63 E6
Kolar, India 66 N11
Kolar Gold Fields, India 66 N11
Kolaras, India 68 G6
Kolari, Finland 8 C20
Kolárovo, Slovak Rep. 27 D10
Kolašin, Montenegro, Yug. 40 D3
Kolayat, India 66 F8
Kolbäck, Sweden 10 E10
Kolbäcksån →, Sweden 10 E10
Kolbermoor, Germany 25 H8
Kolbuszowa, Poland 45 H8
Kolchugino = Leninsk-Kuznetskiy, Russia 50 D9
Kolchugino, Russia 46 D10
Kolda, Senegal 82 C2
Koldegi, Sudan 81 E3
Kolding, Denmark 11 J3
Kolepom = Dolak, Pulau, Indonesia 63 F9
Kolguyev, Ostrov, Russia 50 C5
Kolhapur, India 66 L9
Kolia, Ivory C. 82 D3
Kolín, Czech Rep. 26 A8
Kolind, Denmark 11 H4
Kolkas rags, Latvia 9 H20
Kölleda, Germany 24 D7
Kollum, Neths. 17 A6
Kolmanskop, Namibia 88 D2
Köln, Germany 24 E2
Kolno, Poland 45 E8
Koło, Poland 45 F5
Kołobrzeg, Poland 44 D2
Kolokani, Mali 82 C3
Koloko, Burkina Faso 82 C3
Kololo, Ethiopia 81 F5
Kolomna, Russia 46 E10
Kolomyya, Ukraine 47 H3
Kolondiéba, Mali 82 C3
Kolonodale, Indonesia 63 E6
Kolonowskie, Poland 45 H5
Kolosib, India 67 G18
Kolpashevo, Russia 50 D9
Kolpino, Russia 46 C6
Kolpny, Russia 47 F9
Kolskiy Poluostrov, Russia 50 C4
Kolsva, Sweden 10 E9
Kolubara →, Serbia, Yug. 40 B4
Koluszki, Poland 45 G6
Kolwezi, Dem. Rep. of the Congo 87 E2
Kolyma →, Russia 51 C17
Kolymskoye Nagorye, Russia 51 C16
Kôm Hamâda, Egypt 80 H7
Kôm Ombo, Egypt 80 C3
Komadugu Gana →, Nigeria 83 C7
Komandorskiye Is. = Komandorskiye Ostrova, Russia 51 D17
Komandorskiye Ostrova, Russia 51 D17
Komárno, Slovak Rep. 27 D10
Komárom, Hungary 42 C3
Komárom-Esztergom □, Hungary 42 C3
Komatipoort, S. Africa 89 D5
Komatou Yialou, Cyprus 36 D13
Komatsu, Japan 55 F8
Komatsujima, Japan 55 H7
Kombissiri, Burkina Faso 83 C4
Kombori, Burkina Faso 82 C4
Kombóti, Greece 38 B3
Komen, Slovenia 29 C10
Komenda, Ghana 83 D4
Komi □, Russia 50 C6
Komiža, Croatia 29 E13
Komló, Hungary 42 D3
Kommunarsk = Alchevsk, Ukraine 47 H10
Kommunizma, Pik, Tajikistan 50 F8
Komodo, Indonesia 63 F5
Komoé, Ivory C. 82 D4
Komoran, Pulau, Indonesia 63 F9
Komoro, Japan 55 F9
Komotini, Greece 41 E9
Komovi, Montenegro, Yug. 40 D3
Kompasberg, S. Africa 88 E3
Kompong Bang, Cambodia 65 F5
Kompong Cham, Cambodia 65 F5
Kompong Chhnang = Kampang Chhnang, Cambodia 65 F5
Kompong Chikreng, Cambodia 64 F5
Kompong Kleang, Cambodia 64 F5
Kompong Luong, Cambodia 65 G5
Kompong Pranak, Cambodia 64 F5
Kompong Som = Kampong Saom, Cambodia 65 G4
Kompong Som, Chhung = Kampong Saom, Chaak, Cambodia 65 G4
Kompong Speu, Cambodia 65 G5

Kompong Sralao, Cambodia 64 E5
Kompong Thom, Cambodia 64 F5
Kompong Trabeck, Cambodia 64 F5
Kompong Trabeck, Cambodia 65 G5
Kompong Trach, Cambodia 65 G5
Kompong Tralach, Cambodia 65 G5
Komrat = Comrat, Moldova 43 D13
Komsberg, S. Africa 88 E3
Komsomolets, Ostrov, Russia 51 A10
Komsomolsk, Amur, Russia 51 D14
Komsomolsk, Ivanovo, Russia 46 D11
Komsomolskiy, Russia 48 C7
Kömür Burnu, Turkey 39 C8
Kon Tum, Vietnam 64 E7
Kon Tum, Plateau du, Vietnam 64 E7
Kona, Mali 82 C4
Konakovo, Russia 46 D9
Konarhā □, Afghan. 66 B7
Konārī, Iran 71 D6
Konch, India 69 G8
Konde, Tanzania 86 C4
Kondiá, Greece 39 B7
Kondinin, Australia 93 F2
Kondoa, Tanzania 86 C4
Kondókali, Greece 36 A3
Kondopaga, Russia 46 A8
Kondratyevo, Russia 51 D10
Kondrovo, Russia 46 E8
Konduga, Nigeria 83 C7
Köneürgench, Turkmenistan 50 E6
Konevo, Russia 46 A10
Kong = Khong →, Cambodia 64 F5
Kong, Ivory C. 82 D4
Kong, Koh, Cambodia 65 G4
Kong Christian IX Land, Greenland 4 C6
Kong Christian X Land, Greenland 4 B6
Kong Frederik IX Land, Greenland 4 C5
Kong Frederik VI Kyst, Greenland 4 C5
Kong Frederik VIII Land, Greenland 4 B6
Kong Oscar Fjord, Greenland 4 B6
Kongeå →, Denmark 11 J2
Kongerslev, Denmark 11 H4
Kongju, S. Korea 57 F20
Konglu, Burma 67 F20
Kongola, Namibia 88 B3
Kongolo, Kasai-Or., Dem. Rep. of the Congo 86 D1
Kongolo, Katanga, Dem. Rep. of the Congo 86 D2
Kongor, Sudan 81 F3
Kongoussi, Burkina Faso 83 C4
Kongsberg, Norway 9 G13
Kongsvinger, Norway 9 F15
Kongwa, Tanzania 86 D4
Koni, Dem. Rep. of the Congo 87 E2
Koni, Mts., Dem. Rep. of the Congo 87 E2
Koniakari, Mali 82 C2
Koniecpol, Poland 45 H6
Königs Wusterhausen, Germany 24 C9
Königsberg = Kaliningrad, Russia 9 J19
Königsbrunn, Germany 25 G6
Königslutter, Germany 24 C6
Konin, Poland 45 F5
Konispol, Albania 40 G4
Kónitsa, Greece 38 A2
Konjic, Bos.-H. 42 G2
Konkiep, Namibia 88 D2
Konkouré →, Guinea 82 D2
Könnern, Germany 24 D7
Kono, S. Leone 82 D2
Konongo, Ghana 83 D4
Konosha, Russia 46 B11
Kōnosu, Japan 55 F9
Konotop, Ukraine 47 G7
Konsankoro, Guinea 82 D3
Końskie, Poland 45 G7
Konstancin-Jeziorna, Poland 45 F8
Konstantinovka = Kostyantynivka, Ukraine 47 H9
Konstantinovsk, Russia 49 G5
Konstantynów Łódzki, Poland 45 G6
Konstanz, Germany 25 H5
Kont, Iran 71 E9
Kontagora, Nigeria 83 C6
Kontcha, Cameroon 83 D7
Konya, Turkey 70 B2
Konya Ovası, Turkey 72 C5
Konz, Germany 25 F2
Konza, Kenya 86 C4
Koocanusa, L., Canada 114 B6
Kookynie, Australia 93 E3
Koolyanobbing, Australia 93 F2
Koonibba, Australia 95 E1
Koorawatha, Australia 95 E4
Koorda, Australia 93 F2
Kooskia, U.S.A. 114 C6
Kootenay L., Canada 104 D5
Kootenay Nat. Park, Canada 104 C5
Kootjieskolk, S. Africa 88 E3
Kopanova, Russia 49 G8
Kopaonik, Yugoslavia 40 C4
Kópavogur, Iceland 8 D3
Koper, Slovenia 29 C10
Kopervik, Norway 9 G11

Kopet Dagh, *Asia* 71 B8
Kopi, *Australia* 95 E2
Köping, *Sweden* 10 E10
Köpingsvik, *Sweden* 11 H10
Kopište, *Croatia* 29 F13
Kopliku, *Albania* 40 D3
Köpmanholmen, *Sweden* .. 10 A12
Kopparberg, *Sweden* 10 E9
Kopparbergs län □, *Sweden* 10 C8
Koppeh Dāgh = Kopet
  Dagh, *Asia* 71 B8
Koppies, *S. Africa* 89 D4
Koppom, *Sweden* 10 E6
Koprivlen, *Bulgaria* 40 E7
Koprivnica, *Croatia* 29 B13
Kopřivnice, *Czech Rep.* 27 B11
Koprivshtitsa, *Bulgaria* ... 41 D8
Köprübaşı, *Turkey* 39 C10
Kopychyntsi, *Ukraine* 47 H3
Korab, *Macedonia* 40 E4
Korakiána, *Greece* 36 A3
Koral, *India* 68 J5
Korarou, L., *Mali* 82 B4
Korba, *India* 69 H10
Korbach, *Germany* 24 D4
Korbu, G., *Malaysia* 65 K3
Korça, *Albania* 40 F4
Korce = Korça, *Albania* .. 40 F4
Korčula, *Croatia* 29 F13
Korčulanski Kanal, *Croatia* . 29 E13
Kord Kūy, *Iran* 71 B7
Kord Sheykh, *Iran* 71 D7
Kordestān □, *Iran* 70 C5
Kordofân, *Sudan* 79 F11
Koré Mayroua, *Niger* 83 C5
Korea, North ■, *Asia* 57 E14
Korea, South ■, *Asia* 57 G15
Korea Bay, *Korea* 57 E13
Korea Strait, *Asia* 57 H15
Korem, *Ethiopia* 81 E4
Korenevo, *Russia* 47 G8
Korenovsk, *Russia* 49 H4
Korets, *Ukraine* 47 G4
Korfantów, *Poland* 45 H4
Korgan, *Turkey* 72 B7
Korgus, *Sudan* 80 D3
Korhogo, *Ivory C.* 82 D3
Koribundu, *S. Leone* 82 D2
Korienzé, *Mali* 82 B4
Korinthía □, *Greece* 38 D4
Korinthiakós Kólpos, *Greece* 38 C4
Kórinthos, *Greece* 38 D4
Korioumé, *Mali* 82 B4
Koríssa, Límni, *Greece* ... 36 B3
Kōriyama, *Japan* 54 F10
Korkuteli, *Turkey* 39 D12
Kormakiti, C., *Cyprus* 36 D11
Körmend, *Hungary* 42 C1
Kornat, *Croatia* 29 E12
Korneshty = Corneşti,
  Moldova 43 C13
Korneuburg, *Austria* 27 C9
Kórnik, *Poland* 45 F4
Koro, *Fiji* 91 C8
Koro, *Ivory C.* 82 D3
Koro, *Mali* 82 C4
Koro Sea, *Fiji* 91 C9
Korocha, *Russia* 47 G9
Köroğlu Dağları, *Turkey* .. 72 B5
Korogwe, *Tanzania* 86 D4
Koronadal, *Phil.* 61 H6
Koróni, *Greece* 38 E3
Korónia, Limni, *Greece* ... 40 F7
Koronís, *Greece* 39 D7
Koronowo, *Poland* 45 E4
Koror, *Palau* 63 C8
Körös →, *Hungary* 42 D5
Köröstarcsa, *Hungary* 42 D6
Korosten, *Ukraine* 47 G5
Korostyshev, *Ukraine* 47 G5
Korotoyak, *Russia* 47 G10
Korraraika, Helodranon' i,
  Madag. 89 B7
Korsakov, *Russia* 51 E15
Korsberga, *Sweden* 11 G9
Korshunovo, *Russia* 51 D12
Korsør, *Denmark* 11 J5
Korsun Shevchenkovskiy,
  Ukraine 47 H6
Korsze, *Poland* 44 D8
Korti, *Sudan* 80 D3
Kortrijk, *Belgium* 17 D3
Korucu, *Turkey* 39 B9
Korwai, *India* 68 G8
Koryakskoye Nagorye,
  Russia 51 C18
Koryŏng, *S. Korea* 57 G15
Koryukovka, *Ukraine* 47 G7
Kos, *Greece* 39 E9
Kosa, *Ethiopia* 81 F4
Kosaya Gora, *Russia* 46 E9
Kościan, *Poland* 45 F3
Kościerzyna, *Poland* 44 D4
Kosciusko, *U.S.A.* 113 J10
Kosciuszko, Mt., *Australia* . 95 F4
Kösely →, *Hungary* 42 C6
Kosha, *Sudan* 80 C3
Koshava, *Bulgaria* 40 B7
K'oshih = Kashi, *China* ... 60 C2
Koshiki-Rettō, *Japan* 55 J4
Kosi, *India* 68 F7
Kosi →, *India* 69 E8
Kosice, *Slovak Rep.* 27 C14
Košický □, *Slovak Rep.* ... 27 C14
Kosjerić, *Serbia, Yug.* 40 B3
Köşk, *Turkey* 39 D10
Koskhinoú, *Greece* 36 C10
Koslan, *Russia* 50 C5
Kosŏng, *N. Korea* 57 E15
Kosovo □, *Yugoslavia* 40 D4
Kosovo Polje, *Kosovo, Yug.* 40 D5

Kosovska Kamenica,
  Kosovo, Yug. 40 D5
Kosovska Mitrovica,
  Kosovo, Yug. 40 D4
Kossou, L. de, *Ivory C.* ... 82 D3
Kosta, *Sweden* 11 H9
Kostajnica, *Croatia* 29 C13
Kostanjevica, *Slovenia* ... 29 C12
Kostenets, *Bulgaria* 40 D7
Koster, *S. Africa* 88 D4
Kôstî, *Sudan* 81 E3
Kostinbrod, *Bulgaria* 40 D7
Kostolac, *Serbia, Yug.* 40 B5
Kostopil, *Ukraine* 47 G4
Kostroma, *Russia* 46 D11
Kostromskoye Vdkhr.,
  Russia 46 D11
Kostrzyn, *Lubuskie, Poland* 45 F1
Kostrzyn, *Wielkopolskie,
  Poland* 45 F4
Kostyantynivka, *Ukraine* ... 47 H9
Kostyukovichi =
  Kastsyukovichy, *Belarus* . 46 F7
Koszalin, *Poland* 44 D3
Kőszeg, *Hungary* 42 C1
Kot Addu, *Pakistan* 68 D4
Kot Kapura, *India* 68 D6
Kot Moman, *Pakistan* 68 C5
Kot Sultan, *Pakistan* 68 D4
Kota, *India* 68 G6
Kota Baharu, *Malaysia* ... 65 J4
Kota Barrage, *India* 68 G6
Kota Belud, *Malaysia* 62 C5
Kota Kinabalu, *Malaysia* .. 62 C5
Kota Kubu Baharu, *Malaysia* 65 L3
Kota Tinggi, *Malaysia* 65 M4
Kotaagung, *Indonesia* 62 F2
Kotabaru, *Indonesia* 62 E5
Kotabumi, *Indonesia* 62 E2
Kotamobagu, *Indonesia* ... 63 D6
Kotcho L., *Canada* 104 B4
Kotdwara, *India* 69 E8
Kotelnich, *Russia* 48 A9
Kotelnikovo, *Russia* 49 G6
Kotelnyy, Ostrov, *Russia* .. 51 B14
Kothari →, *India* 68 G6
Köthen, *Germany* 24 D7
Kothi, *Mad. P., India* 69 H10
Kothi, *Mad. P., India* 69 G9
Kotiro, *Pakistan* 68 F2
Kotka, *Finland* 9 F22
Kotlas, *Russia* 50 C5
Kotlenska Planina, *Bulgaria* 41 D10
Kotli, *Pakistan* 68 C5
Kotma, *India* 69 H9
Kotmul, *Pakistan* 69 B6
Koton-Karifi, *Nigeria* 83 D6
Kotonkoro, *Nigeria* 83 C6
Kotor, *Montenegro, Yug.* .. 40 D2
Kotor Varoš, *Bos.-H.* 42 F2
Kotoriba, *Croatia* 29 B13
Kotovo, *Russia* 48 E7
Kotovsk, *Russia* 48 D5
Kotovsk, *Ukraine* 47 J5
Kotputli, *India* 68 F7
Kotri, *Pakistan* 68 G3
Kótronas, *Greece* 38 E4
Kötschach-Mauthen, *Austria* 26 E6
Kottayam, *India* 66 Q10
Kotturu, *India* 66 M10
Kotuy →, *Russia* 51 B11
Kotzebue, *U.S.A.* 100 B3
Koudougou, *Burkina Faso* .. 82 C4
Koufonísi, *Greece* 36 E8
Koufonísia, *Greece* 39 E7
Kougaberge, *S. Africa* 88 E3
Kouibli, *Ivory C.* 82 D3
Kouilou →, *Congo* 84 E2
Koula Moutou, *Gabon* 84 E2
Koulen = Kulen, *Cambodia* 64 F5
Koulikoro, *Mali* 82 C3
Kouloúra, *Greece* 36 A3
Koúm-bournoú, Ákra,
  Greece 36 C10
Koumala, *Australia* 94 C4
Koumankou, *Mali* 82 C3
Koumbia, *Burkina Faso* ... 82 C4
Koumbia, *Guinea* 82 C2
Koumboum, *Guinea* 82 C2
Koumpenntoum, *Senegal* .. 82 C2
Koumra, *Chad* 79 G9
Koun-Fao, *Ivory C.* 82 D4
Koundara, *Guinea* 82 C2
Koundian, *Guinea* 82 C2
Koungheul, *Senegal* 82 C2
Kounradskiy, *Kazakstan* ... 50 E8
Kountze, *U.S.A.* 113 K7
Koupéla, *Burkina Faso* 83 C4
Kouris →, *Cyprus* 36 E11
Kourou, *Fr. Guiana* 125 B8
Kourouba, *Mali* 82 C2
Kouroukoto, *Mali* 82 C2
Kouroussa, *Guinea* 82 C2
Koussané, *Senegal* 82 C2
Kousseri, *Cameroon* 79 F8
Koutiala, *Mali* 82 C3
Kouto, *Ivory C.* 82 D3
Kouvé, *Togo* 83 D5
Kouvola, *Finland* 9 F22
Kovačica, *Serbia, Yug.* 42 E5
Kovel, *Ukraine* 47 G3
Kovin, *Serbia, Yug.* 42 F5
Kovrov, *Russia* 48 B5
Kowal, *Poland* 45 F6

Kowalewo Pomorskie,
  Poland 45 E5
Kowanyama, *Australia* 94 B3
Kowloon, *H.K.* 59 F10
Kowŏn, *N. Korea* 57 E14
Köyceğiz, *Turkey* 39 E10
Köyceğiz Gölü, *Turkey* 39 E10
Koyulhisar, *Turkey* 72 B7
Koyunyeri, *Turkey* 41 F10
Koza, *Japan* 55 L3
Kozak, *Turkey* 39 B9
Kozan, *Turkey* 70 B2
Kozáni, *Greece* 40 F5
Kozáni □, *Greece* 40 F5
Kozara, *Bos.-H.* 29 D14
Kozarac, *Bos.-H.* 29 D13
Kozelets, *Ukraine* 47 G6
Kozelsk, *Russia* 46 E8
Kozhikode = Calicut, *India* 66 P9
Koziegłowy, *Poland* 45 H6
Kozienice, *Poland* 45 G8
Kozje, *Slovenia* 29 B12
Kozloduy, *Bulgaria* 40 C7
Kozlovets, *Bulgaria* 41 C9
Kozlovka, *Russia* 48 C9
Kozlu, *Turkey* 72 B4
Kozluk, *Turkey* 73 C9
Koźmin, *Poland* 45 G4
Kozmodemyansk, *Russia* .. 48 B8
Kożuchów, *Poland* 45 G2
Kozyatyn, *Ukraine* 47 H5
Kpabia, *Ghana* 83 D4
Kpalimé, *Togo* 83 D5
Kpandae, *Ghana* 83 D4
Kpessi, *Togo* 83 D5
Kra, Isthmus of = Kra, Kho
  Khot, *Thailand* 65 G2
Kra, Kho Khot, *Thailand* .. 65 G2
Kra Buri, *Thailand* 65 G2
Kraai →, *S. Africa* 88 E4
Krabi, *Thailand* 65 H2
Kracheh, *Cambodia* 64 F6
Kragan, *Indonesia* 63 G14
Kragerø, *Norway* 9 G13
Kragujevac, *Serbia, Yug.* .. 40 B4
Krajenka, *Poland* 45 E3
Krajina, *Bos.-H.* 29 D13
Krakatau = Rakata, Pulau,
  Indonesia 62 F3
Krakatoa = Rakata, Pulau,
  Indonesia 62 F3
Krakor, *Cambodia* 64 F5
Kraków, *Poland* 45 H6
Kralanh, *Cambodia* 64 F4
Králíky, *Czech Rep.* 27 A9
Kraljevo, *Serbia, Yug.* 40 C4
Královský Chlmec,
  Slovak Rep. 27 C14
Kralupy nad Vltavou,
  Czech Rep. 26 A7
Kramatorsk, *Ukraine* 47 H9
Kramfors, *Sweden* 10 B11
Kraniá, *Greece* 40 G5
Kranía Elassónas, *Greece* .. 38 B4
Kranídhion, *Greece* 38 D5
Kranj, *Slovenia* 29 B11
Kranjska Gora, *Slovenia* ... 29 B10
Krankskop, *S. Africa* 89 D5
Krapina, *Croatia* 29 B12
Krapina →, *Croatia* 29 C12
Krapkowice, *Poland* 45 H4
Kras, *Croatia* 29 C10
Kraskino, *Russia* 51 E14
Krāslava, *Latvia* 46 E4
Kraslice, *Czech Rep.* 26 A5
Krasnaya Gorbatka, *Russia* . 48 C5
Krasnaya Polyana, *Russia* .. 49 J5
Kraśnik, *Poland* 45 H9
Krasnoarmeisk, *Ukraine* ... 47 H9
Krasnoarmeysk, *Russia* ... 48 E7
Krasnoarmeyskiy, *Russia* .. 49 G6
Krasnobrod, *Poland* 45 H10
Krasnodar, *Russia* 49 H4
Krasnodon, *Ukraine* 47 H10
Krasnogorskiy, *Russia* 48 B9
Krasnograd = Krasnohrad,
  Ukraine 47 H8
Krasnogvardeyskoye, *Russia* 49 H5
Krasnogvardyesk, *Ukraine* . 47 K8
Krasnohrad, *Ukraine* 47 H8
Krasnokutsk, *Ukraine* 47 G8
Krasnolesnyy, *Russia* 47 G10
Krasnoperekopsk, *Ukraine* . 47 J7
Krasnorechenskiy, *Russia* . 54 B7
Krasnoselkup, *Russia* 50 C9
Krasnoslobodsk, *Mordvinia,
  Russia* 48 C6
Krasnoslobodsk, *Volgograd,
  Russia* 49 F7
Krasnoturinsk, *Russia* 50 D7
Krasnovodsk =
  Türkmenbashi,
  Turkmenistan 50 E6
Krasnoyarsk, *Russia* 51 D10
Krasnoye = Krasnyy, *Russia* 46 E6
Krasnozavodsk, *Russia* ... 46 D10
Krasny Sulin, *Russia* 47 J11
Krasnystaw, *Poland* 45 H10
Krasnyy, *Russia* 46 E6
Krasnyy Kholm, *Russia* ... 46 C9
Krasnyy Kut, *Russia* 48 E8
Krasnyy Liman, *Ukraine* .. 47 H9
Krasnyy Luch, *Ukraine* ... 47 H10
Krasnyy Profintern, *Russia* 46 D11
Krasnyy Yar, *Astrakhan,
  Russia* 49 G9
Krasnyy Yar, *Samara, Russia* 48 D9
Krasnyy Yar, *Volgograd,
  Russia* 48 E7
Krasnyye Baki, *Russia* 48 B7

Krasnyyoskolske Vdskh.,
  Ukraine 47 H9
Kraszna →, *Hungary* 42 B7
Kratie = Kracheh, *Cambodia* 64 F6
Kratovo, *Macedonia* 40 D6
Krau, *Indonesia* 63 E10
Kravanh, Chuor Phnum,
  Cambodia 65 G4
Krefeld, *Germany* 24 D2
Krémaston, Límni, *Greece* . 38 C3
Kremen, *Croatia* 29 D12
Kremenchug = Kremenchuk,
  Ukraine 47 H7
Kremenchuk, *Ukraine* 47 H7
Kremenchuksk Vdskh.,
  Ukraine 47 H7
Kremenets, *Ukraine* 47 G3
Kremennaya, *Ukraine* 47 H10
Kremges = Svitlovodsk,
  Ukraine 47 H7
Kremmen, *Germany* 24 C9
Kremmling, *U.S.A.* 114 F10
Kremnica, *Slovak Rep.* ... 27 C11
Krems, *Austria* 26 C8
Kremsmünster, *Austria* ... 26 C7
Kretinga, *Lithuania* 9 J19
Krettsy, *Russia* 46 C7
Kreuzberg, *Germany* 25 E5
Kreuztal, *Germany* 24 E4
Kría Vrísi, *Greece* 40 F6
Kribi, *Cameroon* 83 E6
Krichem, *Bulgaria* 41 D8
Krichev = Krychaw, *Belarus* 46 F6
Krim, *Slovenia* 29 C11
Kriós, Ákra, *Greece* 36 D5
Krishna →, *India* 67 M12
Krishnanagar, *India* 69 H13
Kristdala, *Sweden* 11 G10
Kristiansand, *Norway* 9 G13
Kristianstad, *Sweden* 11 H8
Kristiansund, *Norway* 8 E12
Kristiinankaupunki, *Finland* 9 E19
Kristinehamn, *Sweden* 10 E8
Kristinestad =
  Kristiinankaupunki,
  Finland 9 E19
Kríti, *Greece* 36 D7
Kritsá, *Greece* 36 D7
Kriva →, *Macedonia* 40 D5
Kriva Palanka, *Macedonia* . 40 D6
Krivaja →, *Bos.-H.* 42 F3
Krivelj, *Serbia, Yug.* 40 B6
Krivoy Rog = Kryvyy Rih,
  Ukraine 47 J7
Križevci, *Croatia* 29 B13
Krk, *Croatia* 29 C11
Krka →, *Slovenia* 29 C12
Krkonoše, *Czech Rep.* 26 A8
Krnov, *Czech Rep.* 27 A10
Krobia, *Poland* 45 G3
Krokeaí, *Greece* 38 E4
Krokodil →, *Mozam.* 89 D5
Krokom, *Sweden* 10 A8
Krokowa, *Poland* 44 D5
Krolevets, *Ukraine* 47 G7
Kroměříž, *Czech Rep.* 27 B10
Krompachy, *Slovak Rep.* .. 27 C13
Kromy, *Russia* 47 F8
Kronach, *Germany* 25 E7
Krong Kaoh Kong,
  Cambodia 62 B2
Kronoberg län □, *Sweden* . 11 H8
Kronprins Olav Kyst,
  Antarctica 5 C5
Kronshtadt, *Russia* 46 C5
Kroonstad, *S. Africa* 88 D4
Kröpelin, *Germany* 24 A7
Kropotkin, *Russia* 49 H5
Kropp, *Germany* 24 A5
Krosna, *Lithuania* 44 D10
Krośniewice, *Poland* 45 F6
Krosno, *Poland* 45 J8
Krosno Odrzańskie, *Poland* 45 F2
Krotoszyn, *Poland* 45 G4
Krotovka, *Russia* 48 D10
Kroussón, *Greece* 36 D6
Krraba, *Albania* 40 E3
Krško, *Slovenia* 29 C12
Kruger Nat. Park, *S. Africa* 89 C5
Krugersdorp, *S. Africa* ... 89 D4
Kruisfontein, *S. Africa* ... 88 E3
Kruja, *Albania* 40 E3
Krulevshchina =
  Krulyewshchyna, *Belarus* . 46 E4
Krulyewshchyna, *Belarus* .. 46 E4
Kruma, *Albania* 40 D4
Krumbach, *Germany* 25 G6
Krumovgrad, *Bulgaria* 41 E9
Krung Thep = Bangkok,
  Thailand 64 F3
Krupanj, *Serbia, Yug.* 40 B3
Krupina, *Slovak Rep.* 27 C12
Krupinica →, *Slovak Rep.* . 27 C11
Krupki, *Belarus* 46 E5
Kruševac, *Serbia, Yug.* 40 C5
Kruševo, *Macedonia* 40 E5
Kruszwica, *Poland* 45 F5
Krychaw, *Belarus* 46 F6
Krymsk, *Russia* 47 K10
Krymskiy Poluostrov =
  Krymskyy Pivostriv,
  Ukraine 47 K8
Krymskyy Pivostriv, *Ukraine* 47 K8
Krynica, *Poland* 45 J7
Krynica Morska, *Poland* .. 44 D6
Krynki, *Poland* 45 E10
Kryvyy Rih, *Ukraine* 47 J7
Krzepice, *Poland* 45 H5
Krzeszów, *Poland* 45 H9

Krzna →, *Poland* 45 F10
Krzywiń, *Poland* 45 G3
Krzyż Wielkopolski, *Poland* 45 F2
Ksar el Kebir, *Morocco* ... 78 B4
Ksar es Souk = Ar
  Rachidiya, *Morocco* ... 78 B5
Ksiąz Wielkopolski, *Poland* 45 F4
Kstovo, *Russia* 48 B7
Ku, W. el →, *Sudan* 81 E2
Kuala Belait, *Malaysia* 62 D4
Kuala Berang, *Malaysia* ... 65 K4
Kuala Dungun = Dungun,
  Malaysia 65 K4
Kuala Kangsar, *Malaysia* .. 65 K3
Kuala Kelawang, *Malaysia* . 65 L4
Kuala Kerai, *Malaysia* 65 K4
Kuala Lipis, *Malaysia* 65 K4
Kuala Lumpur, *Malaysia* .. 65 L3
Kuala Nerang, *Malaysia* ... 65 J3
Kuala Pilah, *Malaysia* 65 L4
Kuala Rompin, *Malaysia* .. 65 L4
Kuala Selangor, *Malaysia* .. 65 L3
Kuala Sepetang, *Malaysia* . 65 K3
Kuala Terengganu, *Malaysia* 65 K4
Kualajelai, *Indonesia* 62 E4
Kualakapuas, *Indonesia* ... 62 E4
Kualakurun, *Indonesia* ... 62 E4
Kualapembuang, *Indonesia* . 62 E4
Kualasimpang, *Indonesia* .. 62 D1
Kuancheng, *China* 57 D10
Kuandang, *Indonesia* 63 D6
Kuandian, *China* 57 D13
Kuangchou = Guangzhou,
  China 59 F9
Kuanshan, *Taiwan* 59 F13
Kuantan, *Malaysia* 65 L4
Kuba = Quba, *Azerbaijan* . 49 K9
Kuban →, *Russia* 47 K9
Kubenskoye, Ozero, *Russia* 46 C10
Kubokawa, *Japan* 55 H6
Kubrat, *Bulgaria* 41 C10
Kučevo, *Serbia, Yug.* 40 B5
Kucha Gompa, *India* 69 B7
Kuchaman, *India* 68 F6
Kuchenspitze, *Austria* 26 D3
Kuchinda, *India* 69 J11
Kuching, *Malaysia* 62 D4
Kuchino-eruba-Jima, *Japan* 55 J5
Kuchino-Shima, *Japan* ... 55 K4
Kuchinotsu, *Japan* 55 H5
Kuchl, *Austria* 26 D6
Kucing = Kuching, *Malaysia* 62 D4
Kuçovë, *Albania* 40 F3
Küçükbahçe, *Turkey* 39 C8
Küçükköy, *Turkey* 39 B8
Küçükkuyu, *Turkey* 39 B8
Küçükmenderes →, *Turkey* 39 D9
Kud →, *Pakistan* 68 F2
Kuda, *India* 66 H7
Kudat, *Malaysia* 62 C5
Kudirkos Naumiestis,
  Lithuania 44 D9
Kudowa-Zdrój, *Poland* ... 45 H3
Kudus, *Indonesia* 63 G14
Kudymkar, *Russia* 50 D6
Kueiyang = Guiyang, *China* 58 D6
Kufra Oasis = Al Kufrah,
  Libya 79 D10
Kufstein, *Austria* 26 D5
Kugluktuk, *Canada* 100 B8
Kugong I., *Canada* 102 A4
Kūhak, *Iran* 66 F3
Kuhan, *Pakistan* 68 E2
Kūhbonān, *Iran* 71 D8
Kühestak, *Iran* 71 E8
Kuhin, *Iran* 71 B6
Kūhīrī, *Iran* 71 E9
Kuhnsdorf, *Austria* 26 E7
Kūhpāyeh, *Esfahan, Iran* .. 71 C7
Kūhpāyeh, *Kermān, Iran* .. 71 D8
Kührān, Kūh-e, *Iran* 71 E8
Kui Buri, *Thailand* 65 F2
Kuiseb →, *Namibia* 88 C2
Kuito, *Angola* 85 G3
Kuiu I., *U.S.A.* 104 B2
Kujang, *N. Korea* 57 E14
Kujawsko-Pomorskie □,
  Poland 44 E5
Kuji, *Japan* 54 D10
Kujū-San, *Japan* 55 H5
Kukavica, *Serbia, Yug.* 40 D5
Kukawa, *Nigeria* 83 C7
Kukësi, *Albania* 40 D4
Kukmor, *Russia* 48 B10
Kukup, *Malaysia* 65 M4
Kukvidze, *Russia* 48 E6
Kula, *Bulgaria* 40 C6
Kula, *Serbia, Yug.* 42 E4
Kula, *Turkey* 39 C10
Kulachi, *Pakistan* 68 D4
Kulai, *Malaysia* 65 M4
Kulal, Mt., *Kenya* 86 B4
Kulaly, Ostrov, *Kazakstan* . 49 H10
Kulasekarappattinam, *India* 66 Q11
Kulautuva, *Lithuania* 44 D10
Kuldīga □, *Latvia* 44 B8
Kuldja = Yining, *China* ... 50 E9
Kuldu, *Sudan* 81 E2
Kulebaki, *Russia* 48 C6
Kulen, *Cambodia* 64 F5
Kulen Vakuf, *Bos.-H.* 29 D13
Kulgam, *India* 69 C6
Kulgera, *Australia* 94 D1
Kulim, *Malaysia* 65 K3
Kulin, *Australia* 93 F2
Kullen, *Sweden* 11 H6
Kulmbach, *Germany* 25 E7
Kŭlob, *Tajikistan* 50 F7
Kulp, *Turkey* 73 C9
Kulpawn →, *Ghana* 83 D4

Kulsary

Kulsary, *Kazakstan* 50 E6
Kulti, *India* 69 H12
Kulu, *India* 68 D7
Kulu, *Turkey* 72 C5
Kulumbura, *Australia* 92 B4
Kulunda, *Russia* 50 D8
Kulungar, *Afghan.* 68 C3
Kūlvand, *Iran* 71 D7
Kulwin, *Australia* 95 F3
Kulyab = Kŭlob, *Tajikistan* 50 F7
Kuma →, *Russia* 49 H8
Kumafşarı, *Turkey* 39 D11
Kumaganum, *Nigeria* 83 C7
Kumagaya, *Japan* 55 F9
Kumai, *Indonesia* 62 E4
Kumalar Dağı, *Turkey* 39 C12
Kumamba, Kepulauan, *Indonesia* 63 E9
Kumamoto, *Japan* 55 H5
Kumamoto □, *Japan* 55 H5
Kumanovo, *Macedonia* 40 D5
Kumara, *N.Z.* 91 K3
Kumarina, *Australia* 93 D2
Kumasi, *Ghana* 82 D4
Kumayri = Gyumri, *Armenia* 49 K6
Kumba, *Cameroon* 83 E6
Kumbağ, *Turkey* 41 F11
Kumbakonam, *India* 66 P11
Kumbarilla, *Australia* 95 D5
Kumbhraj, *India* 68 G7
Kumbia, *Australia* 95 D5
Kumbo, *Cameroon* 83 D7
Kŭmch'ŏn, *N. Korea* 57 E14
Kumdok, *India* 69 C8
Kume-Shima, *Japan* 55 L3
Kumeny, *Russia* 48 A9
Kumharsain, *India* 68 D7
Kŭmhwa, *S. Korea* 57 E14
Kumi, *Uganda* 86 B3
Kumkale, *Turkey* 41 G10
Kumla, *Sweden* 10 E9
Kumluca, *Turkey* 39 E12
Kummerower See, *Germany* 24 B8
Kumo, *Nigeria* 83 C7
Kumon Bum, *Burma* 67 F20
Kumylzhenskaya, *Russia* 48 F6
Kunágota, *Hungary* 42 D6
Kunashir, Ostrov, *Russia* 51 E15
Kunda, *Estonia* 9 G22
Kunda, *India* 69 G9
Kundar →, *Pakistan* 68 D3
Kundian, *Pakistan* 68 C4
Kundla, *India* 68 J4
Kunga →, *Bangla.* 69 J13
Kungälv, *Sweden* 11 G5
Kunghit I., *Canada* 104 C2
Kungrad = Qŭnghirot, *Uzbekistan* 50 E6
Kungsängen, *Sweden* 10 E11
Kungsbacka, *Sweden* 11 G6
Kungsgården, *Sweden* 10 D10
Kungshamn, *Sweden* 11 F5
Kungsör, *Sweden* 10 E10
Kungur, *Russia* 50 D6
Kunhar →, *Pakistan* 69 B5
Kunhegyes, *Hungary* 42 C5
Kuningan, *Indonesia* 63 G13
Kunlong, *Burma* 58 F2
Kunlun Shan, *Asia* 60 C3
Kunmadaras, *Hungary* 42 C5
Kunming, *China* 58 E4
Kunów, *Poland* 45 H8
Kunsan, *S. Korea* 57 G14
Kunshan, *China* 59 B13
Kunszentmárton, *Hungary* 42 D5
Kunszentmiklós, *Hungary* 42 C4
Kuntaur, *Senegal* 82 C2
Kununurra, *Australia* 92 C4
Kunwari →, *India* 69 F8
Kunya-Urgench = Köneürgench, *Turkmenistan* 50 E6
Künzelsau, *Germany* 25 F5
Kuopio, *Finland* 8 E22
Kupa →, *Croatia* 29 C13
Kupang, *Indonesia* 63 F6
Kupreanof I., *U.S.A.* 104 B2
Kupres, *Bos.-H.* 42 G2
Kupyansk, *Ukraine* 47 H9
Kupyansk-Uzlovoi, *Ukraine* 47 H9
Kuqa, *China* 60 B3
Kür →, *Azerbaijan* 73 C13
Kür Dili, *Azerbaijan* 71 B6
Kura = Kür →, *Azerbaijan* 73 C13
Kuranda, *Australia* 94 B4
Kuranga, *India* 68 H3
Kurashiki, *Japan* 55 G6
Kurayoshi, *Japan* 55 G6
Kürdämir, *Azerbaijan* 49 K9
Kurdistan, *Asia* 73 D10
Kŭrdzhali, *Bulgaria* 41 E9
Kure, *Japan* 55 G6
Küre, *Turkey* 72 B5
Küre Dağları, *Turkey* 72 B6
Kuressaare, *Estonia* 9 G20
Kurgan, *Russia* 50 D7
Kurganinsk, *Russia* 49 H5
Kurgannaya = Kurganinsk, *Russia* 49 H5
Kuri, *India* 68 F4
Kuria Maria Is. = Khurīyā Murīyā, Jazā 'ir, *Oman* 74 D6
Kuridala, *Australia* 94 C3
Kurigram, *Bangla.* 67 G16
Kurikka, *Finland* 9 E20
Kuril Is. = Kurilskiye Ostrova, *Russia* 51 E15
Kuril Trench, *Pac. Oc.* 52 E19
Kurilsk, *Russia* 51 E15
Kurilskiye Ostrova, *Russia* 51 E15
Kurino, *Japan* 55 J5
Kurinskaya Kosa = Kür Dili, *Azerbaijan* 71 B6
Kurkur, *Egypt* 80 C3
Kurlovskiy, *Russia* 48 C5
Kurmuk, *Sudan* 81 E3
Kurnool, *India* 66 M11
Kuro-Shima, *Kagoshima, Japan* 55 J4
Kuro-Shima, *Okinawa, Japan* 55 M2
Kuror, J., *Sudan* 80 C3
Kurow, *N.Z.* 91 L3
Kurów, *Poland* 45 G9
Kurram →, *Pakistan* 68 C4
Kurri Kurri, *Australia* 95 E5
Kurrimine, *Australia* 94 B4
Kursavka, *Russia* 49 H6
Kuršėnai, *Lithuania* 44 B9
Kurshskiy Zaliv, *Russia* 9 J19
Kursk, *Russia* 47 G9
Kuršumlija, *Serbia, Yug.* 40 C5
Kuršumlijska Banja, *Serbia, Yug.* 40 C5
Kurşunlu, *Bursa, Turkey* 41 F13
Kurşunlu, *Çankırı, Turkey* 72 B5
Kurtalan, *Turkey* 73 D9
Kurtbey, *Turkey* 41 E10
Kuru, *Sudan* 81 F2
Kuru, Bahr el →, *Sudan* 81 F2
Kurucaşile, *Turkey* 72 B5
Kuruçay, *Turkey* 70 B3
Kuruktag, *China* 60 B3
Kuruman, *S. Africa* 88 D3
Kuruman →, *S. Africa* 88 D3
Kurume, *Japan* 55 H5
Kurun →, *Sudan* 81 F3
Kurunegala, *Sri Lanka* 66 R12
Kurya, *Russia* 50 C6
Kus Gölü, *Turkey* 41 F11
Kuşadası, *Turkey* 72 D2
Kuşadası Körfezi, *Turkey* 39 D8
Kusatsu, *Japan* 55 F9
Kusawa L., *Canada* 104 A1
Kusel, *Germany* 25 F3
Kushaka, *Nigeria* 83 C6
Kushalgarh, *India* 68 H6
Kushchevskaya, *Russia* 49 G4
Kusheriki, *Nigeria* 83 C6
Kushikino, *Japan* 55 J5
Kushima, *Japan* 55 J5
Kushimoto, *Japan* 55 H7
Kushiro, *Japan* 54 C12
Kushiro-Gawa →, *Japan* 54 C12
Kūshk, *Iran* 71 D8
Kushka = Gushgy, *Turkmenistan* 50 F7
Kūshkī, *Iran* 70 C5
Kushol, *India* 69 C7
Kushtia, *Bangla.* 67 H16
Kushum →, *Kazakstan* 48 F10
Kuskokwim B., *U.S.A.* 100 C3
Kusmi, *India* 69 H10
Kussharo-Ko, *Japan* 54 C12
Kustanay = Qostanay, *Kazakstan* 50 D7
Kut, Ko, *Thailand* 65 G4
Kütahya, *Turkey* 39 B12
Kütahya □, *Turkey* 39 B11
Kutaisi, *Georgia* 49 J6
Kutaraja = Banda Aceh, *Indonesia* 62 C1
Kutch, Gulf of = Kachchh, Gulf of, *India* 68 H3
Kutch, Rann of = Kachchh, Rann of, *India* 68 H4
Kutina, *Croatia* 29 C13
Kutiyana, *India* 68 J4
Kutjevo, *Croatia* 42 E2
Kutkashen, *Azerbaijan* 49 K8
Kutná Hora, *Czech Rep.* 26 B8
Kutno, *Poland* 45 F6
Kutse, *Botswana* 88 C3
Kutu, *Dem. Rep. of the Congo* 84 E3
Kutum, *Sudan* 81 E1
Kúty, *Slovak Rep.* 27 C10
Kuujjuaq, *Canada* 101 C13
Kuujjuarapik, *Canada* 102 A4
Kuŭp-tong, *N. Korea* 57 D14
Kuusamo, *Finland* 8 D23
Kuusankoski, *Finland* 9 F22
Kuvshinovo, *Russia* 46 D8
Kuwait = Al Kuwayt, *Kuwait* 70 D5
Kuwait ■, *Asia* 70 D5
Kuwana, *Japan* 55 G8
Kuwana →, *India* 69 F10
Kuybyshev = Samara, *Russia* 48 D10
Kuybyshev, *Russia* 50 D8
Kuybyshevo, *Ukraine* 47 J9
Kuybyshevskoye Vdkhr., *Russia* 48 C9
Kuye He →, *China* 56 E6
Kūyeh, *Iran* 70 B5
Kūysanjaq, *Iraq* 70 B5
Kuyucak, *Turkey* 39 D10
Kuyumba, *Russia* 51 C10
Kuzey Anadolu Dağları, *Turkey* 72 B7
Kuzmin, *Serbia, Yug.* 42 E4
Kuznetsk, *Russia* 48 D8
Kuzomen, *Russia* 50 C4
Kvænangen, *Norway* 8 A19
Kværndrup, *Denmark* 11 J4
Kvaløy, *Norway* 8 B18
Kvänum, *Sweden* 11 F7
Kvareli = Qvareli, *Georgia* 49 K7
Kvarner, *Croatia* 29 D11
Kvarnerič, *Croatia* 29 D11
Kvicksund, *Sweden* 10 E10
Kvillsfors, *Sweden* 11 G9
Kvismare kanal, *Sweden* 10 E9
Kvissleby, *Sweden* 10 B11
Kwa-Nobuhle, *S. Africa* 85 L5
Kwabhaca, *S. Africa* 89 E4
Kwakhanai, *Botswana* 88 C3
Kwakoegron, *Surinam* 125 B7
Kwale, *Kenya* 86 C4
Kwale, *Nigeria* 83 D6
KwaMashu, *S. Africa* 89 D5
Kwando →, *Africa* 88 B3
Kwangdaeri, *N. Korea* 57 D14
Kwangju, *S. Korea* 57 G14
Kwango →, *Dem. Rep. of the Congo* 77 G5
Kwangsi-Chuang = Guangxi Zhuangzu Zizhiqu □, *China* 58 F7
Kwangtung = Guangdong □, *China* 59 F9
Kwara □, *Nigeria* 83 D6
Kwataboahegan →, *Canada* 102 B3
Kwatisore, *Indonesia* 63 E8
KwaZulu Natal □, *S. Africa* 89 D5
Kweichow = Guizhou □, *China* 58 D6
Kwekwe, *Zimbabwe* 87 F2
Kwidzyn, *Poland* 44 E5
Kwiha, *Ethiopia* 81 E4
Kwinana New Town, *Australia* 93 F2
Kwisa →, *Poland* 45 G2
Kwoka, *Indonesia* 63 E8
Kwolla, *Nigeria* 83 D6
Kyabra Cr. →, *Australia* 95 D3
Kyabram, *Australia* 95 F4
Kyaikto, *Burma* 64 D1
Kyakhta, *Russia* 51 D11
Kyancutta, *Australia* 95 E2
Kyangin, *Burma* 67 K19
Kyaukpadaung, *Burma* 67 J19
Kyaukpyu, *Burma* 67 K18
Kyaukse, *Burma* 67 J20
Kybartai, *Lithuania* 44 D9
Kyburz, *U.S.A.* 116 G6
Kyelang, *India* 68 C7
Kyenjojo, *Uganda* 86 B3
Kyjov, *Czech Rep.* 27 B10
Kyle, *Canada* 105 C7
Kyle Dam, *Zimbabwe* 87 G3
Kyle of Lochalsh, *U.K.* 14 D3
Kyll →, *Germany* 25 F2
Kyllburg, *Germany* 25 E2
Kymijoki →, *Finland* 9 F22
Kyneton, *Australia* 95 F3
Kynuna, *Australia* 94 C3
Kyō-ga-Saki, *Japan* 55 G7
Kyoga, L., *Uganda* 86 B3
Kyogle, *Australia* 95 D5
Kyom →, *Sudan* 81 F2
Kyongju, *S. Korea* 57 G15
Kyongpyaw, *Burma* 67 L19
Kyŏngsŏng, *N. Korea* 57 D15
Kyōto, *Japan* 55 G7
Kyōto □, *Japan* 55 G7
Kyparissovouno, *Cyprus* 36 D12
Kyperounda, *Cyprus* 36 E11
Kyrenia, *Cyprus* 36 D12
Kyrgyzstan ■, *Asia* 50 E8
Kyritz, *Germany* 24 C8
Kyrkhult, *Sweden* 11 H8
Kyrönjoki →, *Finland* 8 E19
Kystatyam, *Russia* 51 C13
Kysucké Nové Mesto, *Slovak Rep.* 27 B11
Kythréa, *Cyprus* 36 D12
Kyunhla, *Burma* 67 H19
Kyuquot Sound, *Canada* 104 D3
Kyurdamir = Kürdämir, *Azerbaijan* 49 K9
Kyūshū, *Japan* 55 H5
Kyūshū □, *Japan* 55 H5
Kyūshū-Sanchi, *Japan* 55 H5
Kyustendil, *Bulgaria* 40 D6
Kyusyur, *Russia* 51 B13
Kyyiv, *Ukraine* 47 G6
Kyyivske Vdskh., *Ukraine* 47 G6
Kyzyl, *Russia* 51 D10
Kyzyl Kum, *Uzbekistan* 50 E7
Kyzyl-Kyya, *Kyrgyzstan* 50 E8
Kyzyl-Orda = Qyzylorda, *Kazakstan* 50 E7

L

La Albuera, *Spain* 35 G4
La Alcarria, *Spain* 32 E2
La Almarcha, *Spain* 32 F2
La Almunia de Doña Godina, *Spain* 32 D3
La Asunción, *Venezuela* 124 A6
La Baie, *Canada* 103 C5
La Banda, *Argentina* 126 B3
La Bañeza, *Spain* 34 C5
La Barca, *Mexico* 118 C4
La Barge, *U.S.A.* 114 E8
La Bastide-Puylaurent, *France* 20 D7
La Baule-Escoubiac, *France* 18 E4
La Belle, *U.S.A.* 109 M5
La Biche →, *Canada* 104 B4
La Biche, L., *Canada* 104 C6
La Bisbal d'Empordà, *Spain* 32 D8
La Bomba, *Mexico* 118 A1
La Bresse, *France* 19 D13
La Bureba, *Spain* 34 C7
La Calera, *Chile* 126 C1
La Campiña, *Spain* 35 H6
La Canal = Sa Canal, *Spain* 37 C7
La Cañiza = A Cañiza, *Spain* 34 C2
La Canourgue, *France* 20 D7
La Capelle, *France* 19 C10
La Carlota, *Argentina* 126 C3
La Carlota, *Phil.* 61 F5
La Carlota, *Spain* 35 H6
La Carolina, *Spain* 35 G7
La Cavalerie, *France* 20 D7
La Ceiba, *Honduras* 120 C2
La Chaise-Dieu, *France* 20 C7
La Chapelle d'Angillon, *France* 19 E9
La Chapelle-St-Luc, *France* 19 D11
La Chapelle-sur-Erdre, *France* 18 E5
La Charité-sur-Loire, *France* 19 E10
La Chartre-sur-le-Loir, *France* 18 E7
La Châtaigneraie, *France* 20 B3
La Châtre, *France* 19 F9
La Chaux-de-Fonds, *Switz.* 25 H2
La Chorrera, *Panama* 120 E4
La Ciotat, *France* 21 E9
La Clayette, *France* 19 F11
La Cocha, *Argentina* 126 B2
La Concepción = Ri-Aba, *Eq. Guin.* 83 E6
La Concepción, *Panama* 120 E3
La Concordia, *Mexico* 119 D6
La Coruña = A Coruña, *Spain* 34 B2
La Coruña □, *Spain* 34 B2
La Côte-St-André, *France* 21 C9
La Courtine-le-Trucq, *France* 20 C6
La Crau, *Bouches-du-Rhône, France* 21 E8
La Crau, *Var, France* 21 E10
La Crescent, *U.S.A.* 112 D9
La Crete, *Canada* 104 B5
La Crosse, *Kans., U.S.A.* 112 F5
La Crosse, *Wis., U.S.A.* 112 D9
La Cruz, *Costa Rica* 120 D2
La Cruz, *Mexico* 118 C3
La Désirade, *Guadeloupe* 121 C7
La Escondida, *Mexico* 118 C5
La Esmeralda, *Paraguay* 126 A3
La Esperanza, *Cuba* 120 B3
La Esperanza, *Honduras* 120 D2
La Estrada = A Estrada, *Spain* 34 C2
La Faouët, *France* 18 D3
La Fayette, *U.S.A.* 109 H3
La Fé, *Cuba* 120 B3
La Fère, *France* 19 C10
La Ferté-Bernard, *France* 18 D7
La Ferté-Gaucher, *France* 19 D10
La Ferté-Macé, *France* 18 D6
La Ferté-St-Aubin, *France* 19 E8
La Ferté-sous-Jouarre, *France* 19 D10
La Ferté-Vidame, *France* 18 D7
La Flèche, *France* 18 E6
La Follette, *U.S.A.* 109 G3
La Fregeneda, *Spain* 34 E4
La Fuente de San Esteban, *Spain* 34 E4
La Gacilly, *France* 18 E4
La Gineta, *Spain* 33 F2
La Grand-Combe, *France* 21 D8
La Grande, *U.S.A.* 114 D4
La Grande →, *Canada* 102 B5
La Grande Deux, Rés., *Canada* 102 B4
La Grande-Motte, *France* 21 E8
La Grande Quatre, Rés., *Canada* 102 B5
La Grande Trois, Rés., *Canada* 102 B4
La Grange, *Calif., U.S.A.* 116 H6
La Grange, *Ga., U.S.A.* 109 J3
La Grange, *Ky., U.S.A.* 108 F3
La Grange, *Tex., U.S.A.* 113 L6
La Grave, *France* 21 C10
La Guaira, *Venezuela* 124 A5
La Guardia = A Guarda, *Spain* 34 D2
La Gudiña = A Gudiña, *Spain* 34 C3
La Guerche-de-Bretagne, *France* 18 E5
La Guerche-sur-l'Aubois, *France* 19 F9
La Habana, *Cuba* 120 B3
La Haye-du-Puits, *France* 18 C5
La Horra, *Spain* 34 D7
La Independencia, *Mexico* 119 D6
La Isabela, *Dom. Rep.* 121 C5
La Jonquera, *Spain* 32 C7
La Junta, *U.S.A.* 113 F3
La Laguna, *Canary Is.* 37 F3
La Libertad, *Guatemala* 120 C1
La Libertad, *Mexico* 118 B2
La Ligua, *Chile* 126 C1
La Línea de la Concepción, *Spain* 35 J5
La Loche, *Canada* 105 B7
La Londe-les-Maures, *France* 21 E10
La Lora, *Spain* 34 C7
La Loupe, *France* 18 D8
La Louvière, *Belgium* 17 D4
La Machine, *France* 19 F10
La Maddalena, *Italy* 30 A2
La Malbaie, *Canada* 103 C5
La Mancha, *Spain* 33 F2
La Mariña, *Spain* 34 B3
La Martre, L., *Canada* 104 A5
La Mesa, *U.S.A.* 117 N9
La Misión, *Mexico* 118 A1
La Mothe-Achard, *France* 18 F5
La Motte, *France* 21 D10
La Motte-Chalançon, *France* 21 D9
La Motte-Servolex, *France* 21 C9
La Moure, *U.S.A.* 112 B5
La Muela, *Spain* 32 D3
La Mure, *France* 21 D9
La Negra, *Chile* 126 A1
La Oliva, *Canary Is.* 37 F6
La Orotava, *Canary Is.* 37 F3
La Oroya, *Peru* 124
La Pacaudière, *France* 19 F10
La Palma, *Canary Is.* 37 F2
La Palma, *Panama* 120 E4
La Palma del Condado, *Spain* 35 H4
La Paloma, *Chile* 126 C1
La Pampa □, *Argentina* 126 D2
La Paragua, *Venezuela* 124 B6
La Paz, *Entre Ríos, Argentina* 126 C4
La Paz, *San Luis, Argentina* 126 C2
La Paz, *Bolivia* 124 G5
La Paz, *Honduras* 120 D2
La Paz, *Mexico* 118 C2
La Paz, *Phil.* 61 D4
La Paz Centro, *Nic.* 120 D2
La Pedrera, *Colombia* 124 D5
La Pérade, *Canada* 103 C5
La Perouse Str., *Asia* 54 B11
La Pesca, *Mexico* 119 C5
La Piedad, *Mexico* 118 C4
La Pine, *U.S.A.* 114 E3
La Plata, *Argentina* 126 D4
La Pobla de Lillet, *Spain* 32 C6
La Pocatière, *Canada* 103 C5
La Pola de Gordón, *Spain* 34 C5
La Porta, *France* 21 F13
La Porte, *Ind., U.S.A.* 108 E2
La Porte, *Tex., U.S.A.* 113 L7
La Presanella, *Italy* 28 B7
La Puebla = Sa Pobla, *Spain* 32 F8
La Puebla de Cazalla, *Spain* 35 H5
La Puebla de los Infantes, *Spain* 35 H5
La Puebla de Montalbán, *Spain* 34 F6
La Puebla del Río, *Spain* 35 H4
La Puerta de Segura, *Spain* 35 G8
La Purísima, *Mexico* 118 B2
La Push, *U.S.A.* 116 C2
La Quiaca, *Argentina* 126 A2
La Réole, *France* 20 D3
La Restinga, *Canary Is.* 37 G2
La Rioja, *Argentina* 126 B2
La Rioja □, *Argentina* 126 B2
La Rioja □, *Spain* 32 C2
La Robla, *Spain* 34 C5
La Roche-Bernard, *France* 18 E4
La Roche-Canillac, *France* 20 C5
La Roche-en-Ardenne, *Belgium* 17 D5
La Roche-sur-Foron, *France* 19 F13
La Roche-sur-Yon, *France* 18 F5
La Rochefoucauld, *France* 20 C4
La Rochelle, *France* 20 B2
La Roda, *Spain* 33 F2
La Roda de Andalucía, *Spain* 35 H6
La Romana, *Dom. Rep.* 121 C6
La Ronge, *Canada* 105 B7
La Rumorosa, *Mexico* 117 N10
La Sabina = Sa Savina, *Spain* 37 C7
La Sagra, *Spain* 33 H2
La Salle, *U.S.A.* 112 E10
La Sanabria, *Spain* 34 C4
La Santa, *Canary Is.* 37 E6
La Sarre, *Canada* 102 C4
La Scie, *Canada* 103 C8
La Selva, *Spain* 32 C7
La Selva Beach, *U.S.A.* 116 J5
La Selva del Camp, *Spain* 32 D6
La Serena, *Chile* 126 B1
La Serena, *Spain* 35 G5
La Seu d'Urgell, *Spain* 32 C6
La Seyne-sur-Mer, *France* 21 E9
La Sila, *Italy* 31 C9
La Solana, *Spain* 35 G7
La Soufrière, *St. Vincent* 121 D7
La Souterraine, *France* 19 F8
La Spézia, *Italy* 28 D6
La Suze-sur-Sarthe, *France* 18 E7
La Tagua, *Colombia* 124 C4
La Teste, *France* 20 D2
La Tortuga, *Venezuela* 121 D6
La Tour-du-Pin, *France* 21 C9
La Tranche-sur-Mer, *France* 18 F5
La Tremblade, *France* 20 C2
La Tuque, *Canada* 102 C5
La Unión, *Chile* 128 E2
La Unión, *El Salv.* 120 D2
La Unión, *Mexico* 118 D4
La Unión, *Spain* 33 H4
La Urbana, *Venezuela* 124 B5
La Vall d'Uixó, *Spain* 32 F4
La Vecilla de Curveño, *Spain* 34 C5
La Vega, *Dom. Rep.* 121 C5
La Vela de Coro, *Venezuela* 124 A5
La Veleta, *Spain* 35 H7
La Venta, *Mexico* 119 D6
La Ventura, *Mexico* 118 C4
La Voulte-sur-Rhône, *France* 21 D8
Laa an der Thaya, *Austria* 27 C9
Laaber, Grosse →, *Germany* 25 G8
Laage, *Germany* 24 B8
Laatzen, *Germany* 24 C5
Laba →, *Russia* 49 H4
Labason, *Phil.* 61 G5
Labastide-Murat, *France* 20 D5
Labastide-Rouairoux, *France* 20 E6
Labbézenga, *Mali* 83 B5

Lastchance Cr.

Labe = Elbe →, *Europe* .. 24 B4
Labé, *Guinea* 82 C2
Laberge, L., *Canada* 104 A1
Labin, *Croatia* 29 C11
Labinsk, *Russia* 49 H5
Labis, *Malaysia* 65 L4
Łabiszyn, *Poland* 45 F4
Labo, *Phil.* 61 D5
Laboe, *Germany* 24 A6
Laborec →, *Slovak Rep.* .. 27 C14
Labouheyre, *France* 20 D3
Laboulaye, *Argentina* 126 C3
Labrador, *Canada* 103 B7
Labrador City, *Canada* 103 B6
Labrador Sea, *Atl. Oc.* 101 C14
Lábrea, *Brazil* 124 E6
Labrède, *France* 20 D3
Labruguière, *France* 20 E6
Labuan, *Malaysia* 62 C5
Labuan, Pulau, *Malaysia* ... 62 C5
Labuha, *Indonesia* 63 E7
Labuhan, *Indonesia* 63 G11
Labuhanbajo, *Indonesia* 63 F6
Labuk, Telok, *Malaysia* 62 C5
Labyrinth, L., *Australia* 95 E2
Labytnangi, *Russia* 50 C7
Laç, *Albania* 40 E3
Lac Bouchette, *Canada* 103 C5
Lac Édouard, *Canada* 102 C5
Lac La Biche, *Canada* 104 C6
Lac la Martre = Wha Ti, *Canada* 100 B8
Lac La Ronge Prov. Park, *Canada* 105 B7
Lac-Mégantic, *Canada* 103 C5
Lac Seul, Res., *Canada* 102 B1
Lac Thien, *Vietnam* 64 F7
Lacanau, *France* 20 D2
Lacanau, Étang de, *France* . 20 D2
Lacantúm →, *Mexico* 119 D6
Lacara →, *Spain* 35 G4
Lacaune, *France* 20 E6
Lacaune, Mts. de, *France* .. 20 E6
Laccadive Is. = Lakshadweep Is., *Ind. Oc.* 52 H11
Lacepede B., *Australia* 95 F2
Lacepede Is., *Australia* 92 C3
Lacerdónia, *Mozam.* 87 F4
Lacey, *U.S.A.* 116 C4
Lachhmangarh, *India* 68 F6
Lachi, *Pakistan* 68 C4
Lachine, *Canada* 102 C5
Lachlan →, *Australia* 95 E3
Lachute, *Canada* 102 C5
Lackawanna, *U.S.A.* 110 D6
Lackawaxen, *U.S.A.* 111 E10
Lacolle, *Canada* 111 A11
Lacombe, *Canada* 104 C6
Lacona, *U.S.A.* 111 C8
Láconi, *Italy* 30 C2
Laconia, *U.S.A.* 111 C13
Lacq, *France* 20 E3
Ladakh Ra., *India* 69 C8
Lądek-Zdrój, *Poland* 45 H3
Ládhon →, *Greece* 38 D3
Ladik, *Turkey* 72 B6
Ladismith, *S. Africa* 88 E3
Ladíspoli, *Italy* 29 G9
Lādīz, *Iran* 71 D9
Ladnun, *India* 68 F6
Ladoga, L. = Ladozhskoye Ozero, *Russia* 46 B6
Ladozhskoye Ozero, *Russia* . 46 B6
Lady Elliott I., *Australia* ... 94 C5
Lady Grey, *S. Africa* 88 E4
Ladybrand, *S. Africa* 88 D4
Ladysmith, *Canada* 104 D4
Ladysmith, *S. Africa* 89 D4
Ladysmith, *U.S.A.* 112 C9
Lae, *Papua N. G.* 96 H6
Laem Ngop, *Thailand* 65 F4
Laem Pho, *Thailand* 65 J3
Læsø, *Denmark* 11 G5
Læsø Rende, *Denmark* 11 G4
Lafayette, *Colo., U.S.A.* 112 F2
Lafayette, *Ind., U.S.A.* 108 E2
Lafayette, *La., U.S.A.* 113 K9
Lafayette, *Tenn., U.S.A.* ... 109 G2
Laferte →, *Canada* 104 A5
Lafia, *Nigeria* 83 D6
Lafiagi, *Nigeria* 83 D6
Lafleche, *Canada* 105 D7
Lafon, *Sudan* 81 F3
Lagan, *Sweden* 11 H7
Lagan →, *Sweden* 11 H6
Lagan →, *U.K.* 15 B6
Lagarfljót →, *Iceland* 8 D6
Lage, *Germany* 24 D4
Lågen →, *Oppland, Norway* 9 F14
Lågen →, *Vestfold, Norway* 9 G14
Lägerdorf, *Germany* 24 B5
Laghouat, *Algeria* 78 B6
Lagnieu, *France* 21 C9
Lagny-sur-Marne, *France* .. 19 D9
Lago, *Italy* 31 C9
Lagôa, *Portugal* 35 H2
Lagoa Vermelha, *Brazil* ... 127 B5
Lagoaça, *Portugal* 34 D4
Lagodekhi, *Georgia* 49 K8
Lagónegro, *Italy* 31 B8
Lagonoy G., *Phil.* 61 E5
Lagos, *Nigeria* 83 D5
Lagos, *Portugal* 35 H2
Lagos □, *Nigeria* 83 D5
Lagos de Moreno, *Mexico* .. 118 C4
Lagrange, *Australia* 92 C3
Lagrange B., *Australia* 92 C3
Laguardia, *Spain* 32 C2
Laguépie, *France* 20 D5
Laguna, *Brazil* 127 B6
Laguna, *U.S.A.* 115 J10
Laguna Beach, *U.S.A.* 117 M9
Laguna de Duera, *Spain* ... 34 D6
Laguna Limpia, *Argentina* .. 126 B4
Laguna Madre, *U.S.A.* 119 B5
Lagunas, *Chile* 126 A2
Lagunas, *Peru* 124 E3
Lahad Datu, *Malaysia* 63 C5
Lahad Datu, Teluk, *Malaysia* 63 D5
Lahan Sai, *Thailand* 64 E4
Lahanam, *Laos* 64 D5
Lahar, *India* 69 F8
Laharpur, *India* 69 F9
Lahat, *Indonesia* 62 E2
Lahewa, *Indonesia* 62 D1
Lāhījān, *Iran* 71 B6
Lahn →, *Germany* 25 E3
Lahnstein, *Germany* 25 E3
Laholm, *Sweden* 11 H7
Laholmsbukten, *Sweden* ... 11 H6
Lahore, *Pakistan* 68 D6
Lahr, *Germany* 25 G3
Lahri, *Pakistan* 68 E3
Lahti, *Finland* 9 F21
Lahtis = Lahti, *Finland* 9 F21
Laï, *Chad* 79 G9
Lai Chau, *Vietnam* 58 F4
Lai'an, *China* 59 A12
Laibin, *China* 58 F7
Laifeng, *China* 58 C7
L'Aigle, *France* 18 D7
Laignes, *France* 19 E11
L'Aiguillon-sur-Mer, *France* 20 B2
Laila = Laylá, *Si. Arabia* .. 74 C4
Laingsburg, *S. Africa* 88 E3
Lainio älv →, *Sweden* 8 C20
Lairg, *U.K.* 14 C4
Laishui, *China* 56 E8
Laissac, *France* 20 D6
Láives, *Italy* 29 B8
Laiwu, *China* 57 F9
Laixi, *China* 57 F11
Laiyang, *China* 57 F11
Laiyuan, *China* 56 E8
Laizhou, *China* 57 F10
Laizhou Wan, *China* 57 F10
Laja →, *Mexico* 118 C4
Lajere, *Nigeria* 83 C7
Lajes, *Brazil* 127 B5
Lajkovac, *Serbia, Yug.* 40 B4
Lajosmizse, *Hungary* 42 C4
Lak Sao, *Laos* 64 C5
Lakaband, *Pakistan* 68 D3
Lakamané, *Mali* 82 C3
Lake Alpine, *U.S.A.* 116 G7
Lake Andes, *U.S.A.* 112 D5
Lake Arthur, *U.S.A.* 113 K8
Lake Cargelligo, *Australia* .. 95 E4
Lake Charles, *U.S.A.* 113 K8
Lake City, *Colo., U.S.A.* ... 115 G10
Lake City, *Fla., U.S.A.* 109 K4
Lake City, *Mich., U.S.A.* ... 108 C3
Lake City, *Minn., U.S.A.* ... 112 C8
Lake City, *Pa., U.S.A.* 110 D4
Lake City, *S.C., U.S.A.* ... 109 J6
Lake Cowichan, *Canada* ... 104 D4
Lake District, *U.K.* 12 C4
Lake Elsinore, *U.S.A.* 117 M9
Lake George, *U.S.A.* 111 C11
Lake Grace, *Australia* 93 F2
Lake Harbour = Kimmirut, *Canada* 101 B13
Lake Havasu City, *U.S.A.* . 117 L12
Lake Hughes, *U.S.A.* 117 L8
Lake Isabella, *U.S.A.* 117 K8
Lake Jackson, *U.S.A.* 113 L7
Lake Junction, *U.S.A.* 114 D8
Lake King, *Australia* 93 F2
Lake Lenore, *Canada* 105 C8
Lake Louise, *Canada* 104 C5
Lake Mead National Recreation Area, *U.S.A.* . 117 K12
Lake Mills, *U.S.A.* 112 D8
Lake Placid, *U.S.A.* 111 B11
Lake Pleasant, *U.S.A.* 111 C10
Lake Providence, *U.S.A.* ... 113 J9
Lake St. Peter, *Canada* 110 A6
Lake Superior Prov. Park, *Canada* 102 C3
Lake Village, *U.S.A.* 113 J9
Lake Wales, *U.S.A.* 109 M5
Lake Worth, *U.S.A.* 109 M5
Lakefield, *Canada* 102 D4
Lakehurst, *U.S.A.* 111 F10
Lakeland, *Australia* 94 B3
Lakeland, *U.S.A.* 109 M5
Lakemba, *Fiji* 91 D9
Lakeport, *Calif., U.S.A.* 116 F4
Lakeport, *Mich., U.S.A.* ... 110 C2
Lakes Entrance, *Australia* .. 95 F4
Lakeside, *Ariz., U.S.A.* 115 J9
Lakeside, *Calif., U.S.A.* 117 N10
Lakeside, *Nebr., U.S.A.* 112 D3
Lakeside, *Ohio, U.S.A.* 110 E2
Lakeview, *U.S.A.* 114 E3
Lakeville, *U.S.A.* 112 C8
Lakewood, *Colo., U.S.A.* ... 112 F2
Lakewood, *N.J., U.S.A.* 111 F10
Lakewood, *N.Y., U.S.A.* ... 110 D5
Lakewood, *Ohio, U.S.A.* ... 110 E3
Lakewood, *Wash., U.S.A.* .. 116 C4
Lakha, *India* 68 F4
Lakhaniá, *Greece* 36 D9
Lakhimpur, *India* 69 F9
Lakhnadon, *India* 69 H8
Lakhonpheng, *Laos* 64 E5
Lakhpat, *India* 68 H3
Läki, *Azerbaijan* 49 K8
Lakin, *U.S.A.* 113 G4
Lakitusaki →, *Canada* 102 B3
Lakki, *Pakistan* 68 C4
Lákkoi, *Greece* 36 D5
Lakonía □, *Greece* 38 E4
Lakonikós Kólpos, *Greece* . 38 E4
Lakor, *Indonesia* 63 F7
Lakota, *Ivory C.* 82 D3
Lakota, *U.S.A.* 112 A5
Laksar, *India* 68 E8
Laksefjorden, *Norway* 8 A22
Lakselv, *Norway* 8 A21
Lakshadweep Is., *Ind. Oc.* . 52 H11
Lakshmanpur, *India* 69 H10
Lakshmikantapur, *India* 69 H13
Lala Ghat, *India* 67 G18
Lala Musa, *Pakistan* 68 C5
Lalago, *Tanzania* 86 C3
Lalapanzi, *Zimbabwe* 87 F3
Lalapaşa, *Turkey* 41 E10
Lalbenque, *France* 20 D5
L'Albufera, *Spain* 33 F4
Lalganj, *India* 69 G11
Lalgola, *India* 69 G13
Lālī, *Iran* 71 C6
Lalibela, *Ethiopia* 81 E4
Lalin, *China* 57 B14
Lalín, *Spain* 34 C2
Lalin He →, *China* 57 B13
Lalinde, *France* 20 D4
Lalitapur = Patan, *Nepal* .. 67 F14
Lalitpur, *India* 69 G8
Lalkua, *India* 69 E8
Lalsot, *India* 68 F7
Lam, *Vietnam* 64 B6
Lam Pao Res., *Thailand* ... 64 D4
Lama Kara, *Togo* 83 D5
Lamaing, *Burma* 67 M20
Lamar, *Colo., U.S.A.* 112 F3
Lamar, *Mo., U.S.A.* 113 G7
Lamas, *Peru* 124 E3
Lamastre, *France* 21 D8
Lambach, *Austria* 26 C6
Lamballe, *France* 18 D4
Lambaréné, *Gabon* 84 E2
Lambasa, *Fiji* 91 C8
Lambay I., *Ireland* 15 C5
Lambert Glacier, *Antarctica* 5 D6
Lambert's Bay, *S. Africa* ... 88 E2
Lambesc, *France* 21 E9
Lambeth, *Canada* 110 D3
Lambi Kyun, *Burma* 65 G2
Lámbia, *Greece* 38 D3
Lambomakondro, *Madag.* .. 89 C7
Lambro →, *Italy* 28 C6
Lame, *Nigeria* 83 C6
Lame Deer, *U.S.A.* 114 D10
Lamego, *Portugal* 34 D3
Lamèque, *Canada* 103 C7
Lameroo, *Australia* 95 F3
Lamesa, *U.S.A.* 113 J4
Lamía, *Greece* 38 C4
Lamitan, *Phil.* 61 H5
Lammermuir Hills, *U.K.* ... 14 F6
Lammhult, *Sweden* 11 G8
Lamoille →, *U.S.A.* 111 B11
Lamon B., *Phil.* 61 D5
Lamont, *Canada* 104 C6
Lamont, *Calif., U.S.A.* 117 K8
Lamont, *Wyo., U.S.A.* 114 E10
Lamotte-Beuvron, *France* .. 19 E9
Lampa, *Peru* 124 G4
Lampang, *Thailand* 64 C2
Lampasas, *U.S.A.* 113 K5
Lampazos de Naranjo, *Mexico* 118 B4
Lampertheim, *Germany* 25 F4
Lampeter, *U.K.* 13 E3
Lampman, *Canada* 105 D8
Lamprechtshausen, *Austria* . 26 D5
Lampung □, *Indonesia* 62 F2
Lamta, *India* 69 H9
Lamu, *Kenya* 86 C5
Lamy, *U.S.A.* 115 J11
Lan Xian, *China* 56 E6
Lan Yu = Hungt'ou Hsü, *Taiwan* 59 F13
Lanai, *U.S.A.* 106 H16
Lanak La, *India* 69 B8
Lanak'o Shank'ou = Lanak La, *India* 69 B8
Lanao, L., *Phil.* 61 H6
Lanark, *Canada* 111 A8
Lanark, *U.K.* 14 F5
Lancang, *China* 58 F2
Lancang Jiang →, *China* .. 58 G3
Lancashire □, *U.K.* 12 D5
Lancaster, *Canada* 111 A10
Lancaster, *U.K.* 12 C5
Lancaster, *Calif., U.S.A.* ... 117 L8
Lancaster, *Ky., U.S.A.* 108 G3
Lancaster, *N.H., U.S.A.* ... 111 B13
Lancaster, *N.Y., U.S.A.* ... 110 D6
Lancaster, *Ohio, U.S.A.* ... 108 F4
Lancaster, *Pa., U.S.A.* 111 F8
Lancaster, *S.C., U.S.A.* ... 109 H5
Lancaster, *Wis., U.S.A.* ... 112 D9
Lancaster Sd., *Canada* 101 A11
Lancelin, *Australia* 93 F2
Lanchow = Lanzhou, *China* 56 F2
Lanciano, *Italy* 29 F11
Lancun, *China* 57 F11
Łańcut, *Poland* 45 H9
Landau, *Bayern, Germany* . 25 G8
Landau, *Rhld-Pfz., Germany* 25 F4
Landeck, *Austria* 26 D3
Lander, *U.S.A.* 114 E9
Lander →, *Australia* 92 D5
Landerneau, *France* 18 D2
Landeryd, *Sweden* 11 G7
Landes, *France* 20 D2
Landes □, *France* 20 E3
Landete, *Spain* 32 F3
Landi Kotal, *Pakistan* 68 B4
Landisburg, *U.S.A.* 110 F7
Landivisiau, *France* 18 D2
Landquart, *Switz.* 25 J5
Landrecies, *France* 19 B10
Land's End, *U.K.* 13 G2
Landsborough Cr. →, *Australia* 94 C3
Landsbro, *Sweden* 11 G8
Landshut, *Germany* 25 G8
Landskrona, *Sweden* 11 J6
Landstuhl, *Germany* 25 F3
Landvetter, *Sweden* 11 G6
Lanesboro, *U.S.A.* 111 E9
Lanester, *France* 18 E3
Lanett, *U.S.A.* 109 J3
Lang Qua, *Vietnam* 64 A5
Lang Shan, *China* 56 D4
Lang Son, *Vietnam* 58 G6
Lang Suan, *Thailand* 65 H2
Langå, *Denmark* 11 H3
La'nga Co, *China* 67 D12
Langådhás, *Greece* 40 F7
Langádhia, *Greece* 38 D4
Långan →, *Sweden* 10 A8
Langano, L., *Ethiopia* 81 F4
Langar, *Iran* 71 C9
Langara I., *Canada* 104 C2
Långås, *Sweden* 11 H6
Langdai, *China* 58 D5
Langdon, *U.S.A.* 112 A5
Långe Jan = Ölands södra udde, *Sweden* 11 H10
Langeac, *France* 20 C7
Langeais, *France* 18 E7
Langeb Baraka →, *Sudan* . 80 D4
Langeberg, *S. Africa* 88 E3
Langeberge, *S. Africa* 88 D3
Langeland, *Denmark* 11 K4
Langelands Bælt, *Denmark* . 11 K4
Langen, *Hessen, Germany* . 25 F4
Langen, *Niedersachsen, Germany* 24 B4
Langenburg, *Canada* 105 C8
Langeneß, *Germany* 24 A4
Langenlois, *Austria* 26 C8
Langeoog, *Germany* 24 B3
Langeskov, *Denmark* 11 J4
Länghem, *Sweden* 11 G7
Langhirano, *Italy* 28 D7
Langholm, *U.K.* 14 F5
Langjökull, *Iceland* 8 D3
Langkawi, Pulau, *Malaysia* . 65 J2
Langklip, *S. Africa* 88 D3
Langkon, *Malaysia* 62 C5
Langlade, *St- P. & M.* 103 C8
Langley, *Canada* 116 A4
Langnau, *Switz.* 25 J3
Langogne, *France* 20 D7
Langon, *France* 20 D3
Langøya, *Norway* 8 B16
Langreo, *Spain* 34 B5
Langres, *France* 19 E12
Langres, Plateau de, *France* 19 E12
Langsa, *Indonesia* 62 D1
Långsele, *Sweden* 10 A11
Långshyttan, *Sweden* 10 D10
Langtry, *U.S.A.* 113 L4
Langu, *Thailand* 65 J2
Languedoc, *France* 20 E7
Languedoc-Roussillon □, *France* 20 E6
Langxi, *China* 59 B12
Langxiangzhen, *China* 56 E9
Langzhong, *China* 58 B5
Lanigan, *Canada* 105 C7
Lankao, *China* 56 G8
Länkäran, *Azerbaijan* 71 B6
Lanmeur, *France* 18 D3
Lannemezan, *France* 20 E4
Lannilis, *France* 18 D2
Lannion, *France* 18 D3
L'Annonciation, *Canada* ... 102 C5
Lanouaille, *France* 20 C5
Lanping, *China* 58 D2
Lansdale, *U.S.A.* 111 F9
Lansdowne, *Australia* 95 E5
Lansdowne, *Canada* 111 B8
Lansdowne, *India* 69 E8
Lansdowne House, *Canada* . 102 B2
L'Anse, *Mich., U.S.A.* 108 B1
L'Anse, *Mich., U.S.A.* 112 B10
L'Anse au Loup, *Canada* .. 103 B8
L'Anse aux Meadows, *Canada* 103 B8
Lansford, *U.S.A.* 111 F9
Lanshan, *China* 59 E9
Lansing, *U.S.A.* 108 D3
Lanslebourg-Mont-Cenis, *France* 21 C10
Lanta Yai, Ko, *Thailand* ... 65 J2
Lantewa, *Nigeria* 83 C7
Lantian, *China* 56 G5
Lanus, *Argentina* 126 C4
Lanusei, *Italy* 30 C2
Lanuza, *Phil.* 61 G7
Lanxi, *China* 59 C12
Lanzarote, *Canary Is.* 37 F6
Lanzhou, *China* 56 F2
Lanzo Torinese, *Italy* 28 C4
Lao →, *Italy* 31 C8
Lao Bao, *Laos* 64 D6
Lao Cai, *Vietnam* 58 F4
Laoag, *Phil.* 61 B4
Laoang, *Phil.* 61 E6
Laoha He →, *China* 57 C11
Laohekou, *China* 59 A8
Laois □, *Ireland* 15 D4
Laon, *France* 19 C10
Laona, *U.S.A.* 108 C1
Laos ■, *Asia* 64 D5
Lapa, *Brazil* 127 B6
Lapai, *Nigeria* 83 D6
Lapalisse, *France* 19 F10
Lapeer, *U.S.A.* 108 D4
Lapeyrade, *France* 20 D3
Lapithos, *Cyprus* 36 D12
Lapland = Lappland, *Europe* 8 B21
Laporte, *U.S.A.* 111 E8
Lapovo, *Serbia, Yug.* 40 B5
Lappeenranta, *Finland* 9 F23
Lappland, *Europe* 8 B21
Laprida, *Argentina* 126 D3
Lapseki, *Turkey* 41 F10
Laptev Sea, *Russia* 51 B13
Lapua, *Finland* 8 E20
Lăpuş →, *Romania* 43 C8
Lapuş, Munţii, *Romania* ... 43 C8
Lăpuşna, *Moldova* 43 D13
Łapy, *Poland* 45 F9
Laqiya Arba'in, *Sudan* 80 C2
Laqiya Umran, *Sudan* 80 D2
L'Áquila, *Italy* 29 F10
Lār, *Āzarbājān-e Sharqī, Iran* 70 B5
Lār, *Fārs, Iran* 71 E7
Larabanga, *Ghana* 82 D4
Laragne-Montéglin, *France* . 21 D9
Laramie, *U.S.A.* 112 E2
Laramie →, *U.S.A.* 114 F11
Laramie Mts., *U.S.A.* 112 E2
Laranjeiras do Sul, *Brazil* .. 127 B5
Larantuka, *Indonesia* 63 F6
Larat, *Indonesia* 63 F8
L'Arbresle, *France* 21 C8
Lärbro, *Sweden* 11 G12
Larde, *Mozam.* 87 F4
Larder Lake, *Canada* 102 C4
Lardhos, Ákra = Líndhos, Ákra, *Greece* 36 C10
Lardhos, Órmos, *Greece* ... 36 C10
Laredo, *Spain* 34 B7
Laredo, *U.S.A.* 113 M5
Laredo Sd., *Canada* 104 C3
Largentière, *France* 21 D8
L'Argentière-la-Bessée, *France* 21 D10
Largo, *U.S.A.* 109 M4
Largs, *U.K.* 14 F4
Lari, *Italy* 28 E7
Lariang, *Indonesia* 63 E5
Larimore, *U.S.A.* 112 B6
Lārīn, *Iran* 71 C7
Larino, *Italy* 29 G11
Lárisa, *Greece* 38 B4
Lárisa □, *Greece* 38 B4
Larkana, *Pakistan* 68 F3
Larnaca, *Cyprus* 36 E12
Larnaca Bay, *Cyprus* 36 E12
Larne, *U.K.* 15 B6
Larned, *U.S.A.* 112 F5
Laroquebrou, *France* 20 D6
Larose, *U.S.A.* 113 L9
Larrimah, *Australia* 92 C5
Larsen Ice Shelf, *Antarctica* 5 C17
Laruns, *France* 20 F3
Larvik, *Norway* 9 G14
Larzac, Causse du, *France* . 20 E7
Las Alpujarras, *Spain* 33 J1
Las Animas, *U.S.A.* 112 F3
Las Anod, *Somali Rep.* 74 F4
Las Arenas, *Spain* 34 B6
Las Aves, Is., *W. Indies* ... 121 C7
Las Brenãs, *Argentina* 126 B3
Las Cabezas de San Juan, *Spain* 35 J5
Las Cejas, *Argentina* 128 B4
Las Chimeneas, *Mexico* 117 N10
Las Cruces, *U.S.A.* 115 K10
Las Flores, *Argentina* 126 D4
Las Heras, *Argentina* 126 C2
Las Lajas, *Argentina* 128 D2
Las Lomitas, *Argentina* 126 A3
Las Marismas, *Spain* 35 H4
Las Minas, *Spain* 33 G3
Las Navas de la Concepción, *Spain* 35 H5
Las Navas del Marqués, *Spain* 34 E6
Las Palmas, *Argentina* 126 B4
Las Palmas, *Canary Is.* 37 F4
Las Palmas →, *Mexico* 117 N10
Las Pedroñas, *Spain* 33 F2
Las Piedras, *Uruguay* 127 C4
Las Pipinas, *Argentina* 126 D4
Las Plumas, *Argentina* 128 E3
Las Rosas, *Argentina* 126 C3
Las Rozas, *Spain* 34 E7
Las Tablas, *Panama* 120 E3
Las Termas, *Argentina* 126 B3
Las Toscas, *Argentina* 126 B4
Las Truchas, *Mexico* 118 D4
Las Varillas, *Argentina* 126 C3
Las Vegas, *N. Mex., U.S.A.* 115 J11
Las Vegas, *Nev., U.S.A.* ... 117 J11
Lasarte, *Spain* 32 B2
Lascano, *Uruguay* 127 C5
Lashburn, *Canada* 105 C7
Lashio, *Burma* 67 H20
Lashkar, *India* 68 F8
Łasin, *Poland* 44 E6
Lasíthi, *Greece* 36 D7
Lasíthi □, *Greece* 36 D7
Lāsjerd, *Iran* 71 C7
Lask, *Poland* 45 G6
Łaskarzew, *Poland* 45 G8
Laško, *Slovenia* 29 B12
Lassay-les-Châteaux, *France* 18 D6
Lassen Pk., *U.S.A.* 114 F3
Lassen Volcanic National Park, *U.S.A.* 114 F3
Last Mountain L., *Canada* . 105 C7
Lastchance Cr. →, *U.S.A.* . 116 E5

Lastoursville

Lastoursville, *Gabon*	84	E2
Lastovo, *Croatia*	29	F13
Lastovski Kanal, *Croatia*	29	F14
Lat Yao, *Thailand*	64	E2
Latacunga, *Ecuador*	124	D3
Latakia = Al Lādhiqīyah, *Syria*	70	C2
Latchford, *Canada*	102	C4
Latehar, *India*	69	H11
Laterza, *Italy*	31	B9
Latham, *Australia*	93	E2
Lathen, *Germany*	24	C3
Lathi, *India*	68	F4
Lathrop Wells, *U.S.A.*	117	J10
Latiano, *Italy*	31	B10
Latina, *Italy*	30	A5
Latisana, *Italy*	29	C10
Latium = Lazio □, *Italy*	29	F9
Laton, *U.S.A.*	116	J7
Latorytsya →, *Slovak Rep.*	27	C14
Latouche Treville, C., *Australia*	92	C3
Latrobe, *Australia*	94	G4
Latrobe, *U.S.A.*	110	F5
Latrónico, *Italy*	31	B9
Latvia ■, *Europe*	9	H20
Lau, *Nigeria*	83	D7
Lau Group, *Fiji*	91	C9
Lauchhammer, *Germany*	24	D9
Lauda-Königshofen, *Germany*	25	F5
Lauenburg, *Germany*	24	B6
Lauf, *Germany*	25	F7
Laughlin, *U.S.A.*	115	J6
Laujar de Andarax, *Spain*	33	H2
Laukaa, *Finland*	9	E21
Launceston, *Australia*	94	G4
Launceston, *U.K.*	13	G3
Laune →, *Ireland*	15	D2
Launglon Bok, *Burma*	64	F1
Laupheim, *Germany*	25	G5
Laura, *Australia*	94	B3
Laureana di Borrello, *Italy*	31	D9
Laurel, *Miss., U.S.A.*	113	K10
Laurel, *Mont., U.S.A.*	114	D9
Laurencekirk, *U.K.*	14	E6
Laurens, *U.S.A.*	109	H4
Laurentian Plateau, *Canada*	103	B6
Lauria, *Italy*	31	B8
Laurie L., *Canada*	105	B8
Laurinburg, *U.S.A.*	109	H6
Laurium, *U.S.A.*	108	B1
Lausanne, *Switz.*	25	J2
Laut, *Indonesia*	65	K6
Laut, Pulau, *Indonesia*	62	E5
Laut Kecil, Kepulauan, *Indonesia*	62	E5
Lauterbach, *Germany*	24	E5
Lauterecken, *Germany*	25	F3
Lautoka, *Fiji*	91	C7
Lauzès, *France*	20	D5
Lauzès, *France*	20	D5
Lavagna, *Italy*	28	D6
Laval, *France*	18	D6
Lavalle, *Argentina*	126	B2
Lavant Station, *Canada*	111	A8
Lāvar Meydān, *Iran*	71	D7
Lávara, *Greece*	41	E10
Lavardac, *France*	20	D4
Lavaur, *France*	20	E5
Lavelanet, *France*	20	F5
Lavello, *Italy*	31	A8
Laverton, *Australia*	93	E3
Lavis, *Italy*	28	B8
Lávkos, *Greece*	38	B5
Lavos, *Portugal*	34	E2
Lavradio, *Portugal*	35	G1
Lavras, *Brazil*	127	A7
Lavre, *Portugal*	35	G2
Lávrion, *Greece*	38	D6
Lávris, *Greece*	36	D6
Lavumisa, *Swaziland*	89	D5
Lawas, *Malaysia*	62	D5
Lawele, *Indonesia*	63	F6
Lawng Pit, *Burma*	67	G20
Lawqah, *Si. Arabia*	70	D4
Lawra, *Ghana*	82	C4
Lawrence, *N.Z.*	91	L2
Lawrence, *Kans., U.S.A.*	112	F7
Lawrence, *Mass., U.S.A.*	111	D13
Lawrenceburg, *Ind., U.S.A.*	108	F3
Lawrenceburg, *Tenn., U.S.A.*	109	H2
Lawrenceville, *Ga., U.S.A.*	109	J4
Lawrenceville, *Pa., U.S.A.*	110	E7
Laws, *U.S.A.*	116	H8
Lawton, *U.S.A.*	113	H5
Lawu, *Indonesia*	63	G14
Lawz, J. al, *Si. Arabia*	80	B4
Laxå, *Sweden*	11	F8
Laxford, L., *U.K.*	14	C3
Laxou, *France*	19	D13
Lay →, *France*	20	B2
Laylá, *Si. Arabia*	74	C4
Laylān, *Iraq*	70	C5
Layon →, *France*	18	E6
Layton, *U.S.A.*	114	F7
Laytonville, *U.S.A.*	114	G2
Lazarevac, *Serbia, Yug.*	40	B4
Lazarevskoye, *Russia*	49	J4
Lazarivo, *Madag.*	89	C8
Lazdijai, *Lithuania*	44	D10
Lazio □, *Italy*	29	F9
Lazo, *Moldova*	43	C13
Lazo, *Russia*	54	C6
Le Beausset, *France*	21	E9
Le Blanc, *France*	20	B5
Le Bleymard, *France*	20	D7
Le Bourgneuf-la-Forêt, *France*	18	D6
Le Bugue, *France*	20	D4

Le Canourgue = La Canourgue, *France*	20	D7
Le Cateau Cambrésis, *France*	19	B10
Le Caylar, *France*	20	E7
Le Chambon-Feugerolles, *France*	21	C8
Le Châtelet, *France*	19	F9
Le Chesne, *France*	19	C11
Le Cheylard, *France*	21	D8
Le Conquet, *France*	18	D2
Le Creusot, *France*	19	F11
Le Croisic, *France*	18	E4
Le Donjon, *France*	19	F10
Le Dorat, *France*	20	B5
Le François, *Martinique*	121	D7
Le Grand-Lucé, *France*	18	E7
Le Grand-Pressigny, *France*	18	F7
Le Grand-Quevilly, *France*	18	C8
Le Havre, *France*	18	C7
Le Lavandou, *France*	21	E10
Le Lion-d'Angers, *France*	18	E6
Le Louroux-Béconnais, *France*	18	E6
Le Luc, *France*	21	E10
Le Lude, *France*	18	E7
Le Mans, *France*	18	E7
Le Mars, *U.S.A.*	112	D6
Le Mayet-de-Montagne, *France*	19	F10
Le Mêle-sur-Sarthe, *France*	18	D7
Le Monastier-sur-Gazeille, *France*	20	D7
Le Monêtier-les-Bains, *France*	21	D10
Le Mont-Dore, *France*	20	C6
Le Mont-St-Michel, *France*	18	D5
Le Moule, *Guadeloupe*	121	C7
Le Muy, *France*	21	E10
Le Palais, *France*	18	E3
Le Perthus, *France*	20	F6
Le Puy-en-Velay, *France*	20	C7
Le Sueur, *U.S.A.*	112	C8
Le Teil, *France*	21	D8
Le Teilleul, *France*	18	D6
Le Theil, *France*	18	D7
Le Thillot, *France*	19	E13
Le Thuy, *Vietnam*	64	D6
Le Touquet-Paris-Plage, *France*	19	B8
Le Tréport, *France*	18	B8
Le Val-d'Ajol, *France*	19	E13
Le Verdon-sur-Mer, *France*	20	C2
Le Vigan, *France*	20	E7
Lea →, *U.K.*	13	F8
Leach, *Cambodia*	65	F4
Lead, *U.S.A.*	112	C3
Leader, *Canada*	105	C7
Leadville, *U.S.A.*	115	G10
Leaf →, *U.S.A.*	113	K10
Leaf Rapids, *Canada*	105	B9
Leamington, *Canada*	102	D3
Leamington, *U.S.A.*	114	G7
Leamington Spa = Royal Leamington Spa, *U.K.*	13	E6
Le'an, *China*	59	D10
Leandro Norte Alem, *Argentina*	127	B4
Leane, L., *Ireland*	15	D2
Learmonth, *Australia*	92	D1
Leask, *Canada*	105	C7
Leatherhead, *U.K.*	13	F7
Leavenworth, *Kans., U.S.A.*	112	F7
Leavenworth, *Wash., U.S.A.*	114	C3
Łeba, *Poland*	44	D4
Łeba →, *Poland*	44	D4
Lebach, *Germany*	25	F2
Lebak, *Phil.*	61	H6
Lebam, *U.S.A.*	116	D3
Lebane, *Serbia, Yug.*	40	D5
Lebanon, *Ind., U.S.A.*	108	E2
Lebanon, *Kans., U.S.A.*	112	F5
Lebanon, *Ky., U.S.A.*	108	G3
Lebanon, *Mo., U.S.A.*	113	G8
Lebanon, *N.H., U.S.A.*	111	C12
Lebanon, *Oreg., U.S.A.*	114	D2
Lebanon, *Pa., U.S.A.*	111	F8
Lebanon, *Tenn., U.S.A.*	109	G2
Lebanon ■, *Asia*	75	B5
Lebec, *U.S.A.*	117	L8
Lebedyan, *Russia*	47	F10
Lebedyn, *Ukraine*	47	G8
Lebel-sur-Quévillon, *Canada*	102	C4
Lebomboberge, *S. Africa*	89	C5
Lębork, *Poland*	44	D4
Lebrija, *Spain*	35	J4
Lebu, *Chile*	126	D1
Leca da Palmeira, *Portugal*	34	D2
Lecce, *Italy*	31	B11
Lecco, *Italy*	28	C6
Lecco, L. di, *Italy*	28	C6
Lécera, *Spain*	32	D4
Lech, *Austria*	26	D3
Lech →, *Germany*	25	G6
Lechang, *China*	59	E9
Lechtaler Alpen, *Austria*	26	D3
Lecontes Mills, *U.S.A.*	110	E6
Lectoure, *France*	20	E4
Łęczna, *Poland*	45	G9
Łęczyca, *Poland*	45	F6
Ledesma, *Spain*	34	D5
Ledong, *China*	64	C7
Leduc, *Canada*	104	C6
Lee, *U.S.A.*	111	D11
Lee →, *Ireland*	15	E3
Lee Vining, *U.S.A.*	116	H7
Leech L., *U.S.A.*	112	B7
Leechburg, *U.S.A.*	110	F5
Leeds, *U.K.*	12	D6
Leeds, *U.S.A.*	109	J2
Leek, *Neths.*	17	A6

Leek, *U.K.*	12	D5
Leeman, *Australia*	93	E1
Leeper, *U.S.A.*	110	E5
Leer, *Germany*	24	B3
Leesburg, *U.S.A.*	109	L5
Leesville, *U.S.A.*	113	K8
Leeton, *Australia*	95	E4
Leetonia, *U.S.A.*	110	F4
Leeu Gamka, *S. Africa*	88	E3
Leeuwarden, *Neths.*	17	A5
Leeuwin, C., *Australia*	93	F2
Leeward Is., *Atl. Oc.*	121	C7
Lefka, *Cyprus*	36	D11
Lefkoniko, *Cyprus*	36	D12
Lefroy, *Canada*	110	B5
Lefroy, L., *Australia*	93	F3
Łęg →, *Poland*	45	H8
Leganés, *Spain*	34	E7
Legazpi, *Phil.*	61	E5
Lège, *France*	20	D2
Lege Hida, *Ethiopia*	81	F5
Legendre I., *Australia*	92	D2
Leghorn = Livorno, *Italy*	28	E7
Legionowo, *Poland*	45	F7
Legnago, *Italy*	29	C8
Legnano, *Italy*	28	C5
Legnica, *Poland*	45	G3
Legrad, *Croatia*	29	B13
Leh, *India*	69	B7
Lehigh Acres, *U.S.A.*	109	M5
Lehighton, *U.S.A.*	111	F9
Lehliu, *Romania*	43	F11
Leho, *Sudan*	81	F3
Lehrte, *Germany*	24	C5
Lehututu, *Botswana*	88	C3
Lei Shui →, *China*	59	D9
Leiah, *Pakistan*	68	D4
Leibnitz, *Austria*	26	E8
Leibo, *China*	58	C4
Leicester, *U.K.*	13	E6
Leicester City □, *U.K.*	13	E6
Leicestershire □, *U.K.*	13	E6
Leichhardt →, *Australia*	94	B2
Leichhardt Ra., *Australia*	94	C4
Leiden, *Neths.*	17	B4
Leie →, *Belgium*	17	C3
Leifers = Láives, *Italy*	29	B8
Leigh Creek, *Australia*	95	E2
Leimen, *Germany*	25	F4
Leine →, *Germany*	24	C5
Leinefelde, *Germany*	24	D6
Leinster, *Australia*	93	E3
Leinster □, *Ireland*	15	C4
Leinster, Mt., *Ireland*	15	D5
Leipalingis, *Lithuania*	44	D10
Leipzig, *Germany*	24	D8
Leiria, *Portugal*	34	F2
Leiria □, *Portugal*	34	F2
Leirvik, *Norway*	9	G11
Leishan, *China*	58	D7
Leisler, Mt., *Australia*	92	D4
Leith, *U.K.*	14	F5
Leith Hill, *U.K.*	13	F7
Leitha →, *Europe*	27	D10
Leitrim, *Ireland*	15	B3
Leitrim □, *Ireland*	15	B4
Leitza, *Spain*	32	B3
Leiyang, *China*	59	D9
Leizhou, *China*	59	G8
Leizhou Bandao, *China*	58	G7
Leizhou Wan, *China*	59	G8
Lek →, *Neths.*	17	C4
Leka, *Norway*	8	D14
Lekáni, *Greece*	41	E8
Lekbibaj, *Albania*	40	D3
Lekeitio, *Spain*	32	B2
Lekhainá, *Greece*	38	D3
Lekoui, *Burkina Faso*	82	C4
Leksand, *Sweden*	10	D9
Lékva Óros, *Greece*	36	D6
Leland, *Mich., U.S.A.*	108	C3
Leland, *Miss., U.S.A.*	113	J9
Lelång, *Sweden*	10	E6
Leleque, *Argentina*	128	E2
Lelystad, *Neths.*	17	B5
Lem, *Denmark*	11	H2
Lema, *Nigeria*	83	C5
Lema Shilindi, *Ethiopia*	81	G5
Léman, L., *Europe*	19	F13
Lemera, *Dem. Rep. of the Congo*	86	C2
Lemery, *Phil.*	61	E4
Lemhi Ra., *U.S.A.*	114	D7
Lemmer, *Neths.*	17	B5
Lemmon, *U.S.A.*	112	C3
Lemon Grove, *U.S.A.*	117	N9
Lemoore, *U.S.A.*	116	J7
Lempdes, *France*	20	C7
Lemvig, *Denmark*	11	H2
Lena →, *Russia*	51	B13
Lenart, *Slovenia*	29	B12
Lenartovce, *Slovak Rep.*	27	C13
Lencloître, *France*	18	F7
Léndas, *Greece*	36	E6
Lendava, *Slovenia*	29	B13
Lendeh, *Iran*	71	D6
Lendinara, *Italy*	29	C8
Lengerich, *Germany*	24	C3
Lenggong, *Malaysia*	65	K3
Lenggries, *Germany*	25	H7
Lengshuijiang, *China*	59	D8
Lengshuitan, *China*	59	D8
Lengua de Vaca, Pta., *Chile*	126	C1
Lengyeltóti, *Hungary*	42	D2
Lenhovda, *Sweden*	11	G9
Lenina, Kanal →, *Russia*	49	J7
Leninabad = Khudzhand, *Tajikistan*	50	E7
Leninakan = Gyumri, *Armenia*	49	K6

Leningrad = Sankt-Peterburg, *Russia*	46	C6
Lenino, *Ukraine*	47	K8
Leninogorsk, *Kazakstan*	50	D9
Leninsk, *Russia*	49	F7
Leninsk-Kuznetskiy, *Russia*	50	D9
Leninskoye, *Russia*	48	A8
Lenk, *Switz.*	25	J3
Lenkoran = Länkäran, *Azerbaijan*	71	B6
Lenmalu, *Indonesia*	63	E8
Lenne →, *Germany*	24	D3
Lennestadt, *Germany*	24	D4
Lennox, *U.S.A.*	112	D6
Lennoxville, *Canada*	111	A13
Leno, *Italy*	28	C7
Lenoir, *U.S.A.*	109	H5
Lenoir City, *U.S.A.*	109	H3
Lenore L., *Canada*	105	C8
Lenox, *U.S.A.*	111	D11
Lens, *France*	19	B9
Lensahn, *Germany*	24	A6
Lensk, *Russia*	51	C12
Lentekhi, *Georgia*	49	J6
Lenti, *Hungary*	42	D1
Lentini, *Italy*	31	E8
Lenwood, *U.S.A.*	117	L9
Lenya, *Burma*	62	B1
Léo, *Burkina Faso*	82	C4
Leoben, *Austria*	26	D8
Leodhas = Lewis, *U.K.*	14	C2
Leola, *U.S.A.*	112	C5
Leominster, *U.K.*	13	E5
Leominster, *U.S.A.*	111	D13
Léon, *France*	20	E2
León, *Mexico*	118	C4
León, *Nic.*	120	D2
León, *Spain*	34	C5
León, *U.S.A.*	112	E8
León □, *Spain*	34	C5
León →, *U.S.A.*	113	K6
León, Montes de, *Spain*	34	C4
Leonardtown, *U.S.A.*	108	F7
Leonardville, *Namibia*	88	C2
Leonberg, *Germany*	25	G5
Leonding, *Austria*	26	C7
Leonessa, *Italy*	29	F9
Leonforte, *Italy*	31	E7
Leongatha, *Australia*	95	F4
Leonídhion, *Greece*	38	D4
Leonora, *Australia*	93	E3
Léopold II, Lac = Mai-Ndombe, L., *Dem. Rep. of the Congo*	84	E3
Leopoldina, *Brazil*	127	A7
Leopoldsburg, *Belgium*	17	C5
Léopoldville = Kinshasa, *Dem. Rep. of the Congo*	84	E3
Leoti, *U.S.A.*	112	F4
Leova, *Moldova*	43	D13
Leoville, *Canada*	105	C7
Lepe, *Spain*	35	H3
Lepel = Lyepyel, *Belarus*	46	E5
Lepenoú, *Greece*	38	C3
Leping, *China*	59	C11
Lépo, L. do, *Angola*	88	B2
Lepontine, Alpi, *Italy*	28	B5
Leppävirta, *Finland*	9	E22
Lepsény, *Hungary*	42	D3
Lequeitio = Lekeitio, *Spain*	32	B2
Lercara Friddi, *Italy*	30	E6
Lerdo, *Mexico*	118	B4
Léré, *Chad*	83	D7
Léré, *Mali*	82	B4
Lere, *Bauchi, Nigeria*	83	D6
Lere, *Kaduna, Nigeria*	83	C6
Leribe, *Lesotho*	89	D4
Lérici, *Italy*	28	D6
Lérins, Îs. de, *France*	21	E11
Lerma, *Spain*	34	C7
Léros, *Greece*	39	D8
Lérouville, *France*	19	D12
Lerum, *Sweden*	11	G6
Lerwick, *U.K.*	14	A7
Leş, *Romania*	42	D6
Les Abrets, *France*	21	C9
Les Andelys, *France*	18	C8
Les Borges Blanques, *Spain*	32	D5
Les Cayes, *Haiti*	121	C5
Les Essarts, *France*	18	F5
Les Herbiers, *France*	18	F5
Les Minquiers, Plateau des, *Chan. Is.*	18	D4
Les Pieux, *France*	18	C5
Les Ponts-de-Cé, *France*	18	E6
Les Riceys, *France*	19	E11
Les Sables-d'Olonne, *France*	20	B2
Les Vans, *France*	21	D8
Lesbos = Lésvos, *Greece*	39	B8
L'Escala, *Spain*	32	C8
Lésina, *Italy*	29	G12
Lésina, L. di, *Italy*	29	G12
Lesjöfors, *Sweden*	10	E8
Lesko, *Poland*	45	J9
Leskovac, *Serbia, Yug.*	40	C5
Leskoviku, *Albania*	40	F4
Leśna, *Poland*	45	G2
Lesna, *Serbia, Yug.*	40	B3
Lesnoye, *Russia*	46	C9
Lesopilnoye, *Russia*	54	A7
Lesotho ■, *Africa*	89	D4
Lesozavodsk, *Russia*	51	E14
Lesparre-Médoc, *France*	20	C3
Lessay, *France*	18	C5
Lesse →, *Belgium*	17	D4

Lessebo, *Sweden*	11	H9
Lesser Antilles, *W. Indies*	121	D7
Lesser Slave L., *Canada*	104	B5
Lesser Sunda Is., *Indonesia*	63	F6
Lessines, *Belgium*	17	D3
Lester, *U.S.A.*	116	C5
Lestock, *Canada*	105	C8
Lesuer I., *Australia*	92	B4
Lésvos, *Greece*	39	B8
Leszno, *Poland*	45	G3
Letaba, *S. Africa*	89	C5
Letälven, *Sweden*	10	E8
Létavértes, *Hungary*	42	C6
Letchworth, *U.K.*	13	F7
Letea, Ostrov, *Romania*	43	E14
Lethbridge, *Canada*	104	D6
Lethem, *Guyana*	124	C7
Leti, Kepulauan, *Indonesia*	63	F7
Leti Is. = Leti, Kepulauan, *Indonesia*	63	F7
Letiahau →, *Botswana*	88	C3
Leticia, *Colombia*	124	D5
Leting, *China*	57	E10
Letjiesbos, *S. Africa*	88	E3
Letlhakane, *Botswana*	88	C4
Letlhakeng, *Botswana*	88	C3
Letong, *Indonesia*	62	D3
Letpadan, *Burma*	67	L19
Letpan, *Burma*	67	K19
Letsôk-aw Kyun, *Burma*	65	G2
Letterkenny, *Ireland*	15	B4
Leu, *Romania*	43	F9
Leucadia, *U.S.A.*	117	M9
Leucate, *France*	20	F7
Leucate, Étang de, *France*	20	F7
Leuk, *Switz.*	25	J3
Leuşeni, *Moldova*	43	D13
Leuser, G., *Indonesia*	62	D1
Leutkirch, *Germany*	25	H6
Leuven, *Belgium*	17	D4
Leuze-en-Hainaut, *Belgium*	17	D3
Lev Tolstoy, *Russia*	46	F10
Levádhia, *Greece*	38	C4
Levanger, *Norway*	8	E14
Levani, *Albania*	40	F3
Levant, Î. du, *France*	21	E10
Lévanto, *Italy*	28	D6
Lévanzo, *Italy*	30	D5
Levelland, *U.S.A.*	113	J3
Leven, *U.K.*	14	E6
Leven, L., *U.K.*	14	E5
Leven, Toraka, *Madag.*	89	A8
Leveque C., *Australia*	92	C3
Leverano, *Italy*	31	B10
Leverkusen, *Germany*	24	D3
Levice, *Slovak Rep.*	27	C11
Lévico Terme, *Italy*	29	C8
Levie, *France*	21	G13
Levier, *France*	19	F13
Levin, *N.Z.*	91	J5
Lévis, *Canada*	103	C5
Levis, L., *Canada*	104	A5
Levítha, *Greece*	39	D8
Levittown, *N.Y., U.S.A.*	111	F11
Levittown, *Pa., U.S.A.*	111	F10
Levka, *Bulgaria*	41	E10
Levkás, *Greece*	38	C2
Levkás □, *Greece*	38	C2
Levkímmi, *Greece*	36	B4
Levkímmi, Ákra, *Greece*	36	B4
Levkôsia = Nicosia, *Cyprus*	36	D12
Levoča, *Slovak Rep.*	27	B13
Levroux, *France*	19	F8
Levski, *Bulgaria*	41	C9
Levskigrad = Karlovo, *Bulgaria*	41	D8
Lewes, *U.K.*	13	G8
Lewes, *U.S.A.*	108	F8
Lewin Brzeski, *Poland*	45	H4
Lewis, *U.K.*	14	C2
Lewis →, *U.S.A.*	116	E4
Lewis, Butt of, *U.K.*	14	C2
Lewis Ra., *Australia*	92	D4
Lewis Range, *U.S.A.*	114	B7
Lewis Run, *U.S.A.*	110	E6
Lewisburg, *Pa., U.S.A.*	110	F8
Lewisburg, *Tenn., U.S.A.*	109	H2
Lewisburg, *W. Va., U.S.A.*	108	G5
Lewisporte, *Canada*	103	C8
Lewiston, *Idaho, U.S.A.*	114	C5
Lewiston, *Maine, U.S.A.*	109	C11
Lewiston, *N.Y., U.S.A.*	110	C5
Lewistown, *Mont., U.S.A.*	114	C9
Lewistown, *Pa., U.S.A.*	110	F7
Lexington, *Ill., U.S.A.*	112	E10
Lexington, *Ky., U.S.A.*	108	F3
Lexington, *Mich., U.S.A.*	110	C2
Lexington, *Mo., U.S.A.*	112	F8
Lexington, *N.C., U.S.A.*	109	H5
Lexington, *N.Y., U.S.A.*	111	D10
Lexington, *Nebr., U.S.A.*	112	E5
Lexington, *Ohio, U.S.A.*	110	F2
Lexington, *Tenn., U.S.A.*	109	H1
Lexington, *Va., U.S.A.*	108	G6
Lexington Park, *U.S.A.*	108	F7
Leyburn, *U.K.*	12	C6
Leye, *China*	58	E6
Leyland, *U.K.*	12	D5
Leyre →, *France*	20	D2
Leyte □, *Phil.*	61	F6
Leyte Gulf, *Phil.*	61	F6
Leżajsk, *Poland*	45	H9
Lezay, *France*	20	B3
Lezha, *Albania*	40	E3
Lezhi, *China*	58	B5
Lézignan-Corbières, *France*	20	E6
Lezoux, *France*	20	C7
Lgov, *Russia*	47	G8
Lhasa, *China*	60	D4
Lhazê, *China*	60	D3
Lhokkruet, *Indonesia*	62	D1

Lhokseumawe, Indonesia .. 62 C1
L'Hospitalet de Llobregat, Spain . 32 D7
Lhuntsi Dzong, India ... 67 F17
Li, Thailand ... 64 D2
Li Shui →, China ... 59 C9
Li Xian, Gansu, China ... 56 G3
Li Xian, Hebei, China 56 E8
Li Xian, Hunan, China 59 C8
Liádhoi, Greece ... 39 E8
Liancheng, China ... 59 E11
Lianga, Phil. ... 61 G7
Liangcheng, Nei Mongol Zizhiqu, China ... 56 D7
Liangcheng, Shandong, China ... 57 G10
Liangdang, China ... 56 H4
Lianghe, China ... 58 E2
Lianghekou, China ... 58 C7
Liangping, China ... 58 B6
Liangpran, Indonesia ... 62 D4
Lianhua, China ... 59 D9
Lianjiang, Fujian, China .. 59 D12
Lianjiang, Guangdong, China 59 G8
Lianping, China ... 59 E10
Lianshan, China ... 59 E9
Lianshanguan, China ... 57 D12
Lianshui, China ... 57 H10
Lianyuan, China ... 59 D8
Lianzhou, China ... 59 E9
Liao He →, China ... 57 D11
Liaocheng, China ... 56 F8
Liaodong Bandao, China .. 57 E12
Liaodong Wan, China 57 D11
Liaoning □, China ... 57 D12
Liaoyang, China ... 57 D12
Liaoyuan, China ... 57 C13
Liaozhong, China ... 57 D12
Liapádhes, Greece ... 38 B1
Liard →, Canada ... 104 A4
Liard River, Canada ... 104 B3
Liari, Pakistan ... 68 G2
Libau = Liepāja, Latvia ... 9 H19
Libby, U.S.A. ... 114 B6
Libenge, Dem. Rep. of the Congo . 84 D3
Liberal, U.S.A. ... 113 G4
Liberec, Czech Rep. ... 26 A8
Liberia, Costa Rica ... 120 D2
Liberia ■, W. Afr. ... 82 D3
Liberty, Mo., U.S.A. ... 112 F7
Liberty, N.Y., U.S.A. ... 111 E10
Liberty, Pa., U.S.A. ... 110 E7
Liberty, Tex., U.S.A. ... 113 K7
Libiąż, Poland ... 45 H6
Lībīya, Sahrâ', Africa ... 79 C10
Libo, China ... 58 E6
Libobo, Tanjung, Indonesia 63 E7
Libode, S. Africa ... 89 E4
Libohava, Albania ... 40 F4
Libourne, France ... 20 D3
Libramont, Belgium ... 17 E5
Librazhdi, Albania ... 40 E4
Libreville, Gabon ... 84 D1
Libya ■, N. Afr. ... 79 C9
Libyan Desert = Lîbîya, Sahrâ', Africa ... 79 C10
Libyan Plateau = Ed-Déffa, Egypt ... 80 A2
Licantén, Chile ... 126 D1
Licata, Italy ... 30 E7
Lice, Turkey ... 73 C9
Licheng, China ... 56 F7
Lichfield, U.K. ... 13 E6
Lichinga, Mozam. ... 87 E4
Lichtenburg, S. Africa ... 88 D4
Lichtenfels, Germany ... 25 E7
Lichuan, Hubei, China ... 58 B7
Lichuan, Jiangxi, China ... 59 D11
Licking →, U.S.A. ... 108 F3
Licosa, Punta, Italy ... 31 B7
Lida, Belarus ... 9 K21
Liden, Sweden ... 10 B10
Lidhoríkion, Greece ... 38 C4
Lidhult, Sweden ... 11 H7
Lidköping, Sweden ... 11 F7
Lido, Italy ... 29 C9
Lido, Niger ... 83 C5
Lido di Roma = Òstia, Lido di, Italy ... 29 G9
Lidzbark, Poland ... 45 E6
Lidzbark Warmiński, Poland 44 D7
Liebenwalde, Germany ... 24 C9
Lieberose, Germany ... 24 D10
Liebig, Mt., Australia ... 92 D5
Liebling, Romania ... 42 E6
Liechtenstein ■, Europe .. 25 H5
Liège, Belgium ... 17 D5
Liège □, Belgium ... 17 D5
Liegnitz = Legnica, Poland 45 G3
Lienart, Dem. Rep. of the Congo . 86 B2
Lienyünchiangshih = Lianyungang, China ... 57 G10
Lienz, Austria ... 26 E5
Liepāja, Latvia ... 9 H19
Liepāja □, Latvia ... 44 B8
Liepājas ezers, Latvia ... 44 B8
Lier, Belgium ... 17 C4
Liernais, France ... 19 E11
Lieşti, Romania ... 43 E12
Liévin, France ... 19 B9
Lièvre →, Canada ... 102 C4
Liezen, Austria ... 26 D7
Liffey →, Ireland ... 15 C5
Lifford, Ireland ... 15 B4
Liffré, France ... 18 D5
Lifudzin, Russia ... 54 B7
Ligao, Phil. ... 61 E5

Lightning Ridge, Australia . 95 D4
Lignano Sabbiadoro, Italy .. 29 C10
Ligny-en-Barrois, France . 19 D12
Ligonier, U.S.A. ... 110 F5
Ligourión, Greece ... 38 D5
Ligueil, France ... 18 E7
Liguria □, Italy ... 28 D5
Ligurian Sea, Medit. S. ... 6 G7
Lihou Reefs and Cays, Australia ... 94 B5
Lihue, U.S.A. ... 106 H15
Lijiang, China ... 58 D3
Likasi, Dem. Rep. of the Congo . 87 E2
Likenäs, Sweden ... 10 D8
Likhoslavl, Russia ... 46 D8
Likhovskoy, Russia ... 47 H11
Likoma I., Malawi ... 87 E3
Likumburu, Tanzania ... 87 D4
L'Île-Bouchard, France ... 18 E7
L'Île-Rousse, France ... 21 F12
Liling, China ... 59 D9
Lilla Edet, Sweden ... 11 F6
Lille, France ... 19 B10
Lille Bælt, Denmark ... 11 J3
Lillebonne, France ... 18 C7
Lillehammer, Norway ... 9 F14
Lillesand, Norway ... 9 G13
Lillhärdal, Sweden ... 10 C8
Lillian Pt., Australia ... 93 E4
Lillo, Spain ... 34 F7
Lillooet, Canada ... 104 C4
Lilloet →, Canada ... 104 D4
Lilongwe, Malawi ... 87 E3
Liloy, Phil. ... 63 C6
Lim →, Bos.-H. ... 40 C3
Lima, Indonesia ... 63 E7
Lima, Peru ... 124 F3
Lima, Mont., U.S.A. ... 114 D7
Lima, Ohio, U.S.A. ... 108 E3
Lima →, Portugal ... 34 D2
Liman, Indonesia ... 63 G14
Liman, Russia ... 49 H8
Limanowa, Poland ... 45 J7
Limassol, Cyprus ... 36 E12
Limavady, U.K. ... 15 A5
Limay →, Argentina ... 128 D3
Limay Mahuida, Argentina . 126 D2
Limbach-Oberfrohna, Germany ... 24 E8
Limbang, Brunei ... 62 D5
Limbara, Mte., Italy ... 30 B2
Limbaži, Latvia ... 9 H21
Limbdi, India ... 68 H4
Limbe, Cameroon ... 83 E6
Limburg, Germany ... 25 E4
Limburg □, Belgium ... 17 C5
Limburg □, Neths. ... 17 C5
Limedsforsen, Sweden ... 10 D7
Limeira, Brazil ... 127 A6
Limenária, Greece ... 41 F8
Limerick, Ireland ... 15 D3
Limerick, U.S.A. ... 111 C14
Limerick □, Ireland ... 15 D3
Limestone, U.S.A. ... 110 D6
Limestone →, Canada ... 105 B10
Limfjorden, Denmark ... 11 H3
Limia = Lima →, Portugal 34 D2
Limín Khersónísou, Greece . 39 D7
Limingen, Norway ... 8 D15
Limmared, Sweden ... 11 G7
Limmen Bight, Australia .. 94 A2
Limmen Bight →, Australia 94 B2
Límni, Greece ... 38 C5
Límnos, Greece ... 39 B7
Limoges, Canada ... 111 A9
Limoges, France ... 20 C5
Limón, Costa Rica ... 120 E3
Limon, U.S.A. ... 112 F3
Limone Piemonte, Italy ... 28 D4
Limousin, France ... 20 C5
Limousin, Plateaux du, France ... 20 C5
Limoux, France ... 20 E6
Limpopo →, Africa ... 89 D5
Limuru, Kenya ... 86 C4
Lin'an, China ... 59 B12
Linapacan I., Phil. ... 61 F3
Linapacan Str., Phil. ... 61 F3
Linares, Chile ... 126 D1
Linares, Mexico ... 119 C5
Linares, Spain ... 35 G7
Linaro, Capo, Italy ... 29 F8
Lincang, China ... 58 F3
Lincheng, China ... 56 F8
Linchuan, China ... 59 D11
Lincoln, Argentina ... 126 C3
Lincoln, N.Z. ... 91 K4
Lincoln, U.K. ... 12 D7
Lincoln, Calif., U.S.A. ... 116 G5
Lincoln, Ill., U.S.A. ... 112 E10
Lincoln, Kans., U.S.A. ... 112 F5
Lincoln, Maine, U.S.A. ... 109 C11
Lincoln, N.H., U.S.A. ... 111 B13
Lincoln, N. Mex., U.S.A. .. 115 K11
Lincoln, Nebr., U.S.A. ... 112 E6
Lincoln City, U.S.A. ... 114 D1
Lincoln Hav = Lincoln Sea, Arctic ... 4 A5
Lincoln Sea, Arctic ... 4 A5
Lincolnshire □, U.K. ... 12 D7
Lincolnshire Wolds, U.K. . 12 D7
Lincolnton, U.S.A. ... 109 H5
L'Incudine, France ... 21 G13
Linda, U.S.A. ... 116 F5
Lindau, Germany ... 25 H5
Linden, Guyana ... 124 B7
Linden, Ala., U.S.A. ... 109 J2

Linden, Calif., U.S.A. ... 116 G5
Linden, Tex., U.S.A. ... 113 J7
Lindenhurst, U.S.A. ... 111 F11
Lindesberg, Sweden ... 10 E9
Lindesnes, Norway ... 9 H12
Líndhos, Greece ... 36 C10
Líndhos, Ákra, Greece ... 36 C10
Lindi, Tanzania ... 87 D4
Lindi □, Tanzania ... 87 D4
Lindi →, Dem. Rep. of the Congo . 86 B2
Lindö, Sweden ... 11 F10
Lindome, Sweden ... 11 G6
Lindoso, Portugal ... 34 D2
Lindow, Germany ... 24 C8
Lindsay, Canada ... 102 D4
Lindsay, Calif., U.S.A. ... 116 J7
Lindsay, Okla., U.S.A. ... 113 H6
Lindsborg, U.S.A. ... 112 F6
Lindsdal, Sweden ... 11 H10
Linesville, U.S.A. ... 110 E4
Linfen, China ... 56 F6
Ling Xian, Hunan, China .. 59 D9
Ling Xian, Shandong, China 56 F9
Lingao, China ... 64 C7
Lingayen, Phil. ... 63 A6
Lingayen G., Phil. ... 61 C4
Lingbi, China ... 57 H9
Lingbo, Sweden ... 10 C10
Lingchuan, Guangxi Zhuangzu, China 59 E8
Lingchuan, Shanxi, China . 56 G7
Lingen, Germany ... 24 C3
Lingga, Indonesia ... 62 E2
Lingga, Kepulauan, Indonesia ... 62 E2
Lingga Arch. = Lingga, Kepulauan, Indonesia ... 62 E2
Linghem, Sweden ... 11 F9
Lingle, U.S.A. ... 112 D2
Lingqiu, China ... 56 E8
Lingshan, China ... 58 F7
Lingshi, China ... 56 F6
Lingshou, China ... 56 E8
Lingshui, China ... 64 C8
Lingtai, China ... 56 G4
Linguère, Senegal ... 82 B1
Lingui, China ... 59 E8
Lingwu, China ... 56 E4
Lingyuan, China ... 57 D10
Lingyun, China ... 58 E6
Linhai, China ... 59 C13
Linhares, Brazil ... 125 G10
Linhe, China ... 56 D4
Linjiang, China ... 57 D14
Linköping, Sweden ... 11 F9
Linkou, China ... 57 B16
Linli, China ... 59 C8
Linnhe, L., U.K. ... 14 E3
Linqi, China ... 56 G7
Linqing, China ... 56 F8
Linqu, China ... 57 F10
Linru, China ... 56 G7
Lins, Brazil ... 127 A6
Linshui, China ... 58 B6
Linta →, Madag. ... 89 D7
Linth →, Switz. ... 25 H5
Linthal, Switz. ... 25 J5
Linton, Ind., U.S.A. ... 108 F2
Linton, N. Dak., U.S.A. ... 112 B4
Lintong, China ... 56 G5
Linwood, Canada ... 110 C4
Linwu, China ... 59 E9
Linxi, China ... 57 C10
Linxia, China ... 60 C5
Linxiang, China ... 59 C9
Linyanti →, Africa ... 88 B4
Linyi, China ... 57 G10
Linz, Austria ... 26 C7
Linz, Germany ... 24 E3
Linzhenzhen, China ... 56 F5
Linzi, China ... 57 F10
Lion, G. du, France ... 20 E7
Lionárisso, Cyprus ... 36 D13
Lioni, Italy ... 31 B8
Lions, G. of = Lion, G. du, France ... 20 E7
Lion's Den, Zimbabwe ... 87 F3
Lion's Head, Canada ... 110 B3
Liozno = Lyozna, Belarus . 46 E6
Lipa, Phil. ... 61 E4
Lipali, Mozam. ... 87 E4
Lipany, Slovak Rep. ... 27 B13
Lípari, Italy ... 31 D7
Lípari, I., Italy ... 31 D7
Lípari, Is. = Eólie, Ís., Italy 31 D7
Lipcani, Moldova ... 43 B11
Lipetsk, Russia ... 47 F10
Lipiany, Poland ... 45 E1
Liping, China ... 58 D7
Lipkany = Lipcani, Moldova 43 B11
Lipljan, Kosovo, Yug. ... 40 D5
Lipník nad Bečvou, Czech Rep. ... 27 B10
Lipno, Poland ... 45 F6
Lipova, Romania ... 42 D6
Lipovcy Manzovka, Russia . 54 B6
Lipovets, Ukraine ... 47 H5
Lippe →, Germany ... 24 D2
Lippstadt, Germany ... 24 D4
Lipscomb, U.S.A. ... 113 G4
Lipsk, Poland ... 44 E10
Lipsko, Poland ... 45 G8
Lipsói, Greece ... 39 D8
Liptovský Hrádok, Slovak Rep. ... 27 B12
Liptovský Milkuláš, Slovak Rep. ... 27 B12
Liptrap C., Australia ... 95 F4
Lipu, China ... 59 E8
Lira, Uganda ... 86 B3

Liri →, Italy ... 30 A6
Liria = Lliria, Spain ... 33 F4
Lisala, Dem. Rep. of the Congo . 84 D4
Lisboa, Portugal ... 35 G1
Lisboa □, Portugal ... 35 F1
Lisbon = Lisboa, Portugal . 35 G1
Lisbon, N. Dak., U.S.A. ... 112 B6
Lisbon, N.H., U.S.A. ... 111 B13
Lisbon, Ohio, U.S.A. ... 110 F4
Lisbon Falls, U.S.A. ... 109 D10
Lisburn, U.K. ... 15 B5
Liscannor B., Ireland ... 15 D2
Liscia →, Italy ... 30 A2
Lishe Jiang →, China ... 58 E3
Lishi, China ... 56 F6
Lishui, Jiangsu, China ... 59 B12
Lishui, Zhejiang, China ... 59 C12
Lisianski I., Pac. Oc. ... 96 E10
Lisichansk = Lysychansk, Ukraine ... 47 H10
Lisieux, France ... 18 C7
Liski, Russia ... 47 G10
L'Isle-Jourdain, Gers, France 20 E5
L'Isle-Jourdain, Vienne, France ... 20 B4
L'Isle-sur-la-Sorgue, France 21 E9
Lisle-sur-Tarn, France ... 20 E5
Lismore, Australia ... 95 D5
Lismore, Ireland ... 15 D4
Lista, Norway ... 9 G12
Lister, Mt., Antarctica ... 5 D11
Liston, Australia ... 95 D5
Listowel, Canada ... 102 D3
Listowel, Ireland ... 15 D2
Lit, Sweden ... 10 A8
Lit-et-Mixe, France ... 20 D2
Litang, Guangxi Zhuangzu, China ... 58 F7
Litang, Sichuan, China ... 58 B3
Litang Qu →, China ... 58 C3
Litani →, Lebanon ... 75 B4
Litchfield, Calif., U.S.A. .. 116 E6
Litchfield, Conn., U.S.A. .. 111 E11
Litchfield, Ill., U.S.A. ... 112 F10
Litchfield, Minn., U.S.A. .. 112 C7
Liteni, Romania ... 43 C11
Líthinon, Ákra, Greece ... 36 E6
Lithuania ■, Europe ... 9 J20
Litija, Slovenia ... 29 B11
Lititz, U.S.A. ... 111 F8
Litókhoron, Greece ... 40 F6
Litoměřice, Czech Rep. ... 26 A7
Litomyšl, Czech Rep. ... 27 B9
Litschau, Austria ... 26 C8
Little Abaco I., Bahamas . 120 A4
Little Barrier I., N.Z. ... 91 G5
Little Belt Mts., U.S.A. ... 114 C8
Little Blue →, U.S.A. ... 112 F6
Little Buffalo →, Canada .. 104 A6
Little Cayman, I., Cayman Is. ... 120 C3
Little Churchill →, Canada . 105 B9
Little Colorado →, U.S.A. . 115 H8
Little Current, Canada ... 102 C3
Little Current →, Canada .. 102 B3
Little Falls, Minn., U.S.A. . 112 C7
Little Falls, N.Y., U.S.A. . 111 C10
Little Fork →, U.S.A. ... 112 A8
Little Grand Rapids, Canada 105 C9
Little Humboldt →, U.S.A. 114 F5
Little Inagua I., Bahamas . 121 B5
Little Karoo, S. Africa ... 88 E3
Little Lake, U.S.A. ... 117 K9
Little Laut Is. = Laut Kecil, Kepulauan, Indonesia ... 62 E5
Little-Mecatina = Petit-Mécatina →, Canada ... 103 B8
Little Minch, U.K. ... 14 D2
Little Missouri →, U.S.A. . 112 B3
Little Ouse →, U.K. ... 13 E9
Little Rann, India ... 68 H4
Little Red →, U.S.A. ... 113 H9
Little River, N.Z. ... 91 K4
Little Rock, U.S.A. ... 113 H8
Little Ruaha →, Tanzania . 86 D4
Little Sable Pt., U.S.A. ... 108 D2
Little Scarcies →, S. Leone 82 D2
Little Sioux →, U.S.A. ... 112 E6
Little Smoky →, Canada ... 104 C5
Little Snake →, U.S.A. ... 114 F9
Little Valley, U.S.A. ... 110 D6
Little Wabash →, U.S.A. .. 108 G1
Little White →, U.S.A. ... 112 D4
Littlefield, U.S.A. ... 113 J3
Littlehampton, U.K. ... 13 G7
Littleton, U.S.A. ... 111 B13
Litvinov, Czech Rep. ... 26 A6
Liu He →, China ... 57 D11
Liu Jiang →, China ... 58 F7
Liuba, China ... 56 H4
Liucheng, China ... 58 E7
Liugou, China ... 57 D10
Liuhe, China ... 57 C13
Liuheng Dao, China ... 59 C14
Liujiang, China ... 58 E7
Liukang Tenggaja = Sabalana, Kepulauan, Indonesia ... 63 F5
Liuli, Tanzania ... 87 E3
Liuwa Plain, Zambia ... 85 G4
Liuyang, China ... 59 C9
Liuzhou, China ... 58 E7
Liuzhuang, China ... 57 H11
Livada, Romania ... 42 C8
Livadherón, Greece ... 40 F5
Livadhion, Cyprus ... 36 E12
Livadhión, Greece ... 38 A4
Livarot, France ... 18 D7

Live Oak, Calif., U.S.A. ... 116 F5
Live Oak, Fla., U.S.A. ... 109 K4
Liveras, Cyprus ... 36 D11
Livermore, U.S.A. ... 116 H5
Livermore, Mt., U.S.A. ... 113 K2
Livermore Falls, U.S.A. ... 109 C11
Liverpool, Canada ... 103 D7
Liverpool, U.K. ... 12 D4
Liverpool, U.S.A. ... 111 C8
Liverpool Bay, U.K. ... 12 D4
Liverpool Plains, Australia . 95 E5
Liverpool Ra., Australia ... 95 E5
Livigno, Italy ... 28 B7
Livingston, Guatemala ... 120 C2
Livingston, U.K. ... 14 F5
Livingston, Ala., U.S.A. ... 109 J1
Livingston, Calif., U.S.A. . 116 H6
Livingston, Mont., U.S.A. . 114 D8
Livingston, S.C., U.S.A. ... 109 J5
Livingston, Tenn., U.S.A. . 109 G3
Livingston, Tex., U.S.A. ... 113 K7
Livingston, L., U.S.A. ... 113 K7
Livingston Manor, U.S.A. . 111 E10
Livingstone, Zambia ... 87 F2
Livingstone Mts., Tanzania . 87 D3
Livingstonia, Malawi ... 87 E3
Livno, Bos.-H. ... 42 G2
Livny, Russia ... 47 F9
Livonia, Mich., U.S.A. ... 108 D4
Livonia, N.Y., U.S.A. ... 110 D7
Livorno, Italy ... 28 E7
Livramento, Brazil ... 127 C4
Livron-sur-Drôme, France . 21 D8
Liwale, Tanzania ... 87 D4
Liwiec →, Poland ... 45 F8
Lixi, China ... 58 D3
Lixian, China ... 58 B4
Lixoúrion, Greece ... 38 C2
Liyang, China ... 59 B12
Lizard I., Australia ... 94 A4
Lizard Pt., U.K. ... 13 H2
Lizzano, Italy ... 31 B10
Ljig, Serbia, Yug. ... 40 B4
Ljubija, Bos.-H. ... 29 D13
Ljubinje, Bos.-H. ... 40 D2
Ljubljana, Slovenia ... 29 B11
Ljubno, Slovenia ... 29 B11
Ljubovija, Serbia, Yug. ... 40 B3
Ljugarn, Sweden ... 11 G12
Ljung, Sweden ... 11 G7
Ljungan →, Sweden ... 10 B11
Ljungaverk, Sweden ... 10 B10
Ljungby, Sweden ... 9 H15
Ljungbyholm, Sweden ... 11 H10
Ljungdalen, Sweden ... 10 B6
Ljungsbro, Sweden ... 11 F9
Ljungskile, Sweden ... 11 F5
Ljusdal, Sweden ... 10 C10
Ljusfallshammar, Sweden . 11 F9
Ljusnan →, Sweden ... 10 C11
Ljusne, Sweden ... 10 C11
Ljutomer, Slovenia ... 29 B13
Llagostera, Spain ... 32 D7
Llancanelo, Salina, Argentina 126 D2
Llandeilo, U.K. ... 13 F4
Llandovery, U.K. ... 13 F4
Llandrindod Wells, U.K. ... 13 E4
Llandudno, U.K. ... 12 D4
Llanelli, U.K. ... 13 F3
Llanes, Spain ... 34 B6
Llangollen, U.K. ... 12 E4
Llanidloes, U.K. ... 13 E4
Llano, U.S.A. ... 113 K5
Llano →, U.S.A. ... 113 K5
Llano Estacado, U.S.A. ... 113 J3
Llanos, S. Amer. ... 122 C3
Llanquihue, L., Chile ... 128 E1
Llanwrtyd Wells, U.K. ... 13 E4
Llebeig, C. des, Spain ... 37 B9
Lleida, Spain ... 32 D5
Lleida □, Spain ... 32 C6
Llentrisca, C., Spain ... 37 C7
Llera, Mexico ... 119 C5
Llerena, Spain ... 35 G5
Lleyn Peninsula, U.K. ... 12 E3
Llico, Chile ... 126 C1
Lliria, Spain ... 33 F4
Llobregat →, Spain ... 32 D7
Llodio, Spain ... 32 B2
Lloret de Mar, Spain ... 32 D7
Lloyd B., Australia ... 94 A3
Lloyd L., Canada ... 105 B7
Lloydminster, Canada ... 105 C7
Llucena del Cid, Spain ... 32 E4
Llucmajor, Spain ... 37 B9
Llullaillaco, Volcán, S. Amer. ... 126 A2
Lo →, Vietnam ... 64 B5
Loa, U.S.A. ... 115 G8
Loa →, Chile ... 126 A1
Loaita I., S. China Sea ... 62 B4
Loange →, Dem. Rep. of the Congo . 84 E4
Loano, Italy ... 28 D5
Lobatse, Botswana ... 88 D4
Löbau, Germany ... 24 D10
Lobenstein, Germany ... 24 E7
Lobería, Argentina ... 126 D4
Lobito, Angola ... 85 G2
Lobo →, Ivory C. ... 82 D3
Lobos, Argentina ... 126 D4
Lobos, I., Mexico ... 118 B2
Lobos, I. de, Canary Is. ... 37 F6
Łobżenica, Poland ... 45 E4
Loc Binh, Vietnam ... 64 B6
Loc Ninh, Vietnam ... 65 G6
Locarno, Switz. ... 25 J4
Loch Baghasdail = Lochboisdale, U.K. ... 14 D1

Loch Garman = Wexford,
  Ireland 15 D5
Loch Nam Madadh =
  Lochmaddy, U.K. 14 D1
Lochaber, U.K. 14 E3
Locharbriggs, U.K. 14 F5
Lochboisdale, U.K. 14 D1
Loche, L. La, Canada 105 B7
Lochem, Neths. 17 B6
Loches, France 18 E7
Lochgilphead, U.K. 14 E3
Lochinver, U.K. 14 C3
Lochmaddy, U.K. 14 D1
Lochnagar, Australia 94 C4
Lochnagar, U.K. 14 E5
Łochów, Poland 45 F8
Lochy, L., U.K. 14 E4
Lock, Australia 95 E2
Lock Haven, U.S.A. 110 E7
Lockeford, U.S.A. 116 G5
Lockeport, Canada 103 D6
Lockerbie, U.K. 14 F5
Lockhart, Australia 95 F4
Lockhart, U.S.A. 113 L6
Lockhart, L., Australia 93 F2
Lockhart River, Australia .. 94 A3
Lockney, U.S.A. 113 H4
Lockport, U.S.A. 110 C6
Locminé, France 18 E4
Locri, Italy 31 D9
Locronan, France 18 D2
Lod, Israel 75 D3
Lodeinoye Pole, Russia 46 B7
Lodève, France 20 E7
Lodge Bay, Canada 103 B8
Lodge Grass, U.S.A. 114 D10
Lodgepole Cr. →, U.S.A. . 112 E2
Lodhran, Pakistan 68 E4
Lodi, Italy 28 C6
Lodi, Calif., U.S.A. 116 G5
Lodi, Ohio, U.S.A. 110 E3
Lodja,
  Dem. Rep. of the Congo . 86 C1
Lodosa, Spain 32 C2
Lödöse, Sweden 11 F6
Lodwar, Kenya 86 B4
Łódź, Poland 45 G6
Łódzkie □, Poland 45 G6
Loei, Thailand 64 D3
Loengo,
  Dem. Rep. of the Congo . 86 C2
Loeriesfontein, S. Africa .. 88 E2
Lofa →, Liberia 83 D2
Lofer, Austria 26 D5
Lofoten, Norway 8 B15
Lofsdalen, Sweden 10 B7
Lofsen →, Sweden 10 B7
Loftahammar, Sweden 11 G10
Loga, Niger 83 C5
Logan, Iowa, U.S.A. 112 E7
Logan, Ohio, U.S.A. 108 F4
Logan, Utah, U.S.A. 114 F8
Logan, W. Va., U.S.A. ... 108 G5
Logan, Mt., Canada 100 B5
Logandale, U.S.A. 117 J12
Logansport, Ind., U.S.A. . 108 E2
Logansport, La., U.S.A. . 113 K8
Logirim, Sudan 81 G3
Logo, Sudan 81 F3
Logone →, Chad 79 F9
Logroño, Spain 32 C2
Logrosán, Spain 35 F5
Løgstør, Denmark 11 H3
Løgumkloster, Denmark .. 11 J2
Lohals, Denmark 11 J4
Lohardaga, India 69 H11
Loharia, India 68 H6
Loharu, India 68 E6
Lohja, Finland 9 F21
Löhne, Germany 24 C4
Lohr, Germany 25 F5
Lohri Wah →, Pakistan .. 68 F2
Loi-kaw, Burma 67 K20
Loimaa, Finland 9 F20
Loir →, France 18 E6
Loir-et-Cher □, France ... 18 E8
Loire □, France 21 C8
Loire →, France 18 E4
Loire-Atlantique □, France 18 E5
Loiret □, France 19 E9
Loitz, Germany 24 B9
Loja, Ecuador 124 D3
Loja, Spain 35 H6
Loji = Kawasi, Indonesia . 63 E7
Løjt Kirkeby, Denmark ... 11 J3
Lojung, China 58 E7
Loka, Sudan 81 G3
Lokandu,
  Dem. Rep. of the Congo . 86 C2
Lokeren, Belgium 17 C3
Lokgwabe, Botswana 88 C3
Lokhvitsa, Ukraine 47 G7
Lokichokio, Kenya 86 B3
Lokitaung, Kenya 86 B4
Lokkan tekojärvi, Finland . 8 C22
Løkken, Denmark 11 G3
Loknya, Russia 46 D6
Loko, Nigeria 83 D6
Lokoja, Nigeria 83 D6
Lokot, Russia 47 F8
Lol →, Sudan 81 F2
Lola, Guinea 82 D3
Lola, Mt., U.S.A. 116 F6
Lolibai, Gebel, Sudan 81 G3
Lolimi, Sudan 81 G3
Loliondo, Tanzania 86 C4
Lolland, Denmark 11 K5
Lollar, Germany 24 E4
Lolo, U.S.A. 114 C6
Lolodorf, Cameroon 83 E7
Lom, Bulgaria 40 C7

Lom →, Bulgaria 40 C7
Lom Kao, Thailand 64 D3
Lom Sak, Thailand 64 D3
Loma, U.S.A. 114 C8
Loma Linda, U.S.A. 117 L9
Lomami →,
  Dem. Rep. of the Congo . 86 B1
Lomas de Zamóra, Argentina 126 C4
Lombadina, Australia 92 C3
Lombárdia □, Italy 28 C6
Lombardy = Lombárdia □,
  Italy 28 C6
Lombez, France 20 E4
Lomblen, Indonesia 63 F6
Lombok, Indonesia 62 F5
Lomé, Togo 83 D5
Lomela,
  Dem. Rep. of the Congo . 84 E4
Lomela →,
  Dem. Rep. of the Congo . 84 E4
Łomianki, Poland 45 F7
Lomma, Sweden 11 J7
Lommel, Belgium 17 C5
Lomond, Canada 104 C6
Lomond, L., U.K. 14 E4
Lomphat, Cambodia 64 F6
Lompobatang, Indonesia . 63 F5
Lompoc, U.S.A. 117 L6
Łomża, Poland 45 E9
Loncoche, Chile 128 D2
Londa, India 66 M9
Londiani, Kenya 86 C4
Londinières, France 18 C8
London, Canada 102 D3
London, U.K. 13 F7
London, Ky., U.S.A. 108 G3
London, Ohio, U.S.A. ... 108 F4
London, Greater □, U.K. . 13 F7
Londonderry, U.K. 15 B4
Londonderry □, U.K. 15 B4
Londonderry, C., Australia . 92 B4
Londonderry, I., Chile ... 128 H2
Londres, Argentina 128 B3
Londrina, Brazil 127 A5
Lone Pine, U.S.A. 116 J8
Lonely Mine, Zimbabwe . 89 B4
Long B., U.S.A. 109 J6
Long Beach, Calif., U.S.A. 117 M8
Long Beach, N.Y., U.S.A. 111 F11
Long Beach, Wash., U.S.A. 116 D2
Long Branch, U.S.A. 111 F11
Long Creek, U.S.A. 114 D4
Long Eaton, U.K. 12 E6
Long I., Australia 94 C4
Long I., Bahamas 121 B4
Long I., Canada 102 B4
Long I., Ireland 15 E2
Long I., U.S.A. 111 F11
Long Island Sd., U.S.A. . 111 E12
Long L., Canada 102 C2
Long Lake, U.S.A. 111 C10
Long Point B., Canada .. 110 D4
Long Prairie, U.S.A. 112 C7
Long Pt., Canada 110 D4
Long Range Mts., Canada 103 C8
Long Reef, Australia 92 B4
Long Spruce, Canada ... 105 B10
Long Str. = Longa, Proliv,
  Russia 4 C16
Long Thanh, Vietnam ... 65 G6
Long Xian, China 56 G4
Long Xuyen, Vietnam ... 65 G5
Longá, Greece 38 E3
Longa, Proliv, Russia ... 4 C16
Long'an, China 58 F6
Longarone, Italy 29 B9
Longbenton, U.K. 12 B6
Longboat Key, U.S.A. ... 109 M4
Longchang, China 58 C5
Longchi, China 58 C4
Longchuan, Guangdong,
  China 59 E10
Longchuan, Yunnan, China 58 E1
Longde, China 56 G4
Longeau, France 19 E12
Longford, Australia 94 G4
Longford, Ireland 15 C4
Longford □, Ireland 15 C4
Longguan, China 56 D8
Longhai, China 59 E11
Longhua, China 57 D9
Longhui, China 59 D8
Longido, Tanzania 86 C4
Longiram, Indonesia 62 E5
Longkou, Jiangxi, China . 59 D10
Longkou, Shandong, China 57 F11
Longlac, Canada 102 C2
Longli, China 58 D6
Longlin, China 58 E5
Longling, China 58 E2
Longmeadow, U.S.A. ... 111 D12
Longmen, China 59 F10
Longming, China 58 F6
Longmont, U.S.A. 112 E2
Longnan, China 59 E10
Longnawan, Indonesia .. 62 D4
Longobucco, Italy 31 C9
Longquan, China 59 C12
Longreach, Australia ... 94 C3
Longshan, China 58 C7
Longsheng, China 59 E8
Longué-Jumelles, France . 18 E6
Longueau, France 19 C9
Longueuil, Canada 111 A11
Longuyon, France 19 C12
Longvic, France 19 E12
Longview, Tex., U.S.A. . 113 J7
Longview, Wash., U.S.A. 116 D4
Longwy, France 19 C12
Longxi, China 56 G3
Longyan, China 59 E11

Longyou, China 59 C12
Longzhou, China 58 F6
Lonigo, Italy 29 C8
Löningen, Germany 24 C3
Lonja →, Croatia 29 C13
Lonoke, U.S.A. 113 H9
Lonquimay, Chile 128 D2
Lons-le-Saunier, France . 19 F12
Lönsboda, Sweden 11 H8
Looe, U.K. 13 G3
Lookout, C., Canada 102 A3
Lookout, C., U.S.A. 109 H7
Loolmalasin, Tanzania .. 86 C4
Loon →, Alta., Canada .. 104 B5
Loon →, Man., Canada . 105 B8
Loon Lake, Canada 105 C7
Loongana, Australia 93 F4
Loop Hd., Ireland 15 D2
Lop Buri, Thailand 64 E3
Lop Nor = Lop Nur, China 60 B4
Lop Nur, China 60 B4
Lopare, Bos.-H. 42 F3
Lopatin, Russia 49 J8
Lopatina, Gora, Russia . 51 D15
Lopaye, Sudan 81 F3
Lopez, Phil. 61 E5
Lopez, U.S.A. 111 E8
Lopez, C., Gabon 84 E1
Lopphavet, Norway 8 A19
Lora →, Afghan. 66 D4
Lora, Hamun-i-, Pakistan 66 E4
Lora Cr. →, Australia .. 95 D2
Lora del Río, Spain 35 H5
Lorain, U.S.A. 110 E2
Loralai, Pakistan 68 D3
Lorca, Spain 33 H3
Lord Howe I., Pac. Oc. . 96 L7
Lord Howe Ridge, Pac. Oc. 96 L8
Lordsburg, U.S.A. 115 K9
Loreto, Brazil 125 E9
Loreto, Italy 29 E10
Loreto, Mexico 118 B2
Lorgues, France 21 E10
Lorhosso, Burkina Faso . 82 C4
Lorient, France 18 E3
Lorn, U.K. 14 E3
Lorn, Firth of, U.K. 14 E3
Lorne, Australia 95 F3
Loronyo, Sudan 81 G3
Lorovouno, Cyprus 36 D11
Lörrach, Germany 25 H3
Lorraine □, France 19 D13
Los, Sweden 10 C9
Los, Îles de, Guinea 82 D2
Los Alamos, Calif., U.S.A. 117 L6
Los Alamos, N. Mex.,
  U.S.A. 115 J10
Los Altos, U.S.A. 116 H4
Los Andes, Chile 126 C1
Los Angeles, Chile 126 D1
Los Angeles, U.S.A. ... 117 M8
Los Angeles, Bahía de,
  Mexico 118 B2
Los Angeles Aqueduct,
  U.S.A. 117 K9
Los Banos, U.S.A. 116 H6
Los Barrios, Spain 35 J5
Los Blancos, Argentina . 126 A3
Los Chiles, Costa Rica . 120 D3
Los Corrales de Buelna,
  Spain 34 B6
Los Cristianos, Canary Is. 37 F3
Los Gallardos, Spain ... 33 H3
Los Gatos, U.S.A. 116 H5
Los Hermanos Is., Venezuela 121 D7
Los Islotes, Canary Is. . 37 E6
Los Llanos de Aridane,
  Canary Is. 37 F2
Los Loros, Chile 126 B1
Los Lunas, U.S.A. 115 J10
Los Mochis, Mexico 118 B3
Los Monegros, Spain ... 32 D4
Los Nietos, Spain 33 H4
Los Olivos, U.S.A. 117 L6
Los Palacios, Cuba 120 B3
Los Palacios y Villafranca,
  Spain 35 H5
Los Reyes, Mexico 118 D4
Los Roques Is., Venezuela 121 D6
Los Santos de Maimona,
  Spain 35 G4
Los Teques, Venezuela .. 124 A5
Los Testigos, Is., Venezuela 124 A6
Los Vilos, Chile 126 C1
Los Yébenes, Spain 35 F7
Łosice, Poland 45 F9
Loskop Dam, S. Africa .. 89 D4
Løsning, Denmark 11 J3
Loßnica, Serbia, Yug. .. 40 B3
Lossiemouth, U.K. 14 D5
Lostwithiel, U.K. 13 G3
Lot □, France 20 D5
Lot →, France 20 D4
Lot-et-Garonne □, France 20 D4
Lota, Chile 126 D1
Lotagipi Swamp, Sudan . 81 G3
Lotfābād, Iran 71 B8
Lothair, S. Africa 89 D5
Lotorp, Sweden 11 F9
Lötschbergtunnel, Switz. . 25 J3
Löttorp, Sweden 11 G11
Lotung, Taiwan 59 E13
Loubomo, Congo 84 E2
Loudéac, France 18 D4
Loudi, China 59 D8
Loudonville, U.S.A. 110 F2
Loudun, France 18 E7
Loue →, France 19 E12
Louga, Senegal 82 B1

Loughborough, U.K. 12 E6
Loughrea, Ireland 15 C3
Loughros More B., Ireland 15 B3
Louhans, France 19 F12
Louis Trichardt, S. Africa 89 C4
Louis XIV, Pte., Canada . 102 B4
Louisa, U.S.A. 108 F4
Louisbourg, Canada 103 C8
Louise I., Canada 104 C2
Louiseville, Canada 102 C5
Louisiade Arch.,
  Papua N. G. 96 J7
Louisiana, U.S.A. 112 F9
Louisiana □, U.S.A. 113 K9
Louisville, Ky., U.S.A. . 108 F3
Louisville, Miss., U.S.A. 113 J10
Louisville, Ohio, U.S.A. 110 F3
Loulay, France 20 B3
Loulé, Portugal 35 H3
Louny, Czech Rep. 26 A6
Loup City, U.S.A. 112 E5
Loups Marins, Lacs des,
  Canada 102 A5
Lourdes, France 20 E3
Lourenço-Marques =
  Maputo, Mozam. 89 D5
Lourinhã, Portugal 35 F1
Lousã, Portugal 34 E2
Louta, Burkina Faso ... 82 C4
Louth, Australia 95 E4
Louth, Ireland 15 C5
Louth, U.K. 12 D7
Louth □, Ireland 15 C5
Loutrá Aidhipsoú, Greece 38 C5
Loutráki, Greece 38 D4
Louvain = Leuven, Belgium 17 D4
Louviers, France 18 C8
Louwsburg, S. Africa ... 89 D5
Lovat →, Russia 46 C6
Lovčen, Montenegro, Yug. 40 D2
Lovech, Bulgaria 41 C8
Lovech □, Bulgaria 41 C8
Loveland, U.S.A. 112 E2
Lovell, U.S.A. 114 D9
Lovelock, U.S.A. 114 F4
Lóvere, Italy 28 C7
Lövestad, Sweden 11 J7
Loviisa, Finland 9 F22
Loving, U.S.A. 113 J2
Lovington, U.S.A. 113 J3
Lovisa = Loviisa, Finland 9 F22
Lovosice, Czech Rep. .. 26 A7
Lovran, Croatia 29 C11
Lovrin, Romania 42 E5
Lövstabruk, Sweden ... 10 D11
Lövstabukten, Sweden . 10 D11
Low, L., Canada 102 B4
Low Pt., Australia 93 F4
Low Tatra = Nízké Tatry,
  Slovak Rep. 27 C12
Lowa,
  Dem. Rep. of the Congo . 86 C2
Lowa →,
  Dem. Rep. of the Congo . 86 C2
Lowell, U.S.A. 111 D13
Lowellville, U.S.A. 110 E4
Löwen →, Namibia 88 D2
Lower Alkali L., U.S.A. . 114 F3
Lower Arrow L., Canada 104 D5
Lower Austria =
  Niederösterreich □,
  Austria 26 C8
Lower California = Baja
  California, Mexico 118 A1
Lower Hutt, N.Z. 91 J5
Lower Lake, U.S.A. 116 G4
Lower Manitou L., Canada 105 D10
Lower Post, Canada 104 B3
Lower Red L., U.S.A. .. 112 B7
Lower Saxony =
  Niedersachsen □,
  Germany 24 C4
Lower Tunguska =
  Tunguska, Nizhnyaya →,
  Russia 51 C9
Lowestoft, U.K. 13 E9
Łowicz, Poland 45 F6
Lowville, U.S.A. 111 C9
Loxton, Australia 95 E3
Loxton, S. Africa 88 E3
Loyalton, U.S.A. 116 F6
Loyalty Is. = Loyauté, Is.,
  N. Cal. 96 K8
Loyang = Luoyang, China 56 G7
Loyauté, Is., N. Cal. ... 96 K8
Loyev = Loyew, Belarus . 47 G6
Loyew, Belarus 47 G6
Loyoro, Uganda 86 B3
Loz, Slovenia 29 C11
Lozère □, France 20 D7
Loznica, Serbia, Yug. .. 40 B3
Lozova, Ukraine 47 H9
Lü Shan, China 59 C11
Lü-Tao, Taiwan 59 F13
Luachimo, Angola 84 F4
Luajan →, India 69 G11
Lualaba →,
  Dem. Rep. of the Congo . 86 B2
Luampa, Zambia 87 F1
Lu'an, China 59 B11
Luan Chau, Vietnam .. 58 G4
Luan He →, China 57 E10
Luan Xian, China 57 E10
Luancheng,
  Guangxi Zhuangzu, China 58 F7
Luancheng, Hebei, China 56 F8
Luanco, Spain 34 B5
Luanda, Angola 84 F2
Luang, Thale, Thailand . 65 J3
Luang Prabang, Laos .. 58 H4
Luangwa, Zambia 87 F3

Luangwa →, Zambia ... 87 E3
Luangwa Valley, Zambia . 87 E3
Luanne, China 57 D9
Luanping, China 57 D9
Luanshya, Zambia 87 E2
Luapula □, Africa 87 E2
Luapula →, Africa 87 D2
Luarca, Spain 34 B4
Luashi,
  Dem. Rep. of the Congo . 87 E1
Luau, Angola 84 G4
Lubaczów, Poland 45 H10
Lubań, Poland 45 G2
Lubana, Ozero = Lubānas
  Ezers, Latvia 9 H22
Lubānas Ezers, Latvia .. 9 H22
Lubang, Phil. 61 E4
Lubang Is., Phil. 63 B6
Lubartów, Poland 45 G9
Lubawa, Poland 44 E6
Lübbecke, Germany ... 24 C4
Lübben, Germany 24 D9
Lübbenau, Germany ... 24 D9
Lubbock, U.S.A. 113 J4
Lübeck, Germany 24 B6
Lübecker Bucht, Germany 24 A6
Lubefu,
  Dem. Rep. of the Congo . 86 C1
Lubefu →,
  Dem. Rep. of the Congo . 86 C1
Lubelskie □, Poland ... 45 G9
Lubero = Luofu,
  Dem. Rep. of the Congo . 86 C2
Lubersac, France 20 C5
Lubicon L., Canada 104 B5
Lubień Kujawski, Poland 45 F6
Lubilash →,
  Dem. Rep. of the Congo . 84 F4
Lubin, Poland 45 G3
Lublin, Poland 45 G9
Lubliniec, Poland 45 H5
Lubnān, Jabal, Lebanon . 75 B4
Lubniewice, Poland ... 45 F2
Lubny, Ukraine 47 G7
Lubomierz, Poland 45 G2
Luboń, Poland 45 F3
Lubongola,
  Dem. Rep. of the Congo . 86 C2
L'ubotín, Slovak Rep. ... 27 B13
Lubraniec, Poland 45 F5
Lubsko, Poland 45 G2
Lübtheen, Germany ... 24 B7
Lubuagan, Phil. 61 C4
Lubudi,
  Dem. Rep. of the Congo . 84 F5
Lubudi →,
  Dem. Rep. of the Congo . 87 D2
Lubuklinggau, Indonesia 62 E2
Lubuksikaping, Indonesia 62 D2
Lubumbashi,
  Dem. Rep. of the Congo . 87 E2
Lubunda,
  Dem. Rep. of the Congo . 86 D2
Lubungu, Zambia 87 E2
Lubuskie □, Poland ... 45 F2
Lubutu,
  Dem. Rep. of the Congo . 86 C2
Luc An Chau, Vietnam . 58 A5
Luc-en-Diois, France .. 21 D9
Lucan, Canada 110 C3
Lucania, Mt., Canada .. 100 B5
Lucas Channel, Canada . 110 A3
Lucban, Phil. 61 D4
Lucca, Italy 28 C4
Lucé, France 18 D8
Luce Bay, U.K. 14 G4
Lucea, Jamaica 120 C4
Lucedale, U.S.A. 109 K1
Lucena, Phil. 61 E4
Lucena, Spain 35 H6
Lučenec, Slovak Rep. .. 27 C12
Lucera, Italy 31 A8
Lucerne = Luzern, Switz. 25 H4
Lucerne, U.S.A. 116 F4
Lucerne Valley, U.S.A. . 117 L10
Lucero, Mexico 118 A3
Luchena →, Spain 33 H3
Lucheng, China 56 F7
Lucheringo →, Mozam. 87 E4
Lüchow, Germany 24 C7
Luchuan, China 59 F8
Lucia, U.S.A. 116 J5
Lucinda, Australia 94 B4
Lucindale, Australia ... 95 F3
Luckau, Germany 24 D9
Luckenwalde, Germany 24 C9
Luckhoff, S. Africa 88 D3
Lucknow, Canada 110 C3
Lucknow, India 69 F9
Luçon, France 20 B2
Lüda = Dalian, China .. 57 E11
Luda Kamchiya →, Bulgaria 41 C11
Ludbreg, Croatia 29 B13
Lüdenscheid, Germany 24 D3
Lüderitz, Namibia 88 D2
Lüderitzbaai, Namibia . 88 D2
Ludhiana, India 68 D6
Ludian, China 58 D4
Luding Qiao, China ... 58 C4
Lüdinghausen, Germany 24 D3
Ludington, U.S.A. 108 D2
Ludlow, U.K. 13 E5
Ludlow, Calif., U.S.A. . 117 L10
Ludlow, Pa., U.S.A. ... 110 E6
Ludlow, Vt., U.S.A. ... 111 C12
Ludus, Romania 43 D9
Ludvika, Sweden 10 D9
Ludwigsburg, Germany 25 G5
Ludwigsfelde, Germany 24 C9
Ludwigshafen, Germany 25 F4
Ludwigslust, Germany . 24 B7

Ludza, *Latvia* 46 D4
Lueki,
  Dem. Rep. of the Congo 86 C2
Luena,
  Dem. Rep. of the Congo 87 D2
Luena, *Zambia* 87 E3
Lüeyang, *China* 56 H4
Lufeng, *Guangdong, China* 59 F10
Lufeng, *Yunnan, China* 58 E4
Lufira →,
  Dem. Rep. of the Congo 87 D2
Lufkin, *U.S.A.* 113 K7
Lufupa,
  Dem. Rep. of the Congo 87 E1
Luga, *Russia* 46 C5
Luga →, *Russia* 46 C5
Lugano, *Switz.* 25 J4
Lugano, L. di, *Switz.* 28 C6
Lugansk = Luhansk, *Ukraine* 47 H10
Lugard's Falls, *Kenya* 86 C4
Lugela, *Mozam.* 87 F4
Lugenda →, *Mozam.* 87 E4
Lugh Ganana, *Somali Rep.* . 74 G3
Lugnaquilla, *Ireland* 15 D5
Lugo, *Italy* 29 D8
Lugo, *Spain* 34 B3
Lugo □, *Spain* 34 C3
Lugoj, *Romania* 42 E6
Lugovoy, *Kazakstan* 50 E8
Luhansk, *Ukraine* 47 H10
Luhe, *China* 59 A12
Luhe →, *Germany* 24 B6
Luhuo, *China* 58 B3
Luiana, *Angola* 88 B3
Luimneach = Limerick,
  Ireland 15 D3
Luing, *U.K.* 14 E3
Luino, *Italy* 28 C5
Luís Correia, *Brazil* 125 D10
Luitpold Coast, *Antarctica* . 5 D1
Luiza,
  Dem. Rep. of the Congo 84 F4
Luizi,
  Dem. Rep. of the Congo 86 D2
Luján, *Argentina* 126 C4
Lujiang, *China* 59 B11
Lukang, *Taiwan* 59 E13
Lukanga Swamp, *Zambia* .. 87 E2
Lukavac, *Bos.-H.* 42 F3
Lukenie →,
  Dem. Rep. of the Congo 84 E3
Lukhisaral, *India* 69 G12
Lŭki, *Bulgaria* 41 E8
Lukolela,
  Dem. Rep. of the Congo 86 D1
Lukosi, *Zimbabwe* 87 F2
Lukovë, *Albania* 40 G3
Lukovit, *Bulgaria* 41 C8
Łuków, *Poland* 45 G9
Lukoyanov, *Russia* 48 C7
Lule älv →, *Sweden* 8 D19
Luleå, *Sweden* 8 D20
Luleburgaz, *Turkey* 41 E11
Luliang, *China* 58 E4
Luling, *U.S.A.* 113 L6
Lulong, *China* 57 E10
Lulonga →,
  Dem. Rep. of the Congo 84 D3
Lulua →,
  Dem. Rep. of the Congo 84 E4
Luluabourg = Kananga,
  Dem. Rep. of the Congo 84 F4
Lumajang, *Indonesia* 63 H15
Lumbala N'guimbo, *Angola* 85 G4
Lumberton, *U.S.A.* 109 H6
Lumbwa, *Kenya* 86 C4
Lumsden, *Canada* 105 C8
Lumsden, *N.Z.* 91 L2
Lumut, *Malaysia* 65 K3
Lumut, Tanjung, *Indonesia* . 62 E3
Luna, *India* 68 H3
Lunan, *China* 58 E4
Lunavada, *India* 68 H5
Lunca, *Romania* 43 C10
Lunca Corbului, *Romania* . 43 F9
Lund, *Sweden* 11 J7
Lundazi, *Zambia* 87 E3
Lunderskov, *Denmark* 11 J3
Lundi →, *Zimbabwe* 87 G3
Lundu, *Malaysia* 62 D3
Lundy, *U.K.* 13 F3
Lune →, *U.K.* 12 C5
Lüneburg, *Germany* 24 B6
Lüneburg Heath =
  Lüneburger Heide,
  Germany 24 B6
Lüneburger Heide, *Germany* 24 B6
Lunel, *France* 21 E8
Lünen, *Germany* 24 D3
Lunenburg, *Canada* 103 D7
Lunéville, *France* 19 D13
Lunga →, *Zambia* 87 E2
Lungi Airport, *S. Leone* ... 82 D2
Lunglei, *India* 67 H18
Luni, *India* 68 G5
Luni →, *India* 68 G4
Luninets = Luninyets,
  Belarus 47 F4
Luning, *U.S.A.* 114 G4
Lunino, *Russia* 48 D7
Luninyets, *Belarus* 47 F4
Lunkaransar, *India* 68 E5
Lunsemfwa →, *Zambia* 87 E3
Lunsemfwa Falls, *Zambia* . 87 E2
Luo He →, *China* 56 G6
Luocheng, *China* 58 E7
Luochuan, *China* 56 G5
Luoci, *China* 58 E4
Luodian, *China* 58 E6
Luoding, *China* 59 F8

Luofu,
  Dem. Rep. of the Congo . 86 C2
Luohe, *China* 56 H8
Luojiang, *China* 58 B5
Luonan, *China* 56 G6
Luoning, *China* 56 G6
Luoshan, *China* 59 A10
Luotian, *China* 59 B10
Luoxiao Shan, *China* 59 D10
Luoyang, *China* 56 G7
Luoyuan, *China* 59 D12
Luozigou, *China* 57 C16
Lupanshui, *China* 58 D5
Lupeni, *Romania* 43 E8
Lupilichi, *Mozam.* 87 E4
Łupków, *Poland* 45 J9
Lupoing, *China* 58 E5
Luquan, *China* 58 E4
Luque, *Paraguay* 126 B4
Lúras, *Italy* 30 B2
Luray, *U.S.A.* 108 F6
Lure, *France* 19 E13
Lurgan, *U.K.* 15 B5
Lusaka, *Zambia* 87 F2
Lusambo,
  Dem. Rep. of the Congo . 86 C1
Lusangaye,
  Dem. Rep. of the Congo . 86 C2
Luseland, *Canada* 105 C7
Lushan, *Henan, China* 56 H7
Lushan, *Sichuan, China* ... 58 B4
Lushi, *China* 56 G6
Lushnja, *Albania* 40 F3
Lushoto, *Tanzania* 86 C4
Lushui, *China* 58 E2
Lüshun, *China* 57 E11
Lusignan, *France* 20 B4
Lusigny-sur-Barse, *France* . 19 D11
Lusk, *U.S.A.* 112 D2
Lussac-les-Châteaux, *France* 20 B4
Lustenau, *Austria* 26 D2
Lūt, Dasht-e, *Iran* 71 D8
Luta = Dalian, *China* 57 E11
Lutherstadt Wittenberg,
  Germany 24 D8
Luton, *U.K.* 13 F7
Luton □, *U.K.* 13 F7
Lutselke, *Canada* 105 A6
Lutsk, *Ukraine* 47 G3
Lützow Holmbukta,
  Antarctica 5 C4
Lutzputs, *S. Africa* 88 D3
Luverne, *Ala., U.S.A.* 109 K2
Luverne, *Minn., U.S.A.* ... 112 D6
Luvua,
  Dem. Rep. of the Congo . 87 D2
Luvua →,
  Dem. Rep. of the Congo . 86 D2
Luvuvhu →, *S. Africa* 89 C5
Luwegu →, *Tanzania* 87 D4
Luwuk, *Indonesia* 63 E6
Luxembourg, *Lux.* 17 E6
Luxembourg □, *Belgium* .. 17 E5
Luxembourg ■, *Europe* ... 7 F7
Luxeuil-les-Bains, *France* .. 19 E13
Luxi, *Hunan, China* 59 C8
Luxi, *Yunnan, China* 58 E4
Luxi, *Yunnan, China* 58 E2
Luxor = El Uqsur, *Egypt* .. 80 B3
Luy-de-Béarn →, *France* .. 20 E3
Luy-de-France →, *France* . 20 E3
Luyi, *China* 56 H8
Luz-St-Sauveur, *France* ... 20 F4
Luzern, *Switz.* 25 H4
Luzern □, *Switz.* 25 H3
Luzhai, *China* 58 E7
Luzhi, *China* 58 D5
Luzhou, *China* 58 C5
Luziânia, *Brazil* 125 G9
Lužnice →, *Czech Rep.* ... 26 B7
Luzon, *Phil.* 61 D4
Luzy, *France* 19 F10
Luzzi, *Italy* 31 C9
Lviv, *Ukraine* 47 H3
Lvov = Lviv, *Ukraine* 47 H3
Lwówek, *Poland* 45 F3
Lwówek Śląski, *Poland* 45 G2
Lyakhavichy, *Belarus* 47 F4
Lyakhovskiye, Ostrova,
  Russia 51 B15
Lyaki = Läki, *Azerbaijan* .. 49 K8
Lyal I., *Canada* 110 B3
Lyallpur = Faisalabad,
  Pakistan 68 D5
Lyaskovets, *Bulgaria* 41 C9
Lybster, *U.K.* 14 C5
Lycaonia, *Turkey* 72 D5
Lychen, *Germany* 24 B9
Lychkova, *Russia* 46 D7
Lycia, *Turkey* 39 E11
Lyckeby, *Sweden* 11 H9
Lycksele, *Sweden* 8 D18
Lycosura, *Greece* 38 D4
Lydda = Lod, *Israel* 75 D3
Lydenburg, *S. Africa* 89 D5
Lydia, *Turkey* 39 C10
Łydynia →, *Poland* 45 F7
Lyell, *N.Z.* 91 J4
Lyell I., *Canada* 104 C2
Lyepyel, *Belarus* 46 E5
Lygnern, *Sweden* 11 G6
Lykens, *U.S.A.* 111 F8
Lyman, *U.S.A.* 114 F8
Lyme B., *U.K.* 13 G5
Lyme Regis, *U.K.* 13 G5
Lymington, *U.K.* 13 G6
Łyna →, *Poland* 9 J19
Lynchburg, *U.S.A.* 108 G6
Lynd →, *Australia* 94 B3
Lynd Ra., *Australia* 95 D4
Lynden, *Canada* 110 C4

Lynden, *U.S.A.* 116 B4
Lyndhurst, *Australia* 95 E2
Lyndon →, *Australia* 93 D1
Lyndonville, *N.Y., U.S.A.* . 110 C6
Lyndonville, *Vt., U.S.A.* .. 111 B12
Lyngen, *Norway* 8 B19
Lynher Reef, *Australia* 92 C3
Lynn, *U.S.A.* 111 D14
Lynn Lake, *Canada* 105 B8
Lynnwood, *U.S.A.* 116 C4
Lynton, *U.K.* 13 F4
Lyntupy, *Belarus* 9 J22
Lynx L., *Canada* 105 A7
Lyon, *France* 21 C8
Lyonnais, *France* 21 C8
Lyons = Lyon, *France* 21 C8
Lyons, *Ga., U.S.A.* 109 J4
Lyons, *Kans., U.S.A.* 112 F5
Lyons, *N.Y., U.S.A.* 110 C8
Lyons →, *Australia* 93 E2
Lyons Falls, *U.S.A.* 111 C9
Lyozna, *Belarus* 46 E6
Lys = Leie →, *Belgium* ... 17 C3
Lysekil, *Sweden* 11 F5
Lyskovo, *Russia* 48 B7
Lysichansk, *Ukraine* 47 H10
Lysva, *Russia* 10 D7
Lysychansk, *Ukraine* 47 H10
Lytham St. Anne's, *U.K.* .. 12 D4
Lyttelton, *N.Z.* 91 K4
Lytton, *Canada* 104 C4
Lyuban, *Russia* 46 C6
Lyubertsy, *Russia* 46 E9
Lyubim, *Russia* 46 C11
Lyubimets, *Bulgaria* 41 E10
Lyuboml, *Ukraine* 47 G3
Lyubotyn, *Ukraine* 47 H8
Lyubytino, *Russia* 46 C7
Lyudinovo, *Russia* 46 F8

M

M.R. Gomez, Presa, *Mexico* 119 B5
Ma →, *Vietnam* 58 H5
Ma'adaba, *Jordan* 75 E4
Maamba, *Zambia* 88 B4
Ma'ān, *Jordan* 75 E4
Ma'ān □, *Jordan* 75 F5
Maanselkä, *Finland* 8 C23
Ma'anshan, *China* 59 B12
Maarianhamina, *Finland* .. 9 F18
Ma'arrat an Nu'mān, *Syria* 70 C3
Maas →, *Neths.* 17 C4
Maaseik, *Belgium* 17 C5
Maasin, *Phil.* 63 B6
Maastricht, *Neths.* 17 D5
Maave, *Mozam.* 89 C5
Mababe Depression,
  Botswana 88 B3
Mabalane, *Mozam.* 89 C5
Mabel L., *Canada* 104 C5
Mabenge,
  Dem. Rep. of the Congo . 86 B1
Maberly, *Canada* 111 B8
Mabian, *China* 58 C4
Mabil, *Ethiopia* 81 E4
Mablethorpe, *U.K.* 12 D8
Mably, *France* 19 F11
Maboma,
  Dem. Rep. of the Congo . 86 B2
Mabonto, *S. Leone* 82 D2
Mabrouk, *Mali* 83 B4
Mac Bac, *Vietnam* 65 H6
Macachín, *Argentina* 126 D3
Macaé, *Brazil* 127 A7
Macael, *Spain* 33 H2
McAlester, *U.S.A.* 113 H7
McAllen, *U.S.A.* 113 M5
MacAlpine L., *Canada* ... 100 B9
Macamic, *Canada* 102 C4
Macao = Macau, *Asia* 59 F9
Macão, *Portugal* 35 F3
Macapá, *Brazil* 125 C8
McArthur →, *Australia* ... 94 B2
McArthur, Port, *Australia* . 94 B2
Macau, *Brazil* 125 E11
Macau, *Asia* 59 F9
McBride, *Canada* 104 C4
McCamey, *U.S.A.* 113 K3
McCammon, *U.S.A.* 114 E7
McCauley I., *Canada* 104 C2
McCleary, *U.S.A.* 116 C3
Macclenny, *U.S.A.* 109 K4
Macclesfield, *U.K.* 12 D5
M'Clintock Chan., *Canada* 100 A9
McClintock Ra., *Australia* . 92 C4
McCloud, *U.S.A.* 114 F2
McClure, *U.S.A.* 110 F7
McCluer I., *Australia* 92 B5
M'Clure Str., *Canada* 4 B2
McClusky, *U.S.A.* 112 B4
McComb, *U.S.A.* 113 K9
McConaughy, L., *U.S.A.* .. 112 E4
McCook, *U.S.A.* 112 E4
McCreary, *Canada* 105 C9
McCullough Mt., *U.S.A.* .. 117 K11
McCusker →, *Canada* 105 B7
McDame, *Canada* 104 B3
McDermitt, *U.S.A.* 114 F5
McDonald, *U.S.A.* 110 F4
Macdonald, L., *Australia* .. 92 D4
McDonald Is., *Ind. Oc.* ... 3 G13
MacDonnell Ranges,
  Australia 92 D5
MacDowell L., *Canada* ... 102 B1

Macduff, *U.K.* 14 D6
Maceda, *Spain* 34 C3
Macedonia, *U.S.A.* 110 E3
Macedonia ■, *Europe* 40 E5
Maceió, *Brazil* 125 E11
Maceira, *Portugal* 34 F2
Macenta, *Guinea* 82 D3
Macerata, *Italy* 29 E10
McFarland, *U.S.A.* 117 K7
McFarlane →, *Canada* 105 B7
Macfarlane, L., *Australia* .. 95 E2
McGehee, *U.S.A.* 113 J9
McGill, *U.S.A.* 114 G6
Macgillycuddy's Reeks,
  Ireland 15 E2
McGraw, *U.S.A.* 111 D8
McGregor, *U.S.A.* 112 D9
McGregor Ra., *Australia* .. 95 D3
Mach, *Pakistan* 66 E5
Māch Kowr, *Iran* 71 E9
Machado = Jiparaná →,
  Brazil 124 E6
Machagai, *Argentina* 126 B3
Machakos, *Kenya* 86 C4
Machala, *Ecuador* 124 D3
Machanga, *Mozam.* 89 C6
Machattie, L., *Australia* ... 94 C2
Machault, *France* 19 C11
Machava, *Mozam.* 89 D5
Machece, *Mozam.* 87 F4
Machecoul, *France* 18 F5
Macheke, *Zimbabwe* 89 B5
Macheng, *China* 59 B10
Machero, *Spain* 35 F6
Machhu →, *India* 68 H4
Machias, *Maine, U.S.A.* .. 109 C12
Machias, *N.Y., U.S.A.* ... 110 D6
Machichi →, *Canada* 105 B10
Machico, *Madeira* 37 D3
Machilipatnam, *India* 67 L12
Machiques, *Venezuela* 124 A4
Machupicchu, *Peru* 124 F4
Machynlleth, *U.K.* 13 E4
Macia, *Mozam.* 89 D5
Maciejowice, *Poland* 45 G8
McIlwraith Ra., *Australia* .. 94 A3
Măcin, *Romania* 43 E13
Macina, *Mali* 82 C4
McInnes L., *Canada* 105 C10
McIntosh, *U.S.A.* 112 C4
McIntosh L., *Canada* 105 B8
Macintosh Ra., *Australia* .. 93 E4
Macintyre →, *Australia* ... 95 D5
Macizo Galaico, *Spain* 34 C3
Mackay, *Australia* 94 C4
Mackay, *U.S.A.* 114 E7
MacKay →, *Canada* 104 B6
Mackay, L., *Australia* 92 D4
McKay Ra., *Australia* 92 D3
McKeesport, *U.S.A.* 110 F5
McKellar, *Canada* 110 A5
McKenna, *U.S.A.* 116 D4
Mackenzie, *Canada* 104 B4
Mackenzie, *U.S.A.* 109 G1
Mackenzie →, *Australia* .. 94 C4
Mackenzie →, *Canada* ... 100 B6
Mackenzie →, *Canada* ... 114 D2
Mackenzie Bay, *Canada* .. 4 B1
Mackenzie City = Linden,
  Guyana 124 B7
Mackenzie Mts., *Canada* .. 100 B6
Mackinaw City, *U.S.A.* ... 108 C3
McKinlay, *Australia* 94 C3
McKinlay →, *Australia* ... 94 C3
McKinley, Mt., *U.S.A.* 100 B4
McKinley Sea, *Arctic* 4 A7
McKinney, *U.S.A.* 113 J6
Mackinnon Road, *Kenya* .. 86 C4
McKittrick, *U.S.A.* 117 K7
Macklin, *Canada* 105 C7
Macksville, *Australia* 95 E5
McLaughlin, *U.S.A.* 112 C4
Maclean, *Australia* 95 D5
McLean, *U.S.A.* 113 H4
McLeansboro, *U.S.A.* 112 F10
McLear →, *Canada* 104 C5
Maclear, *S. Africa* 89 E4
Macleay →, *Australia* 95 E5
McLennan, *Canada* 104 B5
MacLeod, B., *Canada* 105 A7
MacLeod, L., *Australia* ... 93 D1
MacLeod Lake, *Canada* .. 104 C4
McLoughlin, Mt., *U.S.A.* .. 114 E2
McMechen, *U.S.A.* 110 G4
McMinnville, *Oreg., U.S.A.* 114 D2
McMinnville, *Tenn., U.S.A.* 109 H3
McMurdo Sd., *Antarctica* . 5 D11
McMurray = Fort
  McMurray, *Canada* 104 B6
McMurray, *U.S.A.* 116 B4
Macodoene, *Mozam.* 89 C6
Macomb, *U.S.A.* 112 E9
Macomer, *Italy* 30 B1
Mâcon, *France* 19 F11
Macon, *Ga., U.S.A.* 109 J4
Macon, *Miss., U.S.A.* 109 J1
Macon, *Mo., U.S.A.* 112 F8
Macossa, *Mozam.* 87 F3
Macoun L., *Canada* 105 B8
Macovane, *Mozam.* 89 C6
McPherson, *U.S.A.* 112 F6
McPherson Pk., *U.S.A.* ... 117 L7
McPherson Ra., *Australia* . 95 D5
Macquarie →, *Australia* .. 95 E4
Macquarie Harbour,
  Australia 94 G4
Macquarie Is., *Pac. Oc.* ... 96 N7
MacRobertson Land,
  Antarctica 5 D6
Macroom, *Ireland* 15 E3
MacTier, *Canada* 110 A5

Macubela, *Mozam.* 87 F4
Macugnaga, *Italy* 28 C4
Macuiza, *Mozam.* 87 F3
Macuro, *Venezuela* 87 F4
Macusani, *Peru* 124 F4
Macuspana, *Mexico* 119 D6
Mada →, *Nigeria* 83 D6
Madadeni, *S. Africa* 89 D5
Madagali, *Nigeria* 83 C7
Madagascar ■, *Africa* 89 C8
Madā'in Sālih, *Si. Arabia* .. 70 E3
Madama, *Niger* 79 D8
Madame I., *Canada* 103 C7
Madan, *Bulgaria* 41 E8
Madaoua, *Niger* 83 C6
Madara, *Nigeria* 83 C7
Madaripur, *Bangla.* 67 H17
Madauk, *Burma* 67 L20
Madawaska, *Canada* 110 A7
Madawaska →, *Canada* .. 102 C4
Madaya, *Burma* 67 H20
Madbar, *Sudan* 81 F3
Maddalena, *Italy* 30 A2
Maddaloni, *Italy* 31 A7
Madeira, *Atl. Oc.* 37 D3
Madeira →, *Brazil* 122 D5
Madeleine, Îs. de la, *Canada* 103 C7
Maden, *Turkey* 73 C8
Madera, *Mexico* 118 B3
Madera, *Calif., U.S.A.* ... 116 J6
Madera, *Pa., U.S.A.* 110 F6
Madha, *India* 66 L9
Madhavpur, *India* 68 J3
Madhepura, *India* 69 F12
Madhubani, *India* 69 F12
Madhupur, *India* 69 G12
Madhya Pradesh □, *India* . 68 J8
Madian, *China* 59 A11
Madidi →, *Bolivia* 124 F5
Madikeri, *India* 66 N9
Madill, *U.S.A.* 113 H6
Madimba,
  Dem. Rep. of the Congo . 84 E3
Ma'din, *Syria* 70 C3
Madina, *Mali* 82 C3
Madinani, *Ivory C.* 82 D3
Madingou, *Congo* 84 E2
Madirovalo, *Madag.* 89 B8
Madison, *Calif., U.S.A.* ... 116 G5
Madison, *Fla., U.S.A.* 109 K4
Madison, *Ind., U.S.A.* 108 F3
Madison, *Nebr., U.S.A.* .. 112 E6
Madison, *Ohio, U.S.A.* ... 110 E3
Madison, *S. Dak., U.S.A.* . 112 D6
Madison, *Wis., U.S.A.* ... 112 D10
Madison →, *U.S.A.* 114 D8
Madison Heights, *U.S.A.* .. 108 G6
Madisonville, *Ky., U.S.A.* . 108 G2
Madisonville, *Tex., U.S.A.* 113 K7
Madista, *Botswana* 88 C4
Madiun, *Indonesia* 63 G14
Madoc, *Canada* 110 B7
Madol, *Sudan* 81 F2
Madon →, *France* 19 D13
Madona, *Latvia* 9 H22
Madonie, *Italy* 30 E6
Madonna di Campíglio, *Italy* 28 B7
Madra Dağı, *Turkey* 39 B9
Madrakah, Ra's al, *Oman* . 74 D6
Madras = Chennai, *India* . 66 N12
Madras = Tamil Nadu □,
  India 66 P10
Madras, *U.S.A.* 114 D3
Madre, L., *Mexico* 119 C5
Madre, Laguna, *U.S.A.* ... 113 M6
Madre de Dios, I., *Chile* .. 122 J3
Madre del Sur, Sierra,
  Mexico 119 D5
Madre Occidental, Sierra,
  Mexico 118 B3
Madre Oriental, Sierra,
  Mexico 118 C5
Madri, *India* 68 G5
Madrid, *Spain* 34 E7
Madrid, *U.S.A.* 111 B9
Madrid □, *Spain* 34 E7
Madridejos, *Spain* 35 F7
Madrigal de las Altas Torres,
  Spain 34 D6
Madrona, Sierra, *Spain* ... 35 G6
Madroñera, *Spain* 35 F5
Madu, *Sudan* 81 E2
Madura, *Australia* 93 F4
Madura, *Indonesia* 63 G15
Madura, Selat, *Indonesia* . 63 G15
Madurai, *India* 66 Q11
Madurantakam, *India* 66 N11
Madzhalis, *Russia* 49 J8
Mae Chan, *Thailand* 64 B2
Mae Hong Son, *Thailand* . 64 C2
Mae Khlong →, *Thailand* . 64 F3
Mae Phrik, *Thailand* 64 D2
Mae Ramat, *Thailand* 64 D2
Mae Rim, *Thailand* 64 C2
Mae Sot, *Thailand* 64 D2
Mae Suai, *Thailand* 58 H2
Mae Tha, *Thailand* 64 C2
Maebashi, *Japan* 55 F9
Maella, *Spain* 32 D5
Maesteg, *U.K.* 13 F4
Maestra, Sierra, *Cuba* 120 B4
Maevatanana, *Madag.* 89 B8
Mafeking = Mafikeng,
  S. Africa 88 D4
Mafeking, *Canada* 105 C8
Mafeteng, *Lesotho* 88 D4
Maféré, *Ivory C.* 82 D4
Mafeteng, *Lesotho* 88 D4
Maffra, *Australia* 95 F4

Mafia I.

Mafia I., *Tanzania* 86 D4
Mafikeng, *S. Africa* 88 D4
Mafra, *Brazil* 127 A6
Mafra, *Portugal* 35 G1
Mafungabusi Plateau,
　Zimbabwe 87 F2
Magadan, *Russia* 51 D16
Magadi, *Kenya* 86 C4
Magadi, L., *Kenya* 86 C4
Magaliesburg, *S. Africa* ... 89 D4
Magallanes, Estrecho de,
　Chile 122 J3
Magaluf, *Spain* 33 F7
Magangué, *Colombia* 124 B4
Magaria, *Niger* 83 C6
Magburaka, *S. Leone* 82 D2
Magdalen Is. = Madeleine,
　Îs. de la, *Canada* 103 C7
Magdalena, *Argentina* 126 D4
Magdalena, *Bolivia* 124 F6
Magdalena, *Mexico* 118 A2
Magdalena, *U.S.A.* 115 J10
Magdalena →, *Colombia* .. 122 B3
Magdalena →, *Mexico* 118 A2
Magdalena, B., *Mexico* ... 118 C2
Magdalena, Llano de la,
　Mexico 118 C2
Magdeburg, *Germany* 24 C7
Magdelaine Cays, *Australia* . 94 B5
Magdub, *Sudan* 81 E2
Magee, *U.S.A.* 113 K10
Magelang, *Indonesia* 63 G14
Magellan's Str. =
　Magallanes, Estrecho de,
　Chile 122 J3
Magenta, *Italy* 28 C5
Magenta, L., *Australia* 93 F2
Magerøya, *Norway* 8 A21
Maggia →, *Switz.* 25 J4
Maggiorasca, Mte., *Italy* .. 28 D6
Maggiore, Lago, *Italy* 28 C5
Maghâgha, *Egypt* 80 B3
Maghama, *Mauritania* 82 B2
Magherafelt, *U.K.* 15 B5
Maghreb, *N. Afr.* 78 B5
Magione, *Italy* 29 E9
Magistralnyy, *Russia* 51 D11
Maglaj, *Bos.-H.* 42 F3
Magliano in Toscana, *Italy* . 29 F8
Máglie, *Italy* 31 B11
Magnac-Laval, *France* 20 B5
Magnetic Pole (North) =
　North Magnetic Pole,
　Canada 4 B2
Magnetic Pole (South) =
　South Magnetic Pole,
　Antarctica 5 C9
Magnisía □, *Greece* 38 E5
Magnitogorsk, *Russia* 50 D6
Magnolia, Ark., *U.S.A.* ... 113 J8
Magnolia, Miss., *U.S.A.* .. 113 K9
Magny-en-Vexin, *France* .. 19 C8
Magog, *Canada* 103 C5
Magoro, *Uganda* 86 B3
Magosa = Famagusta,
　Cyprus 36 D12
Magouládhes, *Greece* 36 A3
Magoye, *Zambia* 87 F2
Magozal, *Mexico* 119 C5
Magpie, L., *Canada* 103 B7
Magrath, *Canada* 104 D6
Magre →, *Spain* 33 F4
Magrur, *Sudan* 81 E3
Magrur, Wadi →, *Sudan* .. 81 D2
Magta Lahjar, *Mauritania* . 82 B2
Maguan, *China* 58 F5
Maguarinho, C., *Brazil* ... 125 D9
Magude, *Mozam.* 89 D5
Magusa = Famagusta,
　Cyprus 36 D12
Maguse L., *Canada* 105 A9
Maguse Pt., *Canada* 105 A10
Magvana, *India* 68 H3
Magwe, *Burma* 67 J19
Magwe, *Sudan* 81 G3
Maha Sarakham, *Thailand* . 64 D4
Mahābād, *Iran* 70 B5
Mahabharat Lekh, *Nepal* .. 69 E10
Mahabo, *Madag.* 89 C7
Mahadeo Hills, *India* 69 H8
Mahaffey, *U.S.A.* 110 F6
Mahagi,
　Dem. Rep. of the Congo . 86 B3
Mahajamba →, *Madag.* ... 89 B8
Mahajamba, Helodranon' i,
　Madag. 89 B8
Mahajan, *India* 68 E5
Mahajanga, *Madag.* 89 B8
Mahajanga □, *Madag.* 89 B8
Mahajilo →, *Madag.* 89 B8
Mahakam →, *Indonesia* .. 62 E5
Mahalapye, *Botswana* 88 C4
Maḥallāt, *Iran* 71 C6
Māhān, *Iran* 71 D8
Mahan →, *India* 69 H10
Mahanadi →, *India* 67 J15
Mahananda →, *India* 69 G12
Mahanoro, *Madag.* 89 B8
Mahanoy City, *U.S.A.* 111 F8
Maharashtra □, *India* 66 J9
Mahari Mts., *Tanzania* 86 D3
Mahasham, W. →, *Egypt* .. 75 E3
Mahasoa, *Madag.* 89 C8
Mahasolo, *Madag.* 89 B8
Mahattat ash Shīdīyah,
　Jordan 75 F4
Mahattat 'Unayzah, *Jordan* . 75 E4
Mahavavy →, *Madag.* 89 B8
Mahaxay, *Laos* 64 D5
Mahbubnagar, *India* 66 L10
Maḥḍah, *Oman* 71 E7

Mahdia, *Tunisia* 79 A8
Mahe, *India* 69 C8
Mahendragarh, *India* 68 E7
Mahenge, *Tanzania* 87 D4
Maheno, *N.Z.* 91 L3
Mahesana, *India* 68 H5
Maheshwar, *India* 68 H6
Mahgawan, *India* 69 F8
Mahi →, *India* 68 H5
Mahia Pen., *N.Z.* 91 H6
Mahilyow, *Belarus* 46 F6
Mahmiya, *Sudan* 81 D3
Mahmud Kot, *Pakistan* ... 68 D4
Mahmudia, *Romania* 43 E14
Mahmudiye, *Turkey* 39 B12
Mahmutbey, *Turkey* 41 E12
Mahnomen, *U.S.A.* 112 B7
Mahón = Maó, *Spain* 37 B11
Mahone Bay, *Canada* 103 D7
Mahopac, *U.S.A.* 111 E11
Mahuta, *Nigeria* 83 C5
Mahuva, *India* 68 J4
Mahya Daği, *Turkey* 41 E11
Mai-Ndombe, L.,
　Dem. Rep. of the Congo . 84 E3
Mai-Sai, *Thailand* 58 G2
Maia, *Portugal* 34 D2
Maia, *Spain* 32 B3
Maials, *Spain* 32 D5
Maicurú →, *Brazil* 125 D8
Máida, *Italy* 31 D9
Maidan Khula, *Afghan.* ... 68 C3
Maidenhead, *U.K.* 13 F7
Maidstone, *Canada* 105 C7
Maidstone, *U.K.* 13 F8
Maiduguri, *Nigeria* 83 C7
Măieruș, *Romania* 43 E10
Maigatari, *Nigeria* 83 C6
Maignelay Montigny, *France* . 19 C9
Maigo, *Phil.* 61 G5
Maigudo, *Ethiopia* 81 F4
Maihar, *India* 69 G9
Maijdi, *Bangla.* 67 H17
Maikala Ra., *India* 69 E9
Mailani, *India* 69 E9
Maillezais, *France* 20 B3
Mailsi, *Pakistan* 68 E5
Main →, *Germany* 25 F4
Main →, *U.K.* 15 B5
Mainburg, *Germany* 25 G7
Maine, *France* 18 D6
Maine □, *U.S.A.* 109 C11
Maine →, *Ireland* 15 D2
Maine-et-Loire □, *France* .. 18 E6
Maïne-Soroa, *Niger* 83 C7
Maingkwan, *Burma* 67 F20
Mainit, L., *Phil.* 61 G6
Mainland, Orkney, *U.K.* ... 14 C5
Mainland, Shet., *U.K.* 14 A7
Mainoru, *Australia* 94 A1
Mainpuri, *India* 69 F8
Maintal, *Germany* 25 E4
Maintenon, *France* 19 D8
Maintirano, *Madag.* 89 B7
Mainz, *Germany* 25 E4
Maipú, *Argentina* 126 D4
Maiquetía, *Venezuela* 124 A5
Máira →, *Italy* 28 D4
Mairabari, *India* 67 F18
Maisí, *Cuba* 121 B5
Maisí, Pta. de, *Cuba* 121 B5
Maitland, N.S.W., *Australia* . 95 E5
Maitland, S. Austral.,
　Australia 95 E2
Maitland →, *Canada* 110 C3
Maiyema, *Nigeria* 83 C5
Maiyuan, *China* 59 E11
Maíz, Is. del, *Nic.* 120 D3
Maizuru, *Japan* 55 G7
Majalengka, *Indonesia* ... 63 G13
Majene, *Indonesia* 63 E5
Majevica, *Bos.-H.* 42 F3
Maji, *Ethiopia* 81 F4
Majiang, *China* 58 D6
Majorca = Mallorca, *Spain* . 37 B10
Maka, *Senegal* 82 C2
Makaha, *Zimbabwe* 89 B5
Makak, *Cameroon* 83 E7
Makakalamabedi, *Botswana* . 88 C3
Makale, *Indonesia* 63 E5
Makamba, *Burundi* 86 C2
Makari, *Cameroon* 83 C7
Makarikari = Makgadikgadi
　Salt Pans, *Botswana* 88 C4
Makarovo, *Russia* 51 D11
Makarska, *Croatia* 29 E14
Makaryev, *Russia* 48 B6
Makasar = Ujung Pandang,
　Indonesia 63 F5
Makasar, Selat, *Indonesia* . 63 E5
Makasar, Str. of = Makasar,
　Selat, *Indonesia* 63 E5
Makat, *Kazakhstan* 50 E6
Makedonija = Macedonia ■,
　Europe 40 E5
Makena, *U.S.A.* 106 H16
Makeni, *S. Leone* 82 D2
Makeyevka = Makiyivka,
　Ukraine 47 H9
Makgadikgadi Salt Pans,
　Botswana 88 C4
Makhachkala, *Russia* 49 J8
Makharadze = Ozurgeti,
　Georgia 49 K5
Makhmūr, *Iraq* 70 C4
Makian, *Indonesia* 63 D7
Makindu, *Kenya* 86 C4
Makinsk, *Kazakhstan* 50 D8
Makiyivka, *Ukraine* 47 H9

Makkah, *Si. Arabia* 74 C2
Makkovik, *Canada* 103 A8
Makó, *Hungary* 42 D5
Mako, *Senegal* 82 C2
Makokou, *Gabon* 84 D2
Makongo,
　Dem. Rep. of the Congo . 86 B2
Makoro,
　Dem. Rep. of the Congo . 86 B2
Maków Mazowiecki, *Poland* . 45 F8
Maków Podhalański, *Poland* . 45 J6
Makrá, *Greece* 39 E7
Makran Coast Range,
　Pakistan 66 G4
Makrana, *India* 68 F6
Makrai, *India* 66 H10
Mákri, *Greece* 41 F9
Makriyialos, *Greece* 36 D7
Mākū, *Iran* 70 B5
Makunda, *Botswana* 88 C3
Makung, *Taiwan* 59 F12
Makurazaki, *Japan* 55 J5
Makurdi, *Nigeria* 83 D6
Makūyeh, *Iran* 71 D7
Makwassie, *S. Africa* 88 D4
Makwiro, *Zimbabwe* 89 B5
Mâl, *Mauritania* 82 B2
Mala, Pta., *Panama* 120 E3
Mala = Mallow, *Ireland* ... 15 D3
Mala Belozërka, *Ukraine* .. 47 J8
Mala Kapela, *Croatia* 29 D12
Mała Panew →, *Poland* ... 45 H4
Mala Vyska, *Ukraine* 47 H6
Malabang, *Phil.* 61 H6
Malabar Coast, *India* 66 P9
Malabo = Rey Malabo,
　Eq. Guin. 83 E6
Malabon, *Phil.* 61 D4
Malabu, *Nigeria* 83 D7
Malacca, Str. of, *Indonesia* . 65 L3
Malacky, *Slovak Rep.* 27 C10
Malad City, *U.S.A.* 114 E7
Maladeta, *Spain* 32 C5
Maladzyechna, *Belarus* ... 46 E4
Málaga, *Spain* 35 J6
Málaga □, *Spain* 35 J6
Malagarasi, *Tanzania* 86 D3
Malagarasi →, *Tanzania* .. 86 D2
Malagasy Rep. =
　Madagascar ■, *Africa* ... 89 C8
Malagón, *Spain* 35 F7
Malagón →, *Spain* 35 H3
Malahide, *Ireland* 15 C5
Malaimbandy, *Madag.* 89 C8
Malakâl, *Sudan* 81 F3
Malakand, *Pakistan* 68 B4
Malakwal, *Pakistan* 68 C5
Malamala, *Indonesia* 63 E6
Malanda, *Australia* 94 B4
Malang, *Indonesia* 63 G15
Malangen, *Norway* 8 B18
Malanje, *Angola* 84 F3
Mälaren, *Sweden* 10 E11
Malargüe, *Argentina* 126 D2
Malartic, *Canada* 102 C4
Malaryta, *Belarus* 47 G3
Malatya, *Turkey* 70 B3
Malawi ■, *Africa* 87 E3
Malawi, L. = Nyasa, L.,
　Africa 87 E3
Malay Pen., *Asia* 65 J3
Malaya Belozërka = Mala
　Belozërka, *Ukraine* 47 J8
Malaya Vishera, *Russia* ... 46 C7
Malaya Viska = Mala Vyska,
　Ukraine 47 H6
Malaybalay, *Phil.* 61 G6
Malāyer, *Iran* 71 C6
Malaysia ■, *Asia* 65 K4
Malazgirt, *Turkey* 70 B4
Malbaza, *Niger* 83 C6
Malbon, *Australia* 94 C3
Malbooma, *Australia* 95 E1
Malbork, *Poland* 44 D6
Malcésine, *Italy* 28 C7
Malchin, *Germany* 24 B8
Malchow, *Germany* 24 B8
Malcolm, *Australia* 93 E3
Malcolm, Pt., *Australia* ... 93 F3
Malczyce, *Poland* 45 G3
Maldah, *India* 69 G13
Maldegem, *Belgium* 17 C3
Malden, Mass., *U.S.A.* ... 111 D13
Malden, Mo., *U.S.A.* 113 G10
Malden I., *Kiribati* 97 H12
Maldives ■, *Ind. Oc.* 52 J11
Maldonado, *Uruguay* 127 C5
Maldonado, Punta, *Mexico* . 119 D5
Malè, *Italy* 28 B7
Malé, *Maldives* 53 J11
Malé Karpaty, *Slovak Rep.* . 27 C10
Maléa, Ákra, *Greece* 38 E5
Malegaon, *India* 66 J9
Malei, *Mozam.* 87 F4
Malek, *Sudan* 81 F3
Malek Kandī, *Iran* 70 B5
Malela,
　Dem. Rep. of the Congo . 86 C2
Malema, *Mozam.* 87 E4
Máleme, *Greece* 36 D5
Maleny, *Australia* 95 D5
Mälerås, *Sweden* 11 H9
Malerkotla, *India* 68 D6
Máles, *Greece* 36 D7
Malesherbes, *France* 19 D9
Malesína, *Greece* 38 C5
Maleshevska Planina, *Europe* . 40 E7
Malestroit, *France* 18 E4
Malfa, *Italy* 31 D7
Malgobek, *Russia* 49 J7
Malgomaj, *Sweden* 8 D17

Malgrat = Malgrat de Mar,
　Spain 32 D7
Malgrat de Mar, *Spain* 32 D7
Malha, *Sudan* 81 D2
Malhargarh, *India* 68 G6
Malheur →, *U.S.A.* 114 D5
Malheur L., *U.S.A.* 114 E4
Mali, *Guinea* 82 C2
Mali ■, *Africa* 82 B4
Mali →, *Burma* 67 G20
Mali Kanal, *Serbia, Yug.* .. 42 E4
Mali Kyun, *Burma* 64 F2
Malibu, *U.S.A.* 117 L8
Maliku, *Indonesia* 63 E6
Malili, *Indonesia* 63 E6
Målilla, *Sweden* 11 G9
Malimba, Mts.,
　Dem. Rep. of the Congo . 86 D2
Malin, *Russia* 15 A4
Malin Pen., *Ireland* 15 A4
Malindi, *Kenya* 86 C5
Malines = Mechelen,
　Belgium 17 C4
Malino, *Indonesia* 63 D6
Malinyi, *Tanzania* 87 D4
Malipo, *China* 58 F5
Maliqi, *Albania* 40 F4
Malita, *Phil.* 63 C7
Maliwun, *Burma* 62 B1
Maliya, *India* 68 H4
Maljenik, *Serbia, Yug.* 40 C5
Malkara, *Turkey* 41 F10
Malkinia Górna, *Poland* ... 45 F9
Malko Tŭrnovo, *Bulgaria* . 41 E11
Mallacoota Inlet, *Australia* . 95 F4
Mallaig, *U.K.* 14 D3
Mallaoua, *Niger* 83 C6
Mallawan, *India* 69 F9
Mallawi, *Egypt* 80 B3
Mallemort, *France* 21 E9
Málles Venosta, *Italy* 28 B7
Mállia, *Greece* 36 D7
Mallión, Kólpos, *Greece* .. 36 D7
Mallorca, *Spain* 37 B10
Mallorytown, *Canada* 111 B9
Mallow, *Ireland* 15 D3
Malmbäck, *Sweden* 11 G8
Malmberget, *Sweden* 8 C19
Malmédy, *Belgium* 17 D6
Malmesbury, *S. Africa* 88 E2
Malmköping, *Sweden* 10 E10
Malmö, *Sweden* 11 J6
Malmslätt, *Sweden* 11 F9
Malmyzh, *Russia* 48 B10
Malo Konare, *Bulgaria* ... 41 D8
Maloarkhangelsk, *Russia* .. 47 G9
Malolos, *Phil.* 61 D4
Malombe L., *Malawi* 87 E4
Malomice, *Poland* 45 G2
Malomir, *Bulgaria* 41 D10
Malone, *U.S.A.* 111 B10
Malong, *China* 58 E4
Małopolskie □, *Poland* ... 45 J7
Malorad, *Bulgaria* 40 C7
Måløy, *Norway* 9 F11
Maloyaroslovets, *Russia* ... 46 E9
Malpartida, *Spain* 35 F4
Malpaso, Canary Is. 37 G1
Malpelo, I. de, *Colombia* .. 124 C2
Malpica de Bergantiños,
　Spain 34 B2
Malpur, *India* 68 H5
Malpura, *India* 68 F6
Mals = Málles Venosta, *Italy* . 28 B7
Malta, Idaho, *U.S.A.* 114 E7
Malta, Mont., *U.S.A.* 114 B10
Malta ■, *Europe* 36 D2
Maltahöhe, *Namibia* 88 C2
Maltepe, *Turkey* 41 F13
Malton, *Canada* 110 C5
Malton, *U.K.* 12 C7
Maluku, *Indonesia* 63 E7
Maluku □, *Indonesia* 63 E7
Maluku Sea = Molucca Sea,
　Indonesia 63 E6
Malumfashi, *Nigeria* 83 C6
Malung, *Sweden* 10 D7
Malungsfors, *Sweden* 10 D7
Maluwe, *Ghana* 82 D4
Malvan, *India* 66 L8
Malvern, *U.S.A.* 113 H8
Malvern Hills, *U.K.* 13 E5
Malvinas, Is. = Falkland
　Is. □, *Atl. Oc.* 128 G5
Malý Dunaj →, *Slovak Rep.* . 27 D11
Malya, *Tanzania* 86 C3
Malyn, *Ukraine* 47 G5
Malyy Lyakhovskiy, Ostrov,
　Russia 51 B15
Mama, *Russia* 51 D12
Mamadysh, *Russia* 48 C10
Mamanguape, *Brazil* 125 E11
Mamarr Mitlā, *Egypt* 75 E1
Mamasa, *Indonesia* 63 E5
Mambasa,
　Dem. Rep. of the Congo . 86 B2
Mamberamo →, *Indonesia* . 63 E9
Mambilima Falls, *Zambia* . 87 E2
Mambirima,
　Dem. Rep. of the Congo . 87 E2
Mambo, *Tanzania* 86 C4
Mambrui, *Kenya* 86 C5
Mamburao, *Phil.* 61 E4
Mameigwess L., *Canada* .. 102 B2
Mamers, *France* 18 D7
Mamfe, *Cameroon* 83 D6
Mammoth, *U.S.A.* 115 K8
Mammoth Cave National
　Park, *U.S.A.* 108 G3
Mamoré →, *Bolivia* 122 E4

Mamou, *Guinea* 82 C2
Mampatá, *Guinea-Biss.* ... 82 C2
Mampikony, *Madag.* 89 B8
Mampong, *Ghana* 83 D4
Mamry, Jezioro, *Poland* ... 44 D8
Mamuju, *Indonesia* 63 E5
Mamuno, *Botswana* 88 C3
Mamuras, *Albania* 40 E3
Man, *Ivory C.* 82 D3
Man, I. of, *U.K.* 12 C3
Man-Bazar, *India* 69 H12
Man Na, *Burma* 67 H20
Mana →, *Fr. Guiana* 125 B8
Manaar, G. of = Mannar,
　G. of, *Asia* 66 Q11
Manacapuru, *Brazil* 124 D6
Manacor, *Spain* 37 B10
Manado, *Indonesia* 63 D6
Managua, *Nic.* 120 D2
Managua, L. de, *Nic.* 120 D2
Manakara, *Madag.* 89 C8
Manali, *India* 68 C7
Manama = Al Manāmah,
　Bahrain 71 E6
Manambao →, *Madag.* ... 89 B7
Manambato, *Madag.* 89 A8
Manambolo →, *Madag.* ... 89 B7
Manambolosy, *Madag.* ... 89 B8
Mananara, *Madag.* 89 B8
Mananara →, *Madag.* 89 C8
Mananjary, *Madag.* 89 C8
Manankoro, *Mali* 82 C3
Manantenina, *Madag.* 89 C8
Manaos = Manaus, *Brazil* . 124 D7
Manapire →, *Venezuela* ... 124 B5
Manapouri, *N.Z.* 91 L1
Manapouri, L., *N.Z.* 91 L1
Manaqil, *Sudan* 81 E3
Manār, Jabal, *Yemen* 74 E3
Manaravolo, *Madag.* 89 C8
Manas, *China* 60 B3
Manas →, *India* 67 F17
Manaslu, *Nepal* 69 E11
Manasquan, *U.S.A.* 111 F10
Manassa, *U.S.A.* 115 H11
Manaung, *Burma* 67 K18
Manaus, *Brazil* 124 D7
Manavgat, *Turkey* 72 D4
Manawan L., *Canada* 105 B8
Manay, *Phil.* 61 H7
Manbij, *Syria* 70 B3
Mancha Real, *Spain* 35 H7
Manche □, *France* 18 C5
Manchegorsk, *Russia* 50 C5
Manchester, *U.K.* 12 D5
Manchester, Calif., *U.S.A.* . 116 G3
Manchester, Conn., *U.S.A.* . 111 E12
Manchester, Ga., *U.S.A.* .. 109 J3
Manchester, Iowa, *U.S.A.* . 112 D9
Manchester, Ky., *U.S.A.* .. 108 G4
Manchester, N.H., *U.S.A.* . 111 D13
Manchester, N.Y., *U.S.A.* . 110 D7
Manchester, Pa., *U.S.A.* .. 111 F8
Manchester, Tenn., *U.S.A.* . 109 H2
Manchester, Vt., *U.S.A.* .. 111 C11
Manchester L., *Canada* ... 105 A7
Manchuria = Dongbei,
　China 57 D13
Manchurian Plain, *China* .. 52 E16
Manciano, *Italy* 29 F8
Mancifa, *Ethiopia* 81 F5
Mand →, *India* 69 J10
Mand →, *Iran* 71 D7
Manda, Chunya, *Tanzania* . 86 D3
Manda, Ludewe, *Tanzania* . 87 E3
Mandabé, *Madag.* 89 C7
Mandaguari, *Brazil* 127 A5
Mandah = Töhöm, *Mongolia* . 56 B5
Mandal, *Norway* 9 G12
Mandala, Puncak, *Indonesia* . 63 E10
Mandalay, *Burma* 67 J20
Mandale = Mandalay,
　Burma 67 J20
Mandalgarh, *India* 68 G6
Mandalgovi, *Mongolia* 56 B4
Mandalī, *Iraq* 70 C5
Mandan, *U.S.A.* 112 B4
Mandaon, *Phil.* 61 E5
Mandar, Teluk, *Indonesia* . 63 E5
Mándas, *Italy* 30 C2
Mandaue, *Phil.* 61 F5
Mandelieu-la-Napoule,
　France 21 E10
Mandera, *Kenya* 86 B5
Mandi, *India* 68 D7
Mandi Dabwali, *India* 68 E6
Mandiana, *Guinea* 82 C3
Mandimba, *Mozam.* 87 E4
Mandioli, *Indonesia* 63 E7
Mandla, *India* 69 H9
Mandø, *Denmark* 11 J2
Mandorah, *Australia* 92 B5
Mandoto, *Madag.* 89 B8
Mandoúdhion, *Greece* ... 38 C5
Mándra, *Greece* 38 C5
Mandra, *Pakistan* 68 C5
Mandráki, *Greece* 39 E9
Mandrare →, *Madag.* 89 D8
Mandritsara, *Madag.* 89 B8
Mandronarivo, *Madag.* ... 89 C8
Mandsaur, *India* 68 G6
Mandurah, *Australia* 93 F2
Mandúria, *Italy* 31 B10
Mandvi, *India* 68 H3
Mandya, *India* 66 N10
Mandzai, *Pakistan* 68 D2
Mané, *Burkina Faso* 83 C4
Maneh, *Iran* 71 B8
Manengouba, Mts.,
　Cameroon 83 E6

180

Manera, Madag. 89 C7
Manérbio, Italy 28 C7
Maneroo Cr. →, Australia 94 C3
Manfalût, Egypt 80 B3
Manfredonia, Italy 29 G12
Manfredónia, G. di, Italy 29 G13
Manga, Burkina Faso 83 C4
Manga, Niger 83 C7
Mangabeiras, Chapada das, Brazil 125 F9
Mangalia, Romania 43 G13
Mangalore, India 66 N9
Mangan, India 69 F13
Mangaung, S. Africa 85 K5
Mangawan, India 69 G9
Mangaweka, N.Z. 91 H5
Manggar, Indonesia 62 E3
Manggawitu, Indonesia 63 E8
Mangindrano, Madag. 89 A8
Mangkalihat, Tanjung, Indonesia 63 D5
Mangla, Pakistan 68 C5
Mangla Dam, Pakistan 69 C5
Manglaur, India 68 E7
Mangnai, China 60 C4
Mango, Togo 83 C5
Mangoche, Malawi 87 E4
Mangoky →, Madag. 89 C7
Mangole, Indonesia 63 E6
Mangombe, Dem. Rep. of the Congo 86 C2
Mangonui, N.Z. 91 F4
Mangoro →, Madag. 89 B8
Mangrol, Mad. P., India 68 J4
Mangrol, Raj., India 68 G6
Mangualde, Portugal 34 E3
Mangueira, L. da, Brazil 127 C5
Mangum, U.S.A. 113 H5
Mangyshlak Poluostrov, Kazakstan 50 E6
Manhattan, U.S.A. 112 F6
Manhiça, Mozam. 89 D5
Mania →, Madag. 89 B8
Maniago, Italy 29 B9
Manica, Mozam. 89 B5
Manica □, Mozam. 89 B5
Manicaland □, Zimbabwe 87 F3
Manicoré, Brazil 124 E6
Manicouagan →, Canada 103 C6
Manicouagan, Rés., Canada 103 B6
Maniema □, Dem. Rep. of the Congo 86 C2
Manīfah, Si. Arabia 71 E6
Manifold, C., Australia 94 C5
Maniganggo, China 58 B2
Manigotagan, Canada 105 C9
Manigotagan →, Canada 105 C9
Manihari, India 69 G12
Manihiki, Cook Is. 97 J11
Manika, Plateau de la, Dem. Rep. of the Congo 87 E2
Manikpur, India 69 G9
Manila, Phil. 61 D4
Manila, U.S.A. 114 F9
Manila B., Phil. 61 D4
Manilla, Australia 95 E5
Manimpé, Mali 82 C3
Maningrida, Australia 94 A1
Maninian, Ivory C. 82 C3
Manipur □, India 67 G19
Manipur →, Burma 67 H19
Manisa, Turkey 39 C9
Manisa □, Turkey 39 C9
Manistee, U.S.A. 108 C2
Manistee →, U.S.A. 108 C2
Manistique, U.S.A. 108 C2
Manito L., Canada 105 C7
Manitoba □, Canada 105 B9
Manitoba, L., Canada 105 C9
Manitou, Canada 105 D9
Manitou, L., Canada 103 B6
Manitou Is., U.S.A. 108 C3
Manitou Springs, U.S.A. 112 F2
Manitowadge, Canada 102 C2
Manitoulin I., Canada 102 C3
Manitowoc, U.S.A. 108 C2
Manizales, Colombia 124 B3
Manja, Madag. 89 C7
Manjacaze, Mozam. 89 C5
Manjakandriana, Madag. 89 B8
Manjhand, Pakistan 68 G3
Manjil, Iran 71 B6
Manjimup, Australia 93 F2
Manjra →, India 66 K10
Mankato, Kans., U.S.A. 112 F5
Mankato, Minn., U.S.A. 112 C8
Mankayane, Swaziland 89 D5
Mankera, Pakistan 68 D4
Mankim, Cameroon 83 D7
Mankono, Ivory C. 82 D3
Mankota, Canada 105 D7
Manlay = Üydzin, Mongolia 56 B4
Manlleu, Spain 32 C7
Manmad, India 66 J9
Mann Ranges, Australia 93 E5
Manna, Indonesia 62 E2
Mannahill, Australia 95 E3
Mannar, Sri Lanka 66 Q11
Mannar, G. of, Asia 66 Q11
Mannar I., Sri Lanka 66 Q11
Mannheim, Germany 25 F4
Manning, Canada 104 B5
Manning, Oreg., U.S.A. 116 E3
Manning, S.C., U.S.A. 109 J5
Manning Prov. Park, Canada 104 D4
Mannu →, Italy 30 C2
Mannu, C., Italy 30 B1
Mannum, Australia 95 E2
Mano, S. Leone 82 D2
Mano →, Liberia 82 D2
Mano River, Liberia 82 D2

Manoharpur, India 69 H11
Manokwari, Indonesia 63 E8
Manolás, Greece 38 C3
Manombo, Madag. 89 C7
Manono, Dem. Rep. of the Congo 86 D2
Manoppello, Italy 29 F11
Manosque, France 21 E9
Manotick, Canada 111 A9
Manouane →, Canada 103 C5
Manouane, L., Canada 103 B5
Manp'o, N. Korea 57 D14
Manpojin = Manp'o, N. Korea 57 D14
Manpur, Mad. P., India 68 H6
Manpur, Mad. P., India 69 H10
Manresa, Spain 32 D6
Mansa, Gujarat, India 68 H5
Mansa, Punjab, India 68 E6
Mansa, Zambia 87 E2
Månsåsen, Sweden 10 A8
Mansehra, Pakistan 68 B5
Mansel I., Canada 101 B11
Mansfield, Australia 95 F4
Mansfield, U.K. 12 D6
Mansfield, La., U.S.A. 113 J8
Mansfield, Mass., U.S.A. 111 D13
Mansfield, Ohio, U.S.A. 110 F2
Mansfield, Pa., U.S.A. 110 E7
Mansfield, Mt., U.S.A. 111 B12
Mansilla de las Mulas, Spain 34 C5
Mansle, France 20 C4
Mansoa, Guinea-Biss. 82 C1
Manson Creek, Canada 104 B4
Manta, Ecuador 124 D2
Mantalingajan, Mt., Phil. 61 G2
Mantare, Tanzania 86 C3
Manteca, U.S.A. 116 H5
Manteo, U.S.A. 109 H8
Mantes-la-Jolie, France 19 D8
Manthani, India 66 K11
Manti, U.S.A. 114 G8
Manton, U.S.A. 108 C3
Mantorp, Sweden 11 F9
Mántova, Italy 28 C7
Mänttä, Finland 9 E21
Mantua = Mántova, Italy 28 C7
Manturovo, Russia 48 A7
Manu, Peru 124 F4
Manu →, Peru 124 F4
Manua Is., Amer. Samoa 91 B14
Manuel Alves →, Brazil 125 F9
Manui, Indonesia 63 E6
Manuripi →, Bolivia 124 F5
Many, U.S.A. 113 K8
Manyara, L., Tanzania 86 C4
Manyas, Turkey 41 F11
Manych →, Russia 49 G5
Manych-Gudilo, Ozero, Russia 49 G6
Manyonga →, Tanzania 86 C3
Manyoni, Tanzania 86 D3
Manzai, Pakistan 68 C4
Manzala, Bahra el, Egypt 80 H7
Manzanares, Spain 35 F7
Manzaneda, Spain 34 C3
Manzanillo, Cuba 120 B4
Manzanillo, Mexico 118 D4
Manzanillo, Pta., Panama 120 E4
Manzano Mts., U.S.A. 115 J10
Manẓarīyeh, Iran 71 C6
Manzhouli, China 60 B6
Manzini, Swaziland 89 D5
Mao, Chad 79 F9
Maó, Spain 37 B11
Maoke, Pegunungan, Indonesia 63 E9
Maolin, China 57 C12
Maoming, China 59 G8
Maopi T'ou, China 59 G13
Maouri, Dallol →, Niger 83 C5
Maoxian, China 58 B4
Maoxing, China 57 B13
Mapam Yumco, China 60 C3
Mapastepec, Mexico 119 D6
Mapia, Kepulauan, Indonesia 63 D8
Mapimí, Mexico 118 B4
Mapimí, Bolsón de, Mexico 118 B4
Maping, China 59 B9
Mapinga, Tanzania 86 D4
Mapinhane, Mozam. 89 C6
Maple Creek, Canada 105 D7
Maple Valley, U.S.A. 116 C4
Mapleton, U.S.A. 114 D2
Mapuera →, Brazil 124 D7
Mapulanguene, Mozam. 89 C5
Maputo, Mozam. 89 D5
Maputo □, Mozam. 89 D5
Maputo, B. de, Mozam. 89 D5
Maqiaohe, China 57 B16
Maqnā, Si. Arabia 70 D2
Maqueda, Spain 34 E6
Maquela do Zombo, Angola 84 F3
Maquinchao, Argentina 128 E3
Maquoketa, U.S.A. 112 D9
Mar, Serra do, Brazil 127 B6
Mar Chiquita, L., Argentina 126 C3
Mar del Plata, Argentina 126 D4
Mar Menor, Spain 33 H4
Mara, Tanzania 86 C3
Mara □, Tanzania 86 C3
Maraã, Brazil 124 D5
Marabá, Brazil 125 E9
Maracá, I. de, Brazil 125 C8
Maracaibo, Venezuela 124 A4
Maracaibo, L. de, Venezuela 124 B4
Maracaju, Brazil 127 A4
Maracay, Venezuela 124 A5
Maracena, Spain 35 H7
Maradi, Niger 83 C6

Marágheh, Iran 70 B5
Marāh, Si. Arabia 70 E5
Marajó, I. de, Brazil 122 D6
Marākand, Iran 70 B5
Maralal, Kenya 86 B4
Maralinga, Australia 93 F5
Maramasike, Turkey 41 F11
Marampa, S. Leone 82 D2
Maramureş □, Romania 43 C9
Maran, Malaysia 65 L4
Marana, U.S.A. 115 K8
Maranboy, Australia 92 B5
Maranchón, Spain 32 D2
Marand, Iran 70 B5
Marang, Malaysia 65 K4
Maranguape, Brazil 125 D11
Maranhão = São Luís, Brazil 125 D10
Maranhão □, Brazil 125 E9
Marano, L. di, Italy 29 C10
Maranoa →, Australia 95 D4
Marañón →, Peru 122 D3
Marão, Mozam. 89 C5
Maraş = Kahramanmaraş, Turkey 70 B3
Mărăşeşti, Romania 43 E12
Maratea, Italy 31 C8
Marateca, Portugal 35 G2
Marathasa □, Cyprus 36 E11
Marathókambos, Greece 39 D8
Marathon, Australia 94 C3
Marathon, Canada 102 C2
Marathón, Greece 38 C5
Marathon, N.Y., U.S.A. 111 D8
Marathon, N.Y., U.S.A. 111 D8
Marathon, Tex., U.S.A. 113 K3
Marathóvouno, Cyprus 36 D12
Maratua, Indonesia 63 D5
Maravatío, Mexico 118 D4
Marawi City, Phil. 61 G6
Marāwih, U.A.E. 71 E7
Marbella, Spain 35 J6
Marble Bar, Australia 92 D2
Marble Falls, U.S.A. 113 K5
Marblehead, U.S.A. 111 D14
Marburg, Germany 24 E4
Marcal →, Hungary 42 C2
Marcali, Hungary 42 D2
Marcaria, Italy 28 C7
Mărcăuţi, Moldova 43 B12
March, U.K. 13 E8
Marche, France 20 B5
Marche □, Italy 29 E10
Marche-en-Famenne, Belgium 17 D5
Marchena, Spain 35 H5
Marches = Marche □, Italy 29 E10
Marciana Marina, Italy 28 F7
Marcianise, Italy 31 A7
Marcigny, France 19 F11
Marcillat-en-Combraille, France 19 F9
Marck, France 19 B8
Marckolsheim, France 19 D14
Marco, U.S.A. 109 N5
Marcos Juárez, Argentina 126 C3
Marcus I. = Minami-Tori-Shima, Pac. Oc. 96 E7
Marcus Necker Ridge, Pac. Oc. 96 F9
Marcy, Mt., U.S.A. 111 B11
Mardan, Pakistan 68 B5
Mardin, Turkey 70 B4
Mårdsjön, Sweden 10 A9
Marécchia →, Italy 29 D9
Maree, L., U.K. 14 D3
Mareeba, Australia 94 B4
Mareetsane, S. Africa 88 D4
Maremma, Italy 29 F8
Maréna, Mali 82 C2
Maréna, Mali 82 C3
Marengo, U.S.A. 112 E8
Marennes, France 20 C2
Marenyi, Kenya 86 C4
Marerano, Madag. 89 C7
Maréttimo, Italy 30 E5
Mareuil, France 20 C4
Marfa, U.S.A. 113 K2
Marfa Pt., Malta 36 D1
Marganets = Marhanets, Ukraine 47 J8
Margaret →, Australia 92 C4
Margaret Bay, Canada 104 C3
Margaret L., Canada 104 B5
Margaret River, Australia 93 F2
Margarita, I. de, Venezuela 122 B4
Margaritovo, Russia 54 C7
Margate, S. Africa 89 E5
Margate, U.K. 13 F9
Margerie, Mts. de la, France 20 D7
Margherita di Savóia, Italy 31 A9
Marghita, Romania 42 C7
Margonin, Poland 45 F4
Margosatubig, Phil. 61 H5
Marguerite, Canada 104 C4
Marhanets, Ukraine 47 J8
Mari El □, Russia 48 B8
Mari Indus, Pakistan 68 C4
Mari Republic = Mari El □, Russia 48 B8
María, Sa. de, Spain 33 H2
María Elena, Chile 126 A2
María Grande, Argentina 126 C4
Maria I., N. Terr., Australia 94 A2
Maria I., Tas., Australia 94 G4
Maria van Diemen, C., N.Z. 91 F4
Mariager, Denmark 11 H3
Mariager Fjord, Denmark 11 H4

Mariakani, Kenya 86 C4
Marian, Australia 94 C4
Marian L., Canada 104 A5
Mariana Trench, Pac. Oc. 52 H18
Marianao, Cuba 120 B3
Marianna, Ark., U.S.A. 113 H9
Marianna, Fla., U.S.A. 109 K3
Mariannelund, Sweden 11 G9
Mariánské Lázně, Czech Rep. 26 B5
Marias →, U.S.A. 114 C8
Mariato, Punta, Panama 120 E3
Mariazell, Austria 26 D8
Maribo, Denmark 11 K5
Maribor, Slovenia 29 B12
Marico →, Africa 88 C4
Maricopa, Ariz., U.S.A. 115 K7
Maricopa, Calif., U.S.A. 117 K7
Marīdī, Sudan 81 G2
Maridi, Wadi →, Sudan 81 F2
Marié →, Brazil 124 D5
Marie Byrd Land, Antarctica 5 D14
Marie-Galante, Guadeloupe 121 C7
Mariecourt = Kangiqsujuaq, Canada 101 B12
Mariefred, Sweden 10 E11
Marieholm, Sweden 11 J7
Mariembourg, Belgium 17 D4
Marienbad = Mariánské Lázně, Czech Rep. 26 B5
Marienberg, Germany 24 E9
Mariental, Namibia 88 C2
Marienville, U.S.A. 110 E5
Mariestad, Sweden 11 F7
Marietta, Ga., U.S.A. 109 J3
Marietta, Ohio, U.S.A. 108 F5
Marieville, Canada 111 A11
Mariga →, Nigeria 83 C6
Marignane, France 21 E9
Marihatag, Phil. 61 G7
Mariinsk, Russia 50 D9
Mariinskiy Posad, Russia 48 B8
Marijampolė, Lithuania 9 J20
Marijampolė □, Lithuania 44 D10
Marília, Brazil 127 A6
Marín, Spain 34 C2
Marina, U.S.A. 116 J5
Marinduque, Phil. 63 B6
Marine City, U.S.A. 110 D2
Marineo, Italy 30 E6
Marinette, U.S.A. 108 C2
Maringá, Brazil 127 A5
Marinha Grande, Portugal 34 F2
Marino, Italy 29 G9
Marion, Ala., U.S.A. 109 J2
Marion, Ill., U.S.A. 113 G10
Marion, Ind., U.S.A. 108 E3
Marion, Iowa, U.S.A. 112 D9
Marion, Kans., U.S.A. 112 F6
Marion, N.C., U.S.A. 109 H5
Marion, Ohio, U.S.A. 108 E4
Marion, S.C., U.S.A. 109 H6
Marion, Va., U.S.A. 109 G5
Marion, L., U.S.A. 109 J5
Mariposa, U.S.A. 116 H7
Mariscal Estigarribia, Paraguay 126 A3
Maritime Alps = Maritimes, Alpes, Europe 21 D11
Maritimes, Alpes, Europe 21 D11
Maritsa = Évros →, Bulgaria 72 B2
Maritsá, Greece 36 C10
Mariupol, Ukraine 47 J9
Marīvān, Iran 70 C5
Marj 'Uyūn, Lebanon 75 B4
Markam, China 58 C2
Markaryd, Sweden 11 H7
Markazī □, Iran 71 C6
Markdale, Canada 110 B4
Marked Tree, U.S.A. 113 H9
Markelsdorfer Huk, Germany 24 A7
Market Drayton, U.K. 12 E5
Market Harborough, U.K. 13 E7
Market Rasen, U.K. 12 D7
Markham, Canada 110 C5
Markham, Mt., Antarctica 5 E11
Marki, Poland 45 F8
Markleeville, U.S.A. 116 G7
Markoupoulon, Greece 38 D5
Markovac, Serbia, Yug. 40 B5
Markovo, Russia 51 C17
Markoye, Burkina Faso 83 C5
Marks, Russia 48 E8
Marksville, U.S.A. 113 K8
Markt Schwaben, Germany 25 G7
Marktoberdorf, Germany 25 H6
Marktredwitz, Germany 25 E8
Marl, Germany 24 D3
Marla, Australia 95 D1
Marlbank, Canada 110 B7
Marlboro, Mass., U.S.A. 111 D13
Marlboro, N.Y., U.S.A. 111 E11
Marlborough, Australia 94 C4
Marlborough, U.K. 13 F6
Marlborough Downs, U.K. 13 F6
Marle, France 19 C10
Marlin, U.S.A. 113 K6
Marlow, Germany 24 A8
Marlow, U.S.A. 113 H6
Marmagao, India 66 M8
Marmande, France 20 D4
Marmara, Turkey 41 F11
Marmara, Sea of = Marmara Denizi, Turkey 41 F12
Marmara Denizi, Turkey 41 F12
Marmara Gölü, Turkey 39 C10
Marmaris, Turkey 39 E10

Marmaris Limanı, Turkey 39 E10
Marmion, Mt., Australia 93 E2
Marmion L., Canada 102 C1
Marmolada, Mte., Italy 29 B8
Marmolejo, Spain 35 G6
Marmora, Canada 102 D4
Mármora, La, Italy 30 C2
Marnay, France 19 E12
Marne, Germany 24 B5
Marne □, France 19 D11
Marne →, France 19 D9
Marneuli, Georgia 49 K7
Maroala, Madag. 89 B8
Maroantsetra, Madag. 89 B8
Maroelaboom, Namibia 88 B2
Marofandilia, Madag. 89 C7
Marolambo, Madag. 89 C8
Maromandia, Madag. 89 A8
Marondera, Zimbabwe 87 F3
Maroni →, Fr. Guiana 125 B8
Marónia, Greece 41 F9
Maronne →, France 20 C5
Maroochydore, Australia 95 D5
Maroona, Australia 95 F3
Maros →, Hungary 42 D5
Marosakoa, Madag. 89 B8
Maróstica, Italy 29 C8
Marotandrano, Madag. 89 B8
Marotaolano, Madag. 89 A8
Maroua, Cameroon 83 C7
Marovato, Madag. 89 B8
Marovoay, Madag. 89 B8
Marquard, S. Africa 88 D4
Marquesas Is. = Marquises, Is., Pac. Oc. 97 H14
Marquette, U.S.A. 108 B2
Marquise, France 19 B8
Marquises, Is., Pac. Oc. 97 H14
Marra, Djebel, Sudan 79 F10
Marra, Gebel, Sudan 81 F2
Marracuene, Mozam. 89 D5
Marradi, Italy 29 D8
Marrakech, Morocco 78 B4
Marratxi, Spain 32 F7
Marrawah, Australia 94 G3
Marree, Australia 95 D2
Marrero, U.S.A. 113 L9
Marrimane, Mozam. 89 C5
Marromeu, Mozam. 89 B6
Marroquí, Punta, Spain 35 K5
Marrowie Cr. →, Australia 95 E4
Marrubane, Mozam. 87 F4
Marrúbiu, Italy 30 C1
Marrupa, Mozam. 87 E4
Mars Hill, U.S.A. 109 B12
Marsa Alam, Egypt 80 B3
Marsá Matrûh, Egypt 80 A2
Marsa Sha'b, Sudan 80 C4
Marsabit, Kenya 86 B4
Marsala, Italy 30 E5
Marsalforn, Malta 36 C1
Mârşani, Romania 43 F9
Marsberg, Germany 24 D4
Marsciano, Italy 29 F9
Marsden, Australia 95 E4
Marseillan, France 20 E7
Marseille, France 21 E9
Marseilles = Marseille, France 21 E9
Marsh I., U.S.A. 113 L9
Marshall, Liberia 82 D2
Marshall, Ark., U.S.A. 113 H8
Marshall, Mich., U.S.A. 108 D3
Marshall, Minn., U.S.A. 112 C7
Marshall, Mo., U.S.A. 112 F8
Marshall, Tex., U.S.A. 113 J7
Marshall →, Australia 94 C2
Marshall Is. ■, Pac. Oc. 96 G9
Marshalltown, U.S.A. 112 D8
Marshbrook, Zimbabwe 89 B5
Marshfield, Mo., U.S.A. 113 G8
Marshfield, Vt., U.S.A. 111 B12
Marshfield, Wis., U.S.A. 112 C9
Marshūn, Iran 71 B6
Mársico Nuovo, Italy 31 B8
Märsta, Sweden 10 E11
Marstal, Denmark 11 K4
Marstrand, Sweden 11 G5
Mart, U.S.A. 113 K6
Marta →, Italy 29 F8
Martaban, Burma 67 L20
Martaban, G. of, Burma 67 L20
Martano, Italy 31 B11
Martapura, Kalimantan, Indonesia 62 E4
Martapura, Sumatera, Indonesia 62 E2
Marte, Nigeria 83 C7
Martel, France 20 D5
Martelange, Belgium 17 E5
Martellago, Italy 29 C9
Martés, Sierra, Spain 33 F4
Martfü, Hungary 42 C5
Martha's Vineyard, U.S.A. 111 E14
Martigné-Ferchaud, France 18 E5
Martigues, France 21 E9
Martin, Slovak Rep. 27 B11
Martin, S. Dak., U.S.A. 112 D4
Martin, Tenn., U.S.A. 113 G10
Martín →, Spain 32 D4
Martin, L., U.S.A. 109 J3
Martina Franca, Italy 31 B10
Martinborough, N.Z. 91 J5
Martínez, Calif., U.S.A. 116 G4
Martínez, Ga., U.S.A. 109 J4
Martinique ■, W. Indies 121 D7
Martinique Passage, W. Indies 121 C7
Martínon, Greece 38 C5

Martinópolis, *Brazil* 127 A5
Martins Ferry, *U.S.A.* 110 F4
Martinsberg, *Austria* 26 C8
Martinsburg, *Pa., U.S.A.* .. 110 F6
Martinsburg, *W. Va., U.S.A.* 108 F7
Martinsicuro, *Italy* 29 F10
Martinsville, *Ind., U.S.A.* . 108 F2
Martinsville, *Va., U.S.A.* .. 109 G6
Marton, *N.Z.* 91 J5
Martorell, *Spain* 32 D6
Martos, *Spain* 35 H7
Martuni, *Armenia* 49 K7
Maru, *Nigeria* 83 C6
Marudi, *Malaysia* 62 D4
Ma'ruf, *Afghan.* 66 D5
Marugame, *Japan* 55 G6
Marunga, *Angola* 88 B3
Marungu, Mts.,
  Dem. Rep. of the Congo . 86 D3
Marv Dasht, *Iran* 71 D7
Marvast, *Iran* 71 D7
Marvejols, *France* 20 D7
Marvel Loch, *Australia* 93 F2
Marwar, *India* 68 G5
Mary, *Turkmenistan* 50 F7
Maryborough = Port Laoise,
  Ireland 15 C4
Maryborough, *Queens.,*
  Australia 95 D5
Maryborough, *Vic., Australia* 95 F3
Maryfield, *Canada* 105 D8
Maryland □, *U.S.A.* 108 F7
Maryland Junction,
  Zimbabwe 87 F3
Maryport, *U.K.* 12 C4
Mary's Harbour, *Canada* .. 103 B8
Marystown, *Canada* 103 C8
Marysville, *Canada* 104 D5
Marysville, *Calif., U.S.A.* .. 116 F5
Marysville, *Kans., U.S.A.* .. 112 F6
Marysville, *Mich., U.S.A.* .. 110 D2
Marysville, *Ohio, U.S.A.* .. 108 E4
Marysville, *Wash., U.S.A.* . 116 B4
Maryville, *Mo., U.S.A.* 112 E7
Maryville, *Tenn., U.S.A.* .. 109 H4
Marzūq, *Libya* 79 C8
Masahunga, *Tanzania* 86 C3
Masai Steppe, *Tanzania* ... 86 C4
Masaka, *Uganda* 86 C3
Masalembo, Kepulauan,
  Indonesia 62 F4
Masalima, Kepulauan,
  Indonesia 62 F5
Masallı, *Azerbaijan* 73 C13
Masamba, *Indonesia* 63 E6
Masan, *S. Korea* 57 G15
Masandam, Ra's, *Oman* ... 71 E8
Masasi, *Tanzania* 87 E4
Masaya, *Nic.* 120 D2
Masba, *Nigeria* 83 C7
Masbate, *Phil.* 61 E5
Máscali, *Italy* 31 E8
Mascara, *Algeria* 78 A6
Mascota, *Mexico* 118 C4
Masela, *Indonesia* 63 F7
Maseru, *Lesotho* 88 D4
Mashaba, *Zimbabwe* 87 G3
Mashābih, *Si. Arabia* 70 E3
Mashan, *China* 58 F7
Mashar, *Sudan* 81 F2
Mashegu, *Nigeria* 83 D6
Masherbrum, *Pakistan* 69 B7
Mashhad, *Iran* 71 B8
Mashi, *Nigeria* 83 C6
Mashīz, *Iran* 71 D8
Mashkel, Hamun-i, *Pakistan* 66 E3
Mashki Chāh, *Pakistan* 66 E3
Mashonaland, *Zimbabwe* ... 85 H6
Mashonaland Central □,
  Zimbabwe 89 B5
Mashonaland East □,
  Zimbabwe 89 B5
Mashonaland West □,
  Zimbabwe 89 B4
Mashrakh, *India* 69 F11
Mashtaga = Maştağa,
  Azerbaijan 49 K10
Masindi, *Uganda* 86 B3
Masindi Port, *Uganda* 86 B3
Maşīrah, *Oman* 74 C6
Maşīrah, Khalīj, *Oman* 74 C6
Masisi,
  Dem. Rep. of the Congo . 86 C2
Masjed Soleyman, *Iran* ... 71 D6
Mask, L., *Ireland* 15 C2
Maskin, *Oman* 71 F8
Maslen Nos, *Bulgaria* 41 D11
Maslinica, *Croatia* 29 E13
Masnou = El Masnou, *Spain* 32 D7
Masoala, Tanjon' i, *Madag.* 89 B9
Masoarivo, *Madag.* 89 B7
Masohi = Amahai, *Indonesia* 63 E7
Masomeloka, *Madag.* 89 C8
Mason, *Nev., U.S.A.* 116 G7
Mason, *Tex., U.S.A.* 113 K5
Mason City, *U.S.A.* 112 D8
Maspalomas, *Canary Is.* ... 37 G4
Maspalomas, Pta., *Canary Is.* 37 G4
Masqat, *Oman* 74 C6
Massa, *Italy* 28 D7
Massa Maríttima, *Italy* 28 E7
Massachusetts □, *U.S.A.* .. 111 D13
Massachusetts B., *U.S.A.* .. 111 D14
Massafra, *Italy* 31 B10
Massakory, *Chad* 79 F9
Massanella, *Spain* 37 B9
Massangena, *Mozam.* 89 C5
Massango, *Angola* 84 F3
Massat, *France* 20 F5
Massawa = Mitsiwa, *Eritrea* 81 D4
Massena, *U.S.A.* 111 B10

Massénya, *Chad* 79 F9
Masset, *Canada* 104 C2
Masseube, *France* 20 E4
Massiac, *France* 20 C7
Massif Central, *France* 20 D7
Massigui, *Mali* 82 C3
Massillon, *U.S.A.* 110 F3
Massinga, *Mozam.* 89 C6
Massingir, *Mozam.* 89 C5
Mässlingen, *Sweden* 10 B6
Masson, *Canada* 111 A9
Masson I., *Antarctica* 5 C7
Maştağa, *Azerbaijan* 49 K10
Mastanli = Momchilgrad,
  Bulgaria 41 E9
Masterton, *N.Z.* 91 J5
Mastic, *U.S.A.* 111 F12
Mástikho, Ákra, *Greece* ... 39 C8
Mastuj, *Pakistan* 69 A5
Mastung, *Pakistan* 66 E5
Mastūrah, *Si. Arabia* 80 C4
Masty, *Belarus* 46 F3
Masuda, *Japan* 55 G5
Masvingo, *Zimbabwe* 87 G3
Masvingo □, *Zimbabwe* ... 87 G3
Maşyāf, *Syria* 70 C3
Maszewo, *Poland* 44 E2
Matabeleland, *Zimbabwe* .. 85 H5
Matabeleland North □,
  Zimbabwe 87 F2
Matabeleland South □,
  Zimbabwe 87 G2
Matachel →, *Spain* 35 G4
Matachewan, *Canada* 102 C3
Matadi,
  Dem. Rep. of the Congo . 84 F2
Matagalpa, *Nic.* 120 D2
Matagami, *Canada* 102 C4
Matagami, L., *Canada* 102 C4
Matagorda B., *U.S.A.* 113 L6
Matagorda I., *U.S.A.* 113 L6
Matak, *Indonesia* 65 L6
Mátala, *Greece* 36 E6
Matam, *Senegal* 82 B2
Matameye, *Niger* 83 C6
Matamoros, *Campeche,*
  Mexico 119 D6
Matamoros, *Coahuila,*
  Mexico 118 B4
Matamoros, *Tamaulipas,*
  Mexico 119 B5
Ma'ţan as Sarra, *Libya* 79 D10
Matandu →, *Tanzania* 87 D3
Matane, *Canada* 103 C6
Matang, *China* 58 F5
Matankari, *Niger* 83 C5
Matanomadh, *India* 68 H3
Matanzas, *Cuba* 120 B3
Matapa, *Botswana* 88 C3
Matapan, C. = Taínaron,
  Ákra, *Greece* 38 E4
Matapédia, *Canada* 103 C6
Matara, *Sri Lanka* 66 S12
Mataram, *Indonesia* 62 F5
Matarani, *Peru* 124 G4
Mataranka, *Australia* 92 B5
Matarma, Râs, *Egypt* 75 E1
Mataró, *Spain* 32 D7
Matarraña →, *Spain* 32 D5
Mataruška Banja,
  Serbia, Yug. 40 C4
Matatiele, *S. Africa* 89 E4
Mataura, *N.Z.* 91 M2
Matehuala, *Mexico* 118 C4
Mateke Hills, *Zimbabwe* .. 87 G3
Matera, *Italy* 31 B9
Matese, Monti del, *Italy* .. 31 A7
Mátészalka, *Hungary* 42 C7
Matetsi, *Zimbabwe* 87 F2
Matha, *France* 20 C3
Mathis, *U.S.A.* 113 L6
Mathráki, *Greece* 36 A3
Mathura, *India* 68 F7
Mati, *Phil.* 61 H7
Mati →, *Albania* 40 E3
Matiakoali, *Burkina Faso* .. 83 C5
Matiali, *India* 69 F13
Matías Romero, *Mexico* ... 119 D5
Matibane, *Mozam.* 87 E5
Matima, *Botswana* 88 C3
Matiri Ra., *N.Z.* 91 J4
Matjiesfontein, *S. Africa* .. 88 E3
Matla →, *India* 69 J13
Matlamanyane, *Botswana* . 88 B4
Matli, *Pakistan* 68 G3
Matlock, *U.K.* 12 D6
Matna, *Sudan* 81 E4
Mato Grosso □, *Brazil* 125 F8
Mato Grosso, Planalto do,
  Brazil 122 E5
Mato Grosso do Sul □,
  Brazil 125 G8
Matochkin Shar, *Russia* ... 50 B6
Matopo Hills, *Zimbabwe* .. 87 G2
Matopos, *Zimbabwe* 87 G2
Matosinhos, *Portugal* 34 D2
Matour, *France* 19 F11
Maţraḥ, *Oman* 74 C6
Matroosberg, *S. Africa* ... 88 E2
Matsena, *Nigeria* 83 C7
Matsesta, *Russia* 49 J4
Matsu Tao, *Taiwan* 59 E13
Matsue, *Japan* 55 G6
Matsumae, *Japan* 54 D10
Matsumoto, *Japan* 55 F9
Matsusaka, *Japan* 55 G8
Matsutō, *Japan* 55 F8
Matsuura, *Japan* 55 H4
Matsuyama, *Japan* 55 H6
Mattagami →, *Canada* ... 102 B3

Mattancheri, *India* 66 Q10
Mattawa, *Canada* 102 C4
Matterhorn, *Switz.* 25 K3
Mattersburg, *Austria* 27 D9
Matthew Town, *Bahamas* . 121 B5
Matthew's Ridge, *Guyana* . 124 B6
Mattice, *Canada* 102 C3
Mattituck, *U.S.A.* 111 F12
Mattoon, *U.S.A.* 108 F1
Matuba, *Mozam.* 89 C5
Matucana, *Peru* 124 F3
Matūn = Khowst, *Afghan.* . 68 C3
Maturín, *Venezuela* 124 B6
Matveyev Kurgan, *Russia* . 47 J10
Matxitxako, C., *Spain* 32 B2
Mau, *Mad. P., India* 69 F8
Mau, *Ut. P., India* 69 G10
Mau, *Ut. P., India* 69 G9
Mau Escarpment, *Kenya* .. 86 C4
Mau Ranipur, *India* 69 G8
Maubeuge, *France* 19 B10
Maubourguet, *France* 20 E4
Maud, Pt., *Australia* 92 D1
Maude, *Australia* 95 E3
Maudin Sun, *Burma* 67 M19
Maués, *Brazil* 124 D7
Mauganj, *India* 67 G12
Maughold Hd., *U.K.* 12 C3
Mauguio, *France* 20 E7
Maui, *U.S.A.* 106 H16
Maulamyaing = Moulmein,
  Burma 67 L20
Maule □, *Chile* 126 D1
Mauléon-Licharre, *France* . 20 E3
Maumee, *U.S.A.* 108 E4
Maumee →, *U.S.A.* 108 E4
Maumere, *Indonesia* 63 F6
Maumusson, Pertuis de,
  France 20 C2
Maun, *Botswana* 88 C3
Mauna Kea, *U.S.A.* 106 J17
Mauna Loa, *U.S.A.* 106 J17
Maungmagan Is., *Burma* .. 64 E1
Maungmagan Kyunzu,
  Burma 67 N20
Maupin, *U.S.A.* 114 D3
Maure-de-Bretagne, *France* 18 E5
Maurepas, L., *U.S.A.* 113 K9
Maures, *France* 21 E10
Mauriac, *France* 20 C6
Maurice, L., *Australia* 93 E5
Mauricie, Parc Nat. de la,
  Canada 102 C5
Maurienne, *France* 21 C10
Mauritania ■, *Africa* 78 E3
Mauritius ■, *Ind. Oc.* 77 J9
Mauron, *France* 18 D4
Maurs, *France* 20 D6
Mauston, *U.S.A.* 112 D9
Mauterndorf, *Austria* 26 D6
Mauthen, *Austria* 26 E6
Mauvezin, *France* 20 E4
Mauzé-sur-le-Mignon, *France* 20 B3
Mavli, *India* 68 G5
Mavrova, *Albania* 40 F3
Mavuradonha Mts.,
  Zimbabwe 87 F3
Mawa,
  Dem. Rep. of the Congo . 86 B2
Mawai, *India* 69 H9
Mawana, *India* 68 E7
Mawand, *Pakistan* 68 E3
Mawk Mai, *Burma* 67 J20
Mawlaik, *Burma* 67 H19
Mawlamyine = Moulmein,
  Burma 67 L20
Mawqaq, *Si. Arabia* 70 E4
Mawson Coast, *Antarctica* . 5 C6
Max, *U.S.A.* 112 B4
Maxcanú, *Mexico* 119 C6
Maxesibeni, *S. Africa* 89 E4
Maxhamish L., *Canada* ... 104 B4
Maxixe, *Mozam.* 89 C6
Maxville, *Canada* 111 A10
Maxwell, *U.S.A.* 116 F4
Maxwelton, *Australia* 94 C3
May, C., *U.S.A.* 108 F8
May Pen, *Jamaica* 120 C4
Maya →, *Russia* 51 D14
Maya Mts., *Belize* 119 D7
Mayaguana, *Bahamas* 121 B5
Mayagüez, *Puerto Rico* ... 121 C6
Mayahi, *Niger* 83 C6
Mayals = Maials, *Spain* ... 32 D5
Mayámey, *Iran* 71 B7
Mayang, *China* 58 D7
Mayanup, *Australia* 93 F2
Mayapan, *Mexico* 119 C7
Mayari, *Cuba* 121 B4
Maybell, *U.S.A.* 114 F9
Maybole, *U.K.* 14 F4
Maychew, *Ethiopia* 81 E4
Maydān, *Iraq* 70 C5
Maydena, *Australia* 94 G4
Mayen, *Germany* 25 E3
Mayenne, *France* 18 D6
Mayenne □, *France* 18 D6
Mayenne →, *France* 18 E6
Mayer, *U.S.A.* 115 J7
Mayerthorpe, *Canada* 104 C5
Mayfield, *Ky., U.S.A.* 109 G1
Mayfield, *N.Y., U.S.A.* 111 C10
Mayhill, *U.S.A.* 115 K11
Maykop, *Russia* 49 H5
Maymyo, *Burma* 64 A1
Maynard, *Mass., U.S.A.* ... 111 D13
Maynard, *Wash., U.S.A.* .. 116 C4
Maynard Hills, *Australia* .. 93 E2
Mayne →, *Australia* 94 C3
Maynooth, *Ireland* 15 C5
Mayo, *Canada* 100 B6

Mayo □, *Ireland* 15 C2
Mayo Daga, *Nigeria* 83 D7
Mayo Faran, *Nigeria* 83 D7
Mayon Volcano, *Phil.* 61 E5
Mayor I., *N.Z.* 91 G6
Mayorga, *Spain* 34 C5
Mayotte □, *Ind. Oc.* 85 G9
Mayraira Pt., *Phil.* 61 B4
Maysville, *U.S.A.* 108 F4
Mayu, *Indonesia* 63 D7
Mayville, *N. Dak., U.S.A.* . 112 B6
Mayville, *N.Y., U.S.A.* 110 D5
Mayya, *Russia* 51 C14
Mazabuka, *Zambia* 87 F2
Mazagán = El Jadida,
  Morocco 78 B4
Mazagão, *Brazil* 125 D8
Mazamet, *France* 20 E6
Mazán, *Peru* 124 D4
Māzandarān □, *Iran* 71 B7
Mazapil, *Mexico* 118 C4
Mazara del Vallo, *Italy* 30 E5
Mazarrón, *Spain* 33 H3
Mazarrón, G. de, *Spain* ... 33 H3
Mazaruni →, *Guyana* 124 B7
Mazatán, *Mexico* 118 B2
Mazatenango, *Guatemala* . 120 D1
Mazatlán, *Mexico* 118 C3
Mažeikiai, *Lithuania* 9 H20
Māzhān, *Iran* 71 C8
Mazīnān, *Iran* 71 B8
Mazoe, *Mozam.* 87 F3
Mazoe →, *Mozam.* 87 F3
Mazowe, *Zimbabwe* 87 F3
Mazowieckie □, *Poland* ... 45 F8
Mazrūb, *Sudan* 81 E2
Mazu Dao, *China* 59 D12
Mazurian Lakes = Mazurski,
  Pojezierze, *Poland* 44 E7
Mazurski, Pojezierze, *Poland* 44 E7
Mazyr, *Belarus* 47 F5
Mbaba, *Senegal* 82 C1
Mbabane, *Swaziland* 89 D5
Mbagne, *Mauritania* 82 B2
M'bahiakro, *Ivory C.* 82 D4
Mbaïki, *C.A.R.* 84 D3
Mbala, *Zambia* 87 D3
Mbalabala, *Zimbabwe* 89 C4
Mbale, *Uganda* 86 B3
Mbalmayo, *Cameroon* 83 E7
Mbam →, *Cameroon* 83 E7
Mbamba Bay, *Tanzania* ... 87 E3
Mbandaka,
  Dem. Rep. of the Congo . 84 D3
Mbanga, *Cameroon* 83 E6
Mbanza Congo, *Angola* ... 84 F2
Mbanza Ngungu,
  Dem. Rep. of the Congo . 84 F2
Mbarara, *Uganda* 86 C3
Mbashe →, *S. Africa* 89 E4
Mbatto, *Ivory C.* 82 D4
Mbenkuru →, *Tanzania* .. 87 D4
Mberengwa, *Zimbabwe* ... 87 G2
Mberengwa, Mt., *Zimbabwe* 87 G2
Mberubu, *Nigeria* 83 D6
Mbesuma, *Zambia* 87 E3
Mbeya, *Tanzania* 87 D3
Mbeya □, *Tanzania* 87 D3
M'bili, *Sudan* 81 F2
Mbinga, *Tanzania* 87 E4
Mbini □, *Eq. Guin.* 84 D2
Mboki, *C.A.R.* 81 F2
M'bonge, *Cameroon* 83 E6
Mboro, *Senegal* 82 B1
M'boukou Res., *Cameroon* . 83 D7
Mboune, *Senegal* 82 C2
Mbour, *Senegal* 82 C1
Mbout, *Mauritania* 82 B2
Mbuji-Mayi,
  Dem. Rep. of the Congo . 86 D1
Mbulu, *Tanzania* 86 C4
Mburucuyá, *Argentina* 126 B4
Mchinja, *Tanzania* 87 D4
Mchinji, *Malawi* 87 E3
Mdantsane, *S. Africa* 85 L5
Mead, L., *U.S.A.* 117 J12
Meade, *U.S.A.* 113 G4
Meadow Lake, *Canada* ... 105 C7
Meadow Lake Prov. Park,
  Canada 105 C7
Meadow Valley Wash →,
  U.S.A. 117 J12
Meadville, *U.S.A.* 110 E4
Meaford, *Canada* 102 D3
Mealhada, *Portugal* 34 E2
Mealy Mts., *Canada* 103 B8
Meander River, *Canada* ... 104 B5
Meares, C., *U.S.A.* 114 D1
Mearim →, *Brazil* 125 D10
Meath □, *Ireland* 15 C5
Meath Park, *Canada* 105 C7
Meaulne, *France* 19 F9
Meaux, *France* 19 D9
Mebechi-Gawa →, *Japan* . 54 D10
Mecanhelas, *Mozam.* 87 F4
Mecca = Makkah, *Si. Arabia* 74 C2
Mecca, *U.S.A.* 117 M10
Mechanicsburg, *U.S.A.* ... 110 F8
Mechanicville, *U.S.A.* 111 D11
Mechara, *Ethiopia* 81 F5
Mechelen, *Belgium* 17 C4
Mecheria, *Algeria* 78 B5
Mechernich, *Germany* 24 E2
Mechetinskaya, *Russia* ... 49 G5
Mecidiye, *Turkey* 41 F10
Meciözü, *Turkey* 72 B6
Mecklenburg-
  Vorpommern □, *Germany* 24 B8
Mecklenburger Bucht,
  Germany 24 A7

Meconta, *Mozam.* 87 E4
Mecsek, *Hungary* 42 D3
Meda, *Portugal* 34 E3
Medan, *Indonesia* 62 D1
Medanosa, Pta., *Argentina* . 128 C3
Mede, *Italy* 28 C5
Médéa, *Algeria* 78 A6
Mededa, *Bos.-H.* 42 G4
Medellín, *Colombia* 124 B3
Medelpad, *Sweden* 10 B11
Medemblik, *Neths.* 17 B5
Mederdra, *Mauritania* 82 B1
Medford, *Mass., U.S.A.* ... 111 D13
Medford, *Oreg., U.S.A.* ... 114 E2
Medford, *Wis., U.S.A.* 112 C9
Medgidia, *Romania* 43 F13
Medi, *Sudan* 81 F3
Media Agua, *Argentina* ... 126 C2
Media Luna, *Argentina* ... 126 C2
Medianeira, *Brazil* 127 B5
Mediaş, *Romania* 43 D9
Medicina, *Italy* 29 D8
Medicine Bow, *U.S.A.* 114 F10
Medicine Bow Pk., *U.S.A.* . 114 F10
Medicine Bow Ra., *U.S.A.* . 114 F10
Medicine Hat, *Canada* 105 D6
Medicine Lake, *U.S.A.* 112 A2
Medicine Lodge, *U.S.A.* ... 113 G5
Medina = Al Madīnah,
  Si. Arabia 70 E3
Medina, *N. Dak., U.S.A.* .. 112 B5
Medina, *N.Y., U.S.A.* 110 C6
Medina, *Ohio, U.S.A.* 110 E3
Medina →, *U.S.A.* 113 L5
Medina de Pomar, *Spain* .. 34 C7
Medina de Ríoseco, *Spain* . 34 D5
Medina del Campo, *Spain* . 34 D6
Medina L., *U.S.A.* 113 L5
Medina Sidonia, *Spain* 35 J5
Medinaceli, *Spain* 32 D2
Medinipur, *India* 69 H12
Mediterranean Sea, *Europe* 6 H7
Médoc, *France* 20 C3
Medulin, *Croatia* 29 D10
Medveda, *Serbia, Yug.* ... 40 D5
Medvedevo, *Russia* 48 B8
Medveditsa →, *Tver, Russia* 46 D9
Medveditsa →, *Volgograd,*
  Russia 48 F6
Medvedok, *Russia* 48 B10
Medvezhi, Ostrava, *Russia* . 51 B17
Medvezhyegorsk, *Russia* .. 50 C4
Medway →, *U.K.* 13 F8
Medway Towns □, *U.K.* ... 13 F8
Medzev, *Slovak Rep.* 27 C13
Medzilaborce, *Slovak Rep.* . 27 B14
Medžitlija, *Macedonia* 40 F5
Meekatharra, *Australia* ... 93 E2
Meeker, *U.S.A.* 114 F10
Meelpaeg Res., *Canada* ... 103 C8
Meersburg, *Germany* 25 H5
Meerut, *India* 68 E7
Meeteetse, *U.S.A.* 114 D9
Mega, *Ethiopia* 81 G4
Megálo Khório, *Greece* ... 39 E9
Megálo Petalí, *Greece* 38 D6
Megalópolis, *Greece* 38 D4
Meganísi, *Greece* 38 C2
Mégara, *Greece* 38 D5
Megasini, *India* 69 J12
Megdhova →, *Greece* 38 B3
Megève, *France* 21 C10
Meghalaya □, *India* 67 G17
Meghezez, *Ethiopia* 81 F4
Mégiscane, L., *Canada* 102 C4
Megiste, *Greece* 39 E11
Megra, *Russia* 46 B9
Mehadia, *Romania* 42 F7
Meharry, Mt., *Australia* ... 92 D2
Mehedeby, *Sweden* 10 D11
Mehedinţi □, *Romania* 42 F7
Meheisa, *Sudan* 80 D3
Mehlville, *U.S.A.* 112 F9
Mehndawal, *India* 69 F10
Mehr Jān, *Iran* 71 C7
Mehrābād, *Iran* 70 B5
Mehrān, *Iran* 70 C5
Mehrīz, *Iran* 71 D7
Mehun-sur-Yèvre, *France* . 19 E9
Mei Jiang →, *China* 59 E11
Mei Xian, *China* 56 G4
Meicheng, *China* 59 C12
Meichengzhen, *China* 59 C8
Meichuan, *China* 59 B10
Meigu, *China* 58 C4
Meiktila, *Burma* 67 J19
Meinerzhagen, *Germany* .. 24 D3
Meiningen, *Germany* 24 E6
Meira, Serra de, *Spain* 34 B3
Meiringen, *Switz.* 25 J4
Meishan, *China* 58 B4
Meissen, *Germany* 24 D9
Meissner, *Germany* 24 D5
Meitan, *China* 58 D6
Meizhou, *China* 59 E11
Meja, *India* 69 G10
Mejillones, *Chile* 126 A1
Mekdela, *Ethiopia* 81 E4
Mekele, *Ethiopia* 81 E4
Mekhtar, *Pakistan* 66 D6
Meknès, *Morocco* 78 B4
Meko, *Nigeria* 83 D5
Mekong →, *Asia* 65 H6
Mekongga, *Indonesia* 63 E6
Mekrou →, *Benin* 83 C5
Mekvari = Kür →,
  Azerbaijan 73 C13
Mel, *Italy* 29 B9
Melagiri Hills, *India* 66 N10
Melaka, *Malaysia* 65 L4
Melalap, *Malaysia* 62 C5

Millicent

Mélambes, *Greece* 36 D6
Melanesia, *Pac. Oc.* 96 H7
Melbourne, *Australia* 95 F4
Melbourne, *U.S.A.* 109 L5
Melchor Múzquiz, *Mexico* 118 B4
Melchor Ocampo, *Mexico* 118 C4
Méldola, *Italy* 29 D9
Meldorf, *Germany* 24 A5
Melegnano, *Italy* 28 C6
Melenci, *Serbia, Yug.* 42 E5
Melenki, *Russia* 48 C5
Mélèzes →, *Qué., Canada* 101 C12
Mélèzes →, *Qué., Canada* 102 A5
Melfi, *Italy* 31 B8
Melfort, *Canada* 105 C8
Melfort, *Zimbabwe* 87 F3
Melgaço, *Portugal* 34 C2
Melgar de Fernamental, *Spain* 34 C6
Melhus, *Norway* 8 E14
Melide, *Spain* 34 C2
Meligalá, *Greece* 38 D3
Melilla, *N. Afr.* 78 A5
Melilli, *Italy* 31 E8
Melipilla, *Chile* 126 C1
Mélissa, Ákra, *Greece* 36 D6
Mélissa Óros, *Greece* 39 D8
Melita, *Canada* 105 D8
Mélito di Porto Salvo, *Italy* 31 E8
Melitopol, *Ukraine* 47 J8
Melk, *Austria* 26 C8
Mellan Fryken, *Sweden* 10 E7
Mellansel, *Sweden* 8 E18
Mellbystrand, *Sweden* 11 H6
Melle, *France* 20 B3
Melle, *Germany* 24 C4
Mellen, *U.S.A.* 112 B9
Mellerud, *Sweden* 11 F6
Mellette, *U.S.A.* 112 C5
Mellid = Melide, *Spain* 34 C2
Mellieha, *Malta* 36 D1
Mellit, *Sudan* 81 E2
Mellrichstadt, *Germany* 24 E6
Melnik, *Bulgaria* 40 E7
Mělník, *Czech Rep.* 26 A7
Melo, *Uruguay* 127 C5
Melolo, *Indonesia* 63 F6
Melouprey, *Cambodia* 64 F5
Melrose, *Australia* 95 E4
Melrose, *U.K.* 14 F6
Melrose, *Minn., U.S.A.* 112 C7
Melrose, *N. Mex., U.S.A.* 113 H3
Melstone, *U.S.A.* 114 C10
Melsungen, *Germany* 24 D5
Melton Mowbray, *U.K.* 12 E7
Melun, *France* 19 D9
Melut, *Sudan* 81 E3
Melville, *Canada* 105 C8
Melville, C., *Australia* 94 A3
Melville, L., *Canada* 103 B8
Melville B., *Australia* 94 A2
Melville I., *Australia* 92 B5
Melville I., *Canada* 4 B2
Melville Pen., *Canada* 101 B11
Mélykút, *Hungary* 42 D4
Memaliaj, *Albania* 40 F3
Memba, *Mozam.* 87 E5
Memboro, *Indonesia* 63 F5
Membrilla, *Spain* 35 G7
Memel = Klaìpėda, *Lithuania* 9 J19
Memel, *S. Africa* 89 D4
Memmingen, *Germany* 25 H6
Mempawah, *Indonesia* 62 D3
Memphis, *Egypt* 80 J7
Memphis, *Mich., U.S.A.* 110 D2
Memphis, *Tenn., U.S.A.* 113 H10
Memphis, *Tex., U.S.A.* 113 H4
Memphremagog, L., *U.S.A.* 111 B12
Mena, *Ukraine* 47 G7
Mena, *U.S.A.* 113 H7
Mena →, *Ethiopia* 81 F5
Menai Strait, *U.K.* 12 D3
Ménaka, *Mali* 83 B5
Menan = Chao Phraya →, *Thailand* 64 F3
Menarandra →, *Madag.* 89 D7
Menard, *U.S.A.* 113 K5
Menawashei, *Sudan* 81 E1
Mendawai →, *Indonesia* 62 E4
Mende, *France* 20 D7
Mendebo, *Ethiopia* 81 F4
Menden, *Germany* 24 D3
Menderes, *Turkey* 39 C9
Mendez, *Mexico* 119 B5
Mendhar, *India* 69 C6
Mendi, *Ethiopia* 81 F4
Mendip Hills, *U.K.* 13 F5
Mendocino, *U.S.A.* 114 G2
Mendocino, C., *U.S.A.* 114 F1
Mendooran, *Australia* 95 E4
Mendota, *Calif., U.S.A.* 116 J6
Mendota, *Ill., U.S.A.* 112 E10
Mendoza, *Argentina* 126 C2
Mendoza □, *Argentina* 126 C2
Mene Grande, *Venezuela* 124 B4
Menemen, *Turkey* 39 C9
Menen, *Belgium* 17 D3
Menfi, *Italy* 30 E5
Mengdingjie, *China* 58 F2
Mengeš, *Slovenia* 29 B11
Menggala, *Indonesia* 62 E3
Menghai, *China* 58 G3
Mengíbar, *Spain* 35 H7
Mengjin, *China* 56 G7
Mengla, *China* 58 G3
Menglian, *China* 58 F2
Mengshan, *China* 59 E8
Mengyin, *China* 57 G9
Mengzhe, *China* 58 F3
Mengzi, *China* 58 F4
Menihek, *Canada* 103 B6
Menihek L., *Canada* 103 B6
Menin = Menen, *Belgium* 17 D3
Menindee, *Australia* 95 E3
Menindee L., *Australia* 95 E3
Meningie, *Australia* 95 F2
Menlo Park, *U.S.A.* 116 H4
Menominee, *U.S.A.* 108 C2
Menominee →, *U.S.A.* 108 C2
Menomonie, *U.S.A.* 112 C9
Menongue, *Angola* 85 G3
Menorca, *Spain* 37 B11
Mentakab, *Malaysia* 65 L4
Mentawai, Kepulauan, *Indonesia* 62 E1
Menton, *France* 21 E11
Mentor, *U.S.A.* 110 E3
Menzies, *Australia* 93 E3
Meob B., *Namibia* 88 B2
Me'ona, *Israel* 75 B4
Meoqui, *Mexico* 118 B3
Mepaco, *Mozam.* 87 F3
Meppel, *Neths.* 17 B6
Meppen, *Germany* 24 C3
Mequinenza, *Spain* 32 D5
Mequinenza, Embalse de, *Spain* 32 D5
Mer, *France* 18 E8
Merabéllou, Kólpos, *Greece* 36 D7
Merak, *Indonesia* 63 F12
Meramangye, L., *Australia* 93 E5
Meran = Merano, *Italy* 29 B8
Merano, *Italy* 29 B8
Merate, *Italy* 28 C6
Merauke, *Indonesia* 63 F10
Merbein, *Australia* 95 E3
Merca, *Somali Rep.* 74 G3
Mercato Saraceno, *Italy* 29 E9
Merced, *U.S.A.* 116 H6
Merced →, *U.S.A.* 116 H6
Merced Pk., *U.S.A.* 116 H7
Mercedes, *Buenos Aires, Argentina* 126 C4
Mercedes, *Corrientes, Argentina* 126 B4
Mercedes, *San Luis, Argentina* 126 C2
Mercedes, *Uruguay* 126 C4
Mercedes, *U.S.A.* 113 M6
Merceditas, *Chile* 126 B1
Mercer, *N.Z.* 91 G5
Mercer, *U.S.A.* 110 E4
Mercer Island, *U.S.A.* 116 C4
Mercury, *U.S.A.* 117 J11
Mercy C., *Canada* 101 B13
Merdrignac, *France* 18 D4
Mere, *U.K.* 13 F5
Meredith, C., *Falk. Is.* 128 G4
Meredith, L., *U.S.A.* 113 H4
Merefa, *Ukraine* 47 H9
Merei, *Romania* 43 E11
Merga = Nukheila, *Sudan* 80 D2
Mergui, *Burma* 64 F2
Mergui Arch. = Myeik Kyunzu, *Burma* 65 G1
Meriç, *Turkey* 41 E10
Meriç →, *Turkey* 41 F10
Mérida, *Mexico* 119 C7
Mérida, *Spain* 35 G4
Mérida, *Venezuela* 124 B4
Mérida, Cord. de, *Venezuela* 122 C3
Meriden, *U.K.* 13 E6
Meriden, *U.S.A.* 111 E12
Meridian, *Calif., U.S.A.* 116 F5
Meridian, *Idaho, U.S.A.* 114 E5
Meridian, *Miss., U.S.A.* 109 J1
Mérignac, *France* 20 D3
Merimbula, *Australia* 95 F4
Mérinaghène, *Senegal* 82 B1
Merinda, *Australia* 94 C4
Mering, *Germany* 25 G6
Meringa, *Nigeria* 83 C7
Meringur, *Australia* 95 E3
Merir, *Pac. Oc.* 63 D8
Merirumã, *Brazil* 125 C8
Merkel, *U.S.A.* 113 J5
Mermaid Reef, *Australia* 92 C2
Merowe, *Sudan* 80 D3
Merredin, *Australia* 93 F2
Merrick, *U.K.* 14 F4
Merrickville, *Canada* 111 B9
Merrill, *Oreg., U.S.A.* 114 E3
Merrill, *Wis., U.S.A.* 112 C10
Merrimack →, *U.S.A.* 111 D14
Merriman, *U.S.A.* 112 D4
Merritt, *Canada* 104 C4
Merritt Island, *U.S.A.* 109 L5
Merriwa, *Australia* 95 E5
Merry I., *Canada* 102 A4
Merryville, *U.S.A.* 113 K8
Mersa Fatma, *Eritrea* 81 E5
Mersch, *Lux.* 17 E6
Merse →, *Italy* 29 E8
Mersea I., *U.K.* 13 F8
Merseburg, *Germany* 24 D7
Mersey →, *U.K.* 12 D4
Merseyside □, *U.K.* 12 D4
Mersin, *Turkey* 70 B2
Mersing, *Malaysia* 65 L4
Merta, *India* 68 F6
Merta Road, *India* 68 F5
Merthyr Tydfil, *U.K.* 13 F4
Merthyr Tydfil □, *U.K.* 13 F4
Mértola, *Portugal* 35 H3
Mertzon, *U.S.A.* 113 K4
Méru, *France* 19 C9
Meru, *Kenya* 86 B4
Meru, *Tanzania* 86 C4
Merville, *France* 19 B9
Méry-sur-Seine, *France* 19 D10
Merzifon, *Turkey* 72 B6
Merzig, *Germany* 25 F2
Mesa, *U.S.A.* 115 K8
Mesa Verde National Park, *U.S.A.* 115 H9
Mesagne, *Italy* 31 B10
Mesanagrós, *Greece* 36 C9
Mesaoría □, *Cyprus* 36 D12
Mesarás, Kólpos, *Greece* 36 D6
Meschede, *Germany* 24 D4
Mescit, *Turkey* 73 B9
Mesfinto, *Ethiopia* 81 E4
Mesgouez, L., *Canada* 102 B5
Meshchovsk, *Russia* 46 E8
Meshed = Mashhad, *Iran* 71 B8
Meshoppen, *U.S.A.* 111 E8
Meshra er Req, *Sudan* 81 F2
Mesilinka →, *Canada* 104 B4
Mesilla, *U.S.A.* 115 K10
Meslay-du-Maine, *France* 18 E6
Mesocco, *Switz.* 25 J5
Mesolóngion, *Greece* 38 C3
Mesopotamia = Al Jazirah, *Iraq* 70 C5
Mesopotamia, *U.S.A.* 110 E4
Mesopótamon, *Greece* 38 B2
Mesoraca, *Italy* 31 C9
Mésou Volímais = Volímai, *Greece* 38 D2
Mesquite, *U.S.A.* 115 H6
Messac, *France* 18 E5
Messad, *Algeria* 78 B6
Messalo →, *Mozam.* 87 E4
Méssaména, *Cameroon* 83 E7
Messeue, *Greece* 38 D3
Messina, *Italy* 31 D8
Messina, *S. Africa* 89 C5
Messina, Str. di, *Italy* 31 D8
Messíni, *Greece* 38 D4
Messínia □, *Greece* 38 D3
Messiniakós Kólpos, *Greece* 38 E4
Messkirch, *Germany* 25 H5
Messonghi, *Greece* 36 B3
Mesta →, *Bulgaria* 40 E7
Mestá, Ákra, *Greece* 39 C7
Mestanza, *Spain* 35 G6
Mestre, *Italy* 29 C9
Mesudiye, *Turkey* 72 B7
Meta →, *S. Amer.* 122 C4
Meta Incognita Peninsula, *Canada* 101 B13
Metabetchouan, *Canada* 103 C5
Metairie, *U.S.A.* 113 L9
Metalici, Munții, *Romania* 42 D7
Metaline Falls, *U.S.A.* 114 B5
Metallifere, Colline, *Italy* 28 E8
Metán, *Argentina* 126 B3
Metangula, *Mozam.* 87 E3
Metauro →, *Italy* 29 E10
Metema, *Ethiopia* 81 E4
Metengobalame, *Mozam.* 87 E3
Méthana, *Greece* 38 D5
Methóni, *Greece* 38 E3
Methven, *N.Z.* 91 K3
Metil, *Mozam.* 87 F4
Metkovets, *Bulgaria* 40 C7
Metković, *Croatia* 29 E14
Metlakatla, *U.S.A.* 100 C6
Metlika, *Slovenia* 29 C12
Metropolis, *U.S.A.* 113 G10
Métsovon, *Greece* 38 B3
Mettur Dam, *India* 66 P10
Metu, *Ethiopia* 81 F4
Metz, *France* 19 C13
Metzingen, *Germany* 25 G5
Meulaboh, *Indonesia* 62 D1
Meung-sur-Loire, *France* 19 E8
Meureudu, *Indonesia* 62 C1
Meurthe →, *France* 19 D13
Meurthe-et-Moselle □, *France* 19 D13
Meuse □, *France* 19 C12
Meuse →, *Europe* 17 D5
Meuselwitz, *Germany* 24 D8
Mexia, *U.S.A.* 113 K6
Mexiana, I., *Brazil* 125 D9
Mexicali, *Mexico* 117 N11
Mexican Plateau, *Mexico* 98 G9
Mexican Water, *U.S.A.* 115 H9
México, *Mexico* 119 D5
Mexico, *Maine, U.S.A.* 111 B14
Mexico, *Mo., U.S.A.* 112 F9
Mexico, *N.Y., U.S.A.* 111 C8
México □, *Mexico* 119 D5
Mexico ■, *Cent. Amer.* 118 C4
Mexico, G. of, *Cent. Amer.* 119 C7
Mexico B., *U.S.A.* 111 C8
Meydān-e Naftūn, *Iran* 71 D6
Meydani, Ra's-e, *Iran* 71 E8
Meyenburg, *Germany* 24 B8
Meymac, *France* 20 C6
Meymaneh, *Afghan.* 66 B4
Meyrueis, *France* 20 D7
Meyssac, *France* 20 C5
Meyzieu, *France* 21 C8
Mezdra, *Bulgaria* 40 C7
Mèze, *France* 20 E7
Mezen, *Russia* 50 C5
Mezen →, *Russia* 50 C5
Mézenc, Mt., *France* 21 D8
Mezeş, Munţii, *Romania* 42 C8
Mezha →, *Russia* 46 E6
Mezhdurechenskiy, *Russia* 50 D7
Mézidon-Canon, *France* 18 C6
Mézières-en-Brenne, *France* 20 B5
Mézilhac, *France* 21 D8
Mézin, *France* 20 D4
Mezőberény, *Hungary* 42 D6
Mezőfalva, *Hungary* 42 D3
Mezőhegyes, *Hungary* 42 D5
Mezőkövácsháza, *Hungary* 42 D5
Mezőkövesd, *Hungary* 42 C5
Mézos, *France* 20 D2
Mezőtúr, *Hungary* 42 C5
Mezquital, *Mexico* 118 C4
Mezzolombardo, *Italy* 28 B8
Mfolozi →, *S. Africa* 89 D5
Mgeta, *Tanzania* 87 D4
Mglin, *Russia* 47 F7
Mhlaba Hills, *Zimbabwe* 87 F3
Mhow, *India* 68 H6
Miahuatlán, *Mexico* 119 D5
Miajadas, *Spain* 35 F5
Miami, *Fla., U.S.A.* 109 N5
Miami, *Okla., U.S.A.* 113 G7
Miami, *Tex., U.S.A.* 113 H4
Miami Beach, *U.S.A.* 109 N5
Mian Xian, *China* 56 H4
Mianchi, *China* 56 G6
Mīāndarreh, *Iran* 71 C7
Mīāndowāb, *Iran* 70 B5
Miandrivazo, *Madag.* 89 B8
Mīāneh, *Iran* 70 B5
Mianning, *China* 58 C4
Mianwali, *Pakistan* 68 C4
Mianyang, *China* 58 B5
Mianzhu, *China* 58 B5
Miaoli, *Taiwan* 59 E13
Miarinarivo, *Antanarivo, Madag.* 89 B8
Miarinarivo, *Toamasina, Madag.* 89 B8
Miariravaratra, *Madag.* 89 C8
Miass, *Russia* 50 D7
Miasteczko Krajeńskie, *Poland* 45 E4
Miastko, *Poland* 44 E3
Mica, *S. Africa* 89 C5
Micăsasa, *Romania* 43 D9
Michalovce, *Slovak Rep.* 27 C14
Michigan □, *U.S.A.* 108 C3
Michigan, L., *U.S.A.* 108 D2
Michigan City, *U.S.A.* 108 E2
Michika, *Nigeria* 83 C7
Michipicoten I., *Canada* 102 C2
Michoacan □, *Mexico* 118 D4
Michurin, *Bulgaria* 41 D11
Michurinsk, *Russia* 48 D5
Mico, Pta., *Nic.* 120 D3
Micronesia, *Pac. Oc.* 96 G7
Micronesia, Federated States of ■, *Pac. Oc.* 96 G7
Midai, *Indonesia* 65 L6
Midale, *Canada* 105 D8
Middelburg, *Neths.* 17 C3
Middelburg, *Eastern Cape, S. Africa* 88 E4
Middelburg, *Mpumalanga, S. Africa* 89 D4
Middelfart, *Denmark* 11 J3
Middelpos, *S. Africa* 88 E3
Middelwit, *S. Africa* 88 C4
Middle Alkali L., *U.S.A.* 114 F3
Middle Bass I., *U.S.A.* 110 E2
Middle East, *Asia* 52 F7
Middle Fork Feather →, *U.S.A.* 116 F5
Middle I., *Australia* 93 F3
Middle Loup →, *U.S.A.* 112 E5
Middle Sackville, *Canada* 103 D7
Middleboro, *U.S.A.* 111 E14
Middleburg, *Fla., U.S.A.* 109 K5
Middleburg, *N.Y., U.S.A.* 111 D10
Middleburg, *Pa., U.S.A.* 110 F7
Middlebury, *U.S.A.* 111 B11
Middlemount, *Australia* 94 C4
Middleport, *N.Y., U.S.A.* 110 C6
Middleport, *Ohio, U.S.A.* 108 F4
Middlesboro, *U.S.A.* 109 G4
Middlesbrough, *U.K.* 12 C6
Middlesbrough □, *U.K.* 12 C6
Middlesex, *Belize* 120 C2
Middlesex, *N.J., U.S.A.* 111 F10
Middlesex, *N.Y., U.S.A.* 110 D7
Middleton, *Australia* 94 C3
Middleton, *Canada* 103 D6
Middleton Cr. →, *Australia* 94 C3
Middletown, *U.K.* 15 B5
Middletown, *Calif., U.S.A.* 116 G4
Middletown, *Conn., U.S.A.* 111 E12
Middletown, *N.Y., U.S.A.* 111 E10
Middletown, *Ohio, U.S.A.* 108 F3
Middletown, *Pa., U.S.A.* 111 F8
Midhurst, *U.K.* 13 G7
Mīdī, *Yemen* 81 D5
Midi, Canal du →, *France* 20 E5
Midi d'Ossau, Pic du, *France* 20 F3
Midi-Pyrénées □, *France* 20 E5
Midland, *Canada* 102 D4
Midland, *Calif., U.S.A.* 117 M12
Midland, *Mich., U.S.A.* 108 D3
Midland, *Pa., U.S.A.* 110 F4
Midland, *Tex., U.S.A.* 113 K3
Midlands □, *Zimbabwe* 87 F2
Midleton, *Ireland* 15 E3
Midlothian, *U.S.A.* 113 J6
Midlothian □, *U.K.* 14 F5
Midongy, Tangorombohitr' i, *Madag.* 89 C8
Midongy Atsimo, *Madag.* 89 C8
Midou →, *France* 20 E3
Midouze →, *France* 20 E3
Midsayap, *Phil.* 61 H6
Midu, *China* 58 E3
Midway Is., *Pac. Oc.* 96 E10
Midway Wells, *U.S.A.* 117 N11
Midwest, *U.S.A.* 107 B9
Midwest, *Wyo., U.S.A.* 114 E10
Midwest City, *U.S.A.* 113 H6
Midyat, *Turkey* 70 B4
Midzŏr, *Bulgaria* 40 C6
Mie □, *Japan* 55 G8
Miechów, *Poland* 45 H7
Miedwie, Jezioro, *Poland* 45 E1
Międzybórz, *Poland* 45 G4
Międzychód, *Poland* 45 F2
Międzylesie, *Poland* 45 H3
Międzyrzec Podlaski, *Poland* 45 G9
Międzyrzecz, *Poland* 45 F2
Międzyzdroje, *Poland* 44 E1
Miejska Górka, *Poland* 45 G3
Miélan, *France* 20 E4
Mielec, *Poland* 45 H8
Mienga, *Angola* 88 B2
Miercurea-Ciuc, *Romania* 43 D10
Miercurea Sibiului, *Romania* 43 E8
Mieres, *Spain* 34 B5
Mieroszów, *Poland* 45 H3
Mieso, *Ethiopia* 81 F5
Mieszkowice, *Poland* 45 F1
Mifflintown, *U.S.A.* 110 F7
Mifraz Hefa, *Israel* 75 C4
Migennes, *France* 19 E10
Migliarino, *Italy* 29 D8
Miguel Alemán, Presa, *Mexico* 119 D5
Miguelturra, *Spain* 35 G7
Mihăileni, *Romania* 43 C11
Mihăileşti, *Romania* 43 F10
Mihailovca, *Moldova* 43 D13
Mihalgazi, *Turkey* 39 A12
Mihaliççık, *Turkey* 72 C4
Mihara, *Japan* 55 G6
Miheşu de Cîmpie, *Romania* 43 D9
Mijas, *Spain* 35 J6
Mikese, *Tanzania* 86 D4
Mikha-Tskhakaya = Senaki, *Georgia* 49 J6
Mikhailovka = Mykhaylivka, *Ukraine* 47 J8
Mikhaylov, *Russia* 46 E10
Mikhaylovgrad = Montana, *Bulgaria* 40 C7
Mikhaylovka, *Russia* 48 E6
Mikhnevo, *Russia* 46 E9
Mikínai, *Greece* 38 D4
Mikkeli, *Finland* 9 F22
Mikkwa →, *Canada* 104 B6
Mikniya, *Sudan* 81 D3
Mikołajki, *Poland* 44 E8
Míkonos, *Greece* 39 D7
Míkrí Préspa, Límni, *Greece* 40 F5
Míkrón Dhérion, *Greece* 41 E10
Mikstat, *Poland* 45 G4
Mikulov, *Czech Rep.* 27 C9
Mikumi, *Tanzania* 86 D4
Milaca, *U.S.A.* 112 C8
Milagro, *Ecuador* 124 D3
Milagros, *Phil.* 61 E5
Milan = Milano, *Italy* 28 C6
Milan, *Mo., U.S.A.* 112 E8
Milan, *Tenn., U.S.A.* 109 H1
Milang, *Australia* 95 F2
Milange, *Mozam.* 87 F4
Milano, *Italy* 28 C6
Milanoa, *Madag.* 89 A8
Milâs, *Turkey* 39 D9
Mílatos, *Greece* 36 D7
Milazzo, *Italy* 31 D8
Milbank, *U.S.A.* 112 C6
Milbanke Sd., *Canada* 104 C3
Milden, *Canada* 105 C7
Mildenhall, *U.K.* 13 E8
Mildmay, *Canada* 110 B3
Mildura, *Australia* 95 E3
Mile, *China* 58 E4
Miléai, *Greece* 38 B5
Miles, *Australia* 95 D5
Miles City, *U.S.A.* 112 B2
Mileşti, *Moldova* 43 C13
Milestone, *Canada* 105 D8
Mileto, *Italy* 31 D9
Miletto, Mte., *Italy* 31 A7
Miletus, *Turkey* 39 D9
Milevsko, *Czech Rep.* 26 B7
Milford, *Calif., U.S.A.* 116 E6
Milford, *Conn., U.S.A.* 111 E11
Milford, *Del., U.S.A.* 108 F8
Milford, *Mass., U.S.A.* 111 D13
Milford, *N.H., U.S.A.* 111 D13
Milford, *Pa., U.S.A.* 111 E10
Milford, *Utah, U.S.A.* 115 G7
Milford Haven, *U.K.* 13 F2
Milford Sd., *N.Z.* 91 L1
Milḥ, Baḥr al, *Iraq* 70 C4
Milicz, *Poland* 45 G4
Milikapiti, *Australia* 92 B5
Miling, *Australia* 93 F2
Militello in Val di Catánia, *Italy* 31 E7
Milk →, *U.S.A.* 114 B10
Milk, Wadi el →, *Sudan* 80 D3
Milk River, *Canada* 104 D6
Mill I., *Antarctica* 5 C8
Mill Valley, *U.S.A.* 116 H4
Millárs →, *Spain* 32 F4
Millau, *France* 20 D7
Millbridge, *Canada* 110 B7
Millbrook, *Canada* 110 B6
Millbrook, *U.S.A.* 111 E11
Mille Lacs, L. des, *Canada* 102 C1
Mille Lacs L., *U.S.A.* 112 B8
Milledgeville, *U.S.A.* 109 J4
Millen, *U.S.A.* 109 J5
Miller, *U.S.A.* 112 C5
Millerovo, *Russia* 49 F5
Millersburg, *Ohio, U.S.A.* 110 F3
Millersburg, *Pa., U.S.A.* 110 F8
Millerton, *U.S.A.* 111 E11
Millerton L., *U.S.A.* 116 J7
Millevaches, Plat. de, *France* 20 C6
Millheim, *U.S.A.* 110 F7
Millicent, *Australia* 95 F3

Millington, U.S.A. 113 H10
Millinocket, U.S.A. 109 C11
Millmerran, Australia ... 95 D5
Millom, U.K. 12 C4
Mills L., Canada 104 A5
Millsboro, U.S.A. 110 G5
Millville, N.J., U.S.A. 108 F8
Millville, Pa., U.S.A. 111 E8
Millwood L., U.S.A. 113 J8
Milna, Croatia 29 E13
Milne →, Australia 94 C2
Milo, U.S.A. 109 C11
Mílos, Greece 38 E6
Miłosław, Poland 45 F4
Milot, Albania 40 E3
Milparinka, Australia 95 D3
Miltenberg, Germany 25 F5
Milton, N.S., Canada 103 D7
Milton, Ont., Canada 110 C5
Milton, N.Z. 91 M2
Milton, Calif., U.S.A. 116 G6
Milton, Fla., U.S.A. 109 K2
Milton, Pa., U.S.A. 110 F8
Milton, Vt., U.S.A. 111 B11
Milton-Freewater, U.S.A. . 114 D4
Milton Keynes, U.K. 13 E7
Milton Keynes □, U.K. ... 13 E7
Miluo, China 59 C9
Milverton, Canada 110 C4
Milwaukee, U.S.A. 108 D2
Milwaukee Deep, Atl. Oc. . 121 C6
Milwaukie, U.S.A. 116 E4
Mim, Ghana 82 D4
Mimizan, France 20 D2
Mimoň, Czech Rep. 26 A7
Min Jiang →, Fujian, China 59 E12
Min Jiang →, Sichuan,
   China 58 C5
Min Xian, China 56 G3
Mina Pirquitas, Argentina . 126 A2
Mīnā Su'ud, Si. Arabia ... 71 D6
Mīnā'al Aḥmadī, Kuwait .. 71 D6
Minago →, Canada 105 C9
Minaki, Canada 105 D10
Minamata, Japan 55 H5
Minami-Tori-Shima,
   Pac. Oc. 96 E7
Minas, Uruguay 127 C4
Minas, Sierra de las,
   Guatemala 120 C2
Minas Basin, Canada 103 C7
Minas de Rio Tinto = Minas
   de Riotinto, Spain 35 H4
Minas de Riotinto, Spain .. 35 H4
Minas Gerais □, Brazil ... 125 G9
Minatitlán, Mexico 119 D6
Minbu, Burma 67 J19
Minchinabad, Pakistan ... 68 D5
Mincio →, Italy 28 C7
Minčol, Slovak Rep. 27 B13
Mindanao, Phil. 61 H6
Mindanao Sea = Bohol Sea,
   Phil. 63 C6
Mindanao Trench, Pac. Oc. 61 G7
Mindel →, Germany 25 G6
Mindelheim, Germany 25 G6
Minden, Canada 110 B6
Minden, Germany 24 C4
Minden, La., U.S.A. 113 J8
Minden, Nev., U.S.A. 116 G7
Mindiptana, Indonesia ... 63 F10
Mindoro, Phil. 61 E4
Mindoro Str., Phil. 61 E4
Mine, Japan 55 G5
Minehead, U.K. 13 F4
Mineola, N.Y., U.S.A. 111 F11
Mineola, Tex., U.S.A. 113 J7
Mineral King, U.S.A. 116 J8
Mineral Wells, U.S.A. 113 J5
Mineralnyye Vody, Russia . 49 H6
Minersville, U.S.A. 111 F8
Minerva, U.S.A. 110 F3
Minervino Murge, Italy ... 31 A9
Minetto, U.S.A. 111 C8
Mingäçevir, Azerbaijan ... 49 K8
Mingäçevir Su Anbarı,
   Azerbaijan 49 K8
Mingan, Canada 103 B7
Mingechaur = Mingäçevir,
   Azerbaijan 49 K8
Mingechaurskoye Vdkhr. =
   Mingäçevir Su Anbarı,
   Azerbaijan 49 K8
Mingela, Australia 94 B4
Mingenew, Australia 93 E2
Mingera Cr. →, Australia . 94 C2
Minggang, China 59 A10
Mingguang, China 59 A11
Mingin, Burma 67 H19
Mingir, Moldova 43 D13
Minglanilla, Spain 33 F3
Minglun, China 58 E7
Mingo Junction, U.S.A. ... 110 F4
Mingorria, Spain 34 E6
Mingshan, China 58 B4
Mingxi, China 59 D11
Minho = Miño →, Spain .. 34 D2
Minhou, China 59 E12
Miničevo, Serbia, Yug. ... 40 C6
Minidoka, U.S.A. 114 E7
Minigwal, L., Australia ... 93 E3
Minilya →, Australia 93 D1
Minilya Roadhouse,
   Australia 93 D1
Minipi L., Canada 103 B7
Mink L., Canada 104 A5
Minkammen, Sudan 81 F3
Minna, Nigeria 83 D6
Minneapolis, Kans., U.S.A. 112 F6

Minneapolis, Minn., U.S.A. 112 C8
Minnedosa, Canada 105 C9
Minnesota □, U.S.A. 112 B8
Minnesota →, U.S.A. 112 C8
Minnewaukan, U.S.A. 112 A5
Minnipa, Australia 95 E2
Minnitaki L., Canada 102 C1
Mino, Japan 55 G8
Miño →, Spain 34 B2
Miño, Spain 34 B2
Minoa, Greece 39 F7
Minorca = Menorca, Spain 37 B11
Minot, U.S.A. 112 A4
Minqin, China 56 E2
Minqing, China 59 D12
Minsen, Germany 24 B3
Minsk, Belarus 46 F4
Mińsk Mazowiecki, Poland 45 F8
Mintabie, Australia 95 D1
Mintaka Pass, Pakistan ... 69 A6
Minteke Daban = Mintaka
   Pass, Pakistan 69 A6
Minto, Canada 103 C6
Minto, L., Canada 102 A5
Minton, Canada 105 D8
Minturn, U.S.A. 114 G10
Minturno, Italy 30 A6
Minûf, Egypt 80 H7
Minusinsk, Russia 51 D10
Minutang, India 67 E20
Minya el Qamh, Egypt 80 H7
Mionica, Bos.-H. 42 F3
Mionica, Serbia, Yug. 40 B4
Miquelon, Canada 102 C4
Miquelon, St-P. & M. 103 C8
Mir, Niger 83 C7
Mīr Kūh, Iran 71 E8
Mīr Shahdād, Iran 71 E8
Mira, Italy 29 C9
Mira, Portugal 34 E2
Mira →, Portugal 35 H2
Mira por vos Cay, Bahamas 121 B5
Mirabella Eclano, Italy ... 31 A7
Miraj, India 66 L9
Miram Shah, Pakistan 68 C4
Miramar, Argentina 126 D4
Miramar, Mozam. 89 C6
Miramas, France 21 E8
Mirambeau, France 20 C3
Miramichi, Canada 103 C6
Miramichi B., Canada 103 C7
Miramont-de-Guyenne,
   France 20 D4
Miranda, Brazil 125 H7
Miranda →, Brazil 124 G7
Miranda de Ebro, Spain .. 32 C2
Miranda do Corvo, Portugal 34 E2
Miranda do Douro, Portugal 34 D4
Mirande, France 20 E4
Mirandela, Portugal 34 D3
Mirándola, Italy 28 D8
Mirandópolis, Brazil 127 A5
Mirango, Malawi 87 E3
Mirano, Italy 29 C9
Miras, Albania 40 F4
Mirassol, Brazil 127 A6
Mirbāṭ, Oman 74 D5
Mirear, Egypt 80 C4
Mirebeau, Côte-d'Or, France 19 E12
Mirebeau, Vienne, France . 18 F7
Mirecourt, France 19 D13
Mirgorod = Myrhorod,
   Ukraine 47 H7
Miri, Malaysia 62 D4
Miriam Vale, Australia ... 94 C5
Miribel, France 19 G11
Mirim, L., S. Amer. 127 C5
Mirnyy, Russia 51 C12
Miroč, Serbia, Yug. 40 B6
Mirokhan, Pakistan 68 F3
Mirond L., Canada 105 B8
Mirosławiec, Poland 44 E3
Mirpur, Pakistan 69 C5
Mirpur Batoro, Pakistan .. 68 G3
Mirpur Bibiwari, Pakistan . 68 E2
Mirpur Khas, Pakistan ... 68 G3
Mirpur Sakro, Pakistan ... 68 G2
Mirria, Niger 83 C6
Mirsk, Poland 45 H2
Mirtağ, Turkey 70 B4
Mirzaani, Georgia 49 K8
Mirzapur, India 69 G10
Mirzapur-cum-
   Vindhyachal = Mirzapur,
   India 69 G10
Misantla, Mexico 119 D5
Misawa, Japan 54 D10
Miscou I., Canada 103 C7
Mish'āb, Ra's al, Si. Arabia 71 D6
Mishan, China 60 B8
Mishawaka, U.S.A. 108 E2
Mishbih, Gebel, Egypt 80 C3
Mishima, Japan 55 G9
Misión, Mexico 117 N10
Misiones □, Argentina 127 B5
Misiones □, Paraguay 126 B4
Miskah, Si. Arabia 70 E4
Miskitos, Cayos, Nic. 120 D3
Miskolc, Hungary 42 B5
Misoke,
   Dem. Rep. of the Congo . 86 C2
Misool, Indonesia 63 E8
Miṣrātah, Libya 79 B9
Missanabie, Canada 102 C3
Missinaibi →, Canada 102 B3
Missinaibi L., Canada 102 C3
Mission, Canada 104 D4
Mission, S. Dak., U.S.A. .. 112 D4
Mission, Tex., U.S.A. 113 M5
Mission Beach, Australia . 94 B4

Mission Viejo, U.S.A. 117 M9
Missirah, Senegal 82 C1
Missisa L., Canada 102 B2
Missisicabi →, Canada 102 B4
Mississagi →, Canada 102 C3
Mississauga, Canada 110 C5
Mississippi □, U.S.A. 113 J10
Mississippi →, U.S.A. 113 L10
Mississippi L., Canada ... 111 A8
Mississippi River Delta,
   U.S.A. 113 L9
Mississippi Sd., U.S.A. ... 113 K10
Missoula, U.S.A. 114 C7
Missouri □, U.S.A. 112 F8
Missouri →, U.S.A. 112 F9
Missouri City, U.S.A. 113 L7
Missouri Valley, U.S.A. ... 112 E7
Mist, U.S.A. 116 E3
Mistassibi →, Canada 103 B5
Mistassini, Canada 103 C5
Mistassini →, Canada 103 C5
Mistassini, L., Canada ... 102 B5
Mistastin L., Canada 103 A7
Mistelbach, Austria 27 C9
Misterbianco, Italy 31 E8
Mistinibi, L., Canada 103 A7
Mistretta, Italy 31 E7
Misty L., Canada 105 B8
Misurata = Miṣrātah, Libya 79 B9
Mît Ghamr, Egypt 80 H7
Mitatib, Sudan 81 D4
Mitchell, Australia 95 D4
Mitchell, Canada 110 C3
Mitchell, Nebr., U.S.A. ... 112 E3
Mitchell, Oreg., U.S.A. ... 114 D3
Mitchell, S. Dak., U.S.A. . 112 D6
Mitchell →, Australia 94 B3
Mitchell, Mt., U.S.A. 109 H4
Mitchell Ranges, Australia 94 A2
Mitchelstown, Ireland ... 15 D3
Mitha Tiwana, Pakistan .. 68 C5
Mithi, Pakistan 68 G3
Míthimna, Greece 39 B8
Mithrao, Pakistan 68 F3
Mitilíni, Greece 39 B8
Mitilinoí, Greece 39 D8
Mito, Japan 55 F10
Mitrofanovka, Russia 47 H10
Mitrovica = Kosovska
   Mitrovica, Kosovo, Yug. . 40 D4
Mitsinjo, Madag. 89 B8
Mitsiwa, Eritrea 81 D4
Mitsiwa Channel, Eritrea . 81 D5
Mitsukaidō, Japan 55 F9
Mittagong, Australia 95 E5
Mittelberg, Austria 26 D3
Mittelfranken □, Germany 25 F6
Mittellandkanal →,
   Germany 24 C4
Mittenwalde, Germany ... 24 C9
Mittersill, Austria 26 D5
Mitterteich, Germany 25 F8
Mittweida, Germany 24 E8
Mitú, Colombia 124 C4
Mitumba, Tanzania 86 D3
Mitumba, Mts.,
   Dem. Rep. of the Congo . 86 D2
Mitwaba,
   Dem. Rep. of the Congo . 87 D2
Mityana, Uganda 86 B3
Mixteco →, Mexico 119 D5
Miyagi □, Japan 54 E10
Miyah, W. el →, Egypt ... 80 C3
Miyah, W. el →, Syria 70 C3
Miyake-Jima, Japan 55 G9
Miyako, Japan 54 E10
Miyako-Jima, Japan 55 M2
Miyako-Rettō, Japan 55 M2
Miyakonojō, Japan 55 J5
Miyani, India 68 J3
Miyanoura-Dake, Japan .. 55 J5
Miyazaki, Japan 55 J5
Miyazaki □, Japan 55 H5
Miyazu, Japan 55 G7
Miyet, Bahr el = Dead Sea,
   Asia 75 D4
Miyi, China 58 D4
Miyoshi, Japan 55 G6
Miyun, China 56 D9
Miyun Shuiku, China 57 D9
Mizan Teferi, Ethiopia ... 81 F4
Mizdah, Libya 79 B8
Mizen Hd., Cork, Ireland . 15 E2
Mizen Hd., Wick., Ireland 15 D5
Mizhi, China 56 F6
Mizil, Romania 43 F11
Mizoram □, India 67 H18
Mizpe Ramon, Israel 75 E3
Mizusawa, Japan 54 E10
Mjällby, Sweden 11 H8
Mjöbäck, Sweden 11 G6
Mjölby, Sweden 11 F9
Mjörn, Sweden 11 G6
Mjøsa, Norway 9 F14
Mkata, Tanzania 86 D4
Mkokotoni, Tanzania 86 D4
Mkomazi, Tanzania 86 C4
Mkomazi →, S. Africa ... 89 E5
Mkulwe, Tanzania 87 D3
Mkumbi, Ras, Tanzania .. 86 D4
Mkushi, Zambia 87 E2
Mkushi River, Zambia ... 87 E2
Mkuze, S. Africa 89 D5
Mladá Boleslav, Czech Rep. 26 A7
Mladenovac, Serbia, Yug. . 40 B4
Mlala Hills, Tanzania 86 D3
Mlange = Mulanje, Malawi 87 F4
Mlanje, Pic, Malawi 85 H7
Mlava →, Serbia, Yug. ... 40 B5
Mława, Poland 45 E7
Mliniŝte, Bos.-H. 29 D13

Mljet, Croatia 29 F14
Mljetski Kanal, Croatia ... 29 F14
Młynary, Poland 44 D6
Mmabatho, S. Africa 88 D4
Mme, Cameroon 83 D7
Mnichovo Hradiště,
   Czech Rep. 26 A7
Mo i Rana, Norway 8 C16
Moa, Cuba 121 B4
Moa, Indonesia 63 F7
Moa →, S. Leone 82 D2
Moab, U.S.A. 115 G9
Moala, Fiji 91 D8
Moama, Australia 95 F3
Moamba, Mozam. 89 D5
Moapa, U.S.A. 117 J12
Moate, Ireland 15 C4
Moba,
   Dem. Rep. of the Congo . 86 D2
Mobārakābād, Iran 71 D7
Mobaye, C.A.R. 84 D4
Mobayi,
   Dem. Rep. of the Congo . 84 D4
Moberley Lake, Canada ... 104 B4
Moberly, U.S.A. 112 F8
Mobile, U.S.A. 109 K1
Mobile B., U.S.A. 109 K2
Mobridge, U.S.A. 112 C4
Mobutu Sese Seko, L. =
   Albert L., Africa 86 B3
Moc Chau, Vietnam 64 B5
Moc Hoa, Vietnam 65 G5
Mocabe Kasari,
   Dem. Rep. of the Congo . 87 D2
Moçambique □, Mozam. .. 87 F5
Moçâmedes = Namibe,
   Angola 85 H2
Mocanaqua, U.S.A. 111 E8
Mochudi, Botswana 88 C4
Mocimboa da Praia, Mozam. 87 E5
Mociu, Romania 43 D9
Mocoa, Colombia 124 C3
Mococa, Brazil 127 A6
Mocorito, Mexico 118 B3
Moctezuma, Mexico 118 B3
Moctezuma →, Mexico ... 119 C5
Mocuba, Mozam. 87 F4
Mocúzari, Presa, Mexico .. 118 B3
Modane, France 21 C10
Modasa, India 68 H5
Modder →, S. Africa 88 D3
Modderrivier, S. Africa ... 88 D3
Módena, Italy 28 D7
Modena, U.S.A. 115 H7
Modesto, U.S.A. 116 H6
Módica, Italy 31 F7
Mödling, Austria 27 C9
Modo, Sudan 81 F3
Modra, Slovak Rep. 27 C10
Modriča, Bos.-H. 42 F3
Moe, Australia 95 F4
Moebase, Mozam. 87 F4
Moëlan-sur-Mer, France .. 18 E3
Moengo, Surinam 125 B8
Moffat, U.K. 14 F5
Moga, India 68 D6
Mogadishu = Muqdisho,
   Somali Rep. 74 G4
Mogador = Essaouira,
   Morocco 78 B4
Mogadouro, Portugal 34 D4
Mogalakwena →, S. Africa 89 C4
Mogami-Gawa →, Japan . 54 E10
Mogán, Canary Is. 37 G4
Mogaung, Burma 67 G20
Mogente = Moixent, Spain 33 G4
Mogho, Ethiopia 81 G5
Mogi das Cruzes, Brazil .. 127 A6
Mogi-Guaçu →, Brazil ... 127 A6
Mogi-Mirim, Brazil 127 A6
Mogielnica, Poland 45 G7
Mogige, Ethiopia 81 F4
Mogilev = Mahilyow,
   Belarus 46 F6
Mogilev-Podolskiy =
   Mohyliv-Podilskyy,
   Ukraine 47 H4
Mogilno, Poland 45 F4
Mogincual, Mozam. 87 F5
Mogliano Véneto, Italy ... 29 C9
Mogocha, Russia 51 D12
Mogok, Burma 67 H20
Mogollon Rim, U.S.A. ... 115 J8
Mógoro, Italy 30 C1
Mograt, Sudan 80 D3
Moguer, Spain 35 H4
Mogumber, Australia ... 93 F2
Mohács, Hungary 42 E3
Mohales Hoek, Lesotho .. 88 E4
Mohall, U.S.A. 112 A4
Moḥammadābād, Iran ... 71 B8
Mohammedia, Morocco .. 78 B4
Mohana →, India 69 G11
Mohanlalganj, India 69 F9
Mohave, L., U.S.A. 117 K12
Mohawk →, U.S.A. 111 D11
Moheda, Sweden 11 G8
Mohenjodaro, Pakistan .. 68 F3
Mohicanville Reservoir,
   U.S.A. 110 F3
Möhne →, Germany 24 D3
Mohoro, Tanzania 86 D4
Mohyliv-Podilskyy, Ukraine 47 H4
Moia, Sudan 81 F2
Moidart, L., U.K. 14 E3
Moineşti, Romania 43 D11
Moira →, Canada 110 B7
Moirans, France 21 C9

Moirans-en-Montagne,
   France 19 F12
Moíres, Greece 36 D6
Moisaküla, Estonia 9 G21
Moisie, Canada 103 B6
Moisie →, Canada 103 B6
Moissac, France 20 D5
Moita, Portugal 35 G2
Moixent, Spain 33 G4
Möja, Sweden 10 E12
Mojácar, Spain 33 H3
Mojados, Spain 34 D6
Mojave, U.S.A. 117 K8
Mojave Desert, U.S.A. ... 117 L10
Mojiang, China 58 F3
Mojo, Ethiopia 81 F5
Mojkovac, Montenegro, Yug. 40 D3
Mojo, Bolivia 126 A2
Mojo, Ethiopia 81 F4
Mojokerto, Indonesia ... 63 G15
Mokai, N.Z. 91 H5
Mokambo,
   Dem. Rep. of the Congo . 87 E2
Mokameh, India 69 G11
Mokelumne →, U.S.A. ... 116 G5
Mokelumne Hill, U.S.A. .. 116 G6
Mokhós, Greece 36 D7
Mokhotlong, Lesotho 89 D4
Möklinta, Sweden 10 D10
Mokokchung, India 67 F19
Mokolo, Cameroon 83 C7
Mokolo →, S. Africa 89 C4
Mokp'o, S. Korea 57 G14
Mokra Gora, Yugoslavia . 40 D4
Mokronog, Slovenia 29 C12
Moksha →, Russia 48 C6
Mokshan, Russia 48 D7
Mokwa, Nigeria 83 D6
Mol, Belgium 17 C5
Mola di Bari, Italy 31 A10
Molale, Ethiopia 81 E4
Moláoi, Greece 38 E4
Molara, Italy 30 B2
Molat, Croatia 29 D11
Molchanovo, Russia 50 D9
Mold, U.K. 12 D4
Moldava nad Bodvou,
   Slovak Rep. 27 C14
Moldavia = Moldova ■,
   Europe 43 C13
Moldavia, Romania 43 D10
Molde, Norway 8 E12
Moldova ■, Europe 43 C13
Moldova Nouă, Romania . 42 F6
Moldoveanu, Vf., Romania 43 E9
Moldoviţa, Romania 43 C10
Mole →, U.K. 13 F7
Mole Creek, Australia ... 94 G4
Molepolole, Botswana ... 88 C4
Molfetta, Italy 31 A9
Molina de Aragón, Spain . 32 E3
Molina de Segura, Spain . 33 G3
Moline, U.S.A. 112 E9
Molinella, Italy 29 D8
Molinos, Argentina 126 B2
Moliro,
   Dem. Rep. of the Congo . 86 D3
Moliterno, Italy 31 B8
Molkom, Sweden 10 E7
Mölle, Sweden 11 H6
Molledo, Spain 34 B6
Mollendo, Peru 124 G4
Mollerin, L., Australia ... 93 F2
Mollerussa, Spain 32 D5
Mollina, Spain 35 H6
Mölln, Germany 24 B6
Mölltorp, Sweden 11 F8
Mölnlycke, Sweden 11 G6
Molochansk, Ukraine ... 47 J8
Molochnoye, Ozero, Ukraine 47 J8
Molodechno =
   Maladzyechna, Belarus . 46 E4
Molokai, U.S.A. 106 H16
Molong, Australia 95 E4
Molopo →, Africa 88 D3
Mólos, Greece 38 C4
Molotov = Perm, Russia .. 50 D6
Molsheim, France 19 D14
Molson L., Canada 105 C9
Molteno, S. Africa 88 E4
Molu, Indonesia 63 F8
Molucca Sea, Indonesia .. 63 E6
Moluccas = Maluku,
   Indonesia 63 E7
Moma,
   Dem. Rep. of the Congo . 86 C1
Moma, Mozam. 87 F4
Mombasa, Kenya 86 C4
Mombetsu, Japan 54 B11
Mombuey, Spain 34 C4
Momchilgrad, Bulgaria .. 41 E9
Momi,
   Dem. Rep. of the Congo . 86 C2
Mompós, Colombia 124 B4
Møn, Denmark 11 K6
Mon →, Burma 67 J19
Mona, Canal de la, W. Indies 121 C6
Mona, Isla, Puerto Rico .. 121 C6
Mona, Pta., Costa Rica ... 120 E3
Monaca, U.S.A. 110 F4
Monaco ■, Europe 21 E11
Monadhliath Mts., U.K. .. 14 D4
Monadnock, Mt., U.S.A. . 111 D12
Monaghan, Ireland 15 B5
Monaghan □, Ireland ... 15 B5
Monahans, U.S.A. 113 K3
Monapo, Mozam. 87 E5
Monar, L., U.K. 14 D3
Monarch Mt., Canada ... 104 C3
Monashee Mts., Canada .. 104 C5
Monasterevin, Ireland ... 15 C4

Monastir = Bitola, Macedonia 40 E5
Moncada, Phil. 61 D4
Moncalieri, Italy 28 D4
Moncalvo, Italy 28 C5
Moncão, Portugal 34 C2
Moncarapacho, Portugal . 35 H3
Mönchengladbach, Germany 24 D2
Monchique, Portugal ... 35 H2
Moncks Corner, U.S.A. ... 109 J5
Monclova, Mexico 118 B4
Moncontour, France 18 D4
Moncton, Canada 103 C7
Mondariz, Spain 34 C2
Mondego →, Portugal ... 34 E2
Mondego, C., Portugal ... 34 E2
Mondeodo, Indonesia 63 E6
Mondeville, France 18 C6
Mondolfo, Italy 29 E10
Mondoñedo, Spain 34 B3
Mondovì, Italy 28 D4
Mondragon, Phil. 61 E6
Mondragone, Italy 30 A6
Mondrain I., Australia ... 93 F3
Monemvasía, Greece 38 E5
Monessen, U.S.A. 110 F5
Monesterio, Spain 35 G4
Monestier-de-Clermont, France 21 D9
Monett, U.S.A. 113 G8
Moneymore, U.K. 15 B5
Monfalcone, Italy 29 C10
Monflanquin, France ... 20 D4
Monforte, Portugal 35 F3
Monforte de Lemos, Spain 34 C3
Mong Hsu, Burma 58 G2
Mong Kung, Burma 67 J20
Mong Nai, Burma 67 J20
Mong Pawk, Burma 67 H21
Mong Ping, Burma 58 G2
Mong Ton, Burma 67 J21
Mong Wa, Burma 67 J22
Mong Yai, Burma 67 H21
Mongalla, Sudan 81 F3
Mongers, L., Australia ... 93 E2
Monghyr = Munger, India 69 G12
Mongibello = Etna, Italy . 31 E7
Mongo, Chad 79 F9
Mongo →, S. Leone 82 D2
Mongolia ■, Asia 51 E10
Mongonu, Nigeria 83 C7
Mongu, Zambia 85 H4
Môngua, Angola 88 B2
Monifieth, U.K. 14 E6
Monistrol-sur-Loire, France 21 C8
Monkey Bay, Malawi 87 E4
Monkey Mia, Australia .. 93 E1
Monkey River, Belize ... 119 D7
Moński, Poland 44 E9
Monkoto, Dem. Rep. of the Congo . 84 E4
Monkton, Canada 110 C3
Monmouth, U.K. 13 F5
Monmouth, Ill., U.S.A. .. 112 E9
Monmouth, Oreg., U.S.A. 114 D2
Monmouthshire □, U.K. . 13 F5
Mono L., U.S.A. 116 H7
Monolith, U.S.A. 117 K8
Monólithos, Greece 36 C9
Monongahela, U.S.A. ... 110 F5
Monópoli, Italy 31 B10
Monor, Hungary 42 C4
Monóvar, Spain 33 G4
Monreal del Campo, Spain 32 E3
Monreale, Italy 30 D6
Monroe, Ga., U.S.A. 109 J4
Monroe, La., U.S.A. 113 J8
Monroe, Mich., U.S.A. .. 108 E4
Monroe, N.C., U.S.A. ... 109 H5
Monroe, N.Y., U.S.A. ... 111 E10
Monroe, Utah, U.S.A. ... 115 G7
Monroe, Wash., U.S.A. .. 116 C5
Monroe, Wis., U.S.A. ... 112 D10
Monroe City, U.S.A. 112 F9
Monroeton, U.S.A. 111 E8
Monroeville, Ala., U.S.A. 109 K2
Monroeville, Pa., U.S.A. . 110 F5
Monrovia, Liberia 82 D2
Mons, Belgium 17 D3
Møns Klint, Denmark ... 11 K6
Monsaraz, Portugal 35 G3
Monse, Indonesia 63 E6
Monségur, France 20 D4
Monsélice, Italy 29 C8
Mönsterås, Sweden 11 G10
Mont-de-Marsan, France . 20 E3
Mont-Joli, Canada 103 C6
Mont-Laurier, Canada .. 102 C4
Mont-Louis, Canada ... 103 C6
Mont-roig del Camp, Spain 32 D5
Mont-St-Michel, Le = Le Mont-St-Michel, France . 18 D5
Mont Tremblant, Parc Recr. du, Canada 102 C5
Montabaur, Germany ... 24 E3
Montagnac, France 20 E7
Montagnana, Italy 29 C8
Montagu, S. Africa 88 E3
Montagu I., Antarctica .. 5 B1
Montague, Canada 103 C7
Montague, I., Mexico ... 118 A2
Montague Ra., Australia . 93 E2
Montague Sd., Australia . 92 B4
Montaigu, France 18 F5
Montalbán, Spain 32 E3
Montalbano Iónico, Italy . 31 B9
Montalbo, Spain 32 F2
Montalcino, Italy 29 E8
Montalegre, Portugal .. 34 D3

Montalto, Italy 31 D8
Montalto di Castro, Italy . 29 F8
Montalto Uffugo, Italy ... 31 C9
Montalvo, U.S.A. 117 L7
Montamarta, Spain 34 D5
Montana, Bulgaria 40 C7
Montaña, Peru 124 E4
Montana □, Bulgaria ... 40 C7
Montana □, U.S.A. 114 C9
Montaña Clara, I., Canary Is. 37 E6
Montánchez, Spain 35 F4
Montargil, Portugal 35 F2
Montargis, France 19 E9
Montauban, France 20 D5
Montauk, U.S.A. 111 E13
Montauk Pt., U.S.A. ... 111 E13
Montbard, France 19 E11
Montbarrey, France ... 19 E12
Montbéliard, France ... 19 E13
Montblanc, Spain 32 D6
Montbrison, France ... 21 C8
Montceau-les-Mines, France 19 F11
Montcenis, France 21 B8
Montclair, U.S.A. 111 F10
Montcornet, France ... 19 C11
Montcuq, France 20 D5
Montdidier, France ... 19 C9
Monte Albán, Mexico .. 119 D5
Monte Alegre, Brazil .. 125 D8
Monte Azul, Brazil 125 G10
Monte Bello Is., Australia . 92 D2
Monte-Carlo, Monaco .. 21 E11
Monte Caseros, Argentina 126 C4
Monte Comán, Argentina 126 C2
Monte Cristi, Dom. Rep. . 121 C5
Monte Lindo →, Paraguay 126 A4
Monte Patria, Chile 126 C1
Monte Quemado, Argentina 126 B3
Monte Redondo, Portugal 34 F2
Monte Rio, U.S.A. 116 G4
Monte San Giovanni Campano, Italy 30 A6
Monte San Savino, Italy . 29 E8
Monte Sant' Ángelo, Italy 29 G12
Monte Santu, C. di, Italy . 30 B2
Monte Vista, U.S.A. ... 115 H10
Montealegre del Castillo, Spain 33 G3
Montebello, Canada ... 102 C5
Montebello Iónico, Italy . 31 E8
Montebelluna, Italy ... 29 C9
Montebourg, France ... 18 C5
Montecastrilli, Italy ... 29 F9
Montecatini Terme, Italy . 28 E7
Montecito, U.S.A. 117 L7
Montecristo, Italy 28 F7
Montefalco, Italy 29 F9
Montefiascone, Italy ... 29 F9
Montefrío, Spain 35 H7
Montegiórgio, Italy 29 E10
Montego Bay, Jamaica .. 120 C4
Montehermoso, Spain .. 34 E4
Montejicar, Spain 35 H7
Montélimar, France 21 D8
Montella, Italy 31 B8
Montellano, Spain 35 J5
Montello, U.S.A. 112 D10
Montemor-o-Novo, Portugal 35 G2
Montemor-o-Velho, Portugal 34 E2
Montemorelos, Mexico .. 119 B5
Montendre, France 20 C3
Montenegro, Brazil 127 B5
Montenegro □, Yugoslavia 40 D3
Montenero di Bisáccia, Italy 29 G11
Montepuez, Mozam. 87 E4
Montepuez →, Mozam. . 87 E5
Montepulciano, Italy ... 29 E8
Montereale, Italy 29 F10
Montereau-Faut-Yonne, France 19 D9
Monterey, U.S.A. 116 J5
Monterey B., U.S.A. ... 116 J5
Montería, Colombia ... 124 B3
Monteros, Argentina ... 126 B2
Monterotondo, Italy ... 29 F9
Monterrey, Mexico 118 B4
Montes Claros, Brazil .. 125 G10
Montesano, U.S.A. 116 D3
Montesano sulla Marcellana, Italy 31 B8
Montesárchio, Italy 31 A7
Montescaglioso, Italy .. 31 B9
Montesilvano, Italy 29 F11
Montevarchi, Italy 29 E8
Montevideo, Uruguay .. 127 C4
Montevideo, U.S.A. ... 112 C7
Montezuma, U.S.A. ... 112 E8
Montfaucon, France ... 18 E5
Montfaucon-d'Argonne, France 19 C12
Montfaucon-en-Velay, France 21 C8
Montfort, France 18 D5
Montfort-le-Gesnois, France 18 D7
Montgenèvre, France .. 21 D10
Montgomery = Sahiwal, Pakistan 68 D5
Montgomery, U.K. 13 E4
Montgomery, Ala., U.S.A. 109 J2
Montgomery, Pa., U.S.A. 110 E8
Montgomery, W. Va., U.S.A. 108 F5
Montgomery City, U.S.A. 112 F9
Montguyon, France ... 20 C3
Monthermé, France ... 19 C11
Monthey, Switz. 25 J2
Monthois, France 19 C11
Monti, Italy 30 B2

Monticelli d'Ongina, Italy . 28 C6
Monticello, Ark., U.S.A. .. 113 J9
Monticello, Fla., U.S.A. .. 109 K4
Monticello, Ind., U.S.A. .. 108 E2
Monticello, Iowa, U.S.A. . 112 D9
Monticello, Ky., U.S.A. .. 109 G3
Monticello, Minn., U.S.A. 112 C8
Monticello, Miss., U.S.A. . 113 K9
Monticello, N.Y., U.S.A. . 111 E10
Monticello, Utah, U.S.A. . 115 H9
Montichiari, Italy 28 C7
Montier-en-Der, France . 19 D11
Montignac, France 20 C5
Montigny-Metz, France . 19 C13
Montigny-sur-Aube, France 19 E11
Montijo, Portugal 35 G2
Montijo, Spain 35 G4
Montilla, Spain 35 H6
Montivilliers, France ... 18 C7
Montluçon, France 19 F9
Montmagny, Canada ... 103 C5
Montmarault, France .. 19 F9
Montmartre, Canada ... 105 C8
Montmédy, France 19 C12
Montmélian, France ... 21 C10
Montmirail, France ... 19 D10
Montmoreau-St-Cybard, France 20 C4
Montmorillon, France .. 20 B4
Montmort-Lucy, France . 19 D10
Monto, Australia 94 C5
Montoire-sur-le-Loir, France 18 E7
Montório al Vomano, Italy 29 F10
Montoro, Spain 35 G6
Montour Falls, U.S.A. .. 110 D8
Montoursville, U.S.A. .. 110 E8
Montpelier, Idaho, U.S.A. 114 E8
Montpelier, Vt., U.S.A. . 111 B12
Montpellier, France ... 20 E7
Montpezat-de-Quercy, France 20 D5
Montpon-Ménestérol, France 20 D4
Montréal, Canada 102 C5
Montréal, Aude, France .. 20 E6
Montréal, Gers, France . 20 E4
Montreal →, Canada ... 102 C3
Montreal L., Canada ... 105 C7
Montreal Lake, Canada .. 105 C7
Montredon-Labessonnié, France 20 E6
Montrésor, France 18 E8
Montret, France 19 F12
Montreuil, Pas-de-Calais, France 19 B8
Montreuil, Seine-St-Denis, France 19 D9
Montreuil-Bellay, France . 18 E6
Montreux, Switz. 25 J2
Montrevel-en-Bresse, France 19 F12
Montrichard, France ... 18 E8
Montrose, U.K. 14 E6
Montrose, Colo., U.S.A. . 115 G10
Montrose, Pa., U.S.A. .. 111 E9
Monts, Pte. des, Canada . 103 C6
Montsalvy, France 20 D6
Montsant, Serra de, Spain . 32 D6
Montsauche-les-Settons, France 19 E11
Montsec, Serra del, Spain . 32 C5
Montserrat, Spain 32 D6
Montserrat ■, W. Indies . 121 C7
Montuenga, Spain 34 D6
Montuiri, Spain 37 B9
Monywa, Burma 67 H19
Monza, Italy 28 C6
Monze, Zambia 87 F2
Monze, C., Pakistan ... 68 G2
Monzón, Spain 32 D5
Mooers, U.S.A. 111 B11
Mooi →, S. Africa 89 D5
Mooi River, S. Africa .. 89 D4
Moonah →, Australia .. 94 C2
Moonda, L., Australia .. 94 D3
Moonie, Australia 95 D5
Moonie →, Australia .. 95 D4
Moonta, Australia 95 E2
Moora, Australia 93 F2
Moorcroft, U.S.A. 112 C2
Moore →, Australia ... 93 F2
Moore, L., Australia ... 93 E2
Moore Park, Australia .. 94 C5
Moore Reefs, Australia . 94 B4
Moorefield, U.S.A. 108 F6
Moores Res., U.S.A. ... 111 B13
Moorfoot Hills, U.K. ... 14 F5
Moorhead, U.S.A. 112 B6
Moormerland, Germany . 24 B3
Moorpark, U.S.A. 117 L8
Moorreesburg, S. Africa . 88 E2
Moosburg, Germany ... 25 G7
Moose →, Canada 102 B3
Moose →, U.S.A. 111 C9
Moose Creek, Canada .. 111 A10
Moose Factory, Canada . 102 B3
Moose Jaw, Canada ... 105 C7
Moose Jaw →, Canada . 105 C7
Moose Lake, Canada ... 105 C8
Moose Lake, U.S.A. ... 112 B8
Moose Mountain Prov. Park, Canada 105 D8
Moosehead L., U.S.A. .. 109 C11
Mooselookmeguntic L., U.S.A. 109 C10
Moosilauke, Mt., U.S.A. . 111 B13
Moosomin, Canada 105 C8
Moosonee, Canada 102 B3
Moosup, U.S.A. 111 E13
Mopane, S. Africa 89 C4
Mopeia Velha, Mozam. . 87 F4
Mopipi, Botswana 88 C3

Mopoi, C.A.R. 86 A2
Mopti, Mali 82 C4
Moqatta, Sudan 81 E4
Moqor, Afghan. 68 C2
Moquegua, Peru 124 G4
Mór, Hungary 42 C3
Mora, Cameroon 83 C7
Móra, Portugal 35 G2
Mora, Spain 35 F7
Mora, Sweden 10 C8
Mora, Minn., U.S.A. ... 112 C8
Mora, N. Mex., U.S.A. . 115 J11
Mora →, U.S.A. 113 H2
Mora de Ebro = Mòra d'Ebre, Spain 32 D5
Mora de Rubielos, Spain . 32 E4
Mòra d'Ebre, Spain ... 32 D5
Mòra la Nova, Spain ... 32 D5
Morača →, Montenegro, Yug. 40 D3
Moradabad, India 69 E8
Morafenobe, Madag. ... 89 B7
Morąg, Poland 44 E6
Moral de Calatrava, Spain 35 G7
Moraleja, Spain 34 E4
Moramanga, Madag. ... 89 B8
Moran, Kans., U.S.A. .. 113 G7
Moran, Wyo., U.S.A. .. 114 E8
Moranbah, Australia .. 94 C4
Morano Cálabro, Italy .. 31 C9
Morant Cays, Jamaica .. 120 C4
Morant Pt., Jamaica ... 120 C4
Morar, India 68 F8
Morar, L., U.K. 14 E3
Moratalla, Spain 33 G3
Moratuwa, Sri Lanka .. 66 R11
Morava →, Slovak Rep. . 27 C9
Moravia, U.S.A. 111 D8
Moravian Hts. = Českomoravská Vrchovina, Czech Rep. 26 B8
Moravica →, Serbia, Yug. 40 C4
Moraviţa, Romania 42 E6
Moravská Třebová, Czech Rep. 27 B9
Moravské Budějovice, Czech Rep. 26 B8
Morawa, Australia 93 E2
Morawhanna, Guyana .. 124 B7
Moray □, U.K. 14 D5
Moray Firth, U.K. 14 D5
Morbach, Germany ... 25 F3
Morbegno, Italy 28 B6
Morbi, India 68 H4
Morbihan □, France ... 18 E4
Mörbylånga, Sweden .. 11 H10
Morcenx, France 20 D3
Morcone, Italy 31 A7
Mordelles, France 18 D5
Morden, Canada 105 D9
Mordoğan, Turkey 39 C8
Mordovian Republic = Mordvinia □, Russia .. 48 C7
Mordovo, Russia 48 D5
Mordvinia □, Russia ... 48 C7
Mordy, Poland 45 F9
Morea, Greece 6 H10
Moreau →, U.S.A. 112 C4
Morecambe, U.K. 12 C5
Morecambe B., U.K. ... 12 C5
Moree, Australia 95 D4
Morehead, U.S.A. 108 F4
Morehead City, U.S.A. . 109 H7
Morel →, India 68 F7
Morelia, Mexico 118 D4
Morella, Australia 94 C3
Morella, Spain 32 E4
Morelos, Mexico 118 B3
Morelos □, Mexico ... 119 D5
Morena, India 68 F8
Morena, Sierra, Spain .. 35 G7
Moreni, Romania 43 F10
Moreno Valley, U.S.A. . 117 M10
Moresby I., Canada ... 104 C2
Morestel, France 21 C9
Moreton I., Australia .. 95 D5
Moreuil, France 19 C9
Morey, Spain 37 B10
Morez, France 19 F13
Morgan, U.S.A. 114 F8
Morgan City, U.S.A. ... 113 L9
Morgan Hill, U.S.A. ... 116 H5
Morganfield, U.S.A. ... 108 G2
Morganton, U.S.A. 109 H5
Morgantown, U.S.A. .. 108 F6
Morgenzon, S. Africa .. 89 D4
Morges, Switz. 25 J2
Morghak, Iran 71 D8
Morgongåva, Sweden .. 10 E10
Morhange, France 19 D13
Morhar →, India 69 G11
Mori, Italy 28 C7
Moriarty, U.S.A. 115 J10
Moribaya, Guinea 82 D3
Morice L., Canada 104 C3
Moriki, Nigeria 83 C6
Morinville, Canada ... 104 C6
Morioka, Japan 54 E10
Moris, Mexico 118 B3
Morlaàs, France 20 E3
Morlaix, France 18 D3
Mörlunda, Sweden ... 11 G9
Mormanno, Italy 31 C8
Mormant, France 19 D9
Mornington, Australia . 95 F4
Mornington, I., Chile .. 128 F1
Mornington I., Australia 94 B2
Mórnos →, Greece ... 38 C3
Moro, Pakistan 68 F2
Moro, Sudan 81 E3

Moro →, Pakistan 68 E2
Moro G., Phil. 61 H5
Morocco ■, N. Afr. 78 B4
Morogoro, Tanzania ... 86 D4
Morogoro □, Tanzania . 86 D4
Moroleón, Mexico 118 C4
Morombe, Madag. 89 C7
Moron, Argentina 126 C4
Morón, Cuba 120 B4
Morón de Almazán, Spain 32 D2
Morón de la Frontera, Spain 35 H5
Morona →, Peru 124 D3
Morondava, Madag. ... 89 C7
Morondo, Ivory C. 82 D3
Morongo Valley, U.S.A. 117 L10
Moroni, Comoros Is. .. 77 H8
Moroni, U.S.A. 114 G8
Morotai, Indonesia ... 63 D7
Moroto, Uganda 86 B3
Moroto Summit, Kenya 86 B3
Morozov, Bulgaria 41 D9
Morozovsk, Russia ... 49 F5
Morpeth, U.K. 12 B6
Morphou, Cyprus 36 D11
Morphou Bay, Cyprus . 36 D11
Morrilton, U.S.A. 113 H8
Morrinhos, Brazil 125 G9
Morrinsville, N.Z. 91 G5
Morris, Canada 105 D9
Morris, Ill., U.S.A. 112 E10
Morris, Minn., U.S.A. .. 112 C7
Morris, N.Y., U.S.A. ... 111 D9
Morris, Pa., U.S.A. 110 E7
Morris, Mt., Australia . 93 E5
Morrisburg, Canada ... 111 B9
Morristown, Ariz., U.S.A. 115 K7
Morristown, N.J., U.S.A. 111 F10
Morristown, N.Y., U.S.A. 111 B9
Morristown, Tenn., U.S.A. 109 G4
Morrisville, N.Y., U.S.A. 111 D9
Morrisville, Pa., U.S.A. . 111 F10
Morrisville, Vt., U.S.A. . 111 B12
Morro, Pta., Chile 126 B1
Morro Bay, U.S.A. ... 116 K6
Morro del Jable, Canary Is. 37 F5
Morro Jable, Pta. de, Canary Is. 37 F5
Morrosquillo, G. de, Colombia 120 E4
Mörrum, Sweden 11 H8
Morrumbene, Mozam. . 89 C6
Mörrumsån →, Sweden 11 H8
Mors, Denmark 11 H2
Morshansk, Russia ... 48 D5
Mörsil, Sweden 10 A7
Mortagne →, France .. 19 D13
Mortagne-au-Perche, France 18 D7
Mortagne-sur-Gironde, France 20 C3
Mortagne-sur-Sèvre, France 18 F6
Mortain, France 18 D6
Mortara, Italy 28 C5
Morteau, France 19 E13
Morteros, Argentina .. 126 C3
Mortlach, Canada 105 C7
Mortlake, Australia ... 95 F3
Morton, Tex., U.S.A. .. 113 J3
Morton, Wash., U.S.A. 116 D4
Morundah, Australia .. 95 E4
Moruya, Australia 95 F5
Morvan, France 19 E11
Morven, Australia 95 D4
Morvern, U.K. 14 E3
Morwell, Australia ... 95 F4
Moryń, Poland 45 F1
Morzine, France 19 F13
Mosalsk, Russia 46 E8
Mosbach, Germany ... 25 F5
Mošćenice, Croatia ... 29 C11
Mosciano Sant' Ángelo, Italy 29 F10
Moscos Is. = Maungmagan Is., Burma 64 E1
Moscow = Moskva, Russia 46 E9
Moscow, Idaho, U.S.A. 114 C5
Moscow, Pa., U.S.A. .. 111 E9
Mosel →, Europe 19 B14
Moselle = Mosel →, Europe 19 B14
Moselle □, France 19 D13
Moses Lake, U.S.A. ... 114 C4
Mosgiel, N.Z. 91 L3
Moshaweng →, S. Africa 88 D3
Moshi, Tanzania 86 C4
Moshupa, Botswana .. 88 C4
Mosina, Poland 45 F3
Mosjøen, Norway 8 D15
Moskenesøya, Norway . 8 C15
Moskenstraumen, Norway 8 C15
Moskva, Russia 46 E9
Moskva →, Russia ... 46 E10
Moslavačka Gora, Croatia 29 C13
Mosomane, Botswana . 88 C4
Moson-magyaróvár, Hungary 42 C2
Mošorin, Serbia, Yug. . 42 E5
Mospino, Ukraine 47 J9
Mosquera, Colombia .. 124 C3
Mosquero, U.S.A. 113 H3
Mosqueruela, Spain .. 32 E4
Mosquitia, Honduras .. 120 C3
Mosquito Coast = Mosquitia, Honduras .. 120 C3
Mosquito Creek L., U.S.A. 110 E4
Mosquito L., Canada .. 105 A8
Mosquitos, G. de los, Panama 120 E3
Moss, Norway 9 G14
Moss Vale, Australia .. 95 E5
Mossbank, Canada ... 105 D7
Mossburn, N.Z. 91 L2
Mosselbaai, S. Africa .. 88 E3

Mossendjo, *Congo* 84 E2
Mossgiel, *Australia* 95 E3
Mossingen, *Germany* 25 G5
Mossman, *Australia* 94 B4
Mossoró, *Brazil* 125 E11
Mossuril, *Mozam.* 87 E5
Most, *Czech Rep.* 26 A6
Mosta, *Malta* 36 D1
Moṣṭafāābād, *Iran* 71 C7
Mostaganem, *Algeria* 78 A6
Mostar, *Bos.-H.* 42 G2
Mostardas, *Brazil* 127 C5
Mostiska = Mostyska,
  Ukraine 47 H2
Móstoles, *Spain* 34 E7
Mosty = Masty, *Belarus* .. 46 F3
Mostyska, *Ukraine* 47 H2
Mosul = Al Mawṣil, *Iraq* .. 70 B4
Mosúlpo, *S. Korea* 57 H14
Mota, *Ethiopia* 81 E4
Mota del Cuervo, *Spain* ... 33 F2
Mota del Marqués, *Spain* .. 34 D5
Motagua →, *Guatemala* ... 120 C2
Motala, *Sweden* 11 F9
Motaze, *Mozam.* 89 C5
Moțca, *Romania* 43 C11
Moth, *India* 69 G8
Motherwell, *U.K.* 14 F5
Motihari, *India* 69 F11
Motilla del Palancar, *Spain* . 33 F3
Motnik, *Slovenia* 29 B11
Motovun, *Croatia* 29 C10
Motozintla de Mendoza,
  Mexico 119 D6
Motril, *Spain* 35 J7
Motru, *Romania* 42 F7
Motru →, *Romania* 43 F8
Mott, *U.S.A.* 112 B3
Móttola, *Italy* 31 B10
Motueka, *N.Z.* 91 J4
Motueka →, *N.Z.* 91 J4
Motul, *Mexico* 119 C7
Mouchalagane →, *Canada* . 103 B6
Moúdhros, *Greece* 39 B7
Mouding, *China* 58 E3
Moudjeria, *Mauritania* 82 B2
Moudon, *Switz.* 25 J2
Mouila, *Gabon* 84 E2
Moulamein, *Australia* 95 F3
Mouliana, *Greece* 36 D7
Moulins, *France* 19 F10
Moulmein, *Burma* 67 L20
Moulouya, O. →, *Morocco* 78 B5
Moultrie, *U.S.A.* 109 K4
Moultrie, L., *U.S.A.* 109 J5
Mound City, *Mo., U.S.A.* . 112 E7
Mound City, *S. Dak.,
  U.S.A.* 112 C4
Moúnda, Ákra, *Greece* ... 38 C2
Moundou, *Chad* 79 G9
Moundsville, *U.S.A.* 110 G4
Moung, *Cambodia* 64 F4
Mount Airy, *U.S.A.* 109 G5
Mount Albert, *Canada* 110 B5
Mount Barker, *S. Austral.,
  Australia* 95 F2
Mount Barker, *W. Austral.,
  Australia* 93 F2
Mount Beauty, *Australia* .. 95 F4
Mount Brydges, *Canada* .. 110 D3
Mount Burr, *Australia* 95 F3
Mount Carmel, *Ill., U.S.A.* 108 F2
Mount Carmel, *Pa., U.S.A.* 111 F8
Mount Charleston, *U.S.A.* . 117 J11
Mount Clemens, *U.S.A.* .. 110 D2
Mount Coolon, *Australia* .. 94 C4
Mount Darwin, *Zimbabwe* . 87 F3
Mount Desert I., *U.S.A.* .. 109 C11
Mount Dora, *U.S.A.* 109 L5
Mount Edziza Prov. Park,
  Canada 104 B2
Mount Fletcher, *S. Africa* . 89 E4
Mount Forest, *Canada* 102 D3
Mount Gambier, *Australia* . 95 F3
Mount Garnet, *Australia* .. 94 B4
Mount Holly, *U.S.A.* 111 G10
Mount Holly Springs, *U.S.A.* 110 F7
Mount Hope, *N.S.W.,
  Australia* 95 E4
Mount Hope, *S. Austral.,
  Australia* 95 E2
Mount Isa, *Australia* 94 C2
Mount Jewett, *U.S.A.* 110 E6
Mount Kisco, *U.S.A.* 111 E11
Mount Laguna, *U.S.A.* ... 117 N10
Mount Larcom, *Australia* . 94 C5
Mount Lofty Ra., *Australia* 95 E2
Mount Magnet, *Australia* .. 93 E2
Mount Maunganui, *N.Z.* .. 91 G6
Mount Molloy, *Australia* .. 94 B4
Mount Morgan, *Australia* .. 94 C5
Mount Morris, *U.S.A.* 110 D7
Mount Pearl, *Canada* 103 C9
Mount Penn, *U.S.A.* 111 F9
Mount Perry, *Australia* ... 95 D5
Mount Pleasant, *Iowa,
  U.S.A.* 112 E9
Mount Pleasant, *Mich.,
  U.S.A.* 108 D3
Mount Pleasant, *Pa., U.S.A.* 110 F5
Mount Pleasant, *S.C.,
  U.S.A.* 109 J6
Mount Pleasant, *Tenn.,
  U.S.A.* 109 H2
Mount Pleasant, *Tex.,
  U.S.A.* 113 J7
Mount Pleasant, *Utah,
  U.S.A.* 114 G8
Mount Pocono, *U.S.A.* ... 111 E9
Mount Rainier Nat. Park,
  U.S.A. 116 D5

Mount Revelstoke Nat. Park,
  Canada 104 C5
Mount Robson Prov. Park,
  Canada 104 C5
Mount Selinda, *Zimbabwe* . 89 C5
Mount Shasta, *U.S.A.* 114 F2
Mount Signal, *U.S.A.* 117 N11
Mount Sterling, *Ill., U.S.A.* 112 F9
Mount Sterling, *Ky., U.S.A.* 108 F4
Mount Surprise, *Australia* . 94 B3
Mount Union, *U.S.A.* 110 F7
Mount Upton, *U.S.A.* 111 D9
Mount Vernon, *Ill., U.S.A.* 108 F1
Mount Vernon, *Ind., U.S.A.* 112 F10
Mount Vernon, *N.Y.,
  U.S.A.* 111 F11
Mount Vernon, *Ohio,
  U.S.A.* 110 F2
Mount Vernon, *Wash.,
  U.S.A.* 116 B4
Mountain Ash, *U.K.* 13 F4
Mountain Center, *U.S.A.* . 117 M10
Mountain City, *Nev., U.S.A.* 114 F6
Mountain City, *Tenn.,
  U.S.A.* 109 G5
Mountain Dale, *U.S.A.* ... 111 E10
Mountain Grove, *U.S.A.* . 113 G8
Mountain Home, *Ark.,
  U.S.A.* 113 G8
Mountain Home, *Idaho,
  U.S.A.* 114 E6
Mountain Iron, *U.S.A.* ... 112 B8
Mountain Pass, *U.S.A.* ... 117 K11
Mountain View, *Ark.,
  U.S.A.* 113 H8
Mountain View, *Calif.,
  U.S.A.* 116 H4
Mountain View, *Hawaii,
  U.S.A.* 106 J17
Mountainair, *U.S.A.* 115 J10
Mountlake Terrace, *U.S.A.* 116 C4
Mountmellick, *Ireland* 15 C4
Mountrath, *Ireland* 15 D4
Moura, *Australia* 94 C4
Moura, *Brazil* 124 D6
Moura, *Portugal* 35 G3
Mourão, *Portugal* 35 G3
Mourdi, Dépression du,
  Chad 79 E10
Mourdiah, *Mali* 82 C3
Mourenx-Ville-Nouvelle,
  France 20 E3
Mouri, *Ghana* 83 D4
Mourilyan, *Australia* 94 B4
Mourmelon-le-Grand, *France* 19 C11
Mourne →, *U.K.* 15 B4
Mourne Mts., *U.K.* 15 B5
Mourniaí, *Greece* 36 D6
Mournies = Mourniaí,
  Greece 36 D6
Mouscron, *Belgium* 17 D3
Moussoro, *Chad* 79 F9
Mouthe, *France* 19 F13
Moutier, *Switz.* 25 H3
Moûtiers, *France* 21 C10
Moutohara, *N.Z.* 91 H6
Moutong, *Indonesia* 63 D6
Mouy, *France* 19 C9
Mouzáki, *Greece* 38 B3
Mouzon, *France* 19 C12
Movas, *Mexico* 118 B3
Moville, *Ireland* 15 A4
Mowandjum, *Australia* 92 C3
Moy →, *Ireland* 15 B2
Moyale, *Kenya* 81 G4
Moyamba, *S. Leone* 82 D2
Moyen Atlas, *Morocco* 78 B4
Moyne, L. le, *Canada* 103 A6
Moyo, *Indonesia* 62 F5
Moyobamba, *Peru* 124 E3
Moyyero →, *Russia* 51 C11
Moyynty, *Kazakhstan* 50 E8
Mozambique =
  Moçambique, *Mozam.* ... 87 F5
Mozambique ■, *Africa* ... 87 F4
Mozambique Chan., *Africa* 89 B7
Mozdok, *Russia* 49 J7
Mozdūrān, *Iran* 71 B9
Mozhaysk, *Russia* 46 E9
Mozhga, *Russia* 48 B11
Mozhnābād, *Iran* 71 C9
Mozirje, *Slovenia* 29 B11
Mozyr = Mazyr, *Belarus* .. 47 F5
Mpanda, *Tanzania* 86 D3
Mpésoba, *Mali* 82 C3
Mphoengs, *Zimbabwe* 89 C4
Mpika, *Zambia* 87 E3
Mpulungu, *Zambia* 87 D3
Mpumalanga, *S. Africa* ... 89 D5
Mpumalanga □, *S. Africa* . 89 B5
Mpwapwa, *Tanzania* 86 D4
Mqanduli, *S. Africa* 89 E4
Mqinvartsveri = Kazbek,
  Russia 49 J7
Mrągowo, *Poland* 44 E8
Mramor, *Serbia, Yug.* 40 C5
Mrkonjić Grad, *Bos.-H.* .. 42 F2
Mrkopalj, *Croatia* 29 C11
Mrocza, *Poland* 45 E4
Msambansovu, *Zimbabwe* . 87 F3
M'sila →, *Algeria* 78 A6
Msoro, *Zambia* 87 E3
Msta →, *Russia* 46 C6
Mstislavl = Mstsislaw,
  Belarus 46 E6
Mstsislaw, *Belarus* 46 E6
Mszana Dolna, *Poland* 45 J7
Mszczonów, *Poland* 45 G7
Mtama, *Tanzania* 87 E4
Mtamvuna →, *S. Africa* .. 89 E5

Mtilikwe →, *Zimbabwe* .. 87 G3
Mtsensk, *Russia* 46 F9
Mtskheta, *Georgia* 49 K7
Mtubatuba, *S. Africa* 89 D5
Mtwalume, *S. Africa* 89 E5
Mtwara-Mikindani, *Tanzania* 87 E5
Mu Gia, Deo, *Vietnam* ... 64 D5
Mu Us Shamo, *China* 56 E5
Muang Chiang Rai = Chiang
  Rai, *Thailand* 58 H2
Muang Khong, *Laos* 64 E5
Muang Lamphun, *Thailand* . 64 C2
Muang Pak Beng, *Laos* ... 58 H3
Muar, *Malaysia* 65 L4
Muarabungo, *Indonesia* ... 62 E2
Muaraenim, *Indonesia* 62 E2
Muarajuloi, *Indonesia* 62 E4
Muarakaman, *Indonesia* ... 62 E5
Muaratebo, *Indonesia* 62 E2
Muaratembesi, *Indonesia* .. 62 E2
Muaratewe, *Indonesia* 62 E4
Mubarakpur, *India* 69 F10
Mubarraz = Al Mubarraz,
  Si. Arabia 71 E6
Mubende, *Uganda* 86 B3
Mubi, *Nigeria* 83 C7
Mubur, Pulau, *Indonesia* .. 65 L6
Mucajaí →, *Brazil* 124 C6
Muchachos, Roque de los,
  Canary Is. 37 F2
Müchein, *Germany* 24 D7
Muchinga Mts., *Zambia* ... 87 E3
Muchkapskiy, *Russia* 48 E6
Muchuan, *China* 58 C5
Muck, *U.K.* 14 E2
Muckadilla, *Australia* 95 D4
Mucur, *Turkey* 72 C6
Mucuri, *Brazil* 125 G11
Mucusso, *Angola* 88 B3
Muda, *Canary Is.* 37 F6
Mudanjiang, *China* 57 B15
Mudanya, *Turkey* 41 F12
Muddy Cr. →, *U.S.A.* 115 H8
Mudgee, *Australia* 95 E4
Mudjatik →, *Canada* 105 B7
Mudurnu, *Turkey* 72 B4
Muecate, *Mozam.* 87 E4
Mueda, *Mozam.* 87 E4
Mueller Ra., *Australia* 92 C4
Muende, *Mozam.* 87 E3
Muerto, Mar, *Mexico* 119 D6
Mufu Shan, *China* 59 C10
Mufulira, *Zambia* 87 E2
Mufumbiro Range, *Africa* . 86 C2
Mugardos, *Spain* 34 B2
Muge →, *Portugal* 35 F2
Múggia, *Italy* 29 C10
Mughal Sarai, *India* 69 G10
Mughayrā', *Si. Arabia* 70 D3
Mugi, *Japan* 55 H7
Mugia = Muxía, *Spain* 34 B1
Mugila, Mts.,
  Dem. Rep. of the Congo . 86 D2
Muğla, *Turkey* 39 D10
Muğla □, *Turkey* 39 D10
Muglad, *Sudan* 81 E2
Müglizh, *Bulgaria* 41 D9
Mugu, *Nepal* 69 E10
Muhammad, Ras, *Egypt* .. 70 E2
Muhammad Qol, *Sudan* ... 80 C4
Muhammadabad, *India* ... 69 F10
Muhesi →, *Tanzania* 86 D4
Mühlacker, *Germany* 25 G4
Mühldorf, *Germany* 25 G8
Mühlhausen, *Germany* 24 D6
Mühlig Hofmann fjell,
  Antarctica 5 D3
Mühlviertel, *Austria* 26 C7
Muhos, *Finland* 8 D22
Muhu, *Estonia* 9 G20
Muhutwe, *Tanzania* 86 C3
Muine Bheag, *Ireland* 15 D5
Muir, L., *Australia* 93 F2
Mukacheve, *Ukraine* 47 H1
Mukachevo = Mukacheve,
  Ukraine 47 H1
Mukah, *Malaysia* 62 D4
Mukandwara, *India* 68 G6
Mukawwa, Geziret, *Egypt* 80 C4
Mukawwar, *Sudan* 80 C4
Mukdahan, *Thailand* 64 D5
Mukden = Shenyang, *China* 57 D12
Mukerian, *India* 68 D6
Mukhtolovo, *Russia* 48 C6
Mukhtuya = Lensk, *Russia* . 51 C12
Mukinbudin, *Australia* 93 F2
Mukishi,
  Dem. Rep. of the Congo . 87 D1
Mukomuko, *Indonesia* 62 E2
Mukomwenze,
  Dem. Rep. of the Congo . 86 D2
Muktsar, *India* 68 D6
Mukur = Moqor, *Afghan.* . 68 C2
Mukutawa →, *Canada* ... 105 C9
Mukwela, *Zambia* 87 F2
Mula, *Spain* 33 G3
Mula →, *Pakistan* 68 F2
Mulange,
  Dem. Rep. of the Congo . 86 C2
Mulanje, *Malawi* 87 F4
Mulchén, *Chile* 126 D1
Mulde →, *Germany* 24 D8
Mule Creek Junction, *U.S.A.* 112 D2
Muleba, *Tanzania* 86 C3
Mulejé, *Mexico* 118 B2
Muleshoe, *U.S.A.* 113 H3
Muletta, Gara, *Ethiopia* .. 81 F5
Mulgrave, *Canada* 103 C7
Mulhacén, *Spain* 35 H7
Mülheim, *Germany* 24 D2

Mulhouse, *France* 19 E14
Muli, *China* 58 D3
Muling, *China* 57 B16
Mull, *U.K.* 14 E3
Mull, Sound of, *U.K.* 14 E3
Mullaittivu, *Sri Lanka* 66 Q12
Mullen, *U.S.A.* 112 D4
Mullens, *U.S.A.* 108 G5
Muller, Pegunungan,
  Indonesia 62 D4
Mullet Pen., *Ireland* 15 B1
Mullewa, *Australia* 93 E2
Müllheim, *Germany* 25 H3
Mulligan →, *Australia* 94 D2
Mullingar, *Ireland* 15 C4
Mullins, *U.S.A.* 109 H6
Mullsjö, *Sweden* 11 G7
Mullumbimby, *Australia* .. 95 D5
Mulobezi, *Zambia* 87 F2
Mulroy B., *Ireland* 15 A4
Multan, *Pakistan* 68 D4
Mulumbe, Mts.,
  Dem. Rep. of the Congo . 87 D2
Mulungushi Dam, *Zambia* . 87 E2
Mulvane, *U.S.A.* 113 G6
Mulwad, *Sudan* 80 D3
Mumbai, *India* 66 K8
Mumbwa, *Zambia* 87 F2
Mumra, *Russia* 49 H8
Mun →, *Thailand* 64 E5
Muna, *Indonesia* 63 F6
Munabao, *India* 68 G4
Munamagi, *Estonia* 9 H22
Münchberg, *Germany* 25 E7
Müncheberg, *Germany* ... 24 C10
München, *Germany* 25 G7
Munchen-Gladbach =
  Mönchengladbach,
  Germany 24 D2
Muncho Lake, *Canada* 104 B3
Munch'ŏn, *N. Korea* 57 E14
Muncie, *U.S.A.* 108 E3
Muncoonie, L., *Australia* . 94 D2
Mundabbera, *Australia* ... 95 D5
Munday, *U.S.A.* 113 J5
Münden, *Germany* 24 D5
Mundiwindi, *Australia* 92 D3
Mundo →, *Spain* 33 G2
Mundo Novo, *Brazil* 125 F10
Mundra, *India* 68 H3
Mundrabilla, *Australia* 93 F4
Munera, *Spain* 33 F2
Mungallala, *Australia* 95 D4
Mungallala Cr. →, *Australia* 95 D4
Mungana, *Australia* 94 B3
Mungaoli, *India* 68 G8
Mungari, *Mozam.* 87 F3
Mungbere,
  Dem. Rep. of the Congo . 86 B2
Mungeli, *India* 69 H9
Munger, *India* 69 G12
Mungila, Mts.,
  Dem. Rep. of the Congo . 86 D2
Munich = München,
  Germany 25 G7
Munising, *U.S.A.* 108 B2
Munka-Ljungby, *Sweden* .. 11 H6
Munkebo, *Denmark* 11 J4
Munkedal, *Sweden* 11 F5
Munkfors, *Sweden* 10 E7
Munku-Sardyk, *Russia* ... 51 D11
Münnerstadt, *Germany* ... 25 E6
Muñoz Gamero, Pen., *Chile* 128 G2
Munroe L., *Canada* 105 B9
Munsan, *S. Korea* 57 F14
Munster, *France* 19 D14
Munster, *Niedersachsen,
  Germany* 24 C6
Münster,
  *Nordrhein-Westfalen,
  Germany* 24 D3
Munster □, *Ireland* 15 D3
Muntadgin, *Australia* 93 F2
Muntele Mare, Vf., *Romania* 43 D8
Muntok, *Indonesia* 62 E3
Munyama, *Zambia* 87 F2
Munzur Dağları, *Turkey* .. 73 C8
Muong Beng, *Laos* 58 G3
Muong Boum, *Vietnam* ... 58 F4
Muong Et, *Laos* 64 B5
Muong Hai, *Laos* 58 G3
Muong Hiem, *Laos* 58 B4
Muong Houn, *Laos* 58 G3
Muong Hung, *Vietnam* ... 58 G4
Muong Kau, *Laos* 64 E5
Muong Khao, *Laos* 64 C4
Muong Liep, *Laos* 64 C3
Muong May, *Laos* 64 E6
Muong Ngeun, *Laos* 58 G3
Muong Ngoi, *Laos* 58 G4
Muong Nhie, *Vietnam* 58 F4
Muong Nong, *Laos* 64 D6
Muong Ou Tay, *Laos* 58 F3
Muong Oua, *Laos* 64 C3
Muong Peun, *Laos* 58 B4
Muong Phalane, *Laos* 64 D6
Muong Phieng, *Laos* 64 C3
Muong Phine, *Laos* 64 D6
Muong Sai, *Laos* 58 G3
Muong Saiapoun, *Laos* ... 64 C3
Muong Sen, *Vietnam* 64 C5
Muong Sing, *Laos* 58 G3
Muong Son, *Laos* 58 B4
Muong Soui, *Laos* 64 C4
Muong Va, *Laos* 58 G4
Muong Xia, *Vietnam* 64 B5
Muonionjoki →, *Finland* .. 8 C20
Muping, *China* 57 F11
Muqaddam, Wadi →, *Sudan* 80 D3

Muqdisho, *Somali Rep.* .. 74 G4
Mur →, *Austria* 27 E9
Mur-de-Bretagne, *France* . 18 D4
Muradiye, *Manisa, Turkey* . 39 C9
Muradiye, *Van, Turkey* ... 73 C10
Murakami, *Japan* 54 E9
Murallón, Cerro, *Chile* ... 128 F2
Muranda, *Rwanda* 86 C2
Murang'a, *Kenya* 86 C4
Murashi, *Russia* 50 D5
Murat, *France* 20 C6
Murat →, *Turkey* 73 C9
Murat Dağı, *Turkey* 39 C11
Muratlı, *Turkey* 41 E11
Murato, *France* 21 F13
Murau, *Austria* 26 D7
Muravera, *Italy* 30 C2
Murayama, *Japan* 54 E10
Murban, *U.A.E.* 71 F7
Murça, *Portugal* 34 D3
Murchison →, *Australia* .. 93 E1
Murchison, Mt., *Antarctica* . 5 D11
Murchison Falls, *Uganda* .. 86 B3
Murchison Ra., *Australia* .. 94 C1
Murchison Rapids, *Malawi* . 87 F3
Murcia, *Spain* 33 G3
Murcia □, *Spain* 33 H3
Murdo, *U.S.A.* 112 D4
Murdoch Pt., *Australia* ... 94 A3
Mürefte, *Turkey* 41 F11
Mureş □, *Romania* 43 D9
Mureş →, *Romania* 42 D5
Mureşul = Mureş →,
  Romania 42 D5
Muret, *France* 20 E5
Murewa, *Zimbabwe* 89 C5
Murfreesboro, *N.C., U.S.A.* 109 G7
Murfreesboro, *Tenn., U.S.A.* 109 H2
Murgab = Murghob,
  Tajikistan 50 F8
Murgab →, *Turkmenistan* . 71 B9
Murgenella, *Australia* 92 B5
Murgeni, *Romania* 43 D13
Murgha Kibzai, *Pakistan* .. 68 D3
Murghob, *Tajikistan* 50 F8
Murgon, *Australia* 95 D5
Muri, *India* 69 H11
Muria, *Indonesia* 63 G14
Murias de Paredes, *Spain* . 34 C4
Muriel Mine, *Zimbabwe* .. 87 F3
Müritz, *Germany* 24 B8
Murka, *Kenya* 86 C4
Murliganj, *India* 69 G12
Murmansk, *Russia* 50 C4
Murnau, *Germany* 25 H7
Muro, *France* 21 F12
Muro, *Spain* 37 B10
Muro, C. de, *France* 21 G12
Muro de Alcoy, *Spain* 33 G4
Muro Lucano, *Italy* 31 B8
Murom, *Russia* 48 C6
Muroran, *Japan* 54 C10
Muros, *Spain* 34 C1
Muros y de Noya, Ría de,
  Spain 34 C1
Muroto, *Japan* 55 H7
Muroto-Misaki, *Japan* 55 H7
Murowana Goślina, *Poland* 45 F3
Murphy, *U.S.A.* 114 E5
Murphys, *U.S.A.* 116 G6
Murrat, *Sudan* 80 D2
Murrat Wells, *Sudan* 80 D2
Murray →, *Australia* 95 F2
Murray, *Ky., U.S.A.* 109 G1
Murray, *Utah, U.S.A.* 114 F8
Murray →, *Australia* 95 F2
Murray, L., *U.S.A.* 109 H5
Murray Bridge, *Australia* . 95 F2
Murray Harbour, *Canada* . 103 C7
Murraysburg, *S. Africa* ... 88 E3
Murree, *Pakistan* 68 C5
Murrieta, *U.S.A.* 117 M9
Murro di Porco, Capo, *Italy* 31 F8
Murrumbidgee →, *Australia* 95 E3
Murrumburrah, *Australia* . 95 E4
Murrurundi, *Australia* 95 E5
Murshid, *Sudan* 80 C3
Murshidabad, *India* 69 G13
Murska Sobota, *Slovenia* . 29 B13
Murtle L., *Canada* 104 C5
Murtoa, *Australia* 95 F3
Murtosa, *Portugal* 34 E2
Murungu, *Tanzania* 86 C3
Mururoa, *Pac. Oc.* 97 K14
Murwara, *India* 69 H9
Murwillumbah, *Australia* . 95 D5
Mürz →, *Austria* 26 D8
Mürzzuschlag, *Austria* 26 D8
Muş, *Turkey* 70 B4
Mûsa, Gebel, *Egypt* 70 D2
Musa Khel, *Pakistan* 68 D3
Mûsā Qal'eh, *Afghan.* 66 C4
Musaffargarh, *Pakistan* ... 66 D7
Musafirkhana, *India* 69 F9
Musala, *Bulgaria* 40 D7
Musala, *Indonesia* 62 D1
Musan, *N. Korea* 57 C15
Musangu,
  Dem. Rep. of the Congo . 87 D1
Musasa, *Tanzania* 86 C3
Musay'īd, *Qatar* 71 E6
Muscat = Masqat, *Oman* . 74 C6
Muscat & Oman = Oman ■,
  Asia 74 C6
Muscatine, *U.S.A.* 112 E9
Musgrave Harbour, *Canada* 103 C9
Musgrave Ranges, *Australia* 93 E5
Mushie,
  Dem. Rep. of the Congo . 84 E3
Mushin, *Nigeria* 83 D5

Musi →, *Indonesia* 62 E2
Muskeg →, *Canada* 104 A4
Muskegon, *U.S.A.* 108 D2
Muskegon →, *U.S.A.* 108 D2
Muskegon Heights, *U.S.A.* .. 108 D2
Muskogee, *U.S.A.* 113 H7
Muskoka, L., *Canada* 110 B5
Muskwa →, *Canada* 104 B4
Muslīmiyah, *Syria* 70 B3
Musmar, *Sudan* 80 D4
Musofu, *Zambia* 87 E2
Musoma, *Tanzania* 86 C3
Musquaro, L., *Canada* 103 B7
Musquodoboit Harbour,
    Canada 103 D7
Musselburgh, *U.K.* 14 F5
Musselshell →, *U.S.A.* 114 C10
Mussidan, *France* 20 C4
Mussomeli, *Italy* 30 E6
Mussoorie, *India* 68 D8
Mussuco, *Angola* 88 B2
Mustafakemalpaşa, *Turkey* . 41 F12
Mustang, *Nepal* 69 E10
Musters, L., *Argentina* ... 128 F3
Musudan, *N. Korea* 57 D15
Muswellbrook, *Australia* .. 95 E5
Muszyna, *Poland* 45 J7
Mût, *Egypt* 80 B2
Mut, *Turkey* 70 B2
Mutanda, *Mozam.* 89 C5
Mutanda, *Zambia* 87 E2
Mutare, *Zimbabwe* 87 F3
Muting, *Indonesia* 63 F10
Mutoko, *Zimbabwe* 89 B5
Mutoray, *Russia* 51 C11
Mutshatsha,
    Dem. Rep. of the Congo . 87 E1
Mutsu, *Japan* 54 D10
Mutsu-Wan, *Japan* 54 D10
Muttaburra, *Australia* ... 94 C3
Muttalip, *Turkey* 39 B12
Mutton I., *Ireland* 15 D2
Mutuáli, *Mozam.* 87 E4
Mutum Biyu, *Nigeria* 83 D7
Mutumbo,
    Dem. Rep. of the Congo . 87 E1
Muweilih, *Egypt* 75 E3
Muxía, *Spain* 34 B1
Muy Muy, *Nic.* 120 D2
Muyinga, *Burundi* 86 C3
Muynak, *Uzbekistan* 50 E6
Muzaffarabad, *Pakistan* .. 69 B5
Muzaffargarh, *Pakistan* .. 68 D4
Muzaffarnagar, *India* 68 E7
Muzaffarpur, *India* 69 F11
Muzafirpur, *Pakistan* 68 D3
Muzhi, *Russia* 50 C7
Muzillac, *France* 18 E4
Muzūra, *Egypt* 80 J7
Mvölö, *Sudan* 81 F2
Mvuma, *Zimbabwe* 87 F3
Mvurwi, *Zimbabwe* 87 F3
Mwadui, *Tanzania* 86 C3
Mwambo, *Tanzania* 87 E5
Mwandi, *Zambia* 87 F1
Mwanza,
    Dem. Rep. of the Congo . 86 D2
Mwanza, *Tanzania* 86 C3
Mwanza, *Zambia* 87 F1
Mwanza □, *Tanzania* 86 C3
Mwaya, *Tanzania* 87 D3
Mweelrea, *Ireland* 15 C2
Mweka,
    Dem. Rep. of the Congo . 84 E4
Mwenezi, *Zimbabwe* 87 G3
Mwenezi →, *Mozam.* 87 G3
Mwenga,
    Dem. Rep. of the Congo . 86 C2
Mweru, L., *Zambia* 87 D2
Mweza Range, *Zimbabwe* . 87 G3
Mwilambwe,
    Dem. Rep. of the Congo . 86 D2
Mwimbi, *Tanzania* 87 D3
Mwinilunga, *Zambia* 87 E1
My Tho, *Vietnam* 65 G6
Myajlar, *India* 68 F4
Myanaung, *Burma* 67 K19
Myanmar = Burma ■, *Asia* 67 J20
Myaungmya, *Burma* 67 L19
Myeik Kyunzu, *Burma* ... 65 G1
Myers Chuck, *U.S.A.* 104 B2
Myerstown, *U.S.A.* 111 F8
Myingyan, *Burma* 67 J19
Myitkyina, *Burma* 67 G20
Myjava, *Slovak Rep.* 27 C10
Mykhaylivka, *Ukraine* ... 47 J8
Mykines, *Færoe Is.* 8 E9
Mykolayiv, *Ukraine* 47 J7
Mymensingh, *Bangla.* ... 67 G17
Mynydd Du, *U.K.* 13 F4
Mýrdalsjökull, *Iceland* ... 8 E4
Myrhorod, *Ukraine* 47 H7
Myrtle Beach, *U.S.A.* 109 J6
Myrtle Creek, *U.S.A.* 114 E2
Myrtle Point, *U.S.A.* 114 E1
Myrtou, *Cyprus* 36 D12
Mysia, *Turkey* 41 G11
Myślenice, *Poland* 45 J6
Myślibórz, *Poland* 45 F1
Mysłowice, *Poland* 45 H6
Mysore = Karnataka □,
    India 66 N10
Mysore, *India* 66 N10
Mystic, *U.S.A.* 111 E13
Myszków, *Poland* 45 H6
Myszyniec, *Poland* 44 E8
Mytishchi, *Russia* 46 E9
Mývatn, *Iceland* 8 D5
Mže →, *Czech Rep.* 26 B6
Mzimba, *Malawi* 87 E3
Mzimkulu →, *S. Africa* ... 89 E5
Mzimvubu →, *S. Africa* .. 89 E4
Mzuzu, *Malawi* 87 E3

N

Na Hearadh = Harris, *U.K.* 14 D2
Na Noi, *Thailand* 64 C3
Na Phao, *Laos* 64 D5
Na Sam, *Vietnam* 58 F6
Na San, *Vietnam* 64 B5
Naab →, *Germany* 25 F8
Na'am, *Sudan* 81 F2
Na'am →, *Sudan* 81 F2
Naantali, *Finland* 9 F19
Naas, *Ireland* 15 C5
Nababeep, *S. Africa* 88 D2
Nabadwip = Navadwip,
    India 69 H13
Nabari, *Japan* 55 G8
Nabawa, *Australia* 93 E1
Nabberu, L., *Australia* .. 93 E3
Nabburg, *Germany* 25 F8
Naberezhnyye Chelny,
    Russia 48 C11
Nabeul, *Tunisia* 79 A8
Nabha, *India* 68 D7
Nabīd, *Iran* 71 D8
Nabire, *Indonesia* 63 E9
Nabisar, *Pakistan* 68 G3
Nabisipi →, *Canada* 103 B7
Nabiswera, *Uganda* 86 B3
Nablus = Nābulus,
    West Bank 75 C4
Naboomspruit, *S. Africa* . 89 C4
Nabou, *Burkina Faso* ... 82 C4
Nabua, *Phil.* 61 E5
Nābulus, *West Bank* 75 C4
Nacala, *Mozam.* 87 E5
Nacala-Velha, *Mozam.* .. 87 E5
Nacaome, *Honduras* 120 D2
Nacaroa, *Mozam.* 87 E4
Naches, *U.S.A.* 114 C3
Naches →, *U.S.A.* 116 D6
Nachicapau, L., *Canada* . 103 A6
Nachingwea, *Tanzania* .. 87 E4
Nachna, *India* 68 F4
Náchod, *Czech Rep.* 26 A9
Nacimiento L., *U.S.A.* ... 116 K6
Naco, *Mexico* 118 A3
Nacogdoches, *U.S.A.* ... 113 K7
Nácori Chico, *Mexico* ... 118 B3
Nacozari, *Mexico* 118 A3
Nadi, *Sudan* 80 D3
Nadiad, *India* 68 H5
Nădlac, *Romania* 42 D5
Nador, *Morocco* 78 B5
Nadur, *Malta* 36 C1
Nadūshan, *Iran* 71 C7
Nadvirna, *Ukraine* 47 H3
Nadvornaya = Nadvirna,
    Ukraine 47 H3
Nadym, *Russia* 50 C8
Nadym →, *Russia* 50 C8
Nærbø, *Norway* 9 G11
Næstved, *Denmark* 11 J5
Nafada, *Nigeria* 83 C7
Naft-e Safīd, *Iran* 71 D6
Naftshahr, *Iran* 70 C5
Nafud Desert = An Nafūd,
    Si. Arabia 70 D4
Nag Hammâdi, *Egypt* ... 80 B3
Naga, *Phil.* 61 E5
Nagahama, *Japan* 55 G8
Nagai, *Japan* 54 E10
Nagaland □, *India* 67 G19
Nagano, *Japan* 55 F9
Nagano □, *Japan* 55 F9
Nagaoka, *Japan* 55 F9
Nagappattinam, *India* .. 66 P11
Nagar →, *Bangla.* 69 G13
Nagar Parkar, *Pakistan* . 68 G4
Nagasaki, *Japan* 55 H4
Nagasaki □, *Japan* 55 H4
Nagato, *Japan* 55 G5
Nagaur, *India* 68 F5
Nagda, *India* 68 H6
Nagercoil, *India* 66 Q10
Nagina, *India* 69 E8
Nagīneh, *Iran* 71 C8
Nagir, *Pakistan* 69 A6
Naglarby, *Sweden* 10 D9
Nagod, *India* 69 G9
Nagold, *Germany* 25 G4
Nagold →, *Germany* ... 25 G4
Nagoorin, *Australia* ... 94 C5
Nagorno-Karabakh,
    Azerbaijan 70 B5
Nagornyy, *Russia* 51 D13
Nagoya, *Japan* 55 G8
Nagpur, *India* 66 J11
Nagua, *Dom. Rep.* 121 C6
Nagyatád, *Hungary* ... 42 D2
Nagyecsed, *Hungary* .. 42 C7
Nagykálló, *Hungary* ... 42 C6
Nagykanizsa, *Hungary* . 42 D2
Nagykáta, *Hungary* ... 42 C4
Nagykőrös, *Hungary* .. 42 C4
Naha, *Japan* 55 L3
Nahan, *India* 68 D7
Nahanni Butte, *Canada* . 104 A4
Nahanni Nat. Park, *Canada* 104 A4
Nahargarh, Mad. P., *India* 68 G6
Nahargarh, Raj., *India* .. 68 G7
Nahariyya, *Israel* 70 C2
Nahāvand, *Iran* 71 C6
Nahe →, *Germany* 25 F3
Nahîya, W. →, *Egypt* ... 80 B3
Naicá, *Mexico* 118 B3
Naicam, *Canada* 105 C8
Naikoon Prov. Park, *Canada* 104 C2
Naila, *Germany* 25 E7
Naimisharanya, *India* .. 69 F9
Nain, *Canada* 103 A7

Nā'īn, *Iran* 71 C7
Naini Tal, *India* 69 E8
Nainpur, *India* 66 H12
Nainwa, *India* 68 G6
Naipu, *Romania* 43 F10
Nairn, *U.K.* 14 D5
Nairobi, *Kenya* 86 C4
Naissaar, *Estonia* 9 G21
Naita, Mt., *Ethiopia* ... 81 F4
Naivasha, *Kenya* 86 C4
Naivasha, L., *Kenya* ... 86 C4
Najac, *France* 20 D5
Najafābād, *Iran* 71 C6
Nájera, *Spain* 32 C2
Najerilla →, *Spain* 32 C2
Najibabad, *India* 68 E8
Najin, *N. Korea* 57 C16
Najmah, *Si. Arabia* ... 71 E6
Naju, S. *Korea* 57 G14
Nakadōri-Shima, *Japan* . 55 H4
Nakalagba,
    Dem. Rep. of the Congo . 86 B2
Nakaminato, *Japan* 55 F10
Nakamura, *Japan* 55 H6
Nakano, *Japan* 55 F9
Nakano-Shima, *Japan* .. 55 K4
Nakashibetsu, *Japan* .. 54 C12
Nakfa, *Eritrea* 81 D4
Nakhfar al Buşayyah, *Iraq* 70 D5
Nakhichevan = Naxçıvan,
    Azerbaijan 70 B5
Nakhichevan Republic =
    Naxçıvan □, *Azerbaijan* .. 50 F5
Nakhl, *Egypt* 75 F2
Nakhl-e Taqī, *Iran* 71 E7
Nakhodka, *Russia* 51 E14
Nakhon Nayok, *Thailand* . 64 E3
Nakhon Pathom, *Thailand* 64 F3
Nakhon Phanom, *Thailand* . 64 D5
Nakhon Ratchasima,
    Thailand 64 E4
Nakhon Sawan, *Thailand* . 64 E3
Nakhon Si Thammarat,
    Thailand 65 H3
Nakhon Thai, *Thailand* .. 64 D3
Nakhtarana, *India* 68 H3
Nakina, *Canada* 102 B2
Nakło nad Notecią, *Poland* . 45 E4
Nako, *Burkina Faso* ... 82 C4
Nakodar, *India* 68 D6
Nakskov, *Denmark* 11 K5
Naktong →, S. *Korea* .. 57 G15
Nakuru, *Kenya* 86 C4
Nakuru, L., *Kenya* 86 C4
Nakusp, *Canada* 104 C5
Nal →, *Pakistan* 68 F2
Nalázi, *Mozam.* 89 C5
Nalchik, *Russia* 49 J6
Nalęczów, *Poland* 45 G9
Nalerigu, *Ghana* 83 C4
Nalgonda, *India* 66 L11
Nalhati, *India* 69 G12
Naliya, *India* 68 H3
Nallamalai Hills, *India* . 66 M11
Nallıhan, *Turkey* 72 B4
Nalón →, *Spain* 34 B4
Nam Can, *Vietnam* ... 65 H5
Nam-ch'on, *N. Korea* .. 57 E14
Nam Co, *China* 60 C4
Nam Dinh, *Vietnam* ... 58 G6
Nam Du, Hon, *Vietnam* . 65 H5
Nam Ngum Dam, *Laos* .. 64 C4
Nam-Phan = Cochin China,
    Vietnam 65 G6
Nam Phong, *Thailand* .. 64 D4
Nam Tha, *Laos* 58 G3
Nam Tok, *Thailand* 64 E2
Namacunde, *Angola* .. 88 B2
Namacurra, *Mozam.* ... 89 B6
Namak, Daryācheh-ye, *Iran* 71 C7
Namak, Kavir-e, *Iran* .. 71 C8
Namakzār, Daryācheh-ye,
    Iran 71 C9
Namaland, *Namibia* ... 88 C2
Namangan, *Uzbekistan* . 50 E8
Namapa, *Mozam.* 87 E4
Namaqualand, S. *Africa* . 88 E2
Namasagali, *Uganda* .. 86 B3
Namber, *Indonesia* 63 E8
Nambour, *Australia* ... 95 D5
Nambucca Heads, *Australia* 95 E5
Namche Bazar, *Nepal* .. 69 F12
Namchonjōm = Nam-ch'on,
    N. Korea 57 E14
Namecunda, *Mozam.* .. 87 E4
Nameponda, *Mozam.* .. 87 F4
Náměšt' nad Oslavou,
    Czech Rep. 27 B9
Námestovo, *Slovak Rep.* 27 B12
Nametil, *Mozam.* 87 F4
Namew L., *Canada* 105 C8
Namgia, *India* 69 D8
Namhkam, *Burma* 58 E1
Namib Desert =
    Namibwoestyn, *Namibia* . 88 C2
Namibe, *Angola* 85 H2
Namibe □, *Angola* 88 B1
Namibia ■, *Africa* 88 C2
Namibwoestyn, *Namibia* . 88 C2
Namīn, *Iran* 73 C13
Namlea, *Indonesia* 63 E7
Namoi →, *Australia* ... 95 E4
Nampa, *U.S.A.* 114 E5
Nampala, *Mali* 82 B3
Nampo, *N. Korea* 57 E13
Nampō-Shotō, *Japan* .. 55 J10
Nampula, *Mozam.* 87 F4
Namrole, *Indonesia* ... 63 E7

Namse Shankou, *China* .. 67 E13
Namsen →, *Norway* ... 8 D14
Namsos, *Norway* 8 D14
Namtsy, *Russia* 51 C13
Namtu, *Burma* 67 H20
Namtumbo, *Tanzania* .. 87 E4
Namu, *Canada* 104 C3
Namur, *Belgium* 17 D4
Namur □, *Belgium* 17 D4
Namutoni, *Namibia* ... 88 B2
Namwala, *Zambia* 87 F2
Namwŏn, S. *Korea* 57 G14
Namysłów, *Poland* 45 G4
Nan →, *Thailand* 64 C3
Nan-ch'ang = Nanchang,
    China 59 C10
Nan Ling, *China* 59 E8
Nan Xian, *China* 59 C9
Nana, *Romania* 43 F11
Nana Kru, *Liberia* 82 E3
Nanaimo, *Canada* 104 D4
Nanam, *N. Korea* 57 D15
Nanan, *China* 59 E12
Nanango, *Australia* ... 95 D5
Nan'ao, *China* 59 F11
Nanao, *Japan* 55 F8
Nanbu, *China* 58 B6
Nanchang, Jiangxi, *China* 59 C10
Nanchang, Kiangsi, *China* . 59 C10
Nancheng, *China* 59 D11
Nanching = Nanjing, *China* 59 A12
Nanchong, *China* 58 B6
Nanchuan, *China* 58 C6
Nancy, *France* 19 D13
Nanda Devi, *India* 69 D8
Nanda Kot, *India* 69 D9
Nandan, *China* 58 E6
Nandan, *Japan* 55 G7
Nanded, *India* 66 K10
Nandewar Ra., *Australia* . 95 E5
Nandi, *Fiji* 91 C7
Nandigram, *India* 69 H12
Nandurbar, *India* 66 J9
Nandyal, *India* 66 M11
Nanfeng, Guangdong, *China* 59 F8
Nanfeng, Jiangxi, *China* . 59 D11
Nanga-Eboko, *Cameroon* . 83 E7
Nanga Parbat, *Pakistan* . 69 B6
Nangade, *Mozam.* 87 E4
Nangapinoh, *Indonesia* . 62 E4
Nangarhār □, *Afghan.* . 66 B7
Nangatayap, *Indonesia* . 62 E4
Nangeya Mts., *Uganda* . 86 B3
Nangis, *France* 19 D10
Nangong, *China* 56 F8
Nanhua, *China* 58 E3
Nanhuang, *China* 57 F11
Nanhui, *China* 59 B13
Nanjeko, *Zambia* 87 F1
Nanji Shan, *China* 59 D13
Nanjian, *China* 58 E3
Nanjiang, *China* 58 A6
Nanjing, Fujian, *China* . 59 E11
Nanjing, Jiangsu, *China* . 59 A12
Nanjirinji, *Tanzania* .. 87 D4
Nankana Sahib, *Pakistan* . 68 D5
Nankang, *China* 59 E10
Nanking = Nanjing, *China* 59 A12
Nanling, *China* 59 B12
Nanning, *China* 58 F7
Nannup, *Australia* 93 F2
Nanpan Jiang →, *China* . 58 E6
Nanpara, *India* 69 F9
Nanpi, *China* 56 E9
Nanping, Fujian, *China* . 59 D12
Nanping, Henan, *China* . 59 C9
Nanri Dao, *China* 59 E12
Nanripe, *Mozam.* 87 E4
Nansei-Shotō = Ryūkyū-
    rettō, *Japan* 55 M3
Nansen Sd., *Canada* ... 4 A3
Nanshan I., S. *China Sea* . 62 B5
Nansio, *Tanzania* 86 C3
Nant, *France* 20 D7
Nanterre, *France* 19 D9
Nantes, *France* 18 E5
Nantiat, *France* 20 B5
Nanticoke, *U.S.A.* 111 E8
Nanton, *Canada* 104 C6
Nantong, *China* 59 A13
Nantou, *Taiwan* 59 F13
Nantua, *France* 19 F12
Nantucket I., *U.S.A.* ... 108 E10
Nantwich, *U.K.* 12 D5
Nanty Glo, *U.S.A.* 110 F6
Nanuque, *Brazil* 125 G10
Nanusa, Kepulauan,
    Indonesia 63 D7
Nanutarra Roadhouse,
    Australia 92 D2
Nanxi, *China* 58 C5
Nanxiong, *China* 59 E10
Nanyang, *China* 56 H7
Nanyi Hu, *China* 59 B12
Nanyuan, *China* 56 E9
Nanyuki, *Kenya* 86 B4
Nanzhang, *China* 59 B8
Nao, C. de la, *Spain* ... 33 G5
Naococane, L., *Canada* . 103 B5
Náoussa, Imathía, *Greece* 40 F6
Náoussa, Kikládhes, *Greece* 39 D7
Naozhou Dao, *China* ... 59 G8
Napa, *U.S.A.* 116 G4
Napa →, *U.S.A.* 116 G4
Napanee, *Canada* 102 D4
Napanoch, *U.S.A.* 111 E10
Nape, *Laos* 64 C5
Nape Pass = Keo Neua,
    Deo, *Vietnam* 64 C5

Napier, *N.Z.* 91 H6
Napier Broome B., *Australia* 92 B4
Napier Pen., *Australia* .. 94 A2
Napierville, *Canada* ... 111 A11
Naples = Nápoli, *Italy* .. 31 B7
Naples, *U.S.A.* 109 M5
Napo, *China* 58 F5
Napo →, *Peru* 122 D3
Napoleon, N. Dak., *U.S.A.* 112 B5
Napoleon, Ohio, *U.S.A.* . 108 E3
Nápoli, *Italy* 31 B7
Nápoli, G. di, *Italy* ... 31 B7
Napopo,
    Dem. Rep. of the Congo . 86 B2
Naqâda, *Egypt* 80 B3
Naqadeh, *Iran* 73 D11
Naqb, Ra's an, *Jordan* .. 75 F4
Naqqāsh, *Iran* 71 C6
Nara, *Japan* 55 G7
Nara, *Mali* 82 B3
Nara □, *Japan* 55 G8
Nara Canal, *Pakistan* .. 68 G3
Nara Visa, *U.S.A.* 113 H3
Naracoorte, *Australia* .. 95 F3
Naradhan, *Australia* .. 95 E4
Naraini, *India* 69 G9
Narasapur, *India* 67 L12
Narathiwat, *Thailand* .. 65 J3
Narayanganj, *Bangla.* . 67 H17
Narayanpet, *India* 66 L10
Narbonne, *France* 20 E7
Narcea →, *Spain* 34 B4
Nardīn, *Iran* 71 B7
Nardò, *Italy* 31 B11
Narembeen, *Australia* .. 93 F2
Narendranagar, *India* .. 68 D8
Nares Str., *Arctic* 98 A13
Naretha, *Australia* ... 93 F3
Narew →, *Poland* 45 F7
Nari →, *Pakistan* 68 F2
Narin, *Afghan.* 66 A6
Narindra, Helodranon' i,
    Madag. 89 A8
Narita, *Japan* 55 G10
Närke, *Sweden* 10 E8
Narmada →, *India* ... 68 J5
Narman, *Turkey* 73 B9
Narmland, *Sweden* ... 9 F15
Narnaul, *India* 68 E7
Narni, *Italy* 29 F9
Naro, *Ghana* 82 C4
Naro Fominsk, *Russia* . 46 E9
Narodnaya, *Russia* ... 6 B17
Narok, *Kenya* 86 C4
Narón, *Spain* 34 B2
Narooma, *Australia* .. 95 F5
Narowal, *Pakistan* ... 68 C6
Narrabri, *Australia* ... 95 E4
Narran →, *Australia* .. 95 D4
Narrandera, *Australia* . 95 E4
Narrogin, *Australia* ... 93 F2
Narromine, *Australia* .. 95 E4
Narrow Hills Prov. Park,
    Canada 105 C8
Narsimhapur, *India* ... 69 H8
Narsinghgarh, *India* .. 68 H7
Nartes, L. e, *Albania* .. 40 F3
Naruto, *Japan* 55 G7
Narva, *Estonia* 46 C5
Narva →, *Russia* 9 G22
Narva-Jõesuu, *Estonia* . 46 C5
Narvik, *Norway* 8 B17
Narvskoye Vdkhr., *Russia* . 46 C5
Narwana, *India* 68 E7
Naryan-Mar, *Russia* .. 50 C6
Narym, *Russia* 50 D9
Naryn, *Kyrgyzstan* ... 50 E8
Nasa, *Norway* 8 C16
Nasarawa, *Nigeria* ... 83 D6
Năsăud, *Romania* 43 C9
Naseby, *N.Z.* 91 L3
Naselle, *U.S.A.* 116 D3
Naser, Buheirat en, *Egypt* 80 C3
Nashua, Mont., *U.S.A.* .. 114 B10
Nashua, N.H., *U.S.A.* .. 111 D13
Nashville, Ark., *U.S.A.* . 113 J8
Nashville, Ga., *U.S.A.* .. 109 K4
Nashville, Tenn., *U.S.A.* . 109 G2
Našice, *Croatia* 42 E3
Nasielsk, *Poland* 45 F7
Nasik, *India* 66 K8
Nasipit, *Phil.* 61 G6
Nasirabad, *India* 68 F6
Nasirabad, *Pakistan* .. 68 E3
Naskaupi →, *Canada* . 103 B7
Naso, *Italy* 31 D7
Naşrābād, *Iran* 71 C6
Naşrīān-e Pā'īn, *Iran* .. 70 C5
Nass →, *Canada* 104 C3
Nassarawa □, *Nigeria* . 83 D6
Nassau, *Bahamas* 120 A4
Nassau, *U.S.A.* 111 D11
Nassau, B., *Chile* 128 H3
Nasser, L. = Naser, Buheirat
    en, *Egypt* 80 C3
Nasser City = Kôm Ombo,
    Egypt 80 C3
Nassian, *Ivory C.* 82 D4
Nässjö, *Sweden* 11 G8
Nastapoka →, *Canada* . 102 A4
Nastapoka, Is., *Canada* . 102 A4
Nasugbu, *Phil.* 61 D4
Näsum, *Sweden* 11 H8
Näsviken, *Sweden* 10 C10
Nata, *Botswana* 88 C4
Nata →, *Botswana* ... 88 C4
Natal, *Brazil* 125 E11
Natal, *Indonesia* 62 D1
Natal, S. *Africa* 85 K6
Natalinci, *Serbia, Yug.* . 42 F5

Naţanz, *Iran* ... 71 C6
Natashquan, *Canada* ... 103 B7
Natashquan →, *Canada* ... 103 B7
Natchez, *U.S.A.* ... 113 K9
Natchitoches, *U.S.A.* ... 113 K8
Nathalia, *Australia* ... 95 F4
Nathdwara, *India* ... 68 G5
Nati, Pta., *Spain* ... 37 A10
Natimuk, *Australia* ... 95 F3
Nation →, *Canada* ... 104 B4
National City, *U.S.A.* ... 117 N9
Natitingou, *Benin* ... 83 C5
Natividad, I., *Mexico* ... 118 B1
Natkyizin, *Burma* ... 64 E1
Natron, L. el, *Tanzania* ... 86 C4
Natrona Heights, *U.S.A.* ... 110 F5
Natrûn, W. el →, *Egypt* ... 80 H7
Nättraby, *Sweden* ... 11 H9
Natukanaoka Pan, *Namibia* ... 88 B2
Natuna Besar, Kepulauan, *Indonesia* ... 65 L7
Natuna Is. = Natuna Besar, Kepulauan, *Indonesia* ... 65 L7
Natuna Selatan, Kepulauan, *Indonesia* ... 65 L7
Natural Bridge, *U.S.A.* ... 111 B9
Naturaliste, C., *Australia* ... 94 G4
Nau Qala, *Afghan.* ... 68 B3
Naucelle, *France* ... 20 D6
Nauders, *Austria* ... 26 E3
Nauen, *Germany* ... 24 C8
Naugatuck, *U.S.A.* ... 111 E11
Naujoji Akmenė, *Lithuania* ... 44 B9
Naumburg, *Germany* ... 24 D7
Nā'ūr at Tunayb, *Jordan* ... 75 D4
Nauru ■, *Pac. Oc.* ... 96 H8
Naushahra = Nowshera, *Pakistan* ... 66 C8
Naushahro, *Pakistan* ... 68 F3
Naushon I., *U.S.A.* ... 111 E14
Nauta, *Peru* ... 124 D4
Nautanwa, *India* ... 67 F13
Nautla, *Mexico* ... 119 C5
Nava, *Mexico* ... 118 B4
Nava, *Spain* ... 34 B5
Nava del Rey, *Spain* ... 34 D5
Navadwip, *India* ... 69 H13
Navahermosa, *Spain* ... 35 F6
Navahrudak, *Belarus* ... 46 F3
Navajo Reservoir, *U.S.A.* ... 115 H10
Navalcarnero, *Spain* ... 34 E6
Navalmoral de la Mata, *Spain* ... 34 F5
Navalvillar de Pela, *Spain* ... 35 F5
Navan = An Uaimh, *Ireland* ... 15 C5
Navapolatsk, *Belarus* ... 46 E5
Navarino, I., *Chile* ... 128 H3
Navarra □, *Spain* ... 32 C3
Navarre, *U.S.A.* ... 110 F3
Navarro →, *U.S.A.* ... 116 F3
Navas de San Juan, *Spain* ... 35 G7
Navasota, *U.S.A.* ... 113 K6
Navassa I., *W. Indies* ... 121 C5
Nävekvarn, *Sweden* ... 11 F10
Naver →, *U.K.* ... 14 C4
Navia, *Spain* ... 34 B4
Navia →, *Spain* ... 34 B4
Navia de Suarna, *Spain* ... 34 C3
Navibandar, *India* ... 68 J3
Navidad, *Chile* ... 126 C1
Naviraí, *Brazil* ... 127 A5
Navlakhi, *India* ... 68 H4
Navlya, *Russia* ... 47 F8
Năvodari, *Romania* ... 43 F13
Navoi = Nawoiy, *Uzbekistan* ... 50 E7
Navojoa, *Mexico* ... 118 B3
Navolato, *Mexico* ... 118 C3
Návpaktos, *Greece* ... 38 C3
Návplion, *Greece* ... 38 D4
Navrongo, *Ghana* ... 83 C4
Navsari, *India* ... 66 J8
Nawa Kot, *Pakistan* ... 68 E4
Nawab Khan, *Pakistan* ... 68 D3
Nawabganj, *Ut. P., India* ... 69 F9
Nawabganj, *Ut. P., India* ... 69 F8
Nawabshah, *Pakistan* ... 68 F3
Nawada, *India* ... 69 G11
Nawakot, *Nepal* ... 69 F11
Nawalgarh, *India* ... 68 F6
Nawanshahr, *India* ... 69 C6
Nawar, Dasht-i-, *Afghan.* ... 68 C3
Nawi, *Sudan* ... 80 D3
Nawoiy, *Uzbekistan* ... 50 E7
Naxçıvan, *Azerbaijan* ... 70 B5
Naxçıvan □, *Azerbaijan* ... 70 B5
Náxos, *Greece* ... 39 D7
Nay, *France* ... 20 E3
Nay, Mui, *Vietnam* ... 62 B3
Nāy Band, *Būshehr, Iran* ... 71 E7
Nāy Band, *Khorāsān, Iran* ... 71 C8
Nayakhan, *Russia* ... 51 C16
Nayarit □, *Mexico* ... 118 C4
Nayé, *Senegal* ... 82 C2
Nayong, *China* ... 58 D5
Nayoro, *Japan* ... 54 B11
Nayyāl, W. →, *Si. Arabia* ... 70 D3
Nazaré, *Brazil* ... 125 F11
Nazaré, *Portugal* ... 35 F1
Nazaré = Nazerat, *Israel* ... 75 C4
Nazareth, *U.S.A.* ... 111 F9
Nazas, *Mexico* ... 118 B4
Nazas →, *Mexico* ... 118 B4
Nazca, *Peru* ... 124 F4
Naze, The, *U.K.* ... 13 F9
Nazerat, *Israel* ... 75 C4
Nāzīk, *Iran* ... 70 B5
Nazilli, *Turkey* ... 39 D10
Nazir Hat, *Bangla.* ... 67 H17
Nazko, *Canada* ... 104 C4
Nazko →, *Canada* ... 104 C4
Nazret, *Ethiopia* ... 81 F4

Nazwá, *Oman* ... 74 C6
Nchanga, *Zambia* ... 87 E2
Ncheu, *Malawi* ... 87 E3
Ndala, *Tanzania* ... 86 C3
Ndalatando, *Angola* ... 84 F2
Ndali, *Benin* ... 83 D5
Ndareda, *Tanzania* ... 86 C4
Ndélé, *C.A.R.* ... 84 C4
Ndikiniméki, *Cameroon* ... 83 E7
N'Dioum, *Senegal* ... 82 B2
Ndjamena, *Chad* ... 79 F8
Ndola, *Zambia* ... 87 E2
Ndoto Mts., *Kenya* ... 86 B4
Nduguti, *Tanzania* ... 86 C3
Néa Alikarnassós, *Greece* ... 39 F7
Néa Ankhíalos, *Greece* ... 38 B4
Néa Epídhavros, *Greece* ... 38 D5
Néa Flippiás, *Greece* ... 38 B2
Néa Ionia, *Greece* ... 38 B4
Néa Kallikrátia, *Greece* ... 40 F7
Néa Mákri, *Greece* ... 38 C5
Néa Moudhaniá, *Greece* ... 40 F7
Néa Péramos, *Attikí, Greece* ... 38 C5
Néa Péramos, *Kaválla, Greece* ... 41 F8
Néa Víssi, *Greece* ... 41 E10
Néa Zíkhna, *Greece* ... 40 E7
Neagh, Lough, *U.K.* ... 15 B5
Neah Bay, *U.S.A.* ... 116 B2
Neale, L., *Australia* ... 92 D5
Neamţ □, *Romania* ... 43 C11
Neápolis, *Kozáni, Greece* ... 40 F5
Neápolis, *Kríti, Greece* ... 36 D7
Neápolis, *Lakonía, Greece* ... 38 E5
Near Is., *U.S.A.* ... 100 C1
Neath, *U.K.* ... 13 F4
Neath Port Talbot □, *U.K.* ... 13 F4
Nebbou, *Burkina Faso* ... 83 C4
Nebelat el Hagana, *Sudan* ... 81 E2
Nebine Cr. →, *Australia* ... 95 D4
Nebitdag, *Turkmenistan* ... 50 F6
Nebo, *Australia* ... 94 C4
Nebolchy, *Russia* ... 46 C7
Nebraska □, *U.S.A.* ... 112 E5
Nebraska City, *U.S.A.* ... 112 E7
Nébrodi, Monti, *Italy* ... 31 E7
Necedah, *U.S.A.* ... 112 C9
Nechako →, *Canada* ... 104 C4
Neches →, *U.S.A.* ... 113 L8
Neckar →, *Germany* ... 25 F4
Necochea, *Argentina* ... 126 D4
Neda, *Spain* ... 34 B2
Nedelino, *Bulgaria* ... 41 E8
Nedelišće, *Croatia* ... 29 B13
Nédha →, *Greece* ... 38 D3
Needles, *Canada* ... 104 D5
Needles, *U.S.A.* ... 117 L12
Needles, The, *U.K.* ... 13 G6
Ñeembucú □, *Paraguay* ... 126 B4
Neemuch = Nimach, *India* ... 68 G6
Neenah, *U.S.A.* ... 108 C1
Neepawa, *Canada* ... 105 C9
Neftçala, *Azerbaijan* ... 71 B6
Neftegorsk, *Russia* ... 49 H4
Neftekumsk, *Russia* ... 49 H7
Nefyn, *U.K.* ... 12 E3
Négala, *Mali* ... 82 C3
Negapatam = Nagappattinam, *India* ... 66 P11
Negaunee, *U.S.A.* ... 108 B2
Negele, *Ethiopia* ... 81 F4
Negev Desert = Hanegev, *Israel* ... 75 E4
Negoiul, Vf., *Romania* ... 43 E9
Negombo, *Sri Lanka* ... 66 R11
Negotin, *Serbia, Yug.* ... 40 B6
Negotino, *Macedonia* ... 40 E6
Negra, Peña, *Spain* ... 34 C4
Negra, Pta., *Peru* ... 122 D2
Negrais, C. = Maudin Sun, *Burma* ... 67 M19
Negreşti, *Romania* ... 43 D12
Negreşti-Oaş, *Romania* ... 43 C8
Negril, *Jamaica* ... 120 C4
Negro →, *Argentina* ... 122 H4
Negro →, *Brazil* ... 122 D4
Negro →, *Uruguay* ... 127 C4
Negros, *Phil.* ... 61 G5
Negru Vodă, *Romania* ... 43 G13
Neguac, *Canada* ... 103 C6
Nehalem →, *U.S.A.* ... 116 E3
Nehāvand, *Iran* ... 71 C6
Nehbandān, *Iran* ... 71 D9
Nehoiu, *Romania* ... 43 E11
Nei Mongol Zizhiqu □, *China* ... 56 D7
Neijiang, *China* ... 58 C5
Neillsville, *U.S.A.* ... 112 C9
Neilton, *U.S.A.* ... 114 C2
Neiqiu, *China* ... 56 F8
Neiva, *Colombia* ... 124 C3
Neixiang, *China* ... 56 H6
Nejanilini L., *Canada* ... 105 B9
Nejd = Najd, *Si. Arabia* ... 74 B3
Nejo, *Ethiopia* ... 81 F4
Nekā, *Iran* ... 71 B7
Nekemte, *Ethiopia* ... 81 F4
Nêkheb, *Egypt* ... 80 B3
Neksø, *Denmark* ... 11 J9
Nelas, *Portugal* ... 34 E3
Nelia, *Australia* ... 94 C3
Nelidovo, *Russia* ... 46 D7
Neligh, *U.S.A.* ... 112 D5
Nelkan, *Russia* ... 51 D14
Nellore, *India* ... 66 M11
Nelson, *Canada* ... 104 D5
Nelson, *N.Z.* ... 91 J4
Nelson, *U.K.* ... 12 D5
Nelson, *Ariz., U.S.A.* ... 115 J7
Nelson, *Nev., U.S.A.* ... 117 K12
Nelson →, *Canada* ... 105 C9

Nelson, C., *Australia* ... 95 F3
Nelson, Estrecho, *Chile* ... 128 G2
Nelson Bay, *Australia* ... 95 E5
Nelson Forks, *Canada* ... 104 B4
Nelson House, *Canada* ... 105 B9
Nelson L., *Canada* ... 105 B8
Nelspoort, *S. Africa* ... 88 E3
Nelspruit, *S. Africa* ... 89 D5
Néma, *Mauritania* ... 82 B3
Neman, *Russia* ... 9 J20
Neman →, *Lithuania* ... 9 J20
Neméa, *Greece* ... 38 D4
Nemeiben L., *Canada* ... 105 B7
Nemêrçkë, Mal, *Albania* ... 40 F4
Nemira, Vf., *Romania* ... 43 D11
Némiscau, *Canada* ... 102 B4
Némiscau, L., *Canada* ... 102 B4
Nemours, *France* ... 19 D9
Nemšová, *Slovak Rep.* ... 27 C11
Nemunas = Neman →, *Lithuania* ... 9 J20
Nemuro, *Japan* ... 54 C12
Nemuro-Kaikyō, *Japan* ... 54 C12
Nen Jiang →, *China* ... 57 B13
Nenagh, *Ireland* ... 15 D3
Nenasi, *Malaysia* ... 65 L4
Nene →, *U.K.* ... 13 E8
Nénita, *Greece* ... 39 C8
Nenjiang, *China* ... 60 B7
Neno, *Malawi* ... 87 F3
Neodesha, *U.S.A.* ... 113 G7
Neokhórion, *Aitolía kai Akarnanía, Greece* ... 38 C3
Neokhórion, *Árta, Greece* ... 38 B2
Néon Karlovásion, *Greece* ... 39 D8
Néon Petrítsi, *Greece* ... 40 E7
Neosho, *U.S.A.* ... 113 G7
Neosho →, *U.S.A.* ... 113 H7
Nepal ■, *Asia* ... 69 F11
Nepalganj, *Nepal* ... 69 E9
Nepalganj Road, *India* ... 69 E9
Nephi, *U.S.A.* ... 114 G8
Nephin, *Ireland* ... 15 B2
Nepi, *Italy* ... 29 F9
Nepomuk, *Czech Rep.* ... 26 B6
Neptune, *U.S.A.* ... 111 F10
Nera →, *Italy* ... 29 F9
Nera →, *Romania* ... 42 F6
Nérac, *France* ... 20 D4
Nerang, *Australia* ... 95 D5
Neratovice, *Czech Rep.* ... 26 A7
Nerchinsk, *Russia* ... 51 D12
Nereju, *Romania* ... 43 E11
Nerekhta, *Russia* ... 46 D11
Néret, L., *Canada* ... 103 B5
Neretvanski Kanal, *Croatia* ... 29 E14
Neringa, *Lithuania* ... 9 J19
Nerja, *Spain* ... 35 J7
Nerl →, *Russia* ... 46 D11
Nerpio, *Spain* ... 33 G2
Nerva, *Spain* ... 35 H4
Nervi, *Italy* ... 28 D6
Neryungri, *Russia* ... 51 D13
Nescopeck, *U.S.A.* ... 111 E8
Nesebŭr, *Bulgaria* ... 41 D11
Ness, L., *U.K.* ... 14 D4
Ness City, *U.S.A.* ... 112 F5
Nesterov, *Poland* ... 47 G2
Nestórion, *Greece* ... 40 F5
Néstos →, *Greece* ... 41 E8
Nesvady, *Slovak Rep.* ... 27 D11
Nesvizh = Nyasvizh, *Belarus* ... 47 F4
Netanya, *Israel* ... 75 C3
Netarhat, *India* ... 69 H11
Nete →, *Belgium* ... 17 C4
Netherdale, *Australia* ... 94 C4
Netherlands ■, *Europe* ... 17 C5
Netherlands Antilles ■, *W. Indies* ... 124 A5
Neto →, *Italy* ... 31 C10
Netrang, *India* ... 68 J5
Nettancourt, *France* ... 19 D11
Nettetal, *Germany* ... 24 D2
Nettilling L., *Canada* ... 101 B12
Nettuno, *Italy* ... 30 A5
Netzahualcoyotl, Presa, *Mexico* ... 119 D6
Neu-Isenburg, *Germany* ... 25 E4
Neu-Ulm, *Germany* ... 25 G6
Neubrandenburg, *Germany* ... 24 B9
Neubukow, *Germany* ... 24 A7
Neuburg, *Germany* ... 25 G7
Neuchâtel, *Switz.* ... 25 J2
Neuchâtel □, *Switz.* ... 25 J2
Neuchâtel, Lac de, *Switz.* ... 25 J2
Neudau, *Austria* ... 26 D9
Neuenhagen, *Germany* ... 24 C9
Neuenhaus, *Germany* ... 24 C2
Neuf-Brisach, *France* ... 19 D14
Neufahrn, *Bayern, Germany* ... 25 G8
Neufahrn, *Bayern, Germany* ... 25 G7
Neufchâteau, *Belgium* ... 17 E5
Neufchâteau, *France* ... 19 D12
Neufchâtel-en-Bray, *France* ... 18 C8
Neufchâtel-sur-Aisne, *France* ... 19 C11
Neuhaus, *Germany* ... 24 B6
Neuillé-Pont-Pierre, *France* ... 18 E7
Neuilly-St-Front, *France* ... 19 C10
Neukalen, *Germany* ... 24 B8
Neumarkt, *Germany* ... 25 F7
Neumünster, *Germany* ... 24 A5
Neung-sur-Beuvron, *France* ... 19 E8
Neunkirchen, *Austria* ... 26 D9
Neunkirchen, *Germany* ... 25 F3
Neuquén, *Argentina* ... 128 D3
Neuquén □, *Argentina* ... 126 D2
Neuruppin, *Germany* ... 24 C8
Neusäss, *Germany* ... 25 G6
Neuse →, *U.S.A.* ... 109 H7
Neusiedl, *Austria* ... 27 D9

Neusiedler See, *Austria* ... 27 D9
Neuss, *Germany* ... 24 D2
Neussargues-Moissac, *France* ... 20 C7
Neustadt, *Bayern, Germany* ... 25 F8
Neustadt, *Bayern, Germany* ... 25 G7
Neustadt, *Bayern, Germany* ... 25 F6
Neustadt, *Bayern, Germany* ... 25 E7
Neustadt, *Brandenburg, Germany* ... 24 C8
Neustadt, *Hessen, Germany* ... 24 E5
Neustadt, *Niedersachsen, Germany* ... 24 C5
Neustadt, *Rhld.-Pfz., Germany* ... 25 F4
Neustadt, *Sachsen, Germany* ... 24 D10
Neustadt, *Schleswig-Holstein, Germany* ... 24 A6
Neustadt, *Thüringen, Germany* ... 24 E7
Neustrelitz, *Germany* ... 24 B9
Neuvic, *France* ... 20 C6
Neuville-sur-Saône, *France* ... 21 C8
Neuvy-le-Roi, *France* ... 18 E7
Neuvy-St-Sépulchre, *France* ... 19 F8
Neuvy-sur-Barangeon, *France* ... 19 E9
Neuwerk, *Germany* ... 24 B4
Neuwied, *Germany* ... 24 E3
Neva →, *Russia* ... 46 C6
Nevada, *Iowa, U.S.A.* ... 112 D8
Nevada, *Mo., U.S.A.* ... 113 G7
Nevada □, *U.S.A.* ... 114 G5
Nevada, Sierra, *Spain* ... 35 H7
Nevada, Sierra, *U.S.A.* ... 114 G3
Nevada City, *U.S.A.* ... 116 F6
Nevado, Cerro, *Argentina* ... 126 D2
Nevel, *Russia* ... 46 D5
Nevers, *France* ... 19 F10
Nevertire, *Australia* ... 95 E4
Nevesinje, *Bos.-H.* ... 40 C2
Nevinnomyssk, *Russia* ... 49 H6
Nevis, *W. Indies* ... 121 C7
Nevrokop = Gotse Delchev, *Bulgaria* ... 40 E7
Nevşehir, *Turkey* ... 70 B2
New →, *U.S.A.* ... 108 F5
New Aiyansh, *Canada* ... 104 B3
New Albany, *Ind., U.S.A.* ... 108 F3
New Albany, *Miss., U.S.A.* ... 113 H10
New Albany, *Pa., U.S.A.* ... 111 E8
New Amsterdam, *Guyana* ... 124 B7
New Angledool, *Australia* ... 95 D4
New Baltimore, *U.S.A.* ... 110 D2
New Bedford, *U.S.A.* ... 111 E14
New Berlin, *N.Y., U.S.A.* ... 111 D9
New Berlin, *Pa., U.S.A.* ... 110 F8
New Bern, *U.S.A.* ... 109 H7
New Bethlehem, *U.S.A.* ... 110 F5
New Bloomfield, *U.S.A.* ... 110 F7
New Boston, *U.S.A.* ... 113 J7
New Braunfels, *U.S.A.* ... 113 L5
New Brighton, *N.Z.* ... 91 K4
New Brighton, *Pa., U.S.A.* ... 110 F4
New Britain, *Papua N. G.* ... 96 H7
New Britain, *U.S.A.* ... 111 E12
New Brunswick, *U.S.A.* ... 111 F10
New Brunswick □, *Canada* ... 103 C6
New Bussa, *Nigeria* ... 83 D5
New Caledonia ■, *Pac. Oc.* ... 96 K8
New Castile = Castilla-La Mancha □, *Spain* ... 6 H5
New Castle, *Ind., U.S.A.* ... 108 F3
New Castle, *Pa., U.S.A.* ... 110 F4
New City, *U.S.A.* ... 111 E11
New Concord, *U.S.A.* ... 110 G3
New Cumberland, *U.S.A.* ... 110 F4
New Cuyama, *U.S.A.* ... 117 L7
New Delhi, *India* ... 68 E7
New Denver, *Canada* ... 104 D5
New Don Pedro Reservoir, *U.S.A.* ... 116 H6
New England, *U.S.A.* ... 112 B3
New England Ra., *Australia* ... 95 E5
New Forest, *U.K.* ... 13 G6
New Galloway, *U.K.* ... 14 F4
New Glasgow, *Canada* ... 103 C7
New Guinea, *Oceania* ... 52 K17
New Hamburg, *Canada* ... 110 C4
New Hampshire □, *U.S.A.* ... 111 C13
New Hampton, *U.S.A.* ... 112 D8
New Hanover, *S. Africa* ... 89 D5
New Hartford, *U.S.A.* ... 111 C9
New Haven, *Conn., U.S.A.* ... 111 E12
New Haven, *Mich., U.S.A.* ... 110 D2
New Hazelton, *Canada* ... 104 B3
New Hebrides = Vanuatu ■, *Pac. Oc.* ... 96 J8
New Holland, *U.S.A.* ... 111 F8
New Iberia, *U.S.A.* ... 113 K9
New Ireland, *Papua N. G.* ... 96 H7
New Jersey □, *U.S.A.* ... 108 E8
New Kensington, *U.S.A.* ... 110 F5
New Lexington, *U.S.A.* ... 108 F4
New Liskeard, *Canada* ... 102 C4
New London, *Conn., U.S.A.* ... 111 E12
New London, *Ohio, U.S.A.* ... 110 E2
New London, *Wis., U.S.A.* ... 112 C10
New Madrid, *U.S.A.* ... 113 G10
New Martinsville, *U.S.A.* ... 108 F5
New Meadows, *U.S.A.* ... 114 D5
New Melones L., *U.S.A.* ... 116 H6
New Mexico □, *U.S.A.* ... 115 J10
New Milford, *Conn., U.S.A.* ... 111 E11
New Milford, *Pa., U.S.A.* ... 111 E9
New Norcia, *Australia* ... 93 F2
New Norfolk, *Australia* ... 94 G4
New Orleans, *U.S.A.* ... 113 L9
New Philadelphia, *U.S.A.* ... 110 F3
New Plymouth, *N.Z.* ... 91 H5
New Plymouth, *U.S.A.* ... 114 E5

New Port Richey, *U.S.A.* ... 109 L4
New Providence, *Bahamas* ... 120 A4
New Quay, *U.K.* ... 13 E3
New Radnor, *U.K.* ... 13 E4
New Richmond, *Canada* ... 103 C6
New Richmond, *U.S.A.* ... 112 C8
New Roads, *U.S.A.* ... 113 K9
New Rochelle, *U.S.A.* ... 111 F11
New Rockford, *U.S.A.* ... 112 B5
New Romney, *U.K.* ... 13 G8
New Ross, *Ireland* ... 15 D5
New Salem, *U.S.A.* ... 112 B4
New Scone, *U.K.* ... 14 E5
New Siberian I. = Novaya Sibir, Ostrov, *Russia* ... 51 B16
New Siberian Is. = Novosibirskiye Ostrova, *Russia* ... 51 B15
New Smyrna Beach, *U.S.A.* ... 109 L5
New South Wales □, *Australia* ... 95 E4
New Town, *U.S.A.* ... 112 B3
New Tredegar, *U.K.* ... 13 F4
New Ulm, *U.S.A.* ... 112 C7
New Waterford, *Canada* ... 103 C7
New Westminster, *Canada* ... 116 A4
New York, *U.S.A.* ... 111 F11
New York □, *U.S.A.* ... 111 D9
New York Mts., *U.S.A.* ... 115 J6
New Zealand ■, *Oceania* ... 91 J6
Newaj →, *India* ... 68 G7
Newala, *Tanzania* ... 87 E4
Newark, *Del., U.S.A.* ... 108 F8
Newark, *N.J., U.S.A.* ... 111 F10
Newark, *N.Y., U.S.A.* ... 110 C7
Newark, *Ohio, U.S.A.* ... 110 F2
Newark-on-Trent, *U.K.* ... 12 D7
Newark Valley, *U.S.A.* ... 111 D8
Newberg, *U.S.A.* ... 114 D2
Newberry, *Mich., U.S.A.* ... 108 B3
Newberry, *S.C., U.S.A.* ... 109 H5
Newberry Springs, *U.S.A.* ... 117 L10
Newboro L., *Canada* ... 111 B8
Newbridge = Droichead Nua, *Ireland* ... 15 C5
Newburgh, *Canada* ... 110 B8
Newburgh, *U.S.A.* ... 111 E10
Newbury, *U.K.* ... 13 F6
Newbury, *N.H., U.S.A.* ... 111 B12
Newbury, *Vt., U.S.A.* ... 111 B12
Newburyport, *U.S.A.* ... 109 D10
Newcastle, *Australia* ... 95 E5
Newcastle, *N.B., Canada* ... 103 C6
Newcastle, *Ont., Canada* ... 102 D4
Newcastle, *S. Africa* ... 89 D4
Newcastle, *U.K.* ... 15 B6
Newcastle, *Calif., U.S.A.* ... 116 G5
Newcastle, *Wyo., U.S.A.* ... 112 D2
Newcastle Emlyn, *U.K.* ... 13 E3
Newcastle Ra., *Australia* ... 92 C5
Newcastle-under-Lyme, *U.K.* ... 12 D5
Newcastle-upon-Tyne, *U.K.* ... 12 C6
Newcastle Waters, *Australia* ... 94 B1
Newcastle West, *Ireland* ... 15 D2
Newcomb, *U.S.A.* ... 111 C10
Newcomerstown, *U.S.A.* ... 110 F3
Newdegate, *Australia* ... 93 F2
Newell, *Australia* ... 94 B4
Newell, *U.S.A.* ... 112 C3
Newfane, *U.S.A.* ... 110 C6
Newfield, *U.S.A.* ... 111 D8
Newfound L., *U.S.A.* ... 111 C13
Newfoundland, *N. Amer.* ... 98 E14
Newfoundland, *U.S.A.* ... 111 E9
Newfoundland □, *Canada* ... 103 B8
Newhall, *U.S.A.* ... 117 L8
Newhaven, *U.K.* ... 13 G8
Newkirk, *U.S.A.* ... 113 G6
Newlyn, *U.K.* ... 13 G2
Newman, *Australia* ... 92 D2
Newman, *U.S.A.* ... 116 H5
Newmarket, *Canada* ... 110 B5
Newmarket, *Ireland* ... 15 D2
Newmarket, *U.K.* ... 13 E8
Newmarket, *N.H., U.S.A.* ... 111 C14
Newmarket, *N.H., U.S.A.* ... 111 C14
Newnan, *U.S.A.* ... 109 J3
Newport, *Ireland* ... 15 C2
Newport, *I. of W., U.K.* ... 13 G6
Newport, *Newp., U.K.* ... 13 F5
Newport, *Ark., U.S.A.* ... 113 H9
Newport, *Ky., U.S.A.* ... 108 F3
Newport, *N.H., U.S.A.* ... 111 C12
Newport, *N.Y., U.S.A.* ... 111 C9
Newport, *Oreg., U.S.A.* ... 114 D1
Newport, *Pa., U.S.A.* ... 110 F7
Newport, *R.I., U.S.A.* ... 111 E13
Newport, *Tenn., U.S.A.* ... 109 H4
Newport, *Vt., U.S.A.* ... 111 B12
Newport, *Wash., U.S.A.* ... 114 B5
Newport □, *U.K.* ... 13 F4
Newport Beach, *U.S.A.* ... 117 M9
Newport News, *U.S.A.* ... 108 G7
Newport Pagnell, *U.K.* ... 13 E7
Newquay, *U.K.* ... 13 G2
Newry, *U.K.* ... 15 B5
Newton, *Ill., U.S.A.* ... 112 F10
Newton, *Iowa, U.S.A.* ... 112 E8
Newton, *Kans., U.S.A.* ... 113 F6
Newton, *Mass., U.S.A.* ... 111 D13
Newton, *Miss., U.S.A.* ... 113 J10
Newton, *N.C., U.S.A.* ... 109 H5
Newton, *N.J., U.S.A.* ... 111 E10
Newton, *Tex., U.S.A.* ... 113 K8
Newton Abbot, *U.K.* ... 13 G4
Newton Aycliffe, *U.K.* ... 12 C6
Newton Falls, *U.S.A.* ... 110 E4
Newton Stewart, *U.K.* ... 14 G4
Newtonmore, *U.K.* ... 14 D4
Newtown, *U.K.* ... 13 E4
Newtownabbey, *U.K.* ... 15 B6

Newtownards, *U.K.* 15 B6
Newtownbarry = Bunclody, *Ireland* 15 D5
Newtownstewart, *U.K.* 15 B4
Newville, *U.S.A.* 110 F7
Nexon, *France* 20 C5
Neya, *Russia* 48 A6
Neyrīz, *Iran* 71 D7
Neyshābūr, *Iran* 71 B8
Nezhin = Nizhyn, *Ukraine* 47 G6
Nezperce, *U.S.A.* 114 C5
Ngabang, *Indonesia* 62 D3
Ngabordamlu, Tanjung, *Indonesia* 63 F8
N'Gage, *Angola* 84 F3
Ngala, *Nigeria* 83 C7
Ngambé, *Cameroon* 83 D7
Ngambé, *Cameroon* 83 D7
Ngami Depression, *Botswana* 88 C3
Ngamo, *Zimbabwe* 87 F2
Ngangala, *Sudan* 81 G3
Nganglong Kangri, *China* 67 C12
Ngao, *Thailand* 64 C2
Ngaoundéré, *Cameroon* 84 C2
Ngapara, *N.Z.* 91 L3
Ngara, *Tanzania* 86 C3
Ngawi, *Indonesia* 63 G14
Nghia Lo, *Vietnam* 58 G5
Ngoboli, *Sudan* 81 G3
Ngoma, *Malawi* 87 E3
Ngomahura, *Zimbabwe* 87 G3
Ngomba, *Tanzania* 87 D3
Ngop, *Sudan* 81 F3
Ngoring Hu, *China* 60 C4
Ngorkou, *Mali* 82 B4
Ngorongoro, *Tanzania* 86 C4
Ngozi, *Burundi* 86 C2
Ngudu, *Tanzania* 86 C3
Nguigmi, *Niger* 79 F8
Nguila, *Cameroon* 83 E7
Nguiu, *Australia* 92 B5
Ngukurr, *Australia* 94 A1
Ngulu Atoll, *Pac. Oc.* 63 C9
Ngunga, *Tanzania* 86 C3
Nguru, *Nigeria* 83 C7
Nguru Mts., *Tanzania* 86 D4
Nguyen Binh, *Vietnam* 58 F5
Nha Trang, *Vietnam* 65 F7
Nhacoongo, *Mozam.* 89 C6
Nhamaabué, *Mozam.* 87 F4
Nhamundá →, *Brazil* 125 D7
Nhangulaze, L., *Mozam.* 89 C5
Nhill, *Australia* 95 F3
Nho Quan, *Vietnam* 58 G5
Nhulunbuy, *Australia* 94 A2
Nia-nia, *Dem. Rep. of the Congo* 86 B2
Niafounké, *Mali* 82 B4
Niagara Falls, *Canada* 102 D4
Niagara Falls, *U.S.A.* 110 C6
Niagara-on-the-Lake, *Canada* 110 C5
Niah, *Malaysia* 62 D4
Niamey, *Niger* 83 C5
Niandan-Koro, *Guinea* 82 C3
Nianforando, *Guinea* 82 D2
Niangara, *Dem. Rep. of the Congo* 86 B2
Niangbo, *Ivory C.* 82 D3
Niangoloko, *Burkina Faso* 82 C4
Niantic, *U.S.A.* 111 E12
Niaro, *Sudan* 81 E3
Nias, *Indonesia* 62 D1
Niassa □, *Mozam.* 87 E4
Nibāk, *Si. Arabia* 71 E7
Nibe, *Denmark* 11 H3
Nicaragua ■, *Cent. Amer.* 120 D2
Nicaragua, L. de, *Nic.* 120 D2
Nicastro, *Italy* 31 D9
Nice, *France* 21 E11
Niceville, *U.S.A.* 109 K2
Nichicun, L., *Canada* 103 B5
Nichinan, *Japan* 55 J5
Nicholás, Canal, *W. Indies* 120 B3
Nicholasville, *U.S.A.* 108 G3
Nichols, *U.S.A.* 111 D8
Nicholson, *Australia* 92 C4
Nicholson, *U.S.A.* 111 E9
Nicholson →, *Australia* 94 B2
Nicholson L., *Canada* 105 A8
Nicholson Ra., *Australia* 93 E2
Nicholville, *U.S.A.* 111 B10
Nicobar Is., *Ind. Oc.* 52 J13
Nicola, *Canada* 104 C4
Nicolls Town, *Bahamas* 120 A4
Nicopolis, *Greece* 38 B2
Nicosia, *Cyprus* 36 D12
Nicosia, *Italy* 31 E7
Nicótera, *Italy* 31 D8
Nicoya, *Costa Rica* 120 D2
Nicoya, G. de, *Costa Rica* 120 E3
Nicoya, Pen. de, *Costa Rica* 120 E2
Nidd →, *U.K.* 12 D6
Nidda, *Germany* 25 E5
Nidda →, *Germany* 25 E4
Nidwalden □, *Switz.* 25 J4
Nidzica, *Poland* 45 E7
Niebüll, *Germany* 24 A4
Nied →, *Germany* 19 C13
Niederaula, *Germany* 24 E5
Niederbayern □, *Germany* 25 G8
Niederbronn-les-Bains, *France* 19 D14
Niedere Tauern, *Austria* 26 D7
Niederlausitz, *Germany* 24 D9
Niederösterreich □, *Austria* 26 C8
Niedersachsen □, *Germany* 24 C4
Niekerkshoop, *S. Africa* 88 D3
Niellé, *Ivory C.* 82 C3
Niemba, *Dem. Rep. of the Congo* 86 D2

Niemen = Neman →, *Lithuania* 9 J20
Niemodlin, *Poland* 45 H4
Nienburg, *Germany* 24 C5
Niepołomice, *Poland* 45 H7
Niers →, *Germany* 24 D1
Niesky, *Germany* 24 D10
Nieszawa, *Poland* 45 F5
Nieu Bethesda, *S. Africa* 88 E3
Nieu Amsterdam, *Surinam* 125 B7
Nieuw Nickerie, *Surinam* 125 B7
Nieuwoudtville, *S. Africa* 88 E2
Nieuwpoort, *Belgium* 17 C2
Nieves, Pico de las, *Canary Is.* 37 G4
Nièvre □, *France* 19 E10
Niga, *Mali* 82 C3
Niğde, *Turkey* 70 B2
Nigel, *S. Africa* 89 D4
Niger □, *Nigeria* 83 D6
Niger ■, *W. Afr.* 83 B7
Niger →, *W. Afr.* 83 D6
Niger Delta, *Africa* 83 E6
Nigeria ■, *W. Afr.* 83 D6
Nighasin, *India* 69 E9
Nightcaps, *N.Z.* 91 L2
Nigríta, *Greece* 40 F7
Nii-Jima, *Japan* 55 G9
Niigata, *Japan* 54 F9
Niigata □, *Japan* 55 F9
Niihama, *Japan* 55 H6
Niihau, *U.S.A.* 106 H14
Niimi, *Japan* 55 G6
Niitsu, *Japan* 54 F9
Níjar, *Spain* 33 J2
Nijil, *Jordan* 75 E4
Nijkerk, *Neths.* 17 B5
Nijmegen, *Neths.* 17 C5
Nijverdal, *Neths.* 17 B6
Nīk Pey, *Iran* 71 B6
Nike, *Nigeria* 83 D6
Nikiniki, *Indonesia* 63 F6
Nikísiani, *Greece* 41 F8
Nikítas, *Greece* 40 F7
Nikki, *Benin* 83 D5
Nikkō, *Japan* 55 F9
Nikolayev = Mykolayiv, *Ukraine* 47 J7
Nikolayevsk, *Russia* 48 E7
Nikolayevsk-na-Amur, *Russia* 51 D15
Nikolsk, *Russia* 48 D8
Nikolskoye, *Russia* 51 D17
Nikopol, *Bulgaria* 41 C8
Nikopol, *Ukraine* 47 J8
Niksar, *Turkey* 72 B7
Nīkshahr, *Iran* 71 E9
Nikšić, *Montenegro, Yug.* 40 D2
Nîl, Nahr en →, *Africa* 80 H7
Nîl el Abyad →, *Sudan* 81 D3
Nîl el Azraq →, *Sudan* 81 D3
Nila, *Indonesia* 63 F7
Nile = Nîl, Nahr en →, *Africa* 80 H7
Niles, *Mich., U.S.A.* 108 E2
Niles, *Ohio, U.S.A.* 110 E4
Nilüfer →, *Turkey* 41 F12
Nim Ka Thana, *India* 68 F6
Nimach, *India* 68 G6
Nimbahera, *India* 68 G6
Nîmes, *France* 21 E8
Nimfaíon, Ákra = Pínnes, Ákra, *Greece* 41 F8
Nimmitabel, *Australia* 95 F4
Nimule, *Sudan* 81 G3
Nīnawá, *Iraq* 70 B4
Nindigully, *Australia* 95 D4
Nineveh = Nīnawá, *Iraq* 70 B4
Ning Xian, *China* 56 G4
Ning'an, *China* 57 B15
Ningbo, *China* 59 C13
Ningcheng, *China* 57 D10
Ningde, *China* 59 D12
Ningdu, *China* 59 D10
Ninggang, *China* 59 D9
Ningguo, *China* 59 B12
Ninghai, *China* 59 C13
Ninghua, *China* 59 D11
Ningi, *Nigeria* 83 C6
Ningjin, *China* 56 F8
Ningjing Shan, *China* 58 C2
Ninglang, *China* 58 D3
Ningling, *China* 56 G8
Ningming, *China* 58 F6
Ningnan, *China* 58 D4
Ningpo = Ningbo, *China* 59 C13
Ningqiang, *China* 56 H4
Ningshan, *China* 56 H5
Ningsia Hui A.R. = Ningxia Huizu Zizhiqu □, *China* 56 F4
Ningwu, *China* 56 E7
Ningxia Huizu Zizhiqu □, *China* 56 F4
Ningxiang, *China* 59 C9
Ningyang, *China* 56 G9
Ningyuan, *China* 59 E8
Ninh Binh, *Vietnam* 58 G5
Ninh Giang, *Vietnam* 64 B6
Ninh Hoa, *Vietnam* 64 F7
Ninh Ma, *Vietnam* 64 F7
Ninove, *Belgium* 17 D4
Nioaque, *Brazil* 127 A4
Niobrara, *U.S.A.* 112 D6
Niobrara →, *U.S.A.* 112 D6
Niono, *Mali* 82 C3
Nionsamoridougou, *Guinea* 82 D3
Nioro du Rip, *Senegal* 82 C1
Nioro du Sahel, *Mali* 82 B3
Niort, *France* 20 B3

Nipawin, *Canada* 105 C8
Nipfjället, *Sweden* 10 C6
Nipigon, *Canada* 102 C2
Nipigon, L., *Canada* 102 C2
Nipishish L., *Canada* 103 B7
Nipomo, *U.S.A.* 117 K6
Nipton, *U.S.A.* 117 K11
Niquelândia, *Brazil* 125 F9
Nīr, *Iran* 70 B5
Nirasaki, *Japan* 55 G9
Nirmal, *India* 66 K11
Nirmali, *India* 69 F12
Niš, *Serbia, Yug.* 40 C5
Nisa, *Portugal* 35 F3
Niṣāb, *Si. Arabia* 70 D5
Niṣāb, *Yemen* 74 E4
Niscemi, *Italy* 31 E7
Nishinomiya, *Japan* 55 G7
Nishino'omote, *Japan* 55 J5
Nishiwaki, *Japan* 55 G7
Nísíros, *Greece* 39 E9
Niška Banja, *Serbia, Yug.* 40 C6
Niskibi →, *Canada* 102 A2
Nisko, *Poland* 45 H9
Nisporeni, *Moldova* 43 C13
Nisqually →, *U.S.A.* 116 C4
Nissáki, *Greece* 36 A3
Nissan →, *Sweden* 11 H6
Nissum Bredning, *Denmark* 11 H2
Nissum Fjord, *Denmark* 11 H2
Nistru = Dnister →, *Europe* 47 J6
Nisutlin →, *Canada* 104 A2
Nitchequon, *Canada* 103 B5
Niterói, *Brazil* 127 A7
Nith →, *Canada* 110 C4
Nith →, *U.K.* 14 F5
Nitra, *Slovak Rep.* 27 C11
Nitra →, *Slovak Rep.* 27 D11
Nitriansky □, *Slovak Rep.* 27 C11
Nittenau, *Germany* 25 F8
Niuafo'ou, *Tonga* 91 B11
Niue, *Cook Is.* 97 J11
Niulan Jiang →, *China* 58 D4
Niut, *Indonesia* 62 D4
Niutou Shan, *China* 59 C13
Niuzhuang, *China* 57 D12
Nivala, *Finland* 8 E21
Nivelles, *Belgium* 17 D4
Nivernais, *France* 19 E10
Niwas, *India* 69 H9
Nixon, *U.S.A.* 113 L6
Nizamabad, *India* 66 K11
Nizamghat, *India* 67 E19
Nizhne Kolymsk, *Russia* 51 C17
Nizhnegorskiy = Nyzhnohirskyy, *Ukraine* 47 K8
Nizhnekamsk, *Russia* 48 C10
Nizhneudinsk, *Russia* 51 D10
Nizhnevartovsk, *Russia* 50 C8
Nizhniy Chir, *Russia* 49 F6
Nizhniy Lomov, *Russia* 48 D6
Nizhniy Novgorod, *Russia* 48 B7
Nizhniy Tagil, *Russia* 50 D6
Nizhyn, *Ukraine* 47 G6
Nizina Mazowiecka, *Poland* 45 F8
Nizip, *Turkey* 70 B3
Nízké Tatry, *Slovak Rep.* 27 C12
Nízký Jeseník, *Czech Rep.* 27 B10
Nizza Monferrato, *Italy* 28 D5
Njakwa, *Malawi* 87 E3
Njanji, *Zambia* 87 E3
Njegoš, *Montenegro, Yug.* 40 D2
Njinjo, *Tanzania* 87 D4
Njombe, *Tanzania* 87 D3
Njombe →, *Tanzania* 86 D4
Njurundabommen, *Sweden* 10 B11
Nkambe, *Cameroon* 83 D7
Nkana, *Zambia* 87 E2
Nkandla, *S. Africa* 89 D5
Nkawkaw, *Ghana* 83 D4
Nkayi, *Zimbabwe* 87 F2
Nkhotakota, *Malawi* 87 E3
Nkongsamba, *Cameroon* 83 E6
Nkurenkuru, *Namibia* 88 B2
Nkwanta, *Ghana* 82 D4
Nmai →, *Burma* 58 F2
Noakhali = Maijdi, *Bangla.* 67 H17
Nobel, *Canada* 110 A4
Nobeoka, *Japan* 55 H5
Noblejas, *Spain* 34 F7
Noblesville, *U.S.A.* 108 E3
Noce →, *Italy* 28 B8
Nocera Inferiore, *Italy* 31 B7
Nocera Umbra, *Italy* 29 E9
Noci, *Italy* 31 B10
Nocona, *U.S.A.* 113 J6
Noda, *Japan* 55 G9
Nogales, *Mexico* 118 A2
Nogales, *U.S.A.* 115 L8
Nogaro, *France* 20 E3
Nogat →, *Poland* 44 D6
Nōgata, *Japan* 55 H5
Nogent, *France* 19 D12
Nogent-le-Rotrou, *France* 18 D7
Nogent-sur-Seine, *France* 19 D10
Noggerup, *Australia* 93 F2
Noginsk, *Moskva, Russia* 46 E10
Noginsk, *Tunguska, Russia* 51 C10
Nogoa →, *Australia* 94 C4
Nogoyá, *Argentina* 126 C4
Nógrád □, *Hungary* 42 C4
Noguera Pallaresa →, *Spain* 32 D5
Noguera Ribagorzana →, *Spain* 32 D5
Nohar, *India* 68 E6
Nohfelden, *Germany* 25 F3
Nohta, *India* 69 H8
Noia, *Spain* 34 C2

Noire, Montagne, *France* 20 E6
Noire, Mt., *France* 18 D3
Noirétable, *France* 20 C7
Noirmoutier, Î. de, *France* 18 F4
Noirmoutier-en-l'Île, *France* 18 F4
Nojane, *Botswana* 88 C3
Nojima-Zaki, *Japan* 55 G9
Nok Kundi, *Pakistan* 66 E3
Nokaneng, *Botswana* 88 B3
Nokia, *Finland* 9 F20
Nokomis, *Canada* 105 C8
Nokomis L., *Canada* 105 B8
Nol, *Sweden* 11 G6
Nola, *C.A.R.* 84 D3
Nola, *Italy* 31 B7
Nolay, *France* 19 F11
Noli, C. di, *Italy* 28 D5
Nolinsk, *Russia* 48 B9
Noma Omuramba →, *Namibia* 88 B3
Nombre de Dios, *Panama* 120 E4
Nome, *U.S.A.* 100 B3
Nomo-Zaki, *Japan* 55 H4
Nonacho L., *Canada* 105 A7
Nonancourt, *France* 18 D8
Nonda, *Australia* 94 C3
None, *Italy* 28 D4
Nong Chang, *Thailand* 64 E2
Nong Het, *Laos* 64 C4
Nong Khai, *Thailand* 64 D4
Nong'an, *China* 57 B13
Nongoma, *S. Africa* 89 D5
Nonoava, *Mexico* 118 B3
Nonoava →, *Mexico* 118 B3
Nonthaburi, *Thailand* 64 F3
Nontron, *France* 20 C4
Nonza, *France* 21 F13
Noonamah, *Australia* 92 B5
Noonkanbah, *Australia* 92 C3
Noord Brabant □, *Neths.* 17 C5
Noord Holland □, *Neths.* 17 B5
Noordbeveland, *Neths.* 17 C3
Noordoostpolder, *Neths.* 17 B5
Noordwijk, *Neths.* 17 B4
Nootka I., *Canada* 104 D3
Nopiming Prov. Park, *Canada* 105 C9
Nora, *Eritrea* 81 D5
Nora, *Sweden* 10 E9
Noralee, *Canada* 104 C3
Noranda = Rouyn-Noranda, *Canada* 102 C4
Norberg, *Sweden* 10 D9
Nórcia, *Italy* 29 F10
Norco, *U.S.A.* 117 M9
Nord □, *France* 19 B10
Nord-Kivu □, *Dem. Rep. of the Congo* 86 C2
Nord-Ostsee-Kanal, *Germany* 24 A5
Nord-Pas-de-Calais □, *France* 19 B9
Nordaustlandet, *Svalbard* 4 B9
Nordborg, *Denmark* 11 J3
Nordby, *Denmark* 11 J2
Norddeich, *Germany* 24 B3
Nordegg, *Canada* 104 C5
Norden, *Germany* 24 B3
Nordenham, *Germany* 24 B4
Norderney, *Germany* 24 B3
Norderstedt, *Germany* 24 B6
Nordfjord, *Norway* 9 F11
Nordfriesische Inseln, *Germany* 24 A4
Nordhausen, *Germany* 24 D6
Nordhorn, *Germany* 24 C3
Norðoyar, *Faeroe Is.* 8 E9
Nordingrå, *Sweden* 10 B12
Nordjyllands Amtskommune □, *Denmark* 11 G4
Nordkapp, *Norway* 8 A21
Nordkapp, *Svalbard* 4 A9
Nordkinn = Kinnarodden, *Norway* 6 A11
Nordkinn-halvøya, *Norway* 8 A22
Nördlingen, *Germany* 25 G6
Nordrhein-Westfalen □, *Germany* 24 D3
Nordstrand, *Germany* 24 A4
Nordvik, *Russia* 51 B12
Nore →, *Ireland* 15 D4
Norefjell, *Norway* 9 F13
Norfolk, *Nebr., U.S.A.* 112 D6
Norfolk, *Va., U.S.A.* 108 G7
Norfolk □, *U.K.* 13 E8
Norfolk I., *Pac. Oc.* 96 K8
Norfork L., *U.S.A.* 113 G8
Norilsk, *Russia* 51 C9
Norma, Mt., *Australia* 94 C3
Normal, *U.S.A.* 112 E10
Norman, *U.S.A.* 113 H6
Norman →, *Australia* 94 B3
Norman Wells, *Canada* 100 B7
Normanby →, *Australia* 94 A3
Normandin, *Canada* 102 C5
Normandy = Normandie, *France* 18 D7
Normanhurst, Mt., *Australia* 93 E3
Normanton, *Australia* 94 B3
Normétal, *Canada* 102 C4
Norquay, *Canada* 105 C8
Norquinco, *Argentina* 128 E2
Norra Dellen, *Sweden* 10 C10
Norra Ulvön, *Sweden* 10 A12
Norrahammar, *Sweden* 11 G8
Norrbotten □, *Sweden* 8 C19
Nørre Åby, *Denmark* 11 J3
Nørre Nebel, *Denmark* 11 K5
Nørresundby, *Denmark* 11 G3
Norrhult, *Sweden* 11 H9
Norris Point, *Canada* 103 C8
Norristown, *U.S.A.* 111 F9
Norrköping, *Sweden* 11 F10
Norrland, *Sweden* 9 E16

Norrsundet, *Sweden* 10 D11
Norrtälje, *Sweden* 10 E12
Norseman, *Australia* 93 F3
Norsk, *Russia* 51 D14
Norte, Pta. del, *Canary Is.* 37 G2
Norte, Serra do, *Brazil* 124
North, C., *Canada* 103 C7
North Adams, *U.S.A.* 111 D11
North Arm, *Canada* 104 A5
North Augusta, *U.S.A.* 109 J5
North Ayrshire □, *U.K.* 14 F4
North Bass I., *U.S.A.* 110 E2
North Battleford, *Canada* 105 C7
North Bay, *Canada* 102 C4
North Belcher Is., *Canada* 102 A4
North Bend, *Oreg., U.S.A.* 114 E1
North Bend, *Pa., U.S.A.* 110 E7
North Bend, *Wash., U.S.A.* 116 C5
North Bennington, *U.S.A.* 111 D11
North Berwick, *U.K.* 14 E6
North Berwick, *U.S.A.* 111 C14
North C., *Canada* 103 C7
North C., *N.Z.* 91 F4
North Canadian →, *U.S.A.* 113 H7
North Canton, *U.S.A.* 110 F3
North Cape = Nordkapp, *Norway* 8 A21
North Cape = Nordkapp, *Svalbard* 4 A9
North Caribou L., *Canada* 102 B1
North Carolina □, *U.S.A.* 109 H6
North Cascades National Park, *U.S.A.* 114 B3
North Channel, *Canada* 102 C3
North Channel, *U.K.* 14 F3
North Charleston, *U.S.A.* 109 J6
North Chicago, *U.S.A.* 108 D2
North Creek, *U.S.A.* 111 C11
North Dakota □, *U.S.A.* 112 B5
North Downs, *U.K.* 13 F8
North East, *U.S.A.* 110 D5
North East Frontier Agency = Arunachal Pradesh □, *India* 67 F19
North East Lincolnshire □, *U.K.* 12 D7
North Eastern □, *Kenya* 86 B5
North Esk →, *U.K.* 14 E6
North European Plain, *Europe* 6 E10
North Foreland, *U.K.* 13 F9
North Fork, *U.S.A.* 116 H7
North Fork American →, *U.S.A.* 116 G5
North Fork Feather →, *U.S.A.* 116 F5
North Fork Grand →, *U.S.A.* 112 C3
North Fork Red →, *U.S.A.* 113 H5
North Frisian Is. = Nordfriesische Inseln, *Germany* 24 A4
North Gower, *Canada* 111 A9
North Hd., *Australia* 93 F1
North Henik L., *Canada* 105 A9
North Highlands, *U.S.A.* 116 G5
North Horr, *Kenya* 86 B4
North I., *Kenya* 86 B4
North I., *N.Z.* 91 H5
North Kingsville, *U.S.A.* 110 E4
North Knife →, *Canada* 105 B10
North Koel →, *India* 69 G10
North Korea ■, *Asia* 57 E14
North Lakhimpur, *India* 67 F19
North Lanarkshire □, *U.K.* 14 F5
North Las Vegas, *U.S.A.* 117 J11
North Lincolnshire □, *U.K.* 12 D7
North Little Rock, *U.S.A.* 113 H8
North Loup →, *U.S.A.* 112 E5
North Magnetic Pole, *Canada* 4 B2
North Minch, *U.K.* 14 C3
North Moose L., *Canada* 105 C8
North Myrtle Beach, *U.S.A.* 109 J6
North Nahanni →, *Canada* 104 A4
North Olmsted, *U.S.A.* 110 E3
North Ossetia □, *Russia* 49 J7
North Pagai, I. = Pagai Utara, Pulau, *Indonesia* 62 E2
North Palisade, *U.S.A.* 116 H8
North Platte, *U.S.A.* 112 E4
North Platte →, *U.S.A.* 112 E4
North Pole, *Arctic* 4 A
North Portal, *Canada* 105 D8
North Powder, *U.S.A.* 114 D5
North Pt., *U.S.A.* 110 A1
North Rhine Westphalia = Nordrhein-Westfalen □, *Germany* 24 D3
North River, *Canada* 103 B8
North Ronaldsay, *U.K.* 14 B6
North Saskatchewan →, *Canada* 105 C7
North Sea, *Europe* 6 D6
North Seal →, *Canada* 105 B9
North Somercotes, *U.K.* 13 F5
North Sporades = Vóriai Sporádhes, *Greece* 38 B5
North Sydney, *Canada* 103 C7
North Syracuse, *U.S.A.* 111 C8
North Taranaki Bight, *N.Z.* 91 H5
North Thompson →, *Canada* 104 C4
North Tonawanda, *U.S.A.* 110 C6
North Troy, *U.S.A.* 111 B12
North Truchas Pk., *U.S.A.* 115 J11
North Twin I., *Canada* 102 B4
North Tyne →, *U.K.* 12 B5
North Uist, *U.K.* 14 D1
North Vancouver, *Canada* 104 D4
North Vernon, *U.S.A.* 108 F3

North Wabasca L., *Canada* . 104 B6
North Walsham, *U.K.* 12 E9
North-West □, *S. Africa* 88 D4
North West C., *Australia* ... 92 D1
North West Christmas I.
Ridge, *Pac. Oc.* 97 G11
North West Frontier □,
Pakistan 68 C4
North West Highlands, *U.K.* 14 D4
North West River, *Canada* . 103 B7
North Western □, *Zambia* .. 87 E2
North Wildwood, *U.S.A.* ... 108 F8
North York Moors, *U.K.* ... 12 C7
North Yorkshire □, *U.K.* ... 12 C6
Northallerton, *U.K.* 12 C6
Northam, *Australia* 93 F2
Northam, *S. Africa* 88 C4
Northampton, *Australia* ... 93 E1
Northampton, *U.K.* 13 E7
Northampton, *Mass., U.S.A.* 111 D12
Northampton, *Pa., U.S.A.* . 111 F9
Northamptonshire □, *U.K.* . 13 E7
Northbridge, *U.S.A.* 111 D13
Northcliffe, *Australia* 93 F2
Northeast Providence Chan.,
W. Indies 120 A4
Northeim, *Germany* 24 D6
Northern □, *Ghana* 83 D4
Northern □, *Malawi* 87 E3
Northern □, *Uganda* 86 B3
Northern □, *Zambia* 87 E3
Northern Cape □, *S. Africa* 88 D3
Northern Circars, *India* ... 67 L13
Northern Indian L., *Canada* 105 B9
Northern Ireland □, *U.K.* .. 15 B5
Northern Light L., *Canada* . 102 C1
Northern Marianas ■,
Pac. Oc. 96 F6
Northern Province □,
S. Leone 82 D2
Northern Province □,
S. Africa 89 C4
Northern Territory □,
Australia 92 D5
Northfield, *Minn., U.S.A.* .. 112 C8
Northfield, *Vt., U.S.A.* ... 111 B12
Northland □, *N.Z.* 91 F4
Northome, *U.S.A.* 112 B7
Northport, *Ala., U.S.A.* ... 109 J2
Northport, *Wash., U.S.A.* . 114 B5
Northumberland □, *U.K.* .. 12 B6
Northumberland, C.,
Australia 95 F3
Northumberland Is.,
Australia 94 C4
Northumberland Str.,
Canada 103 C7
Northville, *U.S.A.* 111 C10
Northwest Providence
Channel, *W. Indies* 120 A4
Northwest Territories □,
Canada 100 B9
Northwood, *Iowa, U.S.A.* . 112 D8
Northwood, *N. Dak., U.S.A.* 112 B6
Norton, *U.S.A.* 112 F5
Norton, *Zimbabwe* 87 F3
Norton Sd., *U.S.A.* 100 B3
Nortorf, *Germany* 24 A5
Norwalk, *Calif., U.S.A.* ... 117 M8
Norwalk, *Conn., U.S.A.* .. 111 E11
Norwalk, *Iowa, U.S.A.* ... 112 E8
Norwalk, *Ohio, U.S.A.* ... 110 E2
Norway, *Maine, U.S.A.* ... 109 C10
Norway, *Mich., U.S.A.* ... 108 C2
Norway ■, *Europe* 8 E14
Norway House, *Canada* ... 105 C9
Norwegian Sea, *Atl. Oc.* .. 4 C8
Norwich, *Canada* 110 D4
Norwich, *U.K.* 13 E9
Norwich, *Conn., U.S.A.* . 111 E12
Norwich, *N.Y., U.S.A.* ... 111 D9
Norwood, *Canada* 110 B7
Norwood, *U.S.A.* 111 B10
Noshiro, *Japan* 54 D10
Nosivka, *Ukraine* 47 G6
Nosovka = Nosivka, *Ukraine* 47 G6
Noṣraṭābād, *Iran* 71 D8
Noss Hd., *U.K.* 14 C5
Nossebro, *Sweden* 11 F6
Nossob →, *S. Africa* 88 D3
Nossombougou, *Mali* 82 C3
Nosy Barren, *Madag.* 85 H8
Nosy Be, *Madag.* 85 G9
Nosy Boraha, *Madag.* 89 B8
Nosy Lava, *Madag.* 89 A8
Nosy Varika, *Madag.* 89 C8
Noteć →, *Poland* 45 F2
Notikewin →, *Canada* ... 104 B5
Notios Evvoïkos Kólpos,
Greece 38 C5
Noto, *Italy* 31 F8
Noto, G. di, *Italy* 31 F8
Notodden, *Norway* 9 G13
Notre Dame B., *Canada* .. 103 C8
Notre Dame de Koartac =
Quaqtaq, *Canada* 101 B13
Notre-Dame-des-Bois,
Canada 111 A13
Notre Dame d'Ivugivic =
Ivujivik, *Canada* 101 B12
Notre-Dame-du-Nord,
Canada 102 C4
Nottaway →, *Canada* 102 B4
Nottawasaga B., *Canada* .. 110 B4
Nottaway →, *Canada* 102 B4
Nottingham, *U.K.* 12 E6
Nottingham, City of □, *U.K.* 12 E6
Nottingham I., *Canada* ... 101 B12
Nottinghamshire □, *U.K.* . 12 D6
Nottoway →, *U.S.A.* 108 G7
Notwane →, *Botswana* ... 88 C4

Nouâdhibou, *Mauritania* ... 78 D2
Nouâdhibou, Ras,
Mauritania 78 D2
Nouakchott, *Mauritania* ... 82 B1
Nouâmghâr, *Mauritania* ... 82 B1
Nouméa, *N. Cal.* 96 K8
Nouna, *Burkina Faso* 82 C4
Noupoort, *S. Africa* 88 E3
Nouveau Comptoir =
Wemindji, *Canada* 102 B4
Nouvelle-Amsterdam, I.,
Ind. Oc. 3 F13
Nouvelle-Calédonie = New
Caledonia ■, *Pac. Oc.* . 96 K8
Nouzonville, *France* 19 C11
Nová Baňa, *Slovak Rep.* .. 27 C11
Nová Bystřice, *Czech Rep.* . 26 B8
Nova Casa Nova, *Brazil* .. 125 E10
Nova Esperança, *Brazil* .. 127 A5
Nova Friburgo, *Brazil* ... 127 A7
Nova Gaia = Cambundi-
Catembo, *Angola* 84 G3
Nova Gorica, *Slovenia* 29 C10
Nova Gradiška, *Croatia* ... 42 E2
Nova Iguaçu, *Brazil* 127 A7
Nova Iorque, *Brazil* 125 E10
Nova Kakhovka, *Ukraine* . 47 J7
Nova Lamego, *Guinea-Biss.* 82 C2
Nova Lima, *Brazil* 127 A7
Nova Lisboa = Huambo,
Angola 85 G3
Nova Lusitânia, *Mozam.* .. 87 F3
Nova Mambone, *Mozam.* .. 89 C6
Nova Odesa, *Ukraine* 47 J6
Nová Paka, *Czech Rep.* ... 26 A8
Nova Pavova, *Serbia, Yug.* 42 F5
Nova Scotia □, *Canada* ... 103 C7
Nova Siri, *Italy* 31 B9
Nova Sofala, *Mozam.* 89 C5
Nova Varoš, *Serbia, Yug.* . 40 C3
Nova Venécia, *Brazil* 125 G10
Nova Zagora, *Bulgaria* ... 41 D10
Novaci, *Macedonia* 40 E5
Novaci, *Romania* 43 E8
Novaféltria, *Italy* 29 E9
Novaleksandrovskaya =
Novoaleksandrovsk, *Russia* 49 H5
Novannenskiy =
Novoannenskiy, *Russia* .. 48 E6
Novar, *Canada* 110 A5
Novara, *Italy* 28 C5
Novato, *U.S.A.* 116 G4
Novaya Kakhovka = Nova
Kakhovka, *Ukraine* 47 J7
Novaya Kazanka, *Kazakstan* 49 F9
Novaya Ladoga, *Russia* ... 46 B7
Novaya Lyalya, *Russia* 50 D7
Novaya Sibir, Ostrov, *Russia* 51 B16
Novaya Zemlya, *Russia* ... 50 B6
Nové Město, *Slovak Rep.* .. 27 C10
Nové Město na Moravě,
Czech Rep. 26 B9
Nové Město nad Metují,
Czech Rep. 27 A9
Nové Zámky, *Slovak Rep.* . 27 C11
Novelda, *Spain* 33 G4
Novellara, *Italy* 28 D7
Noventa Vicentina, *Italy* .. 29 C8
Novgorod, *Russia* 46 C6
Novgorod-Severskiy =
Novhorod-Siverskyy,
Ukraine 47 G7
Novhorod-Siverskyy, *Ukraine* 47 G7
Novi Bečej, *Serbia, Yug.* .. 42 E5
Novi Iskar, *Bulgaria* 40 D7
Novi Kneževac, *Serbia, Yug.* 42 D5
Novi Lígure, *Italy* 28 D5
Novi Pazar, *Bulgaria* 41 C11
Novi Pazar, *Serbia, Yug.* . 40 C4
Novi Sad, *Serbia, Yug.* ... 42 E4
Novi Slankamen,
Serbia, Yug. 42 E5
Novi Travnik, *Bos.-H.* ... 42 F2
Novi Vinodolski, *Croatia* . 29 C11
Novigrad, *Istra, Croatia* .. 29 C10
Novigrad, *Zadar, Croatia* . 29 D12
Novigradsko More, *Croatia* 29 D12
Nôvo Hamburgo, *Brazil* .. 127 B5
Novo Mesto, *Slovenia* 29 C12
Novo Miloševo, *Serbia, Yug.* 42 E5
Novo Remanso, *Brazil* ... 125 E10
Novoaleksandrovsk, *Russia* 49 H5
Novoannenskiy, *Russia* ... 48 E6
Novoataysk, *Russia* 50 D9
Novoazovsk, *Ukraine* 47 J10
Novocheboksarsk, *Russia* . 48 B8
Novocherkassk, *Russia* ... 49 G5
Novodevichye, *Russia* 48 D9
Novogrudok = Navahrudak,
Belarus 46 F3
Novohrad-Volynskyy,
Ukraine 47 G4
Novokachalinsk, *Russia* .. 54 B6
Novokazalinsk =
Zhangaqazaly, *Kazakstan* 50 E7
Novokhopersk, *Russia* 48 E5
Novokuybyshevsk, *Russia* . 48 D9
Novokuznetsk, *Russia* 50 D9
Novomirgorod, *Ukraine* .. 47 H6
Novomoskovsk, *Russia* ... 46 E10
Novomoskovsk, *Ukraine* . 47 H8
Novopolotsk = Navapolatsk,
Belarus 46 E5
Novorossiysk, *Russia* 47 K9
Novorybnoye, *Russia* 51 B11
Novoselytsya, *Ukraine* ... 47 H4
Novoshakhtinsk, *Russia* .. 47 J10
Novosibirsk, *Russia* 50 D9

Novosibirskiye Ostrova,
Russia 51 B15
Novosil, *Russia* 46 D6
Novosokolniki, *Russia* 46 D6
Novotitarovskaya, *Russia* . 49 H4
Novotroitsk, *Russia* 50 D6
Novoukrayinka, *Ukraine* .. 47 H6
Novouljanovsk, *Russia* ... 48 C9
Novouzensk, *Russia* 48 E9
Novovolynsk, *Ukraine* 47 G3
Novovoronezhskiy, *Russia* 47 G10
Novozybkov, *Russia* 47 F6
Novska, *Croatia* 29 C14
Novvy Urengoy, *Russia* .. 50 C8
Nový Bor, *Czech Rep.* ... 26 A7
Novy Bug = Novyy Buh,
Ukraine 47 J7
Nový Bydžov, *Czech Rep.* 26 A8
Novy Dwór Mazowiecki,
Poland 45 F7
Nový Jičín, *Czech Rep.* .. 27 B11
Novyy Afon, *Georgia* 49 J5
Novyy Buh, *Ukraine* 47 J7
Novyy Oskol, *Russia* 47 G9
Novyy Port, *Russia* 50 C8
Novyy Urengoy = Novvy
Urengoy, *Russia* 50 C8
Now Shahr, *Iran* 71 B6
Nowbarān, *Iran* 71 C6
Nowe, *Poland* 44 E5
Nowe Miasteczko, *Poland* . 45 G2
Nowe Miasto, *Poland* 45 G7
Nowe Miasto Lubawskie,
Poland 44 E6
Nowe Skalmierzyce, *Poland* 45 G4
Nowe Warpno, *Poland* ... 44 E1
Nowghāb, *Iran* 71 C8
Nowgong, *Assam, India* .. 67 F18
Nowgong, *M. P., India* .. 69 G8
Nowogard, *Poland* 44 E2
Nowogród, *Poland* 45 E8
Nowogród Bobrzanski,
Poland 45 G2
Nowogrodziec, *Poland* ... 45 G2
Nowra-Bomaderry, *Australia* 95 E5
Nowshera, *Pakistan* 66 C8
Nowy Dwór Gdański, *Poland* 44 D6
Nowy Sącz, *Poland* 45 J7
Nowy Staw, *Poland* 44 D6
Nowy Targ, *Poland* 45 J7
Nowy Tomyśl, *Poland* 45 F3
Nowy Wiśnicz, *Poland* ... 45 J7
Noxen, *U.S.A.* 111 E8
Noxon, *U.S.A.* 114 C6
Noyabr'sk, *Russia* 50 C8
Noyant, *France* 18 E7
Noyers, *France* 19 E10
Noyon, *France* 19 C9
Noyon, *Mongolia* 56 C2
Nozay, *France* 18 E5
Nqutu, *S. Africa* 89 D5
Nsanje, *Malawi* 87 F4
Nsawam, *Ghana* 83 D4
Nsomba, *Zambia* 87 E2
Nsukka, *Nigeria* 83 D6
Ntui, *Cameroon* 83 E7
Nu Jiang →, *China* 58 E2
Nu Shan, *China* 58 E2
Nuba Mts. = Nubah,
Jibalan, *Sudan* 81 E3
Nubah, Jibalan, *Sudan* .. 81 E3
Nubia, *Africa* 76 D7
Nubian Desert = Nûbîya, Es
Sahrâ en, *Sudan* 80 C3
Nûbîya, Es Sahrâ en, *Sudan* 80 C3
Nubledo, *Spain* 34 B5
Nuboai, *Indonesia* 63 E9
Nubra →, *India* 69 B7
Nucet, *Romania* 42 D7
Nueces →, *U.S.A.* 113 M6
Nueltin L., *Canada* 105 A9
Nueva Asunción □,
Paraguay 126 A3
Nueva Carteya, *Spain* 35 H6
Nueva Gerona, *Cuba* 120 B3
Nueva Palmira, *Uruguay* . 126 C4
Nueva Rosita, *Mexico* ... 118 B4
Nueva San Salvador, *El Salv.* 120 D2
Nueva Tabarca, *Spain* ... 33 G4
Nuéve de Julio, *Argentina* 126 D3
Nuevitas, *Cuba* 120 B4
Nuevo, G., *Argentina* 128 E4
Nuevo Casas Grandes,
Mexico 118 A3
Nuevo Guerrero, *Mexico* . 119 B5
Nuevo Laredo, *Mexico* .. 119 B5
Nuevo León □, *Mexico* .. 118 C5
Nuevo Rocafuerte, *Ecuador* 124 D3
Nugget Pt., *N.Z.* 91 M2
Nugrus, Gebel, *Egypt* ... 80 C3
Nuhaka, *N.Z.* 91 H6
Nuits-St-Georges, *France* . 19 E11
Nukey Bluff, *Australia* ... 95 E2
Nukheila, *Sudan* 80 D2
Nukhuyb, *Iraq* 70 C4
Nuku'alofa, *Tonga* 91 E12
Nukus, *Uzbekistan* 50 E6
Nules, *Spain* 32 F4
Nullagine, *Australia* 92 D3
Nullagine →, *Australia* ... 92 D3
Nullarbor, *Australia* 93 F5
Nullarbor Plain, *Australia* . 93 F4
Numalla, L., *Australia* 95 D3
Numan, *Nigeria* 83 D7
Numata, *Japan* 55 F9
Numatinna →, *Sudan* 81 F2
Numazu, *Japan* 55 G9
Numbulwar, *Australia* ... 94 A2

Numfoor, *Indonesia* 63 E8
Numurkah, *Australia* 95 F4
Nunaksaluk I., *Canada* ... 103 A7
Nunap Isua, *Greenland* ... 4 D5
Nunavut □, *Canada* 101 B11
Nunda, *U.S.A.* 110 D7
Nungarin, *Australia* 93 F2
Nungo, *Mozam.* 87 E4
Nungwe, *Tanzania* 86 C3
Nunivak I., *U.S.A.* 100 B3
Nunkun, *India* 69 C7
Núoro, *Italy* 30 B2
Nure →, *Italy* 28 C6
Nuremberg = Nürnberg,
Germany 25 F7
Nuri, *Mexico* 118 B3
Nuriootpa, *Australia* 95 E2
Nurlat, *Russia* 48 C10
Nurmes, *Finland* 8 E23
Nürnberg, *Germany* 25 F7
Nurpur, *Pakistan* 68 D4
Nurra, La, *Italy* 30 B1
Nurran Lakes, *Australia* .. 93 E5
Nurri, *Italy* 30 C2
Nürtingen, *Germany* 25 G5
Nurzec →, *Poland* 45 F9
Nus, *Italy* 28 C4
Nusa Barung, *Indonesia* .. 63 H15
Nusa Kambangan, *Indonesia* 63 G13
Nusa Tenggara Barat □,
Indonesia 62 F5
Nusa Tenggara Timur □,
Indonesia 63 F6
Nusaybin, *Turkey* 73 D9
Nushki, *Pakistan* 68 E2
Nuuk, *Greenland* 101 B14
Nuwakot, *Nepal* 69 E10
Nuweiba', *Egypt* 70 D2
Nuwerus, *S. Africa* 88 E2
Nuweveldberge, *S. Africa* . 88 E3
Nuyts, C., *Australia* 93 F5
Nuyts, Pt., *Australia* 93 G2
Nuyts Arch., *Australia* ... 95 E1
Nxau-Nxau, *Botswana* ... 88 B3
Nyaake, *Liberia* 82 E3
Nyabing, *Australia* 93 F2
Nyack, *U.S.A.* 111 E11
Nyagan, *Russia* 50 C7
Nyahanga, *Tanzania* 86 C3
Nyahua, *Tanzania* 86 D3
Nyahururu, *Kenya* 86 B4
Nyaingentanglha Shan,
China 60 C4
Nyakanazi, *Tanzania* 86 C3
Nyakrom, *Ghana* 83 D4
Nyâlâ, *Sudan* 81 E1
Nyamandhlovu, *Zimbabwe* 87 F2
Nyambiti, *Tanzania* 86 C3
Nyamwaga, *Tanzania* ... 86 C3
Nyandekwa, *Tanzania* ... 86 C3
Nyanding →, *Sudan* 81 F3
Nyandoma, *Russia* 46 B11
Nyangana, *Namibia* 88 B3
Nyanguge, *Tanzania* 86 C3
Nyanza, *Rwanda* 86 C2
Nyanza □, *Kenya* 86 C3
Nyanza-Lac, *Burundi* 86 C2
Nyaponges, *Sudan* 81 F3
Nyasa, L., *Africa* 87 E3
Nyasvizh, *Belarus* 47 F4
Nyazura, *Zimbabwe* 87 F3
Nyazwidzi →, *Zimbabwe* . 87 G3
Nyborg, *Denmark* 11 J4
Nybro, *Sweden* 11 H9
Nyda, *Russia* 50 C8
Nyeri, *Kenya* 86 C4
Nyerol, *Sudan* 81 F3
Nyhammar, *Sweden* 10 D8
Nyinahin, *Ghana* 82 D4
Nyíradony, *Hungary* 42 C6
Nyírbátor, *Hungary* 42 C6
Nyíregyháza, *Hungary* ... 42 C6
Nykøbing, Storstrøm,
Denmark 11 K5
Nykøbing, Vestsjælland,
Denmark 11 J5
Nykøbing, Viborg, *Denmark* 11 H2
Nyköping, *Sweden* 11 F11
Nykroppa, *Sweden* 10 E8
Nykvarn, *Sweden* 10 E11
Nyland, *Sweden* 10 A11
Nylstroom, *S. Africa* 89 C4
Nymagee, *Australia* 95 E4
Nymburk, *Czech Rep.* ... 26 A8
Nynäshamn, *Sweden* 11 F11
Nyngan, *Australia* 95 E4
Nyoma Rap, *India* 69 C8
Nyoman = Neman →,
Lithuania 9 J20
Nyon, *Switz.* 25 J2
Nyong →, *Cameroon* 83 E6
Nyons, *France* 21 D9
Nyou, *Burkina Faso* 83 C4
Nýřsko, *Czech Rep.* 26 B6
Nysa, *Poland* 45 H4
Nysa →, *Europe* 24 C10
Nysa Kłodzka →, *Poland* 45 H4
Nysäter, *Sweden* 10 E6
Nyssa, *U.S.A.* 114 E5
Nysted, *Denmark* 11 K5
Nyunzu,
Dem. Rep. of the Congo . 86 D2
Nyurba, *Russia* 51 C12
Nyzhnohirskyy, *Ukraine* . 47 K8
Nzébéla, *Guinea* 82 D3

Nzega, *Tanzania* 86 C3
Nzérékoré, *Guinea* 82 D3
Nzeto, *Angola* 84 F2
Nzilo, Chutes de,
Dem. Rep. of the Congo . 87 E2
Nzo →, *Ivory C.* 82 D3
Nzubuka, *Tanzania* 86 C3

O

O Barco, *Spain* 34 C4
O Carballiño, *Spain* 34 C2
O Corgo, *Spain* 34 C3
O Pino, *Spain* 34 C2
O Porriño, *Spain* 34 C2
Ō-Shima, *Japan* 55 G9
Oa, Mull of, *U.K.* 14 F2
Oacoma, *U.S.A.* 112 D5
Oahe, L., *U.S.A.* 112 C4
Oahe Dam, *U.S.A.* 112 C4
Oahu, *U.S.A.* 106 H16
Oak Harbor, *U.S.A.* 116 B4
Oak Hill, *U.S.A.* 108 G5
Oak Ridge, *U.S.A.* 109 G3
Oak View, *U.S.A.* 117 L7
Oakan-Dake, *Japan* 54 C12
Oakdale, *Calif., U.S.A.* .. 116 H6
Oakdale, *La., U.S.A.* 113 K8
Oakes, *U.S.A.* 112 B5
Oakesdale, *U.S.A.* 114 C5
Oakey, *Australia* 95 D5
Oakfield, *U.S.A.* 110 D3
Oakham, *U.K.* 13 E7
Oakhurst, *U.S.A.* 116 H7
Oakland, *U.S.A.* 116 H4
Oakley, *Idaho, U.S.A.* ... 114 E7
Oakley, *Kans., U.S.A.* ... 112 F4
Oakover →, *Australia* ... 92 D3
Oakridge, *U.S.A.* 114 E2
Oakville, *Canada* 110 C5
Oakville, *U.S.A.* 116 D3
Oamaru, *N.Z.* 91 L3
Oancea, *Romania* 43 E12
Oasis, *Calif., U.S.A.* 117 M10
Oasis, *Nev., U.S.A.* 116 H9
Oates Land, *Antarctica* .. 5 C11
Oatlands, *Australia* 94 G4
Oatman, *U.S.A.* 117 K12
Oaxaca, *Mexico* 119 D5
Oaxaca □, *Mexico* 119 D5
Ob →, *Russia* 50 C7
Oba, *Canada* 102 C3
Obala, *Cameroon* 83 E7
Obama, *Japan* 55 G7
Oban, *Nigeria* 83 D6
Oban, *U.K.* 14 E3
Obbia, *Somali Rep.* 74 F4
Obera, *Argentina* 127 B4
Oberammergau, *Germany* . 25 H7
Oberasbach, *Germany* ... 25 F6
Oberbayern □, *Germany* . 25 G7
Oberdrauburg, *Austria* ... 26 E5
Oberfranken □, *Germany* . 25 E7
Oberhausen, *Germany* ... 24 D2
Oberkirch, *Germany* 25 G4
Oberlausitz, *Germany* 24 D10
Oberlin, *Kans., U.S.A.* .. 112 F4
Oberlin, *La., U.S.A.* 113 K8
Oberlin, *Ohio, U.S.A.* ... 110 E2
Obernai, *France* 19 D14
Oberndorf, *Germany* 25 G4
Oberon, *Australia* 95 E4
Oberösterreich □, *Austria* . 26 C7
Oberpfalz □, *Germany* ... 25 F8
Oberpfälzer Wald, *Germany* 25 F8
Oberstdorf, *Germany* 25 H6
Obersel, *Germany* 25 E4
Oberwart, *Austria* 27 D9
Obi, Kepulauan, *Indonesia* . 63 E7
Obi Is. = Obi, Kepulauan,
Indonesia 63 E7
Obiaruku, *Nigeria* 83 D6
Óbidos, *Brazil* 125 D7
Óbidos, *Portugal* 35 F1
Obihiro, *Japan* 54 C11
Obilatu, *Indonesia* 63 E7
Obilnoye, *Russia* 49 G7
Obing, *Germany* 25 G8
Objat, *France* 20 C5
Obluchye, *Russia* 51 E14
Obninsk, *Russia* 46 E9
Obo, *C.A.R.* 86 A2
Oboa, Mt., *Uganda* 86 B3
Obock, *Djibouti* 81 E5
Oborniki, *Poland* 45 F3
Oborniki Śląskie, *Poland* . 45 G3
Oboyan, *Russia* 47 G9
Obozerskaya = Obozerskiy,
Russia 50 C5
Obozerskiy, *Russia* 50 C5
Obrenovac, *Serbia, Yug.* . 40 B4
Obrovac, *Croatia* 29 D12
Obruk, *Turkey* 72 C5
Obshchi Syrt, *Russia* 6 E16
Obskaya Guba, *Russia* ... 50 C8
Obuasi, *Ghana* 83 D4
Obubra, *Nigeria* 83 D6
Obudu, *Nigeria* 83 D6
Obwalden □, *Switz.* 25 J4
Ocala, *U.S.A.* 109 L4
Ocampo, *Chihuahua, Mexico* 118 B3
Ocampo, *Tamaulipas,
Mexico* 119 C5
Ocaña, *Spain* 34 F7
Ocanomowoc, *U.S.A.* ... 112 D10

Occidental, Cordillera, Colombia 122 C3
Ocean City, Md., U.S.A. .. 108 F8
Ocean City, N.J., U.S.A. .. 108 F8
Ocean City, Wash., U.S.A. 116 C2
Ocean Falls, Canada 104 C3
Ocean I. = Banaba, Kiribati 96 H8
Oceano, U.S.A. 117 K6
Oceanport, U.S.A. 111 F10
Oceanside, U.S.A. 117 M9
Ochagavía, Spain 32 C3
Ochakiv, Ukraine 47 J6
Ochamchira, Georgia 49 J5
Ochil Hills, U.K. 14 E5
Ochsenfurt, Germany 25 F6
Ochsenhausen, Germany ... 25 G5
Ocilla, U.S.A. 109 K4
Ockelbo, Sweden 10 D10
Ocmulgee →, U.S.A. 109 K4
Ocna Mureș, Romania 43 D8
Ocna Sibiului, Romania 43 E8
Ocnele Mari, Romania 43 E9
Ocnița, Moldova 43 B12
Oconee →, U.S.A. 109 K4
Oconto, U.S.A. 108 C2
Oconto Falls, U.S.A. 108 C1
Ocosingo, Mexico 119 D6
Ocotal, Nic. 120 D2
Ocotlán, Mexico 118 C4
Ocotlán de Morelos, Mexico 119 D5
Ocreza →, Portugal 35 F3
Octeville, France 18 C5
Oda, Ghana 83 D4
Ōda, Japan 55 G6
Oda, J., Sudan 80 C4
Ódáðahraun, Iceland 8 D5
Ödåkra, Sweden 11 H6
Odate, Japan 54 D10
Odawara, Japan 55 G9
Odda, Norway 9 F12
Odder, Denmark 11 J4
Odei →, Canada 105 B9
Odemira, Portugal 35 H2
Ödemiş, Turkey 39 C9
Odendaalsrus, S. Africa 88 D4
Odensbacken, Sweden 10 E9
Odense, Denmark 11 J4
Odenwald, Germany 25 F5
Oder →, Europe 24 B10
Oder-Havel Kanal, Germany 24 C10
Oderzo, Italy 29 C9
Odesa, Ukraine 47 J6
Ödeshög, Sweden 11 F8
Odessa = Odesa, Ukraine .. 47 J6
Odessa, Canada 111 B8
Odessa, Tex., U.S.A. 113 K3
Odessa, Wash., U.S.A. 114 C4
Odiakwe, Botswana 88 C4
Odiel →, Spain 35 H4
Odienné, Ivory C. 82 D3
Odintsovo, Russia 46 E9
Odiongan, Phil. 61 E4
Odobești, Romania 43 E12
Odolanów, Poland 45 G4
O'Donnell, U.S.A. 113 J4
Odorheiu Secuiesc, Romania 43 D10
Odoyevo, Russia 46 F9
Odra = Oder →, Europe .. 24 B10
Odra →, Spain 34 C6
Odžaci, Serbia, Yug. 42 E4
Odžak, Bos.-H. 42 F3
Odzi, Zimbabwe 89 B5
Odzi →, Zimbabwe 89 B5
Oebisfelde, Germany 24 C6
Oeiras, Brazil 125 E10
Oeiras, Portugal 35 G1
Oelrichs, U.S.A. 112 D3
Oelsnitz, Germany 25 E8
Oelwein, U.S.A. 112 D9
Oenpelli, Australia 92 B5
Oetz, Austria 26 D3
Of, Turkey 73 B9
Ofanto →, Italy 31 A9
Offa, Nigeria 83 D5
Offaly □, Ireland 15 C4
Offenbach, Germany 25 E4
Offenburg, Germany 25 G3
Offida, Italy 29 F10
Ofidhousa, Greece 39 E8
Ofotfjorden, Norway 8 B17
Ōfunato, Japan 54 E10
Oga, Japan 54 E9
Oga-Hantō, Japan 54 E9
Ogaden, Ethiopia 74 F3
Ōgaki, Japan 55 G8
Ogallala, U.S.A. 112 E4
Ogasawara Gunto, Pac. Oc. 52 G18
Ogbomosho, Nigeria 83 D5
Ogden, U.S.A. 114 F7
Ogdensburg, U.S.A. 111 B9
Ogeechee →, U.S.A. 109 K5
Ogilby, U.S.A. 117 N12
Oglio →, Italy 28 C7
Ogmore, Australia 94 C4
Ognon →, France 19 E12
Ogoja, Nigeria 83 D6
Ogoki, Canada 102 B2
Ogoki →, Canada 102 B2
Ogoki L., Canada 102 B2
Ogoki Res., Canada 102 B2
Ogooué →, Gabon 84 E1
Ogosta →, Bulgaria 40 C7
Ogowe = Ogooué →, Gabon 84 E1
Ogr = Sharafa, Sudan 81 E2
Ograźden, Macedonia 40 E6
Ogre, Latvia 9 H21
Ogrein, Sudan 80 D3
Ogulin, Croatia 29 C12

Ogun □, Nigeria 83 D5
Ogurchinskiy, Ostrov, Turkmenistan 71 B7
Oguta, Nigeria 83 D6
Ogwashi-Uku, Nigeria 83 D6
Ogwe, Nigeria 83 E6
Ohai, N.Z. 91 L2
Ohakune, N.Z. 91 H5
Ohata, Japan 54 D10
Ohau, L., N.Z. 91 L2
Ohio □, U.S.A. 110 F2
Ohio →, U.S.A. 108 G1
Ohře →, Czech Rep. 26 A7
Ohre →, Germany 24 C7
Ohrid, Macedonia 40 E4
Ohridsko Jezero, Macedonia 40 E4
Ohrigstad, S. Africa 89 C5
Öhringen, Germany 25 F5
Oi Qu, China 58 C2
Oiapoque, Brazil 125
Oikou, China 57 E9
Oil City, U.S.A. 110 E5
Oil Springs, Canada 110 D2
Oildale, U.S.A. 117 K7
Oinousa, Greece 39 C8
Oise □, France 19 C9
Oise →, France 19 C9
Ōita, Japan 55 H5
Ōita □, Japan 55 H5
Oiticica, Brazil 125 E10
Ojacaliente, Mexico 118 C4
Ojai, U.S.A. 117 L7
Ojinaga, Mexico 118 B4
Ojiya, Japan 55 F9
Ojos del Salado, Cerro, Argentina 126 B2
Oka →, Russia 48 B7
Okaba, Indonesia 63 F9
Okahandja, Namibia 88 C2
Okahukura, N.Z. 91 H5
Okanagan L., Canada 104 C5
Okanogan, U.S.A. 114 B4
Okanogan →, U.S.A. 114 B4
Okány, Hungary 42 D6
Okaputa, Namibia 88 C2
Okara, Pakistan 68 D5
Okarito, N.Z. 91 K3
Okaukuejo, Namibia 88 B2
Okavango Swamps, Botswana 88 B3
Okaya, Japan 55 F9
Okayama, Japan 55 G6
Okayama □, Japan 55 G6
Okazaki, Japan 55 G8
Oke-Iho, Nigeria 83 D5
Okeechobee, U.S.A. 109 M5
Okeechobee, L., U.S.A. ... 109 M5
Okefenokee Swamp, U.S.A. 109 K4
Okehampton, U.K. 13 G4
Okene, Nigeria 83 D6
Oker →, Germany 24 C6
Okha, India 68 H3
Okha, Russia 51 D15
Ókhi Óros, Greece 38 C6
Okhotsk, Russia 51 D15
Okhotsk, Sea of, Asia 51 D15
Okhotskiy Perevoz, Russia 51 C14
Okhtyrka, Ukraine 47 G8
Oki-Shotō, Japan 55 F6
Okiep, S. Africa 88 D2
Okigwi, Nigeria 83 D6
Okija, Nigeria 83 D6
Okinawa □, Japan 55 L4
Okinawa-Guntō, Japan ... 55 L4
Okinawa-Jima, Japan 55 L4
Okino-erabu-Shima, Japan 55 L4
Okitipupa, Nigeria 83 D5
Oklahoma □, U.S.A. 113 H6
Oklahoma City, U.S.A. ... 113 H6
Okmulgee, U.S.A. 113 H7
Oknitsa = Ocnița, Moldova 43 B12
Oko, W. →, Sudan 80 C4
Okolo, Uganda 86 B3
Okolona, U.S.A. 113 J10
Okombahe, Namibia 88 C2
Okonek, Poland 44 B3
Okotoks, Canada 104 C6
Okrika, Nigeria 83 E6
Oksibil, Indonesia 63 E10
Oktabrsk = Oktyabrsk, Kazakstan 50 E6
Oktyabrsk, Kazakstan 50 E6
Oktyabrsk, Russia 48 D9
Oktyabrskiy = Aktsyabrski, Belarus 47 F5
Oktyabrskiy, Russia 49 G5
Oktyabrskoy Revolyutsii, Ostrov, Russia 51 B10
Oktyabrskoye = Zhovtneve, Ukraine 47 J7
Okulovka, Russia 46 C7
Okuru, N.Z. 91 K2
Okushiri-Tō, Japan 54 C9
Okuta, Nigeria 83 D5
Okwa →, Botswana 88 C3
Ola, U.S.A. 113 H8
Ólafsfjörður, Iceland 8 C4
Ólafsvík, Iceland 8 D2
Olaine, Latvia 44 B10
Olancha, U.S.A. 117 J8
Olancha Pk., U.S.A. 117 J8
Olanchito, Honduras 120 C2
Öland, Sweden 11 H10
Ölands norra udde, Sweden 11 G11
Ölands södra udde, Sweden 11 H10
Olargues, France 20 E6
Olary, Australia 95 E3
Olascoaga, Argentina 126 D3
Olathe, U.S.A. 112 F7
Olavarría, Argentina 126 D3
Oława, Poland 45 H4

Olbernhau, Germany 24 E9
Ólbia, Italy 30 B2
Ólbia, G. di, Italy 30 B2
Olching, Germany 25 G7
Olcott, U.S.A. 110 C6
Old Bahama Chan. = Bahama, Canal Viejo de, W. Indies 120 B4
Old Baldy Pk. = San Antonio, Mt., U.S.A. .. 117 L9
Old Castile = Castilla y Leon □, Spain 34 D6
Old Crow, Canada 100 B6
Old Dale, U.S.A. 117 L11
Old Dongola, Sudan 80 D3
Old Forge, N.Y., U.S.A. .. 111 C10
Old Forge, Pa., U.S.A. ... 111 E9
Old Perlican, Canada 103 C9
Old Shinyanga, Tanzania 86 C3
Old Speck Mt., U.S.A. ... 111 B14
Old Town, U.S.A. 109 C11
Old Washington, U.S.A. .. 110 F3
Old Wives L., Canada 105 C7
Oldbury, U.K. 13 F5
Oldcastle, Ireland 15 C4
Oldeani, Tanzania 86 C4
Oldenburg, Niedersachsen, Germany 24 B4
Oldenburg, Schleswig-Holstein, Germany 24 A6
Oldenzaal, Neths. 17 B6
Oldham, U.K. 12 D5
Oldman →, Canada 104 D6
Oldmeldrum, U.K. 14 D6
Olds, Canada 104 C6
Oldziyt, Mongolia 56 B5
Olean, U.S.A. 110 D6
Olecko, Poland 44 D9
Oléggio, Italy 28 C5
Oleiros, Portugal 34 F3
Oleiros, Spain 34 B2
Olekma →, Russia 51 C13
Olekminsk, Russia 51 C13
Oleksandriya, Kirovohrad, Ukraine 47 H7
Oleksandriya, Rivne, Ukraine 47 G4
Oleksandrovka, Ukraine .. 47 H7
Olema, U.S.A. 116 G4
Olenek, Russia 51 C12
Olenek →, Russia 51 B13
Olenino, Russia 46 D7
Oléron, Î. d', France 20 C2
Oleśnica, Poland 45 G4
Olesno, Poland 45 H5
Olevsk, Ukraine 47 G4
Olga, Russia 51 E14
Olga, L., Canada 102 C4
Olga, Mt., Australia 93 E5
Ølgod, Denmark 11 J2
Olhão, Portugal 35 H3
Olib, Croatia 29 D11
Oliena, Italy 30 B2
Oliete, Spain 32 D4
Olifants →, Africa 89 C5
Olifants →, Namibia 88 C2
Olifantshoek, S. Africa ... 88 D3
Ólimbos, Greece 39 F9
Ólimbos, Óros, Greece ... 40 F6
Olímpia, Brazil 127 A6
Olinda, Brazil 125 E12
Olite, Spain 32 C3
Oliva, Argentina 126 C3
Oliva, Spain 33 G4
Oliva, Punta del, Spain ... 34 B5
Oliva de la Frontera, Spain 35 G4
Olivares, Spain 32 F2
Olivehurst, U.S.A. 116 F5
Oliveira de Azeméis, Portugal 34 E2
Oliveira do Douro, Portugal 34 D2
Olivenza, Spain 35 G3
Oliver, Canada 104 D5
Oliver L., Canada 105 B8
Olivet, France 19 E8
Olkhovka, Russia 48 F7
Olkusz, Poland 45 H6
Ollagüe, Chile 126 A2
Olmedo, Spain 34 D6
Olmeto, France 21 G12
Olney, Ill., U.S.A. 108 F1
Olney, Tex., U.S.A. 113 J5
Olofström, Sweden 11 H8
Oloma, Cameroon 83 E7
Olomane →, Canada 103 B7
Olomouc, Czech Rep. ... 27 B10
Olonets, Russia 46 B7
Olongapo, Phil. 61 D4
Olonne-sur-Mer, France . 20 B2
Oloron, Gave d' →, France 20 E2
Oloron-Ste-Marie, France 20 E3
Olot, Spain 32 C7
Olovo, Bos.-H. 42 F3
Olovyannaya, Russia 51 D12
Oloy →, Russia 51 C16
Olsberg, Germany 24 D4
Olshammar, Sweden 11 F8
Olshanka, Ukraine 47 H6
Olshany, Ukraine 47 G8
Olsztyn, Poland 44 E7
Olsztynek, Poland 44 E7
Olt □, Romania 43 F9
Olt →, Romania 43 G9
Olten, Switz. 25 H3
Oltenița, Romania 43 F11
Olton, U.S.A. 113 H3
Oltu, Turkey 73 B9
Oluanpi, Taiwan 59 G13
Olula del Río, Spain 33 H2
Olur, Turkey 73 B10
Olutanga, Phil. 61 H5

Olvega, Spain 32 D2
Olvera, Spain 35 J5
Olymbos, Cyprus 36 D12
Olympia, Greece 38 D3
Olympia, U.S.A. 116 D4
Olympic Dam, Australia .. 95 E2
Olympic Mts., U.S.A. ... 116 C3
Olympic Nat. Park, U.S.A. 116 C3
Olympus, Cyprus 36 E11
Olympus, Mt. = Ólimbos, Óros, Greece 40 F6
Olympus, Mt. = Uludağ, Turkey 41 F13
Olympus, Mt., U.S.A. ... 116 C3
Olyphant, U.S.A. 111 E9
Om →, Russia 50 D8
Om Hajer, Eritrea 81 E4
Om Koi, Thailand 64 D2
Ōma, Japan 54 D10
Ōmachi, Japan 55 F8
Omae-Zaki, Japan 55 G9
Ōmagari, Japan 54 E10
Omagh, U.K. 15 B4
Omagh □, U.K. 15 B4
Omaha, U.S.A. 112 E7
Omak, U.S.A. 114 B4
Omalos, Greece 36 D5
Oman ■, Asia 74 C6
Oman, G. of, Asia 71 E8
Omaruru, Namibia 88 C2
Omaruru →, Namibia .. 88 C1
Omate, Peru 124 G4
Ombai, Selat, Indonesia . 63 F6
Omboué, Gabon 84 E1
Ombrone →, Italy 28 F8
Omdurmân, Sudan 81 D3
Omemee, Canada 110 B6
Omeo, Australia 95 F4
Omeonga, Dem. Rep. of the Congo 86 C1
Ometepe, I. de, Nic. 120 D2
Ometepec, Mexico 119 D5
Ominato, Japan 54 D10
Omineca →, Canada ... 104 B4
Omiš, Croatia 29 E13
Omišalj, Croatia 29 C11
Omitara, Namibia 88 C2
Ōmiya, Japan 55 G9
Ommen, Neths. 17 B6
Ömnögovi □, Mongolia . 56 C3
Omo →, Ethiopia 81 F4
Omodeo, L., Italy 30 B1
Omodhos, Cyprus 36 E11
Omoko, Nigeria 83 D6
Omolon →, Russia 51 C16
Omono-Gawa →, Japan 54 E10
Omsk, Russia 50 D8
Omsukchan, Russia 51 C16
Ōmu, Japan 54 B11
Omul, Vf., Romania 43 E10
Omulew →, Poland 45 E8
Ōmura, Japan 55 H4
Omuramba Omatako →, Namibia 88 B2
Omuramba Ovambo →, Namibia 88 B2
Omurtag, Bulgaria 41 C10
Ōmuta, Japan 55 H5
Oña, Spain 34 C7
Onaga, U.S.A. 112 F6
Onalaska, U.S.A. 112 D9
Onancock, U.S.A. 108 G8
Onang, Indonesia 63 E5
Onaping L., Canada 102 C3
Oñati, Spain 32 B2
Onavas, Mexico 118 B3
Onawa, U.S.A. 112 D6
Oncócua, Angola 88 B1
Onda, Spain 32 F4
Ondaejin, N. Korea 57 D15
Ondangua, Namibia 88 B2
Ondárroa, Spain 32 B2
Ondava →, Slovak Rep. 27 C14
Ondjiva, Angola 88 B2
Ondo, Nigeria 83 D5
Ondo □, Nigeria 83 D6
Öndörhaan, Mongolia .. 54 B6
Öndörshil, Mongolia ... 56 B5
Öndverðarnes, Iceland . 8 D1
One Tree, Australia 95 E3
Onega, Russia 50 C4
Onega →, Russia 6 C13
Onega, G. of = Onezhskaya Guba, Russia 50 C4
Onega, L. = Onezhskoye Ozero, Russia 46 B8
Onehunga, N.Z. 91 G5
Oneida, U.S.A. 111 C9
Oneida L., U.S.A. 111 C9
O'Neill, U.S.A. 112 D5
Onekotan, Ostrov, Russia 51 E16
Onema, Dem. Rep. of the Congo 86 C1
Oneonta, U.S.A. 111 D9
Onești, Romania 43 D11
Onezhskoye Ozero, Russia 46 B8
Ongarue, N.Z. 91 H5
Ongers →, S. Africa ... 88 E3
Ongerup, Australia 93 F2
Ongjin, N. Korea 57 F13
Ongkharak, Thailand .. 64 E3
Ongniud Qi, China 57 C10
Ongoka, Dem. Rep. of the Congo . 86 C2
Ongole, India 66 M12
Ongon = Havirga, Mongolia 56 B7
Ongoka, Georgia 49 J6
Onida, U.S.A. 112 C4
Onilahy →, Madag. ... 89 C7
Onitsha, Nigeria 83 D6
Onoda, Japan 55 G5
Onpyŏng-ni, S. Korea .. 57 H14

Ons, I. de, Spain 34 C2
Onslow, Australia 92 D2
Onslow B., U.S.A. 109 H7
Ontake-San, Japan 55 G8
Ontario, Calif., U.S.A. .. 117 L9
Ontario, Oreg., U.S.A. .. 114 D5
Ontario □, Canada 102 B2
Ontario, L., N. Amer. ... 102 D4
Ontinyent, Spain 33 G4
Ontonagon, U.S.A. 112 B10
Ontur, Spain 33 G3
Onyx, U.S.A. 117 K8
Oodnadatta, Australia .. 95 D2
Ooldea, Australia 93 F5
Oombulgurri, Australia . 92 C4
Oorindi, Australia 94 C3
Oost-Vlaanderen □, Belgium 17 C3
Oostende, Belgium 17 C2
Oosterhout, Neths. 17 C4
Oosterschelde →, Neths. 17 C4
Oosterwolde, Neths. ... 17 B6
Ootacamund = Udagamandalam, India .. 66 P10
Ootsa L., Canada 104 C3
Opaka, Bulgaria 41 C10
Opala, Dem. Rep. of the Congo 86 C1
Opalenica, Poland 45 F3
Opan, Bulgaria 41 D9
Opanake, Sri Lanka 66 R12
Opasatika, Canada 102 C3
Opasquia Prov. Park, Canada 102 B1
Opatija, Croatia 29 C11
Opatów, Poland 45 H8
Opava, Czech Rep. 27 B10
Opelika, U.S.A. 109 J3
Opelousas, U.S.A. 113 K8
Opémisca, L., Canada .. 102 C5
Opheim, U.S.A. 114 B10
Ophthalmia Ra., Australia 92 D2
Opi, Nigeria 83 D6
Opinaca →, Canada ... 102 B4
Opinaca, Rés., Canada . 102 B4
Opinnagau →, Canada . 102 B3
Opiscoteo, L., Canada .. 103 B6
Opobo, Nigeria 83 E6
Opochka, Russia 46 D5
Opoczno, Poland 45 G7
Opol, Phil. 61 G6
Opole, Poland 45 H4
Opole Lubelskie, Poland 45 G8
Opolskie □, Poland 45 H5
Oponono L., Namibia .. 88 B2
Oporto = Porto, Portugal 34 D2
Opotiki, N.Z. 91 H6
Opp, U.S.A. 109 K2
Oppdal, Norway 9 E13
Óppido Mamertina, Italy 31 D8
Opportunity, U.S.A. ... 114 C5
Oprișor, Romania 42 F8
Oprtalj, Croatia 29 C10
Opua, N.Z. 91 F5
Opunake, N.Z. 91 H4
Opuzen, Croatia 29 E14
Ora, Cyprus 36 E12
Oracle, U.S.A. 115 K8
Oradea, Romania 42 C6
Öræfajökull, Iceland ... 8 D5
Orahovac, Kosovo, Yug. 40 D4
Orahovica, Croatia 42 E2
Orai, India 69 G8
Oraison, France 21 E9
Oral = Zhayyq →, Kazakstan 50 E6
Oral, Kazakstan 48 E10
Oran, Algeria 78 A5
Orange, Australia 95 E4
Orange, France 21 D8
Orange, Calif., U.S.A. .. 117 M9
Orange, Mass., U.S.A. . 111 D12
Orange, Tex., U.S.A. ... 113 K8
Orange, Va., U.S.A. ... 108 F6
Orange →, S. Africa ... 88 D2
Orange, C., Brazil 122 C5
Orange Cove, U.S.A. ... 116 J7
Orange Free State = Free State □, S. Africa 88 D4
Orange Grove, U.S.A. .. 113 M6
Orange Walk, Belize ... 119 D7
Orangeburg, U.S.A. ... 109 J5
Orangeville, Canada ... 102 D3
Orango, Guinea-Biss. .. 82 C1
Orani, Phil. 61 D4
Oranienburg, Germany . 24 C9
Oranje = Orange →, S. Africa 88 D2
Oranje Vrystaat = Free State □, S. Africa 88 D4
Oranjemund, Namibia .. 88 D2
Oranjerivier, S. Africa .. 88 D3
Orapa, Botswana 85 J5
Orari →, Sudan 81 F3
Oras, Phil. 61 E6
Orašje, Bos.-H. 42 E3
Orăștie, Romania 43 E8
Orașul Stalin = Brașov, Romania 43 E10
Orava →, Slovak Rep. . 27 B12
Orava, Vodná nádrž, Slovak Rep. 27 B12
Oravița, Romania 42 E6
Orb →, France 20 E7
Orba →, Italy 28 D5
Ørbæk, Denmark 11 J4
Orbe, Switz. 25 J2
Orbec, France 18 C7
Orbetello, Italy 29 F8
Órbigo →, Spain 34 C5
Orbisonia, U.S.A. 110 F7

191

Orbost, Australia 95 F4
Örbyhus, Sweden 10 D11
Orcas I., U.S.A. 116 B4
Orce, Spain 33 H2
Orce →, Spain 33 H2
Orchard City, U.S.A. 115 G10
Orchies, France 19 B10
Orchila, I., Venezuela 121 D6
Órcia →, Italy 29 F8
Orco →, Italy 28 C4
Orcutt, U.S.A. 117 L6
Ord, U.S.A. 112 E5
Ord →, Australia 92 C4
Ord, Mt., Australia 92 C4
Ordenes = Ordes, Spain 34 B2
Orderville, U.S.A. 115 H7
Ordes, Spain 34 B2
Ording = St-Peter-Ording, Germany 24 A4
Ordos = Mu Us Shamo, China 56 E5
Ordu, Turkey 72 B7
Ordubad, Azerbaijan 73 C12
Orduña, Álava, Spain 32 C2
Orduña, Granada, Spain 35 H7
Ordway, U.S.A. 112 F3
Ordzhonikidze = Vladikavkaz, Russia 49 J7
Ordzhonikidze, Ukraine 47 J8
Ore, Dem. Rep. of the Congo 86 B2
Ore Mts. = Erzgebirge, Germany 24 E8
Orebić, Croatia 29 F14
Örebro, Sweden 10 E9
Örebro län □, Sweden 10 E8
Oregon, U.S.A. 112 D10
Oregon □, U.S.A. 114 E3
Oregon City, U.S.A. 116 E4
Öregrund, Sweden 10 D12
Öregrundsgrepen, Sweden 10 D12
Orekhov = Orikhiv, Ukraine 47 J8
Orekhovo-Zuyevo, Russia 46 E10
Orel, Russia 47 F9
Orel →, Ukraine 47 H8
Orellana, Spain 35 F5
Orellana, Canal de, Spain 35 F5
Orellana, Embalse de, Spain 35 F5
Orem, U.S.A. 114 F8
Ören, Turkey 39 D9
Orenburg, Russia 50 D6
Örencik, Turkey 39 B11
Orense = Ourense, Spain 34 C3
Orense □, Spain 34 C3
Orepuki, N.Z. 91 M1
Orestiás, Greece 41 E10
Orestos Pereyra, Mexico 118 B3
Øresund, Europe 11 J6
Orford Ness, U.K. 13 E9
Organà = Organyà, Spain 32 C6
Organos, Pta. de los, Canary Is. 37 F2
Organyà, Spain 32 C6
Orgaz, Spain 35 F7
Orgeyev = Orhei, Moldova 43 C13
Orhaneli, Turkey 41 G12
Orhaneli →, Turkey 41 G12
Orhangazi, Turkey 41 F13
Orhei, Moldova 43 C13
Orhon Gol →, Mongolia 60 A5
Ória, Italy 31 B10
Oriental, Cordillera, Colombia 122 C3
Orientale □, Dem. Rep. of the Congo 86 B2
Oriente, Argentina 126 D3
Orihuela, Spain 33 G4
Orihuela del Tremedal, Spain 32 E3
Orikhiv, Ukraine 47 J8
Oriku, Albania 40 F3
Orillia, Canada 102 D4
Orinoco →, Venezuela 122 C4
Orion, Canada 105 D6
Oriskany, U.S.A. 111 C9
Orissa □, India 67 K14
Orissaare, Estonia 9 G20
Oristano, Italy 30 C1
Oristano, G. di, Italy 30 C1
Orizaba, Mexico 119 D5
Orizare, Bulgaria 41 D11
Orjen, Bos.-H. 40 D2
Orjiva, Spain 35 J7
Orkanger, Norway 8 E13
Örkelljunga, Sweden 11 H7
Örken, Sweden 11 G9
Örkény, Hungary 42 C4
Orkla →, Norway 8 E13
Orkney, S. Africa 88 D4
Orkney □, U.K. 14 B5
Orkney Is., U.K. 14 B6
Orland, U.S.A. 116 F4
Orlando, U.S.A. 109 L5
Orlando, C. d', Italy 31 D7
Orléanais, France 19 E8
Orléans, France 19 E8
Orleans, U.S.A. 111 B12
Orléans, Î. d', Canada 103 C5
Orlice →, Czech Rep. 26 A8
Orlov, Slovak Rep. 27 B13
Orlov Gay, Russia 48 E9
Orlová, Czech Rep. 27 B11
Orlovat, Serbia, Yug. 42 E5
Ormara, Pakistan 66 G4
Ormea, Italy 28 D4
Ormília, Greece 40 F7
Ormoc, Phil. 61 F6
Ormond, N.Z. 91 H6
Ormond Beach, U.S.A. 109 L5
Ormož, Slovenia 29 B13
Ormskirk, U.K. 12 D5

Ormstown, Canada 111 A11
Ornans, France 19 E13
Orne □, France 18 D7
Orne →, France 18 C6
Orneta, Poland 44 D7
Ornö, Sweden 10 E12
Örnsköldsvik, Sweden 10 A12
Oro, N. Korea 57 D14
Oro →, Mexico 118 B3
Oro Grande, U.S.A. 117 L9
Oro Valley, U.S.A. 115 K8
Orobie, Alpi, Italy 28 B6
Orocué, Colombia 124 C4
Orodara, Burkina Faso 82 C4
Orodo, Nigeria 83 D6
Orofino, U.S.A. 114 C5
Orol Dengizi = Aral Sea, Asia 50 E7
Oromocto, Canada 103 C6
Oron, Nigeria 83 E6
Orono, Canada 110 C6
Orono, U.S.A. 109 C11
Oronsay, U.K. 14 E2
Oropesa, Spain 34 F5
Oroquieta, Phil. 61 G5
Orosei, Italy 30 B2
Orosei, G. di, Italy 30 B2
Orosháza, Hungary 42 D5
Oroszlány, Hungary 42 C3
Orotukan, Russia 51 C16
Oroville, Calif., U.S.A. 116 F5
Oroville, Wash., U.S.A. 114 B4
Oroville, L., U.S.A. 116 F5
Orrefors, Sweden 11 H9
Orroroo, Australia 95 E2
Orrville, U.S.A. 110 F3
Orsa, Sweden 10 C8
Orsara di Púglia, Italy 31 A8
Orsasjön, Sweden 10 C8
Orsha, Belarus 46 E6
Örsjö, Sweden 11 H9
Orsk, Russia 50 D6
Orşova, Romania 42 F7
Ørsted, Denmark 11 H4
Örsundsbro, Sweden 10 E11
Orta, L. d', Italy 28 C5
Orta Nova, Italy 31 A8
Ortaca, Turkey 39 E10
Ortakent, Turkey 39 D9
Ortaklar, Turkey 39 D9
Ortaköy, Çorum, Turkey 72 B6
Ortaköy, Niğde, Turkey 72 C6
Orte, Italy 29 F9
Ortegal, C., Spain 34 B3
Orthez, France 20 E3
Ortigueira, Spain 34 B3
Orting, U.S.A. 116 C4
Ortisei, Italy 29 B8
Ortles, Italy 28 B7
Ortón →, Bolivia 124 F5
Ortona, Italy 29 F11
Ortonville, U.S.A. 112 C6
Orūmīyeh, Iran 70 B5
Orūmīyeh, Daryācheh-ye, Iran 70 B5
Orune, Italy 30 B2
Oruro, Bolivia 124 G5
Orust, Sweden 11 F5
Oruzgān □, Afghan. 66 C5
Orvault, France 18 E5
Orvieto, Italy 29 F9
Orwell, N.Y., U.S.A. 111 C9
Orwell, Ohio, U.S.A. 110 E4
Orwell →, U.K. 13 F9
Orwigsburg, U.S.A. 111 F8
Oryakhovo, Bulgaria 40 C7
Orzinuovi, Italy 28 C6
Orzyc →, Poland 45 F8
Orzysz, Poland 44 E8
Osa →, Poland 44 E5
Osa, Pen. de, Costa Rica 120 E3
Osage →, U.S.A. 112 D8
Osage, U.S.A. 112 D8
Osage City, U.S.A. 112 F7
Ōsaka, Japan 55 G7
Osan, S. Korea 57 F14
Osawatomie, U.S.A. 112 F7
Osborne, U.S.A. 112 F5
Osby, Sweden 11 H7
Osceola, Ark., U.S.A. 113 H10
Osceola, Iowa, U.S.A. 112 E8
Oschatz, Germany 24 D9
Oschersleben, Germany 24 C7
Oscoda, U.S.A. 110 B1
Osečina, Serbia, Yug. 40 B3
Ösel = Saaremaa, Estonia 9 G20
Osery, Russia 46 E10
Osgoode, Canada 111 A9
Osh, Kyrgyzstan 50 E8
Oshakati, Namibia 85 H3
Oshawa, Canada 102 D4
Oshigambo, Namibia 88 B2
Oshkosh, Nebr., U.S.A. 112 E3
Oshkosh, Wis., U.S.A. 112 C10
Oshmyany = Ashmyany, Belarus 9 J21
Oshnoviyeh, Iran 70 B5
Oshogbo, Nigeria 83 D5
Oshtorinān, Iran 71 C6
Oshwe, Dem. Rep. of the Congo 84 E3
Osi, Nigeria 83 D6
Osieczna, Poland 45 G3
Osijek, Croatia 42 E3
Ósilo, Italy 30 B1
Ósimo, Italy 29 E10
Osintorf, Belarus 46 E6
Osipenko = Berdyansk, Ukraine 47 J9

Osipovichi = Asipovichy, Belarus 46 F5
Osiyan, India 68 F5
Osizweni, S. Africa 89 D5
Oskaloosa, U.S.A. 112 E8
Oskarshamn, Sweden 11 G10
Oskarström, Sweden 11 H6
Oskélanéo, Canada 102 C4
Öskemen, Kazakstan 50 E9
Oskol →, Ukraine 47 H9
Oslo, Norway 9 G14
Oslob, Phil. 61 G5
Oslofjorden, Norway 9 G14
Osmanabad, India 66 K10
Osmancık, Turkey 72 B6
Osmaniye, Turkey 70 B3
Osmanlı, Turkey 41 E10
Ösmo, Sweden 10 F11
Osnabrück, Germany 24 C4
Ošno Lubuskie, Poland 45 F1
Osoblaha, Czech Rep. 27 A10
Osogovska Planina, Macedonia 40 D6
Osor, Italy 29 D11
Osorio, Brazil 127 B5
Osorno, Chile 128 E2
Osorno, Spain 34 C6
Osoyoos, Canada 104 D5
Osøyro, Norway 9 F11
Ospika →, Canada 104 B4
Osprey Reef, Australia 94 A4
Oss, Neths. 17 C5
Ossa, Mt., Australia 94 G4
Óssa, Óros, Greece 38 B4
Ossa de Montiel, Spain 33 G2
Ossabaw I., U.S.A. 109 K5
Osse →, France 20 D4
Osse →, Nigeria 83 D6
Ossi, Italy 30 B1
Ossining, U.S.A. 111 E11
Ossipee, U.S.A. 111 C13
Ossokmanuan L., Canada 103 B7
Ossora, Russia 51 D17
Ostashkov, Russia 46 D7
Ostavall, Sweden 10 B9
Oste →, Germany 24 B5
Ostend = Oostende, Belgium 17 C2
Oster, Ukraine 47 G6
Osterburg, Germany 24 C7
Osterburg, U.S.A. 110 F6
Osterburken, Germany 25 F5
Österbybruk, Sweden 10 D11
Österbymo, Sweden 11 G9
Österdalälven, Sweden 10 C7
Østerdalen, Norway 9 F14
Österfärnebo, Sweden 10 D10
Osterforse, Sweden 10 A11
Östergötlands län □, Sweden 11 F9
Osterholz-Scharmbeck, Germany 24 B4
Østerild, Denmark 11 G2
Osterode, Germany 24 D6
Östersund, Sweden 10 A8
Östervåla, Sweden 10 D11
Ostfriesische Inseln, Germany 24 B3
Ostfriesland, Germany 24 B3
Östhammar, Sweden 10 D12
Óstia, Lido di, Italy 29 G9
Óstiglia, Italy 29 C8
Östmark, Sweden 10 D6
Östra Husby, Sweden 11 F10
Ostrava, Czech Rep. 27 B11
Ostróda, Poland 44 E6
Ostrogozhsk, Russia 47 G10
Ostroh, Ukraine 47 G4
Ostrołęka, Poland 45 E8
Ostrov, Bulgaria 41 C8
Ostrov, Czech Rep. 26 A5
Ostrov, Romania 43 F12
Ostrov, Russia 46 D5
Ostrów Lubelski, Poland 45 G9
Ostrów Mazowiecka, Poland 45 F8
Ostrów Wielkopolski, Poland 45 G4
Ostrowiec-Świętokrzyski, Poland 45 H8
Ostrožac, Bos.-H. 42 G2
Ostrzeszów, Poland 45 G4
Ostseebad Kühlungsborn, Germany 24 A7
Osttirol □, Austria 26 E5
Ostuni, Italy 31 B10
Osŭm →, Bulgaria 41 C8
Osumi →, Albania 40 F4
Ōsumi-Kaikyō, Japan 55 J5
Ōsumi-Shotō, Japan 55 J5
Osun □, Nigeria 83 D5
Osuna, Spain 35 H5
Oswegatchie →, U.S.A. 111 B9
Oswego, U.S.A. 111 C8
Oswego →, U.S.A. 111 C8
Oswestry, U.K. 12 E4
Oświęcim, Poland 45 H6
Otaci, Moldova 43 B12
Otago □, N.Z. 91 L2
Otago Harbour, N.Z. 91 L3
Ōtake, Japan 55 G6
Otaki, N.Z. 91 J5
Otaru, Japan 54 C10
Otaru-Wan = Ishikari-Wan, Japan 54 C10
Otavalo, Ecuador 124 C3
Otavi, Namibia 88 B2
Otchinjau, Angola 88 B1
Otelec, Romania 42 E5
Otelnuk L., Canada 103 A6
Oţelu Roşu, Romania 42 E7
Otero de Rey = Outeiro de Rei, Spain 34 B3
Othello, U.S.A. 114 C4

Othonoí, Greece 38 B1
Óthris, Óros, Greece 38 B4
Otira Gorge, N.Z. 91 K3
Otjiwarongo, Namibia 88 C2
Otmuchów, Poland 45 H4
Otočac, Croatia 29 D12
Otoineppu, Japan 54 B11
Otok, Croatia 29 E13
Otorohanga, N.Z. 91 H5
Otoskwin →, Canada 102 B2
Otra →, Norway 9 G13
Otradnyy, Russia 48 D10
Otranto, Italy 31 B11
Otranto, C. d', Italy 31 B11
Otranto, Str. of, Italy 31 B11
Otrokovice, Czech Rep. 27 B10
Otse, S. Africa 88 D4
Ōtsu, Japan 55 G7
Ōtsuki, Japan 55 G9
Ottawa = Outaouais →, Canada 102 C5
Ottawa, Canada 102 C4
Ottawa, Ill., U.S.A. 112 E10
Ottawa, Kans., U.S.A. 112 F7
Ottawa Is., Canada 101 C11
Ottélé, Cameroon 83 E7
Ottensheim, Austria 26 C7
Otter Cr. →, U.S.A. 111 B11
Otter L., Canada 105 B8
Otterndorf, Germany 24 B4
Otterup, Denmark 11 J4
Otterville, Canada 110 D4
Ottery St. Mary, U.K. 13 G4
Otto Beit Bridge, Zimbabwe 87 F2
Ottosdal, S. Africa 88 D4
Ottumwa, U.S.A. 112 E8
Otu, Nigeria 83 D5
Otukpa, Nigeria 83 D6
Oturkpo, Nigeria 83 D6
Otway, B., Chile 128 G2
Otway, C., Australia 95 F3
Otwock, Poland 45 F8
Ötztaler Ache →, Austria 26 D3
Ötztaler Alpen, Austria 26 E3
Ou →, Laos 58 B4
Ou Neua, Laos 58 F3
Ou-Sammyaku, Japan 54 E10
Ouachita →, U.S.A. 113 K9
Ouachita, L., U.S.A. 113 H8
Ouachita Mts., U.S.A. 113 H7
Ouagadougou, Burkina Faso 83 C4
Ouahigouya, Burkina Faso 82 C4
Ouahran = Oran, Algeria 78 A5
Oualâta, Mauritania 82 B3
Ouallam, Niger 83 C5
Ouallene, Algeria 78 D6
Ouargaye, Burkina Faso 83 C5
Ouargla, Algeria 78 B7
Ouarkoye, Burkina Faso 82 C4
Ouarzazate, Morocco 78 B4
Ouassou, Mali 83 B5
Ouatagouna, Mali 83 B5
Oubangi →, Dem. Rep. of the Congo 84 E3
Ouche →, France 19 E12
Ouddorp, Neths. 17 C3
Oude Rijn →, Neths. 17 B4
Oudeïka, Mali 83 B4
Oudenaarde, Belgium 17 D3
Oudon →, France 18 E5
Oudtshoorn, S. Africa 88 E3
Ouéllé, Ivory C. 82 D4
Ouémé →, Benin 83 D5
Ouessa, Burkina Faso 82 C4
Ouessant, Î. d', France 18 D1
Ouesso, Congo 84 D3
Ouest, Pte. de l', Canada 103 C7
Ouezzane, Morocco 78 B4
Ougarou, Burkina Faso 83 C5
Oughterard, Ireland 15 C2
Ouidah, Benin 83 D5
Ouidi, Niger 83 C7
Ouistreham, France 18 C6
Oujda, Morocco 78 B5
Oujeft, Mauritania 82 A2
Oulainen, Finland 8 D21
Ould Yenjé, Mauritania 82 B2
Oulins, France 21 C8
Oulu, Finland 8 D21
Oulujärvi, Finland 8 D22
Oulujoki →, Finland 8 D21
Oulx, Italy 28 C3
Oum Chalouba, Chad 79 E10
Oum Hadjer, Chad 79 F9
Oumé, Ivory C. 82 D3
Ounasjoki →, Finland 8 C21
Ounguati, Namibia 88 C2
Ounianga Sérir, Chad 79 E10
Our →, Lux. 17 E6
Ouranópolis, Greece 40 F7
Ourârene, Niger 83 B6
Ouray, U.S.A. 115 G10
Ourense, Spain 34 C3
Ouricuri, Brazil 125 E10
Ourinhos, Brazil 127 A6
Ourique, Portugal 35 H2
Ouro Fino, Brazil 127 A6
Ouro-Ndia, Mali 82 B4
Ouro Prêto, Brazil 127 A7
Ouro Sogui, Senegal 82 B2
Oursi, Burkina Faso 83 C4
Ourthe →, Belgium 17 D5
Ouse →, E. Susx., U.K. 13 G8
Ouse →, N. Yorks., U.K. 12 D7
Oust, France 20 F5
Oust →, France 18 E4
Outaouais →, Canada 102 C5
Outardes →, Canada 103 C6
Outeiro de Rei, Spain 34 B3
Outer Hebrides, U.K. 14 D1

Outes = Serra de Outes, Spain 34 C2
Outjo, Namibia 88 C2
Outlook, Canada 105 C7
Outokumpu, Finland 8 E23
Outreau, France 19 B8
Ouvèze →, France 21 E8
Ouyen, Australia 95 F3
Ouzouer-le-Marché, France 19 E8
Ovada, Italy 28 D5
Ovalau, Fiji 91 C8
Ovalle, Chile 126 C1
Ovamboland = Namibia 88 B2
Ovar, Portugal 34 E2
Overath, Germany 24 E3
Overflakkee, Neths. 17 C4
Overijssel □, Neths. 17 B6
Overland Park, U.S.A. 112 F7
Overton, U.S.A. 117 J12
Övertorneå, Sweden 8 C20
Överum, Sweden 11 F10
Ovid, U.S.A. 111 D8
Ovidiopol, Ukraine 47 J6
Ovidiu, Romania 43 F13
Oviedo, Spain 34 B5
Oviksfjällen, Sweden 10 A7
Oviši, Latvia 9 H19
Ovoot, Mongolia 56 B7
Övör Hangay □, Mongolia 56 B2
Ovoro, Nigeria 83 D6
Øvre Årdal, Norway 9 F12
Øvre Fryken, Sweden 10 E7
Ovruch, Ukraine 47 G5
Owaka, N.Z. 91 M2
Owambo = Ovamboland, Namibia 88 B2
Owasco L., U.S.A. 111 D8
Owase, Japan 55 G8
Owatonna, U.S.A. 112 C8
Owbeh, Afghan. 66 B3
Owego, U.S.A. 111 D8
Owen Falls Dam, Uganda 86 B3
Owen Sound, Canada 102 D3
Owens →, U.S.A. 116 J9
Owens L., U.S.A. 117 J9
Owensboro, U.S.A. 108 G2
Owerri, Nigeria 83 D6
Owl →, Canada 105 B10
Owo, Nigeria 83 D6
Owosso, U.S.A. 108 D3
Owyhee, U.S.A. 114 F5
Owyhee →, U.S.A. 114 E5
Owyhee, L., U.S.A. 114 E5
Ox Mts. = Slieve Gamph, Ireland 15 B3
Öxarfjörður, Iceland 8 C5
Oxbow, Canada 105 D8
Oxelösund, Sweden 11 F11
Oxford, N.Z. 91 K4
Oxford, U.K. 13 F6
Oxford, Mass., U.S.A. 111 D13
Oxford, Miss., U.S.A. 113 H10
Oxford, N.C., U.S.A. 109 G6
Oxford, N.Y., U.S.A. 111 D9
Oxford, Ohio, U.S.A. 108 F3
Oxford L., Canada 105 C9
Oxfordshire □, U.K. 13 F6
Oxía, Greece 38 C3
Oxie, Sweden 11 J7
Oxilithos, Greece 38 C6
Oxnard, U.S.A. 117 L7
Oxsjövålen, Sweden 10 B7
Oxus = Amudarya →, Uzbekistan 50 E6
Oya, Malaysia 62 D4
Oyama, Japan 55 F9
Oyem, Gabon 84 D2
Oyen, Canada 105 C6
Oykel →, U.K. 14 D4
Oymyakon, Russia 51 C15
Oyo □, Nigeria 83 D5
Oyo, Nigeria 83 D5
Oyonnax, France 19 F12
Oyster Bay, U.S.A. 111 F11
Ōyūbari, Japan 54 C11
Özalp, Turkey 73 C10
Ozamiz, Phil. 61 G5
Ozark, Ala., U.S.A. 109 K3
Ozark, Ark., U.S.A. 113 H8
Ozark, Mo., U.S.A. 113 G8
Ozark Plateau, U.S.A. 113 G9
Ozarks, L. of the, U.S.A. 112 F8
Ożarów, Poland 45 H8
Ózd, Hungary 42 B5
Ozernoye, Russia 48 E10
Ozette L., U.S.A. 116 B2
Ozieri, Italy 30 B2
Ozimek, Poland 45 H5
Ozinki, Russia 48 E9
Ozona, U.S.A. 113 K4
Ozorków, Poland 45 G6
Ozren, Bos.-H. 42 G3
Ozuluama, Mexico 119 C5
Ozun, Romania 43 E10
Ozurgeti, Georgia 49 K5

P

Pa, Burkina Faso 82 C4
Pa-an, Burma 67 L20
Pa Mong Dam, Thailand 64 D4
Pa Sak →, Thailand 62 E3
Paamiut, Greenland 4 C5
Paar →, Germany 25 G7
Paarl, S. Africa 88 E2
Paauilo, U.S.A. 106 H17
Pab Hills, Pakistan 68 G2
Pabbay, U.K. 14 D1

Pabianice, Poland 45 G6
Pabna, Bangla. 67 G16
Pabo, Uganda 86 B3
Pacaja →, Brazil 125 D8
Pacaraima, Sa., S. Amer. .. 122 C4
Pacasmayo, Peru 124 E3
Paceco, Italy 30 E5
Pachino, Italy 31 F8
Pachitea →, Peru 124 E4
Pachmarhi, India 69 H8
Pachpadra, India 66 G8
Pachuca, Mexico 119 C5
Pacific, Canada 104 C3
Pacific-Antarctic Ridge,
  Pac. Oc. 97 M16
Pacific Grove, U.S.A. 116 J5
Pacific Ocean, Pac. Oc. .. 97 G14
Pacific Rim Nat. Park,
  Canada 116 B2
Pacifica, U.S.A. 116 H4
Pacitan, Indonesia 63 H14
Packwood, U.S.A. 116 D5
Pacov, Czech Rep. 26 B8
Pacy-sur-Eure, France 18 C8
Padaido, Kepulauan,
  Indonesia 63 E9
Padang, Indonesia 62 E2
Padang Endau, Malaysia ... 65 L4
Padangpanjang, Indonesia . 62 E2
Padangsidempuan, Indonesia 62 D1
Padborg, Denmark 11 K3
Paddle Prairie, Canada 104 B5
Paddockwood, Canada 105 C7
Paderborn, Germany 24 D4
Padeş, Vf., Romania 42 E7
Padina, Romania 43 F12
Padma, India 69 G11
Pádova, Italy 29 C8
Padra, India 68 H5
Padrauna, India 69 F10
Padre I., U.S.A. 113 M6
Padrón, Spain 34 C2
Padstow, U.K. 13 G3
Padua = Pádova, Italy 29 C8
Paducah, Ky., U.S.A. 108 G1
Paducah, Tex., U.S.A. 113 H4
Padul, Spain 35 H7
Paengnyŏng-do, S. Korea .. 57 F13
Paeroa, N.Z. 91 G5
Paesana, Italy 28 D4
Pafúri, Mozam. 89 C5
Pag, Croatia 29 D12
Paga, Ghana 83 C4
Pagadian, Phil. 61 H5
Pagai Selatan, Pulau,
  Indonesia 62 E2
Pagai Utara, Pulau,
  Indonesia 62 E2
Pagalu = Annobón, Atl. Oc. 77 G4
Pagara, India 69 G9
Pagastikós Kólpos, Greece . 38 B5
Pagatan, Indonesia 62 E5
Page, U.S.A. 115 H8
Pagégiai, Lithuania 44 C8
Pago Pago, Amer. Samoa .. 91 B13
Pagosa Springs, U.S.A. ... 115 H10
Pagwa River, Canada 102 B2
Pahala, U.S.A. 106 J17
Pahang →, Malaysia 65 L4
Pahiatua, N.Z. 91 J5
Pahokee, U.S.A. 109 M5
Pahrump, U.S.A. 117 J11
Pahute Mesa, U.S.A. 116 H10
Pai, Thailand 64 C2
Paia, U.S.A. 106 H16
Paicines, U.S.A. 116 J5
Paide, Estonia 9 G21
Paignton, U.K. 13 G4
Paiho, Taiwan 59 F13
Päijänne, Finland 9 F21
Pailani, India 69 G9
Pailin, Cambodia 64 F4
Paimpol, France 18 D3
Painan, Indonesia 62 E2
Painesville, U.S.A. 110 E3
Paint Hills = Wemindji,
  Canada 102 B4
Paint L., Canada 105 B9
Painted Desert, U.S.A. . 115 J8
Paintsville, U.S.A. 108 G4
País Vasco □, Spain 32 C2
Paisley, Canada 110 B3
Paisley, U.K. 14 F4
Paisley, U.S.A. 114 E3
Paita, Peru 124 E2
Paiva →, Portugal 34 D2
Paizhou, China 59 B9
Pajares, Spain 34 B5
Pajares, Puerto de, Spain . 34 C5
Pajęczno, Poland 45 G5
Pak Lay, Laos 64 C3
Pak Phanang, Thailand ... 65 H3
Pak Sane, Laos 64 C4
Pak Song, Laos 64 E6
Pak Suong, Laos 58 H4
Pakaur, India 69 G12
Pakenham, Canada 111 A8
Pákhnes, Greece 36 D6
Pakhuis, S. Africa 88 E2
Pakistan ■, Asia 68 E4
Pakkading, Laos 58 H4
Pakokku, Burma 67 J19
Pakość, Poland 45 F5
Pakowki L., Canada ... 105 D6
Pakpattan, Pakistan .. 68 D5
Pakrac, Croatia 42 E2
Pakruojis, Lithuania . 44 C10
Paks, Hungary 42 D3
Paktīā □, Afghan. 66 C6
Pakwach, Uganda 86 B3

Pakxe, Laos 64 E5
Pal Lahara, India 69 J11
Pala, Chad 79 G9
Pala,
  Dem. Rep. of the Congo . 86 D2
Pala, U.S.A. 117 M9
Palabek, Uganda 86 B3
Palacios, U.S.A. 113 L6
Palafrugell, Spain 32 D8
Palagiano, Italy 31 B10
Palagonía, Italy 31 E7
Palagruža, Croatia 29 F13
Palaiókastron, Greece 36 D8
Palaiokhóra, Greece 36 D5
Pálairos, Greece 38 C2
Palaiseau, France 19 D9
Palam, India 66 K10
Palamás, Greece 38 B4
Palamòs, Spain 32 D8
Palampur, India 68 C7
Palamut, Turkey 39 C9
Palana, Australia 94 F4
Palana, Russia 51 D16
Palanan, Phil. 61 C5
Palanan Pt., Phil. 61 C5
Palandri, Pakistan 69 C5
Palanga, Lithuania 9 J19
Palangkaraya, Indonesia . 62 E4
Palani Hills, India 66 P10
Palanpur, India 68 G5
Palapye, Botswana 88 C4
Palas, Pakistan 69 B5
Palas de Rei, Spain 34 C3
Palashi, India 69 H13
Palasponga, India 69 J11
Palatka, Russia 51 C16
Palatka, U.S.A. 109 L5
Palau, Italy 30 A2
Palau ■, Pac. Oc. 63 C8
Palauk, Burma 64 F2
Palawan, Phil. 61 G3
Palayankottai, India .. 66 Q10
Palazzo, Pte., France . 21 F12
Palazzo San Gervásio, Italy . 31 B8
Palazzolo Acréide, Italy . 31 E7
Paldiski, Estonia 9 G21
Pale, Bos.-H. 42 G3
Paleleh, Indonesia ... 63 D6
Palembang, Indonesia . 62 E2
Palencia, Spain 34 C6
Palencia □, Spain 34 C6
Palenque, Mexico 119 D6
Paleokastrítsa, Greece . 36 A3
Palermo, Italy 30 D6
Palermo, U.S.A. 114 G3
Palestina, Chile 128 A3
Palestine, Asia 75 D4
Palestine, U.S.A. 113 K7
Palestrina, Italy 29 G9
Paletwa, Burma 67 J18
Palghat, India 66 P10
Palgrave, Mt., Australia . 92 D2
Pali, India 68 G5
Palikir, Micronesia . 96 G7
Palinuro, Italy 31 B8
Palinuro, C., Italy .. 31 B8
Palioúrion, Ákra, Greece . 40 G7
Palisades Reservoir, U.S.A. 114 E8
Paliseul, Belgium ... 17 E5
Palitana, India 68 J4
Palizada, Mexico ... 119 D6
Palk Bay, India 66 Q11
Palk Strait, Asia ... 66 Q11
Palkānah, Iraq 70 C5
Palkot, India 69 H11
Palla Road = Dinokwe,
  Botswana 88 C4
Pallanza = Verbánia, Italy . 28 C5
Pallarenda, Australia .. 94 B4
Pallasovka, Russia ... 48 E8
Pallës, Bishti i, Albania . 40 E3
Pallinup →, Australia . 93 F2
Pallisa, Uganda 86 B3
Pallu, India 68 E6
Palm Bay, U.S.A. ... 109 L5
Palm Beach, U.S.A. . 109 M6
Palm Coast, U.S.A. . 109 L5
Palm Desert, U.S.A. 117 M10
Palm Is., Australia . 94 B4
Palm Springs, U.S.A. 117 M10
Palma, Mozam. 87 E5
Palma, B. de, Spain . 37 B9
Palma de Mallorca, Spain . 37 B9
Palma del Río, Spain . 35 H5
Palma di Montechiaro, Italy 30 E6
Palma Soriano, Cuba . 120 B4
Palmares, Brazil 125 E11
Palmas, Brazil 127 B5
Palmas, C., Liberia . 82 E3
Pálmas, G. di, Italy . 30 D1
Palmdale, U.S.A. ... 117 L8
Palmeira das Missões, Brazil 127 B5
Palmeira dos Índios, Brazil . 125 E11
Palmela, Portugal ... 35 G2
Palmer, U.S.A. 100 B5
Palmer →, Australia . 94 B3
Palmer Arch., Antarctica . 5 C17
Palmer Lake, U.S.A. . 112 F2
Palmer Land, Antarctica . 5 D18
Palmerston, Canada .. 110 C4
Palmerston, N.Z. 91 L3
Palmerston North, N.Z. . 91 J5
Palmerton, U.S.A. .. 111 F9
Palmetto, U.S.A. ... 109 M4
Palmi, Italy 31 D8
Palmira, Argentina . 126 C2
Palmira, Colombia . 124 C3
Palmyra = Tudmur, Syria . 70 C3
Palmyra, Mo., U.S.A. . 112 F9

Palmyra, N.J., U.S.A. .. 111 F9
Palmyra, N.Y., U.S.A. .. 110 C7
Palmyra, Pa., U.S.A. ... 111 F8
Palmyra Is., Pac. Oc. .. 97 G11
Palo Alto, U.S.A. 116 H4
Palo Verde, U.S.A. 117 M12
Paloich, Sudan 81 E3
Palompon, Phil. 61 F6
Palopo, Indonesia 63 E6
Palos, C. de, Spain .. 33 H4
Palos de la Frontera, Spain . 35 H4
Palos Verdes, U.S.A. . 117 M8
Palos Verdes, Pt., U.S.A. . 117 M8
Pålsboda, Sweden ... 10 E9
Palu, Indonesia 63 E5
Palu, Turkey 70 B3
Paluke, Liberia 82 D3
Paluzza, Italy 29 B10
Palwal, India 68 E7
Pama, Burkina Faso . 83 C5
Pamanukan, Indonesia . 63 G12
Pamiers, France 20 E5
Pamir, Tajikistan ... 50 F8
Pamlico →, U.S.A. .. 109 H7
Pamlico Sd., U.S.A. . 109 H8
Pampa, U.S.A. 113 H4
Pampa de las Salinas,
  Argentina 126 C2
Pampanua, Indonesia . 63 E6
Pampas, Argentina .. 126 D3
Pampas, Peru 124 F4
Pamphylia, Turkey . 72 D4
Pamplona, Colombia . 124 B4
Pamplona, Spain 32 C3
Pampoenpoort, S. Africa . 88 E3
Pamukçu, Turkey ... 39 B9
Pamukkale, Turkey . 39 D11
Pan Xian, China 58 E5
Pana, U.S.A. 112 F10
Panabo, Phil. 61 H6
Panaca, U.S.A. 115 H6
Panagyurishte, Bulgaria . 41 D8
Panaitan, Indonesia . 63 G11
Panaji, India 66 M8
Panamá, Panama ... 120 E4
Panama ■, Cent. Amer. . 120 E4
Panamá, G. de, Panama . 120 E4
Panama Canal, Panama . 120 E4
Panama City, U.S.A. . 109 K3
Panamint Range, U.S.A. . 117 J9
Panamint Springs, U.S.A. . 117 J9
Panão, Peru 124 E3
Panaon I., Phil. ... 61 F6
Panare, Thailand .. 65 J3
Panarea, Italy 31 D8
Panaro →, Italy ... 29 D8
Panay, Phil. 61 F5
Panay, G., Phil. ... 63 B6
Pančevo, Serbia, Yug. . 42 F5
Panch'iao, Taiwan . 59 E13
Panciu, Romania .. 43 E12
Pancorbo, Desfiladero, Spain 34 C7
Pâncota, Romania . 42 D6
Panda, Mozam. 89 C5
Pandan, Antique, Phil. . 61 F5
Pandan, Catanduanes, Phil. . 61 D6
Pandegelang, Indonesia . 63 G12
Pandhana, India ... 68 J7
Pandharpur, India . 66 L9
Pando, Uruguay ... 127 C4
Pando, L. = Hope, L.,
  Australia 95 D2
Pandokrátor, Greece . 36 A3
Pandora, Costa Rica . 120 E3
Pandrup, Denmark . 11 G3
Panevėžys, Lithuania . 9 J21
Panfilov, Kazakstan . 50 E8
Panfilovo, Russia .. 48 E6
Pang-Long, Burma . 67 H21
Pang-Yang, Burma . 67 H21
Panga,
  Dem. Rep. of the Congo . 86 B2
Pangaíon Óros, Greece . 41 F8
Pangalanes, Canal des =
  Ampangalana,
  Lakandranon', Madag. . 89 C8
Pangani, Tanzania .. 86 D4
Pangani →, Tanzania . 86 D4
Pangfou = Bengbu, China . 57 H9
Pangil,
  Dem. Rep. of the Congo . 86 C2
Pangkah, Tanjung, Indonesia 63 G15
Pangkajene, Indonesia . 63 E5
Pangkalanbrandan, Indonesia 62 D1
Pangkalanbuun, Indonesia . 62 E4
Pangkalpinang, Indonesia . 62 E3
Pangnirtung, Canada . 101 B13
Pangong Tso, India . 68 B8
Panguitch, U.S.A. . 115 H7
Pangutaran Group, Phil. . 61 H4
Panhandle, U.S.A. . 113 H4
Pani Mines, India . 68 H5
Pania-Mutombo,
  Dem. Rep. of the Congo . 86 D1
Panikota I., India . 68 J4
Panipat, India 68 E7
Panjal Range, India . 68 C7
Panjang, Hon, Vietnam . 65 H4
Panjgur, Pakistan . 66 F4
Panjim = Panaji, India . 66 M8
Panjin, China 57 D12
Panjinad Barrage, Pakistan . 66 E7
Panjnad →, Pakistan . 68 E4
Panjwai, Afghan. . 68 D1
Pankshin, Nigeria . 83 D6
Panmunjŏm, N. Korea . 57 F14
Panna, India 69 G9
Panna Hills, India . 69 G9
Pannawonica, Australia . 92 D2
Pano Akil, Pakistan . 68 F3
Pano Lefkara, Cyprus . 36 E12

Pano Panayia, Cyprus ... 36 E11
Panorama, Brazil 127 A5
Pánormon, Greece 36 D6
Pansemal, India 68 J6
Panshan = Panjin, China . 57 D12
Panshi, China 57 C14
Pantanal, Brazil 124 H7
Pantar, Indonesia 63 F6
Pante Macassar, Indonesia . 63 F6
Pantelleria, Italy 30 F4
Pantón, Spain 34 C3
Pánuco, Mexico 119 C5
Panyam, Nigeria 83 D6
Panyu, China 59 F9
Panzhihua, China ... 58 D3
Páola, Italy 31 C9
Paola, Malta 36 D2
Paola, U.S.A. 112 F7
Paonia, U.S.A. 115 G10
Paoting = Baoding, China . 56 E8
Paot'ou = Baotou, China . 56 D6
Paoua, C.A.R. 84 C3
Pápa, Hungary 42 C2
Papa Stour, U.K. .. 14 A7
Papa Westray, U.K. . 14 B6
Papagayo →, Mexico . 119 D5
Papagayo, G. de, Costa Rica 120 D2
Papakura, N.Z. 91 G5
Papantla, Mexico . 119 C5
Papar, Malaysia .. 62 C5
Pápas, Ákra, Greece . 38 C3
Papeete, Tahiti ... 97 J13
Papenburg, Germany . 24 B3
Paphlagonia, Turkey . 72 B5
Paphos, Cyprus .. 36 E11
Papien Chiang = Da →,
  Vietnam 58 G5
Papigochic →, Mexico . 118 B3
Paposo, Chile 126 B1
Papoutsa, Cyprus . 36 E12
Papua New Guinea ■,
  Oceania 96 H6
Papudo, Chile 126 C1
Papuk, Croatia .. 42 E2
Papun, Burma ... 67 K20
Papunya, Australia . 92 D5
Pará = Belém, Brazil . 125 D9
Pará □, Brazil .. 125 D8
Parabcatu, Brazil . 125 G9
Parabburdoo, Australia . 92 D2
Paracale, Phil. .. 61 D5
Paracatu, Brazil . 125 G9
Paracel Is., S. China Sea . 62 A4
Parachilna, Australia . 95 E2
Parachinar, Pakistan . 68 C4
Paradas, Spain .. 35 H5
Paradela, Spain . 34 C3
Paradhísi, Greece . 36 C10
Paradip, India .. 67 J15
Paradise, Calif., U.S.A. . 116 F5
Paradise, Nev., U.S.A. . 117 J11
Paradise →, Canada . 103 B8
Paradise Hill, Canada . 105 C7
Paradise River, Canada . 103 B8
Paradise Valley, U.S.A. . 114 F5
Parado, Indonesia . 63 F5
Paragould, U.S.A. . 113 G9
Paragua →, Venezuela . 124 B6
Paraguaçu →, Brazil . 125 F11
Paraguaçu Paulista, Brazil . 127 A5
Paraguaná, Pen. de,
  Venezuela 124 A5
Paraguarí, Paraguay . 126 B4
Paraguarí □, Paraguay . 126 B4
Paraguay ■, S. Amer. . 126 A4
Paraguay →, Paraguay . 126 B4
Paraíba = João Pessoa,
  Brazil 125 E12
Paraíba □, Brazil . 125 E11
Paraíba do Sul →, Brazil . 127 A7
Parainen, Finland . 9 F20
Paraíso, Mexico . 119 D6
Parak, Iran 71 E7
Parakhino Paddubye, Russia 46 C7
Parakou, Benin . 83 D5
Paralimni, Cyprus . 36 D12
Parálion-Astrous, Greece . 38 D4
Paramaribo, Surinam . 125 B7
Paramithiá, Greece . 38 B2
Paramushir, Ostrov, Russia 51 D16
Paran →, Israel . 75 E4
Paraná, Argentina . 126 C3
Paraná, Brazil .. 125 F9
Paraná □, Brazil . 127 A5
Paraná →, Argentina . 126 C4
Paranaguá, Brazil . 127 B6
Paranaíba, Brazil . 125 G8
Paranaíba →, Brazil . 125 H8
Paranapanema →, Brazil . 127 A5
Paranapiacaba, Serra do,
  Brazil 127 A6
Paranas, Phil. .. 61 F6
Paranavaí, Brazil . 127 A5
Parang, Maguindanao, Phil. . 63 C6
Parang, Sulu, Phil. . 61 J4
Parângul Mare, Vf.,
  Romania 43 E8
Parapóla, Greece . 38 E5
Paraspóri, Ákra, Greece . 39 F9
Paray-le-Monial, France . 19 F11
Parbati →, Mad. P., India . 68 G7
Parbati →, Raj., India . 68 F7
Parbhani, India . 66 K10
Parchim, Germany . 24 B7
Parczew, Poland . 45 G9
Pardes Hanna-Karkur, Israel 75 C3
Pardilla, Spain . 34 D7
Pardo →, Bahia, Brazil . 125 G11
Pardo →, Mato Grosso,
  Brazil 127 A5
Pardubice, Czech Rep. . 26 A8

Pare, Indonesia 63 G15
Pare Mts., Tanzania 86 C4
Parecis, Serra dos, Brazil . 124 F7
Paredes de Nava, Spain .. 34 C6
Paren, Russia 51 C17
Parent, Canada 102 C5
Parent, L., Canada 102 C4
Parentis-en-Born, France .. 20 D2
Parepare, Indonesia 63 E5
Parfino, Russia 46 D6
Párga, Greece 38 B2
Pargo, Pta. do, Madeira .. 37 D2
Pariaguán, Venezuela 124 B6
Paricutín, Cerro, Mexico .. 118 D4
Parigi, Indonesia 63 E6
Parika, Guyana 124 B7
Parikkala, Finland 46 B5
Parima, Serra, Brazil 124 C6
Parinari, Peru 124 D4
Pariñas, Pta., S. Amer. .. 122 D2
Parincea, Romania 43 D12
Parintins, Brazil 125 D7
Pariparit Kyun, Burma ... 67 M18
Paris, Canada 110 C4
Paris, France 19 D9
Paris, Idaho, U.S.A. 114 E8
Paris, Ky., U.S.A. 108 F3
Paris, Tenn., U.S.A. 109 G1
Paris, Tex., U.S.A. 113 J7
Paris, Ville de □, France . 19 D9
Parish, U.S.A. 111 C8
Parishville, U.S.A. 111 B10
Park, U.S.A. 116 B4
Park City, U.S.A. 113 G6
Park Falls, U.S.A. 112 C9
Park Head, Canada 110 B3
Park Hills, U.S.A. 113 G9
Park Range, U.S.A. ... 114 G10
Park Rapids, U.S.A. .. 112 B7
Park River, U.S.A. ... 112 A6
Park Rynie, S. Africa . 89 E5
Parkā Bandar, Iran .. 71 E8
Parkano, Finland ... 9 E20
Parker, Ariz., U.S.A. . 117 L12
Parker, Pa., U.S.A. .. 110 E5
Parker Dam, U.S.A. . 117 L12
Parkersburg, U.S.A. . 108 F5
Parkes, Australia .. 95 E4
Parkfield, U.S.A. .. 116 K6
Parkhill, Canada .. 110 C3
Parkland, Canada . 116 C4
Parkston, U.S.A. . 112 D6
Parksville, Canada . 104 D4
Parla, Spain 34 E7
Pârlița, Moldova . 43 C12
Parma, Italy 28 D7
Parma, Idaho, U.S.A. . 114 E5
Parma, Ohio, U.S.A. . 110 E3
Parma →, Italy .. 28 D7
Parnaguá, Brazil . 125 F10
Parnaíba, Brazil . 125 D10
Parnaíba →, Brazil . 122 D6
Parnassós, Greece . 38 C4
Párnis, Greece .. 38 C5
Párnon Óros, Greece . 38 D4
Pärnu, Estonia .. 9 G21
Paroo →, Australia . 95 E3
Páros, Greece .. 39 D7
Parowan, U.S.A. . 115 H7
Parpaillon, France . 21 D10
Parral, Chile ... 126 D1
Parras, Mexico . 118 B4
Parrett →, U.K. . 13 F4
Parris I., U.S.A. . 109 J5
Parrsboro, Canada . 103 C7
Parry I., Canada . 110 A4
Parry Is., Canada . 4 B2
Parry Sound, Canada . 102 C4
Parsberg, Germany . 25 F7
Parseta →, Poland . 44 D2
Parsnip →, Canada . 104 B4
Parsons, U.S.A. . 113 G7
Parsons Ra., Australia . 94 A2
Partanna, Italy . 30 E5
Parthenay, France . 18 F6
Partinico, Italy . 30 D6
Partizánske, Slovak Rep. . 27 C11
Partridge I., Canada . 102 A2
Paru →, Brazil . 125 D8
Parvān □, Afghan. . 66 B6
Parvatipuram, India . 67 K13
Parvatsar, India . 68 F6
Påryd, Sweden . 11 H9
Parys, S. Africa . 88 D4
Pas, Pta. des, Spain . 37 C7
Pas-de-Calais □, France . 19 B9
Pasada, Spain . 34 B5
Pasadena, Canada . 103 C8
Pasadena, Calif., U.S.A. . 117 L8
Pasadena, Tex., U.S.A. . 113 L7
Pasaje →, Argentina . 126 B3
Paşalimanı, Turkey . 41 F11
Pasay, Phil. . 61 D4
Pascagoula, U.S.A. . 113 K10
Pascagoula →, U.S.A. . 113 K10
Paşcani, Romania . 43 C11
Pasco, U.S.A. . 114 C4
Pasco, Cerro de, Peru . 124 F3
Pasco I., Australia . 92 D2
Pascoag, U.S.A. . 111 E13
Pascua, I. de, Pac. Oc. . 97 K17
Pasewalk, Germany . 24 B9
Pasfield L., Canada . 105 B7
Pasha →, Russia . 46 B7
Pashiwari, Pakistan . 69 B6
Pashmakli = Smolyan,
  Bulgaria 41 E8
Pasinler, Turkey . 73 C9
Pasir Mas, Malaysia . 65 J4
Pasir Putih, Malaysia . 65 K4
Pasirian, Indonesia 63 H15

Pasirkuning, *Indonesia* 62 E2
Påskallavik, *Sweden* 11 G10
Paskūh, *Iran* 71 E9
Pasłęk, *Poland* 44 D6
Pasłęka →, *Poland* 44 D6
Pasley, C., *Australia* 93 F3
Pašman, *Croatia* 29 E12
Pasni, *Pakistan* 66 G3
Paso Cantinela, *Mexico* ... 117 N11
Paso de Indios, *Argentina* . 128 E3
Paso de los Libres, *Argentina* 126 B4
Paso de los Toros, *Uruguay* 126 C4
Paso Robles, *U.S.A.* 115 J3
Paspébiac, *Canada* 103 C6
Pasrur, *Pakistan* 68 C6
Passage West, *Ireland* 15 E3
Passaic, *U.S.A.* 111 F10
Passau, *Germany* 25 G9
Passero, C., *Italy* 31 F8
Passo Fundo, *Brazil* 127 B5
Passos, *Brazil* 125 H9
Passow, *Germany* 24 B10
Passy, *France* 21 C10
Pastavy, *Belarus* 9 J22
Pastaza →, *Peru* 124 D3
Pasto, *Colombia* 124 C3
Pastrana, *Spain* 32 E2
Pasuruan, *Indonesia* 63 G15
Pasym, *Poland* 44 E7
Pásztó, *Hungary* 42 C4
Patagonia, *Argentina* 122 H4
Patagonia, *U.S.A.* 115 L8
Patambar, *Iran* 71 D9
Patan, *Gujarat, India* 66 H8
Patan, *Maharashtra, India* . 68 H5
Patan, *Nepal* 67 F14
Patani, *Indonesia* 63 D7
Pătârlagele, *Romania* 43 E11
Pataudi, *India* 68 E7
Patchewollock, *Australia* .. 95 F3
Patchogue, *U.S.A.* 111 F11
Patea, *N.Z.* 91 H5
Pategi, *Nigeria* 83 D6
Patensie, *S. Africa* 88 E3
Paterna, *Spain* 33 F4
Paternion, *Austria* 26 E6
Paternò, *Italy* 31 E7
Pateros, *U.S.A.* 114 B4
Paterson, *U.S.A.* 111 F10
Paterson Ra., *Australia* ... 92 D3
Pathankot, *India* 68 C6
Pathfinder Reservoir, *U.S.A.* 114 E10
Pathiu, *Thailand* 65 G2
Pathum Thani, *Thailand* ... 64 E3
Pati, *Indonesia* 63 G14
Patía →, *Colombia* 124 C3
Patiala, *Punjab, India* 68 D7
Patiala, *Ut. P., India* 69 F8
Patine Kouka, *Senegal* 82 C2
Patitírion, *Greece* 38 B5
Patkai Bum, *India* 67 F19
Pátmos, *Greece* 39 D8
Patna, *India* 69 G11
Patnos, *Turkey* 73 C10
Pato Branco, *Brazil* 127 B5
Patonga, *Uganda* 86 B3
Patos, *Brazil* 125 E11
Patos, L. dos, *Brazil* 127 C5
Patos, Río de los →,
    Argentina 126 C2
Patos de Minas, *Brazil* 125 G9
Patosi, *Albania* 40 F3
Patquía, *Argentina* 126 C2
Pátrai, *Greece* 38 C3
Pátraikós Kólpos, *Greece* .. 38 C3
Patras = Pátrai, *Greece* ... 38 C3
Patrocínio, *Brazil* 125 G9
Patta, *Kenya* 86 C5
Pattada, *Italy* 30 B2
Pattani, *Thailand* 65 J3
Pattaya, *Thailand* 62 B2
Patten, *U.S.A.* 109 C11
Patterson, *Calif., U.S.A.* .. 116 H5
Patterson, *La., U.S.A.* 113 L9
Patterson, Mt., *U.S.A.* 116 G7
Patti, *Punjab, India* 68 D6
Patti, *Ut. P., India* 69 G10
Patti, *Italy* 31 D7
Pattoki, *Pakistan* 68 D5
Patton, *U.S.A.* 110 F6
Patuakhali, *Bangla.* 67 H17
Patuanak, *Canada* 105 B7
Patuca →, *Honduras* 120 C3
Patuca, Punta, *Honduras* .. 120 C3
Pătulele, *Romania* 42 F7
Pátzcuaro, *Mexico* 118 D4
Pau, *France* 20 E3
Pau, Gave de →, *France* ... 20 E2
Pauillac, *France* 20 C3
Pauk, *Burma* 67 J19
Paul I., *Canada* 103 A7
Paul Smiths, *U.S.A.* 111 B10
Paulatuk, *Canada* 100 B7
Paulhan, *France* 20 E7
Paulis = Isiro,
    Dem. Rep. of the Congo . 86 B2
Paulistana, *Brazil* 125 E10
Paulo Afonso, *Brazil* 125 E11
Paulpietersburg, *S. Africa* . 89 D5
Pauls Valley, *U.S.A.* 113 H6
Pauma Valley, *U.S.A.* 117 M10
Pauri, *India* 69 D8
Pāveh, *Iran* 70 C5
Pavelets, *Russia* 46 F10
Pāvilosta, *Latvia* 9 H19
Pavlikeni, *Bulgaria* 41 C9
Pavlodar, *Kazakstan* 50 D8

Pavlograd = Pavlohrad,
    Ukraine 47 H8
Pavlohrad, *Ukraine* 47 H8
Pavlovo, *Russia* 48 C6
Pavlovsk, *Russia* 48 E5
Pavlovskaya, *Russia* 49 G4
Pavlovskiy-Posad, *Russia* .. 46 E10
Pavullo nel Frignano, *Italy* . 28 D7
Pawayan, *India* 69 E9
Pawhuska, *U.S.A.* 113 G6
Pawling, *U.S.A.* 111 E11
Pawnee, *U.S.A.* 113 G6
Pawnee City, *U.S.A.* 112 E6
Pawtucket, *U.S.A.* 111 E13
Paximádhia, *Greece* 36 E6
Paxoí, *Greece* 38 B2
Paxton, *Ill., U.S.A.* 108 E1
Paxton, *Nebr., U.S.A.* 112 E4
Payakumbuh, *Indonesia* .. 62 E2
Payerne, *Switz.* 25 J2
Payette, *U.S.A.* 114 D5
Paymogo, *Spain* 35 H3
Payne Bay = Kangirsuk,
    Canada 101 B13
Payne L., *Canada* 101 C12
Paynes Find, *Australia* 93 E2
Paynesville, *Liberia* 82 D2
Paynesville, *U.S.A.* 112 C7
Pays de la Loire □, *France* . 18 E6
Paysandú, *Uruguay* 126 C4
Payson, *U.S.A.* 120 D1
Paz →, *Guatemala* 118 D1
Paz, B. la, *Mexico* 118 C2
Pāzanān, *Iran* 71 D6
Pazar, *Turkey* 73 B9
Pazarcık, *Turkey* 72 D7
Pazardzhik, *Bulgaria* 41 D8
Pazarköy, *Turkey* 39 B9
Pazarlar, *Turkey* 39 C11
Pazaryeri, *Turkey* 39 B11
Pazaryolu, *Turkey* 73 B9
Pazin, *Croatia* 29 C10
Pčinja →, *Macedonia* 40 E5
Pe Ell, *U.S.A.* 116 C8
Peabody, *U.S.A.* 111 D14
Peace →, *Canada* 104 B6
Peace Point, *Canada* 104 B6
Peace River, *Canada* 104 B5
Peach Springs, *U.S.A.* 117 J7
Peachland, *Canada* 104 D5
Peachtree City, *U.S.A.* 109 J3
Peak, The = Kinder Scout,
    U.K. 12 D6
Peak District, *U.K.* 12 D6
Peak Hill, *N.S.W., Australia* 95 E4
Peak Hill, *W. Austral.,
    Australia* 93 E2
Peak Ra., *Australia* 94 C4
Peake Cr. →, *Australia* ... 95 D2
Peal de Becerro, *Spain* 35 H7
Peale, Mt., *U.S.A.* 115 G9
Pearblossom, *U.S.A.* 117 L9
Pearl →, *U.S.A.* 113 K10
Pearl City, *U.S.A.* 106 H16
Pearl Harbor, *U.S.A.* 106 H16
Pearl River, *U.S.A.* 111 E10
Pearsall, *U.S.A.* 113 L5
Peary Land, *Greenland* 4 A6
Pease →, *U.S.A.* 113 H5
Peawanuck, *Canada* 101 C11
Pebane, *Mozam.* 87 F4
Pebas, *Peru* 124 D4
Pebble Beach, *U.S.A.* 116 J5
Peć, *Kosovo, Yug.* 40 D4
Péccioli, *Italy* 28 E7
Pechea, *Romania* 43 E12
Pechenga, *Russia* 50 C4
Pechenizhyn, *Ukraine* 47 H3
Pechiguera, Pta., *Canary Is.* 37 F6
Pechnezhskoye Vdkhr.,
    Ukraine 47 G9
Pechora, *Russia* 50 C6
Pechora →, *Russia* 50 C6
Pechorskaya Guba, *Russia* . 50 C6
Pecica, *Romania* 42 D6
Pecka, *Serbia, Yug.* 40 B3
Pécora, C., *Italy* 30 C1
Pečory, *Russia* 9 H22
Pecos, *U.S.A.* 113 K3
Pecos →, *U.S.A.* 113 L3
Pécs, *Hungary* 42 D3
Pedder, L., *Australia* 94 G4
Peddie, *S. Africa* 89 E4
Pédernales, *Dom. Rep.* 121 C5
Pedieos →, *Cyprus* 36 D12
Pedirka, *Australia* 95 D2
Pedra Azul, *Brazil* 125 G10
Pedreguer, *Spain* 33 G5
Pedreiras, *Brazil* 125 D10
Pedro Afonso, *Brazil* 125 E9
Pedro Cays, *Jamaica* 120 C4
Pedro de Valdivia, *Chile* ... 126 A2
Pedro Juan Caballero,
    Paraguay 127 A4
Pedro Muñoz, *Spain* 35 F8
Pedrógão Grande, *Portugal* 34 F2
Pee Dee →, *U.S.A.* 109 J6
Peebinga, *Australia* 95 E3
Peebles, *U.K.* 14 F5
Peekskill, *U.S.A.* 111 E11
Peel, *U.K.* 12 C3
Peel →, *Australia* 95 E5
Peel →, *Canada* 100 B6
Peel Sound, *Canada* 100 A10
Peene →, *Germany* 24 A9
Peera Peera Poolanna L.,
    Australia 95 D2
Peerless Lake, *Canada* 104 B6
Peers, *Canada* 104 C5
Pegasus Bay, *N.Z.* 91 K4
Peggau, *Austria* 26 D8

Pegnitz, *Germany* 25 F7
Pegnitz →, *Germany* 25 F6
Pego, *Spain* 33 G4
Pegu, *Burma* 67 L20
Pegu Yoma, *Burma* 67 K20
Pehčevo, *Macedonia* 40 E6
Pehlivanköy, *Turkey* 41 E10
Pehuajó, *Argentina* 126 D3
Pei Xian = Pizhou, *China* . 56 G9
Peine, *Chile* 126 A2
Peine, *Germany* 24 C6
Peip'ing = Beijing, *China* .. 56 E9
Peipus, L. = Chudskoye,
    Ózero, *Russia* 9 G22
Peissenberg, *Germany* 25 H7
Peitz, *Germany* 24 D10
Peixe, *Brazil* 125 F9
Peixe →, *Brazil* 125 H8
Pek →, *Serbia, Yug.* 40 B5
Pekalongan, *Indonesia* ... 63 G13
Pekan, *Malaysia* 65 L4
Pekanbaru, *Indonesia* 62 D2
Pekang, *Taiwan* 59 F13
Pekin, *U.S.A.* 112 E10
Peking = Beijing, *China* ... 56 E9
Péla, *Guinea* 82 D3
Pelabuhan Kelang, *Malaysia* 65 L3
Pelabuhan Ratu, Teluk,
    Indonesia 63 G12
Pelabuhanratu, *Indonesia* . 63 G12
Pélagos, *Greece* 38 B6
Pelaihari, *Indonesia* 62 E4
Pelat, Mt., *France* 21 D10
Pełczyce, *Poland* 45 E2
Peleaga, Vf., *Romania* 42 E7
Pelée, Mt., *Martinique* 121 D7
Pelee, Pt., *Canada* 102 D3
Pelee I., *Canada* 102 D3
Pelekech, *Kenya* 86 B4
Peleng, *Indonesia* 63 E6
Pélézi, *Ivory C.* 82 D3
Pelham, *U.S.A.* 109 K3
Pelican, *U.S.A.* 104 B1
Pelican L., *Canada* 105 C8
Pelican Narrows, *Canada* .. 105 B8
Peliješac, *Croatia* 29 F14
Pella, *Greece* 40 F6
Pella, *S. Africa* 88 D2
Pella, *U.S.A.* 112 E8
Péla □, *Greece* 40 F6
Pello, *Finland* 8 C21
Pellworm, *Germany* 24 A4
Pelly →, *Canada* 100 B6
Pelly Bay, *Canada* 101 B11
Peloponnese =
    Pelopónnisos □, *Greece* . 38 D4
Pelopónnisos □, *Greece* ... 38 D4
Peloritani, Monti, *Italy* 31 D8
Pelorus Sd., *N.Z.* 91 J4
Pelotas, *Brazil* 127 C5
Pelotas →, *Brazil* 127 B5
Pelovo, *Bulgaria* 41 C8
Pelplin, *Poland* 44 E5
Pelvoux, Massif du, *France* . 21 D10
Pemalang, *Indonesia* 63 G13
Pemanggil, Pulau, *Malaysia* 65 L5
Pematangsiantar, *Indonesia* 62 D1
Pemba, *Mozam.* 87 E5
Pemba, *Zambia* 87 F2
Pemba Channel, *Tanzania* . 86 D4
Pemba I., *Tanzania* 86 D4
Pemberton, *Australia* 93 F2
Pemberton, *Canada* 104 C4
Pembina, *U.S.A.* 112 A6
Pembroke, *Canada* 102 C4
Pembroke, *U.K.* 13 F3
Pembrokeshire □, *U.K.* ... 13 F3
Pen-y-Ghent, *U.K.* 12 C5
Peña, Sierra de la, *Spain* .. 32 C4
Peña de Francia, Sierra de
    la, *Spain* 34 E4
Peñafiel, *Portugal* 34 D2
Peñafiel, *Spain* 34 D6
Peñaflor, *Spain* 35 H5
Peñalara, *Spain* 34 E7
Penamacôr, *Portugal* 34 E3
Penang = Pinang, *Malaysia* 65 K3
Penápolis, *Brazil* 127 A6
Peñaranda de Bracamonte,
    Spain 34 E5
Peñarroya, *Spain* 32 E4
Peñarroya-Pueblonuevo,
    Spain 35 G5
Penarth, *U.K.* 13 F4
Peñas, C. de, *Spain* 34 B5
Penas, G. de, *Chile* 122 H3
Peñas de San Pedro, *Spain* . 33 G3
Peñas del Chache, *Canary Is.* 37 E6
Peñausende, *Spain* 34 D5
Pench'i = Benxi, *China* ... 57 D12
Pend Oreille →, *U.S.A.* ... 114 B5
Pend Oreille, L., *U.S.A.* ... 114 C5
Pendálofon, *Greece* 40 F5
Pendembu, *Eastern,
    S. Leone* 82 D2
Pendembu, *Northern,
    S. Leone* 82 D2
Pender B., *Australia* 92 C3
Pendleton, *Turkey* 41 F13
Pendleton, *U.S.A.* 114 D4
Pendra, *India* 69 H9
Penedo, *Brazil* 125 F11
Penetanguishene, *Canada* . 102 D4
Penfield, *U.S.A.* 110 E6
Peng, Kasai-Or.,
    Dem. Rep. of the Congo . 86 D1
Penge, Sud-Kivu,
    Dem. Rep. of the Congo . 86 C2

Penghu, *Taiwan* 59 F12
Penglai, *China* 57 F11
Pengshan, *China* 58 B4
Pengshui, *China* 58 C7
Penguin, *Australia* 94 G4
Pengxi, *China* 58 B5
Pengze, *China* 59 C11
Penhalonga, *Zimbabwe* ... 87 F3
Peniche, *Portugal* 35 F1
Penicuik, *U.K.* 14 F5
Penida, *Indonesia* 62 F5
Peninnes, Alpes = Pennine,
    Alpi, *Alps* 25 J3
Peninsular Malaysia □,
    Malaysia 65 L4
Peñíscola, *Spain* 32 E5
Penitente, Serra do, *Brazil* . 125 E9
Penkridge, *U.K.* 12 E5
Penmarch, *France* 18 E2
Penmarch, Pte. de, *France* . 18 E2
Penn Hills, *U.S.A.* 110 F5
Penn Yan, *U.S.A.* 110 D7
Penna, Punta della, *Italy* .. 29 F11
Pennant, *Canada* 105 C7
Penne, *Italy* 29 F10
Penner →, *India* 66 M12
Pennine, Alpi, *Alps* 25 J3
Pennines, *U.K.* 12 C5
Pennington, *U.S.A.* 116 F5
Pennington, *Nigeria* 83 E6
Pennsburg, *U.S.A.* 111 F9
Pennsylvania □, *U.S.A.* ... 108 E7
Penny, *Canada* 104 C4
Peno, *Russia* 46 D7
Penobscot →, *U.S.A.* 109 C11
Penobscot B., *U.S.A.* 109 C11
Penola, *Australia* 95 F3
Penong, *Australia* 93 F5
Penonomé, *Panama* 120 E3
Penrith, *Australia* 95 E5
Penrith, *U.K.* 12 C5
Penryn, *U.K.* 13 G2
Pensacola, *U.S.A.* 109 K2
Pensacola Mts., *Antarctica* . 5 E1
Pense, *Canada* 105 C8
Penshurst, *Australia* 95 F3
Penticton, *Canada* 104 D5
Pentland, *Australia* 94 C4
Pentland Firth, *U.K.* 14 C5
Pentland Hills, *U.K.* 14 F5
Penza, *Russia* 48 D7
Penzance, *U.K.* 13 G2
Penzberg, *Germany* 25 H7
Penzhino, *Russia* 51 C17
Penzhinskaya Guba, *Russia* 51 C17
Penzhou, *China* 58 B4
Penzlin, *Germany* 24 B9
Peoria, *Ariz., U.S.A.* 115 K7
Peoria, *Ill., U.S.A.* 112 E10
Pepacton Reservoir, *U.S.A.* 111 D10
Pepani →, *S. Africa* 88 D3
Pepel, *S. Leone* 82 D2
Peqin, *Albania* 40 E3
Pera Hd., *Australia* 94 A3
Perabumulih, *Indonesia* ... 62 E2
Perak →, *Malaysia* 65 K3
Perakhóra, *Greece* 38 C4
Perales de Alfambra, *Spain* 32 E4
Perales del Puerto, *Spain* .. 34 E4
Pérama, *Kérkira, Greece* .. 36 A3
Pérama, *Kríti, Greece* 36 D6
Peräpohjola, *Finland* 8 C22
Perast, *Montenegro, Yug.* .. 40 D2
Percé, *Canada* 103 C7
Perche, *France* 18 D8
Perchtoldsdorf, *Austria* ... 27 C9
Percival Lakes, *Australia* .. 92 D4
Percy, *France* 18 D5
Percy Is., *Australia* 94 C5
Perdido, Mte., *Spain* 32 C5
Perdu, Mt. = Perdido, Mte.,
    Spain 32 C5
Pereira, *Colombia* 124 C3
Perelazovskiy, *Russia* 49 F6
Perenjori, *Australia* 93 E2
Peresecina, *Moldova* 43 C13
Pereslavl-Zalesskiy, *Russia* 46 D10
Pereyaslav-Khmelnytskyy,
    Ukraine 47 G6
Pérez, I., *Mexico* 119 C7
Perg, *Austria* 26 C7
Pergamino, *Argentina* 126 C3
Pergau →, *Malaysia* 65 K3
Pérgine Valsugana, *Italy* ... 29 B8
Pérgola, *Italy* 29 E9
Perham, *U.S.A.* 112 B7
Perhentian, Kepulauan,
    Malaysia 62 C2
Periam, *Romania* 42 D5
Péribonca →, *Canada* 103 C5
Péribonca, L., *Canada* 103 B5
Perico, *Argentina* 126 A2
Pericos, *Mexico* 118 B3
Périers, *France* 18 C5
Périgord, *France* 20 D4
Périgueux, *France* 20 C4
Perijá, Sierra de, *Colombia* . 124 B4
Peristéra, *Greece* 38 B5
Peristerona →, *Cyprus* ... 36 D12
Perito Moreno, *Argentina* . 128 F2
Perivol = Dragovishtitsa,
    Bulgaria 40 D6
Perkasie, *U.S.A.* 111 F9
Perković, *Croatia* 29 E13
Perlas, Arch. de las, *Panama* 120 E4
Perlas, Punta de, *Nic.* 120 D3
Perleberg, *Germany* 24 B7
Perlez, *Serbia, Yug.* 42 E5
Perm, *Russia* 50 D6

Përmeti, *Albania* 40 F4
Pernambuco = Recife, *Brazil* 125 E12
Pernambuco □, *Brazil* 125 E11
Pernatty Lagoon, *Australia* . 95 E2
Pernik, *Bulgaria* 40 D7
Peron Is., *Australia* 92 B5
Peron Pen., *Australia* 93 E1
Péronne, *France* 19 C9
Perosa Argentina, *Italy* ... 28 D7
Perow, *Canada* 104 C3
Perpendicular Pt., *Australia* 95 E5
Perpignan, *France* 20 F6
Perris, *U.S.A.* 117 M9
Perros-Guirec, *France* 18 D3
Perry, *Fla., U.S.A.* 109 K4
Perry, *Ga., U.S.A.* 109 J4
Perry, *Iowa, U.S.A.* 112 E7
Perry, *Okla., U.S.A.* 113 G6
Perryton, *U.S.A.* 113 G4
Perryville, *U.S.A.* 113 G10
Persan, *France* 19 C9
Persberg, *Sweden* 10 E8
Perse □, *Iran* 71 D7
Persembe, *Turkey* 72 B7
Persepolis, *Iran* 71 D7
Pershotravensk, *Ukraine* .. 47 G4
Persia = Iran ■, *Asia* 71 C7
Persian Gulf = Gulf, The,
    Asia 71 E6
Perstorp, *Sweden* 11 H7
Pertek, *Turkey* 73 C8
Perth, *Australia* 93 F2
Perth, *Canada* 102 D4
Perth, *U.K.* 14 E5
Perth & Kinross □, *U.K.* ... 14 E5
Perth Amboy, *U.S.A.* 111 F10
Perth-Andover, *Canada* ... 103 C6
Pertuis, *France* 21 E9
Pertusato, C., *France* 21 G13
Peru, *Ind., U.S.A.* 108 E2
Peru, *N.Y., U.S.A.* 111 B11
Peru ■, *S. Amer.* 124 C4
Peru-Chile Trench, *Pac. Oc.* 124 G3
Perúgia, *Italy* 29 E9
Perušić, *Croatia* 29 D12
Pervomaysk, *Russia* 48 C6
Pervomaysk, *Ukraine* 47 H6
Pervouralsk, *Russia* 50 D6
Pésaro, *Italy* 29 E9
Pescadores = Penghu,
    Taiwan 59 F12
Pescara, *Italy* 29 F11
Pescara →, *Italy* 29 F11
Peschanokopskoye, *Russia* . 49 G5
Péscia, *Italy* 28 E7
Pescina, *Italy* 29 F10
Peshawar, *Pakistan* 68 B4
Peshkopi, *Albania* 40 E4
Peshtera, *Bulgaria* 41 D8
Peshtigo, *U.S.A.* 108 C2
Peski, *Russia* 48 E6
Pêso da Régua, *Portugal* .. 34 D3
Pesqueira, *Brazil* 125 E11
Pessac, *France* 20 D3
Pest □, *Hungary* 42 C4
Pestovo, *Russia* 46 C8
Pestravka, *Russia* 48 D9
Péta, *Greece* 38 B3
Petah Tiqwa, *Israel* 75 C3
Petalídhion, *Greece* 38 E3
Petaling Jaya, *Malaysia* ... 65 L3
Petaloudhes, *Greece* 36 C10
Petaluma, *U.S.A.* 116 G4
Pétange, *Lux.* 17 E5
Petaro, *Pakistan* 68 G3
Petatlán, *Mexico* 118 D4
Petauke, *Zambia* 87 E3
Petawawa, *Canada* 102 C4
Petén Itzá, L., *Guatemala* .. 120 C2
Peter I.s Øy, *Antarctica* ... 5 C16
Peter Pond L., *Canada* 105 B7
Peterbell, *Canada* 102 C3
Peterborough, *Australia* ... 95 E2
Peterborough, *Canada* 102 D4
Peterborough, *U.K.* 13 E7
Peterborough, *U.S.A.* 111 D13
Peterborough □, *U.K.* 13 E7
Peterculter, *U.K.* 14 D6
Peterhead, *U.K.* 14 D7
Peterlee, *U.K.* 12 C6
Petermann Bjerg, *Greenland* 98 B17
Petermann Ranges, *Australia* 92 E5
Petersburg, *Alaska, U.S.A.* . 100 C6
Petersburg, *Pa., U.S.A.* ... 110 F6
Petersburg, *Va., U.S.A.* ... 108 G7
Petersburg, *W. Va., U.S.A.* . 108 F6
Petersfield, *U.K.* 13 F7
Petershagen, *Germany* 24 C4
Petília Policastro, *Italy* 31 C9
Petit Gôave, *Haiti* 121 C5
Petit Jardin, *Canada* 103 C8
Petit Lac Manicouagan,
    Canada 103 B6
Petit-Mécatina →, *Canada* . 103 B8
Petit-Mécatina, I. du,
    Canada 103 B8
Petit Saint Bernard, Col du,
    Italy 21 C10
Petitcodiac, *Canada* 103 C6
Petite Baleine →, *Canada* . 102 A4
Petite Saguenay, *Canada* .. 103 C5
Petitot →, *Canada* 104 A4
Petitsikapau L., *Canada* ... 103 B6
Petlad, *India* 68 H5
Peto, *Mexico* 119 C7
Petone, *N.Z.* 91 J5
Petorca, *Chile* 126 C1
Petoskey, *U.S.A.* 108 C3
Petra, *Jordan* 75 E4
Petra, *Spain* 37 B10
Petra, Ostrova, *Russia* 4 B13
Petra Velikogo, Zaliv, *Russia* 54 C6

Petrel = Petrer, *Spain* 33 G4
Petrella, Monte, *Italy* 30 A6
Petrer, *Spain* 33 G4
Petreto-Bicchisano, *France* . 21 G12
Petrich, *Bulgaria* 40 E7
Petrified Forest National
  Park, *U.S.A.* 115 J9
Petrijanec, *Croatia* 29 B13
Petrikov = Pyetrikaw,
  Belarus 47 F5
Petrila, *Romania* 43 E8
Petrinja, *Croatia* 29 C13
Petrodvorets, *Russia* 46 C5
Petrograd = Sankt-
  Peterburg, *Russia* 46 C6
Petrolândia, *Brazil* 125 E11
Petrolia, *Canada* 102 D3
Petrolina, *Brazil* 125 E10
Petropavl, *Kazakstan* 50 D7
Petropavlovsk = Petropavl,
  Kazakstan 50 D7
Petropavlovsk-Kamchatskiy,
  Russia 51 D16
Petropavlovskiy =
  Akhtubinsk, *Russia* 49 F8
Petrópolis, *Brazil* 127 A7
Petroşani, *Romania* 43 E8
Petrova Gora, *Croatia* ... 29 C12
Petrovac, *Montenegro, Yug.* 40 D2
Petrovac, *Serbia, Yug.* ... 40 B5
Petrovaradin, *Serbia, Yug.* . 42 E4
Petrovsk, *Russia* 48 D7
Petrovsk-Zabaykalskiy,
  Russia 51 D11
Petrovskaya, *Russia* 47 K9
Petrovskoye = Svetlograd,
  Russia 49 H6
Petrozavodsk, *Russia* 46 B8
Petrus Steyn, *S. Africa* ... 89 D4
Petrusburg, *S. Africa* 88 D4
Petzeck, *Austria* 26 E5
Peumo, *Chile* 126 C1
Peureulak, *Indonesia* 62 D1
Pevek, *Russia* 51 C18
Peveragno, *Italy* 28 D4
Peyrehorade, *France* 20 E2
Peyruis, *France* 21 D9
Pézenas, *France* 20 E7
Pezinok, *Slovak Rep.* 27 C10
Pfaffenhofen, *Germany* ... 25 G7
Pfarrkirchen, *Germany* ... 25 G8
Pfeffenhausen, *Germany* .. 25 G7
Pforzheim, *Germany* 25 G4
Pfullendorf, *Germany* 25 H5
Pfungstadt, *Germany* 25 F4
Phagwara, *India* 66 D9
Phaistós, *Greece* 36 D6
Phala, *Botswana* 88 C4
Phalera = Phulera, *India* .. 68 F6
Phalodi, *India* 68 F5
Phalsbourg, *France* 19 D14
Phan, *Thailand* 64 C2
Phan Rang, *Vietnam* 65 G7
Phan Ri = Hoa Da, *Vietnam* 65 G7
Phan Thiet, *Vietnam* 65 G7
Phanae, *Greece* 39 C7
Phanat Nikhom, *Thailand* . 64 F3
Phangan, Ko, *Thailand* ... 65 H3
Phangnga, *Thailand* 65 H2
Phanh Bho Ho Chi Minh,
  Vietnam 65 G6
Phanom Sarakham, *Thailand* 64 F3
Phaphund, *India* 69 F8
Pharenda, *India* 69 F10
Pharr, *U.S.A.* 113 M5
Phatthalung, *Thailand* ... 65 J3
Phayao, *Thailand* 64 C2
Phelps, *U.S.A.* 110 D7
Phelps L., *Canada* 105 B8
Phenix City, *U.S.A.* 109 J3
Phet Buri, *Thailand* 64 F2
Phetchabun, *Thailand* 64 D3
Phetchabun, Thiu Khao,
  Thailand 64 E3
Phetchaburi = Phet Buri,
  Thailand 64 F2
Phi Phi, Ko, *Thailand* ... 65 J2
Phiafay, *Laos* 64 E6
Phibun Mangsahan, *Thailand* 64 E5
Phichai, *Thailand* 64 D3
Phichit, *Thailand* 64 D3
Philadelphia, *Miss., U.S.A.* 113 J10
Philadelphia, *N.Y., U.S.A.* 111 B9
Philadelphia, *Pa., U.S.A.* . 111 G9
Philip, *U.S.A.* 112 C4
Philippeville, *Belgium* ... 17 D4
Philippi, *Greece* 41 E8
Philippi, *U.S.A.* 108 F5
Philippi L., *Australia* 94 C2
Philippines ■, *Asia* 61 F5
Philippolis, *S. Africa* 88 E4
Philippopolis = Plovdiv,
  Bulgaria 41 D8
Philipsburg, *Canada* 111 A11
Philipsburg, *Mont., U.S.A.* 114 C7
Philipsburg, *Pa., U.S.A.* . 110 F6
Philipstown = Daingean,
  Ireland 15 C4
Philipstown, *S. Africa* ... 88 E3
Phillip I., *Australia* 95 F4
Phillips, *U.S.A.* 112 C9
Phillipsburg, *Kans., U.S.A.* 112 F5
Phillipsburg, *N.J., U.S.A.* . 111 F9
Philmont, *U.S.A.* 111 D11
Philomath, *U.S.A.* 114 D2
Phimai, *Thailand* 64 E4
Phitsanulok, *Thailand* ... 64 D3
Phnom Dangrek, *Thailand* . 62 B2
Phnom Penh, *Cambodia* .. 65 G5
Phnum Penh = Phnom Penh,
  Cambodia 65 G5

Phoenicia, *U.S.A.* 111 D10
Phoenix, *Ariz., U.S.A.* ... 115 K7
Phoenix, *N.Y., U.S.A.* ... 111 C8
Phoenix Is., *Kiribati* 96 H10
Phoenixville, *U.S.A.* 111 F9
Phon, *Thailand* 64 E4
Phon Tiou, *Laos* 64 D5
Phong ➤, *Thailand* 64 D4
Phong Saly, *Laos* 58 G4
Phong Tho, *Vietnam* 64 A4
Phonhong, *Laos* 64 C4
Phonum, *Thailand* 65 H2
Phosphate Hill, *Australia* . 94 C2
Photharam, *Thailand* 64 F2
Phra Nakhon Si Ayutthaya,
  Thailand 64 E3
Phra Thong, Ko, *Thailand* . 65 H2
Phrae, *Thailand* 64 C3
Phrom Phiram, *Thailand* . 64 D3
Phrygia, *Turkey* 72 C4
Phu Dien, *Vietnam* 64 C5
Phu Loi, *Laos* 64 B4
Phu Ly, *Vietnam* 58 G5
Phu Quoc, Dao, *Vietnam* . 65 G4
Phu Tho, *Vietnam* 58 G5
Phuc Yen, *Vietnam* 58 G5
Phuket, *Thailand* 65 J2
Phuket, Ko, *Thailand* ... 65 J2
Phul, *India* 68 D6
Phulad, *India* 68 G5
Phulbani, *India* 69 E8
Phulera, *India* 68 F6
Phulpur, *India* 69 G10
Phun Phin, *Thailand* 65 H2
Piacenza, *Italy* 28 C6
Pian Cr. ➤, *Australia* ... 95 E4
Piana, *France* 21 F12
Pianella, *Italy* 29 F11
Pianosa, *Puglia, Italy* ... 29 F12
Pianosa, *Toscana, Italy* .. 28 F7
Piapot, *Canada* 105 D7
Pias, *Portugal* 35 G3
Piaseczno, *Poland* 45 F8
Piaski, *Poland* 45 G9
Piastów, *Poland* 45 F7
Piatra, *Romania* 43 G10
Piatra Neamţ, *Romania* .. 43 D11
Piatra Olt, *Romania* 43 F9
Piauí □, *Brazil* 125 E10
Piauí ➤, *Brazil* 125 E10
Piave ➤, *Italy* 29 C9
Piazza Ármerina, *Italy* ... 31 E7
Pibor ➤, *Sudan* 81 F3
Pibor Post, *Sudan* 81 F3
Picardie, *France* 19 C10
Picardie, Plaine de, *France* 19 C9
Picardy = Picardie, *France* . 19 C10
Picayune, *U.S.A.* 113 K10
Picerno, *Italy* 31 B8
Pichhor, *India* 69 G8
Pichilemu, *Chile* 126 C1
Pichor, *India* 68 G8
Pickerel L., *Canada* 102 C1
Pickering, *U.K.* 12 C7
Pickering, Vale of, *U.K.* . 12 C7
Pickle Lake, *Canada* 102 B1
Pickwick L., *U.S.A.* 109 H1
Pico Truncado, *Argentina* . 128 F3
Picos, *Brazil* 125 E10
Picton, *Australia* 95 E5
Picton, *Canada* 102 D4
Picton, *N.Z.* 91 J5
Pictou, *Canada* 103 C7
Picture Butte, *Canada* ... 104 D6
Picún Leufú, *Argentina* .. 128 D3
Pidurutalagala, *Sri Lanka* . 66 R12
Piechowice, *Poland* 45 H2
Piedmont = Piemonte □,
  Italy 28 D5
Piedmont, *Ala., U.S.A.* .. 109 J3
Piedmont, *S.C., U.S.A.* .. 107 D10
Piedmonte Matese, *Italy* . 31 A7
Piedra ➤, *Spain* 32 D3
Piedrabuena, *Spain* 35 G6
Piedrahita, *Spain* 34 E5
Piedralaves, *Spain* 34 E6
Piedras Blancas, *Spain* .. 34 B5
Piedras Negras, *Mexico* .. 118 B4
Piekary Śląskie, *Poland* .. 45 H5
Pieksämäki, *Finland* 9 E22
Piemonte □, *Italy* 28 D5
Pienaarsrivier, *S. Africa* . 89 D4
Pieniężno, *Poland* 44 D7
Pieńsk, *Poland* 45 G2
Piercefield, *U.S.A.* 111 B10
Pierceland, *Canada* 105 C7
Piería □, *Greece* 40 F6
Pierpont, *U.S.A.* 110 E4
Pierre, *U.S.A.* 112 C4
Pierre-Buffière, *France* .. 20 C5
Pierre-de-Bresse, *France* . 19 F12
Pierrefontaine-les-Varans,
  France 19 E13
Pierrefort, *France* 20 D6
Pierrelatte, *France* 21 D8
Pieštany, *Slovak Rep.* ... 27 C10
Piesting, *Austria* 27 C9
Pieszyce, *Poland* 45 H3
Piet Retief, *S. Africa* 89 D5
Pietarsaari, *Finland* 8 E20
Pietermaritzburg, *S. Africa* 89 D5
Pietersburg, *S. Africa* ... 89 C4
Pietragalla, *Italy* 31 B8
Pietrasanta, *Italy* 28 E7
Pietroşiţa, *Romania* 43 E10
Pietrosul, Vf., *Maramureş,*
  Romania 43 C9
Pietrosul, Vf., *Suceava,*
  Romania 43 C10
Pieve di Cadore, *Italy* ... 29 B9
Pieve di Teco, *Italy* 28 D4

Pievepélago, *Italy* 28 D7
Pigadhítsa, *Greece* 40 G5
Pigeon L., *Canada* 110 B6
Piggott, *U.S.A.* 113 G9
Pigna, *Italy* 28 D4
Pigüe, *Argentina* 126 D3
Pihani, *India* 69 F9
Pihlajavesi, *Finland* 9 F23
Pijijiapan, *Mexico* 119 D6
Pikalevo, *Russia* 46 C8
Pikangikum Berens, *Canada* 105 C10
Pikes Peak, *U.S.A.* 112 F2
Piketberg, *S. Africa* 88 E2
Pikeville, *U.S.A.* 108 G4
Pikou, *China* 57 E12
Pikwitonei, *Canada* 105 B9
Piła, *Poland* 45 E3
Pila, *Spain* 33 G3
Pilaía, *Greece* 40 F6
Pilani, *India* 68 E6
Pilar, *Paraguay* 126 B4
Pilar de la Horadada, *Spain* 33 H4
Pilawa, *Poland* 45 G8
Pilaya ➤, *Bolivia* 124 H6
Pilbara, *Australia* 92 D2
Pilcomayo ➤, *Paraguay* . 126 B4
Pilgrim's Rest, *S. Africa* . 89 C5
Pilgrimstad, *Sweden* 10 B9
Pili, *Greece* 39 E9
Pilibhit, *India* 69 E8
Pilica ➤, *Poland* 45 G8
Pilion, *Greece* 38 B5
Pilis, *Hungary* 42 C4
Pilisvörösvár, *Hungary* .. 42 C3
Pilkhawa, *India* 68 E7
Pilliga, *Australia* 95 E4
Pílos, *Greece* 38 E3
Pilot Mound, *Canada* ... 105 D9
Pilot Point, *U.S.A.* 113 J6
Pilot Rock, *U.S.A.* 114 D4
Pilsen = Plzeň, *Czech Rep.* 26 B6
Pilštanj, *Slovenia* 29 B12
Piltene, *Latvia* 44 A8
Pilzno, *Poland* 45 J8
Pima, *U.S.A.* 115 K9
Pimba, *Australia* 95 E2
Pimenta Bueno, *Brazil* .. 124 F6
Pimentel, *Peru* 124 E3
Pina de Ebro, *Spain* 32 D4
Pinamalayan, *Phil.* 61 E4
Pinang, *Malaysia* 65 K3
Pinar, C. des, *Spain* 37 B10
Pinar del Río, *Cuba* 120 B3
Pınarbaşı, *Çanakkale, Turkey* 39 B8
Pınarbaşı, *Kayseri, Turkey* . 72 C7
Pınarhisar, *Turkey* 41 E11
Pinatubo, Mt., *Phil.* 61 D3
Pincehely, *Hungary* 42 D3
Pinchang, *China* 58 B6
Pincher Creek, *Canada* .. 104 D6
Pinchi L., *Canada* 104 C4
Pinckneyville, *U.S.A.* ... 112 F10
Pińczów, *Poland* 45 H7
Pindar, *Australia* 93 E2
Pindi Gheb, *Pakistan* ... 68 C5
Pindiga, *Nigeria* 83 D7
Pindos Óros, *Greece* 38 B3
Pindus Mts. = Pindos Óros,
  Greece 38 B3
Pine ➤, *B.C., Canada* ... 104 B4
Pine ➤, *Sask., Canada* .. 105 B7
Pine, C., *Canada* 103 C9
Pine Bluff, *U.S.A.* 113 H9
Pine Bluffs, *U.S.A.* 112 E2
Pine City, *U.S.A.* 112 C8
Pine Cr. ➤, *U.S.A.* 110 E7
Pine Creek, *Australia* ... 92 B5
Pine Falls, *Canada* 105 C9
Pine Flat Res., *U.S.A.* .. 116 J7
Pine Grove, *U.S.A.* 111 F8
Pine Pass, *Canada* 104 B4
Pine Point, *Canada* 104 A6
Pine Ridge, *U.S.A.* 112 D3
Pine River, *Canada* 105 C8
Pine River, *U.S.A.* 112 B7
Pine Valley, *U.S.A.* 117 N10
Pinecrest, *U.S.A.* 116 G6
Pinedale, *Calif., U.S.A.* . 116 J7
Pinedale, *Wyo., U.S.A.* .. 114 E9
Pinega ➤, *Russia* 50 C5
Pinehill, *Australia* 94 C4
Pinehouse L., *Canada* ... 105 B7
Pineimuta ➤, *Canada* .. 102 B1
Pinerolo, *Italy* 28 D4
Pineto, *Italy* 29 F11
Pinetop, *U.S.A.* 115 J9
Pinetown, *S. Africa* 89 D5
Piney, *France* 19 D11
Ping ➤, *Thailand* 64 E3
Pingaring, *Australia* 93 F2
Pingba, *China* 58 D6
Pingbian, *China* 58 F4
Pingchuan, *China* 58 D3
Pingding, *China* 56 F7
Pingdingshan, *China* ... 56 H7
Pingdong, *Taiwan* 59 F13
Pingdu, *China* 57 F10
Pingelly, *Australia* 93 F2
Pingguo, *China* 58 F6
Pinghe, *China* 59 E11
Pinghu, *China* 59 B13
Pingle, *China* 59 E8
Pingli, *China* 58 A7
Pingliang, *China* 56 G4
Pinglu, *China* 56 E7
Pingluo, *China* 56 E4
Pingnan, *Fujian, China* .. 59 D12

Pingnan, *Guangxi Zhuangzu,*
  China 59 F8
Pingquan, *China* 57 D10
Pingrup, *Australia* 93 F2
Pingshan, *China* 58 C5
Pingtan, *China* 59 E12
Pingtang, *China* 58 E6
P'ingtung, *Taiwan* 59 F13
Pingwu, *China* 56 H3
Pingxiang,
  Guangxi Zhuangzu, China 58 F6
Pingxiang, *Jiangxi, China* . 59 D9
Pingyao, *China* 56 F7
Pingyi, *China* 57 G9
Pingyin, *China* 56 F9
Pingyuan, *Guangdong, China* 59 E10
Pingyuan, *Shandong, China* 56 F9
Pingyuanjie, *China* 58 F4
Pinhal, *Brazil* 127 A6
Pinhal Novo, *Portugal* .. 35 G2
Pinheiro, *Brazil* 125 D9
Pinheiro Machado, *Brazil* . 127 C5
Pinhel, *Portugal* 34 E3
Pini, *Indonesia* 62 D1
Piniós ➤, *Ilía, Greece* ... 38 D3
Piniós ➤, *Tríkkala, Greece* 38 B4
Pinjarra, *Australia* 93 F2
Pink Mountain, *Canada* . 104 B4
Pinkafeld, *Austria* 27 D9
Pinnacles, *U.S.A.* 116 J5
Pinnaroo, *Australia* 95 F3
Pinneberg, *Germany* 24 B5
Pínnes, Ákra, *Greece* ... 41 F8
Pinon Hills, *U.S.A.* 117 L9
Pinos, *Mexico* 118 C4
Pinos, Mt., *U.S.A.* 117 L7
Pinos Pt., *U.S.A.* 115 H3
Pinos Puente, *Spain* 35 H7
Pinotepa Nacional, *Mexico* 119 D5
Pinrang, *Indonesia* 63 E5
Pins, Pte. aux, *Canada* .. 110 D3
Pinsk, *Belarus* 47 F4
Pintados, *Chile* 124 H5
Pinyang, *China* 59 D13
Pinyug, *Russia* 50 C5
Pioche, *U.S.A.* 115 H6
Piombino, *Italy* 28 F7
Piombino, Canale di, *Italy* . 28 F7
Pioner, Ostrov, *Russia* .. 51 B10
Pionki, *Poland* 45 G8
Piorini, L., *Brazil* 124 D6
Piotrków Trybunalski,
  Poland 45 G6
Piove di Sacco, *Italy* 29 C9
Píp, *Iran* 71 E9
Pipar, *India* 68 F5
Pipar Road, *India* 68 F5
Piparia, *Mad. P., India* .. 68 H8
Piparia, *Mad. P., India* .. 68 J7
Pipéri, *Greece* 38 B6
Pipestone, *U.S.A.* 112 D6
Pipestone ➤, *Canada* ... 102 B2
Pipestone Cr. ➤, *Canada* 105 D8
Piplan, *Pakistan* 68 C4
Piploda, *India* 68 H6
Pipmuacan, Rés., *Canada* . 103 C5
Pippingarra, *Australia* .. 92 D2
Pipriac, *France* 18 E5
Piqua, *U.S.A.* 108 E3
Piquiri ➤, *Brazil* 127 A5
Pir Sohrāb, *Iran* 71 E9
Pira, *Benin* 83 D5
Piracicaba, *Brazil* 127 A6
Piracuruca, *Brazil* 125 D10
Piræus = Piraiévs, *Greece* . 38 D5
Piraiévs, *Greece* 38 D5
Pirajuí, *Brazil* 127 A6
Piram I., *India* 68 J5
Piran, *Slovenia* 29 C10
Pirané, *Argentina* 126 B4
Pirano = Piran, *Slovenia* . 29 C10
Pirapora, *Brazil* 125 G10
Pirawa, *India* 68 G7
Pirdop, *Bulgaria* 41 D8
Pírgos, *Ilía, Greece* 38 D3
Pírgos, *Kríti, Greece* ... 39 F7
Pirgovo, *Bulgaria* 41 C9
Piribebuy, *Paraguay* 126 B4
Pirimapun, *Indonesia* ... 63 F9
Pirin Planina, *Bulgaria* . 40 E7
Pírineos = Pyrénées, *Europe* 20 F4
Piripiri, *Brazil* 125 D10
Pirmasens, *Germany* 25 F3
Pirna, *Germany* 24 E9
Pirot, *Serbia, Yug.* 40 C6
Piru, *Indonesia* 63 E7
Piru, *U.S.A.* 117 L8
Piryatin = Pyryatyn, *Ukraine* 47 G7
Piryí, *Greece* 39 C7
Pisa, *Italy* 28 E7
Pisa ➤, *Poland* 45 E8
Pisagne, *Italy* 28 C7
Pisagua, *Chile* 124 G4
Pisarovina, *Croatia* 29 C12
Pisco, *Peru* 124 F3
Piscu, *Romania* 43 E12
Písek, *Czech Rep.* 26 B7
Pishan, *China* 60 C2
Pīshīn, *Iran* 71 E9
Pishin, *Pakistan* 68 D2
Pishin Lora ➤, *Pakistan* . 68 E1
Pisidia, *Turkey* 72 D4
Pising, *Indonesia* 63 F6
Pismo Beach, *U.S.A.* 117 K6
Piso, L., *Liberia* 82 D2
Pissila, *Burkina Faso* ... 83 C4
Pissis, Cerro, *Argentina* . 126 B2
Pissos, *France* 20 D3
Pissouri, *Cyprus* 36 E11
Pisticci, *Italy* 31 B9
Pistóia, *Italy* 28 E7

Pistol B., *Canada* 105 A10
Pisuerga ➤, *Spain* 34 D6
Pisz, *Poland* 44 E8
Pit ➤, *U.S.A.* 114 F2
Pita, *Guinea* 82 C2
Pitarpunga, L., *Australia* . 95 E3
Pitcairn I., *Pac. Oc.* 97 K14
Pite älv ➤, *Sweden* 8 D19
Piteå, *Sweden* 8 D19
Piterka, *Russia* 48 E8
Piteşti, *Romania* 43 F9
Pithapuram, *India* 67 L13
Pithara, *Australia* 93 F2
Píthion, *Greece* 41 E10
Pithiviers, *France* 19 D9
Pithoragarh, *India* 69 E9
Pithoro, *Pakistan* 68 G3
Pitigliano, *Italy* 29 F8
Pitkyaranta, *Russia* 46 B6
Pitlochry, *U.K.* 14 E5
Pitsilia □, *Cyprus* 36 E12
Pitt I., *Canada* 104 C3
Pittsburg, *Calif., U.S.A.* . 116 G5
Pittsburg, *Kans., U.S.A.* . 113 G7
Pittsburg, *Tex., U.S.A.* . 113 J7
Pittsburgh, *U.S.A.* 110 F5
Pittsfield, *Ill., U.S.A.* ... 112 F9
Pittsfield, *Maine, U.S.A.* . 109 C11
Pittsfield, *Mass., U.S.A.* . 111 D11
Pittsfield, *N.H., U.S.A.* . 111 C13
Pittston, *U.S.A.* 111 E9
Pittsworth, *Australia* ... 95 D5
Pituri ➤, *Australia* 94 C2
Piura, *Peru* 124 E2
Piva ➤, *Montenegro, Yug.* 40 C2
Piwniczna, *Poland* 45 J7
Pixley, *U.S.A.* 116 K7
Piyai, *Greece* 38 B3
Pizarra, *Spain* 35 J6
Pizhou, *China* 56 G9
Pizzo, *Italy* 31 D9
Placentia, *Canada* 103 C9
Placentia B., *Canada* ... 103 C9
Placer, *Masbate, Phil.* .. 61 F5
Placer, *Surigao N., Phil.* . 61 G6
Placerville, *U.S.A.* 116 G6
Placetas, *Cuba* 120 B4
Plačkovica, *Macedonia* .. 40 E6
Plainfield, *N.J., U.S.A.* .. 111 F10
Plainfield, *Ohio, U.S.A.* . 110 F3
Plainfield, *Vt., U.S.A.* .. 111 B12
Plains, *Mont., U.S.A.* ... 114 C6
Plains, *Tex., U.S.A.* 113 J3
Plainview, *Nebr., U.S.A.* . 112 D6
Plainview, *Tex., U.S.A.* . 113 H4
Plainwell, *U.S.A.* 108 D3
Plaisance, *France* 20 E4
Plaistow, *U.S.A.* 111 D13
Pláka, *Greece* 39 B7
Pláka, Ákra, *Greece* 36 D8
Plakenska Planina,
  Macedonia 40 E5
Planá, *Czech Rep.* 26 B5
Plana Cays, *Bahamas* ... 121 B5
Planada, *U.S.A.* 116 H6
Plancoët, *France* 18 D4
Plandište, *Serbia, Yug.* .. 42 E6
Plano, *U.S.A.* 113 J6
Plant City, *U.S.A.* 109 M4
Plaquemine, *U.S.A.* 113 K9
Plasencia, *Spain* 34 E4
Plaški, *Croatia* 29 C12
Plaster City, *U.S.A.* 117 N11
Plaster Rock, *Canada* ... 103 C6
Plastun, *Russia* 54 B8
Plasy, *Czech Rep.* 26 B6
Plata, Río de la, *S. Amer.* . 126 C4
Plátani ➤, *Italy* 30 E6
Plátanos, *Greece* 36 D5
Plateau □, *Nigeria* 83 D6
Platí, Ákra, *Greece* 41 F8
Platte, *U.S.A.* 112 D5
Platte ➤, *Mo., U.S.A.* .. 112 F7
Platte ➤, *Nebr., U.S.A.* . 112 E7
Platteville, *U.S.A.* 112 D9
Plattling, *Germany* 25 G8
Plattsburgh, *U.S.A.* 111 B11
Plattsmouth, *U.S.A.* 112 E6
Plau, *Germany* 24 B8
Plauen, *Germany* 24 E8
Plauer See, *Germany* ... 24 B8
Plav, *Montenegro, Yug.* . 40 D3
Plavinas, *Latvia* 9 H21
Plavnica, *Montenegro, Yug.* 40 D3
Plavno, *Croatia* 29 D13
Plavsk, *Russia* 46 F9
Playa Blanca, *Canary Is.* . 37 F6
Playa Blanca Sur, *Canary Is.* 37 F6
Playa de las Americas,
  Canary Is. 37 F3
Playa de Mogán, *Canary Is.* 37 G4
Playa del Inglés, *Canary Is.* 37 G4
Playa Esmeralda, *Canary Is.* 37 F5
Playgreen L., *Canada* ... 105 C9
Pleasant Bay, *Canada* ... 103 C7
Pleasant Hill, *U.S.A.* ... 116 H4
Pleasant Mount, *U.S.A.* . 111 E9
Pleasanton, *Calif., U.S.A.* 116 H5
Pleasanton, *Tex., U.S.A.* . 113 L5
Pleasantville, *N.J., U.S.A.* 108 F8
Pleasantville, *U.S.A.* ... 111 E8
Pléaux, *France* 20 C6
Plei Ku, *Vietnam* 64 F7
Plélan-le-Grand, *France* . 18 D4
Pléneuf-Val-André, *France* 18 D4
Pleniţa, *Romania* 43 F8
Plenty ➤, *Australia* 94 C2
Plenty, B. of, *N.Z.* 91 G6
Plentywood, *U.S.A.* 112 A2
Plérin, *France* 18 D4
Plessisville, *Canada* 103 C5

Plestin-les-Grèves

Plestin-les-Grèves, *France* 18 D3
Pleszew, *Poland* 45 G4
Pleternica, *Croatia* 42 E2
Plétipi, L., *Canada* 103 B5
Pleven, *Bulgaria* 41 C8
Plevlja, *Montenegro, Yug.* 40 C3
Plevna, *Canada* 110 B8
Plješevica, *Croatia* 29 D12
Ploaghe, *Italy* 30 B1
Plo'ana, *Slovak Rep.* 27 C12
Ploče, *Croatia* 29 E14
Płock, *Poland* 45 F6
Plöckenpass, *Italy* 29 B9
Plöckenstein, *Germany* 25 G9
Ploemeur, *France* 18 E3
Ploërmel, *France* 18 E4
Ploieşti, *Romania* 43 F11
Plomárion, *Greece* 39 C8
Plombières-les-Bains, *France* 19 E13
Plomin, *Croatia* 29 C11
Plön, *Germany* 24 A6
Plonge, Lac la, *Canada* 105 B7
Płońsk, *Poland* 45 F7
Plopeni, *Romania* 43 E10
Plopişului, Munţii, *Romania* 42 C7
Płoty, *Poland* 44 E2
Plouaret, *France* 18 D3
Plouay, *France* 18 E3
Ploučnice →, *Czech Rep.* 26 A7
Ploudalmézeau, *France* 18 D2
Plouescat, *France* 18 D2
Plougasnou, *France* 18 D3
Plougastel-Daoulas, *France* 18 D2
Plouguerneau, *France* 18 D2
Plouha, *France* 18 D4
Plouhinec, *France* 18 E2
Plovdiv, *Bulgaria* 41 D8
Plovdiv □, *Bulgaria* 41 D8
Plum, *U.S.A.* 110 F5
Plum I., *U.S.A.* 111 E12
Plumas, *U.S.A.* 116 F7
Plummer, *U.S.A.* 114 C5
Plumtree, *Zimbabwe* 87 G2
Plungė, *Lithuania* 9 J19
Pluvigner, *France* 18 E3
Plymouth, *U.K.* 13 G3
Plymouth, *Calif., U.S.A.* 116 G6
Plymouth, *Ind., U.S.A.* 108 E2
Plymouth, *Mass., U.S.A.* 111 E14
Plymouth, *N.C., U.S.A.* 109 H7
Plymouth, *N.H., U.S.A.* 111 C13
Plymouth, *Pa., U.S.A.* 111 E9
Plymouth, *Wis., U.S.A.* 108 D2
Plynlimon = Pumlumon Fawr, *U.K.* 13 E4
Plyusa, *Russia* 46 C5
Plyusa →, *Russia* 46 C5
Plyussa = Plyusa, *Russia* 46 C5
Plyussa → = Plyusa →, *Russia* 46 C5
Plzeň, *Czech Rep.* 26 B6
Pniewy, *Poland* 45 F3
Pô, *Burkina Faso* 83 C4
Po →, *Italy* 29 D9
Po, Foci del, *Italy* 29 D9
Po Hai = Bo Hai, *China* 57 E10
Pobé, *Benin* 83 D5
Pobé, *Burkina Faso* 83 C4
Pobeda, *Russia* 51 C15
Pobedy, Pik, *Kyrgyzstan* 50 E8
Pobiedziska, *Poland* 45 F4
Pobla de Segur, *Spain* 32 C5
Pobladura del Valle, *Spain* 34 C5
Pobra de Trives, *Spain* 34 C3
Pocahontas, *Ark., U.S.A.* 113 G9
Pocahontas, *Iowa, U.S.A.* 112 D7
Pocatello, *U.S.A.* 114 E7
Počátky, *Czech Rep.* 26 B8
Pochep, *Russia* 47 F7
Pochinki, *Russia* 48 C7
Pochinok, *Russia* 46 E7
Pöchlarn, *Austria* 26 C8
Pochutla, *Mexico* 119 D5
Pocito Casas, *Mexico* 118 B2
Pocking, *Germany* 25 G9
Pocomoke City, *U.S.A.* 108 F8
Poços de Caldas, *Brazil* 127 A6
Podbořany, *Czech Rep.* 26 A6
Poddębice, *Poland* 45 G5
Poděbrady, *Czech Rep.* 26 A8
Podensac, *France* 20 D3
Podenzano, *Italy* 28 D6
Podgorač, *Croatia* 42 E3
Podgorica, *Montenegro, Yug.* 40 D3
Podgorie, *Albania* 40 F4
Podilska Vysochyna, *Ukraine* 47 H4
Podkarpackie □, *Poland* 45 H9
Podkova, *Bulgaria* 41 E9
Podlapača, *Croatia* 29 D12
Podlaskie □, *Poland* 45 E10
Podoleni, *Romania* 43 D11
Podolínec, *Slovak Rep.* 27 B13
Podolsk, *Russia* 46 E9
Podor, *Senegal* 82 B1
Podporozhye, *Russia* 46 B8
Podu Iloaiei, *Romania* 43 C12
Podu Turcului, *Romania* 43 D12
Podujevo, *Kosovo, Yug.* 40 D5
Poel, *Germany* 24 B6
Pofadder, *S. Africa* 88 D2
Poggiardo, *Italy* 31 B11
Poggibonsi, *Italy* 28 E8
Póggio Mirteto, *Italy* 29 F9
Pogoanele, *Romania* 43 F12
Pogorzela, *Poland* 45 G4
Pogradeci, *Albania* 40 F4
Pogranitšnyi, *Russia* 54 B5
Poh, *Indonesia* 63 E6
P'ohang, *S. Korea* 57 F15
Pohjanmaa, *Finland* 8 E20
Pohnpei, *Micronesia* 96 G7
Pohorelá, *Slovak Rep.* 27 C13
Pohořelice, *Czech Rep.* 27 C9
Pohorje, *Slovenia* 29 B12
Pohri, *India* 68 G6
Poiana Mare, *Romania* 42 G8
Poiana Ruscăi, Munţii, *Romania* 42 E7
Poiana Stampei, *Romania* 43 C10
Poinsett, C., *Antarctica* 5 C8
Point Arena, *U.S.A.* 116 G3
Point Baker, *U.S.A.* 104 B2
Point Edward, *Canada* 102 D3
Point Hope, *U.S.A.* 100 B3
Point L., *Canada* 100 B8
Point Pedro, *Sri Lanka* 66 Q12
Point Pleasant, *N.J., U.S.A.* 111 F10
Point Pleasant, *W. Va., U.S.A.* 108 F4
Pointe-à-Pitre, *Guadeloupe* 121 C7
Pointe-Claire, *Canada* 111 A11
Pointe-Gatineau, *Canada* 111 A9
Pointe-Noire, *Congo* 84 E2
Poio, *Spain* 34 C2
Poirino, *Italy* 28 D4
Poisonbush Ra., *Australia* 92 D3
Poissonnier Pt., *Australia* 92 C2
Poitiers, *France* 18 F7
Poitou, *France* 20 B3
Poitou-Charentes □, *France* 20 B4
Poix-de-Picardie, *France* 19 C8
Poix-Terron, *France* 19 C11
Pojoaque, *U.S.A.* 115 J11
Pokaran, *India* 66 F7
Pokataroo, *Australia* 95 D4
Pokhara, *Nepal* 69 E10
Pokhvistnevo, *Russia* 48 D11
Poko, *Dem. Rep. of the Congo* 86 B2
Poko, *Sudan* 81 F3
Pokrov, *Russia* 46 E10
Pokrovsk = Engels, *Russia* 48 E8
Pokrovsk, *Russia* 51 C13
Pokrovskoye, *Russia* 47 J10
Pola = Pula, *Croatia* 29 D10
Pola, *Russia* 46 D7
Pola de Allande, *Spain* 34 B4
Pola de Lena, *Spain* 34 B5
Pola de Siero, *Spain* 34 B5
Pola de Somiedo, *Spain* 34 B4
Polacca, *U.S.A.* 115 J8
Polan, *Iran* 71 E9
Poland ■, *Europe* 45 G3
Polanica-Zdrój, *Poland* 45 H3
Połaniec, *Poland* 45 H8
Polanów, *Poland* 44 D3
Polar Bear Prov. Park, *Canada* 102 A2
Polatlı, *Turkey* 72 C5
Polatsk, *Belarus* 46 E5
Polcura, *Chile* 126 D1
Połczyn-Zdrój, *Poland* 44 E3
Polessk, *Russia* 9 J19
Polesye = Pripet Marshes, *Europe* 47 F5
Polgar, *Hungary* 42 C6
Pŏlgyo-ri, *S. Korea* 57 G14
Poli, *Cameroon* 83 C7
Políaigos, *Greece* 38 E6
Policastro, G. di, *Italy* 31 C8
Police, *Poland* 44 E1
Polička, *Czech Rep.* 27 B9
Policoro, *Italy* 31 B9
Polignano a Mare, *Italy* 31 A9
Poligny, *France* 19 F12
Políkhnitas, *Greece* 39 B8
Polillo Is., *Phil.* 61 D4
Polillo Strait, *Phil.* 61 D4
Polis, *Cyprus* 36 D11
Polístena, *Italy* 31 D9
Políyiros, *Greece* 40 F7
Polk, *U.S.A.* 110 E5
Polkowice, *Poland* 45 G3
Polla, *Italy* 31 B8
Pollachi, *India* 66 P10
Pollença, *Spain* 37 B10
Pollença, B. de, *Spain* 37 B10
Póllica, *Italy* 31 B8
Pollino, Mte., *Italy* 31 C9
Polna, *Russia* 46 C5
Polnovat, *Russia* 50 C7
Pology, *Ukraine* 47 J9
Polonne, *Ukraine* 47 G4
Polonnoye = Polonne, *Ukraine* 47 G4
Polski Trŭmbesh, *Bulgaria* 41 C9
Polsko Kosovo, *Bulgaria* 41 C9
Polson, *U.S.A.* 114 C6
Poltár, *Slovak Rep.* 27 C12
Poltava, *Ukraine* 47 H8
Põltsamaa, *Estonia* 9 G21
Polunochnoye, *Russia* 50 C7
Põlva, *Estonia* 9 G22
Polynesia, *Pac. Oc.* 97 J11
Polynésie française = French Polynesia ■, *Pac. Oc.* 97 K13
Pomarance, *Italy* 28 E7
Pomaro, *Mexico* 118 D4
Pombal, *Portugal* 34 F2
Pómbia, *Greece* 36 E6
Pomene, *Mozam.* 89 C6
Pomeroy, *Ohio, U.S.A.* 108 F4
Pomeroy, *Wash., U.S.A.* 114 C5
Pomézia, *Italy* 30 A5
Pomichna, *Ukraine* 47 H6
Pomona, *Australia* 95 D5
Pomona, *U.S.A.* 117 L9
Pomorie, *Bulgaria* 41 D11
Pomorskie □, *Poland* 44 D5
Pomorskie, Pojezierze, *Poland* 44 E3
Pomos, *Cyprus* 36 D11
Pomos, C., *Cyprus* 36 D11
Pompano Beach, *U.S.A.* 109 M5
Pompei, *Italy* 31 B7
Pompey, *France* 19 D13
Pompeys Pillar, *U.S.A.* 114 D10
Pompton Lakes, *U.S.A.* 111 F10
Ponape = Pohnpei, *Micronesia* 96 G7
Ponask L., *Canada* 102 B1
Ponca, *U.S.A.* 112 D6
Ponca City, *U.S.A.* 113 G6
Ponce, *Puerto Rico* 121 C6
Ponchatoula, *U.S.A.* 113 K9
Poncheville, L., *Canada* 102 B4
Pond, *U.S.A.* 117 K7
Pond Inlet, *Canada* 101 A12
Pondicherry, *India* 66 P11
Ponds, I. of, *Canada* 103 B8
Ponferrada, *Spain* 34 C4
Pongo, Wadi →, *Sudan* 81 F2
Poniatowa, *Poland* 45 G9
Poniec, *Poland* 45 G3
Ponikva, *Slovenia* 29 B12
Ponnani, *India* 66 P9
Ponnyadaung, *Burma* 67 J19
Ponoka, *Canada* 104 C6
Ponorogo, *Indonesia* 63 G14
Pons = Ponts, *Spain* 32 D6
Pons, *France* 20 C3
Ponsul →, *Portugal* 34 F3
Pont-à-Mousson, *France* 19 D13
Pont-Audemer, *France* 18 C7
Pont-Aven, *France* 18 E3
Pont Canavese, *Italy* 28 C4
Pont-d'Ain, *France* 19 F12
Pont-de-Roide, *France* 19 E13
Pont-de-Salars, *France* 20 D6
Pont-de-Vaux, *France* 19 F11
Pont-de-Veyle, *France* 19 F11
Pont-du-Château, *France* 19 G10
Pont-l'Abbé, *France* 18 E2
Pont-l'Évêque, *France* 18 C7
Pont-St-Esprit, *France* 21 D8
Pont-St-Martin, *Italy* 28 C4
Pont-Ste-Maxence, *France* 19 C9
Pont-sur-Yonne, *France* 19 D10
Ponta do Sol, *Madeira* 37 D2
Ponta Grossa, *Brazil* 127 B5
Ponta Pora, *Brazil* 127 A4
Pontacq, *France* 20 E3
Pontailler-sur-Saône, *France* 19 E12
Pontarlier, *France* 19 F13
Pontassieve, *Italy* 29 E8
Pontaumur, *France* 20 C6
Pontcharra, *France* 21 C10
Pontchartrain L., *U.S.A.* 113 K10
Pontchâteau, *France* 18 E4
Ponte da Barca, *Portugal* 34 D2
Ponte de Sor, *Portugal* 35 F2
Ponte dell'Ólio, *Italy* 28 D6
Ponte di Legno, *Italy* 28 B7
Ponte do Lima, *Portugal* 34 D2
Ponte do Pungué, *Mozam.* 87 F3
Ponte-Leccia, *France* 21 F13
Ponte nelle Alpi, *Italy* 29 B9
Ponte Nova, *Brazil* 127 A7
Ponteareas, *Spain* 34 C2
Pontebba, *Italy* 29 B10
Ponteceso, *Spain* 34 B2
Pontecorvo, *Italy* 30 A6
Pontedeume, *Spain* 34 B2
Ponteix, *Canada* 105 D7
Pontevedra, *Spain* 34 C2
Pontevedra □, *Spain* 34 C2
Pontevedra, R. de →, *Spain* 34 C2
Pontevico, *Italy* 28 C7
Pontiac, *Ill., U.S.A.* 112 E10
Pontiac, *Mich., U.S.A.* 108 D4
Pontian Kecil, *Malaysia* 65 M4
Pontianak, *Indonesia* 62 E3
Pontine Is. = Ponziane, Ísole, *Italy* 30 B5
Pontine Mts. = Kuzey Anadolu Dağları, *Turkey* 72 B7
Pontínia, *Italy* 30 A6
Pontivy, *France* 18 D4
Pontoise, *France* 19 C9
Ponton →, *Canada* 104 B5
Pontorson, *France* 18 D5
Pontrémoli, *Italy* 28 D6
Pontrieux, *France* 18 D3
Ponts, *Spain* 32 D6
Pontypool, *Canada* 110 B6
Pontypool, *U.K.* 13 F4
Ponza, *Italy* 30 B5
Ponziane, Ísole, *Italy* 30 B5
Poochera, *Australia* 95 E1
Poole, *U.K.* 13 G6
Poole □, *U.K.* 13 G6
Poona = Pune, *India* 66 K8
Pooncarie, *Australia* 95 E3
Poopelloe L., *Australia* 95 E3
Poopó, L. de, *Bolivia* 122 E4
Popayán, *Colombia* 124 C3
Poperinge, *Belgium* 17 D2
Popilta L., *Australia* 95 E3
Popina, *Bulgaria* 41 B10
Popio L., *Australia* 95 E3
Poplar, *U.S.A.* 112 A2
Poplar →, *Canada* 105 C9
Poplar Bluff, *U.S.A.* 113 G9
Poplarville, *U.S.A.* 113 K10
Popocatépetl, Volcán, *Mexico* 119 D5
Popokabaka, *Dem. Rep. of the Congo* 84 F3
Pópoli, *Italy* 29 F10
Popovača, *Croatia* 29 C13
Popovo, *Bulgaria* 41 C10
Poppberg, *Germany* 25 F7
Poppi, *Italy* 29 E8
Poprad, *Slovak Rep.* 27 B13
Poprad →, *Slovak Rep.* 27 B13
Porali →, *Pakistan* 68 G2
Porbandar, *India* 66 J6
Porcher I., *Canada* 104 C2
Porcuna, *Spain* 35 H6
Porcupine →, *Canada* 105 B8
Porcupine →, *U.S.A.* 100 B5
Pordenone, *Italy* 29 C9
Pordim, *Bulgaria* 41 C8
Poreč, *Croatia* 29 C10
Poretskoye, *Russia* 48 C8
Pori, *Finland* 9 F19
Porí, *Greece* 38 F5
Porkhov, *Russia* 46 D5
Porlamar, *Venezuela* 124 A6
Porlezza, *Italy* 28 B6
Porma →, *Spain* 34 C5
Pornic, *France* 18 E4
Poronaysk, *Russia* 51 E15
Póros, *Greece* 38 D5
Poroshiri-Dake, *Japan* 54 C11
Poroszló, *Hungary* 42 C5
Poroto Mts., *Tanzania* 87 D3
Porpoise B., *Antarctica* 5 C9
Porquerolles, Î. de, *France* 21 F10
Porrentruy, *Switz.* 25 H3
Porreres, *Spain* 37 B10
Porsangen, *Norway* 8 A21
Porsgrunn, *Norway* 9 G13
Port Alberni, *Canada* 104 D4
Port Alfred, *S. Africa* 88 E4
Port Alice, *Canada* 104 C3
Port Allegany, *U.S.A.* 110 E6
Port Allen, *U.S.A.* 113 K9
Port Alma, *Australia* 94 C5
Port Angeles, *U.S.A.* 116 B3
Port Antonio, *Jamaica* 120 C4
Port Aransas, *U.S.A.* 113 M6
Port Arthur = Lüshun, *China* 57 E11
Port Arthur, *Australia* 94 G4
Port Arthur, *U.S.A.* 113 L8
Port au Choix, *Canada* 103 B8
Port au Port B., *Canada* 103 C8
Port-au-Prince, *Haiti* 121 C5
Port Augusta, *Australia* 95 E2
Port Austin, *U.S.A.* 110 B2
Port Bell, *Uganda* 86 B3
Port Bergé Vaovao, *Madag.* 89 B8
Port Blandford, *Canada* 103 C9
Port-Bouët, *Ivory C.* 82 D4
Port Bradshaw, *Australia* 94 A2
Port Broughton, *Australia* 95 E2
Port Burwell, *Canada* 110 D4
Port Campbell, *Australia* 95 F3
Port Canning, *India* 69 H13
Port-Cartier, *Canada* 103 B6
Port Chalmers, *N.Z.* 91 L3
Port Charlotte, *U.S.A.* 109 M4
Port Chester, *U.S.A.* 111 F11
Port Clements, *Canada* 104 C2
Port Clinton, *U.S.A.* 108 E4
Port Colborne, *Canada* 102 D4
Port Coquitlam, *Canada* 104 D4
Port Credit, *Canada* 110 C5
Port Curtis, *Australia* 94 C5
Port d'Alcúdia, *Spain* 37 B10
Port Dalhousie, *Canada* 110 C5
Port Darwin, *Australia* 92 B5
Port Darwin, *Falk. Is.* 128 G5
Port Davey, *Australia* 94 G4
Port-de-Bouc, *France* 21 E8
Port-de-Paix, *Haiti* 121 C5
Port de Pollença, *Spain* 37 B10
Port de Sóller, *Spain* 37 B9
Port Dickson, *Malaysia* 65 L3
Port Douglas, *Australia* 94 B4
Port Dover, *Canada* 110 D4
Port Edward, *Canada* 104 C2
Port Elgin, *Canada* 102 D3
Port Elizabeth, *S. Africa* 88 E4
Port Ellen, *U.K.* 14 F2
Port-en-Bessin, *France* 18 C6
Port Erin, *U.K.* 12 C3
Port Essington, *Australia* 92 B5
Port Etienne = Nouâdhibou, *Mauritania* 78 D2
Port Ewen, *U.S.A.* 111 E11
Port Fairy, *Australia* 95 F3
Port Fouâd = Bûr Fuad, *Egypt* 80 H8
Port Gamble, *U.S.A.* 116 C4
Port-Gentil, *Gabon* 84 E1
Port Germein, *Australia* 95 E2
Port Gibson, *U.S.A.* 113 K9
Port Glasgow, *U.K.* 14 F4
Port Harcourt, *Nigeria* 83 E6
Port Hardy, *Canada* 104 C3
Port Harrison = Inukjuak, *Canada* 101 C12
Port Hawkesbury, *Canada* 103 C7
Port Hedland, *Australia* 92 D2
Port Henry, *U.S.A.* 111 B11
Port Hood, *Canada* 103 C7
Port Hope, *Canada* 102 D4
Port Hope, *U.S.A.* 110 C2
Port Hope Simpson, *Canada* 103 B8
Port Hueneme, *U.S.A.* 117 L7
Port Huron, *U.S.A.* 110 D2
Port Iliç, *Azerbaijan* 73 C13
Port Jefferson, *U.S.A.* 111 F11
Port Jervis, *U.S.A.* 111 E10
Port-Joinville, *France* 18 F4
Port Katon, *Russia* 47 J10
Port Kelang = Pelabuhan Kelang, *Malaysia* 65 L3
Port Kenny, *Australia* 95 E1
Port-la-Nouvelle, *France* 20 E7
Port Lairge = Waterford, *Ireland* 15 D4
Port Laoise, *Ireland* 15 C4
Port Lavaca, *U.S.A.* 113 L6
Port Leyden, *U.S.A.* 111 C9
Port Lincoln, *Australia* 95 E2
Port Loko, *S. Leone* 82 D2
Port Louis, *France* 18 E3
Port Louis, *Mauritius* 77 H9
Port Lyautey = Kenitra, *Morocco* 78 B4
Port MacDonnell, *Australia* 95 F3
Port McNeill, *Canada* 104 C3
Port Macquarie, *Australia* 95 E5
Port Maria, *Jamaica* 120 C4
Port Matilda, *U.S.A.* 110 F6
Port Mellon, *Canada* 104 D4
Port-Menier, *Canada* 103 C7
Port Moody, *Canada* 116 A4
Port Morant, *Jamaica* 120 C4
Port Moresby, *Papua N. G.* 96 H6
Port Musgrave, *Australia* 94 A3
Port-Navalo, *France* 18 E4
Port Neches, *U.S.A.* 113 L8
Port Nolloth, *S. Africa* 88 D2
Port Nouveau-Québec = Kangiqsualujjuaq, *Canada* 101 C13
Port of Spain, *Trin. & Tob.* 121 D7
Port Orange, *U.S.A.* 109 L5
Port Orchard, *U.S.A.* 116 C4
Port Orford, *U.S.A.* 114 E1
Port Pegasus, *N.Z.* 91 M1
Port Perry, *Canada* 102 D4
Port Phillip B., *Australia* 95 F3
Port Pirie, *Australia* 95 E2
Port Radium = Echo Bay, *Canada* 100 B8
Port Renfrew, *Canada* 104 D4
Port Roper, *Australia* 94 A2
Port Rowan, *Canada* 110 D4
Port Safaga = Bûr Safâga, *Egypt* 70 E2
Port Said = Bûr Sa'îd, *Egypt* 80 H8
Port St. Joe, *U.S.A.* 109 L3
Port St. Johns = Umzimvubu, *S. Africa* 89 E4
Port-St-Louis-du-Rhône, *France* 21 E8
Port St. Lucie, *U.S.A.* 109 M5
Port-Ste-Marie, *France* 20 D4
Port Sanilac, *U.S.A.* 110 C2
Port Severn, *Canada* 110 B5
Port Shepstone, *S. Africa* 89 E5
Port Simpson, *Canada* 104 C2
Port Stanley = Stanley, *Falk. Is.* 128 G5
Port Stanley, *Canada* 102 D3
Port Sudan = Bûr Sûdân, *Sudan* 80 D4
Port Sulphur, *U.S.A.* 113 L10
Port-sur-Saône, *France* 19 E13
Port Talbot, *U.K.* 13 F4
Port Taufiq = Bûr Taufiq, *Egypt* 80 J8
Port Townsend, *U.S.A.* 116 B4
Port-Vendres, *France* 20 F7
Port Vila, *Vanuatu* 96 J8
Port Wakefield, *Australia* 95 E2
Port Washington, *U.S.A.* 108 D2
Port Weld = Kuala Sepetang, *Malaysia* 65 K3
Portadown, *U.K.* 15 B5
Portaferry, *U.K.* 15 B6
Portage, *Pa., U.S.A.* 110 F6
Portage, *Wis., U.S.A.* 112 D10
Portage La Prairie, *Canada* 105 D9
Portageville, *U.S.A.* 113 G10
Portalegre, *Portugal* 35 F3
Portalegre □, *Portugal* 35 F3
Portales, *U.S.A.* 113 H3
Portarlington, *Ireland* 15 C4
Portbou, *Spain* 32 C8
Portel, *Portugal* 35 G3
Porter L., *N.W.T., Canada* 105 A7
Porter L., *Sask., Canada* 105 B7
Porterville, *S. Africa* 88 E2
Porterville, *U.S.A.* 116 J8
Portes-lès-Valence, *France* 21 D8
Porthcawl, *U.K.* 13 F4
Porthill, *U.S.A.* 114 B5
Porthmadog, *U.K.* 12 E3
Portile de Fier, *Europe* 42 F7
Portimão, *Portugal* 35 H2
Portishead, *U.K.* 13 F5
Portiţei, Gura, *Romania* 43 F14
Portknockie, *U.K.* 14 D6
Portland, *N.S.W., Australia* 95 E5
Portland, *Vic., Australia* 95 F3
Portland, *Canada* 111 B8
Portland, *Conn., U.S.A.* 111 E12
Portland, *Maine, U.S.A.* 101 D12
Portland, *Mich., U.S.A.* 108 D3
Portland, *Oreg., U.S.A.* 116 E4
Portland, *Pa., U.S.A.* 111 F9
Portland, *Tex., U.S.A.* 113 M6
Portland, I. of, *U.K.* 13 G5
Portland B., *Australia* 95 F3
Portland Bill, *U.K.* 13 G5
Portland Canal, *U.S.A.* 104 B2
Portmadoc = Porthmadog, *U.K.* 12 E3
Porto, *France* 21 F12
Porto, *Portugal* 34 D2
Porto □, *Portugal* 34 D2
Porto, G. de, *France* 21 F12
Pôrto Alegre, *Brazil* 127 C5
Porto Amboim = Gunza, *Angola* 84 G2
Porto Azzurro, *Italy* 28 F7
Porto Cristo, *Spain* 37 B10
Pôrto de Móz, *Brazil* 125 D8
Porto Empédocle, *Italy* 30 E6
Pôrto Esperança, *Brazil* 124 G7

Place	Pg	Ref
Pôrto Franco, *Brazil*	125	E9
Pórto Lágos, *Greece*	41	E9
Porto Mendes, *Brazil*	127	A5
Pôrto Murtinho, *Brazil*	124	H7
Pórto Nacional, *Brazil*	125	F9
Porto-Novo, *Benin*	83	D5
Porto Petro, *Spain*	37	B10
Porto San Giórgio, *Italy*	29	E10
Porto Sant' Elpídio, *Italy*	29	E10
Porto Santo, *Madeira*	78	B2
Pôrto São José, *Brazil*	127	A5
Pôrto Seguro, *Brazil*	125	G11
Porto Tolle, *Italy*	29	D9
Porto Tórres, *Italy*	30	B1
Pôrto União, *Brazil*	127	B5
Porto-Vecchio, *France*	21	G13
Pôrto Velho, *Brazil*	124	E6
Portobelo, *Panama*	120	E4
Portoferráio, *Italy*	28	F7
Portogruaro, *Italy*	29	C9
Portola, *U.S.A.*	116	F6
Portomaggiore, *Italy*	29	D8
Portoscuso, *Italy*	30	C1
Portovénere, *Italy*	28	D6
Portoviejo, *Ecuador*	124	D2
Portpatrick, *U.K.*	14	G3
Portree, *U.K.*	14	D2
Portrush, *U.K.*	15	A5
Portsmouth, *Domin.*	121	C7
Portsmouth, *U.K.*	13	G6
Portsmouth, *N.H., U.S.A.*	109	D10
Portsmouth, *Ohio, U.S.A.*	108	F4
Portsmouth, *R.I., U.S.A.*	111	E13
Portsmouth, *Va., U.S.A.*	108	G7
Portsmouth □, *U.K.*	13	G6
Portsoy, *U.K.*	14	D6
Portstewart, *U.K.*	15	A5
Porttipahtan tekojärvi, *Finland*	8	B22
Portugal ■, *Europe*	34	F3
Portugalete, *Spain*	32	B1
Portumna, *Ireland*	15	C3
Portville, *U.S.A.*	110	D6
Porvenir, *Chile*	128	G2
Porvoo, *Finland*	9	F21
Porzuna, *Spain*	35	F6
Posada, *Italy*	30	B2
Posada →, *Italy*	30	B2
Posadas, *Argentina*	127	B4
Posadas, *Spain*	35	H5
Poschiavo, *Switz.*	25	J6
Posets, *Spain*	32	C5
Poshan = Boshan, *China*	57	F9
Posht-e-Badam, *Iran*	71	C7
Posídhion, Ákra, *Greece*	40	G7
Posídium, *Greece*	39	F9
Poso, *Indonesia*	63	E6
Posong, *S. Korea*	57	G14
Posse, *Brazil*	125	F9
Possession I., *Antarctica*	5	D11
Pössneck, *Germany*	24	E7
Possum Kingdom L., *U.S.A.*	113	J5
Post, *U.S.A.*	113	J4
Post Falls, *U.S.A.*	114	C5
Postavy = Pastavy, *Belarus*	9	J22
Poste-de-la-Baleine = Kuujjuarapik, *Canada*	102	A4
Postmasburg, *S. Africa*	88	D3
Postojna, *Slovenia*	29	C11
Poston, *U.S.A.*	117	M12
Postville, *Canada*	103	B8
Potamós, Andikíthira, *Greece*	38	F5
Potamós, Kíthira, *Greece*	38	E4
Potchefstroom, *S. Africa*	88	D4
Potcoava, *Romania*	43	F9
Poteau, *U.S.A.*	113	H7
Poteet, *U.S.A.*	113	L5
Potenza, *Italy*	31	B8
Potenza →, *Italy*	29	E10
Potenza Picena, *Italy*	29	E10
Poteriteri, *N.Z.*	91	M1
Potgietersrus, *S. Africa*	89	C4
Poti, *Georgia*	49	J5
Potiskum, *Nigeria*	83	C7
Potlogi, *Romania*	43	F10
Potomac →, *U.S.A.*	108	G7
Potosí, *Bolivia*	124	G5
Potosi Mt., *U.S.A.*	117	K11
Potrerillos, *Chile*	126	B2
Potsdam, *Germany*	24	C9
Potsdam, *U.S.A.*	111	B10
Pottenstein, *Germany*	25	F7
Pottersville, *U.S.A.*	111	C11
Pottery Hill = Abu Ballas, *Egypt*	80	C2
Pottstown, *U.S.A.*	111	F9
Pottsville, *U.S.A.*	111	F8
Pottuvil, *Sri Lanka*	66	R12
P'otzu, *Taiwan*	59	F13
Pouancé, *France*	18	E5
Pouce Coupé, *Canada*	104	B4
Poughkeepsie, *U.S.A.*	111	E11
Pouilly-sur-Loire, *France*	19	E9
Poulaphouca Res., *Ireland*	15	C5
Poulsbo, *U.S.A.*	116	C4
Poultney, *U.S.A.*	111	C11
Poulton-le-Fylde, *U.K.*	12	D5
Pouso Alegre, *Brazil*	127	A6
Pout, *Senegal*	82	C1
Pouthisat, *Cambodia*	64	F4
Pouzauges, *France*	18	F6
Pova de Sta. Iria, *Portugal*	35	G1
Považská Bystrica, *Slovak Rep.*	27	B11
Poverty B., *N.Z.*	91	H7
Povlen, *Serbia, Yug.*	40	B3
Póvoa de Lanhosa, *Portugal*	34	D2
Póvoa de Varzim, *Portugal*	34	D2
Povorino, *Russia*	48	E6
Povungnituk = Puvirnituq, *Canada*	101	B12
Powassan, *Canada*	102	C4
Poway, *U.S.A.*	117	N9
Powder →, *U.S.A.*	112	B2
Powder River, *U.S.A.*	114	E10
Powell, *U.S.A.*	114	D9
Powell, L., *U.S.A.*	115	H8
Powell River, *Canada*	104	D4
Powers, *U.S.A.*	108	C2
Powys □, *U.K.*	13	E4
Poyang Hu, *China*	59	C11
Poyarkovo, *Russia*	51	E13
Poysdorf, *Austria*	27	C9
Poza de la Sal, *Spain*	34	C7
Poza Rica, *Mexico*	119	C5
Pozanti, *Turkey*	72	D6
Požarevac, *Serbia, Yug.*	40	B5
Pozazal, Puerto, *Spain*	34	C6
Požega, *Croatia*	42	E2
Požega, *Serbia, Yug.*	40	C4
Poznań, *Poland*	45	F3
Pozo, *U.S.A.*	117	K6
Pozo Alcón, *Spain*	35	H8
Pozo Almonte, *Chile*	124	H5
Pozo Colorado, *Paraguay*	126	A4
Pozoblanco, *Spain*	35	G6
Pozzallo, *Italy*	31	F7
Pozzomaggiore, *Italy*	30	B1
Pozzuoli, *Italy*	31	B7
Pra →, *Ghana*	83	D4
Prabuty, *Poland*	44	E6
Prača, *Bos.-H.*	42	G3
Prachatice, *Czech Rep.*	26	B6
Prachin Buri, *Thailand*	64	E3
Prachuap Khiri Khan, *Thailand*	65	G2
Pradelles, *France*	20	D7
Prades, *France*	20	F6
Prado, *Brazil*	125	G11
Prado del Rey, *Spain*	35	J5
Pragersko, *Slovenia*	29	B12
Prague = Praha, *Czech Rep.*	26	A7
Praha, *Czech Rep.*	26	A7
Prahecq, *France*	20	B3
Prahova □, *Romania*	43	E10
Prahova →, *Romania*	43	F10
Prahovo, *Serbia, Yug.*	40	B6
Praia, *C. Verde Is.*	77	E1
Práia a Mare, *Italy*	31	C8
Praid, *Romania*	43	D10
Prainha, *Amazonas, Brazil*	124	E6
Prainha, *Pará, Brazil*	125	D8
Prairie, *Australia*	94	C3
Prairie →, *U.S.A.*	114	D4
Prairie City, *U.S.A.*	114	D4
Prairie Dog Town Fork →, *U.S.A.*	113	H5
Prairie du Chien, *U.S.A.*	112	D9
Prairies, L. of the, *Canada*	105	C8
Pramánda, *Greece*	38	B3
Prampram, *Ghana*	83	D5
Pran Buri, *Thailand*	64	F2
Prang, *Ghana*	83	D4
Prapat, *Indonesia*	62	D1
Prasonísi, Ákra, *Greece*	36	D9
Prästmon, *Sweden*	10	A11
Praszka, *Poland*	45	G5
Prata, *Brazil*	125	G9
Pratabpur, *India*	69	H10
Pratapgarh, *Raj., India*	68	G6
Pratapgarh, *Ut. P., India*	69	G9
Prato, *Italy*	28	E8
Prátola Peligna, *Italy*	29	F10
Prats-de-Mollo-la-Preste, *France*	20	F6
Pratt, *U.S.A.*	113	G5
Prattville, *U.S.A.*	109	J2
Pravdinsk, *Russia*	48	B6
Pravets, *Bulgaria*	40	D7
Pravia, *Spain*	34	B4
Praya, *Indonesia*	62	F5
Pré-en-Pail, *France*	18	D6
Precordillera, *Argentina*	126	C2
Predáppio, *Italy*	29	D8
Predazzo, *Italy*	29	B8
Predeal, *Romania*	43	E10
Predejane, *Serbia, Yug.*	40	D6
Preeceville, *Canada*	105	C8
Preetz, *Germany*	24	A6
Pregrada, *Croatia*	29	B12
Preiļi, *Latvia*	9	H22
Preko, *Croatia*	29	D12
Prelog, *Croatia*	29	B13
Prémery, *France*	19	E10
Premià de Mar, *Spain*	32	D7
Premont, *U.S.A.*	113	M5
Premuda, *Croatia*	29	D11
Prenjasi, *Albania*	40	E4
Prentice, *U.S.A.*	112	C9
Prenzlau, *Germany*	24	B9
Preobrazheniye, *Russia*	54	C6
Preparis North Channel, *Ind. Oc.*	67	M18
Preparis South Channel, *Ind. Oc.*	67	M18
Přerov, *Czech Rep.*	27	B10
Prescott, *Ariz., U.S.A.*	115	J7
Prescott, *Ark., U.S.A.*	113	J8
Prescott Valley, *U.S.A.*	115	J7
Preservation Inlet, *N.Z.*	91	M1
Preševo, *Serbia, Yug.*	40	D6
Presho, *U.S.A.*	112	D4
Presicce, *Italy*	31	C11
Presidencia de la Plaza, *Argentina*	126	B4
Presidencia Roque Saenz Peña, *Argentina*	126	B3
Presidente Epitácio, *Brazil*	125	H8
Presidente Hayes □, *Paraguay*	126	A4
Presidente Prudente, *Brazil*	127	A5
Presidio, *Mexico*	118	B4
Presidio, *U.S.A.*	113	L2
Preslav, *Bulgaria*	41	C10
Preslavska Planina, *Bulgaria*	41	C10
Prešov, *Slovak Rep.*	27	B14
Prešovský □, *Slovak Rep.*	27	B13
Prespa, *Bulgaria*	41	E8
Prespa, L. = Prespansko Jezero, *Macedonia*	40	F5
Prespansko Jezero, *Macedonia*	40	F5
Presque I., *U.S.A.*	110	D4
Presque Isle, *U.S.A.*	109	B12
Prestatyn, *U.K.*	12	D4
Prestea, *Ghana*	82	D4
Presteigne, *U.K.*	13	E5
Přeštice, *Czech Rep.*	26	B6
Preston, *Canada*	110	C4
Preston, *U.K.*	12	D5
Preston, *Idaho, U.S.A.*	114	E8
Preston, *Minn., U.S.A.*	112	D8
Preston, C., *Australia*	92	D2
Prestonburg, *U.S.A.*	108	G4
Prestwick, *U.K.*	14	F4
Pretoria, *S. Africa*	89	D4
Preuilly-sur-Claise, *France*	18	F7
Préveza, *Greece*	38	C2
Préveza □, *Greece*	38	B2
Prey Veng, *Cambodia*	65	G5
Priazovskoye, *Ukraine*	47	J8
Pribilof Is., *U.S.A.*	100	C2
Priboj, *Serbia, Yug.*	40	C3
Příbram, *Czech Rep.*	26	B7
Price, *U.S.A.*	114	G8
Price I., *Canada*	104	C3
Prichard, *U.S.A.*	109	K1
Priego, *Spain*	32	E2
Priego de Córdoba, *Spain*	35	H6
Priekule, *Latvia*	9	H19
Prien, *Germany*	25	H8
Prienai, *Lithuania*	9	J20
Prieska, *S. Africa*	88	D3
Priest L., *U.S.A.*	114	B5
Priest River, *U.S.A.*	114	B5
Priest Valley, *U.S.A.*	116	J6
Prievidza, *Slovak Rep.*	27	C11
Prignitz, *Germany*	24	B7
Prijedor, *Bos.-H.*	29	D13
Prijepolje, *Serbia, Yug.*	40	C3
Prikaspiyskaya Nizmennost = Caspian Depression, *Eurasia*	49	G9
Prikro, *Ivory C.*	82	D4
Prikubanskaya Nizmennost, *Russia*	49	H4
Prilep, *Macedonia*	40	E5
Priluki = Pryluky, *Ukraine*	47	G7
Prime Seal I., *Australia*	94	G4
Primorsk, *Russia*	46	B5
Primorsko, *Bulgaria*	41	D11
Primorsko-Akhtarsk, *Russia*	47	J10
Primorskoye, *Ukraine*	47	J9
Primrose L., *Canada*	105	C7
Prince Albert, *Canada*	105	C7
Prince Albert, *S. Africa*	88	E3
Prince Albert Mts., *Antarctica*	5	D11
Prince Albert Nat. Park, *Canada*	105	C7
Prince Albert Pen., *Canada*	100	A8
Prince Albert Sd., *Canada*	100	A8
Prince Alfred, C., *Canada*	4	B1
Prince Charles I., *Canada*	101	B12
Prince Charles Mts., *Antarctica*	5	D6
Prince Edward I. □, *Canada*	103	C7
Prince Edward Is., *Ind. Oc.*	3	G11
Prince Edward Pt., *Canada*	110	C8
Prince George, *Canada*	104	C4
Prince of Wales, C., *U.S.A.*	98	C3
Prince of Wales I., *Australia*	94	A3
Prince of Wales I., *Canada*	100	A10
Prince of Wales I., *U.S.A.*	100	C6
Prince Patrick I., *Canada*	4	B2
Prince Regent Inlet, *Canada*	4	B3
Prince Rupert, *Canada*	104	C2
Princess Charlotte B., *Australia*	94	A3
Princess May Ranges, *Australia*	92	C4
Princess Royal I., *Canada*	104	C3
Princeton, *Canada*	104	D4
Princeton, *Calif., U.S.A.*	116	F4
Princeton, *Ill., U.S.A.*	112	E10
Princeton, *Ind., U.S.A.*	108	F2
Princeton, *Ky., U.S.A.*	108	G2
Princeton, *Mo., U.S.A.*	112	E8
Princeton, *N.J., U.S.A.*	111	F10
Princeton, *W. Va., U.S.A.*	108	G5
Príncipe, I. de, *Atl. Oc.*	76	F4
Principe da Beira, *Brazil*	124	F6
Prineville, *U.S.A.*	114	D3
Prins Harald Kyst, *Antarctica*	5	D4
Prinsesse Astrid Kyst, *Antarctica*	5	D3
Prinsesse Ragnhild Kyst, *Antarctica*	5	D4
Prinzapolca, *Nic.*	120	D3
Prior, C., *Spain*	34	B2
Priozersk, *Russia*	46	B6
Pripet = Prypyat →, *Europe*	47	G6
Pripet Marshes, *Europe*	47	F5
Pripyat Marshes = Pripet Marshes, *Europe*	47	F5
Pripyats = Prypyat →, *Europe*	47	G6
Prislop, Pasul, *Romania*	43	C9
Pristen, *Russia*	47	G9
Prištína, *Kosovo, Yug.*	40	D5
Pritzwalk, *Germany*	24	B8
Privas, *France*	21	D8
Priverno, *Italy*	30	A6
Privolzhsk, *Russia*	48	B5
Privolzhskaya Vozvyshennost, *Russia*	48	E7
Privolzhskiy, *Russia*	48	E8
Privolzhye, *Russia*	48	D9
Priyutnoye, *Russia*	49	G6
Prizren, *Kosovo, Yug.*	40	D4
Prizzi, *Italy*	30	E6
Prnjavor, *Bos.-H.*	42	F2
Probolinggo, *Indonesia*	63	G15
Prochowice, *Poland*	45	G3
Proctor, *U.S.A.*	111	C11
Proddatur, *India*	66	M11
Prodhromos, *Cyprus*	36	E11
Proença-a-Nova, *Portugal*	34	F3
Profítis Ilías, *Greece*	36	C9
Profondeville, *Belgium*	17	D4
Progreso, *Coahuila, Mexico*	118	B4
Progreso, *Yucatán, Mexico*	119	C7
Prokhladnyy, *Russia*	49	J7
Prokletije, *Albania*	40	D3
Prokopyevsk, *Russia*	50	D9
Prokuplje, *Serbia, Yug.*	40	C5
Proletarsk, *Russia*	49	G5
Proletarskaya = Proletarsk, *Russia*	49	G5
Prome = Pyè, *Burma*	67	K19
Prophet →, *Canada*	104	B4
Prophet River, *Canada*	104	B4
Propriá, *Brazil*	125	F11
Propriano, *France*	21	G12
Proserpine, *Australia*	94	C4
Prosna →, *Poland*	45	F4
Prospect, *U.S.A.*	111	C9
Prosser, *U.S.A.*	114	C4
Prostějov, *Czech Rep.*	27	B10
Prostki, *Poland*	44	E9
Proston, *Australia*	95	D5
Próti, *Greece*	38	D3
Provadiya, *Bulgaria*	41	C11
Provence, *France*	21	E9
Provence-Alpes-Côte d'Azur □, *France*	21	D10
Providence, *Ky., U.S.A.*	108	G2
Providence, *R.I., U.S.A.*	111	E13
Providence Bay, *Canada*	102	C3
Providence Mts., *U.S.A.*	117	K11
Providencia, I. de, *Colombia*	120	D3
Provideniya, *Russia*	51	C19
Provins, *France*	19	D10
Provo, *U.S.A.*	114	F8
Provost, *Canada*	105	C6
Prozor, *Bos.-H.*	42	G2
Prudhoe Bay, *U.S.A.*	100	A5
Prudhoe I., *Australia*	94	C4
Prud'homme, *Canada*	105	C7
Prudnik, *Poland*	45	H4
Prüm, *Germany*	25	E2
Prundu, *Romania*	43	F11
Pruszcz Gdański, *Poland*	44	D5
Pruszków, *Poland*	45	F7
Prut →, *Romania*	43	E13
Pruzhany, *Belarus*	47	F3
Prvič, *Croatia*	29	D11
Prydz B., *Antarctica*	5	C6
Pryluky, *Ukraine*	47	G7
Pryor, *U.S.A.*	113	G7
Prypyat →, *Europe*	47	G6
Przasnysz, *Poland*	45	E7
Przedbórz, *Poland*	45	G6
Przedecz, *Poland*	45	F5
Przemków, *Poland*	45	G2
Przemyśl, *Poland*	45	J9
Przeworsk, *Poland*	45	H9
Przewóz, *Poland*	45	G1
Przhevalsk, *Kyrgyzstan*	50	E8
Przysucha, *Poland*	45	G7
Psakhná, *Greece*	38	C5
Psará, *Greece*	39	C7
Psathoúra, *Greece*	38	B6
Psel →, *Ukraine*	47	H7
Pserimos, *Greece*	39	E9
Psíra, *Greece*	36	D7
Pskov, *Russia*	46	D5
Pskovskoye, Ozero, *Russia*	9	H22
Psunj, *Croatia*	42	E2
Ptelón, *Greece*	38	B4
Ptich = Ptsich →, *Belarus*	47	F5
Ptolemaís, *Greece*	40	F5
Ptsich →, *Belarus*	47	F5
Ptuj, *Slovenia*	29	B12
Ptujska Gora, *Slovenia*	29	B12
Pu Xian, *China*	56	F6
Pua, *Thailand*	64	C3
Puán, *Argentina*	126	D3
Pu'an, *China*	58	E5
Puan, *S. Korea*	57	G14
Pubei, *China*	58	F7
Pucallpa, *Peru*	124	E4
Pucheng, *China*	59	D12
Pucheni, *Romania*	43	E10
Puchheim, *Germany*	25	G7
Púchov, *Slovak Rep.*	27	B11
Pucioasa, *Romania*	43	E10
Pučišća, *Croatia*	29	E13
Puck, *Poland*	44	D5
Pudasjärvi, *Finland*	8	D22
Pudozh, *Russia*	46	B9
Pudukkottai, *India*	66	P11
Puebla, *Mexico*	119	D5
Puebla □, *Mexico*	119	D5
Puebla de Alcocer, *Spain*	35	G5
Puebla de Don Fadrique, *Spain*	33	H2
Puebla de Don Rodrigo, *Spain*	35	F6
Puebla de Guzmán, *Spain*	35	H3
Puebla de la Calzada, *Spain*	35	G4
Puebla de Sanabria, *Spain*	34	C4
Puebla de Trives = Pobra de Trives, *Spain*	34	C3
Pueblo, *U.S.A.*	112	G2
Pueblo Hundido, *Chile*	126	B1
Puelches, *Argentina*	126	D2
Puelén, *Argentina*	126	D2
Puente Alto, *Chile*	126	C1
Puente-Genil, *Spain*	35	H6
Puente la Reina, *Spain*	32	C3
Puenteareas = Ponteareas, *Spain*	34	C2
Puentedeume = Pontedeume, *Spain*	34	B2
Puentes de Garcia Rodriguez = As Pontes de García Rodríquez, *Spain*	34	B3
Pu'er, *China*	58	F3
Puerco →, *U.S.A.*	115	J10
Puerto, *Canary Is.*	37	F2
Puerto Aisén, *Chile*	128	F2
Puerto Ángel, *Mexico*	119	D5
Puerto Arista, *Mexico*	119	D6
Puerto Armuelles, *Panama*	120	E3
Puerto Ayacucho, *Venezuela*	124	B5
Puerto Barrios, *Guatemala*	120	C2
Puerto Bermejo, *Argentina*	126	B4
Puerto Bermúdez, *Peru*	124	F4
Puerto Bolívar, *Ecuador*	124	D3
Puerto Cabello, *Venezuela*	124	A5
Puerto Cabezas, *Nic.*	120	D3
Puerto Cabo Gracias á Dios, *Nic.*	120	D3
Puerto Carreño, *Colombia*	124	B5
Puerto Castilla, *Honduras*	120	C2
Puerto Chicama, *Peru*	124	E3
Puerto Coig, *Argentina*	128	G3
Puerto Cortés, *Costa Rica*	120	E3
Puerto Cortés, *Honduras*	120	C2
Puerto Cumarebo, *Venezuela*	124	A5
Puerto de Alcudia = Port d'Alcúdia, *Spain*	37	B10
Puerto de Andraitx, *Spain*	37	B9
Puerto de Cabrera, *Spain*	37	B9
Puerto de Gran Tarajal, *Canary Is.*	37	F5
Puerto de la Cruz, *Canary Is.*	37	F3
Puerto de Mazarrón, *Spain*	33	H3
Puerto de Pozo Negro, *Canary Is.*	37	F6
Puerto de Sóller = Port de Sóller, *Spain*	37	B9
Puerto de Somosierra, *Spain*	34	D7
Puerto del Carmen, *Canary Is.*	37	F6
Puerto del Rosario, *Canary Is.*	37	F6
Puerto Deseado, *Argentina*	128	F3
Puerto Escondido, *Mexico*	119	D5
Puerto Heath, *Bolivia*	124	F5
Puerto Inírida, *Colombia*	124	C5
Puerto Juárez, *Mexico*	119	C7
Puerto La Cruz, *Venezuela*	124	A6
Puerto Leguízamo, *Colombia*	124	D4
Puerto Limón, *Colombia*	124	C4
Puerto Lobos, *Argentina*	128	E3
Puerto Lumbreras, *Spain*	33	H3
Puerto Maldonado, *Peru*	124	F5
Puerto Manotí, *Cuba*	120	B4
Puerto Mazarrón = Puerto de Mazarrón, *Spain*	33	H3
Puerto Montt, *Chile*	128	E2
Puerto Morazán, *Nic.*	120	D2
Puerto Morelos, *Mexico*	119	C7
Puerto Natales, *Chile*	128	G2
Puerto Padre, *Cuba*	120	B4
Puerto Páez, *Venezuela*	124	B5
Puerto Peñasco, *Mexico*	118	A2
Puerto Pinasco, *Paraguay*	126	A4
Puerto Plata, *Dom. Rep.*	121	C5
Puerto Pollensa = Port de Pollença, *Spain*	37	B10
Puerto Princesa, *Phil.*	61	G3
Puerto Quepos, *Costa Rica*	120	E3
Puerto Real, *Spain*	35	J4
Puerto Rico, *Canary Is.*	37	G4
Puerto Rico ■, *W. Indies*	121	C6
Puerto Rico Trench, *Atl. Oc.*	121	C6
Puerto San Julián, *Argentina*	128	F3
Puerto Sastre, *Paraguay*	126	A4
Puerto Serrano, *Spain*	35	J5
Puerto Suárez, *Bolivia*	124	G7
Puerto Vallarta, *Mexico*	118	C3
Puerto Wilches, *Colombia*	124	B4
Puertollano, *Spain*	35	G6
Pueyrredón, L., *Argentina*	128	F2
Puffin I., *Ireland*	15	E1
Pugachev, *Russia*	48	D9
Pugal, *India*	68	E5
Puge, *China*	58	D4
Puge, *Tanzania*	86	C3
Puget Sound, *U.S.A.*	114	C2
Puget-Théniers, *France*	21	E10
Púglia □, *Italy*	31	A9
Pugŏdong, *N. Korea*	57	C16
Pugu, *Tanzania*	86	D4
Pūgūnzī, *Iran*	71	E8
Pui, *Romania*	42	E8
Puiești, *Romania*	43	D12
Puig Major, *Spain*	37	B9
Puigcerdà, *Spain*	32	C6
Puigmal, *Spain*	32	C7
Puigpunyent, *Spain*	37	B9
Puijiang, *China*	58	B4

Puisaye, Collines de la

Puisaye, Collines de la, *France* 19 E10
Puiseaux, *France* 19 D9
Pujehun, *S. Leone* 82 D2
Pujiang, *China* 59 C12
Pujols, *France* 20 D3
Pujon-chŏsuji, *N. Korea* 57 D14
Puka, *Albania* 40 D3
Pukaki L., *N.Z.* 91 L3
Pukapuka, *Cook Is.* 97 J11
Pukaskwa Nat. Park, *Canada* 102 C2
Pukatawagan, *Canada* 105 B8
Pukchin, *N. Korea* 57 D13
Pukch'ŏng, *N. Korea* 57 D15
Pukekohe, *N.Z.* 91 G5
Pukhrayan, *India* 69 F8
Pukou, *China* 59 A12
Pula, *Croatia* 29 D10
Pula, *Italy* 30 C1
Pulacayo, *Bolivia* 124 H5
Pulandian, *China* 57 E11
Pularumpi, *Australia* 92 B5
Pulaski, *N.Y., U.S.A.* 111 C8
Pulaski, *Tenn., U.S.A.* 109 H2
Pulaski, *Va., U.S.A.* 108 G5
Pulau →, *Indonesia* 63 F9
Puławy, *Poland* 45 G8
Pulga, *U.S.A.* 116 F5
Pulicat L., *India* 66 N12
Pullman, *U.S.A.* 114 C5
Pulo-Anna, *Pac. Oc.* 63 D8
Pulog, Mt., *Phil.* 61 C4
Pułtusk, *Poland* 45 F8
Pülümür, *Turkey* 73 C8
Pumlumon Fawr, *U.K.* 13 E4
Puná, I., *Ecuador* 124 D2
Punakha, *Bhutan* 67 F16
Punasar, *India* 68 F5
Punata, *Bolivia* 124 G5
Punch, *India* 69 C6
Punch →, *Pakistan* 68 C5
Punda Maria, *S. Africa* 89 C5
Pune, *India* 66 K8
P'ungsan, *N. Korea* 57 D15
Pungue, Ponte de, *Mozam.* 87 F3
Puning, *China* 59 F11
Punjab □, *India* 68 D7
Punjab □, *Pakistan* 68 E6
Puno, *Peru* 124 G4
Punpun →, *India* 69 G11
Punta Alta, *Argentina* 128 D4
Punta Arenas, *Chile* 128 G2
Punta de Díaz, *Chile* 126 B1
Punta Gorda, *Belize* 119 D7
Punta Gorda, *U.S.A.* 109 M5
Punta Prieta, *Mexico* 118 B2
Punta Prima, *Spain* 37 B11
Punta Umbría, *Spain* 35 H4
Puntarenas, *Costa Rica* 120 E3
Punto Fijo, *Venezuela* 124 A4
Punxsatawney, *U.S.A.* 110 F6
Puqi, *China* 59 C9
Puquio, *Peru* 124 F4
Pur →, *Russia* 50 C8
Purace, Vol., *Colombia* 124 C3
Puračić, *Bos.-H.* 42 F3
Puralia = Puruliya, *India* 69 H12
Puranpur, *India* 69 E9
Purbeck, Isle of, *U.K.* 13 G6
Purcell, *U.S.A.* 113 H6
Purcell Mts., *Canada* 104 D5
Puri, *India* 67 K14
Purmerend, *Neths.* 17 B4
Purnia, *India* 69 G12
Pursat = Pouthisat, *Cambodia* 64 F4
Purukcahu, *Indonesia* 62 E4
Puruliya, *India* 69 H12
Purus →, *Brazil* 122 D4
Puruvesi, *Finland* 46 B5
Purvis, *U.S.A.* 113 K10
Pŭrvomay, *Bulgaria* 41 D9
Purwa, *India* 69 F9
Purwakarta, *Indonesia* 63 G12
Purwodadi, *Indonesia* 63 G14
Purwokerto, *Indonesia* 63 G13
Puryŏng, *N. Korea* 57 C15
Pusa, *India* 69 G11
Pusan, *S. Korea* 57 G15
Pushkin, *Russia* 46 C6
Pushkino, *Moskva, Russia* 46 D9
Pushkino, *Saratov, Russia* 48 E8
Püspökladány, *Hungary* 42 C6
Pustoshka, *Russia* 46 D5
Puszczykowo, *Poland* 45 F3
Putahow L., *Canada* 105 B8
Putao, *Burma* 67 F20
Putaruru, *N.Z.* 91 H5
Putbus, *Germany* 24 A9
Puthein Myit →, *Burma* 67 M19
Putian, *China* 59 E12
Putignano, *Italy* 31 B10
Puting, Tanjung, *Indonesia* 62 E4
Putlitz, *Germany* 24 B8
Putna, *Romania* 43 C10
Putna →, *Romania* 43 E12
Putnam, *U.S.A.* 111 E13
Putnok, *Hungary* 42 B5
Putorana, Gory, *Russia* 51 C10
Puttalam, *Sri Lanka* 66 Q11
Puttgarden, *Germany* 24 A7
Püttlingen, *Germany* 25 F2
Putumayo →, *S. Amer.* 122 D4
Putuo, *China* 59 C14
Putussibau, *Indonesia* 62 D4
Puvirnituq, *Canada* 101 B12
Puy-de-Dôme, *France* 20 C6
Puy-de-Dôme □, *France* 20 C7
Puy-l'Évêque, *France* 20 D5
Puyallup, *U.S.A.* 116 C4
Puyang, *China* 56 G8
Puylaurens, *France* 20 E6
Pūzeh Rīg, *Iran* 71 E8
Pwani □, *Tanzania* 86 D4
Pweto, *Dem. Rep. of the Congo* 87 D2
Pwllheli, *U.K.* 12 E3
Pyana →, *Russia* 48 C8
Pyapon, *Burma* 67 L19
Pyasina →, *Russia* 51 B9
Pyatigorsk, *Russia* 49 H6
Pyatykhatky, *Ukraine* 47 H7
Pydna, *Greece* 40 F6
Pyè, *Burma* 67 K19
Pyetrikaw, *Belarus* 47 F5
Pyhäjoki, *Finland* 8 D21
Pyinmana, *Burma* 67 K20
Pyla, C., *Cyprus* 36 E12
Pymatuning Reservoir, *U.S.A.* 110 E4
Pyŏktong, *N. Korea* 57 D13
Pyŏnggang, *N. Korea* 57 E14
P'yŏngt'aek, *S. Korea* 57 F14
P'yŏngyang, *N. Korea* 57 E13
Pyote, *U.S.A.* 113 K3
Pyramid L., *U.S.A.* 114 G4
Pyramid Pk., *U.S.A.* 117 J10
Pyramids, *Egypt* 80 J7
Pyrénées, *Europe* 20 F4
Pyrénées-Atlantiques □, *France* 20 E3
Pyrénées-Orientales □, *France* 20 F6
Pyryatyn, *Ukraine* 47 G7
Pyrzyce, *Poland* 45 E1
Pyskowice, *Poland* 45 H5
Pytalovo, *Russia* 46 D4
Pyu, *Burma* 67 K20
Pyzdry, *Poland* 45 F4

Q

Qaanaaq, *Greenland* 4 B4
Qabirri →, *Azerbaijan* 49 K8
Qachasnek, *S. Africa* 89 E4
Qa'el Jafr, *Jordan* 75 E5
Qa'emābād, *Iran* 71 D9
Qā'emshahr, *Iran* 71 B7
Qagan Nur, *China* 56 C8
Qahar Youyi Zhongqi, *China* 56 D7
Qahremānshahr = Bākhtarān, *Iran* 70 C5
Qaidam Pendi, *China* 60 C4
Qajarīyeh, *Iran* 71 D6
Qala, Ras il, *Malta* 36 C1
Qala-i-Jadid = Spīn Búldak, *Afghan.* 68 D2
Qala Viala, *Pakistan* 68 D2
Qala Yangi, *Afghan.* 68 B2
Qal'at al Akhḍar, *Si. Arabia* 70 E3
Qal'at Dīzah, *Iraq* 70 B5
Qal'at Ṣaliḥ, *Iraq* 70 D5
Qal'at Sukkar, *Iraq* 70 D5
Qal'eh Shaharak, *Afghan.* 66 B4
Qalyûb, *Egypt* 80 H7
Qamdo, *China* 58 B1
Qamruddin Karez, *Pakistan* 68 D3
Qandahār, *Afghan.* 66 D4
Qandahār □, *Afghan.* 66 D4
Qapān, *Iran* 71 B7
Qapshaghay, *Kazakstan* 50 E8
Qaqortoq, *Greenland* 4 C5
Qâra, *Egypt* 80 B2
Qara Qash →, *India* 69 B8
Qarabutaq, *Kazakstan* 50 E7
Qaraçala, *Azerbaijan* 49 L9
Qaraghandy, *Kazakstan* 50 E8
Qārah, *Si. Arabia* 70 D4
Qarataū, *Kazakstan* 50 E8
Qardud, *Sudan* 81 E2
Qareh →, *Iran* 70 B5
Qareh Tekān, *Iran* 71 B6
Qarqan He →, *China* 60 C3
Qarqaraly, *Kazakstan* 50 E8
Qarrasa, *Sudan* 81 E3
Qarshi, *Uzbekistan* 50 F7
Qartabā, *Lebanon* 75 A4
Qaryat al Gharab, *Iraq* 70 D5
Qaryat al 'Ulyā, *Si. Arabia* 70 E5
Qasr 'Amra, *Jordan* 70 D3
Qaṣr-e Qand, *Iran* 71 E9
Qasr Farâfra, *Egypt* 80 B2
Qatanā, *Syria* 75 B5
Qatar ■, *Asia* 71 E6
Qatlīsh, *Iran* 71 B8
Qattâra, *Egypt* 80 A2
Qattâra, Munkhafed el, *Egypt* 80 B2
Qattâra Depression = Qattâra, Munkhafed el, *Egypt* 80 B2
Qawām al Ḥamzah, *Iraq* 70 D5
Qāyen, *Iran* 71 C8
Qazaqstan = Kazakstan ■, *Asia* 50 E7
Qazimämmäd, *Azerbaijan* 49 K9
Qazvin, *Iran* 71 B6
Qeissan, *Sudan* 81 E3
Qena, *Egypt* 80 B3
Qena, W. →, *Egypt* 80 B3
Qeqertarsuaq, *Greenland* 4 C5
Qeqertarsuaq, *Greenland* 4 C5
Qeshlāq, *Iran* 70 C5
Qeshm, *Iran* 71 E8
Qeys, *Iran* 71 E7
Qezel Owzen →, *Iran* 71 B6
Qezi'ot, *Israel* 75 E3
Qi Xian, *China* 56 G8
Qian Gorlos, *China* 57 B13
Qian Xian, *China* 56 G5
Qiancheng, *China* 58 D7
Qianjiang, *Guangxi Zhuangzu, China* 58 F7
Qianjiang, *Hubei, China* 59 B9
Qianjiang, *Sichuan, China* 58 C7
Qianshan, *China* 59 B11
Qianwei, *China* 58 C4
Qianxi, *China* 58 D6
Qianyang, *Hunan, China* 59 D8
Qianyang, *Shaanxi, China* 56 G4
Qianyang, *Zhejiang, China* 59 B12
Qiaojia, *China* 58 D4
Qibā', *Si. Arabia* 70 E5
Qichun, *China* 59 B10
Qidong, *Hunan, China* 59 D9
Qidong, *Jiangsu, China* 59 B13
Qijiang, *China* 58 C6
Qikiqtarjuaq, *Canada* 101 B13
Qila Safed, *Pakistan* 66 E2
Qila Saifullāh, *Pakistan* 68 D3
Qilian Shan, *China* 60 C4
Qimen, *China* 59 C11
Qin He →, *China* 56 G7
Qin Jiang →, *Guangxi Zhuangzu, China* 58 F7
Qin Jiang →, *Jiangxi, China* 59 D10
Qin Ling = Qinling Shandi, *China* 56 H5
Qin'an, *China* 56 G3
Qing Xian, *China* 56 E9
Qingcheng, *China* 57 F9
Qingdao, *China* 57 F11
Qingfeng, *China* 56 G8
Qinghai □, *China* 60 C4
Qinghai Hu, *China* 60 C5
Qinghecheng, *China* 57 D13
Qinghemen, *China* 57 D11
Qingjian, *China* 56 F6
Qingjiang = Huaiyin, *China* 57 H10
Qingliu, *China* 59 D11
Qinglong, *China* 58 E5
Qingping, *China* 58 D6
Qingpu, *China* 59 B13
Qingshui, *China* 56 G4
Qingshuihe, *China* 56 E6
Qingtian, *China* 59 C13
Qingtongxia Shuiku, *China* 56 F3
Qingxi, *China* 58 D7
Qingxu, *China* 56 F7
Qingyang, *Anhui, China* 59 B11
Qingyang, *Gansu, China* 56 F4
Qingyi Jiang →, *China* 58 C4
Qingyuan, *Guangdong, China* 59 F9
Qingyuan, *Liaoning, China* 57 C13
Qingyuan, *Zhejiang, China* 59 D12
Qingyun, *China* 57 F9
Qingzhen, *China* 58 D6
Qinhuangdao, *China* 57 E10
Qinling Shandi, *China* 56 H5
Qinshui, *China* 56 G7
Qinyang = Jiyuan, *China* 56 G7
Qinyuan, *China* 56 F7
Qinzhou, *China* 58 G7
Qionghai, *China* 64 C8
Qionglai, *China* 58 B4
Qionglai Shan, *China* 58 B4
Qiongzhou Haixia, *China* 64 B8
Qiqihar, *China* 51 E13
Qiraîya, W. →, *Egypt* 75 E3
Qiryat Ata, *Israel* 75 C4
Qiryat Gat, *Israel* 75 D3
Qiryat Mal'akhi, *Israel* 75 D3
Qiryat Shemona, *Israel* 75 B4
Qiryat Yam, *Israel* 75 C4
Qishan, *China* 56 G4
Qitai, *China* 60 B3
Qiubei, *China* 58 E5
Qixia, *China* 57 F11
Qiyang, *China* 59 D8
Qızılağac Körfäzi, *Azerbaijan* 71 B6
Qojūr, *Iran* 70 B5
Qom, *Iran* 71 C6
Qomolangma Feng = Everest, Mt., *Nepal* 69 E12
Qomsheh, *Iran* 71 D6
Qorveh, *Iran* 73 E12
Qostanay, *Kazakstan* 50 D7
Qoṭūr, *Iran* 73 C11
Qu Jiang →, *China* 58 B6
Qu Xian, *China* 58 B6
Quabbin Reservoir, *U.S.A.* 111 D12
Quairading, *Australia* 93 F2
Quakenbrück, *Germany* 24 C3
Quakertown, *U.S.A.* 111 F9
Qualicum Beach, *Canada* 104 D4
Quambatook, *Australia* 95 F3
Quambone, *Australia* 95 E4
Quamby, *Australia* 94 C3
Quan Long = Ca Mau, *Vietnam* 65 H5
Quanah, *U.S.A.* 113 H5
Quang Ngai, *Vietnam* 64 E7
Quang Tri, *Vietnam* 64 D6
Quang Yen, *Vietnam* 58 G6
Quannan, *China* 59 E10
Quantock Hills, *U.K.* 13 F4
Quanzhou, *Fujian, China* 59 E12
Quanzhou, *Guangxi Zhuangzu, China* 59 E8
Qu'Appelle, *Canada* 105 C8
Quaqtaq, *Canada* 101 B13
Quaraí, *Brazil* 126 C4
Quarré-les-Tombes, *France* 19 E11
Quarteira, *Portugal* 35 H2
Quartu Sant'Élena, *Italy* 30 C2
Quartzsite, *U.S.A.* 117 M12
Quatsino Sd., *Canada* 104 C3
Quba, *Azerbaijan* 49 K9
Qūchān, *Iran* 71 B8
Queanbeyan, *Australia* 95 F4
Québec, *Canada* 103 C5
Québec □, *Canada* 103 C6
Quedlinburg, *Germany* 24 D7
Queen Alexandra Ra., *Antarctica* 5 E11
Queen Charlotte City, *Canada* 104 C2
Queen Charlotte Is., *Canada* 104 C2
Queen Charlotte Sd., *Canada* 104 C3
Queen Charlotte Strait, *Canada* 104 C3
Queen Elizabeth Is., *Canada* 98 B10
Queen Elizabeth Nat. Park, *Uganda* 86 C3
Queen Mary Land, *Antarctica* 5 D7
Queen Maud G., *Canada* 100 B9
Queen Maud Land, *Antarctica* 5 D3
Queen Maud Mts., *Antarctica* 5 E13
Queens Chan., *Australia* 92 C4
Queenscliff, *Australia* 95 F3
Queensland □, *Australia* 94 C3
Queenstown, *Australia* 94 G4
Queenstown, *N.Z.* 91 L2
Queenstown, *S. Africa* 88 E4
Queets, *U.S.A.* 116 C2
Queguay Grande →, *Uruguay* 126 C4
Queimadas, *Brazil* 125 F11
Quelimane, *Mozam.* 87 F4
Quellón, *Chile* 128 E2
Quelpart = Cheju do, *S. Korea* 57 H14
Queluz, *Portugal* 35 G1
Quemado, *N. Mex., U.S.A.* 115 J9
Quemado, *Tex., U.S.A.* 113 L4
Quemoy = Chinmen, *Taiwan* 59 E13
Quemú-Quemú, *Argentina* 126 D3
Quequén, *Argentina* 126 D4
Querétaro, *Mexico* 118 C4
Querétaro □, *Mexico* 118 C5
Querfurt, *Germany* 24 D7
Quérigut, *France* 20 F6
Querqueville, *France* 18 C5
Quesada, *Spain* 35 H7
Queshan, *China* 56 H8
Quesnel, *Canada* 104 C4
Quesnel →, *Canada* 104 C4
Quesnel L., *Canada* 104 C4
Questa, *U.S.A.* 115 H11
Questembert, *France* 18 E4
Quetico Prov. Park, *Canada* 102 C1
Quetta, *Pakistan* 68 D2
Quezaltenango, *Guatemala* 120 D1
Quezon City, *Phil.* 61 D4
Qufār, *Si. Arabia* 70 E4
Qui Nhon, *Vietnam* 64 F7
Quibaxe, *Angola* 84 F2
Quibdo, *Colombia* 124 B3
Quiberon, *France* 18 E3
Quiberon, Presqu'île de, *France* 18 E3
Quickborn, *Germany* 24 B5
Quiet L., *Canada* 104 A2
Quiindy, *Paraguay* 126 B4
Quila, *Mexico* 118 C3
Quilán, C., *Chile* 128 E2
Quilcene, *U.S.A.* 116 C4
Quilimarí, *Chile* 126 C1
Quilino, *Argentina* 126 C3
Quill Lakes, *Canada* 105 C8
Quillabamba, *Peru* 124 F4
Quillagua, *Chile* 126 A2
Quillaicillo, *Chile* 126 C1
Quillan, *France* 20 F6
Quillota, *Chile* 126 C1
Quilmes, *Argentina* 126 C4
Quilon, *India* 66 Q10
Quilpie, *Australia* 95 D3
Quilpué, *Chile* 126 C1
Quilua, *Mozam.* 87 F4
Quimilí, *Argentina* 126 B3
Quimper, *France* 18 E2
Quimperlé, *France* 18 E3
Quinault →, *U.S.A.* 116 C2
Quincy, *Calif., U.S.A.* 116 F6
Quincy, *Fla., U.S.A.* 109 K3
Quincy, *Ill., U.S.A.* 112 F9
Quincy, *Mass., U.S.A.* 111 D14
Quincy, *Wash., U.S.A.* 114 C4
Quines, *Argentina* 126 C2
Quinga, *Mozam.* 87 F5
Quingey, *France* 19 E12
Quinns Rocks, *Australia* 93 F2
Quintana de la Serena, *Spain* 35 G5
Quintana Roo □, *Mexico* 119 D7
Quintanar de la Orden, *Spain* 35 F7
Quintanar de la Sierra, *Spain* 32 D2
Quintanar del Rey, *Spain* 33 F3
Quintero, *Chile* 126 C1
Quintin, *France* 18 D4
Quinto, *Spain* 32 D4
Quípar →, *Spain* 33 G3
Quirihue, *Chile* 126 D1
Quirindi, *Australia* 95 E5
Quirinópolis, *Brazil* 125 G8
Quiroga, *Spain* 34 C3
Quissac, *France* 21 E8
Quissanga, *Mozam.* 87 E5
Quissico, *Mozam.* 89 C5
Quitilipi, *Argentina* 126 B3
Quitman, *U.S.A.* 109 K4
Quito, *Ecuador* 124 D3
Quixadá, *Brazil* 125 D11
Quixaxe, *Mozam.* 87 F5
Qujing, *China* 58 E4
Qul'ân, Jazâ'ir, *Egypt* 70 E2
Qumbu, *S. Africa* 89 E4
Quneitra, *Syria* 75 B4
Qŭnghirot, *Uzbekistan* 50 E6
Qu'nyido, *China* 58 B2
Quoin I., *Australia* 92 B4
Quoin Pt., *S. Africa* 88 E2
Quorn, *Australia* 95 E2
Qŭqon, *Uzbekistan* 50 E8
Qurein, *Sudan* 81 E3
Qurnat as Sawdā', *Lebanon* 75 A5
Qûs, *Egypt* 80 B3
Qusar, *Azerbaijan* 49 K9
Quṣaybā', *Si. Arabia* 70 E4
Qusaybah, *Iraq* 70 C4
Quseir, *Egypt* 70 E2
Qūshchī, *Iran* 70 B5
Quthing, *Lesotho* 89 E4
Qūṭīābād, *Iran* 71 C6
Quwo, *China* 56 G6
Quyang, *China* 56 E8
Quynh Nhai, *Vietnam* 64 B4
Quyon, *Canada* 111 A8
Quzhou, *China* 59 C12
Quzi, *China* 56 F4
Qvareli, *Georgia* 49 K7
Qytet Stalin = Kuçovë, *Albania* 40 F3
Qyzylorda, *Kazakstan* 50 E7

R

Ra, Ko, *Thailand* 65 H2
Raab, *Austria* 26 C6
Raahe, *Finland* 8 D21
Raalte, *Neths.* 17 B6
Raasay, *U.K.* 14 D2
Raasay, Sd. of, *U.K.* 14 D2
Rab, *Croatia* 29 D11
Raba, *Indonesia* 63 F5
Rába →, *Hungary* 42 C2
Raba →, *Poland* 45 H7
Rabaçal →, *Portugal* 34 D3
Rabah, *Nigeria* 83 C6
Rabai, *Kenya* 86 C4
Rabak, *Sudan* 81 E3
Rabastens, *France* 20 E5
Rabastens-de-Bigorre, *France* 20 E4
Rabat, *Malta* 36 D1
Rabat, *Morocco* 78 B4
Rabaul, *Papua N. G.* 96 H7
Rābigh, *Si. Arabia* 74 C2
Rabka, *Poland* 45 J6
Râbniţa, *Moldova* 43 C14
Rābor, *Iran* 71 D8
Rača, *Serbia, Yug.* 40 B4
Răcăciuni, *Romania* 43 D11
Răcăşdia, *Romania* 42 F6
Racconigi, *Italy* 28 D4
Race, C., *Canada* 103 C9
Rach Gia, *Vietnam* 65 G5
Rachid, *Mauritania* 82 B2
Raciąż, *Poland* 45 F7
Racibórz, *Poland* 45 H5
Racine, *U.S.A.* 108 D2
Rackerby, *U.S.A.* 116 F5
Radama, Nosy, *Madag.* 89 A8
Radama, Saikanosy, *Madag.* 89 A8
Radan, *Serbia, Yug.* 40 D5
Rădăuţi, *Romania* 43 C10
Rădăuţi-Prut, *Romania* 43 B11
Radbuza →, *Czech Rep.* 26 B6
Radcliff, *U.S.A.* 108 G3
Radebeul, *Germany* 24 D9
Radeburg, *Germany* 24 D9
Radeče, *Slovenia* 29 B12
Radekhiv, *Ukraine* 47 G3
Radekhov = Radekhiv, *Ukraine* 47 G3
Radenthein, *Austria* 26 E6
Radew →, *Poland* 44 D2
Radford, *U.S.A.* 108 G5
Radhanpur, *India* 68 H4
Radhwa, Jabal, *Si. Arabia* 70 E3
Radika →, *Macedonia* 40 E4
Radisson, *Qué., Canada* 102 B4
Radisson, *Sask., Canada* 105 C7
Radium Hot Springs, *Canada* 104 C5
Radlje ob Dravi, *Slovenia* 29 B12
Radnevo, *Bulgaria* 41 D9
Radnice, *Czech Rep.* 26 B6
Radnor Forest, *U.K.* 13 E4
Radolfzell, *Germany* 25 H4
Radom, *Poland* 45 G8
Radomir, *Bulgaria* 40 D6
Radomka →, *Poland* 45 G8
Radomsko, *Poland* 45 G6
Radomyshl, *Ukraine* 47 G5
Radomyśl Wielki, *Poland* 45 H8
Radoszyce, *Poland* 45 G7
Radoviš, *Macedonia* 40 E6
Radovljica, *Slovenia* 29 B11
Radstadt, *Austria* 26 D6
Radstock, C., *Australia* 95 E1
Răducăneni, *Romania* 43 D12
Raduša, *Macedonia* 40 D5
Radviliškis, *Lithuania* 9 J20
Radville, *Canada* 105 D8
Raḍwá, J., *Si. Arabia* 80 C4
Radymno, *Poland* 45 J9
Radzanów, *Poland* 45 F7
Radziejów, *Poland* 45 F5
Radzyń Chełmiński, *Poland* 44 E5
Radzyń Podlaski, *Poland* 45 G9
Rae, *Canada* 104 A5
Rae Bareli, *India* 69 F9
Rae Isthmus, *Canada* 101 B11
Raeren, *Belgium* 17 D6

Raeside, L., Australia 93 E3
Raetihi, N.Z. 91 H5
Rafaela, Argentina 126 C3
Rafah, Gaza Strip 75 D3
Rafai, C.A.R. 86 B1
Raffadali, Italy 30 E6
Raffili, Sudan 81 F2
Rafḥā, Si. Arabia 70 D4
Rafsanjān, Iran 71 D8
Raft Pt., Australia 92 C3
Râga, Sudan 81 F2
Raga →, Sudan 81 F2
Ragachow, Belarus 47 F6
Ragag, Sudan 81 E1
Ragama, Sri Lanka 66 R11
Ragged, Mt., Australia .. 93 F3
Raglan, N.Z. 91 G5
Ragusa, Italy 31 F7
Raha, Indonesia 63 E6
Rahad, Nahr ed →, Sudan 81 E3
Rahaeng = Tak, Thailand . 64 D2
Rahatgarh, India 69 H8
Rahden, Germany 24 C4
Raheita, Eritrea 81 E5
Raḥīmah, Si. Arabia 71 E6
Rahimyar Khan, Pakistan . 68 E4
Rāhjerd, Iran 71 C6
Rahon, India 68 D7
Raichur, India 66 L10
Raiganj, India 69 G13
Raigarh, India 67 J13
Raijua, Indonesia 63 F6
Raikot, India 68 D6
Railton, Australia 94 G4
Rainbow Lake, Canada ... 104 B5
Rainier, U.S.A. 116 D4
Rainier, Mt., U.S.A. ... 116 D5
Rainy L., Canada 105 D10
Rainy River, Canada 105 D10
Raippaluoto, Finland ... 8 E19
Raipur, India 67 J12
Ra'is, Si. Arabia 80 C4
Raisen, India 68 H8
Raisio, Finland 9 F20
Raj Nandgaon, India 67 J12
Raj Nilgiri, India 69 J12
Raja, Ujung, Indonesia ... 62 D1
Raja Ampat, Kepulauan,
  Indonesia 63 E7
Rajahmundry, India 67 L12
Rajang →, Malaysia ... 62 D4
Rajanpur, Pakistan 68 E4
Rajapalaiyam, India 66 Q10
Rajasthan □, India 68 F5
Rajasthan Canal, India .. 68 F5
Rajauri, India 69 C6
Rajgarh, Mad. P., India .. 68 G7
Rajgarh, Raj., India 68 F7
Rajgarh, Raj., India 68 E6
Rajgir, India 69 G11
Rajgród, Poland 44 E9
Rajkot, India 68 H4
Rajmahal Hills, India ... 69 G12
Rajpipla, India 66 J8
Rajpur, India 68 H6
Rajpura, India 68 D7
Rajshahi, Bangla. 67 G16
Rajshahi □, Bangla. 69 G13
Rajula, India 68 J4
Rakaia, N.Z. 91 K4
Rakaia →, N.Z. 91 K4
Rakan, Ra's, Qatar 71 E6
Rakaposhi, Pakistan 69 A6
Rakata, Pulau, Indonesia . 62 F3
Rakhiv, Ukraine 47 H3
Rakhni, Pakistan 68 D3
Rakhni →, Pakistan 68 E3
Rakitnoye, Russia 54 B7
Rakitovo, Bulgaria 41 E8
Rakoniewice, Poland 45 F3
Rakops, Botswana 88 C3
Rakovica, Croatia 29 D12
Rakovník, Czech Rep. ... 26 A6
Rakovski, Bulgaria 41 D8
Rakvere, Estonia 9 G22
Raleigh, U.S.A. 109 H6
Raleigh B., U.S.A. 107 D11
Ralja, Serbia, Yug. 40 B4
Ralls, U.S.A. 113 J4
Ralston, U.S.A. 110 E8
Ram →, Canada 104 A4
Rām Allāh, West Bank ... 75 D4
Ram Hd., Australia 95 F4
Rama, Nic. 120 D3
Ramacca, Italy 31 E7
Ramakona, India 69 J8
Ramales de la Victoria,
  Spain 34 B7
Raman, Thailand 65 J3
Ramanathapuram, India .. 66 Q11
Ramanetaka, B. de, Madag. 89 A8
Ramanujganj, India 69 H10
Ramat Gan, Israel 75 C3
Ramatlhabama, S. Africa . 88 D4
Ramban, India 69 C6
Rambervillers, France ... 19 D13
Rambipuji, Indonesia ... 63 H15
Rambouillet, France 19 D8
Ramechhap, Nepal 69 F12
Ramenskoye, Russia 46 E10
Ramganga →, India 69 F8
Ramgarh, Bihar, India ... 69 H11
Ramgarh, Raj., India 68 F6
Ramgarh, Raj., India 68 F4
Rāmhormoz, Iran 71 D6
Ramīān, Iran 71 B7
Ramingining, Australia .. 94 A2
Ramla, Israel 75 D3
Ramlu, Eritrea 81 E5

Râmna →, Romania 43 E12
Ramnad =
  Ramanathapuram, India . 66 Q11
Ramnagar,
  Jammu & Kashmir, India 69 C6
Ramnagar, Ut. P., India ... 69 E8
Ramnäs, Sweden 10 E10
Râmnicu Sărat, Romania .. 43 E12
Râmnicu Vâlcea, Romania . 43 E9
Ramon, Russia 47 G10
Ramona, U.S.A. 117 M10
Ramonville-St-Agne, France 20 E5
Ramore, Canada 102 C3
Ramos →, Nigeria 83 D6
Ramotswa, Botswana 88 C4
Rampur, H.P., India 68 D7
Rampur, Mad. P., India .. 68 H5
Rampur, Ut. P., India ... 69 E8
Rampur Hat, India 69 G12
Rampura, India 68 G6
Ramrama Tola, India 69 J8
Ramree I. = Ramree Kyun,
  Burma 67 K19
Ramree Kyun, Burma 67 K19
Râmsar, Iran 71 B6
Ramsey, U.K. 12 C3
Ramsey, U.S.A. 111 E10
Ramsey L., Canada 102 C3
Ramsgate, U.K. 13 F9
Ramsjö, Sweden 10 B9
Ramstein, Germany 25 F3
Ramtek, India 66 J11
Ramvik, Sweden 10 B11
Rana Pratap Sagar Dam,
  India 68 G6
Ranaghat, India 69 H13
Ranahu, Pakistan 68 G3
Ranau, Malaysia 62 C5
Rancagua, Chile 126 C1
Rance →, France 18 D5
Rancheria →, Canada ... 104 A3
Ranchester, U.S.A. 114 D10
Ranchi, India 69 H11
Rancho Cucamonga, U.S.A. 117 L9
Randalstown, U.K. 15 B5
Randan, France 19 F10
Randazzo, Italy 31 E7
Randers, Denmark 11 H4
Randers Fjord, Denmark .. 11 H4
Randfontein, S. Africa ... 89 D4
Randle, U.S.A. 116 D5
Randolph, Mass., U.S.A. . 111 D13
Randolph, N.Y., U.S.A. .. 110 D6
Randolph, Utah, U.S.A. .. 114 F8
Randolph, Vt., U.S.A. ... 111 C12
Randsburg, U.S.A. 117 K9
Råne älv →, Sweden ... 8 D20
Rånea, Thailand 65 J3
Rangae, Thailand 65 J3
Rangaunu B., N.Z. 91 F4
Rangeley, U.S.A. 111 B14
Rangeley L., U.S.A. 111 B14
Rangely, U.S.A. 114 F9
Ranger, U.S.A. 113 J5
Rangia, India 67 F17
Rangiora, N.Z. 91 K4
Rangitaiki →, N.Z. ... 91 G6
Rangitata →, N.Z. 91 K3
Rangkasbitung, Indonesia . 63 G12
Rangon →, Burma 67 L20
Rangoon, Burma 67 L20
Rangpur, Bangla. 67 G16
Rangsit, Thailand 64 F3
Ranibennur, India 66 M9
Raniganj, Ut. P., India ... 69 F9
Raniganj, W. Bengal, India 67 H15
Ranikhet, India 69 E8
Raniwara, India 66 G8
Rāniyah, Iraq 70 B5
Ranka, India 69 H10
Ranken →, Australia ... 94 C2
Rankin, U.S.A. 113 K4
Rankin Inlet, Canada 100 B10
Rankins Springs, Australia 95 E4
Rankweil, Austria 26 D2
Rannoch, L., U.K. 14 E4
Rannoch Moor, U.K. 14 E4
Ranobe, Helodranon' i,
  Madag. 89 C7
Ranohira, Madag. 89 C8
Ranomafana, Toamasina,
  Madag. 89 B8
Ranomafana, Toliara,
  Madag. 89 C8
Ranomena, Madag. 89 C8
Ranong, Thailand 65 H2
Ranotsara Nord, Madag. .. 89 C8
Rānsa, Iran 71 C6
Ransiki, Indonesia 63 E8
Rantabe, Madag. 89 B8
Rantauprapat, Indonesia .. 62 D1
Rantemario, Indonesia ... 63 E5
Rantoul, U.S.A. 108 E1
Ranum, Denmark 11 H3
Ranyah, W. →, Si. Arabia 80 C5
Raon l'Étape, France 19 D13
Raoping, China 59 F11
Raoyang, China 56 E8
Rapa, Pac. Oc. 97 K13
Rapallo, Italy 28 D6
Rapar, India 68 H4
Râpch, Iran 71 E8
Raper, C., Canada 101 B13
Rapid City, U.S.A. 112 D3
Rapid River, U.S.A. 108 C2
Rapla, Estonia 9 G21
Rapti →, India 69 F10
Rapu Rapu I., Phil. 61 E6
Raqqa = Ar Raqqah, Syria 70 C3
Raqaba ez Zarqa →, Sudan 81 F2
Raquette →, U.S.A. ... 111 B10
Raquette Lake, U.S.A. ... 111 C10
Rarotonga, Cook Is. 97 K12

Ra's al 'Ayn, Syria 70 B4
Ra's al Khaymah, U.A.E. .. 71 E7
Râs el Mâ, Mali 82 B4
Ras Ghârib, Egypt 80 B3
Ras Mallap, Egypt 80 B3
Râs Timirist, Mauritania .. 82 B1
Rasa, Pta. de la, Canary Is. 37 G3
Rāscani, Moldova 43 C12
Raseiniai, Lithuania 9 J20
Rashad, Sudan 81 E3
Rashîd, Egypt 80 H7
Rashîd, Masabb, Egypt ... 80 H7
Rashmi, India 68 G6
Rasht, Iran 71 B6
Rasi Salai, Thailand 64 E5
Raška, Serbia, Yug. 40 C4
Rason L., Australia 93 E3
Raşova, Romania 43 F12
Rasovo, Bulgaria 40 C7
Rasra, India 69 G10
Rast, Romania 43 G8
Rasskazovo, Russia 48 D5
Rast, Romania 43 G8
Rastatt, Germany 25 G4
Rastede, Germany 24 B4
Răstolita, Romania 43 D9
Rasul, Pakistan 68 C5
Raszków, Poland 45 G4
Rat Buri, Thailand 64 F2
Rat Islands, U.S.A. 100 C1
Rat L., Canada 105 B9
Ratangarh, India 68 E6
Rātansbyn, Sweden 10 B8
Raṭāwī, Iraq 70 D5
Rath, India 69 G8
Rath Luirc, Ireland 15 D3
Rathdrum, Ireland 15 D5
Rathenow, Germany 24 C8
Rathkeale, Ireland 15 D3
Rathlin I., U.K. 15 A5
Rathmelton, Ireland 15 A4
Ratibor = Racibórz, Poland 45 H5
Rätikon, Austria 26 D2
Ratingen, Germany 24 D2
Ratlam, India 68 H6
Ratnagiri, India 66 L8
Ratodero, Pakistan 68 F3
Raton, U.S.A. 113 G2
Rattaphum, Thailand ... 65 J3
Ratten, Austria 26 D8
Rattray Hd., U.K. 14 D7
Rättvik, Sweden 10 D9
Ratz, Mt., Canada 104 B2
Ratzeburg, Germany 24 B6
Raub, Malaysia 65 L3
Rauch, Argentina 126 D4
Raudales de Malpaso,
  Mexico 119 D6
Raufarhöfn, Iceland 8 C6
Raufoss, Norway 9 F14
Raukumara Ra., N.Z. ... 91 H6
Rauma, Finland 9 F19
Raurkela, India 69 H11
Rausu-Dake, Japan 54 B12
Răut →, Moldova 43 C14
Rava-Ruska, Poland 47 G2
Rava Russkaya = Rava-
  Ruska, Poland 47 G2
Ravalli, U.S.A. 114 C6
Ravānsar, Iran 70 C5
Ravanusa, Italy 30 E6
Rāvar, Iran 71 D8
Ravena, U.S.A. 111 D11
Ravenna, Italy 29 D9
Ravenna, Nebr., U.S.A. .. 112 E5
Ravenna, Ohio, U.S.A. .. 110 E3
Ravensburg, Germany ... 25 H5
Ravenshoe, Australia ... 94 B4
Ravensthorpe, Australia . 93 F3
Ravenswood, Australia .. 94 C4
Ravenswood, U.S.A. 108 F5
Ravi →, Pakistan 68 D4
Ravna Gora, Croatia 29 C11
Ravna Reka, Serbia, Yug. . 40 B5
Ravne na Koroškem,
  Slovenia 29 B11
Rawa Mazowiecka, Poland 45 G7
Rawalpindi, Pakistan ... 68 C5
Rawāndūz, Iraq 70 B5
Rawang, Malaysia 65 L3
Rawene, N.Z. 91 F4
Rawicz, Poland 45 G3
Rawka →, Poland 45 F7
Rawlina, Australia 93 F4
Rawlins, U.S.A. 114 F10
Rawlinson Ra., Australia . 93 D4
Rawson, Argentina 128 E3
Raxaul, India 69 F11
Ray, U.S.A. 112 A3
Ray, C., Canada 103 C8
Rayadurg, India 66 M10
Rayagada, India 67 K13
Raychikhinsk, Russia ... 51 E13
Rāyen, Iran 71 D8
Rayleigh, U.K. 13 F8
Raymond, Canada 104 D6
Raymond, Calif., U.S.A. . 116 H7
Raymond, N.H., U.S.A. .. 111 C13
Raymond, Wash., U.S.A. . 116 D3
Raymond Terrace, Australia 95 E5
Raymondville, U.S.A. ... 113 M6
Raymore, Canada 105 C8
Rayón, Mexico 118 B2
Rayong, Thailand 64 F3
Rayville, U.S.A. 113 J9
Raz, Pte. du, France 18 D2
Razan, Iran 71 C6
Ražana, Serbia, Yug. ... 40 B3
Ražanj, Serbia, Yug. 40 C5
Razdelna, Bulgaria 41 C11

Razdel'naya = Rozdilna,
  Ukraine 47 J6
Razdolnoye, Russia 54 C5
Razdolnoye, Ukraine 47 K7
Razeh, Iran 71 C6
Razgrad, Bulgaria 41 C10
Razim, Lacul, Romania .. 43 F14
Razlog, Bulgaria 40 E7
Razmak, Pakistan 68 C3
Ré, Î. de, France 20 B2
Reading, U.K. 13 F7
Reading, U.S.A. 111 F9
Reading □, U.K. 13 F7
Realicó, Argentina 126 D3
Réalmont, France 20 E6
Ream, Cambodia 65 G4
Reata, Mexico 118 B4
Reay Forest, U.K. 14 C4
Rebais, France 19 D10
Rebi, Indonesia 63 F8
Rebiana, Libya 79 D10
Rebun-Tō, Japan 54 B10
Recanati, Italy 29 E10
Recaş, Romania 42 E6
Recco, Italy 28 D6
Recherche, Arch. of the,
  Australia 93 F3
Rechna Doab, Pakistan .. 68 D5
Rechytsa, Belarus 47 F6
Recife, Brazil 125 E12
Recklinghausen, Germany . 17 C7
Reconquista, Argentina ... 126 B4
Recreo, Argentina 126 B2
Recz, Poland 45 E2
Red →, La., U.S.A. 113 K9
Red →, N. Dak., U.S.A. 100 C10
Red Bank, U.S.A. 111 F10
Red Bay, Canada 103 B8
Red Bluff, U.S.A. 114 F2
Red Bluff L., U.S.A. ... 113 K3
Red Cliffs, Australia ... 95 E3
Red Cloud, U.S.A. 112 E5
Red Creek, U.S.A. 111 C8
Red Deer, Canada 104 C6
Red Deer →, Alta., Canada 105 C7
Red Deer →, Man., Canada 105 C8
Red Deer L., Canada 105 C8
Red Hook, U.S.A. 111 E11
Red Indian L., Canada ... 103 C8
Red L., Canada 105 C10
Red Lake, Canada 105 C10
Red Lake Falls, U.S.A. .. 112 B6
Red Lake Road, Canada .. 105 C10
Red Lodge, U.S.A. 114 D9
Red Mountain, U.S.A. ... 117 K9
Red Oak, U.S.A. 112 E7
Red Rock, Canada 102 C2
Red Rock, L., U.S.A. ... 112 E8
Red Rocks Pt., Australia . 93 F4
Red Sea, Asia 74 C2
Red Slate Mt., U.S.A. ... 116 H8
Red Sucker L., Canada ... 102 B1
Red Tower Pass = Turnu
  Roşu, P., Romania 43 E9
Red Wing, U.S.A. 112 C8
Reda, Poland 44 D5
Redang, Malaysia 62 C2
Redange, Lux. 17 E5
Redcar, U.K. 12 C6
Redcar & Cleveland □, U.K. 12 C7
Redcliff, Canada 105 C6
Redcliffe, Australia 95 D5
Redcliffe, Mt., Australia .. 93 E3
Reddersburg, S. Africa ... 88 D4
Redding, U.S.A. 114 F2
Redditch, U.K. 13 E6
Redfield, U.S.A. 112 C5
Redford, U.S.A. 111 B11
Redkino, Russia 46 D9
Redlands, U.S.A. 117 M9
Redmond, Oreg., U.S.A. . 114 D3
Redmond, Wash., U.S.A. . 116 C4
Redon, France 18 E4
Redonda, Antigua 121 C7
Redondela, Spain 34 C2
Redondo, Portugal 35 G3
Redondo Beach, U.S.A. .. 117 M8
Redruth, U.K. 13 G2
Redvers, Canada 105 D8
Redwater, Canada 104 C6
Redwood, U.S.A. 111 B9
Redwood City, U.S.A. ... 116 H4
Redwood Falls, U.S.A. ... 112 C7
Redwood National Park,
  U.S.A. 114 F1
Ree, L., Ireland 15 C3
Reed, L., Canada 105 C8
Reed City, U.S.A. 108 D3
Reedley, U.S.A. 116 J7
Reedsburg, U.S.A. 112 D9
Reedsport, U.S.A. 114 E1
Reedsville, U.S.A. 110 F7
Reefton, N.Z. 91 K3
Rees, Germany 24 D2
Reese →, U.S.A. 114 F5
Refahiye, Turkey 73 C8
Reftele, Sweden 11 G7
Refugio, U.S.A. 113 L6
Rega →, Poland 44 D2
Regalbuto, Italy 31 E7
Regen, Germany 25 G9
Regen →, Germany 25 F8
Regensburg, Germany ... 25 F8
Regenstauf, Germany ... 25 F8
Reggello, Italy 29 E8
Réggio di Calábria, Italy . 31 D8
Réggio nell'Emília, Italy .. 28 D7
Reghin, Romania 43 D9
Regina, Canada 105 C8
Regina Beach, Canada ... 105 C8
Registro, Brazil 127 A6

Reguengos de Monsaraz,
  Portugal 35 G3
Rehar →, India 69 H10
Rehli, India 69 H8
Rehoboth, Namibia 88 C2
Rehovot, Israel 75 D3
Reichenbach, Germany ... 24 E8
Reid, Australia 93 F4
Reidsville, U.S.A. 109 G6
Reigate, U.K. 13 F7
Reillo, Spain 32 F3
Reims, France 19 C11
Reina Adelaida, Arch., Chile 128 G2
Reinbek, Germany 24 B6
Reindeer →, Canada ... 105 B8
Reindeer I., Canada 105 C9
Reindeer L., Canada 105 B8
Reinga, C., N.Z. 91 F4
Reinosa, Spain 34 B6
Reitz, S. Africa 89 D4
Reivilo, S. Africa 88 D3
Rejaf, Sudan 81 G3
Rejmyre, Sweden 11 F9
Rejowiec Fabryczny, Poland 45 G10
Reka →, Slovenia 29 C11
Rekovac, Serbia, Yug. ... 40 C5
Reliance, Canada 105 A7
Rémalard, France 18 D7
Remarkable, Mt., Australia 95 E2
Rembang, Indonesia 63 G14
Remedios, Panama 120 E3
Remeshk, Iran 71 E8
Remetea, Romania 43 D10
Remich, Lux. 17 E6
Remiremont, France 19 D13
Remo, Ethiopia 81 F5
Remontnoye, Russia 49 G6
Remoulins, France 21 E8
Remscheid, Germany ... 17 C7
Ren Xian, China 56 F8
Rende, Italy 31 C9
Rendína, Greece 38 B3
Rendsburg, Germany ... 24 A5
Renfrew, Canada 102 C4
Renfrewshire □, U.K. ... 14 F4
Rengat, Indonesia 62 E2
Rengo, Chile 126 C1
Renhua, China 59 E9
Renhuai, China 58 D6
Reni, Ukraine 47 K5
Renk, Sudan 81 E3
Renmark, Australia 95 E3
Rennell Sd., Canada 104 C2
Renner Springs, Australia . 94 B1
Rennes, France 18 D5
Rennie L., Canada 105 A7
Reno, U.S.A. 116 F7
Reno →, Italy 29 D9
Renovo, U.S.A. 110 E7
Renqiu, China 56 E9
Rens, Denmark 11 K3
Renshou, China 58 C5
Rensselaer, Ind., U.S.A. .. 108 E2
Rensselaer, N.Y., U.S.A. . 111 D11
Rentería, Spain 32 B3
Renton, U.S.A. 116 C4
Réo, Burkina Faso 82 C4
Reocín, Spain 34 B6
Reotipur, India 69 G10
Répcelak, Hungary 42 C2
Republic, Mo., U.S.A. ... 113 G8
Republic, Wash., U.S.A. . 114 B4
Republican →, U.S.A. .. 112 F6
Repulse Bay, Canada 101 B11
Requena, Peru 124 E4
Requena, Spain 33 F3
Réquista, France 20 D6
Reşadiye = Datça, Turkey . 39 E9
Reşadiye, Turkey 72 B7
Reşadiye Yarımadası, Turkey 39 E9
Resavica, Serbia, Yug. ... 40 B5
Resen, Macedonia 40 E5
Reserve, U.S.A. 115 K9
Resht = Rasht, Iran 71 B6
Resistencia, Argentina ... 126 B4
Reşiţa, Romania 42 E6
Resko, Poland 44 E2
Resolution I., Canada ... 101 B13
Resolution I., N.Z. 91 L1
Ressano Garcia, Mozam. . 89 D5
Reston, Canada 105 D8
Reszel, Poland 44 D8
Retalhuleu, Guatemala ... 120 D1
Retenue, L. de,
  Dem. Rep. of the Congo . 87 E2
Retezat, Munţii, Romania .. 42 E8
Retford, U.K. 12 D7
Rethel, France 19 C11
Rethem, Germany 24 C5
Réthímnon, Greece 36 D6
Réthímnon □, Greece ... 36 D6
Reti, Pakistan 68 E3
Retiche, Alpi, Switz. 25 J6
Retiers, France 18 E5
Retortillo, Spain 34 E4
Retournac, France 21 C8
Rétság, Hungary 42 C4
Réunion ■, Ind. Oc. 77 J9
Reus, Spain 32 D6
Reuterstadt Stavenhagen,
  Germany 24 B8
Reutlingen, Germany ... 25 G5
Reutte, Austria 26 D3
Reval = Tallinn, Estonia . 9 G21
Revel, France 20 E6
Revelganj, India 69 G11
Revelstoke, Canada 104 C5
Reventazón, Peru 124 E2
Revigny-sur-Ornain, France 19 D11
Revillagigedo, Is. de,
  Pac. Oc. 118 D2

Revin, France 19 C11
Revúca, Slovak Rep. 27 C13
Revuè →, Mozam. 87 F3
Rewa, India 69 G9
Rewari, India 68 E7
Rexburg, U.S.A. 114 E8
Rey, Iran 71 C6
Rey, I. del, Panama 120 E4
Rey, Rio del →, Nigeria 83 E6
Rey Malabo, Eq. Guin. 83 E6
Reyðarfjörður, Iceland 8 D6
Reyes, Pt., U.S.A. 116 H3
Reyhanlı, Turkey 72 D7
Reykjahlið, Iceland 8 D5
Reykjanes, Iceland 8 E2
Reykjavík, Iceland 8 D3
Reynolds Ra., Australia 92 D5
Reynoldsville, U.S.A. 110 E6
Reynosa, Mexico 119 B5
Rēzekne, Latvia 9 H22
Rezina, Moldova 43 C13
Rezovo, Bulgaria 41 D12
Rezvān, Iran 71 E8
Rgotina, Serbia, Yug. 40 B6
Rhamnus, Greece 38 C6
Rhayader, U.K. 13 E4
Rheda-Wiedenbrück, Germany 24 D4
Rhede, Germany 24 D2
Rhein →, Europe 17 C6
Rhein-Main-Donau-Kanal, Germany 25 F7
Rheinbach, Germany 24 E2
Rheine, Germany 24 C3
Rheinfelden, Germany 25 H3
Rheinhessen-Pfalz □, Germany 25 F3
Rheinland-Pfalz □, Germany 25 F3
Rheinsberg, Germany 24 B8
Rhin = Rhein →, Europe 17 C6
Rhine = Rhein →, Europe 17 C6
Rhinebeck, U.S.A. 111 E11
Rhineland-Palatinate = Rheinland-Pfalz □, Germany 25 E2
Rhinelander, U.S.A. 112 C10
Rhinns Pt., U.K. 14 F2
Rhino Camp, Uganda 86 B3
Rhir, Cap, Morocco 78 B4
Rho, Italy 28 C6
Rhode Island □, U.S.A. 111 E13
Rhodes = Ródhos, Greece 36 C10
Rhodesia = Zimbabwe ■, Africa 87 F3
Rhodope Mts. = Rhodopi Planina, Bulgaria 41 E8
Rhodopi Planina, Bulgaria 41 E8
Rhön, Germany 24 E5
Rhondda, U.K. 13 F4
Rhondda Cynon Taff □, U.K. 13 F4
Rhône □, France 21 C8
Rhône →, France 21 E8
Rhône-Alpes □, France 21 C9
Rhum, U.K. 14 E2
Rhyl, U.K. 12 D4
Ri-Aba, Eq. Guin. 83 E6
Riachão, Brazil 125 E9
Riangnom, Sudan 81 F3
Riaño, Spain 34 C6
Rians, France 21 E9
Riansáres →, Spain 35 F7
Riasi, India 69 C6
Riau □, Indonesia 62 D2
Riau, Kepulauan, Indonesia 62 D2
Riau Arch. = Riau, Kepulauan, Indonesia 62 D2
Riaza, Spain 34 D7
Riaza →, Spain 34 D7
Riba de Saelices, Spain 32 E2
Riba-Roja de Turia, Spain 33 F4
Ribadavia, Spain 34 C2
Ribadeo, Spain 34 B3
Ribadesella, Spain 34 B5
Ribado, Nigeria 83 D7
Ribao, Cameroon 83 D7
Ribas = Ribes de Freser, Spain 32 C7
Ribas do Rio Pardo, Brazil 125 H8
Ribble →, U.K. 12 D5
Ribe, Denmark 11 J2
Ribe Amtskommune □, Denmark 11 J2
Ribeauville, France 19 D14
Ribécourt-Dreslincourt, France 19 C9
Ribeira = Santa Eugenia, Spain 34 C2
Ribeira Brava, Madeira 37 D2
Ribeirão Prêto, Brazil 127 A6
Ribemont, France 19 C10
Ribera, Italy 30 E6
Ribérac, France 20 C4
Riberalta, Bolivia 124 F5
Ribes de Freser, Spain 32 C7
Ribnica, Slovenia 29 C11
Ribnitz-Damgarten, Germany 24 A8
Ričany, Czech Rep. 26 B7
Riccarton, N.Z. 91 K4
Ríccia, Italy 31 A7
Riccione, Italy 29 D9
Rice, U.S.A. 117 L12
Rice L., U.S.A. 110 B6
Rice Lake, U.S.A. 112 C9
Rich, C., U.S.A. 110 B4
Richard Toll, Senegal 82 B1
Richards Bay, S. Africa 89 D5
Richardson →, Canada 105 B6
Richardson Lakes, U.S.A. 108 C10
Richardson Springs, U.S.A. 116 F5
Riche, C., Australia 93 F2

Richelieu, France 18 E7
Richey, U.S.A. 112 B2
Richfield, U.S.A. 115 G8
Richfield Springs, U.S.A. 111 D10
Richford, U.S.A. 111 B12
Richibucto, Canada 103 C7
Richland, Ga., U.S.A. 109 J3
Richland, Wash., U.S.A. 114 C4
Richland Center, U.S.A. 112 D9
Richlands, U.S.A. 108 G5
Richmond, Australia 94 C3
Richmond, N.Z. 91 J4
Richmond, U.K. 12 C6
Richmond, Calif., U.S.A. 116 H4
Richmond, Ind., U.S.A. 108 F3
Richmond, Ky., U.S.A. 108 G3
Richmond, Mich., U.S.A. 110 D2
Richmond, Mo., U.S.A. 112 F8
Richmond, Tex., U.S.A. 113 L7
Richmond, Utah, U.S.A. 114 F8
Richmond, Va., U.S.A. 108 G7
Richmond, Vt., U.S.A. 111 B12
Richmond Hill, Canada 110 C5
Richmond Ra., Australia 95 D5
Richwood, U.S.A. 108 F5
Ricla, Spain 32 D3
Ridder = Leninogorsk, Kazakstan 50 D9
Riddlesburg, U.S.A. 110 F6
Ridgecrest, U.S.A. 117 K9
Ridgefield, Conn., U.S.A. 111 E11
Ridgefield, Wash., U.S.A. 116 E4
Ridgeland, U.S.A. 109 J5
Ridgetown, Canada 102 D3
Ridgewood, U.S.A. 111 F10
Ridgway, U.S.A. 110 E6
Riding Mountain Nat. Park, Canada 105 C9
Ridley, Mt., Australia 93 F3
Riebeek-Oos, S. Africa 88 E4
Ried, Austria 26 C6
Riedlingen, Germany 25 G5
Riedstadt, Germany 25 F4
Rienza →, Italy 29 B8
Riesa, Germany 24 D9
Riesi, Italy 31 E7
Riet →, S. Africa 88 D3
Rietavas, Lithuania 44 C8
Rietbron, S. Africa 88 E3
Rietfontein, Namibia 88 C3
Rieti, Italy 29 F9
Rieupeyroux, France 20 D6
Riez, France 21 E10
Riffe L., U.S.A. 116 D4
Rifle, U.S.A. 114 G10
Rift Valley □, Kenya 86 B4
Rīga, Latvia 9 H21
Riga, G. of, Latvia 9 H20
Rigacikun, Nigeria 83 C6
Rīgān, Iran 71 D8
Rīgas Jūras Līcis = Riga, G. of, Latvia 9 H20
Rigaud, Canada 111 A10
Rigby, U.S.A. 114 E8
Rīgestān □, Afghan. 66 D4
Riggins, U.S.A. 114 D5
Rignac, France 20 D6
Rigolet, Canada 103 B8
Rihand Dam, India 69 G10
Riihimäki, Finland 9 F21
Riiser-Larsen-halvøya, Antarctica 5 C4
Rijau, Nigeria 83 C6
Rijeka, Croatia 29 C11
Rijeka Crnojevića, Montenegro, Yug. 40 D3
Rijssen, Neths. 17 B6
Rike, Ethiopia 81 E4
Rikuzentakada, Japan 54 E10
Rila, Bulgaria 40 D7
Rila Planina, Bulgaria 40 D7
Riley, U.S.A. 114 E4
Rima →, Nigeria 83 C6
Rimah, Wadi ar →, Si. Arabia 70 E4
Rimavská Sobota, Slovak Rep. 27 C13
Rimbey, Canada 104 C6
Rimbo, Sweden 10 E12
Rimersburg, U.S.A. 110 E5
Rimforsa, Sweden 11 F9
Rimi, Nigeria 83 C6
Rímini, Italy 29 D9
Rimouski, Canada 103 C6
Rimrock, U.S.A. 116 D5
Rinca, Indonesia 63 F5
Rincón de la Victoria, Spain 35 J6
Rincón de Romos, Mexico 118 C4
Rinconada, Argentina 126 A2
Rind →, India 69 G9
Ringarum, Sweden 11 F10
Ringas, India 68 F6
Ringe, Denmark 11 J4
Ringim, Nigeria 83 C6
Ringkøbing, Denmark 11 H2
Ringkøbing Amtskommune □, Denmark 11 H2
Ringkøbing Fjord, Denmark 11 H2
Ringsjön, Sweden 11 J7
Ringsted, Denmark 11 J5
Ringvassøy, Norway 8 B18
Ringwood, U.S.A. 111 E10
Rinía, Greece 39 D7
Rinjani, Indonesia 62 F5
Rinteln, Germany 24 C5
Río, Punta del, Spain 33 J2
Rio Branco, Brazil 124 E5
Río Branco, Uruguay 127 C5
Río Bravo del Norte →, Mexico 119 B5

Rio Brilhante, Brazil 127 A5
Rio Claro, Brazil 127 A6
Rio Claro, Trin. & Tob. 121 D7
Río Colorado, Argentina 128 D4
Río Cuarto, Argentina 126 C3
Rio das Pedras, Mozam. 89 C6
Rio de Janeiro, Brazil 127 A7
Rio de Janeiro □, Brazil 127 A7
Rio do Sul, Brazil 127 B6
Río Gallegos, Argentina 128 G3
Rio Grande = Grande, Rio →, U.S.A. 113 N6
Río Grande, Argentina 128 G3
Rio Grande, Brazil 127 C5
Río Grande, Mexico 118 C4
Río Grande, Nic. 120 D3
Río Grande de Santiago →, Mexico 118 C3
Rio Grande do Norte □, Brazil 125 E11
Rio Grande do Sul □, Brazil 127 C5
Rio Hato, Panama 120 E3
Rio Lagartos, Mexico 119 C7
Rio Largo, Brazil 125 E11
Rio Maior, Portugal 35 F2
Rio Marina, Italy 28 F7
Río Mulatos, Bolivia 124 G5
Río Muni = Mbini □, Eq. Guin. 84 D2
Rio Negro, Brazil 127 B6
Rio Pardo, Brazil 127 C5
Rio Rancho, U.S.A. 115 J10
Río Segundo, Argentina 126 C3
Río Tercero, Argentina 126 C3
Rio Tinto, Portugal 34 D2
Rio Verde, Brazil 125 G8
Río Verde, Mexico 119 C5
Río Vista, U.S.A. 116 G5
Ríobamba, Ecuador 124 D3
Ríohacha, Colombia 124 A4
Riom, France 20 C7
Riom-ès-Montagnes, France 20 C6
Rion-des-Landes, France 20 E3
Rionero in Vúlture, Italy 31 B8
Rioni →, Georgia 49 J5
Ríos, Spain 34 D3
Riosucio, Colombia 124 B3
Riou L., Canada 105 B7
Rioz, France 19 E13
Ripatransone, Italy 29 F10
Ripley, Canada 110 B3
Ripley, Calif., U.S.A. 117 M12
Ripley, N.Y., U.S.A. 110 D5
Ripley, Tenn., U.S.A. 113 H10
Ripley, W. Va., U.S.A. 108 F5
Ripoll, Spain 32 C7
Ripon, U.K. 12 C6
Ripon, Calif., U.S.A. 116 H5
Ripon, Wis., U.S.A. 108 D1
Riposto, Italy 31 E8
Risan, Montenegro, Yug. 40 D2
Riscle, France 20 E3
Rishā', W. ar →, Si. Arabia 70 E5
Rishiri-Tō, Japan 54 B10
Rishon le Ziyyon, Israel 75 D3
Risle →, France 18 C7
Rison, U.S.A. 113 J8
Risør, Norway 9 G13
Rita Blanca Cr. →, U.S.A. 113 H3
Riti, Nigeria 83 D6
Ritter, Mt., U.S.A. 116 H7
Rittman, U.S.A. 110 F3
Ritzville, U.S.A. 114 C4
Riva del Garda, Italy 28 C7
Riva Ligure, Italy 28 E4
Rivadavia, Buenos Aires, Argentina 126 D3
Rivadavia, Mendoza, Argentina 126 C2
Rivadavia, Salta, Argentina 126 A3
Rivadavia, Chile 126 B1
Rivarolo Canavese, Italy 28 C4
Rivas, Nic. 120 D2
Rive-de-Gier, France 21 C8
River Cess, Liberia 82 D3
River Jordan, Canada 116 B2
Rivera, Argentina 126 D3
Rivera, Uruguay 127 C4
Riverbank, U.S.A. 116 H6
Riverdale, U.S.A. 116 J7
Riverhead, U.S.A. 111 F12
Riverhurst, Canada 105 C7
Rivers, Canada 105 C8
Rivers □, Nigeria 83 E6
Rivers Inlet, Canada 104 C3
Riversdale, S. Africa 88 E3
Riverside, U.S.A. 117 M9
Riverton, Australia 95 E2
Riverton, Canada 105 C9
Riverton, N.Z. 91 M2
Riverton, U.S.A. 114 E9
Riverton Heights, U.S.A. 116 C4
Rives, France 21 C9
Rivesaltes, France 20 F6
Riviera, U.S.A. 117 K12
Riviera di Levante, Italy 28 D6
Riviera di Ponente, Italy 28 D5
Rivière-au-Renard, Canada 103 C7
Rivière-du-Loup, Canada 103 C6
Rivière-Pentecôte, Canada 103 C6
Rivière-Pilote, Martinique 121 D7
Rivière St. Paul, Canada 103 B8
Rivne, Ukraine 47 G4
Rívoli, Italy 28 C4
Rivoli B., Australia 95 F3
Rixheim, France 19 E14
Riyadh = Ar Riyāḍ, Si. Arabia 70 E5
Rize, Turkey 73 B9
Rizhao, China 57 G10

Rizokarpaso, Cyprus 36 D13
Rizzuto, C., Italy 31 D10
Rjukan, Norway 9 G13
Ro, Greece 39 E11
Roa, Spain 34 D7
Road Town, Virgin Is. 121 C7
Roan Plateau, U.S.A. 114 G9
Roanne, France 19 F11
Roanoke, Ala., U.S.A. 109 J3
Roanoke, Va., U.S.A. 108 G6
Roanoke →, U.S.A. 109 H7
Roanoke I., U.S.A. 109 H8
Roanoke Rapids, U.S.A. 109 G7
Roatán, Honduras 120 C2
Robāt Sang, Iran 71 C8
Robbins I., Australia 94 G4
Robe →, Australia 92 D2
Robe, Australia 95 F2
Robe →, Australia 92 D2
Röbel, Germany 24 B8
Robert Lee, U.S.A. 113 K4
Robertsdale, U.S.A. 110 F6
Robertsganj, India 69 G10
Robertson, S. Africa 88 E2
Robertson I., Antarctica 5 C18
Robertson Ra., Australia 92 D3
Robertsport, Liberia 82 D2
Robertstown, Australia 95 E2
Roberval, Canada 103 C5
Robeson Chan., Greenland 4 A4
Robesonia, U.S.A. 111 F8
Robi, Ethiopia 81 F4
Robinson, U.S.A. 108 F2
Robinson →, Australia 94 B2
Robinson Ra., Australia 93 E2
Robinvale, Australia 95 E3
Robledo, Spain 33 G2
Roblin, Canada 105 C8
Roboré, Bolivia 124 G7
Robson, Canada 104 D5
Robson, Mt., Canada 104 C5
Robstown, U.S.A. 113 M6
Roca, C. da, Portugal 35 G1
Roca Partida, I., Mexico 118 D2
Rocamadour, France 20 D5
Rocas, I., Brazil 125 D12
Rocca San Casciano, Italy 29 D8
Roccadáspide, Italy 31 B8
Roccastrada, Italy 29 F8
Roccella Iónica, Italy 31 D9
Rocha, Uruguay 127 C5
Rochdale, U.K. 12 D5
Rochechouart, France 20 C4
Rochefort, Belgium 17 D5
Rochefort, France 20 C3
Rochefort-en-Terre, France 18 E4
Rochelle, U.S.A. 112 E10
Rocher River, Canada 104 A6
Rochervière, France 18 F5
Rochester, U.K. 13 F8
Rochester, Ind., U.S.A. 108 E2
Rochester, Minn., U.S.A. 112 C8
Rochester, N.H., U.S.A. 111 C14
Rochester, N.Y., U.S.A. 110 C7
Rociu, Romania 43 F10
Rock →, Canada 104 A3
Rock Creek, U.S.A. 110 E4
Rock Falls, U.S.A. 112 E10
Rock Hill, U.S.A. 109 H5
Rock Island, U.S.A. 112 E9
Rock Rapids, U.S.A. 112 D6
Rock Sound, Bahamas 120 B4
Rock Springs, Mont., U.S.A. 114 C10
Rock Springs, Wyo., U.S.A. 114 F9
Rock Valley, U.S.A. 112 D6
Rockall, Atl. Oc. 6 D3
Rockdale, Tex., U.S.A. 113 K6
Rockdale, Wash., U.S.A. 116 C5
Rockefeller Plateau, Antarctica 5 E14
Rockford, U.S.A. 112 D10
Rockglen, Canada 105 D7
Rockhampton, Australia 94 C5
Rockingham, Australia 93 F2
Rockingham, U.S.A. 109 H6
Rockingham B., Australia 94 B4
Rocklake, U.S.A. 112 A5
Rockland, Canada 111 A9
Rockland, Idaho, U.S.A. 114 E7
Rockland, Maine, U.S.A. 109 C11
Rockland, Mich., U.S.A. 112 B10
Rocklin, U.S.A. 116 G5
Rockport, Mass., U.S.A. 111 D14
Rockport, Mo., U.S.A. 112 E7
Rockport, Tex., U.S.A. 113 L6
Rocksprings, U.S.A. 113 K4
Rockville, Conn., U.S.A. 111 E12
Rockville, Md., U.S.A. 108 F7
Rockwall, U.S.A. 113 J6
Rockwell City, U.S.A. 112 D7
Rockwood, Canada 110 C4
Rockwood, Maine, U.S.A. 109 C11
Rockwood, Tenn., U.S.A. 109 H3
Rocky Ford, U.S.A. 112 F3
Rocky Gully, Australia 93 F2
Rocky Harbour, Canada 103 C8
Rocky Island L., Canada 102 C3
Rocky Lane, Canada 104 B5
Rocky Mount, U.S.A. 109 H7
Rocky Mountain House, Canada 104 C6
Rocky Mountain National Park, U.S.A. 114 F11
Rocky Mts., N. Amer. 114 G10
Rocky Point, Namibia 88 B2
Rocroi, France 19 C11
Rod, Pakistan 66 E3
Rødby, Denmark 11 K5
Rødbyhavn, Denmark 11 K5
Roddickton, Canada 103 B8
Rødding, Denmark 11 J3

Rödeby, Sweden 11 H9
Rødekro, Denmark 11 J3
Rodenkirchen, Germany 24 B4
Rodez, France 20 D6
Rodholívos, Greece 40 F7
Rodhópi □, Greece 41 E9
Rodhopoú, Greece 36 D5
Ródhos, Greece 36 C10
Rodi Gargánico, Italy 29 G12
Rodna, Romania 43 C9
Rodnei, Munţii, Romania 43 C9
Rodney, Canada 110 D3
Rodney, C., N.Z. 91 G5
Rodniki, Russia 48 B5
Rodonit, Kepi i, Albania 40 E3
Rodriguez, Ind. Oc. 3 E13
Roe →, U.K. 15 A5
Roebling, U.S.A. 111 F10
Roebourne, Australia 92 D2
Roebuck B., Australia 92 C3
Roermond, Neths. 17 C6
Roes Welcome Sd., Canada 101 B11
Roeselare, Belgium 17 D3
Rogachev = Ragachow, Belarus 47 F6
Rogačica, Serbia, Yug. 40 B3
Rogagua, L., Bolivia 124 F5
Rogaška Slatina, Slovenia 29 B12
Rogatec, Slovenia 29 B12
Rogatica, Bos.-H. 42 G4
Rogatyn, Ukraine 47 H3
Rogdhia, Greece 36 D7
Rogers, U.S.A. 113 G7
Rogers City, U.S.A. 108 C4
Rogersville, Canada 103 C6
Roggan →, Canada 102 B4
Roggan L., Canada 102 B4
Roggeveldberge, S. Africa 88 E3
Roggiano Gravina, Italy 31 C9
Rogliano, France 21 F13
Rogliano, Italy 31 C9
Rogoaguado, L., Bolivia 124 F5
Rogoźno, Poland 45 F3
Rogue →, U.S.A. 114 E1
Rohan, France 18 D4
Rohda, Greece 36 A3
Rohnert Park, U.S.A. 116 G4
Rohri, Pakistan 68 F3
Rohri Canal, Pakistan 68 F3
Rohtak, India 68 E7
Roi Et, Thailand 64 D4
Roja, Latvia 9 H20
Rojas, Argentina 126 C3
Rojiste, Romania 43 F8
Rojo, C., Mexico 119 C5
Rokan →, Indonesia 62 D2
Rokel →, S. Leone 82 D2
Rokiškis, Lithuania 9 J21
Rokitno, Russia 47 G8
Rokycany, Czech Rep. 26 B6
Rolândia, Brazil 127 A5
Rolla, U.S.A. 113 G9
Rolleston, Australia 94 C4
Rollingstone, Australia 94 B4
Rom, Sudan 81 F3
Roma, Australia 95 D4
Roma, Italy 29 G9
Roma, Sweden 11 G12
Roma, U.S.A. 113 M5
Romain C., U.S.A. 109 J6
Romaine, Canada 103 B7
Romaine →, Canada 103 B7
Roman, Bulgaria 40 C7
Roman, Romania 43 D11
Roman-Kosh, Gora, Ukraine 47 K8
Romanche →, France 21 C9
Romang, Indonesia 63 F7
Români, Egypt 75 E1
Romania ■, Europe 43 D10
Romanija, Bos.-H. 42 G3
Romano, Cayo, Cuba 120 B4
Romanovka = Basarabeasca, Moldova 43 D13
Romans-sur-Isère, France 21 C9
Romanshorn, Switz. 25 H5
Rombari, Sudan 81 G3
Romblon, Phil. 61 E5
Rome = Roma, Italy 29 G9
Rome, Ga., U.S.A. 109 H3
Rome, N.Y., U.S.A. 111 C9
Rome, Pa., U.S.A. 111 E8
Rometta, Italy 31 D8
Romilly-sur-Seine, France 19 D10
Romney, U.S.A. 108 F6
Romney Marsh, U.K. 13 F8
Romny, Ukraine 47 G7
Rømø, Denmark 11 J2
Romodan, Ukraine 47 G7
Romodanovo, Russia 48 C7
Romont, Switz. 25 J2
Romorantin-Lanthenay, France 19 E8
Romsdalen, Norway 9 E12
Romsey, U.K. 13 G6
Ron, Vietnam 64 D6
Rona, U.K. 14 D3
Ronan, U.S.A. 114 C6
Roncador, Serra do, Brazil 125 F8
Ronciglione, Italy 29 F9
Ronco →, Italy 29 D9
Ronda, Spain 35 J5
Ronda, Serranía de, Spain 35 J5
Rondane, Norway 9 F13
Rondônia □, Brazil 124 F6
Rondonópolis, Brazil 125 G8
Rong, Koh, Cambodia 65 G4
Rong Jiang →, China 58 E7
Rong Xian, Guangxi Zhuangzu, China 59 F8
Rong Xian, Sichuan, China 58 C5

Rong'an, China 58 E7
Rongchang, China 58 C5
Ronge, L. la, Canada 105 B7
Rongjiang, China 58 E7
Rongshui, China 58 E7
Rønne, Denmark 11 J8
Ronne Ice Shelf, Antarctica . 5 D18
Ronneby, Sweden 11 H9
Ronnebyån →, Sweden 11 H9
Rönneshyttan, Sweden 11 F9
Ronsard, L., Australia 93 E1
Ronse, Belgium 17 D3
Roodepoort, S. Africa 89 D4
Roof Butte, U.S.A. 115 H9
Rooiboklaagte →, Namibia . 88 C3
Roorkee, India 68 E7
Roosendaal, Neths. 17 C4
Roosevelt, U.S.A. 114 F8
Roosevelt →, Brazil 122 D4
Roosevelt, Mt., Canada . . . 104 B3
Roosevelt I., Antarctica 5 D12
Ropczyce, Poland 45 H8
Roper →, Australia 94 A2
Roper Bar, Australia 94 A1
Roque Pérez, Argentina . . . 126 D4
Roquefort, France 20 D3
Roquemaure, France 21 D8
Roquetas de Mar, Spain . . . 33 J2
Roquetes, Spain 32 E5
Roquevaire, France 21 E9
Roraima □, Brazil 124 C6
Roraima, Mt., Venezuela . . 122 C4
Røros, Norway 9 E14
Rorschach, Switz. 25 H5
Rosa, Zambia 87 D3
Rosa, L., Bahamas 121 B5
Rosa, Monte, Italy 28 C4
Rosal de la Frontera, Spain . 35 H3
Rosalia, U.S.A. 114 C5
Rosamond, U.S.A. 117 L8
Rosans, France 21 D9
Rosario, Argentina 126 C3
Rosário, Brazil 125 D10
Rosario, Baja Calif., Mexico 118 B1
Rosario, Sinaloa, Mexico . . 118 C3
Rosario, Paraguay 126 A4
Rosario de la Frontera,
  Argentina 126 B3
Rosario de Lerma, Argentina 126 A2
Rosario del Tala, Argentina 126 C4
Rosário do Sul, Brazil 127 C5
Rosarito, Mexico 117 N9
Rosarno, Italy 31 D8
Rosas = Roses, Spain 32 C8
Roscoe, U.S.A. 111 E10
Roscoff, France 18 D3
Roscommon, Ireland 15 C3
Roscommon □, Ireland 15 C3
Roscrea, Ireland 15 D4
Rose →, Australia 94 A2
Rose Blanche, Canada 103 C8
Rose Pt., Canada 104 C2
Rose Valley, Canada 105 C8
Roseau, Domin. 121 C7
Roseau, U.S.A. 112 A7
Rosebery, Australia 94 G4
Rosebud, S. Dak., U.S.A. . . 112 D4
Rosebud, Tex., U.S.A. 113 K6
Roseburg, U.S.A. 114 E2
Rosedale, U.S.A. 113 J9
Roseland, U.S.A. 116 G4
Rosemary, Canada 104 C6
Rosenberg, U.S.A. 113 L7
Rosendaël, France 19 A9
Rosenheim, Germany 25 H8
Roses, Spain 32 C8
Roses, G. de, Spain 32 C8
Roseto degli Abruzzi, Italy . 29 F11
Rosetown, Canada 105 C7
Rosetta = Rashîd, Egypt . . . 80 H7
Roseville, Calif., U.S.A. . . . 116 G5
Roseville, Mich., U.S.A. . . . 110 D2
Rosewood, Australia 95 D5
Roshkhvār, Iran 71 C8
Rosières-en-Santerre, France 19 C9
Rosignano Marittimo, Italy . 28 E7
Rosignol, Guyana 124 B7
Roșiori de Vede, Romania . . 43 F10
Rositsa, Bulgaria 41 C11
Rositsa →, Bulgaria 41 C9
Roskilde, Denmark 11 J6
Roskilde Amtskommune □,
  Denmark 11 J6
Roskovec, Albania 40 F3
Roslavl, Russia 46 F7
Rosmaninhal, Portugal 34 F3
Rosmead, S. Africa 88 E4
Røsnæs, Denmark 11 J4
Rosolini, Italy 31 F7
Rosporden, France 18 E3
Ross, Australia 94 G4
Ross, N.Z. 91 K3
Ross Béthio, Mauritania . . . 82 B1
Ross I., Antarctica 5 D11
Ross Ice Shelf, Antarctica . . 5 E12
Ross-on-Wye, U.K. 13 F5
Ross River, Australia 94 C1
Ross River, Canada 104 A2
Ross Sea, Antarctica 5 D11
Rossall Pt., U.K. 12 D4
Rossano, Italy 31 C9
Rossburn, Canada 105 C8
Rosseau, Canada 110 A5
Rosseau L., Canada 110 A5
Rosses, The, Ireland 15 A3
Rossignol, L., Canada 102 B5
Rossignol Res., Canada . . . 103 D6
Rossland, Canada 104 D5
Rosslare, Ireland 15 D5

Rosslau, Germany 24 D8
Rosso, Mauritania 82 B1
Rosso, C., France 21 F12
Rossosh, Russia 47 G10
Røssvatnet, Norway 8 D16
Røst, Norway 8 C15
Rosthern, Canada 105 C7
Rostock, Germany 24 A8
Rostov, Don, Russia 47 J10
Rostov, Yaroslavl, Russia . . 46 D10
Rostrenen, France 18 D3
Roswell, Ga., U.S.A. 109 H3
Roswell, N. Mex., U.S.A. . . 113 J2
Rota, Spain 35 J4
Rotan, U.S.A. 113 J4
Rotenburg, Hessen, Germany 24 E5
Rotenburg, Niedersachsen,
  Germany 24 B5
Roth, Germany 25 F7
Rothaargebirge, Germany . . 24 D4
Rothenburg ob der Tauber,
  Germany 25 F6
Rother →, U.K. 13 G8
Rotherham, U.K. 12 D6
Rothes, U.K. 14 D5
Rothesay, Canada 103 C6
Rothesay, U.K. 14 F3
Roti, Indonesia 63 F6
Rotja, Pta., Spain 33 G6
Roto, Australia 95 E4
Rotoroa, L., N.Z. 91 J4
Rotorua, N.Z. 91 H6
Rotorua, L., N.Z. 91 H6
Rott →, Germany 25 G9
Rottenburg, Germany 25 G4
Rottenmann, Austria 26 D7
Rotterdam, Neths. 17 C4
Rotterdam, U.S.A. 111 D10
Rottne, Sweden 11 G8
Rottnest I., Australia 93 F2
Rottumeroog, Neths. 17 A6
Rottweil, Germany 25 G4
Rotuma, Fiji 96 J9
Roubaix, France 19 B10
Roudnice nad Labem,
  Czech Rep. 26 A7
Rouen, France 18 C8
Rouergue, France 20 D5
Rouillac, France 20 C3
Rouleau, Canada 105 C8
Round Mountain, U.S.A. . . 114 G5
Round Mt., Australia 95 E5
Round Rock, U.S.A. 113 K6
Roundup, U.S.A. 114 C9
Rousay, U.K. 14 B5
Rouses Point, U.S.A. 111 B11
Rouseville, U.S.A. 110 E5
Roussillon, Isère, France . . . 21 C8
Roussillon, Pyrénées-Or.,
  France 20 F6
Rouxville, S. Africa 88 E4
Rouyn-Noranda, Canada . . 102 C4
Rovaniemi, Finland 8 C21
Rovato, Italy 28 C7
Rovenki, Ukraine 47 H10
Rovereto, Italy 28 C8
Rovigo, Italy 29 C8
Rovinj, Croatia 29 C10
Rovno = Rivne, Ukraine . . . 47 G4
Rovnoye, Russia 48 E8
Rovuma = Ruvuma →,
  Tanzania 87 E5
Row'ān, Iran 71 C6
Rowena, Australia 95 D4
Rowley Shoals, Australia . . . 92 C2
Roxa, Guinea-Biss. 82 C1
Roxas, Capiz, Phil. 61 F5
Roxas, Isabela, Phil. 61 C4
Roxas, Mind. Or., Phil. 61 E4
Roxboro, U.S.A. 109 G6
Roxburgh, N.Z. 91 L2
Roxbury, U.S.A. 110 F7
Roxen, Sweden 11 F9
Roy, Mont., U.S.A. 114 C9
Roy, N. Mex., U.S.A. 113 H2
Roy, Utah, U.S.A. 114 F7
Royal Canal, Ireland 15 C4
Royal Leamington Spa, U.K. 13 E6
Royal Tunbridge Wells, U.K. 13 F8
Royan, France 20 C2
Roye, France 19 C9
Royston, U.K. 13 E7
Rožaj, Montenegro, Yug. . . . 40 D4
Różan, Poland 45 F8
Rozay-en-Brie, France 19 D9
Rozdilna, Ukraine 47 J6
Rozhyshche, Ukraine 47 G3
Rožmitál pod Třemšínem,
  Czech Rep. 26 B6
Rožňava, Slovak Rep. 27 C13
Rozogi, Poland 44 E8
Rozoy-sur-Serre, France . . . 19 C11
Rozzano, Italy 28 C6
Rrësheni, Albania 40 E3
Rrogozhina, Albania 40 E3
Rtanj, Serbia, Yug. 40 C5
Rtishchevo, Russia 48 D6
Rúa, Caná, Angola 88 B1
Rúa = A Rúa, Spain 34 C3
Ruacana, Angola 88 B1
Ruahine Ra., N.Z. 91 H6
Ruapehu, N.Z. 91 H5
Ruapuke I., N.Z. 91 M2
Ruaha, W. →, Si. Arabia . . . 75 F2
Rub' al Khālī, Si. Arabia . . . 74 D4
Rubeho Mts., Tanzania 86 D4
Rubezhnoye = Rubizhne,
  Ukraine 47 H10
Rubh a' Mhail, U.K. 14 F2
Rubha Hunish, U.K. 14 D2
Rubha Robhanais = Lewis,
  Butt of, U.K. 14 C2

Rubi, Spain 32 D7
Rubicon →, U.S.A. 116 G5
Rubicone →, Italy 29 D9
Rubik, Albania 40 E3
Rubino, Ivory C. 82 D4
Rubio, Venezuela 124 B4
Rubizhne, Ukraine 47 H10
Ruby L., U.S.A. 114 F6
Ruby Mts., U.S.A. 114 F6
Rubyvale, Australia 94 C4
Rucheng, China 59 E9
Ruciane-Nida, Poland 44 E8
Rūd Sar, Iran 71 B6
Ruda, Sweden 11 G10
Ruda Śląska, Poland 45 H5
Rudall, Australia 95 E2
Rudall →, Australia 92 D3
Rüdersdorf, Germany 24 C9
Rudewa, Tanzania 87 E3
Rudkøbing, Denmark 11 K4
Rudna, Poland 45 G3
Rudnik, Bulgaria 41 D11
Rudnik, Poland 45 H9
Rudnik, Serbia, Yug. 40 B4
Rudnya, Russia 46 E6
Rudnyy, Kazakstan 50 D7
Rudo, Bos.-H. 42 G4
Rudolfa, Ostrov, Russia . . . 50 A6
Rudolstadt, Germany 24 E7
Rudong, China 59 A13
Rudozem, Bulgaria 41 E8
Rudyard, U.S.A. 108 B3
Rue, France 19 B8
Rufa'a, Sudan 81 E3
Rufiji →, Tanzania 86 D4
Rufino, Argentina 126 C3
Rufisque, Senegal 82 C1
Rufunsa, Zambia 87 F2
Rugao, China 59 A13
Rugby, U.K. 13 E6
Rugby, U.S.A. 112 A5
Rügen, Germany 24 A9
Rugles, France 18 D7
Ruhengeri, Rwanda 86 C2
Ruhla, Germany 24 E6
Ruhland, Germany 24 D9
Ruhnu, Estonia 9 H20
Ruhr →, Germany 24 D2
Ruhuhu →, Tanzania 87 E3
Rui'an, China 59 D13
Ruichang, China 59 C10
Ruidoso, U.S.A. 115 K11
Ruijin, China 59 E10
Ruili, China 58 E1
Ruivo, Pico, Madeira 37 D3
Ruj, Bulgaria 40 D6
Rujen, Macedonia 40 D6
Rujm Tal'at al Jamā'ah,
  Jordan 75 E4
Ruk, Pakistan 68 F3
Rukhla, Pakistan 68 C4
Ruki →,
  Dem. Rep. of the Congo . 84 E3
Rukwa □, Tanzania 86 D3
Rukwa, L., Tanzania 86 D3
Rulhieres, C., Australia 92 B4
Rum = Rhum, U.K. 14 E2
Rum Cay, Bahamas 121 B5
Rum Jungle, Australia 92 B5
Ruma, Serbia, Yug. 42 E4
Rumāḥ, Si. Arabia 70 E5
Rumania = Romania ■,
  Europe 43 D10
Rumaylah, Iraq 70 D5
Rumbêk, Sudan 81 F2
Rumburk, Czech Rep. 26 A7
Rumford, U.S.A. 109 C10
Rumia, Poland 44 D5
Rumilly, France 21 C9
Rumoi, Japan 54 C10
Rumonge, Burundi 86 C2
Rumson, U.S.A. 111 F11
Rumuruti, Kenya 86 B4
Runan, China 56 H8
Runanga, N.Z. 91 K3
Runaway, C., N.Z. 91 G6
Runcorn, U.K. 12 D5
Rundu, Namibia 88 B2
Rungwa, Tanzania 86 D3
Rungwa →, Tanzania 86 D3
Rungwe, Tanzania 87 D3
Rungwe, Mt., Tanzania 84 F6
Runka, Nigeria 83 C6
Runn, Sweden 10 D9
Runton Ra., Australia 92 D3
Ruokolahti, Finland 46 B5
Ruoqiang, China 60 C3
Rupa, India 67 F18
Rupar, India 68 D7
Rupat, Indonesia 62 D2
Rupea, Romania 43 D10
Rupen →, India 68 H4
Rupert, U.S.A. 114 E7
Rupert →, Canada 102 B4
Rupert B., Canada 102 B4
Rupert House =
  Waskaganish, Canada . . . 102 B4
Rupsa, India 69 J12
Rur →, Germany 24 D1
Rurrenabaque, Bolivia 124 F5
Rus →, Spain 33 F2
Rusambo, Zimbabwe 87 F3
Rusape, Zimbabwe 87 F3
Ruschuk = Ruse, Bulgaria . . 41 C9
Ruse, Bulgaria 41 C9
Ruse □, Bulgaria 41 C10
Ruşeţu, Romania 43 F12
Rush, Ireland 15 C5
Rushan, China 57 F11
Rushden, U.K. 13 E7

Rushmore, Mt., U.S.A. 112 D3
Rushville, Ill., U.S.A. 112 E9
Rushville, Ind., U.S.A. 108 F3
Rushville, Nebr., U.S.A. . . . 112 D3
Russas, Brazil 125 D11
Russell, Canada 105 C8
Russell, Kans., U.S.A. 112 F5
Russell, N.Y., U.S.A. 111 B9
Russell, Pa., U.S.A. 110 E5
Russell L., Man., Canada . . 105 B8
Russell L., N.W.T., Canada 104 A5
Russellkonda, India 67 K14
Russellville, Ala., U.S.A. . . 109 H2
Russellville, Ark., U.S.A. . . 113 H8
Russellville, Ky., U.S.A. . . . 109 G2
Rüsselsheim, Germany 25 F4
Russi, Italy 29 D9
Russia ■, Eurasia 51 C11
Russian →, U.S.A. 116 G3
Russkoye Ustie, Russia 4 B15
Rust, Austria 27 D9
Rustam, Pakistan 68 B5
Rustam Shahr, Pakistan . . . 68 F2
Rustavi, Georgia 49 K7
Rustenburg, S. Africa 88 D4
Ruston, U.S.A. 113 J8
Rutana, Burundi 86 C3
Rute, Spain 35 H6
Ruteng, Indonesia 63 F6
Ruth, U.S.A. 110 C2
Rutherford, U.S.A. 116 G4
Rutland, U.S.A. 111 C12
Rutland □, U.K. 13 E7
Rutland Water, U.K. 13 E7
Rutledge →, Canada 105 A6
Rutledge L., Canada 105 A6
Rutqa, W. →, Syria 73 E9
Rutshuru,
  Dem. Rep. of the Congo . 86 C2
Ruvo di Púglia, Italy 31 A9
Ruvu, Tanzania 86 D4
Ruvu →, Tanzania 86 D4
Ruvuma □, Tanzania 87 E4
Ruvuma →, Tanzania 87 E5
Ruwais, U.A.E. 71 E7
Ruwenzori, Africa 86 B2
Ruya →, Zimbabwe 89 B5
Ruyigi, Burundi 86 C3
Ruyuan, China 59 E9
Ruzayevka, Russia 48 C7
Růzhevo Konare, Bulgaria . 41 D8
Ružomberok, Slovak Rep. . . 27 B12
Rwanda ■, Africa 86 C3
Ryakhovo, Bulgaria 41 C10
Ryan, L., U.K. 14 G3
Ryazan, Russia 46 E10
Ryazhsk, Russia 46 F11
Rybache = Rybachye,
  Kazakstan 50 E9
Rybachye, Kazakstan 50 E9
Rybinsk, Russia 46 C10
Rybinskoye Vdkhr., Russia . 46 C10
Rybnik, Poland 45 H5
Rybnitsa = Râbniţa,
  Moldova 43 C14
Rybnoye, Russia 46 E10
Rychnov nad Kněžnou,
  Czech Rep. 27 A9
Rychwał, Poland 45 F5
Rycroft, Canada 104 B5
Ryd, Sweden 11 H8
Rydaholm, Sweden 11 H8
Ryde, U.K. 13 G6
Ryderwood, U.S.A. 116 D3
Rydzyna, Poland 45 G3
Rye, U.K. 13 G8
Rye →, U.K. 12 C7
Rye Bay, U.K. 13 G8
Rye Patch Reservoir, U.S.A. 114 F4
Ryegate, U.S.A. 114 C9
Ryki, Poland 45 G8
Rylsk, Russia 47 G8
Rylstone, Australia 95 E4
Rymanów, Poland 45 J8
Ryn, Poland 44 E8
Ryn Peski, Kazakstan 49 G9
Ryōtsu, Japan 54 E9
Rypin, Poland 45 E6
Ryssby, Sweden 11 H8
Ryūgasaki, Japan 55 G10
Ryūkyū Is. = Ryūkyū-rettō,
  Japan 55 M3
Ryūkyū-rettō, Japan 55 M3
Rzepin, Poland 45 F1
Rzeszów, Poland 45 H8
Rzhev, Russia 46 D8

S

Sa, Thailand 64 C3
Sa Canal, Spain 37 C7
Sa Conillera, Spain 37 C7
Sa Dec, Vietnam 65 G5
Sa Dragonera, Spain 37 B9
Sa Mesquida, Spain 37 B11
Sa Pobla, Spain 32 F8
Sa Savina, Spain 37 C7
Sa'ādatābād, Fārs, Iran 71 D7
Sa'ādatābād, Hormozgān,
  Iran 71 D7
Sa'ādatābād, Kermān, Iran . 71 D7
Saale →, Germany 24 D7
Saaler Bodden, Germany . . 24 A8
Saalfeld, Germany 24 E7
Saalfelden, Austria 26 D5
Saane →, Switz. 25 H3
Saar →, Europe 17 E6

Saarbrücken, Germany 25 F2
Saarburg, Germany 25 F2
Saaremaa, Estonia 9 G20
Saarijärvi, Finland 9 E21
Saariselkä, Finland 8 B23
Saarland □, Germany 25 F2
Saarlouis, Germany 25 F2
Sab 'Ābar, Syria 70 C3
Saba, W. Indies 121 C7
Šabac, Serbia, Yug. 40 B3
Sabadell, Spain 32 D7
Sabah □, Malaysia 62 C5
Sabak Bernam, Malaysia . . 65 L3
Sabalān, Kūhhā-ye, Iran . . . 70 B5
Sabalana, Kepulauan,
  Indonesia 63 F5
Sábana de la Mar,
  Dom. Rep. 121 C6
Sábanalarga, Colombia . . . 124 A4
Sabang, Indonesia 62 C1
Săbăoani, Romania 43 C11
Sabará, Brazil 125 G10
Sabarmati →, India 68 H5
Sabattis, U.S.A. 111 B10
Sabáudia, Italy 30 A6
Saberania, Indonesia 63 E9
Sabhah, Libya 79 C8
Sabi →, India 68 E7
Sabidana, J., Sudan 80 D4
Sabie, S. Africa 89 D5
Sabinal, Mexico 118 A3
Sabinal, U.S.A. 113 L5
Sabiñánigo, Spain 32 C4
Sabinar, Punta del, Spain . . 33 J2
Sabinas, Mexico 118 B4
Sabinas →, Mexico 118 B4
Sabinas Hidalgo, Mexico . . 118 B4
Sabine →, U.S.A. 113 L8
Sabine L., U.S.A. 113 L8
Sabine Pass, U.S.A. 113 L8
Sabinov, Slovak Rep. 27 B14
Sabinsville, U.S.A. 110 E7
Sabirabad, Azerbaijan 49 K9
Sabkhet el Bardawîl, Egypt . 75 D2
Sablayan, Phil. 61 E4
Sable, Canada 103 A6
Sable, C., Canada 103 D6
Sable, C., U.S.A. 107 E10
Sable I., Canada 103 D8
Sablé-sur-Sarthe, France . . . 18 E6
Sabonkafi, Niger 83 C6
Sabor →, Portugal 34 D3
Sabou, Burkina Faso 82 C4
Sabres, France 20 D3
Sabrina Coast, Antarctica . . 5 C9
Sabugal, Portugal 34 E3
Sabulubbek, Indonesia 62 E1
Sabuncu, Turkey 39 B12
Sabzevār, Iran 71 B8
Sabzvārān, Iran 71 D8
Sac City, U.S.A. 112 D7
Sacedón, Spain 32 E2
Săcele, Romania 43 E10
Sachigo →, Canada 102 A2
Sachigo, L., Canada 102 B1
Sachkhere, Georgia 49 J6
Sachsen □, Germany 24 E9
Sachsen-Anhalt □, Germany 24 D7
Sacile, Italy 29 C9
Sackets Harbor, U.S.A. . . . 111 C8
Sackville, Canada 103 C7
Saco, Maine, U.S.A. 109 D10
Saco, Mont., U.S.A. 114 B10
Sacramento, U.S.A. 116 G5
Sacramento →, U.S.A. 116 G5
Sacramento Mts., U.S.A. . . 115 K11
Sacramento Valley, U.S.A. . 116 G5
Sacratif, C., Spain 35 J7
Săcueni, Romania 42 C7
Sada, Spain 34 B2
Sada-Misaki, Japan 55 H6
Sádaba, Spain 32 C3
Sadabad, India 68 F8
Sadani, Tanzania 86 D4
Sadao, Thailand 65 J3
Sadd el Aali, Egypt 80 C3
Saddle Mt., U.S.A. 116 E3
Sade, Nigeria 83 C7
Sadimi,
  Dem. Rep. of the Congo . 87 D1
Sadiola, Mali 82 C2
Sa'dīyah, Hawr as, Iraq . . . 73 F12
Sado, Japan 54 F9
Sado →, Portugal 35 G2
Sadon, Burma 67 G20
Sadon, Russia 49 J6
Sadra, India 68 H5
Sadri, India 68 G5
Sæby, Denmark 11 G4
Saegertown, U.S.A. 110 E4
Saelices, Spain 32 F2
Safaalan, Turkey 41 E12
Safaga, Egypt 80 B3
Şafājah, Si. Arabia 70 E3
Šafárikovo = Tornal'a,
  Slovak Rep. 27 C13
Säffle, Sweden 10 E6
Safford, U.S.A. 115 K9
Saffron Walden, U.K. 13 E8
Safi, Morocco 78 B4
Şafiābād, Iran 71 B8
Safīd Dasht, Iran 71 C6
Safīd Kūh, Afghan. 66 B3
Safīd Rūd →, Iran 71 B6
Safipur, India 69 F9
Safonovo, Russia 46 E7
Safranbolu, Turkey 72 B5
Saft Rashîn, Egypt 80 J7
Safwān, Iraq 70 D5
Sag Harbor, U.S.A. 111 F12
Saga, Japan 55 H5

Saga □, *Japan* 55 H5
Sagae, *Japan* 54 E10
Sagala, *Mali* 82 C3
Sagamore, *U.S.A.* 110 F5
Sagar, *Karnataka, India* 66 M9
Sagar, *Mad. P., India* 69 H8
Sagay, *Phil.* 61 F5
Sagginaw, *U.S.A.* 108 D4
Saginaw ➔, *U.S.A.* 108 D4
Saginaw B., *U.S.A.* 108 D4
Sagleipie, *Liberia* 82 D3
Saglouc = Salluit, *Canada* .. 101 B12
Sagŏ-ri, *S. Korea* 57 G14
Sagone, *France* 21 F12
Sagone, G. de, *France* 21 F12
Sagres, *Portugal* 35 J2
Sagua la Grande, *Cuba* .. 120 B3
Saguache, *U.S.A.* 115 G10
Saguaro Nat. Park, *U.S.A.* 115 K8
Saguenay ➔, *Canada* 103 C5
Sagunt, *Spain* 32 F4
Sagunto = Sagunt, *Spain* .. 32 F4
Sagwara, *India* 68 H6
Sahagún, *Spain* 34 C5
Saham al Jawlān, *Syria* .. 75 C4
Sahamandrevo, *Madag.* .. 89 C8
Sahand, Kūh-e, *Iran* 70 B5
Sahara, *Africa* 78 D6
Saharan Atlas = Saharien,
  Atlas, *Algeria* 78 B6
Saharanpur, *India* 68 E7
Saharien, Atlas, *Algeria* .. 78 B6
Saharsa, *India* 69 G12
Sahasinaka, *Madag.* 89 C8
Sahaswan, *India* 69 E8
Sahel, *Africa* 78 E5
Sahel, Canal du, *Mali* 82 C3
Sahibganj, *India* 69 G12
Sāḥilīyah, *Iraq* 70 C4
Sahiwal, *Pakistan* 68 D5
Sahneh, *Iran* 70 C5
Sahuaripa, *Mexico* 118 B3
Sahuarita, *U.S.A.* 115 L8
Sahuayo, *Mexico* 118 C4
Šahy, *Slovak Rep.* 27 C11
Sai ➔, *India* 69 G10
Sai Buri, *Thailand* 65 J3
Sa'id Bundās, *Sudan* 81 F1
Sa'īdābād, *Kermān, Iran* 71 D7
Sa'īdābād, *Semnān, Iran* 71 B7
Sa'īdīyeh, *Iran* 71 B6
Saidpur, *Bangla.* 67 G16
Saidpur, *India* 69 G10
Saidu, *Pakistan* 69 B5
Saignes, *France* 20 C6
Saigon = Phanh Bho Ho Chi
  Minh, *Vietnam* 65 G6
Saijō, *Japan* 55 H6
Saikanosy Masoala, *Madag.* 89 B9
Saikhoa Ghat, *India* 67 F19
Saiki, *Japan* 55 H5
Sailana, *India* 68 H6
Saillans, *France* 21 D9
Sailolof, *Indonesia* 63 E8
Saimaa, *Finland* 9 F23
Saimbeyli, *Turkey* 72 D7
Şa'in Dezh, *Iran* 70 B5
St. Abb's Head, *U.K.* 14 F6
St-Affrique, *France* 20 E6
St-Agrève, *France* 21 C8
St-Aignan, *France* 18 E8
St. Alban's, *Canada* 103 C8
St. Albans, *U.K.* 13 F7
St. Albans, *Vt., U.S.A.* .. 111 B11
St. Albans, *W. Va., U.S.A.* 108 F5
St. Alban's Head, *U.K.* .. 13 G5
St. Albert, *Canada* 104 C6
St-Amand-en-Puisaye, *France* 19 E10
St-Amand-les-Eaux, *France* 19 B10
St-Amand-Montrond, *France* 19 F9
St-Amarin, *France* 19 E14
St-Amour, *France* 19 F12
St-André-de-Cubzac, *France* 20 D3
St-André-les-Alpes, *France* 21 E10
St. Andrew's, *Canada* 103 C8
St. Andrews, *U.K.* 14 E6
St-Anicet, *Canada* 111 A10
St. Ann B., *Canada* 103 C7
St. Ann's Bay, *Jamaica* .. 120 C4
St. Anthony, *Canada* 103 B8
St. Anthony, *U.S.A.* 114 E8
St. Antoine, *Canada* 103 C7
St-Antonin-Noble-Val,
  France 20 D5
St-Arnaud, *Australia* 95 F3
St-Astier, *France* 20 C4
St-Aubin-du-Cormier, *France* 18 D5
St-Augustin ➔, *Canada* .. 103 B8
St-Augustin-Saguenay,
  Canada 103 B8
St. Augustine, *U.S.A.* .. 109 L5
St-Aulaye, *France* 20 C4
St. Austell, *U.K.* 13 G3
St-Avold, *France* 19 C13
St. Barbe, *Canada* 103 B8
St-Barthélemy, *W. Indies* 121 C7
St-Béat, *France* 20 F4
St. Bees Hd., *U.K.* 12 C4
St-Benoît-du-Sault, *France* . 20 B5
St-Bonnet, *France* 21 D10
St-Brévin-les-Pins, *France* . 18 E4
St-Brice-en-Coglès, *France* 18 D5
St. Bride's, *Canada* 103 C9
St. Brides B., *U.K.* 13 F2
St-Brieuc, *France* 18 D4
St-Calais, *France* 18 E7
St-Cast-le-Guildo, *France* 18 D4
St. Catharines, *Canada* .. 102 D4
St. Catherines I., *U.S.A.* . 109 K5

St. Catherine's Pt., *U.K.* ... 13 G6
St-Céré, *France* 20 D5
St-Cergue, *Switz.* 25 J2
St-Cernin, *France* 20 C6
St-Chamond, *France* 21 C8
St. Charles, *Ill., U.S.A.* .. 108 E1
St. Charles, *Mo., U.S.A.* .. 112 F9
St. Charles, *Va., U.S.A.* .. 108 F7
St-Chély-d'Apcher, *France* . 20 D7
St-Chinian, *France* 20 E6
St. Christopher-Nevis = St.
  Kitts & Nevis ■, *W. Indies* 121 C7
St-Ciers-sur-Gironde, *France* 20 C3
St. Clair, *Mich., U.S.A.* .. 110 D2
St. Clair, *Pa., U.S.A.* 111 F8
St. Clair ➔, *U.S.A.* 110 D2
St. Clair, L., *Canada* 102 D3
St. Clair, L., *U.S.A.* 110 D2
St. Clairsville, *U.S.A.* .. 110 F4
St-Claud, *France* 20 C4
St. Claude, *Canada* 105 D9
St-Claude, *France* 19 F12
St-Clet, *Canada* 111 A10
St. Cloud, *Fla., U.S.A.* .. 109 L5
St. Cloud, *Minn., U.S.A.* .. 112 C7
St-Cricq, C., *Australia* .. 93 E1
St. Croix, *Virgin Is.* 121 C7
St. Croix ➔, *U.S.A.* 112 C8
St. Croix Falls, *U.S.A.* .. 112 C8
St-Cyprien, *France* 20 F7
St-Cyr-sur-Mer, *France* .. 21 E9
St. David's, *Canada* 103 C8
St. David's, *U.K.* 13 F2
St. David's Head, *U.K.* .. 13 F2
St-Denis, *France* 19 D9
St-Dié, *France* 19 D13
St-Dizier, *France* 19 D11
St-Égrève, *France* 21 C9
St. Elias, Mt., *U.S.A.* .. 100 B5
St. Elias Mts., *Canada* .. 104 A1
St. Elias Mts., *U.S.A.* .. 100 C6
St-Eloy-les-Mines, *France* .. 19 F9
St-Émilion, *France* 20 D3
St-Étienne, *France* 21 C8
St-Étienne-de-Tinée, *France* 21 D10
St-Étienne-du-Rouvray,
  France 18 C8
St. Eugène, *Canada* 111 A10
St. Eustatius, *W. Indies* .. 121 C7
St-Fargeau, *France* 19 E10
St-Félicien, *Canada* 102 C5
St-Florent, *France* 21 F13
St-Florent, G. de, *France* .. 21 F13
St-Florent-sur-Cher, *France* 19 F9
St-Florentin, *France* 19 E10
St-Flour, *France* 20 C7
St. Francis, *U.S.A.* 112 F4
St. Francis ➔, *U.S.A.* .. 113 H9
St. Francis, C., *S. Africa* .. 88 E3
St. Francisville, *U.S.A.* .. 113 K9
St-François, L., *Canada* .. 111 A10
St-Fulgent, *France* 18 F5
St-Gabriel, *Canada* 102 C5
St. Gallen = Sankt Gallen,
  Switz. 25 H5
St-Galmier, *France* 19 G11
St-Gaudens, *France* 20 E4
St-Gaultier, *France* 18 F8
St-Gengoux-le-National,
  France 19 F11
St-Geniez-d'Olt, *France* 20 D6
St. George, *Australia* 95 D4
St. George, *Canada* 103 C6
St. George, *S.C., U.S.A.* .. 109 J5
St. George, *Utah, U.S.A.* .. 115 H7
St. George, C., *Canada* .. 103 C8
St. George, C., *U.S.A.* .. 109 L3
St. George Ra., *Australia* .. 92 C4
St. George's, *Canada* 103 C8
St-Georges, *Canada* 103 C5
St. George's, *Grenada* .. 121 D7
St. George's B., *Canada* .. 103 C8
St. Georges Basin, *N.S.W.,
  Australia* 95 F5
St. Georges Basin,
  W. Austral., Australia 92 C4
St. George's Channel,
  Europe 15 E6
St. Georges Hd., *Australia* . 95 F5
St-Georges-lès-Baillargeaux,
  France 20 B4
St-Germain-de-Calberte,
  France 20 D7
St-Germain-en-Laye, *France* 19 D9
St-Germain-Lembron, *France* 20 C7
St-Gervais-d'Auvergne,
  France 19 F9
St-Gervais-les-Bains, *France* 21 C10
St-Gildas, Pte. de, *France* .. 18 E4
St-Gilles, *France* 21 E8
St-Girons, *Ariège, France* .. 20 F5
St-Girons, *Landes, France* .. 20 E2
St. Gotthard P. = San
  Gottardo, P. del, *Switz.* .. 25 J4
St. Helena, *U.S.A.* 114 G2
St. Helena ■, *Atl. Oc.* .. 76 H3
St. Helena, Mt., *U.S.A.* .. 116 G4
St. Helena B., *S. Africa* .. 88 E2
St. Helens, *Australia* 94 G4
St. Helens, *U.K.* 12 D5
St. Helens, *U.S.A.* 116 E4
St. Helens, Mt., *U.S.A.* .. 116 D4
St. Helier, *France* 13 H5
St-Herblain, *France* 18 E5
St-Hilaire-du-Harcouët,
  France 18 D5
St-Hippolyte, *France* 19 E13
St-Hippolyte-du-Fort, *France* 20 E7
St-Honoré-les-Bains, *France* 19 F10
St-Hubert, *Belgium* 17 D5
St-Hyacinthe, *Canada* .. 102 C5

St. Ignace, *U.S.A.* 108 C3
St. Ignace I., *Canada* 102 C2
St. Ignatius, *U.S.A.* 114 C6
St-Imier, *Switz.* 25 H2
St. Ives, *U.K.* 13 G2
St-James, *France* 18 D5
St. James, *U.S.A.* 112 D7
St-Jean ➔, *Canada* 103 B7
St-Jean, L., *Canada* 103 C5
St-Jean-d'Angély, *France* .. 20 C3
St-Jean-de-Braye, *France* .. 19 E8
St-Jean-de-Luz, *France* .. 20 E2
St-Jean-de-Maurienne,
  France 21 C10
St-Jean-de-Monts, *France* .. 18 F4
St-Jean-de-Gard, *France* .. 20 D7
St-Jean-en-Royans, *France* 21 C9
St-Jean-Pied-de-Port, *France* 20 E2
St-Jean-Port-Joli, *France* .. 103 C5
St-Jean-sur-Richelieu,
  Canada 102 C5
St-Jérôme, *Canada* 102 C5
St. John, *Canada* 103 C6
St. John, *U.S.A.* 113 G5
St. John ➔, *Liberia* 82 D2
St. John ➔, *U.S.A.* 109 C12
St. John, C., *Canada* 103 C6
St. John's, *Antigua* 121 C7
St. John's, *Canada* 103 C9
St. Johns, *Ariz., U.S.A.* .. 115 J9
St. Johns, *Mich., U.S.A.* .. 108 D3
St. Johns ➔, *U.S.A.* 109 K5
St. John's Pt., *Ireland* .. 15 B3
St. Johnsbury, *U.S.A.* .. 111 B12
St. Johnsville, *U.S.A.* .. 111 D10
St. Joseph, *La., U.S.A.* .. 113 K9
St. Joseph, *Mo., U.S.A.* .. 112 F7
St. Joseph ➔, *U.S.A.* .. 108 D2
St. Joseph, I., *Canada* .. 102 C3
St. Joseph, L., *Canada* .. 102 B1
St-Jovite, *Canada* 102 C5
St-Juéry, *France* 20 E6
St-Julien-Chapteuil, *France* 21 C8
St-Julien-de-Vouvantes,
  France 18 E5
St-Julien-en-Genevois,
  France 19 F13
St-Junien, *France* 20 C4
St-Just-en-Chaussée, *France* 19 C9
St-Just-en-Chevalet, *France* 20 C7
St. Kilda, *N.Z.* 91 L3
St. Kitts & Nevis ■,
  W. Indies 121 C7
St. Laurent, *Canada* 105 C9
St-Laurent-de-la-Salanque,
  France 20 F6
St-Laurent-du-Pont, *France* . 21 C9
St-Laurent-en-Grandvaux,
  France 19 F12
St-Laurent-et-Benon, *France* 20 C3
St. Lawrence, *Australia* .. 94 C4
St. Lawrence, *Canada* .. 103 C8
St. Lawrence ➔, *Canada* 103 C6
St. Lawrence, Gulf of,
  Canada 103 C7
St. Lawrence I., *U.S.A.* .. 100 B3
St. Leonard, *Canada* 103 C6
St-Léonard-de-Noblat,
  France 20 C5
St. Lewis ➔, *Canada* .. 103 B8
St-Lô, *France* 18 C5
St-Louis, *France* 19 E14
St. Louis, *Senegal* 82 B1
St. Louis, *U.S.A.* 112 F9
St. Louis ➔, *U.S.A.* .. 112 B8
St-Loup-sur-Semouse, *France* 19 E13
St. Lucia ■, *W. Indies* .. 121 D7
St. Lucia, L., *S. Africa* .. 89 D5
St. Lucia Channel, *W. Indies* 121 D7
St. Maarten, *W. Indies* .. 121 C7
St. Magnus B., *U.K.* 14 A7
St-Maixent-l'École, *France* . 20 B3
St-Malo, *France* 18 D4
St-Malo, G. de, *France* .. 18 D4
St-Mandrier-sur-Mer, *France* 21 E9
St-Marc, *Haiti* 121 C5
St-Marcellin, *France* 21 C9
St-Marcouf, Îs., *France* .. 18 C5
St. Maries, *U.S.A.* 114 C5
St. Martin, *W. Indies* .. 121 C7
St-Martin, L., *Canada* .. 105 C9
St-Martin-de-Crau, *France* . 21 E8
St-Martin-de-Ré, *France* .. 20 B2
St-Martin-d'Hères, *France* . 21 C9
St-Martin-Vésubie, *France* 21 D11
St-Martory, *France* 20 E4
St. Mary Pk., *Australia* .. 95 E2
St. Marys, *Australia* 94 G4
St. Marys, *Canada* 110 C3
St. Marys, *Corn., U.K.* .. 13 H1
St. Mary's, *Orkney, U.K.* .. 14 C6
St. Marys, *Ga., U.S.A.* .. 109 K5
St. Marys, *Pa., U.S.A.* .. 110 E6
St. Mary's, C., *Canada* .. 103 C9
St. Mary's B., *Canada* .. 103 C9
St. Marys Bay, *Canada* .. 103 D6
St-Mathieu, Pte., *France* .. 18 D2
St. Matthew I. = Zadetkyi
  Kyun, *Burma* 65 G1
St-Maurice ➔, *Canada* .. 102 C5
St-Maximin-la-Ste-Baume,
  France 21 E9
St-Médard-en-Jalles, *France* 20 D3
St-Mère-le-Grand, *France* .. 18 C5
St-Mihiel, *France* 19 D12
St. Moritz, *Switz.* 25 J5
St-Nazaire, *France* 18 E4
St. Neots, *U.K.* 13 E7
St-Nicolas-de-Port, *France* 19 D13
St-Niklaas, *Belgium* 17 C4

St-Omer, *France* 19 B9
St-Palais-sur-Mer, *France* .. 20 C2
St-Pamphile, *Canada* 103 C6
St-Pardoux-la-Rivière, *France* 20 C4
St. Pascal, *Canada* 103 C6
St. Paul, *Canada* 104 C6
St. Paul, *Minn., U.S.A.* .. 112 C8
St. Paul, *Nebr., U.S.A.* .. 112 E5
St-Paul ➔, *Canada* 103 B8
St. Paul ➔, *Liberia* 82 D2
St. Paul, I., *Ind. Oc.* 3 F13
St-Paul-de-Fenouillet, *France* 20 F6
St. Paul I., *Canada* 103 C7
St-Paul-lès-Dax, *France* .. 20 E2
St-Péray, *France* 21 D8
St. Peter, *U.S.A.* 112 C8
St-Peter-Ording, *Germany* .. 24 A4
St. Peter Port, *U.K.* 13 H5
St. Peters, *N.S., Canada* .. 103 C7
St. Peters, *P.E.I., Canada* 103 C7
St. Petersburg = Sankt-
  Peterburg, *Russia* 46 C6
St. Petersburg, *U.S.A.* .. 109 M4
St-Philbert-de-Grand-Lieu,
  France 18 E5
St-Pie, *Canada* 111 A12
St-Pierre, *St- P. & M.* .. 103 C8
St-Pierre, L., *Canada* .. 102 C5
St-Pierre-d'Oléron, *France* .. 20 C2
St-Pierre-en-Port, *France* .. 18 C7
St-Pierre et Miquelon □,
  St- P. & M. 103 C8
St-Pierre-le-Moûtier, *France* 19 F10
St-Pol-de-Léon, *France* .. 18 D3
St-Pol-sur-Mer, *France* .. 19 A9
St-Pol-sur-Ternoise, *France* . 19 B9
St-Pons, *France* 20 E6
St-Pourçain-sur-Sioule,
  France 19 F10
St-Priest, *France* 21 C8
St-Quay-Portrieux, *France* .. 18 D4
St. Quentin, *Canada* 103 C6
St. Quentin, *France* 19 C10
St-Rambert-d'Albon, *France* 21 C8
St-Raphaël, *France* 21 E10
St. Regis, *U.S.A.* 114 C6
St-Renan, *France* 18 D2
St-Saëns, *France* 18 C8
St-Savin, *France* 20 B4
St-Savinien, *France* 20 C3
St. Sebastien, Tanjon' i,
  Madag. 89 A8
St-Seine-l'Abbaye, *France* 19 E11
St-Sernin-sur-Rance, *France* 20 E6
St-Sever, *France* 20 E3
St-Siméon, *Canada* 103 C6
St. Simons I., *U.S.A.* 109 K5
St. Simons Island, *U.S.A.* .. 109 K5
St. Stephen, *Canada* 103 C6
St-Sulpice, *France* 20 E5
St-Sulpice-Laurière, *France* . 20 B5
St-Sulpice-les-Feuilles,
  France 20 B5
St-Syprien = St-Cyprien,
  France 20 F7
St-Thégonnec, *France* 18 D3
St. Thomas, *Canada* 102 D3
St. Thomas I., *Virgin Is.* .. 121 C7
St-Tite, *Canada* 102 C5
St-Tropez, *France* 21 E10
St. Troud = St. Truiden,
  Belgium 17 D5
St. Truiden, *Belgium* 17 D5
St-Vaast-la-Hougue, *France* 18 C5
St-Valéry-en-Caux, *France* . 18 C7
St-Valéry-sur-Somme, *France* 19 B8
St-Vallier, *France* 19 F11
St-Vallier-de-Thiey, *France* 21 E10
St-Varent, *France* 18 F6
St-Vaury, *France* 20 B5
St. Vincent, *Italy* 28 C4
St. Vincent, G., *Australia* .. 95 F2
St. Vincent & the
  Grenadines ■, *W. Indies* 121 D7
St-Vincent-de-Tyrosse,
  France 20 E2
St. Vincent Passage,
  W. Indies 121 D7
St-Vith, *Belgium* 17 D6
St-Vivien-de-Médoc, *France* 20 C2
St. Walburg, *Canada* 105 C7
St-Yrieix-la-Perche, *France* . 20 C5
Ste-Adresse, *France* 18 C7
Ste-Agathe-des-Monts,
  Canada 102 C5
Ste-Anne, L., *Canada* .. 103 B6
Ste-Anne-des-Monts, *Canada* 103 C6
Ste-Croix, *Switz.* 25 J2
Ste-Énimie, *France* 20 D7
Ste-Foy-la-Grande, *France* . 20 D4
Ste. Genevieve, *U.S.A.* .. 112 G9
Ste-Hermine, *France* 20 B2
Ste-Livrade-sur-Lot, *France* 20 D4
Ste-Marguerite ➔, *Canada* 103 B6
Ste-Marie, *Martinique* .. 121 D7
Ste-Marie-aux-Mines, *France* 19 D14
Ste-Marie de la Madeleine,
  Canada 103 C5
Ste-Maure-de-Touraine,
  France 18 E7
Ste-Maxime, *France* 21 E10
Ste-Menehould, *France* .. 19 C11
Ste-Mère-Église, *France* .. 18 C5
Ste-Rose, *Guadeloupe* .. 121 C7
Ste. Rose du Lac, *Canada* .. 105 C9
Ste-Savine, *France* 19 D11
Ste-Sigolène, *France* 21 C8
Saintes, *France* 20 C3
Saintes, Î. des, *Guadeloupe* 121 C7

Stes-Maries-de-la-Mer,
  France 21 E8
Saintfield, *U.K.* 15 B6
Saintonge, *France* 20 C3
Saipan, *Pac. Oc.* 96 F6
Sairang, *India* 67 H18
Sairecábur, Cerro, *Bolivia* . 126 A2
Saitama □, *Japan* 55 F9
Saiteli = Kadınhanı, *Turkey* 72 C5
Sajama, *Bolivia* 124 D4
Sajó ➔, *Hungary* 42 C6
Sajószentpéter, *Hungary* .. 42 B5
Sajum, *India* 69 C8
Sak ➔, *S. Africa* 88 E3
Sakaba, *Nigeria* 83 C6
Sakai, *Japan* 55 G7
Sakaide, *Japan* 55 G6
Sakaiminato, *Japan* 55 G6
Sakākah, *Si. Arabia* 70 D4
Sakakawea, L., *U.S.A.* .. 112 B4
Sakami ➔, *Canada* 102 B4
Sakami, L., *Canada* 102 B4
Sâkâne, 'Erg i-n, *Mali* .. 83 A4
Sakania,
  Dem. Rep. of the Congo . 87 E2
Sakaraha, *Madag.* 89 C7
Sakarya, *Turkey* 72 B4
Sakarya ➔, *Turkey* 72 B4
Sakashima-Guntō, *Japan* .. 55 M2
Sakassou, *Ivory C.* 82 D3
Sakata, *Japan* 54 E9
Sakchu, *N. Korea* 57 D13
Sakeny ➔, *Madag.* 89 C8
Sakété, *Benin* 83 D5
Sakha □, *Russia* 51 C13
Sakhalin, *Russia* 51 D15
Sakhalinskiy Zaliv, *Russia* .. 51 D15
Şaki, *Azerbaijan* 49 K8
Šakiai, *Lithuania* 9 J20
Sakon Nakhon, *Thailand* .. 64 D5
Sakrand, *Pakistan* 68 F3
Sakri, *India* 69 F12
Sakrivier, *S. Africa* 88 E3
Sakskøbing, *Denmark* .. 11 K5
Sakti, *India* 69 H10
Sakuma, *Japan* 55 G8
Sakurai, *Japan* 55 G7
Saky, *Ukraine* 47 K7
Sal ➔, *Russia* 49 G5
Sal, *Eritrea* 81 D4
Šal'a, *Slovak Rep.* 27 C10
Sala, *Sweden* 10 E10
Sala ➔, *Eritrea* 81 D4
Sala Consilina, *Italy* 31 B8
Sala-y-Gómez, *Pac. Oc.* .. 97 K17
Salaberry-de-Valleyfield,
  Canada 102 C5
Saladas, *Argentina* 126 B4
Saladillo, *Argentina* 126 D4
Salado ➔, *Buenos Aires,
  Argentina* 126 D4
Salado ➔, *La Pampa,
  Argentina* 128 D3
Salado ➔, *Santa Fe,
  Argentina* 126 C3
Salado ➔, *Mexico* 113 M5
Salaga, *Ghana* 83 D4
Şalāh, *Syria* 75 C5
Sălaj □, *Romania* 42 C9
Sálakhos, *Greece* 36 C9
Salala, *Liberia* 82 D2
Salala, *Sudan* 80 C4
Salālah, *Oman* 74 D5
Salamanca, *Chile* 126 C1
Salamanca, *Spain* 34 E5
Salamanca, *U.S.A.* 110 D6
Salamanca □, *Spain* 34 E5
Salāmatābād, *Iran* 70 C5
Salamis, *Cyprus* 36 D12
Salamís, *Greece* 38 D5
Salar de Atacama, *Chile* .. 126 A2
Salar de Uyuni, *Bolivia* .. 124 H5
Sălard, *Romania* 42 C7
Salas, *Spain* 34 B4
Salas de los Infantes, *Spain* . 34 C7
Salatiga, *Indonesia* 63 G14
Salaverry, *Peru* 124 E3
Salawati, *Indonesia* 63 E8
Salaya, *India* 68 H3
Salayar, *Indonesia* 63 F6
Salazar ➔, *Spain* 32 C3
Salbris, *France* 19 E9
Salcia, *Romania* 43 G9
Sălciua, *Romania* 43 D9
Salcombe, *U.K.* 13 G4
Saldaña, *Spain* 34 C6
Saldanha, *S. Africa* 88 E2
Saldanha B., *S. Africa* .. 88 E2
Saldus □, *Latvia* 9 H20
Saldus □, *Latvia* 44 B9
Sale, *Australia* 95 F4
Sale, *Italy* 28 D5
Salé, *Morocco* 78 B4
Sale, *U.K.* 12 D5
Salekhard, *Russia* 50 C7
Salem, *India* 66 P10
Salem, *Ill., U.S.A.* 108 F1
Salem, *Ind., U.S.A.* 108 F2
Salem, *Mass., U.S.A.* .. 111 D14
Salem, *Mo., U.S.A.* 113 G9
Salem, *N.H., U.S.A.* 111 D13
Salem, *N.J., U.S.A.* 108 F8
Salem, *N.Y., U.S.A.* 111 C11
Salem, *Ohio, U.S.A.* 110 F4
Salem, *Oreg., U.S.A.* .. 114 D2
Salem, *S. Dak., U.S.A.* .. 112 D6
Salem, *Va., U.S.A.* 108 G5
Salemi, *Italy* 30 E5

San Pedro de las Colonias

Sälen, *Sweden* 10 C7
Salernes, *France* 21 E10
Salerno, *Italy* 31 B7
Salerno, G. di, *Italy* 31 B7
Salford, *U.K.* 12 D5
Salgir →, *Ukraine* 47 K8
Salgótarján, *Hungary* 42 B4
Salgueiro, *Brazil* 125 E11
Salibabu, *Indonesia* 63 D7
Salida, *U.S.A.* 106 C5
Salies-de-Béarn, *France* 20 E3
Salihli, *Turkey* 72 C3
Salihorsk, *Belarus* 47 F4
Salima, *Malawi* 85 G6
Salina, *Italy* 31 D7
Salina, *Kans., U.S.A.* 112 F6
Salina, *Utah, U.S.A.* 115 G8
Salina Cruz, *Mexico* 119 D5
Salinas, *Brazil* 125 G10
Salinas, *Chile* 126 A2
Salinas, *Ecuador* 124 D2
Salinas, *U.S.A.* 116 J5
Salinas →, *Guatemala* 119 D6
Salinas →, *U.S.A.* 116 J5
Salinas, B. de, *Nic.* 120 D2
Salinas, Pampa de las, *Argentina* 126 C2
Salinas Ambargasta, *Argentina* 126 B3
Salinas de Hidalgo, *Mexico* 118 C4
Salinas Grandes, *Argentina* 126 C3
Saline →, *Ark., U.S.A.* 113 J8
Saline →, *Kans., U.S.A.* 112 F6
Salines, *Spain* 37 B10
Salines, C. de ses, *Spain* 37 B10
Salinópolis, *Brazil* 125 D9
Salins-les-Bains, *France* 19 F12
Salir, *Portugal* 35 H2
Salisbury = Harare, *Zimbabwe* 87 F3
Salisbury, *U.K.* 13 F6
Salisbury, *Md., U.S.A.* 108 F8
Salisbury, *N.C., U.S.A.* 109 H5
Salisbury I., *Canada* 101 B12
Salisbury Plain, *U.K.* 13 F6
Săliște, *Romania* 43 E8
Salka, *Nigeria* 83 C5
Şalkhad, *Syria* 75 C5
Salla, *Finland* 8 C23
Sallanches, *France* 21 C10
Sallent, *Spain* 32 D6
Salles, *France* 20 D3
Salles-Curan, *France* 20 D6
Salling, *Denmark* 11 H2
Salliq, *Canada* 101 B11
Sallisaw, *U.S.A.* 113 H7
Sallom Junction, *Sudan* 80 D4
Salluit, *Canada* 101 B12
Salmās, *Iran* 70 B5
Salmerón, *Spain* 32 E2
Salmo, *Canada* 104 D5
Salmon, *U.S.A.* 114 D7
Salmon →, *Canada* 104 C4
Salmon →, *U.S.A.* 114 D5
Salmon Arm, *Canada* 104 C5
Salmon Gums, *Australia* 93 F3
Salmon River Mts., *U.S.A.* 114 D6
Salo, *Finland* 9 F20
Salò, *Italy* 28 C7
Salobreña, *Spain* 35 J7
Salome, *U.S.A.* 117 M13
Salon, *India* 69 F9
Salon-de-Provence, *France* 21 E9
Salonica = Thessaloníki, *Greece* 40 F6
Salonta, *Romania* 42 D6
Salor →, *Spain* 35 F3
Salou, *Spain* 32 D6
Salou, C. de, *Spain* 32 D6
Saloum →, *Senegal* 82 C1
Salpausselkä, *Finland* 9 F22
Salsacate, *Argentina* 126 C2
Salses, *France* 20 F6
Salsk, *Russia* 49 G5
Salso →, *Italy* 30 E6
Salsomaggiore Terme, *Italy* 28 D6
Salt, *Spain* 32 D7
Salt →, *Canada* 104 B6
Salt →, *U.S.A.* 115 K7
Salt Lake City, *U.S.A.* 114 F8
Salt Range, *Pakistan* 68 C5
Salta, *Argentina* 126 A2
Salta □, *Argentina* 126 A2
Saltara, *Italy* 29 E9
Saltash, *U.K.* 13 G3
Saltburn by the Sea, *U.K.* 12 C7
Saltcoats, *U.K.* 14 F4
Saltee Is., *Ireland* 15 D5
Saltfjellet, *Norway* 8 C16
Saltfjorden, *Norway* 8 C16
Saltholm, *Denmark* 11 J6
Saltillo, *Mexico* 118 B4
Salto, *Argentina* 126 C3
Salto, *Uruguay* 126 C4
Salto del Guaíra, *Paraguay* 127 A5
Salton City, *U.S.A.* 117 M11
Salton Sea, *U.S.A.* 117 M11
Saltpond, *Ghana* 83 D4
Saltsburg, *U.S.A.* 110 F5
Saltsjöbaden, *Sweden* 10 E12
Saluda →, *U.S.A.* 109 J5
Salûm, *Egypt* 80 A2
Salûm, Khâlig el, *Egypt* 80 A2
Salur, *India* 67 K13
Saluzzo, *Italy* 28 D4
Salvador, *Brazil* 125 F11
Salvador, *Canada* 105 C7
Salvador, L., *U.S.A.* 113 L9
Salvaterra de Magos, *Portugal* 35 F2
Sálvora, I. de, *Spain* 34 C2
Salween →, *Burma* 67 L20
Salyan, *Azerbaijan* 50 F5
Salza →, *Austria* 26 D7
Salzach →, *Austria* 26 C5
Salzburg, *Austria* 26 D6
Salzburg □, *Austria* 26 D6
Salzgitter, *Germany* 24 C6
Salzkotten, *Germany* 24 D4
Salzwedel, *Germany* 24 C7
Sam, *India* 68 F4
Sam Neua, *Laos* 58 G5
Sam Ngao, *Thailand* 64 D2
Sam Rayburn Reservoir, *U.S.A.* 113 K7
Sam Son, *Vietnam* 64 C5
Sam Teu, *Laos* 64 C5
Sama de Langreo = Langreo, *Spain* 34 B5
Samagaltay, *Russia* 51 D10
Samales Group, *Phil.* 61 J4
Samâlût, *Egypt* 80 B3
Samana, *India* 68 D7
Samaná □, *Dom. Rep.* 121 C6
Samana Cay, *Bahamas* 121 B5
Samandağı, *Turkey* 72 D6
Samandıra, *Turkey* 41 F13
Samanga, *Tanzania* 87 D4
Samangwa, *Dem. Rep. of the Congo* 86 C1
Samani, *Japan* 54 C11
Samanli Dağları, *Turkey* 41 F13
Samar, *Phil.* 61 F6
Samara, *Russia* 48 D10
Samara →, *Russia* 48 D10
Samara →, *Ukraine* 47 H8
Samaria = Shōmrōn, *West Bank* 75 C4
Samariá, *Greece* 36 D5
Samarinda, *Indonesia* 62 E5
Samarkand = Samarqand, *Uzbekistan* 50 F7
Samarqand, *Uzbekistan* 50 F7
Sāmarrā, *Iraq* 70 C4
Samastipur, *India* 69 G11
Şamaxi, *Azerbaijan* 49 K9
Samba, *Dem. Rep. of the Congo* 86 C2
Samba, *India* 69 C6
Sambalpur, *India* 67 J14
Sambar, Tanjung, *Indonesia* 62 E4
Sambas, *Indonesia* 62 D3
Sambava, *Madag.* 89 A9
Sambawizi, *Zimbabwe* 87 F2
Sambhal, *India* 69 E8
Sambhar, *India* 68 F6
Sambhar L., *India* 68 F6
Sambiase, *Italy* 31 D9
Sambir, *Ukraine* 47 H2
Sambor, *Cambodia* 64 F6
Samborombón, B., *Argentina* 126 D4
Sambuca di Sicília, *Italy* 30 E6
Samch'ŏk, *S. Korea* 57 F15
Samch'onp'o, *S. Korea* 57 G15
Same, *Tanzania* 86 C4
Samer, *France* 19 B8
Samfya, *Zambia* 87 E2
Sámi, *Greece* 38 C2
Şämkir, *Azerbaijan* 49 K8
Şamlı, *Turkey* 39 B9
Samnah, *Si. Arabia* 70 E3
Samo Alto, *Chile* 126 C1
Samoa = Western Samoa ■, *Pac. Oc.* 91 B13
Samobor, *Croatia* 29 C12
Samoëns, *France* 19 F13
Samokov, *Bulgaria* 40 D7
Šamorín, *Slovak Rep.* 27 C10
Samorogouan, *Burkina Faso* 82 C4
Sámos, *Greece* 39 D8
Samoš, *Serbia, Yug.* 42 E5
Samos, *Spain* 34 C3
Sámos □, *Greece* 39 D8
Samothráki = Mathráki, *Greece* 36 A3
Samothráki, *Greece* 41 F9
Samothráki, *Évros, Greece* 41 F9
Samoylovka, *Russia* 48 E6
Sampa, *Ghana* 82 D4
Sampacho, *Argentina* 126 C3
Sampang, *Indonesia* 63 G15
Samper de Calanda, *Spain* 32 D4
Sampéyre, *Italy* 28 D4
Sampit, *Indonesia* 62 E4
Sampit, Teluk, *Indonesia* 62 E4
Samrong, *Cambodia* 64 E4
Samrong, *Thailand* 64 E3
Samsø, *Denmark* 11 J4
Samsø Bælt, *Denmark* 11 J4
Samsun, *Turkey* 72 B7
Samtredia, *Georgia* 49 J6
Samui, Ko, *Thailand* 65 H3
Samur →, *Russia* 49 K9
Samurskiy Khrebet, *Russia* 49 K8
Samusole, *Dem. Rep. of the Congo* 87 E1
Samut Prakan, *Thailand* 64 F3
Samut Songkhram →, *Thailand* 62 B1
Samwari, *Pakistan* 68 E2
San, *Mali* 82 C4
San →, *Cambodia* 64 F5
San →, *Poland* 45 H8
San Adrián, *Spain* 32 C3
San Adrián, C. de, *Spain* 34 B2
San Agustin, C., *Phil.* 61 H7
San Agustín de Valle Fértil, *Argentina* 126 C2
San Ambrosio, *Pac. Oc.* 122 F3
San Andreas, *U.S.A.* 116 G6
San Andres, *Phil.* 61 E6
San Andrés, I. de, *Caribbean* 120 D3
San Andrês del Rabanedo, *Spain* 34 C5
San Andres Mts., *U.S.A.* 115 K10
San Andrés Tuxtla, *Mexico* 119 D5
San Angelo, *U.S.A.* 113 K4
San Anselmo, *U.S.A.* 116 H4
San Antonio, *Belize* 119 D7
San Antonio, *Chile* 126 C1
San Antonio, *Phil.* 61 D4
San Antonio, *N. Mex., U.S.A.* 115 K10
San Antonio, *Tex., U.S.A.* 113 L5
San Antonio →, *U.S.A.* 113 L6
San Antonio, C., *Argentina* 126 D4
San Antonio, C., *Cuba* 120 B3
San Antonio, C. de, *Spain* 33 G5
San Antonio, Mt., *U.S.A.* 117 L9
San Antonio de los Baños, *Cuba* 120 B3
San Antonio de los Cobres, *Argentina* 126 A2
San Antonio Oeste, *Argentina* 128 E4
San Arcángelo, *Italy* 31 B9
San Ardo, *U.S.A.* 116 J6
San Augustín, *Canary Is.* 37 G4
San Augustine, *U.S.A.* 113 K7
San Bartolomé, *Canary Is.* 37 F6
San Bartolomé de Tirajana, *Canary Is.* 37 G4
San Bartolomeo in Galdo, *Italy* 31 A8
San Benedetto del Tronto, *Italy* 29 F10
San Benedetto Po, *Italy* 28 C7
San Benedicto, I., *Mexico* 118 D2
San Benito, *U.S.A.* 113 M6
San Benito →, *U.S.A.* 116 J5
San Benito Mt., *U.S.A.* 116 J6
San Bernardino, *U.S.A.* 117 L9
San Bernardino Mts., *U.S.A.* 117 L10
San Bernardino Str., *Phil.* 61 E6
San Bernardo, *Chile* 126 C1
San Bernardo, I. de, *Colombia* 124 B3
San Blas, *Mexico* 118 B3
San Blas, Arch. de, *Panama* 120 E4
San Blas, C., *U.S.A.* 109 L3
San Bonifacio, *Italy* 29 C8
San Borja, *Bolivia* 124 F5
San Buenaventura, *Mexico* 118 B4
San Carlos = Butuku-Luba, *Eq. Guin.* 83 E6
San Carlos = Sant Carles, *Spain* 37 B8
San Carlos, *Argentina* 126 C2
San Carlos, *Chile* 126 D1
San Carlos, *Baja Calif. S., Mexico* 118 C2
San Carlos, *Coahuila, Mexico* 118 B4
San Carlos, *Nic.* 120 D3
San Carlos, *Neg. Occ., Phil.* 61 F5
San Carlos, *Pangasinan, Phil.* 61 D4
San Carlos, *Uruguay* 127 C5
San Carlos, *U.S.A.* 115 K8
San Carlos, *Venezuela* 124 B5
San Carlos de Bariloche, *Argentina* 128 E2
San Carlos de Bolívar, *Argentina* 128 D4
San Carlos de la Rápita = Sant Carles de la Ràpita, *Spain* 32 E5
San Carlos del Zulia, *Venezuela* 124 B4
San Carlos L., *U.S.A.* 115 K8
San Cataldo, *Italy* 30 E6
San Celoni = Sant Celoni, *Spain* 32 D7
San Clemente, *Chile* 126 D1
San Clemente, *Spain* 33 F2
San Clemente, *U.S.A.* 117 M9
San Clemente I., *U.S.A.* 117 N8
San Cristóbal = Es Migjorn Gran, *Spain* 37 B11
San Cristóbal, *Argentina* 126 C3
San Cristóbal, *Dom. Rep.* 121 C5
San Cristóbal, *Venezuela* 124 B4
San Cristóbal de la Casas, *Mexico* 119 D6
San Damiano d'Asti, *Italy* 28 D5
San Daniele del Friuli, *Italy* 29 B10
San Diego, *Calif., U.S.A.* 117 N9
San Diego, *Tex., U.S.A.* 113 M5
San Diego, C., *Argentina* 128 G3
San Diego de la Unión, *Mexico* 118 C4
San Dimitri, Ras, *Malta* 36 C1
San Donà di Piave, *Italy* 29 C9
San Estanislao, *Paraguay* 126 A4
San Esteban de Gormaz, *Spain* 32 D1
San Felice Circeo, *Italy* 30 A6
San Felice sul Panaro, *Italy* 29 D8
San Felipe, *Chile* 126 C1
San Felipe, *Mexico* 118 A2
San Felipe, *Venezuela* 124 A5
San Felipe →, *U.S.A.* 117 M11
San Felix, *Chile* 126 B1
San Félix, *Pac. Oc.* 122 F2
San Fernando = Sant Ferran, *Spain* 37 C7
San Fernando, *Chile* 126 C1
San Fernando, *Baja Calif., Mexico* 118 B1
San Fernando, *Tamaulipas, Mexico* 119 C5
San Fernando, *La Union, Phil.* 61 C4
San Fernando, *Pampanga, Phil.* 61 D4
San Fernando, *Spain* 35 J4
San Fernando, *Trin. & Tob.* 121 D7
San Fernando, *U.S.A.* 117 L8
San Fernando de Apure, *Venezuela* 124 B5
San Fernando de Atabapo, *Venezuela* 124 C5
San Fernando di Púglia, *Italy* 31 A9
San Francisco, *Argentina* 126 C3
San Francisco, *U.S.A.* 116 H4
San Francisco →, *U.S.A.* 115 K9
San Francisco, Paso de, *S. Amer.* 126 B2
San Francisco de Macorís, *Dom. Rep.* 121 C5
San Francisco del Monte de Oro, *Argentina* 126 C2
San Francisco del Oro, *Mexico* 118 B3
San Francisco Javier = Sant Francesc de Formentera, *Spain* 37 C7
San Francisco Solano, Pta., *Colombia* 122 C3
San Fratello, *Italy* 31 D7
San Gabriel, *Chile* 126 C1
San Gabriel Mts., *U.S.A.* 117 L9
San Gavino Monreale, *Italy* 30 C1
San Gimignano, *Italy* 28 E8
San Giórgio di Nogaro, *Italy* 29 C10
San Giórgio Iónico, *Italy* 31 B10
San Giovanni Bianco, *Italy* 28 C6
San Giovanni in Fiore, *Italy* 31 C9
San Giovanni in Persiceto, *Italy* 29 D8
San Giovanni Rotondo, *Italy* 29 G12
San Giovanni Valdarno, *Italy* 29 E8
San Giuliano Terme, *Italy* 28 E7
San Gorgonio Mt., *U.S.A.* 117 L10
San Gottardo, P. del, *Switz.* 25 J4
San Gregorio, *Uruguay* 127 C4
San Gregorio, *U.S.A.* 116 H4
San Guiseppe Jato, *Italy* 30 E6
San Ignacio, *Belize* 119 D7
San Ignacio, *Bolivia* 124 G6
San Ignacio, *Mexico* 118 B2
San Ignacio, *Paraguay* 120 C2
San Ignacio, L., *Mexico* 118 B2
San Ildefonso, C., *Phil.* 61 C5
San Isidro, *Argentina* 126 C4
San Isidro, *Phil.* 61 H7
San Jacinto, *U.S.A.* 117 M10
San Jaime = Sant Jaume, *Spain* 37 B11
San Javier, *Misiones, Argentina* 127 B4
San Javier, *Santa Fe, Argentina* 126 C4
San Javier, *Bolivia* 124 G6
San Javier, *Chile* 126 D1
San Javier, *Spain* 33 H4
San Jeronimo Taviche, *Mexico* 119 D5
San Joaquin, *U.S.A.* 116 J6
San Joaquin →, *U.S.A.* 116 G5
San Joaquin Valley, *U.S.A.* 116 J6
San Jon, *U.S.A.* 113 H3
San Jordi = Sant Jordi, *Spain* 37 B9
San Jorge, *Argentina* 126 C3
San Jorge, *Spain* 37 C7
San Jorge, B. de, *Mexico* 118 A2
San Jorge, G., *Argentina* 128 F3
San Jorge, G. of, *Argentina* 122 H4
San José = San Josep, *Spain* 37 C7
San José, *Costa Rica* 120 E3
San José, *Guatemala* 120 D1
San José, *Mexico* 118 C2
San Jose, *Mind. Occ., Phil.* 61 E4
San Jose, *Nueva Ecija, Phil.* 61 D4
San Jose, *U.S.A.* 116 H5
San Jose →, *U.S.A.* 115 J10
San Jose de Buenavista, *Phil.* 63 B6
San José de Chiquitos, *Bolivia* 124 G6
San José de Feliciano, *Argentina* 126 C4
San José de Jáchal, *Argentina* 126 C2
San José de Mayo, *Uruguay* 126 C4
San José del Cabo, *Mexico* 118 C3
San José del Guaviare, *Colombia* 124 C4
San Josep, *Spain* 37 C7
San Juan, *Argentina* 126 C2
San Juan, *Mexico* 118 C4
San Juan, *Phil.* 61 F6
San Juan, *Puerto Rico* 121 C6
San Juan □, *Argentina* 126 C2
San Juan □, *Dom. Rep.* 121 C5
San Juan →, *Argentina* 126 C2
San Juan →, *Nic.* 120 D3
San Juan →, *U.S.A.* 115 H8
San Juan Bautista = Sant Joan Baptista, *Spain* 37 B8
San Juan Bautista, *Paraguay* 126 B4
San Juan Bautista, *U.S.A.* 116 J5
San Juan Bautista Valle Nacional, *Mexico* 119 D5
San Juan Capistrano, *U.S.A.* 117 M9
San Juan Cr. →, *U.S.A.* 116 J5
San Juan de Alicante, *Spain* 33 G4
San Juan de Guadalupe, *Mexico* 118 C4
San Juan de la Costa, *Mexico* 118 C2
San Juan de los Morros, *Venezuela* 124 B5
San Juan del Norte, *Nic.* 120 D3
San Juan del Norte, B. de, *Nic.* 120 D3
San Juan del Río, *Mexico* 119 C5
San Juan del Sur, *Nic.* 120 D2
San Juan I., *U.S.A.* 116 B3
San Juan Mts., *U.S.A.* 115 H10
San Just, Sierra de, *Spain* 32 E4
San Justo, *Argentina* 126 C3
San Kamphaeng, *Thailand* 64 C2
San Lázaro, C., *Mexico* 118 C2
San Lázaro, Sa., *Mexico* 118 C3
San Leandro, *U.S.A.* 116 H4
San Leonardo de Yagüe, *Spain* 32 D1
San Lorenzo = Sant Llorenç des Cardassar, *Spain* 37 B10
San Lorenzo, *Argentina* 126 C3
San Lorenzo, *Ecuador* 124 C3
San Lorenzo, *Paraguay* 126 B4
San Lorenzo →, *Mexico* 118 C3
San Lorenzo, I., *Mexico* 118 B2
San Lorenzo, Mte., *Argentina* 128 F2
San Lorenzo de la Parrilla, *Spain* 32 F2
San Lorenzo de Morunys = Sant Llorenç de Morunys, *Spain* 32 C6
San Lucas, *Bolivia* 124 H5
San Lucas, *Baja Calif. S., Mexico* 118 C3
San Lucas, *Baja Calif. S., Mexico* 118 B2
San Lucas, *U.S.A.* 116 J5
San Lucas, C., *Mexico* 118 C3
San Lúcido, *Italy* 31 C9
San Luis, *Argentina* 126 C2
San Luis, *Cuba* 120 B3
San Luis, *Guatemala* 120 C2
San Luis, *Ariz., U.S.A.* 115 K6
San Luis, *Colo., U.S.A.* 115 H11
San Luis □, *Argentina* 126 C2
San Luis, I., *Mexico* 118 B2
San Luis, Sierra de, *Argentina* 126 C2
San Luis de la Paz, *Mexico* 118 C4
San Luis Obispo, *U.S.A.* 117 K6
San Luis Potosí, *Mexico* 118 C4
San Luis Potosí □, *Mexico* 118 C4
San Luis Reservoir, *U.S.A.* 116 H5
San Luis Río Colorado, *Mexico* 118 A2
San Manuel, *U.S.A.* 115 K8
San Marco, C., *Italy* 30 C1
San Marco Argentano, *Italy* 31 C9
San Marco in Lámis, *Italy* 29 G12
San Marcos, *Guatemala* 120 D1
San Marcos, *Mexico* 118 B2
San Marcos, *Calif., U.S.A.* 117 M9
San Marcos, *Tex., U.S.A.* 113 L6
San Marino, *San Marino* 29 E9
San Marino ■, *Europe* 29 E9
San Martín, *Argentina* 126 C2
San Martin →, *Bolivia* 124 F6
San Martín, L., *Argentina* 128 F2
San Martín de la Vega, *Spain* 34 E7
San Martin de los Andes, *Argentina* 128 E2
San Martín de Valdeiglesias, *Spain* 34 E6
San Mateo = Sant Mateu, *Baleares, Spain* 37 B7
San Mateo = Sant Mateu, *Valencia, Spain* 32 E5
San Mateo, *Phil.* 61 C4
San Mateo, *U.S.A.* 116 H4
San Matías, *Bolivia* 124 G7
San Matías, G., *Argentina* 122 H4
San Miguel = Sant Miquel, *Spain* 37 B7
San Miguel, *El Salv.* 120 D2
San Miguel, *Panama* 120 E4
San Miguel, *U.S.A.* 116 K6
San Miguel →, *Bolivia* 124 F6
San Miguel de Tucumán, *Argentina* 126 B2
San Miguel del Monte, *Argentina* 126 D4
San Miguel I., *U.S.A.* 117 L6
San Miniato, *Italy* 28 E7
San Nicolás, *Canary Is.* 37 G4
San Nicolas, *Phil.* 61 B4
San Nicolás de los Arroyas, *Argentina* 126 C3
San Nicolas I., *U.S.A.* 117 M7
San Onofre, *U.S.A.* 117 M9
San Pablo, *Bolivia* 126 A2
San Pablo, *Phil.* 61 D4
San Pablo, *U.S.A.* 116 H4
San Páolo di Civitate, *Italy* 29 G12
San Pedro, *Buenos Aires, Argentina* 126 C4
San Pedro, *Misiones, Argentina* 127 B5
San Pedro, *Chile* 126 C1
San Pédro, *Ivory C.* 82 E3
San Pedro, *Mexico* 118 C2
San Pedro □, *Paraguay* 126 A4
San Pedro →, *Chihuahua, Mexico* 118 B3
San Pedro →, *Nayarit, Mexico* 118 C3
San Pedro →, *U.S.A.* 115 K8
San Pedro, Pta., *Chile* 126 B1
San Pedro, Sierra de, *Spain* 35 F4
San Pedro Channel, *U.S.A.* 117 M8
San Pedro de Atacama, *Chile* 126 A2
San Pedro de Jujuy, *Argentina* 126 A3
San Pedro de las Colonias, *Mexico* 118 B4

San Pedro de Macorís,
  Dom. Rep. 121 C6
San Pedro del Norte, *Nic.* 120 D3
San Pedro del Pinatar, *Spain* 33 H4
San Pedro del Paraná,
  Paraguay 126 B4
San Pedro Mártir, Sierra,
  Mexico 118 A1
San Pedro Mixtepec, *Mexico* 119 D5
San Pedro Ocampo =
  Melchor Ocampo, *Mexico* 118 C4
San Pedro Sula, *Honduras* 120 C2
San Pietro, *Italy* 30 C1
San Pietro Vernótico, *Italy* 31 B11
San Quintín, *Mexico* 118 A1
San Rafael, *Argentina* 126 C2
San Rafael, *Calif., U.S.A.* 116 H4
San Rafael, *N. Mex., U.S.A.* 115 J10
San Rafael Mt., *U.S.A.* .. 117 L7
San Rafael Mts., *U.S.A.* .. 117 L7
San Ramón de la Nueva
  Orán, *Argentina* 126 A3
San Remo, *Italy* 28 E4
San Roque, *Argentina* 126 B4
San Roque, *Spain* 35 J5
San Rosendo, *Chile* 126 D1
San Saba, *U.S.A.* 113 K5
San Salvador, *El Salv.* .. 120 D2
San Salvador, *Spain* 37 B10
San Salvador de Jujuy,
  Argentina 126 A3
San Salvador I., *Bahamas* 121 B5
San Salvo, *Italy* 29 F11
San Sebastián = Donostia-
  San Sebastián, *Spain* .. 32 B3
San Sebastián, *Argentina* 128 G3
San Sebastian de la Gomera,
  Canary Is. 37 F2
San Serra = Son Serra,
  Spain 37 B10
San Serverino Marche, *Italy* 29 E10
San Severo, *Italy* 29 G12
San Simeon, *U.S.A.* 116 K5
San Simon, *U.S.A.* 115 K9
San Stéfano di Cadore, *Italy* 29 B9
San Stino di Livenza, *Italy* 29 C9
San Telmo = Sant Telm,
  Spain 37 B9
San Telmo, *Mexico* 118 A1
San Tiburcio, *Mexico* 118 C4
San Valentin, Mte., *Chile* . 122 H3
San Vicente de Alcántara,
  Spain 35 F3
San Vicente de la Barquera,
  Spain 34 B6
San Vicente del Raspeig,
  Spain 33 G4
San Vincenzo, *Italy* 28 E7
San Vito, *Costa Rica* 120 E4
San Vito, *Italy* 30 C2
San Vito, C., *Italy* 30 D5
San Vito al Tagliamento,
  Italy 29 C9
San Vito Chietino, *Italy* .. 29 F11
San Vito dei Normanni, *Italy* 31 B10
Sana', *Yemen* 74 D3
Sana →, *Bos.-H.* 29 C13
Sanaba, *Burkina Faso* .. 82 C4
Sanafir, *Si. Arabia* 80 B3
Sanaga →, *Cameroon* .. 83 E6
Sanaloa, Presa, *Mexico* .. 118 C3
Sanana, *Indonesia* 63 E7
Sanand, *India* 68 H5
Sanandaj, *Iran* 70 C5
Sanandita, *Bolivia* 126 A3
Sanary-sur-Mer, *France* .. 21 E9
Sanawad, *India* 68 H7
Sancellas = Sencelles, *Spain* 37 B9
Sancergues, *France* 19 E9
Sancerre, *France* 19 E9
Sancerrois, Collines du,
  France 19 E9
Sancha He →, *China* .. 58 D6
Sanchahe, *China* 57 B14
Sánchez, *Dom. Rep.* 121 C6
Sanchor, *India* 68 G4
Sancoins, *France* 19 F9
Sancti Spíritus, *Cuba* .. 120 B4
Sancy, Puy de, *France* .. 20 C6
Sand →, *S. Africa* 89 C5
Sand Hills, *U.S.A.* 112 D4
Sand Springs, *U.S.A.* .. 113 G6
Sanda, *Japan* 55 G7
Sandakan, *Malaysia* 62 C5
Sandan = Sambor,
  Cambodia 64 F6
Sandanski, *Bulgaria* 40 E7
Sandaré, *Mali* 82 C2
Sandared, *Sweden* 11 G6
Sandarne, *Sweden* 10 C11
Sanday, *U.K.* 14 B6
Sandefjord, *Norway* 9 G14
Sanders, *U.S.A.* 115 J9
Sanderson, *U.S.A.* 113 K3
Sandersville, *U.S.A.* 109 J4
Sandfire Roadhouse,
  Australia 92 C3
Sandfly L., *Canada* 105 B7
Sandfontein, *Namibia* .. 88 C2
Sandhammaren, C., *Sweden* 11 J8
Sandía, *Peru* 124 F5
Sandıklı, *Turkey* 39 C12
Sandila, *India* 69 F9
Sandnes, *Norway* 9 G11
Sandnessjøen, *Norway* .. 8 C15
Sandoa,
  Dem. Rep. of the Congo . 84 F4
Sandomierz, *Poland* 45 H8
Sândominic, *Romania* .. 43 D10
Sandover →, *Australia* .. 94 C2
Sandoway, *Burma* 67 K19

Sandoy, *Færoe Is.* 8 F9
Sandpoint, *U.S.A.* 114 B5
Sandray, *U.K.* 14 E1
Sandringham, *U.K.* 12 E8
Sandu, *China* 58 E6
Sandusky, *Mich., U.S.A.* 110 C2
Sandusky, *Ohio, U.S.A.* 110 E2
Sandvig, *Sweden* 11 J8
Sandviken, *Sweden* 10 D10
Sandwich, C., *Australia* .. 94 B4
Sandwich B., *Canada* .. 103 B8
Sandwich B., *Namibia* .. 88 C1
Sandwip Chan., *Bangla.* .. 67 H17
Sandy, *Oreg., U.S.A.* .. 116 E4
Sandy, *Pa., U.S.A.* 110 E6
Sandy, *Utah, U.S.A.* .. 114 F8
Sandy Bay, *Canada* 105 B8
Sandy Bight, *Australia* .. 93 F3
Sandy C., *Queens., Australia* 94 C5
Sandy C., *Tas., Australia* . 94 G3
Sandy Cay, *Bahamas* .. 121 B4
Sandy Cr. →, *U.S.A.* .. 114 F9
Sandy L., *Canada* 102 B1
Sandy Lake, *Canada* 102 B1
Sandy Valley, *U.S.A.* .. 117 K11
Sanford, *Fla., U.S.A.* .. 109 L5
Sanford, *Maine, U.S.A.* 109 D10
Sanford, *N.C., U.S.A.* .. 109 H6
Sanford →, *Australia* .. 93 E2
Sanford, Mt., *U.S.A.* .. 100 B5
Sang-i-Masha, *Afghan.* .. 68 C2
Sanga, *Mozam.* 87 E4
Sanga →, *Congo* 84 E3
Sangamner, *India* 66 K9
Sangar, *Afghan.* 68 C1
Sangar, *Russia* 51 C13
Sangar Sarai, *Afghan.* .. 68 B4
Sangaredi, *Guinea* 82 C2
Sangarh →, *Pakistan* .. 68 D4
Sangasso, *Mali* 82 C3
Sange,
  Dem. Rep. of the Congo 86 D2
Sangeang, *Indonesia* 63 F5
Sângeorz-Băi, *Romania* .. 43 C9
Sanger, *U.S.A.* 116 J7
Sângera, *Moldova* 43 D13
Sangerhausen, *Germany* .. 24 D7
Sanggan He →, *China* .. 56 E9
Sanggau, *Indonesia* 62 D4
Sanghar, *Pakistan* 68 F3
Sangihe, Kepulauan,
  Indonesia 63 D7
Sangihe, Pulau, *Indonesia* 63 D7
Sangju, *S. Korea* 57 F15
Sangkapura, *Indonesia* .. 62 F4
Sangkhla, *Thailand* 64 E2
Sangkulirang, *Indonesia* .. 62 D5
Sangla, *Pakistan* 68 D5
Sangli, *India* 66 L9
Sangmélima, *Cameroon* .. 83 E7
Sangod, *India* 68 G7
Sangre de Cristo Mts.,
  U.S.A. 113 G2
Sangro →, *Italy* 29 F11
Sangrur, *India* 68 D6
Sangudo, *Canada* 104 C6
Sangue →, *Brazil* 124 F7
Sangüesa, *Spain* 32 C3
Sanguinaires, Îs., *France* . 21 G12
Sangzhi, *China* 59 C8
Sanhala, *Ivory C.* 82 C3
Sanibel, *U.S.A.* 109 M4
Sanirajak, *Canada* 101 B11
Sanjawi, *Pakistan* 68 D3
Sanje, *Uganda* 86 C3
Sanjiang, *China* 58 E7
Sanjo, *Japan* 54 F9
Sankh →, *India* 69 H11
Sankt Andrä, *Austria* .. 26 E7
Sankt Augustin, *Germany* . 24 E3
Sankt Blasien, *Germany* .. 25 H4
Sankt Gallen, *Switz.* 25 H5
Sankt Gallen □, *Switz.* .. 25 H5
Sankt Goar, *Germany* .. 25 E3
Sankt Ingbert, *Germany* .. 25 F3
Sankt Johann im Pongau,
  Austria 26 D6
Sankt Johann in Tirol,
  Austria 26 D5
Sankt-Peterburg, *Russia* .. 46 C6
Sankt Pölten, *Austria* .. 26 C8
Sankt Ulrich = Ortisei, *Italy* 29 B8
Sankt Valentin, *Austria* .. 26 C7
Sankt Veit an der Glan,
  Austria 26 E7
Sankt Wendel, *Germany* .. 25 F3
Sankt Wolfgang, *Austria* .. 26 D6
Sankuru →,
  Dem. Rep. of the Congo 84 E4
Sanliurfa, *Turkey* 70 B3
Sanlúcar de Barrameda,
  Spain 35 J4
Sanluri, *Italy* 30 C1
Sânmartin, *Romania* .. 43 D10
Sanmen, *China* 59 C13
Sanmenxia, *China* 56 G6
Sanming, *China* 59 D11
Sannaspos, *S. Africa* .. 88 D4
Sannicandro Gargánico, *Italy* 29 G12
Sânnicolau Mare, *Romania* 42 D5
Sannieshof, *S. Africa* .. 88 D4
Sannīn, J., *Lebanon* 75 B4
Sanniquellie, *Liberia* .. 82 D3
Sannūr, W. →, *Egypt* .. 80 B3
Sanok, *Poland* 45 J9
Sanquhar, *U.K.* 14 F5
Sansanding, *Mali* 82 C3
Sansepolcro, *Italy* 29 E9

Sansha, *China* 59 D13
Sanshui, *China* 59 F9
Sanski Most, *Bos.-H.* .. 29 D13
Sansui, *China* 58 D7
Sant Antoni Abat, *Spain* .. 37 C7
Sant Boi de Llobregat, *Spain* 32 D7
Sant Carles, *Spain* 37 B8
Sant Carles de la Ràpita,
  Spain 32 E5
Sant Celoni, *Spain* 32 D7
Sant Feliu de Guíxols, *Spain* 32 D8
Sant Feliu de Llobregat,
  Spain 32 D7
Sant Ferran, *Spain* 37 C7
Sant Francesc de
  Formentera, *Spain* 37 C7
Sant Jaume, *Spain* 37 B11
Sant Joan Baptista, *Spain* 37 B8
Sant Jordi, *Spain* 37 B9
Sant Jordi, G. de, *Spain* .. 32 E6
Sant Llorenç de Morunys,
  Spain 32 C6
Sant Llorenç des Cardassar,
  Spain 37 B10
Sant Mateu, *Baleares, Spain* 37 B7
Sant Mateu, *Valencia, Spain* 32 E5
Sant Miquel, *Spain* 37 B7
Sant Telm, *Spain* 37 B9
Sant' Ágata Militello, *Italy* 31 D7
Santa Agnés, *Spain* 37 B7
Santa Ana, *Bolivia* 124 F5
Santa Ana, *El Salv.* 120 D2
Santa Ana, *Mexico* 118 A2
Santa Ana, *U.S.A.* 117 M9
Sant' Ángelo Lodigiano, *Italy* 28 C6
Sant' Antíoco, *Italy* 30 C1
Santa Barbara, *Chile* .. 126 D1
Santa Barbara, *Honduras* 120 D2
Santa Bárbara, *Mexico* .. 118 B3
Santa Bárbara, *Spain* .. 32 E5
Santa Barbara, *U.S.A.* .. 117 L7
Santa Bárbara, Mt., *Spain* 33 H2
Santa Barbara Channel,
  U.S.A. 117 L7
Santa Barbara I., *U.S.A.* 117 M7
Santa Catalina, Gulf of,
  U.S.A. 117 N9
Santa Catalina, I., *Mexico* . 118 B2
Santa Catalina I., *U.S.A.* 117 M8
Santa Catarina □, *Brazil* 127 B6
Santa Catarina, I. de, *Brazil* 127 B6
Santa Caterina di Pittinuri,
  Italy 30 B1
Santa Caterina Villarmosa,
  Italy 31 E7
Santa Cecília, *Brazil* 127 B5
Santa Clara, *Cuba* 120 B4
Santa Clara, *Calif., U.S.A.* 116 H5
Santa Clara, *Utah, U.S.A.* 115 H7
Santa Clara, El Golfo de,
  Mexico 118 A2
Santa Clara de Olimar,
  Uruguay 127 C5
Santa Clarita, *U.S.A.* .. 117 L8
Santa Coloma de Farners,
  Spain 32 D7
Santa Coloma de Gramenet,
  Spain 32 D7
Santa Comba, *Spain* 34 B2
Santa Croce Camerina, *Italy* 31 F7
Santa Croce di Magliano,
  Italy 29 G11
Santa Cruz, *Argentina* .. 128 G3
Santa Cruz, *Bolivia* 124 G6
Santa Cruz, *Chile* 126 C1
Santa Cruz, *Costa Rica* .. 120 D2
Santa Cruz, *Madeira* 37 D3
Santa Cruz, *Phil.* 61 D4
Santa Cruz, *U.S.A.* 116 J4
Santa Cruz →, *Argentina* 128 G3
Santa Cruz de la Palma,
  Canary Is. 37 F2
Santa Cruz de Mudela, *Spain* 35 G7
Santa Cruz de Tenerife,
  Canary Is. 37 F3
Santa Cruz del Norte, *Cuba* 120 B3
Santa Cruz del Retamar,
  Spain 34 E6
Santa Cruz del Sur, *Cuba* 120 B4
Santa Cruz do Rio Pardo,
  Brazil 127 A6
Santa Cruz do Sul, *Brazil* 127 B5
Santa Cruz I., *U.S.A.* .. 117 M7
Santa Cruz Is., *Solomon Is.* 96 J8
Santa Domingo, Cay,
  Bahamas 120 B4
Sant' Egídio alla Vibrata,
  Italy 29 F10
Santa Elena, *Argentina* .. 126 C4
Santa Elena, C., *Costa Rica* 120 D2
Sant' Eufémia, G. di, *Italy* . 31 D9
Sant Eulàlia des Riu, *Spain* 37 C8
Santa Fe, *Argentina* 126 C3
Santa Fe, *Spain* 35 H7
Santa Fe, *U.S.A.* 115 J11
Santa Fé □, *Argentina* .. 126 C3
Santa Fé do Sul, *Brazil* .. 125 H8
Santa Filomena, *Brazil* .. 125 E9
Santa Fiora, *Italy* 29 F8
Santa Gertrudis, *Spain* .. 37 C7
Santa Giustina, *Italy* 29 B9
Santa Inês, *Brazil* 125 F11
Santa Inés, *Spain* 35 G5
Santa Inés, I., *Chile* 122 J3
Santa Isabel = Rey Malabo,
  Eq. Guin. 83 E6
Santa Isabel, *Argentina* .. 126 D2
Santa Isabel, Pico, *Eq. Guin.* 83 E6
Santa Isabel do Morro,
  Brazil 125 F8

Santa Lucía, *Corrientes,
  Argentina* 126 B4
Santa Lucía, *San Juan,
  Argentina* 126 C2
Santa Lucía, *Spain* 33 H4
Santa Lucia, *Uruguay* .. 126 C4
Santa Lucia Range, *U.S.A.* 116 K5
Santa Magdalena, I., *Mexico* 118 C2
Santa Margarita, *Argentina* . 126 D3
Santa Margarita, *Spain* .. 37 B9
Santa Margarita, *U.S.A.* 116 K6
Santa Margarita →, *U.S.A.* 117 M9
Santa Margarita, I., *Mexico* 118 C2
Santa Margherita, *Italy* .. 30 D1
Santa Margherita Ligure,
  Italy 28 D6
Santa María, *Argentina* .. 126 B2
Santa María, *Brazil* 127 B5
Santa Maria, *U.S.A.* .. 117 L6
Santa María →, *Mexico* .. 118 A3
Santa María, B. de, *Mexico* 118 B3
Santa Maria, C. de, *Portugal* 35 J3
Santa Maria Cápua Vétere,
  Italy 31 A7
Santa Maria da Feira,
  Portugal 34 E2
Santa Maria da Vitória,
  Brazil 125 F10
Santa Maria del Camí, *Spain* 37 B9
Santa Maria di Léuca, C.,
  Italy 31 C11
Santa María la Real de
  Nieva, *Spain* 34 D6
Santa Marinella, *Italy* .. 29 F8
Santa Marta, *Colombia* .. 124 A4
Santa Marta, Sierra Nevada
  de, *Colombia* 122 B3
Santa Marta de Tormes,
  Spain 34 E5
Santa Marta Grande, C.,
  Brazil 127 B6
Santa Marta Ortigueira, Ría
  de, *Spain* 34 B3
Santa Maura = Levkás,
  Greece 38 C2
Santa Monica, *U.S.A.* .. 117 M8
Santa Olalla, *Huelva, Spain* 35 H4
Santa Olalla, *Toledo, Spain* 34 E6
Santa Paula, *U.S.A.* .. 117 L7
Santa Pola, *Spain* 33 G4
Santa Ponsa, *Spain* 37 B9
Santa Rita, *U.S.A.* 115 K10
Santa Rosa, *La Pampa,
  Argentina* 126 D3
Santa Rosa, *San Luis,
  Argentina* 126 C2
Santa Rosa, *Brazil* 127 B5
Santa Rosa, *Calif., U.S.A.* 116 G4
Santa Rosa, *N. Mex., U.S.A.* 113 H2
Santa Rosa de Copán,
  Honduras 120 D2
Santa Rosa de Río Primero,
  Argentina 126 C3
Santa Rosa del Sara, *Bolivia* 124 G6
Santa Rosa I., *U.S.A.* .. 117 M6
Santa Rosa Range, *U.S.A.* 114 F5
Santa Rosalía, *Mexico* .. 118 B2
Santa Sylvina, *Argentina* . 126 B3
Santa Tecla = Nueva San
  Salvador, *El Salv.* 120 D2
Santa Teresa, *Argentina* .. 126 C3
Santa Teresa, *Australia* .. 94 C1
Santa Teresa, *Mexico* .. 119 B5
Santa Teresa di Riva, *Italy* . 31 E8
Santa Teresa Gallura, *Italy* . 30 A2
Santa Uxía, *Spain* 34 C2
Santa Vitória do Palmar,
  Brazil 127 C5
Santa Ynez →, *U.S.A.* .. 117 L6
Santa Ynez Mts., *U.S.A.* 117 L6
Santa Ysabel, *U.S.A.* .. 117 M10
Santadi, *Italy* 30 C1
Santaella, *Spain* 35 H6
Santai, *China* 58 B5
Santana, *Madeira* 37 D3
Sântana, *Romania* 42 D6
Santana, Coxilha de, *Brazil* 127 C4
Santana do Livramento,
  Brazil 127 C4
Santander, *Spain* 34 B7
Santander Jiménez, *Mexico* . 119 C5
Santanyí, *Spain* 37 B10
Santaquin, *U.S.A.* 114 G8
Santarcángelo di Romagna,
  Italy 29 D9
Santarém, *Portugal* 35 F2
Santarém □, *Portugal* .. 35 F2
Santaren Channel, *W. Indies* 120 B4
Santee, *U.S.A.* 117 N10
Santee →, *U.S.A.* 109 J6
Santéramo in Colle, *Italy* .. 31 B9
Santerno →, *Italy* 29 D8
Santhià, *Italy* 28 C5
Santiago, *Brazil* 127 B5
Santiago, *Chile* 126 C1
Santiago, *Panama* 120 E3
Santiago, *Phil.* 61 C4
Santiago □, *Chile* 126 C1
Santiago →, *Mexico* 98 G9
Santiago →, *Peru* 124 D3
Santiago, Punta de,
  Eq. Guin. 83 E6
Santiago de Compostela,
  Spain 34 C2
Santiago de Cuba, *Cuba* .. 120 C4
Santiago de los Cabelleros,
  Dom. Rep. 121 C5
Santiago del Estero,
  Argentina 126 B3

Santiago del Estero □,
  Argentina 126 B3
Santiago del Teide,
  Canary Is. 37 F3
Santiago do Cacém, *Portugal* 35 G2
Santiago Ixcuintla, *Mexico* . 118 C3
Santiago Papasquiaro,
  Mexico 118 C3
Santiaguillo, L. de, *Mexico* 118 C4
Santiguila, *Mali* 82 C3
Santillana, *Spain* 34 B6
Santisteban del Puerto, *Spain* 35 G7
Santo Amaro, *Brazil* 125 F11
Santo Anastácio, *Brazil* .. 127 A5
Santo André, *Brazil* 127 A6
Santo Ângelo, *Brazil* 127 B5
Santo Antônio do Içá, *Brazil* 124 D5
Santo Antônio do Leverger,
  Brazil 125 G7
Santo Domingo, *Dom. Rep.* 121 C6
Santo Domingo, *Baja Calif.*,
  Mexico 118 A1
Santo Domingo,
  Baja Calif. S., Mexico .. 118 B2
Santo Domingo, *Nic.* 120 D3
Santo Domingo de la
  Calzada, *Spain* 32 C2
Santo Domingo de los
  Colorados, *Ecuador* .. 124 D3
Santo Domingo Pueblo,
  U.S.A. 115 J10
Santo Stéfano di Camastro,
  Italy 31 D7
Santo Tirso, *Portugal* .. 34 D2
Santo Tomás, *Mexico* .. 118 A1
Santo Tomás, *Peru* 124 F4
Santo Tomé, *Argentina* .. 127 B4
Santo Tomé de Guayana =
  Ciudad Guayana,
  Venezuela 124 B6
Santomera, *Spain* 33 G3
Santoña, *Spain* 34 B7
Santorini = Thíra, *Greece* 39 E7
Santos, *Brazil* 127 A6
Santos, Sierra de los, *Spain* 35 G5
Santos Dumont, *Brazil* .. 127 A7
Sanwer, *India* 68 H6
Sanxenxo, *Spain* 34 C2
Sanyuan, *China* 56 G5
São Bartolomeu de Messines,
  Portugal 35 H2
São Bernardo do Campo,
  Brazil 127 A6
São Borja, *Brazil* 127 B4
São Brás de Alportel,
  Portugal 35 H3
São Carlos, *Brazil* 127 A6
São Cristóvão, *Brazil* .. 125 F11
São Domingos, *Brazil* .. 125 F9
São Domingos, *Guinea-Biss.* 82 C1
São Francisco, *Brazil* .. 125 G10
São Francisco →, *Brazil* 122 E7
São Francisco do Sul, *Brazil* 127 B6
São Gabriel, *Brazil* 127 C5
São Gonçalo, *Brazil* 127 A7
Sao Hill, *Tanzania* 87 D4
São João, *Guinea-Biss.* .. 82 C1
São João da Boa Vista,
  Brazil 127 A6
São João da Madeira,
  Portugal 34 E2
São João da Pesqueira,
  Portugal 34 D3
São João do Araguaia, *Brazil* 125 E9
São João do Piauí, *Brazil* . 125 E10
São Joaquim, *Brazil* 127 B6
São Jorge, Pta. de, *Madeira* 37 D3
São José, *Brazil* 127 B5
São José do Norte, *Brazil* 127 C5
São José do Rio Prêto,
  Brazil 127 A6
São José dos Campos, *Brazil* 127 A6
São Leopoldo, *Brazil* 127 B5
São Lourenço, *Brazil* .. 127 A6
São Lourenço →, *Brazil* 125 G7
São Lourenço, Pta. de,
  Madeira 37 D3
São Lourenço do Sul, *Brazil* 127 C5
São Luís, *Brazil* 125 D10
São Luís Gonzaga, *Brazil* 127 B5
São Marcos →, *Brazil* .. 125 G9
São Marcos, B. de, *Brazil* 125 D10
São Martinho da Cortiça,
  Portugal 34 E2
São Mateus, *Brazil* 125 G11
São Mateus do Sul, *Brazil* 127 B5
São Miguel do Oeste, *Brazil* 127 B5
São Paulo, *Brazil* 127 A6
São Paulo □, *Brazil* 127 A6
São Paulo, I., *Atl. Oc.* .. 2 D8
São Paulo de Olivença,
  Brazil 124 D5
São Pedro do Sul, *Portugal* . 34 E2
São Roque, *Madeira* 37 D3
São Roque, C. de, *Brazil* 125 E12
São Sebastião, I. de, *Brazil* 127 A6
São Sebastião do Paraíso,
  Brazil 127 A6
São Teotónio, *Portugal* .. 35 H2
São Tomé, *Atl. Oc.* 76 F4
São Tomé, C. de, *Brazil* 127 A7
São Tomé & Príncipe ■,
  Africa 77 F4
São Vicente, *Brazil* 127 A6
São Vicente, *Madeira* .. 37 D2
São Vicente, C. de, *Portugal* 35 H1
Saona, I., *Dom. Rep.* .. 121 C6
Saône →, *France* 19 G11
Saône-et-Loire □, *France* . 19 F11
Saonek, *Indonesia* 63 E8

Sápai, Greece ... 41 E9
Sapanca, Turkey ... 72 B4
Saparua, Indonesia ... 63 E7
Sapele, Nigeria ... 83 D6
Sapelo I., U.S.A. ... 109 K5
Şaphane, Turkey ... 39 B11
Sapiéntza, Greece ... 38 E3
Sapone, Burkina Faso ... 83 C4
Saposoa, Peru ... 124 E3
Sapouy, Burkina Faso ... 83 C4
Sapozhok, Russia ... 48 D5
Sapphire, Australia ... 94 C4
Sappho, U.S.A. ... 116 B2
Sapporo, Japan ... 54 C10
Sapri, Italy ... 31 B8
Sapulpa, U.S.A. ... 113 H6
Saqqez, Iran ... 70 B5
Sar Dasht, Iran ... 71 C6
Sar Gachīneh, Iran ... 71 D6
Sar Planina, Macedonia ... 40 E4
Sara, Burkina Faso ... 82 C4
Sara, Phil. ... 61 F5
Sara Buri = Saraburi, Thailand ... 64 E3
Sarāb, Iran ... 70 B5
Sarabadi, Iraq ... 70 C5
Saraburi, Thailand ... 64 E3
Sarada →, India ... 67 F12
Saradiya, India ... 68 J4
Saraféré, Mali ... 82 B4
Saragossa = Zaragoza, Spain ... 32 D4
Saraguro, Ecuador ... 124 D3
Sarai Naurang, Pakistan ... 68 C4
Saraikela, India ... 69 H11
Saraiu, Romania ... 43 F13
Sarajevo, Bos.-H. ... 42 G3
Sarakhs, Turkmenistan ... 71 B9
Saran, Gunung, Indonesia ... 62 E4
Saranac, U.S.A. ... 111 B10
Saranac Lake, U.S.A. ... 111 B10
Saranda, Tanzania ... 86 D3
Sarandë, Albania ... 40 G3
Sarandí del Yi, Uruguay ... 127 C4
Sarandí Grande, Uruguay ... 126 C4
Sarangani B., Phil. ... 61 J6
Sarangani Is., Phil. ... 61 J6
Sarangarh, India ... 67 J13
Saransk, Russia ... 48 C7
Sarapul, Russia ... 50 D6
Sarasota, U.S.A. ... 109 M4
Saratoga, Calif., U.S.A. ... 116 H4
Saratoga, Wyo., U.S.A. ... 114 F10
Saratoga Springs, U.S.A. ... 111 C11
Saratok, Malaysia ... 62 D4
Saratov, Russia ... 48 E7
Saravane, Laos ... 64 E6
Sarawak □, Malaysia ... 62 D4
Saray, Tekirdağ, Turkey ... 41 E11
Saray, Van, Turkey ... 73 C11
Saraya, Guinea ... 82 C2
Saraya, Senegal ... 82 C2
Sarayçık, Turkey ... 39 B11
Sarayköy, Turkey ... 39 D10
Saraylar, Turkey ... 41 F11
Sarayönü, Turkey ... 72 C5
Sarbāz, Iran ... 71 E9
Sarbīsheh, Iran ... 71 C8
Sárbogárd, Hungary ... 42 D3
Sarca →, Italy ... 28 C7
Sarcelles, France ... 19 D9
Sarda = Sarada →, India ... 67 F12
Sardarshahr, India ... 68 E6
Sardegna □, Italy ... 30 B1
Sardhana, India ... 68 E7
Sardina, Pta., Canary Is. ... 37 F4
Sardinia = Sardegna □, Italy ... 30 B1
Sardis, Turkey ... 39 C10
Sārdūīyeh = Dar Mazār, Iran ... 71 D8
S'Arenal, Spain ... 37 B9
Sarentino, Italy ... 29 B8
Saréyamou, Mali ... 82 B4
Sargasso Sea, Atl. Oc. ... 97 D20
Sargodha, Pakistan ... 68 C5
Sarh, Chad ... 79 G9
Sarhala, Ivory C. ... 82 D3
Sārī, Iran ... 71 B7
Sari d'Orcino, France ... 21 F12
Sária, Greece ... 39 F9
Saria, India ... 69 J10
Sariab, Pakistan ... 68 D2
Sarıbeyler, Turkey ... 39 B9
Sarıgöl, Turkey ... 72 C3
Sarıkamış, Turkey ... 73 B10
Sarıkaya, Turkey ... 72 C6
Sarikei, Malaysia ... 62 D4
Sarıköy, Turkey ... 41 F11
Sarila, India ... 69 G8
Sarina, Australia ... 94 C4
Sariñena, Spain ... 32 D4
Sarita, U.S.A. ... 113 M6
Sariwŏn, N. Korea ... 57 E13
Sariyar Baraji, Turkey ... 72 B4
Sarıyer, Turkey ... 41 E13
Sarju →, India ... 69 F9
Sark, U.K. ... 13 H5
Sarkad, Hungary ... 42 D6
Sarkari Tala, India ... 68 F4
Şarkışla, Turkey ... 72 C7
Şarköy, Turkey ... 41 F11
Sarlat-la-Canéda, France ... 20 D5
Sărmaşu, Romania ... 43 D9
Sarmi, Indonesia ... 63 E9
Sarmiento, Argentina ... 128 F3
Sarmizegetusa, Romania ... 42 E7
Särna, Sweden ... 10 C7
Sarnano, Italy ... 29 E10
Sarnen, Switz. ... 25 J4
Sarnia, Canada ... 102 D3
Sarno, Italy ... 31 B7

Sarnthein = Sarentino, Italy ... 29 B8
Särö, Sweden ... 11 G5
Sarolangun, Indonesia ... 62 E2
Saronikós Kólpos, Greece ... 38 D5
Saronno, Italy ... 28 C6
Saros Körfezi, Turkey ... 41 F10
Sárospatak, Hungary ... 42 B6
Sarpsborg, Norway ... 9 G14
Sarracín, Spain ... 34 C7
Sarralbe, France ... 19 D14
Sarre = Saar →, Europe ... 17 E6
Sarre, Italy ... 28 C4
Sarre-Union, France ... 19 D14
Sarrebourg, France ... 19 D14
Sarreguemines, France ... 19 C14
Sarria, Spain ... 34 C3
Sarrión, Spain ... 32 E4
Sarro, Mali ... 82 C3
Sarstedt, Germany ... 24 C5
Sartène, France ... 21 G12
Sarthe □, France ... 18 D7
Sarthe →, France ... 18 E6
Sartilly, France ... 18 D5
Saruhanlı, Turkey ... 39 C9
Săruleşti, Romania ... 43 F11
Saruna →, Pakistan ... 68 F2
Sárvár, Hungary ... 42 C1
Sarvestān, Iran ... 71 D7
Sárviz →, Hungary ... 42 D3
Sarzana, Italy ... 28 D6
Sarzeau, France ... 18 E4
Sasan Gir, India ... 68 J4
Sasebo, Japan ... 55 H4
Saser, India ... 69 B7
Saskatchewan □, Canada ... 105 C7
Saskatchewan →, Canada ... 105 C8
Saskatoon, Canada ... 105 C7
Saskylakh, Russia ... 51 B12
Sasolburg, S. Africa ... 89 D4
Sasovo, Russia ... 48 C5
Sassandra, Ivory C. ... 82 E3
Sassandra →, Ivory C. ... 82 E3
Sássari, Italy ... 30 B1
Sassnitz, Germany ... 24 A9
Sasso Marconi, Italy ... 29 D8
Sassocorvaro, Italy ... 29 E9
Sassoferrato, Italy ... 29 E9
Sasstown, Liberia ... 82 E3
Sassuolo, Italy ... 28 D7
Sástago, Spain ... 32 D4
Sasumua Dam, Kenya ... 86 C4
Sasyk, Ozero, Ukraine ... 47 K5
Sata-Misaki, Japan ... 55 J5
Satadougou, Mali ... 82 C2
Satakunta, Finland ... 9 F20
Satama-Soukoura, Ivory C. ... 82 D4
Satara, India ... 66 L8
Satara, S. Africa ... 89 C5
Satbarwa, India ... 69 H11
Såtenäs, Sweden ... 11 F6
Säter, Sweden ... 10 D9
Satevó, Mexico ... 118 B3
Satilla →, U.S.A. ... 109 K5
Satmala Hills, India ... 66 J9
Satna, India ... 69 G9
Šator, Bos.-H. ... 29 D13
Sátoraljaújhely, Hungary ... 42 B6
Satpura Ra., India ... 66 J10
Satrup, Germany ... 24 A5
Satsuna-Shotō, Japan ... 55 K5
Sattahip, Thailand ... 64 F3
Satu Mare, Romania ... 42 C7
Satu Mare □, Romania ... 42 C8
Satui, Indonesia ... 62 E5
Satun, Thailand ... 65 J3
Saturnina →, Brazil ... 124 F7
Sauce, Argentina ... 126 C4
Sauceda, Mexico ... 118 B4
Saucillo, Mexico ... 118 B3
Sauda, Norway ... 9 G12
Sauðárkrókur, Iceland ... 8 D4
Saugeen →, Canada ... 110 B3
Saugerties, U.S.A. ... 111 D11
Saugues, France ... 20 D7
Saugus, U.S.A. ... 117 L8
Sauk Centre, U.S.A. ... 112 C7
Sauk Rapids, U.S.A. ... 112 C7
Saulgau, Germany ... 25 G5
Saulieu, France ... 19 E11
Sault, France ... 21 D9
Sault Ste. Marie, Canada ... 102 C3
Sault Ste. Marie, U.S.A. ... 101 D11
Saumlaki, Indonesia ... 63 F8
Saumur, France ... 18 E6
Saunders, C., N.Z. ... 91 L3
Saunders I., Antarctica ... 5 B1
Saunders Point, Australia ... 93 E4
Sauri, Nigeria ... 83 C6
Saurimo, Angola ... 84 F4
Sausalito, U.S.A. ... 116 H4
Sauveterre-de-Béarn, France ... 20 E3
Sauzé-Vaussais, France ... 20 B4
Savá, Honduras ... 120 C2
Sava, Italy ... 31 B10
Sava →, Serbia, Yug. ... 42 F5
Savage, U.S.A. ... 112 B2
Savage I. = Niue, Cook Is. ... 97 J11
Savage River, Australia ... 94 G4
Savai'i, W. Samoa ... 91 A12
Savalou, Benin ... 83 D5
Savane, Mozam. ... 87 F4
Savanna, U.S.A. ... 112 D9
Savanna-la-Mar, Jamaica ... 120 C4

Savannah, Ga., U.S.A. ... 109 J5
Savannah, Mo., U.S.A. ... 112 F7
Savannah, Tenn., U.S.A. ... 109 H1
Savannah →, U.S.A. ... 109 J5
Savannakhet, Laos ... 64 D5
Savant L., Canada ... 102 B1
Savant Lake, Canada ... 102 B1
Savanur, India ... 66 M9
Săvârşin, Romania ... 42 D7
Savaştepe, Turkey ... 39 B9
Savé, Benin ... 83 D5
Save →, France ... 20 E5
Save →, Mozam. ... 89 C5
Sāveh, Iran ... 71 C6
Savelugu, Ghana ... 83 D4
Savenay, France ... 18 E5
Săveni, Romania ... 43 C11
Saverdun, France ... 20 E5
Saverne, France ... 19 D14
Savigliano, Italy ... 28 D4
Savigny-sur-Braye, France ... 18 E7
Sávio →, Italy ... 29 D9
Šavnik, Montenegro, Yug. ... 40 D3
Savo, Finland ... 8 E22
Savoie □, France ... 21 C10
Savona, Italy ... 28 D5
Savonlinna, Finland ... 46 B5
Savoy = Savoie □, France ... 21 C10
Şavşat, Turkey ... 73 B10
Sävsjö, Sweden ... 11 G8
Savur, Turkey ... 70 B4
Sawahlunto, Indonesia ... 62 E2
Sawai, Indonesia ... 63 E7
Sawai Madhopur, India ... 68 G7
Sawang Daen Din, Thailand ... 64 D4
Sawankhalok, Thailand ... 64 D2
Sawara, Japan ... 55 G10
Sawatch Range, U.S.A. ... 115 G10
Sawel Mt., U.K. ... 15 B4
Sawi, Thailand ... 65 G2
Sawla, Ghana ... 82 D4
Sawmills, Zimbabwe ... 87 F2
Sawtooth Range, U.S.A. ... 114 E6
Sawu, Indonesia ... 63 F6
Sawu Sea, Indonesia ... 63 F6
Saxby →, Australia ... 94 B3
Saxmundham, U.K. ... 13 E9
Saxony = Sachsen □, Germany ... 24 E9
Saxony, Lower = Niedersachsen □, Germany ... 24 C4
Saxton, U.S.A. ... 110 F6
Say, Mali ... 82 C4
Say, Niger ... 83 C5
Saya, Nigeria ... 83 D5
Sayabec, Canada ... 103 C6
Sayaboury, Laos ... 64 C3
Sayán, Peru ... 124 F3
Sayan, Vostochnyy, Russia ... 51 D10
Sayan, Zapadnyy, Russia ... 51 D10
Saydā, Lebanon ... 75 B4
Sayhandulaan = Oldziyt, Mongolia ... 56 B5
Sayḩūt, Yemen ... 74 D5
Saykhin, Kazakhstan ... 49 F8
Saynshand, Mongolia ... 56 B6
Sayre, Okla., U.S.A. ... 113 H5
Sayre, Pa., U.S.A. ... 111 E8
Sayreville, U.S.A. ... 111 F10
Sayula, Mexico ... 118 D4
Sayward, Canada ... 104 C3
Sazanit, Albania ... 40 F3
Sázava →, Czech Rep. ... 26 B7
Sazin, Pakistan ... 69 B5
Sazlika →, Bulgaria ... 41 E9
Scaër, France ... 18 D3
Scafell Pike, U.K. ... 12 C4
Scalea, Italy ... 31 C8
Scalloway, U.K. ... 14 A7
Scalpay, U.K. ... 14 D3
Scandia, Canada ... 104 C6
Scandiano, Italy ... 28 D7
Scandicci, Italy ... 29 E8
Scandinavia, Europe ... 6 C8
Scansano, Italy ... 29 F8
Scapa Flow, U.K. ... 14 C5
Scappoose, U.S.A. ... 116 E4
Scarámia, Capo, Italy ... 31 F7
Scarba, U.K. ... 14 E3
Scarborough, Trin. & Tob. ... 121 D7
Scarborough, U.K. ... 12 C7
Scariff I., Ireland ... 15 E1
Scarp, U.K. ... 14 C1
Scebeli, Wabi →, Somali Rep. ... 74 G3
Ščedro, Croatia ... 29 E13
Schaal See, Germany ... 24 B6
Schagen, Neths. ... 17 B4
Schaghticoke, U.S.A. ... 111 D11
Schärding, Austria ... 26 C6
Scharhörn, Germany ... 24 B4
Scheessel, Germany ... 24 B5
Schefferville, Canada ... 103 B6
Scheibbs, Austria ... 26 C8
Schelde →, Belgium ... 17 C4
Schell Creek Ra., U.S.A. ... 114 G6
Schellsburg, U.S.A. ... 110 F6
Schenectady, U.S.A. ... 111 D11
Schenevus, U.S.A. ... 111 D10
Scherfede, Germany ... 24 D5
Schesslitz, Germany ... 25 F7
Schiedam, Neths. ... 17 C4
Schiermonnikoog, Neths. ... 17 A6
Schiltigheim, France ... 19 D14
Schio, Italy ... 29 C8
Schladming, Austria ... 26 D6
Schlanders = Silandro, Italy ... 28 B7
Schlei →, Germany ... 24 A5

Schleiden, Germany ... 24 E2
Schleiz, Germany ... 24 E7
Schleswig, Germany ... 24 A5
Schleswig-Holstein □, Germany ... 24 A5
Schlüchtern, Germany ... 25 E5
Schmalkalden, Germany ... 24 E6
Schmölln, Germany ... 24 E8
Schneeberg, Austria ... 26 D8
Schneeberg, Germany ... 24 E8
Schneverdingen, Germany ... 24 B5
Schoharie, U.S.A. ... 111 D10
Schoharie →, U.S.A. ... 111 D10
Scholls, U.S.A. ... 116 E4
Schönberg, Mecklenburg-Vorpommern, Germany ... 24 B6
Schönberg, Schleswig-Holstein, Germany ... 24 A6
Schönebeck, Germany ... 24 C7
Schongau, Germany ... 25 H6
Schöningen, Germany ... 24 C6
Schopfheim, Germany ... 25 H3
Schorndorf, Germany ... 25 G5
Schortens, Germany ... 24 B3
Schouten I., Australia ... 94 G4
Schouten Is. = Supiori, Indonesia ... 63 E9
Schouwen, Neths. ... 17 C3
Schramberg, Germany ... 25 G4
Schrankogel, Austria ... 26 D4
Schreiber, Canada ... 102 C2
Schrems, Austria ... 26 C8
Schrobenhausen, Germany ... 25 G7
Schroon Lake, U.S.A. ... 111 C11
Schroffenstein, Namibia ... 88 D2
Schruns, Austria ... 26 D2
Schuler, Canada ... 105 C6
Schumacher, Canada ... 102 C3
Schurz, U.S.A. ... 114 G4
Schuyler, U.S.A. ... 112 E6
Schuylerville, U.S.A. ... 111 C11
Schuylkill →, U.S.A. ... 111 G8
Schuylkill Haven, U.S.A. ... 111 F8
Schwabach, Germany ... 25 F7
Schwaben □, Germany ... 25 G6
Schwäbisch Gmünd, Germany ... 25 G5
Schwäbisch Hall, Germany ... 25 F5
Schwäbische Alb, Germany ... 25 G5
Schwabmünchen, Germany ... 25 G6
Schwalmstadt, Germany ... 24 E5
Schwandorf, Germany ... 25 F8
Schwaner, Pegunungan, Indonesia ... 62 E4
Schwanewede, Germany ... 24 B4
Schwarmstedt, Germany ... 24 C5
Schwarze Elster →, Germany ... 24 D8
Schwarzenberg, Germany ... 24 E8
Schwarzrand, Namibia ... 88 D2
Schwarzwald, Germany ... 25 G4
Schwaz, Austria ... 26 D4
Schwechat, Austria ... 27 C9
Schwedt, Germany ... 24 B10
Schweinfurt, Germany ... 25 E6
Schweizer-Reneke, S. Africa ... 88 D4
Schwenningen = Villingen-Schwenningen, Germany ... 25 G4
Schwerin, Germany ... 24 B7
Schweriner See, Germany ... 24 B7
Schwetzingen, Germany ... 25 F4
Schwyz, Switz. ... 25 H4
Schwyz □, Switz. ... 25 H4
Sciacca, Italy ... 30 E6
Scicli, Italy ... 31 F7
Scilla, Italy ... 31 D8
Scilly, Isles of, U.K. ... 13 H1
Ścinawa, Poland ... 45 G3
Scione, Greece ... 40 G7
Scioto →, U.S.A. ... 108 F4
Scituate, U.S.A. ... 111 D14
Scobey, U.S.A. ... 112 A2
Scone, Australia ... 95 E5
Scordia, Italy ... 31 E7
Scoresbysund = Illoqqortoormiit, Greenland ... 4 B6
Scorniceşti, Romania ... 43 F9
Scotia, Calif., U.S.A. ... 114 F1
Scotia, N.Y., U.S.A. ... 111 D11
Scotia Sea, Antarctica ... 5 B18
Scotland, Canada ... 110 C4
Scotland □, U.K. ... 14 E5
Scott, C., Canada ... 92 B4
Scott City, U.S.A. ... 112 F4
Scott Glacier, Antarctica ... 5 C8
Scott I., Antarctica ... 5 C11
Scott Is., Canada ... 104 C3
Scott L., Canada ... 105 B7
Scott Reef, Australia ... 92 B3
Scottburgh, S. Africa ... 89 E5
Scottdale, U.S.A. ... 110 F5
Scottsbluff, U.S.A. ... 112 E3
Scottsboro, U.S.A. ... 109 H3
Scottsburg, U.S.A. ... 108 F3
Scottsdale, Australia ... 94 G4
Scottsdale, U.S.A. ... 115 K7
Scottsville, Ky., U.S.A. ... 109 G2
Scottsville, N.Y., U.S.A. ... 110 C7
Scottville, U.S.A. ... 108 D2
Scranton, U.S.A. ... 111 E9
Scugog, L., Canada ... 110 B6
Sculeni, Moldova ... 43 C12
Scunthorpe, U.K. ... 12 D7
Scuol Schuls, Switz. ... 25 J6
Scutari = Üsküdar, Turkey ... 41 F13
Seabrook, Australia ... 93 F2
Seaford, U.K. ... 13 G8

Seaford, U.S.A. ... 108 F8
Seaforth, Australia ... 94 C4
Seaforth, Canada ... 110 C3
Seaforth, L., U.K. ... 14 D2
Seagraves, U.S.A. ... 113 J3
Seaham, U.K. ... 12 C6
Seal →, Canada ... 105 B10
Seal L., Canada ... 103 B7
Sealy, U.S.A. ... 113 L6
Searchlight, U.S.A. ... 117 K12
Searcy, U.S.A. ... 113 H9
Searles L., U.S.A. ... 117 K9
Seascale, U.K. ... 12 C4
Seaside, Calif., U.S.A. ... 116 J5
Seaside, Oreg., U.S.A. ... 116 E3
Seaspray, Australia ... 95 F4
Seattle, U.S.A. ... 116 C4
Seaview Ra., Australia ... 94 B4
Sebago L., U.S.A. ... 111 C14
Sebago Lake, U.S.A. ... 111 C14
Sebastián Vizcaíno, B., Mexico ... 118 B2
Sebastopol = Sevastopol, Ukraine ... 47 K7
Sebastopol, U.S.A. ... 116 G4
Sebba, Burkina Faso ... 83 C5
Sebderat, Eritrea ... 81 D4
Sébékoro, Mali ... 82 C3
Seben, Turkey ... 72 B4
Sebeş, Romania ... 43 E8
Sebeşului, Munţii, Romania ... 43 E8
Sebewaing, U.S.A. ... 108 D4
Sebezh, Russia ... 46 D5
Sebha = Sabhah, Libya ... 79 C8
Sébi, Mali ... 82 B4
Sebinkarahisar, Turkey ... 73 B8
Sebiş, Romania ... 42 D7
Sebnitz, Germany ... 24 E10
Sebring, Fla., U.S.A. ... 109 M5
Sebring, Ohio, U.S.A. ... 110 F3
Sebringville, Canada ... 110 C3
Sebta = Ceuta, N. Afr. ... 78 A4
Sebuku, Indonesia ... 62 E5
Sebuku, Teluk, Malaysia ... 62 D5
Sečanj, Serbia, Yug. ... 42 E5
Secchia →, Italy ... 28 C8
Sechelt, Canada ... 104 D4
Sechura, Desierto de, Peru ... 124 E2
Seclin, France ... 19 B10
Secondigny, France ... 18 F6
Sečovce, Slovak Rep. ... 27 C14
Secretary I., N.Z. ... 91 L1
Secunderabad, India ... 66 L11
Security-Widefield, U.S.A. ... 112 F2
Sedalia, U.S.A. ... 112 F8
Sedan, France ... 19 C11
Sedan, U.S.A. ... 113 G6
Sedano, Spain ... 34 C7
Seddon, N.Z. ... 91 J5
Seddonville, N.Z. ... 91 J4
Sedé Boqér, Israel ... 75 E3
Sedeh, Fārs, Iran ... 71 D7
Sedeh, Khorāsān, Iran ... 71 C8
Séderon, France ... 21 D9
Sderot, Israel ... 75 D3
Sédhiou, Senegal ... 82 C1
Sedico, Italy ... 29 B9
Sedlčany, Czech Rep. ... 26 B7
Sedley, Canada ... 105 C8
Sedona, U.S.A. ... 115 J8
Sedova, Pik, Russia ... 50 B6
Sedro Woolley, U.S.A. ... 116 B4
Šeduva, Lithuania ... 44 C10
Sędziszów, Poland ... 45 H7
Sędziszów Małopolski, Poland ... 45 H8
Seebad Ahlbeck, Germany ... 24 B10
Seefeld in Tirol, Austria ... 26 D4
Seehausen, Germany ... 24 C7
Seeheim, Namibia ... 88 D2
Seeheim-Jugenheim, Germany ... 25 F4
Seeis, Namibia ... 88 C2
Seekoei →, S. Africa ... 88 E4
Seeley's Bay, Canada ... 111 B8
Seelow, Germany ... 24 C10
Sées, France ... 18 D7
Seesen, Germany ... 24 D6
Seevetal, Germany ... 24 B6
Sefadu, S. Leone ... 82 D2
Seferihisar, Turkey ... 39 C8
Séfeto, Mali ... 82 C3
Sefwi Bekwai, Ghana ... 82 D4
Segamat, Malaysia ... 65 L4
Segarcea, Romania ... 43 F8
Ségbana, Benin ... 83 C5
Segbwema, S. Leone ... 82 D2
Seget, Indonesia ... 63 E8
Segonzac, France ... 20 C3
Segorbe, Spain ... 32 F4
Ségou, Mali ... 82 C3
Segovia = Coco →, Cent. Amer. ... 120 D3
Segovia, Spain ... 34 E6
Segovia □, Spain ... 34 E6
Segré, France ... 18 E6
Segre →, Spain ... 32 D5
Séguéla, Ivory C. ... 82 D3
Séguénéga, Burkina Faso ... 83 C4
Seguin, U.S.A. ... 113 L6
Segundo →, Argentina ... 126 C3
Segura →, Spain ... 33 G4
Segura, Sierra de, Spain ... 33 G2
Seh Konj, Kūh-e, Iran ... 71 D8
Seh Qal'eh, Iran ... 71 C8
Sehitwa, Botswana ... 88 C3
Sehore, India ... 68 H7
Sehwan, Pakistan ... 68 F2
Seica Mare, Romania ... 43 D9
Seil, U.K. ... 14 E3
Seiland, Norway ... 8 A20

Seilhac, France 20 C5
Seiling, U.S.A. 113 G5
Seille →, Moselle, France . 19 C13
Seille →, Saône-et-Loire, France 19 F11
Sein, Î. de, France 18 D2
Seinäjoki, Finland 9 E20
Seine →, France 18 C7
Seine, B. de la, France 18 C6
Seine-et-Marne □, France .. 19 D10
Seine-Maritime □, France .. 18 C7
Seine-St-Denis □, France .. 19 D9
Seini, Romania 43 C8
Seirijai, Lithuania 44 D10
Sejerø, Denmark 11 J5
Sejerø Bugt, Denmark 11 J5
Sejny, Poland 44 D10
Seka, Ethiopia 81 F4
Sekayu, Indonesia 62 E2
Seke, Tanzania 86 C3
Sekenke, Tanzania 86 C3
Seki, Turkey 39 E11
Sekondi-Takoradi, Ghana .. 82 E4
Sekota, Ethiopia 81 E4
Seksna, Russia 46 C10
Sekuma, Botswana 88 C3
Selah, U.S.A. 114 C3
Selama, Malaysia 65 K3
Selárgius, Italy 30 C2
Selaru, Indonesia 63 F8
Selb, Germany 25 E8
Selby, U.K. 12 D6
Selby, U.S.A. 112 C4
Selça, Croatia 29 E13
Selçuk, Turkey 39 D9
Selden, U.S.A. 112 F4
Sele →, Italy 31 B7
Selebi-Pikwe, Botswana 89 C4
Selemdzha →, Russia 51 D13
Selendi, Manisa, Turkey ... 39 C10
Selendi, Manisa, Turkey ... 39 C9
Selenga = Selenge
  Mörön →, Asia 60 A5
Selenge Mörön →, Asia 60 A5
Selenica, Albania 40 F3
Selenter See, Germany 24 A6
Sélestat, France 19 D14
Seletan, Tanjung, Indonesia 62 E4
Selevac, Serbia, Yug. 40 B4
Sélibabi, Mauritania 82 B2
Seliger, Ozero, Russia 46 D7
Seligman, U.S.A. 115 J7
Şelim, Turkey 73 B10
Selîma, El Wâhât el, Sudan 80 C2
Selimiye, Turkey 39 D9
Selinda Spillway →,
  Botswana 88 B3
Selinoús, Greece 38 D3
Selinsgrove, U.S.A. 110 F8
Selizharovo, Russia 46 D7
Selkirk, Canada 105 C9
Selkirk, U.K. 14 F6
Selkirk I., Canada 105 C9
Selkirk Mts., Canada 100 C8
Sellama, Sudan 81 E2
Selliá, Greece 36 D6
Sellières, France 19 F12
Sells, U.S.A. 115 L8
Sellye, Hungary 42 E2
Selma, Ala., U.S.A. 109 J2
Selma, Calif., U.S.A. 116 J7
Selma, N.C., U.S.A. 109 H6
Selmer, U.S.A. 109 H1
Selongey, France 19 E12
Selowandoma Falls,
  Zimbabwe 87 G3
Selpele, Indonesia 63 E8
Selsey Bill, U.K. 13 G7
Seltso, Russia 46 F8
Seltz, France 19 D15
Selu, Indonesia 63 F8
Sélune →, France 18 D5
Selva = La Selva del Camp,
  Spain 32 D6
Selva, Argentina 126 B3
Selvas, Brazil 122 D4
Selwyn L., Canada 105 B8
Selwyn Mts., Canada 100 B6
Selwyn Ra., Australia 94 C3
Semani →, Albania 40 F3
Semarang, Indonesia 63 G14
Sembabule, Uganda 86 C3
Şemdinli, Turkey 73 D11
Sémé, Senegal 82 B2
Semeih, Sudan 81 E3
Semenov, Russia 48 B7
Semenovka, Chernihiv,
  Ukraine 47 F7
Semenovka, Kremenchuk,
  Ukraine 47 H7
Semeru, Indonesia 63 H15
Semey, Kazakhstan 50 D9
Semikarakorskiy, Russia ... 49 G5
Semiluki, Russia 47 G10
Seminoe Reservoir, U.S.A. . 114 F10
Seminole, Okla., U.S.A. ... 113 H6
Seminole, Tex., U.S.A. 113 J3
Seminole Draw →, U.S.A. ... 113 J3
Semipalatinsk = Semey,
  Kazakhstan 50 D9
Semirara Is., Phil. 61 F4
Semitau, Indonesia 62 D4
Semiyarka, Kazakhstan 50 D8
Semiyarskoye = Semiyarka,
  Kazakhstan 50 D8
Semmering P., Austria 26 D8
Semnān, Iran 71 C7
Semnān □, Iran 71 C7
Semporna, Malaysia 63 D5
Semuda, Indonesia 62 E4
Semur-en-Auxois, France ... 19 E11

Sen →, Cambodia 62 B3
Senã, Iran 71 D6
Sena, Mozam. 87 H4
Sena Madureira, Brazil 124 E5
Senador Pompeu, Brazil 125 E11
Senaki, Georgia 49 J6
Senanga, Zambia 88 B3
Senatobia, U.S.A. 113 H10
Sencelles, Spain 37 B9
Sendafa, Ethiopia 81 F4
Sendai, Kagoshima, Japan .. 55 J5
Sendai, Miyagi, Japan 54 E10
Sendai-Wan, Japan 54 E10
Senden, Bayern, Germany ... 25 G6
Senden,
  Nordrhein-Westfalen,
  Germany 24 D3
Sendhwa, India 68 J6
Sene →, Ghana 83 D4
Senec, Slovak Rep. 27 C10
Seneca, U.S.A. 109 H4
Seneca Falls, U.S.A. 111 D8
Seneca L., U.S.A. 110 D8
Senecaville L., U.S.A. 110 G3
Senegal ■, W. Afr. 82 C2
Sénégal →, W. Afr. 82 B1
Senegambia, Africa 76 E2
Senekal, S. Africa 89 D4
Senftenberg, Germany 24 D10
Senga Hill, Zambia 87 D3
Senge Khambab = Indus →,
  Pakistan 68 G2
Sengiley, Russia 48 D9
Sengua →, Zimbabwe 87 F2
Senhor-do-Bonfim, Brazil .. 125 F10
Senica, Slovak Rep. 27 C10
Senigállia, Italy 29 E10
Senio →, Italy 29 D9
Senirkent, Turkey 39 C12
Senise, Italy 31 B9
Senj, Croatia 29 D11
Senja, Norway 8 B17
Senkaku-Shotō, Japan 55 L1
Senlis, France 19 C9
Senmonorom, Cambodia 64 F6
Sennâr, Sudan 81 E3
Sennar □, Sudan 81 E3
Senneterre, Canada 102 C4
Senno, Belarus 46 E5
Sénnori, Italy 30 B1
Seno, Laos 64 D5
Senonches, France 18 D8
Senorbì, Italy 30 C2
Senožeče, Slovenia 29 C11
Sens, France 19 D10
Senta, Serbia, Yug. 42 E5
Sentani, Indonesia 63 E10
Sentery,
  Dem. Rep. of the Congo . 86 D2
Sentinel, U.S.A. 115 K7
Šentjur, Slovenia 29 B12
Senya Beraku, Ghana 83 D4
Seo de Urgel = La Seu
  d'Urgell, Spain 32 C6
Seohara, India 69 E8
Seonath →, India 69 J10
Seondha, India 69 F8
Seoni, India 69 H8
Seoni Malwa, India 68 H8
Seoul = Sŏul, S. Korea 57 F14
Sepīdān, Iran 71 D7
Sepo-ri, N. Korea 57 E14
Sępólno Krajeńskie, Poland 44 E4
Sepone, Laos 64 D6
Sepopol, Poland 44 D8
Sept-Îles, Canada 103 B6
Septemvri, Bulgaria 41 D8
Sepúlveda, Spain 34 D7
Sequeros, Spain 34 E4
Sequim, U.S.A. 116 B3
Sequoia National Park,
  U.S.A. 116 J8
Serafimovich, Russia 48 F6
Seraing, Belgium 17 D5
Seraja, Indonesia 65 L7
Serakhis →, Cyprus 36 D11
Seram, Indonesia 63 E7
Seram Sea, Indonesia 63 E7
Seranantsara, Madag. 89 B8
Serang, Indonesia 63 G12
Serasan, Indonesia 65 L7
Seravezza, Italy 28 E7
Şerbettar, Turkey 41 E10
Serbia □, Yugoslavia 40 C5
Şercaia, Romania 43 E10
Serdo, Ethiopia 81 E5
Serdobsk, Russia 48 D7
Sered', Slovak Rep. 27 C10
Seredka, Russia 46 C5
Şereflikoçhisar, Turkey ... 72 C5
Seregno, Italy 28 C6
Seremban, Malaysia 65 L3
Serengeti Plain, Tanzania . 86 C4
Serenje, Zambia 87 E3
Sereth = Siret →, Romania . 43 E12
Sergach, Russia 48 C7
Sergen, Turkey 41 E11
Sergino, Russia 50 C7
Sergipe □, Brazil 125 F11
Sergiyev Posad, Russia 46 D10
Seria, Brunei 62 D4
Serian, Malaysia 62 D4
Seriate, Italy 28 C6
Seribu, Kepulauan, Indonesia 62 F3
Sérifontaine, France 19 C8
Sérifos, Greece 38 D6
Sérignan, France 20 E7
Sérigny →, Canada 103 A6
Serik, Turkey 72 D4
Seringapatam Reef, Australia 92 B3
Serinhisar, Turkey 39 D11

Sermaize-les-Bains, France 19 D11
Sermata, Indonesia 63 F7
Sérmide, Italy 29 C8
Sernovodsk, Russia 48 D10
Sernur, Russia 48 B9
Serock, Poland 45 F8
Serón, Spain 33 H2
Serós, Spain 32 D5
Serov, Russia 50 D7
Serowe, Botswana 88 C4
Serpa, Portugal 35 H3
Serpeddí, Punta, Italy 30 C2
Serpentara, Italy 30 C2
Serpentine Lakes, Australia 93 E4
Serpis →, Spain 33 G4
Serpukhov, Russia 46 E9
Serra de Outes, Spain 34 C2
Serra do Navio, Brazil 125 C8
Serra San Bruno, Italy 31 D9
Serradilla, Spain 34 F4
Sérrai, Greece 40 E7
Sérrai □, Greece 40 E7
Serramanna, Italy 30 C1
Serravalle Scrívia, Italy . 28 D5
Serre-Ponçon, L. de, France 21 D10
Serres, France 21 D9
Serrezuela, Argentina 126 C2
Serrinha, Brazil 125 F11
Sersale, Italy 31 C9
Sertã, Portugal 34 F2
Sertanópolis, Brazil 127 A5
Sêrtar, China 58 A3
Serua, Indonesia 63 F8
Serui, Indonesia 63 E9
Serule, Botswana 88 C4
Sérvia, Greece 40 F6
Serzedelo, Portugal 34 D2
Sese Is., Uganda 86 C3
Sesepe, Indonesia 63 E7
Sesfontein, Namibia 88 B1
Sesheke, Zambia 88 B3
Sésia →, Italy 28 C5
Sesimbra, Portugal 35 G1
S'Espalmador, Spain 37 C7
S'Espardell, Spain 37 C7
Sessa Aurunca, Italy 30 A6
S'Estanyol, Spain 37 B9
Sestao, Spain 32 B2
Sesto Calende, Italy 28 C5
Sesto San Giovanni, Italy . 28 C6
Sestri Levante, Italy 28 D6
Sestriere, Italy 28 D3
Sestroretsk, Russia 46 B6
Sestrunj, Croatia 29 D11
Sestu, Italy 30 C2
Setana, Japan 54 C9
Sète, France 20 E7
Sete Lagôas, Brazil 125 G10
Sétif, Algeria 78 A7
Seto, Japan 55 G8
Setonaikai, Japan 55 G6
Settat, Morocco 78 B4
Séttimo Torinese, Italy ... 28 C4
Setting L., Canada 105 C9
Settle, U.K. 12 C5
Settlement Pt., Bahamas ... 109 M6
Settlers, S. Africa 89 C4
Setúbal, Portugal 35 G2
Setúbal □, Portugal 35 G2
Setúbal, B. de, Portugal .. 35 G2
Seugne →, France 20 C3
Seul, Lac, Canada 100 C10
Seurre, France 19 F12
Sevan, Armenia 49 K7
Sevan, Ozero = Sevana
  Lich, Armenia 49 K7
Sevana Lich, Armenia 49 K7
Sevastopol, Ukraine 47 K7
Seven Sisters, Canada 104 C3
Sever →, Spain 35 F3
Sévérac-le-Château, France 20 D7
Severn →, Canada 102 A2
Severn →, U.K. 13 F5
Severn L., Canada 102 B1
Severnaya Zemlya, Russia .. 51 B10
Severo-Kurilsk, Russia 51 D16
Severo-Yeniseyskiy, Russia 51 C10
Severočeský □, Czech Rep. . 26 A7
Severodonetsk =
  Syeverodonetsk, Ukraine 47 H10
Severodvinsk, Russia 50 C4
Severomoravský □,
  Czech Rep. 27 B10
Sevier, U.S.A. 115 G7
Sevier →, U.S.A. 115 G7
Sevier Desert, U.S.A. 114 G7
Sevier L., U.S.A. 114 G7
Sevilla, Spain 35 H5
Sevilla □, Spain 35 H5
Seville = Sevilla, Spain .. 35 H5
Sevlievo, Bulgaria 41 D9
Sevnica, Slovenia 29 B12
Sèvre-Nantaise →, France .. 18 E5
Sèvre-Niortaise →, France . 20 B3
Sevsk, Russia 47 F8
Sewa →, S. Leone 82 D2
Sewani, India 68 E6
Seward, Alaska, U.S.A. 100 B5
Seward, Nebr., U.S.A. 112 E6
Seward, Pa., U.S.A. 110 F5
Seward Peninsula, U.S.A. .. 100 B3
Sewell, Chile 126 C1
Sewer, Indonesia 63 F8
Sewickley, U.S.A. 110 F4
Sexsmith, Canada 104 B5
Seychelles ■, Ind. Oc. 52 K9
Seyðisfjörður, Iceland 8 D6
Seydişehir, Turkey 72 D4
Seydvān, Iran 70 B5
Seyhan →, Turkey 70 B2
Seyhan Baraji, Turkey 72 D6

Seyitgazi, Turkey 39 B12
Seyitömer, Turkey 39 B11
Seym →, Ukraine 47 G7
Seymen, Turkey 41 E11
Seymour, Australia 95 F4
Seymour, S. Africa 89 E4
Seymour, Conn., U.S.A. 111 E11
Seymour, Ind., U.S.A. 108 F3
Seymour, Tex., U.S.A. 113 J5
Seyne, France 21 D10
Seyssel, France 21 C9
Sežana, Slovenia 29 C10
Sézanne, France 19 D10
Sezze, Italy 30 A6
Sfântu Gheorghe, Covasna,
  Romania 43 E10
Sfântu Gheorghe, Tulcea,
  Romania 43 F14
Sfântu Gheorghe, Brațul →,
  Romania 43 F14
Sfax, Tunisia 79 B8
Sha Xi →, China 59 D12
Sha Xian, China 59 D11
Shaanxi □, China 56 G5
Shaba = Katanga □,
  Dem. Rep. of the Congo . 86 D2
Shabla, Bulgaria 41 C12
Shabogamo L., Canada 103 B6
Shabunda,
  Dem. Rep. of the Congo . 86 C2
Shache, China 60 C2
Shackleton Ice Shelf,
  Antarctica 5 C8
Shackleton Inlet, Antarctica 5 E11
Shādegān, Iran 71 D6
Shadi, China 59 D10
Shadi, India 69 C7
Shadrinsk, Russia 50 D7
Shadyside, U.S.A. 110 G4
Shaffa, Nigeria 83 C7
Shafter, U.S.A. 117 K7
Shaftesbury, U.K. 13 F5
Shagamu, Nigeria 83 D5
Shagram, Pakistan 69 A5
Shah Alizai, Pakistan 68 E2
Shah Bunder, Pakistan 68 G2
Shahabad, Punjab, India ... 68 D7
Shahabad, Raj., India 68 G7
Shahabad, Ut. P., India ... 69 F8
Shahadpur, Pakistan 68 G3
Shahba, Syria 75 C5
Shahdād, Iran 71 D8
Shahdād, Namakzār-e, Iran . 71 D8
Shahdadkot, Pakistan 68 F2
Shahdol, India 69 H9
Shahe, China 56 F8
Shahganj, India 69 F10
Shahgarh, India 66 F6
Shahjahanpur, India 69 F8
Shahpur, India 68 H7
Shahpur, Baluchistan,
  Pakistan 68 E3
Shahpur, Punjab, Pakistan . 68 C5
Shahpur Chakar, Pakistan .. 68 F3
Shahpura, Mad. P., India .. 69 H9
Shahpura, Raj., India 68 G6
Shahr-e Bābak, Iran 71 D7
Shahr-e Kord, Iran 71 C6
Shāhrakht, Iran 71 C9
Shahrig, Pakistan 68 D2
Shahukou, China 56 D7
Shaikhabad, Afghan. 68 B3
Shajapur, India 68 H7
Shakargarh, Pakistan 68 C6
Shakawe, Botswana 88 B3
Shaker Heights, U.S.A. 110 E3
Shakhty, Russia 49 G5
Shakhunya, Russia 48 B8
Shaki, Nigeria 83 D5
Shallow Lake, Canada 110 B3
Shalqar, Kazakhstan 50 E6
Shalskiy, Russia 46 B8
Shaluli Shan, China 58 B2
Shām, Iran 71 E8
Shām, Bādiyat ash, Asia ... 70 C3
Shamāl Bahr el Ghazal □,
  Sudan 81 F2
Shamāl Dârfûr □, Sudan 81 E2
Shamāl Kordofân □, Sudan .. 81 E3
Shamattawa, Canada 102 A1
Shamattawa →, Canada 102 A2
Shambe, Sudan 81 F3
Shambu, Ethiopia 81 F4
Shamīl, Iran 71 E8
Shamkhor = Şämkir,
  Azerbaijan 49 K8
Shāmkūh, Iran 71 C8
Shamli, India 68 E7
Shammar, Jabal, Si. Arabia 70 E4
Shamo = Gobi, Asia 56 C6
Shamo, L., Ethiopia 81 F4
Shamokin, U.S.A. 111 F8
Shamrock, U.S.A. 113 H4
Shamva, Zimbabwe 87 F3
Shan □, Burma 67 J21
Shan Xian, China 56 G9
Shanan →, Ethiopia 81 F5
Shanchengzhen, China 57 C13
Shāndak, Iran 71 D9
Shandon, U.S.A. 116 K6
Shandong □, China 57 G10
Shandong Bandao, China 57 F11
Shang Xian = Shangzhou,
  China 56 H5
Shanga, Nigeria 78 F6
Shangalowe,
  Dem. Rep. of the Congo . 87 E2
Shangani, Zimbabwe 87 F2

Shangani →, Zimbabwe 87 F2
Shangbancheng, China 57 D10
Shangcheng, China 59 B10
Shangchuan Dao, China 59 G9
Shangdu, China 56 D7
Shanggao, China 59 C10
Shanghai, China 59 B13
Shanghai □, China 59 B13
Shanghai Shi □, China 59 B13
Shanghang, China 59 E11
Shanghe, China 57 F9
Shanglin, China 58 F7
Shangnan, China 56 H6
Shangqiu, China 56 G8
Shangrao, China 59 C11
Shangshui, China 56 H8
Shangyou, China 59 E10
Shangyu, China 59 B13
Shangzhi, China 57 B14
Shangzhou, China 56 H5
Shanhetun, China 57 B14
Shani, Nigeria 83 C7
Shannon, N.Z. 91 J5
Shannon →, Ireland 15 D2
Shannon, Mouth of the,
  Ireland 15 D2
Shannon Airport, Ireland .. 15 D3
Shansi = Shanxi □, China .. 56 F7
Shantar, Ostrov Bolshoy,
  Russia 51 D14
Shantipur, India 69 H13
Shantou, China 59 F11
Shantung = Shandong □,
  China 57 G10
Shanwei, China 59 F10
Shanxi □, China 56 F7
Shanyang, China 56 H5
Shanyin, China 56 E7
Shaodong, China 59 D8
Shaoguan, China 59 E9
Shaoshan, China 59 D8
Shaowu, China 59 D11
Shaoxing, China 59 C13
Shaoyang, Hunan, China 59 D8
Shaoyang, Hunan, China 59 D8
Shap, U.K. 12 C5
Shapinsay, U.K. 14 B6
Shaqq el Gi'eifer →, Sudan 81 D2
Shaqra', Si. Arabia 70 E5
Shaqrā', Yemen 74 E4
Sharafa, Sudan 81 E2
Sharafkhāneh, Iran 70 B5
Sharbot Lake, Canada 111 B8
Shari, Japan 54 C12
Sharjah = Ash Shāriqah,
  U.A.E. 71 E7
Shark B., Australia 93 E1
Sharm el Sheikh, Egypt 80 B3
Sharon, Mass., U.S.A. 111 D13
Sharon, Pa., U.S.A. 110 E4
Sharon Springs, Kans.,
  U.S.A. 112 F4
Sharon Springs, N.Y.,
  U.S.A. 111 D10
Sharp Pt., Australia 94 A3
Sharpe L., Canada 102 B1
Sharpsville, U.S.A. 110 E4
Sharq el Istiwa'iya □, Sudan 81 G3
Sharya, Russia 48 A7
Shasha, Ethiopia 81 F4
Shashemene, Ethiopia 81 F4
Shashi, Botswana 89 C4
Shashi, China 59 B9
Shashi →, Africa 87 G2
Shasta, Mt., U.S.A. 114 F2
Shasta L., U.S.A. 114 F2
Shatawi, Sudan 81 E3
Shatsk, Russia 48 C5
Shatt al'Arab →, Iraq 71 D6
Shatura, Russia 46 E10
Shaumyani = Shulaveri,
  Georgia 49 K7
Shaunavon, Canada 105 D7
Shaver L., U.S.A. 116 H7
Shaw →, Australia 92 D2
Shaw I., Australia 94 C4
Shawanaga, Canada 110 A4
Shawano, U.S.A. 108 C1
Shawinigan, Canada 102 C5
Shawnee, U.S.A. 113 H6
Shay Gap, Australia 92 D3
Shayang, China 59 B9
Shaybārā, Si. Arabia 70 E3
Shayib el Banat, Gebel,
  Egypt 80 B3
Shaykh, J. ash, Lebanon ... 75 B4
Shaykh Miskīn, Syria 75 C5
Shaykh Sa'īd, Iraq 70 C5
Shchekino, Russia 46 E9
Shcherbakov = Rybinsk,
  Russia 46 C10
Shchigry, Russia 47 G9
Shchors, Ukraine 47 G6
Shchuchinsk, Kazakhstan ... 50 D8
She Xian, Anhui, China 59 C12
She Xian, Hebei, China 56 F7
Shebekino, Russia 47 G9
Shebele = Scebeli, Wabi →,
  Somali Rep. 74 G3
Sheboygan, U.S.A. 108 D2
Shebshi Mts., Nigeria 83 D7
Shediac, Canada 103 C7
Sheelin, L., Ireland 15 C4
Sheep Haven, Ireland 15 A4
Sheerness, U.K. 13 F8
Sheet Harbour, Canada 103 D7
Sheffield, U.K. 12 D6
Sheffield, Ala., U.S.A. ... 109 H2
Sheffield, Mass., U.S.A. .. 111 D11

Sinegorskiy

Sheffield, *Pa., U.S.A.* 110 E5
Shehojele, *Ethiopia* 81 E4
Shehong, *China* 58 B5
Sheikh Idris, *Sudan* 81 E3
Sheikhpura, *India* 69 G11
Shek Hasan, *Ethiopia* 81 E4
Shekhupura, *Pakistan* 68 D5
Sheki = Şaki, *Azerbaijan* 49 K8
Shelburne, *N.S., Canada* 103 D6
Shelburne, *Ont., Canada* 102 D3
Shelburne, *U.S.A.* 111 B11
Shelburne B., *Australia* 94 A3
Shelburne Falls, *U.S.A.* 111 D12
Shelby, *Mich., U.S.A.* 108 D2
Shelby, *Miss., U.S.A.* 113 J9
Shelby, *Mont., U.S.A.* 114 B8
Shelby, *N.C., U.S.A.* 109 H5
Shelby, *Ohio, U.S.A.* 110 F2
Shelbyville, *Ill., U.S.A.* 112 F10
Shelbyville, *Ind., U.S.A.* 108 F3
Shelbyville, *Ky., U.S.A.* 108 F3
Shelbyville, *Tenn., U.S.A.* 109 H2
Sheldon, *U.S.A.* 112 D7
Sheldrake, *Canada* 103 B7
Shelengo, K. →, *Sudan* 81 E2
Shelikhova, Zaliv, *Russia* 51 D16
Shell Lakes, *Australia* 93 E4
Shellbrook, *Canada* 105 C7
Shellharbour, *Australia* 95 E5
Shelon →, *Russia* 46 C6
Shelter I, *U.S.A.* 111 E12
Shelton, *Conn., U.S.A.* 111 E11
Shelton, *Wash., U.S.A.* 116 C3
Shemakha = Şamaxi, *Azerbaijan* 49 K9
Shemsi, *Sudan* 80 D2
Shen Xian, *China* 56 F8
Shenandoah, *Iowa, U.S.A.* 112 E7
Shenandoah, *Pa., U.S.A.* 111 F8
Shenandoah, *Va., U.S.A.* 108 F6
Shenandoah →, *U.S.A.* 108 F7
Shenandoah National Park, *U.S.A.* 108 F6
Shenchi, *China* 56 E7
Shendam, *Nigeria* 83 D6
Shendî, *Sudan* 81 D3
Shenge, *S. Leone* 82 D2
Shengfang, *China* 56 E9
Shëngjergji, *Albania* 40 E4
Shëngjin, *Albania* 40 E3
Shengzhou, *China* 59 C13
Shenjingzi, *China* 57 B13
Shenmëria, *Albania* 40 D4
Shenmu, *China* 56 E6
Shennongjia, *China* 59 B8
Shenqiu, *China* 56 H8
Shenqiucheng, *China* 56 H8
Shensi = Shaanxi □, *China* 56 G5
Shenyang, *China* 57 D12
Shenzhen, *China* 59 F10
Sheo, *India* 68 F4
Sheopur Kalan, *India* 66 G10
Shepetivka, *Ukraine* 47 G4
Shepetovka = Shepetivka, *Ukraine* 47 G4
Shepparton, *Australia* 95 F4
Sheppey, I. of, *U.K.* 13 F8
Shepton Mallet, *U.K.* 13 F5
Sheqi, *China* 56 H7
Sher Qila, *Pakistan* 69 A6
Sherab, *Sudan* 81 E1
Sherborne, *U.K.* 13 G5
Sherbro →, *S. Leone* 82 D2
Sherbro I., *S. Leone* 82 D2
Sherbrooke, *N.S., Canada* 103 C7
Sherbrooke, *Qué., Canada* 103 C5
Sherburne, *U.S.A.* 111 D9
Shereik, *Sudan* 80 D3
Shergarh, *India* 68 F5
Sherghati, *India* 69 G11
Sheridan, *Ark., U.S.A.* 113 H8
Sheridan, *Wyo., U.S.A.* 114 D10
Sheringham, *U.K.* 12 E9
Sherkin I., *Ireland* 15 E2
Sherkot, *India* 69 E8
Sherman, *U.S.A.* 113 J6
Sherpur, *India* 69 G10
Sherridon, *Canada* 105 B8
Sherwood Forest, *U.K.* 12 D6
Sherwood Park, *Canada* 104 C6
Sheslay →, *Canada* 104 B2
Shethanei L., *Canada* 105 B9
Shetland □, *U.K.* 14 A7
Shetland Is., *U.K.* 14 A7
Shetrunji →, *India* 68 J5
Shewa □, *Ethiopia* 81 F4
Shewa Gimira, *Ethiopia* 81 F4
Sheyenne →, *U.S.A.* 112 B6
Shibām, *Yemen* 74 D4
Shibata, *Japan* 54 F9
Shibecha, *Japan* 54 C12
Shibetsu, *Japan* 54 B11
Shibîn el Kôm, *Egypt* 80 H7
Shibîn el Qanâtir, *Egypt* 80 H7
Shibing, *China* 58 D7
Shibogama L., *Canada* 102 B2
Shibushi, *Japan* 55 J5
Shicheng, *China* 59 D11
Shickshinny, *U.S.A.* 111 E8
Shickshock Mts. = Chic-Chocs, Mts., *Canada* 103 C6
Shidao, *China* 57 F12
Shidian, *China* 58 E2
Shido, *Japan* 55 G7
Shiel, L., *U.K.* 14 E3
Shield, C., *Australia* 94 A2
Shifang, *China* 58 B5
Shiga □, *Japan* 55 G8
Shigu, *China* 58 D2
Shiguaigou, *China* 56 D6
Shihchiachuangi = Shijiazhuang, *China* 56 E8
Shijaku, *Albania* 40 E3
Shijiazhuang, *China* 56 E8
Shijiu Hu, *China* 59 B12
Shikarpur, *India* 68 E8
Shikarpur, *Pakistan* 68 F3
Shikohabad, *India* 69 F8
Shikoku □, *Japan* 55 H6
Shikoku-Sanchi, *Japan* 55 H6
Shiliguri, *India* 67 F16
Shilka, *Russia* 51 D12
Shilka →, *Russia* 51 D13
Shillelagh, *Ireland* 15 D5
Shillington, *U.S.A.* 111 F9
Shillong, *India* 67 G17
Shilo, *West Bank* 75 C4
Shilong, *China* 59 F9
Shilou, *China* 56 F6
Shilovo, *Russia* 48 C5
Shimabara, *Japan* 55 H5
Shimada, *Japan* 55 G9
Shimane □, *Japan* 55 G6
Shimanovsk, *Russia* 51 D13
Shimen, *China* 59 C8
Shimenjie, *China* 59 C11
Shimian, *China* 58 C4
Shimizu, *Japan* 55 G9
Shimodate, *Japan* 55 F9
Shimoga, *India* 66 N9
Shimoni, *Kenya* 86 C4
Shimonoseki, *Japan* 55 H5
Shimpuru Rapids, *Angola* 88 B2
Shimsk, *Russia* 46 C6
Shin, L., *U.K.* 14 C4
Shinan, *China* 58 F7
Shinano-Gawa →, *Japan* 55 F9
Shināş, *Oman* 71 E8
Shīndand, *Afghan.* 66 C3
Shinglehouse, *U.S.A.* 110 E6
Shingū, *Japan* 55 H7
Shingwidzi, *S. Africa* 89 C5
Shinjō, *Japan* 54 E10
Shinkafe, *Nigeria* 83 C6
Shinshār, *Syria* 75 A5
Shinyanga, *Tanzania* 86 C3
Shinyanga □, *Tanzania* 86 C3
Shio-no-Misaki, *Japan* 55 H7
Shiogama, *Japan* 54 E10
Shiojiri, *Japan* 55 F8
Shipchenski Prokhod, *Bulgaria* 41 D9
Shiping, *China* 58 F4
Shipki La, *India* 66 D11
Shippegan, *Canada* 103 C7
Shippensburg, *U.S.A.* 110 F7
Shippenville, *U.S.A.* 110 E5
Shiprock, *U.S.A.* 115 H9
Shiqian, *China* 58 D7
Shiqma, N. →, *Israel* 75 D3
Shiquan, *China* 56 H5
Shiquan He = Indus →, *Pakistan* 68 G2
Shīr Kūh, *Iran* 71 D7
Shiragami-Misaki, *Japan* 54 D10
Shirakawa, *Fukushima, Japan* 55 F10
Shirakawa, *Gifu, Japan* 55 F8
Shirane-San, *Gumma, Japan* 55 F9
Shirane-San, *Yamanashi, Japan* 55 G9
Shiraoi, *Japan* 54 C10
Shīrāz, *Iran* 71 D7
Shirbîn, *Egypt* 80 H7
Shire →, *Africa* 87 F4
Shiretoko-Misaki, *Japan* 54 B12
Shirinab →, *Pakistan* 68 D2
Shiriya-Zaki, *Japan* 54 D10
Shiroishi, *Japan* 54 F10
Shīrvān, *Iran* 71 B8
Shirwa, L. = Chilwa, L., *Malawi* 87 F4
Shishi, *China* 59 E12
Shishou, *China* 59 C9
Shitai, *China* 59 B11
Shivpuri, *India* 68 G7
Shixian, *China* 57 C15
Shixing, *China* 59 E10
Shiyan, *China* 59 A8
Shiyata, *Egypt* 80 B2
Shizhu, *China* 58 C7
Shizong, *China* 58 E5
Shizuishan, *China* 56 E4
Shizuoka, *Japan* 55 G9
Shizuoka □, *Japan* 55 G9
Shklov = Shklow, *Belarus* 46 E6
Shklow, *Belarus* 46 E6
Shkoder = Shkodra, *Albania* 40 D3
Shkodra, *Albania* 40 D3
Shkumbini →, *Albania* 40 E3
Shmidta, Ostrov, *Russia* 51 A10
Shō-Gawa →, *Japan* 55 F8
Shoal L., *Canada* 105 D9
Shoal Lake, *Canada* 105 C8
Shōdo-Shima, *Japan* 55 G7
Sholapur = Solapur, *India* 66 L9
Shologontsy, *Russia* 51 C12
Shōmrōn, *West Bank* 75 C4
Shoreham by Sea, *U.K.* 13 G7
Shori →, *Pakistan* 68 E3
Shorkot Road, *Pakistan* 68 D5
Shoshone, *Calif., U.S.A.* 117 K10
Shoshone, *Idaho, U.S.A.* 114 E6
Shoshone L., *U.S.A.* 114 D8
Shoshone Mts., *U.S.A.* 114 G5
Shoshong, *Botswana* 88 C4
Shoshoni, *U.S.A.* 114 E9
Shostka, *Ukraine* 47 G7
Shou Xian, *China* 59 A11
Shouchang, *China* 59 C12
Shouguang, *China* 57 F10
Shouning, *China* 59 D12
Shouyang, *China* 56 F7
Show Low, *U.S.A.* 115 J9
Shpola, *Ukraine* 47 H6
Shreveport, *U.S.A.* 113 J8
Shrewsbury, *U.K.* 13 E5
Shri Mohangarh, *India* 68 F4
Shrirampur, *India* 69 H13
Shropshire □, *U.K.* 13 E5
Shu, *Kazakstan* 50 E8
Shu →, *Kazakstan* 52 E10
Shuangbai, *China* 58 E3
Shuangcheng, *China* 57 B14
Shuangfeng, *China* 59 D9
Shuanggou, *China* 57 G9
Shuangjiang, *China* 58 F2
Shuangliao, *China* 57 C12
Shuangshanzi, *China* 57 D10
Shuangyang, *China* 57 C13
Shuangyashan, *China* 60 B8
Shubra Khit, *Egypt* 80 H7
Shucheng, *China* 59 B11
Shugozero, *Russia* 46 C8
Shuguri Falls, *Tanzania* 87 D4
Shuiji, *China* 59 D12
Shuiye, *China* 56 F8
Shujalpur, *India* 68 H7
Shukpa Kunzang, *India* 69 B8
Shulan, *China* 57 B14
Shulaveri, *Georgia* 49 K7
Shule, *China* 60 C2
Shumagin Is., *U.S.A.* 100 C4
Shumen, *Bulgaria* 41 C10
Shumerlya, *Russia* 48 C8
Shumikha, *Russia* 50 D7
Shunchang, *China* 59 D11
Shunde, *China* 59 F9
Shungay, *Kazakstan* 49 F8
Shuo Xian = Shuozhou, *China* 56 E7
Shuozhou, *China* 56 E7
Shūr →, *Fārs, Iran* 71 D7
Shūr →, *Kermān, Iran* 71 D8
Shūr →, *Yazd, Iran* 71 D7
Shūr Āb, *Iran* 71 C6
Shūr Gaz, *Iran* 71 D8
Shūrāb, *Iran* 71 C8
Shūrjestān, *Iran* 71 D7
Shurugwi, *Zimbabwe* 87 F3
Shūsf, *Iran* 71 D9
Shūsh, *Iran* 73 F13
Shūshtar, *Iran* 71 D6
Shuswap L., *Canada* 104 C5
Shuya, *Russia* 48 B5
Shuyang, *China* 57 G10
Shūzū, *Iran* 71 D7
Shwebo, *Burma* 67 H19
Shwegu, *Burma* 67 G20
Shweli →, *Burma* 67 H20
Shymkent, *Kazakstan* 50 E7
Shyok, *India* 69 B8
Shyok →, *Pakistan* 69 B6
Si Chon, *Thailand* 65 H2
Si Kiang = Xi Jiang →, *China* 59 F9
Si-ngan = Xi'an, *China* 56 G5
Si Prachan, *Thailand* 64 E3
Si Racha, *Thailand* 64 F3
Si Xian, *China* 57 H9
Siahaf →, *Pakistan* 68 E3
Siahan Range, *Pakistan* 66 F4
Siaksriindrapura, *Indonesia* 62 D2
Sialkot, *Pakistan* 68 C6
Siam = Thailand ■, *Asia* 64 E4
Sian = Xi'an, *China* 56 G5
Sianów, *Poland* 44 D3
Siantan, *Indonesia* 62 D3
Sīāreh, *Iran* 71 D9
Siargao I., *Phil.* 61 G7
Siari, *Pakistan* 69 B7
Siasi, *Phil.* 63 C6
Siasi I., *Phil.* 61 J4
Siátista, *Greece* 40 F5
Siau, *Indonesia* 63 D7
Šiauliai, *Lithuania* 9 J20
Šiauliai □, *Lithuania* 44 C10
Siazan = Siyäzän, *Azerbaijan* 49 K9
Sibâi, Gebel el, *Egypt* 70 E2
Sibayi, L., *S. Africa* 89 D5
Şibdu, *Sudan* 81 E2
Šibenik, *Croatia* 29 E12
Siberia, *Russia* 4 D13
Siberut, *Indonesia* 62 E1
Sibi, *Pakistan* 68 E2
Sibil = Oksibil, *Indonesia* 63 E10
Sibiti, *Congo* 84 E2
Sibiu, *Romania* 43 E9
Sibiu □, *Romania* 43 E9
Sibley, *U.S.A.* 112 D7
Sibolga, *Indonesia* 62 D1
Sibsagar, *India* 67 F19
Sibu, *Malaysia* 62 D4
Sibuco, *Phil.* 61 H5
Sibuguey B., *Phil.* 61 H5
Sibut, *C.A.R.* 84 C3
Sibutu, *Phil.* 63 D5
Sibutu Group, *Phil.* 61 J3
Sibutu Passage, *E. Indies* 63 D5
Sibuyan I., *Phil.* 61 E5
Sibuyan Sea, *Phil.* 61 E5
Sic, *Romania* 43 D8
Sicamous, *Canada* 104 C5
Siccus →, *Australia* 95 E2
Sichuan □, *China* 58 B5
Sichuan Pendi, *China* 58 B5
Sicilia, *Italy* 31 E7
Sicilia □, *Italy* 31 E7
Sicily = Sicilia, *Italy* 31 E7
Sicuani, *Peru* 124 F4
Šid, *Serbia, Yug.* 42 E4
Sidamo □, *Ethiopia* 81 G4
Sidaouet, *Niger* 83 B6
Sidári, *Greece* 36 A3
Siddhapur, *India* 68 H5
Siddipet, *India* 66 K11
Sidensjö, *Sweden* 10 A12
Sidéradougou, *Burkina Faso* 82 C4
Siderno, *Italy* 31 D9
Sidhauli, *India* 69 F9
Sídheros, Ákra, *Greece* 36 D8
Sidhi, *India* 69 G9
Sidhirókastron, *Greece* 40 E7
Sîdi Abd el Rahmân, *Egypt* 80 A2
Sîdi Barrâni, *Egypt* 80 A2
Sidi-bel-Abbès, *Algeria* 78 A5
Sidi Haneish, *Egypt* 80 A2
Sidi Omar, *Egypt* 80 A1
Sidlaw Hills, *U.K.* 14 E5
Sidley, Mt., *Antarctica* 5 D14
Sidmouth, *U.K.* 13 G4
Sidmouth, C., *Australia* 94 A3
Sidney, *Canada* 104 D4
Sidney, *Mont., U.S.A.* 112 B2
Sidney, *N.Y., U.S.A.* 111 D9
Sidney, *Nebr., U.S.A.* 112 E3
Sidney, *Ohio, U.S.A.* 108 E3
Sidney Lanier L., *U.S.A.* 109 H4
Sido, *Mali* 82 C3
Sidoarjo, *Indonesia* 63 G15
Sidon = Saydā, *Lebanon* 75 B4
Sidra, G. of = Surt, Khalīj, *Libya* 79 B9
Siedlce, *Poland* 45 F9
Sieg →, *Germany* 24 E3
Siegburg, *Germany* 24 E3
Siegen, *Germany* 24 E4
Siem Pang, *Cambodia* 64 E6
Siem Reap = Siemreab, *Cambodia* 64 F4
Siemiatycze, *Poland* 45 F9
Siemreab, *Cambodia* 64 F4
Siena, *Italy* 29 E8
Sieniawa, *Poland* 45 H9
Sieradz, *Poland* 45 G5
Sieraków, *Poland* 45 F3
Sierck-les-Bains, *France* 19 C13
Sierning, *Austria* 26 C7
Sierpc, *Poland* 45 F6
Sierra Blanca, *U.S.A.* 115 L11
Sierra Blanca Peak, *U.S.A.* 115 K11
Sierra City, *U.S.A.* 116 F6
Sierra Colorada, *Argentina* 128 E3
Sierra de Yeguas, *Spain* 35 H6
Sierra Gorda, *Chile* 126 A2
Sierra Leone ■, *W. Afr.* 82 D2
Sierra Madre, *Mexico* 119 D6
Sierra Mojada, *Mexico* 118 B4
Sierra Nevada, *U.S.A.* 116 H8
Sierra Vista, *U.S.A.* 115 L8
Sierraville, *U.S.A.* 116 F6
Sierre, *Switz.* 25 J3
Sifani, *Ethiopia* 81 E5
Sifié, *Ivory C.* 82 D3
Sífnos, *Greece* 38 E6
Sifton, *Canada* 105 C8
Sifton Pass, *Canada* 104 B3
Sigean, *France* 20 E6
Sighetu-Marmaţiei, *Romania* 43 C8
Sighişoara, *Romania* 43 D9
Sigli, *Indonesia* 62 C1
Siglufjörður, *Iceland* 8 C4
Sigmaringen, *Germany* 25 G5
Signa, *Italy* 28 E8
Signakhi = Tsnori, *Georgia* 49 K7
Signal, *U.S.A.* 117 L13
Signal Pk., *U.S.A.* 117 M12
Signy-l'Abbaye, *France* 19 C11
Sigsig, *Ecuador* 124 D3
Sigüenza, *Spain* 32 D2
Siguiri, *Guinea* 82 C3
Sigulda, *Latvia* 9 H21
Sihanoukville = Kampong Saom, *Cambodia* 65 G4
Sihora, *India* 69 H9
Sihui, *China* 59 F9
Siikajoki →, *Finland* 8 D21
Siilinjärvi, *Finland* 8 E22
Siirt, *Turkey* 73 D9
Sijarira Ra., *Zimbabwe* 87 F2
Sika, *India* 68 H3
Sikao, *Thailand* 65 J2
Sikar, *India* 68 F6
Sikasso, *Mali* 82 C3
Sikeston, *U.S.A.* 113 G10
Sikhote Alin, Khrebet, *Russia* 51 E14
Sikhote Alin Ra. = Sikhote Alin, Khrebet, *Russia* 51 E14
Sikiá, *Greece* 40 F7
Síkinos, *Greece* 39 E7
Sikkani Chief →, *Canada* 104 B4
Sikkim □, *India* 67 F16
Siklós, *Hungary* 42 E3
Sikotu-Ko, *Japan* 54 C10
Sil →, *Spain* 34 C3
Silacayoapan, *Mexico* 119 D5
Šilalė, *Lithuania* 44 C9
Silandro, *Italy* 28 B7
Silawad, *India* 68 J6
Silay, *Phil.* 61 F5
Silba, *Croatia* 29 D11
Silchar, *India* 67 G18
Şile, *Turkey* 41 E13
Siler City, *U.S.A.* 109 H6
Silgarhi Doti, *Nepal* 69 E9
Silghat, *India* 67 F18
Sili, *Burkina Faso* 82 C4
Silifke, *Turkey* 70 B2
Siliguri = Shiliguri, *India* 67 F16
Siling Co, *China* 60 C3
Silistea Nouă, *Romania* 43 F10
Silistra, *Bulgaria* 41 B11
Silivri, *Turkey* 41 E12
Siljan, *Sweden* 10 D8
Siljansnäs, *Sweden* 10 D8
Silkeborg, *Denmark* 11 H3
Silkwood, *Australia* 94 B4
Silla, *Spain* 33 F4
Sillajhuay, Cordillera, *Chile* 124 G5
Sillamäe, *Estonia* 9 G22
Sillé-le-Guillaume, *France* 18 D6
Silleda, *Spain* 34 C2
Silloth, *U.K.* 12 C4
Sílo, *Greece* 41 E9
Siloam Springs, *U.S.A.* 113 G7
Silopi, *Turkey* 73 D10
Silsbee, *U.S.A.* 113 K7
Şiluko, *Nigeria* 83 D6
Šilutė, *Lithuania* 9 J19
Silva Porto = Kuito, *Angola* 85 G3
Silvan, *Turkey* 73 C9
Silvani, *India* 69 H8
Silver City, *U.S.A.* 115 K9
Silver Cr. →, *U.S.A.* 114 E4
Silver Creek, *U.S.A.* 110 D5
Silver L., *U.S.A.* 116 G6
Silver Lake, *Calif., U.S.A.* 117 K10
Silver Lake, *Oreg., U.S.A.* 114 E3
Silverdalen, *Sweden* 11 G9
Silverton, *Colo., U.S.A.* 115 H10
Silverton, *Tex., U.S.A.* 113 H4
Silves, *Portugal* 35 H2
Silvi Marina, *Italy* 29 F11
Silvies →, *U.S.A.* 114 E4
Silvrettahorn, *Switz.* 28 B7
Silwa Bahari, *Egypt* 80 C3
Silz, *Austria* 26 D3
Simaltala, *India* 69 G12
Simanggang = Bandar Sri Aman, *Malaysia* 62 D4
Simao, *China* 58 F3
Simard, L., *Canada* 102 C4
Şimareh →, *Iran* 73 F12
Simav, *Turkey* 39 B10
Simav →, *Turkey* 41 F12
Simav Dağları, *Turkey* 39 B10
Simba, *Tanzania* 86 C4
Simbach, *Germany* 25 G9
Simbirsk, *Russia* 48 C9
Simbo, *Tanzania* 86 C2
Simcoe, *Canada* 102 D3
Simcoe, L., *Canada* 102 D4
Simdega, *India* 69 H11
Simeonovgrad, *Bulgaria* 41 D9
Simeria, *Romania* 42 E8
Simeto →, *Italy* 31 E8
Simeulue, *Indonesia* 62 D1
Simferopol, *Ukraine* 47 K8
Sími, *Greece* 39 E9
Simi Valley, *U.S.A.* 117 L8
Simikot, *Nepal* 69 E9
Simitli, *Bulgaria* 40 E7
Simla, *India* 68 D7
Simlångsdalen, *Sweden* 11 H7
Şimleu-Silvaniei, *Romania* 42 C7
Simmern, *Germany* 25 F3
Simmie, *Canada* 105 D7
Simmler, *U.S.A.* 117 K7
Simnas, *Lithuania* 44 D10
Simojoki →, *Finland* 8 D21
Simojovel, *Mexico* 119 D6
Simonette →, *Canada* 104 B5
Simonstown, *S. Africa* 88 E2
Simontornya, *Hungary* 42 D3
Simplonpass, *Switz.* 25 J4
Simplontunnel, *Switz.* 25 J4
Simpson Desert, *Australia* 94 D2
Simpson Pen., *Canada* 101 B11
Simpungdong, *N. Korea* 57 D15
Simrishamn, *Sweden* 11 J8
Simsbury, *U.S.A.* 111 E12
Simushir, Ostrov, *Russia* 51 E16
Sin Cowe I., *S. China Sea* 62 C4
Sinabang, *Indonesia* 62 D1
Sinadogo, *Somali Rep.* 74 F4
Sinai = Es Sînâ', *Egypt* 75 F3
Sinai, Mt. = Mûsa, Gebel, *Egypt* 70 D2
Sinai Peninsula, *Egypt* 75 F3
Sinaia, *Romania* 43 E10
Sinaloa □, *Mexico* 118 C3
Sinaloa de Leyva, *Mexico* 118 B3
Sinalunga, *Italy* 29 E8
Sinan, *China* 58 D7
Sînandrei, *Romania* 42 E6
Sinarádhes, *Greece* 36 A3
Sincan, *Turkey* 72 B5
Sincanlı, *Turkey* 39 C12
Sincelejo, *Colombia* 124 B3
Sinch'ang, *N. Korea* 57 D15
Sinchang-ni, *N. Korea* 57 E14
Sinclair, *U.S.A.* 114 F10
Sinclair Mills, *Canada* 104 C4
Sinclair's B., *U.K.* 14 C5
Sinclairville, *U.S.A.* 110 D5
Sincorá, Serra do, *Brazil* 125 F10
Sind, *Pakistan* 68 G3
Sind □, *Pakistan* 68 G3
Sind →, *Jammu & Kashmir, India* 69 B6
Sind →, *Mad. P., India* 69 F8
Sind Sagar Doab, *Pakistan* 68 D4
Sindal, *Denmark* 11 G4
Sindangan, *Phil.* 61 G5
Sindangbarang, *Indonesia* 63 G12
Sinde, *Zambia* 87 F2
Sindelfingen, *Germany* 25 G4
Sındırgı, *Turkey* 39 B10
Sindou, *Burkina Faso* 82 C3
Sindri, *India* 69 H12
Sine →, *Senegal* 82 C1
Sinegorskiy, *Russia* 49 G5

Sinekli, *Turkey* 41 E12
Sinelnikovo = Synelnykove,
  Ukraine 47 H8
Sinendé, *Benin* 83 C5
Sines, *Portugal* 35 H2
Sines, C. de, *Portugal* ... 35 H2
Sineu, *Spain* 37 B10
Sinfra, *Ivory C.* 82 D3
Sing Buri, *Thailand* 64 E3
Singa, *Sudan* 81 E3
Singapore ■, *Asia* 65 M4
Singapore, Straits of, *Asia* . 65 M5
Singaraja, *Indonesia* 62 F5
Singen, *Germany* 25 H4
Singida, *Tanzania* 86 C3
Singida □, *Tanzania* 86 D3
Singitikós Kólpos, *Greece* . 40 F7
Singkaling Hkamti, *Burma* . 67 G19
Singkang, *Indonesia* 63 E6
Singkawang, *Indonesia* ... 62 D3
Singkep, *Indonesia* 62 E2
Singleton, *Australia* 95 E5
Singleton, Mt., *N. Terr.,*
  Australia 92 D5
Singleton, Mt., *W. Austral.,*
  Australia 93 E2
Singö, *Sweden* 10 D12
Singoli, *India* 68 G6
Singora = Songkhla,
  Thailand 65 J3
Singosan, *N. Korea* 57 E14
Sinhung, *N. Korea* 57 D14
Sînî □, *Egypt* 75 F3
Siniátsikon, Óros, *Greece* . 40 F5
Siniscóla, *Italy* 30 B2
Sinj, *Croatia* 29 E13
Sinjai, *Indonesia* 63 F6
Sinjajevina,
  Montenegro, Yug. 40 D3
Sinjār, *Iraq* 70 B4
Sinkat, *Sudan* 80 D4
Sinkiang Uighur = Xinjiang
  Uygur Zizhiqu □, *China* . 60 B3
Sinmak, *N. Korea* 57 E14
Sínnai, *Italy* 30 C2
Sinnamary, *Fr. Guiana* ... 125 B8
Sinni →, *Italy* 31 B9
Sinnuris, *Egypt* 80 J7
Sinoie, Lacul, *Romania* ... 43 F13
Sinop, *Turkey* 72 A6
Sinor, *India* 68 J5
Sinp'o, *N. Korea* 57 E15
Sinsheim, *Germany* 25 F4
Sinsk, *Russia* 51 C13
Sintang, *Indonesia* 62 D4
Sinton, *U.S.A.* 113 L6
Sintra, *Portugal* 35 G1
Sinŭiju, *N. Korea* 57 D13
Sinyukha →, *Ukraine* 47 H6
Sinzig, *Germany* 24 E3
Sio →, *Hungary* 42 D3
Siocon, *Phil.* 61 H5
Siófok, *Hungary* 42 D3
Sioma, *Zambia* 88 B3
Sion, *Switz.* 25 J3
Sion Mills, *U.K.* 15 B4
Sioux City, *U.S.A.* 112 D6
Sioux Falls, *U.S.A.* 112 D6
Sioux Lookout, *Canada* ... 102 B1
Sioux Narrows, *Canada* ... 105 D10
Sipalay, *Phil.* 61 G5
Šipan, *Croatia* 40 D1
Siping, *China* 57 C13
Sipiwesk L., *Canada* 105 B9
Šipovo, *Bos.-H.* 42 F2
Sipra →, *India* 68 H6
Sipura, *Indonesia* 62 E1
Siquia →, *Nic.* 120 D3
Siquijor, *Phil.* 61 G5
Siquirres, *Costa Rica* ... 120 D3
Şīr Banī Yās, *U.A.E.* 71 E7
Sir Edward Pellew Group,
  Australia 94 B2
Sir Graham Moore Is.,
  Australia 92 B4
Sir James MacBrien, Mt.,
  Canada 100 B7
Sira →, *Norway* 9 G12
Siracusa, *Italy* 31 E8
Sirajganj, *Bangla.* 69 G13
Şiran, *Turkey* 73 B8
Sirasso, *Ivory C.* 82 D3
Sirathu, *India* 69 G9
Sīrdān, *Iran* 71 B6
Sirdaryo = Syrdarya →,
  Kazakstan 50 E7
Sire, *Ethiopia* 81 F4
Siren, *U.S.A.* 112 C8
Sirer, *Spain* 37 C7
Siret, *Romania* 43 C11
Siret →, *Romania* 43 E12
Sirghāyā, *Syria* 75 B5
Şiria, *Romania* 42 D6
Sirino, Mte., *Italy* 31 B8
Sirmaur, *India* 69 G9
Şırna, *Greece* 39 E8
Şırnak, *Turkey* 73 D10
Sirohi, *India* 68 G5
Sironj, *India* 68 G7
Síros, *Greece* 38 D6
Sirretta Pk., *U.S.A.* 117 K8
Sīrrī, *Iran* 71 E7
Sirsa, *India* 68 E6
Sirsa →, *India* 69 F8
Siruela, *Spain* 35 G5
Sisak, *Croatia* 29 C13
Sisaket, *Thailand* 64 E5
Sisante, *Spain* 33 F2
Sisargas, Is., *Spain* 34 B2
Sishen, *S. Africa* 88 D3

Sishui, *Henan, China* 56 G7
Sishui, *Shandong, China* . 57 G9
Sisipuk L., *Canada* 105 B8
Sisophon, *Cambodia* 64 F4
Sisseton, *U.S.A.* 112 C6
Sissonne, *France* 19 C10
Sīstān, *Asia* 71 D9
Sīstān, Daryācheh-ye, *Iran* . 66 D2
Sīstān va Balūchestān □,
  Iran 71 E9
Sisteron, *France* 21 D9
Sisters, *U.S.A.* 114 D3
Siswa Bazar, *India* 69 F10
Sitakili, *Mali* 82 C2
Sitamarhi, *India* 69 F11
Sitampiky, *Madag.* 89 B8
Sitapur, *India* 69 F9
Siteki, *Swaziland* 89 D5
Sitges, *Spain* 32 D6
Sithoniá, *Greece* 40 F7
Sitía, *Greece* 36 D8
Sitka, *U.S.A.* 104 B1
Sitoti, *Botswana* 88 C3
Sitra, *Egypt* 80 B2
Sittang Myit →, *Burma* ... 67 L20
Sittard, *Neths.* 17 C5
Sittensen, *Germany* 24 B5
Sittingbourne, *U.K.* 13 F8
Sittona, *Eritrea* 81 E4
Sittoung = Sittang Myit →,
  Burma 67 L20
Sittwe, *Burma* 67 J18
Situbondo, *Indonesia* 63 G16
Siuna, *Nic.* 120 D3
Siuri, *India* 69 H12
Siutghiol, Lacul, *Romania* . 43 F13
Sīvand, *Iran* 71 D7
Sivas, *Turkey* 70 B3
Sivaslı, *Turkey* 39 C11
Siverek, *Turkey* 70 B3
Sivrihisar, *Turkey* 72 C4
Sîwa, *Egypt* 80 B2
Sîwa, El Wâhât es, *Egypt* . 80 B2
Siwa Oasis, *Egypt* 76 D5
Siwalik Range, *Nepal* 69 F10
Siwan, *India* 69 F11
Siwana, *India* 68 G5
Sixmilebridge, *Ireland* .. 15 D3
Sixth Cataract, *Sudan* ... 81 D3
Siyâl, Jazâ'ir, *Egypt* ... 80 C4
Siyäzän, *Azerbaijan* 49 K9
Siziwang Qi, *China* 56 D6
Sjælland, *Denmark* 11 J5
Sjællands Odde, *Denmark* . 11 J5
Sjenica, *Serbia, Yug.* ... 40 C3
Sjöbo, *Sweden* 11 J7
Sjötofta, *Sweden* 11 G7
Sjötorp, *Sweden* 11 F8
Sjumen = Shumen, *Bulgaria* 41 C10
Sjuntorp, *Sweden* 11 F6
Skadarsko Jezero,
  Montenegro, Yug. 40 D3
Skadovsk, *Ukraine* 47 J7
Skælskør, *Denmark* 11 J5
Skærbæk, *Denmark* 11 J2
Skaftafell, *Iceland* 8 D5
Skagafjörður, *Iceland* ... 8 D4
Skagastølstindane, *Norway* . 9 F12
Skagaströnd, *Iceland* 8 D3
Skagen, *Denmark* 11 G4
Skagern, *Sweden* 11 F8
Skagerrak, *Denmark* 11 G2
Skagit →, *U.S.A.* 116 B4
Skagway, *U.S.A.* 100 C6
Skala-Podilska, *Ukraine* . 47 H4
Skala Podolskaya = Skala-
  Podilska, *Ukraine* 47 H4
Skalat, *Ukraine* 47 H3
Skalbmierz, *Poland* 45 H7
Skälderviken, *Sweden* 11 H6
Skalica, *Slovak Rep.* 27 C10
Skallingen, *Denmark* 11 J2
Skalni Dol = Kamenyak,
  Bulgaria 41 C10
Skanderborg, *Denmark* 11 H3
Skåne, *Sweden* 11 J7
Skåne län □, *Sweden* 11 H7
Skaneateles, *U.S.A.* 111 D8
Skaneateles L., *U.S.A.* .. 111 D8
Skänninge, *Sweden* 11 F9
Skanör med Falsterbo,
  Sweden 11 J6
Skantzoúra, *Greece* 38 B6
Skara, *Sweden* 11 F7
Skaraborgs län □, *Sweden* . 11 F7
Skärblacka, *Sweden* 11 F9
Skardu, *Pakistan* 69 B6
Skåre, *Sweden* 10 E7
Skärhamn, *Sweden* 11 G5
Skarszewy, *Poland* 44 D5
Skaryszew, *Poland* 45 G8
Skarżysko-Kamienna, *Poland* 45 G7
Skattkärr, *Sweden* 10 E7
Skattungbyn, *Sweden* 10 C8
Skawina, *Poland* 45 J6
Skebobruk, *Sweden* 10 E12
Skeena →, *Canada* 104 C2
Skeena Mts., *Canada* 104 B3
Skegness, *U.K.* 12 D8
Skeldon, *Guyana* 124 B7
Skeleton Coast Park,
  Namibia 88 C1
Skellefte älv →, *Sweden* . 8 D19
Skellefteå, *Sweden* 8 D19
Skelleftehamn, *Sweden* ... 8 D19
Skender Vakuf, *Bos.-H.* .. 42 F2
Skerries, The, *U.K.* 12 D3
Skhíza, *Greece* 38 E3
Skhoinoúsa, *Greece* 39 E7
Ski, *Norway* 9 G14
Skíathos, *Greece* 38 B5

Skibbereen, *Ireland* 15 E2
Skiddaw, *U.K.* 12 C4
Skidegate, *Canada* 104 C2
Skídhra, *Greece* 40 F6
Skien, *Norway* 9 G13
Skierniewice, *Poland* 45 G7
Skikda, *Algeria* 78 A7
Skillingaryd, *Sweden* 11 G8
Skillinge, *Sweden* 11 J8
Skilloura, *Cyprus* 36 D12
Skipton, *U.K.* 12 D5
Skirmish Pt., *Australia* . 94 A1
Skiropoúla, *Greece* 38 C6
Skíros, *Greece* 38 C6
Skivarp, *Sweden* 11 J7
Skive, *Denmark* 11 H3
Skjálfandafljót →, *Iceland* . 8 D5
Skjálfandi, *Iceland* 8 C5
Skjern, *Denmark* 11 J2
Skoczów, *Poland* 45 J5
Škofja Loka, *Slovenia* ... 29 B11
Skoghall, *Sweden* 10 E7
Skogstorp, *Sweden* 10 E10
Skoki, *Poland* 45 F4
Skole, *Ukraine* 47 H2
Skópelos, *Greece* 38 B5
Skopí, *Greece* 36 D8
Skopin, *Russia* 46 F10
Skopje, *Macedonia* 40 D5
Skórcz, *Poland* 44 E5
Skørping, *Denmark* 11 H3
Skövde, *Sweden* 11 F7
Skovorodino, *Russia* 51 D13
Skowhegan, *U.S.A.* 109 C11
Skradin, *Croatia* 29 E12
Skrea, *Sweden* 11 H6
Skrunda, *Latvia* 44 B9
Skrwa →, *Poland* 45 F6
Skull, *Ireland* 15 E2
Skultorp, *Sweden* 11 F7
Skultuna, *Sweden* 10 E10
Skunk →, *U.S.A.* 112 E9
Skuodas, *Lithuania* 9 H19
Skurup, *Sweden* 11 J7
Skutskär, *Sweden* 10 D11
Skvyra, *Ukraine* 47 H5
Skwierzyna, *Poland* 45 F2
Skye, *U.K.* 14 D2
Skykomish, *U.S.A.* 114 C3
Skyros = Skíros, *Greece* . 38 C6
Skyttorp, *Sweden* 10 D11
Slættaratindur, *Færoe Is.* . 8 E9
Slagelse, *Denmark* 11 J5
Slamet, *Indonesia* 63 G13
Slaney →, *Ireland* 15 D5
Slangberge, *S. Africa* ... 88 E3
Slănic, *Romania* 43 E10
Slano, *Croatia* 40 D1
Slantsy, *Russia* 46 C5
Slaný, *Czech Rep.* 26 A7
Śląskie □, *Poland* 45 H6
Slătbaken, *Sweden* 11 F10
Slate Is., *Canada* 102 C2
Slatina, *Croatia* 42 E2
Slatina, *Romania* 43 F9
Slatina Timiş, *Romania* .. 42 E7
Slatington, *U.S.A.* 111 F9
Slaton, *U.S.A.* 113 J4
Slave →, *Canada* 104 A6
Slave Coast, *W. Afr.* 83 D5
Slave Lake, *Canada* 104 B6
Slave Pt., *Canada* 104 A5
Slavgorod, *Russia* 50 D8
Slavinja, *Serbia, Yug.* .. 40 C6
Slavkov u Brna, *Czech Rep.* 27 B9
Slavonija, *Croatia* 42 E2
Slavonski Brod, *Croatia* . 42 E3
Slavuta, *Ukraine* 47 G4
Slavyanka, *Russia* 54 C5
Slavyanovo, *Bulgaria* 41 C8
Slavyansk = Slovyansk,
  Ukraine 47 H9
Slavyansk-na-Kubani, *Russia* 47 K10
Sława, *Poland* 45 G3
Slawharad, *Belarus* 46 F6
Sławno, *Poland* 44 D3
Sławoborze, *Poland* 44 E2
Sleaford, *U.K.* 12 D7
Sleaford B., *Australia* .. 95 E2
Sleat, Sd. of, *U.K.* 14 D3
Sleeper Is., *Canada* 101 C11
Sleepy Eye, *U.S.A.* 112 C7
Slemon L., *Canada* 104 A5
Ślesin, *Poland* 45 F5
Slide Mt., *U.S.A.* 111 E10
Slidell, *U.S.A.* 113 K10
Sliema, *Malta* 36 D2
Slieve Aughty, *Ireland* .. 15 C3
Slieve Bloom, *Ireland* ... 15 C4
Slieve Donard, *U.K.* 15 B6
Slieve Gamph, *Ireland* ... 15 B3
Slieve Gullion, *U.K.* 15 B5
Slieve Mish, *Ireland* 15 D2
Slievenamon, *Ireland* 15 D4
Sligeach = Sligo, *Ireland* . 15 B3
Sligo, *Ireland* 15 B3
Sligo, *U.S.A.* 110 E5
Sligo □, *Ireland* 15 B3
Sligo B., *Ireland* 15 B3
Slippery Rock, *U.S.A.* ... 110 E4
Slite, *Sweden* 11 G12
Sliven, *Bulgaria* 41 D10
Slivnitsa, *Bulgaria* 40 D7
Sljeme, *Croatia* 29 C12
Sloan, *U.S.A.* 117 K11
Sloansville, *U.S.A.* 111 D10
Slobozia, *Moldova* 43 D14
Slobozia, *Argeş, Romania* . 43 F10
Slobozia, *Ialomiţa, Romania* 43 F12

Slocan, *Canada* 104 D5
Słomniki, *Poland* 45 H7
Slonim, *Belarus* 47 F3
Slough, *U.K.* 13 F7
Slough □, *U.K.* 13 F7
Sloughhouse, *U.S.A.* 116 G5
Slovak Rep. ■, *Europe* ... 27 C13
Slovakia = Slovak Rep. ■,
  Europe 27 C13
Slovenia ■, *Europe* 29 C11
Slovenia = Slovenija ■,
  Europe 29 C11
Slovenj Gradec, *Slovenia* . 29 B12
Slovenska Bistrica, *Slovenia* 29 B12
Slovenské Konjice, *Slovenia* 29 B12
Slovenské Rudohorie,
  Slovak Rep. 27 C12
Slovyansk, *Ukraine* 47 H9
Słubice, *Poland* 45 F1
Sluch →, *Ukraine* 47 G4
Sluis, *Neths.* 17 C3
Slŭnchev Bryag, *Bulgaria* . 41 D11
Slunj, *Croatia* 29 C12
Słupca, *Poland* 45 F4
Słupia →, *Poland* 44 D3
Słupsk, *Poland* 44 D4
Slurry, *S. Africa* 88 D4
Slutsk, *Belarus* 47 F4
Slyne Hd., *Ireland* 15 C1
Slyudyanka, *Russia* 51 D11
Smålandsfarvandet, *Denmark* 11 J5
Smålandsstenar, *Sweden* .. 11 G7
Smalltree L., *Canada* 105 A8
Smallwood Res., *Canada* .. 103 B7
Smara, *Morocco* 78 B4
Smarhon, *Belarus* 46 E4
Smarje, *Slovenia* 29 B12
Smartt Syndicate Dam,
  S. Africa 88 E3
Smartville, *U.S.A.* 116 F5
Smeaton, *Canada* 105 C8
Smederevo, *Serbia, Yug.* . 40 B4
Smederevska Palanka,
  Serbia, Yug. 40 B4
Smedjebacken, *Sweden* 10 D9
Smela = Smila, *Ukraine* .. 47 H6
Smerwick Harbour, *Ireland* . 15 D1
Smethport, *U.S.A.* 110 E6
Smidovich, *Russia* 51 E14
Śmigiel, *Poland* 45 F3
Smila, *Ukraine* 47 H6
Smilyan, *Bulgaria* 41 E8
Smith, *Canada* 104 B6
Smith Center, *U.S.A.* 112 F5
Smith Sund, *Greenland* ... 4 B4
Smithburne →, *Australia* . 94 B3
Smithers, *Canada* 104 C3
Smithfield, *S. Africa* ... 89 E4
Smithfield, *N.C., U.S.A.* . 109 H6
Smithfield, *Utah, U.S.A.* . 114 F8
Smiths Falls, *Canada* 102 D4
Smithton, *Australia* 94 G4
Smithville, *Canada* 110 C5
Smithville, *U.S.A.* 113 K6
Smoky →, *Canada* 104 B5
Smoky Bay, *Australia* 95 E1
Smoky Hill →, *U.S.A.* 112 F6
Smoky Hills, *U.S.A.* 112 F5
Smoky Lake, *Canada* 104 C6
Smøla, *Norway* 8 E13
Smolensk, *Russia* 46 E7
Smolikas, Óros, *Greece* .. 40 F4
Smolník, *Slovak Rep.* 27 C13
Smolyan, *Bulgaria* 41 E8
Smooth Rock Falls, *Canada* 102 C3
Smoothstone L., *Canada* .. 105 C7
Smorgon = Smarhon,
  Belarus 46 E4
Smulţi, *Romania* 43 E12
Smyadovo, *Bulgaria* 41 C11
Smygehamn, *Sweden* 11 J7
Smyrna = İzmir, *Turkey* .. 39 C9
Smyrna, *U.S.A.* 108 F8
Snæfell, *Iceland* 8 D6
Snaefell, *U.K.* 12 C3
Snæfellsjökull, *Iceland* . 8 D2
Snake →, *U.S.A.* 114 C4
Snake I., *Australia* 95 F4
Snake Range, *U.S.A.* 114 G6
Snake River Plain, *U.S.A.* 114 E7
Snåsavatnet, *Norway* 8 D14
Snedsted, *Denmark* 11 H2
Sneek, *Neths.* 17 A5
Sneeuberge, *S. Africa* ... 88 E3
Snejbjerg, *Denmark* 11 H2
Snelling, *U.S.A.* 116 H6
Snezhnoye, *Ukraine* 47 J10
Snežnik, *Slovenia* 29 C11
Śniadowo, *Poland* 45 E8
Śniardwy, Jezioro, *Poland* . 44 E8
Śnieżka, *Europe* 26 A8
Snigirevka = Snihurivka,
  Ukraine 47 J7
Snihurivka, *Ukraine* 47 J7
Snina, *Slovak Rep.* 27 C15
Snizort, L., *U.K.* 14 D2
Snøhetta, *Norway* 9 E13
Snohomish, *U.S.A.* 116 C4
Snoul, *Cambodia* 65 F6
Snow Hill, *U.S.A.* 108 F8
Snow Lake, *Canada* 105 C8
Snow Mt., *Calif., U.S.A.* . 116 F4
Snow Mt., *Maine, U.S.A.* . 111 A14
Snow Shoe, *U.S.A.* 110 E7
Snowbird L., *Canada* 105 A8

Snowdon, *U.K.* 12 D3
Snowdrift →, *Canada* 105 A6
Snowflake, *U.S.A.* 115 J8
Snowshoe Pk., *U.S.A.* 114 B6
Snowtown, *Australia* 95 E2
Snowville, *U.S.A.* 114 F7
Snowy →, *Australia* 95 F4
Snowy Mt., *U.S.A.* 111 C10
Snowy Mts., *Australia* ... 95 F4
Snug Corner, *Bahamas* 121 B5
Snyatyn, *Ukraine* 47 H3
Snyder, *Okla., U.S.A.* ... 113 H5
Snyder, *Tex., U.S.A.* 113 J4
Soahanina, *Madag.* 89 B7
Soalala, *Madag.* 89 B8
Soaloka, *Madag.* 89 B8
Soamanonga, *Madag.* 89 C7
Soan →, *Pakistan* 68 C4
Soanierana-Ivongo, *Madag.* . 89 B8
Soanindrariny, *Madag.* ... 89 B8
Soars, *Romania* 43 E9
Soavina, *Madag.* 89 C8
Soavinandriana, *Madag.* .. 89 B8
Soba, *Nigeria* 83 C6
Sobat, Nahr →, *Sudan* 81 F3
Sobhapur, *India* 68 H8
Sobinka, *Russia* 46 E11
Sobótka, *Poland* 45 H3
Sobra, *Croatia* 29 F14
Sobradinho, Reprêsa de,
  Brazil 125 E10
Sobral, *Brazil* 125 D10
Sobrance, *Slovak Rep.* ... 27 C15
Sobreira Formosa, *Portugal* 34 F3
Soc Giang, *Vietnam* 58 F6
Soc Trang, *Vietnam* 65 H5
Soča →, *Europe* 29 J6
Socastee, *U.S.A.* 109 J6
Soch'e = Shache, *China* .. 60 C2
Sochi, *Russia* 49 J4
Société, Is. de la, *Pac. Oc.* . 97 J12
Society Is. = Société, Is. de
  la, *Pac. Oc.* 97 J12
Socompa, Portezuelo de,
  Chile 126 A2
Socorro, *N. Mex., U.S.A.* . 115 J10
Socorro, *Tex., U.S.A.* ... 115 L10
Socorro, I., *Mexico* 118 D2
Socotra, *Ind. Oc.* 74 E5
Socovos, *Spain* 33 G3
Socuéllamos, *Spain* 33 F2
Soda L., *U.S.A.* 115 J5
Soda Plains, *India* 69 B8
Soda Springs, *U.S.A.* 114 E8
Sodankylä, *Finland* 8 C22
Soddy-Daisy, *U.S.A.* 109 H3
Söderåla, *Sweden* 10 C10
Söderbärke, *Sweden* 10 D9
Söderfors, *Sweden* 10 D11
Söderhamn, *Sweden* 10 C11
Söderköping, *Sweden* 11 F10
Södermanland, *Sweden* 9 G17
Södermanlands län □,
  Sweden 10 E11
Södertälje, *Sweden* 10 E11
Sodiri, *Sudan* 81 E2
Sodo, *Ethiopia* 81 F4
Södra Dellen, *Sweden* 10 C10
Södra Finnskoga, *Sweden* . 10 D6
Södra Sandby, *Sweden* 11 J7
Södra Ulvön, *Sweden* 10 B12
Södra Vi, *Sweden* 11 G9
Sodražica, *Slovenia* 29 C11
Sodus, *U.S.A.* 110 C7
Soekmekaar, *S. Africa* ... 89 C4
Soest, *Germany* 24 D4
Soest, *Neths.* 17 B5
Sofádhes, *Greece* 38 B4
Sofala □, *Mozam.* 89 B5
Sofara, *Mali* 82 C4
Sofia = Sofiya, *Bulgaria* . 40 D7
Sofia →, *Madag.* 89 B8
Sofievka, *Ukraine* 47 H7
Sofikón, *Greece* 38 D5
Sofiya, *Bulgaria* 40 D7
Sofiya □, *Bulgaria* 40 D7
Sōfu-Gan, *Japan* 55 K10
Sogakofe, *Ghana* 83 D5
Sogamoso, *Colombia* 124 B4
Sogār, *Iran* 71 E8
Sögel, *Germany* 24 C3
Sogndalsfjøra, *Norway* ... 9 F12
Søgne, *Norway* 9 G12
Sognefjorden, *Norway* 9 F11
Söğüt, *Bilecik, Turkey* .. 39 A12
Söğüt, *Burdur, Turkey* ... 39 D11
Söğüt Dağı, *Turkey* 39 D11
Söğütköy, *Turkey* 39 E10
Sŏgwipo, *S. Korea* 57 H14
Soh, *Iran* 71 C6
Sohâg, *Egypt* 80 B3
Sohagpur, *India* 68 H8
Sŏhori, *N. Korea* 57 D15
Soignies, *Belgium* 17 D4
Soin, *Burkina Faso* 82 C4
Soira, *Eritrea* 81 E4
Soissons, *France* 19 C10
Sōja, *Japan* 55 G6
Sojat, *India* 68 G5
Sok →, *Russia* 48 D10
Sokal, *Ukraine* 47 G3
Söke, *Turkey* 39 D9
Sokelo,
  Dem. Rep. of the Congo . 87 D1
Sokhós, *Greece* 40 F7
Sokhumi, *Georgia* 49 J5
Soko Banja, *Serbia, Yug.* . 40 C5
Sokodé, *Togo* 83 D5
Sokol, *Russia* 46 C11

Sokolac, Bos.-H. 42 G3
Sokółka, Poland 44 E10
Sokolo, Mali 82 C3
Sokolo, Mali 82 C3
Sokolov, Czech Rep. 26 A5
Sokołów Małopolski, Poland 45 H9
Sokołów Podlaski, Poland .. 45 F9
Sokoły, Poland 45 F9
Sokoto, Nigeria 83 C6
Sokoto □, Nigeria 83 C6
Sokoto →, Nigeria 83 C5
Sol Iletsk, Russia 50 D6
Sola →, Poland 45 H6
Solai, Kenya 86 B4
Solan, India 68 D7
Solano, Phil. 61 C4
Solapur, India 66 L9
Solca, Romania 43 C10
Solda Gölü, Turkey 39 D11
Soldănești, Moldova 43 C13
Soldotna, U.S.A. 100 B4
Soléa □, Cyprus 36 D12
Solec Kujawski, Poland ... 45 E5
Soledad, Colombia 124 A4
Soledad, U.S.A. 116 J5
Soledad, Venezuela 124 B6
Solent, The, U.K. 13 G6
Solenzara, France 21 G13
Solesmes, France 19 B10
Solfonn, Norway 9 F12
Solhan, Turkey 70 B4
Soligorsk = Salihorsk,
   Belarus 47 F4
Solihull, U.K. 13 E6
Solikamsk, Russia 50 D6
Solila, Madag. 89 C8
Solimões = Amazonas →,
   S. Amer. 122 D5
Solin, Croatia 29 E13
Solingen, Germany 24 D3
Sollebrunn, Sweden 11 F6
Sollefteå, Sweden 10 A11
Sollentuna, Sweden 10 E11
Sóller, Spain 37 B9
Sollerön, Sweden 10 D8
Solling, Germany 24 D5
Solnechnogorsk, Russia ... 46 D9
Solo →, Indonesia 63 G15
Solofra, Italy 31 B7
Sologne, France 19 E8
Solok, Indonesia 62 E2
Sololá, Guatemala 120 D1
Solomon, N. Fork →,
   U.S.A. 112 F5
Solomon, S. Fork →,
   U.S.A. 112 F5
Solomon Is. ■, Pac. Oc. .. 96 H7
Solon, China 60 B7
Solon Springs, U.S.A. 112 B9
Solor, Indonesia 63 F6
Solotcha, Russia 46 E10
Solothurn, Switz. 25 H3
Solothurn □, Switz. 25 H3
Solsona, Spain 32 C6
Solt, Hungary 42 D4
Šolta, Croatia 29 E13
Solțānābād, Khorāsān, Iran 71 C8
Solțānābād, Khorāsān, Iran 71 B8
Soltau, Germany 24 C5
Soltsy, Russia 46 C6
Solunska Glava, Macedonia 40 E5
Solvang, U.S.A. 117 L6
Solvay, U.S.A. 111 C8
Sölvesborg, Sweden 11 H8
Solway Firth, U.K. 12 C4
Solwezi, Zambia 87 E2
Sōma, Japan 54 F10
Soma, Turkey 39 B9
Somabhula, Zimbabwe 89 B4
Somali Pen., Africa 76 F8
Somali Rep. ■, Africa 74 F4
Somalia = Somali Rep. ■,
   Africa 74 F4
Sombernon, France 19 E11
Sombor, Serbia, Yug. 42 E4
Sombra, Canada 110 D2
Sombrerete, Mexico 118 C4
Sombrero, Anguilla 121 C7
Șomcuta Mare, Romania 43 C8
Somdari, India 68 G5
Somers, U.S.A. 114 B6
Somerset, Ky., U.S.A. 108 G3
Somerset, Mass., U.S.A. .. 111 E13
Somerset, Pa., U.S.A. 110 F5
Somerset □, U.K. 13 F5
Somerset East, S. Africa . 88 E4
Somerset I., Canada 100 A10
Somerset West, S. Africa . 88 E2
Somersworth, U.S.A. 111 C14
Somerton, U.S.A. 115 K6
Somerville, U.S.A. 111 F10
Someș →, Romania 42 C7
Someșul Mare, Romania 43 C8
Somme □, France 19 C9
Somme →, France 19 B8
Somme, B. de la, France .. 18 B8
Sommen, Jönköping, Sweden 11 F8
Sommen, Östergötland,
   Sweden 11 F9
Sommepy-Tahure, France ... 19 C11
Sömmerda, Germany 24 D7
Sommesous, France 19 D11
Sommières, France 21 E8
Somnath, India 68 J4
Somogy □, Hungary 42 D2
Somogyszob, Hungary 42 D2
Somoto, Nic. 120 D2
Sompolno, Poland 45 F5
Somport, Puerto de, Spain 32 C4
Son →, India 69 G11
Son Ha, Vietnam 64 E7

Son Hoa, Vietnam 64 F7
Son La, Vietnam 58 G4
Son Serra, Spain 37 B10
Son Servera, Spain 32 F8
Son Tay, Vietnam 58 G5
Soná, Panama 120 E3
Sonamarg, India 69 B6
Sonamukhi, India 69 H12
Sonar →, India 69 G8
Sŏnch'ŏn, N. Korea 57 E13
Sondags →, S. Africa 88 E4
Sønder Felding, Denmark .. 11 J2
Sønder Omme, Denmark 11 J2
Sønderborg, Denmark 11 K3
Sønderjyllands
   Amtskommune □,
   Denmark 11 J3
Sondershausen, Germany ... 24 D6
Sóndrio, Italy 28 B6
Sone, Mozam. 87 F3
Sonepur, India 67 J13
Song, Nigeria 83 D7
Song, Thailand 64 C3
Song Cau, Vietnam 64 F7
Song Xian, China 56 G7
Songch'ŏn, N. Korea 57 E14
Songea, Tanzania 87 E4
Songeons, France 19 C8
Songhua Hu, China 57 C14
Songhua Jiang →, China ... 60 B8
Songjiang, China 59 B13
Songjin, N. Korea 57 D15
Songjŏng-ni, S. Korea 57 G14
Songkan, China 58 C6
Songkhla, Thailand 65 J3
Songming, China 58 E4
Songnim, N. Korea 57 E13
Songo, Mozam. 85 H6
Songo, Sudan 79 G10
Songpan, China 58 A4
Songtao, China 58 C7
Songwe,
   Dem. Rep. of the Congo 86 C2
Songwe →, Africa 87 D3
Songxi, China 59 D12
Songzi, China 59 B8
Sonhat, India 69 H10
Sonid Youqi, China 56 C7
Sonipat, India 68 E7
Sonkach, India 68 H7
Sonkovo, Russia 46 D9
Sonmiani, Pakistan 68 G2
Sonmiani B., Pakistan 68 G2
Sonnino, Italy 30 A6
Sono →, Brazil 125 E9
Sonoma, U.S.A. 116 G4
Sonora, Calif., U.S.A. ... 116 H6
Sonora, Tex., U.S.A. 113 K4
Sonora □, Mexico 118 B2
Sonora →, Mexico 118 B2
Sonoran Desert, U.S.A. ... 117 L12
Sonoyta, Mexico 118 A2
Sonqor, Iran 73 E12
Sŏnsan, S. Korea 57 F15
Sonseca, Spain 35 F7
Sonsonate, El Salv. 120 D2
Sonsorol Is., Pac. Oc. ... 63 C8
Sonstorp, Sweden 11 F9
Sonthofen, Germany 25 H6
Soochow = Suzhou, China .. 59 B13
Sooke, Canada 116 B3
Sop Hao, Laos 58 G5
Sop Prap, Thailand 64 D2
Sopelana, Spain 32 B2
Sopi, Indonesia 63 D7
Sopot, Bulgaria 41 D8
Sopot, Poland 44 D5
Sopot, Serbia, Yug. 40 B4
Sopotnica, Macedonia 40 E5
Sopron, Hungary 42 C1
Sopur, India 69 B6
Sør-Rondane, Antarctica .. 5 D4
Sora, Italy 29 G10
Sorah, Pakistan 68 F3
Söråker, Sweden 10 B11
Sorano, Italy 29 F8
Soraon, India 69 G9
Sorbas, Spain 33 H2
Soresina, Italy 28 C6
Sörforsa, Sweden 10 C10
Sórgono, Italy 30 B2
Sorgues, France 21 D8
Sorgun, Turkey 72 C6
Soria, Spain 32 D2
Soria □, Spain 32 D2
Soriano, Uruguay 126 C4
Soriano nel Cimino, Italy 29 F9
Sorkh, Kuh-e, Iran 71 C8
Sorø, Denmark 11 J5
Soro, Guinea 82 C3
Soroca, Moldova 43 B13
Sorocaba, Brazil 127 A6
Soroki = Soroca, Moldova . 43 B13
Sorol Atoll, Pac. Oc. 63 C10
Sorong, Indonesia 63 E8
Soroní, Greece 36 C10
Soroti, Uganda 86 B3
Sørøya, Norway 8 A20
Sørøysundet, Norway 8 A20
Sorraia →, Portugal 35 G2
Sorrell, Australia 94 G4
Sorrento, Italy 31 B7
Sorsele, Sweden 8 D17
Sörsjön, Sweden 10 C7
Sorso, Italy 30 B1

Sorsogon, Phil. 61 E6
Sortavala, Russia 46 B6
Sortino, Italy 31 E8
Sortland, Norway 8 B16
Sorvizhi, Russia 48 B9
Sos = Sos del Rey Católico,
   Spain 32 C3
Sos del Rey Católico, Spain 32 C3
Sŏsan, S. Korea 57 F14
Soscumica, L., Canada 102 B4
Sösdala, Sweden 11 H7
Sosna →, Russia 47 F10
Sosnovka, Kirov, Russia .. 48 B10
Sosnovka, Tambov, Russia . 48 D5
Sosnovyy Bor, Russia 46 C5
Sosnowiec, Poland 45 H6
Sospel, France 21 E11
Sossus Vlei, Namibia 88 C2
Sotkamo, Finland 8 D23
Soto del Barco, Spain 34 B4
Soto la Marina →, Mexico . 119 C5
Soto y Amío, Spain 34 C5
Sotrondio, Spain 34 B5
Sotuta, Mexico 119 C7
Souanké, Congo 84 D2
Soubré, Ivory C. 82 D3
Souderton, U.S.A. 111 F9
Soúdha, Greece 36 D6
Soúdhas, Kólpos, Greece .. 36 D6
Souflíon, Greece 41 E10
Soufrière, St. Lucia 121 D7
Souillac, France 20 D5
Souilly, France 19 C12
Soukhouma, Laos 64 E5
Sŏul, S. Korea 57 F14
Soulac-sur-Mer, France ... 20 C2
Soulougou, Burkina Faso .. 83 C5
Soultz-sous-Forêts, France 19 D14
Sound, The = Øresund,
   Europe 11 J6
Sound, The, U.K. 13 G3
Soúnion, Ákra, Greece 38 D6
Sources, Mt. aux, Lesotho 89 D4
Soure, Brazil 125 D9
Soure, Portugal 34 E2
Souris, Man., Canada 105 D8
Souris, P.E.I., Canada ... 103 C7
Souris →, Canada 112 A5
Sourou →, Africa 82 C4
Soúrpi, Greece 38 B4
Sousa, Brazil 125 E11
Sousel, Portugal 35 G3
Sousse, Tunisia 79 A8
Soustons, France 20 E2
Sout →, S. Africa 88 E2
South Africa ■, Africa ... 88 E3
South America 122 E5
South Atlantic Ocean 122 H7
South Aulatsivik I., Canada 103 A7
South Australia □, Australia 95 E2
South Ayrshire □, U.K. ... 14 F4
South Baldy, U.S.A. 115 J10
South Bass I., U.S.A. 110 E2
South Bend, Ind., U.S.A. . 108 E2
South Bend, Wash., U.S.A. 116 D3
South Boston, U.S.A. 109 G6
South Branch, Canada 103 C8
South Brook, Canada 103 C8
South Carolina □, U.S.A. . 109 J5
South Charleston, U.S.A. . 108 F5
South China Sea, Asia 62 C4
South Dakota □, U.S.A. ... 112 C5
South Deerfield, U.S.A. .. 111 D12
South Downs, U.K. 13 G7
South East C., Australia . 94 G4
South East Is., Australia 93 F3
South Esk →, U.K. 14 E6
South Foreland, U.K. 13 F9
South Fork American →,
   U.S.A. 116 G5
South Fork Feather →,
   U.S.A. 116 F5
South Fork Grand →,
   U.S.A. 112 C3
South Fork Republican →,
   U.S.A. 112 E4
South Georgia, Antarctica 122 J7
South Gloucestershire □,
   U.K. 13 F5
South Hadley, U.S.A. 111 D12
South Haven, U.S.A. 108 D2
South Henik, L., Canada .. 105 A9
South Honshu Ridge,
   Pac. Oc. 96 E6
South Horr, Kenya 86 B4
South I., Kenya 86 B4
South I., N.Z. 91 L3
South Indian Lake, Canada 105 B9
South Invercargill, N.Z. . 91 M2
South Knife →, Canada 105 B10
South Koel →, India 69 H11
South Korea ■, Asia 57 G15
South Lake Tahoe, U.S.A. . 116 G6
South Lanarkshire □, U.K. 14 F5
South Loup →, U.S.A. 112 E5
South Magnetic Pole,
   Antarctica 5 C9
South Milwaukee, U.S.A. .. 108 D2
South Molton, U.K. 13 F4
South Moose L., Canada ... 105 C8
South Nahanni →, Canada .. 104 A4
South Nation →, Canada ... 111 A9
South Natuna Is. = Natuna
   Selatan, Kepulauan,
   Indonesia 65 L7
South Negril Pt., Jamaica 120 C4
South Orkney Is., Antarctica 5 C18
South Ossetia □, Georgia . 49 J7

South Pagai, I. = Pagai
   Selatan, Pulau, Indonesia 62 E2
South Paris, U.S.A. 111 B14
South Pittsburg, U.S.A. .. 109 H3
South Platte →, U.S.A. ... 112 E4
South Pole, Antarctica ... 5 E
South Porcupine, Canada .. 102 C3
South Portland, U.S.A. ... 109 D10
South Pt., U.S.A. 110 B1
South River, Canada 102 C4
South River, U.S.A. 111 F10
South Ronaldsay, U.K. 14 C6
South Sandwich Is.,
   Antarctica 5 B1
South Saskatchewan →,
   Canada 105 C7
South Seal →, Canada 105 B9
South Shetland Is.,
   Antarctica 5 C18
South Shields, U.K. 12 C6
South Sioux City, U.S.A. . 112 D6
South Taranaki Bight, N.Z. 91 H5
South Thompson →,
   Canada 104 C4
South Twin I., Canada 102 B4
South Tyne →, U.K. 12 C5
South Uist, U.K. 14 D1
South West Africa =
   Namibia ■, Africa 88 C2
South West C., Australia . 94 G4
South West Rocks, Australia 95 E5
South Williamsport, U.S.A. 110 E8
South Yorkshire □, U.K. .. 12 D6
Southampton, Canada 102 D3
Southampton, U.K. 13 G6
Southampton, U.S.A. 111 F12
Southampton □, U.K. 13 G6
Southampton I., Canada ... 101 B11
Southaven, U.S.A. 113 H9
Southbank, Canada 104 C3
Southbridge, N.Z. 91 K4
Southbridge, U.S.A. 111 D12
Southend, Canada 105 B8
Southend-on-Sea, U.K. 13 F8
Southend-on-Sea □, U.K. .. 13 F8
Southern □, Malawi 87 F4
Southern □, S. Leone 82 D2
Southern □, Uganda 86 C3
Southern □, Zambia 87 F2
Southern Alps, N.Z. 91 K3
Southern Cross, Australia 93 F2
Southern Indian L., Canada 105 B9
Southern Ocean, Antarctica 5 C6
Southern Pines, U.S.A. ... 109 H6
Southern Uplands, U.K. ... 14 F5
Southington, U.S.A. 111 E12
Southold, U.S.A. 111 E12
Southport, Australia 95 D5
Southport, U.K. 12 D4
Southport, Fla., U.S.A. .. 109 K3
Southport, N.Y., U.S.A. .. 110 D8
Southwest C., N.Z. 91 M1
Southwold, U.K. 13 E9
Soutpansberg, S. Africa .. 89 C4
Souvigny, France 19 F10
Sovata, Romania 43 D10
Soverato, Italy 31 D9
Sovetsk, Kaliningd., Russia 9 J19
Sovetsk, Kirov, Russia ... 48 B9
Sovetskaya Gavan = Vanino,
   Russia 51 E15
Sovicille, Italy 29 E8
Soweto, S. Africa 89 D4
Sōya-Kaikyō = La Perouse
   Str., Japan 54 B11
Sōya-Misaki, Japan 54 B10
Soyaux, France 20 C4
Sozh →, Belarus 47 F6
Sozopol, Bulgaria 41 D11
Spa, Belgium 17 D5
Spain ■, Europe 7 H5
Spalding, Australia 95 E2
Spalding, U.K. 12 E7
Spangler, U.S.A. 110 F6
Spanish, Canada 102 C3
Spanish Fork, U.S.A. 114 F8
Spanish Town, Jamaica 120 C4
Sparks, U.S.A. 116 F7
Sparreholm, Sweden 10 E10
Sparta = Spárti, Greece .. 38 D4
Sparta, Mich., U.S.A. 108 D3
Sparta, N.J., U.S.A. 111 E10
Sparta, Wis., U.S.A. 112 D9
Spartanburg, U.S.A. 109 H5
Spárti, Greece 38 D4
Spartivento, C., Calabria,
   Italy 31 E9
Spartivento, C., Sard., Italy 30 D1
Sparwood, Canada 104 D6
Spas-Demensk, Russia 46 E7
Spas-Klepiki, Russia 46 E11
Spassk Dalniy, Russia 51 E14
Spassk-Ryazanskiy, Russia 46 E11
Spátha, Ákra, Greece 36 D5
Spatsizi →, Canada 104 B3
Spatsizi Plateau Wilderness
   Park, Canada 104 B3
Spean →, U.K. 14 E4
Spearfish, U.S.A. 112 C3
Spearman, U.S.A. 113 G4
Speculator, U.S.A. 111 C10
Speia, Moldova 43 D14
Speightstown, Barbados ... 121 D8
Speke Gulf, Tanzania 86 C3
Spello, Italy 29 F9
Spencer, Idaho, U.S.A. ... 114 D7
Spencer, Iowa, U.S.A. 112 D7
Spencer, N.Y., U.S.A. 111 D8
Spencer, Nebr., U.S.A. ... 112 D5
Spencer, C., Australia ... 95 F2

Spencer B., Namibia 88 D1
Spencer G., Australia 95 E2
Spencerville, Canada 111 B9
Spences Bridge, Canada ... 104 C4
Spennymoor, U.K. 12 C6
Spenser Mts., N.Z. 91 K4
Spentrup, Denmark 11 H4
Sperkhiós →, Greece 38 C4
Sperrin Mts., U.K. 15 B5
Spessart, Germany 25 D5
Spétsai, Greece 38 D5
Spey →, U.K. 14 D5
Speyer, Germany 25 F4
Spezand, Pakistan 68 E2
Spezzano Albanese, Italy . 31 C9
Spiekeroog, Germany 24 B3
Spiez, Switz. 25 J3
Spíli, Greece 36 D6
Spilimbergo, Italy 29 B9
Spin Búldak, Afghan. 68 D2
Spinalónga, Greece 36 D7
Spinazzola, Italy 31 B9
Spineni, Romania 43 F9
Spirit Lake, U.S.A. 116 D4
Spirit River, Canada 104 B5
Spiritwood, Canada 105 C7
Spišská Nová Ves,
   Slovak Rep. 27 C13
Spišské Podhradie,
   Slovak Rep. 27 B13
Spital, Austria 26 D7
Spithead, U.K. 13 G6
Spittal an der Drau, Austria 26 E6
Spitzbergen = Svalbard,
   Arctic 4 B8
Spjelkavik, Norway 9 E12
Split, Croatia 29 E13
Split L., Canada 105 B9
Split Lake, Canada 105 B9
Splitski Kanal, Croatia .. 29 E13
Splügenpass, Switz. 25 J5
Spofford, U.S.A. 113 L4
Spokane, U.S.A. 114 C5
Spoleto, Italy 29 F9
Spooner, U.S.A. 112 C9
Sporyy Navolok, Mys, Russia 50 B7
Sprague, U.S.A. 114 C5
Spratly I., S. China Sea .. 62 C4
Spratly Is., S. China Sea 62 C4
Spray, U.S.A. 114 D4
Spreča →, Bos.-H. 42 F3
Spree →, Germany 24 C9
Spreewald, Germany 24 D9
Spremberg, Germany 24 D10
Sprengisandur, Iceland ... 8 D5
Spring City, U.S.A. 111 F9
Spring Creek, U.S.A. 114 F6
Spring Garden, U.S.A. 116 F6
Spring Hill, U.S.A. 109 L4
Spring Mts., U.S.A. 115 H6
Spring Valley, U.S.A. 117 N10
Springbok, S. Africa 88 D2
Springboro, U.S.A. 110 E4
Springdale, Canada 103 C8
Springdale, U.S.A. 113 G7
Springe, Germany 24 C5
Springer, U.S.A. 113 G2
Springerville, U.S.A. 115 J9
Springfield, Canada 110 D4
Springfield, N.Z. 91 K3
Springfield, Colo., U.S.A. 113 G3
Springfield, Ill., U.S.A. 112 F10
Springfield, Mass., U.S.A. 111 D12
Springfield, Mo., U.S.A. . 113 G8
Springfield, Ohio, U.S.A. 108 F4
Springfield, Oreg., U.S.A. 114 D2
Springfield, Tenn., U.S.A. 109 G2
Springfield, Vt., U.S.A. . 111 C12
Springfontein, S. Africa . 88 E4
Springhill, Canada 103 C7
Springhill, U.S.A. 113 J8
Springhouse, Canada 104 C4
Springs, S. Africa 89 D4
Springsure, Australia 94 C4
Springvale, U.S.A. 111 C14
Springville, Calif., U.S.A. 116 J8
Springville, N.Y., U.S.A. 110 D6
Springville, Utah, U.S.A. 114 F8
Springwater, U.S.A. 110 D7
Spruce-Creek, U.S.A. 110 F6
Spruce Mt., U.S.A. 111 B12
Spur, U.S.A. 113 J4
Spurn Hd., U.K. 12 D8
Spuž, Montenegro, Yug. ... 40 D3
Spuzzum, Canada 104 D4
Squam L., U.S.A. 111 C13
Squamish, Canada 104 D4
Square Islands, Canada ... 103 B8
Squillace, G. di, Italy .. 31 D9
Squinzano, Italy 31 B11
Squires, Mt., Australia .. 93 E4
Srbac, Bos.-H. 42 E2
Srbica, Kosovo, Yug. 40 D4
Srbija = Serbia □,
   Yugoslavia 40 C5
Srbobran, Serbia, Yug. ... 42 E4
Sre Ambel, Cambodia 65 G4
Sre Khtum, Cambodia 65 F6
Sre Umbell = Sre Ambel,
   Cambodia 65 G4
Srebrenica, Bos.-H. 42 F3
Sredinny Ra. = Sredinnyy
   Khrebet, Russia 51 D16
Sredinnyy Khrebet, Russia 51 D16
Središče, Slovenia 29 B13
Sredna Gora, Bulgaria 41 D8
Srednekolymsk, Russia 51 C16
Sredni Rodopi, Bulgaria .. 41 E8
Srednogorie, Bulgaria 41 D8
Śrem, Poland 45 F4

Sremska Mitrovica,
  Serbia, Yug. 42 F4
Sremski Karlovci,
  Serbia, Yug. 42 E4
Srepok →, Cambodia 64 F6
Sretensk, Russia 51 D12
Sri Lanka ■, Asia 66 R12
Srikakulam, India 67 K13
Srinagar, India 69 B6
Środa Śląska, Poland 45 G3
Środa Wielkopolski, Poland 45 F4
Srpska Crnja, Serbia, Yug. . 42 E5
Srpski Itebej, Serbia, Yug. . 42 E5
Staaten →, Australia 94 B3
Staberhuk, Germany 24 A7
Stade, Germany 24 B5
Stadskanaal, Neths. 17 A6
Stadtallendorf, Germany .. 24 E5
Stadthagen, Germany 24 C5
Stadtlohn, Germany 24 D2
Stadtroda, Germany 24 E7
Staffa, U.K. 14 E2
Staffanstorp, Sweden 11 J7
Stafford, U.K. 12 E5
Stafford, U.S.A. 113 G5
Stafford Springs, U.S.A. . 111 E12
Staffordshire □, U.K. 12 E5
Stagnone, Italy 30 E5
Staines, U.K. 13 F7
Stainz, Austria 26 E8
Stakhanov, Ukraine 47 H10
Stalać, Serbia, Yug. 40 C5
Stalingrad = Volgograd,
  Russia 49 F7
Stalinir = Tskhinvali,
  Georgia 49 J7
Stalino = Donetsk, Ukraine 47 J9
Stalinogorsk =
  Novomoskovsk, Russia .. 46 E10
Stalis, Greece 36 D7
Stallarholmen, Sweden 10 E11
Ställdalen, Sweden 10 E8
Stalowa Wola, Poland 45 H9
Stalybridge, U.K. 12 D5
Stamford, Australia 94 C3
Stamford, U.K. 13 E7
Stamford, Conn., U.S.A. . 111 E11
Stamford, N.Y., U.S.A. .. 111 D10
Stamford, Tex., U.S.A. ... 113 J5
Stampriet, Namibia 88 C2
Stamps, U.S.A. 113 J8
Stančevo = Kalipetrovo,
  Bulgaria 41 B11
Standerton, S. Africa 89 D4
Standish, U.S.A. 108 D4
Stanford, S. Africa 88 E2
Stanford, U.S.A. 114 C8
Stånga, Sweden 11 G12
Stanger, S. Africa 89 D5
Stanišić, Serbia, Yug. 42 E4
Stanislaus →, U.S.A. 116 H5
Stanislav = Ivano-Frankivsk,
  Ukraine 47 H3
Stanislav = Ivano-Frankivsk,
  Ukraine 47 H3
Stanisławów, Poland 45 F8
Stanley, Australia 94 G4
Stanley, Canada 105 B8
Stanley, Falk. Is. 128 G5
Stanley, U.K. 12 C6
Stanley, Idaho, U.S.A. ... 114 D6
Stanley, N. Dak., U.S.A. . 112 A3
Stanley, N.Y., U.S.A. 110 D7
Stanovoy Khrebet, Russia . 51 D13
Stanovoy Ra. = Stanovoy
  Khrebet, Russia 51 D13
Stansmore Ra., Australia .. 92 D4
Stanthorpe, Australia 95 D5
Stanton, U.S.A. 113 J4
Stanwood, U.S.A. 116 B4
Staples, U.S.A. 112 B7
Stąporków, Poland 45 G7
Star City, Canada 105 C8
Star Lake, U.S.A. 111 B9
Stará Ľubovňa, Slovak Rep. 27 B13
Stara Moravica, Serbia, Yug. 42 E4
Stara Pazova, Serbia, Yug. . 42 E5
Stara Planina, Bulgaria ... 40 C7
Stará Turá, Slovak Rep. ... 27 C10
Stara Zagora, Bulgaria 41 D9
Starachowice, Poland 45 G8
Staraya Russa, Russia 46 D6
Starbuck I., Kiribati 97 H12
Starchiojd, Romania 43 E11
Stargard Szczeciński, Poland 44 E2
Stari Bar, Montenegro, Yug. 40 D3
Stari Trg, Slovenia 29 C12
Staritsa, Russia 46 D8
Starke, U.S.A. 109 L4
Starnberg, Germany 25 H7
Starnberger See, Germany . 25 H7
Starobilsk, Ukraine 47 H10
Starodub, Russia 47 F7
Starogard Gdański, Poland . 44 E5
Starokonstantinov =
  Starokostyantyniv,
  Ukraine 47 H4
Starokostyantyniv, Ukraine 47 H4
Starominskaya, Russia 47 J10
Staroshcherbinovskaya,
  Russia 47 J10
Start Pt., U.K. 13 G4
Stary Sącz, Poland 45 J7
Staryy Biryuzyak, Russia . 49 H8
Staryy Chartoriysk, Ukraine 47 G3
Staryy Krym, Ukraine 47 K8
Staryy Oskol, Russia 47 G9
Stassfurt, Germany 24 D7
Staszów, Poland 45 H8
State College, U.S.A. 110 F7
Stateline, U.S.A. 116 G7
Staten, I. = Estados, I. de
  Los, Argentina 122 J4

Staten I., U.S.A. 111 F10
Statesboro, U.S.A. 109 J5
Statesville, U.S.A. 109 H5
Stauffer, U.S.A. 117 L7
Staunton, Ill., U.S.A. 112 F10
Staunton, Va., U.S.A. 108 F6
Stavanger, Norway 9 G11
Staveley, N.Z. 91 K3
Stavelot, Belgium 17 D5
Stavern, Norway 9 G14
Stavoren, Neths. 17 B5
Stavropol, Russia 49 H6
Stavrós, Greece 36 D6
Stavrós, Greece 36 D6
Stavrós, Ákra, Greece 36 D6
Stavroúpolis, Greece 41 E8
Stawell, Australia 95 F3
Stawell →, Australia 94 C3
Stawiski, Poland 44 E9
Stawiszyn, Poland 45 G5
Stayner, Canada 110 B4
Stayton, U.S.A. 114 D2
Steamboat Springs, U.S.A. 114 F10
Stebleva, Albania 40 E4
Steele, U.S.A. 112 B5
Steelton, U.S.A. 110 F8
Steen River, Canada 104 B5
Steenkool = Bintuni,
  Indonesia 63 E8
Steens Mt., U.S.A. 114 E4
Steenwijk, Neths. 17 B6
Steep Pt., Australia 93 E1
Steep Rock, Canada 105 C9
Ştefan Vodă, Moldova 43 D14
Ştefăneşti, Romania 43 C12
Stefanie L. = Chew Bahir,
  Ethiopia 81 G4
Stefansson Bay, Antarctica 5 C5
Stege, Denmark 11 K6
Ştei, Romania 42 D7
Steiermark □, Austria 26 D8
Steigerwald, Germany 25 F6
Steilacoom, U.S.A. 116 C4
Steilrandberge, Namibia .. 88 B1
Steinbach, Canada 105 D9
Steinfurt, Germany 24 C3
Steinhausen, Namibia 88 C2
Steinheim, Germany 24 D5
Steinhuder Meer, Germany . 24 C5
Steinkjer, Norway 8 D14
Steinkopf, S. Africa 88 D2
Stellarton, Canada 103 C7
Stellenbosch, S. Africa ... 88 E2
Stelvio, Paso dello, Italy . 28 B7
Stenay, France 19 C12
Stendal, Germany 24 C7
Stende, Latvia 44 A9
Stenhamra, Sweden 10 E11
Stenstorp, Sweden 11 F7
Stenungsund, Sweden 11 F5
Steornabhaigh = Stornoway,
  U.K. 14 C2
Stepanakert = Xankändi,
  Azerbaijan 70 B5
Stepanavan, Armenia 49 K7
Stephens Creek, Australia . 95 E3
Stephens I., Canada 104 C2
Stephens L., Canada 105 B9
Stephenville, Canada 103 C8
Stephenville, U.S.A. 113 J5
Stepnica, Poland 44 E1
Stepnoi = Elista, Russia .. 49 G7
Steppe, Asia 52 D9
Stereá Ellas □, Greece ... 38 C4
Sterkstroom, S. Africa 88 E4
Sterling, Colo., U.S.A. 112 E3
Sterling, Ill., U.S.A. 112 E10
Sterling, Kans., U.S.A. ... 112 F5
Sterling City, U.S.A. 113 K4
Sterling Heights, U.S.A. .. 108 D4
Sterling Run, U.S.A. 110 E6
Sterlitamak, Russia 50 D6
Sternberg, Germany 24 B7
Šternberk, Czech Rep. 27 B10
Stérnes, Greece 36 D6
Sterzing = Vipiteno, Italy . 29 B8
Stettin = Szczecin, Poland . 44 E1
Stettiner Haff, Germany .. 24 B10
Stettler, Canada 104 C6
Steubenville, U.S.A. 110 F4
Stevenage, U.K. 13 F7
Stevens Point, U.S.A. 112 C10
Stevenson, U.S.A. 116 E5
Stevenson L., Canada 105 C9
Stevensville, U.S.A. 114 C6
Stevns Klint, Denmark ... 11 J6
Stewart, B.C., Canada ... 104 B3
Stewart, N.W.T., Canada . 100 B6
Stewart, U.S.A. 116 F7
Stewart, C., Australia 94 A1
Stewart, I., Chile 128 G2
Stewart I., N.Z. 91 M1
Stewarts Point, U.S.A. ... 116 G3
Stewartville, U.S.A. 112 D8
Stewiacke, Canada 103 C7
Steynsburg, S. Africa 88 E4
Steyr, Austria 26 C7
Steyr →, Austria 26 C7
Steytlerville, S. Africa 88 E3
Stia, Italy 29 E8
Stigler, U.S.A. 113 H7
Stigliano, Italy 31 B9
Stigtomta, Sweden 11 F10
Stikine →, Canada 104 B2
Stilfontein, S. Africa 88 D4
Stilís, Greece 38 C4
Stillwater, N.Z. 91 K3
Stillwater, Minn., U.S.A. . 112 C8
Stillwater, N.Y., U.S.A. . 111 D11
Stillwater, Okla., U.S.A. . 113 G6
Stillwater Range, U.S.A. . 114 G4

Stillwater Reservoir, U.S.A. 111 C9
Stilo, Pta., Italy 31 D9
Stilwell, U.S.A. 113 H7
Ştip, Macedonia 40 E6
Stíra, Greece 38 C6
Stirling, Canada 110 B7
Stirling, U.K. 14 E5
Stirling □, U.K. 14 E4
Stirling Ra., Australia 93 F2
Stittsville, Canada 111 A9
Stjernøya, Norway 8 A20
Stjørdalshalsen, Norway .. 8 E14
Stockach, Germany 25 H5
Stockaryd, Sweden 11 G8
Stockerau, Austria 27 C9
Stockholm, Sweden 10 E12
Stockholms län □, Sweden 10 E12
Stockport, U.K. 12 D5
Stocksbridge, U.K. 12 D6
Stockton, Calif., U.S.A. .. 116 H5
Stockton, Kans., U.S.A. .. 112 F5
Stockton, Mo., U.S.A. ... 113 G8
Stockton-on-Tees, U.K. .. 12 C6
Stockton-on-Tees □, U.K. 12 C6
Stockton Plateau, U.S.A. . 113 K3
Stoczek Łukowski, Poland . 45 G8
Stöde, Sweden 10 B10
Stoeng Treng, Cambodia . 64 F5
Stoer, Pt. of, U.K. 14 C3
Stogovo, Macedonia 40 E4
Stoholm, Denmark 11 H3
Stoke-on-Trent, U.K. 12 D5
Stoke-on-Trent □, U.K. .. 12 D5
Stokes Pt., Australia 94 G3
Stokes Ra., Australia 92 C5
Stokksnes, Iceland 8 D6
Stokmarknes, Norway ... 8 B16
Stolac, Bos.-H. 40 C1
Stolberg, Germany 24 E2
Stolbovoy, Ostrov, Russia . 51 D17
Stolbtsy = Stowbtsy, Belarus 46 F4
Stolin, Belarus 47 G4
Stöllet, Sweden 10 D7
Stolnici, Romania 43 F9
Stomíon, Greece 36 D5
Ston, Croatia 29 F14
Stone, U.K. 12 E5
Stoneboro, U.S.A. 110 E4
Stonehaven, U.K. 14 E6
Stonehenge, Australia 94 C3
Stonehenge, U.K. 13 F6
Stonewall, Canada 105 C9
Stony L., Man., Canada .. 105 B9
Stony L., Ont., Canada ... 110 B6
Stony Point, U.S.A. 111 E11
Stony Pt., U.S.A. 111 C8
Stony Rapids, Canada ... 105 B7
Stony Tunguska =
  Tunguska,
  Podkamennaya →, Russia 51 C10
Stonyford, U.S.A. 116 F4
Stopnica, Poland 45 H7
Storå, Sweden 10 E9
Storå →, Denmark 11 H2
Stora Gla, Sweden 10 E6
Stora Le, Sweden 10 E5
Stora Lulevatten, Sweden . 8 C18
Storavan, Sweden 8 D18
Stord, Norway 9 G11
Store Bælt, Denmark 11 J4
Store Heddinge, Denmark . 11 J6
Storebro, Sweden 11 G9
Storfors, Sweden 10 E8
Storlien, Sweden 10 A6
Storm B., Australia 94 G4
Storm Lake, U.S.A. 112 D7
Stormberge, S. Africa 88 E4
Stormsrivier, S. Africa 88 E3
Stornoway, U.K. 14 C2
Storo, Italy 28 C7
Storozhinets = Storozhynets,
  Ukraine 47 H3
Storozhynets, Ukraine 47 H3
Storrs, U.S.A. 111 E12
Storsjön, Gävleborg, Sweden 10 D10
Storsjön, Jämtland, Sweden 10 B7
Storsjön, Jämtland, Sweden . 10 A8
Storstrøms
  Amtskommune □,
  Denmark 11 J5
Storuman, Sweden 8 D17
Storuman, sjö, Sweden ... 8 D17
Storvätteshågna, Sweden . 10 B6
Storvik, Sweden 10 D10
Storvreta, Sweden 10 E11
Stouffville, Canada 110 C5
Stoughton, Canada 105 D8
Stour →, Dorset, U.K. .. 13 G6
Stour →, Kent, U.K. ... 13 F9
Stour →, Suffolk, U.K. . 13 F9
Stourbridge, U.K. 13 E5
Stout L., Canada 105 C10
Stove Pipe Wells Village,
  U.S.A. 117 J9
Støvring, Denmark 11 H3
Stow, U.S.A. 110 E3
Stowbtsy, Belarus 46 F4
Stowmarket, U.K. 13 E9
Strabane, U.K. 15 B4
Stracin, Macedonia 40 D6
Stradella, Italy 28 C6
Strahan, Australia 94 G4
Strajitsa, Bulgaria 41 C9
Strakonice, Czech Rep. ... 26 B6
Straldzha, Bulgaria 41 D10
Stralsund, Germany 24 A9
Strand, S. Africa 88 E2
Stranda, Møre og Romsdal,
  Norway 9 E12
Stranda, Nord-Trøndelag,
  Norway 8 E14

Strandby, Denmark 11 G4
Strangford L., U.K. 15 B6
Strängnäs, Sweden 10 E11
Stranraer, U.K. 14 G3
Strasbourg, Canada 105 C8
Strasbourg, France 19 D14
Strasburg, Germany 24 B9
Stråşeni, Moldova 43 C13
Stråssa, Sweden 10 E9
Stratford, Canada 102 D3
Stratford, N.Z. 91 H5
Stratford, Calif., U.S.A. .. 116 J7
Stratford, Conn., U.S.A. . 111 E11
Stratford, Tex., U.S.A. ... 113 G3
Stratford-upon-Avon, U.K. 13 E6
Strath Spey, U.K. 14 D5
Strathalbyn, Australia 95 F2
Strathaven, U.K. 14 F4
Strathcona Prov. Park,
  Canada 104 D3
Strathmore, Canada 104 C6
Strathmore, U.K. 14 E5
Strathmore, U.S.A. 116 J7
Strathnaver, Canada 104 C4
Strathpeffer, U.K. 14 D4
Strathroy, Canada 102 D3
Strathy Pt., U.K. 14 C4
Strattanville, U.S.A. 110 E5
Stratton, U.S.A. 111 A14
Stratton Mt., U.S.A. 111 C12
Straubing, Germany 25 G8
Straumnes, Iceland 8 C2
Strausberg, Germany 24 C9
Strawberry →, U.S.A. .. 114 F8
Strážnice, Czech Rep. 27 C10
Streaky B., Australia 95 E1
Streaky Bay, Australia ... 95 E1
Streator, U.S.A. 112 E10
Středočeský □, Czech Rep. 26 B7
Streetsboro, U.S.A. 110 E3
Streetsville, Canada 110 C5
Strehaia, Romania 43 F8
Strelcha, Bulgaria 41 D8
Strelka, Russia 51 D10
Streng →, Cambodia 64 F4
Stresa, Italy 28 C5
Streymoy, Færoe Is. 8 E9
Strezhevoy, Russia 50 C8
Stříbro, Czech Rep. 26 A6
Strimón →, Greece 40 F7
Strimonikós Kólpos, Greece 40 F7
Strofádhes, Greece 38 D3
Stroma, U.K. 14 C5
Strómboli, Italy 31 D8
Stromeferry, U.K. 14 D3
Stromness, U.K. 14 C5
Strömsburg, U.S.A. 112 E6
Strömsnäsbruk, Sweden . 11 H7
Strömstad, Sweden 11 F5
Strömsund, Sweden 8 E16
Strongilí, Greece 39 E11
Stróngoli, Italy 31 C10
Strongsville, U.S.A. 110 E3
Stronie Śląskie, Poland ... 45 H3
Stronsay, U.K. 14 B6
Stropkov, Slovak Rep. 27 B14
Stroud, U.K. 13 F5
Stroud Road, Australia ... 95 E5
Stroudsburg, U.S.A. 111 F9
Stroumbi, Cyprus 36 E11
Struer, Denmark 11 H2
Struga, Macedonia 40 E4
Strugi Krasnyye, Russia .. 46 C5
Struma →, Europe 40 E7
Strumica, Macedonia 40 E6
Struthers, Canada 102 C2
Struthers, U.S.A. 110 E4
Stryama, Bulgaria 41 D8
Stryker, U.S.A. 114 B6
Stryków, Poland 45 G6
Stryy, Ukraine 47 H2
Strzegom, Poland 45 H3
Strzelce Krajeńskie, Poland 45 F2
Strzelce Opolskie, Poland . 45 H5
Strzelecki Cr. →, Australia 95 D2
Strzelin, Poland 45 H4
Strzelno, Poland 45 F5
Strzybnica, Poland 45 H5
Strzyżów, Poland 45 J8
Stuart, Fla., U.S.A. 109 M5
Stuart, Nebr., U.S.A. 112 D5
Stuart →, Canada 104 C4
Stuart Bluff Ra., Australia . 92 D5
Stuart L., Canada 104 C4
Stuart Ra., Australia 95 D1
Stubbekøbing, Denmark . 11 K6
Stuben, Austria 26 D3
Studen Kladenets, Yazovir,
  Bulgaria 41 E9
Studenka, Czech Rep. ... 27 B11
Stugun, Sweden 10 A9
Stuhr, Germany 24 B4
Stull L., Canada 102 B1
Stung Treng = Stoeng
  Treng, Cambodia 64 F5
Stupart →, Canada 102 A1
Stupava, Slovak Rep. 27 C10
Stupino, Russia 46 E10
Sturgeon B., Canada 105 C9
Sturgeon Bay, U.S.A. 108 C2
Sturgeon Falls, Canada .. 102 C4
Sturgeon L., Alta., Canada 104 B5
Sturgeon L., Ont., Canada . 102 C1
Sturgeon L., Ont., Canada . 110 B6
Sturgis, Canada 105 C8
Sturgis, Mich., U.S.A. ... 108 E3
Sturgis, S. Dak., U.S.A. . 112 C3
Sturkö, Sweden 11 H9
Štúrovo, Slovak Rep. 27 D11
Sturt Cr. →, Australia ... 92 C4

Stutterheim, S. Africa 88 E4
Stuttgart, Germany 25 G5
Stuttgart, U.S.A. 113 H9
Stuyvesant, U.S.A. 111 D11
Stykkishólmur, Iceland .. 8 D2
Styria = Steiermark □,
  Austria 26 D8
Styrsö, Sweden 11 G5
Su Xian = Suzhou, China . 56 H9
Suakin, Sudan 80 D4
Suan, N. Korea 57 E14
Suaqui, Mexico 118 B3
Subang, Indonesia 63 G12
Subansiri →, India 67 F18
Subarnarekha →, India .. 69 H12
Subayhah, Si. Arabia 70 D3
Subcetate, Romania 42 E8
Subi, Indonesia 65 L7
Subiaco, Italy 29 G10
Subotica, Serbia, Yug. ... 42 D4
Suca, Ethiopia 81 F4
Suceava, Romania 43 C11
Suceava □, Romania 43 C10
Suceava →, Romania 43 C11
Sucha-Beskidzka, Poland . 45 J6
Suchań, Poland 45 E2
Suchan, Russia 54 C6
Suchedniów, Poland 45 G7
Suchitoto, El Salv. 120 D2
Suchou = Suzhou, China . 59 B13
Süchow = Xuzhou, China . 57 G9
Suchowola, Poland 44 E10
Suck →, Ireland 15 C3
Sucre, Bolivia 124 G5
Sućuraj, Croatia 29 E14
Sucuriú →, Brazil 125 H8
Sud, Pte. du, Canada 103 C7
Sud-Kivu □,
  Dem. Rep. of the Congo . 86 C2
Sud-Ouest, Pte. du, Canada 103 C7
Suda →, Russia 46 C9
Sudak, Ukraine 47 K8
Sudan, U.S.A. 113 H3
Sudan ■, Africa 81 E3
Sudbury, Canada 102 C3
Sudbury, U.K. 13 E8
Súðð, Iceland 8 C3
Süderbrarup, Germany .. 24 A5
Süderlügum, Germany ... 24 A4
Süderoogsand, Germany . 24 A4
Sudeten Mts. = Sudety,
  Europe 27 A9
Sudety, Europe 27 A9
Suðuroy, Færoe Is. 8 F9
Sudi, Tanzania 87 E4
Sudirman, Pegunungan,
  Indonesia 63 E9
Sudiţi, Romania 43 F12
Sudogda, Russia 48 C5
Sudr, Egypt 80 B3
Sudzha, Russia 47 G8
Sue →, Sudan 81 F2
Sueca, Spain 33 F4
Südedinenie, Bulgaria ... 41 D8
Suemez I., U.S.A. 104 B2
Suez = El Suweis, Egypt . 80 J8
Suez, G. of = Suweis, Khalig
  el, Egypt 80 J8
Suez Canal = Suweis, Qanâ
  es, Egypt 80 H8
Suffield, Canada 104 C6
Suffolk, U.S.A. 108 G7
Suffolk □, U.K. 13 E9
Şugag, Romania 43 E8
Sugargrove, U.S.A. 110 E5
Sugarive →, India 69 F12
Suğla Gölü, Turkey 72 D5
Sugluk = Salluit, Canada . 101 B12
Suhaia, Lacul, Romania .. 43 G10
Şuḩār, Oman 71 E8
Sühbaatar □, Mongolia .. 56 B8
Suhl, Germany 24 E6
Şuhut, Turkey 39 C12
Sui, Pakistan 68 E3
Sui Xian, China 56 G8
Suica, Bos.-H. 42 G2
Suichang, China 59 C12
Suichuan, China 59 D10
Suide, China 56 F6
Suifenhe, China 57 B16
Suihua, China 60 B7
Suijiang, China 58 C4
Suining, Hunan, China ... 59 D8
Suining, Jiangsu, China .. 57 H9
Suining, Sichuan, China .. 58 B5
Suiping, China 56 H7
Suippes, France 19 C11
Suir →, Ireland 15 D4
Suisun City, U.S.A. 116 G4
Suixi, China 59 G8
Suiyang, Guizhou, China . 58 D6
Suiyang, Heilongjiang, China 57 B16
Suizhong, China 57 D11
Suizhou, China 59 B9
Sujangarh, India 68 F6
Sukabumi, Indonesia 63 G12
Sukadana, Indonesia 65 E4
Sukagawa, Japan 55 F10
Sukaraja, Indonesia 62 E4
Sukarnapura = Jayapura,
  Indonesia 63 E10
Sukch'ŏn, N. Korea 57 E13
Sukhindol, Bulgaria 41 C9
Sukhinichi, Russia 46 E9
Sukhona →, Russia 50 D4
Sukhothai, Thailand 64 D2
Sukhumi = Sokhumi,
  Georgia 49 J5
Sukkur, Pakistan 68 F3
Sukkur Barrage, Pakistan . 68 F3

Sukovo, *Serbia, Yug.* 40 C6
Sukri →, *India* 68 G4
Sukumo, *Japan* 55 H6
Sukunka →, *Canada* 104 B4
Sula →, *Ukraine* 47 H7
Sula, Kepulauan, *Indonesia* 63 E7
Sulaco →, *Honduras* 120 C2
Sulaiman Range, *Pakistan* .. 68 D3
Sulak →, *Russia* 49 J8
Sūlār, *Iran* 71 D6
Sulawesi Sea = Celebes Sea,
  Indonesia 63 D6
Sulawesi Selatan □,
  Indonesia 63 E6
Sulawesi Utara □, *Indonesia* 63 D6
Sulechów, *Poland* 45 F2
Sulęcin, *Poland* 45 F2
Sulejów, *Poland* 45 G6
Sulejówek, *Poland* 45 F8
Süleymanlı, *Turkey* 39 C9
Sulima, *S. Leone* 82 D2
Sulina, *Romania* 43 E14
Sulina, Brațul →, *Romania* 43 E14
Sulingen, *Germany* 24 C4
Sulița, *Romania* 43 C11
Sulitjelma, *Norway* 8 C17
Sułkowice, *Poland* 45 J6
Sullana, *Peru* 124 D2
Süller, *Turkey* 39 C11
Sullivan, *Ill., U.S.A.* 112 F10
Sullivan, *Ind., U.S.A.* 108 F2
Sullivan, *Mo., U.S.A.* 112 F9
Sullivan Bay, *Canada* 104 C3
Sullivan I. = Lambi Kyun,
  Burma 65 G2
Sully-sur-Loire, *France* ... 19 E9
Sulmierzyce, *Poland* 45 G4
Sulmona, *Italy* 29 F10
Süloğlu, *Turkey* 41 E10
Sulphur, *La., U.S.A.* 113 K8
Sulphur, *Okla., U.S.A.* ... 113 H6
Sulphur Pt., *Canada* 104 A6
Sulphur Springs, *U.S.A.* .. 113 J7
Sultan, *Canada* 102 C3
Sultan, *U.S.A.* 116 C5
Sultan Dağları, *Turkey* ... 72 C4
Sultanhisar, *Turkey* 39 D10
Sultaniça, *Turkey* 41 F10
Sultaniye, *Turkey* 41 F12
Sultanpur, *Mad. P., India* .. 68 H8
Sultanpur, *Punjab, India* .. 68 D6
Sultanpur, *Ut. P., India* .. 69 F10
Sulu Arch., *Phil.* 61 J4
Sulu Sea, *E. Indies* 61 G4
Sülüklü, *Turkey* 72 C5
Sululta, *Ethiopia* 81 F4
Suluova, *Turkey* 72 B6
Suluq, *Libya* 79 B10
Sulzbach, *Germany* 25 F3
Sulzbach-Rosenberg,
  Germany 25 F7
Sulzberger Ice Shelf,
  Antarctica 5 D10
Sumalata, *Indonesia* 63 D6
Sumampa, *Argentina* 126 B3
Sumatera □, *Indonesia* ... 62 D2
Sumatera Barat □, *Indonesia* 62 E2
Sumatera Utara □, *Indonesia* 62 D1
Sumatra = Sumatera □,
  Indonesia 62 D2
Sumba, *Indonesia* 63 F5
Sumba, Selat, *Indonesia* ... 63 F5
Sumbawa, *Indonesia* 63 F5
Sumbawa Besar, *Indonesia* . 62 F5
Sumbawanga □, *Tanzania* .. 84 F6
Sumbe, *Angola* 84 G2
Sumburgh Hd., *U.K.* 14 B7
Sumdeo, *India* 69 D8
Sumdo, *India* 69 B8
Sumedang, *Indonesia* 63 G12
Sümeg, *Hungary* 42 D2
Sumeih, *Sudan* 81 F2
Šumen = Shumen, *Bulgaria* 41 C10
Sumenep, *Indonesia* 63 G15
Sumgait = Sumqayıt,
  Azerbaijan 49 K9
Summer L., *U.S.A.* 114 E4
Summerland, *Canada* 104 D5
Summerside, *Canada* 103 C7
Summersville, *U.S.A.* 108 F5
Summerville, *Ga., U.S.A.* .. 109 H3
Summerville, *S.C., U.S.A.* . 109 J5
Summit Lake, *Canada* 104 C4
Summit Peak, *U.S.A.* 115 H10
Sumner, *Iowa, U.S.A.* 112 D8
Sumner, *Wash., U.S.A.* ... 116 C4
Sumoto, *Japan* 55 G7
Šumperk, *Czech Rep.* 27 B9
Sumqayıt, *Azerbaijan* 49 K9
Sumter, *U.S.A.* 109 J5
Sumy, *Ukraine* 47 G8
Sun City, *Ariz., U.S.A.* ... 115 K7
Sun City, *Calif., U.S.A.* ... 117 M9
Sun City Center, *U.S.A.* .. 109 M4
Sun Lakes, *U.S.A.* 115 K8
Sun Valley, *U.S.A.* 114 E6
Sunagawa, *Japan* 54 C10
Sunan, *N. Korea* 57 E13
Sunart, L., *U.K.* 14 E3
Sunburst, *U.S.A.* 114 B8
Sunbury, *Australia* 95 F3
Sunbury, *U.S.A.* 111 F8
Sunchales, *Argentina* 126 C3
Suncho Corral, *Argentina* . 126 B3
Sunch'ŏn, *S. Korea* 57 G14
Suncook, *U.S.A.* 111 C13
Sunda, Selat, *Indonesia* ... 62 F3
Sunda Is., *Indonesia* 52 K14
Sunda Str. = Sunda, Selat,
  Indonesia 62 F3
Sundance, *Canada* 105 B10

Sundance, *U.S.A.* 112 C2
Sundar Nagar, *India* 68 D7
Sundarbans, The, *Asia* ... 67 J16
Sundargarh, *India* 67 H14
Sundays = Sondags →,
  S. Africa 88 E4
Sunderland, *Canada* 110 B5
Sunderland, *U.K.* 12 C6
Sundre, *Canada* 104 C6
Sunds, *Denmark* 11 H3
Sundsvall, *Sweden* 10 B11
Sundsvallsbukten, *Sweden* . 10 B11
Sung Hei, *Vietnam* 65 G6
Sungai Kolok, *Thailand* ... 65 J3
Sungai Lembing, *Malaysia* . 65 L4
Sungai Petani, *Malaysia* ... 65 K3
Sungailiat, *Indonesia* 62 E3
Sungaigerong, *Indonesia* .. 62 E2
Sungaipenuh, *Indonesia* ... 62 E2
Sungari = Songhua
  Jiang →, *China* 60 B8
Sunghua Chiang = Songhua
  Jiang →, *China* 60 B8
Sungikai, *Sudan* 81 E2
Sungurlu, *Turkey* 72 B6
Sunja, *Croatia* 29 C13
Sunland Park, *U.S.A.* 115 L10
Sunnansjö, *Sweden* 10 D8
Sunndalsøra, *Norway* 9 E13
Sunne, *Sweden* 10 E7
Sunnemo, *Sweden* 10 E7
Sunnyside, *U.S.A.* 114 C3
Sunnyvale, *U.S.A.* 116 H4
Suntar, *Russia* 51 C12
Sunyani, *Ghana* 82 D4
Suomenselkä, *Finland* 8 E21
Suomussalmi, *Finland* 8 D23
Suoyarvi, *Russia* 46 A7
Supai, *U.S.A.* 115 H7
Supaul, *India* 69 F12
Superior, *Ariz., U.S.A.* ... 115 K8
Superior, *Mont., U.S.A.* .. 114 C6
Superior, *Nebr., U.S.A.* .. 112 E5
Superior, *Wis., U.S.A.* ... 112 B8
Superior, L., *N. Amer.* ... 102 C2
Supetar, *Croatia* 29 E13
Suphan Buri, *Thailand* ... 64 E3
Suphan Dağı, *Turkey* 70 B4
Supiori, *Indonesia* 63 E9
Suprasl, *Poland* 45 E10
Suprasl →, *Poland* 45 E9
Supung Shuiku, *China* .. 57 D13
Sūq Suwayq, *Si. Arabia* .. 70 E3
Suqian, *China* 57 H10
Sūr, *Lebanon* 75 B4
Sūr, *Oman* 74 C6
Sur, Pt., *U.S.A.* 116 J5
Sura →, *Russia* 48 C8
Surab, *Pakistan* 68 E2
Surabaja = Surabaya,
  Indonesia 63 G15
Surabaya, *Indonesia* 63 G15
Surahammar, *Sweden* 10 E10
Suraia, *Romania* 43 E12
Surakarta, *Indonesia* 63 G14
Surakhany, *Azerbaijan* ... 49 K10
Surat, *Australia* 95 D4
Surat, *India* 66 J8
Surat Thani, *Thailand* 65 H2
Suratgarh, *India* 68 E5
Suraż, *Poland* 45 F9
Surazh, *Belarus* 46 E6
Surazh, *Russia* 47 F7
Surduc, *Romania* 43 C8
Surduc Pasul, *Romania* ... 43 E8
Surdulica, *Serbia, Yug.* ... 40 D6
Surendranagar, *India* 68 H4
Surf, *U.S.A.* 117 L6
Surgères, *France* 20 B3
Surgut, *Russia* 50 C8
Sùria, *Spain* 32 D6
Suriapet, *India* 66 L11
Surigao, *Phil.* 61 G6
Surigao Strait, *Phil.* 61 F6
Surin, *Thailand* 64 E4
Surin Nua, Ko, *Thailand* .. 65 H1
Surinam ■, *S. Amer.* 125 C7
Suriname = Surinam ■,
  S. Amer. 125 C7
Suriname →, *Surinam* ... 125 B7
Sürmaq, *Iran* 71 D7
Sürmene, *Turkey* 73 B9
Surovikino, *Russia* 49 F6
Surrey □, *U.K.* 13 F7
Sursand, *India* 69 F11
Sursar →, *India* 69 F12
Sursee, *Switz.* 25 H4
Sursk, *Russia* 48 D7
Surskoye, *Russia* 48 C8
Surt, *Libya* 79 B9
Surt, Khalīj, *Libya* 79 B9
Surtanahu, *Pakistan* 68 F4
Surte, *Sweden* 11 G6
Surtsey, *Iceland* 8 E3
Suruga-Wan, *Japan* 55 G9
Susa, *Italy* 28 C4
Suså →, *Denmark* 11 J5
Sušac, *Croatia* 29 F13
Susak, *Croatia* 29 D11
Susaki, *Japan* 55 H6
Süsangerd, *Iran* 71 D6
Susanville, *U.S.A.* 114 F3
Susch, *Switz.* 25 J6
Sušice, *Czech Rep.* 26 B6
Susleni, *Moldova* 43 C13
Susner, *India* 68 H7
Susong, *China* 59 B11
Susquehanna, *U.S.A.* 111 E9

Susquehanna →, *U.S.A.* .. 111 G8
Susques, *Argentina* 126 A2
Sussex, *Canada* 103 C6
Sussex, *U.S.A.* 111 E10
Sussex, E. □, *U.K.* 13 G8
Sussex, W. □, *U.K.* 13 G7
Sustut →, *Canada* 104 B3
Susuman, *Russia* 51 C15
Susunu, *Indonesia* 63 E8
Susurluk, *Turkey* 39 B10
Susz, *Poland* 44 E6
Sütçüler, *Turkey* 72 D4
Suțești, *Romania* 43 E12
Sutherland, *S. Africa* 88 E3
Sutherland, *U.S.A.* 112 E4
Sutherland Falls, *N.Z.* 91 L1
Sutherlin, *U.S.A.* 114 E2
Suthri, *India* 68 H3
Sutlej →, *Pakistan* 68 E4
Sutter, *U.S.A.* 116 F5
Sutter Creek, *U.S.A.* 116 G6
Sutton, *Canada* 111 A12
Sutton, *Nebr., U.S.A.* 112 E6
Sutton, *W. Va., U.S.A.* ... 108 F5
Sutton →, *Canada* 102 A3
Sutton Coldfield, *U.K.* ... 13 E6
Sutton in Ashfield, *U.K.* .. 12 D6
Sutton L., *Canada* 102 B3
Suttor →, *Australia* 94 C4
Suttsu, *Japan* 54 C10
Suva, *Fiji* 91 D8
Suva Gora, *Macedonia* ... 40 E4
Suva Planina, *Serbia, Yug.* 40 C6
Suva Reka, *Kosovo, Yug.* .. 40 D4
Suvorov, *Russia* 46 E9
Suvorov Is. = Suwarrow Is.,
  Cook Is. 97 J11
Suvorovo, *Bulgaria* 41 C11
Suwałki, *Poland* 44 D9
Suwannaphum, *Thailand* .. 64 E4
Suwannee →, *U.S.A.* 109 L4
Suwanose-Jima, *Japan* 55 K4
Suwarrow Is., *Cook Is.* ... 97 J11
Suwayq aṣ Ṣuqban, *Iraq* .. 70 D5
Suweis, Khalīg el, *Egypt* .. 80 J8
Suweis, Qanâ es, *Egypt* ... 80 H8
Suwŏn, *S. Korea* 57 F14
Suzdal, *Russia* 46 D11
Suzhou, *Anhui, China* 56 H9
Suzhou, *Jiangsu, China* ... 59 B13
Suzu, *Japan* 55 F8
Suzu-Misaki, *Japan* 55 F8
Suzuka, *Japan* 55 G8
Suzzara, *Italy* 28 D7
Svalbard, *Arctic* 4 B8
Svalöv, *Sweden* 11 J7
Svaneke, *Denmark* 11 J9
Svängsta, *Sweden* 11 H8
Svanskog, *Sweden* 10 E6
Svappavaara, *Sweden* 8 C19
Svärdsjö, *Sweden* 10 D9
Svartå, *Sweden* 10 E8
Svartisen, *Norway* 8 C16
Svartvik, *Sweden* 10 B11
Svatove, *Ukraine* 47 H10
Svatovo = Svatove, *Ukraine* 47 H10
Svay Chek, *Cambodia* 64 F4
Svay Rieng, *Cambodia* 65 G5
Svealand □, *Sweden* 10 D9
Svedala, *Sweden* 11 J7
Sveg, *Sweden* 10 B8
Svendborg, *Denmark* 11 J4
Svenljunga, *Sweden* 11 G7
Svenstavik, *Sweden* 10 B8
Svenstrup, *Denmark* 11 H3
Sverdlovsk = Yekaterinburg,
  Russia 50 D7
Sverdlovsk, *Ukraine* 47 H10
Sverdrup Is., *Canada* 4 B3
Svetac, *Croatia* 29 E12
Sveti Nikola, Prokhad,
  Europe 40 C6
Sveti Nikole, *Macedonia* .. 40 E5
Sveti Rok, *Croatia* 29 D12
Svetlaya, *Russia* 54 A9
Svetlogorsk = Svyetlahorsk,
  Belarus 47 F5
Svetlograd, *Russia* 49 H6
Svetlovodsk = Svitlovodsk,
  Ukraine 47 H7
Svidník, *Slovak Rep.* 27 B14
Svilaja Planina, *Croatia* ... 29 E13
Svilajnac, *Serbia, Yug.* ... 40 B5
Svilengrad, *Bulgaria* 41 E10
Svir →, *Russia* 46 B7
Sviritsa, *Russia* 46 B7
Svishtov, *Bulgaria* 41 C9
Svisloch, *Belarus* 47 F3
Svitava →, *Czech Rep.* ... 27 B9
Svitavy, *Czech Rep.* 27 B9
Svitlovodsk, *Ukraine* 47 H7
Svobodnyy, *Russia* 51 D13
Svoge, *Bulgaria* 40 D7
Svolvær, *Norway* 8 B16
Svratka →, *Czech Rep.* ... 27 B9
Svrljig, *Serbia, Yug.* 40 C6
Svyetlahorsk, *Belarus* 47 F5
Swabian Alps = Schwäbische
  Alb, *Germany* 25 G5
Swainsboro, *U.S.A.* 109 J4
Swakop →, *Namibia* 88 C2
Swakopmund, *Namibia* ... 88 C1
Swale →, *U.K.* 12 C6
Swan →, *Australia* 93 F2
Swan →, *Canada* 105 C8
Swan Hill, *Australia* 95 F3
Swan Hills, *Canada* 104 C5
Swan Is., *W. Indies* 120 C3
Swan L., *Canada* 105 C8
Swan Peak, *U.S.A.* 114 C7

Swan Ra., *U.S.A.* 114 C7
Swan Reach, *Australia* ... 95 E2
Swan River, *Canada* 105 C8
Swanage, *U.K.* 13 G6
Swansea, *Australia* 94 G4
Swansea, *Canada* 110 C5
Swansea, *U.K.* 13 F4
Swansea □, *U.K.* 13 F3
Swar →, *Pakistan* 69 B5
Swartberge, *S. Africa* 88 E3
Swartmodder, *S. Africa* ... 88 D3
Swartnossob →, *Namibia* . 88 C2
Swartruggens, *S. Africa* .. 88 D4
Swarzędz, *Poland* 45 F4
Swastika, *Canada* 102 C3
Swatow = Shantou, *China* . 59 F11
Swaziland ■, *Africa* 89 D5
Sweden ■, *Europe* 9 G16
Swedru, *Ghana* 83 D4
Sweet Home, *U.S.A.* 114 D2
Sweetgrass, *U.S.A.* 114 B8
Sweetwater, *Nev., U.S.A.* . 116 G7
Sweetwater, *Tenn., U.S.A.* 109 H3
Sweetwater, *Tex., U.S.A.* . 113 J4
Sweetwater →, *U.S.A.* ... 114 E10
Swellendam, *S. Africa* 88 E3
Swider →, *Poland* 45 F8
Świdnica, *Poland* 45 H3
Świdnik, *Poland* 45 G9
Świdwin, *Poland* 44 E2
Świebodzice, *Poland* 45 H3
Świebodzin, *Poland* 45 F2
Świecie, *Poland* 44 E5
Świerzawa, *Poland* 45 G2
Świętokrzyski □, *Poland* .. 45 H7
Świętokrzyskie, Góry,
  Poland 45 H7
Swift Current, *Canada* ... 105 C7
Swiftcurrent →, *Canada* .. 105 C7
Swilly, L., *Ireland* 15 A4
Swindon, *U.K.* 13 F6
Swindon □, *U.K.* 13 F6
Swinemünde = Świnoujście,
  Poland 44 E1
Swinford, *Ireland* 15 C3
Świnoujście, *Poland* 44 E1
Switzerland ■, *Europe* ... 25 J4
Swords, *Ireland* 15 C5
Swoyerville, *U.S.A.* 111 E9
Syasstroy, *Russia* 46 B7
Sychevka, *Russia* 46 E8
Syców, *Poland* 45 G4
Sydenham →, *Canada* ... 110 D2
Sydney, *Australia* 95 E5
Sydney, *Canada* 103 C7
Sydney L., *Canada* 105 C10
Sydney Mines, *Canada* ... 103 C7
Sydprøven = Alluitsup Paa,
  Greenland 4 C5
Sydra, G. of = Surt, Khalīj,
  Libya 79 B9
Syeverodonetsk, *Ukraine* .. 47 H10
Syke, *Germany* 24 C4
Sykesville, *U.S.A.* 110 E6
Syktyvkar, *Russia* 50 C6
Sylacauga, *U.S.A.* 109 J2
Sylarna, *Sweden* 8 E15
Sylhet, *Bangla.* 67 G17
Sylt, *Germany* 24 A4
Sylvan Beach, *U.S.A.* 111 C9
Sylvan Lake, *Canada* 104 C6
Sylvania, *U.S.A.* 109 J5
Sylvester, *U.S.A.* 109 K4
Sym, *Russia* 50 C9
Synelnykove, *Ukraine* 47 H8
Synnott Ra., *Australia* ... 92 C4
Syracuse, *Kans., U.S.A.* .. 113 G4
Syracuse, *N.Y., U.S.A.* ... 111 C8
Syracuse, *Nebr., U.S.A.* .. 112 E6
Syrdarya →, *Kazakhstan* .. 50 E7
Syria ■, *Asia* 70 C3
Syrian Desert = Shām,
  Bādiyat ash, *Asia* 70 C3
Syssleback, *Sweden* 10 D6
Syzran, *Russia* 48 D9
Szabolcs-Szatmár-Bereg □,
  Hungary 42 B6
Szadek, *Poland* 45 G5
Szamocin, *Poland* 45 E4
Szamos →, *Hungary* 42 B7
Szamotuły, *Poland* 45 F3
Száraz →, *Hungary* 42 D6
Szarvas, *Hungary* 42 D5
Százhalombatta, *Hungary* . 42 C3
Szczawnica, *Poland* 45 J7
Szczebrzeszyn, *Poland* ... 45 H9
Szczecin, *Poland* 44 E1
Szczecinek, *Poland* 44 E3
Szczeciński, Zalew =
  Stettiner Haff, *Germany* . 24 B10
Szczekociny, *Poland* 45 H6
Szczucin, *Poland* 45 H8
Szczuczyn, *Poland* 44 E9
Szczyrk, *Poland* 45 J6
Szczytna, *Poland* 45 H3
Szczytno, *Poland* 44 E7
Szechwan = Sichuan □,
  China 58 B5
Szécsény, *Hungary* 42 B4
Szeged, *Hungary* 42 D5
Szeghalom, *Hungary* 42 C6
Székesfehérvár, *Hungary* .. 42 C3
Szekszárd, *Hungary* 42 D3
Szendro, *Hungary* 42 B5
Szentendre, *Hungary* 42 C4
Szentes, *Hungary* 42 D5
Szentgotthárd, *Hungary* .. 42 D1
Szentlőrinc, *Hungary* 42 D3
Szerencs, *Hungary* 42 B6
Szigetszentmiklós, *Hungary* 42 C4

Szigetvár, *Hungary* 42 D2
Szikszó, *Hungary* 42 B5
Szklarska Poreba, *Poland* .. 45 H2
Szkwa →, *Poland* 45 E8
Szlichtyngowa, *Poland* ... 45 G3
Szob, *Hungary* 42 C3
Szolnok, *Hungary* 42 C5
Szombathely, *Hungary* ... 42 C1
Szprotawa, *Poland* 45 G2
Sztum, *Poland* 44 E6
Sztutowo, *Poland* 44 D6
Szubin, *Poland* 45 E4
Szydłowiec, *Poland* 45 G7
Szypliszki, *Poland* 44 D10

T

Ta Khli Khok, *Thailand* ... 64 E3
Ta Lai, *Vietnam* 65 G6
Tab, *Hungary* 42 D3
Tabacal, *Argentina* 126 A3
Tabaco, *Phil.* 61 E5
Tabagné, *Ivory C.* 82 D4
Ṭābah, *Si. Arabia* 70 E4
Tabankort, *Niger* 83 B5
Ṭabas, *Khorāsān, Iran* ... 71 C9
Ṭabas, *Khorāsān, Iran* ... 71 C8
Tabasará, Serranía de,
  Panama 120 E3
Tabasco □, *Mexico* 119 D6
Tabāsīn, *Iran* 71 D8
Tabatinga, Serra da, *Brazil* 125 F10
Taber, *Canada* 104 D6
Taberg, *Sweden* 11 G8
Taberg, *U.S.A.* 111 C9
Tabla, *Niger* 83 C5
Tablas I., *Phil.* 61 E5
Tablas Strait, *Phil.* 61 E4
Table B. = Tafelbaai,
  S. Africa 88 E2
Table B., *Canada* 103 B8
Table Mt., *S. Africa* 88 E2
Table Rock L., *U.S.A.* 113 G8
Tabletop, Mt., *Australia* .. 94 C4
Tábor, *Czech Rep.* 26 B7
Tabora, *Tanzania* 86 D3
Tabora □, *Tanzania* 86 D3
Tabou, *Ivory C.* 82 E3
Tabrīz, *Iran* 70 B5
Tabuaeran, *Pac. Oc.* 97 G12
Tabuenca, *Spain* 32 D3
Tabūk, *Si. Arabia* 70 D3
Täby, *Sweden* 10 E12
Tacámbaro de Codallos,
  Mexico 118 D4
Tacheng, *China* 60 B3
Tach'i, *Taiwan* 59 E13
Tachia, *Taiwan* 59 E13
Tach'ing Shan = Daqing
  Shan, *China* 56 D6
Tachov, *Czech Rep.* 26 B5
Tácina →, *Italy* 31 D9
Tacloban, *Phil.* 61 F6
Tacna, *Peru* 124 G4
Tacoma, *U.S.A.* 116 C4
Tacuarembó, *Uruguay* 127 C4
Tademaït, Plateau du,
  Algeria 78 C6
Tadio, L., *Ivory C.* 82 D3
Tadjoura, *Djibouti* 81 E5
Tadjoura, Golfe de, *Djibouti* 81 E5
Tadmor, *N.Z.* 91 J4
Tadoule, L., *Canada* 105 B9
Tadoussac, *Canada* 103 C6
Tadzhikistan = Tajikistan ■,
  Asia 50 F8
Taechŏn-ni, *S. Korea* 57 F14
Taegu, *S. Korea* 57 G15
Taegwan, *N. Korea* 57 D13
Taejŏn, *S. Korea* 57 F14
Tafalla, *Spain* 32 C3
Tafar, *Sudan* 81 F2
Tafelbaai, *S. Africa* 88 E2
Tafermaar, *Indonesia* 63 F8
Tafí Viejo, *Argentina* 126 B2
Tafīhān, *Iran* 71 D7
Tafiré, *Ivory C.* 82 D3
Tafo, *Ghana* 83 D4
Tafresh, *Iran* 71 C6
Taft, *Iran* 71 D7
Taft, *Phil.* 61 F6
Taft, *U.S.A.* 117 K7
Taftān, Kūh-e, *Iran* 71 D9
Taga Dzong, *Bhutan* 67 F16
Taganrog, *Russia* 47 J10
Taganrogskiy Zaliv, *Russia* 47 J10
Tagajō, *Japan* 54 E10
Tagatay, *Phil.* 61 D4
Tagbilaran, *Phil.* 61 G5
Tàggia, *Italy* 28 E4
Tagish, *Canada* 104 A2
Tagish L., *Canada* 104 A2
Tagliacozzo, *Italy* 29 F10
Tagliamento →, *Italy* 29 C10
Táglio di Po, *Italy* 29 D9
Tago, *Phil.* 61 G7
Tagomago, *Spain* 37 B8
Tagourâret, *Mauritania* .. 82 B3
Taguatinga, *Brazil* 125 F10
Tagudin, *Phil.* 61 C4
Tagum, *Phil.* 61 H6
Tagus = Tejo →, *Europe* . 35 G2
Tahakopa, *N.Z.* 91 M2
Tahan, Gunong, *Malaysia* . 65 K4
Tahat, *Algeria* 78 D7
Tāherī, *Iran* 71 E7
Tahiti, *Pac. Oc.* 97 J13
Tahlequah, *U.S.A.* 113 H7

211

Tahoe, L., U.S.A. 116 G6
Tahoe City, U.S.A. 116 F6
Tahoka, U.S.A. 113 J4
Taholah, U.S.A. 116 C2
Tahoua, Niger 83 C6
Tahrūd, Iran 71 D8
Tahsis, Canada 104 D3
Tahta, Egypt 80 B3
Tahtaköprü, Turkey 41 G13
Tahtalı Dağları, Turkey 72 C7
Tahulandang, Indonesia 63 D7
Tahuna, Indonesia 63 D7
Taï, Ivory C. 82 D3
Tai Hu, China 59 B12
Tai Shan, China 57 F9
Tai'an, China 57 F9
Taibei = T'aipei, Taiwan 59 E13
Taibique, Canary Is. 37 G2
Taibus Qi, China 56 D8
Taicang, China 59 B13
Taichung, Taiwan 59 E13
Taieri →, N.Z. 91 M3
Taigu, China 56 F7
Taihang Shan, China 56 G7
Taihape, N.Z. 91 H5
Taihe, Anhui, China 56 H8
Taihe, Jiangxi, China 59 D10
Taihu, China 59 B11
Taijiang, China 58 D7
Taikang, China 56 G8
Tailem Bend, Australia 95 F2
Tailfingen, Germany 25 G5
Tailuko, Taiwan 59 E13
Taimyr Peninsula = Taymyr, Poluostrov, Russia 51 B11
Tain, U.K. 14 D4
T'ainan, Taiwan 59 F13
Taínaron, Ákra, Greece 38 E4
Taining, China 59 D11
T'aipei, Taiwan 59 E13
Taiping, China 59 B12
Taiping, Malaysia 65 K3
Taipingzhen, China 56 H8
Tairbeart = Tarbert, U.K. 14 D2
Taishan, China 59 F9
Taishun, China 59 D12
Taita Hills, Kenya 86 C4
Taitao, Pen. de, Chile 122 H3
T'aitung, Taiwan 59 F13
Taivalkoski, Finland 8 D23
Taiwan ■, Asia 59 F13
Taiwan Strait, Asia 59 E12
Taixing, China 59 A13
Taiyara, Sudan 81 E3
Taïyetos Óros, Greece 38 D4
Taiyiba, Israel 75 C4
Taiyuan, China 56 F7
Taizhong = T'aichung, Taiwan 59 E13
Taizhou, China 59 A12
Taizhou Liedao, China 59 C13
Ta'izz, Yemen 74 E3
Tājābād, Iran 71 D7
Tajikistan ■, Asia 50 F8
Tajima, Japan 55 F9
Tajo = Tejo →, Europe 35 F2
Tajrīsh, Iran 71 C6
Tak, Thailand 64 D2
Takāb, Iran 70 B5
Takachiho, Japan 55 H5
Takachu, Botswana 88 C3
Takada, Japan 55 F9
Takahagi, Japan 55 F10
Takaka, N.Z. 91 J4
Takamatsu, Japan 55 G7
Takaoka, Japan 55 F8
Takapuna, N.Z. 91 G5
Takasaki, Japan 55 F9
Takatsuki, Japan 55 G7
Takaungu, Kenya 86 C4
Takayama, Japan 55 F8
Take-Shima, Japan 55 J5
Takefu, Japan 55 G8
Takengon, Indonesia 62 D1
Takeo, Japan 55 H5
Tākern, Sweden 11 F8
Tākestān, Iran 71 C6
Taketa, Japan 55 H5
Takev, Cambodia 65 G5
Takh, India 69 C7
Takht-Sulaiman, Pakistan 68 D3
Takikawa, Japan 54 C10
Takla L., Canada 104 B3
Takla Landing, Canada 104 B3
Takla Makan = Taklamakan Shamo, China 52 F12
Taklamakan Shamo, China 52 F12
Taku →, Canada 104 B2
Takum, Nigeria 83 D6
Tal Halāl, Iran 71 D7
Tala, Uruguay 127 C4
Talachyn, Belarus 46 E5
Talagang, Pakistan 68 C5
Talagante, Chile 126 C1
Talak, Niger 83 B6
Talamanca, Cordillera de, Cent. Amer. 120 E3
Talant, France 19 E11
Talara, Peru 124 D2
Talas, Kyrgyzstan 50 E8
Talas, Turkey 72 C6
Talâta, Egypt 75 E1
Talata Mafara, Nigeria 83 C6
Talaud, Kepulauan, Indonesia 63 D7
Talaud Is. = Talaud, Kepulauan, Indonesia 63 D7
Talavera de la Reina, Spain 34 F6
Talavera la Real, Spain 35 G4
Talayan, Phil. 61 J5

Talayuela, Spain 34 F5
Talbandh, India 69 H12
Talbert, Sillon de, France 18 D3
Talbot, C., Australia 92 B4
Talbragar →, Australia 95 E4
Talca, Chile 126 D1
Talcahuano, Chile 126 D1
Talcher, India 67 J14
Talcho, Niger 83 C5
Taldy Kurgan = Taldyqorghan, Kazakhstan 50 E8
Taldyqorghan, Kazakhstan 50 E8
Tālesh, Iran 71 B6
Tālesh, Kūhhā-ye, Iran 71 B6
Talguharai, Sudan 80 D4
Tali Post, Sudan 81 F3
Taliabu, Indonesia 63 E6
Talibon, Phil. 63 B6
Talibong, Ko, Thailand 65 J2
Talihina, U.S.A. 113 H7
Talisayan, Phil. 61 G6
Taliwang, Indonesia 62 F5
Tall 'Afar, Iraq 70 B4
Tall Kalakh, Syria 75 A5
Talla, Egypt 80 B3
Talladega, U.S.A. 109 J2
Tallahassee, U.S.A. 109 K3
Tallangatta, Australia 95 F4
Tallard, France 21 D10
Tällberg, Sweden 10 D9
Tallering Pk., Australia 93 E2
Talli, Pakistan 68 E3
Tallinn, Estonia 9 G21
Tallmadge, U.S.A. 110 E3
Tallulah, U.S.A. 113 J9
Tălmaciu, Romania 43 E9
Talmont-St-Hilaire, France 20 B2
Talne, Ukraine 47 H6
Talnoye = Talne, Ukraine 47 H6
Talodi, Sudan 81 E3
Talovaya, Russia 48 E5
Taloyoak, Canada 100 B10
Talpa de Allende, Mexico 118 C4
Talsi, Latvia 9 H20
Talsi □, Latvia 44 A9
Taltal, Chile 126 B1
Taltson →, Canada 104 A6
Talwood, Australia 95 D4
Talyawalka →, Australia 95 E3
Tam Chau, Vietnam 65 G5
Tam Ky, Vietnam 64 E7
Tam Quan, Vietnam 64 E7
Tama, U.S.A. 112 E8
Tamale, Ghana 83 D4
Taman, Russia 47 K9
Tamani, Mali 82 C3
Tamano, Japan 55 G6
Tamanrasset, Algeria 78 D7
Tamaqua, U.S.A. 111 F9
Tamar →, U.K. 13 G3
Tamarinda, Spain 37 B10
Tamarite de Litera, Spain 32 D5
Tamashima, Japan 55 G6
Tamási, Hungary 42 D3
Tamaulipas □, Mexico 119 C5
Tamaulipas, Sierra de, Mexico 119 C5
Tamazula, Mexico 118 C3
Tamazunchale, Mexico 119 C5
Tamba-Dabatou, Guinea 82 C2
Tambacounda, Senegal 82 C2
Tambelan, Kepulauan, Indonesia 62 D3
Tambellup, Australia 93 F2
Tambo, Australia 94 C4
Tambo de Mora, Peru 124 F3
Tambohorano, Madag. 89 B7
Tambora, Indonesia 62 F5
Tambov, Russia 48 D5
Tambre →, Spain 34 C2
Tambuku, Indonesia 63 G15
Tamburâ, Sudan 81 F2
Tâmchekket, Mauritania 82 B2
Tâmega →, Portugal 34 D2
Tamenglong, India 67 G18
Tamgué, Massif du, Guinea 82 C2
Tamiahua, L. de, Mexico 119 C5
Tamil Nadu □, India 66 P10
Tamis →, Serbia, Yug. 42 F5
Tamluk, India 69 H12
Tammerfors = Tampere, Finland 9 F20
Tammisaari, Finland 9 F20
Tämnaren, Sweden 10 D11
Tamo Abu, Pegunungan, Malaysia 62 D5
Tampa, U.S.A. 109 M4
Tampa B., U.S.A. 109 M4
Tampere, Finland 9 F20
Tampico, Mexico 119 C5
Tampin, Malaysia 65 L4
Tamsweg, Austria 26 D7
Tamu, Burma 67 G19
Tamuja →, Spain 35 F4
Tamworth, Australia 95 E5
Tamworth, Canada 110 B8
Tamworth, U.K. 13 E6
Tamyang, S. Korea 57 G14
Tan An, Vietnam 65 G6
Tan-Tan, Morocco 78 C3
Tana →, Kenya 86 C5
Tana →, Norway 8 A23
Tana, L., Ethiopia 81 E4
Tana River, Kenya 86 C4
Tanabe, Japan 55 H7
Tanafjorden, Norway 8 A23
Tanaga, Pta., Canary Is. 37 G1
Tanahbala, Indonesia 62 E1
Tanahgrogot, Indonesia 62 E5
Tanahjampea, Indonesia 63 F6

Tanahmasa, Indonesia 62 E1
Tanahmerah, Indonesia 63 F10
Tanakpur, India 69 E9
Tanakura, Japan 55 F10
Tanami, Australia 92 C4
Tanami Desert, Australia 92 C5
Tanana, U.S.A. 100 B4
Tanana →, U.S.A. 100 B4
Tananarive = Antananarivo, Madag. 89 B8
Tánaro →, Italy 28 D5
Tancheng, China 57 G10
Tanch'ŏn, N. Korea 57 D15
Tanda, Ut. P., India 69 F10
Tanda, Ut. P., India 69 E8
Tanda, Ivory C. 82 D4
Tandag, Phil. 61 G7
Tandaia, Tanzania 87 D3
Tăndărei, Romania 43 F12
Tandaué, Angola 88 B2
Tandil, Argentina 126 D4
Tandil, Sa. del, Argentina 126 D4
Tandlianwala, Pakistan 68 D5
Tando Adam, Pakistan 68 G3
Tando Allahyar, Pakistan 68 G3
Tando Bago, Pakistan 68 G3
Tando Mohommed Khan, Pakistan 68 G3
Tandou L., Australia 95 E3
Tandragee, U.K. 15 B5
Tandsjöborg, Sweden 10 C8
Tane-ga-Shima, Japan 55 J5
Taneatua, N.Z. 91 H6
Tanen Tong Dan, Burma 64 D2
Tanew →, Poland 45 H9
Tanezrouft, Algeria 78 D6
Tang, Koh, Cambodia 65 G4
Tang, Ra's-e, Iran 71 E8
Tang Krasang, Cambodia 64 F5
Tanga, Tanzania 86 D4
Tanga □, Tanzania 86 D4
Tanganyika, L., Africa 86 D3
Tangaza, Nigeria 83 C5
Tanger = Tangier, Morocco 78 A4
Tangerang, Indonesia 63 G12
Tangerhütte, Germany 24 C7
Tangermünde, Germany 24 C7
Tanggu, China 57 E9
Tanggula Shan, China 60 C4
Tanghe, China 56 H7
Tangier, Morocco 78 A4
Tangorin, Australia 94 C3
Tangorombohitr'i Makay, Madag. 89 C8
Tangshan, China 57 E10
Tangtou, China 57 G10
Tanguiéta, Benin 83 C5
Tangxi, China 59 C12
Tangyan He →, China 58 C7
Tanimbar, Kepulauan, Indonesia 63 F8
Tanimbar Is. = Tanimbar, Kepulauan, Indonesia 63 F8
Taninthari = Tenasserim □, Burma 64 F2
Tanjay, Phil. 61 G5
Tanjong Malim, Malaysia 65 L3
Tanjore = Thanjavur, India 66 P11
Tanjung, Indonesia 62 E5
Tanjungbalai, Indonesia 62 D1
Tanjungbatu, Indonesia 62 D5
Tanjungkarang Telukbetung, Indonesia 62 F3
Tanjungpandan, Indonesia 62 E3
Tanjungpinang, Indonesia 62 D2
Tanjungredeb, Indonesia 62 D5
Tanjungselor, Indonesia 62 D5
Tank, Pakistan 68 C4
Tankhala, India 68 J5
Tännäs, Sweden 10 B6
Tannersville, U.S.A. 111 E9
Tannis Bugt, Denmark 11 G4
Tannu-Ola, Russia 51 D10
Tannum Sands, Australia 94 C5
Tano →, Ghana 82 D4
Tanon Str., Phil. 61 F5
Tanout, Niger 83 C6
Tanshui, Taiwan 59 E13
Tansilla, Burkina Faso 82 C4
Tanta, Egypt 80 H7
Tantoyuca, Mexico 119 C5
Tantung = Dandong, China 57 D13
Tanumshede, Sweden 11 F5
Tanunda, Australia 95 E2
Tanus, France 20 D6
Tanzania ■, Africa 86 D3
Tanzilla →, Canada 104 B2
Tao, Ko, Thailand 65 G2
Tao'an = Taonan, China 57 B12
Tao'er He →, China 57 B13
Taohua Dao, China 59 C14
Taolanaro, Madag. 89 D8
Taole, China 56 E4
Taonan, China 57 B12
Taormina, Italy 31 E8
Taos, U.S.A. 115 H11
Taoudenni, Mali 78 D5
Taoyuan, China 59 C8
T'aoyüan, Taiwan 59 E13
Tapa, Estonia 9 G21
Tapa Shan = Daba Shan, China 58 B7
Tapachula, Mexico 119 E6
Tapah, Malaysia 65 K3
Tapajós →, Brazil 122 D5
Tapaktuan, Indonesia 62 D1
Tapanahoni →, Surinam 125 C8
Tapanui, N.Z. 91 L2
Tapauá →, Brazil 124 E6
Tapes, Brazil 127 C5
Tapeta, Liberia 82 D3
Taphan Hin, Thailand 64 D3

Tapia de Casariego, Spain 34 B4
Tapirapecó, Serra, Venezuela 124 C6
Tapolca, Hungary 42 D2
Tapuaenuku, Mt., N.Z. 91 K4
Tapul Group, Phil. 61 J4
Tapurucuará, Brazil 124 D5
Taquara, Brazil 127 B5
Taquari →, Brazil 124 G7
Tara, Australia 95 D5
Tara, Canada 110 B3
Tara, Russia 50 D8
Tara, Zambia 87 F2
Tara →, Montenegro, Yug. 40 C2
Taraba □, Nigeria 83 D7
Taraba →, Nigeria 83 D7
Tarabagatay, Khrebet, Kazakhstan 50 E9
Tarābulus, Lebanon 75 A4
Tarābulus, Libya 79 B8
Taradehi, India 69 H8
Tarajalejo, Canary Is. 37 F5
Tarakan, Indonesia 62 D5
Tarakit, Mt., Kenya 86 B4
Tarama-Jima, Japan 55 M2
Taran, Mys, Russia 9 J18
Taranagar, India 68 E6
Taranaki □, N.Z. 91 H5
Tarancón, Spain 32 E1
Taranga Hill, India 68 H5
Tarankol, U.K. 14 D1
Táranto, Italy 31 B10
Táranto, G. di, Italy 31 B10
Tarapacá, Colombia 124 D5
Tarapacá □, Chile 126 A2
Tarapoto, Peru 124 E3
Tarare, France 21 C8
Tararua Ra., N.Z. 91 J5
Tarascon, France 21 E8
Tarascon-sur-Ariège, France 20 F5
Tarashcha, Ukraine 47 H6
Tarauacá, Brazil 124 E4
Tarauacá →, Brazil 124 E5
Taravo →, France 21 G12
Tarawa, Kiribati 96 G9
Tarawera, N.Z. 91 H6
Tarawera L., N.Z. 91 H6
Tarazona, Spain 32 D3
Tarazona de la Mancha, Spain 33 F3
Tarbat Ness, U.K. 14 D5
Tarbela Dam, Pakistan 68 B5
Tarbert, Arg. & Bute, U.K. 14 F3
Tarbert, W. Isles, U.K. 14 D2
Tarbes, France 20 E4
Tarboro, U.S.A. 109 H7
Tărcău, Munţii, Romania 43 D11
Tarcento, Italy 29 B10
Tarcoola, Australia 95 E1
Tarcoon, Australia 95 E4
Tardets-Sorholus, France 20 E3
Tardoire →, France 20 C4
Taree, Australia 95 E5
Tarfa, W. el →, Egypt 80 B3
Tarfarya, Morocco 78 C3
Tărgoviște, Romania 43 F10
Târgu Bujor, Romania 43 E12
Târgu Cărbuneşti, Romania 43 F8
Târgu Frumos, Romania 43 C12
Târgu-Jiu, Romania 43 E8
Târgu Lăpuş, Romania 43 C8
Târgu Mureş, Romania 43 D9
Târgu Neamţ, Romania 43 C11
Târgu Ocna, Romania 43 D11
Târgu Secuiesc, Romania 43 E11
Târguşor, Romania 43 F13
Tărhăus, Vf., Romania 43 D11
Ţarīf, U.A.E. 71 E7
Tarifa, Spain 35 J5
Tarija, Bolivia 126 A3
Tarija □, Bolivia 126 A3
Tariku →, Indonesia 63 E9
Tarim Basin = Tarim Pendi, China 60 C3
Tarim He →, China 60 C3
Tarim Pendi, China 60 C3
Taritatu →, Indonesia 63 E9
Tarka →, S. Africa 88 E4
Tarkastad, S. Africa 88 E4
Tarkhankut, Mys, Ukraine 47 K7
Tarko Sale, Russia 50 C8
Tarkwa, Ghana 82 D4
Tarlac, Phil. 61 D4
Tarm, Denmark 11 J2
Tarma, Peru 124 F3
Tarn □, France 20 E6
Tarn →, France 20 D5
Tarn-et-Garonne □, France 20 D5
Tårna, Hungary 42 C4
Târnava Mare →, Romania 43 D8
Târnava Mică →, Romania 43 D8
Târnăveni, Romania 43 D9
Tarnica, Poland 45 J9
Tarnobrzeg, Poland 45 H8
Tarnogród, Poland 45 H9
Tarnos, France 20 E2
Târnova, Moldova 43 B12
Târnova, Romania 42 E6
Tarnów, Poland 45 H8
Tarnowskie Góry, Poland 45 H5
Tärnsjö, Sweden 10 D10
Táro →, Italy 28 C7
Ţărom, Iran 71 D7
Taroom, Australia 95 D4
Taroudannt, Morocco 78 B4
Tarp, Germany 24 A5
Tarpon Springs, U.S.A. 109 L4
Tarquínia, Italy 29 F8
Tarragona, Spain 32 D6

Tarragona □, Spain 32 D6
Tarraleah, Australia 94 G4
Tarrasa = Terrassa, Spain 32 D7
Tàrrega, Spain 32 D6
Tarrytown, U.S.A. 111 E11
Tårs, Denmark 11 G4
Tarshiha = Me'ona, Israel 75 B4
Tarso Emissi, Chad 79 D9
Tarsus, Turkey 70 B2
Tartagal, Argentina 126 A3
Tärtär, Azerbaijan 49 K8
Tärtär →, Azerbaijan 49 K8
Tartas, France 20 E3
Tartu, Estonia 9 G22
Ţarţūs, Syria 70 C2
Tarumizu, Japan 55 J5
Tarussa, Russia 46 E9
Tarutao, Ko, Thailand 65 J2
Tarutung, Indonesia 62 D1
Tarvísio, Italy 29 B10
Taseko →, Canada 104 C4
Tash-Kömür, Kyrgyzstan 50 E8
Tash-Kumyr = Tash-Kömür, Kyrgyzstan 50 E8
Tashauz = Dashhowuz, Turkmenistan 50 E6
Tashi Chho Dzong = Thimphu, Bhutan 67 F16
Tashk, Daryācheh-ye, Iran 71 D7
Tashkent = Toshkent, Uzbekistan 50 E7
Tashtagol, Russia 50 D9
Tasiilaq, Greenland 4 C6
Tasikmalaya, Indonesia 63 G13
Tåsinge, Denmark 11 J4
Tåsjön, Sweden 8 D16
Taskan, Russia 51 C16
Tasker, Niger 83 C7
Taşköprü, Turkey 72 B6
Taşlâc, Moldova 43 C14
Tasman B., N.Z. 91 J4
Tasman Mts., N.Z. 91 J4
Tasman Pen., Australia 94 G4
Tasman Sea, Pac. Oc. 96 L8
Tasmania □, Australia 94 G4
Tăşnad, Romania 42 C7
Tassili n'Ajjer, Algeria 78 C7
Tassili Tin-Rerhoh, Algeria 83 A5
Tata, Hungary 42 C3
Tatabánya, Hungary 42 C3
Tatahouine, Tunisia 79 B8
Tatar Republic = Tatarstan □, Russia 48 C10
Tatarbunary, Ukraine 47 K5
Tatarsk, Russia 50 D8
Tatarstan □, Russia 48 C10
Tateyama, Japan 55 G9
Tathlina L., Canada 104 A5
Tathra, Australia 95 F4
Tati →, India 66 J8
Tatinnai L., Canada 105 A9
Tatla L., Canada 104 C4
Tatlısu, Turkey 41 F11
Tatnam, C., Canada 105 B10
Tatra = Tatry, Slovak Rep. 27 B13
Tatry, Slovak Rep. 27 B13
Tatshenshini →, Canada 104 B1
Tatsuno, Japan 55 G7
Tatta, Pakistan 68 G2
Tatuí, Brazil 127 A6
Tatum, U.S.A. 113 J3
Tat'ung = Datong, China 56 D7
Tatvan, Turkey 70 B4
Taubaté, Brazil 127 A6
Tauberbischofsheim, Germany 25 F5
Taucha, Germany 24 D8
Tauern-tunnel, Austria 26 E6
Taufikia, Sudan 81 F3
Taulé, France 18 D3
Taumarunui, N.Z. 91 H5
Taumaturgo, Brazil 124 E4
Taung, S. Africa 88 D3
Taungdwingyi, Burma 67 J19
Taunggyi, Burma 67 J20
Taungup, Burma 67 K19
Taungup Pass, Burma 67 K19
Taungup Taunggya, Burma 67 K18
Taunsa, Pakistan 68 D4
Taunsa Barrage, Pakistan 68 D4
Taunton, U.K. 13 F4
Taunton, U.S.A. 111 E13
Taunus, Germany 25 E4
Taupo, N.Z. 91 H6
Taupo, L., N.Z. 91 H5
Tauragé, Lithuania 9 J20
Tauragé □, Lithuania 44 C9
Tauranga, N.Z. 91 G6
Tauranga Harb., N.Z. 91 G6
Taureau, Rés., Canada 102 C5
Taurianova, Italy 31 D9
Taurus Mts. = Toros Dağları, Turkey 70 B2
Tauste, Spain 32 D3
Tauz = Tovuz, Azerbaijan 49 K7
Tavas, Turkey 39 D11
Tavda, Russia 50 D7
Tavda →, Russia 50 D7
Tavernes de la Valldigna, Spain 33 F4
Taveta, Tanzania 86 C4
Taveuni, Fiji 91 C9
Taviano, Italy 31 C11
Tavignano →, France 21 F13
Tavira, Portugal 35 H3
Tavistock, Canada 110 C4
Tavistock, U.K. 13 G3
Tavolara, Italy 30 B2
Távora →, Portugal 34 D3
Tavoy = Dawei, Burma 64 E2
Tavşanlı, Turkey 39 B11

Taw →, *U.K.* 13 F3
Tawa →, *India* 68 H8
Tawas City, *U.S.A.* 108 C4
Tawau, *Malaysia* 62 D5
Taweisha, *Sudan* 81 E2
Tawitawi, *Phil.* 63 B6
Tawu, *Taiwan* 59 F13
Taxco de Alarcón, *Mexico* 119 D5
Taxila, *Pakistan* 68 C5
Tay →, *U.K.* 14 E5
Tay, Firth of, *U.K.* 14 E5
Tay, L., *Australia* 93 F3
Tay, L., *U.K.* 14 E4
Tay Ninh, *Vietnam* 65 G6
Tayabamba, *Peru* 124 E3
Tayabas Bay, *Phil.* 61 E4
Taylakova, *Russia* 50 D8
Taylakovy = Taylakova, *Russia* 50 D8
Taylor, *Canada* 104 B4
Taylor, *Nebr., U.S.A.* 112 E5
Taylor, *Pa., U.S.A.* 111 E9
Taylor, *Tex., U.S.A.* 113 K6
Taylor, Mt., *U.S.A.* 115 J10
Taylorville, *U.S.A.* 112 F10
Taymā, *Si. Arabia* 70 E3
Taymyr, Oz., *Russia* 51 B11
Taymyr, Poluostrov, *Russia* 51 B11
Tayport, *U.K.* 14 E6
Tayshet, *Russia* 51 D10
Taz →, *Russia* 50 C8
Taza, *Morocco* 78 B5
Tāzah Khurmātū, *Iraq* 70 C5
Tazawa-Ko, *Japan* 54 E10
Tazin →, *Canada* 105 B7
Tazin L., *Canada* 105 B7
Tazovskiy, *Russia* 50 C8
Tbilisi, *Georgia* 49 K7
Tchad = Chad ■, *Africa* 79 E9
Tchad, L., *Chad* 79 F8
Tchaourou, *Benin* 83 D5
Tch'eng-tou = Chengdu, *China* 58 B5
Tchentlo L., *Canada* 104 B4
Tchetti, *Benin* 83 D5
Tchibanga, *Gabon* 84 E2
Tchien, *Liberia* 82 D3
Tchin Tabaraden, *Niger* 83 B6
Tch'ong-k'ing = Chongqing, *China* 58 C6
Tczew, *Poland* 44 D5
Te Anau, L., *N.Z.* 91 L1
Te Aroha, *N.Z.* 91 G5
Te Awamutu, *N.Z.* 91 H5
Te Kuiti, *N.Z.* 91 H5
Te-n-Dghâmcha, Sebkhet, *Mauritania* 82 B1
Te Puke, *N.Z.* 91 G6
Te Waewae B., *N.Z.* 91 M1
Teaca, *Romania* 43 D9
Teague, *U.S.A.* 113 K6
Teano, *Italy* 31 A7
Teapa, *Mexico* 119 D6
Teba, *Spain* 35 J6
Tebakang, *Malaysia* 62 D4
Teberda, *Russia* 49 J5
Tébessa, *Algeria* 78 A7
Tebicuary →, *Paraguay* 126 B4
Tebingtinggi, *Indonesia* 62 D1
Tebintingil, *Indonesia* 62 E2
Tebulos, *Georgia* 49 J7
Tecate, *Mexico* 117 N10
Tecer Dağları, *Turkey* 72 C7
Tech →, *France* 20 F7
Techiman, *Ghana* 82 D4
Techirghiol, *Romania* 43 F13
Tecka, *Argentina* 128 E2
Tecomán, *Mexico* 118 D4
Tecopa, *U.S.A.* 117 K10
Tecoripa, *Mexico* 118 B3
Tecuala, *Mexico* 118 C3
Tecuci, *Romania* 43 E12
Tecumseh, *Canada* 110 D2
Tecumseh, *Mich., U.S.A.* 108 D4
Tecumseh, *Okla., U.S.A.* 113 H6
Tedzhen = Tejen, *Turkmenistan* 50 F7
Tees →, *U.K.* 12 C6
Tees B., *U.K.* 12 C6
Teeswater, *Canada* 110 C3
Tefé, *Brazil* 124 D6
Tefenni, *Turkey* 39 D11
Tegal, *Indonesia* 63 G13
Tegernsee, *Germany* 25 H7
Teggiano, *Italy* 31 B8
Tegid, L. = Bala, L., *U.K.* 12 E4
Tegina, *Nigeria* 83 C6
Tegucigalpa, *Honduras* 120 D2
Teguidda i-n-Tessoum, *Niger* 83 B6
Tehachapi, *U.S.A.* 117 K8
Tehachapi Mts., *U.S.A.* 117 L8
Tehamiyam, *Sudan* 80 D4
Tehilla, *Sudan* 80 D4
Téhini, *Ivory C.* 82 D4
Tehoru, *Indonesia* 63 E7
Tehrān, *Iran* 71 C6
Tehri, *India* 69 D8
Tehuacán, *Mexico* 119 D5
Tehuantepec, *Mexico* 119 D5
Tehuantepec, G. de, *Mexico* 119 D5
Tehuantepec, Istmo de, *Mexico* 119 D6
Teide, *Canary Is.* 37 F3
Teifi →, *U.K.* 13 E3
Teign →, *U.K.* 13 G4
Teignmouth, *U.K.* 13 G4
Teiuș, *Romania* 43 D8
Teixeira Pinto, *Guinea-Biss.* 82 C1
Tejam, *India* 69 E9
Tejen, *Turkmenistan* 50 F7

Tejen →, *Turkmenistan* 71 B9
Tejo →, *Europe* 35 F2
Tejon Pass, *U.S.A.* 117 L8
Tekamah, *U.S.A.* 112 E6
Tekapo, L., *N.Z.* 91 K3
Tekax, *Mexico* 119 C7
Teke, *Turkey* 41 E13
Tekeli, *Kazakstan* 50 E8
Tekeze →, *Ethiopia* 81 E4
Tekija, *Serbia, Yug.* 40 B6
Tekirdağ, *Turkey* 41 F11
Tekirdağ □, *Turkey* 41 E11
Tekirova, *Turkey* 39 E12
Tekkali, *India* 67 K14
Tekke, *Turkey* 72 B7
Tekman, *Turkey* 73 C9
Tekoa, *U.S.A.* 114 C5
Tel Aviv-Yafo, *Israel* 75 C3
Tel Lakhish, *Israel* 75 D3
Tel Megiddo, *Israel* 75 C4
Tela, *Honduras* 120 C2
Telanaipura = Jambi, *Indonesia* 62 E2
Telavi, *Georgia* 49 J7
Telč, *Czech Rep.* 26 B8
Telciu, *Romania* 43 C9
Telde, *Canary Is.* 37 G4
Telegraph Creek, *Canada* 104 B2
Telekhany = Tsyelyakhany, *Belarus* 47 F3
Telemark, *Norway* 9 G12
Telén, *Argentina* 126 D2
Teleneşti, *Moldova* 43 C13
Teleng, *Iran* 71 E9
Teleño, *Spain* 34 C4
Teleorman □, *Romania* 43 G10
Teleorman →, *Romania* 43 G10
Teles Pires →, *Brazil* 122 D5
Telescope Pk., *U.S.A.* 117 J9
Teletaye, *Mali* 83 B5
Telfer Mine, *Australia* 92 C3
Telford, *U.K.* 13 E5
Telford and Wrekin □, *U.K.* 12 E5
Telfs, *Austria* 26 D4
Télimélé, *Guinea* 82 C2
Teljo, J., *Sudan* 81 E2
Telkwa, *Canada* 104 C3
Tell City, *U.S.A.* 108 G2
Tellicherry, *India* 66 P9
Telluride, *U.S.A.* 115 H10
Teloloapán, *Mexico* 119 D5
Telpos Iz, *Russia* 6 C17
Telsen, *Argentina* 128 E3
Telšiai, *Lithuania* 9 H20
Telšiai □, *Lithuania* 44 C9
Teltow, *Germany* 24 C9
Teluk Anson = Teluk Intan, *Malaysia* 65 K3
Teluk Betung = Tanjungkarang Telukbetung, *Indonesia* 62 F3
Teluk Intan, *Malaysia* 65 K3
Telukbutun, *Indonesia* 65 K7
Telukdalem, *Indonesia* 62 D1
Tema, *Ghana* 83 D5
Temax, *Mexico* 119 C7
Temba, *S. Africa* 89 D4
Tembagapura, *Indonesia* 63 E9
Tembe, *Dem. Rep. of the Congo* 86 C2
Tembleque, *Spain* 34 F7
Temblor Range, *U.S.A.* 117 K7
Teme →, *U.K.* 13 E5
Temecula, *U.S.A.* 117 M9
Temerloh, *Malaysia* 62 D2
Teminabuan, *Indonesia* 63 E8
Temir, *Kazakstan* 50 E6
Temirtau, *Kazakstan* 50 D8
Temirtau, *Russia* 50 D9
Temiscamie →, *Canada* 103 B5
Témiscaming, *Canada* 102 C4
Témiscamingue, L., *Canada* 102 C4
Temnikov, *Russia* 48 C6
Temo →, *Italy* 30 B1
Temora, *Australia* 95 E4
Temosachic, *Mexico* 118 B3
Tempe, *U.S.A.* 115 K8
Témpio Pausánia, *Italy* 30 B2
Tempiute, *U.S.A.* 116 H11
Temple, *U.S.A.* 113 K6
Temple B., *Australia* 94 A3
Templemore, *Ireland* 15 D4
Templeton, *U.S.A.* 116 K6
Templeton →, *Australia* 94 C2
Templin, *Germany* 24 B9
Tempoal, *Mexico* 119 C5
Temryuk, *Russia* 47 K9
Temska →, *Serbia, Yug.* 40 C6
Temuco, *Chile* 128 D2
Temuka, *N.Z.* 91 L3
Tenabo, *Mexico* 119 C6
Tenaha, *U.S.A.* 113 K7
Tenakee Springs, *U.S.A.* 104 B1
Tenali, *India* 66 L12
Tenancingo, *Mexico* 119 D5
Tenango, *Mexico* 119 D5
Tenasserim, *Burma* 65 F2
Tenasserim □, *Burma* 64 F2
Tenby, *U.K.* 13 F3
Tenda, Colle di, *France* 21 D11
Tendaho, *Ethiopia* 81 E5
Tende, *France* 21 D11
Tendelti, *Sudan* 81 E3
Tendrovskaya Kosa, *Ukraine* 47 J6
Tendukhera, *India* 69 H8
Teneida, *Egypt* 80 B2
Tenenkou, *Mali* 82 C4
Ténéré, *Niger* 83 B7
Tenerife, *Canary Is.* 37 F3
Tenerife, Pico, *Canary Is.* 37 G1
Teng Xian, *Guangxi Zhuangzu, China* 59 F8
Teng Xian, *Shandong, China* 57 G9

Teng Xian, *Shandong, China* 57 G9
Tengah □, *Indonesia* 63 E6
Tengah, Kepulauan, *Indonesia* 62 F5
Tengchong, *China* 58 E2
Tengchowfu = Penglai, *China* 57 F11
Tenggara □, *Indonesia* 63 E6
Tenggarong, *Indonesia* 62 E5
Tenggol, Pulau, *Malaysia* 65 K4
Tengiz, Ozero, *Kazakstan* 50 D7
Tenhult, *Sweden* 11 G8
Tenino, *U.S.A.* 116 D4
Tenkasi, *India* 66 Q10
Tenke, *Katanga, Dem. Rep. of the Congo* 87 E2
Tenke, *Katanga, Dem. Rep. of the Congo* 87 E2
Tenkodogo, *Burkina Faso* 83 C4
Tenna →, *Italy* 29 E10
Tennant Creek, *Australia* 94 B1
Tennessee □, *U.S.A.* 109 H2
Tennessee →, *U.S.A.* 108 G1
Teno, Pta. de, *Canary Is.* 37 F3
Tenom, *Malaysia* 62 C5
Tenosique, *Mexico* 119 D6
Tenryū-Gawa →, *Japan* 55 G8
Tenterden, *U.K.* 13 F8
Tenterfield, *Australia* 95 D5
Teo, *Spain* 34 C2
Teófilo Otoni, *Brazil* 125 G10
Tepa, *Indonesia* 63 F7
Tepalcatepec →, *Mexico* 118 D4
Tepecik, *Bursa, Turkey* 41 F12
Tepecik, *Kütahya, Turkey* 39 B11
Tepehuanes, *Mexico* 118 B3
Tepelena, *Albania* 40 F4
Tepetongo, *Mexico* 118 C4
Tepic, *Mexico* 118 C4
Teplá, *Czech Rep.* 26 B5
Teplice, *Czech Rep.* 26 A6
Tepoca, C., *Mexico* 118 A2
Tequila, *Mexico* 118 C4
Ter →, *Spain* 32 C8
Ter Apel, *Neths.* 17 B7
Téra, *Niger* 83 C5
Tera →, *Spain* 34 D5
Teraina, *Kiribati* 97 G11
Terak, *Russia* 49 J8
Teramo, *Italy* 29 F10
Terang, *Australia* 95 F3
Terazit, Massif de, *Niger* 83 A6
Tercan, *Turkey* 73 C9
Tercero →, *Argentina* 126 C3
Terebovlya, *Ukraine* 47 H3
Teregova, *Romania* 42 E7
Tereida, *Sudan* 81 E3
Terek →, *Russia* 49 J8
Tereshka →, *Russia* 48 E8
Teresina, *Brazil* 125 E10
Terespol, *Poland* 45 F10
Terewah, L., *Australia* 95 D4
Terges →, *Portugal* 35 H3
Tergnier, *France* 19 C10
Teridgerie Cr. →, *Australia* 95 E4
Terlizzi, *Italy* 31 A9
Terme, *Turkey* 72 B7
Termez = Termiz, *Uzbekistan* 50 F7
Términi Imerese, *Italy* 30 E6
Términos, L. de, *Mexico* 119 D6
Termiz, *Uzbekistan* 50 F7
Térmoli, *Italy* 29 F12
Ternate, *Indonesia* 63 D7
Terneuzen, *Neths.* 17 C3
Terney, *Russia* 51 E14
Terni, *Italy* 29 F9
Ternitz, *Austria* 26 D9
Ternopil, *Ukraine* 47 H3
Ternopol = Ternopil, *Ukraine* 47 H3
Terowie, *Australia* 95 E2
Terpní, *Greece* 40 F7
Terra Bella, *U.S.A.* 117 K7
Terra Nova Nat. Park, *Canada* 103 C9
Terrace, *Canada* 104 C3
Terrace Bay, *Canada* 102 C2
Terracina, *Italy* 30 A6
Terralba, *Italy* 30 C1
Terranova = Ólbia, *Italy* 30 B2
Terrasini, *Italy* 30 D6
Terrassa, *Spain* 32 D7
Terrasson-la-Villedieu, *France* 20 C5
Terre Haute, *U.S.A.* 108 F2
Terrebonne B., *U.S.A.* 113 L9
Terrell, *U.S.A.* 113 J6
Terrenceville, *Canada* 103 C9
Terry, *U.S.A.* 112 B2
Terryville, *U.S.A.* 111 E11
Terschelling, *Neths.* 17 A5
Tersko-Kumskiy Kanal →, *Russia* 49 H7
Tertenia, *Italy* 30 C2
Terter = Tärtär →, *Azerbaijan* 49 K8
Teruel, *Spain* 32 E3
Teruel □, *Spain* 32 E4
Tervel, *Bulgaria* 41 C11
Tervola, *Finland* 8 C21
Teryaweyna L., *Australia* 95 E3
Teshio, *Japan* 54 B10
Teshio-Gawa →, *Japan* 54 B10
Tešica, *Serbia, Yug.* 40 C5
Tesiyn Gol →, *Mongolia* 60 A4
Teslić, *Bos.-H.* 42 F2
Teslin, *Canada* 104 A2

Teslin →, *Canada* 104 A2
Teslin L., *Canada* 104 A2
Tessalit, *Mali* 83 A5
Tessaoua, *Niger* 83 C6
Tessin, *Germany* 24 A8
Tessit, *Mali* 83 B5
Test →, *U.K.* 13 F6
Testa del Gargano, *Italy* 29 G13
Testigos, Is. Las, *Venezuela* 121 D7
Tét, *Hungary* 42 C2
Têt →, *France* 20 F7
Tetachuck L., *Canada* 104 C3
Tetas, Pta., *Chile* 126 A1
Tete, *Mozam.* 87 F3
Tete □, *Mozam.* 87 F3
Teterev →, *Ukraine* 47 G6
Teterow, *Germany* 24 B8
Teteven, *Bulgaria* 41 D8
Tethul →, *Canada* 104 A6
Tetiyev, *Ukraine* 47 H5
Teton →, *U.S.A.* 114 C8
Tétouan, *Morocco* 78 A4
Tetovo, *Macedonia* 40 D4
Tetyushi, *Russia* 48 C9
Teuco →, *Argentina* 126 B3
Teulada, *Italy* 30 D1
Teulon, *Canada* 105 C9
Teun, *Indonesia* 63 F7
Teutoburger Wald, *Germany* 24 C4
Tevere →, *Italy* 29 G9
Teverya, *Israel* 75 C4
Teviot →, *U.K.* 14 F6
Tewantin, *Australia* 95 D5
Tewkesbury, *U.K.* 13 F5
Texada I., *Canada* 104 D4
Texarkana, *Ark., U.S.A.* 113 J8
Texarkana, *Tex., U.S.A.* 113 J7
Texas, *Australia* 95 D5
Texas □, *U.S.A.* 113 K5
Texas City, *U.S.A.* 113 L7
Texel, *Neths.* 17 A4
Texline, *U.S.A.* 113 G3
Texoma, L., *U.S.A.* 113 J6
Teykovo, *Russia* 46 D11
Teza →, *Russia* 48 B5
Tezin, *Afghan.* 68 B3
Teziutlán, *Mexico* 119 D5
Tezpur, *India* 67 F18
Tezzeron L., *Canada* 104 C4
Tha-anne →, *Canada* 105 A10
Tha Deua, *Laos* 64 D4
Tha Deua, *Laos* 64 C3
Tha Pla, *Thailand* 64 D3
Tha Rua, *Thailand* 64 E3
Tha Sala, *Thailand* 65 H2
Tha Song Yang, *Thailand* 64 D1
Thaba Putsoa, *Lesotho* 89 D4
Thabana Ntlenyana, *Lesotho* 89 D4
Thabazimbi, *S. Africa* 89 C4
Thādiq, *Si. Arabia* 70 E5
Thai Binh, *Vietnam* 58 G6
Thai Muang, *Thailand* 65 H2
Thai Nguyen, *Vietnam* 58 G5
Thailand ■, *Asia* 64 E4
Thailand, G. of, *Asia* 65 G3
Thakhek, *Laos* 64 D5
Thal, *Pakistan* 68 C4
Thal Desert, *Pakistan* 68 D4
Thala La, *Burma* 67 E20
Thalabarivat, *Cambodia* 64 F5
Thallon, *Australia* 95 D4
Thalwil, *Switz.* 25 H4
Thames, *N.Z.* 91 G5
Thames →, *Canada* 102 D3
Thames →, *U.K.* 13 F8
Thames →, *U.S.A.* 111 E12
Thames Estuary, *U.K.* 13 F8
Thamesford, *Canada* 110 C4
Thamesville, *Canada* 110 D3
Than, *India* 68 H4
Than Uyen, *Vietnam* 58 G4
Thana Gazi, *India* 68 F7
Thandla, *India* 68 H6
Thane, *India* 66 K8
Thanesar, *India* 68 D7
Thanet, I. of, *U.K.* 13 F9
Thangool, *Australia* 94 C5
Thanh Hoa, *Vietnam* 64 C5
Thanh Hung, *Vietnam* 65 H5
Thanh Pho Ho Chi Minh = Phanh Bho Ho Chi Minh, *Vietnam* 65 G6
Thanh Thuy, *Vietnam* 64 A5
Thanjavur, *India* 66 P11
Thann, *France* 19 E14
Thano Bula Khan, *Pakistan* 68 G2
Thaon-les-Vosges, *France* 19 D13
Thap Sakae, *Thailand* 65 G2
Thap Than, *Thailand* 64 E2
Thar Desert, *India* 68 F5
Tharad, *India* 68 G4
Thargomindah, *Australia* 95 D3
Tharrawaddy, *Burma* 67 L19
Tharthār, Mlaq, *Iraq* 70 C4
Tharthār, W. ath →, *Iraq* 70 C4
Thasopoúla, *Greece* 41 F8
Thásos, *Greece* 41 F8
Thatcher, *Ariz., U.S.A.* 115 K9
Thatcher, *Colo., U.S.A.* 113 G2
Thaton, *Burma* 67 L20
Thau, Bassin de, *France* 20 E7
Thaungdut, *Burma* 67 G19
Thayer, *U.S.A.* 113 G9
Thayetmyo, *Burma* 67 K19
Thazi, *Burma* 67 J20
The Alberga →, *Australia* 95 D2
The Bight, *Bahamas* 121 B4
The Coorong, *Australia* 95 F2
The Dalles, *U.S.A.* 114 D3

The English Company's Is., *Australia* 94 A2
The Frome →, *Australia* 95 D2
The Great Divide = Great Dividing Ra., *Australia* 94 C4
The Hague = 's-Gravenhage, *Neths.* 17 B4
The Hamilton →, *Australia* 95 D2
The Macumba →, *Australia* 95 D2
The Neales →, *Australia* 95 D2
The Officer →, *Australia* 93 E5
The Pas, *Canada* 105 C8
The Range, *Zimbabwe* 87 F3
The Rock, *Australia* 95 F4
The Salt L., *Australia* 95 E3
The Sandheads, *India* 69 J13
The Stevenson →, *Australia* 95 D2
The Warburton →, *Australia* 95 D2
The Woodlands, *U.S.A.* 113 K7
Thebes = Thívai, *Greece* 38 C5
Thebes, *Egypt* 80 B3
Thedford, *Canada* 110 C3
Thedford, *U.S.A.* 112 E4
Theebine, *Australia* 95 D5
Thekulthili L., *Canada* 105 A7
Thelon →, *Canada* 105 A8
Thénezay, *France* 18 F6
Thenon, *France* 20 C5
Theodore, *Australia* 94 C5
Theodore, *Canada* 105 C8
Theodore, *U.S.A.* 109 K1
Theodore Roosevelt National Memorial Park, *U.S.A.* 112 B3
Theodore Roosevelt Res., *U.S.A.* 115 K8
Thepha, *Thailand* 65 J3
Thérain →, *France* 19 C9
Theresa, *U.S.A.* 111 B9
Thermaïkós Kólpos, *Greece* 40 F6
Thermí, *Greece* 39 B8
Thermopolis, *U.S.A.* 114 E9
Thermopylae P., *Greece* 38 C4
Thesprotía □, *Greece* 38 B2
Thessalía □, *Greece* 38 B4
Thessalon, *Canada* 102 C3
Thessaloníki, *Greece* 40 F6
Thessaloníki □, *Greece* 40 F7
Thessaloníki, Gulf of = Thermaïkós Kólpos, *Greece* 40 F6
Thessaly = Thessalía □, *Greece* 38 B4
Thetford, *U.K.* 13 E8
Thetford Mines, *Canada* 103 C5
Theun →, *Laos* 64 C5
Theunissen, *S. Africa* 88 D4
Thevenard, *Australia* 95 E1
Thiámis →, *Greece* 38 B2
Thiberville, *France* 18 C7
Thibodaux, *U.S.A.* 113 L9
Thicket Portage, *Canada* 105 B9
Thief River Falls, *U.S.A.* 112 A6
Thiel Mts., *Antarctica* 5 E16
Thiene, *Italy* 29 C8
Thiérache, *France* 19 C10
Thiers, *France* 20 C7
Thiès, *Senegal* 82 C1
Thiesi, *Italy* 30 B1
Thiet, *Sudan* 81 F2
Thika, *Kenya* 86 C4
Thikombia, *Fiji* 91 B9
Thille-Boubacar, *Senegal* 82 B1
Thimphu, *Bhutan* 67 F16
Thionville, *France* 19 C13
Thíra, *Greece* 39 E7
Thirasía, *Greece* 39 E7
Third Cataract, *Sudan* 80 D3
Thirsk, *U.K.* 12 C6
Thisted, *Denmark* 11 H2
Thistle I., *Australia* 95 F2
Thívai, *Greece* 38 C5
Thiviers, *France* 20 C4
Thizy, *France* 19 F11
þjórsá →, *Iceland* 8 E3
Thlewiaza →, *Man., Canada* 105 B8
Thlewiaza →, *N.W.T., Canada* 105 A10
Thmar Puok, *Cambodia* 64 F4
Tho Vinh, *Vietnam* 64 C5
Thoa →, *Canada* 105 A7
Thoen, *Thailand* 64 D2
Thoeng, *Thailand* 64 C3
Thohoyandou, *S. Africa* 85 J6
Tholdi, *Pakistan* 69 B7
Thomas, *U.S.A.* 113 H5
Thomas, L., *Australia* 95 D2
Thomaston, *U.S.A.* 109 J3
Thomasville, *Ala., U.S.A.* 109 K2
Thomasville, *Ga., U.S.A.* 109 K4
Thomasville, *N.C., U.S.A.* 109 H5
Thompson, *Canada* 105 B9
Thompson, *U.S.A.* 111 E9
Thompson →, *Canada* 104 C4
Thompson →, *U.S.A.* 112 F8
Thompson Falls, *U.S.A.* 114 C6
Thompson Pk., *U.S.A.* 114 F2
Thompson Springs, *U.S.A.* 115 G9
Thompsontown, *U.S.A.* 110 F7
Thomson, *U.S.A.* 109 J4
Thomson →, *Australia* 94 C3
Thomson's Falls = Nyahururu, *Kenya* 86 B4
Thônes, *France* 21 C10
Thonon-les-Bains, *France* 19 F13
Thorez, *Ukraine* 47 H10
þórisvatn, *Iceland* 8 D4
Thornaby on Tees, *U.K.* 12 C6
Thornbury, *Canada* 110 B4
Thorne, *U.K.* 12 D7
Thornhill, *Canada* 104 C3

Thorold, *Canada*	110	C5
Þórshöfn, *Iceland*	8	C6
Thouarcé, *France*	18	E6
Thouars, *France*	18	F6
Thouet →, *France*	18	E6
Thouin, C., *Australia*	92	D2
Thousand Oaks, *U.S.A.*	117	L8
Thrace, *Turkey*	41	F10
Thrakikón Pélagos, *Greece*	41	E8
Three Forks, *U.S.A.*	114	D8
Three Gorges Dam, *China*	59	B8
Three Hills, *Canada*	104	C6
Three Hummock I., *Australia*	94	G3
Three Points, C., *Ghana*	82	E4
Three Rivers, *Calif., U.S.A.*	116	J8
Three Rivers, *Tex., U.S.A.*	113	L5
Three Sisters, *U.S.A.*	114	D3
Three Springs, *Australia*	93	E2
Throssell, L., *Australia*	93	E3
Throssell Ra., *Australia*	92	D3
Thuan Hoa, *Vietnam*	65	H5
Thubun Lakes, *Canada*	105	A6
Thueyts, *France*	21	D8
Thuin, *Belgium*	17	D4
Thuir, *France*	20	F6
Thule = Qaanaaq, *Greenland*	4	B4
Thun, *Switz.*	25	J3
Thunder B., *U.S.A.*	110	B1
Thunder Bay, *Canada*	102	C2
Thunersee, *Switz.*	25	J3
Thung Song, *Thailand*	65	H2
Thunkar, *Bhutan*	67	F17
Thuong Tra, *Vietnam*	64	D6
Thur →, *Switz.*	25	H5
Thurgau □, *Switz.*	25	H5
Thüringen □, *Germany*	24	D6
Thüringer Wald, *Germany*	24	E6
Thurles, *Ireland*	15	D4
Thurn P., *Austria*	26	D5
Thurrock □, *U.K.*	13	F8
Thursday I., *Australia*	94	A3
Thurso, *Canada*	102	C4
Thurso, *U.K.*	14	C5
Thurso →, *U.K.*	14	C5
Thurston I., *Antarctica*	5	D16
Thury-Harcourt, *France*	18	D6
Thutade L., *Canada*	104	B3
Thy, *Denmark*	11	H2
Thyborøn, *Denmark*	11	H2
Thyolo, *Malawi*	87	F4
Thysville = Mbanza Ngungu, *Dem. Rep. of the Congo*	84	F2
Ti-n-Amzi →, *Niger*	83	B5
Ti-n-Barraouene, O. →, *Africa*	83	B5
Ti-n-Zaouatene, *Algeria*	83	B5
Ti Tree, *Australia*	94	C1
Tiadiaye, *Senegal*	82	C1
Tian Shan, *Asia*	60	B3
Tianchang, *China*	59	A12
Tiandeng, *China*	58	F6
Tiandong, *China*	58	F6
Tian'e, *China*	58	E6
Tianhe, *China*	58	E7
Tianjin, *China*	57	E9
Tiankoura, *Burkina Faso*	82	C4
Tianlin, *China*	58	E6
Tianmen, *China*	59	B9
Tianquan, *China*	58	B4
Tianshui, *China*	56	G3
Tiantai, *China*	59	C13
Tianyang, *China*	58	F6
Tianzhen, *China*	56	D8
Tianzhu, *China*	58	D7
Tianzhuangtai, *China*	57	D12
Tiaret, *Algeria*	78	A6
Tiassalé, *Ivory C.*	82	D4
Tibagi, *Brazil*	127	A5
Tibagi →, *Brazil*	127	A5
Tibati, *Cameroon*	83	D7
Tibe, *Ethiopia*	81	F4
Tiber = Tevere →, *Italy*	29	G9
Tiberias = Teverya, *Israel*	75	C4
Tiberias, L. = Yam Kinneret, *Israel*	75	C4
Tibesti, *Chad*	79	D9
Tibet = Xizang Zizhiqu □, *China*	60	C3
Tibet, Plateau of, *Asia*	52	F12
Tibiao, *Phil.*	61	F5
Tibiri, *Niger*	83	C6
Tîbleş, Vf., *Romania*	43	C9
Tîbleşului, Munţii, *Romania*	43	C9
Tibnî, *Syria*	70	C3
Tibooburra, *Australia*	95	D3
Tibro, *Sweden*	11	F8
Tiburón, I., *Mexico*	118	B2
Ticao I., *Phil.*	61	E5
Tîchît, *Mauritania*	82	B3
Ticho, *Ethiopia*	81	F4
Ticino □, *Switz.*	25	K4
Ticino →, *Italy*	25	K5
Ticleni, *Romania*	43	F8
Ticonderoga, *U.S.A.*	111	C11
Ticul, *Mexico*	119	C7
Tidaholm, *Sweden*	11	F7
Tidan, *Sweden*	11	F8
Tiddim, *Burma*	67	H18
Tidioute, *U.S.A.*	110	E5
Tidjikja, *Mauritania*	82	B2
Tidore, *Indonesia*	63	D7
Tiébissou, *Ivory C.*	82	D3
Tiel, *Neths.*	17	C5
Tiel, *Senegal*	82	C1
Tieling, *China*	57	C12
Tielt, *Belgium*	17	C3
Tien Shan → Tian Shan, *Asia*	60	B3
Tien-tsin = Tianjin, *China*	57	E9
Tien Yen, *Vietnam*	64	B6

T'ienching = Tianjin, *China*	57	E9
Tienen, *Belgium*	17	D4
Tiénigbé, *Ivory C.*	82	D3
Tientsin = Tianjin, *China*	57	E9
Tieri, *Australia*	94	C4
Tierp, *Sweden*	10	D11
Tierra Amarilla, *Chile*	126	B1
Tierra Amarilla, *U.S.A.*	115	H10
Tierra Colorada, *Mexico*	119	D5
Tierra de Barros, *Spain*	35	G4
Tierra de Campos, *Spain*	34	C6
Tierra del Fuego, I. Gr. de, *Argentina*	122	J4
Tiétar →, *Spain*	34	F4
Tieté →, *Brazil*	127	A5
Tiffin, *U.S.A.*	108	E4
Tiflis = Tbilisi, *Georgia*	49	K7
Tifton, *U.S.A.*	109	K4
Tifu, *Indonesia*	63	E7
Tighina, *Moldova*	43	D14
Tigil, *Russia*	51	D16
Tignish, *Canada*	103	C7
Tigray □, *Ethiopia*	81	E4
Tigre →, *Peru*	124	D4
Tigre →, *Venezuela*	124	B6
Tigris = Dijlah, Nahr →, *Asia*	70	D5
Tigveni, *Romania*	43	E9
Tigyaing, *Burma*	67	H20
Tîh, Gebel el, *Egypt*	80	B3
Tijara, *India*	68	F7
Tijuana, *Mexico*	117	N9
Tikal, *Guatemala*	120	C2
Tikamgarh, *India*	69	G8
Tikaré, *Burkina Faso*	83	C4
Tikhoretsk, *Russia*	49	H5
Tikhvin, *Russia*	46	C7
Tiko, *Cameroon*	83	E6
Tikrīt, *Iraq*	70	C4
Tiksi, *Russia*	51	B13
Tilamuta, *Indonesia*	63	D6
Tilburg, *Neths.*	17	C5
Tilbury, *Canada*	102	D3
Tilbury, *U.K.*	13	F8
Tilcara, *Argentina*	126	A2
Tilden, *U.S.A.*	112	D6
Tilemses, *Niger*	83	B5
Tilemsi, Vallée du, *Mali*	83	B5
Tilhar, *India*	69	F8
Tilichiki, *Russia*	51	C17
Tílissos, *Greece*	36	D7
Till →, *U.K.*	12	B5
Tillabéri, *Niger*	83	C5
Tillamook, *U.S.A.*	114	D2
Tillberga, *Sweden*	10	E10
Tillia, *Niger*	83	B5
Tillsonburg, *Canada*	102	D3
Tillyeria □, *Cyprus*	36	D11
Tilogne, *Senegal*	82	B2
Tílos, *Greece*	39	E9
Tilpa, *Australia*	95	E3
Tilsit = Sovetsk, *Russia*	9	J19
Tilt →, *U.K.*	14	E5
Tilton, *U.S.A.*	111	C13
Tiltonsville, *U.S.A.*	110	F4
Tim, *Denmark*	11	H2
Timagami, L., *Canada*	102	C3
Timanshevo, *Russia*	48	D10
Timashevsk, *Russia*	49	H4
Timau, *Kenya*	86	B4
Timbákion, *Greece*	36	D6
Timbedgha, *Mauritania*	82	B3
Timber Creek, *Australia*	92	C5
Timber Lake, *U.S.A.*	112	C4
Timber Mt., *U.S.A.*	116	H10
Timbo, *Guinea*	82	C2
Timbo, *Liberia*	82	D3
Timbuktu = Tombouctou, *Mali*	82	B4
Timeiaouine, *Algeria*	83	A5
Timétrine, Mts., *Mali*	83	B4
Timfi Óros, *Greece*	38	B2
Timfristós, Óros, *Greece*	38	C3
Timi, *Cyprus*	36	E11
Tîmia, *Niger*	83	B6
Timimoun, *Algeria*	78	C6
Timiş = Tamis →, *Serbia, Yug.*	42	F5
Timiş □, *Romania*	42	E6
Timişoara, *Romania*	42	E6
Timmersdala, *Sweden*	11	F7
Timmins, *Canada*	102	C3
Timok →, *Serbia, Yug.*	40	B6
Timor, *Indonesia*	63	F7
Timor Sea, *Ind. Oc.*	92	B4
Timor Timur □, *Indonesia*	63	F7
Timrå, *Sweden*	10	B11
Tin Can Bay, *Australia*	95	D5
Tin Ethisane, *Mali*	83	B4
Tin Gornai, *Mali*	83	B4
Tin Mt., *U.S.A.*	116	J9
Tina →, *S. Africa*	89	E4
Tîna, Khalîg el, *Egypt*	80	A3
Tinaca Pt., *Phil.*	61	J6
Tinajo, *Canary Is.*	37	E6
Tinca, *Romania*	42	D6
Tindal, *Australia*	92	B5
Tindouf, *Algeria*	78	C4
Tinée →, *France*	21	E11
Tineo, *Spain*	34	B4
Ting Jiang →, *China*	59	E11
Tinggi, Pulau, *Malaysia*	65	L5
Tingo Maria, *Peru*	124	E3
Tingrela, *Ivory C.*	82	C3
Tingsryd, *Sweden*	11	H9
Tingstäde, *Sweden*	11	G12
Tinh Bien, *Vietnam*	65	G5
Tinnevelly = Tirunelveli, *India*	66	Q10

Tinogasta, *Argentina*	126	B2
Tínos, *Greece*	39	D7
Tiñoso, C., *Spain*	33	H3
Tinpahar, *India*	69	G12
Tintina, *Argentina*	126	B3
Tintinara, *Australia*	95	F3
Tinto →, *Spain*	35	H4
Tioga, *N. Dak., U.S.A.*	112	A3
Tioga, *Pa., U.S.A.*	110	E7
Tioman, Pulau, *Malaysia*	65	L5
Tione di Trento, *Italy*	28	B7
Tionesta, *U.S.A.*	110	E5
Tior, *Sudan*	81	F3
Tipongpani, *India*	67	F19
Tipperary, *Ireland*	15	D3
Tipperary □, *Ireland*	15	D4
Tipton, *Calif., U.S.A.*	116	J7
Tipton, *Iowa, U.S.A.*	112	E9
Tipton Mt., *U.S.A.*	117	K12
Tiptonville, *U.S.A.*	113	G10
Tīrān, *Iran*	71	C6
Tīrān, *Si. Arabia*	80	B3
Tirana, *Albania*	40	E3
Tiranë = Tirana, *Albania*	40	E3
Tirano, *Italy*	28	B7
Tiraspol, *Moldova*	43	D14
Tirdout, *Mali*	83	B4
Tire, *Turkey*	39	C9
Tirebolu, *Turkey*	73	B8
Tiree, *U.K.*	14	E2
Tiree, Passage of, *U.K.*	14	E2
Tîrgovişte = Târgovişte, *Romania*	43	F10
Tîrgu-Jiu = Târgu-Jiu, *Romania*	43	E8
Tîrgu Mureş = Târgu Mureş, *Romania*	43	D9
Tirich Mir, *Pakistan*	66	A7
Tiriolo, *Italy*	31	D9
Tiriro, *Guinea*	82	C3
Tírnavos, *Greece*	38	B4
Tirodi, *India*	66	J11
Tirol □, *Austria*	26	D3
Tirso →, *Spain*	30	C1
Tirstrup, *Denmark*	11	H4
Tiruchchirappalli, *India*	66	P11
Tirunelveli, *India*	66	Q10
Tirupati, *India*	66	N11
Tiruppur, *India*	66	P10
Tiruvannamalai, *India*	66	N11
Tisa, *India*	68	C7
Tisa →, *Serbia, Yug.*	42	E5
Tisdale, *Canada*	105	C8
Tishomingo, *U.S.A.*	113	H6
Tisjön, *Sweden*	10	D7
Tisnaren, *Sweden*	11	F9
Tišnov, *Czech Rep.*	27	B9
Tisovec, *Slovak Rep.*	27	C12
Tisza = Tisa →, *Serbia, Yug.*	42	E5
Tiszaföldvár, *Hungary*	42	D5
Tiszafüred, *Hungary*	42	C5
Tiszalök, *Hungary*	42	B6
Tiszavasvári, *Hungary*	42	C6
Tit-Ary, *Russia*	51	B13
Titaguas, *Spain*	32	F3
Titao, *Burkina Faso*	83	C4
Titel, *Serbia, Yug.*	42	E5
Tithwal, *Pakistan*	69	B5
Titicaca, L., *S. Amer.*	122	E4
Titisee, *Germany*	25	H4
Titiwa, *Nigeria*	83	C7
Tito, *Serbia, Yug.*	31	B8
Titograd = Podgorica, *Montenegro, Yug.*	40	D3
Titova Korenica, *Croatia*	29	D12
Titu, *Romania*	43	F10
Titule, *Dem. Rep. of the Congo*	86	B2
Titusville, *Fla., U.S.A.*	109	L5
Titusville, *Pa., U.S.A.*	110	E5
Tivaouane, *Senegal*	82	C1
Tivat, *Montenegro, Yug.*	40	D2
Tiverton, *U.K.*	13	G4
Tívoli, *Italy*	29	G9
Tiyo, *Eritrea*	81	E5
Tizi-Ouzou, *Algeria*	78	A6
Tizimín, *Mexico*	119	C7
Tjæreborg, *Denmark*	11	J2
Tjällmo, *Sweden*	11	F9
Tjeggelvas, *Sweden*	8	C17
Tjirebon = Cirebon, *Indonesia*	63	G13
Tjörn, *Sweden*	11	F5
Tkibuli = Tqibuli, *Georgia*	49	J6
Tkvarcheli = Tqvarcheli, *Georgia*	49	J5
Tlacotalpan, *Mexico*	119	D5
Tlahualilo, *Mexico*	118	B4
Tlaquepaque, *Mexico*	118	C4
Tlaxcala, *Mexico*	119	D5
Tlaxcala □, *Mexico*	119	D5
Tlaxiaco, *Mexico*	119	D5
Tlemcen, *Algeria*	78	B5
Tłuszcz, *Poland*	45	F8
Tlyarata, *Russia*	49	J8
To Bong, *Vietnam*	64	F7
Toad →, *Canada*	104	B4
Toad River, *Canada*	104	B3
Toamasina, *Madag.*	89	B8
Toamasina □, *Madag.*	89	B8
Toay, *Argentina*	126	D3
Toba, *China*	58	B1
Toba, *Japan*	55	G8
Toba, Danau, *Indonesia*	62	D1
Toba Kakar, *Pakistan*	68	D3
Toba Tek Singh, *Pakistan*	68	D5
Tobago, *W. Indies*	121	D7
Tobarra, *Spain*	33	G3

Tobelo, *Indonesia*	63	D7
Tobermory, *Canada*	102	C3
Tobermory, *U.K.*	14	E2
Tobi, *Pac. Oc.*	63	D8
Tobin, *U.S.A.*	116	F5
Tobin, L., *Australia*	92	D4
Tobin L., *Canada*	105	C8
Toboali, *Indonesia*	62	E3
Tobol →, *Russia*	50	D7
Toboli, *Indonesia*	63	E6
Tobolsk, *Russia*	50	D7
Tobor, *Senegal*	82	C1
Tobruk = Tubruq, *Libya*	79	B10
Tobyhanna, *U.S.A.*	111	E9
Tobyl = Tobol →, *Russia*	50	D7
Tocantinópolis, *Brazil*	125	E9
Tocantins □, *Brazil*	125	F9
Tocantins →, *Brazil*	122	D6
Toccoa, *U.S.A.*	109	H4
Toce →, *Italy*	28	C5
Tochi →, *Pakistan*	68	C4
Tochigi, *Japan*	55	F9
Tochigi □, *Japan*	55	F9
Tocina, *Spain*	35	H5
Toconao, *Chile*	126	A2
Tocopilla, *Chile*	126	A1
Tocumwal, *Australia*	95	F4
Tocuyo →, *Venezuela*	124	A5
Todd →, *Australia*	94	C2
Todeli, *Indonesia*	63	E6
Todenyang, *Kenya*	86	B4
Todgarh, *India*	68	G5
Todi, *Italy*	29	F9
Todos os Santos, B. de, *Brazil*	125	F11
Todos Santos, *Mexico*	118	C2
Todtnau, *Germany*	25	H3
Toe Hd., *U.K.*	14	D1
Toecé, *Burkina Faso*	83	C4
Tofield, *Canada*	104	C6
Tofino, *Canada*	104	D3
Tofua, *Tonga*	91	D11
Tōgane, *Japan*	55	G10
Togba, *Mauritania*	82	B2
Togian, Kepulauan, *Indonesia*	63	E6
Togliatti, *Russia*	48	D9
Togo ■, *W. Afr.*	83	D5
Togtoh, *China*	56	D6
Tohma →, *Turkey*	72	C7
Tōhoku □, *Japan*	54	E10
Töhöm, *Mongolia*	56	B5
Toinya, *Sudan*	81	F2
Toiyabe Range, *U.S.A.*	114	G5
Tojikiston = Tajikistan ■, *Asia*	50	F8
Tojo, *Indonesia*	63	E6
Tōjō, *Japan*	55	G6
Tok, *U.S.A.*	100	B5
Tok-do, *Japan*	55	F5
Tokachi-Dake, *Japan*	54	C11
Tokachi-Gawa →, *Japan*	54	C11
Tokaj, *Hungary*	42	B6
Tokala, *Indonesia*	63	E6
Tōkamachi, *Japan*	55	F9
Tokanui, *N.Z.*	91	M2
Tokar, *Sudan*	80	D4
Tokara-Rettō, *Japan*	55	K4
Tokarahi, *N.Z.*	91	L3
Tokashiki-Shima, *Japan*	55	L3
Tokat □, *Turkey*	72	B7
Tŏkch'ŏn, *N. Korea*	57	E14
Tokeland, *U.S.A.*	116	D3
Tokelau Is. ■, *Pac. Oc.*	96	H10
Tokmak, *Kyrgyzstan*	50	E8
Tokmak, *Ukraine*	47	J8
Toko Ra., *Australia*	94	C2
Tokoro-Gawa →, *Japan*	54	B12
Tokuno-Shima, *Japan*	55	L4
Tokushima, *Japan*	55	G7
Tokushima □, *Japan*	55	H7
Tokuyama, *Japan*	55	G5
Tōkyō, *Japan*	55	G9
Tolaga Bay, *N.Z.*	91	H7
Tolbukhin = Dobrich, *Bulgaria*	41	C11
Toledo, *Brazil*	127	A5
Toledo, *Spain*	34	F6
Toledo, *Ohio, U.S.A.*	108	E4
Toledo, *Oreg., U.S.A.*	114	D2
Toledo, *Wash., U.S.A.*	114	C2
Toledo, Montes de, *Spain*	35	F6
Toledo Bend Reservoir, *U.S.A.*	113	K8
Tolentino, *Italy*	29	E10
Tolfa, *Italy*	29	F8
Tolga, *Australia*	94	B4
Toliara, *Madag.*	89	C7
Toliara □, *Madag.*	89	C8
Tolima, *Colombia*	124	C3
Tolitoli, *Indonesia*	63	D6
Tolkmicko, *Poland*	44	D6
Tollarp, *Sweden*	11	J7
Tollensee, *Germany*	24	B9
Tollhouse, *U.S.A.*	116	H7
Tolmachevo, *Russia*	46	C5
Tolmezzo, *Italy*	29	B10
Tolmin, *Slovenia*	29	B10
Tolna, *Hungary*	42	D3
Tolo, Teluk, *Indonesia*	63	E6
Tolochin = Talachyn, *Belarus*	46	E5
Tolosa, *Spain*	32	B2
Tolox, *Spain*	35	J6
Toluca, *Mexico*	119	D5
Tom Burke, *S. Africa*	89	C4
Tom Price, *Australia*	92	D2
Toma, *Burkina Faso*	82	C4

Tomah, *U.S.A.*	112	D9
Tomahawk, *U.S.A.*	112	C10
Tomai, *Moldova*	43	D13
Tomakomai, *Japan*	54	C10
Tomales, *U.S.A.*	116	G4
Tomales B., *U.S.A.*	116	G3
Tomar, *Portugal*	35	F2
Tómaros, Óros, *Greece*	38	B2
Tomarza, *Turkey*	72	C6
Tomaszów Lubelski, *Poland*	45	H10
Tomaszów Mazowiecki, *Poland*	45	G7
Tomatlán, *Mexico*	118	D3
Tombadonkéa, *Guinea*	82	C2
Tombador, Serra do, *Brazil*	124	F7
Tombe, *Sudan*	81	F3
Tombigbee →, *U.S.A.*	109	K2
Tombouctou, *Mali*	82	B4
Tombstone, *U.S.A.*	115	L8
Tombua, *Angola*	88	B1
Tomé, *Chile*	126	D1
Tomelilla, *Sweden*	11	J7
Tomelloso, *Spain*	35	F7
Tomini, *Indonesia*	63	D6
Tomini, Teluk, *Indonesia*	63	E6
Tominian, *Mali*	82	C4
Tomiño, *Spain*	34	D2
Tomintoul, *U.K.*	14	D5
Tomislavgrad, *Bos.-H.*	42	G2
Tomkinson Ranges, *Australia*	93	E4
Tommot, *Russia*	51	D13
Tomnop Ta Suos, *Cambodia*	65	G5
Tomo →, *Colombia*	124	B5
Toms Place, *U.S.A.*	116	H8
Toms River, *U.S.A.*	111	G10
Tomsk, *Russia*	50	D9
Tomtabacken, *Sweden*	11	G8
Tona, *Spain*	32	D7
Tonalá, *Mexico*	119	D6
Tonale, Passo del, *Italy*	28	B7
Tonantins, *Brazil*	124	D5
Tonasket, *U.S.A.*	114	B4
Tonawanda, *U.S.A.*	110	D6
Tonbridge, *U.K.*	13	F8
Tondano, *Indonesia*	63	D6
Tondela, *Portugal*	34	E2
Tønder, *Denmark*	11	K2
Tondi Kiwindi, *Niger*	83	C5
Tondibi, *Mali*	83	B4
Tondoro, *Namibia*	88	B2
Tone →, *Australia*	93	F2
Tone-Gawa →, *Japan*	55	F9
Tonekābon, *Iran*	71	B6
Tong Xian, *China*	56	E9
Tong'an, *China*	59	E12
Tongareva, Cook Is.	97	H12
Tongatapu, *Tonga*	91	E12
Tongbai, *China*	59	A9
Tongcheng, *Anhui, China*	59	B11
Tongcheng, *Hubei, China*	59	C9
Tongchŏn-ni, *N. Korea*	57	E14
Tongchuan, *China*	56	G5
Tongdao, *China*	58	D7
Tongeren, *Belgium*	17	D5
Tonggu, *China*	59	C10
Tongguan, *China*	56	G6
Tonghai, *China*	58	E4
Tonghua, *China*	57	D13
Tongjiang, *China*	58	B6
Tongjosŏn Man, *N. Korea*	57	E15
Tongking, G. of = Tonkin, G. of, *Asia*	64	B7
Tongliang, *China*	58	C6
Tongliao, *China*	57	C12
Tongling, *China*	59	B11
Tonglu, *China*	59	C12
Tongnae, *S. Korea*	57	G15
Tongnan = Anyue, *China*	58	B5
Tongobory, *Madag.*	89	C7
Tongoy, *Chile*	126	C1
Tongren, *China*	58	D7
Tongsa = Tongeren, *Belgium*	17	D5
Tongsa Dzong, *Bhutan*	67	F17
Tongue, *U.K.*	14	C4
Tongue →, *U.S.A.*	112	B2
Tongwei, *China*	56	G3
Tongxiang, *China*	59	B13
Tongxin, *China*	56	F4
Tongyang, *N. Korea*	57	E14
Tongyu, *China*	57	B12
Tongzi, *China*	58	C6
Tonj, *Sudan*	81	F2
Tonj →, *Sudan*	81	F2
Tonk, *India*	68	F6
Tonkawa, *U.S.A.*	113	G6
Tonkin = Bac Phan, *Vietnam*	64	B5
Tonkin, G. of, *Asia*	64	B7
Tonle Sap, *Cambodia*	64	F5
Tonnay-Charente, *France*	20	C3
Tonneins, *France*	20	D4
Tonnerre, *France*	19	E10
Tönning, *Germany*	24	A4
Tono, *Japan*	54	E10
Tonopah, *U.S.A.*	115	G5
Tonosí, *Panama*	120	E3
Tons →, *Haryana, India*	68	D7
Tons →, *Ut. P., India*	69	D8
Tønsberg, *Norway*	9	G14
Tonya, *Turkey*	73	B8
Toobanna, *Australia*	94	B4
Toodyay, *Australia*	93	F2
Tooele, *U.S.A.*	114	F7
Toompine, *Australia*	95	D3
Toora, *Australia*	95	F4
Toora-Khem, *Russia*	51	D10
Toowoomba, *Australia*	95	D5

Top Springs, *Australia* 92 C5
Topalu, *Romania* 43 F13
Topaz, *U.S.A.* 116 G7
Topeka, *U.S.A.* 112 F7
Topl'a →, *Slovak Rep.* 27 C14
Topley, *Canada* 104 C3
Toplica →, *Serbia, Yug.* .. 40 C5
Topliţa, *Romania* 43 D10
Topocalma, Pta., *Chile* ... 126 C1
Topock, *U.S.A.* 117 L12
Topola, *Serbia, Yug.* 40 B4
Topolčani, *Macedonia* 40 E5
Topol'čany, *Slovak Rep.* .. 27 C11
Topolnitsa →, *Bulgaria* ... 41 D8
Topolobampo, *Mexico* 118 B3
Topoloveni, *Romania* 43 F10
Topolovgrad, *Bulgaria* 41 D10
Topolváţu Mare, *Romania* .. 42 F6
Toppenish, *U.S.A.* 114 C3
Topraisar, *Romania* 43 F13
Topusko, *Croatia* 29 C12
Torà, *Spain* 32 D6
Tora Kit, *Sudan* 81 E3
Toraka Vestale, *Madag.* ... 89 B7
Torata, *Peru* 124 G4
Torbalı, *Turkey* 39 C9
Torbat-e Ḥeydārīyeh, *Iran* . 71 C8
Torbat-e Jām, *Iran* 71 C9
Torbay, *Canada* 103 C9
Torbay □, *U.K.* 13 G4
Torbjörntorp, *Sweden* 11 F7
Tordesillas, *Spain* 34 D6
Töreboda, *Sweden* 11 F8
Torekov, *Sweden* 11 H6
Torelló, *Spain* 32 C7
Toreno, *Spain* 34 C4
Torfaen □, *U.K.* 13 F4
Torgau, *Germany* 24 D8
Torgelow, *Germany* 24 B10
Torhamn, *Sweden* 11 H9
Torhout, *Belgium* 17 C3
Tori, *Ethiopia* 81 F3
Tori-Shima, *Japan* 55 J10
Torigni-sur-Vire, *France* .. 18 C6
Torija, *Spain* 32 E1
Torin, *Mexico* 118 B2
Torit, *Sudan* 81 G3
Torkamān, *Iran* 70 B5
Torkovichi, *Russia* 46 C6
Tormac, *Romania* 42 E6
Tormes →, *Spain* 34 D4
Tornado Mt., *Canada* 104 D6
Tornal'a, *Slovak Rep.* 27 C13
Torne älv →, *Sweden* 8 D21
Torneå = Tornio, *Finland* . 8 D21
Torneträsk, *Sweden* 8 B18
Tornio, *Finland* 8 D21
Tornionjoki →, *Finland* ... 8 D21
Tornquist, *Argentina* 126 D3
Toro, *Baleares, Spain* 37 B11
Toro, *Zamora, Spain* 34 D5
Torö, *Sweden* 11 F11
Toro, Cerro del, *Chile* ... 126 B2
Toro Pk., *U.S.A.* 117 M10
Törökszentmiklós, *Hungary* .42 C5
Toroníios Kólpos, *Greece* . 40 F7
Toronto, *Canada* 102 D4
Toronto, *U.S.A.* 110 F4
Toropets, *Russia* 46 D6
Tororo, *Uganda* 86 B3
Toros Dağları, *Turkey* 70 B2
Torpa, *India* 69 H11
Torquay, *Australia* 95 F3
Torquay, *U.K.* 13 G4
Torquemada, *Spain* 34 C6
Torrance, *U.S.A.* 117 M8
Torrão, *Portugal* 35 G2
Torre Annunziata, *Italy* ... 31 B7
Torre de Moncorvo, *Portugal* 34 D3
Torre del Campo, *Spain* ... 35 H7
Torre del Greco, *Italy* 31 B7
Torre del Mar, *Spain* 35 J6
Torre-Pacheco, *Spain* 33 H4
Torre Péllice, *Italy* 28 D4
Torreblanca, *Spain* 32 E5
Torrecampo, *Spain* 35 G6
Torrecilla en Cameros, *Spain* 32 C2
Torredembarra, *Spain* 32 D6
Torredonjimeno, *Spain* ... 35 H7
Torrejón de Ardoz, *Spain* . 34 E7
Torrejoncillo, *Spain* 34 F4
Torrelaguna, *Spain* 34 E7
Torrelavega, *Spain* 34 B6
Torremaggiore, *Italy* 29 G12
Torremolinos, *Spain* 35 J6
Torrens, L., *Australia* 95 E2
Torrens Cr. →, *Australia* .. 94 C4
Torrens Creek, *Australia* .. 94 C4
Torrent, *Spain* 33 F4
Torrenueva, *Spain* 35 G7
Torreón, *Mexico* 118 B4
Torreperogil, *Spain* 35 G7
Torres, *Brazil* 127 B5
Torres, *Mexico* 118 B2
Torres Novas, *Portugal* ... 35 F2
Torres Strait, *Australia* ... 96 H6
Torres Vedras, *Portugal* ... 35 F1
Torrevieja, *Spain* 33 H4
Torrey, *U.S.A.* 115 G8
Torridge →, *U.K.* 13 G3
Torridon, L., *U.K.* 14 D3
Torrijos, *Spain* 34 F6
Tørring, *Denmark* 11 J3
Torrington, Conn., *U.S.A.* 111 E11
Torrington, Wyo., *U.S.A.* 112 D2
Torroella de Montgrì, *Spain* 32 C8
Torrox, *Spain* 35 J7
Torsås, *Sweden* 11 H9
Torsby, *Sweden* 10 D6
Torshälla, *Sweden* 10 E10

Tórshavn, *Færoe Is.* 8 E9
Torslanda, *Sweden* 11 G5
Torsö, *Sweden* 11 F7
Tortola, *Virgin Is.* 121 C7
Tórtoles de Esgueva, *Spain* . 34 D6
Tortolì, *Italy* 30 C2
Tortona, *Italy* 28 D5
Tortorici, *Italy* 31 D7
Tortosa, *Spain* 32 E5
Tortosa, C., *Spain* 32 E5
Tortosendo, *Portugal* 34 E3
Tortue, I. de la, *Haiti* ... 121 B5
Tortum, *Turkey* 73 B9
Ţorūd, *Iran* 71 C7
Torul, *Turkey* 73 B8
Toruń, *Poland* 45 E5
Torysa →, *Slovak Rep.* 27 C14
Torzhok, *Russia* 46 D8
Torzym, *Poland* 45 F2
Tosa, *Japan* 55 H6
Tosa-Shimizu, *Japan* 55 H6
Tosa-Wan, *Japan* 55 H6
Toscana □, *Italy* 28 E8
Toscano, Arcipelago, *Italy* . 28 F7
Toshkent, *Uzbekistan* 50 E7
Tosno, *Russia* 46 C6
Tossa de Mar, *Spain* 32 D7
Tösse, *Sweden* 11 F6
Tostado, *Argentina* 126 B3
Tostedt, *Germany* 24 B5
Tostón, Pta. de, *Canary Is.* 37 F5
Tosu, *Japan* 55 H5
Tosya, *Turkey* 72 B6
Toszek, *Poland* 45 H5
Totana, *Spain* 33 H3
Totebo, *Sweden* 11 G10
Toteng, *Botswana* 88 C3
Tôtes, *France* 18 C8
Tótkomlós, *Hungary* 42 D5
Totma, *Russia* 50 C5
Totnes, *U.K.* 13 G4
Totness, *Surinam* 125 B7
Toto, *Nigeria* 83 D6
Totonicapán, *Guatemala* .. 120 D1
Totten Glacier, *Antarctica* . 5 C8
Tottenham, *Australia* 95 E4
Tottenham, *Canada* 110 B5
Tottori, *Japan* 55 G7
Tottori □, *Japan* 55 G7
Touaret, *Niger* 83 A6
Touba, *Ivory C.* 82 D3
Touba, *Senegal* 82 C1
Toubkal, Djebel, *Morocco* . 78 B4
Toucy, *France* 19 E10
Tougan, *Burkina Faso* 82 C4
Touggourt, *Algeria* 78 B7
Tougouri, *Burkina Faso* ... 83 C4
Tougué, *Guinea* 82 C2
Toukoto, *Mali* 82 C3
Toul, *France* 19 D12
Toulepleu, *Ivory C.* 82 D3
Toulon, *France* 21 E9
Toulouse, *France* 20 E5
Toummo, *Niger* 79 D8
Toumodi, *Ivory C.* 82 D3
Tounan, *Taiwan* 59 F13
Toungo, *Nigeria* 83 D7
Toungoo, *Burma* 67 K20
Touques →, *France* 18 C7
Touraine, *France* 18 E7
Tourane = Da Nang,
   Vietnam 64 D7
Tourcoing, *France* 19 B10
Touriñán, C., *Spain* 34 B1
Tournai, *Belgium* 17 D3
Tournan-en-Brie, *France* .. 19 D9
Tournay, *France* 20 E4
Tournon-St-Martin, *France* . 18 F7
Tournon-sur-Rhône, *France* 21 C8
Tournus, *France* 19 F11
Tours, *France* 18 E7
Tousidé, Pic, *Chad* 79 D9
Toussora, Mt., *C.A.R.* 84 C4
Touws →, *S. Africa* 88 E3
Touwsrivier, *S. Africa* 88 E3
Tovarkovskiy, *Russia* 46 F10
Tovuz, *Azerbaijan* 49 K7
Towada, *Japan* 54 D10
Towada-Ko, *Japan* 54 D10
Towanda, *U.S.A.* 111 E8
Towang, *India* 67 F17
Tower, *U.S.A.* 112 B8
Towerhill Cr. →, *Australia* . 94 C3
Towner, *U.S.A.* 112 A4
Townsend, *U.S.A.* 114 C8
Townshend I., *Australia* .. 94 C5
Townsville, *Australia* 94 B4
Towson, *U.S.A.* 108 F7
Towuti, Danau, *Indonesia* . 63 E6
Toya-Ko, *Japan* 54 C10
Toyama, *Japan* 55 F8
Toyama □, *Japan* 55 F8
Toyama-Wan, *Japan* 55 F8
Toyohashi, *Japan* 55 G8
Toyokawa, *Japan* 55 G8
Toyonaka, *Japan* 55 G7
Toyooka, *Japan* 55 G7
Toyota, *Japan* 55 G8
Tozeur, *Tunisia* 78 B7
Tqibuli, *Georgia* 49 J6
Tqvarcheli, *Georgia* 49 J5
Trá Li = Tralee, *Ireland* .. 15 D2
Tra On, *Vietnam* 65 H5
Trabancos →, *Spain* 34 D5
Traben-Trarbach, *Germany* 25 F3
Trabzon, *Turkey* 73 B8
Tracadie, *Canada* 103 C7
Tracy, Calif., *U.S.A.* 116 H5
Tracy, Minn., *U.S.A.* 112 C7
Tradate, *Italy* 28 C5

Trade Town, *Liberia* 82 D3
Trafalgar, C., *Spain* 35 J4
Traian, Brăila, *Romania* .. 43 E12
Traian, Tulcea, *Romania* .. 43 E13
Trail, *Canada* 104 D5
Trainor L., *Canada* 104 A4
Trákhonas, *Cyprus* 36 D12
Tralee, *Ireland* 15 D2
Tralee B., *Ireland* 15 D2
Tramore, *Ireland* 15 D4
Tramore B., *Ireland* 15 D4
Tran Ninh, Cao Nguyen,
   Laos 64 C4
Tranås, *Sweden* 11 F8
Tranbjerg, *Denmark* 11 H4
Trancas, *Argentina* 126 B2
Trancoso, *Portugal* 34 E3
Tranebjerg, *Denmark* 11 J4
Tranemo, *Sweden* 11 G7
Trang, *Thailand* 65 J2
Trangahy, *Madag.* 89 B7
Trangan, *Indonesia* 63 F8
Trangie, *Australia* 95 E4
Trångsviken, *Sweden* 10 A7
Trani, *Italy* 31 A9
Tranoroa, *Madag.* 89 C8
Tranqueras, *Uruguay* ... 127 C4
Transantarctic Mts.,
   Antarctica 5 E12
Transilvania, *Romania* ... 43 D9
Transilvanian Alps =
   Carpaţii Meridionali,
   Romania 43 E9
Transtrand, *Sweden* 10 C7
Transtrandsfjällen, *Sweden* 10 C6
Transvaal, *S. Africa* 85 K5
Transylvania = Transilvania,
   Romania 43 D9
Trápani, *Italy* 30 D5
Trapper Pk., *U.S.A.* 114 D6
Traralgon, *Australia* 95 F4
Trarza, *Mauritania* 82 B2
Trăscău, Munţii, *Romania* . 43 D8
Trasimeno, L., *Italy* 29 E9
Träslövsläge, *Sweden* 11 G6
Trasvase Tajo-Segura, Canal
   de, *Spain* 32 E2
Trat, *Thailand* 65 F4
Tratani →, *Pakistan* 68 E3
Traun, *Austria* 26 C7
Traunreut, *Germany* 25 H8
Traunsee, *Austria* 26 D6
Traunstein, *Germany* 25 H8
Travellers L., *Australia* .. 95 E3
Travemünde, *Germany* ... 24 B6
Travers, Mt., *N.Z.* 91 K4
Traverse City, *U.S.A.* ... 108 C3
Travis, L., *U.S.A.* 113 K5
Travnik, *Bos.-H.* 42 F2
Trbovlje, *Slovenia* 29 B12
Trébbia →, *Italy* 28 C6
Trebel →, *Germany* 24 B9
Trébeurden, *France* 18 D3
Třebíč, *Czech Rep.* 26 B8
Trebinje, *Bos.-H.* 40 D2
Trebisacce, *Italy* 31 C9
Trebišnjica →, *Bos.-H.* ... 40 D2
Trebišov, *Slovak Rep.* 27 C14
Trebižat →, *Bos.-H.* 29 E14
Trebnje, *Slovenia* 29 C12
Trebonne, *Australia* 94 B4
Trebujena, *Spain* 35 J4
Trecate, *Italy* 28 C5
Tregaron, *U.K.* 13 E4
Tregnago, *Italy* 29 C8
Tregrosse Is., *Australia* ... 94 B5
Tréguier, *France* 18 D3
Trégunc, *France* 18 E3
Treherne, *Canada* 105 D9
Tréia, *Italy* 29 E10
Treignac, *France* 20 C5
Treinta y Tres, *Uruguay* . 127 C5
Treis-karden, *Germany* ... 25 E3
Treklyano, *Bulgaria* 40 D6
Trelawney, *Zimbabwe* ... 89 B5
Trélazé, *France* 18 E6
Trelew, *Argentina* 128 E3
Trélissac, *France* 20 C4
Trelleborg, *Sweden* 11 J7
Tremadog Bay, *U.K.* 12 E3
Trémiti, *Italy* 29 F12
Tremonton, *U.S.A.* 114 F7
Tremp, *Spain* 32 C5
Trenche →, *Canada* 102 C5
Trenčiansky □, *Slovak Rep.* 27 C11
Trenčín, *Slovak Rep.* 27 C11
Trenggalek, *Indonesia* ... 63 H14
Trenque Lauquen, *Argentina* 126 D3
Trent →, *Canada* 110 B7
Trent →, *U.K.* 12 D7
Trentino-Alto Adige □, *Italy* 29 B8
Trento, *Italy* 28 B8
Trenton, *Canada* 102 D4
Trenton, Mo., *U.S.A.* 112 E8
Trenton, N.J., *U.S.A.* ... 111 F10
Trenton, Nebr., *U.S.A.* .. 112 E4
Trepassey, *Canada* 103 C9
Trepuzzi, *Italy* 31 B11
Tres Arroyos, *Argentina* . 126 D3
Três Corações, *Brazil* 127 A6
Três Lagoas, *Brazil* 125 H8
Tres Lomas, *Argentina* .. 126 D3
Tres Marías, Islas, *Mexico* . 118 C3
Tres Montes, C., *Chile* ... 128 F1
Tres, Pinos, *U.S.A.* 116 J5
Três Pontas, *Brazil* 127 A6
Tres Puentes, *Chile* 126 B1
Tres Puntas, C., *Argentina* 128 F3
Três Rios, *Brazil* 127 A7

Tres Valles, *Mexico* 119 D5
Tresco, *U.K.* 13 H1
Treska →, *Macedonia* 40 E5
Treskavica, *Bos.-H.* 42 G3
Trespaderne, *Spain* 34 C7
Trets, *France* 21 E9
Treuchtlingen, *Germany* .. 25 G6
Treuenbrietzen, *Germany* . 24 C8
Trevi, *Italy* 29 F9
Trevíglio, *Italy* 28 C6
Trevínca, Peña, *Spain* 34 C4
Treviso, *Italy* 29 C9
Trévoux, *France* 21 C8
Trgovište, *Serbia, Yug.* ... 40 D6
Triabunna, *Australia* 94 G4
Triánda, *Greece* 36 C10
Triangle, *Zimbabwe* 89 C5
Triaucourt-en-Argonne,
   France 19 D12
Tribsees, *Germany* 24 A8
Tribulation, C., *Australia* . 94 B4
Tribune, *U.S.A.* 112 F4
Tricárico, *Italy* 31 B9
Tricase, *Italy* 31 C11
Trichinopoly =
   Tiruchchirappalli, *India* . 66 P11
Trichur, *India* 66 P10
Trida, *Australia* 95 E4
Trier, *Germany* 25 F2
Trieste, *Italy* 29 C10
Trieste, G. di, *Italy* 29 C10
Trieux →, *France* 18 D3
Triggiano, *Italy* 31 A9
Triglav, *Slovenia* 29 B10
Trigno →, *Italy* 29 F11
Trigueros, *Spain* 35 H4
Tríkeri, *Greece* 38 B5
Trikhonis, Límni, *Greece* . 38 C3
Tríkkala, *Greece* 38 B3
Tríkkala □, *Greece* 38 B3
Trikomo, *Cyprus* 36 D12
Trikora, Puncak, *Indonesia* . 63 E9
Trilj, *Croatia* 29 E13
Trillo, *Spain* 32 E2
Trim, *Ireland* 15 C5
Trincomalee, *Sri Lanka* .. 66 Q12
Trindade, *Brazil* 125 G9
Trindade, I., *Atl. Oc.* 2 F8
Trinidad, *Bolivia* 124 F6
Trinidad, *Cuba* 120 B4
Trinidad, *Uruguay* 126 C4
Trinidad, *U.S.A.* 113 G2
Trinidad, W. Indies 121 D7
Trinidad →, *Mexico* 119 D5
Trinidad & Tobago ■,
   W. Indies 121 D7
Trinitápoli, *Italy* 31 A9
Trinity, *Canada* 103 C9
Trinity, *U.S.A.* 113 K7
Trinity →, Calif., *U.S.A.* . 114 F2
Trinity →, Tex., *U.S.A.* .. 113 L7
Trinity B., *Canada* 103 C9
Trinity Is., *U.S.A.* 100 C4
Trinity Range, *U.S.A.* ... 114 F4
Trino, *Italy* 28 C5
Trinway, *U.S.A.* 110 F2
Trionto, C., *Italy* 31 C9
Triora, *Italy* 28 D4
Tripoli = Tarābulus,
   Lebanon 75 A4
Tripoli = Tarābulus, *Libya* . 79 B8
Trípolis, *Greece* 38 D4
Tripolitania, *Libya* 76 C5
Tripolitania, N. Afr. 79 B8
Tripura □, *India* 67 H18
Tripylos, *Cyprus* 36 E11
Trischen, *Germany* 24 A4
Tristan da Cunha, *Atl. Oc.* 77 K2
Trisul, *India* 69 D8
Trivandrum, *India* 66 Q10
Trivento, *Italy* 29 G11
Trnava, *Slovak Rep.* 27 C10
Trnavský □, *Slovak Rep.* .. 27 C10
Troarn, *France* 18 C6
Trochu, *Canada* 104 C6
Trodely I., *Canada* 102 B4
Troezen, *Greece* 38 D5
Trogir, *Croatia* 29 E13
Troglav, *Croatia* 29 E13
Tróia, *Italy* 31 A8
Troilus, L., *Canada* 102 B5
Troina, *Italy* 31 E7
Trois-Pistoles, *Canada* .. 103 C6
Trois-Rivières, *Canada* .. 102 C5
Troisdorf, *Germany* 24 E3
Troitsk, *Russia* 50 D7
Troitsko Pechorsk, *Russia* . 50 C6
Troitsko Pechorsk, *Russia* . 50 C6
Trölladyngja, *Iceland* 8 D5
Trollhättan, *Sweden* 11 F6
Trollheimen, *Norway* 8 E13
Trombetas →, *Brazil* ... 125 D7
Tromsø, *Norway* 8 B18
Trona, *U.S.A.* 117 K9
Tronador, Mte., *Argentina* . 128 E2
Trøndelag, *Norway* 8 D14
Trondheim, *Norway* 8 E14
Trondheimsfjorden, *Norway* 8 E14
Trönninge, *Sweden* 11 H6
Tronto →, *Italy* 29 F10
Troodos, *Cyprus* 36 E11
Troon, *U.K.* 14 F4
Tropea, *Italy* 31 D8
Tropic, *U.S.A.* 115 H7
Tropoja, *Albania* 40 D4
Trosa, *Sweden* 11 F11
Trostan, *U.K.* 15 A5
Trostberg, *Germany* 25 G8
Trostyanets, *Ukraine* 47 G8
Trout →, *Canada* 104 A5

Trout L., N.W.T., *Canada* . 104 A4
Trout L., Ont., *Canada* .. 105 C10
Trout Lake, *Canada* 104 B6
Trout Lake, *U.S.A.* 116 E5
Trout River, *Canada* 103 C8
Trout Run, *U.S.A.* 110 E7
Trouville-sur-Mer, *France* . 18 C7
Trowbridge, *U.K.* 13 F5
Troy, *Turkey* 39 B8
Troy, Ala., *U.S.A.* 109 K3
Troy, Kans., *U.S.A.* 112 F7
Troy, Mo., *U.S.A.* 112 F9
Troy, Mont., *U.S.A.* 114 B6
Troy, N.Y., *U.S.A.* 111 D11
Troy, Ohio, *U.S.A.* 108 E3
Troy, Pa., *U.S.A.* 111 E8
Troyan, *Bulgaria* 41 D8
Troyes, *France* 19 D11
Trpanj, *Croatia* 29 E14
Trstenik, *Serbia, Yug.* ... 40 C5
Trubchevsk, *Russia* 47 F7
Truchas Peak, *U.S.A.* ... 113 H2
Trucial States = United
   Arab Emirates ■, *Asia* .. 71 F7
Truckee, *U.S.A.* 116 F6
Trudfront, *Russia* 49 H8
Trudovoye, *Russia* 54 C6
Trujillo, *Honduras* 120 C2
Trujillo, *Peru* 124 E3
Trujillo, *Spain* 35 F5
Trujillo, *U.S.A.* 113 H2
Trujillo, *Venezuela* 124 B4
Truk, *Micronesia* 96 G7
Trumann, *U.S.A.* 113 H9
Trumansburg, *U.S.A.* ... 111 D8
Trumbull, Mt., *U.S.A.* .. 115 H7
Trün, *France* 18 D7
Trun, *France* 40 D6
Trundle, *Australia* 95 E4
Trung-Phan = Annam,
   Vietnam 64 E7
Truro, *Canada* 103 C7
Truro, *U.K.* 13 G2
Truskavets, *Ukraine* 47 H2
Trŭstenik, *Bulgaria* 41 C8
Trustrup, *Denmark* 11 H4
Trutch, *Canada* 104 B4
Truth or Consequences,
   U.S.A. 115 K10
Trutnov, *Czech Rep.* 26 A8
Truxton, *U.S.A.* 111 D8
Truyère →, *France* 20 D6
Tryavna, *Bulgaria* 41 D9
Tryonville, *U.S.A.* 110 E5
Trzcianka, *Poland* 45 E3
Trzciel, *Poland* 45 F2
Trzcińsko Zdrój, *Poland* .. 45 F1
Trzebiatów, *Poland* 44 D2
Trzebiez, *Poland* 44 E1
Trzebnica, *Poland* 45 G4
Trzemeszno, *Poland* 45 F4
Tržič, *Slovenia* 29 B11
Tsagan Aman, *Russia* 49 G8
Tsamandás, *Greece* 38 B2
Tsandi, *Namibia* 88 B1
Tsaratanana, *Madag.* 89 B8
Tsaratanana, Mt. de, *Madag.* 89 A8
Tsarevo = Michurin,
   Bulgaria 41 D11
Tsarevo, *Bulgaria* 41 D9
Tsaritsáni, *Greece* 38 B4
Tsau, *Botswana* 88 C3
Tsebrykove, *Ukraine* 47 J6
Tselinograd = Astana,
   Kazakhstan 50 D8
Tses, *Namibia* 88 D2
Tsetserleg, *Mongolia* 60 B5
Tsévié, *Togo* 83 D5
Tshabong, *Botswana* 88 D3
Tshane, *Botswana* 88 C3
Tshela,
   Dem. Rep. of the Congo . 84 E2
Tshesebe, *Botswana* 89 C4
Tshibeke,
   Dem. Rep. of the Congo . 86 C2
Tshibinda,
   Dem. Rep. of the Congo . 86 C2
Tshikapa,
   Dem. Rep. of the Congo . 84 F4
Tshilenge,
   Dem. Rep. of the Congo . 86 D1
Tshinsenda,
   Dem. Rep. of the Congo . 87 E2
Tshofa,
   Dem. Rep. of the Congo . 86 D2
Tshwane, *Botswana* 88 C3
Tsigara, *Botswana* 88 C4
Tsihombe, *Madag.* 89 D8
Tsiigehtchic, *Canada* ... 100 B6
Tsimlyansk, *Russia* 49 G6
Tsimlyansk Res. =
   Tsimlyanskoye Vdkhr.,
   Russia 49 F6
Tsimlyanskoye Vdkhr.,
   Russia 49 F6
Tsinan = Jinan, *China* 56 F9
Tsineng, *S. Africa* 88 D3
Tsínga, *Greece* 41 E8
Tsinghai = Qinghai □, *China* 60 C4
Tsingtao = Qingdao, *China* 57 F11
Tsinjoarivo, *Madag.* 89 B8
Tsinjomitondraka, *Madag.* . 89 B8
Tsiroanomandidy, *Madag.* . 89 B8
Tsiteli-Tsqaro, *Georgia* ... 49 K8
Tsitondroina, *Madag.* 89 C8
Tsivilsk, *Russia* 48 C8
Tsivory, *Madag.* 89 C8
Tskhinvali, *Georgia* 49 J7
Tsna →, *Russia* 48 D6
Tsnori, *Georgia* 49 K7
Tso Moriri, L., *India* 69 C8

215

Tsobis

Tsobis, *Namibia* 88 B2
Tsodilo Hill, *Botswana* 88 B3
Tsogttsetsiy = Baruunsuu, *Mongolia* 56 C3
Tsolo, *S. Africa* 89 E4
Tsomo, *S. Africa* 89 E4
Tsu, *Japan* 55 G8
Tsu L., *Canada* 104 A6
Tsuchiura, *Japan* 55 F10
Tsuen Wan, *H.K.* 59 F10
Tsugaru-Kaikyō, *Japan* 54 D10
Tsumeb, *Namibia* 88 B2
Tsumis, *Namibia* 88 C2
Tsuruga, *Japan* 55 G8
Tsurugi-San, *Japan* 55 H7
Tsuruoka, *Japan* 54 E9
Tsushima, *Gifu, Japan* 55 G8
Tsushima, *Nagasaki, Japan* 55 G4
Tsuyama, *Japan* 55 G7
Tsvetkovo, *Ukraine* 47 H6
Tsyelyakhany, *Belarus* 47 F3
Tua →, *Portugal* 34 D3
Tual, *Indonesia* 63 F8
Tuam, *Ireland* 15 C3
Tuamotu Arch. = Tuamotu Is., *Pac. Oc.* 97 J13
Tuamotu Is., *Pac. Oc.* 97 J13
Tuamotu Ridge, *Pac. Oc.* 97 K14
Tuanfeng, *China* 59 B10
Tuanxi, *China* 58 D6
Tuao, *Phil.* 61 C4
Tuapse, *Russia* 49 H4
Tuatapere, *N.Z.* 91 M1
Tuba City, *U.S.A.* 115 H8
Tuban, *Indonesia* 63 G15
Tubani, *Botswana* 88 C3
Tubarão, *Brazil* 127 B6
Tūbās, *West Bank* 75 C4
Tubas →, *Namibia* 88 C2
Tübingen, *Germany* 25 G5
Tubruq, *Libya* 79 B10
Tubuai Is., *Pac. Oc.* 97 K13
Tuc Trung, *Vietnam* 65 G6
Tucacas, *Venezuela* 124 A5
T'uch'ang, *Taiwan* 59 E13
Tuchodi →, *Canada* 104 B4
Tuchola, *Poland* 44 E4
Tuchów, *Poland* 45 J8
Tuckanarra, *Australia* 93 E2
Tucson, *U.S.A.* 115 K8
Tucumán □, *Argentina* 126 B2
Tucumcari, *U.S.A.* 113 H3
Tucupita, *Venezuela* 124 B6
Tucuruí, *Brazil* 125 D9
Tucuruí, Reprêsa de, *Brazil* 125 D9
Tuczno, *Poland* 45 E3
Tudela, *Spain* 32 C3
Tudmur, *Syria* 70 C3
Tudor, L., *Canada* 103 A6
Tudora, *Romania* 43 C11
Tuella →, *Portugal* 34 D3
Tugela →, *S. Africa* 89 D5
Tuguegarao, *Phil.* 61 C4
Tugur, *Russia* 51 D14
Tui, *Spain* 34 C2
Tuineje, *Canary Is.* 37 F5
Tukangbesi, Kepulauan, *Indonesia* 63 F6
Tukarak I., *Canada* 102 A4
Tukayyid, *Iraq* 70 D5
Tûkh, *Egypt* 80 H7
Tukobo, *Ghana* 82 D4
Tuktoyaktuk, *Canada* 100 B6
Tukums, *Latvia* 9 H20
Tukums □, *Latvia* 44 B10
Tukuyu, *Tanzania* 87 D3
Tula, *Hidalgo, Mexico* 119 C5
Tula, *Tamaulipas, Mexico* 119 C5
Tula, *Nigeria* 83 D7
Tula, *Russia* 46 E9
Tulancingo, *Mexico* 119 C5
Tulare, *Serbia, Yug.* 40 D5
Tulare, *U.S.A.* 116 J7
Tulare Lake Bed, *U.S.A.* 116 K7
Tularosa, *U.S.A.* 115 K10
Tulbagh, *S. Africa* 88 E2
Tulcán, *Ecuador* 124 C3
Tulcea, *Romania* 43 E13
Tulcea □, *Romania* 43 E13
Tulchyn, *Ukraine* 47 H5
Tūleh, *Iran* 71 C7
Tulemalu L., *Canada* 105 A9
Tulgheş, *Romania* 43 D10
Tuli, *Zimbabwe* 87 G2
Tulia, *U.S.A.* 113 H4
Tuliszków, *Poland* 45 F5
Tulita, *Canada* 100 B7
Ţūlkarm, *West Bank* 75 C4
Tulla, *Ireland* 15 D3
Tullahoma, *U.S.A.* 109 H2
Tullamore, *Australia* 95 E4
Tullamore, *Ireland* 15 C4
Tulle, *France* 20 C5
Tulln, *Austria* 26 C9
Tullow, *Ireland* 15 D5
Tullus, *Sudan* 81 E1
Tully, *Australia* 94 B4
Tully, *U.S.A.* 111 D8
Tulnici, *Romania* 43 E11
Tulovo, *Bulgaria* 41 D9
Tulsa, *U.S.A.* 113 G7
Tulsequah, *Canada* 104 B2
Tulu Milki, *Ethiopia* 81 F4
Tulu Welel, *Ethiopia* 81 F3
Tulua, *Colombia* 124 C3
Tuluceşti, *Romania* 43 E13
Tulun, *Russia* 51 D11
Tulungagung, *Indonesia* 63 H14
Tuma, *Russia* 46 E11
Tuma →, *Nic.* 120 D3
Tumaco, *Colombia* 124 C3
Tumatumari, *Guyana* 124 B7
Tumba, *Sweden* 10 E11
Tumba, L., *Dem. Rep. of the Congo* 84 E3
Tumbarumba, *Australia* 95 F4
Tumbaya, *Argentina* 126 A2
Tumbes, *Peru* 124 D2
Tumbur, *Sudan* 81 G3
Tumbwe, *Dem. Rep. of the Congo* 87 E2
Tumby Bay, *Australia* 95 E2
Tumd Youqi, *China* 56 D6
Tumen, *China* 57 C15
Tumen Jiang →, *China* 57 C16
Tumeremo, *Venezuela* 124 B6
Tumkur, *India* 66 N10
Tump, *Pakistan* 66 F3
Tumpat, *Malaysia* 65 J4
Tumu, *Ghana* 82 C4
Tumucumaque, Serra, *Brazil* 122 C5
Tumut, *Australia* 95 F4
Tumwater, *U.S.A.* 116 C4
Tuna, *India* 68 H4
Tunadal, *Sweden* 10 B11
Tunas de Zaza, *Cuba* 120 B4
Tunbridge Wells = Royal Tunbridge Wells, *U.K.* 13 F8
Tunçbilek, *Turkey* 39 B11
Tunceli, *Turkey* 73 C8
Tuncurry-Forster, *Australia* 95 E5
Tundla, *India* 68 F8
Tundubai, *Sudan* 80 D2
Tunduru, *Tanzania* 87 E4
Tundzha →, *Bulgaria* 41 E10
Tunga Pass, *India* 67 E19
Tungabhadra →, *India* 66 M11
Tungaru, *Sudan* 81 E3
Tungla, *Nic.* 120 D3
Tungsha Tao, *Taiwan* 59 G11
Tungshih, *Taiwan* 59 E13
Tungsten, *Canada* 104 A3
Tunguska, Nizhnyaya →, *Russia* 51 C9
Tunguska, Podkamennaya →, *Russia* 51 C10
Tunica, *U.S.A.* 113 H9
Tunis, *Tunisia* 79 A8
Tunisia ■, *Africa* 79 A7
Tunja, *Colombia* 124 B4
Tunkhannock, *U.S.A.* 111 E9
Tunliu, *China* 56 F7
Tunnsjøen, *Norway* 8 D15
Tunø, *Denmark* 11 J4
Tunungayualok I., *Canada* 103 A7
Tunuyán, *Argentina* 126 C2
Tunuyán →, *Argentina* 126 C2
Tuo Jiang →, *China* 58 C5
Tuolumne, *U.S.A.* 116 H6
Tuolumne →, *U.S.A.* 116 H5
Tūp Āghāj, *Iran* 70 B5
Tupã, *Brazil* 127 A5
Tupelo, *U.S.A.* 109 H1
Tupik, *Russia* 46 E7
Tupinambaranas, *Brazil* 124 D7
Tupiza, *Bolivia* 126 A2
Tupižnica, *Serbia, Yug.* 40 C6
Tupman, *U.S.A.* 117 K7
Tupper, *Canada* 104 B4
Tupper Lake, *U.S.A.* 111 B10
Tupungato, Cerro, *S. Amer.* 126 C2
Tuquan, *China* 57 B11
Túquerres, *Colombia* 124 C3
Tura, *Russia* 51 C11
Turabah, *Si. Arabia* 70 D4
Turabah, *Si. Arabia* 80 C5
Tūrān, *Iran* 71 C8
Turan, *Russia* 51 D10
Ţurayf, *Si. Arabia* 70 D3
Turbacz, *Poland* 45 J7
Turbe, *Bos.-H.* 42 F2
Turčianske Teplice, *Slovak Rep.* 27 C11
Turcoaia, *Romania* 43 E13
Turda, *Romania* 43 D8
Turek, *Poland* 45 F5
Turen, *Venezuela* 124 B5
Turfan = Turpan, *China* 60 B3
Turfan Depression = Turpan Hami, *China* 52 E12
Turgeon →, *Canada* 102 C4
Tŭrgovishte, *Bulgaria* 41 C10
Turgut, *Turkey* 39 D10
Turgutlu, *Turkey* 39 C9
Turgwe →, *Zimbabwe* 89 C5
Turhal, *Turkey* 72 B7
Turia →, *Spain* 33 F4
Turiaçu, *Brazil* 125 D9
Turiaçu →, *Brazil* 125 D9
Turiec →, *Slovak Rep.* 27 B11
Turin = Torino, *Italy* 28 C4
Turkana, L., *Africa* 86 B4
Türkeli, *Turkey* 41 F11
Turkestan = Türkistan, *Kazakstan* 50 E7
Túrkeve, *Hungary* 42 C5
Turkey ■, *Eurasia* 72 C7
Turkey Creek, *Australia* 92 C4
Turki, *Russia* 48 D6
Türkistan, *Kazakstan* 50 E7
Türkmenbashi, *Turkmenistan* 50 E6
Turkmenistan ■, *Asia* 50 F6
Türkmenli, *Turkey* 39 B8
Türkoğlu, *Turkey* 72 D7
Turks & Caicos Is. ■, *W. Indies* 121 B5
Turks Island Passage, *W. Indies* 121 B5
Turku, *Finland* 9 F20
Turkwel →, *Kenya* 86 B4
Turlock, *U.S.A.* 116 H6
Turnagain →, *Canada* 104 B3
Turnagain, C., *N.Z.* 91 J6
Turneffe Is., *Belize* 119 D7
Turner, *U.S.A.* 114 B9
Turner Pt., *Australia* 94 A1
Turner Valley, *Canada* 104 C6
Turners Falls, *U.S.A.* 111 D12
Turnhout, *Belgium* 17 C4
Türnitz, *Austria* 26 D8
Turnor L., *Canada* 105 B7
Turnov, *Czech Rep.* 26 A8
Tŭrnovo = Veliko Tŭrnovo, *Bulgaria* 41 C9
Turnu Măgurele, *Romania* 43 G9
Turnu Roşu, P., *Romania* 43 E9
Turobin, *Poland* 45 H9
Turpan, *China* 60 B3
Turpan Hami, *China* 52 E12
Turrës, Kalaja e, *Albania* 40 E3
Turriff, *U.K.* 14 D6
Tursāq, *Iraq* 70 C5
Tursi, *Italy* 31 B9
Turtle Head I., *Australia* 94 A3
Turtle Is., *S. Leone* 82 D2
Turtle L., *Canada* 105 C7
Turtle Lake, *U.S.A.* 112 B4
Turtleford, *Canada* 105 C7
Turukhansk, *Russia* 51 C9
Turzovka, *Slovak Rep.* 27 B11
Tuscaloosa, *U.S.A.* 109 J2
Tuscánia, *Italy* 29 F8
Tuscany = Toscana □, *Italy* 28 E8
Tuscarawas →, *U.S.A.* 110 F3
Tuscarora Mt., *U.S.A.* 110 F7
Tuscola, *Ill., U.S.A.* 108 F1
Tuscola, *Tex., U.S.A.* 113 J5
Tuscumbia, *U.S.A.* 109 H2
Tuskegee, *U.S.A.* 109 J3
Tustin, *U.S.A.* 117 M9
Tuszyn, *Poland* 45 G6
Tutak, *Turkey* 73 C10
Tutayev, *Russia* 46 D10
Tuticorin, *India* 66 Q11
Tutin, *Serbia, Yug.* 40 D4
Tutóia, *Brazil* 125 D10
Tutong, *Brunei* 62 D4
Tutova →, *Romania* 43 D12
Tutrakan, *Bulgaria* 41 B10
Tuttle Creek L., *U.S.A.* 112 F6
Tuttlingen, *Germany* 25 H4
Tutuala, *Indonesia* 63 F7
Tutuila, *Amer. Samoa* 91 B13
Tutume, *Botswana* 85 J5
Tutun, *Egypt* 80 J7
Tututepec, *Mexico* 119 D5
Tuva □, *Russia* 51 D10
Tuvalu ■, *Pac. Oc.* 96 H9
Tuxer Alpen, *Austria* 26 D4
Tuxpan, *Mexico* 119 C5
Tuxtla Gutiérrez, *Mexico* 119 D6
Tuy = Tui, *Spain* 34 C2
Tuy An, *Vietnam* 64 F7
Tuy Duc, *Vietnam* 65 F6
Tuy Hoa, *Vietnam* 64 F7
Tuy Phong, *Vietnam* 65 G7
Tuya L., *Canada* 104 B2
Tuyen Hoa, *Vietnam* 64 D6
Tuyen Quang, *Vietnam* 58 G5
Tūysarkān, *Iran* 71 C6
Tuz Gölü, *Turkey* 72 C5
Ţūz Khurmātū, *Iraq* 70 C5
Tuzi, *Montenegro, Yug.* 40 D3
Tuzla, *Bos.-H.* 42 F3
Tuzlov →, *Russia* 47 J10
Tuzluca, *Turkey* 73 B10
Tvååker, *Sweden* 11 G6
Tvardiţa, *Moldova* 43 D13
Tver, *Russia* 46 D8
Tvrdošin, *Slovak Rep.* 27 B12
Tvrdošovce, *Slovak Rep.* 27 C11
Tvŭrditsa, *Bulgaria* 41 D9
Twain, *U.S.A.* 116 E5
Twain Harte, *U.S.A.* 116 G6
Twardogóra, *Poland* 45 G4
Tweed, *Canada* 110 B7
Tweed →, *U.K.* 14 F6
Tweed Heads, *Australia* 95 D5
Tweedsmuir Prov. Park, *Canada* 104 C3
Twentynine Palms, *U.S.A.* 117 L10
Twillingate, *Canada* 103 C9
Twin Bridges, *U.S.A.* 114 D7
Twin Falls, *Canada* 103 B7
Twin Falls, *U.S.A.* 114 E6
Twin Valley, *U.S.A.* 112 B6
Twinsburg, *U.S.A.* 110 E3
Twistringen, *Germany* 24 C4
Twitchell Reservoir, *U.S.A.* 117 L6
Two Harbors, *U.S.A.* 112 B9
Two Hills, *Canada* 104 C6
Two Rivers, *U.S.A.* 108 C2
Two Rocks, *Australia* 93 F2
Twofold B., *Australia* 95 F4
Tyachiv, *Ukraine* 47 H2
Tychy, *Poland* 45 H5
Tyczyn, *Poland* 45 J9
Tykocin, *Poland* 45 E9
Tyler, *Minn., U.S.A.* 112 C6
Tyler, *Tex., U.S.A.* 113 J7
Tyligul →, *Ukraine* 47 J6
Týn nad Vltavou, *Czech Rep.* 26 B7
Tynda, *Russia* 51 D13
Tyndall, *U.S.A.* 112 D6
Tyne →, *U.K.* 12 C6
Tyne & Wear □, *U.K.* 12 B6
Týnec nad Sázavou, *Czech Rep.* 26 B7
Tynemouth, *U.K.* 12 B6
Tyre = Sūr, *Lebanon* 75 B4
Tyrifjorden, *Norway* 9 F14
Tyringe, *Sweden* 11 H7
Tyrnyauz, *Russia* 49 J6
Tyrol = Tirol □, *Austria* 26 D3
Tyrone, *U.S.A.* 110 F6
Tyrone □, *U.K.* 15 B4
Tyrrell →, *Australia* 95 F3
Tyrrell, L., *Australia* 95 F3
Tyrrell L., *Canada* 105 A7
Tyrrhenian Sea, *Medit. S.* 6 G8
Tysfjorden, *Norway* 8 B17
Tystberga, *Sweden* 11 F11
Tytuvėnai, *Lithuania* 44 C10
Tyub Karagan, Mys, *Kazakstan* 49 H10
Tyuleni, Ostrova, *Kazakstan* 49 H10
Tyuleniy, *Russia* 49 H8
Tyuleniy, Mys, *Azerbaijan* 49 K10
Tyumen, *Russia* 50 D7
Tywi →, *U.K.* 13 F3
Tywyn, *U.K.* 13 E3
Tzaneen, *S. Africa* 89 C5
Tzermiádhes, *Greece* 36 D7
Tzoumérka, Óros, *Greece* 38 B3
Tzukong = Zigong, *China* 58 C5

U

U Taphao, *Thailand* 64 F3
U.S.A. = United States of America ■, *N. Amer.* 106 C7
Uatumã →, *Brazil* 124 D7
Uaupés, *Brazil* 124 D5
Uaupés →, *Brazil* 124 C5
Uaxactún, *Guatemala* 120 C2
Ub, *Serbia, Yug.* 40 B4
Ubá, *Brazil* 127 A7
Uba, *Nigeria* 83 C7
Ubaitaba, *Brazil* 125 F11
Ubangi = Oubangi →, *Dem. Rep. of the Congo* 84 E3
Ubauro, *Pakistan* 68 E3
Ubaye →, *France* 21 D10
Ubayyiḍ, W. al →, *Iraq* 70 C4
Ube, *Japan* 55 H5
Úbeda, *Spain* 35 G7
Uberaba, *Brazil* 125 G9
Uberlândia, *Brazil* 125 G9
Überlingen, *Germany* 25 H5
Ubiaja, *Nigeria* 83 D6
Ubolratna Res., *Thailand* 64 D4
Ubombo, *S. Africa* 89 D5
Ubon Ratchathani, *Thailand* 64 E5
Ubondo, *Dem. Rep. of the Congo* 86 C2
Ubort →, *Belarus* 47 F5
Ubrique, *Spain* 35 J5
Ubundu, *Dem. Rep. of the Congo* 86 C2
Ucayali →, *Peru* 122 D3
Uchab, *Namibia* 88 B2
Uchiura-Wan, *Japan* 54 C10
Uchquduq, *Uzbekistan* 50 E7
Uchte, *Germany* 24 C4
Uchur →, *Russia* 51 D14
Uckermark, *Germany* 24 B9
Ucluelet, *Canada* 104 D3
Uda →, *Russia* 51 D14
Udagamandalam, *India* 66 P10
Udainagar, *India* 68 H7
Udaipur, *India* 68 G5
Udaipur Garhi, *Nepal* 69 F12
Udala, *India* 69 J12
Udbina, *Croatia* 29 D12
Uddeholm, *Sweden* 10 D7
Uddevalla, *Sweden* 11 F5
Uddjaur, *Sweden* 8 D17
Uden, *Neths.* 17 C5
Udgir, *India* 66 K10
Udhampur, *India* 69 C6
Ụdi, *Nigeria* 83 D6
Údine, *Italy* 29 B10
Udmurtia □, *Russia* 50 D6
Udon Thani, *Thailand* 64 D4
Udupi, *India* 66 N9
Udvoy Balkan, *Bulgaria* 41 D10
Udzungwa Range, *Tanzania* 87 D4
Ueckermünde, *Germany* 24 B10
Ueda, *Japan* 55 F9
Uedineniya, Os., *Russia* 4 B12
Uele →, *Dem. Rep. of the Congo* 84 D4
Uelen, *Russia* 51 C19
Uelzen, *Germany* 24 C6
Uetersen, *Germany* 24 B5
Uetze, *Germany* 24 C6
Ufa, *Russia* 50 D6
Uffenheim, *Germany* 25 F6
Ugab →, *Namibia* 88 C1
Ugalla →, *Tanzania* 86 D3
Uganda ■, *Africa* 86 B3
Ugento, *Italy* 31 C11
Ugep, *Nigeria* 83 D6
Ughelli, *Nigeria* 83 D6
Ugie, *S. Africa* 89 E4
Ugíjar, *Spain* 35 J7
Ugine, *France* 21 C10
Uglegorsk, *Russia* 51 E15
Uglich, *Russia* 46 D10
Ugljan, *Croatia* 29 D12
Ugljane, *Croatia* 29 E13
Ugra →, *Russia* 46 E9
Ugŭrchin, *Bulgaria* 41 C8
Uh →, *Slovak Rep.* 27 C15
Uherské Hradiště, *Czech Rep.* 27 B10
Uherský Brod, *Czech Rep.* 27 B10
Úhlava →, *Czech Rep.* 26 B6
Uhlenhorst, *Namibia* 88 C2
Uhrichsville, *U.S.A.* 110 F3
Uibhist a Deas = South Uist, *U.K.* 14 D1
Uibhist a Tuath = North Uist, *U.K.* 14 D1
Uig, *U.K.* 14 D2
Uíge, *Angola* 84 F2
Uijŏngbu, *S. Korea* 57 F14
Ŭiju, *N. Korea* 57 D13
Uinta Mts., *U.S.A.* 114 F8
Uis, *Namibia* 88 B2
Uitenhage, *S. Africa* 88 E4
Uithuizen, *Neths.* 17 A6
Ujazd, *Poland* 45 H5
Újfehértó, *Hungary* 42 C6
Ujh →, *India* 68 C6
Ujhani, *India* 69 F8
Uji-guntō, *Japan* 55 J4
Ujjain, *India* 68 H6
Ujście, *Poland* 45 E3
Újszász, *Hungary* 42 C5
Ujung Pandang, *Indonesia* 63 F5
Uka, *Russia* 51 D17
Ukara I., *Tanzania* 86 C3
Uke-Shima, *Japan* 55 K4
Ukerewe I., *Tanzania* 86 C3
Ukholovo, *Russia* 48 D5
Ukhrul, *India* 67 G19
Ukhta, *Russia* 50 C6
Ukiah, *U.S.A.* 116 F3
Ukki Fort, *India* 69 C7
Ukmergė, *Lithuania* 9 J21
Ukraine ■, *Europe* 47 H7
Ukwi, *Botswana* 88 C3
Ulaan-Uul, *Mongolia* 56 B6
Ulaanbaatar, *Mongolia* 51 E11
Ulaangom, *Mongolia* 60 A4
Ulaanjirem, *Mongolia* 56 B3
Ulamba, *Dem. Rep. of the Congo* 87 D1
Ulan Bator = Ulaanbaatar, *Mongolia* 51 E11
Ulan Erge, *Russia* 49 G7
Ulan Khol, *Russia* 49 H8
Ulan Ude, *Russia* 51 D11
Ulanów, *Poland* 45 H9
Ulaş, *Sivas, Turkey* 72 C7
Ulaş, *Tekirdağ, Turkey* 41 E11
Ulaya, *Morogoro, Tanzania* 86 D4
Ulaya, *Tabora, Tanzania* 86 C3
Ulcinj, *Montenegro, Yug.* 40 E3
Ulco, *S. Africa* 88 D3
Ulefoss, *Norway* 9 G13
Ulëza, *Albania* 40 E3
Ulfborg, *Denmark* 11 H2
Ulhasnagar, *India* 66 K8
Uliastay, *Mongolia* 60 B4
Ulithi Atoll, *Pac. Oc.* 63 B9
Uljma, *Serbia, Yug.* 42 E6
Ulla →, *Spain* 34 C2
Ulladulla, *Australia* 95 F5
Ullapool, *U.K.* 14 D3
Ullared, *Sweden* 11 G6
Ulldecona, *Spain* 32 E5
Ullswater, *U.K.* 12 C5
Ullŭng-do, *S. Korea* 55 F5
Ulm, *Germany* 25 G5
Ulmarra, *Australia* 95 D5
Ulmeni, *Buzău, Romania* 43 E11
Ulmeni, *Maramureş, Romania* 43 C8
Ulonguè, *Mozam.* 87 E3
Ulricehamn, *Sweden* 11 G7
Ulrika, *Sweden* 11 F9
Ulsan, *S. Korea* 57 G15
Ulsta, *U.K.* 14 A7
Ulster □, *U.K.* 15 B5
Ulstrem, *Bulgaria* 41 D10
Ulubat Gölü, *Turkey* 41 F12
Ulubey, *Turkey* 39 C11
Uluborlu, *Turkey* 39 C12
Uluçinar, *Turkey* 72 D6
Uludağ, *Turkey* 41 F13
Uludere, *Turkey* 73 D10
Uluguru Mts., *Tanzania* 86 D4
Ulukişla, *Turkey* 72 D6
Ulungur He →, *China* 60 B3
Uluru = Ayers Rock, *Australia* 93 E5
Uluru Nat. Park, *Australia* 93 E5
Ulutau, *Kazakstan* 50 E7
Ulva, *U.K.* 14 E2
Ulverston, *U.K.* 12 C4
Ulverstone, *Australia* 94 G4
Ulya, *Russia* 51 D15
Ulyanovsk = Simbirsk, *Russia* 48 C9
Ulyasutay = Uliastay, *Mongolia* 60 B4
Ulysses, *U.S.A.* 113 G4
Umag, *Croatia* 29 C10
Umala, *Bolivia* 124 G5
Uman, *Ukraine* 47 H6
Umaria, *India* 67 H12
Umarkot, *Pakistan* 66 G6
Umarpada, *India* 68 J5
Umatilla, *U.S.A.* 114 D4
Umbagog L., *U.S.A.* 111 B13
Umbakumba, *Australia* 94 A2
Umbértide, *Italy* 29 E9
Umbrella Mts., *N.Z.* 91 L2
Umbria □, *Italy* 29 F9
Ume älv →, *Sweden* 8 E19
Umeå, *Sweden* 8 E19
Umera, *Indonesia* 63 E7
Umfuli →, *Zimbabwe* 87 F2
Umgusa, *Zimbabwe* 87 F2
Umim Urūmah, *Si. Arabia* 80 B4

Vânju Mare

Umka, *Serbia, Yug.* 40 B4
Umkomaas, *S. Africa* 89 E5
Umlazi, *S. Africa* 85 L6
Umm ad Daraj, J., *Jordan* 75 C4
Umm al Qaywayn, *U.A.E.* 71 E7
Umm al Qittayn, *Jordan* 75 C5
Umm Arda, *Sudan* 81 D3
Umm Bāb, *Qatar* 71 E6
Umm Badr, *Sudan* 81 E2
Umm Baiyud, *Sudan* 81 E3
Umm Bel, *Sudan* 81 E2
Umm Birkah, *Si. Arabia* 80 B4
Umm Boim, *Sudan* 81 E2
Umm Dam, *Sudan* 81 E3
Umm Debi, *Sudan* 81 E3
Umm Dubban, *Sudan* 81 D3
Umm el Fahm, *Israel* 75 C4
Umm Gafala, *Sudan* 81 E2
Umm Gimala, *Sudan* 81 E2
Umm Inderaba, *Sudan* 80 D3
Umm Keddada, *Sudan* 81 E2
Umm Koweika, *Sudan* 81 E3
Umm Lajj, *Si. Arabia* 70 E3
Umm Merwa, *Sudan* 80 D3
Umm Qantur, *Sudan* 81 E3
Umm Qurein, *Sudan* 81 F2
Umm Ruwaba, *Sudan* 81 E3
Umm Saiyala, *Sudan* 81 E3
Umm Shanqa, *Sudan* 81 E2
Umm Shutur, *Sudan* 81 F3
Umm Sidr, *Sudan* 81 E2
Umm Zehetir, *Egypt* 80 J8
Umnak I., *U.S.A.* 100 C3
Umniati →, *Zimbabwe* 87 F2
Umpqua →, *U.S.A.* 114 E1
Umreth, *India* 68 H5
Umtata, *S. Africa* 89 E4
Umuahia, *Nigeria* 83 D6
Umuarama, *Brazil* 127 A5
Umurbey, *Turkey* 41 F10
Umvukwe Ra., *Zimbabwe* 87 F3
Umzimvubu, *S. Africa* 89 E4
Umzingwane →, *Zimbabwe* 87 G2
Umzinto, *S. Africa* 89 E5
Una, *India* 68 J4
Una →, *Bos.-H.* 29 D13
Unac →, *Bos.-H.* 29 D13
Unadilla, *U.S.A.* 111 D9
Unalakleet, *U.S.A.* 100 B3
Unalaska, *U.S.A.* 100 C3
Unalaska I., *U.S.A.* 100 C3
'Unayzah, *Si. Arabia* 70 E4
'Unāzah, J., *Asia* 70 C3
Uncastillo, *Spain* 32 C3
Uncía, *Bolivia* 124 G5
Uncompahgre Peak, *U.S.A.* 115 G10
Uncompahgre Plateau, *U.S.A.* 115 G9
Unden, *Sweden* 11 F8
Underbool, *Australia* 95 F3
Undersaker, *Sweden* 10 A7
Unecha, *Russia* 47 F7
Ungarie, *Australia* 95 E4
Ungarra, *Australia* 95 E2
Ungava, Pén. d', *Canada* 101 C12
Ungava B., *Canada* 101 C13
Ungeny = Ungheni, *Moldova* 43 C12
Unggi, *N. Korea* 57 C16
Ungheni, *Moldova* 43 C12
Unguala →, *Ethiopia* 81 F5
Ungwatiri, *Sudan* 81 D4
Uni, *Russia* 48 B10
União da Vitória, *Brazil* 127 B5
Uničov, *Czech Rep.* 27 B10
Uniejów, *Poland* 45 G5
Unije, *Croatia* 29 D11
Unimak I., *U.S.A.* 100 C3
Union, *Miss., U.S.A.* 113 J10
Union, *Mo., U.S.A.* 112 F9
Union, *S.C., U.S.A.* 109 H5
Union City, *Calif., U.S.A.* 116 H4
Union City, *N.J., U.S.A.* 111 F10
Union City, *Pa., U.S.A.* 110 E5
Union City, *Tenn., U.S.A.* 113 G10
Union Gap, *U.S.A.* 114 C3
Union Springs, *U.S.A.* 109 J3
Uniondale, *S. Africa* 88 E3
Uniontown, *U.S.A.* 108 F6
Unionville, *U.S.A.* 112 E8
Unirea, *Romania* 43 F12
United Arab Emirates ■, *Asia* 71 F7
United Kingdom ■, *Europe* 7 E5
United States of America ■, *N. Amer.* 106 C7
Unity, *Canada* 105 C7
Universales, Mtes., *Spain* 32 E3
University Park, *U.S.A.* 115 K10
Unjha, *India* 68 H5
Unna, *Germany* 24 D3
Unnao, *India* 69 F9
Uno, Ilha, *Guinea-Biss.* 82 C1
Unst, *U.K.* 14 A8
Unstrut →, *Germany* 24 D7
Unterfranken □, *Germany* 25 F5
Unterschleissheim, *Germany* 25 G7
Unuk →, *Canada* 104 B2
Ünye, *Turkey* 72 B7
Unzha, *Russia* 48 A7
Unzha →, *Russia* 48 B6
Uozu, *Japan* 55 F8
Upata, *Venezuela* 124 B6
Upemba, L., *Dem. Rep. of the Congo* 87 D2
Upernavik, *Greenland* 4 B5
Upington, *S. Africa* 88 D3
Upleta, *India* 68 J4
Upolu, *W. Samoa* 91 A13
Upper □, *Ghana* 83 C4
Upper Alkali L., *U.S.A.* 114 F3
Upper Arrow L., *Canada* 104 C5
Upper Austria = Oberösterreich □, *Austria* 26 C7
Upper Foster L., *Canada* 105 B7
Upper Hutt, *N.Z.* 91 J5
Upper Klamath L., *U.S.A.* 114 E3
Upper Lake, *U.S.A.* 116 F4
Upper Musquodoboit, *Canada* 103 C7
Upper Red L., *U.S.A.* 112 A7
Upper Sandusky, *U.S.A.* 108 E4
Upper Volta = Burkina Faso ■, *Africa* 82 C4
Upphärad, *Sweden* 11 F6
Uppland, *Sweden* 10 E11
Upplands-Väsby, *Sweden* 10 E11
Uppsala, *Sweden* 10 E11
Uppsala län □, *Sweden* 10 D11
Upshi, *India* 69 C7
Upstart, C., *Australia* 94 B4
Upton, *U.S.A.* 112 C2
Ur, *Iraq* 70 D5
Urad Qianqi, *China* 56 D5
Urakawa, *Japan* 54 C11
Ural = Zhayyq →, *Kazakstan* 50 E6
Ural, *Australia* 95 E4
Ural Mts. = Uralskie Gory, *Eurasia* 50 D6
Uralla, *Australia* 95 E5
Uralsk = Oral, *Kazakstan* 48 E10
Uralskie Gory, *Eurasia* 50 D6
Urambo, *Tanzania* 86 D3
Urana, *Australia* 95 F4
Urandangi, *Australia* 94 C2
Uranium City, *Canada* 105 B7
Uraricoera →, *Brazil* 124 C6
Urawa, *Japan* 55 G9
Uray, *Russia* 50 C7
'Uray'irah, *Si. Arabia* 71 E6
Urbana, *Ill., U.S.A.* 108 E1
Urbana, *Ohio, U.S.A.* 108 E4
Urbánia, *Italy* 29 E9
Urbel →, *Spain* 34 C7
Urbino, *Italy* 29 E9
Urbión, Picos de, *Spain* 32 C2
Urcos, *Peru* 124 F4
Urdinarrain, *Argentina* 126 C4
Urdos, *France* 20 F3
Urdzhar, *Kazakstan* 50 E9
Ure →, *U.K.* 12 C6
Uren, *Russia* 48 B7
Ures, *Mexico* 118 B2
Urfa = Sanliurfa, *Turkey* 70 B3
Urganch, *Uzbekistan* 50 E7
Urgench = Urganch, *Uzbekistan* 50 E7
Ürgüp, *Turkey* 70 B2
Uri, *India* 69 B6
Uri □, *Switz.* 25 J4
Uribia, *Colombia* 124 A4
Uricani, *Romania* 42 E8
Uriondo, *Bolivia* 126 A3
Urique, *Mexico* 118 B3
Urique →, *Mexico* 118 B3
Urk, *Neths.* 17 B5
Urla, *Turkey* 39 C8
Urlați, *Romania* 43 F11
Urmia = Orūmīyeh, *Iran* 70 B5
Urmia, L. = Orūmīyeh, Daryācheh-ye, *Iran* 70 B5
Uroševac, *Kosovo, Yug.* 40 D5
Urshult, *Sweden* 11 H8
Uruaçu, *Brazil* 125 F9
Uruapan, *Mexico* 118 D4
Urubamba →, *Peru* 124 F4
Uruçara, *Brazil* 124 D7
Uruçuí, *Brazil* 125 E10
Uruguai →, *Brazil* 127 B5
Uruguaiana, *Brazil* 126 B4
Uruguay ■, *S. Amer.* 126 C4
Uruguay →, *S. Amer.* 126 C4
Urumchi = Ürümqi, *China* 50 E9
Ürümqi, *China* 50 E9
Urup →, *Russia* 49 H5
Urup, Ostrov, *Russia* 51 E16
Uryupinsk, *Russia* 48 E5
Urzhum, *Russia* 48 B9
Urziceni, *Romania* 43 F11
Usa →, *Russia* 50 C6
Uşak, *Turkey* 39 C11
Uşak □, *Turkey* 39 C11
Usakos, *Namibia* 88 C2
Ušće, *Serbia, Yug.* 40 C4
Usedom, *Germany* 24 B10
Useless Loop, *Australia* 93 E1
'Usfān, *Si. Arabia* 80 C4
Ush-Tobe, *Kazakstan* 50 E8
Ushakova, Ostrov, *Russia* 4 A12
Ushant = Ouessant, Î. d', *France* 18 D1
Ushashi, *Tanzania* 86 C3
Ushat, *Sudan* 81 F2
'Ushayrah, *Si. Arabia* 80 C5
Ushibuka, *Japan* 55 H5
Ushuaia, *Argentina* 128 G3
Ushumun, *Russia* 51 D13
Usk, *Canada* 104 C3
Usk →, *U.K.* 13 F5
Uska, *India* 69 F10
Üsküdar, *Turkey* 41 F13
Uslar, *Germany* 24 D5
Usman, *Russia* 47 F10
Usoke, *Tanzania* 86 D3
Usolye Sibirskoye, *Russia* 51 D11
Usoro, *Nigeria* 83 D6
Uspallata, P. de, *Argentina* 126 C2
Uspenskiy, *Kazakstan* 50 E8
Ussel, *France* 20 C6
Usson-du-Poitou, *France* 20 B4
Ussuri →, *Asia* 54 A7
Ussuriysk, *Russia* 51 E14
Ussurka, *Russia* 54 B6
Ust-Aldan = Batamay, *Russia* 51 C13
Ust-Amginskoye = Khandyga, *Russia* 51 C14
Ust-Bolsheretsk, *Russia* 51 D16
Ust-Buzulukskaya, *Russia* 48 E6
Ust-Chaun, *Russia* 51 C18
Ust-Donetskiy, *Russia* 49 G5
Ust-Ilimpeya = Yukta, *Russia* 51 C11
Ust-Ilimsk, *Russia* 51 D11
Ust-Ishim, *Russia* 50 D8
Ust-Kamchatsk, *Russia* 51 D17
Ust-Kamenogorsk = Öskemen, *Kazakstan* 50 E9
Ust-Khayryuzovo, *Russia* 51 D16
Ust-Kut, *Russia* 51 D11
Ust-Kuyga, *Russia* 51 B14
Ust-Labinsk, *Russia* 49 H4
Ust-Luga, *Russia* 46 C5
Ust-Maya, *Russia* 51 C14
Ust-Mil, *Russia* 51 D14
Ust-Nera, *Russia* 51 C15
Ust-Nyukzha, *Russia* 51 D13
Ust-Olenek, *Russia* 51 B12
Ust-Omchug, *Russia* 51 C15
Ust-Port, *Russia* 50 C9
Ust-Tsilma, *Russia* 50 C6
Ust Urt = Ustyurt Plateau, *Asia* 50 E6
Ustaritz, *France* 20 E2
Uster, *Switz.* 25 H4
Ústí nad Labem, *Czech Rep.* 26 A7
Ústí nad Orlicí, *Czech Rep.* 27 B9
Ustica, *Italy* 30 D6
Ustinov = Izhevsk, *Russia* 50 D6
Ustka, *Poland* 44 D3
Ustroń, *Poland* 45 J5
Ustrzyki Dolne, *Poland* 45 J9
Ustyurt Plateau, *Asia* 50 E6
Ustyuzhna, *Russia* 46 C9
Usu, *China* 60 B3
Usuki, *Japan* 55 H5
Usulután, *El Salv.* 120 D2
Usumacinta →, *Mexico* 119 D6
Usumbura = Bujumbura, *Burundi* 86 C2
Usure, *Tanzania* 86 C3
Usutuo →, *Mozam.* 89 D5
Uta, *Indonesia* 63 E9
Utah □, *U.S.A.* 114 G8
Utah L., *U.S.A.* 114 F8
Utansjö, *Sweden* 10 B11
Utarni, *India* 68 F4
Utatlan, *Guatemala* 120 C1
Ute Creek →, *U.S.A.* 113 H3
Utebo, *Spain* 32 D3
Utena, *Lithuania* 9 J21
Utete, *Tanzania* 86 D4
Uthai Thani, *Thailand* 64 E3
Uthal, *Pakistan* 68 G2
Utiariti, *Brazil* 124 F7
Utica, *N.Y., U.S.A.* 111 C9
Utica, *Ohio, U.S.A.* 110 F2
Utiel, *Spain* 33 F3
Utikuma L., *Canada* 104 B5
Utö, *Sweden* 10 F12
Utopia, *Australia* 94 C1
Utraula, *India* 69 F10
Utrecht, *Neths.* 17 B5
Utrecht, *S. Africa* 89 D5
Utrecht □, *Neths.* 17 B5
Utrera, *Spain* 35 H5
Utsjoki, *Finland* 8 B22
Utsunomiya, *Japan* 55 F9
Uttar Pradesh □, *India* 69 F9
Uttaradit, *Thailand* 64 D3
Uttoxeter, *U.K.* 12 E6
Uummannarsuaq = Nunap Isua, *Greenland* 4 D5
Uusikaarlepyy, *Finland* 8 E20
Uusikaupunki, *Finland* 9 F19
Uva, *Russia* 48 B11
Uvac →, *Serbia, Yug.* 40 C3
Uvalde, *U.S.A.* 113 L5
Uvarovo, *Russia* 48 E6
Uvat, *Russia* 50 D7
Uvinza, *Tanzania* 86 D3
Uvira, *Dem. Rep. of the Congo* 86 C2
Uvs Nuur, *Mongolia* 60 A4
'Uwairidh, Harrat al, *Si. Arabia* 70 E3
Uwajima, *Japan* 55 H6
Uweinat, Jebel, *Sudan* 80 C1
Uxbridge, *Canada* 110 B5
Uxin Qi, *China* 56 E5
Uxmal, *Mexico* 119 C7
Üydzin, *Mongolia* 56 B4
Uyo, *Nigeria* 83 D6
Üyüklü Tepe, *Turkey* 39 D9
Uyûn Mûsa, *Egypt* 75 F1
Uyuni, *Bolivia* 124 H5
Uzbekistan ■, *Asia* 50 E7
Uzen, Bolshoi →, *Kazakstan* 49 F9
Uzen, Mal →, *Kazakstan* 49 F9
Uzerche, *France* 20 C5
Uzès, *France* 21 D8
Uzh →, *Ukraine* 47 G6
Uzhgorod = Uzhhorod, *Ukraine* 47 H2
Uzhhorod, *Ukraine* 47 H2
Užice, *Serbia, Yug.* 40 C3
Uzlovaya, *Russia* 46 F10
Üzümlü, *Turkey* 39 E11
Uzunköprü, *Turkey* 41 E10
Uzunkuyu, *Turkey* 39 C8

V

Vaal →, *S. Africa* 88 D3
Vaal Dam, *S. Africa* 89 D4
Vaalwater, *S. Africa* 89 C4
Vaasa, *Finland* 8 E19
Vabre, *France* 20 E6
Vác, *Hungary* 42 C4
Vacaria, *Brazil* 127 B5
Vacaville, *U.S.A.* 116 G5
Vaccarès, Étang de, *France* 21 E8
Vach = Vakh →, *Russia* 50 C8
Vache, Î. à, *Haiti* 121 C5
Väckelsång, *Sweden* 11 H8
Väddö, *Sweden* 10 D12
Väderstad, *Sweden* 11 F8
Vadnagar, *India* 68 H5
Vado Lígure, *Italy* 28 D5
Vadodara, *India* 68 H5
Vadsø, *Norway* 8 A23
Vadstena, *Sweden* 11 F8
Vaduz, *Liech.* 25 H5
Værøy, *Norway* 8 C15
Vágar, *Færoe Is.* 8 E9
Vaggeryd, *Sweden* 11 G8
Vagney, *France* 19 D13
Vagnhärad, *Sweden* 11 F11
Vagos, *Portugal* 34 E2
Vågsfjorden, *Norway* 8 B17
Váh →, *Slovak Rep.* 27 D11
Vahsel B., *Antarctica* 5 D1
Váï, *Greece* 36 D8
Vaigach, *Russia* 50 B6
Vaiges, *France* 18 D6
Vaihingen, *Germany* 25 G4
Vail, *U.S.A.* 106 C5
Vailly-sur-Aisne, *France* 19 C10
Vaisali →, *India* 69 F8
Vaison-la-Romaine, *France* 21 D9
Vakarel, *Bulgaria* 40 D7
Vakfikebir, *Turkey* 73 B8
Vakh →, *Russia* 50 C8
Vakhtan, *Russia* 48 B8
Vál, *Hungary* 42 C3
Val-de-Marne □, *France* 19 D9
Val-d'Isère, *France* 21 C10
Val-d'Oise □, *France* 19 C9
Val-d'Or, *Canada* 102 C4
Val Marie, *Canada* 105 D7
Valaam, *Russia* 46 B6
Valadares, *Portugal* 34 D2
Valahia, *Romania* 43 F9
Valais □, *Switz.* 25 J3
Valais, Alpes du, *Switz.* 25 J3
Valandovo, *Macedonia* 40 E6
Valašské Meziříčí, *Czech Rep.* 27 B10
Valáxa, *Greece* 38 C6
Vålberg, *Sweden* 10 E7
Valbo, *Sweden* 10 D10
Valbondione, *Italy* 28 B7
Vălcani, *Romania* 42 D5
Vâlcea □, *Romania* 43 F9
Valcheta, *Argentina* 128 E3
Valdagno, *Italy* 29 C8
Valdahon, *France* 19 E13
Valday, *Russia* 46 D7
Valdayskaya Vozvyshennost, *Russia* 46 D7
Valdeazogues →, *Spain* 35 G6
Valdecañas, Embalse de, *Spain* 34 F5
Valdemarsvik, *Sweden* 11 F10
Valdemoro, *Spain* 34 E7
Valdepeñas, *Spain* 35 G7
Valderaduey →, *Spain* 34 D5
Valdérice, *Italy* 30 D5
Valderrobres, *Spain* 32 E5
Valdés, Pen., *Argentina* 122 H4
Valdez, *U.S.A.* 100 B5
Valdivia, *Chile* 128 D2
Valdobbiádene, *Italy* 29 C8
Valdosta, *U.S.A.* 109 K4
Valdoviño, *Spain* 34 B2
Valdres, *Norway* 9 F13
Vale, *Georgia* 49 K6
Vale, *U.S.A.* 114 E5
Vale of Glamorgan □, *U.K.* 13 F4
Valea lui Mihai, *Romania* 42 C7
Valea Mărului, *Romania* 43 E12
Valemount, *Canada* 104 C5
Valença, *Brazil* 125 F11
Valença, *Portugal* 34 C2
Valença do Piauí, *Brazil* 125 E10
Valençay, *France* 19 E8
Valence = Valence d'Agen, *France* 20 D4
Valence, *France* 21 D8
Valence d'Agen, *France* 20 D4
Valencia, *Spain* 33 F4
Valencia, *U.S.A.* 115 J10
Valencia, *Venezuela* 124 A5
Valencia □, *Spain* 33 F4
Valencia, G. de, *Spain* 33 F5
Valencia de Alcántara, *Spain* 35 F3
Valencia de Don Juan, *Spain* 34 C5
Valencia I., *Ireland* 15 E1
Valenciennes, *France* 19 B10
Văleni, *Romania* 43 F9
Vălenii de Munte, *Romania* 43 E11
Valensole, *France* 21 E9
Valentigney, *France* 19 E13
Valentim, Sa. do, *Brazil* 125 E10
Valentin, *Russia* 54 C7
Valentine, *U.S.A.* 113 K2
Valenza, *Italy* 28 C5
Valera, *Venezuela* 124 B4
Valga, *Estonia* 9 H22
Valguarnera Caropepe, *Italy* 31 E7
Valier, *U.S.A.* 114 B7
Valinco, G. de, *France* 21 G12
Valjevo, *Serbia, Yug.* 40 B3
Valka, *Latvia* 9 H21
Valkeakoski, *Finland* 9 F20
Valkenswaard, *Neths.* 17 C5
Vall de Uxó = La Vall d'Uixó, *Spain* 32 F4
Valla, *Sweden* 10 E10
Valladolid, *Mexico* 119 C7
Valladolid, *Spain* 34 D6
Valladolid □, *Spain* 34 D6
Vallata, *Italy* 31 A8
Valldemossa, *Spain* 37 B9
Valle d'Aosta □, *Italy* 28 C4
Valle de Arán, *Spain* 32 C5
Valle de la Pascua, *Venezuela* 124 B5
Valle de las Palmas, *Mexico* 117 N10
Valle de Santiago, *Mexico* 118 C4
Valle de Suchil, *Mexico* 118 C4
Valle de Zaragoza, *Mexico* 118 B3
Valle Fértil, Sierra del, *Argentina* 126 C2
Valle Hermoso, *Mexico* 119 B5
Valledupar, *Colombia* 124 A4
Vallehermoso, *Canary Is.* 37 F2
Vallejo, *U.S.A.* 116 G4
Vallenar, *Chile* 126 B1
Vallentuna, *Sweden* 10 E12
Valleraugue, *France* 20 D7
Vallet, *France* 18 E5
Valletta, *Malta* 36 D2
Valley Center, *U.S.A.* 117 M9
Valley City, *U.S.A.* 112 B6
Valley Falls, *Oreg., U.S.A.* 114 E3
Valley Falls, *R.I., U.S.A.* 111 E13
Valley Springs, *U.S.A.* 116 G6
Valley View, *U.S.A.* 111 F8
Valley Wells, *U.S.A.* 117 K11
Valleyview, *Canada* 104 B5
Valli di Comácchio, *Italy* 29 D9
Vallimanca, Arroyo, *Argentina* 126 D4
Vallo della Lucánia, *Italy* 31 B8
Vallon-Pont-d'Arc, *France* 21 D8
Vallorbe, *Switz.* 25 J2
Valls, *Spain* 32 D6
Valmaseda = Balmaseda, *Spain* 32 B1
Valmiera, *Latvia* 9 H21
Valnera, *Spain* 34 B7
Valognes, *France* 18 C5
Valona = Vlóra, *Albania* 40 F3
Valongo, *Portugal* 34 D2
Valozhyn, *Belarus* 46 E4
Valpaços, *Portugal* 34 D3
Valparaíso, *Chile* 126 C1
Valparaíso, *Mexico* 118 C4
Valparaiso, *U.S.A.* 108 E2
Valparaíso □, *Chile* 126 C1
Valpovo, *Croatia* 42 E3
Valréas, *France* 21 D9
Vals, *Switz.* 25 J5
Vals →, *S. Africa* 88 D4
Vals, Tanjung, *Indonesia* 63 F9
Vals-les-Bains, *France* 21 D8
Valsad, *India* 66 J8
Valtellina, *Italy* 28 B6
Valuyki, *Russia* 47 G10
Valverde, *Canary Is.* 37 G2
Valverde del Camino, *Spain* 35 H4
Valverde del Fresno, *Spain* 34 E4
Vama, *Romania* 43 C10
Vamdrup, *Denmark* 11 J3
Våmhus, *Sweden* 10 C8
Vammala, *Finland* 9 F20
Vámos, *Greece* 36 D6
Van, *Turkey* 70 B4
Van, L. = Van Gölü, *Turkey* 70 B4
Van Alstyne, *U.S.A.* 113 J6
Van Blommestein Meer, *Surinam* 125 C7
Van Buren, *Canada* 103 C6
Van Buren, *Ark., U.S.A.* 113 H7
Van Buren, *Maine, U.S.A.* 109 B11
Van Buren, *Mo., U.S.A.* 113 G9
Van Canh, *Vietnam* 64 F7
Van Diemen, C., *N. Terr., Australia* 92 B5
Van Diemen, C., *Queens., Australia* 94 B2
Van Diemen G., *Australia* 92 B5
Van Gölü, *Turkey* 70 B4
Van Horn, *U.S.A.* 113 K2
Van Ninh, *Vietnam* 64 F7
Van Rees, Pegunungan, *Indonesia* 63 E9
Van Wert, *U.S.A.* 108 E3
Van Yen, *Vietnam* 58 G5
Vanadzor, *Armenia* 49 K7
Vanavara, *Russia* 51 C11
Vancouver, *Canada* 104 D4
Vancouver, *U.S.A.* 116 E4
Vancouver, C., *Australia* 93 G2
Vancouver I., *Canada* 104 D3
Vandalia, *Ill., U.S.A.* 112 F10
Vandalia, *Mo., U.S.A.* 112 F9
Vandenburg, *U.S.A.* 117 L6
Vanderbijlpark, *S. Africa* 89 D4
Vandergrift, *U.S.A.* 110 F5
Vanderhoof, *Canada* 104 C4
Vanderkloof Dam, *S. Africa* 88 E3
Vanderlin I., *Australia* 94 B2
Vänern, *Sweden* 11 F7
Vänersborg, *Sweden* 11 F6
Vang Vieng, *Laos* 64 C4
Vanga, *Kenya* 86 C4
Vangaindrano, *Madag.* 89 C8
Vanguard, *Canada* 105 D7
Vanino, *Russia* 51 E15
Vânju Mare, *Romania* 42 F7

Vanna

Vanna, *Norway* 8 A18
Vännäs, *Sweden* 8 E18
Vannes, *France* 18 E4
Vanoise, *France* 21 C10
Vanrhynsdorp, *S. Africa* 88 E2
Vansbro, *Sweden* 10 D8
Vansittart B., *Australia* 92 B4
Vantaa, *Finland* 9 F21
Vanua Levu, *Fiji* 91 C8
Vanua Mbalavu, *Fiji* 91 C9
Vanuatu ■, *Pac. Oc.* 96 J8
Vanwyksvlei, *S. Africa* 88 E3
Vanzylsrus, *S. Africa* 88 D3
Vapnyarka, *Ukraine* 47 H5
Var □, *France* 21 E10
Var →, *France* 21 E11
Vara, *Sweden* 11 F6
Varades, *France* 18 E5
Varáita →, *Italy* 28 D4
Varallo, *Italy* 28 C5
Varanasi, *India* 69 G10
Varanger-halvøya, *Norway* 8 A23
Varangerfjorden, *Norway* 8 A23
Varano, Lago di, *Italy* 29 G12
Varaždin, *Croatia* 29 B13
Varazze, *Italy* 28 D5
Varberg, *Sweden* 11 G6
Vardar = Axiós →, *Greece* 40 F6
Varde, *Denmark* 11 J2
Varde Å →, *Denmark* 11 J2
Vardø, *Norway* 8 A24
Varel, *Germany* 24 B4
Varella, Mui, *Vietnam* 64 F7
Varėna, *Lithuania* 9 J21
Varennes-sur-Allier, *France* 19 F10
Varennes-Vauzelles, *France* 19 E10
Vareš, *Bos.-H.* 42 F3
Varese, *Italy* 28 C5
Vârfurile, *Romania* 42 D7
Vårgårda, *Sweden* 11 F6
Varginha, *Brazil* 127 A6
Vargön, *Sweden* 11 F6
Varillas, *Chile* 126 A1
Varkaus, *Finland* 9 E22
Värmdölandet, *Sweden* 10 E12
Värmeln, *Sweden* 10 E6
Värmlands Bro, *Sweden* 10 E7
Värmlands län □, *Sweden* 10 E6
Varna, *Bulgaria* 41 C11
Varna □, *Bulgaria* 41 C11
Värnamo, *Sweden* 11 G8
Varnsdorf, *Czech Rep.* 26 A7
Várpalota, *Hungary* 42 C3
Vars, *Canada* 111 A9
Vars, *France* 21 D10
Varto, *Turkey* 73 C9
Varvarin, *Serbia, Yug.* 40 C5
Varysburg, *U.S.A.* 110 D6
Varzaneh, *Iran* 71 C7
Varzi, *Italy* 28 D6
Varzo, *Italy* 28 B5
Varzy, *France* 19 E10
Vas □, *Hungary* 42 C1
Vasa Barris →, *Brazil* 125 F11
Vásárosnamény, *Hungary* 42 B7
Vascão →, *Portugal* 35 H3
Vaşcău, *Romania* 42 D7
Vascongadas = País Vasco □, *Spain* 32 C2
Vasht = Khāsh, *Iran* 66 E2
Vasilevichi, *Belarus* 47 F5
Vasilikón, *Greece* 38 C5
Vasilkov = Vasylkiv, *Ukraine* 47 G6
Vaslui, *Romania* 43 D12
Vaslui □, *Romania* 43 D12
Väsman, *Sweden* 10 D9
Vassar, *Canada* 105 D9
Vassar, *U.S.A.* 108 D4
Västerås, *Sweden* 10 E10
Västerbotten, *Sweden* 8 D18
Västerdalälven →, *Sweden* 10 D8
Västergötland, *Sweden* 11 F7
Västerhaninge, *Sweden* 10 E12
Västervik, *Sweden* 11 G10
Västmanland, *Sweden* 9 G16
Västmanlands län □, *Sweden* 10 E10
Vasto, *Italy* 29 F11
Vasvár, *Hungary* 42 C1
Vasylkiv, *Ukraine* 47 G6
Vatan, *France* 19 E8
Vatersay, *U.K.* 14 E1
Váthia, *Greece* 38 E4
Vatican City ■, *Europe* 29 G9
Vaticano, C., *Italy* 31 D8
Vatili, *Cyprus* 36 D12
Vatin, *Serbia, Yug.* 42 E6
Vatnajökull, *Iceland* 8 D5
Vatoa, *Fiji* 91 D9
Vatólakkos, *Greece* 36 D5
Vatoloha, *Madag.* 89 B8
Vatomandry, *Madag.* 89 B8
Vatra-Dornei, *Romania* 43 C10
Vatrak →, *India* 68 H5
Vättern, *Sweden* 11 F8
Vaucluse □, *France* 21 E9
Vaucouleurs, *France* 19 D12
Vaud □, *Switz.* 25 J2
Vaughn, *Mont., U.S.A.* 114 C8
Vaughn, *N. Mex., U.S.A.* 115 J11
Vaujours L., *Canada* 102 A5
Vaupés = Uaupés →, *Brazil* 124 C5
Vaupes □, *Colombia* 124 C4
Vauvert, *France* 21 E8
Vauxhall, *Canada* 104 C6
Vav, *India* 68 G4
Vavatenina, *Madag.* 89 B8
Vava'u, *Tonga* 91 D12
Vavoua, *Ivory C.* 82 D3
Vawkavysk, *Belarus* 47 F3
Vaxholm, *Sweden* 10 E12
Växjö, *Sweden* 11 H8
Våxtorp, *Sweden* 11 H7
Vaygach, Ostrov, *Russia* 50 C6
Váyia, *Greece* 38 C5
Váyia, Ákra, *Greece* 36 C10
Vechelde, *Germany* 24 C6
Vechta, *Germany* 24 C4
Vechte →, *Neths.* 17 B6
Vecsés, *Hungary* 42 C4
Veddige, *Sweden* 11 G6
Vedea →, *Romania* 43 G10
Vedia, *Argentina* 126 C3
Vedum, *Sweden* 11 F7
Veendam, *Neths.* 17 A6
Veenendaal, *Neths.* 17 B5
Vefsna →, *Norway* 8 D15
Vega, *Norway* 8 D14
Vega, *U.S.A.* 113 H3
Vegadeo, *Spain* 34 B3
Vegorrítis, Límni, *Greece* 40 F5
Vegreville, *Canada* 104 C6
Veinge, *Sweden* 11 H7
Veisiejai, *Lithuania* 44 D10
Vejbystrand, *Sweden* 11 H6
Vejen, *Denmark* 11 J3
Vejer de la Frontera, *Spain* 35 J5
Vejle, *Denmark* 11 J3
Vejle Amtskommune □, *Denmark* 11 J3
Vejle Fjord, *Denmark* 11 J3
Vela Luka, *Croatia* 29 F13
Velas, C., *Costa Rica* 120 D2
Velasco, Sierra de, *Argentina* 126 B2
Velay, Mts. du, *France* 20 D7
Velbert, *Germany* 24 D3
Velddrif, *S. Africa* 88 E2
Velebit Planina, *Croatia* 29 D12
Velebitski Kanal, *Croatia* 29 D11
Veleka →, *Bulgaria* 41 D11
Velencei-tó, *Hungary* 42 C3
Velenje, *Slovenia* 29 B12
Veles, *Macedonia* 40 E5
Velestínon, *Greece* 38 B4
Vélez-Málaga, *Spain* 35 J6
Vélez Rubio, *Spain* 33 H2
Velhas →, *Brazil* 125 G10
Velika, *Croatia* 42 E2
Velika Gorica, *Croatia* 29 C13
Velika Kapela, *Croatia* 29 C12
Velika Kladuša, *Bos.-H.* 29 C12
Velika Kruša, *Kosovo, Yug.* 40 D4
Velika Morava →, *Serbia, Yug.* 40 B5
Velika Plana, *Serbia, Yug.* 40 B5
Velikaya →, *Russia* 46 D5
Velikaya Kema, *Russia* 54 B8
Velikaya Lepetikha, *Ukraine* 47 J7
Veliké Kapušany, *Slovak Rep.* 27 C15
Velike Lašče, *Slovenia* 29 C11
Veliki Jastrebac, *Serbia, Yug.* 40 C5
Veliki Kanal, *Serbia, Yug.* 42 E4
Veliki Popović, *Serbia, Yug.* 40 B5
Velikiye Luki, *Russia* 46 D6
Veliko Gradište, *Serbia, Yug.* 40 B5
Veliko Tŭrnovo, *Bulgaria* 41 C9
Velikonda Range, *India* 66 M11
Vélingara, *Senegal* 82 C2
Vélingara, *Senegal* 82 B2
Velingrad, *Bulgaria* 40 D7
Velino, Mte., *Italy* 29 F10
Velizh, *Russia* 46 E6
Velké Karlovice, *Czech Rep.* 27 B11
Velké Meziříčí, *Czech Rep.* 26 B9
Vel'ký Javorník, *Slovak Rep.* 27 B11
Vel'ký Krtíš, *Slovak Rep.* 27 C12
Vel'ký Meder, *Slovak Rep.* 27 D10
Vel'ký Tribeč, *Slovak Rep.* 27 C11
Velletri, *Italy* 30 A5
Vellinge, *Sweden* 11 J6
Vellmar, *Germany* 24 D5
Vellore, *India* 66 N11
Velsk, *Russia* 46 B11
Velten, *Germany* 24 C9
Velva, *U.S.A.* 112 A4
Velvendós, *Greece* 40 F6
Vemb, *Denmark* 11 H2
Vemdalen, *Sweden* 10 B7
Ven, *Sweden* 11 J6
Venaco, *France* 21 F13
Venado Tuerto, *Argentina* 126 C3
Venafro, *Italy* 31 A7
Venarey-les-Laumes, *France* 19 E11
Venaría, *Italy* 28 C4
Venčane, *Serbia, Yug.* 40 B4
Vence, *France* 21 E11
Vendas Novas, *Portugal* 35 G2
Vendée □, *France* 18 F5
Vendée →, *France* 18 F5
Vendéen, Bocage, *France* 20 B2
Vendeuvre-sur-Barse, *France* 19 D11
Vendôme, *France* 18 E8
Vendrell = El Vendrell, *Spain* 32 D6
Vendsyssel, *Denmark* 11 G4
Venelles, *France* 21 E9
Véneta, L., *Italy* 29 C9
Véneto □, *Italy* 29 C9
Venev, *Russia* 46 E10
Venézia, *Italy* 29 C9
Venézia, G. di, *Italy* 29 C10
Venezuela ■, *S. Amer.* 124 B5
Venezuela, G. de, *Venezuela* 122 B3
Vengurla, *India* 66 M8
Venice = Venézia, *Italy* 29 C9
Venice, *U.S.A.* 109 M4
Vénissieux, *France* 21 C8
Venjansjön, *Sweden* 10 D8
Venkatapuram, *India* 67 K12
Venlo, *Neths.* 17 C6
Vennesla, *Norway* 9 G12
Venosa, *Italy* 31 B8
Venray, *Neths.* 17 C6
Venta, *Lithuania* 44 B9
Venta →, *Latvia* 44 A8
Venta de Baños, *Spain* 34 D6
Venta de Cardeña = Cardeña, *Spain* 35 G6
Ventana, Punta de la, *Mexico* 118 C3
Ventana, Sa. de la, *Argentina* 126 D3
Ventersburg, *S. Africa* 88 D4
Venterstad, *S. Africa* 88 E4
Ventimíglia, *Italy* 28 E4
Ventnor, *U.K.* 13 G6
Ventotène, *Italy* 30 B6
Ventoux, Mt., *France* 21 D9
Ventspils, *Latvia* 9 H19
Ventspils □, *Latvia* 44 A8
Ventuarí →, *Venezuela* 124 C5
Ventucopa, *U.S.A.* 117 L7
Ventura, *U.S.A.* 117 L7
Venus B., *Australia* 95 F4
Vera, *Argentina* 126 B3
Vera, *Spain* 33 H3
Veracruz, *Mexico* 119 D5
Veracruz □, *Mexico* 119 D5
Veraval, *India* 68 J4
Verbánia, *Italy* 28 C5
Verbicaro, *Italy* 31 C8
Verbier, *Switz.* 25 J3
Vercelli, *Italy* 28 C5
Verchovchevo, *Ukraine* 47 H8
Verdalsøra, *Norway* 8 E14
Verde →, *Argentina* 128 E3
Verde →, *Goiás, Brazil* 125 G8
Verde →, *Mato Grosso do Sul, Brazil* 125 H8
Verde →, *Chihuahua, Mexico* 118 B3
Verde →, *Oaxaca, Mexico* 119 D5
Verde →, *Veracruz, Mexico* 118 C4
Verde →, *Paraguay* 126 A4
Verde →, *U.S.A.* 106 D4
Verde, Cay, *Bahamas* 120 B4
Verde Island Pass, *Phil.* 61 E4
Verden, *Germany* 24 C5
Verdhikoúsa, *Greece* 38 B3
Verdi, *U.S.A.* 116 F7
Verdon →, *France* 21 E9
Verdun, *France* 19 C12
Verdun-sur-le-Doubs, *France* 19 F12
Vereeniging, *S. Africa* 89 D4
Verga, C., *Guinea* 82 C2
Vergara, *Uruguay* 127 C5
Vergato, *Italy* 28 D8
Vergemont Cr. →, *Australia* 94 C3
Vergennes, *U.S.A.* 111 B11
Vergt, *France* 20 C4
Verín, *Spain* 34 D3
Verkhnedvinsk = Vyerkhnyadzvinsk, *Belarus* 46 E4
Verkhnevilyuysk, *Russia* 51 C13
Verkhniy Baskunchak, *Russia* 49 F8
Verkhovye, *Russia* 47 F9
Verkhoyansk, *Russia* 51 C14
Verkhoyansk Ra. = Verkhoyanskiy Khrebet, *Russia* 51 C13
Verkhoyanskiy Khrebet, *Russia* 51 C13
Vermenton, *France* 19 E10
Vermilion, *Canada* 105 C6
Vermilion, *U.S.A.* 110 E2
Vermilion →, *Alta., Canada* 105 C6
Vermilion →, *Qué., Canada* 102 C5
Vermilion, B., *U.S.A.* 113 L9
Vermilion Bay, *Canada* 105 D10
Vermilion L., *U.S.A.* 112 B8
Vermillion, *U.S.A.* 112 D6
Vermont □, *U.S.A.* 111 C12
Vermosh, *Albania* 40 D3
Vernal, *U.S.A.* 114 F9
Vernalis, *U.S.A.* 116 H5
Vernazza, *Italy* 28 D6
Verner, *Canada* 102 C3
Verneuil-sur-Avre, *France* 18 D7
Verneukpan, *S. Africa* 88 E3
Vernier, *Switz.* 25 J2
Vérnio, *Italy* 28 D8
Vernon, *Canada* 104 C5
Vernon, *France* 18 C8
Vernon, *U.S.A.* 113 H5
Vernonia, *U.S.A.* 116 E3
Vernouillet, *France* 18 D8
Vero Beach, *U.S.A.* 109 M5
Véroia, *Greece* 40 F6
Véroli, *Italy* 29 G10
Verona, *Canada* 111 B8
Verona, *Italy* 28 C7
Verona, *U.S.A.* 112 D10
Verrès, *Italy* 28 C4
Versailles, *France* 19 D9
Versmold, *Germany* 24 C4
Vert, C., *Senegal* 82 C1
Vertou, *France* 18 E5
Vertus, *France* 19 D11
Verulam, *S. Africa* 89 D5
Verviers, *Belgium* 17 D5
Vervins, *France* 19 C10
Veržej, *Slovenia* 29 B13
Verzy, *France* 19 C11
Vescovato, *France* 21 F13
Veselí nad Lužnicí, *Czech Rep.* 26 B7
Veselie, *Bulgaria* 41 D11
Veselovskoye Vdkhr., *Russia* 49 G5
Veshenskaya, *Russia* 48 F5
Vesle →, *France* 19 C10
Vesoul, *France* 19 E13
Vessigebro, *Sweden* 11 H6
Vesterålen, *Norway* 8 B16
Vestfjorden, *Norway* 8 C15
Vestmannaeyjar, *Iceland* 8 E3
Vestsjællands Amtskommune □, *Denmark* 11 J5
Vestspitsbergen, *Svalbard* 4 B8
Vestvågøy, *Norway* 8 B15
Vesuvio, *Italy* 31 B7
Vesuvius, Mt. = Vesuvio, *Italy* 31 B7
Vesyegonsk, *Russia* 46 C9
Veszprém, *Hungary* 42 C2
Veszprém □, *Hungary* 42 C2
Vésztő, *Hungary* 42 D6
Vetlanda, *Sweden* 11 G9
Vetluga, *Russia* 48 B7
Vetlugu →, *Russia* 48 B8
Vetluzhskiy, *Kostroma, Russia* 48 A7
Vetluzhskiy, *Nizhniy Novgorod, Russia* 48 B7
Vetovo, *Bulgaria* 41 C10
Vetralla, *Italy* 29 F9
Vetren, *Bulgaria* 41 D8
Vettore, Mte., *Italy* 29 F10
Veurne, *Belgium* 17 C2
Veveno →, *Sudan* 81 F3
Vevey, *Switz.* 25 J2
Vévi, *Greece* 40 F5
Veynes, *France* 21 D9
Veys, *Iran* 71 D6
Vézelay, *France* 19 E10
Vézelise, *France* 19 D13
Vézère →, *France* 20 D4
Vezhen, *Bulgaria* 41 D8
Vezirköprü, *Turkey* 72 B6
Vezzani, *France* 21 F13
Vi Thanh, *Vietnam* 65 H5
Viacha, *Bolivia* 124 G5
Viadana, *Italy* 28 D7
Viamão, *Brazil* 127 C5
Viana, *Brazil* 125 D10
Viana, *Spain* 32 C2
Viana do Alentejo, *Portugal* 35 G3
Viana do Bolo, *Spain* 34 C3
Viana do Castelo, *Portugal* 34 D2
Viana do Castelo □, *Portugal* 34 D2
Vianden, *Lux.* 17 E6
Vianópolis, *Brazil* 125 G9
Viar →, *Spain* 35 H5
Viaréggio, *Italy* 28 E7
Viaur →, *France* 20 D5
Vibble, *Sweden* 11 G12
Vibo Valéntia, *Italy* 31 D9
Viborg, *Denmark* 11 H3
Viborg Amtskommune □, *Denmark* 11 H3
Vibraye, *France* 18 D7
Vic, *Spain* 32 D7
Vic, Étang de, *France* 20 E7
Vic-en-Bigorre, *France* 20 E4
Vic-Fézensac, *France* 20 E4
Vic-le-Comte, *France* 19 G10
Vic-sur-Cère, *France* 20 D6
Vícar, *Spain* 33 J2
Vicenza, *Italy* 29 C8
Vich = Vic, *Spain* 32 D7
Vichada →, *Colombia* 124 C5
Vichuga, *Russia* 48 B5
Vichy, *France* 19 F10
Vicksburg, *Ariz., U.S.A.* 117 M13
Vicksburg, *Miss., U.S.A.* 113 J9
Vico, *France* 21 F12
Vico, L. di, *Italy* 29 F9
Vico del Gargano, *Italy* 29 G12
Vicovu de Sus, *Romania* 43 C10
Victor, *India* 68 J4
Victor, *U.S.A.* 110 D7
Victor Harbor, *Australia* 95 F2
Victoria = Labuan, *Malaysia* 62 C5
Victoria, *Argentina* 126 C3
Victoria, *Canada* 104 D4
Victoria, *Chile* 128 D2
Victoria, *Guinea* 82 C2
Victoria, *Malta* 36 C1
Victoria, *Phil.* 61 D4
Victoria, *Romania* 43 E9
Victoria, *Kans., U.S.A.* 112 F5
Victoria, *Tex., U.S.A.* 113 L6
Victoria □, *Australia* 95 F3
Victoria →, *Australia* 92 C4
Victoria, Grand L., *Canada* 102 C4
Victoria, L., *Africa* 86 C3
Victoria, L., *Australia* 95 E3
Victoria Beach, *Canada* 105 C9
Victoria de Durango = Durango, *Mexico* 118 C4
Victoria de las Tunas, *Cuba* 120 B4
Victoria Falls, *Zimbabwe* 87 F2
Victoria Harbour, *Canada* 110 B5
Victoria I., *Canada* 100 A8
Victoria L., *Canada* 103 C8
Victoria Ld., *Antarctica* 5 D11
Victoria Nile →, *Uganda* 86 B3
Victoria River, *Australia* 92 C5
Victoria Str., *Canada* 100 B9
Victoria Taungdeik, *Burma* 67 J18
Victoria West, *S. Africa* 88 E3
Victorias, *Phil.* 61 F5
Victoriaville, *Canada* 103 C5
Victorica, *Argentina* 126 D2
Victorville, *U.S.A.* 117 L9
Vicuña, *Chile* 126 C1
Vicuña Mackenna, *Argentina* 126 C3
Vidal, *U.S.A.* 117 L12
Vidal Junction, *U.S.A.* 117 L12
Vidalia, *U.S.A.* 109 J4
Vidauban, *France* 21 E10
Videbæk, *Denmark* 11 H2
Videle, *Romania* 43 F10
Vídho, *Greece* 36 A3
Vidigueira, *Portugal* 35 G3
Vidin, *Bulgaria* 40 C6
Vidio, C., *Spain* 34 B4
Vidisha, *India* 68 H7
Vidra, *Romania* 43 E11
Viduša, *Bos.-H.* 40 D2
Vidzy, *Belarus* 9 J22
Viechtach, *Germany* 25 F8
Viedma, *Argentina* 128 E4
Viedma, L., *Argentina* 128 F2
Vieira do Minho, *Portugal* 34 D2
Vielha, *Spain* 32 C5
Viella = Vielha, *Spain* 32 C5
Vielsalm, *Belgium* 17 D5
Vienenburg, *Germany* 24 D6
Vieng Pou Kha, *Laos* 58 G3
Vienna = Wien, *Austria* 27 C9
Vienna, *Ill., U.S.A.* 113 G10
Vienna, *Mo., U.S.A.* 112 F9
Vienne, *France* 21 C8
Vienne □, *France* 20 B4
Vienne →, *France* 18 E7
Vientiane, *Laos* 64 D4
Vientos, Paso de los, *Caribbean* 121 C5
Viernheim, *Germany* 25 F4
Viersen, *Germany* 24 D2
Vierwaldstättersee, *Switz.* 25 J4
Vierzon, *France* 19 E9
Vieste, *Italy* 29 G13
Vietnam ■, *Asia* 64 C6
Vieux-Boucau-les-Bains, *France* 20 E2
Vif, *France* 21 C9
Vigan, *Phil.* 61 C4
Vigévano, *Italy* 28 C5
Vigia, *Brazil* 125 D9
Vigía Chico, *Mexico* 119 D7
Víglas, Ákra, *Greece* 36 D9
Vignemale, *France* 20 F3
Vigneulles-lès-Hattonchâtel, *France* 19 D12
Vignola, *Italy* 28 D8
Vigo, *Spain* 34 C2
Vigo, Ría de, *Spain* 34 C2
Vigsø Bugt, *Denmark* 11 G2
Vihiers, *France* 18 E6
Vihowa, *Pakistan* 68 D4
Vihowa →, *Pakistan* 68 D4
Vijayawada, *India* 67 L12
Vík, *Iceland* 8 E4
Vika, *Sweden* 10 D8
Vikarbyn, *Sweden* 10 D9
Vikeke, *Indonesia* 63 F7
Viken, *Skåne, Sweden* 11 H6
Viken, *Skaraborg, Sweden* 11 F8
Viking, *Canada* 104 C6
Vikmanshyttan, *Sweden* 10 D9
Vikna, *Norway* 8 D14
Vila da Maganja, *Mozam.* 87 F4
Vila de João Belo = Xai-Xai, *Mozam.* 89 D5
Vila de Rei, *Portugal* 34 F2
Vila do Bispo, *Portugal* 35 H2
Vila do Conde, *Portugal* 34 D2
Vila Franca de Xira, *Portugal* 35 G2
Vila Gamito, *Mozam.* 87 E3
Vila Gomes da Costa, *Mozam.* 89 C5
Vila Machado, *Mozam.* 87 F3
Vila Mouzinho, *Mozam.* 87 E3
Vila Nova de Famalicão, *Portugal* 34 D2
Vila Nova de Fos Côa, *Portugal* 34 D3
Vila Nova de Foscôa = Vila Nova de Fos Côa, *Portugal* 34 D3
Vila Nova de Gaia, *Portugal* 34 D2
Vila Nova de Ourém, *Portugal* 34 F2
Vila Pouca de Aguiar, *Portugal* 34 D3
Vila Real, *Portugal* 34 D3
Vila Real □, *Portugal* 34 D3
Vila-real de los Infantes, *Spain* 32 F4
Vila Real de Santo António, *Portugal* 35 H3
Vila Vasco da Gama, *Mozam.* 87 E3
Vila Velha, *Brazil* 127 A7
Vila Viçosa, *Portugal* 35 G3
Vilafranca del Maestrat, *Spain* 32 E4
Vilafranca del Penedès, *Spain* 32 D6
Vilagarcía de Arousa, *Spain* 34 C2
Vilaine →, *France* 18 E4
Vilanandro, Tanjona, *Madag.* 89 B7
Vilanculos, *Mozam.* 89 C6
Vilanova de Castelló, *Spain* 33 F4
Vilanova i la Geltrú, *Spain* 32 D6
Vilar Formosa, *Portugal* 34 E4
Vilaseca, *Spain* 32 D6
Vilaseca-Salou = Vilaseca, *Spain* 32 D6
Vilbjerg, *Denmark* 11 H2
Vilches, *Spain* 35 G7
Vileyka, *Belarus* 46 E4
Vilhelmina, *Sweden* 8 D17
Vilhena, *Brazil* 124 F6
Viliga, *Russia* 51 C16
Viliya →, *Lithuania* 9 J21

Viljandi, Estonia 9 G21
Vilkaviškis, Lithuania 44 D10
Vilkija, Lithuania 44 C10
Vilkitskogo, Proliv, Russia .. 51 B11
Vilkovo = Vylkove, Ukraine 47 K5
Villa Abecia, Bolivia 126 A2
Villa Ahumada, Mexico 118 A3
Villa Ana, Argentina 126 B4
Villa Ángela, Argentina 126 B3
Villa Bella, Bolivia 124 F5
Villa Bens = Tarfaya,
  Morocco 78 C3
Villa Cañás, Argentina 126 C3
Villa Cisneros = Dakhla,
  W. Sahara 78 D2
Villa Colón, Argentina 126 C2
Villa Constitución, Argentina 126 C3
Villa de María, Argentina . 126 B3
Villa del Rio, Spain 35 H6
Villa Dolores, Argentina ... 126 C2
Villa Frontera, Mexico 118 B4
Villa Guillermina, Argentina 126 B4
Villa Hayes, Paraguay 126 B4
Villa Iris, Argentina 126 D3
Villa Juárez, Mexico 118 B4
Villa María, Argentina 126 C3
Villa Mazán, Argentina 126 B2
Villa Minozzo, Italy 28 D7
Villa Montes, Bolivia 126 A3
Villa Ocampo, Argentina .. 126 B4
Villa Ocampo, Mexico 118 B3
Villa Ojo de Agua, Argentina 126 B3
Villa San Giovanni, Italy .. 31 D8
Villa San José, Argentina .. 126 C4
Villa San Martín, Argentina 126 B3
Villa Santina, Italy 29 B9
Villa Unión, Mexico 118 C3
Villablino, Spain 34 C4
Villacarlos, Spain 37 B11
Villacarriedo, Spain 34 B7
Villacarrillo, Spain 35 G7
Villacastín, Spain 34 E6
Villach, Austria 26 E6
Villacidro, Italy 30 C1
Villada, Spain 34 C6
Villadiego, Spain 34 C6
Villadóssola, Italy 28 B5
Villafeliche, Spain 32 D3
Villafranca, Spain 32 C3
Villafranca de los Barros,
  Spain 35 G4
Villafranca de los Caballeros,
  Baleares, Spain 37 B10
Villafranca de los Caballeros,
  Toledo, Spain 35 F7
Villafranca del Cid =
  Vilafranca del Maestrat,
  Spain 32 E4
Villafranca del Panadés =
  Vilafranca del Penedès,
  Spain 32 D6
Villafranca di Verona, Italy 28 C7
Villafranca Tirrena, Italy .. 31 D8
Villagrán, Mexico 119 C5
Villaguay, Argentina 126 C4
Villaharta, Spain 35 G6
Villahermosa, Mexico 119 D6
Villahermosa, Spain 33 G2
Villaines-la-Juhel, France . 18 D6
Villajoyosa, Spain 33 G4
Villalba, Spain 34 B3
Villalba de Guardo, Spain . 34 C6
Villalón de Campos, Spain . 34 C5
Villalpando, Spain 34 D5
Villaluenga, Spain 34 E7
Villamanán, Spain 34 C5
Villamartín, Spain 35 J5
Villamayor de Santiago,
  Spain 32 F2
Villamblard, France 20 C4
Villanova Monteleone, Italy 30 B1
Villanueva, U.S.A. 113 H2
Villanueva de Castellón =
  Vilanova de Castelló,
  Spain 33 F4
Villanueva de Córdoba,
  Spain 35 G6
Villanueva de la Fuente,
  Spain 33 G2
Villanueva de la Serena,
  Spain 35 G5
Villanueva de la Sierra,
  Spain 34 E4
Villanueva de los Castillejos,
  Spain 35 H3
Villanueva de los Infantes,
  Spain 35 G7
Villanueva del Arzobispo,
  Spain 33 G2
Villanueva del Fresno, Spain 35 G3
Villanueva y Geltrú =
  Vilanova i la Geltrú, Spain 32 D6
Villaputzu, Italy 30 C2
Villaquilambre, Spain 34 C5
Villar del Arzobispo, Spain . 32 F4
Villar del Rey, Spain 35 F4
Villard-de-Lans, France ... 21 C9
Villarramiel, Spain 34 C6
Villarreal = Vila-real de los
  Infantes, Spain
Villarrica, Chile 128 D2
Villarrica, Paraguay 126 B4
Villarrobledo, Spain 33 F2
Villarroya de la Sierra, Spain 32 D3
Villarrubia de los Ojos,
  Spain 35 F7
Villars-les-Dombes, France . 19 F12
Villasayas, Spain 32 D2
Villaseca de los Gamitos =
  Villaseco de los Gamitos,
  Spain 34 D4

Villaseco de los Gamitos,
  Spain 34 D4
Villasimíus, Italy 30 C2
Villastar, Spain 32 E3
Villatobas, Spain 34 F7
Villavicencio, Argentina ... 126 C2
Villavicencio, Colombia ... 124 C4
Villaviciosa, Spain 34 B5
Villazón, Bolivia 126 A2
Ville-Marie, Canada 102 C4
Ville Platte, U.S.A. 113 K8
Villedieu-les-Poêles, France 18 D5
Villefort, France 20 D7
Villefranche-de-Lauragais,
  France 20 E5
Villefranche-de-Rouergue,
  France 20 D6
Villefranche-du-Périgord,
  France 20 D5
Villefranche-sur-Saône,
  France 21 C8
Villel, Spain 32 E3
Villemur-sur-Tarn, France . 20 E5
Villena, Spain 33 G4
Villenauxe-la-Grande, France 19 D10
Villenave-d'Ornon, France . 20 D3
Villeneuve-d'Ascq, France . 19 B10
Villeneuve-l'Archevêque,
  France 19 D10
Villeneuve-lès-Avignon,
  France 21 E8
Villeneuve-sur-Allier, France 19 F10
Villeneuve-sur-Lot, France . 20 D4
Villeneuve-sur-Yonne,
  France 19 D10
Villeréal, France 20 D4
Villers-Bocage, France 18 C6
Villers-Cotterêts, France .. 19 C10
Villers-sur-Mer, France ... 18 C6
Villersexel, France 19 E13
Villerupt, France 19 C12
Villeurbanne, France 21 C8
Villiers, S. Africa 89 D4
Villingen-Schwenningen,
  Germany 25 G4
Vilna, Canada 104 C6
Vilnius, Lithuania 9 J21
Vils, Austria 26 D3
Vils →, Bayern, Germany . 25 G9
Vils →, Bayern, Germany . 25 F7
Vilsbiburg, Germany 25 G8
Vilshofen, Germany 25 G9
Vilusi, Montenegro, Yug. . 40 D2
Vilvoorde, Belgium 17 D4
Vilyuy →, Russia 51 C13
Vilyuysk, Russia 51 C13
Vimianzo, Spain 34 B1
Vimioso, Portugal 34 D4
Vimmerby, Sweden 11 G9
Vimoutiers, France 18 D7
Vimperk, Czech Rep. 26 B6
Viña del Mar, Chile 126 C1
Vinarós, Spain 32 E5
Vincennes, U.S.A. 108 F2
Vincent, U.S.A. 117 L8
Vinchina, Argentina 126 B2
Vindelälven →, Sweden ... 8 D18
Vindeln, Sweden 8 D18
Vinderup, Denmark 11 H2
Vindhya Ra., India 68 H7
Vineland, U.S.A. 108 F8
Vineuil, France 18
Vinga, Romania 42 D6
Vingåker, Sweden 10 E9
Vinh, Vietnam 64 C5
Vinh Linh, Vietnam 64 D6
Vinh Long, Vietnam 65 G5
Vinh Yen, Vietnam 58 G5
Vinhais, Portugal 34 D3
Vinica, Croatia 29 B13
Vinica, Macedonia 40 E6
Vinica, Slovenia 29 C12
Vinita, U.S.A. 113 G7
Vinkovci, Croatia 42 E3
Vinnitsa = Vinnytsya,
  Ukraine 47 H5
Vinnytsya, Ukraine 47 H5
Vinslöv, Sweden 11 H7
Vintjärn, Sweden 10 D10
Vinton, Calif., U.S.A. 116 F6
Vinton, Iowa, U.S.A. 112 D8
Vinton, La., U.S.A. 113 K8
Vințu de Jos, Romania ... 43 D8
Viöl, Germany 24 A5
Vipava, Slovenia 29 C10
Vipiteno, Italy 29 B8
Vir, Croatia 29 D12
Virac, Phil. 61 E6
Virachei, Cambodia 64 F6
Virago Sd., Canada 104 C2
Viramgam, India 68 H5
Virananşehir, Turkey 70 B3
Virawah, Pakistan 68 G4
Virbalis, Lithuania 44 D9
Virden, Canada 105 D8
Vire, France 18 D6
Vire →, France 18 C5
Vírgenes, C., Argentina .. 128 G3
Virgin →, U.S.A. 115 H6
Virgin Gorda, Virgin Is. .. 121 C7
Virgin Is. (British) ■,
  W. Indies 121 C7
Virgin Is. (U.S.) ■,
  W. Indies 121 C7
Virginia, S. Africa 88 D4
Virginia, U.S.A. 112 B8
Virginia □, U.S.A. 108 G7
Virginia Beach, U.S.A. ... 108 G8
Virginia City, Mont., U.S.A. 114 D8
Virginia City, Nev., U.S.A. 116 F7
Virginia Falls, Canada 104 A3

Virginiatown, Canada 102 C4
Virje, Croatia 29 B13
Viroqua, U.S.A. 112 D9
Virpazar, Montenegro, Yug. 40 D3
Virpur, India 68 J4
Virserum, Sweden 11 G9
Virton, Belgium 17 E5
Virudunagar, India 66 Q10
Vis, Croatia 29 E13
Visalia, U.S.A. 116 J7
Visayan Sea, Phil. 61 F5
Visby, Sweden 11 G12
Viscount Melville Sd.,
  Canada 4 B2
Visé, Belgium 17 D5
Višegrad, Bos.-H. 42 G4
Viseu, Brazil 125 D9
Viseu, Portugal 34 E3
Viseu □, Portugal 34 E3
Vişeu de Sus, Romania ... 43 C9
Vishakhapatnam, India .. 67 L13
Vişina, Romania 43 G9
Vişineşti, Moldova 43 D13
Visingsö, Sweden 11 F8
Viskafors, Sweden 11 G6
Viskan →, Sweden 11 G6
Viški Kanal, Croatia 29 E13
Vislanda, Sweden 11 H8
Visnagar, India 68 H5
Višnja Gora, Slovenia ... 29 C11
Viso, Mte., Italy 28 D4
Viso del Marqués, Spain . 35 G7
Visoko, Bos.-H. 42 G3
Visokoi I., Antarctica 5 B1
Visp, Switz. 25 J3
Vissefjärda, Sweden 11 H9
Visselhövede, Germany .. 24 C5
Vissenbjerg, Denmark ... 11 J4
Vista, U.S.A. 117 M9
Vistonikos, Ormos =
  Vistonís, Límni, Greece . 41 E9
Vistonís, Límni, Greece ... 41 E9
Vistula = Wisła →, Poland 44 D5
Vit →, Bulgaria 41 C8
Vitanje, Slovenia 29 B12
Vitebsk = Vitsyebsk, Belarus 46 E6
Viterbo, Italy 29 F9
Vitez, Bos.-H. 42 F2
Viti Levu, Fiji 91 C7
Vitigudino, Spain 34 D4
Vitim, Russia 51 D12
Vitim →, Russia 51 D12
Vitina, Bos.-H. 29 E14
Vitína, Greece 38 D4
Vítkov, Czech Rep. 27 B10
Vitória, Brazil 125 H10
Vitória da Conquista, Brazil 125 F10
Vitória de São Antão, Brazil 125 E11
Vitoria-Gasteiz, Spain ... 32 C2
Vitré, France 18 D5
Vitry-le-François, France . 19 D11
Vitry-sur-Seine, France .. 19 D9
Vitsand, Sweden 10 D7
Vitsi, Óros, Greece 40 F5
Vitsyebsk, Belarus 46 E6
Vittaryd, Sweden 11 H7
Vitteaux, France 19 E11
Vittel, France 19 D12
Vittória, Italy 31 F7
Vittório Véneto, Italy ... 29 C9
Vittsjö, Sweden 11 H7
Viveiro, Spain 34 B3
Vivian, U.S.A. 113 J8
Viviers, France 21 D8
Vivonne, France 20 B4
Vizcaíno, Desierto de,
  Mexico 118 B2
Vizcaíno, Sierra, Mexico . 118 B2
Vizcaya □, Spain 32 B2
Vize, Turkey 41 E11
Vizianagaram, India 67 K13
Vizille, France 21 C9
Viziñada, Croatia 29 C10
Viziru, Romania 43 E12
Vizzini, Italy 31 E7
Vjosa →, Albania 40 F3
Vlaardingen, Neths. 17 C4
Vlădeasa, Vf., Romania .. 42 D7
Vladičin Han, Serbia, Yug. 40 D6
Vladikavkaz, Russia 49 J7
Vladimir, Russia 46 D11
Vladimir Volynskiy =
  Volodymyr-Volynskyy,
  Ukraine 47 G3
Vladimirci, Serbia, Yug. . 40 B4
Vladimirovac, Serbia, Yug. 42 E5
Vladimirovka, Russia 49 F8
Vladimirovo, Bulgaria ... 40 C7
Vladimorvka, Kazakstan .. 48 E10
Vladislavovka, Ukraine .. 47 K8
Vladivostok, Russia 51 E14
Vlăhiţa, Romania 43 D10
Vlakhiótis, Greece 38 E4
Vlasenica, Bos.-H. 42 F3
Vlašić, Bos.-H. 42 F2
Vlašim, Czech Rep. 26 B7
Vlasinsko Jezero,
  Serbia, Yug. 40 D6
Vlasotince, Serbia, Yug. .. 40 D6
Vlieland, Neths. 17 A4
Vlissingen, Neths. 17 C3
Vlorë, Albania 40 F3
Vlorës, Gjiri i, Albania ... 40 F3
Vltava →, Czech Rep. ... 26 A7
Vo Dat, Vietnam 65 G6
Vobarno, Italy 28 C7
Voćin, Croatia 42 E2
Vöcklabruck, Austria 26 C6
Vodice, Croatia 29 E12
Vodňany, Czech Rep. ... 26 B7

Vodnjan, Croatia 29 D10
Voe, U.K. 14 A7
Vogel Pk., Nigeria 83 D7
Vogelkop = Doberai,
  Jazirah, Indonesia 63 E8
Vogelsberg, Germany 24 E5
Voghera, Italy 28 D6
Vohibinany, Madag. 89 B8
Vohilava, Madag. 89 C8
Vohimarina = Iharana,
  Madag. 89 A9
Vohimena, Tanjon' i,
  Madag. 89 D8
Vohipeno, Madag. 89 C8
Voi, Kenya 86 C4
Void-Vacon, France 19 D12
Voineşti, Iaşi, Romania ... 43 C12
Voineşti, Prahova, Romania 43 E10
Voíotía □, Greece 38 C5
Voiron, France 21 C9
Voisey B., Canada 103 A7
Voitsberg, Austria 26 D8
Vojens, Denmark 11 J3
Vojmsjön, Sweden 8 D17
Vojnić, Croatia 29 C12
Vojnik, Slovenia 29 B12
Vojvodina □, Serbia, Yug. 42 E5
Vokhtoga, Russia 46 C11
Volary, Czech Rep. 26 C6
Volborg, U.S.A. 112 C2
Volcano Is. = Kazan-Rettō,
  Pac. Oc. 96 E6
Volchansk = Vovchansk,
  Ukraine 47 G9
Volchya →, Ukraine 47 H8
Volda, Norway 9 E12
Volga →, Russia 49 G9
Volga, Russia 46 C10
Volga Hts. = Privolzhskaya
  Vozvyshennost, Russia .. 48 E7
Volga-Baltiyskiy Kanal,
  Russia 46 B9
Volgo-Donskoy Kanal,
  Russia 49 F7
Volgodonsk, Russia 49 G6
Volgograd, Russia 49 F7
Volgogradskoye Vdkhr.,
  Russia 48 E8
Volgorechensk, Russia ... 48 B5
Volímai, Greece 38 D2
Volintiri, Moldova 43 D14
Volissós, Greece 39 C7
Volkach, Germany 25 F6
Völkermarkt, Austria 26 E7
Volkhov, Russia 46 C7
Volkhov →, Russia 46 B7
Völklingen, Germany 25 F2
Volkovysk = Vawkavysk,
  Belarus 47 F3
Volksrust, S. Africa 89 D4
Volnansk, Ukraine 47 H8
Volnovakha, Ukraine 47 J9
Volochanka, Russia 51 B10
Volodarsk, Russia 48 B6
Volodymyr-Volynskyy,
  Ukraine 47 G3
Vologda, Russia 46 C10
Volokolamsk, Russia 46 D8
Volokonovka, Russia 47 G9
Vólos, Greece 38 B4
Volosovo, Russia 46 C5
Volovets, Ukraine 47 H2
Volovo, Russia 46 F10
Volozhin = Valozhyn,
  Belarus 46 E4
Volsk, Russia 48 D8
Volta □, Ghana 83 D5
Volta →, Ghana 83 D5
Volta, L., Ghana 83 D5
Volta Blanche = White
  Volta →, Ghana 83 D4
Volta Redonda, Brazil 127 A7
Voltaire, C., Australia 92 B4
Volterra, Italy 28 E7
Voltri, Italy 28 D5
Volturno →, Italy 30 A6
Vólvi, L., Greece 40 F7
Volyně, Czech Rep. 26 B6
Volzhsk, Russia 48 C9
Volzhskiy, Russia 49 F7
Vondrozo, Madag. 89 C8
Vónitsa, Greece 38 C2
Vopnafjörður, Iceland ... 8 D6
Vorarlberg □, Austria ... 26 D2
Vóras Óros, Greece 40 F5
Vorbasse, Denmark 11 J3
Vorchdorf, Austria 26 C6
Vorderrhein →, Switz. .. 25 J5
Vordingborg, Denmark .. 11 J5
Vorë, Albania 40 E3
Voreppe, France 21 C9
Vóriai Sporádhes, Greece . 38 B5
Vórios Aiyaíon □, Greece . 39 C7
Vórios Evvoïkos Kólpos,
  Greece 38 C5
Vorkuta, Russia 50 C7
Vormsi, Estonia 9 G20
Vorona →, Russia 48 E6
Voronezh, Russia 47 G10
Voronezh, Ukraine 47 G7
Voronezh →, Russia 47 G10
Vorontsovo-
  Aleksandrovskoye =
  Zelenokumsk, Russia ... 49 H6
Voroshilovgrad = Luhansk,
  Ukraine 47 H10
Voroshilovsk = Alchevsk,
  Ukraine 47 H10
Vórskla →, Ukraine 47 H8
Võrts Järv, Estonia 9 G22

Võru, Estonia 9 H22
Vosges, France 19 D14
Vosges □, France 19 D13
Voskopoja, Albania 40 F4
Voskresensk, Russia 46 E10
Voskresenskoye, Russia .. 48 B7
Voss, Norway 9 F12
Vostok I., Kiribati 97 J12
Votice, Czech Rep. 26 B7
Votsuri-Shima, Japan 55 M1
Vouga →, Portugal 34 E2
Vouillé, France 18 F7
Voúxa, Ákra, Greece 36 D5
Vouzela, Portugal 34 E2
Vouziers, France 19 C11
Vovchansk, Ukraine 47 G9
Vozhe, Ozero, Russia 46 B10
Vozhega, Russia 46 B11
Voznesensk, Ukraine 47 J6
Voznesenye, Russia 46 B8
Vrå, Denmark 11 G3
Vráble, Slovak Rep. 27 C11
Vračevšnica, Serbia, Yug. . 40 B4
Vrakhnéïka, Greece 38 C3
Vrancea □, Romania 43 E11
Vrancei, Munţii, Romania . 43 E11
Vrangelya, Ostrov, Russia . 51 B19
Vranica, Bos.-H. 42 G2
Vranje, Serbia, Yug. 40 D6
Vranjska Banja, Serbia, Yug. 40 D6
Vranov nad Topľou,
  Slovak Rep. 27 C14
Vransko, Slovenia 29 B11
Vransko Jezero, Croatia .. 29 E12
Vrapčište, Macedonia 40 E4
Vratsa, Bulgaria 40 C7
Vrbas, Serbia, Yug. 42 E4
Vrbas →, Bos.-H. 42 E2
Vrbnik, Croatia 29 C11
Vrbovec, Croatia 29 C13
Vrbovsko, Croatia 29 C12
Vrchlabí, Czech Rep. 26 A8
Vrede, S. Africa 89 D4
Vredefort, S. Africa 88 D4
Vreden, Germany 24 C2
Vredenburg, S. Africa ... 88 E2
Vredendal, S. Africa 88 E2
Vretstorp, Sweden 10 E8
Vrgorac, Croatia 29 E14
Vrhnika, Slovenia 29 C11
Vrídi, Ivory C. 82 D4
Vrigstad, Sweden 11 G8
Vrindavan, India 68 F7
Vríses, Greece 36 D6
Vrnograč, Bos.-H. 29 C12
Vrondádhes, Greece 39 C8
Vrpolje, Croatia 42 E3
Vršac, Serbia, Yug. 42 E6
Vrsacki Kanal, Serbia, Yug. 42 E5
Vrútky, Slovak Rep. 27 B11
Vryburg, S. Africa 88 D3
Vryheid, S. Africa 89 D5
Vsetín, Czech Rep. 27 B11
Vu Liet, Vietnam 64 C5
Vúcha →, Bulgaria 41 D8
Vučitrn, Kosovo, Yug. ... 40 D4
Vukovar, Croatia 42 E3
Vulcan, Canada 104 C6
Vulcan, Romania 43 E8
Vulcăneşti, Moldova 43 E13
Vulcano, Italy 31 D7
Vŭlchedruma, Bulgaria .. 40 C7
Vulkaneshty = Vulcăneşti,
  Moldova 43 E13
Vunduzi →, Mozam. 87 F3
Vung Tau, Vietnam 65 G6
Vŭrbitsa, Bulgaria 41 D10
Vurshets, Bulgaria 40 C7
Vutcani, Romania 43 D12
Vuya, Sudan 81 F2
Vyartsilya, Russia 46 A6
Vyatka = Kirov, Russia .. 50 D5
Vyatka →, Russia 48 C10
Vyatskiye Polyany, Russia 48 B10
Vyazemskiy, Russia 51 E14
Vyazma, Russia 46 E8
Vyazniki, Russia 48 B6
Vyborg, Russia 46 B5
Vychegda →, Russia 50 C5
Vychodné Beskydy, Europe 27 B15
Východočeský □,
  Czech Rep. 26 A8
Vyerkhnyadzvinsk, Belarus 46 E4
Vyksa, Russia 48 C6
Vylkove, Ukraine 47 K5
Vynohradiv, Ukraine 47 H2
Vyrnwy, L., U.K. 12 E4
Vyshniy Volochek, Russia . 46 D8
Vyshzha = imeni 26
  Bakinskikh Komissarov,
  Turkmenistan 71 B7
Vyškov, Czech Rep. 27 B9
Vysoké Mýto, Czech Rep. . 27 B9
Vysokovsk, Russia 46 D9
Vyšší Brod, Czech Rep. .. 26 C7
Vytegra, Russia 46 B9

W

W.A.C. Bennett Dam,
  Canada 104 B4
Wa, Ghana 82 C4
Waal →, Neths. 17 C5
Waalwijk, Neths. 17 C5
Waat, Sudan 81 F3
Wabana, Canada 103 C9
Wabasca →, Canada 104 B5
Wabasca-Desmarais, Canada 104 B6

Wabash, U.S.A. ... 108 E3
Wabash →, U.S.A. ... 108 G1
Wabi →, Ethiopia ... 81 F5
Wabigoon L., Canada ... 105 D10
Wabowden, Canada ... 105 C9
Wąbrzeźno, Poland ... 45 E5
Wabu Hu, China ... 59 A11
Wabuk Pt., Canada ... 102 A2
Wabush, Canada ... 103 B6
Wąchock, Poland ... 45 G8
Wächtersbach, Germany ... 25 E5
Waco, U.S.A. ... 113 K6
Waconichi, L., Canada ... 102 B5
Wad Ban Naqa, Sudan ... 81 D3
Wad Banda, Sudan ... 81 E2
Wad el Haddad, Sudan ... 81 E3
Wad en Nau, Sudan ... 81 E3
Wad Hamid, Sudan ... 81 D3
Wad Medani, Sudan ... 81 E3
Wad Thana, Pakistan ... 68 F2
Wadai, Africa ... 76 E5
Wadayama, Japan ... 55 G7
Waddeneilanden, Neths. ... 17 A5
Waddenzee, Neths. ... 17 A5
Waddington, U.S.A. ... 111 B9
Waddington, Mt., Canada ... 104 C3
Waddy Pt., Australia ... 95 C5
Wadebridge, U.K. ... 13 G3
Wadena, Canada ... 105 C8
Wadena, U.S.A. ... 112 B7
Wädenswil, Switz. ... 25 H4
Wadern, Germany ... 25 F2
Wadeye, Australia ... 92 B4
Wadhams, Canada ... 104 C3
Wādī as Sīr, Jordan ... 75 D4
Wadi Gemāl, Egypt ... 80 C4
Wadi Halfa, Sudan ... 80 C3
Wadian, China ... 59 A9
Wadlew, Poland ... 45 G6
Wadowice, Poland ... 45 J6
Wadsworth, Nev., U.S.A. ... 114 G4
Wadsworth, Ohio, U.S.A. ... 110 E3
Waegwan, S. Korea ... 57 G15
Wafangdian, China ... 57 E11
Wafrah, Si. Arabia ... 70 D5
Wageningen, Neths. ... 17 C5
Wager B., Canada ... 101 B11
Wagga Wagga, Australia ... 95 F4
Waghete, Indonesia ... 63 E9
Wagin, Australia ... 93 F2
Wagner, U.S.A. ... 112 D5
Wagon Mound, U.S.A. ... 113 G2
Wagoner, U.S.A. ... 113 H7
Wagrowiec, Poland ... 45 F4
Wah, Pakistan ... 68 C5
Wahai, Indonesia ... 63 E7
Wahiawa, U.S.A. ... 106 H15
Wāḥid, Egypt ... 75 E1
Wahnai, Afghan. ... 68 C1
Wahni, Ethiopia ... 81 E4
Wahoo, U.S.A. ... 112 E6
Wahpeton, U.S.A. ... 112 B6
Wai, Koh, Cambodia ... 65 H4
Waiau →, N.Z. ... 91 K4
Waibeem, Indonesia ... 63 E8
Waiblingen, Germany ... 25 G5
Waidhofen an der Thaya,
  Austria ... 26 C8
Waidhofen an der Ybbs,
  Austria ... 26 D7
Waigeo, Indonesia ... 63 E8
Waihi, N.Z. ... 91 G5
Waihou →, N.Z. ... 91 G5
Waika,
  Dem. Rep. of the Congo ... 86 C2
Waikabubak, Indonesia ... 63 F5
Waikari, N.Z. ... 91 K4
Waikato →, N.Z. ... 91 G5
Waikerie, Australia ... 95 E3
Waikokopu, N.Z. ... 91 H6
Waikouaiti, N.Z. ... 91 L3
Wailuku, U.S.A. ... 106 H16
Waimakariri →, N.Z. ... 91 K4
Waimate, N.Z. ... 91 L3
Wainganga →, India ... 66 K11
Waingapu, Indonesia ... 63 F6
Waini →, Guyana ... 124 A7
Wainwright, Canada ... 105 C6
Waiouru, N.Z. ... 91 H5
Waipara, N.Z. ... 91 K4
Waipawa, N.Z. ... 91 H6
Waipiro, N.Z. ... 91 H7
Waipu, N.Z. ... 91 F5
Waipukurau, N.Z. ... 91 J6
Wairakei, N.Z. ... 91 H6
Wairarapa, L., N.Z. ... 91 J5
Wairoa, N.Z. ... 91 H6
Waitaki →, N.Z. ... 91 L3
Waitara, N.Z. ... 91 H5
Waitsburg, U.S.A. ... 114 C5
Waiuku, N.Z. ... 91 G5
Wajima, Japan ... 55 F8
Wajir, Kenya ... 86 B5
Waka, Ethiopia ... 81 F4
Wakasa, Japan ... 55 G7
Wakasa-Wan, Japan ... 55 G7
Wakatipu, L., N.Z. ... 91 L2
Wakaw, Canada ... 105 C7
Wakayama, Japan ... 55 G7
Wakayama □, Japan ... 55 H7
Wake Forest, U.S.A. ... 109 H6
Wake I., Pac. Oc. ... 96 F8
WaKeeney, U.S.A. ... 112 F5
Wakefield, N.Z. ... 91 J4
Wakefield, U.K. ... 12 D6
Wakefield, Mass., U.S.A. ... 111 D13
Wakefield, Mich., U.S.A. ... 112 B10
Wakema, Burma ... 67 L19
Wakkanai, Japan ... 54 B10
Wakkerstroom, S. Africa ... 89 D5
Wakool, Australia ... 95 F3

Wakool →, Australia ... 95 F3
Wakre, Indonesia ... 63 E8
Wakuach, L., Canada ... 103 A6
Walamba, Zambia ... 87 E2
Wałbrzych, Poland ... 45 H3
Walbury Hill, U.K. ... 13 F6
Walcha, Australia ... 95 E5
Walcheren, Neths. ... 17 C3
Walcott, U.S.A. ... 114 F10
Wałcz, Poland ... 45 E3
Waldbröl, Germany ... 24 E3
Waldburg Ra., Australia ... 93 D2
Waldeck, Germany ... 24 D5
Walden, Colo., U.S.A. ... 114 F10
Walden, N.Y., U.S.A. ... 111 E10
Waldkirch, Germany ... 25 G3
Waldkirchen, Germany ... 25 G9
Waldkraiburg, Germany ... 25 G8
Waldport, U.S.A. ... 114 D1
Waldron, U.S.A. ... 113 H7
Waldviertel, Austria ... 26 C8
Walebing, Australia ... 93 F2
Walembele, Ghana ... 82 C4
Walensee, Switz. ... 25 H5
Wales □, U.K. ... 13 E3
Walewale, Ghana ... 83 C4
Walgett, Australia ... 95 E4
Walgreen Coast, Antarctica ... 5 D15
Walker, U.S.A. ... 112 B7
Walker, L., Canada ... 103 B6
Walker L., Canada ... 105 C9
Walker L., U.S.A. ... 114 G4
Walkerston, Australia ... 94 C4
Walkerton, Canada ... 102 D3
Wall, U.S.A. ... 112 D3
Walla Walla, U.S.A. ... 114 C4
Wallace, Idaho, U.S.A. ... 114 C6
Wallace, N.C., U.S.A. ... 109 H7
Wallaceburg, Canada ... 102 D3
Wallachia = Valahia,
  Romania ... 43 F9
Wallal, Australia ... 95 D4
Wallam Cr. →, Australia ... 95 D4
Wallambin, L., Australia ... 93 F2
Wallan, Australia ... 95 F3
Wallangarra, Australia ... 95 D5
Wallaroo, Australia ... 95 E2
Walldürn, Germany ... 25 F5
Wallenhorst, Germany ... 24 C4
Wallenpaupack, L., U.S.A. ... 111 E9
Wallingford, U.S.A. ... 111 E12
Wallis & Futuna, Is.,
  Pac. Oc. ... 96 J10
Wallowa, U.S.A. ... 114 D5
Wallowa Mts., U.S.A. ... 114 D5
Walls, U.K. ... 14 A7
Wallula, U.S.A. ... 114 C4
Wallumbilla, Australia ... 95 D4
Walmsley, L., Canada ... 105 A7
Walney, I. of, U.K. ... 12 C4
Walnut Creek, U.S.A. ... 116 H4
Walnut Ridge, U.S.A. ... 113 G9
Walpole, Australia ... 93 F2
Walpole, U.S.A. ... 111 D13
Wals, Austria ... 26 D5
Walsall, U.K. ... 13 E6
Walsenburg, U.S.A. ... 113 G2
Walsh, U.S.A. ... 113 G3
Walsh →, Australia ... 94 B3
Walsrode, Germany ... 24 C5
Walterboro, U.S.A. ... 109 J5
Walters, U.S.A. ... 113 H5
Waltershausen, Germany ... 24 E6
Waltham, U.S.A. ... 111 D13
Waltman, U.S.A. ... 114 E10
Walton, U.S.A. ... 111 D9
Walton-on-the-Naze, U.K. ... 13 F9
Walvis Bay, Namibia ... 88 C1
Walvisbaai = Walvis Bay,
  Namibia ... 88 C1
Wamba,
  Dem. Rep. of the Congo ... 86 B2
Wamba, Kenya ... 86 B4
Wamba, Nigeria ... 83 D6
Wamego, U.S.A. ... 112 F6
Wamena, Indonesia ... 63 E9
Wamsutter, U.S.A. ... 114 F9
Wamulan, Indonesia ... 63 E7
Wan Xian, China ... 56 E8
Wana, Pakistan ... 68 C3
Wanaaring, Australia ... 95 D3
Wanaka, N.Z. ... 91 L2
Wanaka L., N.Z. ... 91 L2
Wan'an, China ... 59 D10
Wanapitei L., Canada ... 102 C3
Wandel Sea = McKinley
  Sea, Arctic ... 4 A7
Wandérama, Ivory C. ... 82 D4
Wanderer, Zimbabwe ... 87 F3
Wandhari, Pakistan ... 68 F2
Wanding, China ... 58 E2
Wandoan, Australia ... 95 D4
Wanfu, China ... 57 D12
Wanga,
  Dem. Rep. of the Congo ... 86 B2
Wangal, Indonesia ... 63 F8
Wanganella, Australia ... 95 F3
Wanganui, N.Z. ... 91 H5
Wangaratta, Australia ... 95 F4
Wangary, Australia ... 95 E2
Wangcang, China ... 58 A6
Wangcheng, China ... 59 C9
Wangdu, China ... 56 E8
Wangen, Germany ... 25 H5
Wangerooge, Germany ... 24 B3
Wangi, Kenya ... 86 C5

Wangiwangi, Indonesia ... 63 F6
Wangjiang, China ... 59 B11
Wangmo, China ... 58 E6
Wangolodougou, Ivory C. ... 82 D3
Wangqing, China ... 57 C15
Wankaner, India ... 68 H4
Wanless, Canada ... 105 C8
Wannian, China ... 59 C11
Wanning, China ... 64 C8
Wanon Niwat, Thailand ... 64 D4
Wanquan, China ... 56 D8
Wanrong, China ... 56 G6
Wanshan, China ... 58 D7
Wanshengchang, China ... 58 C6
Wantage, U.K. ... 13 F6
Wanyuan, China ... 58 A7
Wanzai, China ... 59 C10
Wapakoneta, U.S.A. ... 108 E3
Wapato, U.S.A. ... 114 C3
Wapawekka L., Canada ... 105 C8
Wapikopa L., Canada ... 102 B2
Wapiti →, Canada ... 104 B5
Wappingers Falls, U.S.A. ... 111 E11
Wapsipinicon →, U.S.A. ... 112 E9
Warab □, Sudan ... 81 F2
Warangal, India ... 66 L11
Waraseoni, India ... 69 J9
Waratah, Australia ... 94 G4
Waratah B., Australia ... 95 F4
Warburg, Germany ... 24 D5
Warburton, Vic., Australia ... 95 F4
Warburton, W. Austral.,
  Australia ... 93 E4
Warburton Ra., Australia ... 93 E4
Ward, N.Z. ... 91 J5
Ward →, Australia ... 95 D4
Ward Mt., Australia ... 116 H8
Warden, S. Africa ... 89 D4
Wardha, India ... 66 J11
Wardha →, India ... 66 K11
Ware, Canada ... 104 B3
Ware, U.S.A. ... 111 D12
Waregem, Belgium ... 17 D3
Wareham, U.S.A. ... 111 E14
Waremme, Belgium ... 17 D5
Waren, Germany ... 24 B8
Warendorf, Germany ... 24 D4
Warialda, Australia ... 95 D5
Wariap, Indonesia ... 63 E8
Warin Chamrap, Thailand ... 64 E5
Warka, Poland ... 45 G8
Warkopi, Indonesia ... 63 E8
Warm Springs, U.S.A. ... 115 G5
Warman, Canada ... 105 C7
Warmbad, Namibia ... 88 D2
Warmbad, S. Africa ... 89 C4
Warmińsko-Mazurskie □,
  Poland ... 44 D8
Warminster, U.K. ... 13 F5
Warminster, U.S.A. ... 111 F9
Warnemünde, Germany ... 24 A8
Warner Mts., U.S.A. ... 114 F3
Warner Robins, U.S.A. ... 109 J4
Warnow →, Germany ... 24 A8
Waroona, Australia ... 93 F2
Warracknabeal, Australia ... 95 F3
Warragul, Australia ... 95 F4
Warrego →, Australia ... 95 E4
Warrego Ra., Australia ... 94 C4
Warren, Australia ... 95 E4
Warren, Ark., U.S.A. ... 113 J8
Warren, Mich., U.S.A. ... 108 D4
Warren, Minn., U.S.A. ... 112 A6
Warren, Ohio, U.S.A. ... 110 E4
Warren, Pa., U.S.A. ... 110 E5
Warrenpoint, U.K. ... 15 B5
Warrensburg, Mo., U.S.A. ... 112 F8
Warrensburg, N.Y., U.S.A. ... 111 C11
Warrenton, S. Africa ... 88 D3
Warrenton, U.S.A. ... 116 D3
Warri, Nigeria ... 83 D6
Warrina, Australia ... 95 D2
Warrington, U.K. ... 12 D5
Warrington, U.S.A. ... 109 K2
Warrington □, U.K. ... 12 D5
Warrnambool, Australia ... 95 F3
Warroad, U.S.A. ... 112 A7
Warruwi, Australia ... 94 A1
Warsa, Indonesia ... 63 E9
Warsak Dam, Pakistan ... 68 B4
Warsaw = Warszawa,
  Poland ... 45 F8
Warsaw, Ind., U.S.A. ... 108 E3
Warsaw, N.Y., U.S.A. ... 110 D6
Warsaw, Ohio, U.S.A. ... 110 F3
Warstein, Germany ... 24 D4
Warszawa, Poland ... 45 F8
Warta, Poland ... 45 G5
Warta →, Poland ... 45 F1
Warthe = Warta →, Poland ... 45 F1
Waru, Indonesia ... 63 E8
Warwick, Australia ... 95 D5
Warwick, U.K. ... 13 E6
Warwick, N.Y., U.S.A. ... 111 E10
Warwick, R.I., U.S.A. ... 111 E13
Warwickshire □, U.K. ... 13 E6
Wasaga Beach, Canada ... 110 B4
Wasagaming, Canada ... 105 C9
Wasatch Ra., U.S.A. ... 114 F8
Wasbank, S. Africa ... 89 D5
Wasco, Calif., U.S.A. ... 117 K7
Wasco, Oreg., U.S.A. ... 114 D3
Wase, Nigeria ... 83 D6
Waseca, U.S.A. ... 112 C8
Wasekamio L., Canada ... 105 B7
Wash, The, U.K. ... 12 E8
Washburn, N. Dak., U.S.A. ... 112 B4
Washburn, Wis., U.S.A. ... 112 B9
Washim, India ... 66 J10
Washington, U.K. ... 12 C6

Washington, D.C., U.S.A. ... 108 F7
Washington, Ga., U.S.A. ... 109 J4
Washington, Ind., U.S.A. ... 108 F2
Washington, Iowa, U.S.A. ... 112 E9
Washington, Mo., U.S.A. ... 112 F9
Washington, N.C., U.S.A. ... 109 H7
Washington, N.J., U.S.A. ... 111 F10
Washington, Pa., U.S.A. ... 110 F4
Washington, Utah, U.S.A. ... 115 H7
Washington □, U.S.A. ... 114 C3
Washington, Mt., U.S.A. ... 111 B13
Washington Court House,
  U.S.A. ... 108 F4
Washington I., U.S.A. ... 108 C2
Washougal, U.S.A. ... 116 E4
Wasian, Indonesia ... 63 E8
Wasilków, Poland ... 45 E10
Wasilla, U.S.A. ... 100 B5
Wasior, Indonesia ... 63 E8
Waskaganish, Canada ... 102 B4
Waskaiowaka, L., Canada ... 105 B9
Waskesiu Lake, Canada ... 105 C7
Wasserburg, Germany ... 25 G8
Wasserkuppe, Germany ... 24 E5
Wassy, France ... 19 D11
Waswanipi, Canada ... 102 C4
Waswanipi, L., Canada ... 102 C4
Watampone, Indonesia ... 63 E6
Water Park Pt., Australia ... 94 C5
Water Valley, U.S.A. ... 113 H10
Waterberge, S. Africa ... 89 C4
Waterbury, Conn., U.S.A. ... 111 E11
Waterbury, Vt., U.S.A. ... 111 B12
Waterbury L., Canada ... 105 B8
Waterdown, Canada ... 110 C5
Waterford, Canada ... 110 D4
Waterford, Ireland ... 15 D4
Waterford, Calif., U.S.A. ... 116 H6
Waterford, Pa., U.S.A. ... 110 E5
Waterford □, Ireland ... 15 D4
Waterford Harbour, Ireland ... 15 D5
Waterhen L., Canada ... 105 C9
Waterloo, Belgium ... 17 D4
Waterloo, Ont., Canada ... 102 D3
Waterloo, Qué., Canada ... 111 A12
Waterloo, S. Leone ... 82 D2
Waterloo, Ill., U.S.A. ... 112 F9
Waterloo, Iowa, U.S.A. ... 112 D8
Waterloo, N.Y., U.S.A. ... 110 D8
Watermeet, U.S.A. ... 112 B10
Waterton Lakes Nat. Park,
  U.S.A. ... 114 B7
Watertown, Conn., U.S.A. ... 111 E11
Watertown, N.Y., U.S.A. ... 111 C9
Watertown, S. Dak., U.S.A. ... 112 C6
Watertown, Wis., U.S.A. ... 112 D10
Waterval-Boven, S. Africa ... 89 D5
Waterville, Canada ... 111 A13
Waterville, Maine, U.S.A. ... 109 C11
Waterville, N.Y., U.S.A. ... 111 D9
Waterville, Pa., U.S.A. ... 110 E7
Waterville, Wash., U.S.A. ... 114 C3
Watervliet, U.S.A. ... 111 D11
Wates, Indonesia ... 63 G14
Watford, Canada ... 110 D3
Watford, U.K. ... 13 F7
Watford City, U.S.A. ... 112 B3
Wathaman →, Canada ... 105 B8
Wathaman L., Canada ... 105 B8
Watheroo, Australia ... 93 F2
Wating, China ... 56 G4
Watkins Glen, U.S.A. ... 110 D8
Watling I. = San Salvador I.,
  Bahamas ... 121 B5
Watonga, U.S.A. ... 113 H5
Watrous, Canada ... 105 C7
Watrous, U.S.A. ... 113 H2
Watsa,
  Dem. Rep. of the Congo ... 86 B2
Watseka, U.S.A. ... 108 E2
Watson, Australia ... 93 F5
Watson, Canada ... 105 C8
Watson Lake, Canada ... 104 A3
Watsontown, U.S.A. ... 110 E8
Watsonville, U.S.A. ... 116 J5
Wattiwarriganna Cr. →,
  Australia ... 95 D2
Wattwil, Switz. ... 25 H5
Watuata = Batuata,
  Indonesia ... 63 F6
Watubela, Kepulauan,
  Indonesia ... 63 E8
Watubela Is. = Watubela,
  Kepulauan, Indonesia ... 63 E8
Wau, Sudan ... 77 F6
Waubamik, Canada ... 110 A4
Waubay, U.S.A. ... 112 C6
Wauchope, N.S.W.,
  Australia ... 95 E5
Wauchope, N. Terr.,
  Australia ... 94 C1
Waukarlycarly, L., Australia ... 92 D3
Waukegan, U.S.A. ... 108 D2
Waukesha, U.S.A. ... 108 D1
Waukon, U.S.A. ... 112 D9
Waupaca, U.S.A. ... 112 C10
Waupun, U.S.A. ... 112 D10
Waurika, U.S.A. ... 113 H6
Wausau, U.S.A. ... 112 C10
Wautoma, U.S.A. ... 112 C10
Wauwatosa, U.S.A. ... 108 D2
Waveney →, U.K. ... 13 E9
Waverley, N.Z. ... 91 H5
Waverly, Iowa, U.S.A. ... 112 D8
Waverly, N.Y., U.S.A. ... 111 E8
Wavre, Belgium ... 17 D4
Wāw, Sudan ... 81 F2
Wāw al Kabīr, Libya ... 79 C9
Wawa, Canada ... 102 C3
Wawa, Nigeria ... 83 D5
Wawa, Sudan ... 80 C3

Wawanesa, Canada ... 105 D9
Wawona, U.S.A. ... 116 H7
Waxahachie, U.S.A. ... 113 J6
Way, L., Australia ... 93 E3
Waycross, U.S.A. ... 109 K4
Wayi, Sudan ... 81 F3
Wayland, U.S.A. ... 110 D7
Wayne, Nebr., U.S.A. ... 112 D6
Wayne, W. Va., U.S.A. ... 108 F4
Waynesboro, Ga., U.S.A. ... 109 J4
Waynesboro, Miss., U.S.A. ... 109 K1
Waynesboro, Pa., U.S.A. ... 108 F7
Waynesboro, Va., U.S.A. ... 108 F6
Waynesburg, U.S.A. ... 108 F5
Waynesville, U.S.A. ... 109 H4
Waynoka, U.S.A. ... 113 G5
Wazirabad, Pakistan ... 68 C6
Wda →, Poland ... 44 E5
We, Indonesia ... 62 C1
Weald, The, U.K. ... 13 F8
Wear →, U.K. ... 12 C6
Weatherford, Okla., U.S.A. ... 113 H5
Weatherford, Tex., U.S.A. ... 113 J6
Weaverville, U.S.A. ... 114 F2
Webb City, U.S.A. ... 113 G7
Webequie, Canada ... 102 B2
Webo = Nyaake, Liberia ... 82 E3
Webster, Mass., U.S.A. ... 111 D13
Webster, N.Y., U.S.A. ... 110 C7
Webster, S. Dak., U.S.A. ... 112 C6
Webster City, U.S.A. ... 112 D8
Webster Springs, U.S.A. ... 108 F5
Weda, Indonesia ... 63 D7
Weda, Teluk, Indonesia ... 63 D7
Weddell I., Falk. Is. ... 128 G4
Weddell Sea, Antarctica ... 5 D1
Wedderburn, Australia ... 95 F3
Wedel, Germany ... 24 B5
Wedemark, Germany ... 24 C5
Wedgeport, Canada ... 103 D6
Wedza, Zimbabwe ... 87 F3
Wee Waa, Australia ... 95 E4
Weed, U.S.A. ... 114 F2
Weed Heights, U.S.A. ... 116 G7
Weedsport, U.S.A. ... 111 C8
Weedville, U.S.A. ... 110 E6
Weenen, S. Africa ... 89 D5
Weener, Germany ... 24 B3
Weert, Neths. ... 17 C5
Węgliniec, Poland ... 45 G2
Węgorzewo, Poland ... 44 D8
Węgorzyno, Poland ... 44 E2
Węgrów, Poland ... 45 F9
Wehda □, Sudan ... 81 F3
Wei He →, Hebei, China ... 56 F8
Wei He →, Shaanxi, China ... 56 G6
Weichang, China ... 57 D9
Weichuan, China ... 56 G7
Weida, Germany ... 24 E8
Weiden, Germany ... 25 F8
Weifang, China ... 57 F10
Weihai, China ... 57 F12
Weil, Germany ... 25 H3
Weilburg, Germany ... 24 E4
Weilheim, Germany ... 25 H7
Weimar, Germany ... 24 E7
Weinan, China ... 56 G5
Weingarten, Germany ... 25 H5
Weinheim, Germany ... 25 F4
Weining, China ... 58 D5
Weipa, Australia ... 94 A3
Weir →, Australia ... 95 D4
Weir →, Canada ... 105 B10
Weir River, Canada ... 105 B10
Weirton, U.S.A. ... 110 F4
Weiser, U.S.A. ... 114 D5
Weishan, Shandong, China ... 57 G9
Weishan, Yunnan, China ... 58 E3
Weissenburg, Germany ... 25 F6
Weissenfels, Germany ... 24 D7
Weisswasser, Germany ... 24 D10
Wéitra, Austria ... 26 C8
Weixi, China ... 58 D2
Weixin, China ... 58 D5
Weiyuan, China ... 56 G3
Weiz, Austria ... 26 D8
Weizhou Dao, China ... 58 G7
Wejherowo, Poland ... 44 D5
Wekusko L., Canada ... 105 C9
Welch, U.S.A. ... 108 G5
Weldya, Ethiopia ... 81 E4
Welega □, Ethiopia ... 81 F3
Welkite, Ethiopia ... 81 F4
Welkom, S. Africa ... 88 D4
Welland, Canada ... 102 D4
Welland →, U.K. ... 13 E7
Wellesley Is., Australia ... 94 B2
Wellingborough, U.K. ... 13 E7
Wellington, Australia ... 95 E4
Wellington, Canada ... 110 C7
Wellington, N.Z. ... 91 J5
Wellington, S. Africa ... 88 E2
Wellington, Somst., U.K. ... 13 G4
Wellington,
  Telford & Wrekin, U.K. ... 13 E5
Wellington, Colo., U.S.A. ... 112 E2
Wellington, Kans., U.S.A. ... 113 G6
Wellington, Nev., U.S.A. ... 116 G7
Wellington, Ohio, U.S.A. ... 110 E2
Wellington, Tex., U.S.A. ... 113 H4
Wellington, I., Chile ... 122 H3
Wellington, L., Australia ... 95 F4
Wells, U.K. ... 13 F5
Wells, Maine, U.S.A. ... 111 C14
Wells, N.Y., U.S.A. ... 111 C10
Wells, Nev., U.S.A. ... 114 F6
Wells, L., Australia ... 93 E3
Wells, Mt., Australia ... 92 C4
Wells Gray Prov. Park,
  Canada ... 104 C4

Wells-next-the-Sea, U.K. 12 E8
Wells River, U.S.A. 111 B12
Wellsboro, U.S.A. 110 E7
Wellsburg, U.S.A. 110 F4
Wellsville, N.Y., U.S.A. 110 D7
Wellsville, Ohio, U.S.A. 110 F4
Wellsville, Utah, U.S.A. 114 F8
Wellton, U.S.A. 115 K6
Welmel, Wabi →, Ethiopia 81 F5
Welo □, Ethiopia 81 E4
Wels, Austria 26 C7
Welshpool, U.K. 13 E4
Welwyn Garden City, U.K. 13 F7
Wem, U.K. 12 E5
Wembere →, Tanzania 86 C3
Wemindji, Canada 102 B4
Wen Xian, China 56 G7
Wenatchee, U.S.A. 114 C3
Wenchang, China 64 C8
Wencheng, China 59 D13
Wenchi, Ghana 82 D4
Wenchow = Wenzhou, China 59 D13
Wenchuan, China 58 B4
Wenden, U.S.A. 117 M13
Wendeng, China 57 F12
Wendesi, Indonesia 63 E8
Wendo, Ethiopia 81 F4
Wendover, U.S.A. 114 F6
Weng'an, China 58 D6
Wengcheng, China 59 E9
Wengyuan, China 59 E10
Wenjiang, China 58 B4
Wenling, China 59 C13
Wenlock →, Australia 94 A3
Wenshan, China 58 F5
Wenshang, China 56 G9
Wenshui, Guizhou, China 58 C6
Wenshui, Shanxi, China 56 F7
Wensleydale, U.K. 12 C6
Wensu, China 60 B3
Wensum →, U.K. 12 E8
Wentworth, Australia 95 E3
Wentzel L., Canada 104 B6
Wenut, Indonesia 63 E8
Wenxi, China 56 G6
Wenxian, China 56 H3
Wenzhou, China 59 D13
Weott, U.S.A. 114 F2
Wepener, S. Africa 88 D4
Werda, Botswana 88 D3
Werdau, Germany 24 E8
Werder, Germany 24 C8
Werder, Ethiopia 68 F4
Werdohl, Germany 24 D3
Wereilu, Ethiopia 81 E4
Weri, Indonesia 63 E8
Werneck, Germany 25 F6
Wernigerode, Germany 24 D6
Werra →, Germany 24 D5
Werrimull, Australia 95 E3
Werris Creek, Australia 95 E5
Wertach →, Germany 25 G6
Wertheim, Germany 25 F5
Wertingen, Germany 25 G6
Wesel, Germany 24 D2
Weser →, Germany 24 B4
Weser-Ems □, Germany 24 C3
Weserbergland, Germany 24 C5
Wesiri, Indonesia 63 F7
Weslemkoon L., Canada 110 A7
Wesleyville, Canada 103 C9
Wesleyville, U.S.A. 110 D4
Wessel, C., Australia 94 A2
Wessel Is., Australia 94 A2
Wesselburen, Germany 24 A4
Wessington Springs, U.S.A. 112 C5
West, U.S.A. 113 K6
West →, U.S.A. 111 D12
West Baines →, Australia 92 C4
West Bank □, Asia 75 C4
West Bend, U.S.A. 108 D1
West Bengal □, India 69 H13
West Berkshire □, U.K. 13 F6
West Beskids = Západné Beskydy, Europe 27 B12
West Branch, U.S.A. 108 C3
West Branch Susquehanna →, U.S.A. 111 F8
West Bromwich, U.K. 13 E6
West Burra, U.K. 14 A7
West Canada Cr. →, U.S.A. 111 C10
West Cape Howe, Australia 93 G2
West Chazy, U.S.A. 111 B11
West Chester, U.S.A. 111 G9
West Columbia, U.S.A. 113 L7
West Covina, U.S.A. 117 L9
West Des Moines, U.S.A. 112 E8
West Dunbartonshire □, U.K. 14 F4
West End, Bahamas 120 A4
West Falkland, Falk. Is. 122 J4
West Fargo, U.S.A. 112 B6
West Farmington, U.S.A. 110 E4
West Fjord = Vestfjorden, Norway 8 C15
West Fork Trinity →, U.S.A. 113 J6
West Frankfort, U.S.A. 112 G10
West Hartford, U.S.A. 111 E12
West Haven, U.S.A. 111 E12
West Hazleton, U.S.A. 111 F9
West Helena, U.S.A. 113 H9
West Hurley, U.S.A. 111 E10
West Ice Shelf, Antarctica 5 C7
West Indies, Cent. Amer. 121 D7
West Jordan, U.S.A. 114 F8
West Lorne, Canada 110 D3
West Lothian □, U.K. 14 F5
West Lunga →, Zambia 87 E1
West Memphis, U.S.A. 113 H9
West Midlands □, U.K. 13 E6
West Mifflin, U.S.A. 110 F5
West Milton, U.S.A. 110 E8
West Monroe, U.S.A. 113 J8
West Newton, U.S.A. 110 F5
West Nicholson, Zimbabwe 87 G2
West Palm Beach, U.S.A. 109 M5
West Plains, U.S.A. 113 G9
West Point, N.Y., U.S.A. 111 E11
West Point, Nebr., U.S.A. 112 E6
West Point, Va., U.S.A. 108 G7
West Pt. = Ouest, Pte. de l', Canada 103 C7
West Pt., Australia 95 F2
West Road →, Canada 104 C4
West Rutland, U.S.A. 111 C11
West Schelde = Westerschelde →, Neths. 17 C3
West Seneca, U.S.A. 110 D6
West Siberian Plain, Russia 52 C11
West Sussex □, U.K. 13 G7
West-Terschelling, Neths. 17 A5
West Valley City, U.S.A. 114 F8
West Virginia □, U.S.A. 108 F5
West-Vlaanderen □, Belgium 17 D2
West Walker →, U.S.A. 116 G7
West Wyalong, Australia 95 E4
West Yellowstone, U.S.A. 114 D8
West Yorkshire □, U.K. 12 D6
Westall Pt., Australia 95 E1
Westbrook, U.S.A. 109 D10
Westbury, Australia 94 G4
Westby, U.S.A. 112 A2
Westend, U.S.A. 117 K9
Westerland, Germany 9 J13
Westerly, U.S.A. 111 E13
Western □, Ghana 82 D4
Western □, Kenya 86 B3
Western □, S. Leone 82 D2
Western □, Uganda 86 B3
Western □, Zambia 87 F1
Western Australia □, Australia 93 E2
Western Cape □, S. Africa 88 E3
Western Dvina = Daugava →, Latvia 9 H21
Western Ghats, India 66 N9
Western Isles □, U.K. 14 D1
Western Sahara ■, Africa 78 D3
Western Samoa ■, Pac. Oc. 91 B13
Westernport, U.S.A. 108 F6
Westerschelde →, Neths. 17 C3
Westerstede, Germany 24 B3
Westerwald, Germany 24 E3
Westfield, Mass., U.S.A. 111 D12
Westfield, N.Y., U.S.A. 110 D5
Westfield, Pa., U.S.A. 110 E7
Westhill, U.K. 14 D6
Westhope, U.S.A. 112 A4
Westland Bight, N.Z. 91 K3
Westlock, Canada 104 C6
Westmar, Australia 95 D4
Westmeath □, Ireland 15 C4
Westminster, U.S.A. 108 F7
Westmont, U.S.A. 110 F6
Westmorland, U.S.A. 117 M11
Weston, Oreg., U.S.A. 114 D4
Weston, W. Va., U.S.A. 108 F5
Weston I., Canada 102 B4
Weston-super-Mare, U.K. 13 F5
Westover, U.S.A. 110 F6
Westport, Canada 111 B8
Westport, Ireland 15 C2
Westport, N.Z. 91 J3
Westport, N.Y., U.S.A. 111 B11
Westport, Oreg., U.S.A. 116 D3
Westport, Wash., U.S.A. 116 D2
Westray, Canada 105 C8
Westray, U.K. 14 B5
Westree, Canada 102 C3
Westville, U.S.A. 116 F6
Westwood, U.S.A. 114 F3
Wetar, Indonesia 63 F7
Wetaskiwin, Canada 104 C6
Wete, Tanzania 84 F7
Wetherby, U.K. 12 D6
Wethersfield, U.S.A. 111 E12
Wetteren, Belgium 17 D3
Wetzlar, Germany 24 E4
Wewoka, U.S.A. 113 H6
Wexford, Ireland 15 D5
Wexford □, Ireland 15 D5
Wexford Harbour, Ireland 15 D5
Weyburn, Canada 105 D8
Weyer Markt, Austria 26 D7
Weyhe, Germany 24 C4
Weyib →, Ethiopia 81 F5
Weymouth, Canada 103 D6
Weymouth, U.K. 13 G5
Weymouth, U.S.A. 111 D14
Weymouth, C., Australia 94 A3
Wha Ti, Canada 100 B8
Whakatane, N.Z. 91 G6
Whale →, Canada 103 A6
Whale Cove, Canada 105 A10
Whales, B. of, Antarctica 5 D12
Whalsay, U.K. 14 A8
Whangamomona, N.Z. 91 H5
Whangarei, N.Z. 91 F5
Whangarei Harb., N.Z. 91 F5
Wharfe →, U.K. 12 D6
Wharfedale, U.K. 12 C5
Wharton, N.J., U.S.A. 111 F10
Wharton, Pa., U.S.A. 110 E6
Wharton, Tex., U.S.A. 113 L6
Wheatland, Calif., U.S.A. 116 F5
Wheatland, Wyo., U.S.A. 112 D2
Wheatley, Canada 110 D2
Wheaton, Md., U.S.A. 108 F7
Wheaton, Minn., U.S.A. 112 C6
Wheelbarrow Pk., U.S.A. 116 H10
Wheeler, Oreg., U.S.A. 114 D2
Wheeler, Tex., U.S.A. 113 H4
Wheeler →, Canada 103 A6
Wheeler L., U.S.A. 109 H2
Wheeler Pk., N. Mex., U.S.A. 115 H11
Wheeler Pk., Nev., U.S.A. 115 G6
Wheeler Ridge, U.S.A. 117 L8
Wheeling, U.S.A. 110 F4
Whernside, U.K. 12 C5
Whiskey Jack L., Canada 105 B8
Whistleduck Cr. →, Australia 94 C2
Whistler, Canada 104 C4
Whitby, Canada 110 C6
Whitby, U.K. 12 C7
White →, Ark., U.S.A. 113 J9
White →, Ind., U.S.A. 108 F2
White →, S. Dak., U.S.A. 112 D5
White →, Tex., U.S.A. 113 J4
White →, Utah, U.S.A. 114 F9
White →, Vt., U.S.A. 111 C12
White →, Wash., U.S.A. 116 C4
White, L., Australia 92 D4
White B., Canada 103 C8
White Bird, U.S.A. 114 D5
White Butte, U.S.A. 112 B3
White City, U.S.A. 114 E2
White Cliffs, Australia 95 E3
White Hall, U.S.A. 112 F9
White Haven, U.S.A. 111 E9
White Horse, Vale of, U.K. 13 F6
White I., N.Z. 91 G6
White L., Canada 111 A8
White L., U.S.A. 113 L8
White Mountain Peak, U.S.A. 115 G4
White Mts., Calif., U.S.A. 116 H8
White Mts., N.H., U.S.A. 111 B13
White Nile = Nîl el Abyad →, Sudan 81 D3
White Nile Dam = Khazzân Jabal al Awliyâ, Sudan 81 D3
White Otter L., Canada 102 C1
White Pass, U.S.A. 116 D5
White Plains, U.S.A. 111 E11
White River, Canada 102 C2
White River, S. Africa 89 D5
White River, U.S.A. 112 D4
White Rock, Canada 116 A4
White Russia = Belarus ■, Europe 46 F4
White Sea = Beloye More, Russia 50 C4
White Sulphur Springs, Mont., U.S.A. 114 C8
White Sulphur Springs, W. Va., U.S.A. 108 G5
White Swan, U.S.A. 116 D6
White Volta →, Ghana 83 D4
Whitecliffs, N.Z. 91 K3
Whitecourt, Canada 104 C5
Whiteface Mt., U.S.A. 111 B11
Whitefield, U.S.A. 111 B13
Whitefish, U.S.A. 114 B6
Whitefish L., Canada 105 A7
Whitefish Point, U.S.A. 108 B3
Whitegull, L., Canada 103 A7
Whitehall, Mich., U.S.A. 108 D2
Whitehall, Mont., U.S.A. 114 C7
Whitehall, N.Y., U.S.A. 111 C11
Whitehall, Wis., U.S.A. 112 C9
Whitehaven, U.K. 12 C4
Whitehorse, Canada 104 A1
Whitemark, Australia 94 G4
Whiteplains, Liberia 82 D2
Whiteriver, U.S.A. 115 K9
Whitesand →, Canada 104 A5
Whitesands, S. Africa 88 E3
Whitesboro, N.Y., U.S.A. 111 C9
Whitesboro, Tex., U.S.A. 113 J6
Whiteshell Prov. Park, Canada 105 D9
Whitesville, U.S.A. 110 D7
Whiteville, U.S.A. 109 H6
Whitewater, U.S.A. 108 D1
Whitewater Baldy, U.S.A. 115 K9
Whitewater L., Canada 102 B2
Whitewood, Australia 94 C3
Whitewood, Canada 105 C8
Whithorn, U.K. 14 G4
Whitianga, N.Z. 91 G5
Whitman, U.S.A. 111 D14
Whitney, Canada 102 C4
Whitney, Mt., U.S.A. 115 J8
Whitney Point, U.S.A. 111 D9
Whitstable, U.K. 13 F9
Whitsunday I., Australia 94 C4
Whittier, U.S.A. 117 M8
Whittlesea, Australia 95 F4
Wholdaia L., Canada 105 A8
Whyalla, Australia 95 E2
Wiarton, Canada 102 D3
Wiawso, Ghana 82 D4
Wiay, U.K. 14 D1
Wiązów, Poland 45 H4
Wibaux, U.S.A. 112 B2
Wichian Buri, Thailand 64 E3
Wichita, U.S.A. 113 G6
Wichita Falls, U.S.A. 113 J5
Wick, U.K. 14 C5
Wicked Pt., Canada 110 C7
Wickenburg, U.S.A. 115 K7
Wickepin, Australia 93 F2
Wickham, Australia 92 D2
Wickham, C., Australia 94 F3
Wickliffe, U.S.A. 110 E3
Wicklow, Ireland 15 D5
Wicklow □, Ireland 15 D5
Wicklow Hd., Ireland 15 D6
Wicklow Mts., Ireland 15 C5
Widawa, Poland 45 G8
Widawka →, Poland 45 G5
Widgeegoara Cr. →, Australia 95 D4
Widgiemooltha, Australia 93 F3
Widnes, U.K. 12 D5
Więcbork, Poland 45 E4
Wiehl, Germany 24 E3
Wiek, Germany 24 A9
Wielbark, Poland 44 E7
Wieleń, Poland 45 F3
Wielichowo, Poland 45 F3
Wieliczka, Poland 45 J7
Wielkopolskie □, Poland 45 F4
Wieluń, Poland 45 G5
Wien, Austria 27 C9
Wiener Neustadt, Austria 27 D9
Wieprz →, Poland 45 G8
Wieprza →, Poland 44 D3
Wieruszów, Poland 45 G5
Wiesbaden, Germany 25 E4
Wiesental, Germany 25 F4
Wiesloch, Germany 25 F4
Wiesmoor, Germany 24 B3
Wieżyca, Poland 44 D5
Wigan, U.K. 12 D5
Wiggins, Colo., U.S.A. 112 E2
Wiggins, Miss., U.S.A. 113 K10
Wight, I. of □, U.K. 13 G6
Wigry, Jezioro, Poland 44 D10
Wigston, U.K. 13 E6
Wigton, U.K. 12 C4
Wigtown, U.K. 14 G4
Wigtown B., U.K. 14 G4
Wil, Switz. 25 H5
Wilamowice, Poland 45 J6
Wilber, U.S.A. 112 E6
Wilberforce, Canada 110 A6
Wilberforce, C., Australia 94 A2
Wilburton, U.S.A. 113 H7
Wilcannia, Australia 95 E3
Wilcox, U.S.A. 110 E6
Wildbad, Germany 25 G4
Wildeshausen, Germany 24 C4
Wildon, Austria 26 E8
Wildrose, U.S.A. 117 J9
Wildspitze, Austria 26 E3
Wilga →, Poland 45 G8
Wilge →, S. Africa 89 D4
Wilhelm II Coast, Antarctica 5 C7
Wilhelmsburg, Austria 26 C8
Wilhelmshaven, Germany 24 B4
Wilhelmstal, Namibia 88 C2
Wilkes-Barre, U.S.A. 111 E9
Wilkie, Canada 105 C7
Wilkinsburg, U.S.A. 110 F5
Wilkinson Lakes, Australia 93 E5
Willandra Creek →, Australia 95 E4
Willapa B., U.S.A. 114 C2
Willapa Hills, U.S.A. 116 D3
Willard, N.Y., U.S.A. 110 D8
Willard, Ohio, U.S.A. 110 E2
Willcox, U.S.A. 115 K9
Willemstad, Neth. Ant. 121 D6
Willet, U.S.A. 111 D9
William →, Canada 105 B7
William 'Bill' Dannely Res., U.S.A. 109 J2
William Creek, Australia 95 D2
Williams, Australia 93 F2
Williams, Ariz., U.S.A. 115 J7
Williams, Calif., U.S.A. 116 F4
Williams Harbour, Canada 103 B8
Williams Lake, Canada 104 C4
Williamsburg, Ky., U.S.A. 109 G3
Williamsburg, Pa., U.S.A. 110 F6
Williamsburg, Va., U.S.A. 108 G7
Williamson, N.Y., U.S.A. 110 C7
Williamson, W. Va., U.S.A. 108 G4
Williamsport, U.S.A. 110 E7
Williamston, U.S.A. 109 H7
Williamstown, Australia 95 F3
Williamstown, Ky., U.S.A. 108 F3
Williamstown, Mass., U.S.A. 111 D11
Williamstown, N.Y., U.S.A. 111 C9
Willimantic, U.S.A. 111 E12
Willingboro, U.S.A. 108 E8
Willis Group, Australia 94 B5
Williston, S. Africa 88 E3
Williston, Fla., U.S.A. 109 L4
Williston, N. Dak., U.S.A. 112 A3
Williston L., Canada 104 B4
Willits, U.S.A. 114 G2
Willmar, U.S.A. 112 C7
Willoughby, U.S.A. 110 E3
Willow Bunch, Canada 105 D7
Willow L., Canada 104 A5
Willow Wall, The, China 57 C12
Willowick, U.S.A. 110 E3
Willowlake →, Canada 104 A4
Willowmore, S. Africa 88 E3
Willows, U.S.A. 116 F4
Willowvale = Gatyana, S. Africa 89 E4
Wills, L., Australia 92 D4
Wills Cr. →, Australia 94 C3
Willsboro, U.S.A. 111 B11
Willunga, Australia 95 F2
Wilmette, U.S.A. 108 D2
Wilmington, Australia 95 E2
Wilmington, Del., U.S.A. 108 F8
Wilmington, N.C., U.S.A. 109 H7
Wilmington, Ohio, U.S.A. 108 F4
Wilmington, Vt., U.S.A. 111 D12
Wilpena →, Australia 95 E2
Wilsall, U.S.A. 114 D8
Wilson, N.C., U.S.A. 109 H7
Wilson, N.Y., U.S.A. 110 C6
Wilson, Pa., U.S.A. 111 F9
Wilson →, Australia 92 C4
Wilson Bluff, Australia 93 F4
Wilson Inlet, Australia 93 G2
Wilsons Promontory, Australia 95 F4
Wilster, Germany 24 B5
Wilton, U.S.A. 112 B4
Wilton →, Australia 94 A1
Wiltshire □, U.K. 13 F6
Wiltz, Lux. 17 E5
Wiluna, Australia 93 E3
Wimborne Minster, U.K. 13 G6
Wimereux, France 19 B8
Wimmera →, Australia 95 F3
Winam G., Kenya 86 C3
Winburg, S. Africa 88 D4
Winchendon, U.S.A. 111 D12
Winchester, U.K. 13 F6
Winchester, Conn., U.S.A. 111 E11
Winchester, Idaho, U.S.A. 114 C5
Winchester, Ind., U.S.A. 108 E3
Winchester, Ky., U.S.A. 108 G3
Winchester, N.H., U.S.A. 111 D12
Winchester, Nev., U.S.A. 117 J11
Winchester, Tenn., U.S.A. 109 H2
Winchester, Va., U.S.A. 108 F6
Wind →, U.S.A. 114 E9
Wind River Range, U.S.A. 114 E9
Windau = Ventspils, Latvia 9 H19
Windber, U.S.A. 110 F6
Winder, U.S.A. 109 J4
Windermere, U.K. 12 C5
Windhoek, Namibia 88 C2
Windischgarsten, Austria 26 D7
Windom, U.S.A. 112 D7
Windorah, Australia 94 D3
Window Rock, U.S.A. 115 J9
Windrush →, U.K. 13 F6
Windsor, Australia 95 E5
Windsor, N.S., Canada 103 D7
Windsor, Ont., Canada 102 D3
Windsor, U.K. 13 F7
Windsor, Colo., U.S.A. 112 E2
Windsor, Conn., U.S.A. 111 E12
Windsor, Mo., U.S.A. 112 F8
Windsor, N.Y., U.S.A. 111 D9
Windsor, Vt., U.S.A. 111 C12
Windsor & Maidenhead □, U.K. 13 F7
Windsorton, S. Africa 88 D3
Windward Is., W. Indies 121 D7
Windward Passage = Vientos, Paso de los, Caribbean 121 C5
Winefred L., Canada 105 B6
Winejok, Sudan 81 F2
Winfield, U.S.A. 113 G6
Wingate Mts., Australia 92 B5
Wingham, Australia 95 E5
Wingham, Canada 102 D3
Winisk, Canada 102 A2
Winisk →, Canada 102 A2
Winisk L., Canada 102 B2
Wink, U.S.A. 113 K3
Winkler, Canada 105 D9
Winklern, Austria 26 E5
Winlock, U.S.A. 116 D4
Winneba, Ghana 83 D4
Winnebago, L., U.S.A. 108 D1
Winnecke Cr. →, Australia 92 C5
Winnemucca, U.S.A. 114 F5
Winnemucca L., U.S.A. 114 F4
Winnett, U.S.A. 114 C9
Winnfield, U.S.A. 113 K8
Winnibigoshish, L., U.S.A. 112 B7
Winnipeg, Canada 105 D9
Winnipeg →, Canada 105 C9
Winnipeg, L., Canada 105 C9
Winnipeg Beach, Canada 105 C9
Winnipegosis, Canada 105 C9
Winnipegosis L., Canada 105 C9
Winnipesaukee, L., U.S.A. 111 C13
Winnisquam L., U.S.A. 111 C13
Winnsboro, La., U.S.A. 113 J9
Winnsboro, S.C., U.S.A. 109 H5
Winnsboro, Tex., U.S.A. 113 J7
Winokapau, L., Canada 103 B7
Winona, Minn., U.S.A. 112 C9
Winona, Miss., U.S.A. 113 J10
Winooski, U.S.A. 111 B11
Winooski →, U.S.A. 111 B11
Winschoten, Neths. 17 A7
Winsen, Germany 24 B6
Winsford, U.K. 12 D5
Winslow, Ariz., U.S.A. 115 J8
Winslow, Wash., U.S.A. 116 C4
Winsted, U.S.A. 111 E11
Winston-Salem, U.S.A. 109 G5
Winter Garden, U.S.A. 109 L5
Winter Haven, U.S.A. 109 M5
Winter Park, U.S.A. 109 L5
Winterberg, Germany 24 D4
Winterhaven, U.S.A. 117 N12
Winters, U.S.A. 116 G5
Wintersville, U.S.A. 110 F4
Winterswijk, Neths. 17 C6
Winterthur, Switz. 25 H4
Winthrop, U.S.A. 114 B3
Winton, Australia 94 C3
Winton, N.Z. 91 M2
Wipper →, Germany 24 D7
Wirrulla, Australia 95 E1
Wisbech, U.K. 13 E8
Wisconsin □, U.S.A. 112 C10
Wisconsin →, U.S.A. 112 D9
Wisconsin Rapids, U.S.A. 112 C10
Wisdom, U.S.A. 114 D7
Wishaw, U.K. 14 F5
Wishek, U.S.A. 112 B5
Wisła, Poland 45 J5
Wisła →, Poland 44 D5
Wisłok →, Poland 45 H9

Wisłoka →, Poland 45 H8
Wismar, Germany 24 B7
Wisner, U.S.A. 112 E6
Wissant, France 19 B8
Wissembourg, France 19 C14
Wisznice, Poland 45 G10
Witbank, S. Africa 89 D4
Witdraai, S. Africa 88 D3
Witham, U.K. 13 F8
Witham →, U.K. 12 E7
Withernsea, U.K. 12 D8
Witkowo, Poland 45 F4
Witney, U.K. 13 F6
Witnica, Poland 45 F1
Witnossob →, Namibia 88 D3
Wittdün, Germany 24 A4
Witten, Germany 24 D3
Wittenberge, Germany 24 B7
Wittenburg, Germany 24 B7
Wittenheim, France 19 E14
Wittenoom, Australia 92 D2
Wittingen, Germany 24 C6
Wittlich, Germany 25 F2
Wittmund, Germany 24 B3
Wittow, Germany 24 A9
Wittstock, Germany 24 B8
Witvlei, Namibia 88 C2
Witzenhausen, Germany ... 24 D5
Wkra →, Poland 45 F7
Władysławowo, Poland 44 D5
Wleń, Poland 45 G2
Wlingi, Indonesia 63 H15
Włocławek, Poland 45 F6
Włodawa, Poland 45 G10
Włoszczowa, Poland 45 H6
Woburn, U.S.A. 111 D13
Wodian, China 56 H7
Wodzisław Śląski, Poland .. 45 H5
Wœrth, France 19 D14
Woinbogoin, China 58 A2
Woippy, France 19 C13
Wojcieszow, Poland 45 H2
Wokam, Indonesia 63 F8
Woking, U.K. 13 F7
Wokingham □, U.K. 13 F7
Wolbrom, Poland 45 H6
Wołczyn, Poland 45 G5
Woldegk, Germany 24 B9
Wolf →, Canada 104 A2
Wolf Creek, U.S.A. 114 C7
Wolf L., Canada 104 A2
Wolf Point, U.S.A. 112 A2
Wolfe I., Canada 102 D4
Wolfeboro, U.S.A. 111 C13
Wolfen, Germany 24 D8
Wolfenbüttel, Germany ... 24 C6
Wolfratshausen, Germany . 25 H7
Wolfsberg, Austria 26 E7
Wolfsburg, Germany 24 C6
Wolgast, Germany 24 A9
Wolhusen, Switz. 25 H4
Wolin, Poland 44 E1
Wollaston, Is., Chile 128 H3
Wollaston, L., Canada 105 B8
Wollaston Lake, Canada .. 105 B8
Wollaston Pen., Canada .. 100 B8
Wollongong, Australia 95 E5
Wolmaransstad, S. Africa . 88 D4
Wolmirstedt, Germany 24 C7
Wołomin, Poland 45 F8
Wołów, Poland 45 G3
Wolseley, S. Africa 88 E2
Wolsey, U.S.A. 112 C5
Wolstenholme, C., Canada . 98 C12
Wolsztyn, Poland 45 F3
Wolvega, Neths. 17 B6
Wolverhampton, U.K. 13 E5
Wondai, Australia 95 D5
Wongalarroo L., Australia 95 E3
Wongan Hills, Australia .. 93 F2
Wŏnju, S. Korea 57 F14
Wonosari, Indonesia 63 G14
Wonosobo, Indonesia 63 G13
Wonowon, Canada 104 B4
Wŏnsan, N. Korea 57 E14
Wonthaggi, Australia 95 F4
Wood Buffalo Nat. Park,
   Canada 104 B6
Wood Is., Australia 92 C3
Wood L., Canada 105 B8
Woodah I., Australia 94 A2
Woodbourne, U.S.A. 111 E10
Woodbridge, Canada 110 C5
Woodbridge, U.K. 13 E9
Woodburn, U.S.A. 114 D2
Woodenbong, Australia .. 95 D5
Woodend, Australia 95 F3
Woodford, Australia 95 D5
Woodfords, U.S.A. 116 G7
Woodlake, U.S.A. 116 J7
Woodland, Calif., U.S.A. 116 G5
Woodland, Maine, U.S.A. 109 C12
Woodland, Pa., U.S.A. .. 110 F6
Woodland, Wash., U.S.A. 116 E4
Woodland Caribou Prov.
   Park, Canada 105 C10
Woodridge, Canada 105 D9
Woodroffe, Mt., Australia 93 E5
Woods, L., Australia 94 B1
Woods, L. of the, Canada 105 D10
Woodside, Australia 95 F4
Woodstock, Australia 94 B4
Woodstock, N.B., Canada 103 C6
Woodstock, Ont., Canada 102 D3
Woodstock, U.K. 13 F6
Woodstock, Ill., U.S.A. . 112 D10
Woodstock, Vt., U.S.A. . 111 C12
Woodsville, U.S.A. 111 B13
Woodville, N.Z. 91 J5
Woodville, Miss., U.S.A. 113 K9
Woodville, Tex., U.S.A. . 113 K7

Woodward, U.S.A. 113 G5
Woody, U.S.A. 117 K8
Woody →, Canada 105 C8
Woolamai, C., Australia . 95 F4
Wooler, U.K. 12 B5
Woolgoolga, Australia ... 95 E5
Woomera, Australia 95 E2
Woonsocket, R.I., U.S.A. 111 E13
Woonsocket, S. Dak.,
   U.S.A. 112 C5
Wooramel →, Australia .. 93 E1
Wooramel Roadhouse,
   Australia 93 E1
Wooster, U.S.A. 110 F3
Worcester, S. Africa 88 E2
Worcester, U.K. 13 E5
Worcester, Mass., U.S.A. 111 D13
Worcester, N.Y., U.S.A. 111 D10
Worcestershire □, U.K. .. 13 E5
Wörgl, Austria 26 D5
Workington, U.K. 12 C4
Worksop, U.K. 12 D6
Workum, Neths. 17 B5
Worland, U.S.A. 114 D10
Wormhout, France 19 B9
Worms, Germany 25 F4
Worsley, Canada 104 B5
Wörth, Germany 25 F8
Wortham, U.S.A. 113 K6
Wörther See, Austria 26 E7
Worthing, U.K. 13 G7
Worthington, Minn., U.S.A. 112 D7
Worthington, Pa., U.S.A. 110 F5
Wosi, Indonesia 63 E7
Wou-han = Wuhan, China 59 B10
Wousi = Wuxi, China ... 59 B13
Wowoni, Indonesia 63 E6
Wrangel I. = Vrangelya,
   Ostrov, Russia 51 B19
Wrangell, U.S.A. 104 B2
Wrangell Mts., U.S.A. .. 100 B5
Wrath, C., U.K. 14 C3
Wray, U.S.A. 112 E3
Wrekin, The, U.K. 13 E5
Wrens, U.S.A. 109 J4
Wrexham, U.K. 12 D4
Wrexham □, U.K. 12 D5
Wriezen, Germany 24 C10
Wright = Paranas, Phil. . 61 F6
Wright, U.S.A. 112 D2
Wright Pt., Canada 110 C3
Wrightson Mt., U.S.A. . 115 L8
Wrightwood, U.S.A. ... 117 L9
Wrigley, Canada 100 B7
Wrocław, Poland 45 G4
Wronki, Poland 45 F3
Września, Poland 45 F4
Wschowa, Poland 45 G3
Wu Jiang →, China ... 58 C6
Wu'an, China 56 F8
Wubin, Australia 93 F2
Wubu, China 56 F6
Wuchang, China 57 B14
Wucheng, China 56 F9
Wuchuan, Guangdong,
   China 59 G8
Wuchuan, Guizhou, China 58 C7
Wuchuan,
   Nei Mongol Zizhiqu,
   China 56 D6
Wudi, China 57 F9
Wuding, China 58 E4
Wuding He →, China .. 56 F6
Wudinna, Australia 95 E2
Wudu, China 56 H3
Wufeng, China 59 B8
Wugang, China 59 D8
Wugong Shan, China ... 59 D9
Wuhan, China 59 B10
Wuhe, China 57 H9
Wuhsi = Wuxi, China . 59 B13
Wuhu, China 59 B12
Wujiang, China 59 B13
Wukari, Nigeria 83 D6
Wulajie, China 57 B14
Wular L., India 69 B6
Wulehe, Ghana 83 D5
Wulian, China 57 G10
Wuliang Shan, China .. 58 E3
Wuliaru, Indonesia 63 F8
Wuling Shan, China ... 58 C7
Wulong, China 58 C6
Wulumuchi = Ürümqi,
   China 50 E9
Wum, Cameroon 83 D7
Wuming, China 58 F7
Wun Rog, Sudan 81 F2
Wuning, China 59 C10
Wunnummin L., Canada 102 B2
Wunsiedel, Germany ... 25 E8
Wunstorf, Germany 24 C5
Wuntho, Burma 67 H19
Wuping, China 59 E11
Wuppertal, Germany ... 24 D3
Wuppertal, S. Africa ... 88 E2
Wuqing, China 57 E9
Wurtsboro, U.S.A. 111 E10
Würzburg, Germany ... 25 F5
Wurzen, Germany 24 D8
Wushan, China 56 G3
Wushishi, Nigeria 83 D6
Wusuli Jiang = Ussuri →,
   Asia 54 A7
Wutach →, Germany . 25 H4
Wutai, China 56 E7
Wutingju, China 59 E13
Wuting = Huimin, China 57 F9
Wutong, China 59 E8
Wutonghaolai, China .. 57 C11
Wutongqiao, China 58 C4

Wuwei, Anhui, China ... 59 B11
Wuwei, Gansu, China ... 60 C5
Wuxi, Jiangsu, China ... 59 B13
Wuxi, Sichuan, China ... 58 B7
Wuxiang, China 56 F7
Wuxuan, China 58 F7
Wuxue, China 59 C10
Wuyang, China 56 H7
Wuyi, Hebei, China 56 F8
Wuyi, Zhejiang, China . 59 C12
Wuyi Shan, China 59 D11
Wuyishan, China 59 D12
Wuyo, Nigeria 83 C7
Wuyuan, Jiangxi, China 59 C11
Wuyuan,
   Nei Mongol Zizhiqu,
   China 56 D5
Wuzhai, China 56 E6
Wuzhi Shan, China 64 C7
Wuzhong, China 56 E4
Wuzhou, China 59 F8
Wyaaba Cr. →, Australia 94 B3
Wyalkatchem, Australia 93 F2
Wyalusing, U.S.A. 111 E8
Wyandotte, U.S.A. ... 108 D4
Wyandra, Australia 95 D4
Wyangala Res., Australia 95 E4
Wyara, L., Australia ... 95 D3
Wycheproof, Australia . 95 F3
Wye →, U.K. 13 F5
Wyemandoo, Australia . 93 E2
Wyk, Germany 24 A4
Wymondham, U.K. 13 E9
Wymore, U.S.A. 112 E6
Wyndham, Australia ... 92 C4
Wyndham, N.Z. 91 M2
Wynne, U.S.A. 113 H9
Wynyard, Australia ... 94 G4
Wynyard, Canada 105 C8
Wyola L., Australia ... 93 E5
Wyoming, Canada 110 D2
Wyoming □, U.S.A. .. 114 E10
Wyomissing, U.S.A. .. 111 F9
Wyong, Australia 95 E5
Wyrzysk, Poland 45 E4
Wyśmierzyce, Poland .. 45 G7
Wysoka, Poland 45 E4
Wysokie, Poland 45 H9
Wysokie Mazowieckie,
   Poland 45 F9
Wyszków, Poland 45 F8
Wyszogród, Poland ... 45 F7
Wytheville, U.S.A. 108 G5
Wyżyna Małopolska, Poland 45 H7

X

Xaçmaz, Azerbaijan 49 K9
Xai-Xai, Mozam. 89 D5
Xainza, China 60 C3
Xangongo, Angola 88 B2
Xankändi, Azerbaijan ... 70 B5
Xanlar, Azerbaijan 49 K8
Xanten, Germany 24 D2
Xánthi, Greece 41 E8
Xánthi □, Greece 41 E8
Xanthos, Turkey 39 E11
Xanxerê, Brazil 127 B5
Xapuri, Brazil 124 F5
Xar Moron He →, China 57 C11
Xarrë, Albania 40 G4
Xátiva, Spain 33 G4
Xau, L., Botswana 88 C3
Xavantina, Brazil 127 A5
Xenia, U.S.A. 108 F4
Xeropotamos →, Cyprus 36 E11
Xertigny, France 19 D13
Xhora, S. Africa 89 E4
Xhumo, Botswana 88 C3
Xi Jiang →, China 59 F9
Xi Xian, Henan, China . 59 A10
Xi Xian, Shanxi, China . 56 F6
Xia Xian, China 56 G6
Xiachengzi, China 57 B16
Xiachuan Dao, China ... 59 G9
Xiaguan, China 58 E3
Xiajiang, China 59 D10
Xiajin, China 56 F9
Xiamen, China 59 E12
Xi'an, China 56 G5
Xian Xian, China 56 E9
Xianfeng, China 58 C7
Xiang Jiang →, China . 59 C9
Xiangcheng, Henan, China 56 H8
Xiangcheng, Henan, China 56 H7
Xiangcheng, Sichuan, China 58 C2
Xiangdu, China 58 F6
Xiangfan, China 59 A9
Xianggang = Hong Kong □,
   China 59 F10
Xianghuang Qi, China .. 56 C7
Xiangning, China 56 G6
Xiangquan He = Sutlej →,
   Pakistan 68 E4
Xiangshan, China 59 C13
Xiangshui, China 57 G10
Xiangtan, China 59 D9
Xiangxiang, China 59 D9
Xiangyin, China 59 C9
Xiangyun, China 58 E3
Xiangzhou, China 58 F7
Xianju, China 59 C13
Xianning, China 59 C10
Xianshui He →, China . 58 B3
Xiantao, China 59 B9
Xianyang, China 56 G5

Xianyou, China 59 E12
Xiao Hinggan Ling, China 60 B7
Xiao Xian, China 56 G9
Xiaofeng, China 59 B12
Xiaogan, China 59 B9
Xiaojin, China 58 B4
Xiaoshan, China 59 F9
Xiaoyi, China 59 B13
Xiapu, China 56 F6
Xiawa, China 59 D12
Xiayi, China 57 C11
Xichang, China 56 G9
Xichong, China 58 D4
Xichuan, China 58 B5
Xichuan, China 56 H6
Xide, China 58 C4
Xiemahe, China 59 B8
Xieng Khouang, Laos .. 64 C4
Xifei He →, China 56 H9
Xifeng, Gansu, China .. 56 G4
Xifeng, Guizhou, China 58 D6
Xifeng, Liaoning, China 57 C13
Xifengzhen = Xifeng, China 56 G4
Xigazê, China 60 D3
Xihe, China 56 G3
Xihua, China 56 H8
Xilaganí, Greece 41 F9
Xiliao He →, China ... 57 C12
Xilin, China 58 E5
Xilókastron, Greece 38 C4
Xime, Guinea-Biss. 82 C2
Ximeng, China 58 F2
Xin Jiang →, China ... 59 C11
Xin Xian = Xinzhou, China 56 E7
Xinavane, Mozam. 89 D5
Xinbin, China 57 D13
Xincai, China 59 A10
Xinchang, China 59 C13
Xincheng,
   Guangxi Zhuangzu, China 58 E7
Xincheng, Jiangxi, China 59 D10
Xindu, China 58 B5
Xinfeng, Guangdong, China 59 E10
Xinfeng, Jiangxi, China 59 D11
Xinfeng, Jiangxi, China 59 D11
Xinfengjiang Skuiku, China 59 F10
Xing Xian, China 56 E6
Xing'an, Guangxi Zhuangzu,
   China 59 E8
Xingan, Jiangxi, China . 59 D10
Xingcheng, China 57 D11
Xingguo, China 59 D10
Xinghe, China 56 D7
Xinghua, China 57 H10
Xinghua Wan, China .. 59 E12
Xinglong, China 57 D9
Xingning, China 59 E10
Xingping, China 56 G5
Xingren, China 58 E5
Xingshan, China 59 B8
Xingtai, China 56 F8
Xingu →, Brazil 122 D5
Xingwen, China 58 C5
Xingyang, China 56 G7
Xinhe, China 56 F8
Xinhua, China 59 D8
Xinhuang, China 58 D7
Xinhui, China 59 F9
Xining, China 60 C5
Xinjian, China 59 C10
Xinjiang Uygur Zizhiqu □,
   China 60 B3
Xinjie, China 58 D3
Xinjin = Pulandian, China 57 E11
Xinjin, China 58 B4
Xinkai He →, China ... 57 C12
Xinle, China 56 E8
Xinlitun, China 57 D12
Xinlong, China 58 B3
Xinmin, China 57 D12
Xinning, China 59 D8
Xinping, China 58 E3
Xinshao, China 59 D8
Xintai, China 57 G9
Xintian, China 59 E9
Xinxian, China 59 B10
Xinxiang, China 56 G7
Xinxing, China 59 F9
Xinyang, China 59 A10
Xinye, China 59 A9
Xinyi, China 59 F8
Xinyu, China 59 D10
Xinzheng, China 57 C14
Xinzheng, China 56 G7
Xinzhou, Hubei, China . 59 B10
Xinzhou, Shanxi, China 56 E7
Xinzo de Limia, Spain . 34 C3
Xiong Xian, China 56 E9
Xiongyuecheng, China . 57 D12
Xiping, Henan, China .. 56 H8
Xiping, Henan, China .. 56 H6
Xique-Xique, Brazil 125 F10
Xisha Qundao = Paracel Is.,
   S. China Sea 62 A4
Xishui, Guizhou, China 58 C6
Xishui, Hubei, China .. 59 B10
Xitole, Guinea-Biss. ... 82 C2
Xiu Shui →, China ... 59 C10
Xiuning, China 59 C12
Xiuren, China 59 E8
Xiushan, China 58 C7
Xiushui, China 59 C10
Xiuwen, China 58 D6
Xiuyan, China 57 D12
Xixabangma Feng, China 67 E14
Xixia, China 56 H6
Xixiang, China 56 H4

Xiyang, China 56 F7
Xizang Zizhiqu □, China 60 C3
Xlendi, Malta 36 C1
Xu Jiang →, China ... 59 D11
Xuan Loc, Vietnam ... 65 G6
Xuan'en, China 58 C7
Xuanhan, China 58 B6
Xuanhua, China 56 D8
Xuanwei, China 58 C5
Xuanzhou, China 59 B12
Xuchang, China 56 G7
Xudat, Azerbaijan 49 K9
Xuefeng Shan, China . 59 D8
Xuejiaping, China 59 B8
Xun Jiang →, China . 59 F8
Xun Xian, China 56 G8
Xundian, China 58 E4
Xunwu, China 59 E10
Xunyang, China 56 H5
Xunyi, China 56 G5
Xúquer →, Spain 33 F4
Xushui, China 56 E8
Xuwen, China 59 G8
Xuyen Moc, Vietnam . 65 G6
Xuyong, China 58 C5
Xuzhou, China 57 G9
Xylophagou, Cyprus .. 36 E12

Y

Ya Xian, China 64 C7
Yaamba, Australia 94 C5
Ya'an, China 58 C4
Yaapeet, Australia 95 F3
Yabassi, Cameroon ... 83 E6
Yabelo, Ethiopia 81 G4
Yablanitsa, Bulgaria .. 41 C8
Yablonovy Ra. =
   Yablonovyy Khrebet,
   Russia 51 D12
Yablonovyy Khrebet, Russia 51 D12
Yabrai Shan, China ... 56 E2
Yabrūd, Syria 75 B5
Yacheng, China 64 C7
Yacuiba, Bolivia 126 A3
Yacuma →, Bolivia .. 124 F5
Yadgir, India 66 L10
Yadkin →, U.S.A. ... 109 H5
Yadrin, Russia 48 C8
Yaeyama-Rettō, Japan 55 M1
Yagaba, Ghana 83 C4
Yağcılar, Turkey 39 B10
Yagodnoye, Russia ... 51 C15
Yahila,
   Dem. Rep. of the Congo 86 B1
Yahk, Canada 104 D5
Yahotyn, Ukraine 47 G6
Yahuma,
   Dem. Rep. of the Congo 84 D4
Yahyalı, Turkey 72 C6
Yaita, Japan 55 F9
Yaiza, Canary Is. 37 F6
Yajiang, China 58 B3
Yajua, Nigeria 83 C7
Yakima, U.S.A. 114 C3
Yakima →, U.S.A. .. 114 C3
Yako, Burkina Faso .. 82 C4
Yakobi I., U.S.A. 104 B1
Yakoruda, Bulgaria ... 40 D7
Yakovlevka, Russia ... 54 B6
Yaku-Shima, Japan ... 55 J5
Yakumo, Japan 54 C10
Yakutat, U.S.A. 100 C6
Yakutia = Sakha □, Russia 51 C13
Yakutsk, Russia 51 C13
Yala, Thailand 65 J3
Yale, U.S.A. 110 C2
Yalgoo, Australia 93 E2
Yalinga, C.A.R. 84 C4
Yalkubul, Punta, Mexico 119 C7
Yalleroi, Australia ... 94 C4
Yalobusha →, U.S.A. 113 J9
Yalong Jiang →, China 58 D3
Yalova, Turkey 41 F13
Yalta, Ukraine 47 K8
Yalu Jiang →, China 57 E13
Yalvaç, Turkey 72 C4
Yam Ha Melah = Dead Sea,
   Asia 75 D4
Yam Kinneret, Israel .. 75 C4
Yamada, Japan 55 H5
Yamagata, Japan 54 E10
Yamagata □, Japan .. 54 E10
Yamaguchi, Japan ... 55 G5
Yamaguchi □, Japan . 55 G5
Yamal, Poluostrov, Russia 50 B8
Yamal Pen. = Yamal,
   Poluostrov, Russia .. 50 B8
Yamanashi □, Japan . 55 G9
Yamba, Australia 95 D5
Yamberoora Ra., Australia 92 C5
Yambéring, Guinea ... 82 C2
Yâmbiô, Sudan 81 G2
Yambol, Bulgaria 41 D10
Yamdena, Indonesia .. 63 F8
Yame, Japan 55 H5
Yamethin, Burma 67 J20
Yamma-Yamma, L.,
   Australia 95 D3
Yamoussoukro, Ivory C. 82 D4
Yampa →, U.S.A. ... 114 F9
Yampi Sd., Australia . 92 C3
Yampil, Moldova 47 H5
Yampol = Yampil, Moldova 47 H5
Yamrat, Nigeria 83 C6
Yamrukchal = Botev,
   Bulgaria 41 D8

Yamuna →, India 69 G9
Yamunanagar, India 68 D7
Yamzho Yumco, China .. 60 D4
Yan, Nigeria 83 C7
Yana →, Russia 51 B14
Yanagawa, Japan 55 H5
Yanai, Japan 55 H6
Yan'an, China 56 F5
Yanbian, China 58 D3
Yanbu 'al Baḥr, Si. Arabia . 70 F3
Yanchang, China 56 F6
Yancheng, Henan, China .. 56 H8
Yancheng, Jiangsu, China . 57 H11
Yanchep Beach, Australia .. 93 F2
Yanchi, China 56 F4
Yanchuan, China 56 F6
Yanco, Australia 95 E4
Yanco Cr. →, Australia ... 95 E4
Yandoon, Burma 67 L19
Yanfeng, China 58 E2
Yanfolila, Mali 82 C3
Yang Xian, China 56 H4
Yang-Yang, Senegal 82 B1
Yangambi,
  Dem. Rep. of the Congo . 86 B1
Yangbi, China 58 E2
Yangcheng, China 56 G7
Yangch'ü = Taiyuan, China 56 F7
Yangchun, China 59 F8
Yanggao, China 56 D7
Yanggu, China 56 F8
Yangjiang, China 59 G8
Yangliuqing, China 57 E9
Yangon = Rangoon, Burma 67 L20
Yangping, China 59 B8
Yangquan, China 56 F7
Yangshan, China 59 E9
Yangshuo, China 59 E8
Yangtse = Chang Jiang →,
  China 59 B13
Yangtze Kiang = Chang
  Jiang →, China 59 B13
Yangxin, China 59 C10
Yangyang, S. Korea 57 E15
Yangyuan, China 56 D8
Yangzhong, China 59 A12
Yangzhou, China 59 A12
Yanhe, China 58 C7
Yanji, China 57 C15
Yanjin, China 58 C5
Yanjing, China 58 C2
Yankton, U.S.A. 112 D6
Yanonge,
  Dem. Rep. of the Congo . 86 B1
Yanqi, China 60 B3
Yanqing, China 56 D8
Yanshan, Hebei, China ... 57 E9
Yanshan, Jiangxi, China .. 59 C11
Yanshan, Yunnan, China .. 58 F5
Yanshou, China 57 B15
Yantabulla, Australia 95 D4
Yantai, China 57 F11
Yanting, China 58 B5
Yantra →, Bulgaria 41 C9
Yanwa, China 58 D2
Yanyuan, China 58 D3
Yanzhou, China 56 G9
Yao Xian, China 56 G5
Yao Yai, Ko, Thailand ... 65 J2
Yao'an, China 58 E3
Yaodu, China 58 A5
Yaoundé, Cameroon 83 E7
Yaowan, China 57 G10
Yap I., Pac. Oc. 96 G5
Yapen, Indonesia 63 E9
Yapen, Selat, Indonesia .. 63 E9
Yapero, Indonesia 63 E9
Yappar →, Australia 94 B3
Yaqui →, Mexico 118 B2
Yar-Sale, Russia 50 C8
Yaraka, Australia 94 C3
Yaransk, Russia 48 B8
Yarbasan, Turkey 39 C10
Yardımcı Burnu, Turkey .. 39 E12
Yare →, U.K. 13 E9
Yaremcha, Ukraine 47 H3
Yarensk, Russia 50 C5
Yarfa, Si. Arabia 80 C4
Yarí →, Colombia 124 D4
Yarkand = Shache, China . 60 C2
Yarker, Canada 111 B8
Yarkhun →, Pakistan ... 69 A5
Yarmouth, Canada 103 D6
Yarmūk →, Syria 75 C4
Yaroslavl, Russia 46 D10
Yarqa, W. →, Egypt 75 F2
Yarra Yarra Lakes, Australia 93 E2
Yarram, Australia 95 F4
Yarraman, Australia 95 D5
Yarras, Australia 95 E5
Yartsevo, Sib., Russia ... 51 C10
Yartsevo, Smolensk, Russia . 46 E7
Yarumal, Colombia 124 B3
Yasawa Group, Fiji 91 C7
Yaselda, Belarus 47 F4
Yashi, Nigeria 83 C6
Yashikera, Nigeria 83 D5
Yashkul, Russia 49 G7
Yasin, Pakistan 69 A5
Yasinovataya, Ukraine ... 47 H9
Yasinski, L., Canada 102 B4
Yasinya, Ukraine 47 H3
Yasothon, Thailand 64 E5
Yass, Australia 95 E4
Yatağan, Turkey 39 D10
Yatakala, Niger 83 C5
Yates Center, U.S.A. 113 G7
Yathkyed L., Canada 105 A9
Yatsushiro, Japan 55 H5

Yatta Plateau, Kenya 86 C4
Yavari →, Peru 124 D4
Yávaros, Mexico 118 B3
Yavatmal, India 66 J11
Yavne, Israel 75 D3
Yavoriv, Ukraine 47 H2
Yavorov = Yavoriv, Ukraine 47 H2
Yavuzeli, Turkey 72 D7
Yawatahama, Japan 55 H6
Yawri B., S. Leone 82 D2
Yaxi, China 58 D6
Yazd, Iran 71 D7
Yazd □, Iran 71 D7
Yazd-e Khvāst, Iran 71 D7
Yazıköy, Turkey 39 E9
Yazman, Pakistan 68 E4
Yazoo →, U.S.A. 113 J9
Yazoo City, U.S.A. 113 J9
Ybbs, Austria 26 C8
Yding Skovhøj, Denmark . 11 J3
Ye Xian = Laizhou, China . 57 F10
Ye Xian, China 56 H7
Yebyu, Burma 64 E2
Yechŏn, S. Korea 57 F15
Yecla, Spain 33 G3
Yécora, Mexico 118 B3
Yedintsy = Edineţ, Moldova 43 B12
Yedseram →, Nigeria ... 83 C7
Yefremov, Russia 46 F10
Yeghegnadzor, Armenia .. 73 C11
Yegorlyk →, Russia 49 G5
Yegorlykskaya, Russia ... 49 G5
Yegoryevsk, Russia 46 E10
Yegros, Paraguay 126 B4
Yehuda, Midbar, Israel .. 75 D4
Yei, Sudan 81 G3
Yei, Nahr →, Sudan 81 F3
Yejmiadzin, Armenia 49 K7
Yekaterinburg, Russia ... 50 D7
Yekaterinodar = Krasnodar,
  Russia 47 H4
Yelabuga, Russia 48 C11
Yelan, Russia 48 E6
Yelarbon, Australia 95 D5
Yelatma, Russia 48 C5
Yelets, Russia 47 F10
Yélimané, Mali 82 B2
Yelizavetgrad = Kirovohrad,
  Ukraine 47 H7
Yell, U.K. 14 A7
Yell Sd., U.K. 14 A7
Yellow Sea, China 57 G12
Yellowhead Pass, Canada . 104 C5
Yellowknife, Canada 104 A6
Yellowknife →, Canada .. 104 A6
Yellowstone →, U.S.A. .. 112 B3
Yellowstone L., U.S.A. ... 114 D8
Yellowstone National Park,
  U.S.A. 114 D9
Yelnya, Russia 46 E7
Yelsk, Belarus 47 G5
Yelwa, Nigeria 83 C5
Yemen ■, Asia 74 E3
Yen Bai, Vietnam 58 G5
Yenagoa, Nigeria 83 E6
Yenakiyeve, Ukraine 47 H10
Yenakiyevo = Yenakiyeve,
  Ukraine 47 H10
Yenangyaung, Burma 67 J19
Yenbo = Yanbu 'al Baḥr,
  Si. Arabia 70 F3
Yenda, Australia 95 E4
Yende Millimou, Guinea .. 82 D2
Yendéré, Burkina Faso ... 82 C4
Yendi, Ghana 83 D4
Yéni, Niger 83 C5
Yenice, Ankara, Turkey ... 72 C5
Yenice, Aydın, Turkey ... 39 D10
Yenice, Çanakkale, Turkey . 39 B9
Yenice, Edirne, Turkey ... 41 F10
Yenice →, Turkey 72 D6
Yenifoça, Turkey 39 C8
Yenihisar, Turkey 39 D9
Yeniköy, Bursa, Turkey .. 41 F13
Yeniköy, Çanakkale, Turkey 39 B8
Yeniköy, Kütahya, Turkey . 39 C11
Yenipazar, Turkey 39 D10
Yenisaía, Greece 41 E8
Yenişehir, Turkey 41 F13
Yenisey →, Russia 50 B9
Yeniseysk, Russia 51 D10
Yeniseyskiy Zaliv, Russia . 50 B9
Yennádhi, Greece 36 C9
Yenne, France 21 C9
Yenotayevka, Russia 49 G8
Yenyuka, Russia 51 D13
Yeo →, U.K. 13 G5
Yeo, L., Australia 93 E3
Yeo I., Canada 110 A3
Yeola, India 66 J9
Yeoryioúpolis, Greece ... 36 D6
Yeovil, U.K. 13 G5
Yeppoon, Australia 94 C5
Yeráki, Greece 38 D4
Yerbent, Turkmenistan ... 50 F6
Yerbogachen, Russia 51 C11
Yerevan, Armenia 49 K7
Yerington, U.S.A. 114 G4
Yerkesik, Turkey 39 D10
Yerköy, Turkey 72 C6
Yermak, Kazakstan 50 D8
Yermo, U.S.A. 117 L10
Yerólakkos, Cyprus 36 D12
Yeropol, Russia 51 C17
Yeropótamos →, Greece . 36 D6
Yeroskípos, Cyprus 36 E11
Yershov, Russia 48 E9
Yerushalayim = Jerusalem,
  Israel 75 D4
Yerville, France 18 C7

Yes Tor, U.K. 13 G4
Yesan, S. Korea 57 F14
Yeşilhisar, Turkey 72 C6
Yeşilırmak →, Turkey ... 72 B7
Yeşilkent, Turkey 72 D7
Yeşilköy, Turkey 41 F12
Yeşilova, Turkey 39 D11
Yeşilyurt, Manisa, Turkey . 39 C10
Yeşilyurt, Muğla, Turkey .. 39 D10
Yesnogorsk, Russia 46 E9
Yeso, U.S.A. 113 H2
Yessentuki, Russia 49 H6
Yessey, Russia 51 C11
Yeste, Spain 33 G2
Yetman, Australia 95 D5
Yeu, Î. d', France 18 F4
Yevlakh = Yevlax,
  Azerbaijan 49 K8
Yevlax, Azerbaijan 49 K8
Yevpatoriya, Ukraine ... 47 K7
Yevsk, Russia 47 J10
Yeya →, Russia 47 J10
Yezd = Yazd, Iran 71 D7
Yezerishche, Belarus 46 E5
Yhati, Paraguay 126 B4
Yhú, Paraguay 127 B4
Yi →, Uruguay 126 C4
Yi 'Allaq, G., Egypt 75 E2
Yi He →, China 57 G10
Yi Xian, Anhui, China ... 59 C11
Yi Xian, Hebei, China ... 56 E8
Yi Xian, Liaoning, China . 57 D11
Yialí, Greece 39 E9
Yialiás →, Cyprus 36 D12
Yi'allaq, G., Egypt 80 A3
Yialousa, Cyprus 36 D13
Yiáltra, Greece 38 C4
Yianisádhes, Greece 36 D8
Yiannitsa, Greece 40 F6
Yibin, China 58 C5
Yichang, China 59 B8
Yicheng, Henan, China .. 56 B9
Yicheng, Shanxi, China .. 56 G6
Yichuan, China 56 F6
Yichun, Heilongjiang, China 60 B7
Yichun, Jiangxi, China ... 59 D10
Yidu, China 57 F10
Yidun, China 58 B2
Yifag, Ethiopia 81 E4
Yifeng, China 59 C10
Yihuang, China 59 D11
Yijun, China 56 G5
Yiliang, Yunnan, China .. 58 D5
Yiliang, Yunnan, China .. 58 E4
Yilong, China 58 B6
Yimen, China 58 E4
Yimianpo, China 57 B15
Yinchuan, China 56 E4
Yindarlgooda, L., Australia 93 F3
Ying He →, China 56 H9
Ying Xian, China 56 E7
Yingcheng, China 59 B9
Yingde, China 59 E9
Yingjiang, China 58 E1
Yingjing, China 58 C4
Yingkou, China 57 D12
Yingshan, Henan, China . 56 H9
Yingshan, Hubei, China .. 59 B10
Yingshan, Sichuan, China . 58 B6
Yingshang, China 59 A11
Yingtan, China 59 C11
Yining, China 50 E9
Yinjiang, China 58 C7
Yinmabin, Burma 67 H19
Yiofiros →, Greece 36 D7
Yioúra, Nótios Aiyaíon,
  Greece 38 D6
Yioúra, Thessalía, Greece . 38 B6
Yipinglang, China 58 E3
Yirba Muda, Ethiopia ... 81 F4
Yirga Alem, Ethiopia 81 F4
Yirol, Sudan 81 F3
Yirrkala, Australia 94 A2
Yishan, China 58 E7
Yishui, China 57 G10
Yíthion, Greece 38 E4
Yitiaoshan, China 56 F3
Yitong, China 57 C13
Yiwu, China 59 C13
Yixing, China 59 B12
Yiyang, Henan, China ... 56 G7
Yiyang, Hunan, China ... 59 C9
Yiyang, Jiangxi, China ... 59 C11
Yizhang, China 59 E9
Yizheng, China 59 A12
Yli-Kitka, Finland 8 C23
Ylitornio, Finland 8 C20
Ylivieska, Finland 8 D21
Yngaren, Sweden 11 F10
Yoakum, U.S.A. 113 L6
Yobe □, Nigeria 83 C7
Yog Pt., Phil. 63 B6
Yogan, China 83 D7
Yogyakarta, Indonesia ... 63 G14
Yoho Nat. Park, Canada . 104 C5
Yojoa, L. de, Honduras .. 120 D2
Yŏju, S. Korea 57 F14
Yokadouma, Cameroon .. 84 D2
Yokkaichi, Japan 55 G8
Yoko, Cameroon 83 D7
Yokohama, Japan 55 G9
Yokosuka, Japan 55 G9
Yokote, Japan 54 E10
Yola, Nigeria 83 D7
Yolaina, Cordillera de, Nic. 120 D3
Yoloten, Turkmenistan ... 71 B9
Yom →, Thailand 62 A2
Yonago, Japan 55 G6

Yonaguni-Jima, Japan ... 55 M1
Yŏnan, N. Korea 57 F14
Yonezawa, Japan 54 F10
Yong Peng, Malaysia 65 L4
Yong Sata, Thailand 65 J2
Yongamp'o, N. Korea ... 57 E13
Yong'an, China 59 E11
Yongcheng, China 56 H9
Yŏngch'ŏn, S. Korea ... 57 G15
Yongchun, China 59 E12
Yongde, China 58 E2
Yongding, China 59 E11
Yongdeng, China 56 F2
Yongding, China 59 E11
Yŏngdŏk, S. Korea 57 F15
Yŏngdŭngp'o, S. Korea . 57 F14
Yongfeng, China 59 D10
Yongfu, China 58 E7
Yonghe, China 56 F6
Yŏnghŭng, N. Korea ... 57 E14
Yongji, China 56 G6
Yongjia, China 59 C13
Yongjiu, S. Korea 57 F15
Yongkang, Yunnan, China 58 E2
Yongkang, Zhejiang, China 59 C13
Yongnian, China 56 F8
Yongning,
  Guangxi Zhuangzu, China 58 F7
Yongning, Ningxia Huizu,
  China 56 E4
Yongping, China 58 E2
Yongqing, China 56 E9
Yongren, China 58 D3
Yongshan, China 58 C4
Yongsheng, China 58 D3
Yongshun, China 58 C7
Yongtai, China 59 E12
Yŏngwŏl, S. Korea 57 F15
Yongxin = Jinggangshan,
  China 59 D10
Yongxing, China 59 D9
Yongxiu, China 59 C10
Yongzhou, China 59 D8
Yonibana, S. Leone 82 D2
Yonkers, U.S.A. 111 F11
Yonne □, France 19 E10
Yonne →, France 19 D9
York, Australia 93 F2
York, U.K. 12 D6
York, Ala., U.S.A. 113 J10
York, Nebr., U.S.A. 112 E6
York, Pa., U.S.A. 108 F7
York, C., Australia 94 A3
York, City of □, U.K. ... 12 D6
York, Kap, Greenland ... 4 B4
York, Vale of, U.K. 12 C6
York Haven, U.S.A. 110 F8
York Sd., Australia 92 C4
Yorke Pen., Australia ... 95 E2
Yorketown, Australia ... 95 F2
Yorkshire Wolds, U.K. .. 12 C7
Yorkton, Canada 105 C8
Yorkville, U.S.A. 116 G3
Yoro, Honduras 120 C2
Yoron-Jima, Japan 55 L4
Yorosso, Mali 82 C4
Yos Sudarso, Pulau =
  Dolak, Pulau, Indonesia . 63 F9
Yosemite National Park,
  U.S.A. 116 H7
Yosemite Village, U.S.A. . 116 H7
Yoshkar Ola, Russia 48 B8
Yŏsu, S. Korea 57 G14
Yotvata, Israel 75 F4
You Jiang →, China 58 F6
You Xian, China 59 D9
Youbou, Canada 116 B2
Youghal, Ireland 15 E4
Youghal B., Ireland 15 E4
Youkounkoun, Guinea .. 82 C2
Young, Australia 95 E4
Young, Canada 105 C7
Young, Uruguay 126 C4
Younghusband, L., Australia 95 E2
Younghusband Pen.,
  Australia 95 F2
Youngstown, Canada ... 105 C6
Youngstown, N.Y., U.S.A. 110 C5
Youngstown, Ohio, U.S.A. 110 E4
Youngsville, U.S.A. 110 E5
Youngwood, U.S.A. 110 F5
Youxi, China 59 D12
Youyang, China 58 C7
Youyu, China 56 D7
Yozgat, Turkey 72 C6
Ypané →, Paraguay ... 126 A4
Yport, France 18 C7
Ypres = Ieper, Belgium .. 17 D2
Yreka, U.S.A. 114 F2
Yssingeaux, France 21 C8
Ystad, Sweden 11 J7
Ysyk-Köl, Ozero, Kyrgyzstan 50 E8
Ythan →, U.K. 14 D7
Ytterhogdal, Sweden ... 10 B8
Ytyk Kyuyel, Russia 51 C14
Yu Jiang →, China 58 F7
Yu Xian = Yuzhou, China 56 G7
Yu Xian, Hebei, China .. 56 E8
Yu Xian, Shanxi, China .. 56 E7
Yuan Jiang →, Hunan,
  China 59 C8
Yuan Jiang →, Yunnan,
  China 58 F4
Yuan'an, China 59 B8
Yuanjiang, Hunan, China . 59 C9
Yuanjiang, Yunnan, China . 58 F4
Yuanli, Taiwan 59 F13
Yuanlin, Taiwan 59 F13
Yuanling, China 59 C8
Yuanmou, China 58 E3
Yuanqu, China 56 G6

Yuanyang, Henan, China . 56 G7
Yuanyang, Yunnan, China . 58 F4
Yuba →, U.S.A. 116 F5
Yuba City, U.S.A. 116 F5
Yūbari, Japan 54 C10
Yubdo, Ethiopia 81 F4
Yūbetsu, Japan 54 B11
Yubo, Sudan 81 F2
Yucatán □, Mexico ... 119 C7
Yucatán, Canal de,
  Caribbean 120 B2
Yucatán, Península de,
  Mexico 98 H11
Yucatan Basin, Cent. Amer. 98 H11
Yucatan Str. = Yucatán,
  Canal de, Caribbean ... 120 B2
Yucca, U.S.A. 117 L12
Yucca Valley, U.S.A. ... 117 L10
Yucheng, China 56 F9
Yuci, China 56 F7
Yudu, China 59 E10
Yuechi, China 58 B6
Yuendumu, Australia ... 92 D5
Yueqing, China 59 C13
Yueqing Wan, China ... 59 D13
Yuexi, Anhui, China 59 B11
Yuexi, Sichuan, China ... 58 C4
Yueyang, China 59 C9
Yugan, China 59 C11
Yugoslavia ■, Europe .. 40 C4
Yuhuan, China 59 C13
Yühuan Dao, China 59 C13
Yujiang, China 59 C11
Yukhnov, Russia 46 E8
Yukon →, U.S.A. 100 B3
Yukon Territory □, Canada 100 B6
Yüksekova, Turkey 73 D11
Yukta, Russia 51 C11
Yukuhashi, Japan 55 H5
Yulara, Australia 93 E5
Yule →, Australia 92 D2
Yuleba, Australia 95 D4
Yuli, Nigeria 83 D7
Yuli, Taiwan 59 F13
Yulin, Guangxi Zhuangzu,
  China 59 F8
Yülin, Hainan, China ... 65 C7
Yulin, Shaanxi, China ... 56 E5
Yuma, Ariz., U.S.A. 117 N12
Yuma, Colo., U.S.A. ... 112 E3
Yuma, B. de, Dom. Rep. . 121 C6
Yumbe, Uganda 86 B3
Yumbi,
  Dem. Rep. of the Congo . 86 C2
Yumen, China 60 C4
Yun Gui Gaoyuan, China . 58 E3
Yun Ho →, China 57 E9
Yun Ling, China 58 D2
Yun Xian, Hubei, China .. 59 A8
Yun Xian, Yunnan, China . 58 E3
Yuna, Australia 93 E2
Yunak, Turkey 72 C4
Yunan, China 59 F8
Yuncheng, Henan, China . 56 G8
Yuncheng, Shanxi, China . 56 G6
Yunfu, China 59 F9
Yungas, Bolivia 124 G5
Yungay, Chile 126 D1
Yunhe, China 59 C12
Yunkai Dashan, China .. 59 F8
Yunlin, Taiwan 59 F13
Yunlong, China 58 E2
Yunmeng, China 59 B9
Yunnan □, China 58 E4
Yunquera de Henares, Spain 32 E1
Yunt Dağı, Turkey 39 C9
Yunta, Australia 95 E2
Yunxi, China 56 H6
Yunxiao, China 59 F11
Yuping, China 58 D7
Yupyongdong, N. Korea . 57 D15
Yuqing, China 58 D6
Yurga, Russia 50 D9
Yurimaguas, Peru 124 E3
Yurya, Russia 46 D10
Yuryevets, Russia 48 B6
Yuryung Kaya, Russia .. 51 B12
Yuscarán, Honduras ... 120 D2
Yushan, China 59 C12
Yushanzhen, China 58 C7
Yushe, China 56 F7
Yushu, Jilin, China 57 B14
Yushu, Qinghai, China .. 60 C4
Yusufeli, Turkey 73 B9
Yutai, China 56 G9
Yutian, China 57 E9
Yuxarı Qarabağ = Nagorno-
  Karabakh, Azerbaijan .. 70 B5
Yuxi, China 58 E4
Yuyao, China 59 B13
Yuzawa, Japan 54 E10
Yuzha, Russia 48 B6
Yuzhno-Sakhalinsk, Russia 51 E15
Yuzhou, China 56 G7
Yvelines □, France 19 D8
Yverdon-les-Bains, Switz. . 25 J2
Yvetot, France 18 C7
Yzeure, France 19 F10

Z

Zaanstad, Neths. 17 B4
Zāb al Kabīr →, Iraq ... 70 C4
Zāb aş Şaḡīr →, Iraq ... 70 C4
Žabalj, Serbia, Yug. 42 E5
Žabari, Serbia, Yug. 40 B5
Zabarjad, Egypt 80 C4

Zabaykalsk, Russia 51 E12
Żabki, Poland 45 F8
Ząbkowice Śląskie, Poland .. 45 H3
Žabljak, Montenegro, Yug. .. 40 C3
Żabłudów, Poland 45 F9
Żabno, Poland 45 H7
Zābol, Iran 71 D9
Zābolī, Iran 71 E9
Zabré, Burkina Faso ...., . 83 C4
Zábřeh, Czech Rep. 27 B9
Zabrze, Poland 45 H5
Zabzuga, Ghana 83 D5
Zacapa, Guatemala 120 D2
Zacapu, Mexico 118 D4
Zacatecas, Mexico 118 C4
Zacatecas □, Mexico 118 C4
Zacatecoluca, El Salv. 120 D2
Zachary, U.S.A. 113 K9
Zachodnio-Pomorskie □, Poland ... 44 E2
Zacoalco, Mexico 118 C4
Zacualtipán, Mexico 119 C5
Zadar, Croatia 29 D12
Zadawa, Nigeria 83 C7
Zadetkyi Kyun, Burma 65 G1
Zadonsk, Russia 47 F10
Zafarqand, Iran 71 C7
Zafora, Greece 39 E8
Zafra, Spain 35 G4
Zagań, Poland 45 G2
Zagaoua, Chad 79 E10
Żagaré, Lithuania 44 B10
Zagazig, Egypt 80 H7
Zāgheh, Iran 71 C6
Zaglivérion, Greece 40 F7
Zagnanado, Benin 83 D5
Zagorá, Greece 38 B5
Zagorje, Slovenia 29 B11
Zagórów, Poland 45 F4
Zagorsk = Sergiyev Posad, Russia ... 46 D10
Zagórz, Poland 45 J9
Zagreb, Croatia 29 C12
Zāgros, Kūhhā-ye, Iran 71 C6
Zagros Mts. = Zāgros, Kūhhā-ye, Iran ... 71 C6
Zagubica, Serbia, Yug. 40 B5
Zaguinaso, Ivory C. 82 C3
Zagyva →, Hungary 42 C5
Zāhedān, Fārs, Iran 71 D7
Zāhedān, Sīstān va Balūchestān, Iran ... 71 D9
Zahlah, Lebanon 75 B4
Zahna, Germany 24 D8
Záhony, Hungary 42 B7
Zainsk, Russia 48 C11
Zaïre = Congo →, Africa . 84 F2
Zaječar, Serbia, Yug. 40 C6
Zaka, Zimbabwe 89 C5
Zakamensk, Russia 51 D11
Zakataly = Zaqatala, Azerbaijan ... 49 K8
Zakháro, Greece 38 D3
Zakhodnaya Dzvina = Daugava →, Latvia ... 9 H21
Zākhū, Iraq 70 B4
Zákinthos, Greece 38 D2
Zákinthos □, Greece 38 D2
Zakopane, Poland 45 J6
Zakroczym, Poland 45 F7
Zákros, Greece 36 D8
Zala, Ethiopia 81 F4
Zala □, Hungary 42 D1
Zala →, Hungary 42 D2
Zalaegerszeg, Hungary 42 D1
Zalakomár, Hungary 42 D2
Zalalövö, Hungary 42 D1
Zalamea de la Serena, Spain . 35 G5
Zalamea la Real, Spain 35 H4
Zalău, Romania 42 C8
Žalec, Slovenia 29 B12
Zaleshchiki = Zalishchyky, Ukraine ... 47 H3
Zalew Wiślany, Poland 44 D6
Zalewo, Poland 44 E6
Zalingei, Sudan 79 F10
Zalishchyky, Ukraine 47 H3
Zama L., Canada 104 B5
Zambeke, Dem. Rep. of the Congo . 86 B2
Zambeze →, Africa 87 F4
Zambezi = Zambeze →, Africa ... 87 F4
Zambezi, Zambia 85 G4
Zambezia □, Mozam. 87 F4
Zambia ■, Africa 87 F2
Zamboanga, Phil. 61 H5
Zambrów, Poland 45 F9
Zametchino, Russia 48 D6
Zamfara □, Nigeria 83 C6
Zamfara →, Nigeria 83 C5
Zamora, Mexico 118 D4
Zamora, Spain 34 D5
Zamora □, Spain 34 D5
Zamość, Poland 45 H10
Zamtang, China 58 A3
Zan, Ghana 83 D4
Záncara →, Spain 33 F1
Zandvoort, Neths. 17 B4
Zanesville, U.S.A. 110 G2
Zangābād, Iran 70 B5
Zangue →, Mozam. 87 F4
Zanján, Iran 71 B6
Zanján □, Iran 71 B6
Zanján →, Iran 71 B6
Zannone, Italy 30 B6
Zante = Zákinthos, Greece . 38 D2
Zanthus, Australia 93 F3
Zanzibar, Tanzania 86 D4

Zaouiet El-Kala = Bordj Omar Driss, Algeria 78 C7
Zaouiet Reggane, Algeria ... 78 C6
Zaoyang, China 59 A9
Zaozhuang, China 57 G9
Zap Suyu = Zāb al Kabīr →, Iraq 70 C4
Zapadna Morava →, Serbia, Yug. 40 C5
Zapadnaya Dvina = Daugava →, Latvia 9 H21
Zapadnaya Dvina, Russia ... 46 D7
Západné Beskydy, Europe ... 27 B12
Zapadni Rodopi, Bulgaria ... 40 E7
Západočeský □, Czech Rep. . 26 B6
Zapala, Argentina 128 D2
Zapaleri, Cerro, Bolivia ... 126 A2
Zapata, U.S.A. 113 M5
Zapatón →, Spain 35 F4
Zaporizhzhya, Ukraine 47 J8
Zaporozhye = Zaporizhzhya, Ukraine ... 47 J8
Zaqatala, Azerbaijan 49 K8
Zara, Turkey 70 B3
Zaragoza, Coahuila, Mexico . 118 B4
Zaragoza, Nuevo León, Mexico ... 119 C5
Zaragoza, Spain 32 D4
Zaragoza □, Spain 32 D4
Zarand, Kermān, Iran 71 D8
Zarand, Markazī, Iran 71 C6
Zărandului, Munţii, Romania 42 D7
Zaranj, Afghan. 66 D2
Zarasai, Lithuania 9 J22
Zárate, Argentina 126 C4
Zarautz, Spain 32 B2
Zaraysk, Russia 46 E10
Zard, Kūh-e, Iran 71 C6
Zāreh, Iran 71 C6
Zari, Nigeria 83 C7
Zaria, Nigeria 83 C6
Zarki, Poland 45 H6
Zárkon, Greece 38 B4
Zarneh, Iran 70 C5
Zărneşti, Romania 43 E10
Żarós, Greece 36 D6
Zarów, Poland 45 H3
Zarqā', Nahr az →, Jordan . 75 C4
Zarrīn, Iran 71 C7
Zaruma, Ecuador 124 D3
Żary, Poland 45 G2
Zarza de Granadilla, Spain . 34 E4
Zarzis, Tunisia 79 B8
Zas, Spain 34 B2
Zaskar →, India 69 B7
Zaskar Mts., India 69 C7
Zastron, S. Africa 88 E4
Žatec, Czech Rep. 26 A6
Zaterechnyy, Russia 49 H7
Zator, Poland 45 J6
Zavala, Bos.-H. 40 D1
Zavāreh, Iran 71 C7
Zave, Zimbabwe 89 B5
Zavetnoye, Russia 49 G6
Zavidovići, Bos.-H. 42 F3
Zavitinsk, Russia 51 D13
Zavodovski, I., Antarctica . 5 B1
Zavolzhsk, Russia 48 B6
Zavolzhye, Russia 48 B6
Zawadzkie, Poland 45 H5
Zawichost, Poland 45 H8
Zawidów, Poland 45 G2
Zawiercie, Poland 45 H6
Zāwiyat al Baydā = Al Baydā, Libya 79 B10
Zāwyet Shammas, Egypt ... 80 A2
Zāwyet Um el Rakham, Egypt 80 A2
Zāwyet Ungeîla, Egypt ... 80 A2
Zāyā, Iraq 70 C5
Zāyandeh →, Iran 71 C7
Zaysan, Kazakstan 50 E9
Zaysan, Oz., Kazakstan 50 E9
Zayü, China 58 C1
Zazafotsy, Madag. 89 C8
Zázrivá, Slovak Rep. 27 B12
Zbarazh, Ukraine 47 H3
Zbąszyń, Poland 45 F2
Zbąszynek, Poland 45 F2
Zblewo, Poland 44 E5
Žďár nad Sázavov, Czech Rep. 26 B8
Zdolbuniv, Ukraine 47 G4
Ždrelo, Serbia, Yug. 40 B5
Zduńska Wola, Poland 45 G5
Zduny, Poland 45 G4
Zeballos, Canada 104 D3
Zebediela, S. Africa 89 C4
Zebila, Ghana 83 C4
Zebrugge, Belgium 17 C3
Zeehan, Australia 94 G4
Zeeland □, Neths. 17 C3
Zeerust, S. Africa 88 D4
Zefat, Israel 75 C4
Zege, Ethiopia 81 E4
Zeggerene, Iracher, Mali ... 83 B5
Zégoua, Mali 82 C3
Zehdenick, Germany 24 C9
Zeil, Mt., Australia 92 D5
Zeila, Somali Rep. 74 E3
Zeist, Neths. 17 B5
Zelechów, Poland 45 G8
Zelengora, Bos.-H. 40 C2
Zelenodolsk, Russia 48 C9
Zelenogorsk, Russia 46 B5
Zelenograd, Russia 46 D9
Zelenogradsk, Russia 9 J19
Zelenokumsk, Russia 49 H6

Železná Ruda, Czech Rep. . 26 B6
Železnik, Serbia, Yug. 40 B4
Zelienople, U.S.A. 110 F4
Železovce, Slovak Rep. 27 C11
Zelina, Croatia 29 C13
Zell, Baden-W., Germany ... 25 H3
Zell, Rhld-Pfz., Germany ... 25 E3
Zell am See, Austria 26 D5
Zella-Mehlis, Germany 24 E6
Zelów, Poland 45 G6
Zeltweg, Austria 26 D7
Zémio, C.A.R. 86 A2
Zempléni-hegység, Hungary . 42 B6
Zemplínska šírava, Slovak Rep. 27 C15
Zemun, Serbia, Yug. 40 B4
Zengbé, Cameroon 83 D7
Zengcheng, China 59 F9
Zenica, Bos.-H. 42 F3
Žepče, Bos.-H. 42 F3
Zeraf, Bahr ez →, Sudan ... 81 F3
Zerbst, Germany 24 D8
Żerków, Poland 45 F4
Zermatt, Switz. 25 J3
Zernograd, Russia 49 G5
Zernez, Switz. 25 J6
Zerqani, Albania 40 E4
Zestaponi, Georgia 49 J6
Zetel, Germany 24 B3
Zeulenroda, Germany 24 E7
Zeven, Germany 24 B5
Zevenaar, Neths. 17 C6
Zévio, Italy 28 C8
Zeya, Russia 51 D13
Zeya →, Russia 51 D13
Zeytinbaği, Turkey 41 F12
Zeytindağ, Turkey 39 C9
Zghartā, Lebanon 75 A4
Zgierz, Poland 45 G6
Zgorzelec, Poland 45 G2
Zgurița, Moldova 43 B13
Zhabinka, Belarus 47 F3
Zhailma, Kazakstan 50 D7
Zhambyl, Kazakstan 50 E8
Zhangaly, Kazakstan 49 G10
Zhangaqazaly, Kazakstan ... 50 E7
Zhangbei, China 56 D8
Zhangguangcai Ling, China . 57 B15
Zhangjiakou, China 56 D8
Zhangping, China 59 E11
Zhangpu, China 59 E11
Zhangshu, China 59 C10
Zhangwu, China 57 C12
Zhangye, China 60 C5
Zhangzhou, China 59 E11
Zhanhua, China 57 F10
Zhanjiang, China 59 G8
Zhannetty, Ostrov, Russia . 51 B16
Zhanyi, China 58 E4
Zhanyu, China 57 B12
Zhao Xian, China 56 F8
Zhao'an, China 59 F11
Zhaocheng, China 56 F6
Zhaojue, China 58 C4
Zhaoping, China 59 E8
Zhaoqing, China 59 F9
Zhaotong, China 58 D4
Zhaoyuan, Heilongjiang, China ... 57 B13
Zhaoyuan, Shandong, China 57 F11
Zharkovskiy, Russia 46 E7
Zhashkiv, Ukraine 47 H6
Zhashui, China 56 H5
Zhayyq →, Kazakstan 50 E6
Zhdanov = Mariupol, Ukraine ... 47 J9
Zhecheng, China 56 G8
Zhegao, China 59 B11
Zhejiang □, China 59 C13
Zheleznogorsk, Russia 47 F8
Zheleznogorsk-Ilimskiy, Russia 51 D11
Zheltyye Vody = Zhovti Vody, Ukraine 47 H7
Zhen'an, China 56 H5
Zhenba, China 58 A6
Zhenfeng, China 58 E5
Zheng'an, China 58 C6
Zhengding, China 56 E8
Zhenghe, China 59 D12
Zhengyang, China 59 A10
Zhengzhuguan, China 59 A11
Zhengzhou, China 56 G7
Zhenhai, China 59 C13
Zhenjiang, China 59 A12
Zhenkang, China 58 F2
Zhenlai, China 57 B12
Zhenning, China 58 D5
Zhenping, Henan, China 56 H7
Zhenping, Shaanxi, China ... 58 A7
Zhenxiong, China 58 D5
Zhenyuan, Gansu, China 56 G4
Zhenyuan, Guizhou, China . 58 D7
Zherdevka, Russia 48 E5
Zherong, China 59 D12
Zhetiqara, Kazakstan 50 D7
Zhezqazghan, Kazakstan 50 E7
Zhicheng, China 59 B8
Zhidan, China 56 F5
Zhigansk, Russia 51 C13
Zhigulevsk, Russia 48 D9
Zhijiang, Hubei, China 59 B8
Zhijiang, Hunan, China 58 D7
Zhijin, China 58 D5
Zhilinda, Russia 51 C12
Zhirnovsk, Russia 48 E7
Zhitomir = Zhytomyr, Ukraine 47 G5
Zhizdra, Russia 46 F9
Zhlobin, Belarus 47 F6

Zhmerinka = Zhmerynka, Ukraine 47 H5
Zhmerynka, Ukraine 47 H5
Zhob, Pakistan 68 D3
Zhob →, Pakistan 68 C3
Zhodino = Zhodzina, Belarus 46 E5
Zhodzina, Belarus 46 E5
Zhokhova, Ostrov, Russia . 51 B16
Zhongdian, China 58 D2
Zhongdong, China 58 F6
Zhongdu, China 58 E7
Zhongning, China 56 F3
Zhongshan, Guangdong, China 59 F9
Zhongshan, Guangxi Zhuangzu, China 59 E8
Zhongtiao Shan, China 56 G6
Zhongwei, China 56 F3
Zhongxiang, China 59 B9
Zhongyang, China 56 F6
Zhoucun, China 57 F9
Zhouning, China 59 D12
Zhoushan, China 59 B14
Zhoushan Dao, China 59 C14
Zhouzhi, China 56 G5
Zhovti Vody, Ukraine 47 H7
Zhovtnevoye = Zhovtneve, Ukraine ... 47 J7
Zhovtneve, Ukraine 47 J7
Zhu Jiang →, China 59 F9
Zhuanghe, China 57 E12
Zhucheng, China 57 G10
Zhugqu, China 56 H3
Zhuhai, China 59 F9
Zhuji, China 59 C13
Zhukovka, Russia 46 F7
Zhumadian, China 56 H8
Zhuo Xian = Zhuozhou, China 56 E8
Zhuolu, China 56 D8
Zhuozhou, China 56 E8
Zhuozi, China 56 D7
Zhushan, China 59 A8
Zhuxi, China 58 A7
Zhuzhou, China 59 D9
Zhytomyr, Ukraine 47 G5
Zi Shui →, China 59 C9
Ziārān, Iran 71 B6
Ziarat, Pakistan 68 D2
Zibo, China 57 F10
Zichang, China 56 F5
Zidarovo, Bulgaria 41 D11
Ziębice, Poland 45 H4
Zielona Góra, Poland 45 G2
Zierikzee, Neths. 17 C3
Ziesar, Germany 24 C8
Zifta, Egypt 80 H7
Zigey, Chad 79 F9
Zigong, China 58 C5
Ziguinchor, Senegal 82 C1
Zihuatanejo, Mexico 118 D4
Zijin, China 59 F10
Zile, Turkey 72 B6
Žilina, Slovak Rep. 27 B11
Žilinský □, Slovak Rep. ... 27 B12
Zillah, Libya 79 C9
Zillertaler Alpen, Austria . 26 D4
Zima, Russia 51 D11
Zimapán, Mexico 119 C5
Zimba, Zambia 87 F2
Zimbabwe, Zimbabwe 87 G3
Zimbabwe ■, Africa 87 F3
Zimi, S. Leone 82 D2
Zimnicea, Romania 43 G10
Zimovniki, Russia 49 G6
Zinder, Niger 83 C6
Zinga, Tanzania 87 D4
Zingst, Germany 24 A8
Ziniaré, Burkina Faso 83 C4
Zinnowitz, Germany 24 A9
Zion National Park, U.S.A. . 115 H7
Zirbitzkogel, Austria 26 D7
Zirc, Hungary 42 C2
Žiri, Slovenia 29 B11
Žirje, Croatia 29 E12
Zirl, Austria 26 D4
Zirndorf, Germany 25 F6
Ziros, Greece 36 D8
Zisterdorf, Austria 27 C9
Zitácuaro, Mexico 118 D4
Žitava →, Slovak Rep. 27 C11
Žitište, Serbia, Yug. 42 E5
Zitong, China 58 B5
Zitsa, Greece 38 B2
Zittau, Germany 24 E10
Zitundo, Mozam. 89 D5
Ziway, L., Ethiopia 81 F4
Zixi, China 59 D11
Zixing, China 59 E9
Ziyang, Shaanxi, China 58 A7
Ziyang, Sichuan, China 58 B5
Ziyun, China 58 E6
Zizhong, China 58 C5
Zlarin, Croatia 29 E12
Zlatar, Croatia 29 B13
Zlatar, Serbia, Yug. 40 C3
Zlataritsa, Bulgaria 41 C9
Zlaté Moravce, Slovak Rep. . 27 C11
Zlatibor, Serbia, Yug. 40 C3
Zlatitsa, Bulgaria 41 D8
Zlatna, Romania 43 D8
Zlatna Panega, Bulgaria ... 41 C8
Zlatni Pyasŭtsi, Bulgaria . 41 C12
Zlatograd, Bulgaria 41 E9
Zlatoust, Russia 50 D6

Zletovo, Macedonia 40 E6
Zlín, Czech Rep. 27 B10
Złocieniec, Poland 44 E3
Złoczew, Poland 45 G5
Zlot, Serbia, Yug. 40 B5
Złotoryja, Poland 45 G2
Złotów, Poland 44 E4
Zmeinogorsk, Kazakstan 50 D9
Żmigród, Poland 45 G3
Zmiyev, Ukraine 47 H9
Znamenka = Znamyanka, Ukraine 47 H7
Znamyanka, Ukraine 47 H7
Żnin, Poland 45 F4
Znojmo, Czech Rep. 26 C9
Zobeyrī, Iran 70 C5
Zobia, Dem. Rep. of the Congo . 86 B2
Zoetermeer, Neths. 17 B4
Zogang, China 58 C1
Zogno, Italy 28 C6
Zogqên, China 58 A2
Zolochev = Zolochiv, Ukraine 47 H3
Zolochiv, Ukraine 47 H3
Zolotonosha, Ukraine 47 H7
Zomba, Malawi 87 F4
Zongo, Dem. Rep. of the Congo . 84 D3
Zonguldak, Turkey 72 B4
Zongyang, China 59 B11
Zonqor Pt., Malta 36 D2
Zonza, France 21 G13
Zorgo, Burkina Faso 83 C4
Zorita, Spain 35 F5
Zorleni, Romania 43 D12
Zornitsa, Bulgaria 41 D10
Zorritos, Peru 124 D2
Żory, Poland 45 H5
Zorzor, Liberia 82 D3
Zossen, Germany 24 C9
Zou Xiang, China 56 G9
Zouan-Hounien, Ivory C. ... 82 D3
Zouar, Chad 79 D9
Zouérate = Zouîrât, Mauritania 78 D3
Zouîrât, Mauritania 78 D3
Zourika, Niger 83 B6
Zourma, Burkina Faso 83 C4
Zoushan Dao, China 59 B14
Zoutkamp, Neths. 17 A6
Zrenjanin, Serbia, Yug. ... 42 E5
Zuarungu, Ghana 83 C4
Zuba, Nigeria 83 D6
Zubayr, Yemen 81 D5
Zubtsov, Russia 46 D8
Zuénoula, Ivory C. 82 D3
Zuera, Spain 32 D4
Žufar, Oman 74 D5
Zug □, Switz. 25 H4
Zugdidi, Georgia 49 J5
Zugersee, Switz. 25 H4
Zugspitze, Germany 25 H6
Zuid-Holland □, Neths. 17 C4
Zuidbeveland, Neths. 17 C3
Zuidhorn, Neths. 17 A6
Zújar, Spain 35 H4
Zújar →, Spain 35 G5
Zukowo, Poland 44 D5
Zula, Eritrea 81 D4
Zülpich, Germany 24 E2
Zumaia, Spain 32 B3
Zumárraga, Spain 32 B2
Zumbo, Mozam. 87 F3
Zummo, Nigeria 83 D7
Zumpango, Mexico 119 D5
Zungeru, Nigeria 83 D6
Zunhua, China 57 D9
Zuni, U.S.A. 115 J9
Zunyi, China 58 D6
Zuo Jiang →, China 58 F6
Zuozhou, China 58 F6
Županja, Croatia 42 E3
Žur, Kosovo, Yug. 40 D4
Zurbāţīyah, Iraq 70 C5
Zürich, Switz. 25 H4
Zürich □, Switz. 25 H4
Zürichsee, Switz. 25 H4
Zuromin, Poland 45 E6
Žut, Croatia 29 E12
Zutphen, Neths. 17 B6
Zuwārah, Libya 79 B8
Zūzan, Iran 71 C8
Žužemberk, Slovenia 29 C11
Zvenigorodka = Zvenyhorodka, Ukraine ... 47 H6
Zvenyhorodka, Ukraine 47 H6
Zverinogolovskoye, Russia . 50 D7
Zvezdets, Bulgaria 41 D11
Zvishavane, Zimbabwe 87 G3
Zvolen, Slovak Rep. 27 C12
Zvonce, Serbia, Yug. 40 D6
Zvornik, Bos.-H. 42 F3
Zwedru = Tchien, Liberia . 82 D3
Zweibrücken, Germany 25 F3
Zwenkau, Germany 24 D8
Zwettl, Austria 26 C8
Zwickau, Germany 24 E8
Zwierzyniec, Poland 45 H9
Zwiesel, Germany 25 F9
Zwoleń, Poland 45 G8
Zwolle, Neths. 17 B6
Zwolle, U.S.A. 113 K8
Żychlin, Poland 45 F6
Żyrardów, Poland 45 F7
Zyryan, Kazakstan 50 E9
Zyryanka, Russia 51 C16
Zyryanovsk = Zyryan, Kazakstan 50 E9
Żywiec, Poland 45 J6
Zyyi, Cyprus 36 E12

KEY TO WORLD MAP PAGES

NORTH AMERICA

ARCTIC OCEAN 4

Arctic Circle

8

8-9

14

15

12-13

18-19

34-35

20-21

28-

37

37

32-33

100-101

104-105

102-103

108-109

110-111

116-117

114-115

112-113

118-119

120-121

ATLANTIC

OCEAN

Tropic of Cancer

37

37

78-79

Equator

AFRICA

106

PACIFIC OCEAN 96-97

SOUTH AMERICA

124-125

126-127

Tropic of Capricorn

PACIFIC OCEAN

128